Handbook of Qualitative Research

INTERNATIONAL ADVISORY BOARD

Handbook of Qualitative Research

Norman K. Denzin
Yvonna S. Lincoln
editors

SAGE Publications
International Educational and Professional Publisher
Thousand Oaks London New Delhi

For information address:

SAGE Publications, Inc.
2455 Teller Road
Thousand Oaks, California 91320
E-mail: order@sagepub.com

SAGE Publications Ltd.
6 Bonhill Street
London EC2A 4PU
United Kingdom

SAGE Publications India Pvt. Ltd.
M-32 Market
Greater Kailash I
New Delhi 110 048 India

Printed in the United States of America

Library of Congress Cataloging-in-Publication Data

Main entry under title:

Handbook of qualitative research / edited by Norman K. Denzin, Yvonna
S. Lincoln.
p. cm.
Includes bibliographical references and index.
ISBN 0-8039-4679-1
1. Social sciences—Research. I. Denzin, Norman K. II. Lincoln,
Yvonna S. III. Title: Qualitative research.
H62.H2455 1994
300′.72—dc20 93-36736

98 99 00 01 12 11 10

Sage Production Editor: Astrid Virding

Contents

Preface

Over the past two decades, a quiet methodological revolution has been taking place in the social sciences. A blurring of disciplinary boundaries has occurred. The social sciences and humanities have drawn closer together in a mutual focus on an interpretive, qualitative approach to research and theory. Although these trends are not new ones (see Vidich & Lyman, Chapter 2, and Reason, Chapter 20, this volume), the extent to which the "qualitative revolution" has overtaken the social sciences and related professional fields has been nothing short of amazing.

Where only statistics, experimental designs, and survey research once stood, researchers have opened up to ethnography, unstructured interviewing, textual analysis, and historical studies. Where "We're doing science" was once the watchword, scholars are now experimenting with the boundaries of interpretation, linking research to social change, delving into characteristics of race, ethnicity, gender, age, and culture to understand more fully the relationship of the researcher to the research. In various disciplines in various guises, this implicit critique of the traditional worldview of science and quantitative methods is taking place. All of these trends have fallen under the rubric of "qualitative research."

Reflecting this revolution, a host of textbooks, journals, research monographs, and readers have been published in recent years. In the field of education, a handbook of qualitative research already exists (LeCompte, Millroy, & Preissle, 1992). Yet, to date, there has been no attempt to represent this field in its entirety, to take stock of how far it has come, to make predictions about where it will be a decade from now, to assess and present the major paradigms, histories, strategies, and techniques of inquiry and analysis that qualitative researchers now use.

The *Handbook of Qualitative Research* represents our attempt to address this void. A handbook, as we were told by our publisher, should ideally represent the distillation of knowledge of a field; it should be a benchmark volume that synthesizes an existing literature, helping to define and shape the present and future of that discipline. In metaphoric terms, if you were to take one book on qualitative research with you to a desert island (or to study for a comprehensive graduate examination), you would choose a handbook. With that mandate, we set off in the summer of 1991 to develop this volume.

The "Field" of Qualitative Research

It did not take us long to discover that the "field" of qualitative research is far from a unified set of principles promulgated by networked groups of scholars. In fact, we have discovered that the field of qualitative research is defined primarily by a series of essential tensions, contradictions, and hesitations. These tensions work back and forth among competing definitions and conceptions of the field.

Further, these tensions exist in a less-than-unified arena. We discovered that the issues and concerns of qualitative researchers in nursing are decidedly different from those of researchers in cultural anthropology. Symbolic interactionist sociologists deal with questions that are different from those of interest to critical theorists in educational research. Nor do the disciplinary networks of qualitative researchers necessarily cross each other, speak to each other, or read each other.

Our attempt, then, is to solidify, interpret, and organize a field of qualitative research in the face of essential paradigmatic differences, inherent contradictions among styles and types of research, and barriers of disciplinary, national, racial, cultural, and gender differences. We present our understanding of how these tensions resolved themselves in our introductory and concluding chapters, and in the implicit dialogue we carry on with various authors—many of whom have views of the field quite different from ours—in the introductions to the various sections of the book. For you, the reader, to understand why we resolved these dilemmas as we did, we must first locate ourselves in these tensions and contradictions.

Norman Denzin is committed to a cultural studies, postmodern, poststructural position that stresses the importance of the social text and its construction. Yvonna Lincoln is an avowed constructionist who places great value on theory and paradigm formation. We share a belief in the limitations of positivism and its successor, postpositivism. Lincoln brings to the project the disciplines of education, psychology, and history, whereas Denzin's grounding is in sociology, communications, anthropology, and the humanities. These biases shaped the construction of this volume, and entered directly into our dialogues with one another. Although we do not always agree—for example, on the question of whether paradigms can be crossed or integrated—our two voices are heard often in the following pages. Other editors, working from different perspectives, would define the field and construct this book in different ways, choose different spokespersons for each topic, focus on other concerns, and so on.

Organization of This Volume

The organization of the *Handbook* moves from the general to the specific, the past to the present. Part I locates the field, starting with history, then applied qualitative research traditions, studying the "other," and the politics and ethics of field research. Part II isolates what we regard as the major historical and contemporary paradigms now structuring and influencing qualitative research in the human disciplines. The chapters move from competing paradigms (positivist, postpositivist, constructivist, critical theory) to specific interpretive perspectives.

Part III isolates the major strategies of inquiry—historically the research methods—a researcher can utilize in a concrete study. The question of methods begins with the design of the qualitative research project. This always begins with a socially situated researcher who moves from a research question to a paradigm or perspective, and then to the empirical world. So located, the researcher then addresses the range of methods that can be employed in any study. The history and uses of these strategies are explored extensively in the 10 chapters in Part III.

Part IV examines methods of collecting and analyzing empirical materials. It moves from interviewing to observation, to the use of artifacts, documents, and records from the past, to visual, personal experience, data management, computerized, narrative, content, and semiotic methods of analysis. Part V takes up the art of interpretation, including criteria for judging the adequacy of qualitative materials, the interpretive process, the written text, and policy research and qualitative evaluation. Part VI examines the future of qualitative research.

Preparation of the *Handbook*

The idea of a handbook preceded our participation by several years. Mitch Allen, our editor at Sage, canvassed more than 70 scholars in different disciplines about the need for and feasibility of a handbook. Based upon the positive responses to his inquiries, he approached Norman Denzin to serve as lead editor, with the admonition to "find someone very different from yourself" to serve as coeditor. Our editorial teaming occurred almost by happenstance from a chance meeting at a conference, in Norm's view, or as "the great setup" in Yvonna's. We (and Mitch) shaped the structure of the *Handbook* during a several-day session in 1991 in Urbana-Champaign, the epiphanal moment (Denzin, 1989, p. 15) of the project, in our view.

One thing that became clear in our lengthy discussions was that we needed input from perspectives other than our own. In response, we assembled a highly prestigious international and interdisciplinary editorial board (names of board members are listed at the front of this volume) who assisted us in the selection of equally prestigious authors, the preparation of the table of contents, and the reading of (often multiple) drafts of each chapter. Editorial board members were used as windows into their respective disciplines as we sought information on key topics, perspectives, and controversies that needed to be addressed. In our selection of editorial board members—and chapter authors—we sought to crosscut disciplinary, gender, race, paradigm, and national boundaries. Our hope was to use board members' views to minimize our own disciplinary blinders.

We received extensive feedback from the editorial board, including suggestions for new chapters, slants to take on some of the chapters, and suggestions of authors for different chapters. Each *Handbook* author we sought, internationally recognized in his or her subject matter, was asked to treat such issues as history, epistemology, ontology, exemplary texts, key controversies, competing paradigms, and predictions about the future.

Tales of the *Handbook*

Many of the difficulties in developing this volume are common to any project of this type and magnitude. Others were the result of the essential tensions and contradictions that operate in this field. The "right" chapter author was busy, overcommitted, going overseas for fieldwork. Few overlapping networks cut across the many disciplines we were attempting to cover, so we often entered territory with little knowledge about who should be asked to do what. We confronted disciplinary blinders—including our own—and discovered there were separate traditions surrounding each of our topics within distinct interpretive communities. It was often difficult to know how to bridge these differences, and our "bridges" were often makeshift constructions. We also had to cope with vastly different styles of thinking about a variety of different topics based on disciplinary, epistemological, gender, racial, ethnic, cultural, and national beliefs, boundaries, and ideologies.

In several cases we unwittingly entered into political battles over who should write a chapter, or over how a chapter should be written. These disputes clearly pointed to the political nature of this project and to the fact that each chapter was a potential, if not real, site for multiple interpretations. Many times the politics of meaning came into play, as we attempted to negotiate and navigate our way through areas fraught with high emotion. On more than one occasion we disagreed with both an author and an editorial board member. Regrettably, in some cases we hurt feelings and perhaps even damaged long-standing friendships. With the clarity of hindsight there are many things we would do differently today, and we apologize for any damage we have done.

We (and our authors and advisers) struggled with the meanings we wanted to bring to such terms as *paradigm, epistemology, interpretive framework, empirical materials* versus *data, research strategies,* and *case study.* We discovered that the very term *qualitative research* means different things to many different people.

We confronted the problem that we could not be comprehensive, even with 1,600 manuscript pages. We fought with authors over deadlines, and over the number of pages we would give them. We also fought with authors over how to conceptualize their chapters, and found that what was clear to us was not necessarily clear to anyone else! We fought, too, over when a chapter was finished, and constantly sought the forbearance of our authors as we requested yet another revision.

Reading the *Handbook*

Were we to write our own critique of this book, we would point to the shortcomings we see in it: an overreliance on the perspectives of our two disciplines (sociology and education), underrepresentation of the new ethnographic sensibility developing in anthropology, uneven coverage of applied qualitative work, minimal dialogue among chapter authors, and a shortfall of voices representing people of color and of the Third World, though we worked hard to avoid all of these problems. You, the reader, will certainly have your own response to this book that may highlight other issues we do not see.

This is all in the nature of the *Handbook,* and in the nature of doing qualitative research. This handbook is a social construction, a socially enacted, cocreated entity, and though it exists in a material form, it will no doubt be re-created in subsequent iterations as generations of scholars and graduate students use it, adapt it, and launch from it additional methodological, paradigmatic, theoretical, and practical work. It is not a final statement. It is a starting point, a springboard for new thought and new work, work that is fresh and sensitive and that blurs the boundaries of our disciplines, but always sharpens our understanding of the larger human project.

It is our hope that this *Handbook,* with all its strengths and all its flaws, will contribute to the growing maturity and influence of qualitative research in the human disciplines. And, in keeping with our original mandate, we hope that it convinces you, the reader, that qualitative research now constitutes a field of study in its own right, allowing you to anchor your own work more firmly in the qualitative research tradition.

Acknowledgments

Of course, this *Handbook* would not exist without its authors or the editorial board members, who gave freely, often on very short notice, of their time, advice, and ever-courteous suggestions. We acknowledge en masse the support of the authors and the editorial board members, whose names are listed facing the title page. These individuals were able to offer both long-term, sustained commitments to the project and short-term emergency assistance.

There are other debts as well, intensely personal and closer to home. The *Handbook* would never have been possible without the ever-present help, support, wisdom, and encouragement of our editor, Mitch Allen. His grasp of this field and its history and diversity is extraordinary. His early conceptions of what this project should look like were extremely valuable. His energy kept us moving forward. Not only did he force us to learn to use electronic mail, but whenever we confronted a problem he was there with his assistance and good-natured humor.

We would also like to thank the following individuals and institutions for their assistance, support, insights, and patience: our respective universities and departments, especially Yvonna's dean, Jane Stallings, who made the extraordinary gift of a very special research assistant, Becky Carr, available so that Yvonna could balance the demands of administrative work, teaching, and the *Handbook*. Linda Detman and Becky Carr, our respective graduate assistants, with good humor and grace, kept our ever-growing files in order, and without both of them, we could never have kept this project on course. Eva Ridenour, Betty Barlow, Gina Manning, and Delores Jean Hill at the University of Illinois kept faxes moving among Urbana, Walnut Creek, College Station, and other far-flung worldly places. At Sage Publications, Astrid Virding and Tricia Howell helped move this project through production; we are extremely grateful to them, as well as to the copy editor, Judy Selhorst, and to those, including Rachel Denzin and Linda Detman, whose excellent proofreading and indexing skills have helped to polish this volume. We especially thank Becky Carr for her preparation of the two indices. Finally, our spouses, Katherine Ryan and Egon Guba, helped keep us on track, listened to our complaints, accessed e-mail for at least one of us (Denzin), and generally displayed extraordinary patience, forbearance, and support, especially when we asked ourselves why we ever got into this project in the first place.

Finally, there is another group of people who gave unstintingly of their time and energy to provide us with their expertise and thoughtful reviews when we needed additional guidance. Without the help of these individuals we would often have found ourselves with less-than-complete understanding of the various traditions, perspectives, and methods represented in this volume. We would like to acknowledge the important contributions of the following individuals to this project: Michael Agar, Anthropology, University of Maryland; David Fetterman, Education, Stanford University; Egon G. Guba, Education, Indiana University; Jeffrey M. Johnson, Institute for Marine Affairs, East Carolina University; J. Gary Knowles, Education, University of Michigan; Raymond Lee, Social Policy, University of London; Markku Lonkila, Sociology, University of Helsinki; Matthew B. Miles, Center for Policy Research, New York; John Ogbu, Anthropology, University of California, Berkeley; Dennis Palumbo, Justice Studies, Arizona State University; Renato Rosaldo, Anthropology, Stanford University; Tom Schwandt, Education, Indiana University; John Seidel, Qualis Research Associates, Amherst, Massachusetts; Renata Tesch, Qualitative Research Management, Desert Springs, California; and Henry T. Trueba, Education, University of Wisconsin, Madison.

Norman K. Denzin
University of Illinois at Urbana-Champaign
Yvonna S. Lincoln
Texas A&M University

References

Denzin, N. K. (1989). *Interpretive interactionism.* Newbury Park, CA: Sage.

LeCompte, M. D., Millroy, W. L., & Preissle, J. (Eds.). (1992). *The handbook of qualitative research in education.* New York: Academic Press.

1

Introduction

Entering the Field of Qualitative Research

NORMAN K. DENZIN
YVONNA S. LINCOLN

QUALITATIVE research has a long and distinguished history in the human disciplines. In sociology the work of the "Chicago school" in the 1920s and 1930s established the importance of qualitative research for the study of human group life. In anthropology, during the same period, the pathbreaking studies of Boas, Mead, Benedict, Bateson, Evans-Pritchard, Radcliffe-Brown, and Malinowski charted the outlines of the fieldwork method, wherein the observer went to a foreign setting to study the customs and habits of another society and culture (for a critique of this tradition, see Rosaldo, 1989, pp. 25-45). Soon qualitative research would be employed in other social science disciplines, including education, social work, and communications. The opening chapter in Part I of this volume, by Vidich and Lyman, charts key features of this history.

In this introductory chapter we will briefly define the field of qualitative research, then review the history of qualitative research in the human disciplines, so that this volume and its contents may be located in their proper historical moment. A conceptual framework for reading the qualitative research act as a multicultural, gendered process will be presented. We will then provide a brief introduction to the chapters that follow.

Definitional Issues

Qualitative research is a field of inquiry in its own right. It crosscuts disciplines, fields, and subject matter.[1] A complex, interconnected family of terms, concepts, and assumptions surround the term *qualitative research.* These include the traditions associated with positivism, poststructuralism, and the many qualitative research perspectives, or methods, connected to cultural and interpretive studies (the chapters in Part II take up these paradigms). There are separate and detailed literatures on the many methods and approaches that fall under the category of qualitative research, such as interviewing, participant observation, and visual methods.

Qualitative research operates in a complex historical field that crosscuts five historical moments (we discuss these in detail below). These five

AUTHORS' NOTE: We are grateful to the many people who have helped with this chapter, including Mitch Allen, Katherine E. Ryan, and Harry Wolcott.

moments simultaneously operate in the present. We describe them as the traditional (1900-1950), the modernist or golden age (1950-1970), blurred genres (1970-1986), the crisis of representation (1986-1990), and postmodern or present moments (1990-present). The present moment is defined, Laurel Richardson (1991) argues, by a new sensibility, the core of which "is doubt that any discourse has a privileged place, any method or theory a universal and general claim to authoritative knowledge" (p. 173).

Successive waves of epistemological theorizing move across these five moments. The traditional period is associated with the positivist paradigm. The modernist or golden age and blurred genres moments are connected to the appearance of postpositivist arguments. At the same time, a variety of new interpretive, qualitative perspectives made their presence felt, including hermeneutics, structuralism, semiotics, phenomenology, cultural studies, and feminism.[2] In the blurred genres phase the humanities became central resources for critical, interpretive theory, and the qualitative research project was broadly conceived. The blurred genres phase produced the next stage, the crisis of representation, where researchers struggled with how to locate themselves and their subjects in reflexive texts. The postmodern moment is characterized by a new sensibility that doubts all previous paradigms (see the chapters in Part VI).

Any description of what constitutes qualitative research must work within this complex historical field. *Qualitative research* means different things in each of these moments. Nonetheless, an initial, generic definition can be offered: Qualitative research is multimethod in focus, involving an interpretive, naturalistic approach to its subject matter. This means that qualitative researchers study things in their natural settings, attempting to make sense of, or interpret, phenomena in terms of the meanings people bring to them. Qualitative research involves the studied use and collection of a variety of empirical materials—case study, personal experience, introspective, life story, interview, observational, historical, interactional, and visual texts—that describe routine and problematic moments and meanings in individuals' lives. Accordingly, qualitative researchers deploy a wide range of interconnected methods, hoping always to get a better fix on the subject matter at hand.

The Qualitative Researcher as *Bricoleur*

The multiple methodologies of qualitative research may be viewed as a bricolage, and the researcher as *bricoleur.* Nelson, Treichler, and Grossberg (1992, p. 2), Lévi-Strauss (1966, p. 17), and Weinstein and Weinstein (1991, p. 161) clarify the meaning of these two terms.[3] A *bricoleur* is a "Jack of all trades or a kind of professional do-it-yourself person" (Lévi-Strauss, 1966, p. 17). The *bricoleur* produces a bricolage, that is, a pieced-together, close-knit set of practices that provide solutions to a problem in a concrete situation. "The solution (bricolage) which is the result of the *bricoleur's* method is an [emergent] construction" (Weinstein & Weinstein, 1991, p. 161) that changes and takes new forms as different tools, methods, and techniques are added to the puzzle. Nelson et al. (1992) describe the methodology of cultural studies "as a bricolage. Its choice of practice, that is, is pragmatic, strategic and self-reflexive" (p. 2). This understanding can be applied equally to qualitative research.

The qualitative researcher-as-*bricoleur* uses the tools of his or her methodological trade, deploying whatever strategies, methods, or empirical materials as are at hand (Becker, 1989). If new tools have to be invented, or pieced together, then the researcher will do this. The choice of which tools to use, which research practices to employ, is not set in advance. The "choice of research practices depends upon the questions that are asked, and the questions depend on their context" (Nelson et al., 1992, p. 2), what is available in the context, and what the researcher can do in that setting.

Qualitative research is inherently multimethod in focus (Brewer & Hunter, 1989). However, the use of multiple methods, or triangulation, reflects an attempt to secure an in-depth understanding of the phenomenon in question. Objective reality can never be captured. Triangulation is not a tool or a strategy of validation, but an alternative to validation (Denzin, 1989a, 1989b, p. 244; Fielding & Fielding, 1986, p. 33; Flick, 1992, p. 194). The combination of multiple methods, empirical materials, perspectives and observers in a single study is best understood, then, as a strategy that adds rigor, breadth, and depth to any investigation (see Flick, 1992, p. 194).

The *bricoleur* is adept at performing a large number of diverse tasks, ranging from interviewing to observing, to interpreting personal and historical documents, to intensive self-reflection and introspection. The *bricoleur* reads widely and is knowledgeable about the many interpretive paradigms (feminism, Marxism, cultural studies, constructivism) that can be brought to any particular problem. He or she may not, however, feel that paradigms can be mingled, or synthesized. That is, paradigms as overarching philosophical systems denoting particular ontologies, epistemologies, and methodologies cannot be easily moved between. They represent belief systems that attach the user to a particular worldview. Perspectives, in contrast, are less well developed systems, and can be more easily moved between. The researcher-as-*bricoleur*-theorist works between and within competing and overlapping perspectives and paradigms.

The *bricoleur* understands that research is an interactive process shaped by his or her personal history, biography, gender, social class, race, and ethnicity, and those of the people in the setting. The *bricoleur* knows that science is power, for all research findings have political implications. There is no value-free science. The *bricoleur* also knows that researchers all tell stories about the worlds they have studied. Thus the narratives, or stories, scientists tell are accounts couched and framed within specific storytelling traditions, often defined as paradigms (e.g., positivism, postpositivism, constructivism).

The product of the *bricoleur*'s labor is a bricolage, a complex, dense, reflexive, collagelike creation that represents the researcher's images, understandings, and interpretations of the world or phenomenon under analysis. This bricolage will, as in the case of a social theorist such as Simmel, connect the parts to the whole, stressing the meaningful relationships that operate in the situations and social worlds studied (Weinstein & Weinstein, 1991, p. 164).

Qualitative Research as a Site of Multiple Methodologies and Research Practices

Qualitative research, as a set of interpretive practices, privileges no single methodology over any other. As a site of discussion, or discourse, qualitative research is difficult to define clearly. It has no theory, or paradigm, that is distinctly its own. As Part II of this volume reveals, multiple theoretical paradigms claim use of qualitative research methods and strategies, from constructivism to cultural studies, feminism, Marxism, and ethnic models of study. Qualitative research is used in many separate disciplines, as we will discuss below. It does not belong to a single discipline.

Nor does qualitative research have a distinct set of methods that are entirely its own. Qualitative researchers use semiotics, narrative, content, discourse, archival, and phonemic analysis, even statistics. They also draw upon and utilize the approaches, methods, and techniques of ethnomethodology, phenomenology, hermeneutics, feminism, rhizomatics, deconstructionism, ethnographies, interviews, psychoanalysis, cultural studies, survey research, and participant observation, among others (see Nelson et al., 1992, p. 2).[4] All of these research practices "can provide important insights and knowledge" (Nelson et al., 1992, p. 2). No specific method or practice can be privileged over any other, and none can be "eliminated out of hand" (p. 2).

Many of these methods, or research practices, are also used in other contexts in the human disciplines. Each bears the traces of its own disciplinary history. Thus there is an extensive history of the uses and meanings of ethnography and ethnology in education (Hymes, 1980; LeCompte & Preissle, 1992); participant observation and ethnography in anthropology (Marcus, Chapter 35, this volume), sociology (Atkinson & Hammersley, Chapter 15, this volume), and cultural studies (Fiske, Chapter 11, this volume); textual, hermeneutic, feminist, psychoanalytic, semiotic, and narrative analysis in cinema and literary studies (Lentricchia & McLaughlin, 1990; Nichols, 1985; see also Manning & Cullum-Swan, Chapter 29, this volume); archival, material culture, historical, and document analysis in history, biography, and archaeology (Hodder, Chapter 24, this volume; Smith, Chapter 18, this volume; Tuchman, Chapter 19, this volume); and discourse and conversational analysis in communications and education (Holstein & Gubrium, Chapter 16, this volume).

The many histories that surround each method or research strategy reveal how multiple uses and meanings are brought to each practice. Textual analysis in literary studies, for example, often treat texts as self-contained systems. On the other hand, a researcher employing a cultural studies or feminist perspective would read a text in terms of its location within a historical moment marked by a particular gender, race, or class ideology. A cultural studies use of ethnography would bring a set of understandings from postmodernism and poststructuralism to the project. These understandings would likely not be shared by mainstream postpositivist sociologists (see Atkinson & Hammersley, Chapter 15, and Altheide & Johnson, Chapter 30, this volume). Similarly, postpositivist and poststructural historians bring different understandings and uses to the methods and findings of historical research (see Tuchman, Chapter 19, this volume). These tensions and contradictions are all evident in the chapters presented here.

These separate and multiple uses and meanings of the methods of qualitative research make it difficult for researchers to agree on any essential definition of the field, for it is never just one thing.[5] Still, a definition must be established for use here. We borrow from, and paraphrase, Nelson et al.'s (1992, p. 4) attempt to define cultural studies:

> Qualitative research is an interdisciplinary, transdisciplinary, and sometimes counterdisciplinary field. It crosscuts the humanities and the social and physical sciences. Qualitative research is many things at the same time. It is multiparadigmatic in focus. Its practitioners are sensitive to the value

of the multimethod approach. They are committed to the naturalistic perspective, and to the interpretive understanding of human experience. At the same time, the field is inherently political and shaped by multiple ethical and political positions.

Qualitative research embraces two tensions at the same time. On the one hand, it is drawn to a broad, interpretive, postmodern, feminist, and critical sensibility. On the other hand, it is drawn to more narrowly defined positivist, postpositivist, humanistic, and naturalistic conceptions of human experience and its analysis.

This rather awkward statement means that qualitative research, as a set of practices, embraces within its own multiple disciplinary histories constant tensions and contradictions over the project itself, including its methods and the forms its findings and interpretations take. The field sprawls between and crosscuts all of the human disciplines, even including, in some cases, the physical sciences. Its practitioners are variously committed to modern and postmodern sensibilities and the approaches to social research that these sensibilities imply.

Resistances to Qualitative Studies

The academic and disciplinary resistances to qualitative research illustrate the politics embedded in this field of discourse. The challenges to qualitative research are many. Qualitative researchers are called journalists, or soft scientists. Their work is termed unscientific, or only exploratory, or entirely personal and full of bias. It is called criticism and not theory, or it is interpreted politically, as a disguised version of Marxism, or humanism.

These resistances reflect an uneasy awareness that the traditions of qualitative research commit the researcher to a critique of the positivist project. But the positivist resistance to qualitative research goes beyond the "ever-present desire to maintain a distinction between hard science and soft scholarship" (Carey, 1989, p. 99). The positive sciences (physics, chemistry, economics, and psychology, for example) are often seen as the crowning achievements of Western civilization, and in their practices it is assumed that "truth" can transcend opinion and personal bias (Carey, 1989, p. 99). Qualitative research is seen as an assault on this tradition, whose adherents often retreat into a "value-free objectivist science" (Carey, 1989, p. 104) model to defend their position. They seldom attempt to make explicit, or to critique, the "moral and political commitments in their own contingent work" (Carey, 1989, p. 104). The opposition to positive science by the postpositivists (see below) and the poststructuralists is seen, then, as an attack on reason and truth. At the same time, the positive science attack on qualitative research is regarded as an attempt to legislate one version of truth over another.

This political terrain defines the many traditions and strands of qualitative research: the British tradition and its presence in other national contexts; the American pragmatic, naturalistic, and interpretive traditions in sociology, anthropology, communications, and education; the German and French phenomenological, hermeneutic, semiotic, Marxist, structural, and poststructural perspectives; feminist, African American studies, Latino studies, gay and lesbian studies, and studies of indigenous and aboriginal cultures (Nelson et al., 1992, p. 15). The politics of qualitative research creates a tension that informs each of the above traditions. This tension itself is constantly being reexamined and interrogated, as qualitative research confronts a changing historical world, new intellectual positions, and its own institutional and academic conditions.

To summarize: Qualitative research is many things to many people. Its essence is twofold: a commitment to some version of the naturalistic, interpretive approach to its subject matter, and an ongoing critique of the politics and methods of positivism. We turn now to a brief discussion of the major differences between qualitative and quantitative approaches to research.

Qualitative Versus Quantitative Research

The word *qualitative* implies an emphasis on processes and meanings that are not rigorously examined, or measured (if measured at all), in terms of quantity, amount, intensity, or frequency. Qualitative researchers stress the socially constructed nature of reality, the intimate relationship between the researcher and what is studied, and the situational constraints that shape inquiry. Such researchers emphasize the value-laden nature of inquiry. They seek answers to questions that stress how social experience is created and given meaning. In contrast, quantitative studies emphasize the measurement and analysis of causal relationships between variables, not processes. Inquiry is purported to be within a value-free framework.

Research Styles: Doing the Same Things Differently?

Of course, both qualitative and quantitative researchers "think they know something about society worth telling to others, and they use a variety of forms, media and means to communicate their ideas and findings" (Becker, 1986, p. 122).

Qualitative research differs from quantitative research in five significant ways (Becker, 1993). These points of difference turn on different ways of addressing the same set of issues. They return always to the politics of research, and who has the power to legislate correct solutions to these problems.

Uses of positivism. First, both perspectives are shaped by the positivist and postpositivist traditions in the physical and social sciences (see the discussion below). These two positive science traditions hold to naive and critical realist positions concerning reality and its perception. In the positivist version it is contended that there is a reality out there to be studied, captured, and understood, whereas postpositivists argue that reality can never be fully apprehended, only approximated (Guba, 1990, p. 22). Postpositivism relies on multiple methods as a way of capturing as much of reality as possible. At the same time, emphasis is placed on the discovery and verification of theories. Traditional evaluation criteria, such as internal and external validity, are stressed, as is the use of qualitative procedures that lend themselves to structured (sometimes statistical) analysis. Computer-assisted methods of analysis that permit frequency counts, tabulations, and low-level statistical analyses may also be employed.

The positivist and postpositivist traditions linger like long shadows over the qualitative research project. Historically, qualitative research was defined within the positivist paradigm, where qualitative researchers attempted to do good positivist research with less rigorous methods and procedures. Some mid-century qualitative researchers (e.g., Becker, Geer, Hughes, & Strauss, 1961) reported participant observation findings in terms of quasi-statistics. As recently as 1990, two leaders of the grounded theory approach to qualitative research attempted to modify the usual canons of good (positivistic) science to fit their own postpositivist conception of rigorous research (Strauss & Corbin, 1990; see also Strauss & Corbin, Chapter 17, this volume; but also see Glaser, 1992). Some applied researchers, while claiming to be atheoretical, fit within the positivist or postpositivist framework by default. Spindler and Spindler (1992) summarize their qualitative approach to quantitative materials: "Instrumentation and quantification are simply procedures employed to extend and reinforce certain kinds of data, interpretations and test hypotheses across samples. Both must be kept in their place. One must avoid their premature or overly extensive use as a security mechanism" (p. 69).

Although many qualitative researchers in the postpositivist tradition use statistical measures, methods, and documents as a way of locating a group of subjects within a larger population, they seldom report their findings in terms of the kinds of complex statistical measures or methods to which quantitative researchers are drawn (e.g., path, regression, or log-linear analyses). Much of applied research is also atheoretical.

Acceptance of postmodern sensibilities. The use of quantitative, positivist methods and assumptions has been rejected by a new generation of qualitative researchers who are attached to poststructural, postmodern sensibilities (see below; see also Vidich & Lyman, Chapter 2, and Richardson, Chapter 32, this volume). These researchers argue that positivist methods are but one way of telling a story about society or the social world. They may be no better or no worse than any other method; they just tell a different kind of story.

This tolerant view is not shared by everyone. Many members of the critical theory, constructivist, poststructural, and postmodern schools of thought reject positivist and postpositivist criteria when evaluating their own work. They see these criteria as irrelevant to their work, and contend that these criteria reproduce only a certain kind of science, a science that silences too many voices. These researchers seek alternative methods for evaluating their work, including verisimilitude, emotionality, personal responsibility, an ethic of caring, political praxis, multivoiced texts, and dialogues with subjects. In response, positivists and postpositivists argue that what they do is good science, free of individual bias and subjectivity; as noted above, they see postmodernism as an attack on reason and truth.

Capturing the individual's point of view. Both qualitative and quantitative researchers are concerned about the individual's point of view. However, qualitative investigators think they can get closer to the actor's perspective through detailed interviewing and observation. They argue that quantitative researchers seldom are able to capture the subject's perspective because they have to rely on more remote, inferential empirical materials. The empirical materials produced by the softer, interpretive methods are regarded by many quantitative researchers as unreliable, impressionistic, and not objective.

Examining the constraints of everyday life. Qualitative researchers are more likely than quantitative researchers to confront the constraints of the everyday social world. They see this world in action and embed their findings in it. Quantitative researchers abstract from this world and seldom study it directly. They seek a nomothetic or etic science based on probabilities derived from the study of large numbers of randomly selected cases. These kinds of statements stand above and outside the constraints of everyday life. Qualitative researchers are committed to an emic, idiographic, case-based position, which directs their attention to the specifics of particular cases.

Securing rich descriptions. Qualitative researchers believe that rich descriptions of the social world are valuable, whereas quantitative researchers, with their etic, nomothetic commitments, are less concerned with such detail.

The five points of difference described above (uses of positivism, acceptance of postmodern sensibilities, capturing the individual's point of view, examining the constraints of everyday life, and securing rich descriptions) reflect commitments to different styles of research, different epistemologies, and different forms of representation. Each work tradition is governed by a different set of genres; each has its own classics, its own preferred forms of representation, interpretation, and textual evaluation (see Becker, 1986, pp. 134-135). Qualitative researchers use ethnographic prose, historical narratives, first-person accounts, still photographs, life histories, fictionalized facts, and biographical and autobiographical materials, among others. Quantitative researchers use mathematical models, statistical tables, and graphs, and often write about their research in impersonal, third-person prose.

With the differences between these two traditions understood, we will now offer a brief discussion of the history of qualitative research. We can break this into four historical moments, mindful that any history is always somewhat arbitrary.

The History of Qualitative Research

The history of qualitative research reveals, as Vidich and Lyman remind us in Chapter 2 of this volume, that the modern social science disciplines have taken as their mission "the analysis and understanding of the patterned conduct and social processes of society." The notion that this task could be carried out presupposed that social scientists had the ability to observe this world objectively. Qualitative methods were a major tool of such observations.[6]

Throughout the history of qualitative research, investigators have always defined their work in terms of hopes and values, "religious faiths, occupational and professional ideologies" (Vidich & Lyman, Chapter 2, this volume). Qualitative research (like all research) has always been judged on the "standard of whether the work communicates or 'says' something to us" (Vidich & Lyman, Chapter 2), based on how we conceptualize our reality and our images of the world. *Epistemology* is the word that has historically defined these standards of evaluation. In the contemporary period, as argued above, many received discourses on epistemology have been "disprivileged," or cast into doubt.

The history presented by Vidich and Lyman in Chapter 2 covers the following (somewhat) overlapping stages: early ethnography (to the seventeenth century); colonial ethnography (seventeenth-, eighteenth-, and nineteenth-century explorers); the ethnography of the American Indian as "other" (late nineteenth- and early twentieth-century anthropology); the ethnography of the "civic other," or community studies, and ethnographies of American immigrants (early twentieth century through the 1960s); studies of ethnicity and assimilation (mid-century through the 1980s); and the present, which we call the *fifth moment.*

In each of these eras researchers were and have been influenced by their political hopes and ideologies, discovering findings in their research that confirmed prior theories or beliefs. Early ethnographers confirmed the racial and cultural diversity of peoples throughout the globe and attempted to fit this diversity into a theory about the origin of history, the races, and civilizations. Colonial ethnographers, before the professionalization of ethnography in the twentieth century, fostered a colonial pluralism that left natives on their own as long as their leaders could be coopted by the colonial administration.

European ethnographers studied Africans and other Third World peoples of color. Early American ethnographers studied the American Indian from the perspective of the conqueror, who saw the life world of the primitive as a window to the prehistoric past. The Calvinist mission to save the Indian was soon transferred to the mission of saving the "hordes" of immigrants who entered the United States with the beginnings of industrialization. Qualitative community studies of the ethnic other proliferated from the early 1900s to the 1960s, and included the work of E. Franklin Frazier, Robert Park, and Robert Redfield and their students, as well as William Foote Whyte, the Lynds, August Hollingshead, Herbert Gans, Stanford Lyman, Arthur Vidich, and Joseph Bensman. The post-1960s' ethnicity studies challenged the "melting pot" hypothesis of Park and his followers and corresponded to the emergence of ethnic studies programs that saw Native Americans, Latinos, Asian Americans, and African Americans attempting to take control over the study of their own peoples.

The postmodern challenge emerged in the mid-1980s. It questioned the assumptions that had organized this earlier history, in each of its colonializing moments. Qualitative research that crosses the "postmodern divide" requires one, Vidich and

Lyman argue in Chapter 2, to "abandon all established and preconceived values, theories, perspectives, . . . and prejudices as resources for ethnographic study." In this new era the qualitative researcher does more than observe history; he or she plays a part in it. New tales of the field will now be written, and they will reflect the researcher's direct and personal engagement with this historical period.

Vidich and Lyman's analysis covers the full sweep of ethnographic history. Ours, presented below, is confined to the twentieth century and complements many of their divisions. We begin with the early foundational work of the British and French, as well the Chicago, Columbia, Harvard, and Berkeley schools of sociology and anthropology. This early foundational period established the norms of classical qualitative and ethnographic research.

The Five Moments of Qualitative Research

As noted above, we divide our history of qualitative research in this century into five phases, each of which is described in turn below.

The Traditional Period

We call the first moment the traditional period (this covers Vidich and Lyman's second and third phases). It begins in the early 1900s and continues until World War II. In this period, qualitative researchers wrote "objective," colonializing accounts of field experiences that were reflective of the positivist scientist paradigm. They were concerned with offering valid, reliable, and objective interpretations in their writings. The "other" who was studied was alien, foreign, and strange.

Here is Malinowski (1967) discussing his field experiences in New Guinea and the Trobriand Islands in the years 1914-1915 and 1917-1918:

> Nothing whatever draws me to ethnographic studies. . . . On the whole the village struck me rather unfavorably. There is a certain disorganization . . . the rowdiness and persistence of the people who laugh and stare and lie discouraged me somewhat. . . . Went to the village hoping to photograph a few stages of the *bara* dance. I handed out half-sticks of tobacco, then watched a few dances; then took pictures—but results were poor. . . . they would not pose long enough for time exposures. At moments I was furious at them, particularly because after I gave them their portions of tobacco they all went away. (quoted in Geertz, 1988, pp. 73-74)

In another work, this lonely, frustrated, isolated field-worker describes his methods in the following words:

> In the field one has to face a chaos of facts. . . . in this crude form they are not scientific facts at all; they are absolutely elusive, and can only be fixed by interpretation. . . . Only laws and generalizations are scientific facts, and field work consists only and exclusively in the interpretation of the chaotic social reality, in subordinating it to general rules. (Malinowski, 1916/1948, p. 328; quoted in Geertz, 1988, p. 81)

Malinowski's remarks are provocative. On the one hand they disparage fieldwork, but on the other they speak of it within the glorified language of science, with laws and generalizations fashioned out of this selfsame experience.

The field-worker, during this period, was lionized, made into a larger-than-life figure who went into and then returned from the field with stories about strange people. Rosaldo (1989) describes this as the period of the Lone Ethnographer, the story of the man-scientist who went off in search of his native in a distant land. There this figure "encountered the object of his quest . . . [and] underwent his rite of passage by enduring the ultimate ordeal of 'fieldwork'" (p. 30). Returning home with his data, the Lone Ethnographer wrote up an objective account of the culture he studied. These accounts were structured by the norms of classical ethnography. This sacred bundle of terms (Rosaldo, 1989, p. 31) organized ethnographic texts in terms of four beliefs and commitments: a commitment to objectivism, a complicity with imperialism, a belief in monumentalism (the ethnography would create a museumlike picture of the culture studied), and a belief in timelessness (what was studied never changed). This model of the researcher, who could also write complex, dense theories about what was studied, holds to the present day.

The myth of the Lone Ethnographer depicts the birth of classic ethnography. The texts of Malinowski, Radcliffe-Brown, Margaret Mead, and Gregory Bateson are still carefully studied for what they can tell the novice about fieldwork, taking field notes, and writing theory (see the discussion of Bateson and Mead in Harper, Chapter 25, this volume). Today this image has been shattered. The works of the classic ethnographers are seen by many as relics of the colonial past (Rosaldo, 1989, p. 44). Although many feel nostalgic about this image, others celebrate its passing. Rosaldo (1989) quotes Cora Du Bois, a retired Harvard anthropology professor, who lamented this passing at a conference in 1980, reflecting on the crisis in anthropology: "[I feel a distance] from the complexity and disarray of what I once found a justifiable and challenging discipline. . . . It has been like moving from a distinguished art museum into a garage sale" (p. 44).

Du Bois regards the classic ethnographies as pieces of timeless artwork, such as those contained in a museum. She detests the chaos of the garage sale, which Rosaldo values: "It [the garage sale] provides a precise image of the postcolonial situation where cultural artifacts flow between unlikely places, and nothing is sacred, permanent, or sealed off. The image of anthropology as a garage sale depicts our present global situation" (p. 44). Old standards no longer hold. Ethnographies do not produce timeless truths. The commitment to objectivism is now in doubt. The complicity with imperialism is openly challenged today, and the belief in monumentalism is a thing of the past.

The legacies of this first period begin at the end of the nineteenth century, when the novel and the social sciences had become distinguished as separate systems of discourse (Clough, 1992, pp. 21-22). However, the Chicago school, with its emphasis on the life story and the "slice-of-life" approach to ethnographic materials, sought to develop an interpretive methodology that maintained the centrality of the narrated life history approach. This led to the production of the texts that gave the researcher-as-author the power to represent the subject's story. Written under the mantle of straightforward, sentiment-free social realism, these texts used the language of ordinary people. They articulated a social science version of literary naturalism, which often produced the sympathetic illusion that a solution to a social problem had been found. Like films about the Depression-era juvenile delinquent and other social problems (Roffman & Purdy, 1981), these accounts romanticized the subject. They turned the deviant into a sociological version of a screen hero. These sociological stories, like their film counterparts, usually had happy endings, as they followed individuals through the three stages of the classic morality tale: existence in a state of grace, seduction by evil and the fall, and finally redemption through suffering.

The Modernist Phase

The modernist phase, or second moment, builds on the canonical works of the traditional period. Social realism, naturalism, and slice-of-life ethnographies are still valued. This phase extended through the postwar years to the 1970s; it is still present in the work of many (see Wolcott, 1992, for a review). In this period many texts attempted to formalize qualitative methods (see, for example, Bogdan & Taylor, 1975; Cicourel, 1964; Filstead, 1970; Glaser & Strauss, 1967; J. Lofland, 1971; Lofland & Lofland, 1984).[7] The modernist ethnographer and sociological participant observer attempted rigorous, qualitative studies of important social processes, including deviance and social control in the classroom and society. This was a moment of creative ferment.

A new generation of graduate students, across the human disciplines, encountered new interpretive theories (ethnomethodology, phenomenology, critical theory, feminism). They were drawn to qualitative research practices that would let them give a voice to society's underclass. Postpositivism functioned as a powerful epistemological paradigm in this moment. Researchers attempted to fit the arguments of Campbell and Stanley (1963) about internal and external validity to constructionist and interactionist models of the research act. They returned to the texts of the Chicago school as sources of inspiration (see Denzin, 1970, 1978).

A canonical text from this moment remains *Boys in White* (Becker et al., 1961). Firmly entrenched in mid-century methodological discourse, this work attempted to make qualitative research as rigorous as its quantitative counterpart. Causal narratives were central to this project. This multimethod work combined open-ended and quasi-structured interviewing with participant observation and the careful analysis of such materials in standardized, statistical form. In a classic article, "Problems of Inference and Proof in Participant Observation," Howard S. Becker (1958/1970) describes the use of quasi-statistics:

> Participant observations have occasionally been gathered in standardized form capable of being transformed into legitimate statistical data. But the exigencies of the field usually prevent the collection of data in such a form to meet the assumptions of statistical tests, so that the observer deals in what have been called "quasi-statistics." His conclusions, while implicitly numerical, do not require precise quantification. (p. 31)

In the analysis of data, Becker notes, the qualitative researcher takes a cue from statistical colleagues. The researcher looks for probabilities or support for arguments concerning the likelihood that, or frequency with which, a conclusion in fact applies in a specific situation. Thus did work in the modernist period clothe itself in the language and rhetoric of positivist and postpositivist discourse.

This was the golden age of rigorous qualitative analysis, bracketed in sociology by *Boys in White* (Becker et al., 1961) at one end and *The Discovery of Grounded Theory* (Glaser & Strauss, 1967) at the other. In education, qualitative research in this period was defined by George and Louise Spindler, Jules Henry, Harry Wolcott, and John Singleton. This form of qualitative research is still present in the work of such persons as Strauss and Corbin (1990) and Miles and Huberman (1993), and is represented in their chapters in this volume.

The "golden age" reinforced a picture of qualitative researchers as cultural romantics. Imbued with Promethean human powers, they valorized villains and outsiders as heroes to mainstream society. They embodied a belief in the contingency of self and society, and held to emancipatory ideals for which "one lives and dies." They put in place a tragic and often ironic view of society and self, and joined a long line of leftist cultural romantics that included Emerson, Marx, James, Dewey, Gramsci, and Martin Luther King, Jr. (West, 1989, chap. 6).

As this moment came to an end, the Vietnam War was everywhere present in American society. In 1969, alongside these political currents, Herbert Blumer and Everett Hughes met with a group of young sociologists called the "Chicago Irregulars" at the American Sociological Association meetings held in San Francisco and shared their memories of the "Chicago years." Lyn Lofland (1980) describes the 1969 meetings as a

> moment of creative ferment—scholarly and political. The San Francisco meetings witnessed not simply the Blumer-Hughes event but a "counter-revolution." . . . a group first came to . . . talk about the problems of being a sociologist and a female. . . . the discipline seemed literally to be bursting with new . . . ideas: labelling theory, ethnomethodology, conflict theory, phenomenology, dramaturgical analysis. (p. 253)

Thus did the modernist phase come to an end.

Blurred Genres

By the beginning of the third stage (1970-1986), which we call the moment of blurred genres, qualitative researchers had a full complement of paradigms, methods, and strategies to employ in their research. Theories ranged from symbolic interactionism to constructivism, naturalistic inquiry, positivism and postpositivism, phenomenology, ethnomethodology, critical (Marxist), semiotics, structuralism, feminism, and various ethnic paradigms. Applied qualitative research was gaining in stature, and the politics and ethics of qualitative research were topics of considerable concern. Research strategies ranged from grounded theory to the case study, to methods of historical, biographical, ethnographic action and clinical research. Diverse ways of collecting and analyzing empirical materials were also available, including qualitative interviewing (open-ended and quasi-structured) and observational, visual, personal experience, and documentary methods. Computers were entering the situation, to be fully developed in the next decade, along with narrative, content, and semiotic methods of reading interviews and cultural texts.

Two books by Geertz, *The Interpretation of Cultures* (1973) and *Local Knowledge* (1983), defined the beginning and end of this moment. In these two works, Geertz argued that the old functional, positivist, behavioral, totalizing approaches to the human disciplines were giving way to a more pluralistic, interpretive, open-ended perspective. This new perspective took cultural representations and their meanings as its point of departure. Calling for "thick description" of particular events, rituals, and customs, Geertz suggested that all anthropological writings were interpretations of interpretations. The observer had no privileged voice in the interpretations that were written. The central task of theory was to make sense out of a local situation.

Geertz went on to propose that the boundaries between the social sciences and the humanities had become blurred. Social scientists were now turning to the humanities for models, theories, and methods of analysis (semiotics, hermeneutics). A form of genre dispersion was occurring: documentaries that read like fiction (Mailer), parables posing as ethnographies (Castañeda), theoretical treatises that look like travelogues (Lévi-Strauss). At the same time, many new approaches were emerging: poststructuralism (Barthes), neopositivism (Philips), neo-Marxism (Althusser), micro-macro descriptivism (Geertz), ritual theories of drama and culture (V. Turner), deconstructionism (Derrida), ethnomethodology (Garfinkel). The golden age of the social sciences was over, and a new age of blurred, interpretive genres was upon us. The essay as an art form was replacing the scientific article. At issue now is the author's presence in the interpretive text, or how the researcher can speak with authority in an age when there are no longer any firm rules concerning the text, its standards of evaluation, and its subject matter (Geertz, 1988).

The naturalistic, postpositivist, and constructionist paradigms gained power in this period, especially in education in the works of Harry Wolcott, Egon Guba, Yvonna Lincoln, Robert Stake, and Elliot Eisner. By the end of the 1970s several qualitative journals were in place, from *Urban Life* (now *Journal of Contemporary Ethnography*) to *Qualitative Sociology, Symbolic Interaction,* and *Studies in Symbolic Interaction.*

Crisis of Representation

A profound rupture occurred in the mid-1980s. What we call the fourth moment, or the crisis of representation, appeared with *Anthropology as Cultural Critique* (Marcus & Fischer, 1986), *The Anthropology of Experience* (Turner & Bruner, 1986), *Writing Culture* (Clifford & Marcus, 1986), *Works and Lives* (Geertz, 1988), and *The Predicament of Culture* (Clifford, 1988). These works made research and writing more reflexive, and called into question the issues of gender, class, and race. They articulated the consequences of Geertz's "blurred genres" interpretation of the field in the early 1980s.

New models of truth and method were sought (Rosaldo, 1989). The erosion of classic norms in anthropology (objectivism, complicity with colonialism, social life structured by fixed rituals and customs, ethnographies as monuments to a culture) was complete (Rosaldo, 1989, pp. 44-45). Critical and feminist epistemologies and epistemologies of color now compete for attention in this arena. Issues such as validity, reliability, and objectivity, which had been settled in earlier phases, are once more problematic. Interpretive theories, as opposed to grounded theories, are now more common, as writers continue to challenge older models of truth and meaning (Rosaldo, 1989).

Stoller and Olkes (1987) describe how the crisis of representation was felt in their fieldwork among the Songhay of Niger. Stoller observes: "When I began to write anthropological texts, I followed the conventions of my training. I 'gathered data,' and once the 'data' were arranged in neat piles, I 'wrote them up.' In one case I reduced Songhay insults to a series of neat logical formulas" (p. 227). Stoller became dissatisfied with this form of writing, in part because he learned "everyone had lied to me and . . . the data I had so painstakingly collected were worthless. I learned a lesson: Informants routinely lie to their anthropologists" (Stoller & Olkes, 1987, p. 229). This discovery led to a second, that he had, in following the conventions of ethnographic realism, edited himself out of his text. This led Stoller to produce a different type of text, a memoir, in which he became a central character in the story he told. This story, an account of his experiences in the Songhay world, became an analysis of the clash between his world and the world of Songhay sorcery. Thus did Stoller's journey represent an attempt to confront the crisis of representation in the fourth moment.

Clough (1992) elaborates this crisis and criticizes those who would argue that new forms of writing represent a way out of it:

> While many sociologists now commenting on the criticism of ethnography view writing as "downright central to the ethnographic enterprise" [Van Maanen, 1988, p. xi], the problems of writing are still viewed as different from the problems of method or fieldwork itself. Thus the solution usually offered is experiments in writing, that is a self-consciousness about writing. (p. 136)

However, it is this insistence on the difference between writing and fieldwork that must be analyzed.

In writing, the field-worker makes a claim to moral and scientific authority. These claims allow the realist and the experimental ethnographic text to function as sources of validation for an empirical science. They show, that is, that the world of real lived experience can still be captured, if only in the writer's memoirs, fictional experimentations, or dramatic readings. These works have the danger of directing attention away from the ways in which the text constructs sexually situated individuals in a field of social difference. They also perpetuate "empirical science's hegemony" (Clough, 1992, p. 8), for these new writing technologies of the subject become the site "for the production of knowledge/power . . . [aligned] with . . . the capital/state axis" (Aronowitz, 1988, p. 300, quoted in Clough, 1992, p. 8). Such experiments come up against, and then back away from, the difference between empirical science and social criticism. Too often they fail to engage fully a new politics of textuality that would "refuse the identity of empirical science" (Clough, 1992, p. 135). This new social criticism "would intervene in the relationship of information economics, nation-state politics, and technologies of mass communication, especially in terms of the empirical sciences" (Clough, 1992, p. 16). This, of course, is the terrain occupied by cultural studies.

Richardson, in Chapter 32 of this volume, and Clandinin and Connelly, in Chapter 26, develop the above arguments, viewing writing as a method of inquiry that moves through successive stages of self-reflection. As a series of writings, the field-worker's texts flow from the field experience, through intermediate works, to later work, and finally to the research text that is the public presentation of the ethnographic and narrative experience. Thus do fieldwork and writing blur into one another. There is, in the final analysis, no difference between writing and fieldwork. These two perspectives inform each other throughout every chapter in this volume. In these ways the crisis of representation moves qualitative research in new, critical directions.

A Double Crisis

The ethnographer's authority remains under assault today. A double crisis of representation and legitimation confronts qualitative researchers in the social sciences. Embedded in the discourses of poststructuralism and postmodernism (Vidich & Lyman, Chapter 2, and Richardson, Chapter 32, this volume), these two crises are coded in multiple terms, variously called and associated with the *interpretive, linguistic,* and *rhetorical* turns in social theory. This linguistic turn makes problematic two key assumptions of qualitative research. The first is that qualitative researchers can directly capture lived experience. Such experience, it is now argued, is created in the social text written by the researcher. This is the representational crisis. It confronts the inescapable problem of representation, but does so within a framework that makes the direct link between experience and text problematic.

The second assumption makes the traditional criteria for evaluating and interpreting qualitative research problematic. This is the legitimation crisis. It involves a serious rethinking of such terms as *validity, generalizability,* and *reliability,* terms already retheorized in postpositivist, constructionist-naturalistic (Lincoln & Guba, 1985, p. 36), feminist (Fonow & Cook, 1991, pp. 1-13; Smith, 1992), and interpretive (Atkinson, 1990; Hammersley, 1992; Lather, 1993) discourses. This crisis asks, How are qualitative studies to be evaluated in the poststructural moment? Clearly these two crises blur together, for any representation must now legitimate itself in terms of some set of criteria that allows the author (and the reader) to make connections between the text and the world written about.

The Fifth Moment

The fifth moment is the present, defined and shaped by the dual crises described above; we shall say a great deal about this moment in our last chapter. Theories are now read in narrative terms, as "tales of the field" (Van Maanen, 1988). Preoccupations with the representation of the "other" remain. New epistemologies from previously silenced groups emerge to offer solutions to this problem. The concept of the aloof researcher has been abandoned. More action-, activist-oriented research is on the horizon, as are more social criticism and social critique. The search for grand narratives will be replaced by more local, small-scale theories fitted to specific problems and specific situations (Lincoln, 1993).

Reading History

We draw four conclusions from this brief history, noting that it is, like all histories, somewhat arbitrary. First, each of the earlier historical moments is still operating in the present, either as legacy or as a set of practices that researchers still follow or argue against. The multiple, and fractured, histories of qualitative research now make it possible for any given researcher to attach a project to a canonical text from any of the above-described historical moments. Multiple criteria of evaluation now compete for attention in this field. Second, an embarrassment of choices now characterizes the field of qualitative research. There have never been so many paradigms, strategies of inquiry, or methods of analysis to draw upon and utilize. Third, we are in a moment of discovery and rediscovery, as new ways of looking, interpreting, arguing, and writing are debated and discussed. Fourth, the qualitative research act can no longer be viewed from within a neutral, or objective, positivist perspective. Class, race, gender, and ethnicity shape the process of inquiry, making research a multicultural process. It is to this topic that we next turn.

Qualitative Research as Process

Three interconnected, generic activities define the qualitative research process. They go by a variety of different labels, including *theory, method* and *analysis,* and *ontology, epistemology,* and *methodology.* Behind these terms stands the personal biography of the gendered researcher, who speaks from a particular class, racial, cultural, and ethnic community perspective. The gendered, multiculturally situated researcher approaches the world with a set of ideas, a framework (theory, ontology) that specifies a set of questions (epistemology) that are then examined (methodology, analysis) in specific ways. That is, empirical materials bearing on the question are collected and then analyzed and written about. Every researcher speaks from within a distinct interpretive community, which configures, in its special way, the multicultural, gendered components of the research act.

In this volume we treat these generic activities under five headings, or phases: the researcher and the researched as multicultural subjects, major paradigms and interpretive perspectives, research strategies, methods of collecting and analyzing empirical materials, and the art of interpretation. Behind all of these phases stands the biographically situated researcher. This individual enters the research process from inside an interpretive community that incorporates its own historical research traditions into a distinct point of view. This perspective leads the researcher to adopt particular views of the "other" who is studied. At the same time, the politics and the ethics of research must also be considered, for these concerns permeate every phase of the research process.

The Other as Research Subject

From its turn-of-the-century birth in modern, interpretive form, qualitative research has been haunted by a double-faced ghost. On the one hand, qualitative researchers have assumed that qualified, competent observers can with objectivity, clarity, and precision report on their own observations of the social world, including the experiences of others. Second, researchers have held to a belief in a real subject, or real individual, who is present in the world and able, in some form, to report on his or her experiences. So armed, researchers could blend their observations with the observations provided by subjects through interviews and life story, personal experience, case study, and other documents.

These two beliefs have led qualitative researchers across disciplines to seek a method that would allow them to record their own observations accurately while still uncovering the meanings their subjects bring to their life experiences. This method would rely upon the subjective verbal and written expressions of meaning given by the individuals studied, these expressions being windows into the inner life of the person. Since Dilthey (1900/ 1976), this search for a method has led to a perennial focus in the human disciplines on qualitative, interpretive methods.

Recently, this position and its beliefs have come under attack. Poststructuralists and postmodernists have contributed to the understanding that there is no clear window into the inner life of an individual. Any gaze is always filtered through the lenses of language, gender, social class, race, and ethnicity. There are no objective observations, only observations socially situated in the worlds of the observer and the observed. Subjects, or individuals, are seldom able to give full explanations of their actions or intentions; all they can offer are accounts, or stories, about what they did and why. No single method can grasp the subtle variations in ongoing human experience. As a consequence, as argued above, qualitative researchers deploy a wide range of interconnected interpretive methods, always seeking better ways to make more understandable the worlds of experience that have been studied.

Table 1.1 depicts the relationships we see among the five headings, or phases, that define the research process. Behind all but one of these phases stands the biographically situated researcher. These five levels of activity, or practice, work their way through the biography of the researcher. We take them up briefly in order here; we discuss the phases more fully in the introductions to the individual parts of this volume.

TABLE 1.1 The Research Process

Phase 1: The Researcher as a Multicultural Subject
history and research traditions
conceptions of self and the other
ethics and politics of research
Phase 2: Theoretical Paradigms and Perspectives
positivism, postpositivism
constructivism
feminism(s)
ethnic models
Marxist models
cultural studies models
Phase 3: Research Strategies
study design
case study
ethnography, participant observation
phenomenology, ethnomethodology
grounded theory
biographical method
historical method
action and applied research
clinical research
Phase 4: Methods of Collection and Analysis
interviewing
observing
artifacts, documents, and records
visual methods
personal experience methods
data management methods
computer-assisted analysis
textual analysis
Phase 5: The Art of Interpretation and Presentation
criteria for judging adequacy
the art and politics of interpretation
writing as interpretation
policy analysis
evaluation traditions
applied research

Phase 1: The Researcher

Our remarks above indicate the depth and complexity of the traditional and applied qualitative research perspectives into which a socially situated researcher enters. These traditions locate the researcher in history, both guiding and constraining work that will be done in any specific study. This field has been characterized constantly by diversity and conflict, and these, David Hamilton argues in Chapter 3 of this volume, are its most enduring traditions. As a carrier of this complex and contradictory history, the researcher must also confront the ethics and politics of research. The age of value-free inquiry for the human disciplines is over, and researchers now struggle to develop situational and transsituational ethics that apply to any given research act.

Phase 2: Interpretive Paradigms

All qualitative researchers are philosophers in that "universal sense in which all human beings . . .

TABLE 1.2 Interpretive Paradigms

Paradigm/Theory	*Criteria*	*Form of Theory*	*Type of Narration*
Positivist/postpositivist	internal, external validity	logical-deductive, scientific, grounded	scientific report
Constructivist	trustworthiness, credibility, transferability, confirmability	substantive-formal	interpretive case studies, ethnographic fiction
Feminist	Afrocentric, lived experience, dialogue, caring, accountability, race, class, gender, reflexivity, praxis, emotion, concrete grounding	critical, standpoint	essays, stories, experimental writing
Ethnic	Afrocentric, lived experience, dialogue, caring, accountability, race, class, gender	standpoint, critical, historical	essays, fables, dramas
Marxist	emancipatory theory, falsifiable, dialogical, race, class, gender	critical, historical, economic	historical, economic, sociocultural analysis
Cultural studies	cultural practices, praxis, social texts, subjectivities	social criticism	cultural theory as criticism

are guided by highly abstract principles" (Bateson, 1972, p. 320). These principles combine beliefs about ontology (What kind of being is the human being? What is the nature of reality?), epistemology (What is the relationship between the inquirer and the known?), and methodology (How do we know the world, or gain knowledge of it?) (see Guba, 1990, p. 18; Lincoln & Guba, 1985, pp. 14-15; see also Guba & Lincoln, Chapter 6, this volume). These beliefs shape how the qualitative researcher sees the world and acts in it. The researcher is "bound within a net of epistemological and ontological premises which—regardless of ultimate truth or falsity—become partially self-validating" (Bateson, 1972, p. 314).

This net that contains the researcher's epistemological, ontological, and methodological premises may be termed a *paradigm* (Guba, 1990, p. 17), or interpretive framework, a "basic set of beliefs that guides action" (Guba, 1990, p. 17). All research is interpretive, guided by a set of beliefs and feelings about the world and how it should be understood and studied. Some of these beliefs may be taken for granted, only assumed; others are highly problematic and controversial. However, each interpretive paradigm makes particular demands on the researcher, including the questions that are asked and the interpretations that are brought to them.

At the most general level, four major interpretive paradigms structure qualitative research: positivist and postpositivist, constructivist-interpretive, critical (Marxist, emancipatory), and feminist-poststructural. These four abstract paradigms become more complicated at the level of concrete specific interpretive communities. At this level it is possible to identify not only the constructivist, but also multiple versions of feminist (Afrocentric and poststructural)[8] as well as specific ethnic, Marxist, and cultural studies paradigms. These perspectives, or paradigms, are examined in Part II of this volume.

The paradigms examined in Part II work against and alongside (and some within) the positivist and postpositivist models. They all work within relativist ontologies (multiple constructed realities), interpretive epistemologies (the knower and known interact and shape one another), and interpretive, naturalistic methods.

Table 1.2 presents these paradigms and their assumptions, including their criteria for evaluating research, and the typical form that an interpretive or theoretical statement assumes in the paradigm.[9] Each paradigm is explored in considerable detail in Part II, by Guba (Chapter 6), Schwandt (Chapter 7), Kincheloe and McLaren (Chapter 8), Olesen (Chapter 9), Stanfield (Chapter 10), and Fiske (Chapter 11). The positivist and postpositivist paradigms have been discussed above. They work from within a realist and critical realist ontology and objective epistemologies, and rely upon experimental, quasi-experimental, survey, and rigorously defined qualitative methodologies. Huberman and Miles (Chapter 27) develop elements of this paradigm.

The constructivist paradigm assumes a relativist ontology (there are multiple realities), a subjectivist epistemology (knower and subject create understandings), and a naturalistic (in the natural world) set of methodological procedures. Findings are usually presented in terms of the criteria of grounded theory (see Strauss & Corbin, Chapter 17, this volume). Terms such as *credibility, transferability, dependability,* and *confirmability* replace the usual positivist criteria of *internal* and *external validity, reliability,* and *objectivity.*

Feminist, ethnic, Marxist, and cultural studies models privilege a materialist-realist ontology; that is, the real world makes a material difference in terms of race, class, and gender. Subjectivist epistemologies and naturalistic methodologies (usually ethnographies) are also employed. Empirical materials and theoretical arguments are evaluated in terms of their emancipatory implications. Criteria from gender and racial communities (e.g., African American) may be applied (emotionality and feeling, caring, personal accountability, dialogue).

Poststructural feminist theories emphasize problems with the social text, its logic, and its inability ever to represent fully the world of lived experience. Positivist and postpositivist criteria of evaluation are replaced by others, including the reflexive, multivoiced text that is grounded in the experiences of oppressed peoples.

The cultural studies paradigm is multifocused, with many different strands drawing from Marxism, feminism, and the postmodern sensibility (Richardson, Chapter 32, this volume). There is a tension between humanistic cultural studies stressing lived experiences and more structural cultural studies projects stressing the structural and material determinants (race, class, gender) of experience. The cultural studies paradigm uses methods strategically, that is, as resources for understanding and for producing resistances to local structures of domination. Cultural studies scholars may do close textual readings and discourse analysis of cultural texts (Fiske, Chapter 11, this volume) as well as local ethnographies, open-ended interviewing, and participant observation. The focus is on how race, class, and gender are produced and enacted in historically specific situations.

Paradigm and history in hand, focused on a concrete empirical problem to examine, the researcher now moves to the next stage of the research process, namely, working with a specific strategy of inquiry.

Phase 3: Strategies of Inquiry and Interpretive Paradigms

Table 1.1 presents some of the major strategies of inquiry a researcher may use. Phase 3 begins with research design, which, broadly conceived, involves a clear focus on the research question, the purposes of the study, "what information most appropriately will answer specific research questions, and which strategies are most effective for obtaining it" (LeCompte & Preissle, 1993, p. 30). A research design describes a flexible set of guidelines that connects theoretical paradigms to strategies of inquiry and methods for collecting empirical material. A research design situates researchers in the empirical world and connects them to specific sites, persons, groups, institutions, and bodies of relevant interpretive material, including documents and archives. A research design also specifies how the investigator will address the two critical issues of representation and legitimation.

A strategy of inquiry comprises a bundle of skills, assumptions, and practices that researchers employ as they move from their paradigm to the empirical world. Strategies of inquiry put paradigms of interpretation into motion. At the same time, strategies of inquiry connect the researcher to specific methods of collecting and analyzing empirical materials. For example, the case study method relies on interviewing, observing, and document analysis. Research strategies implement and anchor paradigms in specific empirical sites, or in specific methodological practices, such as making a case an object of study. These strategies include the case study, phenomenological and ethnomethodological techniques, as well as the use of grounded theory, the biographical, historical, action, and clinical methods. Each of these strategies is connected to a complex literature; each has a separate history, exemplary works, and preferred ways for putting the strategy into motion.

Phase 4: Methods of Collecting and Analyzing Empirical Materials

The researcher has several methods for collecting empirical materials,[10] ranging from the interview to direct observation, to the analysis of artifacts, documents, and cultural records, to the use of visual materials or personal experience. The researcher may also use a variety of different methods of reading and analyzing interviews or cultural texts, including content, narrative, and semiotic strategies. Faced with large amounts of qualitative materials, the investigator seeks ways of managing and interpreting these documents, and here data management methods and computer-assisted models of analysis may be of use. Huberman and Miles, in Chapter 27, and Richards and Richards, in Chapter 28, take up these techniques.

Phase 5: The Art of Interpretation

Qualitative research is endlessly creative and interpretive. The researcher does not just leave the field with mountains of empirical materials and then easily write up his or her findings. Qualitative interpretations are constructed. The researcher first creates a field text consisting of field notes and documents from the field, what Roger Sanjek (1990, p. 386) calls "indexing" and David Plath (1990, p. 374) calls "filework." The writer-as-interpreter moves from this text to a research text: notes and interpretations based on the field text. This text is then re-created as a working interpretive document that contains the writer's initial attempts to make sense out of what he or she has learned. Finally, the writer produces the public text that comes to the reader. This final tale of the field may assume several forms: confessional, realist, impressionistic, critical, formal, literary, analytic, grounded theory, and so on (see Van Maanen, 1988).

The interpretive practice of making sense of one's findings is both artful and political. Multiple criteria for evaluating qualitative research now exist, and those we emphasize stress the situated, relational, and textual structures of the ethnographic experience. There is no single interpretive truth. As we argued earlier, there are multiple interpretive communities, each having its own criteria for evaluating an interpretation.

Program evaluation is a major site of qualitative research, and qualitative researchers can influence social policy in important ways. David Hamilton, in Chapter 3 of this volume, traces the rich history of applied qualitative research in the social sciences. This is the critical site where theory, method, praxis, or action, and policy all come together. Qualitative researchers can isolate target populations, show the immediate effects of certain programs on such groups, and isolate the constraints that operate against policy changes in such settings. Action-oriented and clinically oriented qualitative researchers can also create spaces for those who are studied (the other) to speak. The evaluator becomes the conduit for making such voices heard. Greene, in Chapter 33, and Rist, in Chapter 34, develop these topics.

The Fifth Moment: What Comes Next?

Marcus, in Chapter 35, argues that we are already in the post "post" period—post-poststructuralism, post-postmodernism. What this means for interpretive, ethnographic practices is still not clear, but it is certain that things will never be the same. We are in a new age where messy, uncertain, multivoiced texts, cultural criticism, and new experimental works will become more common, as will more reflexive forms of fieldwork, analysis, and intertextual representation. The subject of our final essay in this volume is this "fifth moment." It is true that, as the poet said, the center cannot hold. We can reflect on what should be at a new center.

Thus we come full circle. The chapters in this volume take the researcher through every phase of the research act. The contributors examine the relevant histories, controversies, and current practices associated with each paradigm, strategy, and method. They also offer projections for the future—where specific paradigms, strategies, or methods will be 10 years from now.

In reading the chapters that follow, it is important to remember that the field of qualitative research is defined by a series of tensions, contradictions, and hesitations. This tension works back and forth between the broad, doubting postmodern sensibility and the more certain, more traditional positivist, postpositivist, and naturalistic conceptions of this project. All of the chapters that follow are caught in and articulate this tension.

Notes

1. Qualitative research has separate and distinguished histories in education, social work, communications, psychology, history, organizational studies, medical science, anthropology, and sociology.

2. Definitions of some of these terms are in order here. *Positivism* asserts that objective accounts of the world can be given. *Postpositivism* holds that only partially objective accounts of the world can be produced, because all methods are flawed. *Structuralism* asserts that any system is made up of a set of oppositional categories embedded in language. *Semiotics* is the science of signs or sign systems—a structuralist project. According to *poststructuralism,* language is an unstable system of referents, thus it is impossible ever to capture completely the meaning of an action, text, or intention. *Postmodernism* is a contemporary sensibility, developing since World War II, that privileges no single authority, method, or paradigm. *Hermeneutics* is an approach to the analysis of texts that stresses how prior understandings and prejudices shape the interpretive process. *Phenomenology* is a complex system of ideas associated with the works of Husserl, Heidegger, Sartre, Merleau-Ponty, and Alfred Schutz. *Cultural studies* is a complex, interdisciplinary field that merges critical theory, feminism, and poststructuralism.

3. According to Weinstein and Weinstein (1991), "The meaning of *bricoleur* in French popular speech is 'someone who works with his (or her) hands and uses devious means compared to those of the craftsman' . . . the *bricoleur* is practical and gets the job done" (p. 161). These authors provide a history of this term, connecting it to the works of the German sociologist and social theorist Georg Simmel and, by implication, Baudelaire.

4. Here it is relevant to make a distinction between techniques that are used across disciplines and methods that are used within disciplines. Ethnomethodologists, for example, employ their approach as a method, whereas others selectively borrow that method as a technique for their own applications. Harry Wolcott (personal communication, 1993) suggests this distinction. It is also relevant to make distinctions among topic, method, and resource. Methods can be studied as topics of inquiry—for instance, how a case study gets done. In this ironic, ethnomethodological sense, method is both a resource and a topic of inquiry.

5. Indeed, any attempt to give an essential definition of qualitative research requires a qualitative analysis of the circumstances that produce such a definition.

6. In this sense all research is qualitative, because "the observer is at the center of the research process" (Vidich & Lyman, Chapter 2, this volume).

7. See Lincoln and Guba (1985) for an extension and elaboration of this tradition in the mid-1980s.

8. Olesen (Chapter 9, this volume) identifies three strands of feminist research: mainstream empirical, standpoint and cultural studies, and poststructural, postmodern, placing Afrocentric and other models of color under the cultural studies and postmodern categories.

9. These, of course, are our interpretations of these paradigms and interpretive styles.

10. *Empirical materials* is the preferred term for what are traditionally described as data.

References

Aronowitz, S. (1988). *Science as power: Discourse and ideology in modern society.* Minneapolis: University of Minnesota Press.

Atkinson, P. (1990). *The ethnographic imagination: Textual constructions of reality.* London: Routledge.

Bateson, G. (1972). *Steps to an ecology of mind.* New York: Ballantine.

Becker, H. S. (1970). Problems of inference and proof in participant observation. In H. S. Becker, *Sociological work.* Chicago: Aldine. (Reprinted from *American Sociological Review,* 1958, *23,* 652-660)

Becker, H. S. (1986). *Doing things together.* Evanston, IL: Northwestern University Press.

Becker, H. S. (1989). Tricks of the trade. *Studies in Symbolic Interaction, 10,* 481-490.

Becker, H. S. (1993, June 9). *The epistemology of qualitative research.* Paper presented at the MacArthur Foundation Conference on Ethnographic Approaches to the Study of Human Behavior, Oakland, CA.

Becker, H. S., Geer, B., Hughes, E. C., & Strauss, A. L. (1961). *Boys in white: Student culture in medical school.* Chicago: University of Chicago Press.

Bogdan, R., & Taylor, S. J. (1975). *Introduction to qualitative research methods: A phenomenological approach to the social sciences.* New York: John Wiley.

Brewer, J., & Hunter, A. (1989). *Multimethod research: A synthesis of styles.* Newbury Park, CA: Sage.

Campbell, D. T., & Stanley, J. C. (1963). *Experimental and quasi-experimental designs for research.* Chicago: Rand McNally.

Carey, J. W. (1989). *Communication as culture: Essays on media and society.* Boston: Unwin Hyman.

Cicourel, A. V. (1964). *Method and measurement in sociology.* New York: Free Press.

Clifford, J. (1988). *The predicament of culture: Twentieth-century ethnography, literature, and art.* Cambridge, MA: Harvard University Press.

Clifford, J., & Marcus, G. E. (Eds.). (1986). *Writing culture: The poetics and politics of ethnography.* Berkeley: University of California Press.

Clough, P. T. (1992). *The end(s) of ethnography: From realism to social criticism.* Newbury Park, CA: Sage.

Denzin, N. K. (1970). *The research act.* Chicago: Aldine.

Denzin, N. K. (1978). *The research act* (2nd ed.). New York: McGraw-Hill.

Denzin, N. K. (1989a). *Interpretive interactionism.* Newbury Park, CA: Sage.

Denzin, N. K. (1989b). *The research act* (3rd ed.). Englewood Cliffs, NJ: Prentice Hall.

Dilthey, W. L. (1976). *Selected writings.* Cambridge: Cambridge University Press. (Original work published 1900)

Fielding, N. G., & Fielding, J. L. (1986). *Linking data.* Beverly Hills, CA: Sage.

Filstead, W. J. (Ed.). (1970). *Qualitative methodology.* Chicago: Markham.

Flick, U. (1992). Triangulation revisited: Strategy of validation or alternative? *Journal for the Theory of Social Behaviour, 22,* 175-198.

Fonow, M. M., & Cook, J. A. (1991). Back to the future: A look at the second wave of feminist epistemology and methodology. In M. M. Fonow & J. A. Cook (Eds.), *Beyond methodology: Feminist scholarship as lived research* (pp. 1-15). Bloomington: Indiana University Press.

Geertz, C. (1973). *The interpretation of cultures: Selected essays.* New York: Basic Books.

Geertz, C. (1983). *Local knowledge: Further essays in interpretive anthropology.* New York: Basic Books.

Geertz, C. (1988). *Works and lives: The anthropologist as author.* Stanford, CA: Stanford University Press.

Glaser, B. G. (1992). *Emergence vs. forcing: Basics of grounded theory.* Mill Valley, CA: Sociology Press.

Glaser, B. G., & Strauss, A. L. (1967). *The discovery of grounded theory: Strategies for qualitative research.* Chicago: Aldine.

Guba, E. G. (1990). The alternative paradigm dialog. In E. G. Guba (Ed.), *The paradigm dialog* (pp. 17-30). Newbury Park, CA: Sage.

Hammersley, M. (1992). *What's wrong with ethnography? Methodological explorations.* London: Routledge.

Hymes, D. (1980). Educational ethnology. *Anthropology and Education Quarterly, 11,* 3-8.

Lather, P. (1993). Fertile obsession: Validity after poststructuralism. *Sociological Quarterly, 34*(4), 673-693.

LeCompte, M. D., & Preissle, J. (1992). Toward an ethnology of student life in schools and classrooms: Synthesizing the qualitative research tradition. In M. D. LeCompte, W. L. Millroy, & J. Preissle (Eds.), *The handbook of qualitative research in education* (pp. 815-859). New York: Academic Press.

LeCompte, M. D., & Preissle, J., with Tesch, R. (1993). *Ethnography and qualitative design in educational research* (2nd ed.). New York: Academic Press.

Lentricchia, F., & McLaughlin, T. (Eds.). (1990). *Critical terms for literary study.* Chicago: University of Chicago Press.

Lévi-Strauss, C. (1966). *The savage mind* (2nd ed.). Chicago: University of Chicago Press.

Lincoln, Y. S. (1993, January 27-28). *Notes toward a fifth generation of evaluation: Lessons from the voiceless, or, Toward a postmodern politics of evaluation.* Paper presented at the Fifth Annual Meeting of the Southeast Evaluation Association, Tallahassee, FL.

Lincoln, Y. S., & Guba, E. G. (1985). *Naturalistic inquiry.* Beverly Hills, CA: Sage.

Lofland, J. (1971). *Analyzing social settings: A guide to qualitative observation and analysis.* Belmont, CA: Wadsworth.

Lofland, J., & Lofland, L. H. (1984). *Analyzing social settings: A guide to qualitative observation and analysis* (2nd ed.). Belmont, CA: Wadsworth.

Lofland, L. (1980). The 1969 Blumer-Hughes talk. *Urban Life, 8,* 248-260.

Malinowski, B. (1948). *Magic, science and religion, and other essays.* New York: Natural History Press. (Original work published 1916)

Malinowski, B. (1967). *A diary in the strict sense of the term.* New York: Harcourt Brace.

Marcus, G., & Fischer, M. (1986). *Anthropology as cultural critique: An experimental moment in the human sciences.* Chicago: University of Chicago Press.

Miles, M. B., & Huberman, A. M. (1993). *Qualitative data analysis: A sourcebook of new methods* (2nd ed.). Newbury Park, CA: Sage.

Nelson, C., Treichler, P. A., & Grossberg, L. (1992). Cultural studies. In L. Grossberg, C. Nelson, & P. A. Treichler (Eds.), *Cultural studies* (pp. 1-16). New York: Routledge.

Nichols, B. (Ed.). (1985). *Movies and methods* (Vol. 2). Berkeley: University of California Press.

Plath, D. (1990). Fieldnotes, filed notes, and the conferring of note. In R. Sanjek (Ed.), *Fieldnotes: The makings of anthropology* (pp. 371-384). Albany: State University of New York Press.

Richardson, L. (1991). Postmodern social theory. *Sociological Theory, 9,* 173-179.

Roffman, P., & Purdy, J. (1981). *The Hollywood social problem film.* Bloomington: Indiana University Press.

Rosaldo, R. (1989). *Culture and truth: The remaking of social analysis.* Boston: Beacon.

Sanjek, R. (Ed.). (1990). *Fieldnotes: The makings of anthropology.* Albany: State University of New York Press.

Smith, D. (1992). Sociology from women's perspective: A reaffirmation. *Sociological Theory, 10,* 88-97.

Spindler, G., & Spindler, L. (1992). Cultural process and ethnography: An anthropological perspective. In M. D. LeCompte, W. L. Millroy, & J. Preissle (Eds.), *The handbook of qualitative research in education* (pp. 53-92). New York: Academic Press.

Stoller, P., & Olkes, C. (1987). *In sorcery's shadow: A memoir of apprenticeship among the Songhay of Niger.* Chicago: University of Chicago Press.

Strauss, A. L., & Corbin, J. (1990). *Basics of qualitative research: Grounded theory procedures and techniques.* Newbury Park, CA: Sage.

Turner, V., & Bruner, E. (Eds.). (1986). *The anthropology of experience.* Urbana: University of Illinois Press.

Van Maanen, J. (1988). *Tales of the field: On writing ethnography.* Chicago: University of Chicago Press.

West, C. (1989). *The American evasion of philosophy.* Madison: University of Wisconsin Press.

Weinstein, D., & Weinstein, M. A. (1991). Georg Simmel: Sociological flaneur bricoleur. *Theory, Culture & Society, 8,* 151-168.

Wolcott, H. F. (1992). Posturing in qualitative research. In M. D. LeCompte, W. L. Millroy, & J. Preissle (Eds.), *The handbook of qualitative research in education* (pp. 3-52). New York: Academic Press.

PART I
LOCATING THE FIELD

This part of the *Handbook* begins with history and the socially situated observer, and then turns to the ethics and politics of qualitative research.

History and Tradition

Chapter 2, by Arthur Vidich and Stanford Lyman, and Chapter 3, by David Hamilton, reveal the depth and complexity of the traditional and applied qualitative research perspectives that are consciously and unconsciously inherited by the researcher-as-*bricoleur.*[1] These traditions locate the investigator in history, both guiding and constraining work that will be done in any specific study. They are part of his or her tool kit.

Vidich and Lyman show how the ethnographic tradition extends from the Greeks through the fifteenth- and sixteenth-century interests of Westerners in the origins of primitive cultures, to colonial ethnology connected to the empires of Spain, England, France, and Holland, to several twentieth-century transformations in the United States and Europe. Throughout this history the users of qualitative research have displayed commitments to a small set of beliefs, including objectivism, the desire to contextualize experience, and a willingness to interpret theoretically what has been observed. These beliefs supplement the positivist tradition of complicity with colonialism, commitment to monumentalism, and production of timeless texts discussed in Chapter 1. Recently, of course, as we noted, these beliefs have come under attack.

Hamilton complicates this situation in his examination of applied qualitative research traditions. He begins with Evelyn Jacob's important, but contested, fivefold division of qualitative research traditions (ecological psychology, holistic ethnography, ethnography of communication, cognitive anthropology, symbolic interaction), noting that the history of this approach is several centuries old. The desire to chart and change the course of human history extends back to the ancient Greeks. Hamilton then offers a history of applied research traditions extending from Descartes to the work of Kant, Engels, Dilthey, Booth, and Webb to the Chicago school, and finally to Habermas. This history is not linear and straightforward. It is more like a diaspora, a story of the dispersion and migration of ideas from one spot to another, one thinker to another. Hamilton suggests that this area of inquiry has constantly been characterized by diversity and conflict, and that these are its most enduring traditions.

However, Hamilton notes that in the contemporary period at least three propositions organize applied research: Late twentieth-century democracies should empower all citizens; liberal social practice can never be morally neutral; and research cannot be separated from action and practice. These propositions organize much of action research, the topic of Peter Reason's contribution to this volume (Chapter 20). It is no longer the case that researchers can choose which side they are on, for sides have already been taken (Becker, 1967).

Situating the Other and the Ethics of Inquiry

The contributions of Michelle Fine (Chapter 4) and Maurice Punch (Chapter 5) can be easily fitted to this discussion. Fine argues that a great deal of qualitative research has reproduced a colonizing discourse of the "Other"; that is, the Other is interpreted through the eyes and cultural standards of the researcher. Fine reviews the traditions that have led researchers to speak on behalf of the Other, especially those connected to the belief systems identified by Lyman, Vidich, and Rosaldo. She then examines a set of postmodern texts that interrupt this process. (This theme is elaborated in the Richardson and Marcus chapters at the end of this volume.)

Punch examines the problems of betrayal, deception, and harm in qualitative research. These are problems directly connected to a deception model of ethical practice (see below). Punch argues for a commonsense, collaborative social science research model that makes the researcher responsible to those studied. This perspective supplements recent critical, action, and feminist traditions that forcefully align the ethics of research with a politics of the oppressed. Punch can be easily located within the contextualized-consequentialist model outlined below.

Five Ethical Positions

Clearly, all researchers, as Punch and Fine argue, must immediately confront the ethics and politics of empirical inquiry. Qualitative researchers continue to struggle with the establishment of a set of ethical standards that will guide their research (see Deyhle, Hess, & LeCompte, 1992). Historically, and most recently, one of five ethical stances (absolutist, consequentialist, feminist, relativist, deceptive) has been followed; often these stances merge with one another.

The *absolutist stance* argues that social scientists have no right to invade the privacy of others. Thus disguised research is unethical. However, social scientists have a responsibility to contribute to a society's self-understanding. Any method that contributes to this understanding is thereby justified. However, because invasions of privacy can cause harm, social scientists should study only those behaviors and experiences that occur in the public sphere.

The absolutist model stands in sharp contrast to the *deception model,* which endorses investigative voyeurism in the name of science, truth, and understanding (see Douglas, 1976, chap. 8; see also Mitchell, 1993).[2] In this model the researcher uses any method necessary to obtain greater and deeper understanding in a situation. This may involve telling lies, deliberately misrepresenting oneself, duping others, setting people up, using adversarial interviewing techniques, building friendly trust, and infiltrating settings. These techniques are justified, proponents of this position argue, because frequently people in power, like those out of power, will attempt to hide the truth from the researcher.

The *relativist stance* assumes that researchers have absolute freedom to study what they see fit, but they should study only those problems that flow directly from their own experiences. Agenda setting is determined by personal biography, not by some larger scientific community. The only reasonable ethical standard, accordingly, is the one dictated by the individual's conscience. The relativist stance argues that no single set of ethical standards can be developed, because each situation encountered requires a different ethical stance (see Denzin, 1989, pp. 261-264). However, the researcher is directed to build open, sharing relationships with those investigated, and thus this framework is connected to the feminist and consequentialist models.

Guba and Lincoln (1989, pp. 120-141) review the traditional arguments supporting the absolutist position. Professional scholarly societies and federal law mandate four areas of ethical concern, involving the protection of subjects from harm (physical and psychological), deception, and loss of privacy. Informed consent is presumed to protect the researcher from charges that harm, deception, and invasion of privacy have occurred. Guba and Lincoln analyze the weaknesses of each of these claims, challenging the warrant of science to create conditions that invade private spaces, dupe subjects, and challenge subjects' sense of moral worth and dignity.

Lincoln and Guba (1989) call for an empowering, educative ethic that joins researchers and subjects together in an open, collegial relationship. In such a model deception is removed, and threats of harm and loss of privacy operate as barriers that cannot be crossed.

The *contextualized-consequentialist model* (House, 1990; Smith, 1990) builds on four principles (principles compatible with those espoused by Lincoln and Guba): mutual respect, noncoercion and nonmanipulation, the support of democratic values and institutions, and the belief that every research act implies moral and ethical decisions that are contextual. Every ethical decision, that is, affects others, with immediate and long-range consequences. These consequences involve personal values held by the researcher and those studied. The consequentialist model requires the researcher to build relationships of respect and trust that are noncoercive and that are not based on deception.

The consequentialist model elaborates a feminist ethic that calls for collaborative, trusting, nonoppressive relationships between researchers and those studied (Fonow & Cook, 1991, pp. 8-9). Such a model presumes that investigators are committed to an ethic that stresses personal accountability, caring, the value of individual expressiveness, the capacity for empathy, and the sharing of emotionality (Collins, 1990, p. 216). This is the position we endorse.

Notes

1. Any distinction between applied and nonapplied qualitative research traditions is somewhat arbitrary. Both traditions are scholarly; both have long traditions and long histories, and both carry basic implications for theory and social change. Good nonapplied research should also have applied relevance and implications. On occasion, it is argued that applied research is nontheoretical, but even this conclusion can be disputed, as Peter Reason demonstrates in Chapter 20 of this volume.

2. Mitchell does not endorse deception as a research practice, but points to its inevitability in human (especially research) interactions.

References

Becker, H. S. (1967). Whose side are we on? *Social Problems, 14,* 239-248.

Collins, P. H. (1990). *Black feminist thought: Knowledge, consciousness and the politics of empowerment.* New York: Routledge.

Denzin, N. K. (1989). *The research act* (3rd ed.). Englewood Cliffs, NJ: Prentice Hall.

Deyhle, D. L., Hess, G. A., Jr., & LeCompte, M. D. (1992). Approaching ethical issues for qualitative researchers in education. In M. D. LeCompte, W. L. Millroy, & J. Preissle (Eds.), *The handbook of qualitative research in education* (pp. 597-641). New York: Academic Press.

Douglas, J. D. (1976). *Investigative social research.* Beverly Hills, CA: Sage.

Fonow, M. M., & Cook, J. A. (1991). Back to the future: A look at the second wave of feminist epistemology and methodology. In M. M. Fonow & J. A. Cook (Eds.), *Beyond methodology: Feminist scholarship as lived research* (pp. 1-15). Bloomington: Indiana University Press.

Guba, E. G., & Lincoln, Y. S. (1989). *Fourth generation evaluation.* Newbury Park, CA: Sage.

House, E. R. (1990). An ethics of qualitative field studies. In E. G. Guba (Ed.), *The paradigm dialog* (pp. 158-164). Newbury Park, CA: Sage.

Lincoln, Y. S., & Guba, E. G. (1989). Ethics: The failure of positivist science. *Review of Higher Education, 12,* 221-241.

Mitchell, R. J., Jr. (1993). *Secrecy and fieldwork.* Newbury Park, CA: Sage.

Smith, L. M. (1990). Ethics, field studies, and the paradigm crisis. In E. G. Guba (Ed.), *The paradigm dialog* (pp. 139-157). Newbury Park, CA: Sage.

2

■

Qualitative Methods

Their History in Sociology and Anthropology

ARTHUR J. VIDICH
STANFORD M. LYMAN

MODERN sociology has taken as its mission the analysis and understanding of the patterned conduct and social processes of society, and of the bases in values and attitudes on which individual and collective participation in social life rests. It is presupposed that, to carry out the tasks associated with this mission, the sociologist has the following:

1. The ability to perceive and contextualize the world of his or her own experience as well as the capacity to project a metaempirical conceptualization onto those contexts of life and social institutions with which he or she has not had direct experience. The sociologist requires a sensitivity to and a curiosity about both what is visible and what is not visible to immediate perception—and sufficient self-understanding to make possible an empathy with the roles and values of others.
2. The ability to detach him- or herself from the particular values and special interests of organized groups in order that he or she may gain a level of understanding that does not rest on a priori commitments. For every individual and group, ideologies and faiths define the distinction between good and evil and lead to such nonsociological but conventional orientations as are involved in everyday judging and decision making. The sociologist's task in ethnography is not only to be a part of such thoughts and actions but also to understand them at a higher level of conceptualization.
3. A sufficient degree of social and personal distance from prevailing norms and values to be able to analyze them objectively. Usually, the ability to engage in self-objectification is sufficient to produce the quality of orientation necessary for an individual to be an ethnographic sociologist or anthropologist.

Qualitative ethnographic social research, then, entails an attitude of detachment toward society that permits the sociologist to observe the conduct of self and others, to understand the mechanisms of social processes, and to comprehend and explain why both actors and processes are as they are. The existence of this sociological attitude is presupposed in any meaningful discussion of methods appropriate to ethnographic investigation (see

Adler, Adler, & Fontana, 1991; Hammersley, 1992).

Sociology and anthropology are disciplines that, born out of concern to understand the "other," are nevertheless also committed to an understanding of the self. If, following the tenets of symbolic interactionism, we grant that the other can be understood only as part of a relationship with the self, we may suggest a different approach to ethnography and the use of qualitative methods, one that conceives the observer as possessing a self-identity that by definition is re-created in its relationship with the observed—the other, whether in another culture or that of the observer.

In its entirety, the research task requires both the act of observation and the act of communicating the analysis of these observations to others (for works describing how this is accomplished, see Johnson, 1975; Schatzman & Strauss, 1973; see also Pratt, 1986). The relationships that arise between these processes are not only the determinants of the character of the final research product, but also the arena of sociological methods least tractable to conventionalized understanding. The data gathering process can never be described in its totality because these "tales of the field" are themselves part of an ongoing social process that in its minute-by-minute and day-to-day experience defies recapitulation. To take as one's objective the making of a total description of the method of gathering data would shift the frame of ethnological reference, in effect substituting the means for the end. Such a substitution occurs when exactitude in reporting research methods takes priority over the solution to substantive sociological problems.

In fact, a description of a particular method of research usually takes place as a retrospective account, that is, a report written after the research has been completed. This all-too-often unacknowledged fact illustrates the part of the research process wherein the acts of observation are temporally separated from the description of how they were accomplished. Such essays in methodology are reconstructions of ethnographic reality; they take what was experienced originally and shrink it into a set of images that, although purporting to be a description of the actual method of research, exemplify a textbook ideal.

The point may be clarified through a comparison of the world of a supposedly "scientific" sociologist with that of such artists as painters, novelists, composers, poets, dancers, or chess masters. Viewing a painting, listening to music, reading a novel, reciting a poem, watching a chess game, or attending to the performance of a ballerina, one experiences a finished production, the "front region," as Goffman (1959, p. 107) puts it. The method seems to be inherent in the finished form (Goffman, 1949, pp. 48-77). More appropriately, we might say that the method—of composing, writing, painting, performing, or whatever—is an intrinsic part of the creator's craftsmanship, without which the creation could not be made. If the artist were to be asked, "How did you do it? Tell me your method," his or her answer would require an act of ex post facto reconstruction: the method of describing the method. However, the original production would still retain its primordial integrity; that cannot be changed, whatever conclusions are to be drawn from later discussions about how it was accomplished. Speaking of sociological methods, Robert Nisbet (1977) recalls:

> While I was engaged in exploration of some of the sources of modern sociology [it occurred to me] that none of the great themes which have provided continuing challenge and also theoretical foundation for sociologists during the last century was ever reached through anything resembling what we are to-day fond of identifying as "scientific method." I mean the kind of method, replete with appeals to statistical analysis, problem design, hypothesis, verification, replication, and theory construction, that we find described in textbooks and courses on methodology. (p. 3)

From Nisbet's pointed observation we may conclude that the method-in-use for the production of a finished sociological study is unique to that study and can be neither described nor replicated as it actually occurred. That societal investigators may choose to use different kinds of material as their data—documents for the historian, quantified reports for the demographer, or direct perception of a portion of society for the ethnographer—does not alter the fact that social scientists are observers. As observers of the world they also participate in it; therefore, they make their observations within a mediated framework, that is, a framework of symbols and cultural meanings given to them by those aspects of their life histories that they bring to the observational setting. Lurking behind each method of research is the personal equation supplied to the setting by the individual observer (Clifford, 1986). In this fundamental sense all research methods are at bottom qualitative and are, for that matter, equally objective; the use of quantitative data or mathematical procedures does not eliminate the intersubjective element that underlies social research. Objectivity resides not in a method, per se, but in the framing of the research problem and the willingness of the researchers to pursue that problem wherever the data and their hunches may lead (Vidich, 1955; see also Fontana, 1980; Goffman, 1974).[1] If, in this sense, all research is qualitative—because the observer is at the center of the research process—does this mean that the findings produced by the method are no more than the peculiar reality of each observer (Atkinson, 1990)?

One simple answer is that we judge for ourselves on the standard of whether the work communicates or "says" something to us—that is, does it connect with our reality?[2] Does it provide us with insights that help to organize our own observations? Does it resonate with our image of the world? Or does it provide such a powerful incursion on the latter that we feel compelled to re-examine what we have long supposed to be true about our life world?

Or, put another way, if the method used is not the issue, by what standards are we able to judge the worth of sociological research (Gellner, 1979)? Each is free to judge the work of others and to accept it or reject it if it does not communicate something meaningful about the world; and what is meaningful for one person is not necessarily meaningful for another.

In the present and for the foreseeable future, the virtually worldwide disintegration of common values and a deconstruction of consensus-based societies evoke recognition of the fact that there exist many competing realities, and this fact poses problems not previously encountered by sociology. In effect, this situation sets up a condition wherein the number of possible theoretical perspectives from which the world, or any part of it, may be viewed sociologically is conditioned only by the number of extant scientific worldviews. As for the potential subjects of investigation, their outlooks are limited only by the many religious faiths, occupational and professional ideologies, and other *Weltanschauungen* that arise to guide or upset their lives. At the time of this writing, a new outlook on epistemology has come to the fore. It disprivileges all received discourses and makes discourse itself a topic of the sociology of knowledge.[3]

The history of qualitative research suggests that this has not always been the case (Douglas, 1974). In the past, the research problems for many investigators were given to them by their commitment to or against a religious faith or an ethnic creed, or by their identification with or opposition to specific national goals or socioeconomic programs. In the historical account of the use of qualitative methods that follows, we shall show that their use has been occasioned by more than the perspective of the individual observer, but also that the domain assumptions that once guided qualitative research have lost much of their force. However, the faiths, creeds, and hopes that had given focus to the work of our predecessors have not disappeared altogether from the sociologist's mental maps (Luhmann, 1986). Rather, they remain as a less-than-conscious background, the all-too-familiar furniture of the sociological mind. Milan Kundera (1988) has pointed to a central issue in our present dilemma in *The Art of the Novel*: "But if God is gone and man is no longer the master, then who is the master? The planet is moving through the void without any master. There it is, the unbearable lightness of being" (p. 41).

Throughout all of the eras during which social science made use of observational methods, researchers have entered into their studies with problems implicitly and, in some cases, explicitly defined by hopes and faiths. Focusing on the substance of these problems and their ideational adumbrations, we shall confine our discussion of this history to the qualitative methods used by anthropologists and sociologists in ethnographic research, that is, the direct observation of the social realities by the individual observer. Our history proceeds along a continuum that begins with the first encounters of early ethnographers with the New World and ends with the practical and theoretical problems facing the work of our contemporaries.

Early Ethnography: The Discovery of the Other

Ethnos, a Greek term, denotes a people, a race or cultural group (A. D. Smith, 1989, pp. 13-18). When *ethno* as a prefix is combined with *graphic* to form the term *ethnographic,* the reference is to the subdiscipline known as descriptive anthropology—in its broadest sense, the science devoted to describing ways of life of humankind. *Ethnography,* then, refers to a social scientific description of a people and the cultural basis of their peoplehood (Peacock, 1986). Both descriptive anthropology and ethnography are thought to be atheoretical, to be concerned solely with description. However, the observations of the ethnographer are always guided by world images that determine which data are salient and which are not: An act of attention to one rather than another object reveals one dimension of the observer's value commitment, as well as his or her value-laden interests.

Early ethnography grew out of the interests of Westerners in the origins of culture and civilization and in the assumption that contemporary "primitive" peoples, those thought by Westerners to be less civilized than themselves, were, in effect, living replicas of the "great chain of being" that linked the Occident to its prehistoric beginnings (Hodgen, 1964, pp. 386-432). Such a mode of ethnography arose in the fifteenth and sixteenth centuries as a result of fundamental problems that had grown out of Columbus's and later explorers' voyages to the Western hemisphere, the so-called New World, and to the island cultures of the South Seas.

The discovery of human beings living in non-Occidental environments evoked previously unimagined cosmological difficulties for European intellectuals, who felt it necessary to integrate the new fact into the canon of received knowledge and understanding.[4] Because the Bible, especially the book of Genesis, was taken to be the only valid source on which to rely for an understanding of the history of geography and processes of creation, and because it placed the origin of humankind in the Garden of Eden—located somewhere in what is today called the Middle East—all human beings were held to be descended from the first pair, and, later, in accordance with flood ethnography (Numbers, 1992) from the descendants of Noah and his family, the only survivors of a worldwide deluge. Linking Columbus's encounter with what we now know as the Taino, Arawak, and Carib (Keegan, 1992; Rouse, 1992) peoples in the New World to the biblical account proved to be difficult. Specifically, the existence of others outside the Christian brotherhood revealed by his "discovery" posed this question: How had the ancestors of these beings reached the Americas in pre-Columbian times? Any thesis that they had not migrated from Eurasia or Africa was held to be heresy and a claim that humankind might have arisen from more than one creative act by God.

In general, the racial and cultural diversity of peoples throughout the globe presented post-Renaissance Europeans with the problem of how to account for the origins, histories, and development of a multiplicity of races, cultures, and civilizations (see Baker, 1974; Barkan, 1992; Trinkhaus & Shipman, 1993). Not only was it necessary for the cosmologist to account for the disconcerting existence of the "other,"[5] but such a scholar was obliged to explain how and why such differences in the moral values of Europeans and these "others" had arisen. In effect, such a profusion of values, cultures, and ways of life challenged the monopolistic claim on legitimacy and truth of the doctrines of Christianity. Such practices as infanticide, cannibalism, human sacrifice, and what at first appeared as promiscuity reopened the problem of contradictions among cultural values and the inquiry into how these contradictions might be both explained and resolved (Oakes, 1938).

These issues of value conflicts were conflated with practical questions about the recruitment, organization, and justification for the division of labor in the Spanish settlements in the Americas, and these confusions are to be found in the debates of Bartolome de Las Casas with Juan Gines de Sepulveda at the Council of Valladolid. Sepulveda, "who used Aristotle's doctrine of natural slavery in order to legitimize Spanish behavior against the Indians" (Hosle, 1992, p. 238) in effect won the day against Las Casas, who insisted that the peoples we now call Native Americans were "full fellow human beings, possessing valid traditions, dignity and rights" (Marty, 1992, p. xiii). Today, despite or perhaps because of the new recognition of cultural diversity, the tension between universalistic and relativistic values remains an unresolved conundrum for the Western ethnographer (Hosle, 1992).[6] In practice, it becomes this question: By which values are observations to be guided? The choices seem to be either the values of the ethnographer or the values of the observed—that is, in modern parlance, either the *etic* or the *emic* (Pike, 1967; for an excellent discussion, see Harré, 1980, pp. 135-137). Herein lies a deeper and more fundamental problem: How is it possible to understand the other when the other's values are not one's own? This problem arises to plague ethnography at a time when Western Christian values are no longer a surety of truth and, hence, no longer the benchmark from which self-confidently valid observations can be made.

Colonial Mentalities and the Persistence of the Other

Before the professionalization of ethnography, descriptions and evaluations of the races and cultures of the world were provided by Western missionaries, explorers, buccaneers, and colonial administrators. Their reports, found in church, national, and local archives throughout the world and, for the most part, not known to contemporary ethnologists, were written from the perspective of, or by the representatives of, a conquering civilization, confident in its mission to civilize the world (for pertinent discussion of this issue, see Ginsburg, 1991, 1993). Some of the seventeenth-, eighteenth-, and nineteenth-century explorers, missionaries, and administrators have provided thick descriptions of those practices of the "primitives" made salient to the observer by his Christian value perspective.[7] For societies studied by these observers (see, for example, Degerando, 1800/1969), the author's ethnographic report is a reversed mirror image of his own ethnocultural ideal. That these early ethnographies reveal as much about the West as about their objects of study may explain why they have not been recovered and reanalyzed by contemporary anthropologists: Present-day ethnographers hope to separate themselves from the history of Western conquest and reject the earlier ethnographies as hopelessly biased (see "Symposium on Qualitative Methods," 1993). Recently they have begun to take seriously the accounts the natives have given of their Western "discoverers" and to "decenter" or "disprivilege" the reports presented by the latter (Abeyesekere, 1992; Salmond, 1991; Todorov, 1984).

A rich resource, through which one can discern the effects that this early ethnographic literature had on the subjugation of these peoples, is to be found in the works of latter-day colonial administrators (e.g., Olivier, 1911/1970). Ethnology arose out of the reports written by administrators of the long-maintained seaborne empires of the Spanish, English, French, and Dutch (Maunier, 1949). These empires provided opportunities for amateur and, later, professional ethnologists not only to examine hosts of "native" cultures,[8] but also to administer the conditions of life affecting the "cultural advancement" of peoples over whom their metropole exercised domination (Gray, 1911/1970, pp. 79-85). In respect to the seaborne empires, European interest was often confined to exploiting the labor power of the natives, utilizing their territory for extractive industry and/or establishing it in terms of the strategic military advantage it provided them in their struggles against imperialist rivals (for some representative examples, see Aldrich, 1990; Boxer, 1965; Duffy, 1968; Gullick, 1956; Suret-Canale, 1988a, 1988b). Hence the anthropology that developed under colonial administrators tended toward disinterest in the acculturation of the natives and encouragement for the culturally preservative effects of indirect rule. Their approach came to be called pluralistic development (M. G. Smith, 1965). Colonial pluralism left the natives more or less under the authority of their own indigenous leaders so long as these leaders could be co-opted in support of the limited interests of the colonial administration (Lugard, 1922/1965). This tendency led to the creation of a market economy at the center of colonial society (Boeke, 1946; Furnivall, 1956) surrounded by a variety of local culture groups (Boeke, 1948), some of whose members were drawn willy-nilly into the market economy and suffered the effects of marginalized identity (Sachs, 1947).

Ethnographers who conducted their field studies in colonialized areas were divided with respect to their attitudes toward cultural and/or political nationalism and self-determination. A few became champions of ethnocultural liberation and anticolonial revolt. Some respected the autonomy of the traditional culture and opposed any tendency among natives in revolt against colonialism to seek further modernization of their lifestyles. The latter, some of whom were Marxists, admired the anticolonial movement but were concerned to see that the natives remained precapitalist. Some of these might have imagined that precapitalist natives would practice some form of primitive communism (see Diamond, 1963, 1972) as described by Friedrich Engels (1884) in *The Origins of the Family, Private Property and the State.* Engels, in fact, had derived his idea of primitive communism from Lewis Henry Morgan's (1877/1964) *Ancient Society,* an original study in the Comtean ethnohistorical tradition of American aborigines that conceived of the latter as "ancestors" to the ancient Greeks (for a recent critique, see Kuper, 1988). Others, no longer concerned to prove that "mother-right" preceded "father-right" by presenting ethnographic accounts of Melanesians, Tasmanians, Bantus, or Dayaks (for a fine example, see Hartland, 1921/1969), turned their attention to acculturation, and, unsure of how long the process might take and how well the formerly colonized subjects would take to Occidental norms, reinvoked "the doctrine of survivals" (Hodgen, 1936) to account for elements of the natives' culture that persisted (see, e.g., Herskovitz, 1958, 1966), or marveled at how well some native peoples had traded "new lives for old" (Mead, 1956/1975). These diverse value and ideological orientations are pervasive in the work of early professional ethnologists and provided anthropology the grounding for most of its theoretical debates.

The "Evolution" of Culture and Society: Comte and the Comparative Method

Even before the professionalization of anthropology engulfed the discipline, the enlightened ethnographer had abandoned any attitude that might be associated with that of a merciless conqueror and replaced it with that of an avatar of beneficent evolutionary progress. Value conflicts arising within anthropology from the history of colonialism, and with the moral relativism associated with them were, in part, replaced by theories of social evolution. The application of Darwinian and Spencerian principles to the understanding of how societies and cultures of the world have developed over eons freed the ethnographer from the problems presented by moral relativism; it permitted the assertion that there existed a spatiotemporal hierarchy of values. These values were represented synchronically in the varieties of cultures to be found in the world, but might be classified diachronically according to the theory of developmental advance.

This new approach to comprehending how the lifeways of the Occident related to those of the others had first been formally proposed by Auguste Comte and was soon designated the "comparative method" (Bock, 1948, pp. 11-36). According to Comte and his followers (see Lenzer, 1975), the study of the evolution of culture and civilization would postulate three stages of culture and would hold fast to the idea that the peoples and cultures of the world are arrangeable diachronically, forming "a great chain of being" (Lovejoy, 1936/1960). Moreover, these stages are interpretable as orderly links in that chain, marking the epochs that occurred as human societies moved from conditions of primitive culture to those of modern civilization.[9] By using technological as well as social indicators, ethnographers could discover where a particular people belonged on the "chain" and thus give that people a definite place in the evolution of culture. (For a recent discussion and critique of Comte as a theorist of history and evolution, see R. Brown, 1984, pp. 187-212.) The seemingly inconvenient fact that all of these different cultures coexisted in time—that is, the time in which the ethnographer conducted his or her field study—was disposed of by applying the theory of "uneven evolution," that is, the assertion, in the guise of an epistemological assumption, that all cultures except that of Western Europe had suffered some form of arrested development (Sanderson, 1990; Sarana, 1975). In this way, and in the absence of documentary historical materials, ethnographers could utilize their on-the-spot field studies to contribute to the construction of the prehistory of civilization and at the same time put forth a genealogy of morals. Following Comte, this diachrony of civilizational development was usually characterized as having three progressive and irreversible stages: savagery, barbarism, and civilization. The peoples assigned to each of these stages corresponded to a color-culture hierarchical diachrony and fitted the ethnocentric bias of the Occident (Nisbet, 1972).

In the nineteenth century, Comte had formalized this mode of thinking for both anthropologists and sociologists by designating as epochs of moral growth (Comte's terms) three stages that, he averred, occurred in the development of religion. The ethnologists' adaptation of Comte's comparative method to their own efforts provided them with a set of a priori assumptions on the cultures of "primitives"—assumptions that vitiated the need to grant respect to these cultures in their own terms—that is, from the perspective of those who are its participants (for a countervailing perspective, see Hill-Lubin, 1992). The imposition of a preconceived Eurocentric developmental framework made the work of the ethnographer much simpler;[10] the task became that of a classifier of cultural traits in transition, or in arrest. Ultimately, this approach was institutionalized in the Human Relations Area Files (HRAF) housed at Yale University, which became the depository for an anthropological data bank and the resource for a vast project dedicated to the classification and cross-classification of virtually all the extant ethnographic literature—in the drawers of the HRAF any and all items of culture found a secure classificatory niche (Murdock, 1949/1965). A Yale-produced handbook of categories provided the ethnographer with guidelines to direct his or her observations and provided the basis for the classification of these and other collections of cultural traits.[11] The trait data in the Yale cross-cultural files represent ethnography in a form disembodied from that of a lived social world in which actors still exist. They are a voluminous collection of disparate cultural items that represent the antithesis of the ethnographic method.

Twentieth-Century Ethnography: Comteanism and the Cold War

Two twentieth-century developments have undermined both the various "colonial" anthropological perspectives and evolutionary schemes. Within 30 years of the termination of World War II, the several decolonization movements in Africa and Asia succeeded in ending the direct forms of Western global colonialism. As part of the same movements, an anticolonial assault on Western ethnocentrism led to a critical attack on the idea of "the primitive" and on the entire train of ethnological thought that went with it (Montagu, 1968). In effect, by the 1960s anthropologists had begun not only to run out of "primitive" societies to study but also to abandon the evolutionary epistemology that had justified their very existence in the first place.

A new term, *underdeveloped,* tended to replace *primitive.* The colonial powers and their supporters became defendants in an academic prosecution of those who were responsible for the underdevelopment of the newly designated "Third World" and who had neglected to recognize the integrity of "black culture" and that of other peoples of color in the United States (see Willis, 1972).[12] Ethnologists discovered that their basic orientation was under attack. Insofar as that orientation had led them or their much-respected predecessors to cooperate with imperial governments in the suppression and exploitation of natives, or with the American military and its "pacification" programs in Vietnam, anthropologists began to suffer from the effects of a collective and intradisciplinary guilt complex (see Nader, 1972).[13]

Changes in what appeared to be the direction of world history led anthropologists to retool their approach to ethnography. Because, by definition, there were few, if any, primitives available for study, and because the spokespersons for the newly designated Third World of "underdeveloped" countries often held anthropologists to have contributed to the latter condition, access to tribal societies became more difficult than it had been. As opportunities for fieldwork shrank, recourse was had to the study of linguistics, to the data banks of the Yale files, or to the discovery of the ethnographic possibilities for anthropological examinations of American society. Anthropology had come full circle, having moved back to a study of its own society, the point of departure—as well as the benchmark—for its investigation of more "primitive" cultures. Linguistics and data banks lend themselves to the study of texts, as does the study of Western society, with its rich literary and historical archives. These tendencies opened ethnography to the modernist and, later, the postmodernist approaches to the study of exotic peoples and to the investigation of alien culture bearers residing within industrial societies of the Occident.

However, even as anthropology was convulsed by decolonization movements and constrained by restricted access to its traditional fieldwork sites, the Cold War gave to sociology an opportunity to revive Comte's and Spencer's variants of evolutionary doctrine in modernist form and to combine them with a secular theodicy harking back to America's Puritan beginnings.

Talcott Parsons's (1966, 1971) two-volume study of the development of society restored the Calvinist-Puritan imagery, applying the latter to those "others" not yet included in the Christian brotherhood of the Occident. Written during the decades of the U.S. global contest with the Soviet Union, it arranged selected nations and societies in a schema according to which the United States was said to have arrived at the highest stage of societal development; other peoples, cultures, and civilizations were presumed to be moving in the direction plotted by America, "the first new nation" (Lipset, 1979; for a critique, see Lyman, 1975), or to be suffering from an arrest of advancement that prevented them from doing so. That developmental scheme held to the idea that economic progress was inherent in industrialization and that nation building coincided with capitalism, the gradual extension of democratization, and the orderly provision of individual rights. Despite the pointed criticisms of the comparative method that would continue to be offered by the school of sociohistorical thought associated with Frederick J. Teggart (1941) and his followers (Bock, 1952, 1956, 1963, 1974; Hodgen, 1974; Nisbet, 1969, 1986; for a critical discussion of this school, see Lyman, 1978; see also Kuper, 1988), a Comtean outlook survived within sociology in the work of Talcott Parsons and his macrosociological epigoni.

Social scientific literature during the Cold War included such titles as Robert Heilbroner's *The Great Ascent,* A. F. K. Organski's *The Stages of Political Development,* and W. W. Rostow's *The Stages of Economic Growth.* The American political economy and a democratic social order replaced earlier images of the ultimate stage of cultural evolution. Changes in the rest of the nations of the world that seemed to herald movement toward adoption of an American social, political, and economic institutional structure became the standard by which social scientists could measure the "advance" of humankind. This standard provided the analyst-ethnographer with a new measure for evaluating the "progress" of the "other" (which, after 1947, included the peoples and cultures of the Soviet Union as well as those of the "underdeveloped" world). The matter reached epiphany in the early 1990s, when students and scholars of the cosmological, moral, economic, and military problems faced by claimants of the right to spread a benevolent variant of Christianized Western civilization throughout the world began to rejoice over the collapse of communism, the disintegration of the Soviet Union, and the decomposition of its allies and alliances in Eastern Europe (Gwertzman & Kaufman, 1992). But for some there arose a new apprehension: worry over whether these events signaled the very end of history itself (see Fukuyama, 1992).[14]

The end of the Cold War and the deconstruction of the Soviet Union revived nationalist and ethnic claims in almost every part of the world. In such a newly decentered world, cultural pluralism has become a new watchword, especially for all those who hope to distinguish themselves from ethnonational "others." The dilemmas once posed by cultural relativism have been replaced by the issues arising out of the supposed certainties of primordial descent. Ethnographers now find themselves caught in the cross fire of incommensurable but competing values.

The Ethnography of the American Indian: An Indigenous "Other"

In the United States, the Calvinist variant of the Protestant errand into the wilderness began with the arrival of the Puritans in New England. Convinced of their own righteousness and of their this-worldly mission to bring to fruition God's kingdom on the "new continent," the Puritans initially set out to include the so-called Indians in their covenant of faith. But, having misjudged both the Indians' pliability and their resistance to an alien worldview, the Puritans did not succeed in their attempt (Calloway, 1991, pp. 57-90; A. T. Vaughan, 1965). Nevertheless, they continued their missionary endeavors throughout the nineteenth and twentieth centuries (Coleman, 1985; Keller, 1983; Milner & O'Neil, 1985). American political and jurisprudential policy toward the Indian, as well as the ethnographic work on the cultures of Native Americans, derive from this failure and shape its results. As one consequence, the several tribes of North American aborigines would remain outside the ethnographic, moral, and cultural pale of both European immigrant enclaves and settled white American communities.

From the seventeenth through the nineteenth centuries—that is, during the period of westward expansion across the American continent—ethnographic reports on Indian cultures were written from the perspective of the Euro-American conqueror and his missionary allies (Bowden, 1981). Even more than the once-enslaved Africans and their American-born descendants, the Indians have remained in a special kind of "otherness." One salient social indicator of this fact is their confinement to reservations of the mind as well as the body. In the conventional academic curriculum, the study of Native Americans is a part of the cultural anthropology of "primitive" peoples, whereas that of European and Asian immigrants and American blacks is an institutionalized feature of sociology courses on "minorities" and "race and ethnic relations."

In the United States a shift in ethnographic perspective from that written by missionaries and military conquerors to that composed exclusively by anthropologists arose with the establishment of the ethnology section of the Smithsonian Institution (Hinsley, 1981). However, ethnographies of various Indian "tribes" had been written earlier by ethnologists in service to the Bureau of Indian Affairs (BIA) (Bieder, 1989; two representative examples of pre-Smithsonian Amerindian ethnography are found in McKenney & Hall, 1836/1972; Schoolcraft, 1851/1975). In addition to being "problem peoples" for those theorists who wished to explain Indian origins in America and to construct their ancestry in terms consistent with the creation and flood myths of the Bible, the presence of the Indians within the borders of the United States posed still another problem: their anomalous status in law (R. A. Williams, 1990). Politically, the Indian "tribes" regarded themselves as separate sovereign nations and, for a period, were dealt with as such by the colonial powers and the U.S. government. However, in 1831, their legal status was redesignated in a Supreme Court case, *Cherokee Nation v. Georgia* (1831). In his decision, Chief Justice Marshall declared the Indians to occupy a unique status in law. They form, he said, "a domestic dependent nation." As such, he went on, they fell into a special "ward" relationship to the federal government. The latter had already established the Bureau of Indian Affairs to deal with them. Within the confines and constraints of this decision, the BIA administered the affairs of the Indian. From the special brand of anthropology that it fostered, American ethnography developed its peculiar outlook on Native Americans.[15]

The BIA and later the Smithsonian Institution employed ethnographers to staff the various reservation agencies and to study the ways of the Indians. The focus of study for this contingent of observers was not the possible conversion of Indians, but rather the depiction of their cultures—ceremonies recorded, kinship systems mapped, technology described, artifacts collected—all carried out from a secular and administrative point of view.[16] The theoretical underpinning of the BIA's perspective was the civilized/primitive dichotomy that had already designated Indians as preliterates. In effect, the tribal lands and reservation habitats of these "domestic, dependent nationals" became a living anthropological museum from which ethnologists could glean descriptions of the early stages of primitive life. In those parts of the country where Indians lived in large numbers—especially the Southwest[17]—and where archaeological artifacts were numerous, the Comtean evolutionary perspective was used to trace the ancestry of existing tribes back to an origin that might be found by paleontological efforts. From the beginning, however, the Southwest would also be the setting where debates—over how ethnography was to be carried out, and what purpose it ought to serve—would break out and divide anthropologists not only from missionaries and from federal agents, but from one another (Dale, 1949/1984; Dockstader, 1985).

The life world of "the primitive" was thought to be a window through which the prehistoric past could be seen, described, and understood. At its most global representation, this attitude had been given the imprimatur of ethnological science at the St. Louis World's Fair in 1904, when a scientifically minded missionary, Samuel Phillips Verner, allowed Ota Benga, a pygmy from the Belgian Congo, to be put on display as a living specimen of primitivism. A year later, Ota Benga was exhibited at the Monkey House of the Bronx Zoo (Bradford & Blume, 1992). In 1911, the American anthropologist Alfred Kroeber took possession of Ishi, the last surviving member of the Yahi tribe, and placed him in the Museum of Anthropology at the University of California. In the two years before his death, Ishi dwelled in the museum and, like Ota Benga before him, became, in effect, a living artifact, a primitive on display, one to be viewed by the civilized in a manner comparable to their perspective on the presentation of Indians in American museum dioramas (see Kroeber, 1962, 1965; for contemporary accounts in newspapers and other media, see Heizer & Kroeber, 1979).

Although U.S. Indian policy established both the programs and the perspectives under which most ethnographers worked, its orthodoxy was not accepted by all of the early field-workers. Among these heterodoxical ethnologists, perhaps the most important was Frank Hamilton Cushing (1857-1900), who became a Zuni shaman and a war chief while working as an ethnologist for the Smithsonian Institution (see Cushing, 1920/1974, 1979, 1901/1988, 1990; see also Culin, 1922/1967).[18] Cushing's case stands out because, though he was an active participant in Zuni life, he continued to be a professional ethnographer who tried to describe both Zuni culture and the Zuni worldview from an indigenous perspective. Moreover, Cushing joined with R. S. Culin in proposing the heterodoxical thesis that America was the cradle of Asia, that is, that in pre-Columbian times the ancestors of the Zuni had migrated to Asia and contributed significantly to the development of Chinese, Japanese, Korean, and other Asiatic civilizations that in turn had been diffused over the centuries into Africa and Europe (Lyman, 1979, 1982a, 1982b).

Without attempting to become a native himself, Paul Radin (1883-1959) devoted a lifetime to the ethnographic study of the Winnebago Indians (see Radin, 1927, 1927/1957a, 1937/1957b, 1920/1963, 1933/1966, 1953/1971b, 1923/1973, 1956/1976).[19] Maintaining that an inner view of an alien culture could be accomplished only through a deep learning of its language and symbol system, Radin documented the myths, rituals, and poetry in Winnebago and, in his reports, provided English translations of these materials. Taking Cushing's and Radin's works as a standard for Amerindian ethnography, their perspective could be used to reinterpret the works of earlier ethnographers; they might enable future field investigators to comprehend the cultural boundedness of American Indian ethnography and at the same time provide the point of departure for a critical sociology of ethnological knowledge (Vidich, 1966). But, in addition, their work recognizes both the historicity of preliterate cultures and the problems attendant upon understanding the world of the other from the other's point of view. In this, as in the work of Thucydides and in the Weberian conception of a sociology of understanding (*verstehende* sociology), Cushing and Radin transcended the problem of value incommensurability.

The Ethnography of the Civic Other: The Ghetto, the Natural Area, and the Small Town

The Calvinist mission to save and/or include the Indian found its later counterpart in a mission to bring to the urban ghetto communities of blacks and Asian and European immigrants the moral and communitarian values of Protestantism. That these immigrants had carried their Catholic, Judaic, or Buddhist religious cultures to the United States and that the lifestyles of the recently emancipated blacks did not accord with those of the white citizens of the United States were causes for concern among representatives of the older settled groups, who feared for the future integrity of America's Protestant civilization (Contosta, 1980, pp. 121-144; Hartmann, 1948/1967; Jones, 1992, pp. 49-166). Initially, efforts to include these groups focused on Protestant efforts to preach and practice a "social gospel" that found its institutionalization in the settlement houses that came to dot the urban landscape of immigrant and ghetto enclaves (Holden, 1922/1970; Woods & Kennedy, 1922/1990).

About three decades after the Civil War, when it became clear that the sheer number and cultural variety of the new urban inhabitants had become too great to be treated by individual efforts, recourse was had to the statistical survey. It would provide a way to determine how many inhabitants from each denomination, nationality, and race there were in any one place, and to describe each group's respective problems of adjustment (C. A. Chambers, 1971; Cohen, 1981; McClymer, 1980). In this manner, the "other" was transformed into a statistical aggregate and reported in a tabular census of exotic lifestyles. These quantified reports, sponsored in the first years by various churches in eastern cities of the United States, were the forerunners of the corporate-sponsored surveys of immigrants and Negroes and of the massive government-sponsored surveys of European, Asian, Mexican, and other immigrant laborers in 1911 (Immigration Commission, 1911/1970). The church surveys and their corporate and sociological successors were designed to facilitate the "moral reform" and social adjustment of newcomer and ghetto populations. What is now known as qualitative research in sociology had its origins in this Christian mission (see Greek, 1978, 1992).

It was out of such a movement to incorporate the alien elements within the consensual community that the first qualitative community study was carried out. W. E. B. Du Bois's (1899/1967) *The Philadelphia Negro,* a survey of that city's seventh ward, was supported by Susan B. Wharton, a leader of the University of Pennsylvania's college settlement. To Wharton, Du Bois, and their colleagues, the "collection and analysis of social facts were as much a religious as a scientific activity offered as a form of prayer for the redemption of dark-skinned people" (Vidich & Lyman, 1985, p. 128). This study, which included 5,000 interviews conducted by Du Bois, aimed not only at description, but also at the uplift of Philadelphia's Negro population by the Quaker community that surrounded it. The tone of noblesse oblige that inspires the final pages of Du Bois's book are a stark reminder of the paternalistic benevolence underlying this first ethnographic study of a community.

Church- and corporate-sponsored survey methods continued to dominate social research until the early 1920s (see Burgess, 1916), when Helen and Robert Lynd began their study of Middletown. Robert Lynd, a newly ordained Protestant minister, was selected by the Council of Churches, then concerned about the moral state of Christian communities in industrial America, to examine the lifeways of what was thought to be a typical American community. Rather suddenly catapulted into the position of a two-person research team, the Lynds consulted the anthropologist Clark Wissler (1870-1947), then on the staff of the American Museum of Natural History,[20] for advice on how to conduct such a survey and how to report it once the data had been gathered. Wissler provided them with what was then known as the cultural inventory, a list of standard categories used by anthropologists to organize field data (see Wissler, 1923, chaps. 5, 7). Those categories—getting a living, making a home, training the young, using leisure, engaging in religious practices, engaging in community activities—became the organizing principle of Lynd and Lynd's (1929/1956) book and provided them with a set of cues for their investigation. Although the Middletown study was designed to provide its church sponsors with information that might be used to set church policy, the Lynds approached the Middletown community in the manner of social anthropologists. As Wissler (1929/1956) states in his foreword to the published volume of the study, "To most people anthropology is a mass of curious information about savages, and this is so far true, in that most of its observations are on the less civilized. . . . The authors of this volume have approached an American community as an anthropologist does a primitive tribe" (p. vi). In Middletown, the "other" of the anthropologist found its way into American sociological practice and purpose. Moreover, from the point of view of the policy makers in the central church bureaucracy, he who had once been assumed to be the civic "brother" had to all intents and purposes become the "other," an ordinary inhabitant of Muncie, Indiana.

Shortly after the publication of *Middletown* in 1929, the Great Depression set in. Soon, the Lynds were commissioned to do a restudy of Muncie. Published in 1937 as *Middletown in Transition: A Study in Cultural Conflicts,* this investigation reflected not only changes in the town, but also a transformation in the outlook of its two ethnographers. During the early years of the Depression, Robert Lynd, a church progressive, had begun to look to the Soviet Union for answers to the glaring contradictions of capitalism that seemed to have manifested themselves so alarmingly in Depression-ridden America. This new political orientation was reflected in both what the Lynds observed and how they reported it. Where the first volume had made no mention of the Ball family's domination of what was a virtual "company town," or of the family's philanthropic sponsorship of Ball State University and the local library and hospital, or its control over the banks, *Middletown in Transition* included a chapter titled "The X Family: A Pattern of Business-Class Control," and an appendix titled "Middletown's Banking Institutions in Boom and Depression." Responding to what they believed to be the utter failure of America's laissez-faire, free market economy, the Lynds abandoned the ethnographic categories they had used in *Middletown.* Choosing instead to employ categories and conceptualizations derived from their own recently acquired Marxist outlook, they shifted the sociological focus from religious to political values.

Middletown in Transition would become a standard and much-praised work of sociological ethnography for the next half century. At Columbia University, where Robert Lynd taught generations of students, explicit Christian values and rhetoric were replaced by those of an ethically inclined political radicalism. With the radicalization of many Columbia-trained youths (as well as of their fellow students at City College, many of whom would later become prominent sociologists), variants of Marxism would provide a counterperspective to that of the anthropologically oriented ethnographic observer of American communities. Ironically, however, Middletown's second restudy, conducted by a team of non-Marxist sociologists nearly 50 years after *Middletown in Transition* was published, returned the focus to the significance of kinship and family that had characterized the early anthropological perspective, combining it with the kind of concern for Protestant religiosity that had been the stock-in-trade of the earlier American sociological orientation (Caplow, Bahr, Chadwick, Hill, & Williamson, 1982, 1983).

Even before the Lynds' original study, ethnography as a method of research had become identified with the University of Chicago's Department of Sociology. The first generation of Chicago sociologists, led by Albion W. Small, supposed that the discipline they professed had pledged itself to reassert America's destiny—the nation that would be "the city upon a hill." America would become a unified Christian brotherhood, committed to a covenant through which the right and proper values would be shared by all (Vidich & Lyman, 1985, p. 179). Small sought a sociological means to impress the values and morals of Protestantism upon the inhabitants of the newer ethnic, racial, and religious ghettos then forming in Chicago. However, this explicitly Christian attitude—in service to which the University of Chicago had been brought into existence by John D. Rockefeller in 1892—did not survive at Chicago. It was discarded after Robert E. Park, Ernest W. Burgess, W. I. Thomas, and Louis Wirth had become the guiding professoriat of Chicago's sociology, and after Park's son-in-law, Robert Redfield, had become an important figure in that university's anthropology program. Park's secular conceptualization of the "natural area" replaced the Christian locus of the unchurched in the city, while, at the same time, and in contradistinction to Park's point of view, Redfield's formulation of the morally uplifting "little community" introduced a counterimage to that of the metropolis then emerging in Chicago.

Park (1925/1967) conceived the city to be a social laboratory containing a diversity and heterogeneity of peoples, lifestyles, and competing and contrasting worldviews. To Park, for a city to be composed of others, ghettoized or otherwise, was intrinsic to its nature. Under his and Ernest W. Burgess's direction or inspiration, a set of ethnographic studies emerged focusing on singular descriptions of one or another aspect of human life that was to be found in the city. Frequently, these studies examined urban groups whose ways of life were below or outside the purview of the respectable middle classes. In addition to providing descriptions of the myriad and frequently incompatible values by which these groups lived, these ethnographies moved away from the missionary endeavor that had characterized earlier studies. Instead, Park and his colleagues occupied themselves with documenting the various forms of civil otherhood that they perceived to be emerging in the city (see Burgess & Bogue, 1967).

Central to Park's vision of the city was its architectonic as a municipal circumscription of a number of "natural areas," forming a mosaic of minor communities, each strikingly different from the other, but each more or less typical of its kind. Park (1952a) observed, "Every American city has its slums; its ghettos; its immigrant colonies, regions which maintain more or less alien and exotic cultures. Nearly every large city has its bohemias and hobohemias, where life is freer, more adventurous and lonely than it is elsewhere. These are called natural areas of the city" (p. 196). For more than three decades, urban ethnography in Chicago's sociology department focused on describing such "natural areas" as the Jewish ghetto (Wirth, 1928/1956), Little Italy (Nelli, 1970), Polonia (Lopata, 1967; Thomas & Znaniecki, 1958, pp. 1511-1646), Little Germany (Park, 1922/1971), Chinatown (Lee, 1978; Siu, 1987; Wu, 1926), Bronzeville and Harlem (Drake & Cayton, 1962; Frazier, 1931, 1937a, 1937b), the gold coast and the slum (Zorbaugh, 1929), hobo jungles (N. Anderson, 1923/1961), single-room occupants of furnished rooms (Zorbaugh, 1968), enclaves of cultural and social dissidents (Ware, 1935/1965),[21] the urban ecology of gangdom (Thrasher, 1927/1963), and the urban areas that housed the suicidal (Cavan, 1928/1965), the drug addicted (Dai, 1937/1970), and the mentally disturbed (Faris & Dunham, 1939/1965), and on the social and economic dynamics of real estate transactions and the human and metropolitical effects arising out of the occupational interests of realtors as they interfaced with the state of the economy (Hughes, 1928; McCluer, 1928; Schietinger, 1967). Park's (1952b, 1952c) orientation was that of Montesquieu; he emphasized the freedom that the city afforded to those who would partake of the "romance" and "magic" of its sociocultural multiverse.

Some of Park's students, on the other hand, following up an idea developed by Louis Wirth (1938), all too often took to contrasting its forms of liberty in thought and action—that is, its encouragement of "segmented" personalities and role-specific conduct and its fostering of impersonality, secondary relationships, and a blasé attitude (see Roper, 1935, abstracted in Burgess & Bogue, 1967, pp. 231-244)—with what they alleged was the sense of personal security—that is, the gratification that came from conformity to custom, the comfort that arose out of familiar face-to-face contacts, the wholesomeness of whole personalities, and the companionability of primary relationships—to be found among the people who dwelt in rural, ethnoracially homogeneous small towns (see Bender, 1978, pp. 3-27; Redfield & Singer, 1973; see also M. P. Smith, 1979). For those who idealized the "folk society," and who conflated it with concomitant idealizations of the "little community," "primitive" primordialism, pastoral peace, and the small town, the impending urbanization of the countryside—heralded by the building of highways (Dansereau, 1961; McKenzie, 1968), the well-documented trend of young people departing to the city (for early documentation of this phenomenon, see Weber, 1899/1967), and the intrusion of the automobile (Bailey, 1988; Rae, 1965), the telephone (Ball, 1968; de Sola Poole, 1981), and the radio (Gist & Halbert, 1947, pp. 128, 505-507) on rural folkways—was a portent not merely of change but of irredeemable tragedy (see Blake, 1990; Gusfield, 1975; Lingeman, 1980; Tinder, 1980). On the other hand, for those ethnographers who concluded on the basis of their own field experiences that the processes as well as the anomalies of America's inequitable class structure had already found their way into and become deeply embedded within the language and customs of the nation's small towns, there was an equally portentous observation: America's Jeffersonian ideals were professed but not practiced in the very communities that had been alleged to be their secure repository. As August B. Hollingshead (1949/1961) would point out on the basis of his ethnographic study of "Elmtown's youth": "The . . . American class system is extra-legal . . . [but] society has other dimensions than those recognized in law. . . . It is the culture which makes men face toward the facts of the class system and away from the ideals of the American creed" (pp. 448, 453).

Ethnographic studies that followed in this tradition were guided by a nostalgia for nineteenth-century small-town values, an American past that no longer existed, but during the heyday of which—so it was supposed—there had existed a society in which all had been brothers and sisters.

However, neither the civil otherhood conceived by Park nor the classless brotherhood sought by Hollingshead could account for American society's resistance to the incorporation of blacks. It was to address this point that E. Franklin Frazier (1894-1962) would stress the "otherhood" of the American Negro. Building on the teachings of both Park and Du Bois, Frazier began his sociological studies in Chicago with an analysis of the various lifeways within the black ghetto. In the process, he discovered both the ghetto's separateness and its isolation from the larger social and political economy. In his later evaluation of the rise of the "black bourgeoisie" (1957a) he saw it as a tragic, although perhaps inevitable, outcome of the limited economic and social mobility available to the black middle classes. Based on his observations of largely university-based black middle classes, Frazier presented their lifestyle as an emulation of the lifestyle of the white middle classes: as such, his monograph on the subject should be regarded as much as a study of the white bourgeoisie as of the black. Frazier's ethnographic studies were based on almost a lifetime of observation, not only of this specific class, but also of African American ghetto dwellers in Harlem and Chicago, of black families in the rural South and the urban North, and of Negro youths caught up in the problems of their socioeconomic situation (see Frazier, 1925, 1957b, 1963, 1939/1966, 1940/1967, 1968). Frazier's work stands apart, not only because it points to the exclusion of blacks from both the American ideal of brotherhood and the then-emerging civic otherhood, but also because its research orientation drew on the life histories of his subjects and on his own experience.

The importance of personal experience in ethnographic description and interpretation is implicit in all of Frazier's work. His methodology and chosen research sites are comparable to those employed by a very different kind of ethnographer—Thorstein Veblen. In such studies of American university ghettos as *The Higher Learning in America: A Memorandum on the Conduct of Universities by Businessmen,* Veblen (1918/1965) drew on his own experiences at the University of Chicago, Stanford University, and the University of Missouri, three sites that provided the raw materials for his highly organized and prescient examination of the bureaucratic transformations then occurring in American universities.[22] Frazier's and Veblen's oeuvres are, in effect, examples of qualitative research based on data acquired over the course of rich and varied life experiences. In these studies it is impossible to disentangle the method of study from either the theory employed or the person employing it. Such a method would appear to be the ultimate desideratum of ethnographic research.

The ethnographic orientation at the University of Chicago was given a new twist by William Foote Whyte. Whyte made what was designed to be formal research into part of his life experience and called it "participant observation." The Chicago Sociology Department provided Whyte with an opportunity to report, in *Street Corner Society* (1943a, 1955, 1981), his findings about Italian Americans residing in the North End of Boston. That work, initially motivated by a sense of moral responsibility to uplift the slum-dwelling masses, has become the exemplar of the techniques appropriate to participant observation research: Whyte lived in the Italian neighborhood and in many but not all ways became one of the "Cornerville" boys.[23] Although he presents his findings about Cornerville descriptively, Whyte's theoretical stance remains implicit. The book has an enigmatic quality, because Whyte presents his data from the perspective of his relationships with his subjects. That is, Whyte is as much a researcher as he is a subject in his own book; the other had become the brother of Italian ghetto dwellers.

Anthropology at the University of Chicago was also informed by a qualitative orientation. Until 1929, anthropology and ethnology at that university had been subsumed under "historical sociology" in a department called the Department of Social Science and Anthropology. Anthropological and ethnological studies were at first directed by Frederick A. Starr, formerly head of ethnology at the American Museum of Natural History (Diner, 1975). Starr became a Japanophile after his first trip to Japan, while he was on assignment to bring a few of the Ainu people to be displayed, like Ota Benga, at the St. Louis World's Fair in 1904 (Statler, 1983, pp. 237-255). A separate Department of Anthropology was established in 1929, but, unlike Starr's, it reflected the orientation developed by the sociologists W. I. Thomas and Ellsworth Faris (see Faris, 1970, p. 16). One year before the advent of the new department, Robert Redfield presented his dissertation, *A Plan for the Study of Tepoztlan, Mexico* (1928). Borrowing from Tonnies's (1887/1957) dichotomous paradigm, gemeinschaft-gesellschaft, and drawing upon Von Wiese's and Becker's (1950/1962, 1932/1974) sacred-secular continuum, Redfield asserted the virtues of "the folk culture" and what he would later call "the little community" (Redfield, 1962, pp. 143-144; see also Redfield, 1930, 1941, 1960, 1950/1962b; Redfield & Rojas, 1934/1962a).

Regarding the metropolis as a congeries of unhappy and unfulfilled others, Redfield stood opposed to the values associated with urban life and industrial civilization. He extolled the lifestyles of those nonindustrial peoples and small communities that had resisted incorporation into the globally emerging metropolitan world. In his final essay, written in 1958, the year of his death, describing an imaginary conversation with a man from outer space, Redfield (1963) abjured the condition of mutually assured destruction that characterized the Cold War, despaired of halting the march of technocentric progress, conflated the pastoral with the premodern, and concluded by lamenting the rise of noncommunal life in the metropolitan city. Redfield's orientation, Rousseauean in its ethos, would provide a generation of anthropologists with a rustic outlook—a postmissionary attitude that sought to preserve and protect the lifeways of the primitive. His was the antiurban variant of Puritanism, a point of view that held small-scale, face-to-face communities to be superior to all others. To those ethnologists who followed in the ideological footsteps of Redfield, these communal values seemed representative of primordial humanity.[24]

A counterimage to that of ethnography's romance with small-town, communitarian and primordial values of primitivism was offered in 1958 when Arthur J. Vidich and Joseph Bensman published their ethnographic account of "Springdale," a rural community in Upstate New York.[25] As their title forewarned, this was a "small town in mass society."[26] Its situation, moreover, was typical of other American towns. Springdale's much-vaunted localism, its claims to societal, economic, and political autonomy, were illusions of a bygone era. Their "central concern," the authors observed in their introduction to a revised edition released 10 years after the original publication of their monograph, "was with the processes by which the small town (and indirectly all segments of American society) are continuously and increasingly drawn into the central machinery, processes and dynamics of the total society" (Vidich & Bensman, 1968, p. xi).

In so presenting their findings, Vidich and Bensman reversed the direction and exploded what was left of the mythology attendant upon the gemeinschaft-gesellschaft (Parsons, 1937/1949, 1973) and folk-urban continua in American sociological thought (Duncan, 1957; Firey, Loomis, & Beegle, 1950; Miner, 1952). Although the theoretical significance of their study was often neglected in the wake of the controversy that arose over its publication and the charge that they had not done enough to conceal the identities of the town's leading citizens (Vidich & Bensman, 1968, pp. 397-476), their concluding observations—namely, that there had occurred a middle-class revolution in America, that the rise and predominance of the new middle classes had altered the character and culture of both the cities and towns of America, and that "governmental, business, religious and educational super-bureaucracies far distant from the rural town formulate policies to which the rural world can respond only with resentment" (p. 323; see also Bensman & Vidich, 1987)—challenged the older paradigms guiding field research on community life.

By 1963, Roland L. Warren would take note of what he called "the 'great change' in American communities" and point out how a developing division of labor, the increasing differentiation of interests and associations, the growing systemic relations to the larger society, a transfer of local functions to profit enterprises and to state and federal governments, urbanization and suburbanization, and the shifts in values that were both cause and consequences of these changes had been accompanied by a "corresponding decline in community cohesion and autonomy" (see Warren, 1972, pp. 53-94). In effect, community ethnography would not only have to adjust to the encroachment of the city and the suburb on the town, but also enlarge its outlook to embrace the effects of the state and the national political economy on the towns and villages of the Third World as well as of the United States (see, e.g., the ethnographies collected in Toland, 1993; see also Marcus, 1986). ("The point is," Maurice Stein [1964, p. 230] observed in his reflection on nearly six decades of American community studies, "that both the student of the slum and of the suburb [and, he might have added, the small town] require some sort of total picture of the evolution of American communities and of emerging constellations and converging problems"; p. 230. Had the practitioners of American community studies taken their point of departure from Otto von Gierke's, 1868/1990, or Friedrich Ratzel's, 1876/1988, orientations, they might have been more critical of the "Rousseauean" variant of Tonnies's outlook from the beginning of their research. [See McKinney, 1957])[27]

The Ethnography of Assimilation: The Other Remains an Other

A breakdown in another fundamental paradigm affected the ethnographic study of ethnic and racial minorities. Until the 1960s, much of the sociological outlook on race and ethnic relations had focused on the processes and progress of assimilation, acculturation, and amalgamation among America's multiverse of peoples. Guided by the cluster of ideas and notions surrounding the ideology of the "melting pot," as well as by the prediction of the eventual assimilation of everyone that accompanied the widely held understanding of Robert E. Park's theory of the racial cycle, ethnographers of America's many minority groups at first sought to chart each people's location on a continuum that began with "contact," passed consecutively through stages of "competition and conflict" and "accommodation," and eventually culminated in "assimilation" (for critical evaluations of Park's cycle, see Lyman, 1972, 1990b, 1992b). Although by 1937 Park had come to despair of his earlier assertion that the cycle was progressive and irreversible (see Park, 1937/1969b), his students and followers would not give up their quest for a pattern and process that promised to bring an ultimate and beneficent end to interracial relations and their attendant problems.

When the ethnic histories of particular peoples in the United States seemed to defy the unidirectional movement entailed in Park's projected sequence—for example, when Etzioni's (1959) restudy of the Jewish ghetto showed little evidence that either religion or custom would be obliterated, even after many years of settlement in America; when Lee's (1960) discovery that Chinatowns and their old world-centered institutions persisted despite a decline in Sinophobic prejudices; when Woods's (1972) careful depiction of how 10 generations of settlement in America had failed to erode either the traditions or the ethnoracial identity of a marginalized people, the Letoyant Creoles of Louisiana (see also Woods, 1956); and, more generally, when Kramer (1970) had documented the many variations in minority community adaptation in America—there arose a cacophony of voices lamenting the failure of assimilation and calling for a resurgence of WASP hegemony (Brookhiser, 1991, 1993), or expressing grave apprehension about America's ethnocultural future (Christopher, 1989; Schlesinger, 1991; Schrag, 1973).

Even before popularizers and publicists announced the coming of an era in which there would be a "decline of the WASP" (Schrag, 1970) and a rise of the "unmeltable ethnics" (Novak, 1972), some sociologists had begun to reexamine their assumptions about ethnicity in America and to rethink their own and their predecessors' findings on the matter. In 1952, Nathan Glazer caused Marcus Lee Hansen's (1938/1952) hitherto overlooked work on the "law of third generation return" to be republished,[28] sparking a renewed interest in documenting whether, how, and to what extent the grandchildren of immigrants retained, reintroduced, rediscovered, or invented the customs of their old-world forebears in modern America (Kivisto & Blanck, 1990). Stanford M. Lyman (1974, 1986) combined participant observation with documentary and historical analyses to show that the solidarity and persistence over time of territorially based Chinatowns was related in great measure to persistent intracommunity conflict and to the web of traditional group affiliations that engendered both loyalty and altercation. Kramer and Leventman (1961) provided a picture of conflict resolution among three generations of American Jews who had retained many but not all aspects of their ethnoreligious traditions despite, or perhaps because of, the fact that the third generation had become "children of the gilded ghetto." Richard Alba (1985, 1989, 1990) reopened the questions of whether and how European ethnic survival had occurred in the United States, pointing to the several dimensions of its presentation, representation, and disintegration, and carrying out, once more, a study of Italian Americans, a group often chosen by sociologists for ethnographic studies seeking to support, oppose, modify, or reformulate the original assimilation thesis (see, e.g., Covello, 1967; Gans, 1962; Garbaccia, 1984; Landesco, 1968; Lopreato, 1970; Tricarico, 1984; Whyte, 1943a, 1943b).

The reconsideration of assimilation theory in general and Park's race relations cycle in particular produced a methodological critique so telling that it cast doubt on the substance of that hypothesis. In 1950, Seymour Martin Lipset observed that "by their very nature, hypotheses about the inevitability of cycles, whether they be cycles of race relations or the rise and fall of civilization, are not testable at all" (p. 479). Earlier, some ethnographers of racial minority groups in America had attempted to construct lengthier or alternative cycles that would be able to accommodate the findings of their field investigations. Bogardus's (1930, 1940; Ross & Bogardus, 1940) three distinctive cycles for California's diversified Japanese communities and Masuoka's (1946) warning that three generations would be required for the acculturation of Japanese in America and that the third generation would still be victims of "a genuine race problem" evidence the growing disappointment with assimilation's promise. Others, including W. O. Brown (1934), Clarence E. Glick (1955), Stanley Lieberson (1961), and Graham C. Kinloch (1974, pp. 205-209) came to conclusions similar to that of Park's 1937 reformulation—namely, that assimilation was but one possible outcome of sustained interracial contact, and that isolation, subordination, nationalist or nativist movements, and secession ought also to be considered.

Those seeking to rescue the discredited determinism of Park's original cycle from its empirically minded critics turned to policy proposals or hortatory appeals in its behalf. Wirth (1945) urged the adoption of programs that would alleviate the frustration experienced by members of minority groups who had been repeatedly rebuffed in their attempts to be incorporated within a democratic America; Lee (1960, pp. 429-430) converted her uncritical adherence to Park's prophecy into a plaintive plea that Chinese ghetto dwellers live up to it—that is, that they assimilate themselves as rapidly as possible (see also Lyman, 1961-1962, 1963). Still others resolved the ontological and epistemological problems in Park's cycle by treating it as a "logical" rather than "empirical" perspective. Frazier (1953) suggested that, rather than occurring chronologically, the stages in the theory might be spatiotemporally coexistent: "They represent logical steps in a systematic sociological analysis of the subject." Shibutani and Kwan (1965), after examining the many studies of integrative and disintegrative social processes in racial and ethnic communities, concurred, holding that although there were many exceptions to its validity as a descriptive theory, Park's stages provided a "useful way of ordering data on the manner in which immigrants become incorporated into an already-established society" (see pp. 116-135). Geschwender (1978) went further, holding that Park's race relations cycle was "an abstract model of an 'ideal type' sequence which might develop" (p. 25).

In 1918, Edward Byron Reuter had defined America's race issue as "the problem of arriving at and maintaining mutually satisfactory working relations between members of two nonassimilable groups which occupy the same territory" (Reuter, 1918/1969, p. 18). After a half century of sociological studies had seemed to demonstrate that virtually none of the racial or ethnic groups had traversed the cyclical pathway to complete assimilation, America's race problem seemed not only to be immense, but also to have defied as well as defined the basic problematic of sociological theory. Such, at any rate, was the position taken by the ethnological anthropologist Brewton Berry (1963), whose field investigations would eventually include studies of various peoples in Latin America as well as several communities of previously unabsorbed racial hybrids in the United States (see also Lyman, 1964). Having shown that none of the proposed cycles of race relations could claim universal validity on the basis of available evidence, Berry and Tischler (1978) observed, "Some scholars . . . question the existence of any universal pattern, and incline rather to the belief that so numerous and so various are the components that enter into race relations that each situation is unique, and [that] the making of generalizations is a hazardous procedure" (p. 156). Berry's thesis, though not necessarily intended in this direction, set the tone for the subsequent plethora of ethnographies that offered little in the way of theoretical advancements but much more of the detail of everyday life among minorities and other human groups.

During the two decades after 1970, ethnological studies of African American, Amerindian, Mexican American, and Asian peoples also cast considerable doubt on whether, when, and to whose benefit the much-vaunted process of ethnocultural meltdown in America would occur. Ethnographies and linguistic studies of black enclaves, North and South, slave and free, suggested that the tools employed in earlier community analyses had not been honed sufficiently for sociologists to be able to discern the cultural styles and social practices that set African American life apart from that of other segments of the society (see, e.g., Abrahams, 1964, 1970, 1992; E. Anderson, 1978; Bigham, 1987; Blassingame, 1979; Duneier, 1992; Evans & Lee, 1990; Joyner, 1984; Liebow, 1967; for an overview, see Blackwell, 1991). Other critics observed that sociological studies of the "American dilemma" had paid insufficient attention to politics, civil rights, and history (Boxhill, 1992; Button, 1989; Jackson, 1991; Lyman, 1972; V. J. Williams, 1989). Anthropological studies of the culture-preserving and supposedly isolated Native American nations and tribes had to give way in the face of a rising ethnoracial consciousness (Cornell, 1988; Martin, 1987; Sando, 1992), selective demands for the return of Amerindian museum holdings (Berlo, 1992; Clifford, 1990; Messenger, 1991; Milson, 1991-1992; "A Museum Is Set," 1993), Indian recourse to American courts in quest of redress and treaty rights (see T. L. Anderson, 1992; Jaimes, 1992), and political alliances and the tracing of ethnohistorical descent that would connect Amerindians with Hispanics, African Americans, and Jews (Forbes, 1973, 1988; Gutierrez, 1991; Tobias, 1990; Vigil, 1980). Mexican American studies moved from early historical institutional studies through ethnographies of farmworkers, and in the 1980s became part of the new postmodernist revolution.[29] To the Amerasian peoples conventionally treated by ethnographic sociologists—namely, the Chinese and Japanese—were added more recent arrivals, including Koreans, Thais, Vietnamese, Cambodians, Laotians, and the Hmong (see, e.g., Chan, 1991; Hune et al., 1991; Knoll, 1982; Nomura et al., 1989; Okihiro et al., 1988; Takaki, 1989). And, as in the instance of Mexican American ethnographers, a shift in issues and methods is beginning to emerge—moving away from debates about whether and how to measure assimilation and acculturation and toward such postmodern topics as the character, content, and implications of racial discourse about Asians in America (e.g., K. J. Anderson, 1991; Okihiro, 1988). As East Indians, Burmese, Oceanians, Malaysians, and other peoples of what used to be called "the Orient" began to claim common cause with the earlier-established Asian groups (Espiritu, 1992; Ignacio, 1976; Mangiafico, 1988), but insisted on each people's sociocultural and historical integrity, as well as the right of each to choose its own path within U.S. society, it became clear that the trend toward ethnographic postmodernism would continue (see, e.g., Hune et al., 1991; Leonard, 1992).

In 1980, Harvard University Press issued its mammoth *Harvard Encyclopedia of American Ethnic Groups* (Thernstrom, 1980), a work that includes not only separate entries for "Africans" and "Afro-Americans" but also individual essays devoted to each of 173 different tribes of American Indians and reports on each of the Asian peoples coming to the United States from virtually all the lands east of Suez. Harold J. Abrahamson's entry, "Assimilation and Pluralism," in effect announces American sociology's awakening not only from its dream of the eventual assimilation of every people in the country, but also from its conflation of assimilation with Americanization: "American society . . . is revealed as a composite not only of many ethnic backgrounds but also of many different ethnic responses. . . . There is no one single response or adaptation. The variety of styles in pluralism and assimilation suggest that ethnicity is as complex as life itself" (p. 160; see also Gleason, 1980; Novak, 1980; Walzer, 1980).

For the moment, pluralism had won its way onto paradigmatic center stage.[30] But even that orientation did not exhaust the possibilities or dispose of the problems arising out of the presence of diverse races and peoples in America. In 1993, together with Rita Jalali, Seymour Martin Lipset, who had criticized Park's formulation of an inevitable cycle leading to assimilation four decades earlier, observed that "race and ethnicity provide the most striking example of a general failure among experts to anticipate social developments in varying types of societies" (Jalali & Lipset, 1992-1993, p. 585). Moreover, the celebration of pluralism that now prevails in social thought obscures recognition of a fundamental problem: the self-restraint to be placed upon the competitive claims put forward by each ethnic and racial group.

Ethnography Now: The Postmodern Challenge

Historically, the ethnographic method has been used by both anthropologists and sociologists. The guiding frameworks for those who have used this method in the past have all but been abandoned by contemporary ethnographers. The social-historical transformations of society and consciousness in the modern world have undermined the theoretical and value foundations of the older ethnography.

With the present abandonment of virtually every facet of what might now be recognized as the interlocked, secular, eschatological legacies of Comte, Tönnies, Wissler, Redfield, Park, and Parsons—that is, the recognition that the "comparative method" and the anthropology of primitivism is inherently flawed by both its Eurocentric bias and its methodological inadequacies; the determination that the gemeinschaft of the little community has been subverted by the overwhelming force of the national political economy of the gesellschaft; the discovery that assimilation is not inevitable; and the realization that ethnic sodalities and the ghettos persist over long periods of time (sometimes combining deeply embedded internal disharmonies with an outward display of sociocultural solidarity, other times existing as "ghost nations," or as hollow shells of claimed ethnocultural distinctiveness masking an acculturation that has already eroded whatever elementary forms of existence gave primordial validity to that claim, or, finally, as semiarticulated assertions of a peoplehood that has moved through and "beyond the melting pot" without having been fully dissolved in its fiery cauldron)—ethnography and ethnology could emerge on their own terms.[31]

No longer would ethnography have to serve the interests of a theory of progress that pointed toward the breakup of every ethnos. No longer would ethnology have to describe the pastoral peacefulness, proclaim the moral superiority, or document the psychic security supposed to be found in the villages of the nonliterate, the folk societies of non-Western peoples, the little communities of the woods and forests, the small towns of America, or the urban ethnic enclaves of U.S. or world metropolises. No longer would ethnography have to chart the exact position of each traditional and ascriptively based status group as it moved down the socioculturally determined pathway that would eventually take it into a mass, class, or civil society, and recompose it in the process.

Liberated from these conceptual and theoretical constraints, ethnography and ethnology are, for the first time as it were, in a position to act out their own versions of the revolution of "life" against "the forms of life"—a cultural revolution of the twentieth century that Simmel (1968) foresaw as both imminent and tragic. Just as Simmel predicted that the cultural revolutionaries that he saw emerging in pre-World War I Europe would oppose both marriage and prostitution on the grounds that each was a form of the erotic and that they wished to emancipate the erotic from all forms of itself, so the new ethnographers proclaim themselves to be self-liberated from the weight of historical consciousness, relieved of the anxiety of influence (see Bloom, 1979),[32] and, in effect, content to become witnesses to and reporters of the myriad scenes in the quixotic world that has emerged out of the ruins of both religion and secular social theory (see Kundera, 1988).

The proclamation of ethnography as a self-defining orientation and practice in sociology and anthropology and the importation of the postmodernist outlook into it took place recently, irregularly, and in somewhat disorderly moves. Aleksandr Solzhenitsyn (1993) once pointed out that "no new work of art comes into existence (whether consciously or unconsciously) without an organic link to what was created earlier" (p. 3). Such also remains the case in social science, as will be shown with the new developments in sociological and anthropological ethnography.

One beginning of the emancipatory movement in ethnographic methodology is to be found in Peter Manning's seminal essay, "Analytic Induction" (1982/1991). Seeking to set ethnography on an even firmer foundation of the symbolic interactionist perspective and hoping to reinforce its connections to the classical period of the "Chicago school," Manning sought first to warn any practitioners of the sociological enterprise against employing any "concepts and theories developed to deal with the problems of such other disciplines as behavioristic psychology, economics, medicine, or the natural or physical sciences." He identified analytic induction as a procedure derivable from George Herbert Mead's and Florian Znaniecki's writings on scientific method, and he observed that it had been employed with greater or lesser precision by such classical Chicago ethnographers as Thomas and Znaniecki, and, later, by Robert Cooley Angell, Alfred Lindesmith, and Donald Cressey. Distinguishable from deductive, historical-documentary, and statistical approaches, analytic induction was "a nonexperimental qualitative sociological method that employs an exhaustive examination of cases in order to prove universal, causal generalizations." The case method was to be the critical foundation of a revitalized qualitative sociology.

The claim to universality of the causal generalizations is—in the example offered by Manning as exemplary of the method[33]—the weakest, for it is derived from the examination of a single case studied in light of a preformulated hypothesis that might be reformulated if the hypothesis does not fit the facts. And "practical certainty" of the (reformulated) hypothesis is obtained "after a small number of cases has been examined." Discovery of a single negative case is held to disprove the hypothesis and to require its reformulation. After "certainty" has been attained, "for purposes of proof, cases outside the area circumscribed by the definition are examined to determine whether or not the final hypothesis applies to them." If it does, it is implied, there is something wrong with the hypothesis, for "scientific generalizations consist of descriptions of conditions which are always present when the phenomenon is present but which are never present when the phenomenon is absent." The two keys to the entire procedure, Manning points out, are the definition of the phenomenon under investigation and the formulation of the tentative hypothesis. Ultimately, however, as Manning concedes, despite its aim, analytic induction does not live up to the scientific demand that its theories "understand, predict, and control events." After a careful and thoroughgoing critique of the procedure he has chosen over its methodological competitors, Manning asserts, "Analytic induction is not a means of prediction; it does not clearly establish causality; and it probably cannot endure a principled examination of its claims to [be] making universal statements." Indeed, Manning goes further, pointing out that, "according to the most demanding ideal standards of the discipline, analytic induction as a distinctive, philosophical, methodological perspective is less powerful than either enumerative induction or axiomatic-modelling methods." Manning's essay seems about to eject a method intrinsic to ethnography from the scientific community.

Manning's frank appraisal of the weaknesses of analytic induction is "drawn from a positivistic, deductive model of the scientific endeavor, a model seizing on a selected group of concerns." The proponents of that model seek to set the terms and limits of the social sciences according to its criteria. In fact, though few American scholars seem to know much about either the long history or the irresolution of debates over epistemological matters in the social sciences, the very issues of those debates are central to the questions the positivists are raising (see, in this regard, Rorty, 1982, pp. 191-210).

In his defense of analytic induction, Manning invokes an unacknowledged earlier critique by Sorokin (1965), namely, "that what is taken to be [appropriate] methodology at a given time is subject to fads, fashions, and foibles." Manning goes on to credit analytic induction with being a "viable source of data and concepts" and with helping investigators to sort out "the particulars of a given event [and to distinguish them from] those things that are general and theoretical." Erving Goffman, surely a sociological practitioner whose methodological orientation is akin to but not the same as analytic induction, goes even further, however. Opposing, in a defense of his own brand of ethnographic sociology, both system building and enumerative induction, in 1961 he wrote, "At present, if sociological concepts are to be treated with affection, each must be traced back to where it best applies, followed from there wherever it seems to lead, and pressed to disclose the rest of its family. Better, perhaps, different coats to clothe the children well than a single splendid tent in which they all shiver" (p. xiv). A decade later, Goffman (1971) dismissed the scientific claims of positivistic sociologists altogether: "A sort of sympathetic magic seems to be involved, the assumption being that if you go through the motions attributable to science then science will result. But it hasn't" (p. xvi).

With the waning of interest in, support for, or faith in the older purposes for doing ethnology, by the 1970s there had also arisen a concomitant discontent with the epistemological claims as well as the latent or secretive political usages—(see Diamond, 1992; Horowitz, 1967)—of the mainstream perspectives of both sociology—(see Vidich, Lyman, & Goldfarb, 1981)—and anthropology—(e.g., Clifford & Marcus, 1986; Fox, 1991; Manganaro, 1990). An outlook that could be used to carry out research projects and at the same time to treat the very resources of each discipline as a topic to be investigated critically was needed. Postmodernism appeared and seemed to fill that need.

Toward the end of his essay, Manning hints at the issue that would explode on the pages of almost every effort to come to terms with postwar and post-Cold War America: "In an age of existentialism, self-construction is as much a part of sociological method as theory construction." What he would later perceive as a reason for developing a formalistic and semiotic approach to doing fieldwork (Manning, 1987, pp. 7-24, 66-72) was that each construction would come to be seen as inextricably bound up with the other and that each would be said to provide a distorted mirror image of both the body (Cornwell, 1992; Featherstone, Hepworth, & Turner, 1991; Feher, 1989; Sheets-Johnstone, 1990, pp. 112-133; 1992) and the self (Kotarba & Fontana, 1987; Krieger, 1991; Zaner, 1981), of both one's *Umwelt* and the world of the other (the concept of *Umwelt* is developed by Gurwitsch, 1966). But for those who accepted the critique but rejected neoformalism as a technique for ethnography, there opened up a new field of investigation—representation. Hence some of the best postmodern ethnography has focused on the media that give imagery to real life (Bhabha, 1990b; Early, 1993; Gilman, 1991; Minh-ha, 1991). Justification for turning from the fields of lived experience to what is represented as such is the assumption that the former is itself perceived holographically, calling for the thematization of representation as a problem in the construction of "persuasive fictions" (Baudrillard, 1988a, pp. 27-106; Norris, 1990).

The postmodern ethnographer takes Simmel's tragedy of culture to be a fait accompli: It is not possible at the present time to emancipate free-floating life from all of its constraining forms (Strathern, 1990). The postmodern sociologist-ethnographer and his or her subjects are situated in a world suspended between illusory memories of a lost innocence and millennial dreams of a utopia unlikely to be realized. From such a position, not only is the standpoint of the investigator problematic (Lemert, 1992; Weinstein & Weinstein, 1991), but also that of the people to be investigated. Each person has in effect been "touched by the mass media, by alienation, by the economy, by the new family and child-care systems, by the unceasing technologizing of the social world, and by the threat of nuclear annihilation" (Denzin, 1989, p. 139). And, if the anthropologist-ethnographer is to proceed in accordance with the postmodern perspective, he or she must, on the one hand, become less fearful about "going primitive" (Torgovnick, 1990) and, on the other, contend with the claim that Eurocentric imagery has attended virtually all previous reports from the "primitive" world (Beverly, 1992; Bhabha, 1990a; Dirlik, 1987; Turner, 1992; West, 1992). For these ethnographers, Helmut Kuzmics (1988) observes, "The claim that the 'evolutionary gradualism' of the theory of civilization renders it incapable of explaining the simultaneous appearance of civilization (in a narrower sense than is presupposed by the highest values of the Enlightenment) and 'barbarism' still needs to be confronted more thoroughly" (p. 161).

As analytic induction advocates propose, let us begin with a definition of the new outlook—the postmodern. Charlene Spretnak (1991), a critic of much of the postmodernism she surveys, provides one that is comprehensive and useful:

> A sense of detachment, displacement, and shallow engagement dominates deconstructive-postmodern aesthetics because groundlessness is the only constant recognized by this sensibility. The world is considered to be a repressive labyrinth of "social production," a construction of pseudoselves who are pushed and pulled by cultural dynamics and subtly diffused "regimes of power." Values and ethics are deemed arbitrary, as is "history," which is viewed by deconstructive postmodernists as one group or another's self-serving selection of facts. Rejecting all "metanarratives," or supposedly universal representations of reality, deconstructive postmodernists insist that the making of every aspect of human existence is culturally created and determined in particular, localized circumstances about which no generalizations can be

made. Even particularized meaning, however, is regarded as relative and temporary. (pp. 13-14)

Spretnak's definition permits us to see how the postmodern ethnographer proceeds. The postmodernist ethnographer enters into a world from which he or she is methodologically required to have become detached and displaced. Such an ethnographer is in effect reconstituted as Simmel's (1950) "stranger" (see also Frisby, 1992) and Park's (1929/1969a) and Stonequist's (1937/1961) "marginalized" person (see also Wood, 1934/1969, pp. 245-284). Like those ideal-typical ethnographers-in-spite-of-themselves, this social scientist begins work as a self-defined newcomer to the habitat and life world of his or her subjects (see Agar, 1980; Georges & Jones, 1980; D. Rose, 1989). He or she is a citizen-scholar (Saxton, 1993) as well as a participant observer (Vidich, 1955). Older traditions and aims of ethnography, including especially the quest for valid generalizations and substantive conclusions, are temporarily set aside in behalf of securing "thick descriptions" (Geertz, 1973) that will in turn make possible "thick interpretations"—joining ethnography to both biography and lived experience (Denzin, 1989, pp. 32-34). History is banished from the ethnographic enterprise except when and to the effect that local folk histories enter into the vocabularies of motive and conduct employed by the subjects.[34] Because crossing the postmodern divide (Borgmann, 1992; I. Chambers, 1990) requires one to abandon all established and preconceived values, theories, perspectives, preferences, and prejudices as resources for ethnographic study, the ethnographer must bracket these, treating them as if they are arbitrary and contingent rather then hegemonic and guiding (Rosenau, 1992, pp. 25-76). Hence the postmodernist ethnographer takes seriously the aim of such deconstructionists as Derrida (e.g., 1976, 1981), Lyotard (e.g., 1989), and Baudrillard (e.g., 1981, 1983, 1988b), namely, to disprivilege all received texts and established discourses in behalf of an all-encompassing critical skepticism about knowledge. In so doing, the ethnographer displaces and deconstructs his or her own place on the hierarchy of statuses that all too often disguise their invidious character as dichotomies (see Bendix & Berger, 1959; for a postmodern analysis of a dichotomy, see Lyman, 1992a). To all of these, instead, is given contingency—the contingencies of language, of selfhood, and of community (Rorty, 1989; C. Taylor, 1989).

For anthropologists, the new forms for ethnography begin with a recognition of their irreducible limitation: the very presentation of ethnographic information in a monograph is a "text" and therefore subject to the entire critical apparatus that the postmodern perspective brings to bear on any text.[35] The ethnographic enterprise is to be conceived as a task undertaken all too often by an unacculturated stranger who is guided by whatever the uneasy mix of poetry and politics gives to his or her efforts to comprehend an alien culture. Above all, an ethnography is now to be regarded as a piece of writing—as such, it cannot be said either to present or to represent what the older and newly discredited ideology of former ethnography claimed for itself: an unmodified and unfiltered record of immediate experience and an accurate portrait of the culture of the "other."

The postmodern critique has engendered something of a crisis among present-day anthropologists. As in the response to other crises, a new self-and-other consciousness has come to the fore, and the imperatives of reflexivity have shifted attention onto the literary, political, and historical features of ethnography as well as onto career imperatives, all of which have hitherto been overlooked. Engaging themselves with these issues, such disciplinary leaders as Clifford Geertz, Mary Douglas, Claude Lévi-Strauss, and the late Victor Turner have blurred the old distinction between art and science and challenged the very basis of the claim to exacting rigor, unblinking truth telling, and unbiased reporting that marked the boundary separating one from the other.

Rereading the works in the classical ethnographic canon has now become a critical task of the highest importance. A new form of structuralist method must be devised if we are to dig beneath the works and uncover both their hidden truths and their limiting blinders. That canon is now to be seen as a product of the age of Occidental colonialism and to have been methodologically constrained by the metropole ideologies and literary conventions that gave voice and quality to them. Yet these ethnographies are not to be relegated to the historical dustbin of a rejectable epoch of disciplinary childhood by today's and tomorrow's anthropologists. Rather, in consideration of the fact that few of the latter will follow career trajectories like those of Malinowski or Powdermaker—that is, either spending decades of their lives in residence with a nonliterate Oceanic people or moving from the ethnographic task of observing at close range a group of South Africans to another, living among blacks in a segregated Mississippi town, and then to still another, closely examining how the Hollywood film industry became a "dream factory,"—the ethnologist of the present age and the immediate future is likely to do but one ethnography—a dissertation that stakes his or her claim to the title of ethnologist and to the perquisites of an academic life spent largely away from the field. Moreover, career considerations are not the only element affecting ethnology. The "field" itself has become constricted by the march of decolonization and the modernization that has overtaken once "primitive" peoples. For these reasons, rereading old ethnographies becomes a vicarious way to experience the original ways of the discipline, whereas criticizing them provides the ethnologist with a way to distance him- or herself from modernist foibles. Except for the dissertation ethnography and for those anthropologists who choose to move in on the turf of the equally postmodern sociological ethnographers of urban and industrial settings, the ethnographic task of anthropology may become one devoted to reading texts and writing critiques. The "field" may be located in one's library or one's study.

Given the postmodern ethnographers' epistemological stance and disprivileged social status, two fundamental problems for the sociological version of the new ethnography are its relationship to social change and social action, and the applicable scope of its representations of reality.

The first problem has been posed as well as answered by Michael Burawoy et al. (1992) in their conception of "ethnography unbound" and the role of the "extended case method." They direct the ethnographer toward the macropolitical, economic, and historical contexts in which directly observed events occur, and perceive in the latter fundamental issues of domination and resistance (see also Feagin, Orum, & Sjoberg, 1991). Norman Denzin (1989), a leader of postmodern approaches to ethnography, approaches the generality issue in two distinct though related ways. His advice to ethnographers is that they first immerse themselves in the lives of their subjects and, after achieving a deep understanding of these through rigorous effort, produce a contextualized reproduction and interpretation of the stories told by the subjects. Ultimately, an ethnographic report will present an integrated synthesis of experience and theory. The "final interpretive theory is multivoiced and dialogical. It builds on native interpretations and in fact simply articulates what is implicit in those interpretations" (p. 120). Denzin's strategic move out of the epistemological cul-de-sac presented by such daunting observations as Berry's specific skepticism about the possibility of making valid generalizations in an ethnoracially pluralist society, or by the growing skepticism about the kind and quality of results that sociologists' adherence to positivistic and natural science models will engender (T. R. Vaughan, 1993, p. 120), is to take the onset of the postmodern condition as the very occasion for presenting a new kind of ethnography. He encourages, in effect, an ethnographic attitude of engagement with a world that is ontologically absurd but always meaningful to those who live in it (see Lyman & Scott, 1989). Thus he concludes his methodological treatise by claiming that the world has now entered its Fourth Epoch (following Antiquity, the Middle Ages, and the Modern Age), and that this latest epoch is in fact the "postmodern period" (Denzin, 1989, p. 138). The ethnographic method appropriate to this period, Denzin goes on, is one that is dedicated "to understanding how this historical moment universalizes itself in the lives of interesting individuals" (p. 189). Method and substance are joined in the common recognition that everyone shares in the same world and responds to it somehow. The study of the common condition and the uncovering of the uncommon response become the warp and woof of the fragile but not threadbare sociological skein of the postmodern era.

The postmodern is a cultural form as well as an era of history. As the former, like all the forms noted by Simmel, it invites and evokes its counteracting and rebellious tendencies. It too, then, is likely to suffer the penultimate tragedy of culture—the inability to emancipate life from all of its forms (Weinstein & Weinstein, 1990). However, in this era, the sociologist-ethnographer will not merely observe that history; he or she will participate in its everlasting quest for freedom, and be a partner in and a reporter on "the pains, the agonies, the emotional experiences, the small and large victories, the traumas, the fears, the anxieties, the dreams, fantasies and the hopes" of the lives of the peoples. These constitute this era's ethnographies—true tales of the field (Van Maanen, 1988).

The methods of ethnography have become highly refined and diverse, and the reasons for doing ethnography have multiplied. No longer linked to the values that had guided and focused the work of earlier ethnographers, the new ethnography ranges over a vastly expanded subject matter, limited only by the varieties of experience in modern life; the points of view from which ethnographic observations may be made are as great as the choices of lifestyles available in modern society. It is our hope that the technological refinement of the ethnographic method will find its vindication in the discovery of new sets of problems that lead to a greater understanding of the modern world.

Although it is true that at some level all research is a uniquely individual enterprise—not part of a sacrosanct body of accumulating knowledge—it is also true that it is always guided by values that are not unique to the investigator: We are all creatures of our own social and cultural pasts. However, in order to be meaningful to others, the uniqueness of our own research experience gains significance when it is related to the theories of our predecessors and the research of our contemporaries. Social and cultural understanding can be found by ethnographers only if they are aware of the sources of the ideas that motivate them and are willing to confront them—with all that such a confrontation entails.

Notes

1. For a discussion of the fundamental similarities between so-called quantitative and qualitative methods, see Vidich and Bensman (1968, chap. 13).

2. Here we merely gloss a serious problem in the philosophy and epistemology of the social sciences and present one possible approach to it. Some of the issues are discussed and debated in such recent works as those by C. W. Smith (1979), Rabinow and Sullivan (1979), G. Morgan (1983), Fiske and Schweder (1986), Hare and Blumberg (1988), Ashmore (1989), Minnich (1990), Bohman (1991), Sadri (1992, pp. 3-32, 105-142), and Harré (1984).

3. Many of the issues raised by this new outlook are treated in the essays collected in A. Rose (1988).

4. The following draws on Lyman (1990a).

5. This orientation differs from that used by Thucydides (1972) in *History of the Peloponnesian War.* His observations were made from the perspective of a participant who detached himself from the norms of both warring sides while never making explicit his own values. His book has confounded legions of scholars who have attempted to find his underlying themes, not understanding that the work is replete with ambiguities that do not lend themselves to a single viewpoint. For various perspectives on Thucydides' work, see Kitto (1991, pp. 136-152), Kluckhohn (1961, pp. 4, 34-35, 55, 64-66), Humphreys (1978, pp. 94, 131, 143, 227-232, 300-307), and Grant (1992, pp. 5, 45, 148-149).

6. When discussing the crimes committed by the Spaniards against the Indians, Hosle (1992) states: "It is certainly not easy to answer the following question: Were the priests who accompanied the conquistadors also responsible, even if they condemned the violence committed, insofar as their presence in a certain sense legitimized the enterprise? It is impossible to deny that by their mere presence they contributed to Christianity appearing as an extremely hypocritical religion, which spoke of universal love and nevertheless was the religion of brutal criminals. Yet it is clear that without the missionaries' presence even more cruelties would have been committed. Hypocrisy at least acknowledges in theory certain norms, and by so doing gives the oppressed the possibility to claim certain rights. Open brutality may be more sincere, but sincerity is not the only value. Sincere brutality generates nothing positive; hypocrisy, on the other side, bears in itself the force which can overcome it" (p. 236). If it does anything, Hosle's defense of Christianity reveals the difficulty still remaining in debates over universalistic as opposed to relativistic values and leaves wide open any resolution of the problem. See also Lippy, Choquette, and Poole (1992). For further history and discussion of the de Las Casas-Sepulveda dispute and its implications for ethnohistory and ethnology of the Americas, see Hanke (1949/1965, 1959/1970, 1974).

7. A fine example is the ethnographic study by Bishop Robert Henry Codrington (1891) titled *The Melanesians.* Codrington's study provided the sole source for Yale University anthropologist Loomis Havemeyer's (1929) chapter on the Melanesians (pp. 141-160). See Codrington (1974) for an excerpt from *The Melanesians* titled "Mana." See also the critical discussion in Kuper (1988, pp. 152-170).

8. A good example that also illustrates the anthropologists' despair over the disastrous effects of missionary endeavor on native life and culture is to be found in the last published work of William Hale R. Rivers (1922/1974).

9. Thus if the reader wishes to peruse one well-known exposition of "primitive" culture, George Peter Murdock's (1934) *Our Primitive Contemporaries,* as an example of one aspect of the "comparative method," he or she will discover therein ethnographies of 18 peoples who occupy time and space coincident to that of the author, arranged in terms of geography, but—with the term *primitive* as the descriptive adjective in use throughout—making the title of the book historically (that is, diachronically) oxymoronic. For a thoughtful critique, see Bock (1966).

10. Two exceptions to this mode of ethnocentric expression are worthy of note: William Graham Sumner (1840-1910), who coined the term *ethnocentrism,* seemed also to suggest that the failure of either Congress or the courts to do anything to halt the lynching of Negroes in the South signaled something less than that nation's rise to perfected civilization that other ethnologists were willing to credit to America and to other republics of the Occident: "It is unseemly that anyone should be burned at the stake in a modern civilized state" (Sumner, 1906/1940, p. 471; see also Sumner, 1905/1969). Thorstein Veblen (1857-1929) used such categories as "savagery" and "barbarism" tongue-in-cheek, often treating the moral codes and pecuniary values of the peoples so labeled as superior to those of the peoples adhering to the Protestant ethic or the spirit of capitalism, and disputing the claims of Aryan superiority so much in vogue in his day (see Veblen, 1899/1959, 1914/1990, 1919/1961a, 1919/1961b; see also A. K. Davis, 1980; Diggins, 1978; Tilman, 1991).

11. The Human Relations Area Files were reproduced, marketed, and distributed to anthropology departments in other universities. This not only added an element of standardization and uniformity to culture studies, but also made it possible for the analyst of ethnography to forgo a trip to the field. That this approach is still in vogue is illustrated by two researches by the Harvard sociologist Orlando Patterson (1982). Patterson relies on Murdock's "World Sample" of 61 slaveholding societies (out of a total of 186 societies), which are arranged geographically, but rearranges them temporally to make them serve a developmentalist thesis

that seeks to uncover the variations in as well as the functional origins of slavery. On the basis of this method, it is not surprising to find that in the sequel to his study Patterson (1991) believes he can show that "the Tupinamba, the ancient Greeks and Romans, and the southerners of the United States, *so markedly different in time, place, and levels of sociocultural development,* nonetheless reveal the remarkable tenacity of this culture-character complex" (p. 15; emphasis added).

12. For the conceptualization of a sector of the world's peoples as belonging to the Third World, as well as for the conceptualization of "developed" and "undeveloped" or "underdeveloped" societies, see Worsley (1964, 1984).

13. That capitalism had contributed to underdevelopment in both the European overseas empires and America's homegrown "ghetto colonialism" became an assumption and even an article of faith that could shape the perspective of posttraditional ethnography (see Blauner, 1972; Marable, 1983; see also Hechter, 1975).

14. For a historical view on eschatological, millennial, sacred, and secular "end-times" theories, as well as other modes of chronologizing events, see Paolo Rossi (1987).

15. It should be noted that American ethnography up to the beginnings of World War II focused almost exclusively on American Indians and the aboriginal inhabitants of American colonies. Anthropologists' interests in the high cultures of Central and South America were archaeologically oriented and were designed both to fill in the "prehistoric record" and to fill museums. Some ethnographic work was carried out in the U.S.-controlled Pacific Islands (in association with the Bernice P. Bishop Museum in Hawaii). Margaret Mead worked on American Samoa and is one of the earliest of the nonmissionaries to ethnograph a Pacific Island. Her work, aimed in part at criticizing the Puritanical sexual mores of America, overstated the actual situation in Oceania and eventually led to a counterstatement (see Freeman, 1983; Holmes, 1987; Mead, 1928/1960a, 1930/1960b, 1949/1960c, 1935/1960d).

16. This was the same perspective used by anthropologists who administered the Japanese relocation centers during World War II and who had had some of their training on the reservation. For accounts by those anthropologists who moved from Amerindian to Japanese American incarceration ethnography and administration, see Leighton (1945), Wax (1971), Spicer, Hansen, Luomala, and Opler (1969), and Myer (1971). For a spirited critique, see Drinnon (1987).

17. For some representative ethnographies of the southwestern Amerindian peoples, see Schwatka (1893/1977), Nordenskiold (1893/1979), McGee (1899/1971), Goddard (1913/1976), White (1933/1974), Spier (1933/1978), and Kluckhohn (1944). See also Eggan (1966, pp. 112-141).

18. A recent ethnography of the Zuni by Tedlock (1992) both reflects upon and critically appraises Cushing's work among that tribe.

19. Radin (1935/1970, 1936/1971a) also did fieldwork among the Italians and Chinese of San Francisco.

20. Clark Wissler (1940/1966a, 1938/1966b) established his credentials on the basis of a lifetime in service to ethnohistorical and ethnographic study of the United States.

21. Although not carried out at the University of Chicago, this study bears the stamp of that school's approach.

22. In that report, he was the first to see the new role of the university president as an administrative "Captain of Erudition," the beginnings of university public relations designed to protect the image of learning, and the business foundations in real estate and fund-raising (endowments) of the university system in the United States.

23. In 1992, when new questions were raised about the ethnocultural and ethical aspects of Whyte's study of "Cornerville," a symposium reviewed the matter extensively (see "*Street Corner Society* Revisited," 1992).

24. A social variant of Redfield's perspective found its way into some of the urban community, ethnic enclave, and small-town studies of America that were conducted or supervised by anthropologists or Chicago sociologists (see Hannerz, 1980; Lyon, 1987; Suttles, 1972, pp. 3-20). (A revival of ecological studies rooted in the idea that the uses of space are socially constructed was begun with the publication of Lyman & Scott, 1967; see also Ericksen, 1980.) As early as 1914, M. C. Elmer, a promising graduate student at the University of Chicago, had written a Ph.D. dissertation on social surveys in urban communities that reflected the shift from the church to the "scientific" survey tradition in both the social gospel movement and the discipline of sociology; seven years later, Raleigh Webster Stone (1921) in effect signaled that the transition to a newer orientation was well under way when he offered *The Origin of the Survey Movement* as his Ph.D. dissertation at Chicago. In 1933, Albert Bailie Blumenthal submitted *A Sociological Study of a Small Town* as his doctoral dissertation at the same university (Faris, 1970, pp. 135-140). However, the central thrust of ethnological studies in Chicago's sociology department after Robert E. Park had joined its faculty concerned community and subcommunity organization within the city (see, e.g., N. Anderson, 1959), and, for some, how the gemeinschaft could be reconstituted in the metropolis (see Fishman, 1977; Quandt, 1970).

25. That ethnographies of small towns and large cities adopted an approach more or less consistent with the macropolitical-economic orientation emphasized by Vidich and Bensman is evidenced in works by P. Davis (1982), Wallace (1987), Arsenault (1988), Campbell (1992), Moorhouse (1988), and Reid (1992).

26. Earlier, Vidich (1952, 1980) had contributed to the reconsideration of anthropological approaches to so-called primitive societies, reconceiving such studies as requiring an orientation that focused on the effects of global colonialism and its rivalries on the structure

and process of colonialized societies. For the connections between his anthropological study of Palau under various colonial administrations and the study of "Springdale," see Vidich (1986).

27. British approaches to the historical sociology of small towns did not adopt Tönnies's theoretical stance (see, e.g., Abrams & Wrigley, 1979).

28. See also Glazer (1954). "Hansen's law" was the basis for work by Kennedy (1944) and Herberg (1960).

29. For monographs illustrating the stages in the evolution of these studies, see Blackman (1891/1976), P. S. Taylor (1930/1970, 1983), Gamio (1930/1969, 1931/1971), Bogardus (1934/1970), and Galarza (1964, 1970, 1977). For community studies in New Mexico, see Gonzalez (1967), Sanchez (1967), and Forrest (1989). For Arizona, see Sheridan (1986); for Texas, see Rubel (1971); for Indiana, see Lane and Escobar (1987); for Chicago, see Padilla (1985). For general and historical studies, see Burma (1985), Officer (1987), and D. J. Weber (1992). For the shift from eth-class to postmodern analysis, see Barrera (1979, 1988).

30. Subsequent works (e.g., Fuchs, 1990; Keyes, 1982; Kivisto, 1984, 1989; Lieberson, 1980; Lieberson & Waters, 1988; Royce, 1982; Steinberg, 1981; Waters, 1990) emphasized pluralism, contingency, and the voluntary and social constructionist aspects of race and ethnicity.

31. In anthropology, the shift toward a new outlook included a critical reevaluation and commentary on virtually every aspect of ethnology and ethnography in what has thus far produced seven volumes of essays edited by George W. Stocking, Jr. (1983, 1984, 1985, 1986, 1988, 1989, 1991). A turn toward the classics of antiquity and their relation to modern and postmodern anthropology was appraised by Redfield's son (see J. Redfield, 1991).

32. One element of intellectual and moral influence has given rise to anxiety, recriminations, and rhetorical attempts to excuse, justify, or escape from the burden it lays on those who believe that postmodernism is a countercultural orientation of the Left, namely, the accusation that its preeminent philosophical founders—Heidegger and de Man—were sympathetic to and supporters of the Hitler regime and Nazism. For debates on this far-from-resolved issue, see Habermas (1983), Farias (1989), Neske and Kettering (1990), Ferry and Renaut (1990), Lyotard (1990), Rockmore (1992), Derrida (1992), Hamacher, Hertz, and Keenan (1989), and Lehman (1992). Another important contributor to postmodernism, Michel Foucault, has aroused apprehension over the extent to which his sexual preferences and promiscuous lifestyle affected his philosophical perspective. For various opinions on the matter, see Poster (1987-1988), Foucault (1992), Eribon (1991), Miller (1993); and Nikolinakos (1990). See also Paglia (1991).

33. The procedural example used by Manning is from Cressey (1953, p. 16).

34. For a discussion of the several issues involved in the relationship of history to ethnography, see Comaroff and Comaroff (1992); compare Natanson (1962).

35. The following draws on the essays and commentaries in Clifford and Marcus (1986).

References

Abeyesekere, G. (1992). *The apotheosis of Captain Cook: European mythmaking in the Pacific.* Princeton, NJ: Princeton University Press.

Abrahams, R. D. (1964). *Deep down in the jungle: Negro narrative folklore from the streets of Philadelphia.* Hatboro, PA: Folklore Associates.

Abrahams, R. D. (1970). *Positively black.* Englewood Cliffs, NJ: Prentice Hall.

Abrahams, R. D. (1992). *Singing the master: The emergence of African American culture in the plantation South.* New York: Pantheon.

Abrahamson, H. J. (1980). Assimilation and pluralism. In S. Thernstrom (Ed.), *Harvard encyclopedia of American ethnic groups.* Cambridge, MA: Harvard University Press.

Abrams, P., & Wrigley, E. A. (Eds.). (1979). *Towns and societies: Essays in economic history and historical sociology.* Cambridge, UK: Cambridge University Press.

Adler, P. A., Adler, P., & Fontana, A. (1987). Everyday life sociology. In K. Plummer (Ed.), *Symbolic interactionism: Vol. 1. Foundations and history* (pp. 436-454). Brookfield, VT: Edward Elgar.

Agar, M. H. (1980). *The professional stranger: An informal introduction to ethnography.* New York: Academic Press.

Alba, R. (1985). *Italian Americans: Into the twilight of ethnicity.* Englewood Cliffs, NJ: Prentice Hall.

Alba, R. (Ed.). (1989). *Ethnicity and race in the U.S.A.: Toward the twenty-first century.* New York: Routledge, Chapman Hall.

Alba, R. (1990). *Ethnic identity: The transformation of white America.* New Haven, CT: Yale University Press.

Aldrich, R. (1990). *The French presence in the South Pacific, 1842-1940.* Honolulu: University of Hawaii Press.

Anderson, E. (1978). *A place on the corner.* Chicago: University of Chicago Press.

Anderson, K. J. (1991). *Vancouver's Chinatown: Racial discourse in Canada, 1875-1980.* Montreal: McGill-Queen's University Press.

Anderson, N. (1959). *The urban community: A world perspective.* New York: Henry Holt.

Anderson, N. (1961). *The hobo: The sociology of the homeless man.* Chicago: University of Chicago Press. (Original work published 1923)

Anderson, T. L. (Ed.). (1992). *Property rights and Indian economics.* Lanham, MD: Rowman & Littlefield.

Arsenault, R. (1988). *St. Petersburg and the Florida dream, 1888-1950.* Norfolk, VA: Donning.

Ashmore, M. (1989). *The reflexive thesis: Writing sociology of scientific knowledge.* Chicago: University of Chicago Press.

Atkinson, P. (1990). *The ethnographic imagination: Textual constructions of reality.* London: Routledge.

Bailey, B. L. (1988). *From front porch to back seat: Courtship in twentieth century America.* Baltimore: Johns Hopkins University Press.

Baker, J. R. (1974). *Race.* New York: Oxford University Press.

Ball, D. W. (1968). Toward a sociology of telephones and telephoners. In M. Truzzi (Ed.), *Sociology and everyday life* (pp. 59-75). Englewood Cliffs, NJ: Prentice Hall.

Barkan, E. (1992). *The retreat of scientific racism: Changing concepts of race in Britain and the United States.* Cambridge, UK: Cambridge University Press.

Barrera, M. (1979). *Race and class in the Southwest: A theory of racial inequality.* Notre Dame, IN: University of Notre Dame Press.

Barrera, M. (1988). *Beyond Aztlan: Ethnic autonomy in comparative perspective.* Notre Dame, IN: University of Notre Dame Press.

Baudrillard, J. (1981). *For a critique of the political economy of the sign* (C. Levin, Trans.). St. Louis, MO: Telos.

Baudrillard, J. (1983). *In the shadow of the silent majorities, or, the end of the social and other essays* (P. Foss, J. Johnston, & P. Patton, Trans.). New York: Semiotext(e).

Baudrillard, J. (1988a). *America* (C. Turner, Trans.). London: Verso.

Baudrillard, J. (1988b). *The ecstasy of communication* (S. Lotringer, Ed.; B. Schutze & C. Schutze, Trans.). New York: Semiotext(e).

Becker, H. (1962). *Through values to social interpretation: Essays on social contexts, actions, types, and prospects.* New York: Greenwood. (Original work published 1950)

Becker, H. (1974). *Systematic sociology: On the basis of the* Beziehungslehre *and* Begildlehre *of Leopold von Wiese.* New York: Arno. (Original work published 1932)

Bender, T. (1978). *Community and social change in America.* New Brunswick, NJ: Rutgers University Press.

Bendix, R., & Berger, B. (1959). Images of society and problems of concept formation in sociology. In L. Gross (Ed.), *Symposium on sociological theory* (pp. 92-118). Evanston, IL: Row, Peterson.

Bensman, J., & Vidich, A. J. (1987). *American society: The welfare state and beyond* (2nd ed.). Amherst, MA: Bergin & Garvey.

Berlo, J. C. (Ed.). (1992). *The early years of Native American art history: The politics of scholarship and collecting.* Seattle: University of Washington Press.

Berry, B. (1963). *Almost white.* New York: Macmillan.

Berry, B., & Tischler, H. (1978). *Race and ethnic relations* (4th ed.). Boston: Houghton Mifflin.

Beverly, J. (1992). The margin at the center: On *testimonio* (testimonial narrative). In S. Smith & J. Watson (Eds.), *De/colonizing the subject: The politics of gender in women's autobiography.* Minneapolis: University of Minnesota Press.

Bhabha, H. K. (Ed.). (1990a). *Nation and narration.* London: Routledge.

Bhabha, H. K. (1990b). The other question: Differences, discrimination and the discourse of colonialism. In R. Ferguson et al. (Eds.), *Out there: Marginalization and contemporary cultures* (pp. 71-88). Cambridge: MIT Press.

Bieder, R. E. (1989). *Science encounters the Indian, 1820-1880: The early years of American ethnology.* Norman: University of Oklahoma Press.

Bigham, D. E. (1987). *We ask only a fair trial: A history of the black community of Evansville, Indiana.* Bloomington: Indiana University Press/University of Southern Indiana.

Blackman, F. M. (1976). *Spanish institutions of the Southwest.* Glorieta, NM: Rio Grande. (Original work published 1891)

Blackwell, J. E. (1991). *The black community: Diversity and unity* (3rd ed.). New York: HarperCollins.

Blake, C. N. (1990). *Beloved community: The cultural criticism of Randolph Bourne, Van Wyck Brooks, Waldo Frank, and Lewis Mumford.* Chapel Hill: University of North Carolina Press.

Blassingame, J. W. (1979). *The slave community: Plantation life in the antebellum South* (rev. ed.). New York: Oxford University Press.

Blauner, R. (1972). *Racial oppression in America.* New York: Harper & Row.

Bloom, H. (1979). *The anxiety of influence: A theory of poetry.* London: Oxford University Press.

Blumenthal, A. B. (1933). *A sociological study of a small town.* Unpublished doctoral dissertation, University of Chicago.

Bock, K. E. (1948). *The comparative method.* Unpublished doctoral dissertation, University of California, Berkeley.

Bock, K. E. (1952). Evolution and historical process. *American Anthropologist, 54,* 486-496.

Bock, K. E. (1956). *The acceptance of histories: Toward a perspective for social science.* Berkeley: University of California Press.

Bock, K. E. (1963). Evolution, function and change. *American Sociological Review, 27,* 229-237.

Bock, K. E. (1966). The comparative method of anthropology. *Comparative Studies in Society and History, 8,* 269-280.

Bock, K. E. (1974). Comparison of histories: The contribution of Henry Maine. *Comparative Studies in Society and History, 16,* 232-262.

Boeke, J. H. (1946). *The evolution of the Netherlands Indies economy.* New York: Institute of Pacific Relations.

Boeke, J. H. (1948). *The interests of the voiceless Far East: Introduction to Oriental economics.* Leiden, Netherlands: Universitaire Pers Leiden.

Bogardus, E. S. (1930). A race relations cycle. *American Journal of Sociology, 35,* 612-617.

Bogardus, E. S. (1940). Current problems of Japanese Americans. *Sociology and Social Research, 25,* 63-66.

Bogardus, E. S. (1970). *The Mexican in the United States.* New York: Arno/New York Times. (Original work published 1934)

Bohman, J. (1991). *New philosophy of social science.* Cambridge: MIT Press.

Borgmann, A. (1992). *Crossing the postmodern divide.* Chicago: University of Chicago Press.

Boxer, C. R. (1965). *Portuguese society in the tropics: The municipal councils of Goa, Macao, Bahia, and Luanda.* Madison: University of Wisconsin Press.

Boxhill, B. R. (1992). *Blacks and social justice* (rev. ed.). Lanham, MD: Rowman & Littlefield.

Bradford, P. V., & Blume, H. (1992). *Ota Benga: The Pygmy in the zoo.* New York: St. Martin's.

Brookhiser, R. (1991). *The way of the WASP: How it made America, and how it can save it, so to speak.* New York: Free Press.

Brookhiser, R. (1993, March 1). The melting pot is still simmering. *Time,* p. 72.

Brown, R. (1984). *The nature of social laws: Machiavelli to Mill.* Cambridge: Cambridge University Press.

Brown, W. O. (1934). Culture contact and race conflict. In E. B. Reuter (Ed.), *Race and culture contacts* (pp. 34-47). New York: McGraw-Hill.

Bowden, H. W. (1981). *American Indians and Christian missions: Studies in cultural conflict.* Chicago: University of Chicago Press.

Burawoy, M., Burton, A., Ferguson, A. A., Fox, K. J., Gamson, J., Gartrell, N., Hurst, L., Kurzman, C., Salzinger, L., Schiffman, J., & Ui, S. (Eds). (1992). *Ethnography unbound: Power and resistance in the modern metropolis.* Berkeley: University of California Press.

Burgess, E. W. (1916). The social survey: A field for constructive service by departments of sociology. *American Journal of Sociology, 21,* 492-500.

Burgess, E. W., & Bogue, D. J. (Eds.). (1967). *Contributions to urban sociology.* Chicago: University of Chicago Press.

Burma, J. H. (Ed.). (1985). *Mexican-Americans in comparative perspective.* Washington, DC: Urban Institute.

Button, J. W. (1989). *Blacks and social change: Impact of the civil rights movement in southern communities.* Princeton, NJ: Princeton University Press.

Calloway, C. G. (Ed.). (1991). *Dawnland encounters: Indians and Europeans in northern New England.* Hanover, NH: University Press of New England.

Campbell, W. D. (1992). *Providence.* Atlanta: Longstreet.

Caplow, T., Bahr, H. M., Chadwick, B. A., Hill, R., & Williamson, M. H. (1982). *Middletown families: Fifty years of change and continuity.* Minneapolis: University of Minnesota Press.

Caplow, T., Bahr, H. M., Chadwick, B. A., Hill, R., & Williamson, M. H. (1983). *All faithful people: Change and continuity in Middletown's religion.* Minneapolis: University of Minnesota Press.

Cavan, R. S. (1965). *Suicide.* New York: Russell & Russell. (Original work published 1928)

Chambers, C. A. (1971). *Paul U. Kellogg and the survey: Voices for social welfare and social justice.* Minneapolis: University of Minnesota Press.

Chambers, I. (1990). *Border dialogues: Journeys into postmodernity.* London: Routledge.

Chan, S. (1991). *Asian Americans: An interpretive history.* Boston: Twayne.

Cherokee Nation v. Georgia, 30 U.S. (5 Pet.) 1 (1831).

Christopher, R. C. (1989). *Crashing the gates: The de-WASPing of America's power elite.* New York: Simon & Schuster.

Clifford, J. (1986). On ethnographic self-fashioning: Conrad and Malinowski. In T. C. Heller, M. Sosna, & D. E. Wellbery (Eds.), *Reconstructing individualism: Autonomy, individuality, and the self in Western thought* (pp. 140-162). Stanford, CA: Stanford University Press.

Clifford, J. (1990). On collecting art and culture. In R. Ferguson et al. (Eds.). *Out there: Marginalization and contemporary cultures* (pp. 1-169). Cambridge: MIT Press.

Codrington, R. H. (1891). *The Melanesians.* Oxford: Clarendon.

Codrington, R. H. (1974). Mana. In A. Montagu (Ed.), *Frontiers of anthropology* (pp. 255-259). New York: G. P. Putnam's Sons. (Reprinted from *The Melanesians,* Oxford: Clarendon, 1891)

Cohen, S. R. (1981). *Reconciling industrial conflict and democracy: The Pittsburgh survey and the growth of social research in the United States.* Unpublished doctoral dissertation, Columbia University.

Coleman, M. C. (1985). *Presbyterian missionary attitudes toward American Indians, 1837-1893.* Jackson: University Press of Mississippi.

Comaroff, J., & Comaroff, J. (1992). *Ethnography and the historical imagination.* Boulder, CO: Westview.

Contosta, D. R. (1980). *Henry Adams and the American experiment.* Boston: Little, Brown.

Cornell, S. (1988). The transformation of tribe: Organization and self-concept in Native American ethnicities. *Ethnic and Racial Studies, 11,* 27-47.

Cornwell, R. (1992). Interactive art: Touching the "body in the mind." *Discourse: Journal for Theoretical Studies in Media and Culture, 14,* 203-221.

Covello, L. (1967). The social background of the Italo-American school child: A study of the southern Italian family mores and their effect on the school situation in Italy and America (F. Cordesco, Ed.). Leiden, Netherlands: E. J. Brill.

Cressey, D. (1953). *Other people's money.* New York: Free Press.

Culin, S. (1967). Zuni pictures. In E. C. Parsons (Ed.), *American Indian life* (pp. 175-178). Lincoln: University of Nebraska Press. (Original work published 1922)

Cushing, F. H. (1974). *Zuni breadstuff.* New York: Museum of the American Indian, Keye Foundation. (Original work published 1920)

Cushing, F. H. (1979). *Zuni: Selected writings of Frank Hamilton Cushing* (J. Green, Ed.). Lincoln: University of Nebraska Press.

Cushing, F. H. (1988). *Zuni folk tales.* Tucson: University of Arizona Press. (Original work published 1901)

Cushing, F. H. (1990). *Cushing at Zuni: The correspondence and journals of Frank Hamilton Cushing, 1878-1884* (J. Green, Ed.). Albuquerque: University of New Mexico Press.

Dai, B. (1970). *Opium addiction in Chicago.* Montclair, NJ: Patterson Smith. (Original work published 1937)

Dale, E. E. (1984). *The Indians of the Southwest: A century of development under the United States.* Norman: University of Oklahoma Press. (Original work published 1949)

Dansereau, H. K. (1961). Some implications of modern highways for community ecology. In G. A. Theodorsen (Ed.), *Studies in human ecology* (pp. 175-187). Evanston, IL: Row, Peterson.

Davis, A. K. (1980). *Thorstein Veblen's social theory.* New York: Arno.

Davis, P. (1982). *Hometown: A contemporary American chronicle.* New York: Simon & Schuster.

de Sola Poole, I. (Ed.). (1981). *The social impact of the telephone.* Cambridge: MIT Press.

Degerando, J.-M. (1969). *The observation of savage peoples* (F. C. T. Moore, Trans.). London: Routledge & Kegan Paul. (Original work published 1800)

Denzin, N. (1989). *Interpretive Interactionism.* Newbury Park, CA: Sage.

Derrida, J. (1976). *Of grammatology* (G. C. Spivak, Trans.). Baltimore: Johns Hopkins University Press.

Derrida, J. (1981). *Positions* (A. Bass, Trans.). Chicago: University of Chicago Press.

Derrida, J. (1992). *The other heading: Reflections on today's Europe* (P.-A. Brault & M. B. Naas, Trans.). Bloomington: Indiana University Press.

Diamond, S. (1963). The search for the primitive. In I. Goldston (Ed.), *Man's image in medicine and anthropology* (pp. 62-115). New York: International University Press.

Diamond, S. (1972). Anthropology in question. In D. Hymes (Ed.), *Reinventing anthropology* (pp. 401-429). New York: Pantheon.

Diamond, S. (1992). *Compromised campus: The collaboration of universities with the intelligence community, 1945-1955.* New York: Oxford University Press.

Diggins, J. P. (1978). *The bard of savagery: Thorstein Veblen and modern social theory.* New York: Seabury.

Diner, S. J. (1975). Department and discipline: The Department of Sociology at the University of Chicago, 1892-1920. *Minerva, 13,* 518-519, 538.

Dirlik, A. (1987). Culturalism as hegemonic ideology and liberating practice. *Cultural Critique, 6,* 13-50.

Dockstader, F. J. (1985). *The Kachina and the white man: The influences of white culture on the Hopi Kachina religion* (rev. ed.). Albuquerque: University of New Mexico Press.

Douglas, J. (1974). A brief history of sociologists of everyday life. In J. Douglas et al. (Eds.), *Introduction to the sociologies of everyday life* (pp. 182-210). Boston: Allyn & Bacon.

Drake, S. C., & Cayton, H. R. (1962). *Black metropolis: A study of Negro life in a northern city* (rev. ed., Vols. 1-2). New York: Harper Torchbooks.

Drinnon, R. (1987). *Keeper of concentration camps: Dillon S. Myer and American racism.* Berkeley: University of California Press.

Du Bois, W. E. B. (1967). *The Philadelphia Negro: A social study.* New York: Benjamin Blom. (Original work published 1899)

Duffy, J. (1959). *Portuguese Africa.* Cambridge, MA: Harvard University Press.

Duncan, O. D. (1957). Community size and the rural-urban continuum. In P. K. Hatt & A. J. Reiss, Jr. (Eds.), *Cities and society: The revised reader in urban sociology* (pp. 35-45). Glencoe, IL: Free Press.

Duneier, M. (1992). *Slim's table: Race, respectability, and masculinity.* Chicago: University of Chicago Press.

Early, G. (Ed.). (1993). *Lure and loathing: Essays on race, identity, and the ambivalence of assimilation.* New York: Allen Lane/Penguin.

Eggan, F. (1966). *The American Indian: Perspectives for the study of social change* (The Lewis Henry Morgan Lectures). Cambridge, UK: Cambridge University Press.

Elmer, M. C. (1914). *Social surveys of urban communities.* Unpublished doctoral dissertation, University of Chicago.

Engels, F. (1884). *The origins of the family, private property and the state.* Moscow: Foreign Languages.

Eribon, D. (1991). *Michel Foucault* (B. Wing. Trans.). Cambridge, MA: Harvard University Press.

Ericksen, E. G. (1980). *The territorial experience: Human ecology as symbolic interaction.* Austin: University of Texas Press.

Espiritu, Y. L. (1992). *Asian American panethnicity: Bridging institutions and identities.* Philadelphia: Temple University Press.

Etzioni, A. (1959). The ghetto: A re-evaluation. *Social Forces, 37,* 255-262.

Evans, A. S., & Lee, D. (1990). *Pearl City, Florida: A black community remembers.* Boca Raton: Florida Atlantic University Press.

Farias, V. (1989). *Heidegger and Nazism* (J. Margolis & T. Rickmore, Eds.; P. Burrell & G. Ricci, Trans.). Philadelphia: Temple University Press.

Faris, R. E. L. (1970). *Chicago sociology, 1920-1932.* Chicago: University of Chicago Press.

Faris, R. E. L., & Dunham, H. W. (1965). *Mental disorders in urban areas: An ecological study of schizophrenia and other psychoses.* Chicago: University of Chicago Press. (Original work published 1939)

Feagin, J. R., Orum, A., & Sjoberg, G. (1991). The present crisis in U.S. sociology. In J. R. Feagin, A. M. Orum, & G. Sjoberg, *A case for the case study* (pp. 269-278). Chapel Hill: University of North Carolina Press.

Featherstone, M., Hepworth, M., & Turner, B. S. (Eds.). (1991). *The body: Social process and cultural theory.* London: Sage.

Feher, M. (Ed.). (1989). *Fragments for a history of the human body* (Vols. 1-3). Cambridge: MIT Press/Zone.

Ferry, L., & Renaut, A. (1990). *Heidegger and modernity* (F. Philip, Trans.). Chicago: University of Chicago Press.

Firey, W., Loomis, C. P., & Beegle, J. A. (1950). The fusion of urban and rural. In J. Labatut & W. J. Lane (Eds.), *Highways in our national life: A symposium* (pp. 154-163). Princeton, NJ: Princeton University Press.

Fishman, R. (1977). *Urban utopias in the twentieth century: Ebenezer Howard, Frank Lloyd Wright, and Le Corbusier.* New York: Basic Books.

Fiske, D. W., & Schweder, R. A. (Eds.). (1986). *Metatheory in social science: Pluralism and subjectivities.* Chicago: University of Chicago Press.

Fontana, A. (1974). Toward a complex universe: Existential sociology. In J. Douglas et al. (Eds.), *Introduction to the sociologies of everyday life* (pp. 155-181). Boston: Allyn & Bacon.

Forbes, J. D. (1973). *Aztecs del norte: The Chicanos of Aztlan.* Greenwich, CT: Fawcett.

Forbes, J. D. (1988). *Black Africans and Native Americans: Color, race and caste in the evolution of red-black peoples.* New York: Basil Blackwell.

Forrest, S. (1989). *The preservation of the village: New Mexico's Hispanics and the New Deal.* Albuquerque: University of New Mexico Press.

Foucault, M. (1992). *Michel Foucault, philosopher* (T. J. Armstrong, Ed. & Trans.). New York: Routledge, Chapman & Hall.

Fox, R. G. (Ed.). (1991). *Recapturing anthropology: Working in the present.* Santa Fe, NM: School of American Research Press.

Frazier, E. F. (1925). Durham: Capital of the black middle class. In A. Locke (Ed.), *The new Negro* (pp. 333-340). New York: Albert & Charles Boni.

Frazier, E. F. (1931). *The Negro family in Chicago.* Unpublished doctoral dissertation, University of Chicago.

Frazier, E. F. (1937a). The impact of urban civilization upon Negro family life. *American Sociological Review, 2,* 609-618.

Frazier, E. F. (1937b). Negro Harlem: An ecological study. *American Journal of Sociology, 43,* 72-88.

Frazier, E. F. (1953). The theoretical structure of sociology and sociological research. *British Journal of Sociology, 4,* 292-311.

Frazier, E. F. (1957a). *Black bourgeoisie: The rise of a new middle class in the United States.* Glencoe, IL: Free Press/Falcon's Wing.

Frazier, E. F. (1957b). *The Negro in the United States* (rev ed.). New York: Macmillan.

Frazier, E. F. (1963). *The Negro church in America.* New York: Schocken.

Frazier, E. F. (1966). *The Negro family in the United States* (rev ed.). Chicago: University of Chicago Press/Phoenix. (Original work published 1939)

Frazier, E. F. (1967). *Negro youth at the crossways: Their personality development in the middle states.* New York: Schocken. (Original work published 1940)

Frazier, E. F. (1968). *E. Franklin Frazier on race relations: Selected papers* (G. F. Edwards, Ed.). Chicago: University of Chicago Press.

Freeman, D. (1983). *Margaret Mead and Samoa: The making and unmaking of an anthropological myth.* Cambridge, MA: Harvard University Press.

Frisby, D. (1992). *Simmel and since: Essays on Georg Simmel's social theory.* London: Routledge.

Fuchs, L. H. (1990). *The American kaleidoscope: Race, ethnicity, and the civic culture.* Hanover, NH: University Press of New England.

Fukuyama, F. (1992). *The end of history and the last man.* New York: Free Press.

Furnivall, J. S. (1948). *Colonial policy and practice: A comparative study of Burma and Netherlands India.* New York: New York University Press.

Galarza, E. (1964). *Merchants of labor: The Mexican bracero story—an account of the managed migration of Mexican farm workers in California, 1942-1960.* San Jose, CA: Rosicrucian.

Galarza, E. (1970). *Spiders in the house and workers in the field.* Notre Dame, IN: University of Notre Dame Press.

Galarza, E. (1977). *Farm workers and agri-business in California, 1947-1960.* Notre Dame, IN: University of Notre Dame Press.

Gamio, M. (1969). *Mexican immigration to the United States: A study of human migration and adjustment.* New York: Arno/New York Times. (Original work published 1930)

Gamio, M. (1971). *The life story of the Mexican immigrant: Autobiographic documents.* New York: Dover. (Original work published 1931)

Gans, H. J. (1962). *The urban villagers: Group and class in the life of Italian-Americans.* New York: Free Press.

Garbaccia, D. R. (1984). *From Sicily to Elizabeth Street: Housing and social change among Italian immigrants, 1880-1930.* Albany: State University of New York Press.

Geertz, C. (1973). Thick description: Toward an interpretive theory of culture. In C. Geertz, *The inter-*

pretation of cultures: Selected essays (pp. 3-32). New York: Basic Books.

Gellner, E. (1979). Beyond truth and falsehood, or no method in my madness. In E. Gellner, *Spectacles and predicaments: Essays in social theory* (pp. 182-198). Cambridge, UK: Cambridge University Press.

Georges, R. A., & Jones, M. O. (1980). *People studying people: The human element in fieldwork.* Berkeley: University of California Press.

Geschwender, J. A. (1978). *Racial stratification in America.* Dubuque, IA: William C. Brown.

Gilman, S. L. (1991). *Inscribing the other.* Lincoln: University of Nebraska Press.

Ginsburg, C. (1991). *Ecstasies: Deciphering the witches' sabbath* (R. Rosenthal, Trans.). New York: Pantheon.

Ginsburg, C. (1993). The European (re)discovery of the shamans. *London Review of Books, 15,* 2.

Gist, N. P., & Halbert, L. A. (1947). *Urban society* (2nd ed.). New York: Thomas Y. Crowell.

Glazer, G. (1954). Ethnic groups in America: From national culture to ideology. In M. Berger, T. Able, & C. H. Page (Eds.), *Freedom and control in modern society* (pp. 158-173). New York: D. Van Nostrand.

Gleason, P. (1980). American identity and Americanization. In S. Thernstrom (Ed.), *Harvard encyclopedia of American ethnic groups* (pp. 31-58). Cambridge, MA: Harvard University Press.

Glick, C. E. (1955). Social roles and social types in race relations. In W. A. Lind (Ed.), *Race relations in world perspective* (pp. 239-262). Honolulu: University of Hawaii Press.

Goddard, P. E. (1976). *Indians of the Southwest.* Glorieta, NM: Rio Grande. (Original work published 1913)

Goffman, E. (1949). *Some characteristics of response to depicted experience.* Master's thesis, University of Chicago.

Goffman, E. (1959). *The presentation of self in everyday life.* Garden City, NY: Doubleday.

Goffman, E. (1961). *Asylums: Essays on the social situation of mental patients and other inmates.* Garden City, NY: Doubleday.

Goffman, E. (1971). *Relations in public: Microstudies of the public order.* New York: Basic Books.

Goffman, E. (1974). Frame analysis: An essay on the organization of experience. New York: Harper Colophon.

Gonzalez, N. L. (1967). *The Spanish Americans of New Mexico: A heritage of pride.* Albuquerque: University of New Mexico Press.

Grant, M. (1992). *A social history of Greece and Rome.* New York: Charles Scribner's Sons.

Gray, J. (1970). The intellectual standing of different races and their respective opportunities for culture. In G. Spiller (Ed.), *Papers on inter-racial problems communicated to the First Universal Race Congress, University of London, July 26-29, 1911* (pp. 79-85). New York: Citadel. (Original work published 1911)

Greek, C. E. (1978). The social gospel movement and early American sociology, 1870-1915. *Graduate Faculty Journal of Sociology, 3*(1), 30-42.

Greek, C. E. (1992). *The religious roots of American sociology.* New York: Garland.

Gullick, J. M. (1956). *The story of early Kuala Lumpur.* Singapore: Donald Moore.

Gurwitsch, A. (1966). The last work of Edmund Husserl. In A. Gurwitsch, *Studies in phenomenology and psychology.* Evanston, IL: Northwestern University Press.

Gusfield, J. R. (1975). *Community: A critical response.* New York: Harper Colophon.

Gutierrez, R. A. (1991). *When Jesus came the corn mothers went away: Marriage, sexuality and power in New Mexico, 1500-1846.* Stanford, CA: Stanford University Press.

Gwertzman, B., & Kaufman, M. T. (Eds.). (1992). *The decline and fall of the Soviet empire.* New York: New York Times.

Habermas, J. (1983). Martin Heidegger: The great influence (1959). In J. Habermas, *Philosophical-political profiles* (F. G. Lawrence, Trans.) (pp. 53-60). Cambridge: MIT Press.

Hamacher, W., Hertz, N., & Keenan, T. (Eds.). (1989). *On Paul de Man's wartime journalism.* Lincoln: University of Nebraska Press.

Hammersley, M. (1992). *What's wrong with ethnography? Methodological explorations.* London: Routledge.

Hanke, L. (1965). *The Spanish struggle for justice in the conquest of America.* Boston: Little, Brown. (Original work published 1949)

Hanke, L. (1970). *Aristotle and the American Indians: A study in race prejudice in the modern world.* Bloomington: Indiana University Press. (Original work published 1959)

Hanke, L. (1974). *All mankind is one: A study of the disputation between Bartolome de Las Casas and Juan Gines de Sepulveda on the religious and intellectual capacity of the American Indians.* De Kalb: Northern Illinois University Press.

Hannerz, U. (1980). *Exploring the city: Inquiries toward an urban anthropology.* New York: Columbia University Press.

Hansen, M. L. (1952). The problem of the third generation immigrant. *Commentary, 14,* 492-500. (Original work published 1938)

Hare, A. P., & Blumberg, H. H. (1988). *Dramaturgical analysis of social interaction.* New York: Praeger.

Harré, R. (1980). *Social being: A theory for social psychology.* Totowa, NJ: Rowan & Littlefield.

Harré, R. (1984). *Personal being: A theory for individual psychology.* Cambridge, MA: Harvard University Press.

Hartland, E. S. (1969). *Primitive society: The beginnings of the family and the reckoning of descent.* New York: Harper & Row. (Original work published 1921)

Hartmann, E. G. (1967). *The movement to Americanize the immigrant.* New York: AMS. (Original work published 1948)

Havemeyer, L. (1929). *Ethnography.* Boston: Ginn.

Hechter, M. (1975). *Internal colonialism: The Celtic fringe in British national development, 1536-1966.* London: Routledge & Kegan Paul.

Heizer, R. F., & Kroeber, T. (Eds.). (1979). *Ishi the last Yahi: A documentary history.* Berkeley: University of California Press.

Herberg, W. (1960). *Protestant-Catholic-Jew: An essay in American religious sociology.* Garden City, NY: Doubleday.

Herskovitz, M. (1958). *The myth of the Negro past.* Boston: Beacon. (Original work published 1941)

Herskovitz, M. (1966). *The new world Negro: Selected papers in Afroamerican studies* (F. S. Herskovitz, Ed.). Bloomington: Indiana University Press.

Hill-Lubin, M. A. (1992). "Presence Africaine": A voice in the wilderness, a record of black kinship. In V. Y. Mudimbe (Ed.), *The surreptitious speech: Presence Africaine and the politics of otherness, 1947-1987* (pp. 157-173). Chicago: University of Chicago Press.

Hinsley, C. M., Jr. (1981). *Savages and scientists: The Smithsonian Institution and the development of American anthropology, 1846-1910.* Washington, DC: Smithsonian Institution Press.

Hodgen, M. T. (1936). *The doctrine of survivals: A chapter in the history of scientific method in the study of man.* London: Allenson.

Hodgen, M. T. (1964). *Early anthropology in the sixteenth and seventeenth centuries.* Philadelphia: University of Pennsylvania.

Hodgen, M. T. (1974). *Anthropology, history and cultural change.* Tucson: University of Arizona Press/ Wenner-Gren Foundation for Anthropological Research.

Holden, A. C. (1970). *The settlement idea: A vision of social justice.* New York: Arno/New York Times. (Original work published 1922)

Hollingshead, A. B. (1961). *Elmtown's youth: The impact of social classes on adolescents.* New York: Science Editions. (Original work published 1949)

Holmes, L. D. (1987). *Quest for the real Samoa: The Mead/ Freeman controversy and beyond.* South Hadley, MA: Bergin & Garvey.

Horowitz, I. L. (Ed.). (1967). *The rise and fall of Project Camelot: Studies in the relationship between social science and practical politics.* Cambridge: MIT Press.

Hosle, V. (1992). The Third World as a philosophical problem. *Social Research, 59,* 230-262.

Hughes, E. C. (1928). *A study of a secular institution: The Chicago Real Estate Board.* Unpublished doctoral dissertation, University of Chicago.

Humphreys, S. C. (1978). *Anthropology and the Greeks.* London: Routledge & Kegan Paul.

Hune, S., et al. (Eds.). (1991). *Asian Americans: Comparative and global perspectives.* Pullman: Washington State University Press.

Ignacio, L. F. (1976). *Asian Americans and Pacific Islanders (Is there such an ethnic group?).* San Jose, CA: Pilipino Development Associates.

Immigration Commission (W. P. Dillingham, Chair). (1970). *Immigrants in industry* (25 parts). New York: Arno/New York Times. (Original work published 1911)

Jackson, J. S. (Ed.). (1991). *Life in black America.* Newbury Park, CA: Sage.

Jaimes, M. E. (Ed.). (1992). *The state of Native America: Genocide, colonization and resistance.* Boston: South End.

Jalali, R., & Lipset, S. M. (1992-1993). Racial and ethnic conflicts: A global perspective. *Political Science Quarterly, 107*(4), 585-606.

Johnson, J. M. (1975). *Doing field research.* New York: Free Press.

Jones, J. (1992). *Soldiers of light and love: Northern teachers and Georgia blacks, 1865-1873.* Athens: University of Georgia Press.

Joyner, C. (1984). *Down by the riverside: A South Carolina slave community.* Urbana: University of Illinois Press.

Keegan, W. F. (1992). *The people who discovered Columbus: The prehistory of the Bahamas.* Gainesville: University Press of Florida.

Keller, R. W., Jr. (1983). *American Protestantism and United States Indian policy, 1869-1882.* Lincoln: University of Nebraska Press.

Kennedy, R. J. R. (1944). Single or triple melting pot: Intermarriage trends in New Haven, 1870-1940. *American Journal of Sociology, 44,* 331-339.

Keyes, C. F. (Ed.). (1982). *Ethnic change.* Seattle: University of Washington Press.

Kinloch, G. C. (1974). *The dynamics of race relations.* New York: McGraw-Hill.

Kitto, H. D. F. (1951). *The Greeks.* London: Penguin.

Kivisto, P. (1984). *Immigrant socialists in the United States: The case of Finns and the Left.* Cranbury, NJ: Associates University Presses.

Kivisto, P. (Ed.). (1989). *The ethnic enigma: The salience of ethnicity for European-origin groups.* Philadelphia: Balch Institute Press.

Kivisto, P., & Blanck, D. (Eds.). (1990). *American immigrants and their generations: Studies and commentaries on the Hansen thesis after fifty years.* Urbana: University of Illinois Press.

Kluckhohn, C. (1944). *Navajo witchcraft.* Boston: Beacon.

Kluckhohn, C. (1961). *Anthropology and the classics: The Colver Lectures in Brown University, 1960.* Providence, RI: Brown University Press.

Knoll, T. (1982). *Becoming Americans: Asian sojourners, immigrants and refugees in the western United States.* Portland, OR: Coast to Coast.

Kotarba, J. A., & Fontana, A. (Eds.). (1987). *The existential self in society.* Chicago: University of Chicago Press.

Kramer, J. R. (1970). *The American minority community.* New York: Thomas Y. Crowell.

Kramer, J. R., & Leventman, S. (1961). *Children of the gilded ghetto: Conflict resolutions of three generations of American Jews.* New Haven, CT: Yale University Press.

Krieger, S. (1991). *Social science and the self: Personal essays as an art form.* New Brunswick, NJ: Rutgers University Press.

Kroeber, T. (1962). *Ishi in two worlds: A biography of the last wild Indian in North America.* Berkeley: University of California Press.

Kroeber, T. (1965). *Ishi: Last of his tribe.* New York: Bantam.

Kundera, M. (1988). *The art of the novel* (L. Ascher, Trans.). New York: Grove.

Kuper, A. (1988). *The invention of primitive society: Transformations of an illusion.* London: Routledge.

Kuzmics, H. (1988). The civilizing process (H. G. Zilian, Trans.). In J. Keane (Ed.), *Civil society and the state: New European perspectives.* London: Verso.

Landesco, J. (1968). *Organized crime in Chicago* (Part 3 of the Illinois Crime Survey, 1929). Chicago: University of Chicago Press.

Lane, J. B., & Escobar, E. J. (Eds.). (1987). *Forging a community: The Latino experience in Northwest Indiana, 1919-1975.* Chicago: Cattails.

Lee, R. H. (1960). *The Chinese in the United States of America.* Hong Kong: Hong Kong University Press.

Lee, R. H. (1978). *The growth and decline of Chinese communities in the Rocky Mountain region.* New York: Arno.

Lehman, D. (1992). Signs of the times: Deconstruction and the fall of Paul de Man. *Contention: Debates in Society, Culture and Science, 1*(2), 23-38.

Leighton, A. H. (1945). *The governing of men: General principles and recommendations based on experience at a Japanese relocation camp.* Princeton, NJ: Princeton University Press.

Lemert, C. (1992). Subjectivity's limit: The unsolved riddle of the standpoint. *Sociological Theory, 10,* 63-72.

Lenzer, G. (Ed.). (1975). *Auguste Comte and positivism: The essential writings.* New York: Harper Torchbooks.

Leonard, K. I. (1992). *Making ethnic choices: California's Punjabi Mexican Americans.* Philadelphia: Temple University Press.

Lieberson, S. (1961). A societal theory of race and ethnic relations. *American Sociological Review, 26,* 902-910.

Lieberson, S. (1980). *A piece of the pie: Blacks and white immigrants since 1880.* Berkeley: University of California Press.

Lieberson, S., & Waters, M. C. (1988). *From many strands: Ethnic and racial groups in contemporary America.* New York: Russell Sage Foundation.

Liebow, E. (1967). *Tally's corner: A study of Negro street corner men.* Boston: Little, Brown.

Lingeman, R. (1980). *Small town America: A narrative history, 1620-the present.* New York: G. P. Putnam's Sons.

Lippy, C. H., Choquette, R., & Poole, S. (1992). *Christianity comes to the Americas, 1492-1776.* New York: Paragon.

Lipset, S. M. (1950, May). Changing social status and prejudice: The race theories of a pioneering American sociologist. *Commentary, 9,* 475-479.

Lipset, S. M. (1963). *The first new nation: The United States in historical and comparative perspective.* New York: Basic Books.

Lipset, S. M. (1979). *The first new nation: The United States in historical and comparative perspective* (rev. ed.). New York: W. W. Norton.

Lopata, H. Z. (1967). The function of voluntary associations in an ethnic community: "Polonia." In E. W. Burgess & D. J. Bogue (Eds.), *Contributions to urban sociology* (pp. 203-223). Chicago: University of Chicago Press.

Lopreato, J. (1970). *Italian Americans.* New York: Random House.

Lovejoy, A. O. (1960). *The great chain of being: A study of the history of an idea.* New York: Harper Torchbooks.

Lugard, L. (1965). *The dual mandate in British tropical Africa.* Hamden, CT: Archon/Shoe String. (Original work published 1922)

Luhmann, N. (1986). The individuality of the individual: Historical meanings and contemporary problems. In T. C. Heller, M. Sosna, & D. E. Wellbery (Eds.), *Reconstructing individualism: Autonomy, individuality, and the self in Western thought* (pp. 313-328). Stanford, CA: Stanford University Press.

Lyman, S. M. (1961-1962). Overseas Chinese in America and Indonesia: A review article. *Pacific Affairs, 34,* 380-389.

Lyman, S. M. (1963). Up from the "hatchet man." *Pacific Affairs, 36,* 160-171.

Lyman, S. M. (1964). The spectrum of color. *Social Research, 31,* 364-373.

Lyman, S. M. (1972). *The black American in sociological thought: A failure of perspective.* New York: G. P. Putnam's Sons.

Lyman, S. M. (1974). Conflict and the web of group affiliation in San Francisco's Chinatown, 1850-1910. *Pacific Historical Review, 43,* 473-499.

Lyman, S. M. (1975). Legitimacy and consensus in Lipset's America: From Washington to Watergate. *Social Research, 42,* 729-759.

Lyman, S. M. (1978). The acceptance, rejection, and reconstruction of histories. In R. H. Brown & S. M. Lyman (Eds.), *Structure, consciousness and history* (pp. 53-105). New York: Cambridge University Press.

Lyman, S. M. (1979). Stuart Culin and the debate over trans-Pacific migration. *Journal for the Theory of Social Behaviour, 9,* 91-115.

Lyman, S. M. (1982a). Stewart Culin: The earliest American Chinatown studies and a hypothesis about pre-Columbian migration. *Annual Bulletin of the Research Institute for Social Science* (Ryukoku University, Kyoto, Japan), 12, 142-162.

Lyman, S. M. (1982b). Two neglected pioneers of civilizational analysis: The cultural perspectives of R.

Stewart Culin and Frank Hamilton Cushing. *Social Research, 44,* 690-729.

Lyman, S. M. (1986). *Chinatown and Little Tokyo: Power, conflict and community among Chinese and Japanese immigrants in America.* Millwood, NJ: Associated Faculty.

Lyman, S. M. (1990a). Asian American contacts before Columbus: Alternative understandings for civilization, acculturation, and ethnic minority status in America. In S. M. Lyman, *Civilization: Contents, discontents, malcontents and other essays in social theory.* Fayetteville: University of Arkansas Press.

Lyman, S. M. (1990b). *Civilization: Contents, discontents, malcontents and other essays in social theory.* Fayetteville: University of Arkansas Press.

Lyman, S. M. (1992a). The assimilation-pluralism debate: Toward a postmodern resolution of the American ethnoracial dilemma. *International Journal of Politics, Culture and Society, 6,* 181-210.

Lyman, S. M. (1992b). *Militarism, imperialism and racial accommodation: An analysis and interpretation of the early writings of Robert E. Park.* Fayetteville: University of Arkansas Press.

Lyman, S. M., & Scott, M. B. (1967). Territoriality: A neglected sociological dimension. *Social Problems, 15,* 236-248.

Lyman, S. M., & Scott, M. B. (1989). *A sociology of the absurd* (2nd ed.). Dix Hills, NY: General Hall.

Lynd, R. S., & Lynd, H. M. (1937). *Middletown in transition: A study in cultural conflicts.* New York: Harcourt, Brace.

Lynd, R. S., & Lynd, H. M. (1956). *Middletown: A study in modern American culture.* New York: Harcourt, Brace. (Original work published 1929)

Lyon, L. (1987). *The community in urban society.* Chicago: Dorsey.

Lyotard, J.-F. (1989). The sign of history. In A. Benjamin (Ed.), *The Lyotard reader* (pp. 393-411). Cambridge, MA: Basil Blackwell.

Lyotard, J.-F. (1990). *Heidegger and "the jews"* (A. Michel & M. Roberts, Trans.). Minneapolis: University of Minnesota Press.

Manganaro, M. (1990). Textual play, power, and cultural critique: An orientation to modernist anthropology. In M. Manganaro (Ed.), *Modern anthropology: From fieldwork to text* (pp. 3-47). Princeton, NJ: Princeton University Press.

Mangiafico, L. (1988). *Contemporary American immigrants: Patterns of Filipino, Korean, and Chinese settlement in the United States.* New York: Praeger.

Manning, P. K. (1987). *Semiotics and fieldwork.* Newbury Park, CA: Sage.

Manning, P. K. (1991). Analytic induction. In K. Plummer (Ed.), *Symbolic interactionism: Vol. 2. Contemporary issues* (pp. 401-430). Brookfield, VT: Edward Elgar. (Reprinted from R. Smith & P. K. Manning, Eds., *Qualitative methods,* Cambridge, MA: Ballinger, 1982)

Marable, M. (1983). *How capitalism underdeveloped black America: Problems in race, political economy, and society.* Boston: South End.

Marcus, G. E. (1986). Contemporary problems of ethnography in the modern world system. In J. Clifford & G. E. Marcus (Eds.), *Writing culture: The poetics and politics of ethnography* (pp. 165-193). Berkeley: University of California Press.

Martin, C. (Ed.). (1987). *The American Indian and the problem of history.* New York: Oxford University Press.

Marty, M. E. (1992). Foreword. In Bartolome de Las Casas, *In defense of the Indians: The defense of the most reverend Lord, Don Fray Bartolome de Las Casas, of the Order of Preachers, late Bishop of Chiapa, against the persecutors and slanderers of the peoples of the New World discovered across the seas* (C. M. S. Poole, Ed. & Trans.) (original work published 1552). De Kalb: Northern Illinois University Press.

Masuoka, J. (1946). Race relations and Nisei problems. *Sociology and Social Research, 30,* 452-459.

Maunier, R. (1949). *The sociology of colonies: An introduction to the study of race contact* (Vols. 1-2) (E. O. Lorimer, Ed. & Trans.). London: Routledge & Kegan Paul.

McCluer, F. L. (1928). *Living conditions among wage-earning families in forty-one blocks in Chicago.* Unpublished doctoral dissertation, University of Chicago.

McClymer, J. F. (1980). *War and welfare: Social engineering in America, 1890-1925.* Westport, CT: Greenwood.

McGee, W. J. (1971). *The Seri Indians of Bahia Kino and Sonora, Mexico* (Seventeenth Annual Report of the Bureau of American Ethnology to the Secretary of the Smithsonian Institution, 1895-1896, part 1). Glorieta, NM: Rio Grande. (Original work published 1899)

McKenney, T. L., & Hall, J. (1972). *The Indian Tribes of North America—with biographical sketches and anecdotes of the principal chiefs* (Vols. 1-3). Totowa, NJ: Rowman & Littlefield. (Original work published 1836)

McKenzie, R. D. (1968). *On human ecology: Selected writings* (A. H. Hawley, Ed.). Chicago: University of Chicago Press.

McKinney, J. C., in collaboration with Loomis, C. P. (1957). The application of *Gemeinschaft* and *Gesellschaft* as related to other typologies. In F. Tonnies, *Community and society (Gemeinschaft und Gesellschaft)* (C. P. Loomis, Ed. & Trans.) (pp. 12-29). East Lansing: Michigan State University Press.

Mead, M. (1960a). *Coming of age in Samoa: A psychological study of primitive youth for Western civilization.* New York: Mentor. (Original work published 1928)

Mead, M. (1960b). *Growing up in New Guinea: A comparative study of primitive education.* New York: Mentor. (Original work published 1930)

Mead, M. (1960c). *Male and female: A study of the sexes in a changing world.* New York: Mentor. (Original work published 1949)

Mead, M. (1960d). *Sex and temperament in three primitive societies.* New York: Mentor. (Original work published 1935)

Mead, M. (1975). *New lives for old: Cultural transformation—Manau, 1928-1953.* New York: William Morrow. (Original work published 1956)

Messenger, P. M. (Ed.). (1991). *The ethics of collecting cultural property: Whose culture? Whose property?* Albuquerque: University of New Mexico Press.

Miller, J. (1993). *The passion of Michel Foucault.* New York: Simon & Schuster.

Milner, C. A., II, & O'Neil, F. A. (Eds.). (1985). *Churchmen and the Western Indians, 1820-1920.* Norman: University of Oklahoma Press.

Milson, K. (1991-1992). (En)countering imperialist nostalgia: The Indian reburial issue. *Discourse: Journal for Theoretical Studies in Media and Culture, 14,* 58-74.

Miner, H. (1952). The folk-urban continuum. *American Sociological Review, 17,* 529-537.

Minh-ha, T. T. (1991). *When the moon waxes red: Representation, gender and cultural politics.* New York: Routledge.

Minnich, E. K. (1990). *Transforming knowledge.* Philadelphia: Temple University Press.

Montagu, A. (Ed.). (1968). The concept of the primitive. New York: Free Press.

Morgan, G. (Ed.). (1983). *Beyond method: Strategies for social research.* Beverly Hills, CA: Sage.

Morgan, L. H. (1964). *Ancient society* (L. White, Ed.). Cambridge, MA: Belknap.

Moorhouse, G. (1988). *Imperial city: New York.* New York: Henry Holt.

Murdock, G. P. (1965). *Social structure.* New York: Free Press. (Original work published 1949)

Murdock, G. P. (1934). *Our primitive contemporaries.* New York: Macmillan.

A museum is set to part with its Indian treasures. (1993, February 19). *New York Times,* p. A12.

Myer, D. S. (1971). *Uprooted Americans: The Japanese Americans and the War Relocation Authority during World War II.* Tucson: University of Arizona Press.

Nader, L. (1972). Up the anthropologist: Perspectives gained from studying up. In D. Hymes (Ed.), *Reinventing anthropology* (pp. 284-311). New York: Pantheon.

Natanson, M. (1962). History as a finite province of meaning. In H. Natanson, *Literature, philosophy and the social sciences: Essays in existentialism and phenomenology* (pp. 172-178). The Hague: Martinus Nijhoff.

Nelli, H. S. (1970). *The Italians in Chicago, 1880-1930.* New York: Oxford University Press.

Neske, G., & Kettering, E. (1990). *Martin Heidegger and National Socialism: Questions and answers* (L. Harries & J. Neugroschel, Trans.). New York: Paragon House.

Nikolinakos, D. D. (1990). Foucault's ethical quandary. *Telos, 23,* 123-140.

Nisbet, R. A. (1969). *Social change and history: Aspects of the Western theory of development.* New York: Oxford University Press.

Nisbet, R. A. (1972). Ethnocentrism and the comparative method. In A. R. Desai (Ed.), *Essays on modernization of underdeveloped societies* (Vol. 1, pp. 95-114). New York: Humanities Press.

Nisbet, R. A. (1977). *Sociology as an art form.* New York: Oxford University Press.

Nisbet, R. A. (1986). Developmentalism: A critical analysis. In R. A. Nisbet, *The making of modern society* (pp. 33-69). New York: New York University Press.

Nomura, G. M., et al. (Eds.). (1989). *Frontiers of Asian American studies: Writing, research and commentary.* Pullman: Washington State University Press.

Nordenskiold, G. (1979). *The cliff dwellers of the Mesa Verde* (O. L. Morgan, Trans.). Glorieta, NM: Rio Grande. (Original work published 1893)

Norris, C. (1990). Lost in the funhouse: Baudrillard and the politics of postmodernism. In R. Boyne & A. Rattansi (Eds.), *Postmodernism and society* (pp. 119-153). New York: St. Martin's.

Novak, M. (1972). *The rise of the unmeltable ethnics: Politics and culture in the seventies.* New York: Macmillan.

Novak, M. (1980). Pluralism: A humanistic perspective. In S. Thernstrom (Ed.), *Harvard encyclopedia of American ethnic groups* (pp. 772-781). Cambridge, MA: Harvard University Press.

Numbers, R. (1992). *The creationists: The evolution of scientific creationism.* New York: Alfred A. Knopf.

Oakes, K. B. (1938). *Social theory in the early literature of voyage and exploration in Africa.* Unpublished doctoral dissertation, University of California, Berkeley.

Officer, J. E. (1987). *Hispanic Arizona, 1536-1856.* Tucson: University of Arizona Press.

Okihiro, G. Y. (1988). The idea of community and a "particular type of history." In G. Y. Okihiro et al. (Eds.), *Reflections on shattered windows: Promises and prospects for Asian American studies* (pp. 175-183). Pullman: Washington State University Press.

Okihiro, G. Y., et al. (Eds.). (1988). *Reflections on shattered windows: Promises and prospects for Asian American studies.* Pullman: Washington State University Press.

Olivier, S. (1970). The government of colonies and dependencies. In G. Spiller (Ed.), *Papers on interracial problems communicated to the First Universal Race Congress, University of London, July 26-29, 1911* (pp. 293-312). New York: Citadel. (Original work published 1911)

Padilla, F. M. (1985). *Latino ethnic consciousness: The case of Mexican Americans and Puerto Ricans in*

Chicago. Notre Dame, IN: University of Notre Dame Press.

Paglia, C. (1991). Junk bonds and corporate raiders: Academe in the hour of the wolf. *Arion: A Journal of Humanities and the Classics* (third series), *1*(2), 139-212.

Park, R. E. (1952a). *The collected papers of Robert Ezra Park: Vol. 2. Human communities: The city and human ecology* (E. C. Hughes et al., Eds.). Glencoe, IL: Free Press.

Park, R. E. (1952b). Community organization and the romantic temper. In R. E. Park, *The collected papers of Robert Ezra Park: Vol. 2. Human communities: The city and human ecology* (E. C. Hughes et al., Eds.) (pp. 64-72). Glencoe, IL: Free Press.

Park, R. E. (1952c). Magic, mentality and city life. In R. E. Park, *The collected papers of Robert Ezra Park: Vol. 2. Human communities: The city and human ecology* (E. C. Hughes et al., Eds.) (pp. 102-117). Glencoe, IL: Free Press.

Park, R. E. (1967). The city: Suggestions for the investigation of human behavior in the urban environment. In R. E. Park, E. W. Burgess, & R. D. McKenzie (Eds.), *The city* (pp. 1-46). Chicago: University of Chicago Press. (Original work published 1925)

Park, R. E. (1969a). Human migration and the marginal man. In E. W. Burgess (Ed.), *Personality and the social group* (pp. 64-77). Freeport, NY: Books for Libraries Press. (Original work published 1929)

Park, R. E. (1969b). Introduction. In R. Adams, *Interracial marriage in Hawaii: A study of mutually conditioned responses to acculturation and amalgamation* (pp. xiii-xiv). Montclair, NJ: Patterson Smith. (Original work published 1937)

Park, R. E. (1971). *The immigrant press and its control: The acculturation of immigrant groups into American society.* Montclair, NJ: Patterson Smith. (Original work published 1922)

Parsons, T. (1949). *The structure of social action: A study on social theory with special reference to a group of recent European writers.* Glencoe, IL: Free Press. (Original work published 1937)

Parsons, T. (1966). *Societies: Evolutionary and comparative perspectives.* Englewood Cliffs, NJ: Prentice Hall.

Parsons, T. (1971). *The system of modern societies.* Englewood Cliffs, NJ: Prentice Hall.

Parsons, T. (1973). Some afterthoughts on *Gemeinschaft* and *Gesellschaft.* In W. J. Cahnman (Ed.), *Ferdinand Tonnies: A new evaluation* (pp. 140-150). Leiden, Netherlands: E. J. Brill.

Patterson, O. (1982). *Slavery and social death: A comparative study.* Cambridge, MA: Harvard University Press.

Patterson, O. (1991). *Freedom: Vol. 1. Freedom in the making of Western culture.* New York: Basic Books.

Peacock, J. L. (1986). *The anthropological lens: Harsh lights, soft focus.* Cambridge, UK: Cambridge University Press.

Pike, K. (1967). *Language in relation to a unified theory of the structure of human behaviour.* The Hague: Mouton.

Poster, M. (1987-1988). Foucault, the present and history. *Cultural Critique, 8,* 105-121.

Pratt, M. L. (1986). Fieldwork in common places. In J. Clifford & G. E. Marcus (Eds.), *Writing culture: The poetics and politics of ethnography.* Berkeley: University of California Press.

Quandt, J. B. (1970). *From the small town to the great community: The social thought of the progressive intellectuals.* New Brunswick, NJ: Rutgers University Press.

Rabinow, P., & Sullivan, W. M. (Eds.). (1979). *Interpretive social science: A reader.* Berkeley: University of California Press.

Radin, P. (1927). *The story of the American Indian.* New York: Boni & Liveright.

Radin, P. (1957a). *Primitive man as philosopher.* New York: Dover. (Original work published 1927)

Radin, P. (1957b). *Primitive religion: Its nature and origin.* New York: Dover. (Original work published 1937)

Radin, P. (1963). *The autobiography of a Winnebago Indian: Life, ways, acculturation, and the peyote cult.* New York: Dover. (Original work published 1920)

Radin, P. (1966). *The method and theory of ethnology: An essay in criticism.* New York: Basic Books. (Original work published 1933)

Radin, P. (1970). *The Italians of San Francisco: Their adjustment and acculturation.* San Francisco: R & E Research Associates. (Original work published 1935)

Radin, P. (Ed.). (1971a). *The golden mountain: Chinese tales told in California, collected by Jon Lee.* Taipei: Caves. (Original work published 1936)

Radin, P. (1971b). *The world of primitive man.* New York: Dutton. (Original work published 1953)

Radin, P. (1973). *The Winnebago tribe.* Lincoln: University of Nebraska Press. (Original work published 1923)

Radin, P. (1976). *The trickster: A study in American Indian mythology.* New York: Schocken. (Original work published 1956)

Rae, J. B. (1965). *The American automobile: A brief history.* Chicago: University of Chicago Press.

Ratzel, F. (1988). *Sketches of urban and cultural life in North America* (S. A. Stehlin, Ed. & Trans.). New Brunswick, NJ: Rutgers University Press. (Original work published 1876)

Redfield, J. (1991). Classics and anthropology. *Arion: A Journal of Humanities and the Classics* (third series), *1*(2), 5-23.

Redfield, R. (1928). *A plan for the study of Tepoztlan, Mexico.* Unpublished doctoral dissertation, University of Chicago.

Redfield, R. (1930). *Tepoztlan—A Mexican village: A study of folk life.* Chicago: University of Chicago Press.

Redfield, R. (1941). *The folk culture of Yucatan.* Chicago: University of Chicago Press.

Redfield, R. (1960). *The little community and peasant society and culture.* Chicago: University of Chicago Press.

Redfield, R. (1962a). The folk society and civilization. In M. P. Redfield (Ed.), *The papers of Robert Redfield: Vol. 1. Human nature and the study of society.* Chicago: University of Chicago Press.

Redfield, R. (1962b). *A village that chose progress: Chan Kom revisited.* Chicago: University of Chicago Press. (Original work published 1950)

Redfield, R. (1963). Talk with a stranger. In M. P. Redfield (Ed.), *The papers of Robert Redfield: Vol. 2. The social uses of social science* (pp. 270-284). Chicago: University of Chicago Press.

Redfield, R. & Rojas, A. V. (1962). *Chan Kom: A Maya village.* Chicago: University of Chicago Press. (Original work published 1934)

Redfield, R., & Singer, M. B. (1973). The cultural role of the cities: Orthogenetic and heterogenetic change. In G. Germani (Ed.), *Modernization, urbanization, and the urban crisis* (pp. 61-71). Boston: Little, Brown.

Reid, D. (Ed.). (1992). *Sex, death and God in L.A.* New York: Pantheon.

Reuter, E. B. (1969). *The mulatto in the United States: Including a study of the role of mixed-blood races throughout the world.* New York: Negro Universities Press. (Original work published 1918)

Rivers, W. H. R. (1974). The psychological factor. In A. Montagu (Ed.), *Frontiers of anthropology* (pp. 391-409). New York: G. P. Putnam's Sons. (Reprinted from W. H. R. Rivers, Ed., *Essays on the depopulation of Melanesia,* Cambridge, UK: Cambridge University Press, 1922)

Rockmore, T. (1992). *On Heidegger's Nazism and philosophy.* Berkeley: University of California Press.

Roper, M. W. (1935). *The city and the primary group.* Unpublished doctoral dissertation, University of Chicago.

Rorty, R. (1982). *Consequences of pragmatism: Essays, 1972-1980.* Minneapolis: University of Minnesota Press.

Rorty, R. (1989). *Contingency, irony and solidarity.* Cambridge, UK: Cambridge University Press.

Rose, A. (Ed.). (1988). *Universal abandon? The politics of postmodernism.* Minneapolis, MN: University of Minnesota.

Rose, D. (1989). *Patterns of American culture: Ethnography and estrangement.* Philadelphia: University of Pennsylvania Press.

Rosenau, P. M. (1992). *Post-modernism and the social sciences: Insights, inroads, and intrusions.* Princeton, NJ: Princeton University Press.

Ross, R. H., & Bogardus, E. S. (1940). The third generation race relations cycle: A study in Issei-Nisei relationships. *Sociology and Social Research, 24,* 357-363.

Rossi, P. (1987). *The dark abyss of time: The history of the earth and the history of nations from Hooke to Vico* (L. G. Cochrane, Trans.). Chicago: University of Chicago Press.

Rouse, I. (1992). *The Tainos: Rise and decline of the people who greeted Columbus.* New Haven, CT: Yale University Press.

Royce, P. (1982). *Ethnic identity: Strategies of diversity.* Bloomington: Indiana University Press.

Rubel, A. J. (1971). *Across the tracks: Mexican Americans in a Texas city.* Austin: University of Texas Press.

Sachs, W. (1947). *Black anger.* New York: Grove.

Sadri, A. (1992). *Max Weber's sociology of intellectuals.* New York: Oxford University Press.

Salmond, A. (1991). *Two worlds: First meetings between Maori and Europeans, 1642-1772.* Honolulu: University of Hawaii Press.

Sanchez, G. S. (1967). *Forgotten people: A study of New Mexicans.* Albuquerque: Calvin Horn.

Sanderson, S. K. (1990). *Social evolutionism: A critical history.* Cambridge, UK: Basil Blackwell.

Sando, J. S. (1992). *Pueblo nations: Eight centuries of Pueblo Indian history.* Santa Fe, NM: Clear Light.

Sarana, G. (1975). *The methodology of anthropological comparison: An analysis of comparative methods in social and cultural anthropology.* Tucson: University of Arizona Press.

Saxton, S. L. (1993). Sociologist as citizen-scholar: A symbolic interactionist alternative to normal sociology. In T. R. Vaughan, G. Sjoberg, & L. J. Reynolds (Eds.). *A critique of contemporary American sociology* (pp. 232-251). Dix Hills, NY: General Hall.

Schatzman, L., & Strauss, A. L. (1973). *Field research: Strategies for a natural sociology.* Englewood Cliffs, NJ: Prentice Hall.

Schietinger, E. F. (1967). Racial succession and changing property values in residential Chicago. In E. W. Burgess & D. J. Bogue (Eds.), *Contributions to urban sociology* (pp. 86-99). Chicago: University of Chicago Press.

Schlesinger, A. M., Jr. (1991). *The disuniting of America: Reflections on a multicultural society.* Knoxville, TN: Whittle.

Schoolcraft, H. R. (1975). *Personal memoirs of a residence of thirty years with the Indian tribes of the American frontiers, with brief notices of passing events, facts and opinions, A.D. 1812 to A.D. 1842.* New York: Arno. (Original work published 1851)

Schrag, P. (1970). *The decline of the WASP.* New York: Simon & Schuster.

Schrag, P. (1973). *The end of the American future.* New York: Simon & Schuster.

Schwatka, F. (1977). *In the land of cave and cliff dwellers.* Glorieta, NM: Rio Grande. (Original work published 1893)

Sheets-Johnstone, M. (1990). *The roots of thinking.* Philadelphia: Temple University Press.

Sheets-Johnstone, M. (Ed.). (1992). *Giving the body its due*. Albany: State University of New York Press.
Sheridan, T. E. (1986). *Los Tucsonenses: The Mexican community in Tucson, 1854-1941*. Tucson: University of Arizona Press.
Shibutani, T., & Kwan, K. M.(1965). *Ethnic stratification: A comparative approach*. New York: Macmillan.
Simmel, G. (1950). The stranger. In G. Simmel, *The sociology of Georg Simmel* (K. H. Wolff, Ed. & Trans.) (pp. 402-408). Glencoe, IL: Free Press.
Simmel, G. (1968). *The conflict in modern culture and other essays* (K. P. Etzkorn, Ed. & Trans.). New York: Teachers College Press.
Siu, P. C. P. (1987). *The Chinese laundrymen: A study of social isolation* (J. K. W. Tchen, Ed.). New York: New York University Press.
Smith, A. D. (1989). *The ethnic origin of nations*. New York: Basil Blackwell.
Smith, C. W. (1979). *A critique of sociological reasoning: An essay in philosophical sociology*. Oxford: Basil Blackwell.
Smith, M. G. (1965). *The plural society in the British West Indies*. Berkeley: University of California.
Smith, M. P. (1979). *The city and social theory*. New York: St. Martin's.
Solzhenitsyn, A. (1993, February 7). The relentless cult of novelty and how it wrecked the century. *New York Times Book Review*, p. 3.
Sorokin, P. (1965). *Fads and foibles in modern sociology and related sciences*. Chicago: Henry Regnery-Gateway.
Spicer, E. A., Hansen, A. T., Luomala, K., & Opler, M. K. (1969). *Impounded people: Japanese-Americans in the relocation centers*. Tucson: University of Arizona Press.
Spier, L. (1978). *Yuman tribes of the Gila River*. New York: Dover. (Original work published 1933)
Spretnak, C. (1991). *States of grace: The recovery of meaning in the postmodern age*. New York: HarperCollins.
Statler, O. (1983). *Japanese pilgrimage*. New York: William Morrow.
Stein, M. (1964). The eclipse of community: Some glances at the education of a sociologist. In A. J. Vidich, J. Bensman, & M. Stein (Eds.), *Reflections on community studies*. New York: John Wiley.
Steinberg, S. (1981). *The ethnic myth: Race, ethnicity, and class in America*. New York: Atheneum.
Stocking, G. W., Jr. (Ed.). (1983). *Observers observed: Essays on ethnographic field work*. Madison: University of Wisconsin Press.
Stocking, G. W., Jr. (Ed.). (1984). *Functionalism historicized: Essays on British social anthropology*. Madison: University of Wisconsin Press.
Stocking, G. W., Jr. (Ed.). (1985). *Objects and others: Essays on museums and material culture*. Madison: University of Wisconsin Press.
Stocking, G. W., Jr. (Ed.). (1986). *Malinowski, Rivers, Benedict and others: Essays on culture and personality*. Madison: University of Wisconsin Press.
Stocking, G. W., Jr. (Ed.). (1988). *Bones, bodies, behavior: Essays on biological anthropology*. Madison: University of Wisconsin Press.
Stocking, G. W., Jr. (Ed.). (1989). *Romantic motives: Essays on anthropological sensibility*. Madison: University of Wisconsin Press.
Stocking, G. W., Jr. (Ed.). (1991). *Colonial situations: Essays on the contextualization of ethnographic knowledge*. Madison: University of Wisconsin Press.
Stone, R. W. (1921). *The origin of the survey movement*. Unpublished doctoral dissertation, University of Chicago.
Stonequist, E. V. (1961). *The marginal man: A study in personality and culture conflict*. New York: Russell & Russell. (Original work published 1937)
Strathern, M. (1990). Out of context: The persuasive fictions of anthropology, with comments by I. C. Jarvie, Stephen A. Tyler and George E. Marcus. In M. Manganaro (Ed.), *Modern anthropology: From fieldwork to text* (pp. 80-130). Princeton, NJ: Princeton University Press.
Street corner society revisited [Special issue]. (1992). *Journal of Contemporary Ethnography, 21*(1), 3-132.
Sumner, W. G. (1940). *Folkways: A study of the sociological importance of usages, manners, customs, mores, and morals*. Boston: Ginn. (Original work published 1906)
Sumner, W. G. (1969). Foreword. In J. E. Cutler, *Lynch-law: An investigation into the history of lynching in the United States* (p. v). Montclair, NJ: Patterson Smith. (Original work published 1905)
Suret-Canale, J. (1988a). The end of chieftancy in Guinea. In J. Suret-Canale, *Essays on African history: From the slave trade to neocolonialism* (C. Hurst, Trans.). Trenton, NJ: Africa World.
Suret-Canale, J. (1988b). Guinea in the colonial system. In J. Suret-Canale, *Essays on African history: From the slave trade to neocolonialism* (C. Hurst, Trans.). Trenton, NJ: Africa World.
Suttles, G. D. (1972). *The social construction of communities*. Chicago: University of Chicago Press.
Symposium on qualitative methods. (1993, January). *Contemporary Sociology, 22*(1), 1-15.
Takaki, R. (1989). *Strangers from a different shore: A history of Asian Americans*. New York: Penguin.
Taylor, C. (1989). *Sources of the self: The making of modern identity*. Cambridge, MA: Harvard University Press.
Taylor, P. S. (1970). *Mexican labor in the United States* (Vols. 1-2). New York: Arno/New York Times. (Original work published 1930)
Taylor, P. S. (1983). *On the ground in the thirties*. Salt Lake City: Peregrine Smith.
Tedlock, B. (1992). *The beautiful and the dangerous: Encounters with the Zuni Indians*. New York: Viking.
Teggart, F. J. (1941). *The theory and processes of history*. Berkeley: University of California Press.
Thernstrom, S. (Ed.). (1980). *Harvard encyclopedia of American ethnic groups*. Cambridge, MA: Harvard University Press.

Thomas, W. I., & Znaniecki, F. (1958). *The Polish peasant in Europe and America.* New York: Dover.

Thrasher, F. M. (1963). *The gang: A study of 1,313 gangs in Chicago.* Chicago: University of Chicago Press. (Original work published 1927)

Thucydides. (1972). *History of the Peloponnesian War* (R. Warner, Trans.). Harmondsworth: Penguin.

Tilman, R. (1991). *Thorstein Veblen and his critics, 1891-1963.* Princeton, NJ: Princeton University Press.

Tinder, G. (1980). *Community: Reflections on a tragic ideal.* Baton Rouge: Louisiana State University Press.

Tobias, H. J. (1990). *A history of the Jews in New Mexico.* Albuquerque: University of New Mexico Press.

Todorov, T. (1984). *The conquest of America* (R. Howard, Trans.). New York: Harper & Row.

Toland, J. D. (Ed.). (1993). *Ethnicity and the state.* New Brunswick, NJ: Transaction.

Tönnies, F. (1957). *Community and society (Gemeinschaft und Gesellschaft)* (C. P. Loomis, Ed. & Trans.). East Lansing: Michigan State University Press. (Original work published 1887)

Torgovnick, M. (1990). *Gone primitive: Savage intellects, modern lives.* Chicago: University of Chicago Press.

Tricarico, D. (1984). *The Italians of Greenwich Village: The social structure and transformation of an ethnic community.* Staten Island, NY: Center for Migration Studies of New York.

Trinkhouse, E., & Shipman, P. (1993). *The Neanderthals: Changing the image of mankind.* New York: Alfred A. Knopf.

Turner, V. (1992). African ritual and Western literature: Is a comparative symbology possible? In V. Turner, *Blazing the trail: Way marks in the exploration of symbols* (E. Turner, Ed.) (pp. 66-88). Tucson: University of Arizona Press.

Van Maanen, J. (1988). *Tales of the field: On writing ethnography.* Chicago: University of Chicago Press.

Vaughan, A. T. (1965). *New England frontier: Puritans and Indians, 1620-1675.* Boston: Little, Brown.

Vaughan, T. R. (1993). The crisis in contemporary American sociology: A critique of the discipline's dominant paradigm. In T. R. Vaughan, G. Sjoberg, & L. J. Reynolds (Eds.), *A critique of contemporary American sociology.* Dix Hills, NY: General Hall.

Veblen, T. (1959). *The theory of the leisure class.* New York: Mentor. (Original work published 1899)

Veblen, T. (1961a). The blond race and the Aryan culture. In T. Veblen, *The place of science in modern civilization and other essays.* New York: Russell & Russell. (Original work published 1919)

Veblen, T. (1961b). The mutation theory and the blond race. In T. Veblen, *The place of science in modern civilization and other essays.* New York: Russell & Russell. (Original work published 1919)

Veblen, T. (1965). *The higher learning in America: A memorandum on the conduct of universities by businessmen.* New York: Augustus M. Kelley. (Original work published 1918)

Veblen, T. (1990). *The instinct of workmanship and the state of the industrial arts.* New Brunswick, NJ: Transaction. (Original work published 1914)

Vidich, A. J. (1952). *The political impact of colonial administration.* Unpublished doctoral dissertation, Harvard University, Boston.

Vidich, A. J. (1955). Participant observation and the collection and interpretation of data. *American Journal of Sociology, 60,* 335-360.

Vidich, A. J. (1966). Introduction. In P. Radin, *The method and theory of ethnology: An essay in criticism* (pp. vii-cxv). New York: Basic Books.

Vidich, A. J. (1980). *The political impact of colonial administration.* New York: Arno.

Vidich, A. J. (1986). *Anthropology and truth: Some old problems.* Paper presented at the annual meeting of the American Anthropological Society, Philadelphia.

Vidich, A. J., & Bensman, J. (1968). *Small town in mass society: Class, power and religion in a rural community* (2nd ed.). Princeton, NJ: Princeton University Press.

Vidich, A. J., & Lyman, S. M. (1985). *American sociology: Worldly rejections of religion and their directions.* New Haven, CT: Yale University Press.

Vidich, A. J., Lyman, S. M., & Goldfarb, J. C. (1981). Sociology and society: Disciplinary tensions and professional compromises. *Social Research, 48,* 322-361.

Vigil, J. D. (1980). *From Indians to Chicanos: The dynamics of Mexican American culture.* Prospect Heights, IL: Waveland.

von Gierke, O. (1990). *Community in historical perspective: A translation of selections from Das Deutsche Genossenschaftsrecht (the German law of fellowship)* (A. Black, Ed.; M. Fischer, Trans.). Cambridge, UK: Cambridge University Press. (Original work published 1868)

Wallace, A. F. C. (1987). *St. Clair: A nineteenth-century coal town's experience with a disaster-prone industry.* New York: Alfred A. Knopf.

Walzer, M. (1980). Pluralism: A political perspective. In S. Thernstrom (Ed.), *Harvard encyclopedia of American ethnic groups* (pp. 781-787). Cambridge, MA: Harvard University Press.

Ware, C. (1965). *Greenwich Village, 1920-1930: A comment on American civilization in the post-war years.* New York: Harper Colophon. (Original work published 1935)

Warren, R. L. (1963). *The community in America.* Chicago: Rand McNally.

Warren, R. L. (1972). *The community in America* (2nd ed.). Chicago: Rand McNally.

Waters, M. C. (1990). *Ethnic options: Choosing identities in America.* Berkeley: University of California Press.

Wax, R. H. (1971). *Doing fieldwork: Warnings and advice.* Chicago: University of Chicago Press.

Weber, A. F. (1967). *The growth of cities in the nineteenth century: A study in statistics.* Ithaca, NY: Cornell University Press. (Original work published 1899)

Weber, D. J. (1992). *The Spanish frontier in North America.* New Haven, CT: Yale University Press.

Weinstein, D., & Weinstein, M. A. (1990). Dimensions of conflict: Georg Simmel on modern life. In M. Kaern, B. H. Phillips, & R. S. Cohen (Eds.), *Georg Simmel and contemporary sociology* (pp. 341-356). Dordrecht, Netherlands: Kluwer.

Weinstein, D., & Weinstein, M. A. (1991). Simmel and the theory of postmodern society. In B. S. Turner (Ed.), *Theories of modernity and postmodernity* (pp. 75-87). London: Sage.

West, C. (1992). Diverse new world. In P. Berman (Ed.), *Debating P.C.: The controversy over political correctness on college campuses* (pp. 326-332). New York: Dell.

White, L. A. (1974). *The A'Coma Indians: People of the sky city* (Forty-Seventh Annual Report of the Bureau of American Ethnology to the secretary of the Smithsonian Institution, 1929-1930). Glorieta, NM: Rio Grande. (Original work published 1933)

Williams, R. A., Jr. (1990). *The American Indian in Western legal thought: The discourses of conquest.* New York: Oxford University Press.

Williams, V. J., Jr. (1989). *From a caste to a minority: Changing attitudes of American sociologists toward Afro-Americans, 1896-1945.* Westport, CT: Greenwood.

Willis, W. S., Jr. (1972). Skeletons in the anthropological closet. In D. Hymes (Ed.), *Reinventing anthropology* (pp. 121-152). New York: Pantheon.

Wirth, L. (1938). Urbanism as a way of life. *American Journal of Sociology, 44,* 1-24.

Wirth, L. (1945). The problem of minority groups. In R. Linton (Ed.), *The science of man in the world crisis* (pp. 347-372). New York: Columbia University Press.

Wirth, L. (1956). *The ghetto.* Chicago: University of Chicago Press. (Original work published 1928)

Wissler, C. (1923). *Man and culture.* New York: Thomas Y. Crowell.

Wissler, C. (1956). Foreword. In R. S. Lynd & H. M. Lynd, *Middletown: A study in modern American culture.* New York: Harcourt, Brace. (Original work published 1929)

Wissler, C. (1966a). *Indians of the United States* (rev. ed.). Garden City, NY: Doubleday. (Original work published 1940)

Wissler, C. (1966b). *Red man reservations.* New York: Collier. (Original work published 1938)

Wood, M. M. (1969). *The stranger: A study in social relationships.* New York: AMS. (Original work published 1934)

Woods, F. J. (1956). *Cultural values of American ethnic groups.* New York: Harper & Brothers.

Woods, F. J. (1972). *Marginality and identity: A colored creole family through ten generations.* Baton Rouge: Louisiana State University Press.

Woods, R. A., & Kennedy, A. J. (1990). *The settlement horizon.* New Brunswick, NJ: Transaction. (Original work published 1922)

Wu, C. C. (1926). *Chinese immigration in the Pacific area.* Unpublished doctoral dissertation, University of Chicago.

Whyte, W. F. (1943a). *Street corner society: The social structure of an Italian slum.* Chicago: University of Chicago Press.

Whyte, W. F. (1943b). A slum sex code. *American Journal of Sociology, 49,* 24-31.

Whyte, W. F. (1955). *Street corner society: The social structure of an Italian slum* (2nd ed.). Chicago: University of Chicago Press.

Whyte, W. F. (1981). *Street corner society: The social structure of an Italian slum* (3rd ed.). Chicago: University of Chicago Press.

Zaner, R. M. (1981). *The context of self: A phenomenological inquiry using medicine as a clue.* Athens: Ohio University Press.

Zorbaugh, H. W. (1929). *The Gold Coast and the slum.* Chicago: University of Chicago Press.

Zorbaugh, H. W. (1968). The dweller in furnished rooms: An urban type. In E. W. Burgess (Ed.), *The urban community: Selected papers from the Proceedings of the American Sociological Society, 1925* (pp. 98-105). Westport, CT: Greenwood.

3

Traditions, Preferences, and Postures in Applied Qualitative Research

DAVID HAMILTON

ACROSS the Tuscan hills, Florence is less than 200 kilometers from the seaport of Genoa. Two fifteenth-century contemporaries—Niccolò Machiavelli (1469-1527) and Christopher Columbus (c1450-1506)—were born in those respective cities. Their work is widely remembered and, on occasion, even deservedly celebrated. Machiavelli identified a terrain for positive human action; Columbus began the exploitation of such terrain. Together, they set off a chain of political, economic, and intellectual reverberations the impacts of which can still be registered in the late twentieth century. Such was the dawn of Western applied science.

Machiavelli's supreme contribution was to identify a third force in the shaping of the postmedieval world. Conventionally, earlier thinkers had attributed the shaping of nature to two force fields: the hand of God and the hand of Fortuna (Lady Luck). Machiavelli acknowledged these causal constraints, but added a third. In the twenty-fifth chapter of *The Prince,* he suggested, "I am disposed to hold that fortune is the arbiter of half our actions but that it lets us control roughly the other half" (Machiavelli, 1513/1988, p. 85). Henceforth, Machiavelli implied, the world could be steered according to navigational plans drawn up by human beings, albeit within the confines of God's Grand Design. It is no accident, therefore, that the Renaissance world of Columbus and Machiavelli is also remembered as the age of humanism.

The work of Machiavelli and Columbus engendered immense optimism, itself recorded in the architecture and other expressive arts of the late Renaissance. But how was this optimism to be translated into other humanist ideals? In short, where was humanism going?

Within a century of Columbus's death, answers to this question became available. In the meantime, the world of knowledge had been mapped (see, for example, Strauss, 1966) and new methods of science had been established. As Francis Bacon wrote in the final paragraph of his *Novum Organum* (1620), these innovations would lead to an "improvement in man's estates" and an "enlargement of his power over nature." Bacon's vision, however, portrayed a false dawn. Later seventeenth-century scientists suggested the world was more complicated than it appeared. Alternative maps, encyclopedias, and taxonomies of knowledge were proposed (see, for instance, Slaughter, 1982).

The substance, form, significance, and application of knowledge became a contested domain. The optimism of the Renaissance was tempered by the skepticism of human inquiry. Different maps of knowledge prefigured many different futures. Indeed, the cartographic and taxonomic problems raised by 200 years of Baconian science were eventually satirized in Borges's description of a "certain Chinese encyclopedia," where animals are divided into: (a) belonging to the Emperor, (b) embalmed, (c) tame, (d) sucking pigs, (e) sirens, (f) fabulous, (g) stray dogs, (h) included in the present classification, (i) frenzied, (j) innumerable, (k) drawn with a fine camelhair brush, (l) *et cetera,* (m) having just broken the water pitcher, (n) that from a long way off look like flies. (quoted in Foucault, 1973, p. xv)

Structure or Diaspora?

Much the same turbulent history could be written of recent efforts to map the terrain of qualitative research. In 1987, for instance, Evelyn Jacob wrote of a fivefold division of "qualitative research traditions" (ecological psychology, holistic ethnography, ethnography of communication, cognitive anthropology, symbolic interaction). Subsequently, however, she also registered the claim that these were "not the only alternative traditions" (p. 39). By this disclaimer, of course, Jacob left her argument wide open to counterclaims.

Already, in fact, the uncertainty of her original portrayal had provoked a critical response. Three British researchers, Atkinson, Delamont, and Hammersley (1989), problematized Jacob's 1987 model and, in turn, drew rejoinders from U.S. researchers (Buchmann & Floden, 1989; Lincoln, 1989). In fact, Atkinson et al. did not engage in taxonomic revisionism. Rather, they took a skeptical view of the whole enterprise. They underlined the difficulty of producing unambiguous or noncontroversial intellectual maps. Attempts to compile taxonomies of tradition, they felt, may even be counterproductive—generating emotional heat rather than intellectual light. They could foreshadow an atavistic return to the disputatious scholasticism that Machiavelli and his contemporaries sought to overthrow.

More recently, Harry Wolcott (1992) has offered a resolution of the navigational and taxonomic problems surrounding the Jacob debate. In "Posturing in Qualitative Inquiry" he seeks to aid "researchers new to qualitative inquiry." His efforts hinge upon the fact that the verb *to posture* can be used in two senses, positive or negative. *Posturing* in a negative sense refers to the adoption of an affected or artificial pose, whereas in the positive sense (and with reference to the *Random House Dictionary*), to posture is to "position, especially strategically"; "to develop a policy or stance," for oneself or one's group; or "to adopt an attitude or take an official position" (Wolcott, 1992, p. 4).

Within this conceptual framework, Wolcott's novitiate researchers are encouraged to take up "strategic position[s]" vis-à-vis the "many alternatives" presented by qualitative inquiry. Thereafter, Wolcott claims, beginners are better able to "find their [own] way" in the prosecution of their inquiries (p. 4). In effect, Wolcott offers an eclectic, pluralist, and syncretic prescription. Researchers, he suggests, assemble their theoretical assumptions and working practices from a "marketplace of ideas" (p. 5). Traditions, therefore, serve as preferences. They are not so much inherited as compiled or "invented" (see Hobsbawm & Ranger, 1984).

This last distinction, I feel, captures the separation of the ideas of Atkinson and his colleagues from those advanced by Jacob. Atkinson et al.'s argument accepts an evolutionary or historical view of tradition. A tradition is deemed to be a messy social movement, one that is structured as much by recombination of different activities as by their differentiation, divergence, and continuity.

Jacob, on the other hand, uses a more static image. Nevertheless, her argument has an impressive pedigree. It draws upon the work of Thomas Kuhn, reported in *The Structure of Scientific Revolutions* (1962, 1970). Kuhn suggests that every scientific movement (e.g., Newtonian physics, Lamarckian biology, Freudian psychology) has characteristic ways of achieving the advancement of knowledge. Further, these serve as the building blocks that make up the frameworks, scaffolding, traditions, and paradigms of research. They furnish the preferred modes of working.

Jacob's position, therefore, is comparable to the Kuhnian stance taken by Larry Laudan (1977). A "tradition," according to Laudan, is "a set of general assumptions about the entities and processes in a domain of study, and about the appropriate methods to be used for investigating the problems and constructing the theories in that domain" (p. 81). From the standpoint adopted by Laudan and Jacob, traditions are bounded rather than evolving phenomena. They constitute a "disciplinary matrix" (Kuhn, 1970, p. 182) of interrelating constituent elements. Indeed, Jacob (1989, p. 229) quotes directly from Kuhn (1970, p. 175) to the effect that a disciplinary matrix is "the entire constellation of beliefs, values, techniques and so on shared by members of a given community." Moreover, Jacob explicitly conflates tradition and paradigm: "I use the concept [of paradigm] in the sense of disciplinary matrix as a heuristic framework for examining the social sciences. To signal this modification I use the term tradition rather than paradigm" (p. 229). If the sciences operate with paradigms, the social sciences are steered by traditions.

As with all structural analyses, however, this view of knowledge is problematic. The constituent elements of a tradition or paradigm may be clearly defined. They occupy different positions in conceptual space, and they coexist in harmony.

But how does one paradigm become replaced by another—as geocentric cosmologies were replaced by heliocentric worldviews? Certainly, Kuhn addresses this problem as central to the history of science. But can the same argument be applied to the social sciences? Or is it the case that traditions do not replace each other but, rather, emerge spontaneously and coexist alongside each other?

Jacob's efforts pose this problem. They are an innovative, if provocative, attempt to map the qualitative research field without reference to its origins. The outcome is a tidy, easily reproduced map of knowledge. Traditions are represented as separate subfields, each sustained by its own matrix of normative assumptions. Portrayed in such terms, traditions appear as placid archetypes. Unfortunately, however, such formulations are conceptually and practically remote from the swirling currents and posturings of applied science.

This backwater image of tradition is discussed by Ed Shils in *Tradition* (1981). Appeals to tradition have, Shils believes, fallen into "disrepute" among social scientists. That is, the normative—or steering—potential of past research practice has "become very faint," almost "extinguished as an intellectual argument" (p. 1). To explain this atrophy, Shils suggests that the concept of tradition lost its formative value in the eighteenth-century Enlightenment. Knowledge accepted "on the authority of elders" was replaced by "scientific procedure based on the experience of the senses and its rational criticism" (p. 4). "Rational social scientists," Shils wryly observes, "do not mention tradition" (p. 7).

Shils has not been alone in his worries. Alastair MacIntyre (1988) has also suggested that "the standpoint of traditions is necessarily at odds" with the Enlightenment assumptions about the transparency of all knowledge (p. 327). MacIntyre, however, does not let the matter rest at this point. He turns Shils's argument upside down. He resurrects the notion of tradition and reconciles it with the problem identified by Shils:

> Liberalism, beginning as a repudiation of tradition in the name of abstract, universal principles of reason, turned itself into a politically embodied power, whose inability to bring its debates on the nature and context of these universal principles to a conclusion has had the unintended effect of transforming liberalism into a tradition. (p. 349)

If MacIntyre's assertion is accepted, post-Enlightenment traditions share a common feature. They survive because their debates are inconclusive and their disciplinary matrices feature discord rather than harmony. Indeed, a similar conclusion can be reached from a modern reading of the etymology of the term *tradition.*

Like the word *trading, tradition* comes from the Latin root *tradere*—to hand over, deliver. According to the *Oxford English Dictionary, tradition* connotes the handing over of ecclesiastical artifacts and practices from officebearer to officebearer. Conventionally, it was expected that the sacred practices and artifacts would fall into the right hands. But ecclesiastical courts recognized that this might not always be the case. Hence, if the artifacts (e.g., canonical texts) fell into the wrong hands, the courts could deem that a sin had been committed. Indeed, it was by reference to these normative assumptions that the word *surrender* also came to mean hand over, or relinquish.

From this etymological perspective, traditions have three elements: practitioner-guardians, practices, and artifacts. Equally, etymological precedent—affinities between *trading* and *surrendering*—allows rejection of conservative interpretations of tradition. Just like medieval churches, traditions can be invented, established, ransacked, corrupted, and eliminated. The elements of a tradition are just as easily scattered as they are preserved intact. The history of traditions, therefore, is as much a narrative of diaspora as it is a chronicle of successful parallel cohabitation.

The remainder of this chapter adopts a diasporic view of tradition. It recounts the history of qualitative social science as the genesis and dispersal of a constellation of ideas against which social scientists have positioned themselves (compare Wolcott's "posturing"). Further, this chapter assumes that traditions did not emerge spontaneously, but, instead, from the intellectual heritage of Western thought.

Quantity or Quality?

Qualitative research can be traced back to an eighteenth-century disruption that occurred in the fortunes of quantitative research. For the sake of this account, the most notable innovators were René Descartes (1596-1650) and Immanuel Kant (1724-1804).

Descartes's work, notably *Discourse on Method* (1637), founded the quantitative research field. Descartes (1968) argued that natural philosophy should be refocused around the "certainty and self-evidence" of mathematics (p. 31) and that, in the search for truth, investigators should stand back from those elements of the world that might otherwise corrupt their analytic powers. At the risk of oversimplification, Descartes proclaimed the importance of mathematics and objectivity in the search for truth.

Not all philosophical arguments, however, supported Descartes's stance. The seventeenth and eighteenth centuries were as much an epoch of high controversy as they were an era for the dissemination of Cartesian absolutism. Probably the most significant post-Cartesian intervention came from Immanuel Kant, a philosopher who self-consciously sought to resolve the tensions that had arisen among the Cartesians and the skeptics. Stimulated late in life by the writings of Hume, Kant reworked earlier thought and published his observations in the *Critique of Pure Reason* (1781). By these means, Kant unpacked a range of fundamental ideas—the ultimate source of qualitative thinking—that have proved pivotal in the history of Western thought.

Kant proposed, in effect, that perception is more than seeing. Human perception derives not only from the evidence of the senses but also from the mental apparatus that serves to organize the incoming sense impressions. Kant, therefore, broke sharply with Cartesian objectivism. Human knowledge is ultimately based on understanding, an intellectual state that is more than just a consequence of experience. Thus, for Kant, human claims about nature cannot be independent of inside-the-head processes of the knowing subject.

Kant's model of human rationality, therefore, built the process of knowing and the emergence of knowledge upon an epistemology that transcended the limits of empirical inquiry. In turn, this transcendental perspective (see, for instance, Roberts, 1990) opened the door to epistemologies that allowed, if not celebrated, inside-the-head processes. Such epistemologies are totally at variance with Cartesian objectivism. They include versions of subjectivism, idealism, perspectivism, and relativism (see, e.g., Buchdahl, 1969, p. 481; Ermath, 1978, pp. 38-44; Scruton, 1983).

A Kantian perspective on the creation of knowledge, therefore, must take full cognizance of the investigator. It must concede the significance of interpretation and understanding. But there is another side to Kantian thought that is also central to the social sciences. Given his attention to cognitive processing, Kant was able to posit a distinction between "scientific reason" and "practical reason" (Ermath, 1978, p. 42). The world of nature known by science is a world of strict causal determinism, whereas the world of moral freedom (e.g., applied social research) is "governed by autonomous principles which man prescribes to himself" (p. 42). Knowing the truth about the workings of the world is one thing; knowing what to do about it is something else.

Kant revived a distinction, found in Aristotle, between theoretical and practical knowledge. *Theoretical knowledge* refers to states of affairs whose existence can be checked, tested, and accepted. *Practical knowledge,* on the other hand, refers to decision making. Can humans ever know what to do, with the same kind of certainty that they know the truth? Or does human action merely derive from inclination, passion, or desire? Is there a rationality applicable to the establishment of decisions as there is to the establishment of truths?

At this point, Kantian thought harks back to Machiavelli. The capacity of human beings to make decisions suggests they can play a part in their own self-determination. Further, from a Kantian perspective, decision making presumes human freedom. Likewise, every situation that requires practical action has an empirical status and a moral status. Practical reasoning—or applied social science—relates, therefore, to the application of moral judgments in the realm of human action. What to do relates not only to what is, but also to inseparable notions of what ought to be. It is perhaps no accident that the French word *morale* means both "social" and "ethical," and that, over much of Europe, the social sciences are intimately linked with the moral and political sciences.

Having been inducted into the terms of the debate, Kant's heirs branched off in two opposing new-Kantian directions. Dialecticians, inspired by notions of freedom and practical reasoning, explored the links among the social sciences, social change, and social emancipation, whereas members of the other stream—romantic existentialists such as Kierkegaard (1813-1855) and Nietzsche (1844-1900)—were highly skeptical of claims about the association of planned social change with the unfolding of history and the inevitability of human progress (Roberts, 1990, pp. 283-284).

Explanation or Understanding?

The epistemology of qualitative research, therefore, had its origins in an epistemological crisis of the late eighteenth century (see also Erickson, 1986, p. 122). Kant's arguments may have ushered in the possibility of qualitative inquiry, but other factors eventually brought it into being. In fact, it emerged from the attention given to the collection of data on the human condition. It was assumed that important political lessons could be learned from such descriptive information—typically described as "statistical" (see, for instance, Hacking, 1990).

During the 1830s, statistical inquiry became embroiled in fieldwork. Descriptive data were repeatedly used to illustrate the social and economic disruptions caused by the switch to steam-powered production in urban areas. Investigators from statistical societies served as field-workers for these portrayals. Their portraits of social dislocation had a rhetorical intent: to provoke new government policies with respect, for instance, to poverty and schooling.

One of the classic accounts of British urban life was written, in German, by an intellectual—and dialectical—descendant of Kant, Friedrich Engels. *The Condition of the Working Class in England* (1845/1969) was compiled by Engels from "personal observations and authentic sources" relating to Manchester, a notable center of statistical inquiry. Note the neo-Kantian doubts expressed by Engels in the opening sentences of his dedication (written in English):

> Working Men! To you I dedicate a work, in which I have tried to lay before my German Countrymen a faithful picture of your conditions, of your sufferings and struggles, of your hopes and prospects. I have lived long enough amidst you to know something about your circumstances; I have devoted to their knowledge my most serious attention. I have studied the various official and non-official documents as far as I was able to get hold of them—I have not been satisfied with this, I wanted more than a mere *abstract* knowledge of my subject. I wanted to see you in your own homes, to observe you in your every-day life, to chat with you on your conditions and grievances, to witness your struggles against the social and political power of your oppressors. (p. 323)

Engels's work, therefore, fell within a naturalistic, interpretive, and field study framework. His close-up narrative style was part of a nineteenth-century journalistic literary genre whose boundaries stretched at least from Charles Dickens (1812-1870) to Emile Zola (1840-1902).

In a wider sense, the penetration of Kantian ideas in modern scientific thought can also be demonstrated by two further publications of the 1830s and 1840s: Auguste Comte's *Cours de Philosophie Positiviste* (6 volumes, 1830-1842) and John Stuart Mill's *A System of Logic* (1843). Comte argued that the history of the human mind and human society had passed through three stages—the theological, the metaphysical, and the positive. He believed that human action—Comte coined the term *sociology*—would undergo a similar transformation in the not-too-distant future.

A System of Logic was also seminal. Like Comte's proposals, it also responded to the demand that the practice of all sciences—natural or moral/social—should be dedicated to the identification of lawlike patterns. Yet Mill did not entirely follow Comte's reductionism. For Mill, then, analyses of human activity required reference to psychological facts as well as material truths. The dualism implicit in Mill's analysis had a double consequence that still remains controversial. Some social investigators sought to bring the moral/social sciences within the sphere of the physical sciences, whereas others deepened Mill's dualism.

Wilhelm Dilthey (1833-1911) was a notable member of the latter school of thought. He believed that the sciences had emancipated themselves from Comtean metaphysics, yet that they were still struggling to identify themselves with reference to the natural sciences. Accordingly, Dilthey felt that Mill was too much in the thrall of Comtean scientific thinking. In turn, he trenchantly criticized the reductionist and objectivist positions espoused by positivists and empiricists. They were, Dilthey felt, corrupted by the Cartesian belief that "the connection of all phenomena according to the principle of causality" is a "precondition for a knowledge of the laws of thought and society." Dilthey's rejection of empiricism stemmed directly from Kantian theory. Positivists, he suggested, believed that "the self-active 'I' " is "an illusion" (quoted in Ermath, 1978, pp. 72-73).

Dilthey took this opportunity to distinguish sharply between two kinds of knowledge or science: *Naturwissenschaft* and *Geisteswissenschaft.* Following Kant, Dilthey argued that the thing-in-itself—nature apart from human consciousness—is unknowable in the realm of the natural sciences. The same argument, however, could not be applied to the *Geisteswissenschaften.* The data of the human sciences—historical social realities—include the data of consciousness, which, again following Kant, can be known directly.

Against this background of controversy in the social sciences, German neo-Kantianism rose strongly in the 1860s and 1870s. It stressed the uniquely transcendental dimensions of mind. Dilthey, for instance, emphasized the role of understanding (*Verstehen*), contrasting it with the pre-Kantian, Cartesian practices of explanation (*Erklärung*).

More important, however, was Dilthey's attention to the concept of *Erlebnis.* Roughly translated as "lived experience," *Erlebnis* was "central to Dilthey's project" (Ermath, 1978, p. 219). Every lived experience, Dilthey believed, occurs within historical social reality. It also lies beyond the immediate awareness of mind but, nonetheless, can be brought to consciousness. Thus *Erlebnis* relates to the intimate relationship between the inner and outer states and consequences of human existence.

Further, Dilthey's appreciation of lived experience included a notable stance with respect to human freedom. He accepted that all humans have a will of their own, yet he did not reduce human freedom to voluntarism, nor to determinism. Dilthey stipulated that the human will is not so much free "from" conditions as free "to" respond to a multiplicity of circumstances. Human freedom, therefore, was defined by Dilthey in terms of "a range of possible responses and choices within a concrete situation" (Ermath, 1978, p. 121).

Finally, Dilthey viewed *Erlebnis* as an empirical rather than a metaphysical concept. The relationships between individuals and the social, historical, and cultural matrix of their lives were phenomena that could be explored by the social (or human) sciences.

Dilthey's interest in *Erlebnis* was primarily historical—to comprehend the changes in the human condition and human spirit that had been brought about by the upheavals of the Enlightenment. Dilthey's successors, however, gradually relocated the relationship between lived experience and human existence from the field of history to the field of sociology (see Antoni, 1962).

During the latter part of the nineteenth century, neo-Kantian thought spread widely in the United States and the United Kingdom. One illustration of this influence, for instance, was Charles Booth's "passion to understand" the continuing social and economic disruptions wrought by late nineteenth-century industrialization (Simey, 1969, p. 99). Although Booth is sometimes recalled as a mere fact gatherer, his studies of the London urban poor between 1887 and 1902 were closely linked to the ideas of one of his assistants, Beatrice Webb (1856-1943). Webb grew up in a household frequented by the social Darwinian theorist Herbert Spencer. "He taught me," she reports in her autobiographical account of the craft of the social investigator, "to look on all social institutions exactly as if they were plants or animals—things that could be observed, classified and explained, and the action of which could to some extent be foretold if one knew enough about them" (Webb, 1979, p. 38). Subsequently, Webb adopted a different outlook, one that suggests the influence of German thought:

> From my diary entries [which followed a visit to mainland Europe in 1882] I infer that I should have become, not a worker in the field of sociology, but a descriptive psychologist; either in the novel, to which I was from time to time tempted; or (if I had been born thirty years later) in a scientific analysis of the mental make-up of individual men and women, and their behaviour under particular conditions. (p. 109)

America or Germany?

By the end of the nineteenth century, the kind of census taking pioneered in Europe began to come to terms with a new set of historical circumstances in the United States. Anglo-Saxon social Darwinism jostled with neo-Kantian ideas brought back to the United States by students who had studied in Germany. Furthermore, both currents of thought had to come to terms with homegrown Progressive ideals. Together, the interaction of these currents in intellectual thought did much to induce the "Americanization of social science" (Manicas, 1987, p. 11).

Social Darwinists in the United States transposed the theories of Charles Darwin to the realm of civil society. They believed that the evolution of society should be left to the free play of market forces. As in nature, that is, social evolution should be left to the survival of the fittest. On the other hand, the Progressives took a contrary stance. They argued that, unlike other animals, human beings had the capacity, akin to Kant's "freedom of practical reason," to define and achieve their own futures.

Accordingly, the social Darwinists and the Progressives differed on the responsibilities they allocated to government. The social Darwinists felt that government should intervene only to remove barriers that limited laissez-faire economic practices, whereas the Progressives regarded government as an agency that should sponsor—ideologically, legally, and financially—the pursuit of social progress.

In the end, the Progressive current in social thought achieved dominance. Progressive politicians promoted policies that had major repercussions for all research. First, they endorsed the value of social research—encouraging nongovernment agencies to fund social research. Second, they raised the intellectual status of social science in the universities—rendering them the policy think tanks of Progressivism. And third, they created a new social stratum—welfare professionals who serviced the organs of the Progressive state.

Professionals and academics struggled with the think-tank mission of the universities. The promissory notes issued by Descartes, Newton, and Comte were repeatedly invoked in attempts to create free-floating technologies of social progress. Henceforth, social life was to be rational and rule governed, with the rules to be derived from scientific inquiry. A slogan used to publicize the 1933 Chicago World's Fair neatly captures this technocratic aspiration: "Science Explores: Technology Executes: Mankind Conforms."

But the diversity of higher education in the United States also allowed other standpoints to survive. Besides looking to Descartes, Newton, and Comte, Progressivism had another side. Its belief in the capacity of human beings to define and achieve their own futures also found common cause with Kantian ideals about human freedom and the deployment of practical reason. Verstehen inquiry, therefore, had a legitimate place in the Progressive pantheon. Typically, such work reached back to the anthropological research of

Franz Boas in the 1890s, or to work in the Sociology Department of the University of Chicago, which also came into being in the 1890s. Indeed, higher education in the United States has retained long-standing links with Germany—through student sojourns at German universities (see Manicas, 1987, p. 213), through sanctuary offered to German refugees from Nazism (e.g., Theodore Adorno, Herbert Marcuse), and through the co-authoring and translation of theoretical texts in the 1960s and 1970s (e.g., Berger & Luckmann's *The Social Construction of Reality,* 1966; Habermas's *Knowledge and Human Interests,* 1972).

As noted, however, neo-Kantianism has always been a very broad church. Throughout, its adherents and sympathizers in the United States have duly diversified, forming their own intellectual subcultures, specialist terminologies, and social boundaries. Indeed, as suggested above, their fissiparous and hybridization proclivities (or posturings) have provided endless source material for taxonomically inclined commentators.

Indeed, it is at this juncture that Evelyn Jacob (1987) composed her original exploration of the "assumptions about human nature and society" that underpin qualitative research traditions (p. 3). Note, for instance, that each of the selected traditions stems from an *Erlebnis* rationale. Ecological psychology has "psychological habitat" as one of its foci (p. 5), holistic ethnography concerns the "culture shared by particular bounded groups of individuals" (p. 11), ethnography of communication focuses on "patterns of social interaction among members of a cultural group or among members of different cultural groups" (p. 18), cognitive anthropology assumes that "each bounded group in individuals has a unique system for perceiving and organizing the world about them" (p. 23), and symbolic interactionists are interested in understanding how "interpretations [of individuals' experiences] are developed and used by individuals in specific situations of interaction" (p. 27).

Equally, all qualitative research traditions give as much attention to the inner as well as the outer states of human activity. Jacob (1987, table 1), for instance, notes the "subjective perceptions," "emotions," "reflective interpretations," and "mental standards" that can be included within the "characteristics" of qualitative research (see also Bogdan & Biklen, 1982; Sanday, 1983; Wolcott, 1992).

Another way to comprehend the traditions of qualitative inquiry is to note its convergence with Dilthey's interest in ethnographic research. In the United States, anthropological and sociological practitioners gradually annexed a shared territory that they labeled *ethnography,* a term that comes from a Greek root meaning writing about others (Erickson, 1986, p. 123). In the North American case, such "others" had arisen both within and beyond the mainstream culture.

One important consequence of the ethnographic synthesis has been substantial cross-fertilization between the domains of anthropology and sociology. The study of schooling provides a good example. Schooling is a feature of so-called modern societies, whereas anthropology has its roots in the investigation of premodern societies. The examination of schooling through anthropology (see, for instance, Spindler & Spindler, 1992) might, therefore, appear contradictory. Nevertheless, it has done much to remind educationists that there is more to education than schooling. This broader view of education is demonstrated in Margaret Mead's *Coming of Age in Samoa* (1928), and in subsequent institutional studies such as Howard Becker, Blanche Geer, Everett Hughes, and Anselm Strauss's *Boys in White: Student Culture in Medical School* (1961), Jules Henry's *Culture Against Man* (1963), Philip Jackson's *Life in Classrooms* (1968), Harry Wolcott's *The Man in the Principal's Office* (1973), and Hugh Mehan's *Learning Lessons* (1979).

In an important sense, too, recent ethnographies have also resonated with another feature of Dilthey's presumption that *Erlebnis* is an empirical concept. The "how it actually was" of the 1820s (which Leopold Ranke proclaimed as the task of history; see Kreiger, 1977, p. 4) resurfaced in the 1960s as "telling it like it is"; just as the "new" journalism of the 1960s (e.g., Wolfe & Johnson, 1975) had much in common with the magazine-format, muckraking, narrative journalism of the 1890s and earlier.

But the 1960s and 1970s were not the 1890s or even the 1820s. Qualitative research was reactivated by a new intellectual interest. The Cartesian/Newtonian paradigm had begun to lose its intellectual luster. It slipped off the academy's gold standard. Its devaluation not only followed external criticism (see Kuhn, 1962, 1970), it also arose from internalist critiques of science, themselves reminiscent of Beatrice Webb's revaluation of Herbert Spencer's prescriptions.

Two crucial internalist interventions were Donald Campbell and Julian Stanley's "Experimental and Quasi-Experimental Designs for Research on Teaching" (1963) and Lee J. Cronbach's "Beyond the Two Disciplines of Scientific Psychology" (1975). Campbell and Stanley reviewed earlier Cartesian/Newtonian attempts to devise experimental designs that would yield unambiguous results. Their conclusion, prefigured in the title of their paper, was that social research is an impure art. At best, it can only aspire to the organization of quasi-experiments conducted via the imprecision of quasi-control.

Cronbach offered similar reflections on the received paradigm. In 1957 he had written, "Our job is to invent constructs and to form a network of laws which permits prediction" (p. 681). By 1975, however, he confessed that the "line of investigation I advocated in 1957 no longer seems sufficient" (p. 116). "The goal of our work," he concluded in 1975, is "not to amass generalizations atop which a theoretical tower can someday be erected. The special task of the social scientist in each generation is to pin down the contemporary facts" (p. 126).

In an important sense, then, the boundaries between qualitative and quantitative research became blurred in the 1970s. The inherent uncertainty surrounding neo-Kantian research was joined by similar anxieties about the Cartesian paradigm—and both have been forcefully reviewed, for instance, in David Bloor's *Knowledge and Social Imagery* (1976).

Observer or Observed?

Perhaps the most noteworthy outcome of the epistemological disarray of the 1970s has been a return to Kant's concern with human freedom and social emancipation. There has been a significant reexamination of the observer-observed dyad erected by Descartes and redefined by Kant. Both the observer-observed dualism favored by Cartesians and the observer-observed dialectic activated by neo-Kantians have been questioned. In extreme cases, critics have sought to reduce the observer-observed dyad to a unity.

The freedom of thought and action of the privileged observer is transferred to the less privileged subject of the observation. Similarly, the assumed disinterest of the observer is rejected, along with the passivity of the practitioner (or operative). There is a distinct emancipatory sentiment, for instance, in such works as *Action and Knowledge: Breaking the Monopoly With Participatory Action-Research* (Fals-Borda & Rahman, 1992), *The Reflective Practitioner* (Schön, 1983), *Authority, Education and Emancipation* (Stenhouse, 1983), *Participatory Action Research* (Whyte, 1991), and *Becoming Critical: Education, Knowledge and Action* (Carr & Kemmis, 1986).

At least three propositions seem to have been adopted by this movement. First, late twentieth-century democracies should empower all citizens, not just privileged elites. Second, liberal social practice can never be morally or politically disinterested. And third, the managerial separation of conception (research) from execution (practice) is psychologically, socially, and economically inefficient.

Sophisticated rationales for action or participatory research are beginning to emerge from this theoretical conjuncture. One popular source, also with Kantian roots, has been the work of Jürgen Habermas (see, especially, his 1965 Inaugural Lecture, "Knowledge and Human Interests: A General Perspective," reprinted in Habermas, 1972). Like many recent reviewers of social theory, Habermas (1972) points to the "objectivist illusion" of pure theory. Instead, he espouses the Kantian posture that there are indissoluble links among knowledge, methodology, and human interests (p. 309). Not surprisingly, therefore, Habermas explicitly eschews the objectivism of Cartesian science, with its attempts to describe the "universe theoretically in its law-like order, just as it is" (p. 303).

As a representative of the dialectical strand of neo-Kantian thought, Habermas holds that "unreflected consciousness" could, through "self-reflection," serve "emancipatory" cognitive interests such that "knowledge and interest are one" (pp. 310, 314). Habermas has repeatedly returned to the "unmasking of the human sciences" (1987, p. 295). He has suggested, in Kantian terms for instance, that the "objectifying attitude in which the knowing subject regards itself as it would entities in the external world is no longer *privileged*," and that the Cartesian "paradigm of the philosophy of consciousness" be replaced with the "paradigm of mutual understanding" (1987, p. 296).

From Habermas's perspective, social research is an interactive rather than a controlling process. Participants aim for mutual understanding over the coordination of their subsequent actions (see, for instance, Brand, 1990; Kemmis, in press). Applied research, therefore, is not about social conformity but about social justice.

By these considerations, the Renaissance project of Machiavelli and Columbus is joined to the Enlightenment project of Kant and to the Progressive project espoused by Webb and Adorno. Applied research, action research, qualitative research, humanist research, and their consociates become the pursuit of democratic forms of communication that, in their turn, prefigure planned social change.

One Tradition or Many?

This chapter has outlined the diversity of intellectual movements and social practices that have activated applied research since the Enlightenment. From a basis laid down in the Renaissance, Western science has embraced the application of rationality to the furtherance of human endeavor. By the Enlightenment, however, Western rationality began to prove less assured than its founders had imagined. It was reactivated and replenished by a range of new ideas.

Each new generation has drawn from this well, has become the practitioner-guardian of its own postures and traditions, and has replenished the well with its own sweet water of fresh ideas. If nothing else, the dynamism of this intellectual community assures its own future. Indeed, its commitment to participate rationally in the prosecution of worthwhile, even emancipatory, social change is probably the most enduring tradition of qualitative research.

References

Antoni, C. (1962). *From history to sociology: The transition in German historical thinking* (H. V. White, Trans.). London: Merlin.

Atkinson, P., Delamont, S., & Hammersley, M. (1989). Qualitative research traditions: A British response to Jacob. *Review of Educational Research, 58,* 231-250.

Becker, H. S., Geer, B., Hughes, E., & Strauss, A. (1961). *Boys in white: Student culture in medical school.* Chicago: University of Chicago Press.

Berger, P., & Luckmann, T. (1966). *The social construction of reality.* Garden City, NY: Doubleday.

Bloor, D. (1976). *Knowledge and social imagery.* Chicago: University of Chicago Press.

Bogdan, R. C., & Biklen, S. K. (1982). *Qualitative research for education: An introduction to theory and methods.* Boston: Allyn & Bacon.

Brand, A. (1990). *The force of reason: An introduction to Habermas' theory of communicative action.* Sydney: Allen & Unwin.

Buchdahl, G. (1969). *Metaphysics and the philosophy of science.* Cambridge: MIT Press.

Buchmann, M., & Floden, R. E. (1989). Research traditions, diversity and progress. *Review of Educational Research, 59,* 241-248.

Campbell, D., & Stanley, J. (1963). Experimental and quasi-experimental designs for research on teaching. In N. Gage (Ed.), *Handbook for research on teaching* (pp. 171-246). Chicago: Rand McNally.

Carr, W., & Kemmis, S. (1986). *Becoming critical: Education, knowledge and action.* London: Falmer.

Cronbach, L. J. (1957). The two disciplines of scientific psychology. *American Psychologist, 12,* 671-684.

Cronbach, L. J. (1975). Beyond the two disciplines of scientific psychology. *American Psychologist, 30,* 116-126.

Descartes, R. (1968). *Discourse on method and the meditations.* Harmondsworth: Penguin.

Engels, F. (1969). *The condition of the working class in England.* London: Panther. (Original work published 1845)

Erickson, F. (1986). Qualitative methods in research on teaching. In M. C. Wittrock (Ed.), *Handbook of research on teaching* (3rd ed., pp. 119-161). New York: Macmillan.

Ermath, M. (1978). *Wilhelm Dilthey: The critique of historical reason.* Chicago: University of Chicago Press.

Fals-Borda, O., & Rahman, M. A. (1991). *Action and knowledge: Breaking the monopoly with participatory action-research.* New York: Apex.

Foucault, M. (1973). *The order of things: An archaeology of the human sciences.* New York: Vintage.

Habermas, J. (1972). *Knowledge and human interests* (J. J. Shapiro, Trans.). London: Heinemann.

Habermas, J. (1987). *The philosophical discourse of modernity: Twelve lectures* (F. Lawrence, Trans.). Cambridge: Polity.

Hacking, I. (1990). *The taming of chance.* Cambridge, UK: Cambridge University Press.

Henry, J. (1963). *Culture against man.* New York: Random House.

Hobsbawm, E., & Ranger, T. (Eds.). (1984). *The invention of tradition.* Cambridge, UK: Cambridge University Press.

Jackson, P. (1968). *Life in classrooms.* New York: Holt, Rinehart & Winston.

Jacob, E. (1987). Qualitative research traditions: A review. *Review of Educational Research, 57,* 1-50.

Jacob, E. (1989). Qualitative research: A defense of traditions. *Review of Educational Research, 59,* 229-235.

Kemmis, S. (in press). Foucault, Habermas and evaluation. *Curriculum Studies.*

Kreiger, L. (1977). *Ranke: The meaning of history.* Chicago: University of Chicago Press.

Kuhn, T. S. (1962). *The structure of scientific revolutions.* Chicago: University of Chicago Press.

Kuhn, T. S. (1970). *The structure of scientific revolutions* (2nd ed.). Chicago: University of Chicago Press.

Laudan, L. (1977). *Progress and its problems: Toward a theory of scientific growth.* Berkeley: University of California Press.

Lincoln, Y. (1989). Qualitative research: A response to Atkinson, Delamont and Hammersley. *Review of Educational Research, 59,* 237-239.

Machiavelli, N. (1988). *The prince* (Q. Skinner & R. Price, Eds.). Cambridge: Cambridge University Press.

MacIntyre, A. (1988). *Whose justice? Which rationality?* London: Duckworth.

Manicas, P. T. (1987). *A history and philosophy of the social sciences.* New York: Basil Blackwell.

Mead, M., (1928). *Coming of age in Samoa: A psychological study of primitive youth for Western civilization.* New York: William Morrow.

Mehan, H. (1979). *Learning lessons: Social organization in the classroom.* Cambridge, MA: Harvard University Press.

Roberts, J. (1990). *German philosophy: An introduction.* Cambridge, UK: Polity.

Sanday, P. R. (1983). The ethnographic paradigm(s). In J. Van Maanen (Ed.), *Qualitative methodology*. Beverly Hills, CA: Sage.

Schön, D. (1983). *The reflective practitioner: How professionals think in action*. New York: Basic Books.

Scruton, R. (1983). *Kant*. Oxford: Oxford University Press.

Shils, E. (1981). *Tradition*. Boston: Faber & Faber.

Simey, T. S. (1969). Charles Booth. In T. Raison (Ed.), *The founding fathers of social science* (pp. 92-99). Harmondsworth: Penguin.

Slaughter, M. (1982). *Universal languages and scientific taxonomy in the seventeenth century*. Cambridge, UK: Cambridge University Press.

Spindler, G., & Spindler, L. (1992). Cultural process and ethnography: An anthropological perspective. In M. D. LeCompte, W. L. Millroy, & J. Preissle (Eds.), *The handbook of qualitative research in education* (pp. 53-92). New York: Academic Press.

Stenhouse, L. (1983). *Authority, education and emancipation*. London: Heinemann.

Strauss, G. (1966). A sixteenth-century encyclopedia. Sebastian Munster's *Cosmography* and its editions. In C. H. Cater (Ed.), *From the Renaissance to the Counter-Reformation: Essays in honour of Garrett Mattingly* (pp. 145-163). London: Cape.

Webb, B. (1979). *My apprenticeship*. Cambridge, UK: Cambridge University Press.

Whyte, W. F. (1991). *Participatory action research*. London: Sage.

Wolcott, H. F. (1973). *The man in the principal's office: An ethnography*. New York: Holt, Rinehart & Winston.

Wolcott, H. F. (1992). Posturing in qualitative inquiry. In M. D. LeCompte, W. L. Millroy, & J. Preissle (Eds.), *The handbook of qualitative research in education* (pp. 3-52). New York: Academic Press.

Wolfe, T., & Johnson, E. W. (Eds.). (1975). *The new journalism*. London: Pan.

4

Working the Hyphens

Reinventing Self and Other in Qualitative Research

MICHELLE FINE

> I am waiting for them to stop talking about the "Other," to stop even describing how important it is to be able to speak about difference. It is not just important what we speak about, but how and why we speak. Often this speech about the "Other" is also a mask, an oppressive talk hiding gaps, absences, that space where our words would be if we were speaking, if there were silence, if we were there. This "we" is that "us" in the margins, that "we" who inhabit marginal space that is not a site of domination but a place of resistance. Enter that space. Often this speech about the "Other" annihilates, erases: "no need to hear your voice when I can talk about you better than you can speak about yourself. No need to hear your voice. Only tell me about your pain. I want to know your story. And then I will tell it back to you in a new way. Tell it back to you in such a way that it has become mine, my own. Re-writing you, I write myself anew. I am still author, authority. I am still the colonizer, the speak subject, and you are now at the center of my talk." Stop. (hooks, 1990, pp. 151-152)

Much of qualitative research has reproduced, if contradiction-filled, a colonizing discourse of the "Other." This essay is an attempt to review how qualitative research projects have *Othered* and to examine an emergent set of activist and/or post-modern texts that interrupt *Othering*. First, I examine the hyphen at which Self-Other join in the politics of everyday life, that is, the hyphen that both separates and merges personal identities with our inventions of Others. I then take up how qualitative researchers work this hyphen. Here I gather a growing set of works on "inscribing the Other," viewing arguments that critical, feminist, and/or Third World scholars have posed about social science as a tool of domination. This section collects a messy series of questions about methods, ethics, and epistemologies as we rethink how researchers have spoken "of" and "for" Others while occluding ourselves and our own investments, burying the contradictions that percolate at the Self-Other hyphen.

A renewed sense of possibility breathes in the next section, in which I present discussion of qualitative research projects designed for social change. Here readers engage narratives written against Othering, analyzing not just the decontextualized voices of Others, but the very structures, ideologies, contexts, and practices that constitute Othering (Bhavnani, 1992). Qualitative researchers interested in self-consciously working the hyphen—

AUTHOR'S NOTE: My appreciation to Julie Blackman, Norman Denzin, and Yvonna Lincoln for careful reading and comments. Credit is also owed to L. Mun Wong, Cindy Kublik, Sarah Ingersoll, Judi Addelston, and Kim Mizrahi for helping me develop these notions.

that is, unpacking notions of scientific neutrality, universal truths, and researcher dispassion—will be invited to imagine how we can braid critical and contextual struggle back into our texts (Burawoy et al., 1992; Fine & Vanderslice, 1992).

This essay is designed to rupture the textual laminations within which Others have been sealed by social scientists, to review the complicity of researchers in the construction and distancing of Others, and to identify transgressive possibilities inside qualitative texts.

Selves-Others: Co-constructions at the Hyphen

> In September 1989, my niece was sexually assaulted by a department store security officer. He caught her shoplifting and then spent two hours threatening her with prison, legal repercussions, and likely abuse at the hands of other women in prison. She had just turned 16, and half believed him. Filled with terror, she listened for 90 minutes of what would later be determined "unlawful detainment." He offered her a deal, "Give me what women give men and I'll let you go." Surprised, shocked, understanding but not fully, she asked, "What do you mean?" She refused. For another 30 minutes he persisted. Tears, threats, and terror were exchanged. She agreed, ultimately, after he showed her a photo album of "girls who did it." Sheepishly, and brilliantly, she requested that he "get a condom."
>
> March 5, 1992. We won the criminal case for sexual assault, and we are pursuing a civil suit against the department store. Tomorrow my niece is going to be deposed by the store's lawyers. She is, by now, 19, a new mother, living with her longtime boyfriend/father of the baby. She is Latina, and was adopted from Colombia into our middle-class Jewish family 12 years ago.

Writing this essay, I find myself ever conscious about how I participate in constructing Others. Tonight I listen to myself collude in the splitting of Jackie, my niece—the dissection of her adolescent, Latina, female body/consciousness. Family, friends, lawyers, and unsolicited advisers subtly, persistently, and uncomfortably work to present her as white/Jewish (not Latina), sexually innocent (not mother), victim (not shoplifter), the object of male aggression. Stories of her new baby, sexuality, reproductive history, desires, and pains, we all nod across cities, should probably be avoided in her testimony.

At some point in the phone call I realize our collusion in her Othering, and I realize that Jackie has long since grown accustomed to this dynamic. Her life has been punctuated by negotiations at the zippered borders of her gendered, raced, and classed Otherhood. As the good (adopted) granddaughter, daughter, and niece, she always has, and does again, split for us. In a flash I remember that when she was picked up for shoplifting she gave her Spanish name to the police, not the English name she had used for nine years.

Sitting within and across alienating borders, Jackie is now being asked to draw her self-as-good-middle-class-white-woman and to silence her Other-as-bad-Latina-unwed-mother. Valerie Smith (1991) would call these "split affinities." Jackie the Latina street girl had to stay out of court because Jackie the white middle-class young lady was escorted in. That night on the phone we were all circling to find a comfortable (for whom?) space for representation. We struggled with what bell hooks (1990) would call a *politics of location*:

> Within a complex and ever shifting realities of power relations, do we position ourselves on the side of colonizing mentality? Or do we continue to stand in political resistance with the oppressed, ready to offer our ways of seeing and theorizing, of making culture, toward that revolutionary effort which seeks to create space where there is unlimited access to pleasure and power of knowing, where transformation is possible? (p. 145)

No surprise, Jackie danced through the deposition shining with integrity, style, and passion. She told all as proud mother, lover, daughter, niece, and survivor. With a smile and a tear, she resisted their, and she resisted our, Othering.

Jackie mingled her autobiography with our surveilled borders on her Self and the raced and gendered legal interpretations of her Other by which she was surrounded. She braided them into her story, her deposition, which moved among "hot spots" and "safe spots." She slid from victim to survivor, from naive to coy, from deeply experienced young woman to child. In her deposition she dismantled the very categories I so worried we had constructed as sedimented pillars around her, and she wandered among them, pivoting her identity, her self-representations, and, therefore, her audiences. She became neither the Other nor the Same. Not even zippered. Her mobile positioning of contradictions could too easily be written off to the inconsistencies of adolescence. Maybe that's why she ultimately won the settlement for damages. But she would better be viewed as an honest narrator of multiple poststructural selves speaking among themselves, in front of an audience searching relentlessly for pigeonholes.

I think again about Jackie as I read a recent essay on ethnicity, identity, and difference written by Stuart Hall. Hall (1991) takes up this conversation by reviewing the representations that have seasoned his autobiography:

> History changes your conception of yourself. Thus, another critical thing about identity is that it is partly the relationship between you and the Other. Only when there is an Other can you know who you are. To discover the fact is to discover and unlock the whole enormous history of nationalism and of racism. Racism is a structure of discourse and representation that tried to expel the Other symbolically—blot it out, put it over there in the Third World, at the margin. (p. 16)

Hall traces the strands of his "self" through his raced and classed body. Recognizing that representations of his selves are always politically situated, he sees them also as personally negotiated. For Hall, the Self constructs as the Other is invented. In this passage, however, Hall appears to slide between two positions. In one, he sees Self and Other as fluid. The other requires the fixing of an Other in order for Self to be constituted. Ironically, by stipulating the binary opposition, Hall reproduces the separation and detours away from investigating what is "between." Unearthing the blurred boundaries "between," as Jackie understood, constitutes a critical task for qualitative researchers.

Biddy Martin and Chandra Talpade Mohanty (1986) extend this conversation when they take up an analysis of *home* as a site for constituting Self and for expelling Others. They write:

> The tension between the desire for home, for synchrony, for sameness and the realization of the repressions and violence that make home, harmony, sameness imaginable, and that enforce it, is made clear in the movement of the narrative by very careful and effective reversals which do not erase the positive desire for unit, for Oneness, but destabilize and undercut it. . . .
>
> The relationship between the loss of community and the loss of self is crucial. To the extent that identity is collapsed with home and community and based on homogeneity and comfort, on skin, blood and heart, the giving up of home will necessarily mean the giving up of self and vice versa (pp. 208-209)

These writers acknowledge that Self and Other reside on opposite sides of the same door. Home and the "real world" are successfully split. The former codes comfort, whereas the latter flags danger. Othering helps us deny the dangers that loiter inside our homes. Othering keeps us from seeing the comforts that linger outside.

As I write this essay, the *New York Times* lands on the front porch. Another perverse splitting of Identity and Othering explodes on the front page. Lesbian women and gay men in New York City have been informed that they will not be allowed to march in this year's St. Patrick's Day parade. One parade marshal explained, "To be Irish is to know the difference between men and women's characteristics." Ethnic community is being consolidated, whitewashed, through sexual exclusion. At a time when white working-class men and women are struggling to define themselves as whole, to locate their terror outside, and hold some Other responsible for their plight at the hands of late capitalism, we witness public rituals of race purification. A fragile collective identity is secured through promiscuous assaults on Others (African Americans? Asian Americans? women? lesbian women? gay men?) (see Weis, 1990). The exploitations endured today are protected/projected onto Others of varied colors, classes, sexualities, and bodies.

Self and Other are knottily entangled. This relationship, as lived between researchers and informants, is typically obscured in social science texts, protecting privilege, securing distance, and laminating the contradictions. Despite denials, qualitative researchers are always implicated at the hyphen. When we opt, as has been the tradition, simply to write *about* those who have been Othered, we deny the hyphen. Slipping into a contradictory discourse of individualism, personalogic theorizing, and decontextualization, we inscribe the Other, strain to white out Self, and refuse to engage the contradictions that litter our texts.

When we opt, instead, to engage in social struggles *with* those who have been exploited and subjugated, we work the hyphen, revealing far more about ourselves, and far more about the structures of Othering. Eroding the fixedness of categories, we and they enter and play with the blurred boundaries that proliferate.

By *working the hyphen,* I mean to suggest that researchers probe how we are in relation with the contexts we study and with our informants, understanding that we are all multiple in those relations. I mean to invite researchers to see how these "relations between" get us "better" data, limit what we feel free to say, expand our minds and constrict our mouths, engage us in intimacy and seduce us into complicity, make us quick to interpret and hesitant to write. Working the hyphen means creating occasions for researchers and informants to discuss what is, and is not, "happening between," within the negotiated relations of whose story is being told, why, to whom, with what interpretation, and whose story is being shadowed, why, for whom, and with what consequence.

Inscribing the Other

> Studies which have as their focal point the alleged deviant attitudes and behaviors of Blacks are

grounded within the racist assumptions and principles that only render Blacks open to further exploitation. The challenge to social scientists for a redefinition of the basic problem has been raised in terms of the "colonial analogy." It has been argued that the relationship between the researcher and his subjects, by definition, resembles that of the oppressor and the oppressed, because it is the oppressor who defines the problem, the nature of the research, and, to some extent, the quality of interaction between him and his subjects. This inability to understand and research the fundamental problem, neo-colonialism, prevents most social researchers from being able accurately to observe and analyze Black life and culture and the impact racism and oppression have upon Blacks. Their inability to understand the nature and effects of neo-colonialism in the same manner as Black people is rooted in the inherent bias of the social sciences. (Ladner, 1971, p. vii)

Joyce Ladner warned us more than 20 years ago about the racism, bred and obscured, at the Self-Other hyphen of qualitative research. Ladner knew then that texts that sought the coherence of Master Narratives needed, and so created, Others. The clean edges of those narratives were secured by the frayed borders of the Other. The articulate professional voice sounded legitimate against the noisy dialect of the Other. The rationality of the researcher/writer domesticated the outrage of the Other. These texts sought to close contradictions, and by so doing they tranquilized the hyphen, ousting the Other.

Master Narratives seek to preserve the social order while obscuring the privileged stances/investments of writers:

> Within the discourse of modernity, the Other not only sometimes ceases to be a historical agent, but is often defined within totalizing and universalistic theories that create a transcendental rational White, male Eurocentric subject that both occupies the centers of power while simultaneously appearing to exist outside of time and space. Read against this Eurocentric transcendental subject, the Other is shown to lack any redeeming community traditions collective voice of historical weight—and is reduced to the imagery of the colonizer. (Giroux, 1991, p. 7)

The imperialism of such scholarship is evident in terms of whose lives get displayed and whose lives get protected by social science. Put another way, why don't we know much about how the rich live? Why don't we study whiteness? How do "their" and "our" lives get investigated (and not)? Whose stories are presented as if "naturally" self-revealing and whose stories are surrounded by "compensatory" theory? Whose "dirty linen," as Yvonna Lincoln would put it, gets protected by such work?

Two years ago, a student of mine, Nancy Porter, asked me if she could design a dissertation around the gendered and classed lives of elite white women. I was embarrassed that I had somehow set up an expectation among students that poverty was "in." Could I really have conveyed that wealth was a bore? Nonetheless, with my blessings and to her delight, she, a professional golfer with lots of access, proceeded to conduct deep qualitative interviews with rich, "registered" Main Line women of Philadelphia, only to learn that the very discourse of wealthy women constricts and betrays few wrinkles, problems, or any outstanding features. These women describe themselves as if they were "typical," don't talk about money, and rarely reveal any domestic or interpersonal difficulties. Only if divorced will they discuss heterosexuality and gender relations critically. Nancy and I soon began to understand that there had been a collusion between social researchers committed to sanitizing/neglecting the elite through scholarly omission *and* an elite discourse of comfort and simplicity which conveys a relatively bump-free story of their lives. Protected then, twice, by the absence of social surveillance—in welfare offices, from public agencies, through social researchers—and the absence of a scholarly discourse on their dysfunctionality, the elite, with their "new class" academic colleagues, retain a corpus of social science material that fingers Them while it powders the faces of Us.

The social sciences have been, and still are, long on texts that inscribe some Others, preserve other Others from scrutiny, and seek to hide the researcher/writer under a veil of neutrality or objectivity. With the publication of Clifford and Marcus's *Writing Culture* (1986) came an explosion of attention to the domination encoded in such texts, and to the troubling transparency of ethnographers and writers. Although it is most problematic that Clifford and Marcus exclude the work of feminists, the essays in their volume confirm the costs in theory and praxis that devolve from the insistence that ethnographic distance be preferred over authentic engagement. By so doing, *Writing Culture* marks a significant moment in the biography of studying Others, documenting the complicity of ethnographic projects in the narration of colonialism.

A close look at these tensions is offered in Mary Louise Pratt's (1985) analysis of early travel journals. Pratt argues that within these texts, "natives" were portrayed through multiple discourses, typically as if they were "amenable to domination" and had great "potential as a labor pool" (p. 139). Written to "capture" the essence of "natives," these journals allowed little interruption and less evidence of leakage, sweat, pleasure, oppression, rude or polite exchanges in the creation of the manuscripts. These journals were written as if there were no constructing narrators. Disinterested translators simply photographed local practices and customs. Pratt (1985) reproduces John Mandeville's *Travels* (circa 1350):

> Men and women of that isle have heads like hounds; and they are called Cynocephales. This folk, thereof all they be of such shape, yet they are fully reasonable and subtle of wit. . . . And they gang all naked but a little cloth before their privy members. They are large of stature and good warriors, and they bear a great target, with which they cover all their body, and a long spear in their hand. (p. 139)

Pratt comments:

> Any reader recognizes here a familiar, widespread, and stable form of "othering." The people to be othered are homogenized into a collective "they," which is distilled even further into an iconic "he" (the standardized adult male specimen). This abstracted "he"/"they" is the subject of verbs in a timeless present tense, which characterizes anything "he" is or does not as a particular historical event but as an instance of pregiven custom or trait. (p. 139)

Qualitative researchers then, and most now, produce texts through Donna Haraway's (1988) "god trick," presuming to paint the Other from "nowhere." Researchers/writers self-consciously carry no voice, body, race, class, or gender and no interests into their texts. Narrators seek to shelter themselves in the text, as if they were transparent (Spivak, 1988). They recognize no hyphen.

Analogous to Pratt's project on travel journals, sociologist Herb Gans has written and worried about the more recent dense body of work produced on "the underclass." This flourishing area of research has legitimated the category, even amidst multiple slippery frames. Poor adults and children have been codified as Others, as the broader culture is being prepared for a permanent caste of children and adults beyond redemption. Social science has been the intellectual handmaiden for this project, serving to anesthetize the culture with cognitive distinctions that help split the species. These same constructions may, of course, be producing their own subversions, resistances, and transgressions, but, for the moment, "we" don't have to see, smell, hear, feel, or respond to "them." The material and discursive hyphens, again, are being denied.

Michael Katz (1993) narrates a similar story about the historic encoding, within social scientific debates, of the "(un)deserving poor." Katz traces representations of the poor across social science debates and public policies. He argues that social scientists have insinuated moral boundaries of deservingness that thread research and policy, enabling researchers, policy makers, and the public to believe that we can distinguish (and serve) those who are "deserving" and neglect honorably those who are "undeserving" and poor.

We confront, then, one legacy of social research that constructs, legitimates, and distances Others, banishing them to the margins of the culture. Sometimes these texts are used to deprive Them of services; always to rob Them of whole, complex, humanity. Although these portraits of subjugation may be internally slippery, they cohere momentarily around deficiencies, around who they are not. These Others are represented as unworthy, dangerous, and immoral, or as pitiable, victimized, and damaged.

There is, too, a growing postcolonial critique of Othering directed at those literatures written presumably "for" Others. Homi Bhabha (1990), for instance, unravels "nation-centered" discourses that weave ideologies of "common culture." To assure their hermetic seals, he argues these cultures are written in ways that essentialize and silence women's bodies and stories. Like Cornel West (1988) and Kimberle Crenshaw (1992), Bhabha takes affront at "common culture" discourses made coherent by "the subsumption or sublation of social antagonism, . . . the repression of social divisions, . . . the power to authorize an 'impersonal' holistic or universal discourse on the representation of the social that naturalizes cultural difference and turns it into a 'second' nature argument" (p. 242). Thus even "for" Others there are growing, stifling discourses that essentialize to map culture.

At the root of this argument, whether Othering is produced "on" or "for," qualitative researchers need to recognize that our work stands in some relation to Othering. We may self-consciously or not decide *how* to work the hyphen of Self and Other, how to gloss the boundaries between, and within, slippery constructions of Others. But when we look, get involved, demur, analyze, interpret, probe, speak, remain silent, walk away, organize for outrage, or sanitize our stories, and when we construct our texts in or on their words, we decide how to nuance our relations with/for/despite those who have been deemed Others. When we write essays about subjugated Others as if *they* were a homogeneous mass (of vice or virtue), free-floating and severed from contexts of oppression, and as if we were neutral transmitters of voices and stories, we tilt toward a narrative strategy that reproduces Othering on, despite, or even "for." When we construct texts collaboratively, self-consciously examining our relations with/for/despite those who have been contained as Others, we move against, we enable resistance to, Othering.

This is no simple binary opposition of Self and Other, nor of texts that inscribe and texts that resist. There is no easy narrative litmus for Othering. Contradictions litter all narrative forms. And all narratives about Others both inscribe and resist othering. Yet in becoming self-conscious of work at the hyphen, researchers can see a history of qualitative research that has been deeply colonial, surveilling, and exotic (Clifford & Marcus, 1986; Pratt, 1985, 1992; Rosaldo, 1989). Now that the subjects of U.S. ethnography have come home, qualitative accounts of urban and rural, poverty-stricken and working-class, white and of color America flourish. Through these texts, the Other survives next door. But the privileges, interests, biographies, fetishes, and investments of researchers typically remain subtext, buried, protected (Harding, 1987; Haraway, 1988).

Renato Rosaldo (1989) contends that there are no "innocent" ethnographers. When innocence is sought, Rosaldo writes, the "eye of ethnography [often connects with] the I of imperialism" (p. 41). The project at hand is to unravel, critically, the blurred boundaries in our relation, and in our texts; to understand the political work of our narratives; to decipher how the traditions of social science serve to inscribe; and to imagine how our practice can be transformed to resist, self-consciously, acts of othering. As these scenes of translation vividly convey, qualitative researchers are chronically and uncomfortably engaged in ethical decisions about how deeply to work with/for/despite those cast as Others, and how seamlessly to represent the hyphen. Our work will never "arrive" but must always struggle "between."

Writing Against Othering

> I too think the intellectual should constantly disturb, should bear witness to the misery of the world, should be provocative by being independent, should rebel against all hidden and open pressures and manipulations, should be the chief doubter of systems, of power and its incantations, should be the witness to their mendacity. . . . An intellectual is always at odds with hard and fast categories, because these tend to be instruments used by the victors. (Havel, 1990, p. 167)

In contrast to "hard and fast" texts that inscribe and commodify Others, we move now to a set of texts that self-consciously interrupt Othering, that force a radical rethinking of the ethical and political relations of qualitative researchers to the objects/subjects of our work. In this section I review three chunks of work that write against Othering. First, I present those texts that insert "uppity" voices, stances, and critiques to interrupt Master Narratives (see Austin, 1989; Fanon, 1965; Fine, 1992; hooks, 1989; Rollins, 1985). Often, but not always, these are essays written about and by women of color, situated at the intersection of race and gender oppression (Crenshaw, 1992).

Second, I examine texts in which qualitative researchers dissect elites' constructions of Self and Other. Listening to elites as they manicure them-Selves through Othering, we hear the voices of white fraternity brothers interviewed by Peggy Sanday (1990), white high school boys in Lois Weis's (1990) analysis of "working class without work," and nondisabled researchers' analysis of persons with disabilities, projecting their existential and aesthetic anxieties onto the bodies of disabled Others (Hahn, 1983). In each instance, the words of elites are analyzed by researchers as they evince a discourse of Othering. This work enables us to eavesdrop on privileged consciousness as it seeks to peel Self off of Other.

The third chunk of writing against Othering comprises those texts that press social research for social activism. Engaged with struggles of social transformation, these researchers raise questions about the ethics of involvement and the ethics of detachment, the illusions of objectivity and the borders of subjectivity, and the possibilities of collaborative work and the dilemmas of collusion (Burawoy et al., 1992; Fine & Vanderslice, 1992; Kitzinger, 1991; Lykes, 1989).

From the qualitative works discussed here surfaces the next generation of ethical and epistemological questions for qualitative researchers committed to projects of social justice. These writers/researchers mark a space of analysis in which the motives, consciousness, politics, and stances of informants and researchers/writers are rendered contradictory, problematic, and filled with transgressive possibilities.

Scene 1: Rupturing Texts With Uppity Voices

Gayatri Chakravorty Spivak (1988) contends that academics/researchers can do little to correct the "material wrongs of colonialism." She argues that "in the face of the possibility that the intellectual is complicit in the persistent constitution of Other as the Self's shadow, a possibility of political practice for the intellectual would be to put the economic 'under erasure' " (p. 280). Like bell hooks and Joan Scott, Spivak asks that researchers stop trying to *know* the Other or *give voice to* the Other (Scott, 1991) and listen, instead, to the plural voices of those Othered, as constructors and agents of knowledge.

Although I would quibble with Spivak's sense of the diminished capacity of researchers to participate in the interruption/transformation of social conditions, central to Spivak's and Scott's project is the notion that researchers/writers need to listen and also reveal. As researchers, we need to position ourselves as no longer transparent, but as classed, gendered, raced, and sexual subjects who construct our own locations, narrate these locations, and negotiate our stances with relations of domination (Giroux, 1991). But toward what end?

Chantal Mouffe (1988) would implore activist academics to "determine what conditions are necessary for specific forms of subordination to produce struggles that seek their abolishment and to fuse these as links in a 'chain of equivalence' " (p. 99). Like Mouffe, Cornel West (1988) details a liberatory agenda for social research in which we undertake inquiry into the supremacist logics of domination, into the micropractices of daily subjugation, and into the macrostructural dynamics of class and political exploitation. Urging us to document evidence of struggle, resistance, and counterhegemony (p. 22), West presses for a research agenda steeped in movements for social justice.

How engaged researchers become with, for, against, despite Othering constitutes a political decision that is never resolved simply "in the neutral" by "not getting involved" and "doing science" instead. As Stanley Aronowitz (1988) has written, "Science purports to separate the domination of nature from human domination and regards itself as ideologically neutral" (p. 527).

The decision to retreat from scenes of domination in the name of science is oxymoronic witnessing injustice without outrage. The Other is constituted. The Self is shadowed. Science is preserved. Prevailing politics prospers. Objectivity is assumed. As Spivak (1988) warns, the benevolent "construc[tion of] a homogeneous Other" only reassures "our own place in the seat of the Same or the Self" (p. 288). Although most qualitative work has refused to engage intentionally with the politics of justice, a few texts have imported Others to crack the binary oppositional discourses within social science and the law. Much of this work comes from African American women writing at the *intersection,* as Kimberle Crenshaw (1992) explains:

> The particular experience of Black women in the dominant culture ideology of American society can be conceptualized as *intersectional.* Intersectionality captures the way in which the particular location of Black women in dominant American social relations is unique and in some sense unassimilable to the discursive paradigms of gender and race domination. (p. 2)

Using the Anita Hill/Clarence Thomas hearings as the ground for her analysis of intersectionality, Crenshaw maintains that although Anita Hill sat at the nexus of race/gender oppression, she was presented "as if" she were the prototype white woman harassment victim pitted against the prototype black man accused of rape. Crenshaw uses these images to explode, as both theoretically inadequate and strategically problematic, the narrow cultural frames that have contained *race* as black and male and *gender* as white and female. Contending that black women's experiences are not binary but profoundly intersectional, and therefore radically threatening to existing frames, Crenshaw sees Anita Hill's status as "situated within two fundamental hierarchies of social power (gender and race)," and says that "the central disadvantage that Hill faced was the lack of available and widely comprehended narratives to communicate the reality of her experience as a Black woman to the world" (p. 2). Crenshaw argues that the double marginality of black women, suppressed within both gender and race narratives, is exacerbated by the silencing of black women within the pact of race solidarity between black women and men. Hill had to be deraced to be recognized as a survivor of sexual harassment, and, Crenshaw contends, this is why so many women of color rejected her story as authentic.

Repositioning Hill as the renegade survivor resisting at the intersection of race and gender codes, unwilling to be silenced, Crenshaw slits open white feminism and black solidarity as cultural narratives that fundamentally marginalize the experience, complexity, and critique of black women. Crenshaw concludes, "The vilification of Anita Hill and the embracing of Clarence Thomas reveals that a Black woman breaking ranks to complain of sexual harassment is a much greater threat than a Black man who breaks ranks over race policy" (p. 32).

In *Sapphire Bound!*, a text authored some three years earlier, Regina Austin (1989) makes visible those ideologies surrounding black women's bodies and minds as they are buried in seemingly coherent legal texts. Austin first inserts autobiographic outrage:

> When was the last time someone told you that your way of approaching problems . . . was all wrong? You are too angry, too emotional, too subjective, too pessimistic, too political, too anecdotal and too instinctive? I never know how to respond to such accusations. How can I legitimate my way of thinking? I know that I am not used to flying off the handle, seeing imaginary insults and problems where there are none. I am not a witch solely by nature, but by circumstance and choice as well. I suspect that what my critics really want to say is that I am being too self consciously black

(brown, yellow, red) and/or female to suit their tastes and should "lighten up" because I am making them feel very uncomfortable, and that is not nice. And I want them to think that I am nice, don't I or "womanish"? . . . The chief sources of our theory should be black women's critiques of a society that is dominated by and structured to favor white men of wealth and power. We should also find inspiration in the modes of resistance black women mount, individually and collectively. (p. 540)

Austin then details the legal case in which Crystal Chambers, an African American adult woman, single and pregnant, was fired from Omaha Girls' Club because, as the justices argued, "while a single pregnant woman may indeed provide a good example of hard work and independence, the same person may be a negative role model with respect to the girls' club objective of diminishing the number of teenage pregnancies" (p. 551). Austin writes:

> A black feminist jurisprudential analysis of Chambers must seriously consider the possibility that young, single, sexually active, fertile and nurturing black women are being viewed ominously because they have the temerity to attempt to break out of the rigid, economic, social and political categories that a racist, sexist and less stratified society would impose upon them. . . . Like a treasonous recruit, Crystal turns up unmarried and pregnant. As such, she embodied the enemy . . . to the cause of black cultural containment. (p. 551)

With the body of Crystal Chambers, Austin levers a critical analysis of African American women as they collectively embody the Other in the law. Austin writes against Othering through autobiography, and through the embodied story of Crystal Chambers. In an extension of this stance, Austin (1992) argues in a more recent paper, titled *"The Black Community," Its Lawbreakers and a Politics of Identification,* for what she calls a "politics of identification," in which there is critical engagement of lawbreakers by the black middle class, in an effort to invent and resuscitate, discursively and materially, "the [black] community" (p. 1815).

Mari Matsuda (1989), another critical feminist legal scholar of color, self-consciously writes against Othering by reimagining a legal canon written out of the experience of Others. By analyzing how the law buries victims' voices and how it protects an abusive elite, Matsuda invents legal text that would privilege the experiences of victims. She not only legitimates voices of subjugation, but presumes them to be the most substantive wellspring for critical legal knowledge:

> There is an outsider's jurisprudence growing and thriving alongside mainstream jurisprudence in American law schools. The new feminist jurisprudence is a lively example of this. A related, and less celebrated outsider jurisprudence is that belonging to people of color. What is it that characterizes the new jurisprudence of people of color? First is a methodology grounded in the particulars of their social reality and experience. This method is consciously both historical and revisionist, attempting to know history from the bottom. From the fear and namelessness of the slave, from the broken treaties of the indigenous Americans, the desire to know history from the bottom has forced these scholars to sources often ignored: journals, poems, oral histories and stories from their own experiences of life in a hierarchically arranged world. . . .
>
> Outsiders thus search for what Anne Scales has called the ratchet—legal tools that have progressive effect, defying the habit of neutral principals to entrench exiting power. (p. 11)

Crenshaw, Austin, and Matsuda force readers to hear subjugated voices not as Others but as primary informants on Othering and as the source for radical rethinking of the law. Like these legal theorists, sociologist Judith Rollins (1985) studies domination enacted by elite white women on the women of color who work for them as domestics. Committed to the theoretical inversion of Othering, Rollins interrupts what a white reader would recognize as the traditional equipment of narrative legitimacy. Rollins delivers her analysis from the vantage of the women employed as domestics. Reversing who would typically be relied upon to tell the "real" story and who would be portrayed as Other, Rollins allows readers to hear how much subjugated women know about them-Selves and about Others. At the same time, she analyzes how privileged women lack knowledge of Self and knowledge of those who work for them:

> Thus, domestics' stronger consciousness of the Other functions not only to help them survive in the occupation but also to maintain their self response. The worker in the home has a level of knowledge about familial and personal problems that few outsiders do. It is not surprising that domestic workers do not take the insulting attitudes and judgments of employers seriously; they are in a position to make scathing judgments of their own. (p. 215)

Jean Baker Miller, in her book *Toward a New Psychology of Women* (1976), argues a point similar to that made by Rollins. In colonizing relations, what Miller calls "dominant-subordinate relations," subordinates spend much time studying the Other. They carry, therefore, substantial knowledge about Self and dominants. Given their need to anticipate and survive, they contain this knowledge and remain silent about the extent to which dominants depend on them. Rarely do they display/flaunt their knowledge of the Other. At the same time, the dominant Other suffers for lack of knowledge of self or others.

Patricia Hill Collins (1990) develops standpoint theory (see also Dorothy Smith, 1987, 1992) through African American women, who have been positioned as "outsiders within" the academy and thereby enjoy a "peculiar marginality." She urges women to venture into this marginality and unearth a "collective self defined Black feminist consciousness" by listening to black women's stories as they confront and resist images of themselves as Other. Collins recognizes that dominant groups have a "vested interest in suppressing such thought," and for that reason she encourages women to engage in just such subversive work—in contexts where we're wanted and not, in communities that feel comforting, and in those we know to be strange and dangerous.

Rupturing narratives allow us to hear the uppity voices of informants and researchers who speak against structures, representations, and practices of domination. In these texts, researchers are working the hyphen, reconciling the slippery constructions of Self and Other and the contexts of oppression in which both are invented.

Scene 2: Probing the Consciousness of Dominant Others

This second slice of scholarship written self-consciously against Othering probes how individuals inhabiting a space of dominance construct their sense of Self through the denigration of Others. These social researchers unpack how dominants manufacture and conceptualize their relations with subordinated Others through violence, denigration, and exploitation.

For instance, Peggy Sanday (1990) has studied how white fraternity brothers create a collective sense of brotherhood through acts of homophobia, racism, and sexism, which enables them to deny their homoeroticism. By studying these young men as elites who abuse power over women and over men of color, Sanday articulates the psychodynamics of collective homophobia as it breeds "out-group" violence, allows "in-group" homoeroticism, and hyperconfirms "the brothers'" public heterosexuality.

In parallel intellectual form, disability scholar Harlan Hahn (1983) has reviewed the works of nondisabled researchers of disability, only to conclude that by reading their work we learn more about these researchers' terror of disability than we do about the persons with disabilities about whom they presumably have written. Hahn theorizes that nondisabled researchers carry existential and aesthetic anxieties about bodily dis-integrity that they project onto the bodies of persons with disabilities. Their narratives are laced with anxieties as if they were simply in the bodies of "them" rather than (un)settled within the (un)consciousness of the researchers.

As a last example, I draw upon the work of ethnographer Lois Weis, who has spent much time interviewing white working-class adolescent males in a town whose economy has been ravaged by deindustrialization. Weis (1990) argues that these young men, who would have generated social identities through the trade union movement in previous decades, now develop identities instead along the lines of race and gender antagonism. Having "lost" identities that were once available to their fathers and grandfathers, they narrate white, working-class, male identities saturated with "virulent racism and sexism." In an effort to solidify Self, the young men in Sanday's and Weis's texts, like the researchers in Hahn's work, rehearse publicly their ownership and degradation of Others—women, men of color, and persons with disabilities, respectively.

These researchers study the perversions of Othering that constitute a consciousness of domination. This genre of work seeks to understand how individuals carve out contradictory social identities that sculpt, harass, and repel Others within and outside themselves. Deploying what might be called *technologies of Othering* (borrowing from deLauretis, 1987), those studied seem to narrate collective, homogeneous identities by constructing collective, homogeneous identities for Others. Less well understood, or narrated, are the incoherent threads of these men as individuals struggling to construct Self.

In this cavern of critical, qualitative work, social researchers excavate voices of privilege to understand how Othering works as contradictory identity formation. When we read Sanday or Weis, we hear researchers listening to relatively high-power informants seeking desperately a Self, by constructing and expelling Others. In these works, and my own analysis in *Framing Dropouts* (Fine, 1991) could be included here, qualitative researchers practice what might be called *doubled splitting*. We split ourselves from elite informants as though they and we are contained, stable, and separable. We then study the splitting that they produce with/against subjugated Others. We stabilize, essentialize, and render our elite informants' Other. Norman Denzin (personal communication, February 1992) has written to me, concerned that in the study of power elites there remains a tendency to

> create self (colonizer) and other (colonized) as dichotomous categories, oppositions defined out of clearly defined cultural, ethnic, racial, and gendered differences. Such treatments (after Derrida and Bakhtin) fail to treat the complexities and contradictions that define membership in each category. Fixed immutable ethnic (gendered, etc.) identities are thereby inscribed. A picture of a homogeneous culturally dominant group is pitted against a picture of an equally homogeneous group of outsiders on the periphery. The internal oppositional nature of ethnic and cultural life is thereby minimized. A fixed stereotypical picture of an isolated minority group is pitted against a "coherent white-American, male power structure," etc. The image of overlapping, conflicting, de-centered circles of ethnic (gendered, etc.) identities is never considered.

By creating flat caricatures we may indeed be undermining an opportunity for ourselves as social researchers to "come clean" about the contradictory stances, politics, perspectives, and histories we import to our work. Rendering fluid, and not fixed, our constructions of Selves and Others, and the narratives produced as qualitative research, can reveal our partialities and pluralities.

Endings: Social Research for Social Change

Rereading Malinowski's *Argonauts of the Western Pacific* (1922), I can hear an ethnographer searching for a text superior to "mere journalism," a method of science designed to "capture" native life, and a narrative style able to re-present "savagery" through the eyes of an intelligent member, "whereas in a native society there are none of them." Malinowski invites readers to imagine him, a white man unwilling to retreat to the company of other white men, drinking, reading, lonely, and ultimately enjoying the company of "savagery." His portraits are painted entirely of Them, introducing "order" into the "chaos" of their lives.

Malinowski details the recipe for qualitative Othering. Early in the century, 'twas noble to write of the Other for the purposes of creating what was considered knowledge. Perhaps it still is. But now, much qualitative research is undertaken for what may be an even more terrifying aim—to "help" Them. In both contexts the effect may be Othering: muted voices; "structure" imported to local "chaos"; Others represented as extracted from their scenes of exploitation, social relationships, and meaningful communities. If they survive the decontextualization, they appear socially bereft, isolated, and deficient, with insidious distinctions drawn among the good and the bad Thems (Austin, 1992). Distinctions from Us are understood.

From such texts we often learn little about Others, except their invented shapes and texts, and less about the writers/researchers, except their projections. Domination and distance get sanitized inside science. Portraits of disdain, pity, need, strength, or all of the above are delivered for public consumption. New programs may, or may not, be spawned to "remedy" them—the problem. Either way, Others have been yanked out of the contexts of late capitalism, racism, sexism, and economic decline. The public is left with embodied stories of Them, who, in their own words, can't seem to get better.

More recently, however, and more interestingly, qualitative researchers have begun to interrupt Othering by forcing subjugated voices in context to the front of our texts and by exploiting privileged voices to scrutinize the technologies of Othering. Emerging in some spaces is this cadre of qualitative researchers who see their work with those who have been cut out as Others, on struggles of social injustice, in ways that disrupt Othering and provoke a sense of possibility (Bhavnani, 1992).

Ethnographies produced by Michael Burawoy and colleagues in *Ethnography Unbound* (1992) represent such a collection designed for social theory and action. The chapters in Bookman and Morgan's *Women and the Politics of Empowerment* (1990) were written for and about the struggles pursued by everyday activist women in the politics of housing, education, and health care organizing. Rhoda Linton and Michelle Whitman (1982) have written through qualitative research to further feminist peace movements. Brinton Lykes (1989), writing for and with Guatemalan "indigenous" women, seeks to create an archive of political resistance of a culture in exile. All of these texts are instances of writing on/with/for political change. But lest writing/researching for change appears too facile, I'll end with one specific, self-conscious, and yet imperial instance of research for social change that embodies many of the contradictions addressed thus far. Profoundly a moment of Inscribing the Other, this work cracks open a space for our critical gaze and invites the next round of conversations about ethics, praxis, and qualitative work. Here I refer to those qualitative research projects in which researchers self-consciously translate "for" Others in order to promote social justice.

Sometimes explicitly trading on race/class privilege, in these instances researchers understand the hyphen all too well. Bartering privilege for justice, we re-present stories told by subjugated Others, stories that would otherwise be discarded. And we get a hearing. My own work with high school dropouts exemplifies this politically tense form of ethnography (Fine, 1991).

Here, at the Self-Other border, it is not that researchers are absented and Others fronted. Instead, the class politics of translation demands that a researcher is doused quite evidently in status and privilege as the Other sits domesticated. I (white, academic, elite woman) represent the words and voices of African American and Latino, working-class and poor adolescents who have dropped out of high school, in texts, in court, and in public policy debates (Fine, 1991), and it becomes scholarship. Some even find it compelling. My raced and classed translation grants authority to their "native" and "underarticulated" narratives. My race and class are coded as "good science" (Kitzinger, 1991). The power of my translation comes far more from my whiteness, middle-classness, and education than from the stories I tell.

But my translation also colludes in structures of domination. I know that when dropouts speak, few listen. When African American, Latino, Asian, or Native American scholars do the same kinds of work as I, they are more likely to be heard as biased, self-interested, or without distanced perspective (see Cook & Fine, in press). Edward Said (1978) has written to this point:

> Since the Orientals cannot represent themselves, they must therefore be represented by others who know more about Islam than Islam knows about itself. Now it is often the case that you can be known by others in different ways than you know yourself, and that valuable insights might be generated accordingly. But that it is quite different than pronouncing it as immutable law that outsiders *ipso facto* have a better sense of you as an insider than you do yourself. Note that there is no question of an *exchange* between Islam's views and an outsider's: no dialogue, no discussion, no mutual recognition. There is a flat assertion of quality, which the Western policymaker, or his faithful servant, possesses by virtue of his being Western, Shite, non-Muslim. (p. 97)

The stakes are even higher when we move qualitative translation out of academic journals and into the courts. Consider a most complicated instance of scholarly translation located precisely at the hyphen of Othering—the brilliant work of Julie Blackman. A white social psychologist who works as an expert witness for battered women—white, Latina, and/or African American—who have killed their abusers, Blackman enters courtrooms and retells the stories these women have told her, this time in Standard English. She psychologizes and explains away the contradictions. She makes them acceptable. Blackman's project is to get these women a hearing from a jury of their peers. She has an impressive success rate for keeping these women out of jail (Blackman, 1993).

Draped in white colonizing science, Julie and I, and many others, cut a deal: *Listen to the story as long as the teller is not the Other.* Cut with the knives of racism and classism. Should we refuse? Do we merely reproduce power by playing to power? Do we regenerate the Other as we try to keep her from going to jail? Do we erase and silence as we trade on white/elite privilege?

Herein lie the very profound contradictions that face researchers who step out, who presume to want to make a difference, who are so bold or arrogant as to assume we might. Once out beyond the picket fence of illusory objectivity, we trespass all over the classed, raced, and otherwise stratified lines that have demarcated our social legitimacy for publicly telling their stories. And it is then that ethical questions boil.

I would not argue that only those "in the experience" can tell a story of injustice. Indeed, privileging raw (?) experience over analysis, as if they are separate, is simply a sign of (understandable) political desperation (see Scott, 1991). At some point, people decide, I'm tired of hearing you speak for me. Only I can speak for myself. I'll speak for my people, and these issues. As a white, nondisabled, academic woman, I have been on both sides of this tension. Sometimes I'm telling men to stop speaking for me. Sometimes I'm being told to stop speaking "for"—for adolescents, women of color, women with disabilities, and so on. And yet we all have genders and races, classes, sexualities, dis-abilities, and politics. If poststructuralism has taught us anything, it is to beware the frozen identities and the presumption that the hyphen is real, to suspect the binary, to worry the clear distinctions. If these "virtues" are assumed floating and political signifiers (Omi & Winant, 1986), then it is surely essentialist to presume that only women can/should "do" gender; only people of color can/should do race work; only lesbians and gays can/should "do" sexuality; only women in violence can tell the stories of violence.

Yet the risk for qualitative researchers has been and continues to be imperial translation. Doing the work of social change, as Blackman does, within a context committed to discrediting all women's voices means that social researchers have to be negotiating how, when, and why to situate and privilege whose voices. Those of us who do this work need to invent communities of friendly critical informants who can help us think through whose voices and analyses to front, and whose to foreground.

At the same time, another risk surfaces. This risk lies in the romanticizing of narratives and the concomitant retreat from analysis. In the name of ethical, democratic, sometimes feminist methods, there is a subtle, growing withdrawal from interpretation. Nancie Caraway (1991) writes to this point when she describes "some of the assumptions hidden in standpoint/margin/center claims: beliefs that people act rationally in their own interest, that the oppressed are not in fundamental ways damaged by their marginality, and that they themselves are somehow removed from a will to power" (p. 181).

Caraway is a white woman who worries about the stance of some scholars who claim that no one may speak for Others. She struggles in *Segregated Sisterhood* (1991) to produce a text through and about race among/between women. Relying primarily on the theoretical works of women of color, she, like Blackman and others, argues the responsibility of white women to be engaged in "crossover tracks," in critical, democratic conversations about race and racism. If we recognize race, class, gender, and sexuality to be socially and historically contingent (Hall, 1991), then silence, retreat, and engagement all pose ethical dilemmas. All are tangled with ethics of knowing, writing, and acting (see Richardson, Chapter 32, this volume).

In the early 1990s, the whispers of a collective of activist researchers can be heard struggling with these tensions. Seeking to work with, but not romanticize, subjugated voices, searching for moments of social justice, they are inventing strategies of qualitative analysis and writing against Othering. As this corpus of work ages, it too will become a contested site. Residues of domination linger heavily within these qualitative texts. But today these works constitute the next set of critical conversations among qualitative social researchers, eroding fixed categories and provoking possibilities for qualitative research that is designed *against* Othering, *for* social justice, and pivoting identities of Self and Other *at* the hyphen.

References

Aronowitz, S. (1988). The production of scientific knowledge. In C. Nelson & L. Grossberg (Eds.), *Marxism and the interpretation of culture* (pp. 519-538). Urbana: University of Illinois Press.

Austin, R. (1989). Sapphire bound! *Wisconsin Law Review, 3,* 539-578.

Austin, R. (1992). *"The black community," its lawbreakers and a politics of identification.* Unpublished manuscript.

Bhabha, H. (1990). *Nation and narration.* New York: Routledge.

Bhavnani, K. (1992). Talking racism and editing women's studies. In D. Richardson & V. Robinson (Eds.), *Thinking feminist* (pp. 27-48). New York: Guilford.

Blackman, J. (1993). [Master lecture on legal issues affecting women]. Lecture presented at the annual meeting of the American Psychological Association, Toronto.

Bookman, A., & Morgan, S. (Eds.). (1990). *Women and the politics of empowerment.* Philadelphia: Temple University Press.

Burawoy, M., Burton, A., Ferguson, A. A., Fox, K. J., Gamson, J., Gartrell, N., Hurst, L., Kurzman, C., Salzinger, L., Schiffman, J., & Ui, S. (Eds.). (1992). *Ethnography unbound: Power and resistance in the modern metropolis.* Berkeley: University of California Press.

Caraway, N. (1991). *Segregated sisterhood.* Knoxville: University of Tennessee Press.

Clifford, J., & Marcus, G. E. (Eds.). (1986). *Writing culture: The poetics and politics of ethnography.* Berkeley: University of California Press.

Collins, P. H. (1990). *Black feminist thought: Knowledge, consciousness and the politics of empowerment.* New York: Routledge.

Cook, D., & Fine, M. (in press). Motherwit. In B. Swadener & S. Lubeck (Eds.), *Families and children at promise.* Albany: State University of New York Press.

Crenshaw, K. (1992). *Intersectionality of race and sex.* Unpublished manuscript.

deLauretis, T. (1987). *Technologies of gender: Essays on theory, film, and fiction.* Bloomington: Indiana University Press.

Fanon, F. (1965). *A dying colonialism.* New York: Grove.

Fine, M. (1991). *Framing dropouts.* Albany: State University of New York Press.

Fine, M. (1992). *Disruptive voices.* Ann Arbor: University of Michigan Press.

Fine, M., & Vanderslice, V. (1992). Reflections on qualitative research. In E. Posavac (Ed.), *Methodological issues in applied social psychology.* New York: Plenum.

Giroux, H. (1991). Postmodernism as border pedagogy. In H. Giroux (Ed.), *Postmodernism, feminism, and cultural politics.* Albany: State University of New York Press.

Hahn, H. (1983, March-April). Paternalism and public policy. *Society,* pp. 36-44.

Hall, S. (1991). Ethnicity, identity and difference. *Radical America, 3,* 9-22.

Haraway, D. (1988). Situated knowledge. *Feminist Studies, 14,* 575-599.

Harding, S. (Ed.). (1987). *Feminism and methodology: Social science issues.* Bloomington: Indiana University Press.

Havel, V. (1990). *Disturbing the peace.* New York: Vintage.

hooks, b. (1989). *Talking back: Thinking feminist, thinking black.* Boston: South End.

hooks, b. (1990). *Yearning: Race, gender, and cultural politics.* Boston: South End.

Katz, M. (Ed.). (1993). *The underclass debate.* Princeton, NJ: Princeton University Press.

Kitzinger, C. (1991). Feminism, psychology and the paradox of power. *Feminism and Psychology, 1,* 111-130.

Ladner, J. (1971). *Tomorrow's tomorrow.* Garden City, NY: Doubleday.

Linton, R., & Whitman, M. (1982). With mourning, rage, empowerment, and defiance: The 1981 Women's Pentagon Action. *Socialist Review, 12*(3-4), 11-36.

Lykes, B. (1989). Dialogue with Guatemalan women. In R. Unger (Ed.), *Representations: Social constructions of gender* (pp. 167-184). Amityville, NY: Baywood.

Malinowski, B. (1922). *Argonauts of the western Pacific.* London: Routledge & Kegan Paul.

Martin, B., & Mohanty, C. T. (1986). Feminist politics: What's home got to do with it? In T. deLauretis (Ed.), *Feminist studies/critical studies.* Bloomington: Indiana University Press.

Matsuda, M. (1993). Public response to racist speech: Considering the victim's story. In M. Matsuda, C. Lawrence, R. Delgado, K. Crenshaug (Eds.), *Words that wound* (pp. 17-52). Boulder: Westview.

Miller, J. B. (1976). *Toward a new psychology of women.* Boston: Beacon.

Mouffe, C. (1988). Hegemony and new political subjects: Toward a new concept of democracy. In C. Nelson & L. Grossberg (Eds.), *Marxism and the interpretation of culture.* Urbana: University of Illinois Press.

Omi, M., & Winant, H. (1986). *Racial formation in the United States.* New York: Routledge.

Pratt, M. (1985). Scratches on the face of the country. In H. Gates (Ed.), *"Race," writing, and difference* (pp. 138-162). Chicago: University of Chicago Press.

Pratt, M. (1992). *Imperial eyes.* New York: Routledge.

Rollins, J. (1985). *Between women: Domestics and their employers.* Philadelphia: Temple University Press.

Rosaldo, R. (1989). *Culture and truth: The remaking of social analysis.* Boston: Beacon.

Said, E. (1978). *Orientalism.* New York: Pantheon.

Sanday, P. (1990). *Fraternity gang rape: Sex, brotherhood and privilege on campus.* New York: New York University Press.

Scott, J. (1991). Deconstructing equality versus difference. In M. Hirsch & E. Keller (Eds.), *Conflicts in feminism.* New York: Routledge.

Smith, D. E. (1987). *The everyday world as problematic.* Boston: Northeastern University Press.

Smith, D. E. (1992). Sociology from women's experience: A reaffirmation. *Sociological Theory, 10,* 88-98.

Smith, V. (1991). Split affinities. In M. Hirsch & E. Keller (Eds.), *Conflicts in feminism* (pp. 271-287). New York: Routledge.

Spivak, G. C. (1988). Can the subaltern speak? In C. Nelson & L. Grossberg (Eds.), *Marxism and the interpretation of culture* (pp. 280-316). Urbana: University of Illinois Press.

Weis, L. (1990). *Working class without work.* New York: Routledge.

West, C. (1988). Marxist theory and the specificity of Afro-American oppression. In C. Nelson & L. Grossberg (Eds.), *Marxism and the interpretation of culture* (pp. 17-29). Urbana: University of Illinois Press.

5

Politics and Ethics in Qualitative Research

MAURICE PUNCH

"Just Do It!"

FIELDWORK is fun; it is easy; anyone can do it; it is salutary for young academics to flee the nest; and they should be able to take any moral or political dilemmas encountered in their stride. There has always been a somewhat pragmatic, if not reductionist, tradition in qualitative research that was exemplified by Everett Hughes's "fly on your own" strategy for students at Chicago (Gans, 1967, p. 301). Of course, the classical anthropologists engaged in long and lonely involvement in distant settings and had to solve their problems individually and on site (Clarke, 1975, p. 105), and something of this tradition—geared to the solo researcher, absent for a considerable period of time, and cut off from the university—was conveyed by the precepts of the Chicago school. This style of qualitative research holds that it is healthy and wholesome for students and aspiring social scientists to get "the seats of their pants dirty by *real* research" (Park, quoted in Burgess, 1982, p. 6; emphasis in original). They should abandon the classroom in order to knock on doors, troop the streets, and join groups; they should just "get in there and see what is going on" (as Howard Becker advised a bemused British student asking what "paradigm" he should employ in the field; Atkinson, 1977, p. 32).

In contrast, there are voices that alert us to the inherent moral pitfalls of participant observation and that warn us of the essentially "political" nature of all field research. In this model, qualitative research is seen as potentially volatile, even hazardous, requiring careful consideration and preparation before someone should be *allowed* to enter the field. Without adequate training and supervision, the neophyte researcher can unwittingly become an unguided projectile bringing turbulence to the field, fostering personal traumas (for researcher and researched), and even causing damage to the discipline. This position was powerfully argued by John Lofland at an ASA seminar on participant observation, where he virtually demanded a certification of competence before the researcher be let loose in the field. During the past decade, moreover, these two divergent stances have been challenged by the impact of feminist, racial, and ethnic discourse that has not only made visible new research areas but also has raised critical issues related to a politically engaged research dialectic (Welch, 1991). These have profound implications for the ethics and politics of research (Fonow & Cook, 1991; Grossberg, Nelson, & Treichler, 1992; Reinharz, 1992).

AUTHOR'S NOTE: I would like to thank the editors of this volume, and the two readers for this chapter, for their valuable comments on my first draft. I also wish to extend my gratitude to Derek Phillips, Peter K. Manning, Hans Werdmolder, and John Van Maanen for their critical advice while I was preparing this chapter.

My position in this chapter will be to argue forcibly for the "get out and do it" perspective. Understandably, no one in his or her right mind would support a carefree, amateuristic, and unduly naive approach to qualitative research. But, at the same time, I would warn against leaning too far toward a highly restrictive model for research that serves to prevent academics from exploring complex social realities that are not always amenable to more formal methods. My sympathies for this view have been powerfully shaped by my own background as a sociologist who engaged in research that painfully raised a whole range of largely unexpected political and ethical issues (Punch, 1986, 1989), related to stress in the field situation, research fatigue, confidentiality, harm, privacy and identification, and spoiling the field. In two projects that commenced with supportive sponsors, I encountered an accumulation of unanticipated difficulties, such as varying interpretations of the research bargain over time, disputes about contractual obligations, restrictions on secondary access, intimidation via the law, disagreement on publication, and even an (in my view unethical) appeal to professional ethics in an attempt to limit my research. Those issues are not exclusive to projects employing observation, but perhaps they are most likely to occur in an acute way there than in other styles of work.

Furthermore, I trust that many of the views presented in this chapter are also applicable to other styles of qualitative research. Qualitative research covers a spectrum of techniques—but central are observation, interviewing, and documentary analysis—and these may be used in a broad range of disciplines. Indeed, contemporary researchers are to be found within an extensive spectrum of groups and institutions involving differing time spans and types of personal engagement (Burgess, 1982; Hammersley & Atkinson, 1983; Shaffir & Stebbins, 1991). It is probably the case, however, that in Anglo-American universities (with an "apprenticeship" model of graduate education unlike that in most continental European institutes), most researchers will first encounter fieldwork while engaged on a dissertation that is mostly a solo enterprise with relatively unstructured observation, deep involvement in the setting, and a strong identification with the researched. This can mean that the researcher is unavoidably vulnerable and that there is a considerably larger element of risk and uncertainty than with more formal methods.

There is here too an absolutely central point that much field research is dependent on one person's perception of the field situation at a given point in time, that that perception is shaped both by personality and by the nature of the interaction with the researched, and that this makes the researcher his or her own "research instrument." This is fundamentally different from more formal models of research, and it also bedevils our evaluation of what "really" happened because we are almost totally reliant on one person's portrayal of events. This is amplified if we further accept that there are a number of potentially distorting filters at work that militate against full authenticity on methods, and that censor material on the relationships with the human "subjects" concerned.

Here I am assuming that qualitative fieldwork employs participant observation as its central technique and that this involves the researcher in prolonged immersion in the life of a group, community, or organization in order to discern people's habits and thoughts as well as to decipher the social structure that binds them together (McCall & Simmons, 1969; Van Maanen, 1979). Far more than with other styles of social research, then, this implies that the investigator engages in a close, if not intimate, relationship with those he or she observes. Crucial to that relationship is access and acceptance, and elsewhere I have spoken of "infiltration" as a key technique in fieldwork (Punch, 1986, p. 11) even though the concept is negatively associated with spying and deception (Erikson, quoted in Bulmer, 1982, p. 150). Entry and departure, distrust and confidence, elation and despondency, commitment and betrayal, friendship and abandonment—all are as fundamental here as are dry discussions on the techniques of observation, taking field notes, analyzing the data, and writing the report. Furthermore, acute moral and ethical dilemmas may be encountered while a semiconscious political process of negotiation pervades all fieldwork. And both elements, political and ethical, often have to be resolved *situationally,* and even spontaneously, without the luxury of being able to turn first to consult a more experienced colleague. The dynamics and dilemmas associated with this area of fieldwork can be summarized crudely in terms of getting in and getting out, and of one's social and moral conduct in relation to the political constraints of the field.

On the Politics of Fieldwork

To a greater or lesser extent, politics suffuses all social scientific research (Guba & Lincoln, 1989, p. 125). By *politics* I mean everything from the micropolitics of personal relations to the cultures and resources of research units and universities, the powers and policies of government research departments, and ultimately even the hand (heavy or otherwise) of the central state itself (Bell & Newby, 1977; Hammond, 1964). All of these contexts and constraints crucially influence the design, implementation, and outcomes of research (Gubrium & Silverman, 1989). This is important to convey to fledgling researchers, who may imbibe a false view of the research process as smooth and unproblematic ("The unchanging researcher makes a unilinear journey through a static setting"; Hunt, 1984, p. 285), whereas we should be drawing their attention to the political perils and ethical pitfalls of actually carrying out research. An additional motive for doing this is to espouse the view that fieldwork is definitely not a soft option, but, rather, represents a *demanding* craft that involves both coping with multiple negotiations and continually dealing with ethical dilemmas.

But perhaps collectively we are ourselves largely responsible for the "conspiracy" in selling the neat, packaged, unilinear view of research. Successful studies attract the limelight; failures are often neglected. Dilemmas in the field are glossed over in an anodyne appendix, and it may even be deemed inappropriate for the "scientist" to abandon objectivity and detachment in recounting descriptions of personal involvement and political battles in the field setting. This can be reinforced by the strictures of publishers, who may find personal accounts anecdotal, trivial, and scarcely worthy of space (Punch, 1989, p. 203). As Clarke (1975) observes, "A large area of knowledge is systematically suppressed as 'non-scientific' by the limitations of prevailing research methodologies" (p. 96).

In contrast, some accounts of field research touch on the stress, the deep personal involvement, the role conflicts, the physical and mental effort, the drudgery and discomfort—and even the danger—of observational studies for the researcher. Yablonsky (1968) was threatened with violence in a commune, and Thompson (1967) was beaten up by Hell's Angels; Schwartz (1964) was attacked verbally and physically during his study in a mental hospital, where he was seen as a "spy" by both patients and staff; and Vidich and Bensman (1968) were caricatured, in a Fourth of July procession in the town they had studied, by an effigy bending over a manure spreader. Wax (1971) was involved in dangerous and stressful situations in Japanese relocation camps, and she was denounced as a "communist agitator" during research on Native American reservations. Burns (1977) was refused publication for his study of the BBC; Wallis (1977) was tailed and harassed by members of the Scientology movement; and, in a project within a police department, a researcher "literally had to block a file-cabinet with his body to keep two armed internal affairs officers from taking observers' records. Meanwhile the principal investigator was frantically contacting the chief of police to get internal affairs called off" (Florez & Kelling, 1979, p. 17).

These examples could be multiplied by horror stories gleaned from the academic circuit, where "tales of the field" (Van Maanen, 1988) abound of obstructionist gatekeepers, vacillating sponsors, factionalism in the field setting that forces the researcher to choose sides, organizational resistance, respondents subverting the research role, sexual shenanigans, and disputes about publication and the veracity of findings. Such pitfalls and predicaments can rarely be anticipated, yet they may fundamentally alter the whole nature and purpose of the research.

These personal and anecdotal accounts form an oral culture of moral and practical warnings; they are not widely written of, according to John Van Maanen (personal communication, 1993), largely because we have failed to develop a "genre or narrative convention within our standard works" that would shape a taken-for-granted imperative that field-workers own up to the manner in which they solved such issues during their research (but see Sanjek, 1990, on "fieldnotes"). In contrast, there is a stream of thought that does make exposure of affectivity and of the research process central and that is represented by feminist research (Roberts, 1981). This not only attacks traditional methodology as an instrument of repression but also, in some cases, argues for "total immersion" in the field; this new "epistemology of insiderness" (Reinharz, 1992, p. 259) has led feminist scholars to an attempt "to rescue emotion from its discarded role in the creation of knowledge" (Fonow & Cook, 1991, p. 11). This powerful and significant contribution to the recent debate on the politics of research is in reaction to the patriarchal nature of academic life and the "research infrastructure" allied to an effort to construct a feminist epistemology and methodology. Fonow and Cook (1991) focus on a number of themes in the literature on feminist methods: "reflexivity; an action orientation; attention to the affective components of research; and use of the situation-in-hand" (pp. 1-5).

In essence, much research is informed by the experience of oppression owing to sexism, and the research process may well contain an element of "consciousness-raising," of emotional catharsis, and of increased politicization and activism. As the aim of certain strands of feminist research is praxis leading to liberation (Mies, 1991), this has profound implications for "the statement of purpose, topic selection, theoretical orientation, choice of method, view of human nature, and definitions of the researcher's role" (Fonow & Cook, 1991, p. 5). This action component is shared with black studies, Marxism, and gay and lesbian studies and permeates research with an explicitly *political* agenda. Research by women on women to assist women has undoubtedly opened up fresh new arenas largely inaccessible to males, and this enrichment has frequently been embedded within qualitative research precisely because this is held to be more compatible than formal, quantitative methods with feminist scholarship (Hammersley, 1993; Jayaratne & Stewart, 1991; Reinharz, 1992). Feminist research has, for instance, fostered studies of obscene telephone calls, violence against women (shelters for battered females), single-gender college residences, sexual harassment, pornography, AIDS clinics, abortion, and discrimination in the workplace. In effect, the impact of feminist research has been to awaken the whole issue of gender in research activities and to politicize the debate on the conduct of research; similar arguments have been raised about race and ethnicity.

In some cases there is an openness to "complete transformation" through total participation and a belief that consciousness-raising will become the "ground work for friendship, shared struggle and identity change" (Reinharz 1992, p. 68). This has aided in bringing affectivity into accounts of research and has also exposed the reality that much qualitative, observational work was conducted by privileged white males. There are profound epistemological and methodological issues here that I cannot possibly tackle within the confines of this chapter, but I suspect that many traditional ethnographers, brought up in a scholarly convention of "openness" to the field setting and "objectivity" with regard to data, would be concerned that explicitly ideological and political research would overly predetermine the material gleaned in observational studies. This, in turn, would doubtless lead to a riposte about the disingenuousness of believing in objectivity through the eyes of white male academics. My point is that the traditionalists tended to eschew "politics," to avoid "total immersion," and to be wary of "going native," all of which, in contrast, are elements of feminist methods. This debate has illuminated certain research dilemmas in an acute and fresh way that needs to be taken into account in all that follows below. Rather than enter that debate, which poses issues at the ideological and institutional levels, I shall focus here on those practical and mundane elements that continually influence the "politics" of fieldwork in many research projects.

Hence I wish simply to focus on certain features that are not always clearly articulated in accounts but that have a material impact on qualitative research in general and fieldwork in particular and that shape the politics of research.

Researcher personality. The personality of the researcher helps to determine his or her selection of topics, his or her intellectual approach, and his or her ability in the field (Clarke, 1975, p. 104). But often we are left in the dark as to the personal and intellectual path that led researchers to drop one line of inquiry or to pursue another topic. We require more intellectual autobiographies to clarify why academics end up studying what they do (Okely & Callaway, 1992). Family circumstances can be important in terms of absences and travel, and spouse's support, or lack of it, can prove crucial to the continuation of a field project.

Geographic proximity. One simple factor that is often glossed over in terms of selecting topics and field settings is geographic proximity. There may be something romantic about Evans-Pritchard, Malinowski, and Boas setting off stoically into the bush, where they lived in relative isolation and virtuous celibacy, but some researchers just travel conveniently down the road to the nearest morgue, mental hospital, or action group.

Nature of the research object. The nature of the research object—be it a community, a formal organization, or an informal group—is of significance for access, research bargains, funding, and the likelihood of polarity and conflict in the research setting (Punch, 1989; Spencer, 1973).

Researcher's institutional background. The reputation of the researcher's institutional background can be of considerable importance in opening or closing doors. The backing of prestigious academic institutions and figureheads may be vital to access in some settings but irrelevant, or even harmful, in others. For instance, Platt (1976, p. 45) records a case in which researchers in Britain were able to get a member of Parliament to organize a speech in the House of Commons that led to certain doors being opened for them.

Gatekeepers. Gatekeepers can be crucial in terms of access and funding (Argyris, 1969). The determination of some watchdogs to protect their institutions may ironically be almost inversely related to the willingness of members to accept research. Klein (1976) remarks, "Social science is not engaged by 'industry' or organizations, but by individuals in gatekeeping or sponsorship or client roles. The outcome, therefore, is always mediated through the needs, resources, and roles of such individuals" (p. 225). Researchers may suffer by being continually seen as extensions of their political sponsors within the setting despite their denials to the contrary. Furthermore, gatekeepers need not be construed only in terms of government agencies and corporate representatives, but can also be found in scientific funding bodies, among publishers, and within academia. The intellectual development of the discipline, academic imperialism, the institutional division of labor, the selection and availability of specific supervisors, backstage bargaining, precontract lobbying, departmental distribution of perks (research assistance, travel money, typing support), and patronage can all play roles in determining the status of, and resources for, field research, and in specifying why some projects are launched and others buried (Dingwall, Payne, & Payne, 1980; Sharrock & Anderson, 1980; Shils, 1982). It is somewhat encouraging to read that even Whyte had difficulty in publishing his now-classic 1943 book *Street Corner Society,* in having it reviewed and taken seriously, and fluctuating sales have reflected the fads and fashions of postwar sociology. The acceptance of his research for a Ph.D. at Chicago was also contingent on Hughes's championing of him against a critical Wirth (Whyte, 1981, p. 356).

Status of field-workers. The impact that the presence of researchers has on the setting is related to the status and visibility of the field-workers. The "lone wolf" often requires no funding, gains easy access, and melts away into the field. The "hired hand," in contrast, may come with a team of people, be highly visible, be tied to contractual obligations, and be expected to deliver the goods within a specified period of time (Wycoff & Kelling, 1978).

Expectations in team research. A feature of research that has rarely been examined is the variety of expectations and roles in *team* research that can hinder behavior in the field and lead to conflict about outcomes. In team research, leadership, supervision, discipline, morale, status, salaries, career prospects, and the intellectual division of labor can promote unexpected tensions in the field and lead to disputes about publication. Junior assistants may fear that a senior researcher will prematurely publish to increase his or her academic status while cynically exploiting their data, spoiling the field, and ruining their chances of collecting separate data for a dissertation. A love affair breaking up between team members can also spell disaster and undermine timetables and deadlines. Workloads, ownership of data, rights of publication, and career and status issues are all affected by the constraints of team research. Al Reiss, Jr., in operating a team investigating police behavior, had to make it clear that serious "deviance" by a team member might threaten the whole project, and that he also had an employer-employee relationship with them that meant he was prepared to dismiss people if necessary (statements made at an ASA seminar on field research). Bell (1977) presents a graphic portrait of the problems that beset the restudy of the community of Banbury in Britain. The project leader was rarely present, the team never really jelled as a unit, the field supervisor left early to take up an academic appointment, and the two research assistants wanted to collect data for their dissertations as well as for the project; further, data were withheld from the supervisor because the others were worried that he "would in some way run off with the data and publish separately" (p. 55).

The structural and status frustrations of the hired hand (particularly the temporary research assistant virtually abandoned to the field) may mean that he or she suffers from poor morale, becomes estranged from the parent organization, is strongly tempted toward co-optation, becomes secretive toward supervisors, and is a "bother" requiring "unusually intense and patient supervision" (Florez & Kelling, 1979, p. 12). He or she is particularly in danger of "going native."

Other factors affecting research in the field. The actual conduct of research and success in the field can be affected by myriad factors, including age, gender, status, ethnic background, overidentification, rejection, factionalism, bureaucratic obstacles, accidents, and good fortune. But, again, we rarely hear of failures, although Diamond (1964) recounts how he was ejected from the field in Nigeria, and Clarke (1975) speaks of field-workers who nearly went insane, panicked, or got cold feet and never actually got to the field, "but we are systematically denied public information on what happens" (p. 106). Observational studies are often associated with young people (graduate students, research assistants), and some settings may require a youthful appearance and even physical stamina (as in Reimer's 1979 study of construction workers).

Gender, and race, close some avenues of inquiry but clearly open up others. Martin (1980), in her study of women in policing, could not penetrate the world of the policemen's locker room or out-of-work socializing. In masculine worlds the female researcher may have to adopt various ploys to deal with prejudice, sexual innuendo, and unwelcome advances. Hunt (1984) realized that she was operating in a culture where several features of her identity—white, female, educated outsider—were impediments to developing rapport and trust with different categories within the police and had to engage in a transformation from "untrustworthy feminine spy" to "street woman researcher" whereby she renegotiated gender to combine elements of masculinity and femininity. The compromises this involved would doubtless enrage many contemporary feminists, but they force the female field-worker to get out or else accept a measure of "interactional shitwork" (Reinharz, 1992). The limitations associated with views on race and gender mean that it is impossible in many police forces for a white female to patrol alone with a black male officer. Women often have to cope too with the conflict between their desire and need to continue research (e.g., for career purposes) and their encountering "sexual harassment, physical danger, and sexual stereotyping"; furthermore, in a society that is "ageist, sexist, and hetero-sexist, the young, female researcher may be defined as a sexual object to be seduced by heterosexual males" (Reinharz, 1992, p. 58).

A young student, however, may be perceived as nonthreatening and may even elicit a considerable measure of sympathy from respondents. But rather than concluding that fieldwork is not for the "over 40s," one could also argue that advancing age and increased status can open doors to fruitful areas of inquiry, such as senior management in business. Personality, appearance, and luck may all play roles in exploiting unexpected avenues or overcoming unanticipated obstacles in the field.

Publishing. A harmonious relationship in the field may come unstuck at the moment of writing an impending publication where the researcher's material appears in cold print. The subjects of research suddenly see themselves summarized and interpreted in ways that may not match up with their own partial perspectives on the natural setting. Where the research bargain includes an implicit or explicit obligation to consult the group or institution on publication, severe differences of opinion can arise. These may be almost completely unanticipated by the researcher, in the sense that it is difficult to predict what organizational representatives will find objectionable (Burns, 1977). Vidich and Bensman's (1968) study of "Springdale" provoked a scandalized reaction that raised fundamental issues related to invasion of privacy, the ethics of research (on identity, harm, ownership of data, and so on), and responsibilities to Cornell University, which had sponsored the research (and which proved unduly sensitive to the outcry from the community). There were also protests from other *academics.* Progressive and radical institutions, highly critical of the establishment and ideologically committed to openness and publication, may themselves be highly sensitive to criticism because of their marginality, susceptibility to discrediting, and desire for legitimacy (Punch, 1986, pp. 49-70).

Social and moral obligations. Finally, what social and moral obligations are generated by fieldwork? This issue forms a major part of what follows in this chapter and can be viewed as having two central parts. On the one hand, there is the nature of the researcher's personal relationships with people he or she encounters in the field. On the other hand, there are the moral and ethical aspects related to the purpose and conduct of research itself. In effect, how far can you go?

Ethical Features of Qualitative Research

Issues

The view that science is intrinsically neutral and essentially beneficial disappeared with the revelations at the Nuremberg trials (recounting the Nazis' "medical experiments" on concentration camp inmates) and with the role of leading scientists in the Manhattan Project, which led to the dropping of atomic bombs on Japan in 1945. Controlling science, however, raises resilient practical, ethical, and legal issues that are a matter of constant debate. The questions involved confront us with fundamental dilemmas, such as the protection of the subjects versus the freedoms to conduct research and to publish research findings. An understanding of this area needs to be rooted in knowledge of a number of studies that have given rise to moral and ethical questions.

In medical research, for instance, actual physical harm can be done to subjects, as in the Tuskegee Syphilis Study and in the Willowbrook Hepatitis Experiment, and patients' rights can be violated, as when live cancer cells were injected beneath the skin of nonconsenting geriatrics (Barber, 1976; Brandt, 1978; Katz, 1972). This background is important because, for a number of reasons, the attempt to control *biomedical* research, and to protect its subjects, has also become the model for the social sciences (Reiss, 1979). In social science, frequent reference is made to a number of studies that have raised blood pressures on ethical aspects of research. The revelations of Vidich and Bensman (1968) about the community of "Springdale" caused a furor among the townspeople and also fellow academics in relation to identification, harm, sponsorship, and professional ethics. Festinger, Riecken, and Schachter's (1956) work on membership in a sect involved a measure of deception and also implicit if not explicit affirmation for the group that could scarcely be described as nondirective. In the 1960s, American academics were shocked on discovering CIA involvement in the source of funding for "Project Camelot" (Horowitz, 1970). The CIA was also responsible for secretly distributing LSD to visitors to a brothel and then filming the results using a hidden camera; one person committed suicide while under the influence of the LSD (Sieber, 1992, p. 68).

In the Wichita Jury Study, microphones were hidden to record juries' deliberations. Milgram's (1963) renowned psychological experiment on authority required unwitting subjects to think that they were causing "pain" to others in a laboratory situation. Disguise and deception were used in La Pierre's (1934) pioneering study of prejudice, when he entered restaurants and hotels accompanied by a Chinese couple, and also in Lofland and Lejeune's (1960) study of reactions of aspiring members of Alcoholics Anonymous, in which students posed as alcoholics. There is also the well-known, if not now notorious, research of Laud Humphreys (1970, 1972) on homosexuals, whom he observed in a public toilet and later questioned in their homes under the guise of a different project. (He recorded their car license plate numbers on first encounter and traced them to their homes; he then changed his hairstyle, clothes, and car and claimed he was conducting a "social health survey.") On the one hand, he received the coveted C. Wright Mills Award from the SSSP, but on the other hand there were efforts undertaken to revoke his Ph.D. (and an irate Alvin Gouldner socked him on the jaw!). For more details and further debate on these studies, the reader is referred to Klockars and O'Connor (1979) and Bulmer (1982), and also to texts dealing with ethical issues in research, such as Sjoberg (1968), Barnes (1979), Diener and Crandall (1978), Boruch and Cecil (1983), Rynkiewich and Spradley (1976), and special issues of *American Sociologist* (1978) and *Social Problems* (1973, 1980).

In essence, most concern revolves around issues of harm, consent, deception, privacy, and confidentiality of data. And, in a sense, we are all still suffering for the sins of Milgram. His controversial research methods in laboratory experiments, allied to the negative reactions to revelations about medical tests on captive, vulnerable, and nonconsenting populations, led to the construction of various restrictions on social research. Academic associations have formulated codes of professional conduct and of ethics, and some research funding is dependent on researchers' ascribing to ethical guidelines. This codification presents a number of dilemmas, particularly for researchers who engage in fieldwork. For instance, the concept of consent would seem to rule out covert research, but how "honest" do you actually have to be about your research purpose? And the conflict orientation of some scholars—in terms of Becker's (1967) call to take sides or Douglas's (1979) demand that we deceive the establishment in order to expose it—seems to force moral choices upon us. There is a further dimension related to research on "deviants" who may engage in criminal and violent behavior: Does conscience allow us to witness this? Would we be prepared to protect people engaged in illegality from the authorities? The generality of codes often does not help us to make the fine distinctions that arise at the *interactional* level in participant observation studies, where the reality of the field setting may feel far removed from the refinements of scholarly debate and ethical niceties.

These issues have raised fundamental debate about the very nature of the academic enterprise and about the relationships among social science and research ethics, bureaucratic protection and secrecy, political control and individual rights and obligations (Wilkins, 1979, p. 113). Does the end of seeking knowledge justify the scientific means (Homan & Bulmer, 1982, p. 114)? What is public and what is private? When can research be said to be "harming" people? Does the researcher enjoy any immunity from the law when he or she refuses to disclose information? In what way can one institutionalize ethical norms—such as respect, beneficence, and justice (Reiss, 1979)—to ensure accountability and responsibility in the use and control of information on human subjects? And to what extent do betrayal of trust, deception, and invasion of privacy damage field relationships, make the researcher cynical and devious, enrage the "participants" in research, harm the reputation of social scientific research, and lead to malpractice in the wider society? All of these points generate ethical, moral, legal, professional, and practical problems and positions that continue to reverberate at conferences, during discussions, and in print. Here I intend to examine these issues in terms of a number of practical problems encountered, particularly in fieldwork situations that generate an ethical component. Again, I wish to clarify that my focus is predominantly sociological and anthropological and that I have in mind largely the lone researcher engaged in an observational study, where a personal involvement with the "subjects" in the field continually poses moral and ethical dilemmas.

At a more ideological, methodological, and institutional level, however, I wish first to touch on three developments that have materially affected the ethical dimension in research. First, the women's movement has brought forth a scholarship that emphasizes identification, trust, empathy, and nonexploitive relationships. Feminist research by women on women implies a "standpoint epistemology" that not only colors the ethical and moral component of research related to the power imbalances in a sexist and racist environment, but also inhibits deception of the research "subjects." Indeed, the gender and ethnic solidarity between researcher and researched welds that relationship into one of cooperation and collaboration that represents a personal commitment and also a contribution to the interests of women in general (e.g., in giving voice to "hidden women," in generating the "emancipatory praxis," and in seeing the field settings as "sites of resistance"). In this sense the personal is related to the ethical, the moral, and the political standpoint. And you do not rip off your sisters.

Second, the stream of evolutionist and interventionist work, or "action" research, has developed to a phase where "subjects" are seen as partners in the research process. To dupe them in any way would be to undermine the very processes one wants to examine. Rather, they are seen as "respondents, participants, stakeholders" in a constructivist paradigm that is based on avoidance of harm, fully informed consent, and the need for privacy and confidentiality. If "action research" actually seeks to empower participants, then one must be open and honest with them; as two leading proponents of "fourth-generation evaluation" research put it:

> If evaluators cannot be clear, direct, and undeceptive regarding their wish to know how stakeholders make sense of their contexts, then stakeholders will be unclear, indirect, and probably misleading regarding how they do engage in sense-making and what their basic values are. Thus deception is not only counter to the posture of a constructivist evaluator, in that it destroys dignity, respect, and agency, but it also is counterproductive to the major goals of a fourth generation evaluation. Deception is worse than useless to a nonconventional evaluator; it is destructive of the effort's ultimate intent. (Guba & Lincoln, 1989, p. 122)

Third, and last, the concern with harm, consent, confidentiality, and so on has led some government agencies to insist that financing of research be contingent upon an ethical statement in the research proposal and that academic departments set up review and monitoring bodies to oversee the ethical component in funded research (Kimmel, 1988; Sieber, 1992). In brief, these three forces have had a powerful impact on consciousness about ethics in research and have, in particular, argued against deception and for taking the interests of the research "subjects" into account.

Codes and Consent

One significant element in such codes is the concept of "informed consent," by which the subjects of research have the right to be informed that they are being researched and also about the nature of the research. Federal agencies in the United States follow the rule for sponsored research "that the potential research subject understand the intention of the research and sign an 'informed consent' form, which incidentally must specify that the subject may withdraw from the research project at any time" (Weppner, 1977, p. 41). The key question here is, To what extent is this appropriate to much participant observation research? As Weppner (1977) observes, this threatens the continued existence of much "street-style" ethnography. When Powdermaker (1966), for instance, came face-to-face with a lynch mob in the Deep South, was she supposed to flash an academic identity card at the crowd and coolly outline her presence? In these and comparable circumstances, gaining consent is quite inappropriate, because activity is taking place that cannot be interrupted. In much fieldwork there seems to be no way around the predicament that informed consent—divulging one's identity and research purpose to all and sundry—will kill many a project stone dead.

And there are simply no easy answers provided by general codes to these situational ethics in fieldwork. For instance, researchers often confess to professional "misdemeanors" while in the field (Wax, 1971, p. 168). Malinowski (1967) socked a recalcitrant informant on the jaw; Powdermaker (1966) ceased to concern herself with the ethics of recording events in Hollywood unknown to the participants; Dalton (1964) fed information on salaries to a secretary in exchange for information on her male friend that was necessary for his research; and Bowen (1964) deliberately manipulated the research situation when it became impossible for her to maintain personal objectivity. The doyen of qualitative researchers, Whyte (1955, pp. 333-336), broke the law by "repeating" at elections, engaged in "retrospective falsification," and admits to having violated professional ethics (see also Whyte, 1984). What sanctions should we impose for these breaches of "professional" standards? Should we ignominiously drum these miscreants out of the profession? That seems a rather severe punishment for coming clean on their predicaments in the field.

My position is that a professional code of ethics is beneficial as a *guideline* that alerts researchers to the ethical dimensions of their work, particularly *prior* to entry. I am not arguing that the field-worker should abandon all ethical considerations once he of she has gotten in, but rather that informed consent is unworkable in some sorts of observational research. Furthermore, Reiss (1979, pp. 72, 77) notes that consent often serves to *reduce* participation and, although "definitive evidence is lacking," refusals seem more frequent from high-status, powerful people than from low-status, less powerful individuals. The ethicist might rail at my placing practical handicaps above ethical ideals, but I am seriously concerned that a strict application of codes will restrain and restrict a great deal of informal, innocuous research in which students and others study groups and activities that are unproblematic but where explicitly enforcing rules concerning informed consent will make the research role simply untenable.

Deception

What is plain is that codes and consent are opposed to deception. In contrast, the proponents of conflict methodology, which sometimes closely resembles investigative journalism (Wallraff, 1979), would argue that it is perfectly legitimate to expose nefarious institutions by using a measure of deceit. However, a number of studies that were not inspired by conflict methodology have employed some element of deception. In a neglected classic titled *Men Who Manage,* Dalton (1959) recounts how he investigated management in a number of firms by working covertly as a manager over a period of years. He used secretaries to gain information, employed out-of-work socializing to observe the significance of club membership for managers, utilized malcontents for their grievances against the organization, and manipulated intimates as "catalytic agents" to gain data (Dalton, 1964). In other projects, a researcher has joined a Pentecostal sect as if a novitiate; used plastic surgery, lost weight, lied about age, and adopted a "new personality" in order to study Air Force recruits (Sullivan, Queen, & Patrick, 1958); and entered a mental hospital as if a patient (Caudill, 1958). In other words, researchers have been prepared to use disguise, deception, and dissimulation in order to conduct research.

And perhaps *some* measure of deception is acceptable in *some* areas where the benefits of knowledge outweigh the harms that have been minimized by following convention on confidentiality and identity (and I fully acknowledge the sort of rationalizations this could lead to). One need not always be brutally honest, direct, and explicit about one's research purpose, but one should not normally engage in disguise. One should not steal documents. One should not directly lie to people. And, although one may disguise identity to a certain extent, one should not break promises made to people. Academics, in weighing up the balancing edge between overt-covert, and between openness-less than open, should take into account the consequences for the subjects, the profession, and, not least, for themselves.

I base this position on the view that subjects should not be harmed but also the pragmatic perspective that some dissimulation is intrinsic to social life and, therefore, also to fieldwork. Gans (1962) expresses this latter view neatly: "If the researcher is completely honest with people about his activities, they will try to hide actions and attitudes they consider undesirable, and so will be dishonest. Consequently, the researcher must be dishonest to get honest data" (p. 46). The crux of the matter is that some deception, passive or active, enables you to get at data not obtainable by other means. There are frequent references in the literature to field-workers as "spies" or "voyeurs," and an experienced researcher advises us to enter the field with a nebulous explanation of our purpose, to be careful that our deception is not found out until after we have left, and states that it is not "ethically necessary, nor methodologically sound, to make known specific hypotheses, background assumptions, or particular areas of interest" (Van Maanen, 1978, p. 334). So much for informed consent! Or, as a senior American academic at an ASA seminar on field methods put it bluntly, "You do lie through your teeth."

This is an extremely knotty area, because some academics argue precisely that researchers should be concerned with documenting abuses in public and business life. This is because they feel that convention on privacy, harm, and confidentiality should be waived when an institution is seen to be evading its public accountability (Holdaway, 1980, p. 324). Marx (1980) echoes this view when he suggests that perhaps different standards apply with respect to deception, privacy, informed consent, and avoiding harm to the researched against organizations that themselves engage in "deceitful, coercive and illegal activities" and are publicly accountable (p. 41). Can we salve our academic conscience by arguing that certain institutions deserve what they get? There seems to be no answer to this issue because it is impossible to establish a priori which institutions are "pernicious." One could visualize endless and fruitless debate as to which organizations should be included, particularly as many public bureaucracies of a relatively mundane sort are secretive and protective. The argument that they are also accountable is a telling one. But using covert research methods against them is likely only to close doors rather than to open them. The balance on this matter is ultimately a question for the individual researcher and his or her conscience in relation to feelings of responsibility to the profession and to "subjects." And it seems to be somewhat specious that academics can employ deception with high moral purpose against those they accuse of deception.

It is interesting, and even ironic, that social scientists espouse some of the techniques normally associated with morally polluted professions, such as policing and spying, and enjoy some of the moral ambivalence surrounding those occupations. The ironies and ambivalences are magnified when researchers study "deviants" and run the danger of what Klockars (1979) calls getting "dirty hands" (p. 269). In getting at the dirt, one may get dirty oneself (Marx, 1980, p. 27). Klockars (1979) is clear on this; in research on deviants the academic promises *not* to blow the whistle and maintains "the immediate, morally unquestionable, and compelling good end of keeping one's promise to one's subjects" (p. 275; see also Polsky, 1969). His argument is that researchers *must* be prepared to get their hands dirty, but also that they protect themselves by approaching subjects as "decent human beings," and by engaging in *talk*. By discussing moral dilemmas openly, researchers can avoid the danger of concealing dirty means for "good" ends. Here I would fully support Klockars's (1979) standpoint:

> The implication for field-work is to be most wary of any and all attempts to fashion rules and regulations, general guidelines, codes of ethics, or standards of professional conduct which would allow well-meaning bureaucrats and concerned colleagues to mobilize punishments for morally dubious behavior. Doing so will, I think, only have the effect of forcing decent fieldworkers to lie, deceive, wear masks, misrepresent themselves,

> hide the methods of their work, and otherwise dirty their hands more than their vocation now makes morally necessary. (p. 279)

In short, my position is to reject "conflict methodology" as a generally inappropriate model for social science. At the same time, I would accept some moderate measure of field-related deception providing the interests of the subjects are protected. A number of academics, however, take a very strong line on this area. Douglas's claim that basically "anything goes" is firmly opposed by Kai Erikson (cited in Bulmer, 1982). Among others, Erikson argues that it is unethical to misrepresent one's identity deliberately to gain entry into private domains one would otherwise be denied. It is also unethical to misrepresent deliberately the character of one's research. Bulmer (1982) supports the contention that the use of covert observation as a method is "neither ethically justified, nor practically necessary, nor in the best interest of sociology as an academic pursuit" (p. 217). This does not mean that it is *never* justified, but "its use requires most careful consideration in the light of ethical and practical considerations."

Bulmer (1982) then goes on to summarize his position in this debate usefully by arguing that the rights of subjects override the rights of science; that anonymity and confidentiality are necessary but not sufficient for subjects of research (we cannot predict the consequences of publication); and that covert observation is harmful to subjects, researchers, and the discipline. He adds that the need for covert research is exaggerated and that more attention should be paid to access as "overt insider." Also, for Bulmer, the role of "covert outsider" is less reprehensible than that of "covert insider and masquerading as a true participant." And, finally, social scientists should look outside their own profession for ethical guidance and should consider carefully the ethical implications of research before embarking on it. Much of this is sound advice, but it does mean closing avenues to certain types of research. And who is to perform the moral calculus that tells us what to research and what to leave alone?

Privacy, Harm, Identification, and Confidentiality

Conventional practice and ethical codes espouse the view that various safeguards should protect the privacy and identity of research subjects. As Bulmer (1982) puts it, "Identities, locations of individuals and places are concealed in published results, data collected are held in anonymized form, and all data kept securely confidential" (p. 225). The last of these may require considerable ingenuity in these days of computer hackers. In general, there is a strong feeling among fieldworkers that settings and respondents should not be identifiable in print and that they should not suffer harm or embarrassment as a consequence of research. There are powerful arguments for respecting persons (see the "Belmont Report" on ethical principles governing research, discussed in O'Connor, 1979) and their dignity, and also for not invading their privacy. Exposing people's private domains to academics raises imagery of "Peeping Toms" and "Big Brother" (Mead, 1961). It does seem to be going a bit far to lie under beds in order to eavesdrop on conversations (Bulmer, 1982, p. 116). But what about attending meetings of Alcoholics Anonymous? Can we assume that alcoholics are too distressed to worry about someone observing their predicament (or that their appearance at A.A. meetings signals their willingness to be open about their problem in the company of others)? To a large extent, I feel that we can become too sensitive on this issue. There is no simple distinction between "public" and "private" while observation in many public and semipublic places is tolerable even when the subjects are not aware of being observed. Some areas are nonproblematic, such as observing the work of flight attendants while one is traveling, and others may be related to serious social problems, where some benefit may emerge from focusing on the issue (Weppner, 1977).

The major safeguard to place against the invasion of privacy is the assurance of confidentiality. But even such assurances are not watertight, and "sociologists themselves have often flagrantly betrayed confidence, undoing all the work of covers, pseudonyms, and deletions" (Rock, 1979). I mentioned earlier the tendency to choose sites close to one's university; pseudonyms can often be punctured by looking up the researcher's institutional affiliation at the time of the project. Everyone now knows that "Middletown" was Muncie, Indiana; that "Rainfall West" was Seattle; and that "Westville" was Oakland, California. Holdaway (1982) painstakingly uses a pseudonym for his research police station, but then refers in his bibliography to publications that make it plain that he studied the Metropolitan Police of London. And how do you disguise research conducted in readily identifiable cities such as London, New York, or Amsterdam? In addition, the cloak of anonymity for characters may not work with insiders who can easily locate the individuals concerned or, what is even worse, *claim* that they can recognize them when they are, in fact, wrong. Many institutions and public figures are almost impossible to disguise, and, if they cooperate in research, may have to accept a considerable measure of exposure, particularly if the popular media pick up on the research.

This makes it sometimes precarious to assert that no harm or embarrassment will come to the researched (Reiss, 1979, p. 70). In the Cambridge-Somerville Youth Study there were apparently long-term negative consequences that emerged only when an evaluation study was conducted *30 years* after the original project (Kimmel, 1988, pp. 18-20). It is extremely difficult to predict to what uses one's research will be put; Wallis (1977) states that we must not cause "undeserved harm," but who is to define "deserved" and "undeserved" harm? Even people who have cooperated in research may feel hurt or embarrassed when the findings appear in print (e.g., the reactions in "Cornerville"—i.e., the North Side of Boston—to the publication of *Street Corner Society*; Whyte, 1955, p. 346). Indeed, Whyte has recently faced more controversy about his research, some 50 years after the fieldwork; he has been accused, among other things, of misleading respondents about publication (Boelen, 1992). Whyte (1992) has convincingly defended himself and has been supported by some of the original participants in the research (see Orlandella, 1992; Orlandella was "Sam Franco" in *Street Corner Society*). If there has been some element of betrayal on reading or learning of the publication, then the respondents will feel that "they have been cheated and misled by someone in whom they reposed trust and confidence" (Bulmer, 1982, p. 15). Respondents may not be fully aware at the time of the research that its findings may be published. Graduate students who speak vaguely of a dissertation may not make it clear that this is also a public document lodged in a library and open to all (Wallis, 1977, p. 159). The more "deviant" and secretive the activity, the more likely it is that subjects will fear consequences, and "the single most likely source of harm in social science inquiry is that the disclosure of private knowledge can be damaging" (Reiss, 1979, p. 73).

Trust and Betrayal

One major theme running through the ethical debate on research is that academics should not spoil the field for others. This is reflected among field-workers, where there are strong norms not to "foul the nest." But given that replications are rare in social science, that field-workers continually seek new and more esoteric settings, and that institutions frequently find one piece of research enough, there is a general tendency to hop from topic to topic. This makes spoiling the field less problematic for prospective researchers who look elsewhere rather than follow in someone's footsteps. It may well be problematic, however, for the researched. They may be left seething with rage and determined to skin alive the next aspiring ethnographer who seeks access. In fact, I would be curious to know how many of us have actually made it *easier* for colleagues to gain access to institutions or groups. It is already the case that anthropologists are not welcome in some Third World countries because they are associated with espionage, which is why some have turned to urban anthropology as opportunities abroad diminish. Indeed, one of the most fundamental objections to conflict methodology is that it will effectively close doors to further research.

This is particularly the case in qualitative research, compared with more formal and socially distant methods, because the academic enters into a relatively close relationship with the researched. First, in order to conduct research the field-worker has to break through to some form of social acceptance with a group. Second, full or near full involvement in the setting may bring an almost total identification with the group. This may be reinforced in deviant subcultures, where the illegal nature of the group's activities necessarily cements a close relationship, both as a necessary mechanism of entry and as a continued guarantee of collusion and of silence to outsiders. In a number of studies use was made of involvement in the role as a full participant (during employment, on vacations, as a student, or in early career employment, e.g., Becker as a jazz musician, Ditton as a bread salesman, and Van Maanen at Disneyland). Indeed, the actual or pretended full commitment to the role may be essential to gaining legitimacy and acceptance from the researched. But, third, and crucially, the researcher is essentially a transient who at some stage will abandon the field and will reenter an alternative social reality that is generally far more comforting and supportive. Anderson "became" a hobo, but he did not *remain* one; in fact, he posed as one and, like many researchers, acted out a role. In the end, we leave the researched behind in the field setting, and this can lead to acute feelings of abandonment and betrayal.

For instance, I conducted research with the Amsterdam police, and over a period of six years I became increasingly conscious of the social processes involved that gradually began to contain a covert element. Elsewhere, I wrote of my growing unease as I began to see through the pretense that I shared a common experience with ordinary policemen while I became uncomfortably aware of the manipulative element in the relationships built in the field. This brought me to the notion of *mutual deceit* as virtually inherent to the deeply engaged fieldwork role:

> If a latent aim of field-work is to create trust in the researcher then what was the aim of that trust? And did not the relationship involve a double betrayal: first by them of me but then by me of them? In short, I felt that in field-work the subjects are conning you until you can gain their trust

> and then, once you have their confidence, you begin conning them. In other words, I could not escape the realization that deceit and dissemblance were part of the research role and I did not feel ethically comfortable with that insight. Lies, deceit, concealment, and bending the truth are mentioned in many reports of field-work. Indeed, Berreman (1964: 18) states that "participant observation, as a form of social interaction, always involves impression management. Therefore, as a research technique, it inevitably entails some secrecy and some dissimulation." At the time I found this all genuinely distressing and confusing. (Punch, 1979, p. 189)

My experiences and views on the mutual conning in the field are perhaps more generally true of research involving deep and long commitment to the setting and close, if not intimate, relationships with the research subjects. And it is precisely in such research that the departure of the researcher, and the subsequent publications of his or her findings, may lead to painful feelings of abandonment and betrayal. There may also be an emotional rejection of the published portrait of the research setting and interaction. In using one's personality to enter the field situation, and in acting out a transient role, one has to face the personal and emotionally charged accusations that not infrequently accompany this style of work. This can, for instance, prove an especially painful dilemma for feminists when they feel caught between solidarity in the field and the professional need to depart and start writing up their experiences for academic consumption (see Fonow & Cook, 1991, p. 9).

Conclusion

I have endeavored here to sketch an overview of those elements that researchers need to consider in pondering the ethics and politics of qualitative research. I recognize, however, that this area is a swamp and that I have provided no map. Each individual will have to trace his or her own path. This is because there is no consensus or unanimity on what is public and private, what constitutes harm, and what the benefits of knowledge are. Also, at the individual level there is no effective control to prevent a new Laud Humphreys from employing devious methods to conduct research. Indeed, the conflict methodologists would actually encourage us to use murky means in order to expose powerful institutions (while arguing that professional ethics are "scientific suicide"; Douglas, 1979, p. 32); feminists would condemn with passion and with anger certain offensive practices *prior* to researching them (or probably not researching them at all); and frequently we have been enjoined to "take sides" (with such spokespersons as Becker and Goffman, when the latter was president of the American Sociological Association, arguing for an engaged and committed profession that unmasks the forces of power and oppression); for where you stand will doubtless help to determine not only what you will research but also how you will research it.

In the past, particularly in medical research and psychological experimentation, there was a considerable amount of deception and, in some cases, a demonstrable element of harm. Attempts to control this have also had an impact on social science in general. Some federally funded research in the United States, for instance, must conform to ethical standards and to auditing by review boards, and professional associations have espoused codes of conduct. A number of disparate forces, including feminism and action research, have emphasized that deceptive and/or exploitive research is inimical to treating "subjects" as partners, collaborators, and stakeholders. Feminists express solidarity with the researched, reach a highly emotive empathy with them, and are committed to emancipating the oppressed; deception and exploitation would be diametrically opposed to their ideology and methods. Here the personal is both political and ethical. In other styles of research, such as interventionist or community-based research, any attempt to dupe or mislead the researched would prove counterproductive because it would undermine the very purpose of the project. In essence, there is a strong argument, reinforced from disparate but powerful forces, that "sound ethics and sound methodology go hand in hand" (Sieber, 1992, p. 4).

Finally, it is possible to examine these issues at the societal, institutional, and professional levels. I have preferred to focus more on how certain aspects of politics and ethics impinge on the individual researcher approaching fieldwork as a relative newcomer. But that does not occur in a vacuum and, fortunately, there are available experienced and wise mentors, academic debates on moral and ethical dilemmas in the field, and professional publications and guidelines on good research practice. In general, serious academics in a sound academic community will espouse trust, reject deception, and abhor harm. They will be wary of spoiling the field, of closing doors to research, and of damaging the reputation of their profession—both as a matter of principle and out of self-interest. In practice, however, professional codes and sound advice may not be all that clear and unambiguous in the field setting, in all its complexity and fluidity. This is because participant observation, as Ditton (1977) notes, is *inevi-*

tably unethical "by virtue of being interactionally deceitful" (p. 10). At the situational and interactional level, then, it may be unavoidable that there is a degree of impression management, manipulation, concealment, economy with the truth, and even deception. I would maintain that we have to accept much of this as being in good faith, providing the researchers come clean about their "muddy boots" (Fielding, 1982, p. 96) and "grubby hands" (Marx, 1980, p. 27). Not to do so would unduly restrict observational and qualitative studies. In essence, I echo Hughes's and Becker's summons to "simply go out and do it." But I would add that before you go you should stop and reflect on the political and ethical dimensions of what you are about to experience. Just do it by all means, but think a bit first.

References

American Sociologist. (1978). [Special issue on regulation of research]. Vol. *13*(3).

Argyris, C. (1969). Diagnosing defenses against the outsider. In G. J. McCall & J. L. Simmons (Eds.), *Issues in participant observation* (pp. 115-127). Reading, MA: Addison-Wesley.

Atkinson, M. (1977). Coroners and the categorisation of deaths as suicides: Changes in perspective as features of the research process. In C. Bell & H. Newby (Eds.), *Doing sociological research* (pp. 31-46). London: Allen & Unwin.

Barber, B. (1976). The ethics of experimentation with human subjects. *Scientific American, 234*(2), 25-31.

Barnes, J. A. (1979). *Who should know what? Social science, privacy and ethics.* Harmondsworth: Penguin.

Becker, H. S. (1967). Whose side are we on? *Social Problems, 14,* 239-247.

Bell, C. (1977). Reflections on the Banbury restudy. In C. Bell & H. Newby (Eds.), *Doing sociological research* (pp. 47-66). London: Allen & Unwin.

Bell, C., & Newby, H. (Eds.). (1977). *Doing sociological research.* London: Allen & Unwin.

Boelen, W. A. M. (1992). *Street corner society*: Cornerville revisited. In *Street corner society* revisited [Special issue]. *Journal of Contemporary Ethnography, 21,* 11-51.

Boruch, R. F., & Cecil, J. S. (1983). *Solutions to ethical and legal problems in social research.* New York: Academic Press.

Bowen, E. S. (1964). *Return to laughter.* New York: Random House. (Published under pseudonym L. Bohannon)

Brandt, A. M. (1978). *Racism, research and the Tuskegee Syphilis Study* (Report No. 8). New York: Hastings Center.

Bulmer, M. (Ed.). (1982). *Social research ethics.* London: Macmillan.

Burgess, R. G. (Ed.). (1982). *Field research: A source book and field manual.* London: Allen & Unwin.

Burns, T. (1977). *The B.B.C.* London: Macmillan.

Caudill, W. (1958). *The psychiatric hospital as a small society.* Cambridge, MA: Harvard University Press.

Clarke, M. (1975). Survival in the field: Implications of personal experience in field-work. *Theory and Society, 2,* 95-123.

Dalton, M. (1959). *Men who manage.* New York: John Wiley.

Dalton, M. (1964). Preconceptions and methods in *Men who manage.* In P. Hammond (Ed.), *Sociologists at work* (pp. 50-95). New York: Basic Books.

Diamond, S. (1964). Nigerian discovery: The politics of field-work. In A. J. Vidich, J. Bensman, & M. R. Stein (Eds.), *Reflections on community studies* (pp. 119-154). New York: Harper & Row.

Diener, E., & Crandall, R. (1978). *Ethics in social and behavioral research.* Chicago: University of Chicago Press.

Dingwall, R., Payne, G., & Payne, J. (1980). *The development of ethnography in Britain.* Mimeo, Centre for Socio-Legal Studies, Oxford.

Ditton, J. (1977). *Part-time crime.* London: Macmillan.

Douglas, J. D. (1979). Living morality versus bureaucratic fiat. In C. B. Klockars & F. W. O'Connor (Eds.), *Deviance and decency: The ethics of research with human subjects* (pp. 13-33). Beverly Hills, CA: Sage.

Festinger, L., Riecken, H. W., & Schachter, S. (1956). *When prophecy fails.* New York: Harper & Row.

Fielding, N. (1982). Observational research on the national front. In M. Bulmer (Ed.), *Social research ethics* (pp. 80-104). London: Macmillan.

Florez, C. P., & Kelling, G. L. (1979). *Issues in the use of observers in large scale program evaluation: The hired hand and the lone wolf.* Unpublished manuscript, Harvard University, Kennedy School of Government.

Fonow, M. M., & Cook, J. A. (Eds.). (1991). *Beyond methodology: Feminist scholarship as lived research.* Bloomington: Indiana University Press.

Gans, H. J. (1962). *The urban villagers: Group and class in the life of Italian-Americans.* New York: Free Press.

Gans, H. J. (1967). *The Levittowners: Ways of life and politics in a new suburban community.* London: Allen Lane.

Grossberg, L., Nelson, C., & Treichler, P. A. (Eds.). (1992). *Cultural studies.* New York: Routledge.

Guba, E. G., & Lincoln, Y. S. (1989). *Fourth generation evaluation.* Newbury Park, CA: Sage.

Gubrium, J. F., & Silverman, D. (Eds.). (1989). *The politics of field research: Beyond enlightenment.* Newbury Park, CA: Sage.

Hammersley, M. (Ed.). (1993). *Social research: Philosophy, politics and practice.* London: Sage.

Hammersley, M., & Atkinson P. (1983). *Ethnography: Principles in practice.* London: Tavistock.

Hammond, P. (Ed.). (1964). *Sociologists at work.* New York: Basic Books.

Holdaway, S. (1980). *The occupational culture of urban policing: An ethnographic study.* Unpublished doctoral dissertation, University of Sheffield.

Holdaway, S. (1982). "An inside job": A case study of covert research on the police. In M. Bulmer (Ed.), *Social research ethics* (pp. 59-79). London: Macmillan.

Homan, R., & Bulmer, M. (1982). On the merits of covert methods: A dialogue. In M. Bulmer (Ed.), *Social research ethics* (pp. 105-124). London: Macmillan.

Horowitz, I. L. (1970). Sociological snoopers and journalistic moralizers. *Transaction, 7,* 4-8.

Humphreys, L. (1970). *Tearoom trade: Impersonal sex in public places.* Chicago: Aldine.

Humphreys, L. (1972). *Out of the closet.* Englewood Cliffs, NJ: Prentice Hall.

Hunt, J. (1984). The development of rapport through the negotiation of gender in field work among police. *Human Organization, 43,* 283-296.

Jayaratne, T. E., & Stewart, A. J. (1991). Quantitative and qualitative methods in the social sciences: Current feminist issues and practical strategies. In M. M. Fonow & J. A. Cook (Eds.), *Beyond methodology: Feminist scholarship as lived research* (pp. 85-106). Bloomington: Indiana University Press.

Katz, J. (1972). *Experimentation with human beings.* New York: Russell Sage.

Kimmel, A. J. (1988). *Ethics and values in applied social research.* Newbury Park, CA: Sage.

Klein, L. (1976). *A social scientist in industry.* London: Gower.

Klockars, C. B. (1979). Dirty hands and deviant subjects. In C. B. Klockars & F. W. O'Connor (Eds.), *Deviance and decency: The ethics of research with human subjects* (pp. 261-282). Beverly Hills, CA: Sage.

Klockars, C. B., & O'Connor, F. W. (Eds.). (1979). *Deviance and decency: The ethics of research with human subjects.* Beverly Hills, CA: Sage.

La Pierre, R. T. (1934). Attitudes vs. actions. *Social Forces, 13,* 230-237.

Lofland, J. F., & Lejeune, R. A. (1960). Initial interaction of newcomers in Alcoholics Anonymous. *Social Problems, 8,* 102-111.

Malinowski, B. (1967). *A diary in the strict sense of the term.* New York: Harcourt Brace.

Martin, S. E. (1980). *Breaking and entering: Policewomen on patrol.* Berkeley: University of California Press.

Marx, G. (1980). *Notes on the discovery, collection and assessment of hidden and dirty data.* Paper presented at the annual meeting of the Society for the Study of Social Problems, New York.

McCall, G. J., & Simmons, J. L. (Eds.). (1969). *Issues in participant observation.* Reading, MA: Addison-Wesley.

Mead, M. (1961). The human study of human beings. *Science, 133,* 163-165.

Mies, M. (1991). Women's research or feminist research: The debate surrounding feminist science and methodology. In M. M. Fonow & J. A. Cook (Eds.), *Beyond methodology: Feminist scholarship as lived research* (pp. 60-84). Bloomington: Indiana University Press.

Milgram, S. (1963). Behavioral study of obedience. *Journal of Abnormal and Social Psychology, 67,* 371-378.

O'Connor, F. W. (1979). The ethical demands of the Belmont Report. In C. B. Klockars & F. W. O'Connor (Eds.), *Deviance and decency: The ethics of research with human subjects* (pp. 225-258). Beverly Hills, CA: Sage.

Okely, J., & Callaway, H. (Eds.). (1992). *Anthropology and autobiography.* New York: Routledge.

Orlandella, A. R. (1992). Boelen may know Holland, Boelen may know Barzini, but Boelen "doesn't know diddle about the North End!" In *Street corner society* revisited [Special issue]. *Journal of Contemporary Ethnography, 21,* 69-79.

Platt, J. (1976). *The realities of social research.* London: University of Sussex Press.

Polsky, N. (1969). *Hustlers, beats and others.* Chicago: Aldine.

Powdermaker, H. (1966). *Stranger and friend: The way of an anthropologist.* New York: W. W. Norton.

Punch, M. (1986). *The politics and ethics of fieldwork.* Beverly Hills, CA: Sage.

Punch, M. (1989). Researching police deviance: A personal encounter with the limitations and liabilities of field-work. *British Journal of Sociology, 40,* 177-204.

Reimer, J. W. (1979). *Hard hats.* Beverly Hills, CA: Sage.

Reinharz, S. (1992). *Feminist methods in social research.* New York: Oxford University Press.

Reiss, A. J., Jr. (1979). Governmental regulation of scientific inquiry: Some paradoxical consequences. In C. B. Klockars & F. W. O'Connor (Eds.), *Deviance and decency: The ethics of research with human subjects* (pp. 61-95). Beverly Hills, CA: Sage.

Roberts, H. (Ed.). (1981). *Doing feminist research.* London: Routledge.

Rock, P. (1979). *The making of symbolic interactionism.* London: Macmillan.

Rynkiewich, M. A., & Spradley, J. (Eds.). (1976). *Ethics and anthropology: Dilemmas in fieldwork.* New York: John Wiley.

Sanjek, R. (Ed.). (1990). *Fieldnotes: The makings of anthropology.* Albany: State University of New York Press.

Schwartz, M. (1964). The mental hospital: The researched person in the disturbed world. In A. J. Vidich, J. Bensman, & M. R. Stein (Eds.), *Reflections on community studies* (pp. 85-117). New York: Harper & Row.

Shaffir, W. B., & Stebbins, R. A. (Eds.). (1991). *Experiencing fieldwork: An inside view of qualitative research.* Newbury Park, CA: Sage.
Sharrock, W., & Anderson, R. (1980). *Ethnomethodology and British sociology: Some problems of incorporation.* Paper presented at the annual meeting of the British Sociological Association, University of Lancaster.
Shils, E. (1982). Social enquiry and the autonomy of the individual. In M. Bulmer (Ed.), *Social research ethics* (pp. 125-141). London: Macmillan.
Sieber, J. E. (1992). *Planning ethically responsible research.* Newbury Park, CA: Sage.
Sjoberg, G. (Ed.). (1968). *Ethics, politics, and social research.* Cambridge, MA: Schenkman.
Social Problems. (1973). [Special issue on the social control of social research]. Vol. *21*(1).
Social Problems. (1980). [Special issue on ethical problems of field-work]. Vol. *27*(3).
Spencer, G. (1973). Methodological issues in the study of bureaucratic elites: A case of West Point. *Social Problems, 21,* 90-102.
Sullivan, M. A., Queen, S. A., & Patrick, R. C. (1958). Participant observation as employed in the study of a military training program. *American Sociological Review, 23,* 610-667.
Thompson, H. (1967). *Hell's Angels.* Harmondsworth: Penguin.
Van Maanen, J. (1978). On watching the watchers. In P. K. Manning & J. Van Maanen (Eds.), *Policing: A view from the street* (pp. 309-349). Santa Monica, CA: Goodyear.
Van Maanen, J. (Ed.). (1979). Qualitative methodology [Special issue]. *Administrative Science Quarterly, 24,* 519-680.
Van Maanen, J. (1988). *Tales of the field: On writing ethnography.* Chicago: University of Chicago Press.
Vidich, A. J., & Bensman, J. (1968). *Small town in mass society: Class, power and religion in a rural community* (2nd ed.). Princeton, NJ: Princeton University Press.
Wallis, R. (1977). The moral career of a research sociologist. In C. Bell & H. Newby (Eds.), *Doing sociological research* (pp. 149-169). London: Allen & Unwin.
Wallraff, G. (1979). *Beeld van bild.* Amsterdam: Van Gennep.
Wax, R.H. (1971). *Doing fieldwork: Warnings and advice.* Chicago: University of Chicago Press.
Welch, S. (1991). An ethic of solidarity. In H. Giroux (Ed.), *Postmodernism, feminism, and cultural politics* (pp. 83-99). Albany: State University of New York Press.
Weppner, R. S. (1977). *Street ethnography.* Beverly Hills, CA: Sage.
Whyte, W. F. (1943). *Street corner society: The social structure of an Italian slum.* Chicago: University of Chicago Press.
Whyte, W. F. (1955). *Street corner society: The social structure of an Italian slum* (2nd ed.). Chicago: University of Chicago Press.
Whyte, W. F. (1981). *Street corner society: The social structure of an Italian slum* (3rd ed.). Chicago: University of Chicago Press.
Whyte, W. F. (1984). *Learning from the field: A guide from experience.* Beverly Hills, CA: Sage.
Whyte, W. F. (1992). In defense of *Street corner society.* In *Street corner society* revisited [Special issue]. *Journal of Contemporary Ethnography, 21,* 52-68.
Wilkins, L. T. (1979). Human subjects—whose subjects? In C. B. Klockars & F. W. O'Connor (Eds.), *Deviance and decency: The ethics of research with human subjects* (pp. 99-123). Beverly Hills, CA: Sage.
Wycoff, M. A., & Kelling, G. L. (1978). *The Dallas experience: Organizational reform.* Washington, DC: Police Foundation.
Yablonsky, L. (1968). *The hippy trip.* Harmondsworth: Penguin.

PART II
MAJOR PARADIGMS AND PERSPECTIVES

In our introductory chapter, following Guba (1990, p. 17), we defined a paradigm as a basic set of beliefs that guide action. Paradigms deal with first principles, or ultimates. They are human constructions. They define the worldview of the researcher-as-*bricoleur.* These beliefs can never be established in terms of their ultimate truthfulness. Perspectives, in contrast, are not as solidified, or as well unified, as paradigms, although a perspective may share many elements with a paradigm, such as a common set of methodological commitments.

A paradigm encompasses three elements: epistemology, ontology, and methodology. *Epistemology* asks, How do we know the world? What is the relationship between the inquirer and the known? *Ontology* raises basic questions about the nature of reality. *Methodology* focuses on how we gain knowledge about the world. Part II of this volume examines the major paradigms and perspectives that now structure and organize qualitative research: positivism, postpositivism, constructivism, and critical theory and related positions.

Alongside these paradigms are the perspectives of feminism, ethnic models of inquiry, and cultural studies. Each of these perspectives adopts its own criteria, assumptions, and methodological practices that are applied to disciplined inquiry within that framework. (Tables 6.1 and 6.2 in Chapter 6, by Guba and Lincoln, outline the major differences among the positivist, postpositivist, critical theory, and constructivist paradigms.) We have provided a brief discussion of each paradigm and perspective in Chapter 1; here we elaborate them in considerably more detail.

The Positivist Legacy: Epistemology, Ontology, Methodology

Of course, the positivist and postpositivist paradigms provide the backdrop against which other paradigms and perspectives operate. In Chapter 6, Egon Guba and Yvonna Lincoln analyze these two traditions in considerable detail.

Conventional positivist social science applies four criteria to disciplined inquiry: *internal validity,* the degree to which findings correctly map the phenomenon in question; *external validity,* the degree to which findings can be generalized to other settings similar to the one in which the study occurred; *reliability,* the extent to which findings can be replicated, or reproduced, by another inquirer; and *objectivity,* the extent to which findings are free from bias.

The received positivist and postpositivist views have recently come under considerable attack. Guba and Lincoln review these criticisms, including the arguments that these paradigms are unable to deal adequately with the issues surrounding the etic, emic, nomothetic, and idiographic dimensions of inquiry. Too many local (emic), case-based (idiographic) meanings are excluded by the generalizing (etic) nomothetic, positivist position. At the same time, the nomothetic, etic approaches fail to address satisfactorily the theory- and value-laden nature of facts, the interactive nature of inquiry, and the fact that the same set of "facts" can support more than one theory.

Constructivism and Critical Theory

Constructivism, as presented by Guba and Lincoln, adopts a relativist (relativism) ontology, a transactional epistemology, and a hermeneutic, dialectical methodology. The inquiry aims of this paradigm are oriented to the production of reconstructed understandings, wherein the traditional positivist criteria of internal and external validity are replaced by the terms *trustworthiness* and *authenticity.*

Thomas Schwandt's subtle analysis in Chapter 7 of constructivist, interpretivist approaches identifies major differences and strands of thought within these approaches, which are unified by their opposition to positivism and their commitment to the study of the world from the point of view of the interacting individual. Yet these perspectives, as Schwandt argues, are distinguished more by their commitment to questions of knowing and being than by their specific methodologies, which basically enact an emic, idiographic approach to inquiry. Schwandt traces out the theoretical and philosophical foundations of constructivist, interpretivist traditions, connecting them back to the works of Schutz, Weber, Mead, Blumer, Winch, Heidegger, Gadamer, Geertz, Ricoeur, Gergen, Goodman, Guba, and Lincoln. The constructivist tradition, as Schwandt notes, is rich, deep, and complex.

A similarly complicated field describes the multiple critical theory, Marxist models that now circulate within the discourses of qualitative research (see Kincheloe & McLaren, Chapter 8, this volume; see also Nelson & Grossberg, 1988). In Guba and Lincoln's framework this paradigm, in its many forms, articulates an ontology based on historical realism, an epistemology that is transactional, and a methodology that is dialogic and dialectical. In their chapter, Joe Kincheloe and Peter McLaren trace the history of critical research (and Marxist theory) from the Frankfurt school through their most recent transformations in poststructural, postmodern, feminist, and cultural studies theory. They develop a "resistance" version of postmodernism that is joined with critical theory and critical ethnography. An added bonus is their treatment of the Birmingham school of cultural studies and the recent critical work of Cornel West and others on women, the Third World, and race. They outline several ways that critical theory-based research can lead to worker empowerment. Critical theorists seek to produce transformations in the social order, producing knowledge that is historical and structural, judged by its degree of historical situatedness and its ability to produce praxis, or action.

There are, however, some critical theorists (see, e.g., Carspecken & Apple, 1992, pp. 547-548) who work to build testable, falsifiable social theory. Others—for example, materialist ethnographers such as Roman (1992)—reject the postpositivist features of these arguments, as do Dorothy Smith (1992, 1993) and Henry Giroux (1992). Other critical theorists and Marxists work more closely from within a traditional, qualitative, grounded theory approach to validity and theory construction (Burawoy, 1992), stressing the extended case study as the focus of analysis.

Interpretive Perspectives

Each of the three feminisms identified by Virginia Olesen in Chapter 9 (standpoint epistemology, empiricist, and postmodernism-cultural studies), takes a different stance toward the postpositivist tradition. Standpoint epistemologists reject "standard good social scientific methodologies [because they] produce people as objects . . . if [sociologists] work with standard methods of thinking and inquiry, they import the relations of ruling into the texts they produce. . . . this is not an issue of quantitative versus qualitative method" (Smith, 1992, p. 91). Using case studies, participant observation, interviewing, and the critical analysis of social texts, Smith deploys a critical, poststructural epistemology and methodology that continually explores the connections between texts and relations of ruling (but see Clough, 1993a, 1993b). Standpoint epistemologists are, then, close to the critical paradigm while sharing certain features with the constructivist paradigm (hermeneutical, dialogic inquiry).

In contrast, empiricist feminisms are aligned with a postpositivist language of validity, reliability, credibility, multimethod research strategies, and so on (see Reinharz, 1992). There is an emphasis on some version of realism, a modified objectivist epistemology, a concern for hypothesis testing, explanation, prediction, cause-effect linkages, and conventional benchmarks of rigor, including internal and external validity. Here the intent is to apply the full range of qualitative methodologies to feminist issues.

Postmodern, cultural studies feminists merge their work with the postmodern, ethnographic turn in anthropology (see Marcus, Chapter 35, this volume; also Morris, 1988) while exploring autoethnography and other new writing forms (see Franklin, Lury, & Stacey, 1991, p. 181; Wolf, 1992; see also Richardson, Chapter 32, this volume). This tradition draws on the critical and constructivist paradigms, especially in a commitment to relativism and historical realism, transactional epistemologies, dialogic methodologies, and social critique, as well as historically situated and trustworthy empirical materials. However, cultural studies feminists both supplement and at times challenge the more explicit standpoint epistemology projects (Clough, 1993a, 1993b).

Feminist theory and thought is restructuring qualitative research practices. This is especially the case for those approaches shaped by the standpoint epistemology and cultural studies models. From them are coming new ethical and epistemological criteria for evaluating research. At the same time, these perspectives are making lived experience central to qualitative inquiry and developing criteria of evaluation based on ethics of caring, personal responsibility, and open dialogue.

These criteria, as articulated by scholars such as Patricia Hill Collins (1990, p. 219), embody a standpoint epistemology that is fully compatible with the cultural studies paradigm. This is especially the case when these criteria are joined with an emphasis on reflexive textuality (Richardson, Chapter 32, this volume) and an understanding that there is no dividing line between empirical research activity and the process of theorizing. Theory is interpretation, just as it is also criticism and critique.

Ethnic models of inquiry also move in at least three different directions at the same time (see Stanfield, Chapter 10, this volume). Traditional ethnic empiricists utilize participant observation, interviewing, and case study methods to examine the lived experiences of specific ethnic minorities. They assess their findings in terms quite compatible with the postpositivist project. Marxist ethnic models (Collins, 1990) build upon the standpoint epistemologies of Smith and others to examine explicitly how local cultures and "local knowledges can counteract the hegemonic tendencies of objectified knowledge" (Collins, 1992, p. 74). Postmodern ethnic models (West, 1989) elaborate a variety of different cultural studies models (see below) to examine the ways in which race and ethnicity are repressively inscribed in daily social life. It is possible, then, as with feminism, to map the ethnic models into the postpositivist, critical, and constructivist paradigms.

As John Stanfield observes in Chapter 10, these three models confront a common set of problems, involving the normalization of ethnicity as a way of life in the United States, the hegemonic character of American social science, and the white middle-class origins of this enterprise. Historically, critical ethnic models of qualitative inquiry have been excluded from social science discourse, for example, the work of Carter G. Woodson, William E. B. Du Bois, Horace Mann Bond, and, until recently, Zora Neale Hurston. This has made it more difficult for minority scholars to develop their own paradigms, free of the biases and prejudices of race, positivism, and postpositivism.

Stanfield outlines one version of this project, drawing attention to the neglected historical and participant observation research traditions in the Afro-American scholarly community. He anticipates future debates over the insider-outsider issue in social research, noting that minority scholars have traditionally been treated as outsiders, forced to study their own ethnic communities from the Eurocentric perspective. He also reviews feminist research approaches to race and ethnicity. Stanfield discusses much of the revisionist work in this area that has been shaped by Eurocentric biases and outlines a new ethnic paradigm grounded in the global experiences of people of color. This paradigm is holistic, relational, qualitative, and sensitive to gender, kinship, spirituality, and the oral communicative traditions so central to the experiences of Afro-Americans and other people of color in the United States and elsewhere. A great deal is at issue in this area. Historically, racial and ethnic minorities have lacked the power "to represent themselves to themselves and others as complex human beings" (West, 1990, p. 27). Stanfield shows how this situation can be changed radically. Indeed, all of the chapters in this volume address this problem, in one way or another.

Cultural studies cannot be contained within a single framework. There are multiple cultural studies projects, including those connected to the Birmingham school and to the work of Stuart Hall and his associates (see, e.g., Grossberg, 1989, 1992; Hall, 1992). The generic focus of each version involves an examination of how the history people live is produced by structures that have been handed down from the past. Each version is joined by a threefold concern with cultural texts, lived experience, and the articulated relationship between texts and everyday life. Within the cultural text tradition, some scholars examine the mass media and popular culture as sites where history, ideology, and subjective experiences come together, as John Fiske does in Chapter 11. These scholars produce critical ethnographies of the audience in relation to particular historical moments. Other scholars read texts (see Manning & Cullum-Swan, Chapter 29, this volume) as sites where hegemonic meanings are produced, distributed, and consumed (Giroux, 1992). Within the ethnographic tradition, there is a postmodern concern for the social text and its production.

The open-ended nature of the cultural studies project leads to a perpetual resistance against attempts to impose a single paradigm over the entire project. There are critical-Marxist, constructionist, and postpositivist paradigmatic strands within the formation, as well as emergent feminist and ethnic models. Scholars within the cultural studies project are drawn to historical realism and relativism as their ontology, and to transactional epistemologies and dialogic methodologies, while remaining committed to a historical and structural framework that is praxis and action based.

Fiske's chapter is an example of the text-based, ethnographic, and audience research tradition in cultural studies. He notes that he does not speak for cultural studies in his text. He offers, instead, a review of recent studies of television audiences, showing how these qualitative, ethnographic investigations contribute to the cultural studies project. He argues that his work is not "scientific." It is interpretive, based on discourse analysis, and is not systematic in its model of validation. The data Fiske uses are empirical because they derive from material experience. They are not empiricist; that is, he makes no claim that "the material plane has an objective existence that provides the terms of its own significance." Fiske's work has elements that align it with the critical and constructionist paradigms discussed by Guba and Lincoln in Chapter 6.

In Conclusion

The researcher-as-*bricoleur* cannot afford to be a stranger to any of the paradigms discussed in this part of the *Handbook.* He or she must understand the basic ontological, epistemological, and methodological assumptions of each, and be able to engage them in dialogue (Guba, 1990). The differences between paradigms have significant and important implications at the practical, everyday, empirical level. A resolution of paradigm differences, Guba and Lincoln cogently note in Chapter 6, is most likely to occur "if and when proponents of these several [paradigms] come together to discuss their differences, not to argue the sanctity of their views."

References

Burawoy, M. (1992). The extended case method. In M. Burawoy, A. Burton, A. A. Ferguson, K. J. Fox, J. Gamson, N. Gartrell, L. Hurst, C. Kurzman, L. Salzinger, J. Schiffman, & S. Ui (Eds.), *Ethnography unbound: Power and resistance in the modern metropolis* (pp. 271-290). Berkeley: University of California Press.

Carspecken, P. F., & Apple, M. (1992). Critical research: Theory, methodology, and practice. In M. D. LeCompte, W. L. Millroy, & J. Preissle (Eds.), *The handbook of qualitative research in education* (pp. 507-554). New York: Academic Press.

Clough, P. T. (1993a). On the brink of deconstructing sociology: A critical reading of Dorothy Smith's standpoint epistemology. *Sociological Quarterly, 34,* 169-182.

Clough, P. T. (1993b). Response to Smith. *Sociological Quarterly, 34,* 193-194.

Collins, P. H. (1990). *Black feminist thought: Knowledge, consciousness and the politics of empowerment.* New York: Routledge.

Collins, P. H. (1992). Transforming the inner circle: Dorothy Smith's challenge to sociological theory. *Sociological Theory, 10,* 73-80.

Franklin, S., Lury, C., & Stacey, J. (1991). Feminism and cultural studies: Pasts, presents, and futures. *Media, Culture & Society, 13,* 171-192.

Giroux, H. (1992). *Border crossings: Cultural workers and the politics of education.* New York: Routledge.

Grossberg, L. (1989). The formations of cultural studies: An American in Birmingham. *Strategies, 2,* 114-149.

Grossberg, L. (1992). *We gotta get out of this place: Popular conservatism and postmodern culture.* New York: Routledge.

Guba, E. G. (1990). The alternative paradigm dialog. In E. G. Guba (Ed.), *The paradigm dialog* (pp. 17-30). Newbury Park, CA: Sage.

Hall, S. (1992). Cultural studies and its theoretical legacies. In L. Grossberg, C. Nelson, & P. A. Treichler (Eds.), *Cultural studies* (pp. 277-294). New York: Routledge.

Morris, M. (1988). Henry Parkes Motel. *Cultural Studies, 2,* 10-47.

Nelson, C., & Grossberg, L. (Eds.). (1988). *Marxism and the interpretation of culture.* Urbana: University of Illinois Press.

Reinharz, S. (1992). *Feminist methods in social research.* New York: Oxford University Press.

Roman, L. G. (1992). The political significance of other ways of narrating ethnography: A feminist materialist approach. In M. D. LeCompte, W. L. Millroy, & J. Preissle (Eds.), *The handbook of qualitative research in education* (pp. 555-594). New York: Academic Press.

Smith, D. E. (1992). Sociology from women's experience: A reaffirmation. *Sociological Theory, 10,* 88-98.

Smith, D. E. (1993). High noon in Textland: A critique of Clough. *Sociological Quarterly, 34,* 183-192.

West, C. (1989). *The American evasion of philosophy.* Madison: University of Wisconsin Press.

West, C. (1990). The new cultural politics of difference. In R. Ferguson, M. Geverr, T. T. Minh-ha, & C. West (Eds.). *Out there: Marginalization and contemporary cultures* (pp. 19-36). Cambridge: MIT Press.

Wolf, M. (1992). *A thrice-told tale: Feminism, postmodernism, and ethnographic responsibility.* Stanford, CA: Stanford University Press.

6

Competing Paradigms in Qualitative Research

EGON G. GUBA
YVONNA S. LINCOLN

IN this chapter we analyze four paradigms that currently are competing, or have until recently competed, for acceptance as the paradigm of choice in informing and guiding inquiry, especially qualitative inquiry: positivism, postpositivism, critical theory and related ideological positions, and constructivism. We acknowledge at once our own commitment to constructivism (which we earlier called "naturalistic inquiry"; Lincoln & Guba, 1985); the reader may wish to take that fact into account in judging the appropriateness and usefulness of our analysis.

Although the title of this volume, *Handbook of Qualitative Research,* implies that the term *qualitative* is an umbrella term superior to the term *paradigm* (and, indeed, that usage is not uncommon), it is our position that it is a term that ought to be reserved for a description of types of methods. From our perspective, both qualitative and quantitative methods may be used appropriately with any research paradigm. Questions of method are secondary to questions of paradigm, which we define as the basic belief system or worldview that guides the investigator, not only in choices of method but in ontologically and epistemologically fundamental ways.

It is certainly the case that interest in alternative paradigms has been stimulated by a growing dissatisfaction with the patent overemphasis on quantitative methods. But as efforts were made to build a case for a renewed interest in qualitative approaches, it became clear that the metaphysical assumptions undergirding the conventional paradigm (the "received view") must be seriously questioned. Thus the emphasis of this chapter is on paradigms, their assumptions, and the implications of those assumptions for a variety of research issues, not on the relative utility of qualitative versus quantitative methods. Nevertheless, as discussions of paradigms/methods over the past decade have often begun with a consideration of problems associated with overquantification, we will also begin there, shifting only later to our predominant interest.

The Quantitative/Qualitative Distinction

Historically, there has been a heavy emphasis on quantification in science. Mathematics is often termed the "queen of sciences," and those sciences, such as physics and chemistry, that lend themselves especially well to quantification are generally known as "hard." Less quantifiable arenas, such as biology (although that is rapidly changing) and particularly the social sciences, are

AUTHORS' NOTE: We are grateful to Henry Giroux and Robert Stake for their very helpful critiques of an earlier draft of this chapter.

referred to as "soft," less with pejorative intent than to signal their (putative) imprecision and lack of dependability. Scientific maturity is commonly believed to emerge as the degree of quantification found within a given field increases.

That this is the case is hardly surprising. The "received view" of science (positivism, transformed over the course of this century into postpositivism; see below) focuses on efforts to verify (positivism) or falsify (postpositivism) a priori hypotheses, most usefully stated as mathematical (quantitative) propositions or propositions that can be easily converted into precise mathematical formulas expressing functional relationships. Formulaic precision has enormous utility when the aim of science is the prediction and control of natural phenomena. Further, there is already available a powerful array of statistical and mathematical models. Finally, there exists a widespread conviction that only quantitative data are ultimately valid, or of high quality (Sechrest, 1992).

John Stuart Mill (1843/1906) is said to have been the first to urge social scientists to emulate their older, "harder" cousins, promising that if his advice were followed, rapid maturation of these fields, as well as their emancipation from the philosophical and theological strictures that limited them, would follow. Social scientists took this counsel to heart (probably to a degree that would greatly surprise Mill if he were alive today) for other reasons as well. They were the "new kids on the block"; if quantification could lead to the fulfillment of Mill's promise, status and political leverage would accrue that would enormously profit the new practitioners. Imitation might thus lead both to greater acceptance and to more valid knowledge.

Critiques of the Received View

In recent years, however, strong counterpressures against quantification have emerged. Two critiques, one internal to the conventional paradigm (that is, in terms of those metaphysical assumptions that define the nature of positivist inquiry) and one external to it (that is, in terms of those assumptions defining alternative paradigms), have been mounted that seem not only to warrant a reconsideration of the utility of qualitative data but to question the very assumptions on which the putative superiority of quantification has been based.

Internal (Intraparadigm) Critiques

A variety of implicit problems have surfaced to challenge conventional wisdom; several of these are described below.

Context stripping. Precise quantitative approaches that focus on selected subsets of variables necessarily "strip" from consideration, through appropriate controls or randomization, other variables that exist in the context that might, if allowed to exert their effects, greatly alter findings. Further, such exclusionary designs, while increasing the theoretical rigor of a study, detract from its *relevance,* that is, its applicability or generalizability, because their outcomes can be properly applied only in other similarly truncated or contextually stripped situations (another laboratory, for example). Qualitative data, it is argued, can redress that imbalance by providing contextual information.

Exclusion of meaning and purpose. Human behavior, unlike that of physical objects, cannot be understood without reference to the meanings and purposes attached by human actors to their activities. Qualitative data, it is asserted, can provide rich insight into human behavior.

Disjunction of grand theories with local contexts: The etic/emic dilemma. The etic (outsider) theory brought to bear on an inquiry by an investigator (or the hypotheses proposed to be tested) may have little or no meaning within the emic (insider) view of studied individuals, groups, societies, or cultures. Qualitative data, it is affirmed, are useful for uncovering emic views; theories, to be valid, should be qualitatively grounded (Glaser & Strauss, 1967; Strauss & Corbin, 1990). Such grounding is particularly crucial in view of the mounting criticism of social science as failing to provide adequate accounts of nonmainstream lives (the "other") or to provide the material for a criticism of our own Western culture (Marcus & Fischer, 1986).

Inapplicability of general data to individual cases. This problem is sometimes described as the nomothetic/idiographic disjunction. Generalizations, although perhaps statistically meaningful, have no applicability in the individual case (the fact, say, that 80% of individuals presenting given symptoms have lung cancer is at best incomplete evidence that a particular patient presenting with such symptoms has lung cancer). Qualitative data, it is held, can help to avoid such ambiguities.

Exclusion of the discovery dimension in inquiry. Conventional emphasis on the verification of specific, a priori hypotheses glosses over the source of those hypotheses, usually arrived at by what is commonly termed the discovery process. In the received view only empirical inquiry deserves to be called "science." Quantitative normative methodology is thus privileged over the insights of creative and divergent thinkers. The call for qualitative inputs is expected to redress this imbalance.

External (Extraparadigm) Critiques

The intraparadigm problems noted above offer a weighty challenge to conventional methodology, but could be eliminated, or at least ameliorated, by greater use of qualitative data. Many critics of the received view are content to stop at that point; hence many of the calls for more qualitative inputs have been limited to this methods-level accommodation. But an even weightier challenge has been mounted by critics who have proposed *alternative paradigms* that involve not only qualification of approaches but fundamental adjustments in the basic assumptions that guide inquiry altogether. Their rejection of the received view can be justified on a number of grounds (Bernstein, 1988; Guba, 1990; Hesse, 1980; Lincoln & Guba, 1985; Reason & Rowan, 1981), but chief among them are the following.[1]

The theory-ladenness of facts. Conventional approaches to research involving the verification or falsification of hypotheses assume the independence of theoretical and observational languages. If an inquiry is to be objective, hypotheses must be stated in ways that are independent of the way in which the facts needed to test them are collected. But it now seems established beyond objection that theories and facts are quite *interdependent*—that is, that facts are facts only within some theoretical framework. Thus a fundamental assumption of the received view is exposed as dubious. If hypotheses and observations are not independent, "facts" can be viewed only through a theoretical "window" and objectivity is undermined.

The underdetermination of theory. This problem is also known as the problem of induction. Not only are facts determined by the theory window through which one looks for them, but different theory windows might be equally well supported by the same set of "facts." Although it may be possible, given a coherent theory, to derive by deduction what facts ought to exist, it is never possible, given a coherent set of facts, to arrive by *induction* at a single, ineluctable theory. Indeed, it is this difficulty that led philosophers such as Popper (1968) to reject the notion of theory *verification* in favor of the notion of theory *falsification.* Whereas a million white swans can never establish, with complete confidence, the proposition that all swans are white, one black swan can completely falsify it. The historical position of science that it can, by its methods, ultimately converge on the "real" truth is thus brought sharply into question.

The value-ladenness of facts. Just as theories and facts are not independent, neither are values and facts. Indeed, it can be argued that theories are themselves value statements. Thus putative "facts" are viewed not only through a theory window but through a value window as well. The value-free posture of the received view is compromised.

The interactive nature of the inquirer-inquired into dyad. The received view of science pictures the inquirer as standing behind a one-way mirror, viewing natural phenomena as they happen and recording them objectively. The inquirer (when using proper methodology) does not influence the phenomena or vice versa. But evidence such as the Heisenberg uncertainty principle and the Bohr complementarity principle have shattered that ideal in the hard sciences (Lincoln & Guba, 1985); even greater skepticism must exist for the social sciences. Indeed, the notion that findings are created through the interaction of inquirer and phenomenon (which, in the social sciences, is usually people) is often a more plausible description of the inquiry process than is the notion that findings are discovered through objective observation "as they *really* are, and as they *really* work."

The intraparadigm critiques, although exposing many inherent problems in the received view and, indeed, proposing some useful responses to them, are nevertheless of much less interest—or weight—than the extraparadigm critiques, which raise problems of such consequence that the received view is being widely questioned. Several alternative paradigms have been proposed, some of which rest on quite unconventional assumptions. It is useful, therefore, to inquire about the nature of paradigms and what it is that distinguishes one inquiry paradigm from another.

The Nature of Paradigms

Paradigms as Basic Belief Systems Based on Ontological, Epistemological, and Methodological Assumptions

A paradigm may be viewed as a set of *basic beliefs* (or metaphysics) that deals with ultimates or first principles. It represents a *worldview* that defines, for its holder, the nature of the "world," the individual's place in it, and the range of possible relationships to that world and its parts, as, for example, cosmologies and theologies do.[2] The beliefs are basic in the sense that they must be accepted simply on faith (however well argued); there is no way to establish their ultimate truthfulness. If there were, the philosophical debates reflected in these pages would have been resolved millennia ago.

Inquiry paradigms define for *inquirers* what it is they are about, and what falls within and outside the limits of legitimate inquiry. The basic beliefs that define inquiry paradigms can be summarized by the responses given by proponents of any given paradigm to three fundamental questions, which are interconnected in such a way that the answer given to any one question, taken in any order, constrains how the others may be answered. We have selected an order that we believe reflects a logical (if not necessary) primacy:

1. *The ontological question.* What is the form and nature of reality and, therefore, what is there that can be known about it? For example, if a "real" world is assumed, then what can be known about it is "how things really are" and "how things really work." Then only those questions that relate to matters of "real" existence and "real" action are admissible; other questions, such as those concerning matters of aesthetic or moral significance, fall outside the realm of legitimate scientific inquiry.
2. *The epistemological question.* What is the nature of the relationship between the knower or would-be knower and what can be known? The answer that can be given to this question is constrained by the answer already given to the ontological question; that is, not just *any* relationship can now be postulated. So if, for example, a "real" reality is assumed, then the posture of the knower must be one of objective detachment or value freedom in order to be able to discover "how things really are" and "how things really work." (Conversely, assumption of an objectivist posture implies the existence of a "real" world to be objective about.)
3. *The methodological question.* How can the inquirer (would-be knower) go about finding out whatever he or she believes can be known? Again, the answer that can be given to this question is constrained by answers already given to the first two questions; that is, not just *any* methodology is appropriate. For example, a "real" reality pursued by an "objective" inquirer mandates control of possible confounding factors, whether the methods are qualitative (say, observational) or quantitative (say, analysis of covariance). (Conversely, selection of a manipulative methodology—the experiment, say—implies the ability to be objective and a real world to be objective about.) The methodological question cannot be reduced to a question of methods; methods must be fitted to a predetermined methodology.

These three questions serve as the major foci around which we will analyze each of the four paradigms to be considered.

Paradigms as Human Constructions

We have already noted that paradigms, as sets of basic beliefs, are not open to proof in any conventional sense; there is no way to elevate one over another on the basis of ultimate, foundational criteria. (We should note, however, that that state of affairs does not doom us to a radical relativist posture; see Guba, 1992.) In our opinion, any given paradigm represents simply the most informed and sophisticated view that its proponents have been able to devise, given the way they have chosen to respond to the three defining questions. And, we argue, the sets of answers given are in *all* cases *human constructions*; that is, they are all inventions of the human mind and hence subject to human error. No construction is or can be incontrovertibly right; advocates of any particular construction must rely on *persuasiveness* and *utility* rather than *proof* in arguing their position.

What is true of paradigms is true of our analyses as well. Everything that we shall say subsequently is *also* a human construction: ours. The reader cannot be compelled to accept our analyses, or our arguments, on the basis of incontestable logic or indisputable evidence; we can only hope to be persuasive and to demonstrate the utility of our position for, say, the public policy arena (Guba & Lincoln, 1989; House, 1977). We do ask the reader to suspend his or her disbelief until our argument is complete and can be judged as a whole.

The Basic Beliefs of Received and Alternative Inquiry Paradigms

We begin our analysis with descriptions of the responses that we believe proponents of each paradigm would make to the three questions outlined above. These responses (as constructed by us) are displayed in Table 6.1, which consists of three rows corresponding to the ontological, epistemological, and methodological questions, and four columns corresponding to the four paradigms to be discussed. The term *positivism* denotes the "received view" that has dominated the formal discourse in the physical and social sciences for some 400 years, whereas *postpositivism* repre-

TABLE 6.1 Basic Beliefs (Metaphysics) of Alternative Inquiry Paradigms

Item	*Positivism*	*Postpositivism*	*Critical Theory et al.*	*Constructivism*
Ontology	naive realism—"real" reality but apprehendable	critical realism—"real" reality but only imperfectly and probabilistically apprehendable	historical realism—virtual reality shaped by social, political, cultural, economic, ethnic, and gender values; crystallized over time	relativism—local and specific constructed realities
Epistemology	dualist/objectivist; findings true	modified dualist/objectivist; critical tradition/community; findings probably true	transactional/subjectivist; value-mediated findings	transactional/subjectivist; created findings
Methodology	experimental/manipulative; verification of hypotheses; chiefly quantitative methods	modified experimental/manipulative; critical multiplism; falsification of hypotheses; may include qualitative methods	dialogic/dialectical	hermeneutical/dialectical

sents efforts of the past few decades to respond in a limited way (that is, while remaining within essentially the same set of basic beliefs) to the most problematic criticisms of positivism. The term *critical theory* is (for us) a blanket term denoting a set of several alternative paradigms, including additionally (but not limited to) neo-Marxism, feminism, materialism, and participatory inquiry. Indeed, critical theory may itself usefully be divided into three substrands: poststructuralism, postmodernism, and a blending of these two. Whatever their differences, the common breakaway assumption of all these variants is that of the value-determined nature of inquiry—an epistemological difference. Our grouping of these positions into a single category is a judgment call; we will not try to do justice to the individual points of view. The term *constructivism* denotes an alternative paradigm whose breakaway assumption is the move from ontological realism to ontological relativism. These positions will become clear in the subsequent exposition.

Two important caveats need to be mentioned. First, although we are inclined to believe that the paradigms we are about to describe can have meaning even in the realm of the physical sciences, we will not defend that belief here. Accordingly, our subsequent comments should be understood to be limited to the *social sciences* only. Second, we note that except for positivism, the paradigms discussed are all still in formative stages; no final agreements have been reached even among their proponents about their definitions, meanings, or implications. Thus our discussion should be considered tentative and subject to further revision and reformulation.

We will first look down the columns of Table 6.1 to illustrate the positions of each paradigm with respect to the three questions, following with a look across rows to compare and contrast the positions of the paradigms.[3] Limitations of space make it impossible for us to develop our assertions in any depth. The reader will be able to find other evidence, pro and con, in other chapters of this volume, particularly in Chapters 7-11.

Intraparadigm Analyses (Columns of Table 6.1)

Column 1: Positivism

Ontology: realism (commonly called "naive realism"). An apprehendable reality is assumed to exist, driven by immutable natural laws and mechanisms. Knowledge of the "way things are" is conventionally summarized in the form of time- and context-free generalizations, some of which take the form of cause-effect laws. Research can, in principle, converge on the "true" state of affairs. The basic posture of the paradigm is argued to be both reductionist and deterministic (Hesse, 1980).

Epistemology: Dualist and objectivist. The investigator and the investigated "object" are assumed to be independent entities, and the investigator to be capable of studying the object without influencing it or being influenced by it. When influence in either direction (threats to validity) is recognized, or even suspected, various strategies are followed to reduce or eliminate it. Inquiry takes place as through a one-way mirror. Values and biases are prevented from influencing outcomes, so long as the prescribed procedures are rigorously followed. Replicable findings are, in fact, "true."

Methodology: Experimental and manipulative. Questions and/or hypotheses are stated in propositional form and subjected to empirical test to verify them; possible confounding conditions must be carefully controlled (manipulated) to prevent outcomes from being improperly influenced.

Column 2: Postpositivism

Ontology: Critical realism. Reality is assumed to exist but to be only imperfectly apprehendable because of basically flawed human intellectual mechanisms and the fundamentally intractable nature of phenomena. The ontology is labeled as critical realism (Cook & Campbell, 1979) because of the posture of proponents that claims about reality must be subjected to the widest possible critical examination to facilitate apprehending reality as closely as possible (but never perfectly).

Epistemology: Modified dualist/objectivist. Dualism is largely abandoned as not possible to maintain, but objectivity remains a "regulatory ideal"; special emphasis is placed on external "guardians" of objectivity such as critical traditions (Do the findings "fit" with preexisting knowledge?) and the critical community (such as editors, referees, and professional peers). Replicated findings are *probably* true (but always subject to falsification).

Methodology: Modified experimental/manipulative. Emphasis is placed on "critical multiplism" (a refurbished version of triangulation) as a way of falsifying (rather than verifying) hypotheses. The methodology aims to redress some of the problems noted above (intraparadigm critiques) by doing inquiry in more natural settings, collecting more situational information, and reintroducing discovery as an element in inquiry, and, in the social sciences particularly, soliciting emic viewpoints to assist in determining the meanings and purposes that people ascribe to their actions, as well as to contribute to "grounded theory" (Glaser & Strauss, 1967; Strauss & Corbin, 1990). All these aims are accomplished largely through the increased utilization of qualitative techniques.

Column 3: Critical Theory
and Related Ideological Positions

Ontology: Historical realism. A reality is assumed to be apprehendable that was once plastic, but that was, over time, shaped by a congeries of social, political, cultural, economic, ethnic, and gender factors, and then crystallized (reified) into a series of structures that are now (inappropriately) taken as "real," that is, natural and immutable. For all practical purposes the structures *are* "real," a virtual or historical reality.

Epistemology: Transactional and subjectivist. The investigator and the investigated object are assumed to be interactively linked, with the values of the investigator (and of situated "others") inevitably influencing the inquiry. Findings are therefore *value mediated.* Note that this posture effectively challenges the traditional distinction between ontology and epistemology; what can be known is inextricably intertwined with the interaction between a *particular* investigator and a *particular* object or group. The dashed line separating the ontological and epistemological rows of Table 6.1 is intended to reflect this fusion.

Methodology: Dialogic and dialectical. The transactional nature of inquiry requires a dialogue between the investigator and the subjects of the inquiry; that dialogue must be dialectical in nature to transform ignorance and misapprehensions (accepting historically mediated structures as immutable) into more informed consciousness (seeing how the structures might be changed and comprehending the actions required to effect change), or, as Giroux (1988) puts it, "as transformative intellectuals, . . . to uncover and excavate those forms of historical and subjugated knowledges that point to experiences of suffering, conflict, and collective struggle; . . . to link the notion of historical understanding to elements of critique and hope" (p. 213). Transformational inquirers demonstrate "transformational leadership" (Burns, 1978).

(For more discussion of critical theory, see the contributions in this volume by Olesen, Chapter 9; Stanfield, Chapter 10; and Kincheloe & McLaren, Chapter 8.)

Column 4: Constructivism

Ontology: Relativist. Realities are apprehendable in the form of multiple, intangible mental constructions, socially and experientially based, local and specific in nature (although elements are often shared among many individuals and even across cultures), and dependent for their form and content on the individual persons or groups holding the constructions. Constructions are not more or less "true," in any absolute sense, but simply more or less informed and/or sophisticated. Constructions are alterable, as are their associated "realities." This position should be distinguished from both nominalism and idealism (see Reese, 1980, for an explication of these several ideas).

Epistemology: Transactional and subjectivist. The investigator and the object of investigation are assumed to be interactively linked so that the "findings" are *literally created* as the investigation proceeds. The conventional distinction between ontology and epistemology disappears, as in the case of critical theory. Again, the dashed line of Table 6.1 reflects this fact.

Methodology: Hermeneutical and dialectical. The variable and personal (intramental) nature of social constructions suggests that individual constructions can be elicited and refined only through interaction *between and among* investigator and respondents. These varying constructions are interpreted using conventional hermeneutical techniques, and are compared and contrasted through a dialectical interchange. The final aim is to distill a consensus construction that is more informed and sophisticated than any of the predecessor constructions (including, of course, the etic construction of the investigator).

(For more about constructivism, see also Schwandt, Chapter 7, this volume.)

Cross-Paradigm Analyses (Rows of Table 6.1)

Having noted briefly the positions that proponents of each paradigm might take with respect to the three paradigm-defining questions, it is useful to look across rows to compare and contrast those positions among the several paradigms.

Ontology

Moving from left to right across Table 6.1, we note the move from

1. positivism's position of naive realism, assuming an objective external reality upon which inquiry can converge; to
2. postpositivism's critical realism, which still assumes an objective reality but grants that it can be apprehended only imperfectly and probabilistically; to
3. critical theory's historical realism, which assumes an apprehendable reality consisting of historically situated structures that are, in the absence of insight, as limiting and confining as if they were real; to
4. constructivism's relativism, which assumes multiple, apprehendable, and sometimes conflicting social realities that are the products of human intellects, but that may change as their constructors become more informed and sophisticated.

It is the ontological position that most differentiates constructivism from the other three paradigms.

Epistemology

We note the move from

1. positivism's dualist, objectivist assumption that enables the investigator to determine "how things really are" and "how things really work"; to
2. postpositivism's modified dualist/objectivist assumption that it is possible to approximate (but never fully know) reality; to
3. critical theory's transactional/subjectivist assumption that knowledge is value mediated and hence value dependent; to
4. constructivism's somewhat similar but broader transactional/subjectivist assumption that sees knowledge as created in interaction among investigator and respondents.

It is their epistemological positions that most differentiate critical theory and constructivism from the other two paradigms.

Methodology

We note the move from

1. positivism's experimental/manipulative methodology that focuses on verification of hypotheses; to
2. postpositivism's modified experimental/manipulative methodology invested in critical multiplism focusing on falsification of hypotheses; to

TABLE 6.2 Paradigm Positions on Selected Practical Issues

Issue	*Positivism*	*Postpositivism*	*Critical Theory et al.*	*Constructivism*
Inquiry aim	explanation: prediction and control		critique and transformation; restitution and emancipation	understanding; reconstruction
Nature of knowledge	verified hypotheses established as facts or laws	nonfalsified hypotheses that are probable facts or laws	structural/historical insights	individual reconstructions coalescing around consensus
Knowledge accumulation	accretion—"building blocks" adding to "edifice of knowledge"; generalizations and cause-effect linkages		historical revisionism; generalization by similarity	more informed and sophisticated reconstructions; vicarious experience
Goodness or quality criteria	conventional benchmarks of "rigor": internal and external validity, reliability, and objectivity		historical situatedness; erosion of ignorance and misapprehensions; action stimulus	trustworthiness and authenticity
Values	excluded—influence denied		included—formative	
Ethics	extrinsic; tilt toward deception		intrinsic; moral tilt toward revelation	intrinsic; process tilt toward revelation; special problems
Voice	"disinterested scientist" as informer of decision makers, policy makers, and change agents		"transformative intellectual" as advocate and activist	"passionate participant" as facilitator of multi-voice reconstruction
Training	technical and quantitative; substantive theories	technical; quantitative and qualitative; substantive theories	resocialization; qualitative and quantitative; history; values of altruism and empowerment	
Accommodation	commensurable		incommensurable	
Hegemony	in control of publication, funding, promotion, and tenure		seeking recognition and input	

3. critical theory's *dialogic/dialectical* methodology aimed at the reconstruction of previously held constructions; to
4. constructivism's hermeneutic/dialectic methodology aimed at the reconstruction of previously held constructions.

Implications of Each Paradigm's Position on Selected Practical Issues (Rows of Table 6.2)

Differences in paradigm assumptions cannot be dismissed as mere "philosophical" differences; implicitly or explicitly, these positions have important consequences for the practical conduct of inquiry, as well as for the interpretation of findings and policy choices. We have elected to discuss these consequences for ten salient issues.

The entries in Table 6.2, which consists of four columns corresponding to the four paradigms and ten rows corresponding to the ten issues, summarize our interpretation of the major implications. The reader will note that the first four issues (inquiry aim, nature of knowledge, knowledge accumulation, and quality criteria) are among those deemed especially important by positivists and postpositivists; they are therefore the issues on which alternative paradigms are most frequently attacked. The fifth and sixth (values and ethics) are issues taken seriously by all paradigms, although conventional and emergent responses are quite different. Finally, the last four issues (voice, training, accommodation, and hegemony) are those deemed especially important by alternative proponents; they represent areas on which the received view is considered particularly vulnerable. The entries in the table are based only in part on public positions, given that not all issues have been addressed by all paradigms' proponents. In some cases, therefore, we have supplied entries that we believe follow logically from the basic metaphysical (ontological, epistemological, and methodological) postures of the paradigms. To take one example, the issue of voice is rarely addressed directly by positivists or postpositivists, but we believe the entry "disinterested scientist" is one that would be given by those proponents were they to be challenged on this matter.

An immediately apparent difference between Table 6.1 and Table 6.2 is that whereas in the former case it was possible to make a distinct entry for every cell, in the case of Table 6.2 there is considerable overlap within rows, particularly for the positivist and postpositivist columns. Indeed, even for those issues in which the entries in those two columns are different, the differences appear to be minor. In contrast, one may note the major differences found between these two paradigms and the critical theory and constructivist paradigms, which tend also to differ among themselves.

We have formulated the issues as questions, which follow.

Row 1: What is the aim or purpose of inquiry?

Positivism and postpositivism. For both these paradigms the aim of inquiry is *explanation* (von Wright, 1971), ultimately enabling the *prediction and control* of phenomena, whether physical or human. As Hesse (1980) has suggested, the ultimate criterion for progress in these paradigms is that the capability of "scientists" to predict and control should improve over time. The reductionism and determinism implied by this position should be noted. The inquirer is cast in the role of "expert," a situation that seems to award special, perhaps even unmerited, privilege to the investigator.

Critical theory. The aim of inquiry is the *critique and transformation* of the social, political, cultural, economic, ethnic, and gender structures that constrain and exploit humankind, by engagement in confrontation, even conflict. The criterion for progress is that over time, restitution and emancipation should occur and persist. Advocacy and activism are key concepts. The inquirer is cast in the role of instigator and facilitator, implying that the inquirer understands a priori what transformations are needed. But we should note that some of the more radical stances in the criticalist camp hold that judgment about needed transformations should be reserved to those whose lives are most affected by transformations: the inquiry participants themselves (Lincoln, in press).

Constructivism. The aim of inquiry is *understanding and reconstruction* of the constructions that people (including the inquirer) initially hold, aiming toward consensus but still open to new interpretations as information and sophistication improve. The criterion for progress is that over time, everyone formulates more informed and sophisticated constructions and becomes more aware of the content and meaning of competing constructions. Advocacy and activism are also key concepts is this view. The inquirer is cast in the role of participant and facilitator in this process, a position that some critics have faulted on the grounds that it expands the inquirer's role beyond reasonable expectations of expertise and competence (Carr & Kemmis, 1986).

Row 2: What is the nature of knowledge?

Positivism. Knowledge consists of verified hypotheses that can be accepted as facts or laws.

Postpositivism. Knowledge consists of nonfalsified hypotheses that can be regarded as probable facts or laws.

Critical theory. Knowledge consists of a series of structural/historical insights that will be transformed as time passes. Transformations occur when ignorance and misapprehensions give way to more informed insights by means of a dialectical interaction.

Constructivism. Knowledge consists of those constructions about which there is relative consensus (or at least some movement toward consensus) among those competent (and, in the case of more arcane material, trusted) to interpret the substance of the construction. Multiple "knowledges" can coexist when equally competent (or trusted) interpreters disagree, and/or depending on social, political, cultural, economic, ethnic, and gender factors that differentiate the interpreters. These constructions are subject to continuous revision, with changes most likely to occur when relatively different constructions are brought into juxtaposition in a dialectical context.

Row 3: How does knowledge accumulate?

Positivism and postpositivism. Knowledge accumulates by a process of accretion, with each fact (or probable fact) serving as a kind of building block that, when placed into its proper niche, adds to the growing "edifice of knowledge." When the facts take the form of generalizations or cause-effect linkages, they may be used most efficiently for prediction and control. Generalizations may then be made, with predictable confidence, to a population of settings.

Critical theory. Knowledge does not accumulate in an absolute sense; rather, it grows and changes through a dialectical process of historical revision that continuously erodes ignorance and misapprehensions and enlarges more informed insights. Generalization can occur when the mix of social, political, cultural, economic, ethnic, and gender circumstances and values is similar across settings.

Constructivism. Knowledge accumulates only in a relative sense through the formation of ever more informed and sophisticated constructions via the hermeneutical/dialectical process, as varying constructions are brought into juxtaposition. One important mechanism for transfer of knowledge from one setting to another is the provision of vicarious experience, often supplied by case study reports (see Stake, Chapter 14, this volume).

Row 4: What criteria are appropriate for judging the goodness or quality of an inquiry?

Positivism and postpositivism. The appropriate criteria are the conventional benchmarks of "rigor": internal validity (isomorphism of findings with reality), external validity (generalizability), reliability (in the sense of stability), and objectivity (distanced and neutral observer). These criteria depend on the realist ontological position; without the assumption, isomorphism of findings with reality can have no meaning, strict generalizability to a parent population is impossible, stability cannot be assessed for inquiry into a phenomenon if the phenomenon itself can change, and objectivity cannot be achieved because there is nothing from which one can be "distant."

Critical theory. The appropriate criteria are historical situatedness of the inquiry (i.e., that it takes account of the social, political, cultural, economic, ethnic, and gender antecedents of the studied situation), the extent to which the inquiry acts to erode ignorance and misapprehensions, and the extent to which it provides a stimulus to action, that is, to the transformation of the existing structure.

Constructivism. Two sets of criteria have been proposed: the *trustworthiness* criteria of credibility (paralleling internal validity), transferability (paralleling external validity), dependability (paralleling reliability), and confirmability (paralleling objectivity) (Guba, 1981; Lincoln & Guba, 1985); and the *authenticity* criteria of fairness, ontological authenticity (enlarges personal constructions), educative authenticity (leads to improved understanding of constructions of others), catalytic authenticity (stimulates to action), and tactical authenticity (empowers action) (Guba & Lincoln, 1989). The former set represents an early effort to resolve the quality issue for constructivism; although these criteria have been well received, their parallelism to positivist criteria makes them suspect. The latter set overlaps to some extent those of critical theory but goes beyond them, particularly the two of ontological authenticity and educative authenticity. The issue of quality criteria in constructivism is nevertheless not well resolved, and further critique is needed.

Row 5: What is the role of values in inquiry?

Positivism and postpositivism. In both these paradigms values are specifically excluded; indeed, the paradigm is claimed to be "value free" by virtue of its epistemological posture. Values are seen as confounding variables that cannot be allowed a role in a putatively objective inquiry (even when objectivity is, in the case of postpositivism, but a regulatory ideal).

Critical theory and constructivism. In both these paradigms values have pride of place; they are seen as ineluctable in shaping (in the case of constructivism, creating) inquiry outcomes. Furthermore, even if it were possible, excluding values would not be countenanced. To do so would be inimical to the interests of the powerless and of "at-risk" audiences, whose original (emic) constructions deserve equal consideration with those of other, more powerful audiences and of the inquirer (etic). Constructivism, which sees the inquirer as orchestrator and facilitator of the inquiry process, is more likely to stress this point than is critical theory, which tends to cast the inquirer in a more authoritative role.

Row 6: What is the place of ethics in inquiry?

Positivism and postpositivism. In both these paradigms ethics is an important consideration, and it is taken very seriously by inquirers, but it is *extrinsic* to the inquiry process itself. Hence ethical behavior is formally policed by *external* mechanisms, such as professional codes of conduct and human subjects committees. Further, the realist ontology undergirding these paradigms provides a tilt toward the use of deception, which, it is argued in certain cases, is warranted to determine how "things *really* are and work" or for the sake of some "higher social good" or some "clearer truth" (Bok, 1978, 1982; Diener & Crandall, 1978).

Critical theory. Ethics is more nearly *intrinsic* to this paradigm, as implied by the intent to erode ignorance and misapprehensions, and to take full account of values and historical situatedness in the inquiry process. Thus there is a moral tilt that the inquirer be revelatory (in the rigorous meaning of "fully informed consent") rather than deceptive. Of course, these considerations do not *prevent* unethical behavior, but they do provide some process barriers that make it more difficult.

Constructivism. Ethics is *intrinsic* to this paradigm also because of the inclusion of participant values in the inquiry (starting with respondents' existing constructions and working toward increased information and sophistication in their constructions as well as in the inquirer's construction). There is an incentive—a *process tilt*—for revelation; hiding the inquirer's intent is destructive of the aim of uncovering and improving constructions. In addition, the hermeneutical/dialectical methodology itself provides a strong but not infallible safeguard against deception. However, the close personal interactions required by the methodology may produce special and often sticky problems of confidentiality and anonymity, as well as other interpersonal difficulties (Guba & Lincoln, 1989).

Row 7: What "voice" is mirrored in the inquirer's activities, especially those directed at change?

Positivism and postpositivism. The inquirer's voice is that of the "disinterested scientist" informing decision makers, policy makers, and change agents, who independently use this scientific information, at least in part, to form, explain, and justify actions, policies, and change proposals.

Critical theory. The inquirer's voice is that of the "transformative intellectual" (Giroux, 1988) who has expanded consciousness and so is in a position to confront ignorance and misapprehensions. Change is facilitated as individuals develop greater insight into the existing state of affairs (the nature and extent of their exploitation) and are stimulated to act on it.

Constructivism. The inquirer's voice is that of the "passionate participant" (Lincoln, 1991) actively engaged in facilitating the "multivoice" reconstruction of his or her own construction as well as those of all other participants. Change is facilitated as reconstructions are formed and individuals are stimulated to act on them.

Row 8: What are the implications of each paradigm for the training of novice inquirers?

Positivism. Novices are trained primarily in technical knowledge about measurement, design, and quantitative methods, with less but substantial emphasis on formal theories of the phenomena in their substantive specialties.

Postpositivism. Novices are trained in ways paralleling the positivist mode, but with the addition of qualitative methods, often for the purpose of ameliorating the problems noted in the opening paragraphs of this chapter.

Critical theory and constructivism. Novices must first be resocialized from their early and usually intense exposure to the received view of science. That resocialization cannot be accomplished without thorough schooling in the postures and techniques of positivism and postpositivism. Students must come to appreciate paradigm differences (summarized in Table 6.1) and, in that context, to master both qualitative and quantitative methods. The former are essential because of their role in carrying out the dialogic/dialectical or hermeneutical/dialectical methodologies; the latter because they can play a useful informational role in all paradigms. They must also be helped to understand the social, political, cultural, economic, ethnic, and gender history and structure that serve as the surround for their inquiries, and to incorporate the values of altruism and empowerment in their work.

Row 9: Are these paradigms necessarily in conflict? Is it possible to accommodate these several views within a single conceptual framework?

Positivism and postpositivism. Proponents of these two paradigms, given their foundational orientation, take the position that all paradigms can be accommodated—that is, that there exists, or will be found to exist, some common rational structure to which all questions of difference can be referred for resolution. The posture is reductionist and assumes the possibility of point-by-point comparisons (commensurability), an issue about which there continues to be a great deal of disagreement.

Critical theory and constructivism. Proponents of these two paradigms join in affirming the basic incommensurability of the paradigms (although they would agree that positivism and postpositivism are commensurable, and would probably agree that critical theory and constructivism are commensurable). The basic beliefs of the paradigms are believed to be essentially contradictory. For constructivists, either there is a "real" reality or there is not (although one might wish to resolve this problem differently in considering the physical versus the human realms), and thus constructivism and positivism/postpositivism cannot be logically accommodated anymore than, say, the ideas of flat versus round earth can be logically accommodated. For critical theorists and constructivists, inquiry is either value free or it is not; again, logical accommodation seems impossible. Realism and relativism, value freedom and value boundedness, cannot coexist in any internally consistent metaphysical system, which condition of consistency, it is stipulated, is essentially met by each of the candidate paradigms. Resolution of this dilemma will necessarily await the emergence of a metaparadigm that renders the older, accommodated paradigms not less true, but simply irrelevant.

Row 10: Which of the
paradigms exercises hegemony over
the others? That is,
which is predominantly influential?

Positivism and postpositivism. Proponents of positivism gained hegemony over the past several centuries as earlier Aristotelian and theological paradigms were abandoned. But the mantle of hegemony has in recent decades gradually fallen on the shoulders of the postpositivists, the "natural" heirs of positivism. Postpositivists (and indeed many residual positivists) tend to control publication outlets, funding sources, promotion and tenure mechanisms, dissertation committees, and other sources of power and influence. They were, at least until about 1980, the "in" group, and continue to represent the strongest voice in professional decision making.

Critical theory and constructivism. Proponents of critical theory and constructivism are still seeking recognition and avenues for input. Over the past decade, it has become more and more possible for them to achieve acceptance, as attested by increasing inclusion of relevant papers in journals and professional meetings, the development of new journal outlets, the growing acceptability of "qualitative" dissertations, the inclusion of "qualitative" guidelines by some funding agencies and programs, and the like. But in all likelihood, critical theory and constructivism will continue to play secondary, although important and progressively more influential, roles in the near future.

Conclusion

The metaphor of the "paradigm wars" described by Gage (1989) is undoubtedly overdrawn. Describing the discussions and altercations of the past decade or two as wars paints the matter as more confrontational than necessary. A resolution of paradigm differences can occur only when a new paradigm emerges that is more informed and sophisticated than any existing one. That is most likely to occur if and when proponents of these several points of view come together to discuss their differences, not to argue the sanctity of their views. Continuing dialogue among paradigm proponents of all stripes will afford the best avenue for moving toward a responsive and congenial relationship.

We hope that in this chapter we have illustrated the need for such a discussion by clearly delineating the differences that currently exist, and by showing that those differences have significant implications at the practical level. Paradigm issues are crucial; no inquirer, we maintain, ought to go about the business of inquiry without being clear about just what paradigm informs and guides his or her approach.

Notes

1. Many of the objections listed here were first enunciated by positivists themselves; indeed, we might argue that the postpositivist position represents an attempt to transform positivism in ways that take account of these same objections. The naive positivist position of the sixteenth through the nineteenth centuries is no longer held by anyone even casually acquainted with these problems. Although we would concede that the postpositivist position, as enunciated, for example, by Denis Phillips (1987, 1990a, 1990b), represents a considerable improvement over classic positivism, it fails to make a clean break. It represents a kind of "damage control" rather than a reformulation of basic principles. The notion that these problems required a paradigm shift was poorly recognized until the publication of Thomas Kuhn's landmark work, *The Structure of Scientific Revolutions* (1962, 1970), and even then proceeded but slowly. Nevertheless, the contributions of pre-Kuhnian critics should be recognized and applauded.

2. We are reminded by Robert Stake (personal communication, 1993) that the view of paradigms that we present here should not "exclude a belief that there are

worlds within worlds, unending, each with its own paradigms. Infinitesimals have their own cosmologies."

3. It is unlikely that a practitioner of any paradigm would agree that our summaries closely describe what he or she thinks or does. Workaday scientists rarely have either the time or the inclination to assess what they do in philosophical terms. We do contend, however, that these descriptions are apt as broad brush strokes, if not always at the individual level.

References

Bernstein, R. (1988). *Beyond objectivism and relativism.* Philadelphia: University of Pennsylvania Press.

Bok, S. (1978). *Lies: Moral choice in public and private life.* New York: Random House.

Bok, S. (1982). *Secrets: On the ethics of concealment and revelation.* New York: Pantheon.

Burns, J. (1978). *Leadership.* New York: Harper.

Carr, W., & Kemmis, S. (1986). *Becoming critical: Education, knowledge and action research.* London: Falmer.

Cook, T., & Campbell, D. T. (1979). *Quasi-experimentation: Design and analysis issues for field settings.* Chicago: Rand McNally.

Diener, E., & Crandall, R. (1978). *Ethics in social and behavioral research.* Chicago: University of Chicago Press.

Gage, N. (1989). The paradigm wars and their aftermath: A "historical" sketch of research and teaching since 1989. *Educational Research, 18,* 4-10.

Giroux, H. (1988). *Schooling and the struggle for public life: Critical pedagogy in the modern age.* Minneapolis: University of Minnesota Press.

Glaser, B. G., & Strauss, A. L. (1967). *The discovery of grounded theory: Strategies for qualitative research.* Chicago: Aldine.

Guba, E. G. (1981). Criteria for assessing the trustworthiness of naturalistic inquiries. *Educational Communication and Technology Journal, 29,* 75-92.

Guba, E. G. (Ed.). (1990). *The paradigm dialog.* Newbury Park, CA: Sage.

Guba, E. G. (1992). Relativism. *Curriculum Inquiry, 22,* 17-24.

Guba, E. G., & Lincoln, Y. S. (1989). *Fourth generation evaluation.* Newbury Park, CA: Sage.

Hesse, E. (1980). *Revolutions and reconstructions in the philosophy of science.* Bloomington: Indiana University Press.

House, E. (1977). *The logic of evaluative argument.* Los Angeles: University of California, Center for the Study of Evaluation.

Kuhn, T. S. (1962). *The structure of scientific revolutions.* Chicago: University of Chicago Press.

Kuhn, T. S. (1970). *The structure of scientific revolutions* (2nd ed.). Chicago: University of Chicago Press.

Lincoln, Y. S. (1991). *The detached observer and the passionate participant: Discourses in inquiry and science.* Paper presented at the annual meeting of the American Educational Research Association, Chicago.

Lincoln, Y. S. (in press). I and thou: Method and voice in research with the silenced. In D. McLaughlin & W. Tierney (Eds.), *Naming silenced lives.* New York: Praeger.

Lincoln, Y. S., & Guba, E. G. (1985). *Naturalistic inquiry.* Beverly Hills, CA: Sage.

Marcus, G., & Fischer, M. (1986). *Anthropology as cultural critique: An experimental moment in the human sciences.* Chicago: University of Chicago Press.

Mill, J. S. (1906). *A system of logic.* London: Longmans Green. (Original work published 1843)

Phillips, D. C. (1987). *Philosophy, science, and social inquiry.* Oxford: Pergamon.

Phillips, D. C. (1990a). Postpositivistic science: Myths and realities. In E. G. Guba (Ed.), *The paradigm dialog* (pp. 31-45). Newbury Park, CA: Sage.

Phillips, D. C. (1990b). Subjectivity and objectivity: An objective inquiry. In E. Eisner & A. Peshkin (Eds.), *Qualitative inquiry in education* (pp. 19-37). New York: Teachers College Press.

Popper, K. (1968). *Conjectures and refutations.* New York: Harper & Row.

Reason, P., & Rowan, J. (1981). *Human inquiry.* New York: John Wiley.

Reese, W. (1980). *Dictionary of philosophy and religion.* Atlantic Highlands, NJ: Humanities Press.

Sechrest, L. (1992). Roots: Back to our first generations. *Evaluation Practice, 13,* 1-8.

Strauss, A. L., & Corbin, J. (1990). *Basics of qualitative research: Grounded theory procedures and techniques.* Newbury Park, CA: Sage.

von Wright, G. (1971). *Explanation and understanding.* London: Routledge & Kegan Paul.

7

Constructivist, Interpretivist Approaches to Human Inquiry

THOMAS A. SCHWANDT

CONSTRUCTIVIST, constructivism, interpretivist, and *interpretivism* are terms that routinely appear in the lexicon of social science methodologists and philosophers. Yet, their particular meanings are shaped by the intent of their users. As general descriptors for a loosely coupled family of methodological and philosophical persuasions, these terms are best regarded as sensitizing concepts (Blumer, 1954). They steer the interested reader in the general direction of where instances of a particular kind of inquiry can be found. However, they "merely suggest directions along which to look" rather than "provide descriptions of what to see" (p. 7).[1]

Proponents of these persuasions share the goal of understanding the complex world of lived experience from the point of view of those who live it. This goal is variously spoken of as an abiding concern for the life world, for the emic point of view, for understanding meaning, for grasping the actor's definition of a situation, for *Verstehen.* The world of lived reality and situation-specific meanings that constitute the general object of investigation is thought to be constructed by social actors. That is, particular actors, in particular places, at particular times, fashion meaning out of events and phenomena through prolonged, complex processes of social interaction involving history, language, and action.

The constructivist or interpretivist believes that to understand this world of meaning one must interpret it. The inquirer must elucidate the process of meaning construction and clarify what and how meanings are embodied in the language and actions of social actors. To prepare an interpretation is itself to construct a reading of these meanings; it is to offer the inquirer's construction of the constructions of the actors one studies.

Although they share this general framework for human inquiry, constructivist and interpretivist persuasions are unique in the manner in which each answers these questions: What is the purpose and aim of human inquiry (as distinct from inquiry into the physical world)? How can we know about the world of human action? Each particular persuasion offers a somewhat different conceptualization of what we are about when we inquire into the world of social agents and historical actors.

Furthermore, what is unusual about these approaches cannot be explained through an examination of their methods.[2] They are principally concerned with matters of knowing and being, not method per se. As Harry Wolcott (1988, 1992) and Frederick Erickson (1986) have noted, not

AUTHOR'S NOTE: Thanks to Colleen Larson, John K. Smith, Harry Wolcott, Norman Denzin, and Yvonna Lincoln for their comments on an earlier draft of this chapter.

only are methods the most unremarkable aspect of interpretive work, but a focus on methods (techniques for gathering and analyzing data) often masks a full understanding of the relationship between method and inquiry purpose. The aim of attending carefully to the details, complexity, and situated meanings of the everyday life world can be achieved through a variety of methods. Although we may feel professionally compelled to use a special language for these procedures (e.g., participant observation, informant interviewing, archival research), at base, all interpretive inquirers watch, listen, ask, record, and examine. How those activities might best be defined and employed depends on the inquirer's purpose for doing the inquiry. Purpose, in turn, is shaped by epistemological and methodological commitments.[3]

Mindful of the risk of drawing too fine a distinction between interpretivist and constructivist perspectives that share a common intellectual heritage, I have nonetheless chosen to discuss the two separately. In the first section of this chapter I examine interpretivism, beginning with a general sketch of some critical issues in social science epistemology that shape this family of persuasions. I then single out several particular interpretivist approaches for a closer look at how each defines the purpose of human inquiry. These include Clifford Geertz's view of interpretive anthropology, the Herbert Blumer-G. H. Mead version of symbolic interactionism, and Norman Denzin's reformulation of interpretive interactionism.

In the second section, I introduce constructivist thinking through the work of Nelson Goodman. I then discuss Ernst von Glasersfeld's radical constructivism, Kenneth Gergen's social constructionism, feminist standpoint epistemologies, Egon Guba and Yvonna Lincoln's constructivist paradigm, and Elliot Eisner's aesthetic approach to educational inquiry as illustrations of constructivist thinking.[4] I conclude the chapter with an overview of several kinds of criticisms often made of both constructivist and interpretivist approaches.

Interpretivist Thinking

Overview

Painted in broad strokes, the canvas of interpretivism is layered with ideas stemming from the German intellectual tradition of hermeneutics and the *Verstehen* tradition in sociology, the phenomenology of Alfred Schutz, and critiques of scientism and positivism in the social sciences influenced by the writings of ordinary language philosophers critical of logical empiricism (e.g., Peter Winch, A. R. Louch, Isaiah Berlin).[5] Historically, at least, interpretivists argued for the uniqueness of human inquiry. They crafted various refutations of the naturalistic interpretation of the social sciences (roughly the view that the aims and methods of the social sciences are identical to those of the natural sciences). They held that the mental sciences (*Geisteswissenschaften*) or cultural sciences (*Kulturwissenschaften*) were different in kind than the natural sciences (*Naturwissenschaften*): The goal of the latter is scientific explanation (*Erklären*), whereas the goal of the former is the grasping or understanding (*Verstehen*) of the "meaning" of social phenomena.[6]

Owing in part to unresolved tensions between their rationalist and romanticist roots, interpretivists wrestle with maintaining the opposition of subjectivity and objectivity, engagement and objectification (Denzin, 1992; Hammersley, 1989). They celebrate the permanence and priority of the real world of first-person, subjective experience. Yet, in true Cartesian fashion, they seek to disengage from that experience and objectify it.[7] They struggle with drawing a line between the object of investigation and the investigator. The paradox of how to develop an objective interpretive science of subjective human experience thus arises. This grappling with a synthesis of phenomenological subjectivity and scientific objectivity is evident in Wilhelm Dilthey's bid to find a basis for the *scientific* investigation of meaning, in Max Weber's struggles with the relationship between the interpretation of meaning and causal explanations and the separation of facts and values in social inquiry, and in Alfred Schutz's analysis of the operation of *Verstehen*.

Contemporary theoretical descendants of these interpretivist founders have addressed this paradox in several ways. Hammersley (1992a, 1992b) is representative of interpretivists who pursue a synthesis between social realism and constructivism. LeCompte and Preissle (1993) and Kirk and Miller (1986) seek refuge in methods as error-elimination strategies. John K. Smith (1989, p. 158) calls this the "middle ground" of methodology: It rejects certain negative characteristics of empiricist thinking but simultaneously holds that inquirers must avoid the subjectivity and error of naive inquiry through the judicious use of method.[8]

A third response is to deny the opposition of subjectivity and objectivity and overcome it by fully accepting the hermeneutical character of existence. Paul Rabinow and William Sullivan (1987) endorse this view, following a line of argument advanced by Martin Heidegger, Hans-Georg Gadamer, and Charles Taylor. They claim that the activity of interpretation is not simply a methodological option open to the social scientist, but rather the very condition of human inquiry itself: "The interpretive turn is not simply a new methodology, but rather a challenge to the very idea that inquiry into the social world and the value of the understanding that results is to be determined by methodology" (p. 20).

This third interpretivist position assumes that the defining characteristic of an *ontological* hermeneutics is that linguisticality (*Sprachlichkeit*) and historicality (*Geschichtlichkeit*) are constitutive of being human (Wachterhauser, 1986). In other words, we do not simply live out our lives *in* time and *through* language; rather, we *are* our history. The fact that language and history are both the condition and the limit of understanding is what makes the process of meaning construction hermeneutical.

Philosophical Anthropology

Viewed from the perspective of philosophical anthropology (the study of the basic categories in which humans and human behavior are to be described and explained) interpretivism holds that human behavior is purposive (Bruner, 1990; Magoon, 1977). Interpretivists repudiate mechanistic, neobehaviorist, associationist (i.e., acquisition of associated connections between stimuli and responses) explanations of behavior in favor of teleological explanations. Social agents are considered autonomous, intentional, active, goal directed; they construe, construct, and interpret their own behavior and that of their fellow agents.[9]

Not surprisingly, given that they reject the unity of the sciences argument, interpretivists, in general, disavow much of the empiricist epistemology and methodology that is intimately associated with a neobehaviorist psychology and philosophical anthropology. For example, they reject the notions of a theory-neutral data language, operationism, and the covering law model of explanation.

Because they focus on meaning as primary, interpretivists construe the nature of social reality quite differently from those who support empiricist social science frameworks. As Taylor (1971/1987) explains, for the empiricist, social reality comprises a set of social facts that include the overt acts (behaviors) of individuals that can be defined physically or institutionally and the beliefs, affective states, and so forth that describe the motivations for behavior. Both of these kinds of facts are thought to be brute data—data that are identifiable and verifiable in such a way so as not to be subject to further interpretation. In this way, the empiricist accounts for both human behaviors and the meanings of those behaviors for the agents involved.

Interpretivist persuasions are predicated on the assumption that the empiricist's picture of social reality omits something most important, namely, intersubjective, common meanings—"ways of experiencing action in society which are expressed in the language and descriptions constitutive of institutions and practices" (Taylor, 1971/1987, p. 75). Accordingly, constructivists and interpretivists in general focus on the processes by which these meanings are created, negotiated, sustained, and modified within a specific context of human action. The means or process by which the inquirer arrives at this kind of interpretation of human action (as well as the ends or aim of the process) is called *Verstehen* (understanding).[10]

Phenomenological Interpretation of *Verstehen*

Although Weber is credited with elevating the importance of *Verstehen* as a process of sociological interpretation, his (and Dilthey's) conceptualization of *Verstehen* as a subjective process led to much confusion. Neopositivists (e.g., Abel, 1948; Rudner, 1966) seized on the subjective nature of *Verstehen.* They argued that it must mean an act of sympathetic imagination or empathic identification on the part of inquirers that allowed them to grasp the psychological state (i.e., motivation, belief, intention, or the like) of an individual actor. By getting inside the head of another, so to speak, the inquirer could hazard a guess as to the meaning of the actor's behavior; this hypothesis could then be subject to a more rigorous empirical test. In this way, the neopositivists identified *Verstehen* as (at best) a prescientific, heuristic device useful in the context of discovery but without value in the context of justification.

Defenders of the process of *Verstehen* as the key to understanding what is unique about the human sciences countered the latent psychologism of this neopositivist understanding. They claimed that *Verstehen* is less like a process of getting inside the actor's head than it is a matter of grasping intersubjective meanings and symbolizing activities that are constitutive of social life.[11] For example, Schutz (1967) sought to clear up confusion surrounding Weber's notion of *Verstehen* by distinguishing among three senses of the term. In the first sense, *Verstehen* refers to "the experiential form of common-sense knowledge of human affairs" (p. 57). It has nothing to do with introspection or pointing to the subjective states of actors; rather, it refers to the intersubjective character of the world and the complex process by which we come to recognize our own actions and those of our fellow actors as meaningful.

According to Schutz, *Verstehen* could also be explored as an epistemological problem. The central issue here is how *Verstehen* is possible. Schutz's analysis drew on Husserl's notion of the *Lebenswelt* (life world) as ontologically prior or as the grounds from which all inquiry starts and from within which it can only be carried out. Finally, *Verstehen* could be viewed as a method peculiar to the human sciences. Here, Schutz distinguished between two senses of the term. A first-order sense refers to *Verstehen* as the process by which we make sense of or interpret our everyday world. Schutz (1967) argued that, unlike the world of nature, which does not "mean" anything to molecules, electrons, and atoms that inhabit it, "the observational field of the social scientist—social reality—has a specific meaning and relevance structure for the human beings living, acting, and thinking within it. . . . It is these thought objects of theirs which determine their behavior by motivating it" (p. 59). A second-order sense refers to the process by which the social scientist attempts to make sense of the first:

> The thought objects constructed by the social scientist, in order to grasp this social reality, have to be founded upon the thought objects constructed by the common-sense thinking of men, living their daily life within their social world. Thus the constructs of the social sciences are constructs of the second degree . . . constructs of the constructs made by actors on the social scene. (p. 59)

Hermeneutical Interpretation of *Verstehen*

These efforts to give a phenomenological interpretation to *Verstehen* must be sharply distinguished from the hermeneutical position noted earlier. Taylor (1971/1987), for example, defined the activity of interpretation (and the human sciences more generally) as a hermeneutical undertaking analogous to the interpretation of a text. He argued that interpretive inquirers attempt to establish a certain reading or interpretation of the meaning of social action, and that what they appeal to as the warrant for this interpretation can only be other interpretations. Stated somewhat differently, inquirers not only have no "transcendental ground from which to contemplate the process of which [they are] irretrievably a part" (Bauman, 1978, p. 17), but they participate in the very production of meaning via participation in the circle of readings or interpretations (Gadamer, 1989; Taylor, 1971/1987).

This hermeneutical understanding of *Verstehen* in some interpretivist persuasions draws on a distinction between two kinds of hermeneutics (Bauman, 1978; Bleicher, 1980; Madison, 1988). The objective, validation hermeneutics of (the early) Dilthey, Betti, and Hirsch is an epistemology or methodology (with realist pretensions) for understanding the objectifications (e.g., arts, language, institutions, religions) of the human mind. It assumes that meaning is a determinate, objectlike entity waiting to be discovered in a text, a culture, or the mind of a social actor. In this view, hermeneutics is a particular exegetical method for identifying and explicating these objective meanings. The hermeneutical circle is a *methodological* device (in which one considers the whole in relation to its parts and vice versa) that provides a means for inquiry in the human sciences.

In contrast, the philosophical hermeneutics of Heidegger, Gadamer, and Taylor is concerned with ontology (being). The hermeneutical condition is a fact of human existence, and philosophical hermeneutics is concerned with a phenomenological (i.e., existential) explication of *Dasein* (condition of existence or being-in-the-world). The hermeneutical circle here is an "*ontological* condition of understanding; [it] proceeds from a communality that binds us to tradition in general and that of our object of interpretation in particular; [it] provides the link between finality and universality, and between theory and praxis" (Bleicher, 1980, p. 267; emphasis added).

Interpretivist persuasions aligned with ontological hermeneutics transcend the phenomenologist's concern with "capturing" the actors' point of view, with verification, with discriminating between emic and etic perspectives. Taylor (1971/1987) points to the bid to go beyond dualisms of this kind: He claims that if our interpretations seem implausible or if they are not understood by our interlocutors, "there is no verification procedure we can fall back on. We can only continue to offer interpretations; we are in an interpretative circle" (p. 75).[12]

Method Redefined

But what then of method and procedure in interpretivist persuasions of this kind? Although ontological hermeneutics is not a methodology per se, it does suggest an understanding of method that is at odds with the conception of scientific method associated with logical empiricist social science. G. B. Madison (1988, pp. 28-29) explains that *scientific* method is best characterized as an abstract, formal sense of method. In this sense, method is predicated on the elimination of personal, subjective judgment. As Madison explains "one has only to learn the method itself, in and for itself; it is an intellectual technique. Having done so, one has only to apply it to whatever subject matter one chooses; the only criterion in applying the method is *correctness* of application. . . . one's guide is the method itself, not the subject matter to which it is applied" (p. 28). This sense of method supports a belief in the power of demonstrative reasoning and the value of instrumental rationality and aims at achieving exactitude.

In sharp contrast, ontological hermeneutics supports a *normative* sense of method. This conceptualization reflects a belief in persuasive or practical reasoning (where *practical* is understood in the classic sense of involving both contemplation of the good and means of achieving same). A normative sense of method, according to Madison "far from supplanting personal, subjective judgment, or eliminating the need for it, is meant as an aid to good judgment" (1988, p. 28).

Madison argues that the understanding of method here is less like the application of rules and more like the casuistic activity of using ethical principles to guide the making of an ethical decision (interpretation) in a concrete situation (Jonsen & Toulmin, 1988). One seeks to make a responsible decision and to give good reasons for one's action, but the application of ethical principles does not permit the elimination of judgment on the part of the decision maker. In fact, to be rational in this situation demands or *requires* the exercise of judgment (not the following of procedures or rules) and the making of an interpretation. The interpretation or decision one makes cannot properly be said to be verifiable or testable. Rather, at best, we can appraise the interpretation by applying norms or criteria that are compatible with the very condition that demands we interpret in the first place. Hence to judge an interpretation we might use criteria such as thoroughness, coherence, comprehensiveness, and so forth, and ask whether the interpretation is useful, worthy of adoption, and so on.[13]

Conceiving of the activity of interpretation in terms of an ontological condition (i.e., as a fundamental grounds of our being-in-the-world) rather than as a methodological device is what puts the inquirer on the same plane of understanding, so to speak, as those he or she inquires into. To understand through interpretation is to accept a particular model of being or way of life (Shapiro, 1981). That way of being-in-the-world requires a redefinition of method along the lines suggested by Madison. In this way, the earlier comment by Rabinow and Sullivan (1987) about the significance of interpretive work comes into full relief: "For the human sciences both the object of investigation—the web of language, symbol, and institutions that constitutes signification—and the tools by which the investigation is carried out share inescapably the same pervasive context that is the human world" (p. 6).

Two Examples of Interpretivist Persuasions

Interpretivist alternatives to logical empiricist epistemology abound. Three in particular are described here. Geertz's version of interpretive anthropology blends both phenomenological and hermeneutical perspectives on interpretivism. The form of *Verstehende Soziologie* known as symbolic interactionism as represented by Blumer and Mead reflects a tough-minded respect for the reality of the world of experience. Denzin's reconceptualization of interpretive interactionism draws on insights from both critical hermeneutics and poststructuralism to repudiate what he regards as a soft positivism inherent in the Blumer-Mead version of symbolic interactionism.

Interpretive Anthropology

Clifford Geertz's interpretive anthropology is an interpretive theory of culture. It arises in direct opposition to the program of cultural analysis defined by a set of theoretical models known as structuralism or, more specifically, ethnoscience or cognitive anthropology. The structuralist program is firmly rooted in the logical empiricists' bid to find the "real" meaning of myth, ceremony, and other cultural artifacts. For the structuralist, the categories and structures of culture provide powerful explanatory devices accounting for the behaviors of members of a group or society. Structural-functional research frameworks are reductionist in that they claim to discover the one true interpretation lying behind or beneath the complexity of appearances. Geertz (1973) objects to this understanding of the goal of anthropology, preferring to define the analysis of human action as an "interpretive science in search of meaning, not an experimental science in search of laws" (p. 5).

He rejects the philosophical anthropology assumed by ethnoscientific models. He objects to a methodology that aims to reify the world of lived experience in a specialized language of science. For example, his assessment of the literary features of the works of the structuralist Lévi-Strauss reveal more than a critique of that author's prose:

> The marking characteristic of all of Levi-Strauss's work, one upon which almost everyone who deals with it sooner or later remarks [is] its extraordinary air of abstracted self-containment. "Aloof," "closed," "cold," "airless," "cerebral"—all the epithets that collect around any sort of literary absolutism collect around it. Neither picturing lives nor evoking them, neither interpreting them nor explaining them, but rather arranging and rearranging the materials the lives have somehow left behind into formal systems of correspondences—his books seem to exist behind glass, self-sealing disclosures into which jaguars, semen, and rotting meat are admitted to become oppositions, inversions, isomorphisms. (Geertz, 1988, p. 48)

Culture, for Geertz, is a more complicated, less bloodless, more ideational, and, fundamentally, an irreducibly interactive, hermeneutical phenomenon that begs for interpretation, not causal explanation. *Pace* the structuralists, Geertz (1973) argues: "As interworked systems of construable signs (what, ignoring provincial usages, I would call symbols), culture is not a power, something to which social events, behaviors, institutions, or processes can be causally attributed; it is a context, something within which they can be intelligibly—that is *thickly*—described" (p. 14).

A distinguishing feature of Geertz's understanding of both the object of the anthropologist's gaze and the method of his or her gazing is that both are semiotic and hermeneutical phenomena. The language and other symbols in a culture do not simply refer to objects but are constitutive of them, hence, Geertz (1973) claims, "man is an animal suspended in webs of significance he himself has spun" (p. 5). The actions of members of a culture (and the actions and writing of the anthropologist qua ethnographer) both construct and signify meaning. Following Ricoeur (1971), Geertz argues that the ways in which meanings are constituted in a culture must be read or interpreted by the ethnographer in much the same manner as one would read or interpret a complicated text.

Geertz further explains *what* it is that the ethnographer reads and *how* this activity of reading should be construed. For Geertz (1973), there is no world of social facts "out there" waiting to be observed, recorded, described, and analyzed by the inquirer. Rather, the inquirer constructs a reading of the meaning-making process of the people he or she studies. What the ethnographer does is "trace the curve of social discourse; fixing it into respectable form" (p. 19). What the activity of writing "fixes" is the "said" of an event the ethnographer observes—the meaning, the gist, the thought of a speech event—not the event itself. In so doing, the inquirer rescues the activity of participants' meaning making, changing it "from a passing event, which exists only in its own moment of occurrence, into an account, which exists in its inscriptions and can be consulted" (p. 19).

Access to the meaning of an event is not to be had through some process of empathic identification with an informant or respondent, getting inside the person's head, so to speak. Geertz (1983) rejects this neopositivist interpretation of *Verstehen,* arguing that ethnographers cannot claim "some unique form of psychological closeness, a sort of transcultural identification, with our subjects" (p. 56). Rather, the activity of understanding (*Verstehen*) unfolds as one looks over one's respondents' shoulders at what they are doing: "The trick is not to get yourself into some inner correspondence of spirit with your informants. Preferring, like the rest of us, to call their souls their own, they are not going to be altogether keen about such an effort anyhow. The trick is to figure out what the devil they think they are up to" (p. 58).

For example, Geertz (1983) explains that in his study of selfhood in Javanese, Moroccan, and Balinese societies, "I have tried to get at this most intimate of notions not by imagining myself someone else, a rice peasant or a tribal sheikh, and then seeing what I thought, but by searching out and analyzing the symbolic forms—words, images, institutions, behaviors—in terms of which, in each place, people actually represented themselves to themselves and to one another" (p. 58). The task of ethnography is not observation and description, but the inscription or thick description of these meanings of human action.

Because the activity of ethnographic analysis is not a matter of discovering the "Continent of Meaning and mapping out its bodiless landscape" (Geertz, 1973, p. 20) but rather one of "inscribing," writing, fashioning meaning, Geertz blurs the distinction between science and literature in anthropology. Echoing Schutz's understanding of *Verstehen,* Geertz argues that the anthropologist inscribes a text that is itself a second- or third-order interpretation of respondents' interpretations.

This text is built upon the delicate interplay of experience-near and experience-distant concepts: "Confinement to experience-near concepts leaves an ethnographer awash in immediacies, as well as entangled in vernacular. Confinement to experience-distant ones leaves him stranded in abstractions and smothered in jargon" (Geertz, 1983, p. 57).[14] Finally, this text offers a theoretical formulation or interpretation, a statement of what the "meaning particular social actions have for the actors whose actions they are . . . demonstrates about the society in which it is found and, beyond that, about social life as such" (Geertz, 1973, p. 27). Yet, Geertz understands theory (interpretation) to be always grounded and local, not speculative and abstract. He explains that "theoretical formulations hover so low over the interpretations they govern that they don't make much sense or hold much interest apart from them" (1973, p. 25).

Symbolic Interactionism

Another interpretive science in search of portraying and understanding the process of meaning making is the social psychological theory of symbolic interactionism. This approach to the study of human action is difficult to summarize briefly because of the many theoretical and methodological variants of the position (for summaries, see Denzin, 1992; Hammersley, 1989; Meltzer, Petras, & Reynolds, 1975; Plummer, 1991). I offer a characterization of the Blumer-Mead model of symbolic interactionism, followed by an outline of a postmodern version of the approach, namely, Norman Denzin's interpretive interactionism.

Drawing on the work of G. H. Mead, Herbert Blumer (1969, p. 2) claims that symbolic interactionism rests on three premises: First, human beings act toward the physical objects and other beings in their environment on the basis of the meanings that these things have for them. Second, these meanings derive from the social interaction (communication, broadly understood) between and among individuals. Communication is symbolic because we communicate via languages and other symbols; further, in communicating we create or produce significant symbols. Third, these meanings are established and modified through an interpretive process: "The actor selects, checks, suspends, regroups, and transforms the meanings in light of the situation in which he is placed and the direction of his action. . . . meanings are used and revised as instruments for the guidance and formation of action" (p. 5).

The Blumer-Mead version of symbolic interactionism regards human beings as purposive agents. They engage in "minded," self-reflexive behavior (Blumer, 1969, p. 81); they confront a world that they must interpret in order to act rather than a set of environmental stimuli to which they are forced to respond. Despite disavowing a substantive or philosophical behaviorism, symbolic interactionism does endorse a kind of methodological behaviorism (Denzin, 1971, p. 173).[15] In other words, the symbolic interactionist holds that a necessary (although not sufficient) condition for the study of social interaction is careful attention to the overt behaviors and behavior settings of actors and their interaction (i.e., "behavior specimens"; see Denzin, 1989c, pp. 79ff.). Thus symbolic interactionists evince a profound respect for the empirical world. Whether they overestimate the obduracy of that world or imagine that it can be directly apprehended is a matter of some dispute (Blumer, 1980; Denzin, 1989c; Hammersley, 1989).

In much the same way that Geertz rejects a structural-functional approach to the study of human action, Blumer (1969) objects to methodologies in which "participants in . . . a societal organization are logically merely media for the play and expression of the forces or mechanisms of the system itself; [in which] one turns to such forces or mechanisms to account for what takes place" (pp. 57-58). On the contrary, symbolic interactionism requires that the inquirer actively enter the worlds of people being studied in order to "see the situation as it is seen by the actor, observing what the actor takes into account, observing how he interprets what is taken into account" (p. 56). The process of actors' interpretation is rendered intelligible not merely through the description of word and deed, but by taking that rich description as a point of departure for formulating an interpretation of what actors are up to.

As Denzin (1971) explains, symbolic interactionists begin with a "sensitizing image of the interaction process" (p. 168) built around such concepts as self, language, social setting, social object, and joint act. The inquirer then "moves from sensitizing concepts to the immediate world of social experience and permits that world to shape and modify his conceptual framework [and, in this way, the inquirer] moves continually between the realm of the more general social theory and the worlds of native people" (p. 168). Symbolic interactionists seek explanations of that world, although, like Geertz, they view explanatory theories as interpretive, grounded, and hovering low over the data (Denzin, 1989c).

Pragmatism informs the philosophical anthropology, epistemology, and social philosophy of the Blumer-Mead version of symbolic interactionism. Like Dewey, Mead and Blumer criticize associationist theories of cognition that reduce action to environmentally determined conduct. They view human beings as acting (not responding) organisms who construct social action (Blumer, 1969). Consequently, such epistemological terms as *truth* and *meaning* are not expressions of relationships of correspondence to reality, but refer to the consequences of a purposeful action. Mead's political pragmatism also shaped the symbolic interactionist persuasion. Denzin (1992), for one, claims that Mead's political philosophy was more culturally conservative and less critical than Dewey's and often issued in a "conservative cultural romanticism which turned the modern self and its interactional experiences into a moral hero" (p. 6).[16]

Interpretive Interactionism

Denzin finds several faults with the Blumer-Mead version of symbolic interactionism: a naive empirical realism, a romantic conception of the "other," and a conservative social philosophy.[17] He thinks it important that Blumer's respect for the empirical world—his call for "close and reasonably full familiarity with area[s] of life under study" (Blumer, 1969, p. 37)—remain at the heart of symbolic interactionism. However, he is keen on developing a postmodern politics of "interpretive interactionism" (Denzin, 1989a, 1989b) that does not offer inscription in the place of description; present a romantic realist picture of human actors; or obscure, decontextualize, or overtheorize the presentation of the voices, emotions, and actions—that is, the lived experience—of respondents.[18]

To become more self-consciously "interpretive," symbolic interactionism must, in Denzin's view, shed its pretensions to ethnographic realism and adopt insights from poststructural philosophy, principally work in cultural and feminist studies. The former facilitates connecting the study of meaning making in social interaction to the communication process and the communication industry "that produce and shape the meanings that circulate in everyday life" (Denzin, 1992, p. 96). Cultural studies directs the interpretive interactionist toward a critical appraisal of "how interacting individuals connect their lived experiences to the cultural representations of those experiences" (p. 74). From feminist studies, the interactionist learns that the language and activity of both inquirer and respondent must be read in gendered, existential, biographical, and classed ways. As a result, a "phenomenologically, existentially driven view of humans and society positions self, emotionality, power, ideology, violence, and sexuality at the center of the interactionist's interpretive problems [and] [t]hese are the topics that an interactionist cultural studies aims to address" (p. 161).

Finally, in Denzin's (1992) reformulation, interpretive interactionism must explicitly engage in cultural criticism. He argues that this can be accomplished through the development of an "oppositional cultural aesthetic" (p. 151) crafted through a rereading of the pragmatic tradition and an appropriation of insights from critical theory. In true deconstructionist fashion, this approach (a) "aims to always subvert the meaning of a text, to show how its dominant and negotiated meanings can be opposed"; (b) "expose[s] the ideological and political meanings that circulate within the text, particularly those which hide or displace racial, class, ethnic and gender biases"; and (c) "analyze[s] how texts address the problems of presence, lived experience, the real and its representations, and the issues of subjects, authors, and their intentionalities" (p. 151).

Constructivist Thinking

Constructivism, at least in the social sciences, is of more recent vintage than interpretivist thinking, although its roots reach back to the earliest philosophical arguments over a rational foundation for knowledge. Constructivists are preoccupied with related but somewhat different concerns from those of their interpretivist counterparts. As described earlier, interpretivism was conceived in reaction to the effort to develop a natural science of the social. Its foil was largely logical empiricist methodology and the bid to apply that framework to human inquiry.

Constructivists share this concern, and they resonate with the interpretivists' emphasis on the world of experience as it is lived, felt, undergone by social actors. Yet, their particular foils are the notions of objectivism, empirical realism, objective truth, and essentialism. Karin Knorr-Cetina (1981) explains that "to the objectivist, the world is composed of facts and the goal of knowledge is to provide a literal account of what the world is like" (p. 1). And Kenneth Gergen (1991) adds: "Modernism was deeply committed to the view that the facts of the world are essentially *there* for study. They exist independently of us as observers, and if we are rational we will come to know the facts as they are" (p. 91).

Constructivists are deeply committed to the contrary view that what we take to be objective knowledge and truth is the result of perspective. Knowledge and truth are created, not discovered by mind. They emphasize the pluralistic and plastic character of reality—pluralistic in the sense that reality is expressible in a variety of symbol and language systems; plastic in the sense that reality is stretched and shaped to fit purposeful acts of intentional human agents. They endorse the claim that, "contrary to common-sense, there is no unique 'real world' that preexists and is independent of human mental activity and human symbolic language" (Bruner, 1986, p. 95). In place of a realist view of theories and knowledge, constructivists emphasize the instrumental and practical function of theory construction and knowing.

Constructivists are antiessentialists. They assume that what we take to be self-evident kinds (e.g., man, woman, truth, self) are actually the product of complicated discursive practices. Accordingly, as Diana Fuss (1989) explains,

> what is at stake for the constructionist are systems of representations, social and material practices, laws of discourses, and ideological effects. In short, constructionists are concerned above all with the *production* and *organization* of differences, and they therefore reject the idea that any essential or natural givens precede the process of social determination. (p. 3)

Everyday Constructivist Thinking

In a fairly unremarkable sense, we are all constructivists if we believe that the mind is active in the construction of knowledge. Most of us would agree that knowing is not passive—a simple imprinting of sense data on the mind—but active; mind does something with these impressions, at the very least forms abstractions or concepts. In this sense, constructivism means that human beings do not find or discover knowledge so much as construct or make it. We invent concepts, models, and schemes to make sense of experience and, further, we continually test and modify these constructions in the light of new experience.

However, as Kenneth Strike (1987) points out, "the claim that people are active in learning or knowledge construction is rather uninteresting. It is uninteresting because no one, beyond a few aberrant behaviorists, denies it" (p. 483). Even the logical positivists, the favorite target of many who currently claim the label "constructivist," were themselves constructivists in the sense sketched above. They held that theoretical terms were in fact abstractions, human inventions that were simply convenient devices for managing and expressing the relations among observables.

Further, one need not be an antirealist to be a constructivist. One can reasonably hold that concepts and ideas are invented (rather than discovered) yet maintain that these inventions correspond to something in the real world. The logical empiricist picture of theory described by Herbert Feigl—a set of human constructs that have meaning by virtue of their relation to the "soil of experience"—is just such a view.[19] Likewise, the notion that knowledge is invented and error-prone (epistemological fallibilism) cohabits quite comfortably with a belief in a real world independent of human knowledge of same (ontological realism) in the evolutionary epistemology of Donald Campbell and in the Popperian philosophy of social science characteristic of D. C. Phillips.

Given that, by their own admission, the constructivists discussed below would indeed make odd bedfellows with the likes of Feigl, Campbell, Phillips, and the ghosts of the logical empiricists, the former group must be staking a claim to something more than this trivial sense of constructivism. Yet the terrain of constructivist approaches is marked by multiple uses of the term. The sketch of constructivist persuasions that follows can at least alert the reader to the kind of intellectual spadework necessary to come to terms with this concept.

Defining the Contours of Constructivist Philosophy

The philosopher most responsible for defining the contours of a constructivist theory of reality and cognition is Nelson Goodman (1984).[20] He characterizes his view as "irrealism," a kind of rigorously constrained radical relativism that "does not hold that everything or even anything is irreal, but sees the world melting into versions and versions making worlds, finds ontology evanescent, and inquires into what makes a version right and a world well-built" (p. 29). Irrealism is not a doctrine that seeks to takes its place alongside realist and idealist accounts of the world, but rather "an attitude of unconcern with most issues between such doctrines" (p. 43). Goodman (1978) quotes the worldly philosopher Woody Allen to make this point:

> Can we actually "know" the universe? My God, it's hard enough finding your way around Chinatown. The point, however, is: Is there anything out there? And why? And must they be so noisy? Finally, there can be no doubt that the one characteristic of "reality" is that it lacks essence. That is not to say it has no essence, but merely lacks it. (The reality I speak of here is the same one Hobbes described, but a little smaller.) (p. 97)

Or, in Goodman's words, the point is "never mind mind, essence is not essential, and matter doesn't matter" (p. 97). Goodman seeks to transcend the debates of realism versus idealism by reconceptualizing philosophy.

Goodman's constructivist philosophy is pluralistic and pragmatic.[21] Through our nonverbal and verbal symbol systems we create many versions of the world in the sciences, the arts, and the humanities. Our process of inquiry is not a matter of somehow getting in touch with the ready-made world; rather, "worldmaking as we know it always starts from worlds already on hand; the making is a remaking" (Goodman, 1978, p. 6). These "remakings" are not simply different interpretations of the same world, but literally different world versions. Stated somewhat differently, our frames of interpretation (versions) belong both to what is interpreted (worlds) and to a system of interpretation. How we go about the business of making and judging world versions is Goodman's principal concern.

We are inclined to judge claims, interpretations, statements, and world versions for their "truth" (usually understood as correspondence between a claim and some ready-made world) and "certainty." But, in Goodman's view, these are excessively restricted concepts beset with trouble (see Goodman & Elgin, 1988). He proposes that we adopt the more pragmatic notion of "rightness," a term with "greater reach" than truth. *Rightness* is defined as an act of fitting and working but "not a fitting *onto*—a correspondence or matching or mirroring of independent Reality—but a fitting *into* a context or discourse or standing complex of other symbols" (p. 158). He claims that the notion of certainty—"a pretentious muddle of the psychological and the pseudological—is unsalvageable" and proposes instead that we use the term *adoption*: "We can adopt habits, strategies, vocabularies, styles, as well as statements" (p. 159).

Accordingly, the cognitive endeavor is not to be taken as the pursuit of knowledge that seeks "to arrive at an accurate and comprehensive description of 'the real' readymade world" (p. 163).

Rather, cognition is reconceptualized as the advancement of understanding wherein we begin "from what happens to be currently adopted and proceed to integrate and organize, weed out and supplement, not in order to arrive at truth about something already made but in order to make something right—to construct something that works cognitively, that fits together and handles new cases, that may implement further inquiry and invention" (p. 163).

Radical Constructivism

The contrast between a view of mind as the vessel for the acquisition, storage, and retrieval of information and an instrumentalist notion of mind as an active creator and manipulator of symbols is taken up in a version of constructivist thinking called "radical constructivism" as defined by the psychologist Ernst von Glasersfeld,[22] who is concerned with the nature of knowledge and what it means to know. He argues that radical constructivism signals a particular relationship between mind and world. Following the arguments advanced by the skeptics, von Glasersfeld claims that we cannot know such a thing as an independent, objective world that stands apart from our experience of it. Hence we cannot speak of knowledge as somehow corresponding to, mirroring, or representing that world.

Radical constructivism rejects the notion that "knowledge ought to be a veridical 'representation' of a world as it 'exists' prior to being experienced" (von Glasersfeld, 1991, p. 16). In von Glasersfeld's view, knowledge is not a particular kind of product (i.e., a representation) that exists independent of the knower, but an activity or process. He believes that this process is best understood in Piagetian terms of adaptation and equilibration (von Glasersfeld, 1989, 1991). Correspondingly, criteria for evaluating knowledge claims are revised: The validity of a knowledge claim is not to be found in the relationship of reference or correspondence to an independently existing world; rather, a claim is thought to be valid if it is viable or if it provides functional fit, that is, if it works to achieve a goal. The relationship between knowledge and reality is instrumental, not verificative: To know is "to possess ways and means of acting and thinking that allow one to attain the goals one happens to have chosen" (von Glasersfeld, 1991, p. 16).[23]

Social Constructionism

Kenneth and Mary Gergen also challenge the idea of some objective basis for knowledge claims and examine the process of knowledge construction. But, instead of focusing on the matter of individual minds and cognitive processes, they turn their attention outward to the world of intersubjectively shared, social constructions of meaning and knowledge. Acknowledging a debt to the phenomenology of Peter Berger and Alfred Schutz, Kenneth Gergen (1985) labels his approach "social constructionism" because it more adequately reflects the notion that the world that people create in the process of social exchange is a reality *sui generis*.

The social constructionist approach is predicated on the assumption that "the terms by which the world is understood are social artifacts, products of historically situated interchanges among people" (Gergen, 1985, p. 267). Knowledge is one of the many coordinated activities of individuals and as such is subject to the same processes that characterize any human interaction (e.g., communication, negotiation, conflict, rhetoric). As Gergen and Gergen (1991) explain: "Accounts of the world . . . take place within shared systems of intelligibility—usually a spoken or written language. These accounts are not viewed as the external expression of the speaker's internal processes (such as cognition, intention), but as an expression of relationships among persons" (p. 78). Contrary to the emphasis in radical constructivism, the focus here is not on the meaning-making activity of the individual mind but on the collective generation of meaning as shaped by conventions of language and other social processes.

Although both von Glasersfeld and Gergen emphasize that their versions of constructivist philosophy are concerned with epistemology (knowing) not ontology (being), each also takes a stand on the latter. Von Glasersfeld (1991) does not deny that there is an ontological reality, but claims that we cannot in any sense know a "real" world. He sounds very much like an ontological idealist when he says, "I claim that we cannot even imagine what the word 'to exist' might mean in an ontological context, because we cannot conceive of 'being' without the notions of space and time, and these two notions are among the first of our conceptual constructs" (p. 17).

Gergen's theory of reality is both idealist and relative. He claims that "there are no independently identifiable, real-world referents to which the language of social description [or explanation, for that matter] are cemented" (1986, p. 143). Further, he at least implies that language is the only reality we can know, hence his view borders on the radical linguistic relativism or contextualist theory of reality characteristic of Stanley Fish (1989).[24] According to Fish, reality *is* the result of the social processes accepted as normal in a specific context, and knowledge claims are intelligible and debatable only within a particular context or community.

Feminist Standpoint Epistemologies

These constructivist persuasions blend the phenomenological interpretive perspective with critical hermeneutics.[25] They are concerned with portraying the lived reality of women's lives. As Riger (1992) explains, "Giving voice to women's perspectives means identifying ways women create meaning and experience life from their particular position in the social hierarchy" (p. 734). Feminist standpoint persuasions argue that women's life experiences are not captured in existing conceptual schemes (e.g., Belenky, Clinchy, Goldberger, & Tarule, 1986; Gilligan, 1982; D. Smith, 1987), and thus they focus in particular on the ways in which gender is socially constructed, treating it as an analytic category in its own right.[26]

In her review of perspectives in feminist anthropology, Micaela di Leonardo (1991) explains that social constructionists regard language seriously as more than a transparent representational medium. Studies by Susan Gal (1991) on women's speech and silence, Emily Martin (1987) on women's discourse about their own reproductive processes compared with the dominant discourse of medical science, and Jane Radway (1984) on the social event of reading popular romance novels are examples of sociolinguistic analyses of how verbal practices in social interaction construct gender. However, discourse analysis does not replace social analysis. Reflecting the influence of critical theorists of the Frankfurt school, feminist social constructionists evince profound concern for the material conditions of women's lives. Analysis of discourse is thus often combined with political economic research.[27]

Another feature of these persuasions that they share, in part, with recent developments in postmodern ethnography is the careful, public scrutiny of the inquirer's history, values, and assumptions. Although there is a vast fieldwork literature on researcher-respondent relations, feminist standpoint epistemologies are particularly keen on exploring the social construction of the research encounter (e.g., Mies, 1983; Oakley, 1981; Reinharz, 1992; Stacey, 1988).

The social, dialogic nature of inquiry is central to the constructivist thinking of Gergen and Gergen (1991) and Guba and Lincoln (1989) (discussed below) as well. For them, inquiry methodology requires attending both to the inquirer's own self-reflective awareness of his or her own constructions and to the *social* construction of individual constructions (including that of the inquirer). For example, Gergen and Gergen (1991) sketch an interactive approach to inquiry called the "reflexive elaboration of the event," in which the researcher and participants open a sociopsychological phenomenon to inspection and through dialogue generate a process of continuous reflexivity, thereby "enabling new forms of linguistic reality to emerge" (p. 88). The overall aim of this approach is "to expand and enrich the vocabulary of understanding."

Guba and Lincoln (1989) echo a similar view. They believe that the best means of developing joint constructions is the "hermeneutic-dialectic" process, so called because it is interpretive and fosters comparing and contrasting divergent constructions in an effort to achieve a synthesis of same. They strongly emphasize that the goal of constructivist inquiry is to achieve a consensus (or, failing that, an agenda for negotiation) on issues and concerns that define the nature of the inquiry.

A "Constructivist Paradigm"

Egon Guba and Yvonna Lincoln's "constructivist paradigm" is a wide-ranging eclectic framework. They originally discussed their approach under the heading of "naturalistic inquiry" (Lincoln & Guba, 1985). However, recently they have begun using the term *constructivism* to characterize their methodology (Guba & Lincoln, 1989, p. 19), although they acknowledge that constructivist, interpretive, naturalistic, and hermeneutical are all similar notions. They propose their constructivist paradigm as a replacement for what they label the conventional, scientific, or positivist paradigm of inquiry, and they have spelled out in detail the epistemological and ontological assumptions, aims, procedures, and criteria of their approach.

Their constructivist philosophy is idealist; that is, they assume that what is real is a construction in the minds of individuals (Lincoln & Guba, 1985, p. 83).[28] It is also pluralist and relativist: There are multiple, often conflicting, constructions, and all (at least potentially) are meaningful. For Guba and Lincoln, the question of which or whether constructions are true is sociohistorically relative. Truth is a matter of the best-informed and most sophisticated construction on which there is consensus at a given time.

Like those who espouse the feminist standpoint epistemologies noted above, Guba and Lincoln assume that the observer cannot (should not) be neatly disentangled from the observed in the activity of inquiring into constructions. Hence the findings or outcomes of an inquiry are themselves a literal creation or construction of the inquiry process. Constructions, in turn, are resident in the minds of individuals: "They do not exist outside of the persons who create and hold them; they are not part of some 'objective' world that exists apart from their constructors" (Guba & Lincoln, 1989, p. 143).

The act of inquiry begins with issues and/or concerns of participants and unfolds through a "dialectic" of iteration, analysis, critique, reiteration, reanalysis, and so on that leads eventually to a joint (among inquirer and respondents) construction of a case (i.e., findings or outcomes). The joint constructions that issue from the activity of inquiry can be evaluated for their "fit" with the data and information they encompass; the extent to which they "work," that is, provide a credible level of understanding; and the extent to which they have "relevance" and are "modifiable" (Guba & Lincoln, 1989, p. 179).

The properties of constructions can be further elaborated as follows (Guba & Lincoln, 1989):

1. Constructions are attempts to make sense of or to interpret experience, and most are self-sustaining and self-renewing.
2. The nature or quality of a construction that can be held depends upon "the range or scope of information available to a constructor, and the constructor's sophistication in dealing with that information" (p. 71).
3. Constructions are extensively shared, and some of those shared are "disciplined constructions," that is, collective and systematic attempts to come to common agreements about a state of affairs, for example, science (p. 71).
4. Although all constructions must be considered meaningful, some are rightly labeled "malconstruction" because they are "incomplete, simplistic, uninformed, internally inconsistent, or derived by an inadequate methodology" (p. 143).
5. The judgment of whether a given construction is malformed can be made only with reference to the "paradigm out of which the constructor operates" (p. 143); in other words, criteria or standards are framework specific, "so for instance a religious construction can only be judged adequate or inadequate utilizing the particular theological paradigm from which it is derived" (p. 143).
6. One's constructions are challenged when one becomes aware that new information conflicts with the held construction or when one senses a lack of intellectual sophistication needed to make sense of new information.

Educational Connoisseurship and Criticism

Elliot Eisner's version of constructivism is grounded in the work of Suzanne Langer and Michael Polanyi, and in John Dewey's aesthetic theory. It is proposed as an alternative to qualitative approaches to educational studies stemming from ethnographic traditions in social science. Acknowledging a partial debt to Goodman's philosophy of cognition and his philosophy of art, Eisner assumes that perception is framework or theory dependent and that knowledge is a constructed (versus discovered) form of experience. His methodology is concerned with how inquirers develop an enhanced capacity to perceive the qualities that comprise the educational experience and, further, how they can develop the skills to render those perceptions in representational forms that portray, interpret, and appraise educational phenomena. The selection of representational forms is critical because, in Eisner's (1991) view, "the selection of a form through which the world is to be represented not only influences what we can say, it also influences what we are likely to experience" (p. 8).

Connoisseurship is the art of apperception. It is grounded in the "consummatory function" of aesthetic knowing—"the developed ability to experience the subtleties of form" (Eisner, 1985, p. 28). What the connoisseur perceives or experiences are qualities—the sensory features of a phenomenon. Yet perception of qualities is not mere impression of sense data on the mind; rather, the act of perception is a framework- or schema-dependent cognitive act. For the connoisseur, perceiving or experiencing is a kind of heightened awareness or educated perception—a particular kind of attention to nuance and detail, to multiple dimensions or aspects—that comes from intimate familiarity with the phenomenon being examined. The connoisseur's eye (as metaphor for all the senses) is in a state of enlightenment.

What the connoisseur "sees" he or she must eventually "say," and the act of rendering apperception in some publicly available form is the task of criticism. Here, Eisner (1985, p. 28) draws on what he calls the "referential function" of aesthetic knowing—its function of pointing to some aspect of the world beyond our immediate ken, thereby allowing us to experience some phenomenon via vicarious participation. The inquirer as connoisseur-turned-critic reconstructs or transforms his or her perceptions into some representational form that "illuminates, interprets, and appraises the qualities that have been experienced" (Eisner, 1991, p. 86). This form is most typically some kind of narrative that is presentational rather than representational. In other words, the narrative is not an iconic image or mirror of reality but a poetic, expressive form that is a reconstrual or reconstitution of the experience from which it originates. The critic describes, interprets, and appraises the phenomenon and thereby aids in the reeducation of the reader's perception. This narrative, storied mode of re-presenting the connoisseur's experience is particularly significant because it points to the importance of an aesthetic (versus scientific or propositional) form of knowing in human inquiry. These narrative accounts can themselves be evaluated or appraised for their "rightness" through the judgment of their coherence, referential adequacy, and instrumental utility (Eisner, 1991, pp. 53ff.).

On Common Criticisms and Future Directions

Interpretivist and constructivist persuasions have been somewhat artificially disentangled here to afford a closer look at salient aspects of each. Yet it should be apparent that current work in these methodologies reflects the synthetic impulse of the postmodern zeitgeist. Decades from its origins in challenges to scientism and efforts to restore to human inquiry a principal focus on the everyday world of lived experience, the phenomenological-interpretive perspective is now being blended with insights from constructivist epistemology, feminist methodologies, poststructuralism, postmodernism, and critical hermeneutics.[29] This bid to redescribe and reconceptualize makes for an often bewildering array of conflicting considerations, yet it also signals that in-house controversies are now far more intellectually vital and exciting than the simplistic debates between so-called quantitative and qualitative methodologies that continue to be waged in some quarters of the academy. These challenges from within that demand our attention are principally centered on four issues in interpretive work—the perdurable problems of criteria and objectivity, the lack of a critical purchase, the problem of inquirer authority and privilege, and the confusion of psychological and epistemological claims.

The Problem of Criteria

The issue is deceptively simple: What is an adequate warrant for a subjectively mediated account of intersubjective meaning?[30] In the absence of some set of criteria, such accounts are subject to the charges of solipsism (they are only *my* accounts) and relativism (all accounts are equally good or bad, worthy or unworthy, true or false, and so on). Contemporary interpretivists and constructivists are not likely to hold that there are unquestioned *foundations* for any interpretation. They are nonfoundationalists who have given up the quest for objectivism (Bernstein, 1976), hence a solution to the problem of criteria is not likely to be found in this venue.

Nonfoundational resolutions to the problem have arisen in the following ways. One is to claim the middle ground of methodology, as noted at the beginning of this chapter. The notion of an appeal to procedural criteria as grounds for judging the goodness of interpretations is strong. It is evident in the painstaking attention to goodness criteria in the otherwise constructivist frame of reference of Guba and Lincoln.

A second effort issues from arguments for subtle realism. This resolution stems from a bid to rescue an important realist intuition from otherwise incoherent correspondence theories of truth (Matthews, 1992). The intuition is that the truth, worth, or value of a claim, theory, interpretation, construction, and so forth is ultimately determined by something *beyond* the claim, theory, interpretation, construction. Hammersley (1992b), for example, argues that interpretivists investigate independent, knowable, actor-constructed phenomena, but denies that we have an unmediated grasp of or access to those phenomena. He maintains that there can be "multiple, non-contradictory descriptive and explanatory claims about any phenomenon" (Hammersley, 1989, p. 135), "without denying that if those interpretations are accurate they must correspond in relevant aspects to the phenomena described" (p. 194).

A third resolution is to give up the worry about a separation of mind and world and focus instead on intentional, meaningful behavior that is by definition historically, socially, and culturally relative. It acknowledges that a human inquirer is permanently engaged in a discourse with his or her own object, "a discourse in which the object and subject of study employ essentially the same resources" (Bauman, 1978, p. 234; see also Giddens, 1976). Interpretive accounts (efforts to make clear what seems to be confused, unclear) are to be judged on the pragmatic grounds of whether they are useful, fitting, generative of further inquiry, and so forth.

The Lack of a Critical Purchase

This problem is variously identified as one of descriptivism, of the lack of a critical purchase, and of privileging the views of actors. The principal objection here is that interpretive accounts lack any critical interest or the ability to critique the very accounts they produce. Burrell and Morgan (1979), for example, note that interpretive theoretical frameworks reflect a politics that they call the "sociology of regulation" as opposed to a "sociology of radical change" (p. 254). In their view, these frameworks "present a perspective in which individual actors negotiate, regulate, and live their lives within the context of the *status quo*" (p. 254). A similar kind of concern underlies

Denzin's critique of the Blumer-Mead version of symbolic interactionism. Also, as noted above, some feminist social constructionists address this challenge by drawing on the critical theory tradition.

This criticism is, in part, traceable to the origins of the image of the social inquirer as disinterested theorist—one whose practice is defined by the careful separation of empirical from normative concerns, descriptive theory from prescriptive theory (see Berger & Kellner, 1981; Bernstein, 1976; Clifford, 1983). Weber's insistence on the separation of facts and values (the ethics of responsibility versus the ethics of conviction) in interpretive sociology, and Schutz's distinction between the fundamental interests of the individual as ordinary citizen and the individual as scientist are central sources of this idea.

For example, Schutz (1967) held that the world of social scientific investigation constituted a particular finite province of meaning (one of many such finite provinces or multiple realities) that demanded a particular relevance structure, cognitive style, and attitude.[31] The individual-as-social-scientist operates with the attitude of the disinterested observer and abides by the rules for evidence and objectivity within the scientific community. Whereas the individual-as-citizen legitimately has a practical (in a classic sense), pragmatic, interested attitude, the individual-turned-social-scientist brackets out that attitude and adopts the posture of objective, disinterested, empirical theorist. This disinterested attitude is readily evident, for example, in traditional ethnography, where the inquirer is warned not to become more than a marginal native and to discipline his or her subjectivity. Critics hold that it is precisely because of this distancing of oneself as inquirer that interpretivists cannot engage in an explicitly critical evaluation of the social reality they seek to portray.

The Problem of Authority

A third set of criticisms is directed at what might be called the "dangers of high interpretive science" and the "overly sovereign" authoritative stance of the interpreter as inscriber (Rabinow, 1986, p. 258).[32] Postmodern ethnographers (e.g., Clifford, 1983, 1990; Clifford & Marcus, 1986; Rabinow, 1977) argue that defining interpretation as act of inscription vests authority and control in the anthropologist as inscriber and suppresses the dialogic dimension of constructing interpretations of human action. A related worry expressed by some critics of this linguistic, textualist turn, particularly in anthropology (e.g., Jackson, 1989), is that quarrels over whether anthropology is best viewed as an analytic or interpretive science are making for both a bad science and a bad art of anthropological investigation.

The Making of Epistemological Claims

A special set of criticisms is directed at the constructivists' bid to argue from a psychological claim to an epistemological conclusion (Matthews, 1992; Strike, 1987). Recall that the constructivist makes the claim, in Eisner's (1991) words, that there is no "pristine, unmediated grasp of the world as it is" (p. 46) and, further, that no sharp distinction can be drawn between knower and known, between accounts of the world and those doing the accounting. Taken as a *psychological* claim, this is not particularly problematic, even for those who call themselves empiricists. It is a belief that knowledge is not simply the impression of sense data on the mind, but instead is actively constructed.

Yet many constructivists are not making simply a psychological claim, they are making an *epistemological* claim as well. That is, they argue that knowledge does not discover a preexisting, independent, real world outside the mind of the knower, that the process of making or constructing meaning cannot be connected to an "independent world 'out there,' but [only] to our own constructing processes" (Steier, 1991, p. 2).

The difficulty here is how to account for the fact of knowledge as a form of theoretical production, the fact that knowledge is somehow available to individuals, and the fact that knowledge is shared and transmitted. To borrow some language from Guba and Lincoln (1989), if constructions "are resident in the minds of individuals" (p. 143)—that is, they cannot be said to exist outside the self-reflective capacity of an individual mind—then how is it possible that they can be "extensively shared" (p. 71), and that "a range [and] scope of information [knowledge] is available to a constructor" (p. 71) such that constructions can be modified, changed, or abandoned?

One way in which this problem has been addressed, as we have seen, is to emphasize the *social* construction of knowledge. Yet the tension between claiming that knowledge is the property of individual minds and the view that knowledge can be publicly shared is evident.[33]

Future Directions

Having surveyed the contemporary scene and appraised the arguments for nonfoundationalist, antiessentialist thinking, Richard Rorty (1982) concludes that we stand at the head of two paths. One is the path of Dewey, with his liberal social hope; the other is the path of Foucault, with his despair over the prison house of language. I for one can find little comfort in a form of interpretivism that degenerates into nihilism, where we do nothing but engage in endless parasitical deconstruction and deny the existence of social order and our very selves.

To be sure, the future of interpretivist and constructivist persuasions rests on the acceptance of the implications of dissolving long-standing dichotomies such as subject/object, knower/known, fact/value. It rests on individuals being comfortable with the blurring of lines between the science and art of interpretation, the social scientific and the literary account (Geertz, 1980). Yet, in rejecting these rigid distinctions, we need not, as Michael Jackson (1989) argues, dissolve the lived *experience* of inquirer or respondents into the anonymous field of discourse.

We can reject dichotomous thinking on pragmatic grounds: Such distinctions simply are not very useful anymore. We can continue to respect the bid to make sense of the conditions of our lives without claiming that either inquirer or actor is the final arbiter of understanding. The interpretive undertaking thus becomes, in Jackson's (1989) words, the practice of "*actively* debating and exchanging points of view with our informants. It means placing our ideas on a par with theirs, testing them not against predetermined standards of rationality but against the immediate exigencies of life" (p. 14).

I read this union of the interpretive turn and the tradition of practical philosophy, with its defense of the Socratic virtues and its emphasis on our fundamental character as dialogic, conversational, questioning beings, to be a most promising and hopeful development. The interpretivists' profound respect for and interest in socially constructed meaning and practice is consonant with the turn toward the moral-practical (*phronesis*) and away from *theoria* (as explored, although in very different ways, by Bernstein, 1986, 1992; Rorty, 1982; Sullivan, 1986).[34]

The thesis of this chapter is that what marks constructivist or interpretivist work as a unique form of human inquiry is a set of theoretical commitments and philosophical assumptions about the way the world must be in order that we can know it. In reviewing the philosophical roots of this work and in summarizing the kinds of epistemological problems it raises, my intent has not been to make all those who claim the title "constructivist" or "interpretivist" inquirer into philosophers. Rather, my goal has been to enhance the level of awareness of the kind of philosophical investigation that is entailed in proposing alternatives to an empiricist social science. My purpose has been at least partially accomplished if the reader has been drawn to further investigation of the issues raised here.

Notes

1. Following a distinction developed by Stake (1991), I prefer the term *persuasions* or *approaches* to *models*. *Models* overpromises because it suggests that the student of interpretive inquiry would find guidance in the discussions of these methodologies for answering the question of what a completed inquiry should look like. It suggests that these statements are blueprints that should be followed. Yet models are not found in discussions of methodology but in the published accounts of various forms of interpretive inquiry. The term *persuasions,* on the contrary, connotes that what we are dealing with here are statements of particular commitments, purviews, and concerns.

2. A comparison with feminist methodologies is instructive here. In some cases, differences in method *do* help explain what is different about feminist approaches to human inquiry; however, this claim is contested (see, for example, Harding, 1987; Reinharz, 1992; Riger, 1992).

3. This caveat drawing attention to the distinction between methodological commitments and methods is warranted in view of the persistent mistaken belief that making the interpretive turn in the social sciences is principally a matter of employing different means of collecting and analyzing data. Understanding constructivist or interpretivist approaches to the study of human action (or any of the other approaches examined in this volume) is not simply a matter of mastering technique, copying a method, or following a model. Rather, understanding is to be had through an examination of the epistemological assumptions and claims of a methodology, through study of its conceptualization of what we are about when we inquire. This is a philosophical inquiry.

4. Other interpretive and constructivist persuasions are explained elsewhere in this volume: Holstein and Gubrium discuss ethnomethodology in Chapter 16; Greene explores constructivist thinking in evaluation in Chapter 33; Stake, in Chapter 14, notes the influence of interpretivist and constructivist thinking in shaping notions of case study strategies; and Atkinson and Hammersley, in Chapter 15, discuss how the interpretivist's goal for human inquiry is manifest in ethnography.

5. For different accounts of these roots, see Bauman (1978), Bernstein (1976), and Bleicher (1980).

6. See Richard J. Bernstein's (1976) discussion of the definition of scientific explanation in mainstream social science.

7. See Taylor (1989, pp. 159ff.) for a thorough discussion of the tensions between Romanticist and Cartesian notions of the self. Although his work is an exercise in moral philosophy, much of his argument is relevant to understanding the tension referred to here. See also Gergen (1991, chap. 2).

8. According to Smith (1989), advocates of this solution hold that "although the ideas of objectivity, detachment, and methodological constraints as defined by empiricists are a fiction, interpretive inquiry must be made more systematic and rigorous. The claim here is that methods cannot eliminate researcher subjectivity but that they can certainly minimize it; they are thereby the criteria against which to judge that some results are more objective than others" (p. 157).

9. See Taylor (1964) for an account of both kinds of explanations. Interpretivists typically use the term *human action* (as opposed to *behavior*) to signal not only that intentions of the actor are relevant but that these intentions and the behavior itself are socially, temporally, and culturally situated and constituted. See also Bruner (1990, p. 19) and Erickson (1990, p. 98).

10. The bid to explicate the nature of interpretation is directed, in part, at the naturalists' claim that the aim (and form) of causal explanation in the natural sciences applies equally well to the social sciences. To argue that we "understand" human action *by means of interpretation* is to argue for an altogether different aim of the social sciences. Erickson (1990) explains this shift as follows: "If people take action on the grounds of their interpretations of the actions of others, then meaning-interpretations themselves are causal for humans. This is not true in nature. . . . The billiard ball does not make sense of its environment. But the human actor in society does, and different humans make sense differently. They impute symbolic meaning to other's actions and take their own actions in accord with the meaning interpretations they have made" (p. 98).

11. For an example of the difference this interpretation of *Verstehen* makes in humanistic and hermeneutical psychology, see Sass (1988).

12. Critical hermeneutics (e.g., Abel and Habermas) challenges the idealist assumptions of this commitment to interpretation as ontological hermeneutics and points to its failure to consider the extralinguistic considerations that constitute the world of thought and action. In the discussion of feminist standpoint epistemologies that appears later in this chapter these concerns are revisited. See also Chapter 9, by Olesen, and Chapter 10, by Stanfield, in this volume.

13. This reconceptualization of criteria for appraisal is evident in constructionist thinking. See below and Eisner (1991, pp. 53ff.), Goodman and Elgin (1988, pp. 153ff.), and Gergen (1991, pp. 226ff.)

14. Experience-near and experience-distant concepts are roughly analogous to emic and etic perspectives, respectively.

15. For a brief discussion of the difference between philosophical and methodological behaviorism, see Nagel (1961, p. 480).

16. Joas (1987) argues that the Chicago school of symbolic interactionism only partially realized the full promise of a social philosophy of pragmatism.

17. Denzin's (1989a, 1989b, 1992) recent work is in the main a deconstruction of the texts that form the tradition of symbolic interactionism. It is a highly synthetic, complex reformulation of the interactionist project that draws on insights from postmodern ethnography, feminist critiques of positivism, hermeneutical and existential phenomenology, cultural studies, and poststructuralist thought of Foucault and Derrida, as well as a recovery of a critically engaged social pragmatism.

18. For an examination of the ways in which realism is inscribed in a fieldwork text, see Clifford (1983), Clifford and Marcus (1986), Van Maanen (1988).

19. Furthermore, as Stephen Toulmin (1982) has argued, natural scientists are also in the business of construing reality, and the regulative ideals of objectivity and rationality are not necessarily at odds with a constructivist point of view.

20. Goodman is not principally concerned with applying his insights to social science, and furthermore, understanding Goodman is not easy going; by his own admission he disdains writing "flatfooted philosophy." Hence few who label their methodologies constructivist (with the notable exception of Eisner and Bruner) make any reference to Goodman's work. Eisner is discussed below. Bruner (1986, 1990) acknowledges Goodman's influence on his own account of cultural psychology, which takes seriously the activity of meaning making and the intentional states of social agents. Bruner's recent work is a redescription of the cognitive enterprise grounded in the examination of how meaning is constructed. It stands as a corrective to accounts of cognitive science shaped by the metaphors of computation and information processing.

21. See Cornel West (1989) for a brief discussion of Goodman's contribution to the philosophy of American pragmatism.

22. Radical constructivist thinking informs much current work in curriculum inquiry in mathematics and science education (e.g., Bodner, 1986; Cobb & Steffe, 1983; Cobb, Yackel, & Wood, 1992; Davis, Maher, & Noddings, 1990; Driver & Oldham, 1986; Novak, 1987). It is becoming something of a rallying cry for reformulating theories of teaching and learning among instructional technologists and educational psychologists (e.g., Duffy & Jonassen, 1991). As Matthews (1992) has noted, the emphasis here is not on knowledge as something that tells us about the world, but knowledge as something that tells us about our experiences and the best ways to organize them. Learning is redefined as a process of experiencing and developing the knowledge construction process, and teaching becomes less a matter of communicating content (i.e., a transmission model) and more a matter of facilitating a process.

23. Of course, an instrumentalist view of theory and knowledge was also characteristic of the logical empiricists' view. They would no doubt have taken great delight in von Glasersfeld's (1991) choice of the title "Knowing Without Metaphysics."

24. Gergen (1991) claims that "words are not maps of reality. Rather, words gain their meaning through their use in social interchange, within the 'language games' of the culture. We don't use words like *perception, thought,* and *memory* because they accurately map

a world we call mental. Rather, such terms gain their meaning from the way they are used in social life" (p. 102).

25. See Harding (1986) and Riger (1992) for an overview of different feminist epistemologies.

26. See also the chapters in this volume by Olesen (Chapter 9), Stanfield (Chapter 10), and Fiske (Chapter 11).

27. Di Leonardo (1991) argues that social constructionism need not degenerate into the nihilist stance of poststructuralism that denies the existence of social order, declares the death of the subject, and levels the distinctions between truth and falsehood.

28. It should be noted that Lincoln and Guba (1985, pp. 83-87) are somewhat equivocal on this issue. They claim to be drawn to the position that all reality is created by mind, yet are willing to settle for a less radical view of "constructed realities." They hold that constructions are invented or created, yet those constructions are related to "tangible entities"—events, persons, objects. If these tangible entities are not solely creations of mind, then they must be ontically "real." The distinction they draw here seems to be one of a difference between experiential reality (constructions) and ontological reality (tangible entities).

29. See di Leonardo (1991) and Rosenau (1992) for discussions of the difference between postmodernism and poststructuralism.

30. See also J. K. Smith (1989, chap. 7) for an extended discussion of this issue.

31. Schutz's (1967) idea of multiple realities is often wrongly interpreted. He describes the world of science, the world of mythology, the world of religion, the world of dreams, and so forth as multiple realities, or more specifically as "finite provinces of meaning" (p. 230). Yet he does not claim that these are literally different realities: "We speak of provinces of *meaning* . . . because it is the meaning of our experiences and not the ontological structure of the objects [in a given province] which constitutes reality." He views these multiple realities as "merely names for different tensions in one and the same life, unbroken from birth to death, which is attended to in different modifications" (p. 258).

32. See, for example, Crapanzano's (1986) unmasking of Geertz's authority as ethnographer in the study of the Balinese cockfight.

33. Following Matthews (1992), we might hazard the explanation that this tension arises from the fact that constructivism rightly criticizes empiricist assumptions yet clings to an empiricist epistemological paradigm. One alternative is a nonempiricist, objectivist epistemology of Matthews (1992) and Chalmers (1982). Another is the analysis of practices wherein the epistemology of hermeneutics is not detached from the sociology of communication (see, e.g., Giddens, 1976, 1984; Habermas, 1972).

34. This development is also supported by the growing interest in narrative and storytelling as a means of shaping, organizing, and understanding human experience (see MacIntyre, 1977, 1981; Sarbin, 1986).

References

Abel, T. (1948). The operation called *Verstehen*. *American Journal of Sociology, 54,* 211-218.

Bauman, Z. (1978). *Hermeneutics and social science.* London: Hutchinson.

Belenky, M. F., Clinchy, B. M., Goldberger, N. R., & Tarule, J. M. (1986). *Women's ways of knowing: The development of self, voice and mind.* New York: Basic Books.

Berger, P. L., & Kellner, H. (1981). *Sociology reinterpreted: An essay on method and vocation.* Garden City, NY: Anchor.

Bernstein, R. J. (1976). *The restructuring of social and political theory.* Philadelphia: University of Pennsylvania Press.

Bernstein, R. J. (1986). What is the difference that makes a difference? Gadamer, Habermas, and Rorty. In B. R. Wachterhauser (Ed.), *Hermeneutics and modern philosophy* (pp. 343-376). Albany: State University of New York Press.

Bernstein, R. J. (1992). *The new constellation.* Cambridge: MIT Press.

Bleicher, J. (1980). *Contemporary hermeneutics: Hermeneutics as method, philosophy and critique.* London: Routledge & Kegan Paul.

Blumer, H. (1954). What is wrong with social theory? *American Sociological Review, 19,* 3-10.

Blumer, H. (1969). *Symbolic interactionism: Perspective and method.* Englewood Cliffs, NJ: Prentice Hall.

Blumer, H. (1980). Mead and Blumer: The convergent methodological perspectives of social behaviorism and symbolic interactionism. *American Sociological Review, 45,* 409-419.

Bodner, G. M. (1986). Constructivism: A theory of knowledge. *Journal of Chemical Education, 63,* 873-878.

Bruner, J. (1986). *Actual minds, possible worlds.* Cambridge, MA: Harvard University Press.

Bruner, J. (1990). *Acts of meaning.* Cambridge, MA: Harvard University Press.

Burrell, G., & Morgan, G. (1979). *Sociological paradigms and organizational analysis.* London: Heinemann.

Chalmers, A. F. (1982). *What is this thing called science?* St. Lucia: University of Queensland Press.

Clifford, J. (1983). On ethnographic authority. *Representations, 1,* 118-146.

Clifford, J. (1990). Notes on (field)notes. In R. Sanjek (Ed.), *Fieldnotes: The makings of anthropology* (pp. 47-70). Albany: State University of New York Press.

Clifford, J., & Marcus, G. E. (Eds.). (1986). *Writing culture: The poetics and politics of ethnography.* Berkeley: University of California Press.

Cobb, P., & Steffe, L. (1983). The constructivist researcher as teacher and model builder. *Journal for Research in Mathematics Education, 14*(2), 83-94.

Cobb, P., Yackel, E., & Wood, T. (1992). A constructivist alternative to the representational view of mind in mathematics education. *Journal for Research in Mathematics Education, 23*(1), 2-34.

Crapanzano, V. (1986). Hermes' dilemma: The masking of subversion in ethnographic description. In J. Clifford & G. E. Marcus (Eds.), *Writing culture: The poetics and politics of ethnography* (pp. 51-76). Berkeley: University of California Press.

Davis, R. B., Maher, C. A., & Noddings, N. (Eds.). (1990). *Constructivist views on the teaching and learning of mathematics.* Reston, VA: National Council of Teachers of Mathematics.

Denzin, N. K. (1971). The logic of naturalistic inquiry. *Social Forces, 50,* 166-182.

Denzin, N. K. (1989a). *Interpretive biography.* Newbury Park, CA: Sage.

Denzin, N. K. (1989b). *Interpretive interactionism.* Newbury Park, CA: Sage.

Denzin, N. K. (1989c). *The research act: A theoretical introduction to sociological methods* (3rd ed.). Englewood Cliffs, NJ: Prentice Hall.

Denzin, N. K. (1992). *Symbolic interactionism and cultural studies.* Cambridge, UK: Basil Blackwell.

di Leonardo, M. (1991). Introduction: Gender, culture and political economy: Feminist anthropology in historical perspective. In M. di Leonardo (Ed.), *Gender at the crossroads of knowledge: Feminist anthropology in the postmodern era* (pp. 1-48). Berkeley: University of California Press.

Driver, R., & Oldham, V. (1986). A constructivist approach to curriculum development in science. *Studies in Science Education, 13,* 105-122.

Duffy, T. A., & Jonassen, D. H. (Eds.). (1991). Continuing the dialogue on the implications of constructivism for educational technology [Special issue]. *Educational Technology, 31*(9), 9-48.

Eisner, E. (1985). Aesthetic modes of knowing. In E. Eisner (Ed.), *Learning and teaching the ways of knowing: Eighty-fourth yearbook of the National Society for the Study of Education* (Part 2, pp. 23-36). Chicago: National Society for the Study of Education.

Eisner, E. (1991). *The enlightened eye: Qualitative inquiry and the enhancement of educational practices.* New York: Macmillan.

Erickson, F. (1986). Qualitative methods. In M. C. Wittrock (Ed.), *Handbook of research on teaching* (3rd ed., pp. 119-161). New York: Macmillan.

Erickson, F. (1990). Qualitative methods. In *Research in teaching and learning* (Vol. 2, pp. 77-194). New York: Macmillan.

Fish, S. (1989). *Doing what comes naturally: Change, rhetoric, and the practice of theory in literary and legal studies.* Durham, NC: Duke University Press.

Fuss, D. (1989). *Essentially speaking: Feminism, nature, and difference.* London: Routledge.

Gadamer, H. G. (1989). *Truth and method* (2nd rev. ed.). (J. Weinsheimer & D. G. Marshall, Trans.). New York: Crossroads.

Gal, S. (1991). Between speech and silence: The problematics of research on language and gender. In M. di Leonardo (Ed.), *Gender at the crossroads of knowledge: Feminist anthropology in the postmodern era* (pp. 175-203). Berkeley: University of California Press.

Geertz, C. (1973). *The interpretation of cultures: Selected essays.* New York: Basic Books.

Geertz, C. (1980). Blurred genres: The refiguration of social thought. *American Scholar, 49,* 165-179.

Geertz, C. (1983). *Local knowledge: Further essays in interpretive anthropology.* New York: Basic Books.

Geertz, C. (1988). *Works and lives: The anthropologist as author.* Stanford, CA: Stanford University Press.

Gergen, K. J. (1985). The social constructionist movement in modern psychology. *American Psychologist, 40,* 266-275.

Gergen, K. J. (1986). Correspondence versus autonomy in the language of understanding human action. In D. W. Fiske & R. A. Shweder (Eds.), *Metatheory in social science.* Chicago: University of Chicago Press.

Gergen, K. J. (1991). *The saturated self: Dilemmas of identity in contemporary life.* New York: Basic Books.

Gergen, K. J., & Gergen, M. M. (1991). Toward reflexive methodologies. In F. Steier (Ed.), *Research and reflexivity* (pp. 76-95). Newbury Park, CA: Sage.

Giddens, A. (1976). *New rules of sociological method: A positive critique of interpretative sociologies.* New York: Basic Books.

Giddens, A. (1984). *The constitution of society.* Berkeley: University of California Press.

Gilligan, C. (1982). *In a different voice: Psychological theory and women's development.* Cambridge: Harvard University Press.

Goodman, N. (1978). *Ways of worldmaking.* Indianapolis: Hackett.

Goodman, N. (1984). *Of mind and other matters.* Cambridge, MA: Harvard University Press.

Goodman, N., & Elgin, C. (1988). *Reconceptions in philosophy and other arts and sciences.* Indianapolis: Hackett.

Guba, E. G., & Lincoln, Y. S. (1989). *Fourth generation evaluation.* Newbury Park, CA: Sage.

Habermas, J. (1972). *Knowledge and human interests* (T. McCarthy, Trans.). Boston: Beacon.

Hammersley, M. (1989). *The dilemma of qualitative method: Herbert Blumer and the Chicago tradition.* London: Routledge.

Hammersley, M. (1992a). Some reflections on ethnography and validity. *International Journal of Qualitative Studies in Education, 5,* 195-203.

Hammersley, M. (1992b). *What's wrong with ethnography? Methodological explorations.* London: Routledge.

Harding, S. (1986). *The science question in feminism.* Ithaca, NY: Cornell University Press.

Harding, S. (1987). Is there a feminist method? In S. Harding (Ed.), *Feminism and methodology: Social science issues* (pp. 1-14). Bloomington: Indiana University Press.

Jackson, M. (1989). *Paths toward a clearing: Radical empiricism and ethnographic inquiry.* Bloomington: Indiana University Press.

Joas, H. (1987). Symbolic interactionism. In A. Giddens & J. Turner (Eds.), *Social theory today* (pp. 82-115). Stanford, CA: Stanford University Press.

Jonsen, A. R., & Toulmin, S. (1988). *The abuse of casuistry: A history of moral reasoning.* Berkeley: University of California Press.

Kirk, J., & Miller, M. L. (1986). *Reliability and validity in qualitative research.*Newbury Park, CA: Sage.

Knorr-Cetina, K. D. (1981). *The manufacture of knowledge: An essay on the constructivist and contextual nature of science.* New York: Pergamon.

LeCompte, M. D., & Preissle, J., with Tesch, R. (1993). *Ethnography and qualitative design in educational research* (2nd ed.). New York: Academic Press.

Lincoln, Y. S., & Guba, E. G. (1985). *Naturalistic inquiry.* Beverly Hills, CA: Sage.

MacIntyre, A. (1977). Epistemological crises, dramatic narrative and the philosophy of science. *Monist, 60,* 453-472.

MacIntyre, A. (1981). *After virtue.* Notre Dame, IN: University of Notre Dame Press.

Madison, G. B. (1988). *The hermeneutics of postmodernity.* Bloomington: Indiana University Press.

Magoon, A. J. (1977). Constructivist approaches in educational research. *Review of Educational Research, 47,* 651-693.

Martin, E. (1987). *The woman in the body.* Boston: Beacon.

Matthews, M. R. (1992, March). *Old wine in new bottles: A problem with constructivist epistemology.* Paper presented at the annual meeting of the Philosophy of Education Society, Denver, CO.

Meltzer, B. N., Petras, J. W., & Reynolds, L. T. (1975). *Symbolic interactionism: Genesis, varieties and criticism.* London: Routledge & Kegan Paul.

Mies, M. (1983). Towards a methodology for feminist research. In G. Bowles & R. Duelli-Klein (Eds.), *Theories of women's studies* (pp. 117-139). London: Routledge & Kegan Paul.

Nagel, E. (1961). *The structure of science.* New York: Harcourt Brace.

Novak, J. D. (Ed.). (1987). *Proceedings of the second international seminar: Misconceptions and educational strategies in science and mathematics* (Vols. 1-3). Ithaca, NY: Cornell University Press.

Oakley, A. (1981). Interviewing women: A contradiction in terms. In H. Roberts (Ed.), *Doing feminist research* (pp. 30-61). London: Routledge.

Plummer, K. (Ed.). (1991). *Symbolic interactionism: Vols. 1 and 2. Classic and contemporary issues.* Hauts, England: Edward Elgar.

Rabinow, P. (1977). *Reflections on fieldwork in Morocco.* Berkeley: University of California Press.

Rabinow, P. (1986). Representations are social facts: Modernity and post-modernity in anthropology. In J. Clifford & G. E. Marcus (Eds.), *Writing culture: The poetics and politics of ethnography* (pp. 234-261). Berkeley: University of California Press.

Rabinow, P., & Sullivan, W. M. (1987). The interpretive turn: A second look. In P. Rabinow & W. M. Sullivan (Eds.), *Interpretive social science: A second look* (pp. 1-30). Berkeley: University of California Press.

Radway, J. (1984). *Reading the romance: Feminism and the representation of women in popular culture.* Chapel Hill: University of North Carolina Press.

Reinharz, S. (1992). *Feminist methods in social research.* New York: Oxford University Press.

Ricoeur, P. (1971). The model of the text: Meaningful action considered as a text. *Social Research, 38,* 529-562.

Riger, S. (1992). Epistemological debates, feminist voices: Science, social values, and the study of women. *American Psychologist, 47,* 730-740.

Rorty, R. (1982). *Consequences of pragmatism.* Minneapolis: University of Minnesota Press.

Rosenau, P. M. (1992). *Post-modernism and the social sciences: Insights, inroads, and intrusion.* Princeton, NJ: Princeton University Press.

Rudner, R. (1966). *Philosophy of social science.* Englewood Cliffs, NJ: Prentice Hall.

Sarbin, T. (Ed.). (1986). *Narrative psychology: The storied nature of human conduct.* New York: Praeger.

Sass, L. A. (1988). Humanism, hermeneutics, and the concept of the human subject. In S. B. Messer, L. A. Sass, & R. L. Woolfolk (Eds.), *Hermeneutics and psychological theory* (pp. 222-271). New Brunswick, NJ: Rutgers University Press.

Schutz, A. (1967). *Collected papers* (Vol. 1, M. Natanson, Ed.). The Hague: Martinus Nijhoff.

Shapiro, M. J. (1981). *Language and political understanding: The politics of discursive practices.* New Haven, CT: Yale University Press.

Smith, D. (1987). *The everyday world as problematic.* Boston: Northeastern University Press.

Smith, J. K. (1989). *The nature of social and educational inquiry: Empiricism versus interpretation.* Norwood, NJ: Ablex.

Stacey, J. (1988). Can there be a feminist ethnography? *Women's Studies International Forum, 11,* 21-27.

Stake, R. E. (1991). Retrospective on "The countenance of educational evaluation." In M. W. McLaughlin & D. C. Phillips (Eds.), *Evaluation and education at the quarter century: Ninetieth yearbook of the National Society for the Study of Education* (Part 2, pp. 67-88). Chicago: University of Chicago Press.

Steier, F. (1991). Introduction: Research as self-reflexivity, self-reflexivity as social process. In F. Steier (Ed.), *Research and reflexivity* (pp. 1-11). Newbury Park, CA: Sage.

Strike, K. A. (1987). Toward a coherent constructivism, In J. D. Novak (Ed.), *Proceedings of the second international seminar: Misconceptions and educa-*

tional strategies in science and mathematics (Vol. 1, pp. 481-489). Ithaca, NY: Cornell University Press.

Sullivan, W. (1986). *Reconstructing public philosophy.* Berkeley: University of California Press.

Taylor, C. (1964). *The explanation of behaviour.* London: Routledge & Kegan Paul.

Taylor, C. (1987). Interpretation and the sciences of man. In P. Rabinow & W. M. Sullivan (Eds.), *Interpretive social science: A second look* (pp. 33-81). Berkeley: University of California Press. (Reprinted from *Review of Metaphysics,* 1971, *25,* 3-51)

Taylor, C. (1989). *Sources of the self.* Cambridge, MA: Harvard University Press.

Toulmin, S. (1982). The construal of reality: Criticism in modern and postmodern science. In W. J. T. Mitchell (Ed.), *The politics of interpretation* (pp. 99-117). Chicago: University of Chicago Press.

Van Maanen, J. (1988). *Tales of the field: On writing ethnography.* Chicago: University of Chicago Press.

von Glasersfeld, E. (1989). Cognition, construction of knowledge, and teaching. *Synthese, 80,* 121-140.

von Glasersfeld, E. (1991). Knowing without metaphysics: Aspects of the radical constructivist position. In F. Steier (Ed.), *Research and reflexivity* (pp. 12-29). Newbury Park, CA: Sage.

Wachterhauser, B. R. (1986). Introduction: History and language in understanding. In B. R. Wachterhauser (Ed.), *Hermeneutics and modern philosophy* (pp. 5-61). Albany: State University of New York Press.

West, C. (1989). *The American evasion of philosophy: A genealogy of pragmatism.* Madison: University of Wisconsin Press.

Wolcott, H. F. (1988). Ethnographic research in education. In R. M. Jaeger (Ed.), *Complementary methods for research in education* (pp. 187-249). Washington, DC: American Educational Research Association.

Wolcott, H. F. (1992). Posturing in qualitative inquiry. In M. D. LeCompte, W. L. Millroy, & J. Preissle (Eds.), *The handbook of qualitative research in education* (pp. 3-52). New York: Academic Press.

8

Rethinking Critical Theory and Qualitative Research

JOE L. KINCHELOE
PETER L. McLAREN

The Roots of Critical Research

SOME 70 years after its development in Frankfurt, Germany, critical theory retains its ability to disrupt and challenge the status quo. In the process, it elicits highly charged emotions of all types—fierce loyalty from its proponents, vehement hostility from its detractors. Such vibrantly polar reactions indicate at the very least that critical theory still matters. We can be against critical theory or for it, but, especially at the present historical juncture, we cannot be without it. Indeed, qualitative research that frames its purpose in the context of critical theoretical concerns still produces, in our view, undeniably dangerous knowledge, the kind of information and insight that upsets institutions and threatens to overturn sovereign regimes of truth.

Critical theory is a term that is often evoked and frequently misunderstood. It usually refers to the theoretical tradition developed by the Frankfurt school, a group of writers connected to the Institute of Social Research at the University of Frankfurt. However, none of the Frankfurt school theorists ever claimed to have developed a unified approach to cultural criticism. In its beginnings, Max Horkheimer, Theodor Adorno, and Herbert Marcuse initiated a conversation with the German tradition of philosophical and social thought, especially Marx, Kant, Hegel, and Weber. From the vantage point of these critical theorists, whose political sensibilities were influenced by the devastations of World War I, postwar Germany with its economic depression marked by inflation and unemployment, and the failed strikes and protests in Germany and Central Europe in this same period, the world was in urgent need of reinterpretation. From this perspective, they defied Marxist orthodoxy while deepening their belief that injustice and subjugation shaped the lived world (Bottomore, 1984; Gibson, 1986; Held, 1980; Jay, 1973). Focusing their attention on the changing nature of capitalism, the early critical theorists analyzed the mutating forms of domination that accompanied this change (Giroux, 1983; McLaren, 1989).

Only a decade after the Frankfurt school was established, the Nazis controlled Germany. The danger posed by the exclusive Jewish membership of the Frankfurt school, and its association with Marxism, convinced Horkheimer, Adorno,

AUTHORS' NOTE: Thanks to Yvonna Lincoln and Norman Denzin for their helpful suggestions on an earlier draft of this chapter.

and Marcuse to leave Germany. Eventually locating themselves in California, these critical theorists were shocked by American culture. Offended by the taken-for-granted empirical practices of American social science researchers, Horkheimer, Adorno, and Marcuse were challenged to respond to the social science establishment's belief that their research could describe and accurately measure any dimension of human behavior. Piqued by the contradictions between progressive American rhetoric of egalitarianism and the reality of racial and class discrimination, these theorists produced their major work while residing in the United States. In 1953, Horkheimer and Adorno returned to Germany and reestablished the Institute of Social Research. Significantly, Herbert Marcuse stayed in the United States, where he would find a new audience for his work in social theory. Much to his own surprise, Marcuse skyrocketed to fame as the philosopher of the student movements of the 1960s. Critical theory, especially the emotionally and sexually liberating work of Marcuse, provided the philosophical voice of the New Left. Concerned with the politics of psychological and cultural revolution, the New Left preached a Marcusian sermon of political emancipation (Gibson, 1986; Wexler, 1991).

Many academicians who had come of age in the politically charged atmosphere of the 1960s focused their scholarly attention on critical theory. Frustrated by forms of domination emerging from a post-Enlightenment culture nurtured by capitalism, these scholars saw in critical theory a method of temporarily freeing academic work from these forms of power. Impressed by critical theory's dialectical concern with the social construction of experience, they came to view their disciplines as manifestations of the discourses and power relations of the social and historical contexts that produced them. The "discourse of possibility" implicit within the constructed nature of social experience suggested to these scholars that a reconstruction of the social sciences could eventually lead to a more egalitarian and democratic social order. New poststructuralist conceptualizations of human agency and their promise that men and women can at least partly determine their own existence offered new hope for emancipatory forms of social research when compared with orthodox Marxism's assertion of the iron laws of history, the irrevocable evil of capitalism, and the proletariat as the privileged subject and anticipated agent of social transformation. For example, when Henry Giroux and other critical educators criticized the argument made by Marxist scholars Samuel Bowles and Herbert Gintis—that schools were capitalist agencies of social, economic, cultural, and bureaucratic reproduction—they contrasted the deterministic perspectives of Bowles and Gintis with the idea that schools, as venues of hope, could become sites of resistance and democratic possibility through concerted efforts among teachers and students to work within a liberatory pedagogical framework. Giroux (1988), in particular, maintained that schools can become institutions where forms of knowledge, values, and social relations are taught for the purpose of educating young people for critical empowerment rather than subjugation.

Partisan Research in a "Neutral" Academic Culture

In the space available here it is impossible to do justice to all of the critical traditions that have drawn inspiration from Marx, Kant, Hegel, Weber, the Frankfurt school theorists, continental social theorists such as Foucault, Habermas, and Derrida, Latin American thinkers such as Paulo Freire, French feminists such as Irigaray, Kristeva, or Cixous, or Russian sociolinguists such as Bakhtin and Vygotsky—most of whom regularly find their way into the reference lists of contemporary critical researchers. Today there are criticalist schools in many fields, and even a superficial discussion of the most prominent of these schools would demand much more space than we have available.

The fact that numerous books have been written about the often-virulent disagreements among members of the Frankfurt school only heightens our concern with "packaging" the different criticalist schools. Critical theory should not be treated as a universal grammar of revolutionary thought objectified and reduced to discrete formulaic pronouncements or strategies. We have chosen to define the critical tradition very broadly and heuristically, and this will undoubtedly trouble many researchers who identify themselves as criticalists. We have decided to place our stress on the underlying commonality among these schools of thought, at the expense of focusing on their differences. This, of course, is always risky business in terms of suggesting a false unity or consensus where none exists, but such concerns are unavoidable in a survey chapter such as this. We are defining a criticalist as a researcher or theorist who attempts to use her or his work as a form of social or cultural criticism and who accepts certain basic assumptions: that all thought is fundamentally mediated by power relations that are social and historically constituted; that facts can never be isolated from the domain of values or removed from some form of ideological inscription; that the relationship between concept and object and between signifier and signified is never stable or fixed and is often mediated by the social relations of capitalist production and consumption; that language is central to the formation of subjectivity (conscious and unconscious awareness); that certain groups in any society are privileged over others and, although the reasons for this privileging may vary widely, the oppression that characterizes contemporary societies is most forcefully reproduced when subordinates accept their social status as natural, necessary, or inevitable; that oppression has many faces and that focusing on only one at the expense of others (e.g., class oppression versus racism) often elides the interconnections among them; and, finally, that mainstream research practices are generally, although most often unwittingly, implicated in the reproduction of systems of class, race, and gender oppression.

In today's climate of blurred disciplinary genres, it is not uncommon to find literary theorists doing anthropology and anthropologists writing about literary theory, or political scientists trying their hand at ethnomethodological analysis, or philosophers doing Lacanian film criticism. We offer this observation not as an excuse to be wantonly eclectic in our treatment of the critical tradition but to make the point that any attempts to delineate critical theory as discrete schools of analysis will fail to capture the hybridity endemic to contemporary criticalist analysis.

Readers familiar with the criticalist traditions will recognize essentially four different "emergent" schools of social inquiry in this chapter: the neo-Marxist tradition of critical theory associated most closely with the work of Horkheimer, Adorno, and Marcuse; the genealogical writings of Michel Foucault; the practices of poststructuralist deconstruction associated with Derrida; and postmodernist currents associated with Derrida, Foucault, Lyotard, Ebert, and others. In our view, critical ethnography has been influenced by all of these perspectives in different ways and to different degrees. From critical theory, researchers inherit a forceful criticism of the positivist conception of science and instrumental rationality, especially in Adorno's idea of *negative dialectics,* which posits an unstable relationship of contradiction between concepts and objects; from Derrida, researchers are given a means for deconstructing objective truth or what is referred to as "the metaphysics of presence." For Derrida, the meaning of a word is constantly deferred because it can have meaning only in relation to its difference from other words within a given system of language; Foucault invites researchers to explore the ways in which discourses are implicated in relations of power and how power and knowledge serve as dialectically reinitiating practices that regulate what is considered reasonable and true. We have characterized much of the work influenced by these writers as the "ludic" and "resistance" postmodernist theoretical perspectives.

Critical research can be best understood in the context of the empowerment of individuals. Inquiry that aspires to the name *critical* must be connected to an attempt to confront the injustice of a particular society or sphere within the society. Research thus becomes a transformative endeavor unembarrassed by the label "political" and unafraid to consummate a relationship with an emancipatory consciousness. Whereas traditional researchers cling to the guard rail of neutrality, critical researchers frequently announce their partisanship in the struggle for a better world. Traditional researchers see their task as the description, interpretation, or reanimation of a slice of reality, whereas critical researchers often regard their work as a first step toward forms of political action that can redress the injustices found in the field site or constructed in the very act of research itself. Horkheimer (1972) put it succinctly when he argued that critical theory and research are never satisfied with merely increasing knowledge (see also Giroux, 1983, 1988; Quantz, 1992).

Research in the critical tradition takes the form of self-conscious criticism—self-conscious in the sense that researchers try to become aware of the ideological imperatives and epistemological presuppositions that inform their research as well as their own subjective, intersubjective, and normative reference claims. Thus critical researchers enter into an investigation with their assumptions on the table, so no one is confused concerning the epistemological and political baggage they bring with them to the research site. Upon detailed analysis these assumptions may change. Stimulus for change may come from the critical researchers' recognition that such assumptions are not leading to emancipatory actions. The source of this emancipatory action involves the researcher's ability to expose the contradictions of world of appearances accepted by the dominant culture as natural and inviolable (Giroux, 1983; McLaren, 1989, 1992a, in press). Such appearances may, critical researchers contend, conceal social relationships of inequality and injustice. For instance, if we view the violence we find in classrooms not as random or isolated incidents created by aberrant individuals willfully stepping out of line in accordance with a particular form of social pathology, but as narratives of transgression and resistance, then this could indicate that the "political unconscious" lurking beneath the surface of everyday classroom life is not unrelated to issues of race, class, and gender oppression.

There exists among critical researchers a firm recognition that ideologies are not simply deceptive and imaginary mental relations that individuals and groups live out relative to their material conditions of existence, but are also very much inscribed in the materiality of social and institutional practices (Kincheloe, 1993; McLaren, 1989, in press). For instance, people act *as if* certain social and cultural relations were true even when they know them not to be true. They choose, in other words, essentially to misrecognize these relations of power (e.g., state power exists only because we obey its rules). Generally speaking, people do not necessarily want to give up this misrecognition (Zizek, 1990) because of the power it affords them as dominant groups, or, in the case of subordinate groups, because "the ruled accept their subordinate position for the sake of a degree of freedom that indulges certain libidinal drives, sutures fissured egos, fulfills fantasies, and so forth" (San Juan, 1992, p. 114). This willful misrecognition on the part of both dominant and subordinate groups creates a quarantined site where the political dimensions of everyday life can be shrouded by commonsense knowledge and, in effect, rhetorically disengaged. This also explains how the ascendancy of a historic bloc of forces is able to reproduce its economies of power and privilege hegemonically (Gramsci, 1971). Hegemony is secured when the virulence of oppression, in its many guises (e.g., race, gender, class, sexual orientation), is accepted as consensus.

Critical Ethnography: Reclaiming the Marxist Legacy in an Age of Socialist Decline

Still in its infancy as a research approach that has developed within the qualitative tradition over the past 20 years, and lacking that obviousness of meaning that would secure its disciplinary status, critical ethnography continues to redefine itself through its alliances with recent theoretical currents. As a nascent transdisciplinary project, it is more readily identified with its celebrated exponents and coprotagonists (e.g., Paul Willis, George Marcus, Christine Griffin, James Clifford, and Michael Taussig) than with the way it has spawned innumerable alliances with leftist political agendas in general and neo-Marxian ones in particular in both Britain and the United States. It is hardly surprising, then, that its distinctive mode of entry into mainstream anthropological and sociological discourses has been stalled because of the quickening predicament generated by the recent demise of Marxism following the collapse of Soviet communism.

The loss of favor accorded to Marxist theory is certainly a partial explanation for critical ethnography's current—and sometimes narcissistic—infatuation with certain inflections and mutative combinations of postmodern social theory that have found their way into the writings of critical ethnographers. We are not suggesting that the turn to high-vogue postmodernism and the fashionable apostasy of deconstruction among some critical ethnographers is simply a substitute for the flagging credibility of Marxism. Rather, we are in basic agreement with Cornel West (1991), who notes that the "fashionable trashing of Marxist thought in the liberal academy" is primarily the result of the misunderstanding that vulgar Marxist thought (monocausal accounts of history, essentialist concepts of society, or reductionist accounts of history) somehow exhausts the entire Marxist tradition. West argues that the epistemic skepticism found in some strands of faddish deconstructive criticism and the explanatory agnosticism, or nihilism, associated with the work of descriptivist anthropologists and historians have made the "category mistake" of collapsing epistemological concerns of justification in philosophy into methodological concerns of explanation in social theory. This has caused ironic skeptics to avoid any theory that promotes purposeful social action for social and economic transformation. This category mistake has also caused the aesthetic historicists to illuminate the contingency and indeterminacy of social life "with little concern with how and why change and conflict take place" (p. xxii).

We follow West in arguing that, although nationalism, racism, gender oppression, homophobia, and ecological devastation have not been adequately understood by many Marxist theorists, Marxist theory nevertheless "proceeds within the boundaries of warranted assertable claims and rationally acceptable conclusions" and that it has helped to explain how "the dynamic processes of capital accumulation and the commodification of labor condition social, and cultural practices in an *inescapable* manner" (p. xxiii).

Douglas Kellner (1993) has recently argued that blaming the failure of Soviet communism on the work of Marx is highly unwarranted, dishonest, misleading, and, ultimately, philosophically indefensible. This is especially the case when one recognizes that Marx's writings support the claim that he was a consistent democrat, argued for workers' self-activity as the locus of popular sovereignty, and refused to advocate a party state or communist bureaucracy. Instead, Marx argued passionately and lucidly for a free society and democratically empowered citizenry. In fact, Kellner maintains, rather convincingly in our view, that the ideas of Rousseau and those of the Right Hegelians actually go much further in legitimating forms of societal oppression and the modern totalitarian state than Marx's theoretical work. Further, Kellner maintains that it is precisely the case that Marxian theorists have themselves produced some of the most trenchant and powerful criticisms of the repressive incarnations of socialism in the Soviet Union, such as the work of the Frankfurt school theorists. Admittedly, however, one of the serious flaws of Marxist discourse is that it regularly fails to incorporate the work of bourgeois revolutionary traditions (i.e., bourgeois traditions of rights and individual liberty) and the Marxian revolutionary socialist heritage into its system.

We suggest that there is nothing inconsistent in the critical and historical impulses of Marxian thought that would preclude the formation of a theoretical alliance with some of the more political strands of postmodern social theory. In fact, postmodern social theory could help to deepen and extend current incarnations of Marxian criticalist thinking significantly by helping to problematize what Stuart Hall (1990) refers to as "the disappearance of unified agency, like the 'ruling class' or 'the state,' as the instrumentality of oppression" (p. 31). In our view, postmodern criticism does not so much weaken the Marxian tradition as help to expand the Marxian critique of capitalist social relations by addressing the ambiguity currently surrounding the reconstituted nature of classes and class consciousness and by interrogating "the cultural logic of late capitalism" (to cite the now-famous phrase coined by Frederic Jameson to describe the postmodern condition). According to Jameson (1990), arguably the most important Marxian literary critic in the United States, "Democracy must involve more than political consultation. There must be forms of economic democracy and popular control in other ways, some of them are very problematic, like workers' management" (p. 31). The popular sovereignty practiced by the Paris Commune and celebrated by Marx and Engels as a democratic mode of worker self-management is a good example of what Jameson means by "economic democracy."

We agree with Jameson that the Marxian tradition still has an indispensable role to play in the reconstitution and reformation of capitalist democracy. We further share Kellner's (1993) sentiment that "only with genuine democracy can socialism provide a real alternative to the democratic capitalist societies of the West and East" (p. 34). The current crisis of Marxism suggests to us not that Marxist discourse is dead and should be displayed, like Lenin, in a glass case as an embalmed reminder of our debt to the founding fathers of the communist state. Nor in a more postmodern sense do we feel it to be destined to lie frozen like the corpse of Walt Disney, hidden away in a theme park vault, waiting to be reanimated at some future moment during the technological triumph of late capitalism. Rather, we believe that a Marxian-inspired critical ethnography deepened by a critical engagement with new currents of postmodern social theory has an important if not crucial role to play in the project of constructing new forms of socialist democracy.

Babes in Toyland: Critical Theory in Hyperreality

Postmodern Culture

In a contemporary era marked by the delegitimation of the grand narratives of Western civilization, a loss of faith in the power of reason, and a shattering of traditional religious orthodoxies, scholars continue to debate what the term *postmodernism* means, generally positing it as a periodizing concept following modernism. Indeed, scholars have not agreed if this epochal break with the "modern" era even constitutes a discrete period. In the midst of such confusion it seems somehow appropriate that scholars are fighting over the application of the term *postmodernism* to the contemporary condition. Accepting postmodernism as an apt moniker for the end of the twentieth century, a major feature of critical academic work has involved the exploration of what happens when critical theory encounters the postmodern condition, or hyperreality. *Hyperreality* is a term used to describe an information society socially saturated with ever-increasing forms of representation: filmic, photographic, electronic, and so on. These have had a profound effect on constructing the cultural narratives that shape our identities. The drama of living has been portrayed so often on television that individuals, for the most part, are increasingly able to predict the outcomes and consider such outcomes to be the "natural" and "normal" course of social life (Gergen, 1991).

As many postmodern analysts have put it, we become pastiches, imitative conglomerations of one another. In such a condition we approach life with low affect, with a sense of postmodern ennui and irremissible anxiety. Our emotional bonds are diffused as television, computers, VCRs, and stereo headphones assault us with representations that have shaped our cognitive and affective facilities in ways that still remain insufficiently understood. In the political arena, traditionalists circle their cultural wagons and fight off imagined bogeymen such as secular humanists, "extreme liberals," and utopianists, not realizing the impact that postmodern hyperreality exerts on their hallowed institutions. The nuclear family, for example, has declined in importance not because of the assault of "radical feminists" but because the home has been redefined through the familiar presence of electronic communication systems. Particular modes of information put individual family members in constant contact with specific subcultures. While they are physically in the home, they exist emotionally outside of it through the mediating effects of various forms of communication (Gergen, 1991; McLaren, in press; Poster, 1989). We increasingly make sense of the social world and judge other cultures through conventional and culture-bound television genres. Hyperreality has presented us with new forms of literacy that do not simply refer to discrete skills but rather constitute social skills and relations of symbolic power. These new technologies cannot be seen apart from the social and institutional contexts in which they are used and the roles they play in the family, the community, and the workplace. They also need to be seen in terms of how "viewing competencies" are socially distributed and the diverse social and discursive practices in which these new media literacies are produced (Buckingham, 1989).

Electronic transmissions generate new formations of cultural space and restructure experiences of time. We often are motivated to trade community membership for a sense of psuedobelonging to the mediascape. Residents of hyperreality are temporarily comforted by proclamations of community offered by "media personalities" on the 6 o'clock *Eyewitness News*. "Bringing news of your neighbors in the Tri-State community home to you," media marketers attempt to soften the edges of hyperreality, to soften the emotional effects of the social vertigo. The world is not brought into our homes by television as much as television brings its viewers to a quasi-fictional place—hyperreality (Luke, 1991).

Postmodern Social Theory

We believe that it is misleading to identify postmodernism with poststructuralism. Although there are certainly similarities involved, they cannot be considered discrete homologies. We also believe that it is a mistake to equate *postmodernism* with *postmodernity* or that these terms can be contrasted in some simple equivalent way with *modernism* and *modernity*. As Michael Peters (1993) notes, "To do so is to frame up the debate in strictly (and naively) modernist terminology which employs exhaustive binary oppositions privileging one set of terms against the other" (p. 14). We are using the term *postmodernity* to refer to the postmodern condition that we have described as *hyperreality* and the term *postmodern theory* as an umbrella term that includes antifoundationalist writing in philosophy and the social sciences. Again, we are using the term in a very general sense that includes poststructuralist currents.

Postmodern theoretical trajectories take as their entry point a rejection of the deeply ingrained assumptions of Enlightenment rationality, traditional Western epistemology, or any supposedly "secure" representation of reality that exists outside of discourse itself. Doubt is cast on the myth of the autonomous, transcendental subject, and the concept of praxis is marginalized in favor of rhetorical undecidability and textual analysis of social practices. As a species of criticism, intended, in part, as a central requestioning of the humanism and anthropologism of the early 1970s, postmodernist social theory rejects Hegel's ahistorical state of absolute knowledge and resigns itself to the impossibility of an ahistorical, transcendental, or self-authenticating version of truth. The reigning conviction that knowledge is knowledge only if it reflects the world as it "really" exists has been annihilated in favor of a view in which reality is socially constructed or semiotically posited. Furthermore, normative agreement on what should constitute and guide scientific practice and argumentative consistency has become an intellectual target for epistemological uncertainty.

Postmodern criticism takes as its starting point the notion that meaning is constituted by the continual playfulness of the signifier, and the thrust of its critique is aimed at deconstructing Western metanarratives of truth and the ethnocentrism implicit in the European view of history as the unilinear progress of universal reason. Postmodern theory is a site of both hope and fear, where there exists a strange convergence between critical theorists and political conservatives, a cynical complicity with status quo social and institutional relations and a fierce criticism of ideological manipulation and the reigning practices of subjectivity in which knowledge takes place.

Ludic and Resistance Postmodernism

Postmodernist criticism is not monolithic, and for the purposes of this essay we would like to distinguish between two theoretical strands. The first has been astutely described by Teresa Ebert (1991) as "ludic postmodernism" (p. 115)—an approach to social theory that is decidedly limited in its ability to transform oppressive social and political regimes of power. Ludic postmodernism generally occupies itself with a reality that is constituted by the continual playfulness of the signifier and the heterogeneity of differences. As such, ludic postmodernism (see, e.g., Lyotard, Derrida, Baudrillard) constitutes a moment of self-reflexivity in deconstructing Western metanarratives, asserting that "meaning itself is self-divided and undecidable" (Ebert, in press).

We want to argue that critical researchers should assume a cautionary stance toward ludic postmodernism critique because, as Ebert (1991, p. 115) notes, it tends to reinscribe the status quo and reduce history to the supplementarity of signification or the free-floating trace of textuality. As a mode of critique, it rests its case on interrogating specific and local enunciations of oppression, but often fails to analyze such enunciations in relation to larger dominating structures of oppression (Aronowitz & Giroux, 1991; McLaren, in press).

The kind of postmodern social theory we want to pose as a counterweight to skeptical and spectral postmodernism has been referred to as "oppositional postmodernism" (Foster, 1983), "radical critique-al theory" (Zavarzadeh & Morton, 1991), "postmodern education" (Aronowitz & Giroux, 1991), "resistance postmodernism" (Ebert, 1991, in press), and "critical postmodernism" (Giroux, 1992; McLaren, 1992b, in press; McLaren & Hammer, 1989). These forms of critique are not alternatives to ludic postmodernism but appropriations and extensions of this critique. Resistance postmodernism brings to ludic critique a form of materialist intervention, because it is not solely based on a textual theory of difference but rather on one that is also social and historical. In this way, postmodern critique can serve as an interventionist and transformative critique of Western culture. Following Ebert (1991), resistance postmodernism attempts to show that "textualities (significations) are material practices, forms of conflicting social relations" (p. 115). The sign is always an arena of material conflict and competing social relations as well as ideas. From this perspective we can "rewrite the sign as an ideological process formed out of a signifier standing in relation to a matrix of historically possible or suspended signifieds" (Ebert, in press). In other words, difference is politicized by being situated in real social and historical conflicts.

Resistance postmodernism does not abandon the undecidability or contingency of the social altogether; rather, the undecidability of history is understood as related to class struggle, the institutionalization of asymmetrical relations of power and privilege, and the way historical accounts are contested by different groups (Giroux, 1992; McLaren & Hammer, 1989; Zavarzadeh & Morton, 1991). On this matter Ebert (1991) remarks, "We need to articulate a theory of difference in which the differing, deferring slippage of signifiers is not taken as the result of the immanent logic of language but as the effect of the social conflicts traversing signification" (p. 118).

The synergism of the conversation between resistance postmodern and critical theory involves an interplay between the praxis of the critical and the radical uncertainty of the postmodern. As it invokes its strategies for the emancipation of meaning, critical theory provides the postmodern critique with a normative foundation (i.e., a basis for distinguishing between oppressive and liberatory social relations). Without such a foundation the postmodern critique is ever vulnerable to nihilism and inaction. Indeed, the normatively ungrounded postmodern critique is incapable of providing an ethically challenging and politically transformative program of action. Aronowitz, Giroux, and McLaren argue that if the postmodern critique is to make a valuable contribution to the notion of schooling as an emancipatory form of cultural politics, it must make connections to those egalitarian impulses of modernism that contribute to an emancipatory democracy. In doing this, the project of an emancipatory democracy and the schooling that supports it can be extended by new understandings of how power operates and by incorporating groups who had been excluded by their race, gender, or class (Aronowitz & Giroux, 1991; Codd, 1984; Godzich, 1992; Lash, 1990; McLaren, 1986, in press; Morrow, 1991; Rosenau, 1992; Welch, 1991; Yates, 1990).

A Step Beyond the Empirical: Critical Research

Critical research has never been reluctant to point out the limitations of empirical research, calling attention to the inability of traditional models of inquiry to escape the boundaries of a narrative realism. The rigorous methodological approaches of empirical inquiry often preclude larger interpretations of the forces that shape both the researcher and the researched. Empirical observation cannot supplant theoretical analysis and critical reflection. The project of critical research is not simply the empirical re-presentation of the world but the transgressive task of posing the research itself as a set of ideological practices. Empirical analysis needs to be interrogated in order to uncover the contradictions and negations embodied in any objective description. Critical researchers maintain that the meaning of an experience or an observation is not self-evident. The meaning of any experience will depend on the struggle over the interpretation and definition of that experience (Giroux, 1983; McLaren, 1986; Weiler, 1988).

Kincheloe (1991) argues that the way we analyze and interpret empirical data is conditioned by the way it is theoretically framed. It is also dependent upon the researcher's own ideological assumptions. The empirical data derived from any study cannot be treated as simple irrefutable facts. They represent hidden assumptions—assumptions the critical researcher must dig out and expose. As Einstein and Heisenberg pointed out long ago, what we see is not what we see but what we perceive. The knowledge that the world yields has to be interpreted by men and women who are a part of that world. What we call information always involves an act of human judgment. From a critical perspective this act of judgment is an interpretive act. The interpretation of theory, critical analysts contend, involves understanding the relationship between the particular and the whole and between the subject and the object of analysis. Such a position contradicts the traditional empiricist contention that theory is basically a matter of classifying objective data.

One of the most important sites of theoretical production in the history of critical research has been the Centre for Contemporary Cultural Studies (CCCS) at the University of Birmingham. Attempting to connect critical theory with the particularity of everyday experience, the CCCS researchers have argued that all experience is vulnerable to ideological inscription. At the same time, they have maintained that theorizing outside of everyday experience results in formal and deterministic theory. An excellent representative of the CCCS's perspectives is Paul Willis, who published *Learning to Labour: How Working Class Kids Get Working Class Jobs* in 1977, seven years after Colin Lacey's *Hightown Grammar* (1970). Redefining the nature of ethnographic research in a critical manner, *Learning to Labour* inspired a spate of critical studies: David Robins and Philip Cohen's *Knuckle Sandwich: Growing Up in the Working-Class City* in 1978, Paul Corrigan's *Schooling the Smash Street Kids* in 1979, and Dick Hebdige's *Subculture: The Meaning of Style* in 1979.

Also following Willis's work were critical feminist studies, including an anthology titled *Women Take Issue* (Centre for Contemporary Culture Studies, 1978). In 1985 Christine Griffin published *Typical Girls?*, the first extended feminist study produced by the CCCS. Conceived as a response to Willis's *Learning to Labour, Typical Girls?* analyzes adolescent female consciousness as it is constructed in a world of patriarchy. Through their recognition of patriarchy as a major disciplinary technology in the production of subjectivity, Griffin and the members of the CCCS gender study group move critical research in a multicultural direction. In addition to the examination of class, gender and racial analyses are beginning to gain in importance (Quantz, 1992). Poststructuralism frames power not simply as one aspect of a society, but as the basis of society. Thus patriarchy is not simply one isolated force among many with which women must contend; patriarchy informs all aspects of the social and effectively shapes women's lives.

Cornel West pushes critical research even further into the multicultural domain as he focuses critical attention on women, the Third World, and race. Adopting theoretical advances in neo-Marxist postcolonialism criticism and cultural studies, he is able to shed greater light on the workings of power in everyday life.

In *Schooling as a Ritual Performance,* Peter McLaren (1986) integrates poststructuralist and postcolonial criticism theory with the project of critical ethnography. He grounds his theoretical analysis in the poststructuralist claim that the connection of signifier and signified is arbitrary yet shaped by historical, cultural, and economic forces. The primary cultural narrative that defines school life is the resistance by students to the school's attempts to marginalize their street culture and street knowledge. McLaren analyzes the school as a cultural site where symbolic capital is struggled over in the form of ritual dramas. *Schooling as a Ritual Performance* adopts the position that researchers are unable to grasp themselves or others introspectively without social mediation through their positionalities with respect to race, class, gender, and other configurations. The visceral, bodily forms of knowledge, and the rhythms and gestures of the street culture of the students, are distinguished from the formal abstract knowledge of classroom instruction. Knowledge as it is constructed informally outside of the culture of school instruction is regarded by the teachers as threatening to the universalist and decidedly Eurocentric ideal of high culture that forms the basis of the school curriculum.

As critical researchers pursue this synergism between critical theory and postmodernism, they are confronted with postmodernism's redefinition of critical notions of democracy in terms of the concepts of multiplicity and difference. Traditional notions of community often privilege unity over diversity in the name of Enlightenment values. Poststructuralists in general and poststructuralist feminists in particular see this communitarian dream as politically disabling because of the suppression of race, class, and gender differences and the exclusion of subaltern voices and marginalized groups whom community members are loath to engage. What begins to emerge in this instance is the movement of feminist theoretical concerns to the center of critical theory. Indeed, after the feminist critique critical theory can never return to a paradigm of inquiry in which the concept of social class is antiseptically privileged and exalted as the master concept in the Holy Trinity of Race, Class, and Gender. A critical theory reconceptualized by poststructuralism and feminism promotes a politics of difference that refuses to pathologize or exoticize the Other. In this context, communities are more prone to revitalization; peripheralized groups in the thrall of a condescending Eurocentric gaze are able to edge closer to the borders of respect, and "classified" objects of research potentially acquire the characteristics of subjecthood. Kathleen Weiler's *Women Teaching for Change: Gender, Class, and Power* (1988) serves as a good example of critical research framed by feminist theory. Weiler shows not only how feminist theory can extend critical research, but how the concept of emancipation can be reconceptualized in light of a feminist epistemology (Aronowitz & Giroux, 1991; Lugones, 1987; Morrow, 1991; Weiler, 1988; Young, 1990).

As a "postmodernized" critical theory comes to grasp the particularity of oppression more adequately, it realizes that such particularity cannot be explained away by abstract theories of political and cultural systems that exalt the fixed virtues of cultural rootedness over the instability and uncertainty of cultural struggle. At the same time, the concept of totality, which locates the particularity of experience in wider totalities such as patriarchy and capitalism, must not be forsaken (Giroux, 1993; McLaren, 1993a). Feminists such as Britzman (1991), Fine (1988), Benhabib and Cornell (1987), Flax (1990), Pagano (1990), Hutcheon (1989), Kipnis (1988), and Morris (1988), and analysts of gender and race such as hooks (1989), Fox-Genovese (1988), Jordan (1985), and Walker (1983), have taught critical theorists that whereas larger social forces clearly exert a profound impact on society at large, their impact on individuals and localities is ambiguous and idiosyncratic. In this same context Joe Kincheloe and William Pinar's theory of place in *Curriculum as Social Psychoanalysis: Essays on the Significance of Place* (1991a) expands the notion of particularity and its relationship to wider, discursive regimes in the context of critical social theory and the politics of curriculum theory.

In light of this work in gender, race, and place, the traditional critical concept of emancipation cannot remain unaffected. The narrative of emancipation is not forsaken, but it no longer becomes a determining master narrative. Rather, it takes the form of a contingent foundation out of which further dialogue can develop that is attentive to the contextual specificity of the local and the overdetermining characteristics of larger institutional and social structures (Butler, 1990). Further, critical researchers understand that individual identity and human agency form such a chaotic knot of intertwined articulations that no social theorist can ever completely disentangle them. Without such a cautionary stance, any critical theory is vulnerable to the rationalistic tendency to develop a road map to a "logical future," a direct turnpike to the Emerald City of emancipation. Foucault, of course, placed the final postmodern obstacle in the road to emancipation in his prescient exegesis on the relationship between power and discourse. By arguing that power is innate to the structure of discourse, Foucault shed important light on the naive utopian thinking that would annul power relations (Luke, 1991; Morrow, 1991). If history is traveling to some emancipated and unitary community, then subjectivity must become unified and coherent. Postmodernist critical perspectives deny such a simplistic view of identity (postidentity). Thus modernist conceptions of critical emancipation are defrocked as the "blessed redeemer" of sociopolitical life. After this poststructuralist confrontation, the modernist deployment of the term *emancipation* can never escape questioning; it can never "hide out" in the form of a grand (usually phallocentric) narrative guarding the vital ingredients of the Western Enlightenment and supplanting and transcending the postmodern emphasis on social and cultural particularity—a particularity always in dialogue with the totality of social relations.

An Example: Workers as Critical Researchers

An example of how qualitative research grounded in postmodern critical theory might be employed involves a discussion of workers as critical researchers. Here in this traditionally class-driven category, how might postmodern theory help researchers reconceptualize critical inquiry? Many of us have been conditioned to believe that work is improving in terms of both job satisfaction and worker involvement in the administration of the workplace. Management-dominated media assure the public that the field of management has become more self-reflective about the ideologies that inform its own procedural norms, that is, top-down authoritarian management styles and low-skill labor policy. The service and information-based economy, we are told, with its high-tech innovations and computerization, is producing empowered white-collar workers. Such claims do not hold up under examination. First of all, service and information jobs are primarily low-skill, low-paying positions. Contrary to the media message, even goods-producing jobs demand higher pay than service and information jobs. Second, women hold more than half the jobs in the service and information economy, and females have traditionally received less money and decision-making power in the workplace than have males. This feminization of service and information jobs does not bode well for the long-term prospects for democratizing work (Harris, 1981; Wirth, 1983).

Embracing critical postmodern goals of empowerment, workers can use qualitative research to uncover the way power operates to construct their everyday commonsense knowledge and undermine their autonomy as professionals. As they explore the market-driven objectives that shape the ways their jobs are defined, workers can begin to see themselves in relation to the world around them, and to perceive the workplace as a site within larger economies of power and privilege. Such explorations can serve as invitations to workers to understand both the way the workplace is "governed" by a top-down series of directives and the way power is utilized on a day-to-day basis. They come to see the language of the marketplace as a tradition of mediation that defines whose knowledge is most legitimate and whose voices count the most. In the workplace of the late industrial era, workers as critical qualitative researchers are encouraged to challenge their positionality as reified objects of administration defined by prevailing discourses of what counts as "work" and "being a worker." As critical workers uncover the regimes of discourse that construct the meaning of work within the context of a post-Fordist global economy and workplace and the organizational hierarchy that supports them, they can begin to realize that the systems of discourse that interpellate them as workers operate within a milieu driven by the logic of capital. Further, questions of production and profit take precedence over questions of justice and humanity. Workers as researchers discover that concerns with the intellectual or moral development of the workforce often cannot be granted serious consideration in the "no-nonsense" ambience of business discourse. The democratic vision of critical workers who are capable of evaluating a job in terms of its social significance or its moral effects becomes, from the perspective of management, the talk of an impractical and quixotic group of workers too removed from the demands of economic survival in a global marketplace (Feinberg & Horowitz, 1990; Ferguson, 1984).

Confronted by the antidemocratic features of the postmodern condition, workers as critical qualitative researchers become translators of democracy in a hegemonically expanding landscape. In their struggle to translate and interpret the conditions that define their own labor, critical workers recognize capital's growing control over information flow. They come to understand that fewer and fewer corporations control more and more of the production of information. They discover that the postmodern corporation frequently regards the advertising of products to be secondary to the promotion of a positive corporate image. Controlling information in this way enhances the corporation's power, as it engages the public in relating positively to the goals and the "mission" of the corporation. In this way corporations can better shape government policy, control public images of labor-management relations, and portray workers in a way that enhances the self-interest of management. As a result, corporate taxes are minimized, wages are lowered, mergers are deregulated, corporate leaders are lionized, and managerial motives are unquestioned (Harvey, 1989).

So powerful is this corporate control over information flow that other social institutions often defer to its authority. Because of the fear of corporate reprisals, television news often covers only the consequences, and not the causes, of news events. In its coverage of unemployment, for example, TV news has typically avoided analysis of miscalculated corporate policies or managerial attempts to discipline employees. Fearful of corporate charges of bias, broadcasters frame explanations of unemployment within a "times are tough" motif. The current situation victimizes workers, but, reporters assure us, bad times will pass. Unemployment is thus causeless, the capricious result of a natural sequence of events. There is nothing we can do about it. This is the point of intervention for worker researchers; critical workers attempt to uncover the causes of unemployment unaddressed by the media. As these researchers demand access to the airwaves, the public comes to understand that unemployment is not as natural a process as it has been portrayed. A democratic debate about national economic policy is initiated (Apple, 1992).

Bringing a number of postmodern discourses to the negotiating table, critical worker researchers question the productivist biases of a post-Fordist industrial capitalism. In place of a model of unlimited growth and ever-increasing productivity, critical worker researchers propose an ecological model grounded in attempts to limit growth in order to improve the quality of life. Thus workers as critical researchers begin to push on the walls of modernity with their concerns for autonomy and self-reflection in opposition to the instrumental rationality of scientific management (Kellner, 1989).

This notion of self-reflection is central to the understanding of the nature of critically grounded qualitative research. As critical researchers attempt to restructure social relations of domination, they search for insights into an ever-evolving notion of social theory and the understanding it brings to their struggle for self-location in the net of larger and overlapping social, cultural, and economic contexts. As worker researchers analyze their location in the hierarchy of the workplace, they uncover ways in which they are controlled by the diagnostic and prescriptive discourse of managerial experts in their quest for the perfectly controlled workplace. Workers as critical researchers draw upon critical social theory to help them employ their understanding of their location in the corporate hierarchy in an effort to restructure the workplace. Social theory in this case becomes a vehicle for resistance, a means of social transformation through collective participation. In line with the project of critical research, worker researchers attempt not simply to describe the reality of work but to change it (Brosio, 1985; Ferguson, 1984; Zavarzadeh, 1989).

Not only do workers as critical researchers attempt to change the demeaning reality of work, but they also endeavor to change themselves. Critical worker researchers view their own roles as historical agents as a significant focus of their research. Analyzing the various discourses that shape their subjective formation, critical workers attend to the effects of the disjunctures in the social fabric. These disjunctures reveal themselves in routine actions, unconscious knowledge, and cultural memories. Workers trace the genealogies of their subjectivities and the origins of their personal concerns. At this point in their self-analysis, critical workers acquaint themselves with the postmodern condition and its powerful mobilization of affect. Workers study the postmodern condition's consumer-driven production of desire, its culture of manipulation, and its electronic surveillances by large organizations. Fighting against the social amnesia of a media-driven hyperreality, critical worker researchers assess the damage inflicted on them as well as the possibilities presented by the postmodern condition (Collins, 1989; Giroux, 1992; Hammersley & Atkinson, 1983).

Indeed, the postmodern workplace co-opts the language of democracy, as workers are positioned within by TQM (total quality management) programs and other "inclusive," "worker-friendly," and "power-sharing" plans. Workers as critical researchers are forced to develop new forms of demystification that expose the power relations of the "democratic" plans. Upon critical interrogation, workers find that often "the elimination of we/they perceptions" means, as it did in the Staley corn processing plant in Decatur, Illinois, increased worker firings as disciplinary action, required "state of the plant" meetings marked by managerial lectures to workers about the needs of the plant, the development of new contracts outlining "management rights," the introduction of 12-hour shifts without overtime pay, and the formation of work teams that destroy seniority. Whereas the managerial appeal to efficiency is a guise in the modernist workplace to hide worker control strategies, worker researchers find that in the postmodern workplace *cooperation* becomes the word *du jour*. Add to this illusion of cooperation the appearance of upward mobility of a few workers into the ranks of management, and attention is deflected from insidious forms of managerial supervision and hoarding of knowledge about the work process (Cockburn, 1993; Ferguson, 1984; Giroux, 1993).

The only way to address this degradation of worker dignity is to make sure that worker researchers are empowered to explore alternative workplace arrangements and to share in decision making concerning production and distribution of products. Workers distribute their research findings so that the general public understands how the present organization of work has served to concentrate wealth and power in the hands of industrial leaders. Worker researchers explore alternatives to present forms of bureaucratic control.

One of the best sources for such alternatives involves recent feminist research (Brosio, 1985; Cook & Fonow, 1990; Eiger, 1982; Wirth, 1983). Feminist research illustrates how traditional grand narratives that rely on class analysis of the workplace are insufficient. Modernist radical literature frequently used class as a unitary conceptual frame, and as a consequence the androcentric and patriarchal structures of the worker worldview were left uninterrogated. Postmodern forms of critical analysis drawing upon feminist reconceptualizations of research alert critical researchers to the multiple subject positions they hold in relation to the class, race, and gender dimensions of their lives. Critical worker researchers, for example, come to understand that the speaking subject in the discourse of the workplace is most often male, whereas the silent and passive object is female. Only recently has the analysis of workplace oppression foregrounded the special forms of oppression constructed around gender and race. Issues of promotion and equal pay for women and nonwhites and sexual harassment are relatively new elements in the public conversation about work (Fraser & Nicholson, 1990).

One of the most traumatic experience workers have to face involves the closing of a plant. Taking advantage of postmodern technology, factory managers have engaged in "outsourcing" and moved plants to "more attractive" locales with lower business taxes and open shops (often in Third World countries, where it becomes easier to exploit workers). Because more attractive locales exist only for management, workers have few options and typically have to scramble for new lower-paying jobs in the old venue. Worker researchers caught in such situations analyze alternatives to closings or relocations. Worker researchers in plants marked for closing from Detroit to the British Midlands have researched the causes of shutdowns as well as the feasibility of the production of alternate product lines, employee ownership, or government intervention to save their jobs. In relation to the causes of shutdowns, worker researchers employ what feminist researchers call "situation-at-hand" inquiry. Such research takes an already given situation as a focus for critical sociological inquiry. Researchers who find themselves in an already given situation possess little or no ability to control events because they have already happened or have happened for reasons that have nothing to do with the research study. Plant managers would probably be far more guarded about offhand comments made about plant closings if they were taking part in traditional interviews or completing questionnaires. Finding themselves in sensitive and controversial situations in which millions of dollars may be involved, critical worker researchers can make good use of situation-at-hand inquiry as a germane and creative way of uncovering data (Cook & Fonow, 1990; Eiger, 1982).

Critical postmodern research refuses to accept worker experience as unproblematic and beyond interrogation. Critical worker researchers respect their participation in the production of their craft as they collect and document their experiences; at the same time, however, they aver that a significant aspect of the critical research process involves challenging the ideological assumptions that inform the interpretation of their experiences. Simon and Dippo (1987) argue that critical workers must challenge the notion that experience is the best teacher. In this context, critical theoretical research must never be allowed to confirm simply what we already know. As Joan Scott (1992) says: "Experience is a subject's history. Language is the site of history's enactment" (p. 34). Foucault echoes this sentiment in arguing that the experience gained in everyday struggle can, upon examination, yield critical insights into the ways in which power works and the process by which knowledge is certified. In this process, conditions of everyday life mean first of all uncovering the assumptions that privilege particular interpretations of everyday experience (Foucault, 1980; Simon & Dippo, 1987; Simon, Dippo, & Schenke, 1991).

Experience, McLaren (1992b) has written elsewhere, never speaks for itself. Experience is an understanding derived from a specific interpretation of a certain "engagement with the world of symbols, social practices, and cultural forms" (p. 332). Particular experiences, critical researchers maintain, must be respected but always made theoretically problematic. Kincheloe and Pinar (1991b) address this concept in their theory of place, which brings particular experience into focus, but in a way that grounds it contextually through a consideration of the larger political, economic, social, and linguistic forces that shape it. Kincheloe and Steinberg (1993) extend this notion in their critically grounded theory of postformal cognition. Here, theoretical interpretations of experience are contextualized by the particularity of visceral experience. Such experience grounded in lust, fear, joy, love, and hate creates a synergistic interaction between theoretical understanding and the intimacy of the researchers' own autobiography. Critical workers acting on these insights gain the ability to place themselves theoretically within the often messy web of power relations without losing touch with the emotion of their everyday lives.

Drawing upon some ideas promoted by European labor organizations, critical workers can form research and study circles to explore important labor issues. In Sweden, for instance, workers have created 150,000 study circles involving 1.4 million participants. Buoyed by the possibilities held out by the Swedish example, critical workers imagine cooperatives that organize interpretations of everyday events in the economy and the workplace (Eiger, 1982). Motivated by the preponderance of management perspectives on television news programs, critical worker researchers offer alternative views of how workers are positioned in larger material, symbolic, and economic relations and how critical theory can serve to restructure such relations. As workers connect their individual stories of oppression to the larger historical framework, social as well as institutional memory is created (Harrison, 1985). This social memory can be shared with other study circles and with teachers, artists, intellectuals, social workers, and other cultural workers. At a time when few progressive labor voices are heard, worker research and study circles can make an important contribution to the creation of a prodemocracy movement.

Critical theory-based research can be exceedingly practical and can contribute to progressive change on a variety of levels. Below we summarize some of the progressive and empowering outcomes offered by critical theory-based worker research.

Production of more useful and relevant research on work. Worker research provides an account of the world from the marginal perspective of the workers, taking into consideration perspectives of both business and labor (Hartsock, 1989). Research from the margins is more relevant to those who have been marginalized by the hierarchical discourse of mainstream science, with its cult of the expert. Worker researchers ask questions about labor conditions that are relevant to other workers (Garrison, 1989).

Legitimation of worker knowledge. The discourse of traditional modernist science regulates what can be said under the flag of scientific authority and who can say it. Needless to say, workers and the practical knowledge they have accumulated about their work are excluded from this discourse (Collins, 1989). Worker research grounded in critical postmodern theory helps legitimate worker knowledge by pointing out the positionality and limitations of "expert research." James Garrison (1989) contends that practitioner research tends to distort reality less often than expert research because the practitioner is closer to the purposes, cares, everyday concerns, and interests of work. For this reason, critical worker research benefits from the multiplicity of ethnographic approaches available, such as worker sociodramas, life histories/ autobiographies, journaling, personal narratives, writing-as-method, and critical narratology (McLaren, 1993b). With the growth of worker research in Scandinavia, analysts report that the gap between scientists and workers is being diminished. Such reports point to the progressive impact of worker research and the value of such inquiry in the movement toward a more egalitarian community (Eiger, 1982).

Empowerment of workers. Critical worker research operates under the assumption that the validation of workers' knowledge can lead to their empowerment (Garrison, 1989). But worker researchers must not be satisfied simply with producing a catalog of incidents of worker exploitation. Worker researchers must produce a provisional vision of empowerment as part of a larger critical project. This provisional vision must decide which concepts from the present study are essential for worker empowerment (Cook & Fonow, 1990) and which can be extended and elaborated for larger consideration such as the development of a socialist democracy.

Forced reorganization of the workplace. Western science has produced a set of fixed hierarchical binarisms, including the knower and the known, the researcher and the researched, the scientific expert and the practitioner. Critical worker research subverts the existing hierarchical arrangement of the workplace as it challenges the assumptions upon which the cult of the expert and scientific management are based. Without a Cartesian epistemological structure to justify them, the hierarchical binarisms of modernist science are significantly weakened (Butler, 1990; Garrison, 1989; McLaren, 1992a).

Inspiration of the democratization of science. As John Dewey maintained decades ago, science narrowly conceived as a technique puts the power of inquiry in the hands of those at the top of the hierarchy who, by way of their education or status, are pronounced most qualified. These elites engage in research, turning over the data (the product), not the methods (the process), of their inquiries to low-status practitioners who follow their directions. When workers take part in research and legitimate their own knowledge, then scientific research will be better able to serve progressive democratic goals (Garrison, 1989).

Undermining of technical rationality. Technical rationality is an epistemology of worker practice derived from modernist Cartesian science. Technical rationality maintains that workers are rationalistic problem solvers who apply scientifically tested procedures to workplace situations. Well-trained workers solve well-formed problems by applying techniques derived from expert-produced knowledge. Worker researchers have learned, however, that the problems encountered in the workplace are not reducible to simple propositions or assertions. For instance, workers in a garbage recycling plant must decide to balance environmental concerns with business survival demands. They must not only know what waste materials cause environmental damage but what materials bring high market prices. When extraction costs are calculated into this problem, it becomes apparent that no simple technical procedure exists that can lead workers to the solution of problems that confront such a workplace. The relationship between worker competence and expert knowledge needs to be flip-flopped. In the modernist workplace hierarchy, managers start with research provided by "experts" and train workers in accordance with such findings. A critical workplace would start instead with research by the workers themselves on the conditions of their labor. For instance, worker researchers could document the forms of intelligence competent workers exhibit. An important aspect of the worker's job would be to help create nonexploitive conditions that promote such competence (Feinberg & Horowitz, 1990; Raizen, 1989; Schön, 1987).

Promotion of an awareness of worker cognition. Critical worker research encourages a relationship to worker production that is expressed in aesthetic appreciation for the process and product of one's labor, awareness of the relationship between work and world, and solidarity with other workers. In addition, this critical productive orientation highlights an awareness of reality by way of both logic and emotion. Critical research holds many cognitive benefits that transcend Piagetian forms of formal analytic reasoning. As workers as researchers transcend procedural logic, they move to a critical realm of knowledge production. In this realm, researchers organize and interpret information, no longer caught in the hierarchy as passive receivers of "expert" knowledge. As critical researchers, workers learn to teach themselves. In this context, learning in the workplace becomes a way of life, a part of the job. Workers as researchers come to see events in a deconstructive manner, in ways that uncover privileged binary oppositions within logocentric discourses not necessarily apparent before critical reflection (Feinberg & Horowitz, 1990; Kincheloe, 1993; Wirth, 1983).

Critical Postmodern Research: Further Considerations

As much as critical researchers may claim to see meanings that others miss, critical postmodern research respects the complexity of the social world. Humility in this context should not be self-deprecating, nor should it involve the silencing of the researcher's voice; research humility implies a sense of the unpredictability of the sociopolitical microcosm and the capriciousness of the consequences of inquiry. This critical humility is an inescapable feature of a postmodern condition marked by a loss of faith in an unreconceptualized narrative emancipation and the possibility of a privileged frame of reference. A postmodernized critical theory accepts the presence of its own fallibility as well as its contingent relation to progressive social change (Aronowitz, 1983; McLaren, in press; Morrow, 1991; Ruddick, 1980).

In light of this reflective humility, critical researchers do not search for some magic method of inquiry that will guarantee the validity of their findings. As Henry Giroux (1983) maintains, "methodological correctness" will never guarantee valid data, nor does it reveal power interests within a body of information (p. 17). Traditional research argues that the only way to produce valid information is through the application of a rigorous research methodology, that is, one that follows a strict set of objective procedures that separate researchers from those researched. To be meaningful, the argument goes, social inquiry must be rigorous. The pursuit of rigor thus becomes the shortest path to validity. Rigor is a commitment to the established rules for conducting inquiry. Traditional modernist research has focused on rigor to the neglect of the dynamics of the lived world—not to mention the pursuit of justice in the lived world. Habermas and Marcuse maintain that post-Enlightenment science has focused research on the how and the form of inquiry, to the neglect of the what and the substance of inquiry. Thus social research has largely become a technology that has focused on reducing human beings to taken-for-granted social outcomes. These outcomes typically maintain existing power relationships, Habermas (1971, 1973) and Marcuse (1964) argue, as they disregard the ways in which current sociopolitical relationships affect human life. We do not want to suggest that an absolute dialogism is possible, but we support attempts to create conditions of rational social discourse and the establishment of normative claims, noncoerced discussion, and debate.

Because of critical research's agenda of social critique, special problems of validity are raised. How do you determine the validity of information if you reject the notion of methodological correctness and your purpose is to free men and women from sources of oppression and domination? Where traditional verifiability rests on a rational proof built upon literal intended meaning, a critical qualitative perspective always involves a less certain approach characterized by participant reaction and emotional involvement. Some analysts argue that *validity* may be an inappropriate term in a critical research context, as it simply reflects a concern for acceptance within a positivist concept of research rigor. To a critical researcher, validity means much more than the traditional definitions of internal and external validity usually associated with the concept. Traditional research has defined *internal validity* as the extent to which a researcher's observations and measurements are true descriptions of a particular reality; *external validity* has been defined as the degree to which such descriptions can be accurately compared with other groups. *Trustworthiness,* many have argued, is a more appropriate word to use in the context of critical research. It is helpful because it signifies a different set of assumptions about research purposes than does *validity.* What criteria might be used to assess the trustworthiness of critical research (Anderson, 1989; Lincoln & Guba, 1985; Reinharz, 1979)?

One criterion for critical trustworthiness involves the credibility of portrayals of constructed realities. Critical researchers reject the notion of internal validity that is based on the assumption that a tangible, knowable, cause-and-effect reality exists and that research descriptions are able to portray that reality accurately. Critical researchers award credibility only when the constructions are plausible to those who constructed them, and even then there may be disagreement, for the researcher may see the effects of oppression in the constructs of those researched—effects that those researched may not see. Thus it becomes extremely difficult to measure the trustworthiness of critical research; no TQ (trustworthiness quotient) can be developed.

A second criterion for critical trustworthiness can be referred to as *anticipatory accommodation.* Here critical researchers reject the traditional notion of external validity. The ability to make pristine generalizations from one research study to another accepts a one-dimensional, cause-effect universe. Kincheloe (1991) points out that in traditional research all that is needed to ensure transferability is to understand with a high degree of internal validity something about, say, a particular school classroom and to know that the makeup of this classroom is representative of another classroom to which the generalization is being applied. Many critical researchers have argued that this traditionalist concept of external validity is far too simplistic and assert that if generalizations are to be made—that is, if researchers are to be able to apply findings in context A to context B—then we must make sure that the contexts being compared are similar. The Piagetian notion of cognitive processing is instructive because it suggests that in everyday situations men and women do not make generalizations in the ways implied by external validity. Piaget's notion of accommodation seems appropriate in this context, as it asserts that humans reshape cognitive structures to accommodate unique aspects of what they perceive in new contexts. In other words, through their knowledge of a variety of comparable contexts, researchers begin to learn their similarities and differences—they learn from their comparisons of different contexts (Donmoyer, 1990; Kincheloe, 1991).

As critical researchers transcend regressive and counterintuitive notions of validating the knowledge uncovered by research, they remind themselves of their critical project—the attempt to move beyond assimilated experience, the struggle to expose the way ideology constrains the desire for self-direction, and the effort to confront the way power reproduces itself in the construction of human consciousness. Given such purposes, Patti Lather (1991) extends our position with her notion of catalytic validity. Catalytic validity points to the degree to which research moves those it studies to understand the world and the way it is shaped in order for them to transform it. Noncritical researchers who operate within an empiricist framework will perhaps find catalytic validity to be a strange concept. Research that possesses catalytic validity will not only display the reality-altering impact of the inquiry process, it will also direct this impact so that those under study will gain self-understanding and self-direction (Lather, 1991).

Recent attempts by critical researchers to move beyond the objectifying and imperialist gaze associated with the Western anthropological tradition (which fixes the image of the so-called informant from the colonizing perspective of the knowing subject), although laudatory and well-intentioned, are not without their shortcomings (Bourdieu & Wacquaat, 1992). As Fuchs (1993) has so presciently observed, serious limitations plague recent efforts to develop a more reflective approach to ethnographic writing. The challenge here can be summarized in the following questions: How does the knowing subject come to know the Other? How can researchers respect the perspective of the Other and invite the Other to speak?

Although recent confessional modes of ethnographic writing attempt to treat so-called informants as "participants" in an attempt to avoid the objectification of the Other (usually referring to the relationship between Western anthropologists and non-Western culture), there is a risk that uncovering colonial and postcolonial structures of domination may, in fact, unintentionally validate and consolidate such structures as well as reassert liberal values through a type of covert ethnocentrism. Fuchs (1993) warns that the attempt to subject researchers to the same approach to which other societies are subjected could lead to an " 'othering' of one's own world" (p. 108). Such an attempt often fails to question existing ethnographic methodologies and therefore unwittingly extends their validity and applicability while further objectifying the world of the researcher.

Michel Foucault's approach to this dilemma is to "detach" social theory from the epistemology of his own culture by criticizing the traditional philosophy of reflection. However, Foucault falls into the trap of ontologizing his own methodological argumentation and erasing the notion of prior understanding that is linked to the idea of an "inside" view (Fuchs, 1993). Louis Dumont fares somewhat better by arguing that cultural texts need to be viewed simultaneously from the inside and from the outside (Fuchs, 1993, p. 112). However, in trying to affirm a "reciprocal interpretation of various societies among themselves" (Fuchs, 1993, p. 113) through identifying both transindividual structures of consciousness and transsubjective social structures, Dumont aspires to a universal framework for the comparative analysis of societies. Whereas Foucault and Dumont attempt to "transcend the categorical foundations of their own world" (Fuchs, 1993, p. 118) by refusing to include themselves in the process of objectification, Pierre Bourdieu integrates himself as a social actor into the social field under analysis. Bourdieu achieves such integration by "epistemologizing the ethnological content of his own presuppositions" (Fuchs, 1993, p. 121). But the self-objectification of the observer (anthropologist) is not unproblematic. Fuchs (1993) notes, after Bourdieu, that the chief difficulty is "forgetting the difference between the theoretical and the practical relationship with the world and of imposing on the object the theoretical relationship one maintains with it" (p. 120). Bourdieu's approach to research does not fully escape becoming, to a certain extent, a "confirmation of objectivism," but at least there is an earnest attempt by the researcher to reflect on the preconditions of his own self-understanding—an attempt to engage in an "ethnography of ethnographers" (p. 122).

Postmodern ethnography—and we are thinking here of works such as Paul Rabinow's *Reflections on Fieldwork in Morocco* (1977), James Boon's *Other Tribes, Other Scribes* (1982), and Michael Taussig's *Shamanism, Colonialism, and the Wild Man* (1987)—shares the conviction articulated by Marc Manganaro (1990) that "no anthropology is apolitical, removed from ideology and hence from the capacity to be affected by or, as crucially, to effect social formations. The question ought not to be if an anthropological text is political, but rather, what kind of sociopolitical affiliations are tied to particular anthropological texts" (p. 35).

Judith Newton and Judith Stacey (1992-1993) note that the current postmodern textual experimentation of ethnography credits the "postcolonial predicament of culture as the opportunity for anthropology to reinvent itself" (p. 56). Modernist ethnography, according to these authors, "constructed authoritative cultural accounts that served, however inadvertently, not only to establish the authority of the Western ethnographer over native 'others,' but also to sustain Western authority over colonial cultures." They argue (following James Clifford) that ethnographers can and should try to escape

> the recurrent allegorical genre of colonial ethnography—the pastoral, a nostalgic, redemptive text that preserves a primitive culture on the brink of extinction for the historical record of its Western conquerors. The narrative structure of this "salvage text" portrays the native culture as a coherent, authentic, and lamentably "evading past," while its complex, inauthentic, Western successors represent the future. (p. 56)

Postmodern ethnographic writing faces the challenge of moving beyond simply the reanimation of local experience, an uncritical celebration of cultural difference (including figural differentiations within the ethnographer's own culture), and the employment of a framework that espouses universal values and a global role for interpretivist anthropology (Silverman, 1990). What we have described as resistance postmodernism can help qualitative researchers challenge dominant Western research practices that are underwritten by a foundational epistemology and a claim to universally valid knowledge at the expense of local, subjugated knowledges (Peters, 1993). The choice is not one between modernism and postmodernism, but one of whether or not to challenge the presuppositions that inform the normalizing judgments one makes as a researcher. Vincent Crapanzano (1990) warns that "the anthropologist can assume neither the Orphic lyre nor the crown of thorns, although I confess to hear salvationist echoes in his desire to protect his people" (p. 301).

The work of James Clifford, which shares an affinity with ethnographic work associated with Georges Bataille, Michel Lerris, and the College de Sociologie, is described by Connor (1992) as not simply the "writing of culture" but rather "the interior disruption of categories of art and culture correspond[ing] to a radically dialogic form of ethnographic writing, which takes place across and between cultures" (p. 251). Clifford (1992) describes his own work as an attempt "to multiply the hands and discourses involved in 'writing culture' . . . not to assert a naive democracy of plural authorship, but to loosen at least somewhat the monological control of the executive writer/anthropologist and to open for discussion ethnography's hierarchy and negotiation of discourses in power-charged, unequal situations" (p. 100). Citing the work of Marcus and Fisher (1986), Clifford warns against modernist ethnographic practices of "representational essentializing" and "metonymic freezing" in which one aspect of a group's life is taken to represent them as a whole; instead, Clifford urges forms of multilocale ethnography to reflect the "transnational political, economic and cultural forces that traverse and constitute local or regional worlds" (p. 102). Rather than fixing culture into reified textual portraits, culture needs to be better understood as displacement, transplantation, disruption, positionality, and difference.

Although critical ethnography allows, in a way conventional ethnography does not, for the relationship of liberation and history, and although its hermeneutical task is to call into question the social and cultural conditioning of human activity and the prevailing sociopolitical structures, we do not claim that this is enough to restructure the social system. But it is certainly, in our view, a necessary beginning. We follow Patricia Ticineto Clough (1992) in arguing that "realist narrativity has allowed empirical social science to be the platform and horizon of social criticism" (p. 135). Ethnography needs to be analyzed critically not only in terms of its field methods but also as reading and writing practices. Data collection must give way to "rereadings of representations in every form" (p. 137). In the narrative construction of its authority as empirical science, ethnography needs to face the unconscious processes upon which it justifies its canonical formulations, processes that often involve the disavowal of oedipal or authorial desire and the reduction of differences to binary oppositions. Within these processes of binary reduction, the male ethnographer is most often privileged as the guardian of "the factual representation of empirical positivities" (p. 9).

Critical research traditions have arrived at the point where they recognize that claims to truth are always discursively situated and implicated in relations of power. Yet, unlike some claims made within "ludic" strands of postmodernist research, we do not suggest that because we cannot know truth absolutely that truth can simply be equated with an effect of power. We say this because truth involves regulative rules that must be met for some statements to be more meaningful than others. Otherwise, truth becomes meaningless and, if this is the case, liberatory praxis has no purpose other than to win for the sake of winning (Carspecken, 1993). As Phil Carspecken (1993) remarks, every time we act, in every instance of our behavior, we presuppose some normative or universal relation to truth. Truth is internally related to meaning in a pragmatic way through normative referenced claims, intersubjective referenced claims, subjective referenced claims, and the way we deictically ground or anchor meaning in our daily lives.

Carspecken explains that researchers are able to articulate the normative evaluative claims of others when they begin to see them in the same way as their participants by living inside the cultural and discursive positionalities that inform such claims. Claims to universality must be recognized in each particular normative claim and questions must be raised about whether such norms represent the entire group. When the limited claim of universality is seen to be contradictory to the practices under observation, power relations become visible. What is crucial here, according to Carspecken, is that researchers recognize where they are ideologically located in the normative and identity claims of others and at the same time be honest about their own subjective referenced claims and not let normative evaluative claims interfere with what is observed. Critical research continues to problematize normative and universal claims in a way that does not permit them to be analyzed outside of a politics of representation, divorced from the material conditions in which they are produced, or outside of a concern with the constitution of the subject in the very acts of reading and writing.

A critical postmodern research requires researchers to construct their perception of the world anew, not just in random ways but in a manner that undermines what appears natural, that opens to question what appears obvious (Slaughter, 1989). Oppositional and insurgent researchers as maieutic agents must not confuse their research efforts with the textual suavities of an avant-garde academic posturing in which they are awarded the sinecure of representation for the oppressed without actually having to return to those working-class communities where their studies took place. Rather, they need to locate their work in a transformative praxis that leads to the alleviation of suffering and the overcoming of oppression. Rejecting the arrogant reading of metropolitan critics and their imperial mandates governing research, insurgent researchers ask questions about how what is has come to be, whose interests are served by particular institutional arrangements, and where our own frames of reference come from. Facts are no longer simply "what is"; the truth of beliefs is not simply testable by their correspondence to these facts. To engage in critical postmodern research is to take part in a process of critical world making, guided by the shadowed outline of a dream of a world less conditioned by misery, suffering, and the politics of deceit. It is, in short, a pragmatics of hope in an age of cynical reason.

References

Anderson, G. (1989). Critical ethnography in education: Origins, current status, and new directions. *Review of Educational Research, 59,* 249-270.

Apple, M. (1992). *Constructing the captive audience: Channel one and the political economy of the text.* Unpublished manuscript.

Aronowitz, S. (1983, December 27). The relativity of theory. *Village Voice,* p. 60.

Aronowitz, S., & Giroux, H. (1991). *Postmodern education: Politics, culture, and social criticism.* Minneapolis: University of Minnesota Press.

Benhabib, S., & Cornell, D. (1987). *Feminism as critique.* Minneapolis: University of Minnesota Press.

Boon, J. (1982). *Other tribes, other scribes: Symbolic anthropology in the comparative study of cultures, histories, religions, and texts.* Cambridge, UK: Cambridge University Press.

Bottomore, T. (1984). *The Frankfurt school.* London: Tavistock.

Bourdieu, P., & Wacquaat, L. (1992). *An invitation to reflexive sociology.* Chicago: University of Chicago Press.

Britzman, D. (1991). *Practice makes practice: A critical study of learning to teach.* Albany: State University of New York Press.

Brosio, R. (1985). *A bibliographic essay on the world of work.* Paper presented at the annual meeting of the American Educational Studies Association, Chicago.

Buckingham, D. (1989). Television literacy: A critique. *Radical Philosophy, 51,* 12-25.

Butler, J. (1990). *Gender trouble: Feminism and the subversion of identity.* New York: Routledge.

Carspecken, P. (1993). *Power, truth, and method: Outline for a critical methodology.* Unpublished manuscript.

Centre for Contemporary Culture Studies. (1978). *Women take issue: Aspects of women's subordination.* Birmingham, England: University of Birmingham, Women's Studies Group.

Clifford, J. (1992). Traveling cultures. In L. Grossberg, C. Nelson, & P. A. Treichler (Eds.), *Cultural studies* (pp. 96-116). New York: Routledge.

Clough, P. T. (1992). *The end(s) of ethnography: From realism to social criticism.* Newbury Park, CA: Sage.

Cockburn, A. (1993). Clinton and labor: Reform equals rollback. *The Nation, 256,* 654-655.

Codd, J. (1984). Introduction. In J. Codd (Ed.), *Philosophy, common sense, and action in educational administration* (pp. 8-28). Victoria, Australia: Deakin University Press.

Collins, J. (1989). *Uncommon cultures: Popular culture and postmodernism.* New York: Routledge.

Connor, S. (1992). *Theory and cultural value.* Cambridge, UK: Basil Blackwell.

Cook, J. A., & Fonow, M. M. (1990). Knowledge and women's interests: Issues of epistemology and methodology in feminist sociological research. In J. Nielsen (Ed.), *Feminist research methods: Exemplary reading in the social sciences* (pp. 69-93). Boulder, CO: Westview.

Corrigan, P. (1979). *Schooling the Smash Street kids.* London: Macmillan.

Crapanzano, V. (1990). Afterword. In M. Manganaro (Ed.), *Modernist anthropology: From fieldwork to text* (pp. 300-308). Princeton, NJ: Princeton University Press.

Donmoyer, R. (1990). Generalizability and the single-case study. In E. Eisner & A. Peshkin (Eds.), *Qualitative inquiry in education: The continuing debate* (pp. 175-200). New York: Teachers College Press.

Ebert, T. (1991). Political semiosis in/or American cultural studies. *American Journal of Semiotics, 8,* 113-135.

Ebert, T. (in press). Writing in the political: Resistance (post) modernism. *Critical Theory.*

Eiger, N. (1982). The workplace as classroom for democracy: The Swedish experience. *New York University Education Quarterly, 17,* 16-23.

Feinberg, W., & Horowitz, B. (1990). Vocational education and the equality of opportunity. *Journal of Curriculum Studies, 22,* 188-192.

Ferguson, K. (1984). *The feminist case against bureaucracy.* Philadelphia: Temple University Press.

Fine, M. (1988). Sexuality, schooling, and adolescent females: The missing discourse of desire. *Harvard Educational Review, 58,* 29-53.

Flax, J. (1990). Postmodernism and gender relations in feminist theory. In L. Nicholson (Ed.), *Feminism/postmodernism* (pp. 39-62). New York: Routledge.

Foster, H. (Ed.). (1983). *The anti-aesthetic: Essays on postmodern culture.* Port Townsend, WA: Bay.

Foucault, M. (1980). *Power/knowledge: Selected interviews and other writings* (C. Gordon, Ed.). New York: Pantheon.

Fox-Genovese, E. (1988). *Within the plantation household: Black and white women of the Old South.* Chapel Hill: University of North Carolina Press.

Fraser, N., & Nicholson, L. (1990). Social criticism without philosophy: An encounter between feminism and postmodernism. In L. Nicholson (Ed.), *Feminism/postmodernism* (pp. 19-38). New York: Routledge.

Fuchs, M. (1993). The reversal of the ethnological perspective: Attempts at objectifying one's own cultural horizon. Dumont, Foucault, Bourdieu? *Thesis Eleven, 34,* 104-125.

Garrison, J. (1989). The role of postpositivistic philosophy of science in the renewal of vocational education research. *Journal of Vocational Education Research, 14*(3), 39-51.

Gergen, K. J. (1991). *The saturated self: Dilemmas of identity in contemporary life.* New York: Basic Books.

Gibson, R. (1986). *Critical theory and education.* London: Hodder & Stroughton.

Giroux, H. (1983). *Theory and resistance in education: A pedagogy for the opposition.* South Hadley, MA: Bergin & Garvey.

Giroux, H. (1988). Critical theory and the politics of culture and voice: Rethinking the discourse of educational research. In R. Sherman & R. Webb (Eds.), *Qualitative research in education: Focus and methods* (pp. 190-210). New York: Falmer.

Giroux, H. (1992). *Border crossings: Cultural workers and the politics of education.* New York: Routledge.

Giroux, H. (1993). *Living dangerously: Multiculturalism and the politics of difference.* New York: Peter Lang.

Godzich, W. (1992). Afterword: Reading against literacy. In J. F. Lyotard, *The postmodern explained.* Minneapolis: University of Minnesota Press.

Gramsci, A. (1971). *Selections from the prison notebooks* (Q. Hoare & G. Nowell Smith, Eds. & Trans.). New York: International.

Griffin, C. (1985). *Typical girls? Young women from school to the job market.* London: Routledge & Kegan Paul.

Habermas, J. (1971). *Knowledge and human interests* (J. Shapiro, Trans.). Boston: Beacon.

Habermas, J. (1973). *Theory and practice* (J. Viertel, Trans.). Boston: Beacon.

Hall, S. (1990, September). A conversation with F. Jameson: Clinging to the wreckage. *Marxism Today,* pp. 28-31.

Hammersley, M., & Atkinson P. (1983). *Ethnography: Principles in practice.* London: Tavistock.

Harris, M. (1981). *America now.* New York: Simon & Schuster.

Harrison, B. (1985). *Making the connections: Essays in feminist social ethics.* Boston: Beacon.

Hartsock, N. (1989). Foucault on power: A theory for women? In L. Nicholson (Ed.), *Feminism/postmodernism* (pp. 83-106). New York: Routledge.

Harvey, D. (1989). *The condition of postmodernity.* Cambridge, UK: Basil Blackwell.

Hebdige, D. (1979). *Subculture: The meaning of style.* London: Methuen.

Held, D. (1980). *Introduction to critical theory: Horkheimer to Habermas.* Berkeley: University of California Press.

hooks, b. (1989). *Talking back: Thinking feminist, thinking black.* Boston: South End.

Horkheimer, M. (1972). *Critical theory.* New York: Seabury.

Hutcheon, L. (1989). *The politics of postmodernism.* New York: Routledge.

Jameson, F. (1990, September). A conversation with S. Hall: Clinging to the wreckage. *Marxism Today,* pp. 28-31.

Jay, M. (1973). *The dialectical imagination: A history of the Frankfurt school and the Institute of Social Research 1923-1950.* Boston: Little, Brown.

Jordan, J. (1985). *On call: Political essays.* Boston: South End.

Kellner, D. (1989). *Critical theory, Marxism, and modernity.* Baltimore: Johns Hopkins University Press.

Kellner, D. (1993). *The obsolescence of Marxism?* Unpublished manuscript.

Kincheloe, J. (1991). *Teachers as researchers: Qualitative paths to empowerment.* London: Falmer.

Kincheloe, J. (1993). *Toward a critical politics of teacher thinking: Mapping the postmodern.* Granby, MA: Bergin & Garvey.

Kincheloe, J., & Pinar, W. (1991a). *Curriculum as social psychoanalysis: Essays on the significance of place.* Albany: State University of New York Press.

Kincheloe, J., & Pinar, W. (1991b). Introduction. In J. Kincheloe & W. Pinar, *Curriculum as social psychoanalysis: Essays on the significance of place* (pp. 1-23). Albany: State University of New York Press.

Kincheloe, J., & Steinberg, S. (1993). A tentative description of post-formal thinking: The critical confrontation with cognitive theory. *Harvard Educational Review, 63,* 296-320.

Kipnis, L. (1988). Feminism: The political conscience of postmodernism. In A. Ross (Ed.), *Universal abandon? The politics of postmodernism* (pp. 149-166). Minneapolis: University of Minnesota Press.

Lacey, C. (1970). *Hightown Grammar: The school as a social system.* London: Routledge & Kegan Paul.

Lash, S. (1990). Learning from Leipzig . . . or politics in the semiotic society. *Theory, Culture & Society, 7*(4), 145-158.

Lather, P. (1991). *Getting smart: Feminist research and pedagogy with/in the postmodern.* New York: Routledge.

Lincoln, Y. S., & Guba, E. G. (1985). *Naturalistic inquiry.* Beverly Hills, CA: Sage.

Lugones, M. (1987). Playfulness, "world"-traveling, and loving perception. *Hypatia, 2*(2), 3-19.

Luke, T. (1991). Touring hyperreality: Critical theory confronts informational society. In P. Wexler (Ed.), *Critical theory now* (pp. 1-26). New York: Falmer.

Manganaro, M. (1990). Textual play, power, and cultural critique: An orientation to modernist anthropology. In M. Manganaro (Ed.), *Modernist anthropology: From fieldwork to text* (pp. 3-47). Princeton, NJ: Princeton University Press.

Marcus, G., & Fischer, M. (1986). *Anthropology as cultural critique: An experimental moment in the human sciences.* Chicago: University of Chicago Press.

Marcuse, H. (1964). *One dimensional man.* Boston: South End.

McLaren, P. (1986). *Schooling as a ritual performance: Toward a political economy of educational symbols and gestures.* London: Routledge & Kegan Paul.

McLaren, P. (1989). *Life in schools.* New York: Longman.

McLaren, P. (1992a). Collisions with otherness: "Traveling" theory, post-colonial criticism, and the politics of ethnographic practice—the mission of the wounded ethnographer. *Qualitative Studies in Education, 5*(1), 77-92.

McLaren, P. (1992b). Literacy research and the postmodern turn: Cautions from the margins. In R. Beach, J. Green, M. Kamil, & T. Shanahan (Eds.), *Multidisciplinary perspectives on research.* Urbana, IL: National Council of Teachers of English.

McLaren, P. (1993a). Border disputes: Multicultural narrative, identity formation, and critical pedagogy in postmodern America. In W. Tierney & D. McLaughlin (Eds.), *Naming silenced lives.* New York: Routledge.

McLaren, P. (1993b). Multiculturalism and the postmodern critique: Towards a pedagogy of resistance and transformation. *Cultural Critique, 7,* 118-146.

McLaren, P. (Ed.). (in press). *Postmodernism, postcolonialism and pedagogy.* Albert Park, Australia: James Nicholas.

McLaren, P., & Hammer, R. (1989). Critical pedagogy and the postmodern challenge. *Educational Foundations, 3*(3), 29-69.

Morris, M. (1988). Tooth and claw: Tales of survival and Crocodile Dundee. In A. Ross (Ed.), *Universal abandon? The politics of postmodernism* (pp. 105-127). Minneapolis: University of Minnesota Press.

Morrow, R. (1991). Critical theory, Gramsci and cultural studies: From structuralism to post-structuralism. In P. Wexler (Ed.), *Critical theory now* (pp. 27-69). New York: Falmer.

Newton, J., & Stacey, J. (1992-1993). Learning not to curse, or, feminist predicaments in cultural criticism by men: Our movie date with James Clifford and Stephen Greenblatt. *Cultural Critique, 23,* 51-82.

Pagano, J. (1990). *Exiles and communities.* Albany: State University of New York Press.

Peters, M. (1993). *Against Finkielkraut's la defaite de la pensee: Culture, postmodernism and education.* Unpublished manuscript.

Poster, M. (1989). *Critical theory and poststructuralism: In search of a context.* Ithaca, NY: Cornell University Press.

Quantz, R. A. (1992). On critical ethnography (with some postmodern considerations). In M. D. LeCompte, W. L. Millroy, & J. Preissle (Eds.), *The handbook of qualitative research in education* (pp. 447-505). New York: Academic Press.

Rabinow, P. (1977). *Reflections on fieldwork in Morocco.* Berkeley: University of California Press.

Raizen, S. (1989). *Reforming education for work: A cognitive science perspective.* Berkeley, CA: National Center for Research in Vocational Education.

Reinharz, S. (1979). *On becoming a social scientist.* San Francisco: Jossey-Bass.

Robins, D., & Cohen, P. (1978). *Knuckle sandwich: Growing up in the working-class city.* Harmondsworth: Penguin.

Rosenau, P. M. (1992). *Post-modernism and the social sciences: Insights, inroads, and intrusion.* Princeton, NJ: Princeton University Press.

Ruddick, S. (1980). Material thinking. *Feminist Studies, 6,* 342-367.

San Juan, E., Jr. (1992). *Articulations of power in ethnic and racial studies in the United States.* Atlantic Highlands, NJ: Humanities Press.

Schön, D. (1987). *Educating the reflective practitioner: Toward a new design for teaching and learning in the professions.* San Francisco: Jossey-Bass.

Scott, J. W. (1992). Experience. In J. Butler & J. W. Scott (Eds.), *Feminists theorize the political* (pp. 22-40). New York: Routledge.

Silverman, E. K. (1990). Clifford Geertz: Towards a more "thick" understanding? In C. Tilley (Ed.), *Reading material culture* (pp. 121-159). Cambridge, UK: Basil Blackwell.

Simon, R., & Dippo, D. (1987). What schools can do: Designing programs for work education that challenge the wisdom of experience. *Journal of Education, 169*(3), 101-116.

Simon, R., Dippo, D., & Schenke, A. (1991). *Learning work: A critical pedagogy of work education.* South Hadley, MA: Bergin & Garvey.

Slaughter, R. (1989). Cultural reconstruction in the post-modern world. *Journal of Curriculum Studies, 3,* 255-270.

Taussig, M. (1987). *Shamanism, colonialism, and the wild man: A study in terror and healing.* Chicago: University of Chicago Press.

Walker, A. (1983). *In search of our mothers' gardens: Womanist prose.* San Diego, CA: Harcourt Brace Jovanovich.

Weiler, K. (1988). *Women teaching for change: Gender, class, and power.* South Hadley, MA: Bergin & Garvey.

Welch, S. (1991). An ethic of solidarity and difference. In H. Giroux (Ed.), *Postmodernism, feminism, and cultural politics: Redrawing educational boundaries* (pp. 83-99). Albany: State University of New York Press.

West, C. (1991). *The ethical dimensions of Marxist thought.* New York: Monthly Review Press.

Wexler, P. (1991). Preface. In P. Wexler (Ed.), *Critical theory now.* New York: Falmer.

Willis, P. (1977). *Learning to labour: How working class kids get working class jobs.* Farnborough, England: Saxon House.

Wirth, A. (1983). *Productive work—in industry and schools.* Lanham, MD: University Press of America.

Yates, T. (1990). Jacques Derrida: "There is nothing outside of the text." In C. Tilley (Ed.), *Reading material culture* (pp. 206-280). Cambridge, UK: Basil Blackwell.

Young, I. (1990). The ideal of community and the politics of difference. In L. Nicholson (Ed.), *Feminism/postmodernism* (pp. 300-323). New York: Routledge.

Zavarzadeh, M. (1989). Theory as resistance. *Rethinking Marxism, 2,* 50-70.

Zavarzadeh, M., & Morton, D. (1991). *Theory, (post) modernity, opposition.* Washington, DC: Maison-neuve.

Zizek, S. (1990). *The sublime object of ideology.* London: Verso.

9

Feminisms and Models of Qualitative Research

VIRGINIA OLESEN

AT this highly labile moment in the history of feminist thought this chapter attempts to outline feminist qualitative research even as the context and contours of both feminism and qualitative research are shifting. To accomplish this I will review briefly how current complexities emerged, indicate the scope of work, detail some models of research, and discuss issues feminist researchers face.[1]

I emphasize here that there are many feminisms, hence many views, some conflicting (Devault, 1993; Reinharz, 1992; Stanley & Wise, 1990, p. 47; Tong, 1989). Whatever the qualitative research style, and whether or not self-consciously defined as feminist, these many voices share the outlook that it is important to center and make problematic women's diverse situations and the institutions and frames that influence those situations, and then to refer the examination of that problematic to theoretical, policy, or action frameworks in the interest of realizing social justice for women (Eichler, 1986, p. 68). Feminists use a variety of qualitative styles, but share the assumptions held generally by qualitative or interpretive researchers that interpretive human actions, whether found in women's reports of experience or in the cultural products of reports of experience (film and so on), can be the focus of research.

Emergent Complexities in Feminists' Research

Early in the second phase of the women's movement in the United States (1960s onward), one could roughly categorize qualitative feminist researchers in terms of their political views—liberal, radical or Marxist (Fee, 1983)—their academic disciplines (for those few who had made it into the male-dominated academy), or their preferred research styles. These distinctions have blurred: Political orientations are no longer as clear and are characterized by internal divisions within feminist thought; scholars in the social sciences borrow freely from other fields, particularly literary criticism, cultural studies, and history; many researchers mix qualitative methods or attempt to create new styles (see Table 9.1 for a summary of the elements that make up the growing complexity in feminist research). Concomitantly, views of women's lives and the assumptions about their subjectivity, once seen by some as universally homogeneous, have been sharpened and differentiated dramatically (Devault, 1990; Ferguson, 1993). This has led to a highly reflexive stance among many about the conduct of the research, the feminist's place in it, the researcher's

---

AUTHOR'S NOTE: The editors of this handbook, Norman Denzin and Yvonna Lincoln, as well as Michelle Fine and Meaghan Morris provided very help criticisms.

TABLE 9.1 Elements in the Growing Complexity of Feminist Research and Representative Texts

1. Absent and invisible
   Finch and Groves (1982), Lorber (1975), Nakano Glenn (1990)
2. Who can know?
   Cook and Fonow (1986), Jordan (1977), MacKinnon (1982), Ruzek (1978)
3. Frameworks unframed
   a. frames and their critics
      male oriented: Gilligan (1982), Lewin and Olesen (1981), Smith (1974)
      white feminist oriented: Collins (1986), Davis (1978), Dill (1979), Garcia (1989), Green (1990), Hurtado (1989), Zavella (1987), Zinn (1982)
      Western feminist oriented: Mohanty (1988), Spivak (1988)
      able-bodied female: Fine (1992)
      heterosexual: Hall and Stevens (1991), Lewin (1993), Stanley and Wise (1990)
   b. intellectual style
      postmodernism: Clough (1992), Flax (1987), Haraway (1991), Hekman (1990), Nicholson (1990)

relationship to participants, the philosophical location and nature of knowledge and the handling of the report, and the impact of feminist research on the researcher's discipline, issues to be discussed shortly.

Women: Absent and Invisible

In the 1970s and for some time, research concerns were quite straightforward, though nevertheless politically charged. These focused on the absence of women in certain contexts and the invisibility of women in other contexts where they are in fact ubiquitous. Concerned about inequities derived from male dominance rooted in the gender and economic spheres, investigators critically examined contexts such as medicine (Lorber, 1975) and law (Epstein, 1981), where there were few or no women. (These studies led to the later recognition that in female-free contexts "add women and stir" would not redress issues of access or inequity, which lay in deeper interactional and structural problems, a point vividly made in Darlene Clarke Hine's 1989 analysis of African American women and the nursing profession.)

Somewhat later, research from Britain and the United States made visible the widespread caring for children, the ill, and the elderly and exposed the taken-for-grantedness of such work, its oppressiveness, and also its value to women and their societies (Abel & Nelson, 1990; Finch & Groves, 1982; Graham, 1985; Nelson, 1990). Such work highlighted this aspect of women's lives as worthy of analysis and prompted a prominent British feminist sociologist to question the male-framed sociological division of labor (M. Stacey, 1981). Hochschild and Machung (1989) further differentiate the working wife's labor at home with the finding that such labor is embedded in the political economy of domestic emotion.

Later studies on women's preparation of food by Anne Murcott (1983) on Welsh households and Marjorie Devault (1991) on U.S. homes added to the complexity with revelations of the oppression and satisfactions as well as gender-creating activities in the act of women's cooking. With the exception of Phyllis Palmer's (1989) historical analysis of domestic service, the expansion of feminist research to the critical and previously invisible topic of women who do paid domestic work was accomplished by women of color: Evelyn Nakano Glenn's (1990) analysis of Japanese American women who did domestic service between 1905 and 1940, based on interviews and historical labor market data, spells out how the women transcended contradictions in the various forms of oppression they experienced. Judith Rollins's (1985) participant observation research on black women working for white women (she herself did such work) revealed racial dominance within the female sphere, as did Mary Romero's (1992) interview study of Latina domestic workers. These studies are notable for their analysis of class as well as racial issues, an analytic approach feminist researchers stress (Sacks, 1989) but often find difficult to implement (Cannon, Higginbotham, & Leung, 1991; Ferguson, 1993).

Who Can Know?

Simultaneously, the fundamental question of who can be a knower (Code, 1991, p.xi), a query referential both to women as participants and women as researchers, motivated feminist inquiries, thanks to the influences of "consciousness-raising" described by legal scholar Catherine MacKinnon (1982, p. 535; 1983), among others, as *the* basis of feminist methodology (see also Cook & Fonow, 1986). Sheryl Ruzek's (1978) analysis of the rise of the women's health movement took the feminist concern for women as knowers and illustrated how *feminist* research on a social movement differs from standard sociological inquiry. She carefully attended to a familiar sociological issue, professionalization in medicine, but grounded her work and analysis in women's experience and knowledge of medical practice, particularly gynecology, to show how relationships emergent from collective discontent eventuated in social organization, the gynecological self-help clinic. In a phenomenological vein, Brigitte Jordan (1977) showed how women's knowledge of their own bodies enabled them to be competent judges of being pregnant, even in the face of medical refusal to acknowledge this state without scientific tests.

Frameworks Unframed

If topic and knower were becoming problematized, so too were interpretive frameworks, particularly those embedded in studies of men's lives. Carol Gilligan's (1982) well-known study of moral development showed that young girls were not flawed or stunted in their development, as frameworks based on the lives of young boys would suggest, but displayed a pattern appropriate for them. Ellen Lewin and I demonstrated the inadequacy of male-based concepts of success as an endless vertical rise. In our study, nurses viewed lateral career patterns that were characterized by autonomy and satisfaction as success (Lewin & Olesen, 1981).

Male-oriented and -influenced frameworks were not the only perspectives crumbling. Steadily rising incisive criticisms from women of color, Third World feminists, disabled women, and lesbian women decentered and fractured white feminists' formulations of women's place in the world. White feminists' unexamined use of a woman or women who stood for all women came under fire early from African American scholars Angela Davis (1978) and Bonnie Thornton Dill (1979). They argued that the impact of slavery in the United States created a sharply different past and present for black women, with more complex gender relationships than had been seen or understood by white feminists. Twenty years after these critiques, legal scholar Kimberly Crenshaw (1992), commenting on the 1991 Clarence Thomas hearings, found it necessary to reiterate and update this criticism.

This body of criticism, expressed by Maxine Baca Zinn (1982), Aida Hurtado (1989), and Esther Garcia (1989) concerning Latina women, Esther Chow (1987) about Chinese American women, and Rayna Green (1990) about Native American women, decried the tendency to construct, speak for, and, in bell hooks's (1990) incisive words, "to know us better than we know ourselves" (p. 22). Citing research by African American sociologists and literary critics, Patricia Hill Collins (1986) further refines these views when she reminds sociologists in general and feminists in particular how "Black women's family experiences represent a clear case of the workings of race, gender and class oppression in shaping family life" (p. 529). Patricia Zavella's (1987) study of Mexican American women who do cannery work affirmed this.

Powerful critiques by Third World feminists further dissolved the conceptualization of "woman." Their criticisms, along with those of women of color and feminists attuned to postcolonial deconstructionism, anticipated much of the critique of "defining the Other" (invidious, oppressive, and unthinking definition of persons with whom research is done), which was to become influential in the hands of critics of postcolonial anthropology (Clifford, 1986; Marcus & Fisher, 1986), who initially seemed quite unaware of this body of feminist writing. It also became clear that Western feminist frameworks would not work in many Third World contexts because "differences could not simply be absorbed into dominant frameworks" (Kirby, 1991, p. 398). Along with questions of research authority, the very question of asking research questions became problematic, with Gayatri Chakravorty Spivak (1988) posing the hard question of whether the subordinated can speak at all, a point also made by Chandra Mohanty (1988).

Other, more refined, conceptualizations of women's lives emerged from women, who by virtue of deeply rooted American stigma around physical disability and nonheterosexuality, had been rendered invisible by male-dominated frames, and by feminists blinded by these cultural norms. Michelle Fine (1992, p. 142), reviewing the emergence of disabled women as a problematic issue, insightfully noted that even sympathetic research on disabilities tended to overlook disabled women's multiple statuses and instead viewed them only in terms of their specific disabilities. Stanley and Wise's (1990, pp. 29-34) parallel criticism regarding lack of attention to or understanding of lesbians heralded lesbian feminist research, which has refined views of lesbians, for instance Patricia Stevens and Joanne Hall's (1991) historical analysis of how medicine has invidiously framed lesbianism and Ellen Lewin's (1993) interview study of lesbian mothers in America and the surpassing importance to them of the maternal role.

The potentially unsettling and fundamental question of the meaning and construction of gender, largely the concern of feminist anthropologists (Ortner & Whitehead, 1981) and more recently philosophers (J. Butler, 1990) and sociologists (West & Zimmerman, 1987), has emerged to provide some fundamental challenges, as yet not fully explored, to feminist research assumptions. Parallel to and often intersecting with these disruptive criticisms is the steadily growing influence of deconstructive and postmodern studies, which often unsettles not only taken-for-granted male-originated frames but the feminist frames as well.[2] As Jane Flax (1987) succinctly states, "Postmodern discourses are all 'deconstructive' in that they seek to distance us from and make us skeptical about beliefs concerning truth, knowledge, power, the self and language that are often taken for granted within and serve as legitimation for Western culture" (p. 624). Among the provocative consequences of these modes of thinking is a proliferation of conceptualizations of women's subjectivity that attempt to grapple with the potential for multiple sources of women's identity as women without sliding into essentialism (Ferguson, 1993, p. 154).

As this too-brief review suggests, the topic of women's lives has become increasingly differentiated. Before I present a discussion of models and issues that have arisen from that differentiation, it will be useful to outline the scope of research in terms of level of inquiry (phenomenological, relational, structural, policy).

The Scope of Qualitative Feminist Work

Subjectivity

Though one may think that qualitative feminist research would focus on subjectivity and interpersonal relationship, an assumption that reflects the flaws and inaccurate criticism that qualitative work cannot deal with structure or larger issues, the by now substantial body of feminist research ranges over all these levels and utilizes the full span of qualitative methods (for a densely rich compendium that details many of these, see Reinharz, 1992).

Some of the most skillful work on women's subjectivity and experiences has been done in the area of women's health, in ways that unsettle the frames just mentioned and lead to theoretical or pragmatic consequences. Using interviews with women patients who did not follow doctor's orders, Linda Hunt, Brigitte Jordan, and Carole Browner (1989) found that the women were not difficult, noncompliant cranks, but acted for reasons that made sense in their own lives. Robin Saltonstall's (1993) analysis of in-depth interviews with men and women shows important gender differences in embodiment and the construction of health. Using narratives from women who had been battered but were able to seek and find help, Lora Bex Lempert (1992) depicts the women's difficulties in interpreting this experience to themselves and, critically, to others who did not always believe their stories. Susan Bell's (1988) narrative analysis of DES daughters shows the connection between personal problems and collective action.

Relationships and Interaction

Feminists have also looked at women's relationships and interactions with others to reveal aspects of male control lodged in linguistic and conversational structures. Utilizing discourse analysis, Alexandra Dundes Todd (1989) and Sue Fisher (1988) outline the extent to which maleness dominates interaction between female patients and male doctors and significantly influences diagnosis and care. With conversational analysis, Candace West (1988) demonstrates how gender supersedes professional status where the patient is male and the physician female, a finding that reveals the replication of gender dominance.

Women's interactions and relationships have also been examined in a variety of work settings. Maria Patricia Fernandez-Kelly's (1983) participation and observation in border factories unveiled lives of Mexican-American women working there. Anne Game (1991) details the patriarchal nature of secretarial work in Australia. Frances Katsuranis and I have shown how temporary clerical workers, thought by some feminists to be powerless and without agency, exert control of their work assignments and link their work to their private lives (Olesen & Katsuranis, 1978). Arlene Daniels's (1988) interview study of upper-class female volunteers and their work discloses how these women's interactions sustain and create class position.

Social Movements, Organizations, Structures

Analysis of interaction is also central in feminist research on larger units, such as social movements and social organizations, but these rely on historical analysis of structures as well. Dorothy Broom's (1991) account of the emergence of state-sponsored women's health clinics in Australia explicates contradictions faced by feminists interested in reform and transformation of the health care system while working within the system. In a historical analysis of states' laws on informed consent for breast cancer patients undergoing treatment and interviews with key leaders, Theresa Montini (1991) found that medical interests partially co-opted the women's goals. Of interest and perhaps concern to feminists interested in feminist movements, she also found that the activists themselves, although willing to borrow feminist principles, would not define themselves or their work as "feminist." Brandy Britton's (1993) examination of the political economy of the battered women's movement also utilizes historical analysis and interviews that reveal state or federal funding's sometimes pernicious effects on members of movement organizations in terms of race, class, and sexual orientation. All three of these studies attempted to bridge the so-called gap between microinteractional studies and inquiries that look at macro or larger sociological units.

This work borders on an emerging style of analysis within symbolic interactionism that Clarke (1990) calls "meso analysis." This refers to analysis of the "mesostructure" or "how societal and institutional forces mesh with human activity" (Maines, 1982, p. 10). Adele Clarke's (1990; Clarke & Montini, 1993) historical research shows how these processes play out in the arena of women's reproductive health around such issues as production of contraceptives. Where meso analysts have looked at gender and science in the case of technologies, these studies elevate the question of research for women to an important critique of contemporary and historical male-dominated science and its control not only of women but also of the policy process.

Policy

In her review of qualitative analysis and policy in Britain, Janet Finch (1986, p. 127) optimistically argues that feminist qualitative research can make an important contribution to the understanding and making of policy. Though issue- or topic-oriented feminist qualitative research has had small impact on U.S. policy makers, probably because of their preference for quantitative research, it has productively exposed aspects and consequences of the policy-making process. Using aging as their topic, Carroll Estes and Beverly Edmonds (1981) articulate a symbolic interactionist model for understanding how emergent policy issues become framed. They recognize that ambiguousness characterizes much policy activity and that the "transformation of intentions" (their definition of policy) turns on who frames and controls the definitions emergent from the ambiguities.

Joyce Gelb and Marian Lief Palley (1987) detail histories of feminist organizations in such policy issues as credit discrimination, Title IX, and reproductive choice. How deeply divided viewpoints about policy issues can be is shown by Patricia Kaufert and Sonja McKinlay (1985), who used content analysis of scientific and lay publications to display divergent views of clinicians and medical researchers. Shelley Romalis's (1988) ethnographic/interview study of Canadian physicians and women who wanted to have home births outlines the dynamics of policy conflict in the context of home and hospital. Feminist studies from Britain on health (McIntyre, 1985), education (Stanworth, 1985), and housing (Austerberry & Watson, 1985) also excel in showing constructions of and contentions within policy issues, as does Rosalind Petchesky's (1985) analysis of how women's health is framed by feminists and others in the abortion debate and Amanda Rittenhouse's (1991) examination of why premenstrual syndrome emerged as a social problem.

However, feminist researchers have yet to explore other critical areas, for example, policy making (exceptions include Margaret Stacey's 1992 observational research on the British Medical Council and Susan Chase's 1992 narrative studies with female school administrators), how feminist-inspired policies are implemented (Craddock & Reid's 1993 participatory work with a well-woman clinic is an example), or the state's definition and control of women, such as political scientist Wendy Brown (1992) has done in questioning Barbara Ehrenreich and Frances Fox Piven's (1983) positive feminist view of the state for women. These papers, like Nancy Fraser's (1989) examination of women's needs, are a type of theoretical-analytic research importantly oriented as critiques of the state and state systems.

Models of Feminists' Research

The lability noted at the outset of this chapter deeply characterizes more than scope. It is definitely the hallmark of reflections on the nature of feminist research. In 1987 Sandra Harding, a philosopher, described certain social science models as reflecting transitional epistemologies, a characterization that would still apply to feminists both in the social or behavioral sciences and in history and literary studies. Here I will discuss these models, feminist standpoint research, feminist empiricism, and postmodernism, including the rapidly developing area of feminist cultural studies. My discussion may make these viewpoints seem more discrete than they are, but I wish to sharpen core attributes in order to highlight certain criticisms of the approaches and to lead to issues that feminist qualitative researchers face. The labile moment noted previously calls for rethinking these categories, a task not possible in the confines of this chapter.

Feminist Standpoint Research

Reflecting long-standing feminist criticisms of the absence of women from or marginalized reports of women in research accounts, research done from the perspective of standpoint theories stresses a particular view that builds on and from women's experiences (Harding, 1987, p. 184). The work of sociologist Dorothy Smith (1974, 1989, p. 34), who conceptualized women's "perspective," and Marxist political scientist Nancy Hartsock (1983, 1985) exemplifies research starting from women's actual experience in everyday life within the material division of labor (Stanley & Wise, 1990, p. 34). Because Smith's agenda springs from a serious critique of traditional sociology, I will detail her views more fully; this is not intended to slight Hartsock's important contributions to the genre of standpoint theory and research. Much of the feminist work cited earlier could be defined as standpoint work, though not all proceeds from a Marxist orientation and not all self-consciously examines the researcher's place "in the relations of ruling," as Dorothy Smith urges. A body of work by feminist legal scholars (Ashe, 1988; Bartlett, 1990; Fry, 1992; MacKinnon 1982, 1983; Matsuda 1992) that utilizes content analysis also falls within this genre.

Blending Marxist, phenomenological, and ethnomethodological perspectives, Dorothy Smith (1987) moves well beyond widely accepted understandings of the importance of intersubjectivity in qualitative work such as ethnography, participant observation, and interview. Aware of women's exclusions and silencing in many realms, not the least of which are academic disciplines, she conceptualizes the everyday world as a problematic, that is, continually created, shaped, and known by women within it and its organization, which is shaped by external material factors or textually mediated relations (p. 91). To understand that everyday world of women as it is known by the women who continually create and shape it within the materialist context, the researcher herself must not create it as an object for study as would be done traditionally in sociology, which would divide subject and object. She must, instead, "be able to work very differently than she is able to with established sociological strategies of thinking and inquiry" (Smith, 1992, p. 96) that are not outside the relations of ruling. This clearly demands a high degree of reflexivity from the feminist qualitative researcher and a recognition of how feminist sociologists "participate as subjects in the orders of ruling" (p. 96), an example of which is her own work with Alison Griffith on mothers' work on children's schooling (Griffith & Smith, 1987), which discloses how she and her colleague found in their own discussions the effects of the North American discourse on mothering of the 1920s and 1930s (Smith, 1992, p. 97).

For feminist researchers the standpoint position, particularly as powerfully set forth by Nancy Hartsock and subtly argued by Dorothy Smith, stimulates thought, work in this style (for other examples, see Smith, 1992, p. 97), and, importantly, doubts and questions: Is there an essential tone, for example, an overarching inference, as to the nature of woman (Lemert, 1992, p. 69)? Does relativism rear its head (Harding, 1987, p. 187)? Is the model of knowledge generated from women's position simplistic (Hawkesworth, 1989, p. 347)? Does it neglect alternative traditions of knowledge, such as those of women of color (Collins, 1992, p. 77)? Does it raise anew the problem of "validity" (Ramazanoglu, 1989)? Assuming that women's lives are fragmented, can the standpoint researcher understand these fragmented identities (Lemert, 1992, p. 68)? Is "experience" an untenable focus for feminist investigation when it, too, is continually mediated and constructed from unconscious desire (Clough, 1993a)? In these questions lie debates about the nature of disciplines, especially sociology, the vexed issues of experience and text, passion, and rationality, which I will discuss more fully in the section on issues, below.

Feminist Empiricism

These researchers work with thoughtful adherence to the standards of the current norms of qualitative inquiry, whatever the discipline. Their work proceeds on the assumptions of intersubjectivity and commonly created meanings and "realities" between researcher and participants (Olesen, 1992a). Much of the research noted in the discussion of complexities and scope is of this type (Harding, 1987, p. 182). However, some, instead of applying the research standards in their field—which, being male based, produce androcentric findings—self-consciously try to create new, but rigorous, research practices to give their findings credibility.

Just as with standpoint research, questions arise about feminist empiricism: In spite of concern and respect for women's lived experiences, do these studies nevertheless replicate old disciplinary practices and women's subordinated status? How is it possible to achieve the "neutrality/objectivity demanded in standard qualitative procedures whilst recognizing subjectivity, and, more importantly, intersubjectivity between researcher and participants" (Hawkesworth, 1989, p. 329)? Is it even possible to attempt to find a "truth about reality" (Hawkesworth, 1989, p. 330)? Can validity or its shadow cousins in qualitative work, credibility and adequacy, ever be realized? (We will return to this question in the section on issues.) Does the emphasis on subjectivity come "too close . . . to a total elimination of intersubjective validation of description and explanation" (Komarovsky, 1988, p. 592; 1991)?

Postmodernism

Concerned with the difficulties of ever producing more than a partial story of women's lives in oppressive contexts, postmodernist feminist researchers regard "truth" as a destructive illusion. The endless play of signs, the shifting sands of interpretation, language that obscures—all prompt these feminists to view the world as endless stories or texts, many of which sustain the integration of power and oppression and actually "constitute us as subjects in a determinant order" (Hawkesworth, 1989, p. 349). Their focus is therefore narrative and "the nebulous distinction between text and reality" (Hawkesworth, 1989, p. 348). In such a view gender is no longer privileged.

Nowhere has the postmodern debate among feminist qualitative researchers in the social sciences occurred with more vigor and sophistication than in anthropology and political science. Mary Hawkesworth (1989), a political scientist, argues that neither feminist empiricism (commitment to traditional research methods) nor feminist standpoint research (taking women's view as particular and privileged) can deal with what she calls "the politics of knowledge" (p. 346), by which she means the utilization of "the mode of analysis appropriate to a specific problem" (p. 346). Similarly, she criticizes postmodern thought as too relativistic and overlooking life's real problems, which get lost in the emphasis on textuality. Her solution: a critical feminist analysis to demonstrate rationally "deficiencies of alternative explanations" about women's situation. Her fear, like that of others, concerning postmodernism is that "in a world of radical inequality, relativist resignation enforces the status quo" (p. 351). (For replies to Hawkesworth, see Hawkesworth, 1990a, 1990b; Hekman, 1990a; Shogan, 1990.)

Expressing similar worries, anthropologists Frances E. Mascia-Lees, Patricia Sharpe, and Colleen Ballerino Cohen (1989) point out that the postmodern or "new" ethnography, because of its lack of centeredness, "directs attention away from the fact that ethnography is more than 'writing it up' " (p. 33); it can obscure power relationships. (For a reply, see Kirby, 1991; see also Mascia-Lees, Sharpe, & Cohen, 1991.) Agneta M. Johannsen (1992) further characterizes postmodern anthropological ethnographers with her claim that they let "the people" speak for themselves, which neither addresses problems nor represents a cultural system.

Carrying the imprint of feminist forebears from deconstructionism and postmodernism (French feminists such as Cixous and Irigaray, and Foucault, Lyotard, Baudrillard), feminist research in the rapidly developing area of cultural studies stresses representation and text. This area is intellectually particularly complex, for scholars working within it utilize Marxist theorizing from Althusser, French feminist theory (Irigaray, Cixous, and so on), psychoanalytic views (Lacan—though by no means do all feminists agree on Lacan's utility for feminism; see Ferguson, 1993, p. 212, n. 3), literary criticism, and historical analysis.

Three types of inquiry are of interest. First is "the production, distribution, consumption and exchange of cultural objects and their meanings" (Denzin 1992, p. 80), such as video, film, music, and the body itself (Balsamo, 1993; deLauretis, 1987; Morris, 1992). Second is "the textual analysis of these cultural objects, their meanings, and the practices that surround them" (Denzin, 1992, p. 81), including various discourses (Game, 1991) and the work of other feminists or sociologists (Clough, 1992). Third is "the study of lived cultures and experiences, which are shaped by the cultural meanings that circulate in everyday life" (Denzin, 1992, p. 81). Here will be found the by now voluminous (and growing) work in gender and science, where science, the sacred cow of the Enlightenment, modernity, and the contemporary moment, is dismembered as a culture to reveal its practices, discourses, and implications for control of women's lives (Haraway, 1991; Jacobus, Keller, & Shuttleworth, 1990). Research about women's reproductive health, an issue central to feminist research from the start and productive of sociological and historical works regarded as classics in feminist inquiry (Gordon, 1976; Luker, 1984), is moving into the gender and science arena.

Within cultural studies some feminists, following Foucault and Lacan, emphasize text and the point that "desire" is produced and replicated through various discourses. More precisely, as Patricia Clough (1993a) has argued, "The textuality never refers to a text, but to the processes of desire elicited and repressed, projected and introjected in the activity of reading and writing" (p. 175). The term *desire* seems to include (a) passion, (b) the mischievous and mysterious contributions of the unconscious, (c) libidinal resources not squeezed out of us by childhood and adult socialization, and (d) the sexuality and sexual politics of cultural life and its reproduction and representation (e.g., films, video, magazines).

This type of work is not easily classified, for multidisciplinary borrowing, both of content and method, is widespread, legitimate, and, indeed, encouraged as new forms and understandings are sought (Grossberg, Nelson, & Treichler, 1992). Compared with customary qualitative feminist work, these studies are apt to appear as hybrids, radical (in terms of form, content, and substance) and, for some, threatening and subversive, not merely of male dominance but of feminism itself.

Even as standpoint and empiricist perspectives have excited and worried feminist researchers, so has the work of feminists doing cultural studies:

Is the world nothing more than text (Hawkesworth, 1989, p. 349)? Are there only stories, no action, no "progress" (Harding, 1987, p. 188)? Does focus on the text obscure enduring oppressive institutions and practices (Hawkesworth, 1989, p. 350)? Which academic disciplines are prepared to accept such "unusual" work and recognize it?

Emergence of these three models and the growing complexity of qualitative feminist research has prompted highly self-conscious examination (O. Butler, 1986; Collins, 1986; Fine, 1992; Fonow & Cook, 1991; Lather, 1991; Mies, 1982; Moore, 1988; Nielsen, 1990; Reinharz, 1992; Roberts, 1981; Stanley, 1990; Stanley & Wise, 1983; Tom, 1989). This has led to the realization that embedded in all three models are troublesome issues for feminist researchers, though researchers in the three traditions, if they can be called that at this point, do not necessarily confront all of these. These issues derive from criticisms of empirical qualitative work, such as bias, questions about adequacy or credibility, relationships with persons in the research, and ethical implications. Others emerge from the impact of postcolonial deconstructive thought and postmodernism, such as whose voices are heard and how, and whether text or experience should be created, and by whom. Discussion of these issues takes us to the question of how and whether qualitative feminist research addresses boundaries and content of current disciplines, and to some concluding observations.

Issues Derived From Criticisms of Qualitative Research

Bias

Concern with bias, a concept from logicopositivist work, has been a long-standing criticism of qualitative research (Huber, 1973; Denzin, 1992, pp. 49-52). To the charges that the researcher brings her own biases, qualitative feminist researchers would reply that bias is a misplaced term. To the contrary, these are resources and, if the researcher is sufficiently reflexive about her project, she can evoke these as resources to guide data gathering or creating and for understanding her own interpretations and behavior in the research, as Arlene Daniels's (1983) candid account of her fieldwork mistakes in her studies of military psychiatrists and upper-class volunteers shows.

What is required, they would argue, is sufficient reflexivity to uncover what may be deep-seated but poorly recognized views on issues central to the research and a full account of the researcher's views, thinking, and conduct. Commenting on the self in fieldwork, Nancy Scheper-Hughes (1992) writes, "We cannot rid ourselves of the cultural self we bring with us into the field any more than we can disown the eyes, ears and skin through which we take in our intuitive perceptions about the new and strange world we have entered" (p. 28). However, the researcher still needs to be reflexive about her views: Sherry Gorelick (1991) specifically identifies potential problems when inductivist feminist researchers who espouse a Marxist framework "fail to take account of the hidden structure of oppression (the research participant is not omniscient) and the hidden relations of oppression (the participant may be ignorant of her relative privilege over and difference from other women)" (p. 461). Scheper-Hughes (1983) asks whether feminist researchers in anthropology may unwittingly replicate androcentric perspectives.

Speaking directly to questions of bias around race and class that might be introduced by researchers' failure to recognize or incorporate diversity, and anticipating Kathy Ferguson's (1993, p. 168) later criticisms of the underthematizing of class in feminist theory and research, Cannon et al. (1991) draw attention to the problems faced by qualitative studies, which are typically smaller than quantitative projects and hence face greater difficulties in recruiting women of color and of different classes.

Bias is related to the central issue of subjectivity in feminist research and the concomitant problem of objectivity in empirical research. Jennifer Ring (1987) proposes dialectics (following Hegel) as a solution to the problems of subjectivity and objectivity: "Dialectical thought contains the possibility for a radical departure from an empiricist conception of objectivity when it refuses to allow the border between objectivity and subjectivity to rest long enough to take a static form" (p. 771).

Adequacy and Credibility

Perhaps no issue is as challenging to feminist empiricist researchers as that of adequacy or credibility, the parallel to validity in quantitative work (Hall & Stevens, 1991). Because they often problematize taken-for-granted situations, raise difficult and uncomfortable questions about women's contexts, and stress the importance of subjectivity, feminist empiricists working in the qualitative mode are particularly vulnerable to positivists' criticisms about credibility.

Feminist empiricists have struggled with this in a number of ways. Janet Finch and Jennifer Mason (1990) meticulously detail their use of theoretical sampling to find "negative cases" with which to refute or amend their interpretations, a strategy from grounded theory (Strauss & Corbin, 1990). Catherine Kohler Riessman (1990) explicates her analysis and her worries about the sociologist's interpretive voice and the integration of respondents' voices, as many methodologists urge (Burgess, 1984, pp. 209-219). Many of the accounts noted earlier (e.g., Devault, 1991; Ruzek, 1978) detail how the research problem emerged and how different data sources were "triangulated" or how the researcher conducted herself (Rollins, 1985; Warren, 1988). Although "taking the account back to respondents" has been widely discussed, along with cautions about its use (Bloor, 1983; Emerson & Pollner, 1988; Hammersley & Atkinson, 1983), it has not been used as often as perhaps one might expect in feminist research, where concern for respondents is emphasized.

One attempt to achieve this, however, that recognizes the dual task of seeking "objectivity" while dealing with the relations between the researcher and the researched, a task not always easily realized, was made by Joan Acker, Kate Barry, and Johanna Esseveld (1991, pp. 142-150). They tried to create new criteria for adequacy, such as being sure the subjects' voices are heard, accounting for the investigators as well as those participating, and revealing conditions that result in the daily lives being studied, but they also recognize that "it is impossible to create a research process that erases the contradictions (in power and consciousness) between researcher and researched" (p. 150). These struggles with the tension between intersubjective understanding and the goal of objective reporting in feminist qualitative research foreground ethical issues.

Ethical Concerns

Feminists have sharpened the numerous discussions in anthropology and sociology on ethical issues. They draw on the theme that at once characterizes feminist qualitative research and leads to ethical dilemmas, namely, concern for and even involvement with the participating persons. Janet Finch (1984) delineates a part of this problem in her insightful comments on interviewing lonely or isolated women hungry for contact with other people who may be unwittingly manipulated by the researcher. Judith Stacey's (1988) widely cited paper on the fundamental contradictions in feminist ethnography reminds feminist qualitative researchers that their methods can be as worrisome as those of quantitative researchers. More specifically, she calls attention to the uncomfortable question of getting data from respondents as a means to an end and the difficult compromises that may be involved in promising respondents control over the report. Feminist nurse researchers have pointed out that additional ethical dilemmas arise when doing research in one's own professional culture, where the researcher and professional roles may conflict (Field, 1991). These issues emerge with even more urgency in studies where participants are also researchers.

Degree of Participants' Involvement in the Research

All feminist qualitative research shares with interpretive work in general the assumption of intersubjectivity between researcher and participant and the mutual creation of data. In a certain sense, participants are always "doing" research, for they, along with the researchers, construct the meanings that become "data" for later interpretation by the researcher (Olesen, 1992a). Qualitative researchers in general have differed in the extent to which participants are involved as researchers in the inquiry and the nature of the involvement when they are.

Some feminists, however, have undertaken projects in which participants whose lives and situations are the focus of the work become coresearchers, in the interests of not exploiting women as research "subjects" and of empowering women to do research for themselves on issues of interest to them. Participants as researchers are generally found in action-oriented research projects, where the nature of participation ranges from researcher consultation with participants regarding topics and research instruments such as questionnaires, through training women to do research under the direction of a feminist researcher (Lather, 1986, 1988), to participants and researchers working together on all phases of the project (Cancian, 1992; Craddock & Reid, 1993).

Nancy Kleiber and Linda Light's (1978; Light & Kleiber, 1981) early study of a Vancouver women's health collective is an instance of the last of these styles, termed interactive or participatory research. Kleiber and Light describe their conversion from traditional field-workers to coresearchers with the members of the women's health collective and the difficulties of closing the distance between researchers and participants when both engage in the research. Their text, a traditional, not experimental, account written by themselves and their participants, reflects many voices, for the data gathering, analysis, and writing are collective.

Working out modes of participant research in consultation with participants, rather than as an afterthought, challenges feminist researchers on many levels: assumptions about women's knowledge; representations of women; modes of data gathering, analysis, interpretation, and writing the account; relationships between researcher and participants and, critically, diversity among women's views about women, particularly where views are not similar to feminist outlooks (Hess, 1990); and the risk of appropriating participant-generated data to or along the lines of the researcher's interests (Opie, 1992).

Issues Posed by Deconstructionism and Postmodernism

Voice and the Account

Deeply implicated in the very foundations of feminist research lies the question of voice and, by implication, the account. Forcefully stated by women of color and Third World feminists (see earlier sections of the chapter) and reiterated in critical comments on postcolonial research practices, this question concerns how voices of participants are to be heard, with what authority, and in what form. This concern has moved far beyond postmodernism and deconstructionism and has become lodged in the worries of feminist qualitative researchers in general. They are highly conscious of the absence of women's voices, distortions, and the charge that preparing the account in the usual social science modes only replicates hierarchical conditions found in the parent discipline, where women are outside the account (Smith, 1989, p. 34).

Working with the intertwined problem of realizing as fully as possible women's voices in data gathering and preparing an account that transmits those voices poses some difficult questions, though a number of creative attempts have been made. Regarding difficulties, Ellen Lewin (1991) has pointed out that merely letting the tape recorder run to achieve full representation overlooks the fact that respondents' accounts are already mediated when they come into the interview. Michelle Fine (1992) delineates some worrisome issues about use of voices (use of pieces of narrative, taking individual voices to reflect group behavior, assuming that voices are free of power relations, failure to make clear the researcher's own position in relationship to the voices) and forcefully urges feminist researchers to "articulate how, how not, and within what limits" voices are used (pp. 217-219). Borrowing literary devices to express voices may also contain hidden problems of control (Mascia-Lees et al., 1989, p. 30).

Some feminists have developed some innovative ways to reflect and present voice, though not all would be free of the problems Fine discusses (for an extensive roster of new ethnographic accounts, see Mascia-Lees et al., 1989, pp. 7-8, n. 1). Two contrasting examples: Marjorie Shostak (1981) gives a verbatim dialogic account of her voice and that of Nisa, a !Kung woman. In Susan Krieger's (1983) fieldwork report of a lesbian community in the Midwest, members' voices are heard as a polyphonic chorus on various issues, but Susan Krieger's voice as narrator is absent, though she clearly selected the materials for the account.

Margery Wolf (1992) presents three different versions of an event in her fieldwork in Taiwan: a piece of fiction, her anthropological field notes, and a social science article. Ruth Behar (1993) explodes the traditional anthropological form of life history to intertwine the voice of her cocreator with her own in an extended double-voiced text. Her apt title, *Translated Woman,* reflects Behar as researcher and narrator as much as it does her cocreator, "Esperanza."

Calling for new textual and presentational practices, Laurel Richardson (1991, 1992) has utilized poetry; Michael McCall and Howard Becker (1990) have given dramatic readings, a technique also suggested by the late Marianne Paget (1990). Carolyn Ellis and Art Bochner (1992) have used the technique of telling personal stories. (For greater detail on textual practice, see Richardson, Chapter 32, this volume.) Though sessions at meetings of academic disciplines where unusual presentations are given are lively and well attended, and many feminist journals publish creative presentations, the worrisome question remains, given the style and framing of mainstream academic journals, how feminist qualitative researchers can alter present publication practices to realize greater receptivity to these new forms. Is the solvent of feminist scholarship sufficient to break through the ossified academic structures?

Experience and Analysis

Although much research in the empiricist and standpoint styles takes women's experience as the core concern, largely on the basis of women's having been excluded from male-dominated versions of "reality" (Gregg, 1987), some critics have highlighted the unstable nature of a concept of "experience" and have advocated as well analysis of conditions that produce "experience." Feminists in both history (e.g., Scott, 1991) and psychology (e.g., Morawski, 1990) argue that merely taking experience into account does not reflect on how that experience came to be. In short, oppressive systems are replicated rather then criticized in the unquestioning reliance on "experience." As Joan Scott (1991) comments, "Experience is at once always already an interpretation *and* in need of interpretation" (p. 779). Several feminist research accounts both report experience and interpret economic or class influences on the framing of experience. Examples include Arlie Hochschild's (1983) analysis of the experience of flight attendants' management of emotion in the context of the workings of the airline industry, Nona Glazer's (1991) examination of racism and classism in professional nursing, and Nancy Scheper-Hughes's (1992) exploration of motherhood and poverty in northeastern Brazil.

Other feminist researchers, such as Patricia Clough (1993a, p. 179), who look to deconstruction or psychoanalytic feminist semiotics disavow any attention to actual experience on the grounds that, irrespective of how close the researcher, experience is always created in discourse and textuality. Text takes primacy here, constituting the bases for incisive analyses of text production as a fundamental mode of social criticism (Clough, 1992).

Consequences: Disciplines Bounded and Unbounded

How comfortable are feminist qualitative researchers with their own disciplines, and do they see transformation of the discipline as a part of the agenda that urges research for women? Whether the types of qualitative feminist research noted here and the theoretical and epistemological assumptions supporting it can alter, much less transform, the disciplines in which these researchers work cannot be easily answered: Sectors of different disciplines, such as sociology and psychology, hold tenaciously to positivistic outlooks, and there are diverse theoretical views within disciplines that blunt or facilitate feminist transformation (Stacey & Thorne, 1985). Moreover, it is simplistic to think of a single feminist research impact, for as I have tried to show in this chapter, qualitative feminist research is not homogeneous but highly differentiated and complex, with different potentials for influence on the disciplines.

Within anthropology, Lila Abu-Lughod (1990) and Ruth Behar (1993) argue that dissolving the self/other, subject/object distinctions fundamental to traditional ethnography holds the promise of "unsettling boundaries" (Abu-Lughod, 1990, p. 26) and liberating the discipline from "the colonizing domination" of its colonial past (Behar, 1993, p. 302). Writing about the "awkward relationship between anthropology and feminism," Marilyn Strathern (1987, p. 292), however, has contended that feminist and anthropological views are not paradigms that can be shifted, but are so fundamental to the practice of each that they are not open to conscious challenge and in fact "mock" rather than challenge one another.

Calls from feminists for overhaul of their disciplines reflect the diverse views on research noted in this chapter as well as the intellectual inertia and embedded resistance in various fields (Stacey & Thorne, 1985). Dorothy Smith's (1987, 1989, 1990a, 1990b) radical critique of sociology (radical in the sense of "going to the roots" and an orientation to the left politically), initially put forth in 1974 and enriched in subsequent rethinking, formulated a way, unutilized in sociology, to discover women's experience and to link it to the "politics and practice of progressive struggle" (Smith, 1992, p. 88).

In a long-overdue review of Smith's work, several theorists highlight the potential of her thinking for the alteration of sociology, the concept of subjectivity pushed to its limit (Lemert, 1992, p. 71), the integral part of knowledge in "the relations of ruling for contemporary capitalism" (Collins, 1992, p. 73), and the "problematizing of [sociology's] practical underpinnings" (Connell, 1992, p. 81). (Some of their criticisms are noted in the earlier section on standpoint research.) For some, however, Smith has not gone far enough in deconstructing sociology as a dominant discourse of experience (Clough, 1993a, p. 169), a view Smith (1993) herself rejects as overly oriented to text and neglecting experience (see Clough, 1993b, for a reply to Smith).

Other feminist researchers' work strains at the boundaries and hammers at foundations of sociology in particular and the social sciences in general. Patricia Hill Collins's (1986, 1990) analysis of black feminists in sociology raises questions about the impact of dualistic thought in the discipline and its pernicious contribution to the continuance of racism and argues that sociologists should attend more carefully to the anomalies introduced into their discipline by their own biographies. Two feminists, writing in a deconstructive vein, have offered different criticisms. Patricia Clough (1992), through the lens of psychoanalytic semiotics, urges the task of social criticism and asks that feminists and sociologists strip privilege away from observation and "factual" description, hallmarks of traditional ethnography, and turn to "rereadings of representations in every form of information processing," be it literature or empirical science (p. 137). In a similar deconstructive mode, Australian Ann Game (1991, p. 47) rejects the sacred concept of the "social" in favor of discourses as the sociological focus.

In spite of, or perhaps because of, their gloomy assessment of the extent to which feminist psychologists have made or can make an impact on their discipline, Fine and Gordon (1992, p. 25) ask that feminist psychologists work in the space between the personal and the political to reconstitute psychology and urge activist research in feminist psychology.[3]

Whether the subversive potential of feminist cultural studies will influence disciplinary boundaries (Denzin, 1992, p. 75) may well be answered in a trade-off between the rapid growth of this area, including the intellectually exciting gender and science arena, and the constraints of the 1990's fiscal crisis in American universities, a crisis that will also influence the impact of other qualitative feminist research on disciplinary focus and boundaries.

Future Questions for Qualitative Feminist Research

The diversity of approaches, methods, topics and epistemologies noted here suggests that a major future question for qualitative feminist research will be the degree to which these various approaches speak effectively to a sociology for rather than about women. This question is crucial, quite aside from its centrality in the qualitative feminist research agenda, for it raises the issue of audiences and contexts. From the 1970s through the 1990s there has been an unslaked thirst for feminist publications, both theoretical and empirical, but that audience has been largely academic. The extent to which the new participatory forms, discussed here, and the traditional styles or the experimental work reach beyond the academy, and in what mode, will influence feminist qualitative research. It is unlikely, given the range of feminisms, that any orthodoxy, traditional or postmodern, will prevail—nor indeed, in my view, should it. The complexities and problems of women's lives, whatever the context, are sufficiently great that multiple approaches via qualitative research are required.

Notes

1. What you, the reader, will see here is constructed by and filtered through my research experience as a socialist feminist sociologist interested in women's health and women in health and healing systems. I have worked primarily within the emergent or Blumerian wing of the interactionist-social constructionist tradition (Denzin, 1992, pp. 1-21), though I also start with keen interest in the study of cultural products by virtue of a long-ago career in journalism and early graduate study in mass media of communication (Olesen, 1956). I am sympathetic to postmodern currents in both interactionism and feminism, which encourage provocative and productive unpacking of taken-for-grantedness about women in specific historical and material contexts, and I deeply appreciate all attempts to respect women in the research process and to give voice to the voiceless. However, I still believe that research for rather than merely about women is possible through qualitative modes and theoretical writings, imperfect and transitory though they may be and irrespective of researcher's locale. Both experiential and text-oriented styles in combination ought to be utilized. I see that feminist work sets the stage for other research, other actions (I here refer to community, policy, and so on) that transcend and transform (Olesen, 1993). For me, feminist inquiry is dialectical, with different standpoints fusing to produce new syntheses that in turn become the grounds for further work (Nielsen, 1990, p. 29; Westkott, 1979, p. 430). Most of all, feminist qualitative researchers, in making women's lives problematic, should not turn away from rendering their own practices problematic in the interests of more fully realized research for women. If one's own work is overturned or altered by another researcher with a different, more effective approach, then one should rejoice and move forward.

2. The literature on deconstructionism, postmodernism, and feminism is voluminous. For readers starting to explore this area, the following works are helpful: the entire spring 1988 issue of *Feminist Studies,* Nicholson (1990), Hekman (1990b), Flax (1990), and Rosenau (1992).

3. Feminist activist researchers not only work on issues of concern to women, but themselves engage various arenas on women's behalf, participating as lay members of the Food and Drug Administration or its advisory boards (Sheryl Ruzek and Jane Zones) or testifying on behalf of battering women (Julie Blackman; see Blackman, 1989).

References

Abel, E. K., & Nelson, M. K. (1990). *Circles of care: Work and identity in women's lives.* Albany: State University of New York Press.

Abu-Lughod, L. (1990). Can there be a feminist ethnography? *Women and Performance, 5,* 7-27.

Acker, J., Barry, K., & Esseveld, J. (1991). Objectivity and truth: Problems in doing feminist research. In M. M. Fonow & J. A. Cook (Eds.), *Beyond methodology: Feminist scholarship as lived research* (pp. 133-153). Bloomington: Indiana University Press.

Ashe, M. (1988). Law-language of maternity: Discourse holding nature in contempt. *New England Law Review, 521,* 44-70.

Austerberry, H., & Watson, S. (1985). A woman's place: A feminist approach to housing in Britain. In C. Ungerson (Ed.), *Women and social policy* (pp. 91-108). London: Macmillan.

Balsamo, A. (1993). On the cutting edge: Cosmetic surgery and the technological production of the gendered body. *Camera Obscura, 28,* 207-237.

Bartlett, K. (1990). Feminist legal methods. *Harvard Law Review, 103,* 45-50.

Behar, R. (1993). *Translated woman: Crossing the border with Esperanza's story.* Boston: Beacon.

Bell, S. (1988). Becoming a political woman: The reconstruction and interpretation of experience through stories. In A. D. Todd & S. Fisher (Eds.), *Gender and discourse: The power of talk* (pp. 97-123). Norwood, NJ: Ablex.

Blackman, J. (1989). *Intimate violence: A study of injustice.* New York: Columbia University Press.

Bloor, M. J. (1983). Notes on member validation. R. M. Emerson (Ed.), *Contemporary field research* (pp. 156-172). Boston: Little, Brown.

Britton, B. M. (1993). *The battered women's movement in the U.S. c1973-1993: A micro-macro analysis.* Unpublished doctoral dissertation, University of California, San Francisco, School of Nursing, Department of Social and Behavioral Sciences.

Broom, D. (1991). *Damned if we do: Contradictions in women's health care.* Sydney: Allen & Unwin.

Brown, W. (1992). Finding the man in the state. *Feminist Studies, 18,* 7-34.

Burgess, R. (1984). *In the field: An introduction to field research.* Boston: Unwin Hyman.

Butler, O. (1986). *Feminist experiences in feminist research.* Manchester, UK: University of Manchester Press.

Butler, J. (1990). *Gender trouble: Feminism and the subversion of identity.* London: Routledge.

Cancian, F. (1992). Participatory research. In E. F. Borgatta & M. Borgatta (Eds.), *Encyclopedia of sociology* (pp. 1427-1432). New York: Macmillan.

Cannon, L. W., Higginbotham, E., & Leung, M. L. A. (1991). Race and class bias in qualitative research on women. In M. M. Fonow & J. A. Cook (Eds.), *Beyond methodology: Feminist scholarship as lived research* (pp. 107-118). Bloomington: Indiana University Press.

Chase, S. E. (1992). *Narrative practices: Understanding power and subjection and women's work narratives.* Paper presented at the Qualitative Analysis Conference, Carleton University, Ottawa.

Chow, E. N. (1987). The development of feminist consciousness among Asian American women. *Gender & Society, 1,* 284-299.

Clarke, A. (1990). A social worlds research adventure: The case of reproductive science. In S. E. Cozzens & T. F. Gieryn (Eds.), *Theories of science in society* (pp. 15-43). Bloomington: Indiana University Press.

Clarke, A., & Montini, T. (1993). The many faces of RU486: Tales of situated knowledges and technological considerations. *Science, Technology and Human Values, 18,* 42-78.

Clifford, J., & Marcus, G. E. (Eds.). (1986). *Writing culture: The poetics and politics of ethnography.* Berkeley: University of California Press.

Clough, P. T. (1992). *The end(s) of ethnography: From realism to social criticism.* Newbury Park, CA: Sage.

Clough, P. T. (1993a). On the brink of deconstructing sociology: A critical reading of Dorothy Smith's standpoint epistemology. *Sociological Quarterly, 34,* 169-182.

Clough, P. T. (1993b). Response to Smith. *Sociological Quarterly, 34,* 193-194.

Code, L. (1991). *What can she know? Feminist theory and the construction of knowledge.* Ithaca, NY: Cornell University Press.

Collins, P. H. (1986). Learning from the outsider within: The sociological significance of black feminist thought. *Social Problems, 33,* 514-532.

Collins, P. H. (1990). *Black feminist thought: Knowledge, consciousness and the politics of empowerment.* New York: Routledge.

Collins, P. H. (1992). Transforming the inner circle: Dorothy Smith's challenge to sociological theory. *Sociological Theory, 10,* 73-80.

Connell, R. W. (1992). A sober anarchism. *Sociological Theory, 10,* 81-87.

Cook, J. A., & Fonow, M. M. (1986). Knowledge and women's interests: Issues of epistemology and methodology in feminist sociological research. *Sociological Inquiry, 56,* 22-29.

Craddock, E., & Reid, M. (1993). Structure and struggle: Implementing a social model of a well woman clinic in Glasgow. *Social Science and Medicine, 19,* 35-45.

Crenshaw, K. (1992). Whose story is it, anyway? Feminist and antiracist appropriations of Anita Hill. In T. Morrison (Ed.), *Race-ing justice, en-gendering power* (pp. 402-440). New York: Pantheon.

Daniels, A. K. (1983). Self-deception and self-discovery in field work. *Qualitative Sociology, 6,* 195-214.

Daniels, A. K. (1988). *Invisible careers: Civic leaders from the volunteer world.* Chicago: University of Chicago Press.

Davis, A. Y. (1978). Rape, racism and the capitalist setting. *Black Scholar, 9,* 24-30.

deLauretis, T. (1987). *Technologies of gender: Essays on theory, film, and fiction.* Bloomington: Indiana University Press.

Denzin, N. K. (1992). *Symbolic interactionism and cultural studies.* Newbury Park, CA: Sage.

Devault, M. L. (1990). Talking and listening from women's standpoint: Feminist strategies for interviewing and analysis. *Social Problems, 37,* 96-116.

Devault, M. L. (1991). *Feeding the family: The social organization of caring as gendered work.* Chicago: University of Chicago Press.

Devault, M. L. (1993). Different voices: Feminists' methods of social research. *Qualitative Sociology, 16,* 77-83.

Dill, B. T. (1979). The dialectics of black womanhood. *Signs, 4,* 543-555.

Ehrenreich, B., & Fox Piven, F. (1983). Women and the welfare state. In I. Howe (Ed.), *Alternatives: Proposals for America from the democratic left* (pp. 30-45). New York: Pantheon.

Eichler, M. (1986). The relationship between sexist, nonsexist, woman-centered and feminist research. *Studies in Communication, 3,* 37-74.

Ellis, C., & Bochner, A. P. (1992). Telling and performing personal stories. In C. Ellis & M. G. Flaherty (Eds.), *Investigating subjectivity: Research on lived experience* (pp. 79-101). Newbury Park, CA: Sage.

Emerson, R., & Pollner, M. (1988). On the use of members' responses to researchers' accounts. *Human Organization, 47,* 189-198.

Epstein, C. F. (1981). *Women in law.* New York: Basic Books.

Estes, C. L., & Edmonds, B. C. (1981). Symbolic interaction and social policy analysis. *Symbolic Interaction, 4,* 75-86.

Fee, E. (1983). Women and health care: A comparison of theories. In E. Fee (Ed.), *Women and health: The politics of sex in medicine* (pp. 17-34). Englewood Cliffs, NJ: Baywood.

Ferguson, K. (1993). *The man question: Visions of subjectivity in feminist theory.* Berkeley: University of California Press.

Fernandez-Kelly, M. P. (1983). *For we are sold: I and my people.* Albany: State University of New York Press.

Field, P. A. (1991). Doing fieldwork in your own culture. In J. M. Morse (Ed.), *Qualitative nursing research: A contemporary dialogue* (rev. ed., pp. 91-104). Newbury Park, CA: Sage.

Finch, J. (1984). It's great to have someone to talk to. In C. Bell & H. Roberts (Eds.), *Social researching: Politics, problems, practice* (pp. 70-87). London: Routledge & Kegan Paul.

Finch, J. (1986). *Research and policy: The uses of qualitative research in social and educational research.* London: Falmer.

Finch, J., & Groves, D. (1982). *A labour of love: Women, work and caring.* London: Routledge & Kegan Paul.

Finch, J., & Mason, J. (1990). Decision taking in the fieldwork process: Theoretical sampling and collaborative working. In R. G. Burgess (Ed.), *Studies in qualitative methodology: Vol. 2. Reflections on field experience* (pp. 25-50). Greenwich, CT: JAI.

Fine, M. (1992). Passions, politics and power: Feminist research possibilities. In M. Fine (Ed.), *Disruptive voices* (pp. 205-232). Ann Arbor: University of Michigan Press.

Fine, M., & Gordon, S. M. (1992). Feminist transformations of/despite psychology. In M. Fine (Ed.), *Disruptive voices* (pp. 1-25). Ann Arbor: University of Michigan Press.

Fisher, S. (1988). *In the patient's best interest: Women and the politics of medical decisions.* New Brunswick, NJ: Rutgers University Press.

Flax, J. (1987). Postmodernism and gender relations in feminist theory. *Signs, 14,* 621-643.

Flax, J. (1990). *Thinking fragments: Psychoanalysis, feminism and postmodernism in the contemporary West.* Berkeley: University of California Press.

Fonow, M. M., & Cook, J. A. (Eds.). (1991). *Beyond methodology: Feminist scholarship as lived research.* Bloomington: Indiana University Press.

Fraser, N. (1989). Struggle over needs: Outline of a socialist-feminist critical theory of late capitalist political culture. In N. Fraser, *Unruly practices: Power, discourse and gender in contemporary social theory* (pp. 161-187). Minneapolis: University of Minnesota Press.

Fry, M. J. (1992). *Postmodern legal feminism.* London: Routledge.

Game, A. (1991). *Undoing the social: Towards a deconstructive sociology.* Milton Keynes, UK: Open University Press.

Garcia, A. M. (1989). The development of Chicana feminist discourse 1970-1980. *Gender & Society, 3,* 217-238.

Gelb, J., & Palley, M. L. (1987). *Women and public policies* (rev. ed.). Princeton, NJ: Princeton University Press.

Gilligan, C. (1982). *In a different voice: Psychological theory and women's development.* Cambridge: Harvard University Press.

Glazer, N. Y. (1991). "Between a rock and a hard place": Women's professional organizations in nursing and class, racial, and ethnic inequalities. *Gender & Society, 5,* 351-372.

Gordon, L. (1976). *Women's body, women's right.* New York: Grossman.

Gorelick, S. (1991). Contradictions of feminist methodology. *Gender & Society, 5,* 459-477.

Graham, H. (1985). Providers, negotiators and mediators: Women as the hidden carers. In E. Lewin & V. Olesen (Eds.), *Women, health and healing: Toward a new perspective* (pp. 25-52). London: Tavistock.

Green, R. (1990). The Pocahontas perplex: The image of Indian Women in American culture. In E. C. DuBois & V. L. Ruiz (Eds.), *Unequal sisters: A multi-cultural reader in U.S. women's history* (pp. 15-21). London: Routledge.

Gregg, N. (1987). Reflections on the feminist critique of objectivity. *Journal of Communication Inquiry, 11,* 8-18.

Griffith, A., & Smith, D. E. (1987). Constructing knowledge: Mothering as discourse. In J. Gaskell & A. McLaren (Eds.), *Women and education* (pp. 87-103). Calgary: Detselig.

Grossberg, L., Nelson, C., & Treichler, P. A. (Eds.). (1992). *Cultural studies.* New York: Routledge.

Hall, J. M., & Stevens, P. E. (1991). Rigor in feminist research. *Advances in Nursing Science, 13,* 16-29.

Hammersley, M., & Atkinson, P. (1983). *Ethnography: Principles in practice.* London: Tavistock.

Haraway, D. J. (1991). *Simians, cyborgs and women: The reinvention of nature.* London: Routledge.

Harding, S. (1987). Conclusion: Epistemological questions. In S. Harding (Ed.), *Feminism and methodology: Social science issues* (pp. 181-190). Bloomington: Indiana University Press.

Hartsock, N. (1983). The feminist standpoint: Developing the ground for a specifically feminist historical materialism. In S. Harding & M. B. Hintikka (Eds.),

Discovering reality (pp. 283-310). Amsterdam: D. Reidel.

Hartsock, N. (1985). *Money, sex and power: Towards a feminist historical materialism.* Boston: Northeastern University Press.

Hawkesworth, M. E. (1989). Knowers, knowing, known: Feminist theory and claims of truth. In M. R. Malson, J. F. O'Barr, S. Westphal Wihl, & M. Wyer (Eds.), *Feminist theory in practice and process* (pp. 327-351). Chicago: University of Chicago Press. (Reprinted from *Signs,* 1989, *14,* 533-557)

Hawkesworth, M. E. (1990a). Reply to Hekman. *Signs, 15,* 420-423.

Hawkesworth, M. E. (1990b). Reply to Shogan. *Signs, 15,* 426-428.

Hekman, S. (1990a). Comment on Hawkesworth's "Knowers, knowing, known: Feminist theory and claims of truth." *Signs, 15,* 417-419.

Hekman, S. (1990b). *Gender and knowledge: Elements of a postmodern feminism.* Boston: Northeastern University Press.

Hess, B. (1990). Beyond dichotomy: Drawing distinctions and embracing differences. *Sociological Forum, 5,* 75-94.

Hine, D. C. (1989). *Black women in white: Racial conflict and cooperation in the nursing profession, 1890-1950.* Bloomington: Indiana University Press.

Hochschild, A. R. (1983). *The managed heart: Commercialization of human feeling.* Berkeley: University of California Press.

Hochschild, A. R., & Machung, A. (1989). *The second shift: Inside the two-job marriage.* New York: Avon.

hooks, b. (1990). The politics of radical black subjectivity. In b. hooks, *Yearning: Race, gender, and cultural politics* (pp. 15-22). Boston: South End.

Huber, J. (1973). Symbolic interaction as a pragmatic perspective: The bias of emergent theory. *American Sociological Review, 38,* 274-284.

Hunt, L. M., Jordan, B., & Browner, C. H. (1989). Compliance and the patient's perspective. *Culture, Medicine and Psychiatry, 13,* 315-334.

Hurtado, A. (1989). Relating to privilege: Seduction and rejection in the subordination of white women and women of color. *Signs, 14,* 833-855.

Jacobus, M., Keller, E. F., & Shuttleworth, S. (1990). *Body/politics: Women and the discourses of science.* New York: Routledge.

Johannsen, A. M. (1992). Applied anthropology and post-modernist ethnography. *Human Organization, 51,* 71-81.

Jordan, B. (1977). The self-diagnosis of early pregnancy: An investigation of lay competence. *Medical Anthropology, 2,* 20-35.

Kaufert, P. A., & McKinlay, S. M. (1985). Estrogen-replacement therapy: The production of medical knowledge and the emergence of policy. In E. Lewin & V. Olesen (Eds.), *Women, health and healing: Toward a new perspective* (pp. 113-138). London: Tavistock.

Kirby, V. (1991). Comment on Mascia-Lees, Sharpe and Cohen's "The postmodernist turn in anthropology: Cautions from a feminist perspective." *Signs, 16,* 394-400.

Kleiber, N., & Light, L. (1978). *Caring for ourselves: An alternative structure for health care.* Vancouver: University of British Columbia, School of Nursing.

Komarovsky, M. (1988). The new feminist scholarship: Some precursors and polemics. *Journal of Marriage and the Family, 50,* 585-593.

Komarovsky, M. (1991). Some reflections on the feminist scholarship in sociology. *Annual Review of Sociology, 17,* 1-25.

Krieger, S. (1983). *The mirror dance: Identity in a woman's community.* Philadelphia: Temple University Press.

Lather, P. (1986). Research as praxis. *Harvard Educational Review, 56,* 257-277.

Lather, P. (1988). Feminist perspectives on empowering research methodologies. *Women's Studies International Forum, 11,* 569-581.

Lather, P. (1991). *Getting smart: Feminist research and pedagogy with/in the postmodern.* New York: Routledge.

Lemert C. (1992). Subjectivity's limit: The unsolved riddle of the standpoint. *Sociological Theory, 10,* 63-72.

Lempert, L. B. (1992). *The crucible: Battered women's experiences in help seeking.* Unpublished doctoral dissertation, University of California, San Francisco, School of Nursing, Department of Social and Behavioral Sciences.

Lewin, E. (1991). Writing gay and lesbian culture: What the natives have to say for themselves. *American Ethnologist, 18,* 786-792.

Lewin, E. (1993). *Lesbian mothers.* Ithaca, NY: Cornell University Press.

Lewin, E., & Olesen, V. (1981). Lateralness in women's work: New views on success. *Sex Roles, 6, 619-629.*

Light, L., & Kleiber, N. (1981). Interactive research in a feminist setting. In D. A. Messerschmidt (Ed.), *Anthropologists at home in North America: Methods and issues in the study of one's own society* (pp. 167-184). Cambridge, UK: Cambridge University Press.

Lorber, J. (1975). Women and medical sociology: Invisible professionals and ubiquitous patients. In M. M. Millman & R. M. Kanter (Eds.), *Another voice: Feminist perspectives on social life and social science* (pp. 75-105). Garden City, NY: Anchor.

Luker, K. (1984). *Abortion and the politics of motherhood.* Berkeley: University of California Press.

MacKinnon, C. (1982). Feminism, Marxism, method and the state: An agenda for theory. *Signs, 7,* 515-544.

MacKinnon, C. (1983). Feminism, Marxism and the state: Toward feminist jurisprudence. *Signs, 8,* 635-658.

Maines, D. (1982). In search of the mesostructure: Studies in the negotiated order. *Urban Life, 11,* 267-279.

Marcus, G., & Fischer, M. (1986). *Anthropology as cultural critique: An experimental moment in the human sciences.* Chicago: University of Chicago Press.

Mascia-Lees, F. E., Sharpe, P., & Cohen, C. B. (1989). The postmodernist turn in anthropology: Cautions from a feminist perspective. *Signs, 15,* 7-33.

Mascia-Lees, F. E., Sharpe, P., & Cohen, C. B. (1991). Reply to Kirby. *Signs, 16,* 401-408.

Matsuda, M. (1992). *Called from within: Early women lawyers of Hawaii.* Honolulu: University of Hawaii Press.

McCall, M., & Becker, H. (1990). Performance science. *Social Problems, 37,* 117-132.

McIntyre, S. (1985). Gynaecologist/woman interaction. In C. Ungerson (Ed.), *Women and social policy* (pp. 175-184). London: Macmillan.

Mies, M. (1982). *Fighting on two fronts.* The Hague: Institute of Social Studies.

Mohanty, C. (1988). Under Western eyes: Feminist scholarship and colonial discourses. *Feminist Review, 30,* 60-88.

Montini, T. (1991). *The informed consent for breast cancer patients' movement.* Unpublished doctoral dissertation, University of California, San Francisco, School of Nursing, Department of Social and Behavioral Sciences.

Moore, H. (1988). *Feminism and anthropology.* London: Polity.

Morawski, J. (1990). Toward the unimagined: Feminism and epistemology in psychology. In R. Hare-Mustin & J. Marecek (Eds.), *Making a difference: Psychology and the construction of gender* (pp. 159-183). New Haven, CT: Yale University Press.

Morris, M. (1992). On the beach. In L. Grossberg, C. Nelson, & P. A. Treichler (Eds.), *Cultural studies* (pp. 450-472). New York: Routledge.

Murcott, A. (1983). "It's a pleasure to cook for him . . . ": Food mealtimes and gender in South Wales households. In E. Garmarnikov, J. Purvis, D. Taylorson, & D. Morgan (Eds.), *The public and the private* (pp. 1-19). London: Heinemann.

Nakano Glenn, E. (1990). The dialectics of wage work: Japanese-American women and domestic service, 1905-1940. In E. C. DuBois & V. L. Ruiz (Eds.), *Unequal sisters: A multi-cultural reader in U.S. women's history* (pp. 345-372). London: Routledge.

Nelson, M. K. (1990). *Negotiated care: The experience of family day care givers.* Philadelphia: Temple University Press.

Nicholson, L. (Ed.). (1990). *Feminism/postmodernism.* London: Routledge.

Nielsen, J. M. (Ed.). (1990). *Feminist research methods: Exemplary readings in the social sciences.* Boulder, CO: Westview.

Olesen, V. (1956). *Pre-school children's television viewing.* Unpublished master's thesis, University of Chicago, Committee on Communication.

Olesen, V., & Katsuranis, F. (1978). Urban nomads: Temporary clerical service workers. In A. Stromberg & S. Harkess (Eds.), *Women working* (pp. 20-32). Palo Alto, CA: Mayfield.

Olesen, V. (1992). *Re-writing ethnography, re-writing ourselves: Whose text is it?* Paper presented at the Qualitative Analysis Conference, Carleton University, Ottawa.

Olesen, V. (1993). Unfinished business: The problematics of women, health and healing. *The Science of Caring, 5,* 3-6.

Opie, A. (1992). Qualitative research, appropriation of the "other" and empowerment. *Feminist Review, 40,* 52-69.

Ortner, S. B., & Whitehead, H. (1981). *Sexual meanings: The cultural construction of gender and sexuality.* London: Cambridge University Press.

Paget, M. (1990). Performing the text. *Journal of Contemporary Ethnography, 19,* 136-155.

Palmer, P. (1989). *Domesticity and dirt: Housewives and domestic servants in the U.S. 1920-1945.* Philadelphia: Temple University Press.

Petchesky, R. P. (1985). Abortion in the 1980's: Feminist morality and women's health. In E. Lewin & V. Olesen (Eds.), *Women, health and healing: Toward a new perspective* (pp. 139-173). London: Tavistock.

Ramazanoglu, C. (1989). Improving on sociology: The problems of taking a feminist standpoint. *Sociology, 23,* 427-442.

Reinharz, S. (1992). *Feminist methods in social research.* New York: Oxford University Press.

Richardson, L. (1991). Postmodern social theory: Representational practices. *Sociological Theory, 9,* 173-179.

Richardson, L. (1992). The consequences of poetic representation: Writing the other, rewriting the self. In C. Ellis & M. G. Flaherty (Eds.), *Investigating subjectivity: Research on lived experience* (pp. 125-140). Newbury Park, CA: Sage.

Riessman, C. K. (1990). *Divorce talk: Women and men make sense of personal relationships.* New Brunswick, NJ: Rutgers University Press.

Ring, J. (1987). Toward a feminist epistemology. *American Journal of Political Science, 31,* 753-772.

Rittenhouse, C. A. (1991). The emergence of pre-menstrual syndrome as a social problem. *Social Problems, 38,* 15-25.

Roberts, H. (Ed.). (1981). *Doing feminist research.* London: Routledge.

Rollins, J. (1985). *Between women: Domestics and their employers.* Philadelphia: Temple University Press.

Romalis, S. (1985). Struggle between providers and recipients: The case of birth practices. In E. Lewin & V. Olesen (Eds.), *Women, health and healing: Toward a new perspective* (pp. 174-208). London: Tavistock.

Romero, M. (1992). *Maid in the U.S.A.* London: Routledge.

Rosenau, P. M. (1992). *Post-modernism and the social sciences: Insights, inroads and intrusions.* Princeton, NJ: Princeton University Press.

Ruzek, S. R. (1978). *The women's health movement: Feminist alternatives to medical care.* New York: Praeger.

Sacks, K. (1989). Toward a unified theory of class, race and gender. *American Ethnologist, 16,* 534-550.

Saltonstall, R. (1993). Healthy bodies: Gendered constructions of health and illness. *Social Science and Medicine, 19,* 45-52.

Scheper-Hughes, N. (1983). Introduction: The problem of bias in androcentric and feminist anthropology. *Women's Studies, 19,* 109-116.

Scheper-Hughes, N. (1992). *Death without weeping: The violence of everyday life in Brazil.* Berkeley: University of California Press.

Scott, J. (1991). The evidence of experience. *Critical Inquiry, 17,* 773-779.

Shogan, D. (1990). Comment on Hawkesworth's "Knowers, knowing, known: Feminist theory and claims of truth." *Signs, 15,* 424-425.

Shostak, M. (1981). *Nisa: The life and words of a !Kung woman.* Cambridge, MA: Harvard University Press.

Smith, D. E. (1974). Women's perspective as a radical critique of sociology. *Sociological Inquiry, 4,* 1-13.

Smith, D. E. (1987). *The everyday world as problematic.* Boston: Northeastern University Press.

Smith, D. E. (1989). Sociological theory: Methods of writing patriarchy. In R. A. Wallace (Ed.), *Feminism and sociological theory* (pp. 34-64). Newbury Park, CA: Sage.

Smith, D. E. (1990a). *The conceptual practices of power: A feminist sociology of knowledge.* Boston: Northeastern University Press.

Smith, D. E. (1990b). *Texts, facts and femininity: Exploring the relations of ruling.* London: Routledge.

Smith, D. E. (1992). Sociology from women's experience: A reaffirmation. *Sociological Theory, 10,* 88-98.

Smith, D. E. (1993). High noon in Textland: A critique of Clough. *Sociological Quarterly, 34,* 183-192.

Spivak, G. C. (1988). Subaltern studies: Deconstructing historiography. In G. C. Spivak, *In other worlds: Essays in cultural politics* (pp. 197-221). London: Routledge.

Stacey, J. (1988). Can there be a feminist ethnography? *Women's Studies International, 11,* 21-27.

Stacey, J., & Thorne, B. (1985). The missing feminist revolution in sociology. *Social Problems, 32,* 301-316.

Stacey, M. (1981). The division of labor revisited or overcoming the two Adams: The special problems of people work. In P. Abrams, R. Deem, J. Finch, & P. Rock (Eds.), *Practice and progress: British sociology 1950-1980* (pp. 172-204). London: George Allen & Unwin.

Stacey, M. (1992). *Regulating British medicine: The General Medical Council.* New York: John Wiley.

Stanley, L., & Wise, S. (1983). *Breaking out: Feminist consciousness and feminist research.* London: Routledge & Kegan Paul.

Stanley, L., & Wise, S. (1990). Method, methodology and epistemology in feminist research processes. In L. Stanley (Ed.), *Feminist praxis: Research, theory and epistemology in feminist sociology* (pp. 20-60). London: Routledge.

Stanley, L. (Ed.). (1990). *Feminist praxis: Research, theory and epistemology in feminist sociology.* London: Routledge.

Stanworth, M. (1985). "Just three quiet girls." In C. Ungerson (Ed.), *Women and social policy* (pp. 137-148). London: Macmillan.

Stevens, P. E., & Hall, J. H. (1991). A critical historical analysis of the medical construction of lesbianism. *International Journal of Health Services, 21,* 271-307.

Strathern, M. (1987). An awkward relationship: The case of feminism and anthropology. *Signs, 12,* 276-292.

Strauss, A. L., & Corbin, J. (1990). *Basics of qualitative research: Grounded theory procedures and techniques.* Newbury Park, CA: Sage.

Todd, A. D. (1989). *Intimate adversaries: Cultural conflict between doctors and patients.* Bloomington: Indiana University Press.

Tom, W. (1989). *Effects of feminist research on research methods.* Toronto: Wilfred Laurier.

Tong, R. (1989). *Feminist thought: A comprehensive introduction.* Boulder, CO: Westview.

Warren, C. A. B. (1988). *Gender issues in field research.* Newbury Park, CA: Sage.

West, C. (1988). *Routine complications: Troubles with talk between doctors and patients.* Bloomington: Indiana University Press.

West, C., & Zimmerman, D. (1987). Doing gender. *Gender & Society, 1,* 125-151.

Westkott, M. (1979). Feminist criticism of the social sciences. *Harvard Educational Review, 4,* 422-430.

Wolf, M. (1992). *A thrice-told tale: Feminism, postmodernism and ethnographic responsibility.* Stanford, CA: Stanford University Press.

Zavella, P. (1987). *Women's work and Chicano families: Cannery workers of the Santa Clara Valley.* Ithaca, NY: Cornell University Press.

Zinn, M. B. (1982). Mexican-American women in the social sciences. *Signs, 8,* 259-272.

10

Ethnic Modeling in Qualitative Research

JOHN H. STANFIELD II

IN this essay, *ethnicity* denotes the synthesis of biological and fictive ancestry and cultural elements. As a social phenomenon, ethnicity should not be confused with tribalism and race, even though it is intrinsically related to the formation of both culturally and politically constructed categories. That is, although tribes are localized forms of social organization with an emphasis on ancestry rights and "the camp" or "the village," there is also, obviously, the presence of a localized culture reproduced and at times transformed intergenerationally. Races are constructed categories of populations that gain social and cultural relevance when random human qualities such as intellectual abilities, moral fiber, personalities, aesthetic tastes, and physical abilities become fixed and systematized through their association with phenotypical attributes. Ethnicity is a critical attribute of race in that it is a basis of diversity within and between racial categories. For instance, although "Hispanic American" constitutes a "racial category" in the United States, there is great ethnic diversity among those of Cuban, Puerto Rican, Mexican, and Central American descent, as well as within even those more specific anthropological formations.

Whereas race and tribe are special forms of social organization and stratification associated with certain historical and political economic conditions, ethnicity is a more universal human attribute. In short, we all have ethnicity, even though it may be entangled with status and social organizational attributes such as class, gender, age, ethnoregionalism, and religion.

There are certain corners of Western life, such as the modern social sciences and sciences in general, in which the fundamental influences of ethnicity in shaping interpretations of reality are ignored or given only minimal attention. Thus, more clearly, it is difficult for many to understand or to see that even the most "rational" modes of scientific thought are fundamentally ethnic products (Stanfield, 1993a, 1993b).

In this essay, I will discuss several ways in which the conventional concerns regarding racialized ethnicity and related status categories in qualitative research can be understood better when contextualized in critical analytic frameworks. I will then present suggestions as to how we can best create qualitative research methods indigenous to the experiences of Afro-Americans and other people of color in the United States and elsewhere.

Some Conventional Considerations

Usually, when we think about the roles of ascribed status—such as race, ethnicity, and tribe—

AUTHOR'S NOTE: I wish to thank the editors of this handbook as well as Mitch Allen and Rutledge Dennis for their comments on earlier versions of this chapter.

in research methods, several issues come to mind, depending upon the aspect of the research process we choose as a focus. When it comes to qualitative research methods, whether we focus on the researcher, the examined human beings, data analysis, or knowledge dissemination, the point is that ascribed status influences the meanings of subjective experiences. Scholars who have written about the impacts of the ascribed status of qualitative researchers such as ethnographers, oral historians, and archival experts have commented on the insider and outsider dilemmas investigators experience in the research process. What is at least implicit in the insider/outsider researcher debate is that the autobiographies, cultures, and historical contexts of researchers matter; these determine what researchers see and do not see, as well as their ability to analyze data and disseminate knowledge adequately. Although the rule has been that it is possible for researchers of traditional dominant status (meaning white, usually male) to develop value-free methodological procedures to study outsider persons, recently such traditional outsiders with professional credentials have begun to challenge that sacred presumption.

People of color, women, and others traditionally outside the domain of research authority have argued that only those researchers emerging from the life worlds of their "subjects" can be adequate interpreters of such experiences. Dominant researchers (whites and traditional outsiders who embrace mainstream perspectives) have argued fervently against the claims of those outsider scholars claiming to have an insider monopoly on the production of knowledge regarding the life worlds from which they hail. This response on the part of dominant researchers to outsider claims has been especially apparent in the negative treatment of Afrocentric scholarship in the mainstreams of sociology and other social sciences (Asante, 1987; Basu et al., 1980; Hamnett, Porter, Singh, & Kumar, 1984; Hymes, 1972; Kuper, 1983; Ladner, 1973; Magubane & Faris, 1985; Merton, 1972).

It should be noted that, ironically, scholars have yet to debate the outsider/insider knowledge controversy from the standpoint of traditional outsiders, such as people of color, conducting research on traditionally dominant subjects, that is, whites. This issue will become increasing important as a growing number of traditional outsiders begin to break out of the molds of studying "their own," because of choice or career tracking, and begin to gain the access and professional authority necessary to study whites.

When the focus shifts from the researcher to the examined human beings in racialized ethnic concerns in qualitative research, we find studies that mention at least in passing the impact of the skin color and nationality of the researcher on the behavior of those under investigation. Some researchers, for instance, have noticed how the white skin of dominant researchers adds to the authoritative posture of European-descent ethnographers. Others, writing from the perspective of people of color, note the ways in which phenotypical and cultural similarity between ethnographer and subjects in non-Western settings create interesting interaction roles and subject perceptions of the researcher (Sudarkasa, 1986; Whitehead, 1986; R. Williams, 1990). Scholars have also noted the profound human rights problems that continue to haunt qualitative research on people of color, especially those in low socioeconomic status populations. The growing participatory research movement is a partial solution to the historical tendency for people of color to be abused and otherwise exploited as "subjects" in research processes. I consider the participatory research movement only a partial solution because, although participatory research attempts to empower examined human beings and their social organizations, rarely do researchers share career rewards with "subjects" of color, such as coauthorships and access to authoritative credentializing processes.

Conventional concerns about data interpretation and knowledge dissemination have focused on the ethnocentrism tradition that drives so much American and other Western social research on people of color, including those perspectives that claim to be radical and liberating. The tendency for Western researchers to impose even their most enlightened cultural constructs on Others rather than creating indigenized theories and methods to grasp the ontological essences of people of color is, of course, legendary. Another growing concern is the politics of knowledge distribution, that is, the maldistribution of processed knowledge products (specialized information) and knowledge technologies in the world society. It is more than apparent, in other words, that many if not most people of color in Western nation-states and in the so-called Third World reside in oppressed communities and institutions that do not receive the same quality or quantity of specialized information as do (affluent) Eurocentric communities and institutions.

The basic problem with the extensive conventional literature on racialized ethnicity and related status categories in qualitative research is that nowhere is there a conceptual framework for understanding the structures that organize and even marginalize and exclude knowledge production regarding Afro-Americans and other people of color. In the next section I attempt to introduce and apply such a framework before moving on to some suggestions concerning ways to create indigenous paradigms rooted in the experiences of people of color.

Some Radical Musings

I have been asked by the editors of this volume to give some advice about how to do "ethnic" qualitative research. As I am an Afro-American sociologist who has extensive qualitative research experience in Afro-American and African institutions and communities, my remarks are drawn from such African-descent studies. But before embarking on the discussion in question, I must attempt to clarify the matter of the political problematics of truly culturally diversified qualitative research strategies with people of color in the mainstream of qualitative research in the social sciences. Below I shall emphasize, with some detail, using Afro-American experiences as the major case in point, that the ethnic hegemonic character of American and other Eurocentric traditions in the social sciences has made quite problematic the legitimation of competitive, empowering research questions and strategies in work with people of color. I will elaborate a bit and then give examples of how, historically, even though Afro-American intellectuals have developed their own unique qualitative research methods and research results, the more empowering and normality-revealing aspects of their work have been ignored, marginalized, or reinterpreted to fit into the more orthodox norms of social scientific communities (Stanfield, 1985, 1993a, 1993b). I will end with suggestions regarding the development of indigenous qualitative methods that draw from the cosmos of people of color, such as African-descent populations.

In multiracial/multiethnic nation-states such as the United States, Canada, Brazil, Great Britain, Australia, South Africa, and the Netherlands, correlating perceived intellectual abilities, behavior, personality, and moral fiber with real or imagined phenotypical attributes is fundamental to human developmental issues such as self-concept, concepts of others, organizing daily life, and making routine and critical life decisions (such as mate selection, residence, church affiliation, friendship selection, and legitimating authority in politics and employment) (Stanfield, 1991). Thus, whether residents in a multiracial/multiethnic nation are aware of it or not, and despite their personal preferences and political beliefs, they are socialized in their homes and schools and by the mass media and popular and material culture to assume that ethnicity defined in racial terms is normal. Social scientists reared in such societies are not exempt from what Herbert Blumer once called "group feeling." Multiethnic/multiracial nation-states are segmented societies held together through rigid forms of sociocultural and political hegemony.

At least in this essay, *sociocultural and political hegemony* denotes an oligarchical status that the dominant ethnic population enjoys through maintaining virtually exclusive control over political, cultural, social, and technological resources and institutions. The sociocultural and political hegemony of the dominant is legitimated and reproduced through the imposition, if not the diffusion, of particular ethnic cultural attributes throughout the nation-state. What makes hegemony such a powerful source of social and political control is that the imposition and diffusion of the ethnic cultural particulars of the dominant create and institutionalize impressions in public culture and life that there is a societal consensus that the culture of the dominant is universalistic rather than particularistic. Hegemonic racialized ethnic expressions include civil religious practices, conventional historical interpretations of the nation-state, and, related to the point at hand (Stanfield, 1992), the formation of sciences and humanities as institutions and as knowledge producers and disseminators (Stanfield, 1993a, 1993b).

We cannot divorce the history of American social sciences, let alone of course the individual life histories of social scientists, from the origins and transformation of a normative multiethnic/multiracial society. Although there have long been class critiques of the social sciences as middle-class knowledge institutions and producers (Furner, 1975; Haskell, 1977; Hinkle, 1954), only recently have we begun to understand the racialized ethnic character of social sciences as institutions and practices. The social sciences in the United States and in comparable nations are hegemonic racialized ethnic social organizations and forms of knowing and interpreting life worlds.

The hegemonic character of the social sciences in the United States is apparent in many ways. It is apparent in the historical Euro-American dominance in defining and constructing the organizational configurations of social science knowledge production and disciplinary public culture. *Organizational configurations* refers to credentializing settings, such as graduate school programs, professional associations, and invisible colleges. *Disciplinary public culture* is what Merton long ago called the ethos of science: rules of evidence, community norms and values, criticism privileges, and so on.

When it comes to qualitative research as an academic enterprise cutting across disciplines, the sociocultural and politic hegemony of Eurocentric interests and ontology is quite obvious. Qualitative research methods textbooks and handbooks rarely touch upon racialized ethnic diversity issues (Ashworth, Giorgi, & de Koning, 1986; Atkinson, 1992; Burgess, 1985; Crabtree & Miller, 1992; Filstead, 1970; Gilgren, Daly, & Handel, 1992; Goetz & LeCompte, 1984; LeCompte, Millroy, & Preissle, 1992; Merriam, 1988; Seidman, 1991; Shaffir & Stebbins, 1991; Strauss, 1987;

Tesch, 1990; Walker, 1985). When racialized ethnic diversity issues are discussed, it is usually within the confines of orthodox (conventional or radical) Eurocentric perspectives, such as symbolic interactionism, phenomenology, or Marxism, rather than as attempts to develop ethnic diversity in logics of inquiry grounded in the indigenous experiences of people of color. This neglect or marginalization of racialized cultural diversity as logic of inquiry issues has continued to be the case in the post-1980s, as qualitative research has increasingly become the dominion of education scholars (Goetz & LeCompte, 1984; LeCompte et al., 1992). Considering the central presence of racialized ethnic diversity in education, the absence of an emerging body of methodological literature that attempts to de-Europeanize approaches to issues concerning people of color through the introduction of more indigenous approaches is, to say the least, curious.

When we grasp the political history of the ethnic hegemony of American and comparable social science communities, it becomes apparent why there continues to be an absence of diverse racialized ethnic approaches in qualitative and quantitative research perspectives in the mainstreams of such disciplines. This is especially the case when it comes to research strategies designed and applied by nonwhite scholars that approach people of color as normal human beings or in power and privilege terms.

To the extent that ethnic models of research have filtered through the mainstreams of social sciences, they have mirrored pathological and culture-of-poverty interpretations of people of color and of the poor in conformity with historically specific folk beliefs in the dominant societal culture. The work of Clyde Kluckhohn (1944) on Native Americans, Oscar Lewis (1966) on Mexicans and Chicanos, and qualitative studies of Afro-American experiences by E. Franklin Frazier (1967, 1968), Kenneth Clark (1965), Lee Rainwater (1970a, 1970b), Elliot Liebow (1967), William J. Wilson (1974), Elijah Anderson (1978, 1990), Joyce Ladner (1971), and Carol Stack (1974) have all contributed to the forging of mainstream ethnic models. Also, historically, professional and mass-media review organs have contributed greatly to conservative ethnic models in mainstream social sciences through the selection and interpretation of bits and pieces of the works of more critical-minded scholars of color that seem to reconfirm dominant pathological assumptions about people of color.

Besides this mainstream conservative ethnic modeling tradition in American social sciences, more radical traditions of qualitative research have been ignored or misinterpreted, and these should be discussed. This can be done by recovering texts in two senses of the word: first, discovering the works of scholars of color who have been excluded from discipline historical memories because of their critical perspectives on social structure and processes; and second, rereading the texts of scholars of color who have enjoyed some degree of historical immortality but have had the more conservative aspects of their work applauded and remembered even as their more radical statements have been ignored or distorted.

There are two historical traditions in Afro-American scholarship that stand out as critical examples of the use of qualitative research to collect and interpret data in anti-status quo fashions. First, among generations of Afro-American intellectuals such as Carter G. Woodson, William E. B. Du Bois, Charles S. Johnson, and Ida B. Wells, there has been the use of historical documents to critique the origins and dynamics of social domination and social and political economic conflict. Second, Afro-American scholars such as Du Bois, Johnson, St. Clair Drake, Horace Cayton, E. Franklin Frazier, Zora Neale Hurston, Joyce Ladner, Judith Rollins, and Karen Fields used participant observation and oral history techniques to explore the normality of Afro-Americans and their daily struggles to survive in oppressed environments. In both historical traditions there are excluded Afro-American scholars and those who are more mainstream but who have had the more critical edges of their works ignored or distorted in dominant discipline discourse.

There have also been a number of epistemological critiques of conventional approaches to the study of Afro-Americans and other people of color. These approaches are qualitative only in the sense that they offer attempts to demonstrate the flaws in conventional theories and methods and argue for the utilization of perspectives stressing subjective interpretations of human experiences. What is most fascinating about these approaches is that many of their proponents are theologians and literary figures rather than credentialed social scientists. Their importance lies more in their offering a critical critique of logical positivism than in their developing models of research. This is crucial to point out, because my goal in discussing the following individuals is not to offer examples of models of research, but to demonstrate the importance of understanding radical opposition to the conventions of how social research on Afro-Americans and other people of color is usually done.

First, we have the theological critiques of social scientific research done on Afro-Americans advanced by scholars such as Cornel West (1982, 1988). These critiques offer a brilliant synthesis of moral theories of social justice and Marxism as the means to advocate liberation strategies for Afro-Americans. In the process of making their case, West and other theologians of like cloth inevitably get involved in the epistemological and ideological flaws that limit the value of orthodox social sciences in understanding the plight of the racially oppressed or, more important, in participating in efforts to liberate the oppressed from their bondage.

Ralph Ellison's *Shadow and Act* (1964), which offered a commentary on Gunnar Myrdal's *An American Dilemma* (1944), was probably the first comprehensive effort by a literary figure to critique conventional quantitative approaches to Afro-American experiences. In a most eloquent fashion, Ellison argued that Afro-Americans and their experiences, as rich as they are, cannot be reduced to statistical tables, which seemed to be the fad in race relations research during the 1940s and 1950s (although it should be pointed out that earlier journalists, such as Ida B. Wells, Walter White, and Carl Sandburg, along with such literary figures as James Weldon Johnson, Langston Hughes, and Richard Wright, offered humanistic "qualitative" approaches to sociological interpretations of Afro-American experiences well before the quantitative movement in the social sciences began to institutionalize in the 1940s and 1950s—see, e.g., Johnson, 1945, 1979.)

The literary critique of orthodox social scientific perspectives on Afro-American experiences would reappear in powerful force in the 1980s and 1990s as part of the rise of the feminist movement among women of color. Intentionally or unintentionally, bell hooks, Gloria Hull, Toni Morrison, Alice Walker, Paule Marshall, and Paula Giddings all have offered radical alternatives to viewing the lives of women of color as studied in the social sciences and interpreted in literature. Although bell hooks is closest to Cornel West's Marxist critique of social scientific constructions of Afro-Americans, Gloria Hull offers insights in doing literary oral histories through using the diaries and personal correspondence of prominent Afro-American women writers to reconstruct and interpret black female life worlds. Toni Morrison's urban sociological imagination serves as a context of Afro-American women's development in ways that parallel the rural sociological contexts of Alice Walker (and of her literary anthropological "mentor," Zora Neale Hurston). Paule Marshall's brilliant comparative historical sociological sense of Afro-American womanhood in America and in the West Indies and Paula Giddings's sociological history of Afro-American women are additional examples of Afro-American feminist literary approaches that at least remind us of the limitations of both orthodox social scientific and literary analyses. More needs to be said about the rise of feminist thought in relation to ethnic modeling in critical qualitative research, this time in reference to feminism in social sciences.

On the other hand, in the social sciences, feminist critics of Western social sciences from anthropology through sociology (to be alphabetical) have brilliantly exposed the sociological and political bare wires of what used to be viewed as universal forms of objective knowledge and objective methods of inquiry (Abramowitz, 1982; Bernick, 1991; Christman, 1988; Currie, 1988; Devault, 1990; Ergas, 1978-1979; Grant & Ward, 1987; Lather, 1986; Marburg, 1981; Mascia-Lees, Sharpe, & Cohen, 1989; McKeganey & Bloor, 1991; Peplau & Conrad, 1989; Rapp, 1988; Sprague & Zimmerman, 1989; Warren, 1988; A. Williams, 1987, 1990). They have demonstrated in thought-provoking ways how cultural and social elements of male-centric cosmologies silently and more explicitly shape the epistemologies, theories, methods, and other paradigmatic attributes of modern social scientific disciplines and their classical antecedents. We learn through their work how the predominance of patriarchal and hierarchical presumptions and assumptions of male-centric norms and values influence not only the contents of research but, perhaps more important, the conduct of research as a structured power relationship and as an intricate process of creating, interpreting, and disseminating knowledge.

When it comes to qualitative research methods such as ethnography, participant observation, and oral history, feminists have been quick to point out and document how much the hierarchical power relations between researcher and subject or respondent is a cultural product of a male-centric cosmos. This has lead to the revision of classical ethnographic texts steeped in male-centric conceptions of the world and in hierarchical research processes (di Leonardo, 1991). Such feminist critiques have also encouraged power-sharing approaches to ethnographic research that have converged quite well with growing concerns about the human rights of subjects and the growing resistance and awareness on the part of heavily researched populations.

Perhaps the major Achilles' heel of feminist interpretations of how to conduct qualitative research is the absence of a central racialized ethnic component. Once again, we all have ethnicity, just as we all have gender. Indeed, ethnicity, in its subtle and explicit ways, compounded by other synchronic status variables, gives biological sex categories their historical, cultural, social, and political economic meanings. When we speak of ethnic hegemony in the history of qualitative research as well as in the social sciences in general, we must remember that we must consider the female as well as the male dimensions of this unique social inequality problem. As underprivileged as white females have been in comparison with white males in social science historiography, we cannot forget that their gendered interpretations of the world are derived from European-descent experiences (Cannon, 1988; Collins, 1990; Facio, 1993; Hurston, 1969a, 1969b, 1971a, 1971b, 1990; Marks, 1993; Rollins, 1985; Sudarkasa, 1986; Terrell, 1980). Although white women were discriminated against and still continue to be in the structures and processes of knowledge production, they have always enjoyed more political weight and access privileges than have women of color and people of color in general. Only recently have feminist social scientists, especially anthropologists and, to a lesser extent, sociologists, begun to acknowledge their places of white privilege, especially in relation to women of color.

The problem here is how to untangle the gender and ethnic attributes of the historical formation of dominant patterns of research in the social sciences. One way to do this is to argue that, most fundamentally, attributes of orthodox research designs, such as hierarchical relations between researchers and their subjects, are gender issues embedded within a particular ethnic sphere. The development of twentieth-century orthodox social scientific thought, in other words, has been drawn largely from the cosmos of upper-middle-class WASP (white Anglo-Saxon Protestant) and WIE (white immigrant ethnic) males. They created and institutionalized their authority as preeminent reality interpreters by controlling access to credentializing processes and dominating the academic and professional agencies, media, and reward systems that define the "nature of knowing and knowledge." Issues such as deviance and social control in sociology, life-cycle development in psychology, voting behavior and political philosophy in political science, kinship in anthropology, and market behavior in economics all are rooted in the ethnic experiences of privileged whites. The extent to which people of color, no matter their national context, have been absorbed into the confines of orthodox social sciences has been well within the norms and values of the dominant ethnic ways of interpreting and constructing realities (Stanfield, 1993a). Only recently have people of color in some disciplines, the humanities in particular, been allowed to speak in different legitimated voices (Baker, 1980, 1984, 1989, 1991; Carby, 1987; hooks, 1981, 1984, 1989, 1990, 1991, 1992). For the most part, however, post-1970s Western and Westernized academic disciplines, particularly in most social sciences, continue to marginalize and exclude ethnically diverse interpretations of reality and styles of knowing in relation to mainstream normative knowledge creation and reproduction. To the extent to which feminists have engaged in oppositional discourses regarding orthodox social sciences, their struggles have usually been "in the ethnic family" debates. Most of their preoccupations have been with matters related to white maleness, which in many cases are not applicable to nonwhite maleness. For instance, the entire issue of patriarchal hierarchies is a matter of historical and political dominance enjoyed by white men wherever they conquered and settled; this is not so easily attributed to men of color. Aggressiveness, assertiveness, societal and political control, and economic productivity are additional attributes of white male masculinity that have been penalized or discouraged when found among men of color. This is obvious in scholarly studies and in the popular press in multiracial nation-states such as the United States, Great Britain, South Africa, and Australia, which document the negative imagery of men of color who act too much like white men.

Although literary figures are way ahead of us, social scientists sensitive to the issues of women of color are finally beginning to study the sociological and political aggravations that women of color experience (Collins, 1990; Rollins, 1985; Sudarkasa, 1986; Warren, 1988). The more we do so, the more apparent it becomes that even the most revisionist feminist studies of women of color in the social sciences have been conducted within the context of Eurocentric as well as malecentric reasoning. The use of phenomenological concepts and methods of inquiry in understanding how women of color construct their worldviews and identities (Collins, 1990) ignores how much the voluntaristic presumptions of social constructions of reality are very much notions of social privilege. Although the powerful—be they men, whites, or adults—have had the luxury of constructing their realities, a characteristic of the oppressed—women, Afro-Americans and other people of color, and children—has been the sociopolitical controls that have limited the reality construction choices they can choose from and enjoy. This is what makes the work of interpretive social scientists such as Schutz, Geertz, Goffman, and Berger and Luckmann so problematic when applied to the experiences of the oppressed. The problem becomes particularly cumbersome when it comes to populations experiencing two or more subordinate statuses, such as women of color in the United States and in other multiracial nation-states.

The racialized ethnic differences between white women and women of color in multiracial nation-states must be taken into consideration if one is to understand the erroneous ways in which concepts drawn from the experiences of white women are imposed on the experiences of nonwhite women. It has been a common mistake, for instance, to assume that power relations and distributions in (middle-class) white gender relations can be readily applied to Afro-American experiences. Cultural concepts such as masculinity and femininity are often articulated as universals and applied without critical revision to Afro-American male and female gender role development. This misappropriated generalization pattern has been stretched to Western impositions of notions of femininity and masculinity on non-Western, ex-colonial societies and regions. Thus what is missed or not understood properly are the socialization processes in Afro-American and other populations of color, which do not so neatly package and dichotomize femininity and masculinity as social and cultural qualities attributed to females and males.

The external political and economic factors that blur the dichotomy between masculinity and femininity in Afro-American socialization processes, such as the racialization of labor markets and the gender biases of welfare policies, also contribute to the racialized ethnic and social differences between white males and females and Afro-American males and females. Concretely, historically, Afro-American men have experienced employment patterns in which they perform jobs that traditionally have been viewed as female-dominated service work. The extensive underemployment and unemployment many Afro-American men experience creates a cultural scenario in Afro-American communities that actually feminizes Afro-American males as seen in gendered stereotypes in indigenous and broader public cultures.

On the other hand, dire economic conditions and imbalanced sex ratios have prevented many Afro-American women from developing the helpless, passive personal characteristics usually attributed to femininity. As an economic imperative, Afro-American women across classes have historically participated in labor markets and have frequently served as breadwinners and as community leaders.

In white middle-class terms, not a few Afro-American women have masculine cultural attributes, whereas African American men tend to be feminized. But, actually, Afro-American gender socialization processes are much more complicated and paradoxical than the reversal of traditional male/female roles idealized in white contexts. There is a need to study such human experiences within their unique cultural contexts rather than employing alien cognitive maps (i.e., paradigms) for research design and data interpretation.

To sum up, it is no accident that the most powerful historical and contemporary attacks on orthodox reasoning in the social sciences in respect to racial and ethnic studies have been carried out by intellectuals outside the social sciences. Although within their own disciplines and intellectual spheres such outsiders may be greatly celebrated, within the hegemonic walls of the social sciences their work tends to be ignored or marginalized. As is the case for critical epistemological and theoretical perspectives in general in American academic life (especially in the most distinguished circles), conventional reasoning rather than reflective analysis holds center stage when it comes to the study of the souls of black folks and other people of color.

Thus, if the marginal career of Oliver C. Cox is any clue (Hare, 1965; Hunter & Abraham, 1987), those who dare to critique racial orthodoxy from within the lion's den find their work ridiculed as militant, unscientific, and otherwise unworthy of significant attention. The case of Afro-American feminists is a contemporary example of how radical work from within and outside the social sciences may have the attention of other marginals in the academy, such as culturally enlightened women's studies academics, but not the needed professional acknowledgment of those who guard the highest gates of the professional discipline.

As much as it is important to point to and document normality-revealing and empowering studies of people of color within and outside the borders of discussions on qualitative research in the social sciences, such analyses tend to remain within the pale of conventional assumptions and arguments. In the next section I discuss why and how this is the case even when it comes to the most radical thinking going on today about people of color in research processes. More important, I outline some ways to step beyond even the most radical edges of orthodox thinking regarding issues concerning people of color in qualitative research. My thoughts in the next section were influenced mostly by Bernal (1987), Boahen (1987), Chinweizu (1975), Daniel and Renfrew (1988), Das (1935), Du Bois (1965, 1968), Hodgkin (1960), Khaldun (1981), Kuhn (1962), Mbiti (1970), Mudimbe (1988), Nandy (1988), Nkrumah (1973), Nsamenang (1992), O'Connor (1986), Polkinghorne (1988), Said (1978), Suret-Canale (1988), Vansina (1988), and Zaslavsky (1973).

Creating Indigenous Qualitative Methods

A paradigm is a cognitive road map (Kuhn, 1962). In the case of sciences and humanities, paradigms are taken-for-granted assumptions, norms, values, and traditions that create and institutionalize the ontological roots of knowledge definitions and productions. The experiences that construct paradigms in sciences and humanities are derivatives of cultural baggage imported into intellectual enterprises by privileged residents of historically specific societies and world systems. This is important to point out, because it is common for scholars to lapse into internal analyses while discussing paradigms and thus to ignore the rather commonsense fact that sciences and humanities are products of specific cultural and historical contexts that shape the character of intellectual work.

Paradigms, in the sense being articulated here, are actually the cultural foundations of sciences and humanities, because they are really the experiential places in which the realities of the intellectual enterprise are created and given legitimated expression, such as language, conceptions of human nature and the universe, and beliefs about what can and cannot be known. As cultural foundations, paradigms are the guides to more explicit intellectual activities, most fundamentally, theory construction, methodological strategizing, data interpretation, and knowledge dissemination.

When it comes to criticizing the knowledge contents of science and humanities disciplines, there are two levels of analysis. The first of these is the paradigmatic critique, which is the attempt to critique and perhaps revise the cognitive map of a particular discipline or cluster of disciplines. The second level of analysis is the knowledge production critique, which involves examination and perhaps revision of formal epistemologies, theories, methods, data interpretation styles, and patterns of knowledge dissemination.

When we review the critical literature related to ethnicity, race, and tribe in qualitative research, we cannot help but notice that most of them are knowledge production critiques with little or no in-depth concern for paradigmatic critiques. So we have, for instance, Afrocentric scholars (Asante, 1987) who may call for more culturally relevant approaches to Afro-American experiences in the social sciences and humanities but who do so while embracing and even advocating the most sacred norms of logical positivistic reasoning. This results in Afrocentrists' contradicting themselves by claiming to be producing knowledge sensitive to the experiences of African-descent peoples as a unique cultural population even as they insist on using Eurocentric logics of inquiry that reduce the knowable to the measurable or to evolutionary or linear variables.

This peculiar contradictory thinking in Afrocentric scholarship is most prevalent among Afrocentric psychologists (e.g., Hale-Benson and Hilliard) who promote their cultural views by advocating the refining of standardized testing instruments and applying evolutionary concepts of human development to Afro-American experiences, such as Afrocentric childhood studies. In sociology there is the additional problem of Afrocentric scholars attempting to apply phenomenological and symbolic interaction theoretical and methodological principles to Afro-American experiences without realizing the cultural limitations of the conception of voluntary action (i.e., reality construction) when applied to oppressed populations. More specifically, oppressed peoples, whether they be Americanized people of color, women, the differently abled, or the poor, have had little opportunity to construct realities meaningful and empowering in their lives. At worst, the socially constructed realities of the oppressed as official status categories and definitions are the intrusively imposed views of the dominant and at least partially internalized by not a few of the oppressed (Fanon, 1967; Memmi, 1965). At best, the oppressed can construct their own worlds as modes of action in private spheres only, hidden from the eyes and ears of the dominant, such as in racially oppressed communities and institutions. But such private reality constructions of the oppressed are restricted by the parameters of "objective realities" constructed and entrenched by the dominant.

Thus, no matter how people of color define themselves, there are still the more powerful stereotypes embedded in public culture that define their status and identities within the cosmos of the dominant. This is the racialized ethnic dimension of what Frankfurt school theorists refer to as the chronic discrepancies between an intrusive capitalistic (multiethnic/racial) state bent on defining its (racialized ethnically diverse) citizenry in "objective terms" and the growing repression of subjective meanings of individual and collective identities created by its citizenry. It has been the political and cultural interpretation of the persistent discrepancy between the objective and subjective realities on the part of the racially oppressed and of (in terms of temporal sequence) women, the differently abled, and lesbians and gays during the past 40 years that has fueled the emergence of the civil rights and other liberation movements redefining the United States.

Cultural studies proponents also tend to engage in knowledge production critiques with little or no consideration of paradigmatic or societal contexts. In Afro-American and African studies, cultural studies scholars have spent most of their time and energy offering Marxist and postmodern critiques of African-descent experiences via textual analyses. Although cultural studies scholars attempt to draw experiential comparisons between Americanized Africans and indigenous Africans, most cultural studies scholars concentrate on African-descent experiences in the Western Hemisphere, with the focus on the United States and, to a lesser extent, the Caribbean.

Besides a reified fixation on textual discourse analysis, a serious flaw in cultural studies logic of inquiry is the dependence on European theorists. In this regard, cultural studies scholars are well within the American intellectual tradition of receiving most of their inspiration from distinguished European thinkers such as Karl Marx, Foucault, Stuart Hall, and the Frankfurt school. This love affair with European-derived theorizing about the nature of human beings and their collective inventions—institutions, communities, societies, socialization, and so on—has resulted in the failure of even the most astute cultural studies theorists to realize how culturally limiting the work of otherwise brilliant thinkers, such as Alfred Schutz, Karl Marx, and Michel Foucault, is when applied to the United States and, most important, to the experiences of populations such as Americanized people of color who deviate from what we used to call mainstream (i.e., white middle-class) America.

The same criticism can be applied to cultural studies theorists who uncritically embrace American theorists and unintentionally extend folk wisdoms into their work. Perhaps the major example here is the tendency for cultural studies scholars to adopt a highly routinized functional view of American society. Unwittingly, even those who insist that they value and understand cultural diversity as an integral aspect of American society do not differ from most others socialized in the United States in their assumptions that there is, basically, one American society. At most, multiculturalism as a topic of discussion and debate is treated as a growing phenomenon sitting uncomfortably on top of a "singular social system." Needless to say, this causes a number of dilemmas and contradictions in cultural studies scholarship, such as the celebration, on one hand, of racialized ethnic diversity through the recovery and interpretation of the texts of the racially oppressed and, on the other, the attempt to explain the texts as extensions of mainstream canons instead of as culturally unique canons reflective of the normal plural character of the United States. To give a concrete example, cultural studies scholars specializing in Harlem Renaissance literary figures more often than not attempt to use the works of these seminal intellectuals to demonstrate cultural deviations from accepted paradigms of American literature (canons), rather than as examples of paradigms reflecting the normal ethnic pluralism of the United States.

What I wish to suggest here is that ethnic modeling in qualitative research must involve calling into serious question the vast warehouse of knowledge that researchers of European descent have been accumulating and legitimating as ways of knowing and seeing. Until we engage in radical efforts to criticize and revise the paradigms underlying qualitative research strategies and, more important, to create and legitimate new ones, the more secondary traditions of critiquing racialized ethnic theories, methods, styles of data interpretation, and patterns of knowledge dissemination will remain grossly incomplete.

In recent decades, the pendulum in qualitative social science research on people of color in Western nation-states and in the so-called Third World has been swinging gradually toward a greater sensitivity to social and cultural differences in research processes. A growing number of researchers are redefining their relationships with "subjects" and their communities, stressing less hierarchal approaches. Scholarship on "how to" develop participatory bridges between researchers and "subjects" has been increasing dramatically over the past decade.

But with all this said, there is still little comprehensive work being published on how to develop indigenous "ethnic" models of qualitative research. At most we have a developing literature for dominant researchers on how to be more sensitive in doing qualitative research in settings involving people of color. That is not, of course, the same thing as creating novel indigenous paradigms grounded distinctly in the experiences of people of color.

The purpose of establishing such qualitative research paradigms is twofold. First, and most apparent, research paradigms grounded in the experiences of people of color will isomorphize rather than impose cognitive map criteria that structure theory development, methodological strategies, data interpretations, and knowledge dissemination. This would eliminate the dilemmas, contradictions, and distortions generated when researchers involved in work with people of color operate on Eurocentric cognitive map criteria, no matter how progressive and liberating.

Second, although much has been written about the use of Eurocentric cognitive map criteria in examining people of color, to date no one has published a comprehensive text discussing what happens when the tables are turned—when the life worlds of the dominant are investigated and interpreted through the paradigmatic lenses of people of color. In other words, what would, say, anthropology or sociology "look like" as intellectual enterprises if they were invented by native West Africans and applied to Western contexts? Suppose classical qualitative texts on American issues by Lloyd Warner, Hortense Powdermaker, W. I. Thomas, Robert E. Park, Elliot Liebow, E. Franklin Frazier, Joyce Ladner, and Robert Lynd had been written by West Africans unexposed to Western norms of professional education. What would have been different in the cognitive map ingredients the African intellectuals would have drawn upon to develop outsider perspectives on American social issues? This question is not so far-fetched; in fact, the concept can even be studied through examination of the diaries, autobiographies, and travelers' accounts of West Africans who have spent time observing American life since the colonial period and even before. There are also ample qualitative documents about views of British society left by Africans who have resided in the United Kingdom for centuries. The most striking classical African intellectual who created an indigenous qualitative research paradigm to study his world and that of Europeans was the fourteenth-century Arab scholar Ibn Khaldun. In later times, up through the early 1900s, there were West Africans writing indigenous sociological analyses, such as Ghanian Casey Haywood's comparative legal institutions and double-consciousness scholarship, and Liberian Edward Blyden's and Sierra Leonean James Horton's theories of cultural nationalism. These intellectuals preceded and influenced mid-twentieth-century African new nation leaders such as Kwame Nkrumah, who wrote in a distinct indigenous vein about the United States and the general West (much of Nkrumah's thinking about the United States was influenced by his years in America during the 1930s, when he was a student at Lincoln University).

Much more recently, a number of African intellectuals with social scientific imaginations if not credentials have begun not only to criticize Western paradigms but to go beyond them, introducing indigenous cognitive maps to interpret African worldviews and the West. Much of this critique and indigenizing work has involved African intellectuals pointing out not only how Western documentation of African experiences (such as missionary and professional anthropological ethnographies) has often been part of an effort to rationalize and reinforce Eurocentric domination on the continent but, more important, how Western production of knowledge about Africa has more often than not deceived African researchers depending upon such records to interpret their own cultures and societies.

In weaving an indigenous paradigm, it becomes apparent that phenomena such as time, space, spirituality, and human relationships with nature are culture bound. So are the most fundamental configurations and contents of human communication and interaction in a culture. In the Western cosmos, time is linear and is viewed as a commodity—something to be used up for a profit. Time is also viewed as a horizontal sequence of events, such as the life cycle and the aging process. Space tends to have a privatized, individualistic definition and function in Western worldviews. Up until very recently, American and other Western intellectuals tended to define spirituality in institutional terms (i.e., religion) and to view it suspiciously as something inherently separate from human affairs. Thus issues such as relationships with dead ancestors have been viewed in mainstream Western social science as not relevant for serious research. Until the environmental consciousness movement of the post-1970s, Western social scientists, steeped in Judeo-Christian presumptions, viewed human beings as separate from and "naturally" dominant over their environments.

We do not want to make the common mistake of Afrocentrists, of approaching Africa as a simplistic geographic place with no cultural and social diversity. But it has been noticed and documented that there are major differences between the ways in which Africans, with their various historical and cultural backgrounds, and Westerners, with their various historical and cultural backgrounds, socially construct interpretations of realities about themselves and others. Culturally indigenous Africans do not tell time or count the same way Westerners or perhaps Westernized Africans do, nor do they embrace individualized conceptions of space and property. Time in many, if not most, indigenous African cultures is qualitative rather than quantitative and is not viewed as "money spent." Ancestors are viewed as central to family life in many African cultures, including in the kinship systems of Africans who have been converted to Christianity or Islam. In general, spirituality is central rather than marginal or absent in the way Africans explain human development, as opposed to in the West, where up until recently social scientists have tended to shy away from studying spirituality as an integral part of social and emotional well-being and as an explanation for human fortunes and misfortunes.

It used to be claimed that cultures depending upon oral rather than written communication were primitive or underdeveloped. Although this ethnocentric perspective may still be held by some, it is becoming apparent in the most sophisticated circles of intellectuals searching for human understanding that oral communication-based cultures are *different from* rather than *inferior to* written word-based cultures. The oral basis of most African cultures and among aboriginal peoples around the world offers a major challenge, because adequate study of such cultures requires a different portfolio of skills from what researchers reared in written word-based cultures acquire easily. For one thing, in oral-based cultures the records from which data are to be collected come in the form of poems, songs, testimonies, stories, performing arts, and proverbs, rather than diaries, newspapers, census reports, and surveys (Johnson, 1987).

Oral-based cultures, I should add, can also be found in otherwise written-word nation-states. In societal contexts such as that in the United States, oral-based cultures are derived from (a) surviving historical aboriginal social organizations; (b) the marginalization and exclusion of populations from centers of capitalistic modes of production, such as inner-city residents and Appalachians; (c) the imported cultural baggage of voluntary and involuntary non-Western immigrants; and (d) the convergence of b and c. Oral communication research strategies are often more valuable for understanding the nature of people within these four oral culture categories than are methodologies dependent upon written responses. Folklorists of Afro-American life, for instance, have long understood the value of examining sociological and anthropological aspects of inner-city Afro-Americans through the study of the oral traditions and games of "ghetto dwellers." It is also possible to use data from oral traditions to track the quality of life experiences of those living in poor white or Afro-American communities. Testimony in Afro-American churches that serve the inner-city poor can be valuable sources of data about health care, labor market activities, and child rearing.

Given that so many non-Western cultures within and outside industrial nation-states are oral communication based, it would make sense to suggest a generalizable qualitative methods epistemology for people of color structured around verbal communication. As so many non-Westerners view the social, the emotional, and the spiritual as integral parts of a whole person linked to a physical environment, it would also be crucial for such a qualitative methods epistemology to be grounded in holistic rather than fragmented and dichotomized notions of human beings. Operationally, this would be done through the collection of oral histories that allow the examined people of color to articulate holistic explanations about how they construct their realities. This means, among other things, that American researchers would have to discard their usual dislike of religious topics and realize that many Afro-Americans and other people of color (especially aboriginal populations) cannot be understood fully unless the central place of spirituality in their lives is given serious consideration. Other cultural constructs, such as time and space, as paradigmatic principles, which I do not have latitude to discuss here, also have profound implications for developing qualitative research methods derived from paradigms for people of color.

The purpose of creating the new baby is not to bury the old one, but instead to create a family of qualitative research paradigms and derived theories, methodologies, and styles of data interpretation that more adequately reflects the plural character of American society and the global community. Thus, as much as researchers concerned with meaning and realities as social and cultural constructions should continue the noble task of confessing their human biases up front, we need to be about the more complex task of creating paradigms grounded in the experiences of people of color that offer more adequate knowledge production about non-Europeans and that offer fascinating turns of the table in which those of European descent are viewed from the standpoints of "the usually studied."

References

Abramowitz, S. I. (1982). The sexual politics of sex bias in psychotherapy research. *Micropolitics, 2*(1), 21-34.

Anderson, E. (1978). *A place on the corner.* Chicago: University of Chicago Press.

Anderson, E. (1990). *Streetwise: Race, class, and change in an urban community.* Chicago: University of Chicago Press.

Asante, M. K. (1987). *The Afrocentric idea.* Philadelphia: Temple University Press.

Ashworth, P. D., Giorgi, A., & de Koning, A. J. J. (1986). *Qualitative research in psychology.* Pittsburgh, PA: Duquesne University Press.

Atkinson, P. (1992). *Understanding ethnographic texts.* Newbury Park, CA: Sage.

Baker, H. A. (1980). *The journey back: Issues in black literature and criticism.* Chicago: University of Chicago Press.

Baker, H. A. (1984). *Blues, ideology, and Afro-American literature: A vernacular theory.* Chicago: University of Chicago Press.

Baker, H. A. (1989). *Afro-American literary study in the 1990s.* Chicago: University of Chicago Press.

Baker, H. A. (1991). *Workings of the spirit: The poetics of Afro-American women's writing.* Chicago: University of Chicago Press.

Basu, A., Biswas, S. K., Balakrishnan, V., Chattopadhyay, H., Pollitzer, W. S., & Tripathi, T. P. (1980). Is Indian anthropology dead/dying? *Journal of the Indian Anthropological Society, 15,* 4-14

Bernal, M. (1987). *Black Athena.* New Brunswick, NJ: Rutgers University Press.

Bernick, S. E. (1991). Toward a value-laden theory: Feminism and social science. *Hypatia, 6,* 118-136.

Boahen, A. A. (1987). *African perspectives on colonialism.* Baltimore: Johns Hopkins University Press.

Burgess, R. G. (1985). *Strategies of educational research.* Philadelphia: Falmer.

Cannon, L. W. (1988). Race and class bias in qualitative research on women. *Gender & Society, 2,* 449-462.

Carby, H. V. (1987). *Reconstructing womanhood: The emergence of the Afro-American woman novelist.* Wellesley, MA: Wellesley College, Center for Research on Women.

Chinweizu. (1975). *The West and the rest of us: White predators, black slavers, and the African elite.* New York: Vintage.

Christman, J. B. (1988). Working in the field as the female friend. *Anthropology and Education Quarterly, 19*(2), 70-85.

Clark, K. B. (1965). *Dark ghetto: Dilemmas of social power.* New York: Harper & Row.

Collins, P. H. (1990). *Black feminist thought: Knowledge, consciousness and the politics of empowerment.* New York: Routledge.

Crabtree, B. F., & Miller, W. L. (Eds.). (1992). *Doing qualitative research.* Newbury Park, CA: Sage.

Currie, D. (1988). Re-thinking what we do and how we do it: A study of reproductive decisions. *Canadian Review of Sociology and Anthropology, 25,* 231-253.

Daniel, G., & Renfrew, C. (1988). *The idea of prehistory.* Edinburgh: Edinburgh University Press.

Das, B. (1935). *The laws of Manu.* Adyar, Madras, India: Theosophical Publishing House.

Devault, M. L. (1990). Talking and listening from women's standpoint: Feminist strategies for interviewing and analysis. *Social Problems, 37,* 96-116.

di Leonardo, M. (1991). *Gender at the crossroads of knowledge: Feminist anthropology in the post-modern era.* Berkeley: University of California Press.

Du Bois, W. E. B. (1965). *The world and Africa: An inquiry into the part which Africa has played in world history.* New York: International.

Du Bois, W. E. B. (1968). *Atlanta University publications* (No. 7-11—1902-1906). New York: Octagon.

Ellison, R. (1964). *Shadow and act.* New York: Random House.

Ergas, Y. (1978-1979). Feminism and sociology: Cultivating the garden of women's studies or constructing a cultural perspective? *Critica Sociologica, 48,* 29-39.

Facio, E. (1993). Ethnography as personal experience. In J. H. Stanfield II & R. M. Dennis (Eds.), *Race and ethnicity in research methods* (pp. 75-91). Newbury Park, CA: Sage.

Fanon, F. (1967). *Black skin, white masks.* New York: Grove.

Filstead, W. J. (Ed.). (1970). *Qualitative methodology: Firsthand involvement with the social world.* Chicago: Markham.

Frazier, E. F. (1967). *Negro youth at the crossways: Their personality development in the middle states.* New York: Schocken.

Frazier, E. F. (1968). *E. Franklin Frazier on race relations: Selected writings.* Chicago: University of Chicago Press.

Furner, M. O. (1975). *Advocacy and objectivity: A crisis in the professionalization of American social science, 1865-1905.* Lexington: University Press of Kentucky.

Gilgren, J., Daly, K., & Handel, G. (Eds.). (1992). *Qualitative methods in family research.* Newbury Park, CA: Sage.

Goetz, J. P., & LeCompte, M. D. (1984). *Ethnography and qualitative design in educational research.* New York: Academic Press.

Grant, L., & Ward, K. (1987). Is there an association between gender and methods in sociological research? *American Sociological Review, 52,* 856-862.

Hamnett, M., Porter, D. J., Singh, A., & Kumar, K. (1984). *Ethics, politics, and international social science research.* Honolulu: University of Hawaii Press.

Hare, N. (1965). *The black Anglo-Saxons.* New York: Marzani & Munsell.

Haskell, T. L. (1977). *The emergence of professional social science: The American Social Science Association and the nineteenth-century crisis of authority.* Urbana: University of Illinois Press.

Hinkle, R. C. (1954). *The development of modern sociology: Its nature and growth in the United States.* Garden City, NY: Doubleday.

Hodgkin, T. (1960). *Nigerian perspectives: An historical anthology.* London: Oxford University Press.

hooks, b. (1981). *Ain't I a woman: Black women and feminism.* Boston: South End.

hooks, b. (1984). *Feminist theory from margin to center.* Boston: South End.

hooks, b. (1989). *Talking back: Thinking feminist, thinking black.* Boston: South End.

hooks, b. (1990). *Yearning: Race, gender, and cultural politics.* Boston: South End.

hooks, b. (1991). *Breaking bread: Insurgent black intellectual life.* Boston: South End.

hooks, b. (1992). *Black looks: Race and representation.* Boston: South End.

Hunter, H. M., & Abraham, S. Y. (Eds.). (1987). *Race, class, and the world system: The sociology of Oliver C. Cox.* New York: Monthly Review Press.

Hurston, Z. N. (1969a). *Mules and men.* New York: Negro Universities Press.

Hurston, Z. N. (1969b). *Their eyes were watching God.* New York: Negro Universities Press.

Hurston, Z. N. (1971a). *Dust tracks on a road: An autobiography.* Philadelphia: J. B. Lippincott.

Hurston, Z. N. (1971b). *Jonah's gourd vine.* Philadelphia: J. B. Lippincott.

Hurston, Z. N. (1990). *Tell my horse: Voodoo and life in Haiti and Jamaica.* New York: Perennial Library.

Johnson, C. F. (1987). Bitter canaan (John Stanfield, Ed.) New Brunswick: Transaction Books.

Johnson, J. W. (1945). *Along this way: The autobiography of James Weldon Johnson.* New York: Viking.

Johnson, J. W. (1979). *The autobiography of an ex-coloured man.* New York: A. A. Knopf.

Khaldun, I. (1981). *The Muqaddimah* (N. J. Dawood, Ed.; F. Rosenthal, Trans.). Princeton, NJ: Princeton University Press.

Kluckhohn, C. (1944). *Navajo witchcraft.* Boston: Beacon.

Kuper, A. (1983). *Anthropology and anthropologists: The modern British school.* London: Routledge & Kegan Paul.

Ladner, J. A. (1971). *Tomorrow's tomorrow: The black woman.* Garden City, NY: Anchor.

Ladner, J. A. (1973). *The death of white sociology.* New York: Random House.

Lather, P. (1986). Issues of validity in openly ideological research: Between a rock and a soft place. *Interchange, 17*(4), 63-84.

LeCompte, M. D., Millroy, W. L., & Preissle, J. (Eds.). (1992). *The handbook of qualitative research in education.* New York: Academic Press.

Lewis, O. (1966). *La vida.* New York: Random House.

Liebow, E. (1967). *Tally's corner: A study of Negro street corner men.* Boston: Little, Brown.

Magubane, B., & Faris, J. C. (1985). On the political relevance of anthropology. *Dialectical Anthropology, 9,* 91-104.

Marburg, S. L. (1981, April 19-22). *Paradigms of production: Theoretical basis for bias? A history of the idea "man's role, woman's place: in geography."* Paper presented at the annual meeting of the Association of American Geographers, Los Angeles.

Marks, C. C. (1993). Demography and race. In J. H. Stanfield II & R. M. Dennis (Eds.), *Race and ethnicity in research methods* (pp. 159-171). Newbury Park, CA: Sage.

Mascia-Lees, F. E., Sharpe, P., & Cohen, C. B. (1989). The postmodernist turn in anthropology: Cautions from a feminist perspective. *Signs, 15,* 7-33.

Mbiti, J. S. (1970). *African religions and philosophy.* Garden City, NY: Anchor.

McKeganey, N., & Bloor, M. (1991). Spotting the invisible man: The influence of male gender on fieldwork relations. *British Journal of Sociology, 42,* 195-210.

Memmi, A. (1965). *The Colonizer and the colonized.* Boston: Beacon.

Merriam, S. B. (1988). *Case study research in education.* San Francisco: Jossey-Bass.

Merton, R. K. (1972). Insiders and outsiders: A chapter in the sociology of knowledge. *American Journal of Sociology, 78,* 44-47.

Mudimbe, V. Y. (1988). *The invention of Africa: Gnosis, philosophy, and the order of knowledge.* Bloomington: Indiana University Press.

Myrdal, G., with Sterner, R., & Rose, A. (1944). *An American dilemma: The Negro problem and modern democracy.* New York: Harper & Row.

Nandy, A. (Ed.). (1988). *Science, hegemony and violence.* Tokyo: United Nations University.

Nkrumah, K. (1973). *Autobiography of Kwame Nkrumah.* London: Panaf.

Nsamenang, A. B. (1992). *Human development in cultural context: A Third World perspective.* Newbury Park, CA: Sage.

O'Connor, A. (1986). *The African city.* London: Hutchinson University Library for Africa.

Peplau, L. A., & Conrad, E. (1989). Beyond nonsexist research: The perils of feminist methods in psychology. *Psychology of Women Quarterly, 13,* 379-400.

Polkinghorne, D. E. (1988). *Narrative knowing and the human sciences.* Albany: State University of New York Press.

Rainwater, L. (1970a). *Behind ghetto walls: Black families in a federal slum.* Chicago: Aldine.

Rainwater, L. (1970b). *Soul.* Chicago: Aldine.

Rapp, R. (1988). Is the legacy of second wave feminism postfeminism? *Socialist Review, 18,* 31-37.

Rollins, J. (1985). *Between women: Domestics and their employers.* Philadelphia: Temple University Press.

Said, E. W. (1978). *Orientalism.* London: Penguin.

Seidman, I. E. (1991). *Interviewing as qualitative research.* New York: Teachers College Press.

Shaffir, W. B., & Stebbins, R. A. (Eds.). (1991). *Experiencing fieldwork.* Newbury Park, CA: Sage.

Sprague, J., & Zimmerman, M. K. (1989). Quality and quantity: Reconstructing feminist methodology. *American Sociologist, 20,* 71-86.

Stack, C. B. (1974). *All our kin: Strategies for survival in a black community.* New York: Harper Colophon.

Stanfield, J. H., II. (1985). *Philanthropy and Jim Crow in American social science.* Westport, CT: Greenwood.

Stanfield, J. H., II. (1991). Racism in America and in other race-centered nation-states: Synchronic considerations. *International Journal of Comparative Sociology, 32,* 243-260.

Stanfield, J. H., II. (1992). Ethnic pluralism and civic responsibility in post-Cold War America. *Journal of Negro Education, 61*(3).

Stanfield, J. H., II. (1993a). Epistemological considerations. In J. H. Stanfield II & R. M. Dennis (Eds.), *Race and ethnicity in research methods* (pp. 16-36). Newbury Park, CA: Sage.

Stanfield, J. H., II. (1993b). Methodological reflections: An introduction. In J. H. Stanfield II & R. M. Dennis (Eds.), *Race and ethnicity in research methods* (pp. 3-15). Newbury Park, CA: Sage.

Strauss, A. L. (1987). *Qualitative analysis for social scientists.* New York: Cambridge University Press.

Sudarkasa, N. (1986). In a world of women: Field work in a Toruba community. In P. Golde (Ed.), *Women in the field: Anthropological experiences* (pp. 47-64). Berkeley: University of California Press.

Suret-Canale, J. (1988). *Essays on African history: From the slave trade to neocolonialism.* Trenton, NJ: Africa World Press.

Terrell, M. C. (1980). *A colored woman in a white world: Mary Church Terrell.* New York: Arno.

Tesch, R. (1990). *Qualitative research.* New York: Falmer.

Vansina, J. (1988). *Oral tradition as history.* London: James Currey.

Walker, R. (Ed.). (1985). *Applied qualitative research.* Hants, England: Gower.

Warren, C. A. B. (1988). *Gender issues in field research.* Newbury Park, CA: Sage.

West, C. (1982). *Prophesy deliverance! An Afro-American revolutionary Christianity.* Philadelphia: Westminster.

West, C. (1988). *Prophetic fragments.* Grand Rapids, MI/Trenton, NJ: Eerdmans/Africa World Press.

Whitehead, T. L. (1986). Breakdown, resolution and coherence: The fieldwork experiences of a big, brown pretty-talking man in a West Indian community. In T. L. Whitehead & M. E. Conaway (Eds.), *Self, sex and gender in cross-cultural fieldwork* (pp. 213-239). Urbana: University of Illinois Press.

Williams, A. (1987). Reading feminism in fieldnotes. *Studies in Sexual Politics, 16,* 100-109.

Williams, A. (1990). Reflections on the making of an ethnographic text. *Studies in Sexual Politics, 29,* 1-63.

Williams, R. (1990). *Culture and society.* London: Hogarth.

Wilson, W. J. (1974). The new black sociology: Reflections on the "insiders and outsiders" controversy. In W. J. Wilson, *Black sociologist* (pp. 322-338). Chicago: University of Chicago Press.

Zaslavsky, C. (1973). *Africa counts: Number and pattern in African culture*. Boston: Prindle, Weber & Schmidt.

11

■

Audiencing

Cultural Practice and Cultural Studies

JOHN FISKE

CULTURAL studies is such a contested and currently trendy term that I must disclaim any attempt to either define or speak for it. There have been a number of recent studies of television's audiences and ways of watching that have contributed to the field, and I list some of them in the appendix to this chapter. What I wish to do here is to give an example of one way of understanding television watching that falls within "cultural studies," and through that example to highlight some theoretical and methodological issues by which this sort of cultural studies differs from other critical modes of analysis, and from positivist or scientific approaches.

I propose to tell a story about a particular program and a particular group of young people who watched it. I choose such a specific example because the attempt to understand the particularity of experience is one of the priorities of the approach I am illustrating. The program is *Married . . . With Children*; the audience, a group of teenage students who gathered together regularly to watch it.

Married . . . With Children is a situation comedy that premiered in the United States in April 1987 on the new Fox network. By January 1989 it was Fox's top-rated show, with an estimated 21 million viewers, and, as 1989 is the year of the show's major cultural impact, it forms the focus of my study. This, incidentally, signals another difference from many scientific studies, which, because they typically aim for human universals, do not find their dates of particular significance. The date is, however, significant for cultural studies, and it is for this chapter.

By the late 1980s the dominance of the three major networks was cracking. New technologies, particularly cable, but also VCRs, video games, and home computers, had weakened the networks' grip on domestic leisure activities. Statistics here are very suspect, because they are supplied by a commercial organization, the Nielsen Group, to the networks primarily to determine the advertising rates for each time slot and to sell each slot to advertisers. It is therefore in the interests of the networks to use a counting system that keeps the ratings as high as possible and that overlooks defections. And it is in Nielsen's interests to serve the networks' interests. But arguments over stray percentage points could not disguise the steady erosion of the network audience.

New technologies do not in themselves produce social change, however, though they can and do facilitate it. These new technologies met the marketing strategies of late capitalist industries, which can be summarized briefly as ones of market segmentation rather than mass marketing. Advertisers now increasingly target their products to specified social groups or market segments, and do not wish to pay for their messages to reach nontarget groups. The networks, however, grew and prospered by attracting the largest possible audiences whose internal differentiations were kept to the broadest social categories with the weakest categorical boundaries. So although cop/adventure shows might have appealed primarily to men, women were important too, so female characters and "feminine" appeal were featured as strongly as the producers thought was possible without alienating the men. The consequence was that advertisers for razors paid to reach a non-shaving audience. But on a cable channel devoted to sports, they would pay much less and target their advertising dollars more accurately.

But, however dominant the market economy is, our society is not determined by it entirely. Market segmentation is an economic transformation of changes in the social order at large. Throughout the 1970s and 1980s, people's sense of social differences began to challenge the homogenization of consensus more and more openly. The women's movement was one key player, as it asserted women's rights to control not only their economic and domestic relations, but also the sense of the feminine and thus the meaning of feminine identity. Very similar demands were made by the black power movement, and gays and lesbians began to assert their difference from the mainstream. As Reaganism widened the gaps between rich and poor, men and women, whites and those of color, the sense of social differences sharpened and became conflictual. Race, gender, and class were far from the only players in the scene; regional differences became marked, as did those between the urban and the rural, the religious and the secular, the traditionally married and the rest. In this essay the key axis of social difference is one not yet mentioned—that of age.

New information technologies were developed by marketing companies to track the intersections of all these axes of social difference and thus to target market segments more accurately than ever before. Market research found, for instance, that a product aimed at reproducing the old-fashioned satisfaction of baking from scratch would have its strongest appeal among married women with more than two children who lived in the rural South, attended church regularly, did not have full-time jobs outside the home, and watched *Cops* and *Rescue 911* because these programs melodramatized the everyday dangers of the outside world.

This conjuncture of forces, technological, economic, and sociocultural, left the three networks looking like dinosaurs wondering what to do with a changing world. Rupert Murdoch, Fox's owner, thought he knew. He wanted to develop a fourth network that combined the big three's traditional wide geographic reach with a new ability to deliver accurately segmented audiences, particularly ones that lay outside the massed middle America that the other networks vied for. So Fox launched its new network on weekends with a schedule aimed at the teenage and young adult nonfamily audience. (Of course, many teenagers lived in families while wishing, for some of the time at least, that they did not.) With programs such as *The Tracey Ullman Show* and *It's Garry Shandling's Show,* Fox gained a core audience in its targeted segment, but *Married . . . With Children* and *The Simpsons,* which followed soon after, were its first shows to achieve general ratings that challenged those of the big three. It was the high visibility of these shows, as much as their content or audiences, that made them controversial.

Since its origin in the 1950s, the category of "the teenager" has been a site of trouble and anxiety for adult America. As this was the social formation that Fox wished to turn into an audience that it could sell to advertisers, the programs designed for this strategy were predictably controversial. T-shirts showing Bart Simpson and his slogan, "Underachiever—and proud of it" have been banned from schools, and Bart has been identified as one of the causes of the poor record of U.S. schools. *Married . . . With Children* has been similarly controversial, and it is upon this controversy that I wish to focus (Fiske, 1994).

The program was widely seen by adult America as offensive and as sending a "wrong" message to teenagers; by publicly inverting the norms of the "good" family, it offended those whose social interests were inscribed in the family and appealed to those who identified themselves as outside-the-family. The carnivalesque offense of the show runs along a continuum in which offensive bodies extend into offensive family relationships and thence into offensive social relations.

Bodies and bodily functions are its main vehicles for representing the identities and relationships of the Bundy family. Al, the father/husband, has a body that smells and an ugly face that is given to grotesque expressions; he inverts the social norms of masculine power by being economically and sexually inadequate and by being incapable of controlling his children or his wife. Peg, the wife/mother, is oversexed, overcoiffed, over-made-up, and overdressed. Her body movements, gestures, and expressions mock by exaggeration the conventions of feminine attractiveness normally used in patriarchy to discipline the bodies of its women. As she teeters across the room, her high heels thrust her bosom and buttocks into prominence while restricting her movements to those that are sexually attractive but ineffective practically. She exposes to mocking laughter the patriarchal control over feminine bodies and behavior that is applied in the design of high-heeled shoes. Her overblown lips and overblown hair serve a similar parodic function. Her mocking of the feminine body in patriarchy is also accompanied by an inversion of normal social relations. She never provides for the family and neither buys nor prepares food, and in every way is the opposite of the nurturing wife/mother figure. Kelly and Bud, the two teenage children, are similarly defined by their bodily appearances and appetites. They are constantly hungry for both food and sex; in their search for sexual pleasure, Kelly is an excessive success, Bud an excessive failure. She parodies the body and behavior of the "dumb blonde," whereas he is constantly trying to convince himself and others that his inadequate teenage body is that of a macho stud.

The relationships among the family members conflict across gender and age differences. The language in which they are conducted is scatological and often emphasizes their bodily and sexual attributes as markers of identity and of social relationships. The normative family in which gender and age differences are contained within a consensual harmony is simultaneously mocked and inverted by the show.

The show attracted a large and devoted audience of teenagers and young adults to the new Fox network when it was first aired. Many of my students called it the most "realistic" show on television, and they used its carnivalesque elements as ways of expressing the difference between their experience of family life and that proposed for them by the dominant social norms.

One of my graduate students, David Brean, spent a season watching the show with a typical audience of young people. They were undergraduates, mainly freshmen and sophomores, of both sexes who attended a Catholic university and met after evening Mass, which many attended, each Sunday in one or another of their apartments. Some of the group had known each other through high school, others were more recent members, but the group's communitas was organized around the shared taste for *Married . . . With Children.*

The seven members who attended one particular Sunday met in Mick and John's apartment, the main room of which had once been the living room of the single-family house that was now converted into student apartments. The furniture was an eclectic mix of whatever they had been able to scrounge from their families. The couch, for instance, carried the scars of its history, during which it had moved from living room to family room to kids' basement, to student apartment. Its stains and tears spoke against the domestic order still faintly discernible in the traces of what it used to be. During the show, beer was spilled on it and nobody cared, a half-eaten hamburger on a thin piece of paper was set down on it with no thought of grease or ketchup stains seeping through, and, later on, John and Sarah lay on it in a body-hugging embrace that would have sent their parents into conniptions had the couch still been in the family living room.

The walls were decorated with posters of pop and film stars that may have been tolerated at home, though not in the living room, and with signs advertising beer, which almost certainly would have been prohibited, particularly as they had clearly been stolen from a bar, not purchased from a store. Nobody in the apartment had reached the legal drinking age, so the signs were doubly illicit.

The theme music of the show, "Love and Marriage," a Frank Sinatra number from their parents' generation, provoked the group into singing along in vacuous parody of both its "older" style and "older" sentiments. A similar parody of their parents' taste (as they saw it) hung on the wall—a somewhat moth-eaten painting of Elvis on black velvet. The "bad taste" of the picture was different from the "bad taste" of the program, for it was their view of teenage culture then as opposed to now. The picture was a site for experiencing the differences between their parents-as-teenagers and themselves, just as the program enabled them to mock the differences between their parents now and themselves. These differences were not shown on the screen, but were constructed in the process of audiencing and only there: The Bundys did not represent the teenagers' parents, but the teenagers' view of the Bundys and the comedy lay in the difference between parents-as-seen-by-teenagers (represented on the screen) and parents-as-seen-by-themselves (known by the audience, and brought to the screen by them, but never shown on it).

Watching the program involved a series of interactive comments that took every opportunity the show offered to draw disrespectful parallels between it and the families the teenagers had so recently left. These comments ranged from delight in representations of a counterknowledge ("My Dad does that"—said of an action that a father would disown as typically his but that a teenager would know differently) to more engaged family politics ("I wish Mom had seen that").

The show enabled the teenagers to engage in and reconfigure the age politics of their relations with their absent parents: equally, they used it to engage in gender politics with their present partners. The gender conflicts between the parents and the children consisted of verbal punches and counterpunches in which, generally, the females outpointed the males. This caused few problems for the men in this particular audience, and though both sexes would cheer the punches thrown by their own sides, they also gained great pleasure from any well-aimed riposte. When a girl nudged her boyfriend at a remark on the TV, she brought their own interpersonal history to the program just as significantly as the Fox network brought the program to them.

This particular audience, or rather group of people who came together to "audience" the show, is best understood not as a social category, though its members clearly belonged to one (that of white middle-class youth), but as a social formation. As a social unit they were formed around a TV program and a set of social interests. The members of this formation did not experience all their social relations in this antifamily mode, nor even did they necessarily spend much time together as a social formation with other interests in common. Indeed, it is quite possible that some of them were members of other formations that entered more conservative and complicit relations with the social order (some did, after all, attend Mass immediately before watching the show). They did not appear to align themselves with the class identities of the blue-collar Bundys, but confined their observable alignments to ones of gender and age. The fact that no class alignments were observable does not necessarily mean that none were made, but it probably indicates that, if made, they were either secondary or displacements by which class disempowerment was made to stand for age disempowerment. Indeed, it is quite possible that some members of the group were class snobs, but that their social competencies developed to cope with such elaborately transected societies as ours enabled them to experience a comfortable fit between what an objective analysis would describe as contradictory political positions. Audiencing the show as this group did involved a tactical alliance of age interests and little more. Those who formed this alliance may well have been typical of the social category that was the core of Fox's target audience, but the alliance was not coterminous with the category (many of whose members would have shared neither the alliance's tastes nor its interests). A social category holds its members constantly within its conceptual grip; a social formation is formed and dissolved more fluidly, according to its contextual conditions. It is identified by what its members do rather than by what they are, and as such is better able to account nonreductively for the complexities and contradictions of everyday life in a highly elaborated society.

The show's carnivalesque inversions of official family values and its emphasis on the bodily pleasures of eating, drinking, and sexuality reproduced and were reproduced in the practices of this audience formation. Out of them, they produced a cultural experience within which the show, the behavior of watching it, and the place where it was watched were all mobilized to produce social identities and social relations that were within their control as opposed to, and in emancipation from, those institutionalized for them in the officially approved family. The carnivalesque offensiveness of these practices differentiated them from what was officially approved, but it did not in itself do anything positive. It opened up a gap in top-down power that this particular social formation was able to fill with the social identities/relations it produced for itself. The carnivalesque can do no more than open up spaces; it is upon what fills them that we should base our analysis and evaluation.

But the creation of gaps is enough to provoke the power bloc to rush to repair its system. The show provoked wide-ranging and vehement criticism from official, profamily voices. None of them was concerned about what might be used to fill these gaps; rather, it was the attack on family values, that is, the gaps themselves, that concerned them. Terry Rakolta, for example, a wealthy housewife, gained much publicity for her campaign to persuade advertisers to withdraw from the show on the grounds that it resembled softcore pornography and contained "blatant exploitation of women and sex, and anti-family attitudes" (Dell, 1990). According to a front-page story in the *New York Times* (March 2, 1989), Procter & Gamble, McDonald's, Tambrands, and Kimberly-Clark all withdrew advertising support or promised to monitor the show's values more carefully in the future. Procter & Gamble cited the show's "negative portrayal of American family life"; the chairman of Coca-Cola in a letter to Rakolta wrote that he was "corporately, professionally and privately embarrassed" that ads for Coke had appeared on the show; and Gary Lieberman, chairman of Columbia Pictures Television, which produced the show, offered Rakolta "our sincere apology" (*Los Angeles Times,* March 4, 1989). Rakolta's husband was president of a family-owned construction firm worth $400 million (which gives a particular inflection to the term *family values*), so the social positions of those forming this set of allegiances within the power bloc were particularly close. Rakolta attempted to broaden the allegiance, but not its intent, by enlisting the support of lobbying groups within conservative "middle America," specifically, Concerned Women of America and the American Family Association (which had started life as the National Federation for Decency, an organization founded by a fundamentalist minister, the Reverend Donald Wildmon). Rakolta's rallying cry, around which this allegiance was forged, was "Free TV is the last bastion for the American family, or anybody who wants decent programming."

Initially, the press reaction to her campaign was favorable. The *Detroit News* (her local newspaper) was typical in applauding "Mrs. Rakolta's stand for decency" (March 3, 1989). (It is noteworthy how frequently the concept of "decency" is used to disguise class taste and power under the mask of universally agreed-upon standards.) But the press support for the alliance weakened as its narrow social base and repressive strategy became clearer: In the months that followed, the typical line became "If the show offends you, switch it off, don't try and censor it" (*Denver Post,* March 8, 1989; *Detroit News,* July 24, 1989; and *Wall Street Journal,* July 31, 1989; all cited in Dell, 1990). Ironically, the longer-term result of Rakolta's campaign was to increase the show's ratings and expose an alliance of the power bloc to popular rejection.

Rakolta's campaign against the program did not originate in her own living room only; it was part of a sociocultural context in which "family values" had become a crucial political battlefield. Throughout the 1980s, the gap between the ideological norm of "the family" and the material conditions in which people actually lived widened to the extent that less than one-third of U.S. children were growing up in families that would be considered "normal." When the abnormal outnumbers the normal by more than two to one, the ideological power to produce the normal is put under immense pressure, and conflicts become sharpened and multifrontal.

So the conflict over "family values" has been central in every political campaign for the past decade. The high divorce rate, the increasing number of single-parent families, the growth of same-sex parenting—all are taken as evidence of the collapse of the normal family and therefore of danger to the social order in general. Vice President Dan Quayle provided a perfect example of this when he linked the 1992 Los Angeles riots with the collapse of family values and the decision of sitcom character Murphy Brown to become a single mother. When the media reported that Quayle thought Murphy Brown was the cause of the riots, they (typically) oversimplified his argument but did not categorically distort it: He did say that the program's legitimation of single motherhood was one of the causes of the collapse of family values that underlay the riots.

Family values are continuous with social values, for the family is seen as both a miniaturization of society and the building block with which the social order is constructed. The family is not only the foundation of today's social order, it is also the seed ground of tomorrow's. Parental discipline is the politics of the future, and any form of youth culture that appears to oppose or disrupt it is consequently viewed as socially threatening.

Culture is the social circulation of meanings, pleasures, and values, and the cultural order that results is inextricably connected with the social order within which it circulates. Culture may secure the social order and help to hold it in place, or it may destabilize it and work toward changing it, but it is never either neutral or detached. The social circulation of meanings is always a maelstrom, full of conflicting currents, whirlpools, and eddies. The mainstream attempts to keep its current as smooth and inexorable as possible, but around its edges there are always rough, intransigent rocks and promontories that disrupt or divert it.

The cultural analyst cannot possibly chart all of this maelstrom—not only is it so complex as to defy total description, but much of it occurs far beneath the surface and beyond analytic access. The analyst, then, has to select sites of analysis when this circulation of meanings becomes accessible and use them as points from which to theorize the inaccessible undercurrents. Audiences and texts are two of those sites, but neither is sufficient in itself, nor are they together. The social meanings of *Married . . . With Children* will have been circulated as much by those who never saw the show but who read or talked about the controversy it provoked as by those who watched it. The meaning of *Married . . . With Children* is produced at a variety of intersections, with the general "crisis of the family" at the macro social level as well as at the huge number of encounters with it at the micro level of particular viewings, one of which was Terry Rakolta's viewing of one episode in the company of her daughters (which was the origin of her campaign) and another of which was this group of students on this Sunday night. The conflict of interests between socioethical alliances within the power bloc that wish to maintain the nuclear family (itself a product of the capitalism they endorse) and economic alliances that wish to profit from oppositional or subordinate interests reproduces within the power bloc the dinner-table arguments between parents and teenagers—and neither could take the form that it does without the other.

We have been looking at three ways of understanding the audience: Fox's economic category of a market segment defined by its consumer preferences and buying power; Rakolta's sense of it as a site of the inculcation of values; and the students' audiencing as the process of producing, through lived experience, their own sense of their social identities and social relations, and of the pleasures that this process gave them. There are both overlaps and contradictions among these ways of constructing "the audience," but the most significant theoretically are the contradictory relations. Fox and Rakolta struggle over the construction of "the teenager." For Fox, the teenager is a market segment to be differentiated from the adult; for Rakolta, the teenager is a child to be kept under adult control within the family. Between Rakolta and this one student audience there is a struggle over the meanings of the family, over the age and gender politics within it, and thus over the social identities of those who occupy different roles within its structure of relationships. And between Fox and the teenage audience there is the struggle between incorporation and excorporation, in which the industry constantly seeks to incorporate the tastes and practices of subordinate social formations whose members, in their turn, scan the products of the culture industries looking for elements that they can excorporate and use to promote their own sociocultural interests.

The definition of "the audience" depends upon the way it is positioned in the social order. Located within the economic system, the audience is a market segment to be reached and, simultaneously, a commodity to be traded; located within the socioethical system, the audience is a site of acculturation or socialization; and located in the materiality of everyday life, the audience stops being a social category and becomes a process, a constituent element in a way of living. John and Sarah were members of all three "audiences" (and of others, not yet analyzed), but each audience is distinguished from the others only in the process of analysis: In lived culture there are no boundaries between categories, but only a complex of continuities. These different "audiences" merge into each other at the micro level of John and Sarah as social beings, and at the macro level of the social order of late capitalism at a particular point and place in its history.

The cultural analyst faces the inevitable paradox that categories and the distinctions between them are necessary tools in the process of analysis, but they distort the object of analysis, for culture works not in categorically distinct ways but as "a whole way of life" (to use one of Raymond Williams's definitions). What makes a way of life whole is the production of continuities across domains of experience that the analyst may choose to categorize as different. "Specimens" taken out of these continuities for microscopic analysis (a text, an audience, a marketing strategy) are distorted by the extraction, for any extraction disqualifies certain elements and relations in the cultural process while privileging others. And although the analyst is careful to return the specimen to the organic process from which it was taken, extraction and return are productive, not objective, practices.

As an analyst, I extract a specimen—let us say John's laying down a half-eaten hamburger on a sofa that was once in a family living room as he watches Peg Bundy "failing" to produce a family meal. I can never describe fully the relations that make that moment culturally significant. On most Sundays the hamburger will have been bought from a nearby McDonald's, but if John feels particularly self-indulgent and wishes to reward himself he will have gone further afield to buy a "better" burger at a small one-off burger joint. Which burger he bought will be connected to whether or not he finished a class paper he had to write, or whether or not he and Sarah had had a minor tiff, or whatever. The continuities among hamburgers, beer, *Married . . . With Children,* and Sarah in John's Sunday night stretch through into their relationships of not-school, not-church, not-family. Whether the hamburger was one-off or mass produced by McDonald's connects not only with John's sense of the week or day that has passed, but also with the fact that McDonald's advertises on the show, that the local burger joint does not, and that the McDonald's advertising campaign promotes the restaurants as places for the family, particularly for parents and children, and thus with Rakolta's letter-writing campaign and McDonald's (temporary) withdrawal of advertising from the program. McDonald's advertising image of itself as a "family place" is, of course, designed to counter the perception that fast food is opposed to the family dinner table, and that it is itself a sign of and an agent in the breakdown of family values, particularly of the maternal responsibilities within them. The hamburger is much more than ground beef. This complex of continuities, still inadequately traced, will not exist in total in John's consciousness, but the continuities do exist in the culture, and in audiencing the program John activates them (and others not yet described) in a particular configuration more or less consciously, more or less emphatically.

My analysis of the hamburger on the sofa could go further, but my point here is that in extracting it as a specimen I have deformed it. I have set it into cultural relations (with a multinational corporation and a letter-writing upper-middle-class housewife) that are highly significant to me-as-analyst but that may have signified little in John's mouthful in front of the TV set. So in returning that specimen for his second bite, I have changed it, if not for him, then certainly for the reader of this analysis. The analyst's experience of that mouthful is quite different from that of the young man who took the bite in the first place. These differences do not invalidate the analysis, nor do they define John's experience of his own culture as inadequate, nor do they privilege the superiority of theory. They indicate the incompleteness of any understanding (experiential or theoretical) and the need for an academic modesty that acknowledges that the aim of analysis is not to reveal the truth but to contribute to a process of understanding, and to provoke other, probably contradictory, contributions.

A cultural analysis of audiences or audiencing is not, then, "scientific," and for the final section of this essay, I would like to indicate some of the differences between the two paradigms (obviously privileging the cultural, I make no claim to being unbiased) (Fiske, 1991).

The model underlying cultural analysis is one drawn from discourse analysis, and is systemic, not representative, in its model of validation. Its data are empirical but not empiricist. So, the hamburger is not representative of the audience-as-a-whole of *Married . . . With Children*; it is significant regardless of whether or not John is the only audience member in the universe who eats hamburgers while watching, just as the significance of a sentence does not depend on how many people speak it. It is significant because it is a practice of a system, not because it reproduces other practices. In discourse analysis, no utterance is representative of other utterances, though of course it shares structural features with them; a discourse analyst studies utterances in order to understand how the potential of the linguistic system can be activated when it intersects at its moments of use with a social system. The utterance is an actualization in a historical social relationship of the linguistic potential. So the cultural analyst studies instances of culture in order to understand both the system that structures "the whole way of life" and the ways of living that people devise within it.

This study of this audience, or rather example of audiencing, was not an ethnography in the anthropological or social scientific sense of the term; it did not aim to attain a full or objective understanding of the teenagers' whole way of life, for that would be impossible. Rather, it was an attempt to get glimpses of culture in practice that could be set in systemic relationship to other glimpses such as those afforded by Terry Rakolta or by Fox's economic strategy. Insofar as these glimpses, or sites of analysis, come from widely different points in the social order, the systematicity that links them and makes them part of a whole way of life is a generalized one. What links the empirical detail to the general and thus establishes its theoretical significance is a systemic relationship and not a representative one. The data then are empirical in that they derive from a material experience, but not empiricist in that there is no claim that the material plane has an objective existence that provides the terms of its own significance. Their significance is produced only at their intersection with another ontological plane—that of the system, or the structuring principle.

The term *structure,* or *structural,* is common to both positivist and systemic models, but there are crucial differences in the ways in which each uses it. For positivism (e.g., content analysis), a structure is a coherent patterning of empirical data that is part of the larger social reality theoretically derived from the data. Such a structure may be related to more abstract, less empirically derived structures in that social reality (particularly value structures, as in Gerbner's cultivation theory). So a content analysis of gender portrayal on television revealing that women are portrayed less frequently than men and in a narrower range of occupations and settings may be convincingly related to the more abstract values of patriarchy. The tracing of such interstructural relationships is common to both systemic models and positivist ones, but the similarity ends there. Systemic theories of structure go further than do positivist ones, for systemic structures, such as language, are generative, whereas positivist structures are descriptive. Systemic structures generate the practices by which they are used and are, in their turn, modified by those practices. Positivist structures, however, have effects, not practices, and the relationship between structure and effect is one-way. In positivism, structures have no practice.

The structure of language, on the other hand, has a mutually informing relationship with the utterances that are its practices. The system is produced in part, at least, by its practices, as the practices are produced in part, at least, by the system. Systems and practices both structure each other and are structured by each other; structuration is a two-way process, though not an equal one. Because positivism does not theorize structures in relationship to practice, it does not have a theory of either how they change or how they can act as agents of change. Bourdieu (1984) makes the point that theoretical methods are better able to account for social change than those of quantitative positivism, for these produce snapshots of a social system as a particular moment, and positivism therefore tends to model social differences as social stratification. Theory, however (and for Bourdieu the word seems to be a code for Marxist critical theory), is better able to trace social struggle, for that occurs over time as part of the dialectic of history; consequently, this type of theory models social differences not as stratification but as struggle.

When positivism models the differences in the social order as relatively stable and/or harmonious, its policies tend toward liberal pluralism; when it evacuates that social order from the research agenda altogether (as in much TV effects research), its politics shift toward the reactionary. Some of the differences between liberal pluralist positivism and cultural studies emerge in the debate around "the active audience." The "active audience" of uses and gratifications (a positivist theory) differs significantly from that of cultural theory, particularly in its claim that active uses of the media actually gratify needs. This is not the case in cultural studies. Here the needs (for more material or symbolic resources, for more power and control) can be met only by social action; the activity of the media user is that of articulating those needs within the social relations that both produce and frustrate them and of establishing and validating a social identity that is a bottom-up product rather than a top-down one. Audience activity is an engagement in social relations across social inequality; the satisfaction in the process lies in control over the terms of that engagement, but there is no satisfaction of the needs generated by the inequality.

Equally, the psychological brand of positivism assumes that the audience is not just where the effects of television occur but is itself an effect of television. There is no sense that the audience precedes or outlasts the effects of watching. But John and Sarah were social beings and members of social formations long before they watched *Married . . . With Children,* and their experiences of family life affected the ways they watched the program just as much as the program affected their sense of "family values," if not more. In this sense, the meanings of the program are an effect of their social behavior, rather than their social behavior being an effect of the program. Programs, the industry that makes them, and the people who watch them are all active agents in the circulation of meanings, and the relationships among them are not ones of cause and effect, in which one precedes another, but of systematicity.

The word *audience* suggests a priority that is misleading, for an audience can exist only when hearing something. This sense of precedence lies not only in the model of the process (in which the imagined procedure is from message to audience) but also in the history of the chosen word, which originally referred to subjects being summoned to an audience with the monarch or pope. This discursive construction of the audience as the disempowered empty receptacle waiting for the message underlies both Rakolta's fear of *Married . . . With Children* and the whole tradition of effects research.

In a systemic model, in one set of relations "the audience" can be seen to precede the message. The social category of "the teenager" preceded Fox's attempts to turn it into a market segment. Within it there were already tastes and practices, social relations and social identities, ways of living within a social order that entered relations of opposition to some of its structuring forces and of complicity with others. All this not only preceded the first episode of *Married . . . With Children,* but it constituted the social goal at which the text was aimed. The text is an effect of this audience, and the skill of its producers lies in their ability to respond to the ways of living within the category of "the teenager."

In calling the text an effect of the audience, I am attempting to score a point in a debate, not to provide an essential definition, for a text is no more nor less an effect of the audience than is the audience of the text. The relationships between them are not ones of cause and effect, in which one spatially, temporally, or epistemologically takes precedence over the other; the relations are systemic ones of a complex of reciprocities in which contradictions and complicities struggle to gain ground over one another.

In media studies, positivism has tended to produce a normative epistemology; cultural studies, however, does not. It does not assume that what is statistically most normal is therefore most significant. Instead, discourse analysts (like poets) often find that marginal and abnormal uses of language are highly significant because they reveal, in a way that more normal linguistic usages do not, the extremes of which a system is capable. Systems are often more susceptible to change or modification at their margins than at their centers; social change typically originates in marginalized or subordinated minorities and, as cultural studies has a political stake in social change, it requires a model that allows the marginal, the deviant, and the abnormal to be always granted significance and at times major significance. History may show that the 29% of women who were not represented on television as housewives, stewardesses, or models may be more significant than the 71% who were (Dominick & Rauch, 1972).

Let us return to our hamburger for a moment, for we have now refigured it into a statement, not a commodity. This identifies another point of difference between cultural studies and other forms of critical (Marxist) theory, of which I wish to refer to two main schools, broadly known as political economy and ideology theory. The hamburger, as a theoretical construct, is a different cultural object in each theory.

Political economy sees the hamburger as a commodity, and thus in consuming it (in both senses of the word) John is inserted into one set of social relations that override all others—the economic relations of producer and consumer that are specific to capitalism (*mass* production and consumption): The functions of John's dollar bill are first to produce capital for McDonald's and thus to underwrite corporate capitalism, and second to fix him as a consumer and therefore reproducer of capitalism. The more he eats at McDonald's, the more his needs are commodified, and the more his needs that cannot be met by a commodity are extinguished. As a commodity, the hamburger is economic (it transfers money from the subordinate to capital) and it is political—it represses human and social needs that the capitalist social order cannot turn to a profit and thus produces those who eat it into consumers. McDonald's advertisements work in exactly the same way; they promote those family values that can be met in its restaurants and repress the rest. Fox's television programs are equally commodities: *Married . . . With Children* promotes only those identities and behaviors within the category of "teenager" that it can commodify; it recognizes that teenagers do have some say in who they are and what they do, but it always seeks to produce a commodity by which they can say it. In this view, consumption is a reproduction of capitalism, and the function of the media is to ensure that the whole of social life, particularly in the realm of leisure, is turned into an enormous site of consumption. Through its ubiquity, the commodity extinguishes non-capitalist ways of thinking, behaving, relating, and identifying.

Cultural studies accuses political economy of mistaking the strategy for its effectiveness. Political economy does a fine job in analyzing a central (it would claim *the* central) strategic force in capitalism, and it properly identifies the comprehensiveness, the energy, and the enormous resources with which that strategy is applied. It is limited because it limits its terrain of analysis to the macro level; it cannot recognize social difference because social differences are brought into play beneath its level of analysis.

One of the earliest breaks between cultural studies and political economy centered on the text: Cultural studies wished to understand what sort of texts and what semiotic work within texts were characteristic of capitalism, and to devise ways of critically evaluating texts, that is, of distinguishing between them, not as aesthetic objects but as sociopolitical agents. In defining the text as a cultural commodity, political economy left little room for criticism, evaluation, and differentiation. But cultural studies and political economy do agree that texts are political.

Ideology theory joins in this agreement, but again cultural studies differs. Like political economy, ideology theory, particularly in its Althusserian mode, emphasizes one social force over all others. In ideology theory, subjectivity plays the role that the commodity does in political economy. Capitalism reproduces itself, in this account, in the way that its dominant ideology makes all who live under it into "subjects-in-ideology." This concept implies that the overridingly effective part of our consciousness, of our ways of understanding our identities, social relations, and social experiences, is a totally pervasive ideology. This ideology and its ways of working is *institutionalized* into the "ideological state apparatuses"—the law, education, the media, the political system, and so on—and in the ways they go about their daily operations; it is *internalized* into the consciousness, or rather subconsciousness, of the individuals who live within that society and its institutions. The socially colonized consciousness that results is called *subjectivity*. Subjectivity works in the domain of ideology (that is, of meanings, identities, and social relations) in the same way as does the commodity in that of political economy, and similarly, the totality of its pervasiveness is all too easily elided into the totality of its effectiveness.

Althusser brought psychoanalysis into the ideological picture, and this proved particularly fruitful for a powerful school of feminism. Ideology theory had class domination at its center, but central to psychoanalytic theory was sexuality. The combination of the two enabled feminism to develop a theory and mode of analysis that revealed the pervasiveness of patriarchy through all social domains from the institutional to the subconscious. It also showed how capitalism and patriarchy were inextricably intertwined and interdependent.

Cultural studies found both to be helpful, for both provided incisive methodologies for analyzing texts and social behavior, and both provided convincing theoretical paradigms by which to link texts and behavior with individual subjectivity on the one hand and the social system on the other.

But their totalizing tendency still caused problems for cultural studies: In both ideology and psychoanalytic theories, texts became agents of domination. Cultural studies attempts to be multilevel in its methodology and in particular to explore the interface between the structuring conditions that determine our social experience and the ways of living that people devise within them. What has been called "the turn to Gramsci" identifies the crucial difference between cultural studies and the macro-level, determinist, and reductionist tendencies of some other critical theories.

Stuart Hall is largely responsible for drawing our attention to Gramsci and Volosinov. Both these theorists emphasized struggle—Gramsci in the realm of politics and social life, Volosinov in that of language and meaning. Hegemony theory (Gramsci's contribution) argues that ideology has to work by means of negotiation and struggle to win the consent of the subordinates to the system that subordinates them. It does not impose itself on them, but has to take some account (as little as possible) of subordinate social interests in order to secure temporary consent. Such points of consent are never fixed, but can be shifted in one direction or another according to historical conditions and the conjuncture of forces within them. Hegemony is thus a constant process of unequal struggle between unequal social forces. The social struggle is continued in language and texts as the struggle for meaning. Here texts are neither commodities nor agents of the dominant ideology, but sites of struggle where the subordinate can engage in contested relations with the social interests that attempt to subordinate them. Texts always carry the interests of the dominant classes, for those interests have developed the conditions of production, and the conditions of production are necessarily inscribed in the product. Commodification, capitalist ideology, and patriarchy are powerful forces at work within texts, but describing those forces does not describe the totality of ways in which texts can be put to work.

Although cultural studies differs from other critical theories, it shares with them the most important characteristic of all—the critical. The basic assumption of all critical theories is that the inequalities of capitalism need to be changed and that the world would be a better place if we could change them. There are three interrelated reasons for studying capitalism—to expose its mechanisms of inequality, to motivate people to change them, and to reveal sites and methods by which change might be promoted. The differences among forms of critical theory are ones of tactics, not of strategy. Between critical theory and positivism, however, the differences are strategic.

Audiencing is a concept that can exist only in critical theory aimed exclusively at exposing the structural working of capitalism. Audiencing understands consumption, whether of the text or the hamburger, to be an act of micro-level clandestine production, not of reproduction. This clandestine production is a practice: It produces meanings, not objects (whether a commodity or a text); it exists as process rather than product, and can thus escape our notice. Its low visibility, however, should not be translated into low significance. Indeed, the interests of subordinated social formations may well be served by keeping much of their practice unseen and out of the reach of incorporating tentacles.

Dominant interests are most effectively promoted in social domains on the macro level, that is, that of structure, which is why macro-level social theories are best at analyzing the structural strategies of domination; equally, it is why macro social theories often cannot see beyond them to the level of practice. Subordinate culture is one where practice at the micro level engages with these macro-level forces in particular social conditions. Indeed, one of the key locations where social and semiotic struggles are entered, where the weak engage with the strong, is this interface between practice and structure. This is also where social differences of identity and social relations can be struggled over, where the top-down or bottom-up control over such difference can be contested. It is a crucial site of the hegemonic process, and it can be analyzed only by a theory that grants particularities a greater significance than do macro-level critical theories.

The system by which meanings are circulated in a society resembles a maelstrom rather than an engineering diagram. It is a system of conflicting currents in which the slope of the ground always favors one set, but whose flow can be disrupted and even diverted if the terrain is rocky enough. Audiencing is part of this flow and eddy—sometimes part of the mainstream flow, sometimes part of an upstream eddy. The audience that positivism tries to extract and hold still in the calm of its laboratory or in the fixity of its statistical relations is not an audience that cultural studies recognizes. Equally, cultural studies does not recognize the audience pacified and massified, one whose identities and differences have been homogenized through either commodification or ideology: Audiencing is a variety of practices, an activity, not a social category or a site of a victory.

Appendix: Selected Further Reading

Ang, I. (1985). *Watching Dallas.* London: Routledge.

Ang, I. (1991). *Desperately seeking the audience.* London: Routledge.

Lewis, J. (1991). *The ideological octopus: An exploration of television and its audience.* New York: Routledge.

Lull, J. (1990). *Inside family viewing.* New York: Routledge.

Morley, D. (1988). *Family television.* New York: Routledge.

Morley, D. (1993). *Television, audiences and cultural studies.* London: Routledge.

Press, A. (1991). *Women watching television.* Philadelphia: University of Pennsylvania Press.

Seiter, E., Kreutzner, G., Warth, E. M., & Borchers, H. (Eds.). (1989). *Remote control: Television, audiences and cultural power.* London: Routledge.

References

Bourdieu, P. (1984). *Distinction: A social critique of the judgment of taste.* Cambridge, MA: Harvard University Press.

Dell, C. (1990). Married . . . with children *and the press: Sex, lies and reading strategies.* Paper presented at the annual meeting of the Popular Culture Association, Toronto.

Dominick, J. R., & Rauch, G. E. (1972). The image of women in network TV commercials. *Journal of Broadcasting, 16,* 259-265.

Fiske, J. (1991). For cultural interpretation: A study of the culture of homelessness. *Critical Studies in Mass Communication, 8,* 455-474.

Fiske, J. (1994). *Media matters.* Minneapolis: University of Minnesota Press.

PART III
STRATEGIES OF INQUIRY

Qualitative researchers think historically, interactionally, and structurally. They attempt to identify the varieties of men and women who prevail in a given historical period (Mills, 1959, p. 7). Such scholars seek to examine the major public and private issues and personal troubles that define a particular historical moment. Qualitative researchers self-consciously draw upon their own experiences as a resource in their inquiries. They always think reflectively, historically, and biographically. They seek strategies of empirical inquiry that will allow them to make connections among lived experience, larger social and cultural structures, and the here and now. These connections are forged out the empirical materials that are gathered in any given investigation.

Empirical inquiry, of course, is shaped by paradigm commitments and by the recurring questions that any given paradigm, or interpretive perspective, asks about human experience. Critical theorists, for example examine the material conditions and systems of ideology that reproduce class structures. Ethnic and feminist researchers examine the stereotypes, prejudices, and injustices connected to race, ethnicity, and gender.

The researcher-as-*bricoleur* is always already in the empirical world of experience. Still, this world is confronted, in part, through the lens that the scholar's paradigm, or interpretive perspective, provides. In turn, the world so conceived ratifies the individual's commitment to the paradigm in question. However, as specific investigations are planned and carried out, two issues must be confronted immediately: research design and choice of strategy of inquiry.[1] We take them up in order. Each resolves into a variety of related questions and issues that must also be addressed.

Research Design

The research design, as discussed in Chapter 1 of this volume and as analyzed by Valerie Janesick in Chapter 12, situates the investigator in the empirical world.[2] Four basic questions structure the issue of design: (a) How will the design connect to the paradigm being used? That is, how will empirical materials be informed by and interact with the paradigm in question? (b) Who or what will be studied? (c) What strategies of inquiry will be used? (d) What methods or research tools will be used for collecting and analyzing empirical materials? (These questions are examined in detail in Part IV.)

Paradigm, Perspective, and Metaphor

The positivist, postpositivist, constructionist, and critical paradigms dictate, with varying degrees of freedom, the design of a qualitative research investigation. This can be looked at as a continuum, with rigorous design principles on one end and emergent, less well structured directives on the other. Positivist research designs place a premium on the early identification and development of a research question and a set of hypotheses, choice of a research site, and establishment of sampling strategies, as well as a specification of the research strategies and methods of analysis that will be employed. A research proposal may be written that lays out the stages and phases of the study. These phases may be conceptualized in terms of those outlined by Janice Morse in Chapter 13 (reflection, planning, entry, data collection, withdrawal from the field, analysis, and write-up). This proposal may also include a budget, a review of the relevant literature, a statement concerning protection of human subjects, a copy of consent forms, interview schedules, and a timeline. Positivist designs attempt to anticipate all of the problems that may arise in a qualitative study. Such designs provide rather well defined road maps for the researcher. The scholar working in this tradition hopes to produce a work that finds its place in the literature on the topic being studied.

In contrast, much greater ambiguity is associated with postpositivist and nonpositivist designs—those based, for example, on the constructivist or critical theory paradigms or the ethnic, feminist, or cultural studies perspectives. In studies shaped by these paradigms and perspectives there is less emphasis on formal grant proposals, well-formulated hypotheses, tightly defined sampling frames, structured interview schedules, and predetermined research strategies and methods and forms of analysis. The researcher follows a path of discovery, using as a model qualitative works that have achieved the status of classics in the field. Enchanted, perhaps, by the myth of the Lone Ethnographer, the scholar hopes to produce a work that has the characteristics of a study done by one of the giants of the past (Malinowski, Mead, Bateson, Goffman, Becker, Strauss, Wolcott).

The Dance of Design

Janesick, in Chapter 12, presents a fluid view of the design process. Influenced by Martha Graham, Elliot Eisner, and John Dewey, she approaches the problem of research design from an aesthetic, artistic, and metaphoric perspective. With Dewey and Eisner, she sees research design as a work of art:

as an event, a process, with phases connected to different forms of problematic experience, and their interpretation and representation. Art molds and fashions experience. In its dance form, art becomes a choreographed production, with distinct phases: warming up, exercises and design decisions, cooling down, interpretation, evaluation, and criticism.

Qualitative research design decisions parallel the warm-up, exercise, and cool-down periods of dance. Just as dance mirrors and creates life, so too do research designs adapt, change, and mold the very phenomena they are intended to examine. Janesick fits traditional design questions (research questions, research sites, timelines, research strategies) into this framework. She then addresses the problems involved in pilot studies, interdisciplinary triangulation, and alternative views of validity, reliability, and generalizability, criticizing the "methodolatry" (preoccupation with method) of many traditional, positivist approaches to these topics.

Thus do paradigms shape the interpretive imaginations of qualitative researchers.

Who and What Will Be Studied?

The who and what of qualitative studies involve cases, or instances of phenomena and/or social processes (see Huberman & Miles, Chapter 27, this volume). Three generic approaches may be taken to the question of who or what will be studied. First, a single case, or single process, may be studied, what Robert Stake, in Chapter 14, calls the intrinsic case study. Here the researcher examines in detail a single case or instance of the phenomenon in question—for example, a classroom, or the process of death and dying as given in the single case of a dying patient (see Glaser & Strauss, 1967). Fiske's discussion, in Chapter 11, of his study of the weekly media viewing patterns of a group of college students living in the same house is another example of the single-case, single-process approach. His research design took him to a site and told him what questions to ask and what methods to use in answering them. This is what any research design does.

Second, the researcher may focus on a number of cases, in what Stake calls the collective case approach. These cases are then analyzed in terms of their specific and generic properties. Third, the researcher can examine multiple instances of a process as that process is displayed in a variety of different cases. For instance, Denzin's (1987) study of relapse in the careers of recovering alcoholics examined types of relapses across several different types of recovering careers. This process approach is then grounded or anchored in specific cases.

Research designs vary, of course, depending on the needs of multifocus or single-focus case and process inquiries. Different sampling issues arise in each situation. These needs and issues also vary according to the paradigm being employed.

Every instance of a case or process bears the stamp of the general class of phenomena it belongs to. However, any given instance is likely to be particular and unique. Thus, for example, any given classroom is like all classrooms, but no two classrooms are the same.

For these reasons, many postpositivist, constructionist, and critical theory qualitative researchers employ theoretical or purposive, and not random, sampling models (Glaser & Strauss, 1967, pp. 62-65). They seek out groups, settings, and individuals where (and for whom) the processes being studied are most likely to occur. At the same time, a process of constant comparison (Glaser & Strauss, 1967, pp. 101-115) among groups, concepts, and observations is necessary, as the researcher seeks to develop an understanding that encompasses all instances of the process, or case, under investigation. A focus on negative cases is a key feature of this process.

These sampling and selection issues would be addressed differently by a postmodern ethnographer in the cultural studies tradition. This investigator would be likely to place greater stress on the intensive analysis of a small body of empirical materials (cases and processes), arguing, after Sartre (1981, p. ix) that no individual or case is ever just an individual or a case. He or she must be studied as a single instance of more universal social experiences and social processes. The person, Sartre (1981) states, is "summed up and for this reason universalized by his epoch, he in turn resumes it by reproducing himself in it as a singularity" (p. ix). Thus to study the particular is to study the general. For this reason, any case will necessarily bear the traces of the universal; consequently, there is less interest in the traditional positivist and postpositivist concerns with negative cases, generalizations, and case selection. The researcher assumes that readers will be able, as Robert Stake argues, to generalize subjectively from the case in question to their own personal experiences.

Strategies of Inquiry

The *strategy of inquiry* comprises the skills, assumptions, and practices used by the researcher-as-*bricoleur* when moving from a paradigm and a research design to the collection of empirical materials. Strategies of inquiry connect researchers to specific approaches and methods for collecting and analyzing empirical materials. The case study, for example, relies on interviewing, observing, and document analysis. Research strategies locate paradigms in specific empirical sites and in specific methodological practices—for example, making a case an object of study (Stake, Chapter 14).

We turn now to a brief review of the strategies discussed in this volume. Each is connected to a complex literature with its own history, its own exemplary works, and its own set of preferred ways for putting the strategy into motion. Each strategy also has its own set of problems involving the positivist, postpositivist, and postmodern legacies.

The Case Study

Stake argues that not all case studies are qualitative, although many are. Focusing on those that are attached to the naturalistic, holistic, cultural, and phenomenological paradigms, he contends that the case study is not a methodological choice, but a choice of object to be studied, such as a child or a classroom (for other views of this method, see the essays in Feagin, Orum, & Sjoberg, 1991; for arguments over what a case is, see the chapters in Ragin & Becker, 1992).[3]

Ultimately, the researcher is interested in a process, or a population of cases, not an individual case. Stake, as noted above, identifies several types of case studies (intrinsic, instrumental, collective) and outlines the uses, varieties, and problems (bias, theory, triangulation, telling the story, case selection, ethics) of each. He notes that case researchers routinely provide information on such topics as the nature of the case, its historical background, and its relation to contexts and other cases, as well as on their informants.

Ethnography and Participant Observation

Ethnography is perhaps the most hotly contested site in qualitative research today. Traditionalists (positivists), postpositivists, and postmodernists compete over the definitions of this field, the criteria that are applied to its texts, and the reflexive place of the researcher in the interpretive process (see Bruner, 1993). Many argue that the ethnographic text is a fiction fashioned out of the researcher's engagement with the world studied. Accordingly, such texts can be evaluated only in terms of their ability to create a sense of verisimilitude for the reader. Others set forth rigorous criteria for the production and evaluation of ethnographic texts (see also, in this volume, Altheide & Johnson, Chapter 30; Denzin, Chapter 31; Richardson, Chapter 32; Lincoln & Denzin, Chapter 36).

In Chapter 15, Paul Atkinson and Martyn Hammersley steer a careful course down the middle of these several controversies. They argue that ethnographic methods rely chiefly on participant observation. Such methods are characterized by the collection of relatively unstructured empirical materials, a small number of cases, and a writing and style of analysis that are primarily interpretive, involving descriptions of phenomena. Atkinson and Hammersley sketch the history of this method, from Malinowski to the present. They also outline contemporary problems surrounding ethnography, including the so-called science of ethnography, how ethnographic texts represent lived experience, ethnographic authority, the ethical issues involved in studying the "Other," and the literary turn in recent anthropological work (see also Atkinson, 1992; Hammersley, 1992).

Noting the literary turn in ethnography, Atkinson and Hammersley caution against a wholesale relativism that treats all texts as fiction. In turn, they reject a naive realism that says texts easily represent reality. At the same time, they reject many postpositivist criteria for evaluating texts, arguing that these criteria often fail to make clear distinctions between the means and the procedures for establishing the goals of reliability and validity. Although they do not fully develop it in their contribution to this volume, Atkinson and Hammersley have in other work articulated a subtle realism that sets forth two criteria: validity, which asks how truthful, plausible, and credible an account is; and relevance, or whether an account has relevance for theory or social policy (see, e.g., Hammersley, 1992, pp. 69-78).

Phenomenology, Ethnomethodology, and Interpretive Practice

In Chapter 16, James Holstein and Jaber Gubrium examine that family of qualitative research approaches concerned with reality-constituting interpretive practices (phenomenology, ethnomethodology). These approaches examine how human beings construct and give meaning to their actions in concrete social situations (this chapter is profitably read alongside Schwandt's contribution in Part II of the *Handbook*). Many researchers in this tradition use participant observation and interviewing as ways of studying the interpretive practices persons use in their daily lives. Other scholars, those more firmly rooted in the ethnomethodological tradition, criticize the use of any method as a tool, seeing methods instead as practices that produce verifiable findings for any given paradigm.

Holstein and Gubrium draw attention to the interpretive procedures and practices that give structure and meaning to everyday life. These practices are both the topic of and the resources for qualitative inquiry. All knowledge is always local, situated in a local culture and embedded in organizational sites. This local culture embodies cultural stereotypes and ideologies, including understandings about race, class, and gender, and is part of what Dorothy Smith (1993) calls the ruling apparatuses and relations of ruling of society. Holstein and Gubrium show how Smith's project concretely articulates a critical theory of discourse and social structure. Smith's feminist standpoint epistemology (discussed by Olesen in Part II) connects the ethnomethodological project to critical, feminist, Marxist theory.

The emphasis on interpretive resources, local cultures, and the artful production of meaning connects ethnomethodology, Holstein and Gubrium argue, to deconstructionism and the postmodern context. Such a connection also enlivens the reflexive and reflective turn in qualitative research, calling attention, again and again, to the situated practices that constitute and define this project.

Grounded Theory

In Chapter 17, Anselm Strauss and Juliet Corbin give an overview of the origins, purposes, and uses of grounded theory, which is a general methodology for developing theory that is grounded in data systematically gathered and analyzed. Grounded theory may be the most widely employed interpretive strategy in the social sciences today. It gives the researcher a specific set of steps to follow that are closely aligned with the canons of "good science." Strauss and Corbin compare this methodology with other approaches to qualitative research, noting that a major difference lies in the explicit commitment to theory development and theory verification. (This methodology can be used in both qualitative and quantitative studies.) Basic strategies include theoretical sampling, systematic coding, and guidelines for achieving conceptual density, variation, and integration. A conditional matrix is used to connect and specify the place of micro and macro conditions and consequences in a resulting theory.

Critics have argued that grounded theory has yet to feel the direct influence of the newer, feminist, postmodern arguments, although Strauss and Corbin disagree. Some critics have suggested that the authors remain vague on how verification is accomplished, and many have questioned the status of data and the actor's perspective within the theory. Others have commented on the perceived tendency of researchers to impose their own order on empirical materials (for a review of these criticisms, see Denzin, Chapter 31, this volume; see also Glaser, 1992). As presented by Strauss and Corbin, grounded theory methodology remains firmly entrenched within the modernist, postpositivist tradition.

The Biographical Method

Louis Smith (like Hodder, Chapter 24, and Tuchman, Chapter 19, this volume) reminds us in Chapter 18 that every text is biographical, as he outlines the biographical method, which seeks to report on and document the history of a person's life. All methods are biographical in the sense that they work outward and inward from the personal histories of the researcher and those studied. Smith shows how the biographical method cuts across all social science disciplines, creating its own subject matter as it goes along. Writers, that is, create the lives they write about. This method takes many different forms: objective, historical, artistic, narrative, personal, collective, institutional, fictional. The method is filled with problems when put into use, including the factual status of the materials utilized; how these materials are retrieved, organized, and then used; the conventions that structure the genre itself; and how and where the biographer is located in the biographical text.

Every qualitative study involves the intersection of public and private lives and biographies. Many researchers study problems anchored in their personal biographies. How these biographical materials can become part of the research process is a topic more fully explored in Chapter 26 of this volume, by Clandinin and Connelly.

The Historical Method

In Chapter 19, Gaye Tuchman, echoing Smith, argues that social phenomena must be studied in their historical context. This involves the use of historical documents and written records of the past, including diaries, letters, newspapers, census tract data, novels and other popular literature, and popular culture documents. To understand historical documents one must have an interpretive point of view, and this point of view in turn shapes how one gathers, reads, and analyzes historical materials. Tuchman outlines several interpretive approaches to historical materials (functional, cliometric, Marxist, feminist), showing that a historian's account of the past is a social text that constructs and reconstructs the realities of the past.

Couched within the postmodern perspective, Tuchman argues, with Hodder (Chapter 24), that history is always the story of lived experience. The stories that tell history are always biased; none can ever document "the truth." Together, they present a revealing montage that should speak to us today. But how history speaks reveals the politics of power, for history is not purely referential; it is constructed by the historian. Thus, as Tuchman argues, quoting Joan Scott (1989), written history both reflects and creates relations of power. Today's struggles are, then, about how we shall know the past, and how the past will be constituted in the present. Every historical method thus implies a different way of telling these stories.

Applied and Action Research

Peter Reason, in Chapter 20, moves participatory research and action inquiry, perhaps the most humanistic of the traditions considered in the *Handbook,* up against the postmodern and poststructural perspectives. Work in this tradition attempts to make qualitative research more humanistic, holistic, and relevant to the lives of human beings. This worldview sees human beings as cocreating their reality through participation, experience, and action. This participative worldview is present in three action research traditions: cooperative inquiry, participatory action research, and action inquiry. Reason examines each of these traditions, showing their humanistic commonalities and differences.

It is this humanistic emphasis that Reason sees clashing with the postmodern point of view. He correctly reads these positions as saying that raw, lived experience can be accessed only through text-mediated discourse. However, he then argues that any attempt at experiential knowing is rendered impossible from the start. This carries the implication, he contends, of silencing the voices of people already oppressed.

We share Reason's commitment to lived experience and its expression. However, we disagree with this interpretation of the postmodern position. In destabilizing all privileged positions, the postmodern sensibility creates the spaces for those voices Reason wishes to be heard. Although this is not an infrequent criticism of the postmodern position, we regard it as essentially incorrect. It is our hope that there will be a closer alignment between these two perspectives in the fifth moment of qualitative research. We will discuss this in our concluding chapter.

Clinical Models

Applied and action research has a natural affinity with clinical methods. Each tradition reflects a commitment to change, although clinical research displays a greater concern with diagnosis and treatment than with large-scale social change per se. Historically, the positivist and postpositivist paradigms have dominated clinical, medical research. William Miller and Benjamin Crabtree present a qualitative alternative approach in Chapter 21 that locates clinical research in the tradition of postpositivist applied anthropology. They outline an experience-based, interpretive view of clinical practice, a view that makes the clinical practitioner and the patient coparticipants in the realities of medical treatment. On this point they are quite close to the arguments advanced by Reason in Chapter 20. Their perspective stresses research design; experimental, survey, documentary, and field methods; and the uses of grounded theory, personal experience methods, clinical interviews, and participant observation. They rely heavily on the data management methods and techniques developed by Tesch and by Miles and Huberman, offering an innovative model of rigorous analysis for qualitative materials.

The multimethod approach that Miller and Crabtree advocate represents an attempt to bring about radical change in biomedical culture, which historically has been very quantitative and critical of nonquantitative research. They, like Reason, speak to the politics of qualitative research. In the clinical as in other areas of qualitative research, the multimethod approach is often the only avenue to a more interpretive conception of the research process.

More is going on here in the chapters by Reason and Miller and Crabtree. It involves using research and the social text to effect social change. That is, can social texts, or text-mediated systems of discourse, to use Dorothy Smith's phrase, change social situations? Reason says no, preferring to develop a model that links research directly to political action. Miller and Crabtree want to change consciousness in the medical setting by changing the language and the paradigm that physicians now use. The tools that these authors advocate are powerful agents for social change, and they can be easily supplemented with the discourse, or text-mediated, position. Modifying Smith (1993), it can be argued that qualitative research is discourse and practice. Our business as qualitative researchers is to write the ongoing activities and experiences of people "into the texts of that discourse" (p. 183). With Smith, we understand that there is a place for people outside the text, but that our project is to find a place for them in the texts that are written. Thus the "notion of a standpoint outside discourse holds a place in discourse for she who has not yet spoken, not yet declared herself, not yet disinterred her buried life" (p. 183).

There are matters that need to be written that discourse has not yet addressed, matters such as those discussed by Olesen, Reason, and Miller and Crabtree in this volume. But once they are heard, and then written, voices that were previously silenced can speak as agents of social change and personal destiny. In such texts research is connected to political action, systems of language and meaning are changed, and paradigms are challenged. How to hear these voices is the topic of Part IV of the *Handbook*. In the meantime, listen to the voices in Part III.

Notes

1. We have included two chapters on design in this section. Janice Morse presents a treatment of this topic that is directly fitted to the needs of those researchers who write grant proposals for traditional funding agencies. Valerie Janesick presents another version of the design process that is less geared to such audiences.

2. Mitch Allen's comments have significantly shaped our treatment of the relationship between paradigms and research designs.

3. Ragin (1992, p. 9) offers a framework for distinguishing four fundamentally different approaches to case-based research. This framework involves two dichotomies: Is the case considered to be a theoretical or empirical unit? and Is it an example of general or specific phenomena? Thus a case as an empirical unit can be found (invisible communities) or treated as an object, or ongoing event (a family), whereas a case as a theoretical unit can be constructed (modern tyranny) or treated as a convention (gang).

References

Atkinson, P. (1992). *Understanding ethnographic texts.* Newbury Park, CA: Sage.

Bruner, E. M. (1993). Introduction: The ethnographic self and the personal self. In P. Benson (Ed.), *Anthropology and literature* (pp. 1-26). Urbana: University of Illinois Press.

Denzin, N. K. (1987). *The recovering alcoholic.* Newbury Park, CA: Sage.

Feagin, J. R., Orum, A. M., & Sjoberg, G. (1991). *A case for the case study.* Chapel Hill: University of North Carolina Press.

Glaser, B. G. (1992). *Basics of grounded theory.* Mill Valley, CA: Sociology Press.

Glaser, B. G., & Strauss, A. L. (1967). *The discovery of grounded theory: Strategies for qualitative research.* Chicago: Aldine.

Hammersley, M. (1992). *What's wrong with ethnography?* London: Routledge.

Mills, C. W. (1959). *The sociological imagination.* New York: Oxford University Press.

Ragin, C. C. (1992). Introduction: Cases of "What is a case?" In C. C. Ragin & H. S. Becker (Eds.), *What is a case?* New York: Cambridge University Press.

Ragin, C. C., & Becker, H. S. (Eds.). (1992). *What is a case?* New York: Cambridge University Press.

Sartre, J.-P. (1981). *The family idiot: Gustave Flaubert, 1821-1857* (Vol. 1). Chicago: University of Chicago Press.

Smith, D. E. (1993). High noon in Textland: A critique of Clough. *Sociological Quarterly, 34,* 183-192.

12

The Dance of Qualitative Research Design

Metaphor, Methodolatry, and Meaning

VALERIE J. JANESICK

Every dance is to some greater or lesser extent a kind of fever chart, a graph of the heart.

—Martha Graham

WHEN Martha Graham, the dance world's at once most famous and infamous dancer and dance maker, was asked to describe dance, she said these words to capture the essence of dance. In this chapter, I would like to discuss the essence of qualitative research design. I have selected the metaphor of dance for two reasons. First, dance is the art form to which I am most devoted, having been a dancer and choreographer for more than 25 years. I began dance classes as a child. My mother was a dancer in USO shows, and she had a strong influence on me. I became a choreographer as a natural evolution, following in the footsteps of many of my adored and influential teachers. In dance, a vibrant mentor-protégé system is in place. I have choreographed modern dance, ballet, ethnic and folk dances, and dances for musicals for the Ann Arbor Civic Theater and for various university and regional dance companies. Because I was a teacher, I also did choreography for various school districts in Michigan and Ohio. I directed my own dance company, in Ann Arbor, East Lansing, and Bowling Green, Ohio. In Ohio, I received grants, along with the Bowling Green University Dancers, from the Ohio Council for the Arts, to bring dance in the schools' programs into Ohio. I spent summers in New York City, studying technique at the schools of Martha Graham, Merce Cunningham, Alvin Ailey, and Erick Hawkins.[1] While studying at Michigan State University, at the Institute for Research on Teaching, I taught all levels of modern dance, choreography, dance history, and anatomy for the dancers at Lansing Community College in addition to my research internship. In fact, it was this simultaneous experience in dance and research studies that prepared me for my academic career as an ethnographic researcher and teacher of qualitative research methods.

A second reason I have selected the metaphor of dance is simply because of its power. Metaphor in general creeps up on you and surprises. It defies the boilerplate approach to a topic. I can only wholeheartedly agree with Eisner (1991) when he discusses metaphor:

> What is ironic is that in the professional socialization of educational researchers, the use of metaphor is regarded as a sign of imprecision; yet, for making public the ineffable, nothing is more precise than the artistic use of language. Metaphoric precision is the central vehicle for revealing the qualitative aspects of life. (p. 227)

Consequently, I invite the reader to embrace this metaphor of dance, often called the mother of the arts. Dance, as a true art form, is a useful reference point for recalling Dewey's (1934/1958) notion that there is no work of art apart from human experience. For Dewey, the work of art is an event. He sees art as engaging and developing experience with a sense of meaning. Even in the art world, meaning can be lost in the event of objectification of the art. For example, the dance world is filled with wheelers and dealers, aestheticians, foot doctors, managers, advertisers, promoters, and charming eccentrics. At any intersection of the work of art with some individuals, the work of art can be decontextualized and objectified. But it is in the Deweyan sense that I speak of dance. Because dance is about lived experience, it seems to me the perfect metaphor for qualitative research design.

In addition, the qualitative researcher is very much like an artist at various stages in the design process, in terms of situating and recontextualizing the research project within the shared experience of the researcher and the participants in the study. Dewey sees art as the bridge between the experience of individuals and the community. In other words, art forces us to think about how human beings are related to each other in their respective worlds. How appropriate to view dance as an expressively dynamic art form that connects the cultural meanings of dancers, choreographer, and community. Like Dewey (1934/1958), who notes that the actual work of art is what the product does with and in experience, the qualitative researcher, as designer of a project, recognizes the potential of design. The design serves as a foundation for the understanding of the participants' worlds and the meaning of shared experience between the researcher and participants in a given social context. Dance is an interpretive art form, and I see qualitative research design as interpretive as well.

Qualitative Research Design as Choreography

All dances make a statement and begin with the question, What do I want to say in this dance? In much the same way, the qualitative researcher begins with a similar question: What do I want to know in this study? This is a critical beginning point. Regardless of point of view, and quite often because of our point of view, we construct and frame a question for inquiry. After this question is clear, we select the most appropriate methodology to proceed with the research project. I am always surprised by doctoral students and colleagues who forthrightly state that they wish to do a qualitative study without any question in mind. They ask about books and references to learn all the steps. They are taken aback when I give them a reading list, because over the past 25 years or so, in education alone, there has been published quite an impressive and lengthy list of methods texts and articles in journals with illustrative studies using qualitative methods. The next question becomes, Yes, but which one tells me exactly what to do, step by step? You see the point. They are not ready to design qualitative projects, for they have no research question from which to choose appropriate methods. Some go even further, saying, I have pages of data from teachers, how do I make this into a qualitative study? Again, there is no question to guide the inquiry. It is difficult to take such an approach seriously.

Qualitative research design begins with a question. Of course, qualitative researchers design a study with real individuals in mind, and with the intent of living in that social setting over time. They study a social setting to understand the meaning of participants' lives in the participants' own terms. I mention this to contrast it to the quantitative paradigm, which is perfectly comfortable with aggregating large numbers of people without communicating with them face to face. So the questions of the qualitative researcher are quite different from those of the quantitative researcher. Elsewhere in the literature, the reader may find information on the kinds of questions suited to qualitative methods (Erickson, 1986; Janesick, 1983). In general, questions that are suited to qualitative inquiry have long been the questions of many curriculum researchers and theorists. For example:

1. questions concerning the quality of a given curriculum, innovation, or program
2. questions regarding meaning or interpretation about some component of curriculum
3. questions that relate to curriculum in terms of its sociolinguistic aspects
4. questions related to the whole system, as in a classroom, school, or school district
5. questions regarding the political, economic, or sociopsychological aspects of schooling
6. questions regarding the hidden curriculum
7. questions pertaining to the social context of schooling
8. questions pertaining to teachers' implicit theories about teaching and curriculum

This list is not meant to be exhaustive; it serves only to illustrate the basic areas where research has been completed in the field of education and has employed qualitative techniques because of, among other things, the suitability of the technique and the question.

Just as the dancer begins with a warm-up of the body, follows through with floor exercises, and then moves to a cool-down period, I like to think of qualitative design as made up of three stages. First there is the warm-up stage, or design decisions made at the beginning of the study; second is the total workout stage, during which design decisions are made throughout the study; and third is the cool-down stage, when design decisions are made at the end of the study. Just as the dancer relies on the spine for the power and coherence of the dance, so the qualitative researcher relies on the design of the study. Both are elastic. Like the dancer who finds her center from the base of the spine and the connection between the spine and the body, the qualitative researcher is centered by a series of design decisions. A dancer who is centered may tilt forward and backward and from side to side, yet always returns to the center, the core of the dancer's strength. If one thinks of the design of the study as the spine and the base of the spine as the beginning of the warm-up in dance, the beginning decisions in a study are very much like the lower-spine warm-up, the beginning warm-up for the dancer.

Warming Up: Design Decisions at the Beginning of the Study

The first set of design decisions have to do with what is studied, under what circumstances, for what duration of time, and with whom. I always start with a question. For example, when I studied deaf culture in Washington, D.C., over a four-year period (Janesick, 1990), my basic question was, How do some deaf adults manage to succeed academically and in the workplace given the stigma of deafness in our society? This basic question informed all my observations and interviews, and led me to use focus groups and oral history techniques later in the study. Both the focus groups and oral histories evolved after I came to know the perspectives on deafness of the twelve individuals in my study. I then used theoretical sampling techniques to select three individuals to participate in an oral history component of the study.[2] I use this example to illustrate the elasticity of qualitative design. Focus groups allowed me to moderate and observe interactions among three of my participants on their perspectives on deafness, something I could not have planned in the first days in the field. Neither could I have realized at the beginning of the study the value of incorporating these techniques. These techniques allowed me to capture a richer interpretation of participants' perspectives on deafness.

Simultaneous with the question that guides the study, the qualitative researcher needs to select a site according to some rationale. Access and entry are sensitive components in qualitative research, and the researcher must establish trust, rapport, and authentic communication patterns with participants. By establishing trust and rapport at the beginning of the study, the researcher is better able to capture the nuance and meaning of each participant's life from the participant's point of view. This also ensures that participants will be more willing to share everything, warts and all, with the researcher. Maintaining trust and rapport continues through the length of the study and long after, in fact. Yet it must begin at the beginning. It would be difficult to imagine establishing trust, say, six months into a study. Any of us who have done fieldwork know how critical initial interactions in the field are as a precursor to establishing trust and rapport.

Once the researcher has a question, a site, a participant or a number of participants, and a reasonable time period to undertake the study, he or she needs to decide on the most appropriate data collection strategies suited to the study. The selection of these strategies is intimately connected to how the researcher views the purpose of the work, that is, how to understand the social setting under study. Most often, qualitative researchers use some combination of participant observation, interviews, and document analysis. The literature on approaches and strategies used in qualitative studies is extensive (e.g., Bogdan & Biklen, 1992; Denzin, 1989; Goetz & LeCompte, 1984; LeCompte, Millroy, & Priessle, 1992; Lincoln & Guba, 1985; Spradley, 1979, 1980; Strauss & Corbin, 1990). For example, in education over the past three decades, case study methods, oral history, including narrative and life history approaches, grounded theory, literary criticism, and ethnographic approaches to research have been discovered and used for their fit with questions in education and human services. This makes sense, as these are the very approaches that allow researchers to deal with individuals.

Summary

The warm-up period, or the period of making decisions at the beginning of the study, includes decisions regarding the following:

1. the questions that guide the study
2. selection of a site and participants

3. access and entry to the site and agreements with participants
4. timeline for the study
5. selection of appropriate research strategies, which may include some of the following (this list is not meant to be inclusive of all possibilities)
   a. ethnography
   b. life history
   c. oral history
   d. ethnomethodology
   e. case study
   f. participant observation
   g. field research or field study
   h. naturalistic study
   i. phenomenological study
   j. ecological descriptive study
   k. descriptive study
   l. symbolic interactionist study
   m. microethnography
   n. interpretive research
   o. action research
   p. narrative research
   q. historiography
   r. literary criticism
6. the place of theory in the study
7. identification of the researcher's own biases and ideology
8. identification of appropriate informed consent procedures and willingness to deal with ethical issues as they present themselves

In terms of the last two items, I would like to point out that qualitative researchers accept the fact that research is ideologically driven. There is no value-free or bias-free design. The qualitative researcher early on identifies his or her biases and articulates the ideology or conceptual frame for the study. By identifying one's biases, one can see easily where the questions that guide the study are crafted. This is a big difference among paradigms. As we try to make sense of our social world and give meaning to what we do as researchers, we continually raise awareness of our own biases. There is no attempt to pretend that research is value free. Likewise, qualitative researchers, because they deal with individual persons face-to-face on a daily basis, are attuned to making decisions regarding ethical concerns, because this is part of life in the field. From the beginning moments of informed consent decisions, to other ethical decisions in the field, to the completion of the study, qualitative researchers need to allow for the possibilities of recurring ethical dilemmas and problems.

In addition to the decisions made at the beginning of the study, it is helpful to consider some characteristics of qualitative design. Again, the following list is not meant to be exhaustive; it is offered merely as a heuristic tool.

1. Qualitative design is holistic. It looks at the larger picture, the whole picture, and begins with a search for understanding of the whole.
2. Qualitative design looks at relationships within a system or culture.
3. Qualitative design refers to the personal, face-to-face, and immediate.
4. Qualitative design is focused on understanding a given social setting, not necessarily on making predictions about that setting.
5. Qualitative design demands that the researcher stay in the setting over time.
6. Qualitative design demands time in analysis equal to the time in the field.
7. Qualitative design demands that the researcher develop a model of what occurred in the social setting.
8. Qualitative design requires the researcher to become the research instrument. This means the researcher must have the ability to observe behavior and must sharpen the skills necessary for observation and face-to-face interview.
9. Qualitative design incorporates informed consent decisions and is responsive to ethical concerns.
10. Qualitative design incorporates room for description of the role of the researcher as well as description of the researcher's own biases and ideological preference.
11. Qualitative design requires ongoing analyses of the data.

Other chapters in this volume discuss many of the above characteristics in depth, and the reader will benefit from those discussions. Once the researcher begins the study and is in the field, another set of decision points emerges.

Exercises: The Pilot Study and Ongoing Design Decisions

Before devoting oneself to the arduous and significant time commitment of a qualitative study, it is a good idea to do a pilot study. Preinterviews with selected key participants and a brief period of observation and document review can assist the researcher in a number of ways. The pilot study allows the researcher to focus on particular areas that may have been unclear previously. In addition, pilot interviews may be used to test certain questions. Still further, this initial time frame allows the researcher to begin to develop and solidify rapport with participants as well as to establish effective communication patterns. By including some time for the review of records and documents, the researcher may uncover some insight into the shape of the study that previously was not apparent. Again to use an example from my study on deaf culture, prior to my interviews with participants, I spent time in the Gallaudet University archives, reading journals, looking at newspaper clippings, and viewing videotapes, all of which were helpful for my understanding of the historical influences that led to the "Deaf President Now" movement.[3] I saw, in retrospect, common themes and categories in the subsequent interview transcripts that made perfect sense given a series of historical situations in a 125-year period prior to the selection of Gallaudet University's first deaf president. Thus the time invested in a pilot study can be valuable and enriching for later phases in the study.

Other decisions made during the study usually concern effective use of time, participants' issues, and researcher issues. Because working in the field is unpredictable a good deal of the time, the qualitative researcher must be ready to adjust schedules, to be flexible about interview times and about adding or subtracting observations or interviews, to replace participants in the event of trauma or tragedy, and even to rearrange terms of the original agreement. My own experiences in conducting long-term ethnographic studies have led me to refine and readjust the design constantly as I proceed through the study, especially at this phase. Being totally immersed in the immediate and local actions and statements of belief of participants, the researcher must be ready to deal with the substantive focus of the study and with the researcher's own presuppositions. Simply observing and interviewing does not ensure that the research is qualitative, for the qualitative researcher must also interpret the beliefs and behaviors of participants. In a sense, while in the field, the researcher is constantly immersed in a combination of deliberate decisions about hypotheses generated and tested on the one hand and intuitive reactions on the other. The researcher finds in the vast literature of sociology, anthropology, and education common rules of thumb on which most researchers agree:

1. Look for the meaning and perspectives of the participants in the study.
2. Look for relationships regarding the structure, occurrence, and distribution of events over time.
3. Look for points of tension: What does not fit? What are the conflicting points of evidence in the case?

As Erickson (1986) so eloquently reminds us, the use of qualitative techniques does not necessarily mean that the research being conducted is qualitative. What makes the research qualitative is a matter of "substantive focus and intent." Erickson uses the example of narrative description. A quantitative researcher may use this technique and come up with a product that is a very different product from that arrived at by a qualitative researcher in the same setting:

> It is important to emphasize at the outset that the use of continuous narrative description as a technique—what can less formally be called "writing like crazy"—does not necessarily mean that the research being conducted is interpretive or qualitative, in a fundamental sense. What makes such work interpretive or qualitative is a matter of substantive focus and intent, rather than of procedure in data collection, that is, a research *technique* does not constitute a research *method.* The technique of continuous narrative description can be used by researchers with a positivist and behaviorist orientation that deliberately excludes from research interest the immediate meanings of actions from the actors' point of view. Continuous narrative description can also be used by researchers with a nonpositivist, interpretive orientation, in which the immediate (often intuitive) meanings of actions to the actors involved are of central interest. The presuppositions and conclusions of these two types of research are very different, and the content of the narrative description that is written differs as well. If two observers with these differing orientations were placed in the same spot to observe what was ostensibly the "same" behavior performed by the "same" individuals, the observers would write substantively differing accounts of what had happened, choosing differing kinds of verbs, nouns, adverbs, and adjectives to characterize the actions that were described. (pp. 119-120)

Furthermore, he argues that the state of the art in research on teaching, for example, is one of rival theories, rival research programs, and rival uses of techniques. The qualitative researcher needs to come to grips with this in a practical sense at some point during the research project. Erickson (1986) puts it this way:

> The current conflict in research on teaching is not one of competing paradigms, I would argue, not because the competing views do not differ ontologically, but simply because as Lakatos (1978) and others have argued for the natural sciences—and especially for the social sciences—paradigms do not actually compete in scientific discourse. Old paradigms are rarely replaced by falsification. Rather the older and the newer paradigms tend to coexist, as in the survival of Newtonian physics, which can be used for some purposes, despite the competition of the Einsteinian physics, which for other purposes has superseded it. Especially in the social sciences, paradigms don't die; they develop varicose veins and get fitted with cardiac pacemakers. The perspective of standard research on teaching and the interpretive perspective are indeed rival theories—rival research programs—even if it is unlikely that the latter will totally supersede the former. (p. 120)

It is much the same in the dance world. Although the Graham technique represented a paradigm shift from ballet into modern dance, elements of ballet are still used within the idiom of modern dance. Furthermore, modern dance has embraced multiple competing and rival techniques, such as those of Cunningham and Tharp. Basically, the qualitative researcher as designer of the research project will be making decisions at all stages of the project. Warm-up decisions made before entering the field constitute the first set of decisions. Exercises, the second stage of decisions, occur within the period of data collection in the field. The third stage of design decisions consists of those made at the end of the study, after leaving the field—what I call cooling down.

Cooling Down: Design Decisions Made at the End of the Study

Design decisions at the end of the study are similar to the cool-down portion of the dance movement. The researcher must decide when to leave the field setting, often an emotional and traumatic event because of the close rapport that can develop during the course of a study. I usually ease out of the setting much as I would cool down after the exercise of dance. For example, in my study of a teacher's classroom perspective (Janesick, 1982), after observing on a daily basis for six months, I started staggering my observations and interviews in the seventh month of fieldwork from five days per week to three days to once per week and then to meetings with the teacher to go over interview transcripts at his convenience.

Following the process of leaving the field, final data analysis can begin. Of course, the qualitative researcher has been developing categories from the data through constant comparative analysis over the entire time frame of the study.[4] The process of reduction of data into a manageable model constitutes an end goal of qualitative research design. There is a continual reassessment and refining of concepts as the fieldwork proceeds. The researcher purposely seeks negative examples because they may disprove some initial hypothetical constructs. As the analysis proceeds, the researcher develops working models that explain the behavior under study. As the analysis continues, the researcher can identify relationships that connect portions of the description with the explanations offered in the working models. The researcher attempts to determine the significance of the various elements in the working models and to verify these by checking through field notes, interview transcripts, and documents.

Following the construction of a model, the next component of the process is the presentation of the data in narrative form supported by evidence from the statements and behaviors recorded in the notes and interviews. In other words, the researcher makes empirical assertions supported by direct quotations from notes and interviews. The researcher also needs to provide some interpretive commentary framing the key findings in the study. The theoretical discussion should be traceable in the data. In addition, the researcher should describe his or her own role thoroughly, so that the reader understands the relationship between the researcher and participants. This allows the researcher to confront the major assertions in the study with credibility while surveying the full range of evidence. Because qualitative work recognizes early on in the study the perspective of the researcher as it evolves through the study, the description of the role of the researcher is a critical component in the writing of the report of the study.

Triangulation

The researcher often relies on triangulation, or the use of several kinds of methods or data. Denzin (1978) identifies four basic types of triangulation:

1. *data triangulation:* the use of a variety of data sources in a study

2. *investigator triangulation:* the use of several different researchers or evaluators
3. *theory triangulation:* the use of multiple perspectives to interpret a single set of data
4. *methodological triangulation:* the use of multiple methods to study a single problem

I would like to add a fifth type to this list: *interdisciplinary triangulation.* Interdisciplinary triangulation will help to lift us up out of the dominant trench of psychology. In education, at least, psychology has dominated the discourse altogether. Not only is the dominance seen in the quantitative arena, but in fact a good deal of the discourse in qualitative research is heavily influenced by underlying psychometric views of the world. The prevailing myths about aggregating numbers and, more tragically, aggregating individuals into sets of numbers have moved us away from our understanding of lived experience. By using other disciplines, such as art, sociology, history, dance, architecture, and anthropology to inform our research processes, we may broaden our understanding of method and substance.

Triangulation is meant to be a heuristic tool for the researcher. Although the term was originally used by land surveyors to describe the use of three points to locate oneself at particular intersections, it is not to be taken literally, as a student of mine once asked, "Does triangulation mean that you can only use three types of methods or perspectives?" Clearly this limit does not apply in qualitative research. For further elaboration of Denzin's construct, see Patton's (1990) adaptation of it for the evaluation researcher.

Major Considerations in Writing the Narrative

The qualitative researcher uses inductive analysis, which means that categories, themes, and patterns come from the data. The categories that emerge from field notes, documents, and interviews are not imposed prior to data collection. Early on, the researcher will develop a system of coding and categorizing the data. There is no one best system for analysis. The researcher may follow rigorous guidelines described in the literature (see Eisner, 1991; Fetterman, 1989; Goetz & LeCompte, 1984; Lincoln & Guba, 1985; Miles & Huberman, 1984; Patton, 1990), but the ultimate decisions about the narrative reside with the researcher. Like the choreographer, the researcher must find the most effective way to tell the story, to convince the audience. Staying close to the data is the most powerful means of telling the story, just as in dance the story is told through the body itself. As in the quantitative arena, the purpose of conducting a qualitative study is to produce findings. The methods and strategies used are not ends in themselves. There is a danger in becoming so taken up with methods that the substantive findings are obscured.

Methodolatry

I use the term *methodolatry,* a combination of *method* and *idolatry,* to describe a preoccupation with selecting and defending methods to the exclusion of the actual substance of the story being told. Methodolatry is the slavish attachment and devotion to method that so often overtakes the discourse in the education and human services fields. In my lifetime I have witnessed an almost constant obsession with the trinity of validity, reliability, and generalizability. It is always tempting to become overinvolved with method and, in so doing, separate experience from knowing. Methodolatry is another way to move away from understanding the actual experience of participants in the research project. In the final stage of writing up the project, it is probably wise to avoid being overly preoccupied with method. In other words, the qualitative researcher should immediately focus on the substance of the findings. Qualitative research depends on the presentation of solid descriptive data, so that the researcher leads the reader to an understand of the meaning of the experience under study.

In classic terms, sociologists and anthropologists have shown us that finding categories and the relationships and patterns between and among categories leads to completeness in the narrative. Spradley (1980) suggests searching for cultural themes or domains. Denzin (1989) follows Husserl's earlier conception of bracketing, which is to hold the phenomenon up to serious inspection, and suggests the following steps:

1. Locate within the personal experience, or self-story, key phrases and statements that speak directly to the phenomenon in question.
2. Interpret the meanings of these phrases as an informed reader.
3. Obtain the participants' interpretation of these findings, if possible.
4. Inspect these meanings for what they reveal about the essential, recurring features of the phenomenon being studied.
5. Offer a tentative statement or definition of the phenomenon in terms of the essential recurring features identified in Step 4.

So, in the process of bracketing, the researcher has the opportunity to treat the data in all its forms equally. Then the researcher may categorize, group, and cluster the data in order to interpret them. The researcher uses constant comparative analysis to look for statements and indices of behavior that occur over time and in a variety of periods during the study. In addition, bracketing allows the researcher to find points of tension and conflict and what does not fit. After total immersion in the setting, the researcher requires time for analysis and contemplation of the data. By allowing sufficient time to go over the data carefully, the researcher opens up possibilities for uncovering the meaning in participants' lives. I have found Moustakis (1990) helpful in providing a heuristic approach here. He offers room to use inductive analysis through five phases. First, immersion in the setting starts the inductive process. Second, the incubation process allows for thinking, becoming aware of nuance and meaning in the setting, and capturing intuitive insights, to achieve understanding. Third, there is a phase of illumination that allows for expanding awareness. Fourth, and most understandably, there is a phase of explication that includes description and explanation to capture the experience of individuals in the study. Finally, creative synthesis enables one to bring together as a whole the individual's story, including the meaning of the lived experience.

The purposes of these disciplined approaches to analysis are of course to describe and to explain the essence of experience and meaning in participants' lives. Patton (1990) suggests a balance between description and interpretation. Denzin (1989) elaborates further by suggesting that thick description makes thick interpretation possible. Endless description is not useful if the researcher is to present a powerful narrative. Analysis and interpretation effectively balance description.

The Issue of Credibility

The qualitative research literature contains many valuable and useful treatments of the issue of credibility (see, e.g., Eisner, 1991; Lincoln & Guba, 1985; Patton, 1990). Basically, qualitative researchers have been patiently responding to questions, usually formulated from a psychometric perspective. As Patton (1990) puts it, a credible qualitative study addresses three questions:

1. What techniques and methods were used to ensure the integrity, validity, and accuracy of the findings?
2. What does the researcher bring to the study in terms of experience and qualifications?
3. What assumptions undergird the study?

Qualitative researchers may find these questions a useful guide in writing up the narrative.

Validity, Generalizability, and Reliability

In responding to the issues of validity, generalizability, and reliability, I rely on experience and the literature. Description of persons, places, and events has been the cornerstone of qualitative research. I believe it will remain the cornerstone, because this is the qualitative researcher's reason for being. What has happened recently, as Wolcott (1990) reminds us, is that the term *validity,* which is overspecified in one domain, has become confusing because it is reassigned to another. *Validity* in the quantitative arena has a set of technical microdefinitions of which the reader is most likely well aware. Validity in qualitative research has to do with description and explanation, and whether or not a given explanation fits a given description. In other words, is the explanation credible?

By applying the suggestions of Lincoln and Guba (1985) and others, we may cross-check our work through member checks and audit trails. As a rule, in writing up the narrative, the qualitative researcher must decide what form the member check will take. For example, quite often, participants in a study move, leave the area, or request that they omit being part of the member check. The researcher needs to find a way to allow for the participants to review the material one way or another. For years, anthropologists and sociologists have incorporated a kind of member check by having an outsider read their field notes and interview transcripts. This current variation is a good one, for education research is always public, open to the public, and in many cases funded under federal mandates. Implicit in the member check directive, however, is the psychometric assumption that the trinity of validity, generalizability, and reliability, all terms from the quantitative paradigm, are to be adhered to in research. I think it is time to question the trinity.

Wolcott (1990) provides a provocative discussion about seeking and rejecting validity. He argues for understanding the absurdity of validity by developing a case for no single "correct" interpretation. Similarly, Donmoyer (1990) makes an even stronger case for rejecting traditional notions of generalizability for those researchers in education and human services who are concerned with individuals and the meaning in their lives. He argues that traditional ways of thinking about generalizability are inadequate. He does not eschew generalizability altogether, however. Bureaucrats and policy makers, for example, seem to prefer aggregated numbers about certain social conditions, and for their needs generalizability seems to make sense. On the other hand, for those of us interested in questions of meaning and interpretation in individual cases, the kind of research done in education and human services, traditional thinking about generalizability falls short. The traditional view of generalizability limits the ability of the researcher to reconceptualize the role of social science in education and human services. In addition, the whole history of case study research in anthropology, education, sociology, and history stands solidly on its merits. In fact, the value of the case study is its uniqueness; consequently, reliability in the traditional sense of replicability is pointless here. I hope that we can move beyond discussions of this trinity of psychometrica and get on with the discussion of powerful statements from carefully done, rigorous long-term studies that uncover the meanings of events in individuals' lives.

Somehow we have lost the human and passionate element of research. Becoming immersed in a study requires passion: passion for people, passion for communication, and passion for understanding people. This is the contribution of qualitative research, and it can only enhance educational and human services practice. For too long we have allowed psychometrics to rule our research and thus to decontextualize individuals. In depersonalizing the most personal of social events, education, we have lost our way. Now it is time to return to a discourse on the personal, on what it means to be alive.

Meaning and the Dance Metaphor

Isn't it remarkable that the entire history of dance has been characterized by a deep division? What might we learn from this? All arts and sciences draw upon tradition, and a first step in understanding them is to understand their past. Dance and choreography are tied to the past in a peculiar way. Dance and choreography derive from one element of society, the courts of kings and queens. Dance, a type of storytelling, has always fulfilled a basic need in society, expressing happiness, sadness, fears, joy, and wishes. As societies developed and organized, dividing into tribes, nations, and classes, the function of dance became much more complicated. Its language, steps, and movements no longer represented primitive classless tribes. Dance became divided.

One form of this division survives as folk dance from the ancient primitive thread of communal dances. The other emerged from society's ruling class, the court, center of social power. It was not long before ballet became an official lexicon of the court and the court dances a definite class and status symbol. It was not until this century that the ruling influence in dance, ballet, was challenged by a determined, frail woman from Vermont, Martha Graham. The field today in dance is well into a postmodern era, mostly, but not exclusively, owing to Merce Cunningham's artistry. Essentially, Cunningham made the following claims (Banes, 1980, p. 6):

1. Any movement can be material for dance.
2. Any procedure can be valid.
3. Any part or parts of the body can be used, subject to nature's limitation.
4. Music, costume, lighting, and dancing have their own separate logics and identities.
5. Any dancer in a company may be a soloist.
6. Any space may be danced in.
7. Dancing can be about anything, but it is fundamentally and primarily about the human body and its movements, beginning with walking.

Cunningham's dances decentralize space and stretch out time. They do away with what is familiar and easy. They are unpredictable. They sometimes do not even turn out as planned. He may use chance methods, such as tossing coins (Banes, 1980, points out that although this was to be random, the dancers' movements were determined by this chance event). Chance subverts habits and allows for new combinations and interpretations. Cunningham truly makes the word *radical,* returning to the root, come alive. He preserves continuity and a physical logic to his search for meaning in movement and the desire to tell a story. In thinking about dance as a metaphor for qualitative research design, the meaning for me lies in the fact that the substance of dance is the familiar; walking, running, any movement of the body. The qualitative researcher is like the dancer, then, in seeking to describe, explain, and make understandable the familiar in a contextual, personal, and passionate way. As Goethe has told us, "The hardest thing to see is what is in front of your eyes."

Summary and Afterthoughts

The qualitative researcher's design decisions can be thought of as similar to the dancer's three stages of warm-up, exercises, and cool-down. The qualitative researcher makes a series of decisions at the beginning, middle, and end of the study. Qualitative research design has an elastic quality, much like the elasticity of the dancer's spine. Just as dance mirrors and adapts to life, qualitative design is adapted, changed, and redesigned as the study proceeds, because of the social realities of doing research among and with the living. The qualitative researcher focuses on description and explanation, and all design decisions ultimately relate to these acts. Built into qualitative research design is a system of checks and balances that includes staying in a setting over time and capturing and interpreting the meaning in individuals' lives. By staying in a setting over time, the researcher has the opportunity to use data triangulation, investigator triangulation, theory triangulation, methodological triangulation, and interdisciplinary triangulation. This allows for multiple views of framing the problem, selecting research strategies, and extending discourse across several fields of study. This is exactly the opposite of the quantitative approach, which relies on one mind-set, the psychometric, and which prefers to aggregate numbers that are one or more steps removed from social reality. The qualitative researcher is uncomfortable with methodolatry and prefers to capture the lived experience of participants in order to understand their meaning perspectives. Finally, the qualitative researcher is like the choreographer, who creates a dance to make a statement. For the researcher, the story told is the dance in all its complexity, context, originality, and passion.

Notes

1. I went to New York because it is the center of the dance world and all levels and varieties of technique are taught in the various dance schools there. I was originally trained in Graham technique, so I naturally went to that school first. In the first day, first class, I was totally bored. I had outgrown the vocabulary of the method and asked if anyone was questioning this approach. Another student in class told me that Erick Hawkins and Merce Cunningham had resisted, rebelled, and broken away from Graham and started their own schools. I found an opening at the Hawkins school and from that point my life was changed. From Erick Hawkins I learned that creativity and the body/mind are one, and I was introduced to Eastern thought. There is no need to separate one's creative self from living. He and all his teachers were inspiring and brilliant teachers. I decided that I would perfect both the art and craft of teaching as a dance instructor and an arts educator. From Merce Cunningham and the teachers at Westbeth, I learned to trust the body and to draw upon lived experience in my work as a choreographer. For Cunningham, dance is a chance encounter among movement, sound, and light through space. The viewer makes of it what the viewer will. Cunningham pursues the process of dance Zen-like. He has been called the anarchist of modern dance as well as the beginning point of the postmodern movement in dance. All dances are grounded in some experience, and all stories that are told about that experience rely on the body, that is, the research instrument. The body is the instrument through which life is lived. In dance, the body cannot deny the impulse to express the lived experience. It is virtually impossible for the body to tell a lie or to cover up the truth in the dance. The downside of this, of course, is that the body is bounded by the aging process. There is a place for vicarious experience in the dance world, but it is always secondary to lived experience. Merce Cunningham, for example, is in his 70s and still teaching, but only now is he writing about the process of doing choreography and only recently are his dances being videotaped and/or filmed. For the dancer, one has to dance (see Cunningham, 1985).

2. I first learned of theoretical sampling in my training as an ethnographer of the symbolic interactionist school, by reading Glaser and Strauss (1967). Theoretical sampling is the heart of grounded theory approaches to research. It allows for using the constant comparative method in data collection and analysis. Theoretical sampling allows for direction in the study and allows the researcher to have confidence in his or her categories as they emerge from the data and are constantly and selectively reformulated along the way. The data in any study do not speak for themselves. The researcher must make sense of the data in a meaningful way, and this technique allows the researcher to find an active way of searching the data.

3. Gallaudet University is the only liberal arts college dedicated to educating deaf individuals. Dr. I. King Jordan became Gallaudet's first deaf president after the "Deaf President Now" campaign was realized. This grassroots movement, involving both students and faculty members, closed the institution during deliberations on the selection of a president. Gallaudet University has approximately 2,000 students; all of the undergraduate student population is deaf (about 1,500 students) and, of the 500 graduate students, approximately 100 are deaf. Established in 1864 through the efforts of President Lincoln, Gallaudet had only hearing presidents until Dr. Jordan was inaugurated.

4. Constant comparative analysis allows the researcher to develop grounded theory. A grounded theory is one inductively derived from the study. Data collection, analysis, and theory are related reciprocally. One grounds the theory in the data from statements of belief and behavior of participants in the study. See Glaser and Strauss (1967) and Strauss and Corbin (1990) for a more detailed description of grounded theory. It is basically opposite to the use of theory in the quantitative paradigm. Instead of proving a theory, the qualitative researcher studies a setting over time and develops

theory grounded in the data. This is a well-established methodology in social psychology and sociology. Educational researchers are beginning to use grounded theory more and more, because it makes sense given the types of questions we ask.

References

Banes, S. (1980). *Terpsichore in sneakers: Post-modern dance.* Boston: Houghton Mifflin.

Bogdan, R. C., & Biklen, S. K. (1992). *Qualitative research for education: An introduction to theory and methods.* Boston: Allyn & Bacon.

Cunningham, M. (1985). *The dancer and the dance.* New York: Marion Boyars.

Denzin, N. K. (1978). *The research act: A theoretical introduction to sociological methods* (2nd ed.). New York: McGraw-Hill.

Denzin, N. K. (1989). *Interpretive interactionism.* Newbury Park, CA: Sage.

Dewey, J. (1958). *Art as experience.* New York: G. P. Putnam's Sons. (Original work published 1934)

Donmoyer, R. (1990). Generalizability and the single-case study. In E. W. Eisner & A. Peshkin (Eds.), *Qualitative inquiry in education: The continuing debate* (pp. 175-200). New York: Teachers College Press.

Eisner, E. (1991). *The enlightened eye: Qualitative inquiry and the enhancement of educational practices.* New York: Macmillan.

Erickson, F. (1986). Qualitative methods in research on teaching. In M. C. Wittrock (Ed.), *Handbook of research on teaching* (3rd ed., pp. 119-161). New York: Macmillan.

Fetterman, D. M. (1989). *Ethnography: Step by step.* Newbury Park, CA: Sage.

Glaser, B. G., & Strauss, A. L. (1967). *The discovery of grounded theory: Strategies for qualitative research.* Chicago: Aldine.

Goetz, J., & LeCompte, M. D. (1984). *Ethnography and qualitative design in educational research.* New York: Academic Press.

Janesick, V. J. (1982). Of snakes and circles: Making sense of classroom group processes through a case study. *Curriculum Inquiry, 12,* 161-185.

Janesick, V. J. (1983). Reflections on teaching ethnographic research methods. *Anthropology and Education Quarterly, 14,* 198-202.

Janesick, V. J. (1990). *Proud to be deaf: An ethnographic study of deaf culture.* Paper presented at the Qualitative Research in Education Conference, University of Georgia, Athens.

LeCompte, M. D., Millroy, W. L., & Preissle, J. (Eds.). (1992). *The handbook of qualitative research in education.* New York: Academic Press.

Lincoln, Y. S., & Guba, E. G. (1985). *Naturalistic inquiry.* Beverly Hills, CA: Sage.

Miles, M. B., & Huberman, A. M. (1984). *Qualitative data analysis: A sourcebook of new methods.* Beverly Hills, CA: Sage.

Moustakis, C. (1990). *Heuristic research design, methodology, and applications.* Newbury Park, CA: Sage.

Patton, M. Q. (1990). *Qualitative evaluation and research methods.* Newbury Park, CA: Sage.

Spradley, J. P. (1979). *The ethnographic interview.* New York: Holt, Rinehart & Winston.

Spradley, J. P. (1980). *Participant observation.* New York: Holt, Rinehart & Winston.

Strauss, A. L., & Corbin, J. (1990). *Basics of qualitative research: Grounded theory procedures and techniques.* Newbury Park, CA: Sage.

Wolcott, H. F. (1990). On seeking and rejecting validity in qualitative research. In E. W. Eisner & A. Peshkin (Eds.), *Qualitative inquiry in education: The continuing debate* (pp. 121-152). New York: Teachers College Press.

13

■

Designing Funded Qualitative Research

JANICE M. MORSE

MY purposes in this chapter are to identify and describe the major design issues in the planning stage of a qualitative project and to suggest practical ways for the researcher to overcome the paradoxes inherent in qualitative inquiry. I provide a guide to the planning of qualitative proposals and include suggestions for avoiding the pitfalls inherent in the research process. I have chosen to organize the chapter in the same sequence one would use when planning to conduct a qualitative project. Therefore, I begin with the stage of reflection, in which the project is merely a good idea, and proceed to the stage of planning (including writing the proposal) and the stage of entry, or beginning the fieldwork. When data collection is going well and is fruitful, the researcher enters the stage of productive data collection. Next is the stage of withdrawal, which is followed by the most important stage of all, the stage of writing.

The Stage of Reflection

Identifying the Topic

Recognizing that selection of a topic or research question is a fairly long-term commitment (and one that will require intensive effort) is often stressful enough to put student investigators into a state of panic. Students cannot think of researchable topics or think of anything of sufficient interest to make the time commitment required to complete the project. The additional requirement that the research should investigate a relatively new area or innovative question further increases the fear that they will not be able to come up with an original and promising topic.

The key to selecting a qualitative research topic is to identify something that will hold one's interest over time. New investigators can best identify such a topic by reflecting on what is of *real* personal interest to them. Surprisingly, these topics may not be among those on which an individual has already written. Enticing topics may be those that distract a person in the library; they may be topics that preoccupy a person and draw him or her into interesting conversations with others. Identifying such topics often requires some self-reflection and critical self-examination. The topic identified may be an area of interest rather than a more narrowly defined problem or question per se, and, at this stage, it is almost never an elegantly worded research question.

Research questions may also arise from a problem noted in the course of clinical practice, or from a significant experience that occurs in the course of everyday living. Researchable questions may also be "assigned" in consultation with other researchers, or identified in the technical literature (Strauss & Corbin, 1990). Joining a research project and taking responsibility for a "piece" often provides the novice researcher with supportive colleagues who can provide advice and encouragement, and may even provide funding or transcribing services to help with the research. If a research topic arises from suggested recommendations at the end of a published research article, it is wise for the researcher to consult with the author(s) of that article. Considerable time will have elapsed between the completion of the first project and its publication, and the author(s) may have already conducted the particular study that logically extends from the first project. In any case, the author(s) may have important advice about how to proceed with the new investigation.

Finally, researchable questions often become apparent when one reads the literature. For instance, a student interested in breast-feeding may be seeking information to assist mothers coping with breast expression and find that the information in the literature consists entirely of prescriptive accounts on *how* to express the breasts, or maintain lactation. The discovery of a gap, of instances where no information is available, is an exciting indicator that a topic would be good candidate for qualitative study. Similarly, if the reader has a hunch that the information available is poor or biased, or that the theory is wrong, then a qualitative study may also be indicated.

Having identified a topic, the researcher's next step is to go to the library to read in the general area of the research topic. At this stage, the researcher should become familiar with the literature, with what has been done generally in the area, and with the "state of the art." He or she should develop a comfortable knowledge base without spending an extraordinary amount of time on minute details or chasing obscure references. As qualitative inquiry at this stage is unfocused, and as the researcher has the opportunity to return to the library later in the study, when he or she better understands the direction of inquiry, it is inappropriate to spend too much time in the library at this point. As a reminder of the perils of getting bogged down in the library at this stage, I have students read about the fictitious plight of the young man who spent his entire research career in the library trying to learn all that was known about the evil eye (van Gennep, 1967/1992).

Researchers select topics for various reasons, and it is helpful at this stage for the researcher to recognize why he or she has selected a particular topic for study: Why does it hold his or her interest? Often, one reason a topic is selected is that the researcher has had personal or professional experiences related to the subject and has residual personal unmet needs or strong feelings stemming from these experiences. For example, a student may be interested in the experience of abortion because she herself has experienced one; another may be interested in survivors of suicide because he had a sibling or close friend who died that way. Using such personal experiences as the impetus for a research study is not *wrong,* but it is best if the researcher is aware of his or her possible motives for conducting the study, as such experiences may give the study a particular bias. Of even more concern is the possibility that the researcher, when meeting and interviewing participants who have had the same experience, may have many unresolved feelings emerge and may be emotionally unable to continue with the study.

Identifying Paradigmatic Perspectives

Wolcott (1992) identifies three "postures" underlying qualitative research: theory-driven (for example, cultural theory underlies ethnography), concept-driven (such as focusing on the concept of care in a clinical ethnography), and "reform-focused" or "problem-focused" ideas, in which the underlying purpose of the project is political, with predetermined goals, such as feminist research (Code, 1991; Devault, 1990; Harding, 1987; Reinharz, 1992) or critical theory (Anderson, 1989; Campbell, 1991; Quantz, 1992). Although the techniques and methods used in these approaches are similar to other qualitative techniques, they differ in their levels of abstraction, their foci, and their outcomes. For instance, feminist research challenges the social science research status quo by claiming that research historically conducted by men portrays only the male perspective, the paternalistic life world, and has virtually—and deliberately—excluded women's perspective and contributions. Using the same techniques as other qualitative research, feminist researchers collect data to ensure that the female perspective has been elicited and analyzed, that the feminist perspective is primarily presented. The feminist research agenda is to fill the void of decades of social science research that has ignored women informants, women's work, women's roles, and women's contribution to society.

It is actually a misnomer to label research theory or concept "driven," for if theory actually guided data collection and analysis, inductive assumptions of qualitative research would be violated. Rather, in qualitative inquiry the theory is used to focus the inquiry and give it boundaries for comparison in facilitating the development of the theoretical or conceptual outcomes. The theory or concept of interest at best may be considered a conceptual template with which to compare and contrast results, rather than to use as a priori categories into which to force the analysis.

At this stage of planning the project, it is also helpful to examine the research questions in light of the expected results, considering the potential audience and aims of the research. For instance, can the study be conducted with the explicit aim of improving *nursing* practice, and will the results be read by nurse educators? Or is the study being conducted to assist patients' families, and the research will reach an essentially lay readership? Keeping in mind the end results or purpose—even before the study question is refined—places the study in the broader picture; by so doing, the researcher will help refine the question, the focus of data collection and analysis, and guide the style of presentation of the final report.

The Stage of Planning

Planning involves many elements, including selection of a site and a research strategy, the investigator's preparation, creation and refinement of the research question, the writing of the proposal, and, if necessary, obtaining clearance from an institutional review board (IRB). These are discussed in turn below.

Selecting a Site

The possible setting in which the study will be conducted must be identified, and the access to and characteristics of possible participants considered. It is foolish for the researcher to put too much work into a study that must be conducted in one particular setting unless he or she can be assured that access will not be denied. The researcher should visit a possible setting and tentatively sound out administrators to determine if the proposed project would be welcomed and if researchers would be tolerated on site. Administrators may, for example, be wary of a project that will essentially evaluate their personnel or institution, if they have no control over the research outcomes, or if they feel that the results may be detrimental to the organization, even if the researcher assures them that the site will not be identified in the final report. Evaluation research is more typically conducted at the request of administration, as contract research.

Considering alternatives. Much research could feasibly be conducted in several settings, such as in one of several schools or hospitals. This does not mean that the investigator necessarily has the opportunity to choose among settings, but rather that he or she must decide which setting to approach. In these instances, it is best for the researcher to visit each institution and put out feelers to see which is most receptive to having the project conducted there. The researcher should talk to the staff and see if, given the opportunity, they would participate. If possible, he or she should talk to other researchers who have previously worked in the institution to see if the environment is receptive and facilitative.

Selecting a research setting is an important step, and as negotiations for entry are often time-consuming (frequently involving human subjects review and administrative review to assess any costs to the institution), it must be done early. The researcher should solicit letters of support from the clinical setting and from the president of the institution to include with his or her proposal. He or she should also meet with the staff in the setting in which data will actually be collected to ensure their cooperation.

Frequently two settings are selected for the distinct purpose of comparing and contrasting the populations. This design is most commonly used in anthropology, where the behaviors or practices of two cultures or subcultures are of interest. At first glance, such a strategy appears to increase the *work* of research. However, as the process of comparing and contrasting may ease the process of data analysis by making significant factors more readily apparent, the duration of the research may not be unduly lengthened, and the product may be much stronger than if only one group is studied.

The last factor in selecting a research setting is the consideration of available resources, which are always limited. Is the study feasible without a research grant, or will the continuation of the project be contingent on the receipt of funding? If funding must be obtained, the researcher needs to identify the possible sources at this time and obtain the organizations' terms of references (and even establish contact with the agencies) to make sure that his or her project is within their areas of interest for funding purposes. The researcher must note the deadlines for applications and draw up a schedule so that he or she can prepare and submit all the necessary approvals on time.

One final word of warning: It is not wise for an investigator to conduct a qualitative study in a setting in which he or she is already employed and has a work role. The dual roles of investigator and employee are incompatible, and they may place the researcher in an untenable position. The expectations of coworkers will make it difficult for the researcher to stop work to do participant observation, to write notes, or to interview. Collecting data may also place the investigator in an awkward position in which the roles of employee and data collector are in conflict; for instance, the researcher may learn confidential information that should be reported by a loyal employee but that should be kept confidential by an ethical researcher.

The flip side of this is the consideration of how the researcher fits into the setting and how those in the setting perceive him or her. These perceptions affect the types of data informants share and even the kinds of information reported to the researcher during interviews. For instance, when a researcher conducts participant observation in a classroom, his or her perceived role will influence the data he or she can collect. If the students, teachers, and parents perceive the researcher *as a teacher,* the information they offer will focus largely on topics they think will most interest and be most helpful to teachers. In a clinical setting, if participants view the observer as a nurse, then the information will focus on the "medical" aspects of care (such as details about treatments and symptoms) rather than the day-to-day coping with illness. Breaking through such perceptual stereotypes takes a great deal of effort on the part of the researcher. Wearing a uniform identifies the researcher as an employee of the institution, and this may also restrict his or her access to some types of information. Another disadvantage is that the researcher may find him- or herself expected to work (rather than to observe), and these expectations, once met, are difficult for the researcher to change; clearly, this will impede data collection. In light of this, it is best for the researcher to dress somewhat ambiguously—for example, to wear a uniform of a different color if a uniform is called for, or to wear both a scrub suit and a lab coat—as a signal to staff that he or she does not really belong in that setting and is there to collect data, and not to act as an employee.

Selecting a Strategy

The research strategy is determined by the nature of the research question (Field & Morse, 1991). Research strategies are merely *tools*; it is the researcher's responsibility to understand the variety available and the different purposes of each strategy, to appreciate in advance the ramifications of selecting one method over another, and to become astute in the selection of one method over another. Each qualitative strategy offers a particular and unique perspective that illuminates certain aspects of reality more easily than others and produces a type of results more suited for some applications than others. Some qualitative strategies are designed for particular types of data; for instance, they facilitate the management of certain types of observations. Finally, the link between the question and the method chosen will determine the types of results obtained and ultimately the *usefulness of the results,* or the pragmatic application of the study findings. Therefore, the competent researcher is versatile enough to view a setting and recognize the restrictions in the types of data that can be collected and the possibilities that will enable the achievement of his or her research aims. A good researcher is not confined methodologically by being trained in—and limited to—a single strategy (for instance, "I only 'do' ethnography"). Such a restriction limits the types of questions the researcher may ask and the types of results he or she can obtain, and restricts the strength of the research.

Table 13.1 links the major types of qualitative research questions with the research strategies and methods used. Although the table is by no means comprehensive, it provides a beginning guide for research planning. Note that the qualitative strategy used in the study is largely determined by the purpose of the study, the nature of the research questions, and the skills and resources available to the investigator. For instance, if the research question concerns the *meaning* of a phenomenon, then the method that would best answer the question is phenomenology. If the question concerns the *nature* of the phenomenon, then the answer is best obtained using ethnography. If the question concerns an experience and the phenomenon in question is a process, the method of choice for addressing the question is grounded theory.

Another helpful tactic in proposal writing is to *imagine* what one wants to find out. By projecting the research outcome, the researcher may begin to conceptualize the question, the sample size, the feasibility of the study, the data sources, and so forth. A variation of this exercise may be demonstrated in the classroom: A topic of interest may be suggested and the students walked through steps in the research process examining, in particular, the different results that would be obtained with different questions and different strategies. For instance, consider a mock project with the title "Arrivals and Departures: Patterns of Human Attachment." We could imagine we are studying human attachment at the local airport, watching passengers leave relatives or be greeted by relatives. Then, by listing various questions that would be best asked using different qualitative strategies, we quickly discover the differences in the main types of qualitative strategies. Students can participate in these hypothetical research projects by imagining who would be best to interview as participants in each project, or, if an observational method is selected for discussion, where and when the observations could be conducted. Students can explore issues of sample size and modes of data analysis. Finally, they can clearly see, through the construction of a comparative grid such as that shown in Table 13.2, how qualitative strategies vary and how different types of strategies produce very different results.

This type of "planning" is crucial to the development of a solid and enticing proposal. The mental walk-through that the researcher takes in envisioning research plans may even ease some of the researcher anxiety that is invariably a part of entering the setting.

TABLE 13.1 Comparison of the Major Types of Qualitative Strategies

Type of Research Questions	*Strategy*	*Paradigm*	*Method*	*Other Data Sources*	*Major References*
Meaning questions—eliciting the essence of experiences	phenomenology	philosophy (phenomenology)	audiotaped "conversations"; written anecdotes of personal experiences	phenomenological literature; philosophical reflections; poetry; art	Bergum (1991), Giorgi (1970), van Manen (1984, 1990)
Descriptive questions—of values, beliefs, practices of cultural group	ethnography	anthropology (culture)	unstructured interviews; participant observation; field notes	documents; records; photography; maps; genealogies; social network diagrams	Ellen (1984), Fetterman (1989), Grant & Fine (1992), Hammersley & Atkinson (1983), Hughes (1992), Sanjek (1990), Spradley (1979), Werner & Schoepfle (1987a, 1987b)
"Process" questions—experience over time or change, may have stages and phases	grounded theory	sociology (symbolic interactionism)	interviews (tape-recorded)	participant observation; memoing; diary	Chenitz & Swanson (1986), Glaser (1978, 1992), Glaser & Strauss (1967), Strauss (1987), Strauss & Corbin (1990)
Questions regarding verbal interaction and dialogue	ethnomethodology; discourse analysis	semiotics	dialogue (audio/video recording)	observation; field notes	Atkinson (1992), Benson & Hughes (1983), Denzin (1970, 1989), Douglas (1970), Heritage (1984), Leiter (1980), Rogers (1983)
Behavioral questions					
macro	participant observation	anthropology	observation; field notes	interviews; photography	Jorgensen (1989), Spradley (1980)
micro	qualitative ethology	zoology	observation	videotaped; note taking	Eibl-Eibesfeldt (1989), Morse & Bottorff (1990), Scherer & Ekman (1982)

Methodological Triangulation

Because different "lenses" or perspectives result from the use of different methods, often more than one method may be used within a project so the researcher can gain a more holistic view of the setting. Two or more qualitative methods may be used sequentially or simultaneously, provided the analysis is kept separate and the methods are not muddled (Stern, 1994). For example, Wilson and Hutchinson (1991) compared the use of grounded theory and Heideggerian hermeneutics to illustrate how the philosophical and methodological features of each method are distinct, yet complementary. The main methods of Heideggerian hermeneutics (thick description, paradigm cases, and exemplars) enable the researcher to elicit and interpret the meaning of lived experience. On the other hand, the technique of grounded theory incorporates other sources of data (such as document review and observational data along with unstructured interviews) and aims to develop a basic social process and a more abstract, midrange theory.

TABLE 13.2 A Comparison of Strategies in the Conduct of a Hypothetical Project: "Arrivals and Departures: Patterns of Human Attachment"

Strategy	*Research Question/ Focus*	*Participants/ Informants*[a]	*Sample Size*[b]	*Data Collection Methods*	*Type of Results*
Phenomenology	What is the meaning of arriving home?	travelers arriving home; phenomenological literature; art, poetry, and other descriptions	approximately six participants	in-depth conversations	in-depth reflective description of the experience of "what it feels like to come home"
Ethnography	What is the arrival gate like when an international plane arrives?	travelers, families, others who observe the setting, such as skycaps, rental car personnel, cleaning staff, security guards, and so forth	approximately 30-50 interviews	interviews; participant observation; other records, such as airport statistics	description of the day-to-day events at the arrival gate of the airport
Grounded theory	Coming home: reuniting the family	travelers, family members	approximately 30-50	in-depth interviews; observations	description of the social psychological process in the experience of returning home
Ethnoscience	What are types of travelers?	those who observe the setting daily—skycaps, rental car personnel, cleaning staff, security guards, and so forth	approximately 30-50	interviews to elicit similarities and differences of travelers, card sorts	taxonomy and description of types and characteristics of travelers
Qualitative ethology	What are the greeting behaviors of travelers and their families?	travelers and their families	units—numbers of greetings—100-200	photography, video; coded	description of the patterns of greeting behaviors

NOTES: a. Examples only.
b. Number depends on saturation.

Qualitative research may also incorporate quantitative methods into the design to answer particular questions. Of most importance to this chapter is the incorporation of quantitative research into a qualitative project (that is, qualitatively *driven*) (see Morse, 1991a). In this case the nature of the qualitative sample (with a small *n* and purposely selected) violates the assumptions of size and random selection of quantitative research and cannot be used for quantitative data collection. However, if the quantitative measure is standardized (i.e., normative results are available), then a quantitative measure may be administered to the qualitative sample and the results compared with the standardized norms. Such procedures provide important additional information. For example, rather than describing the participants in a qualitative sample as "highly anxious," the researcher can describe exactly *how* anxious they are, compared with a normal population. However, if the quantitative measure is not standardized, then sequential triangulation techniques must be employed, with the researcher administering the instrument to a separate, larger and randomly selected, sample following the completion of the qualitative data analysis.

Investigator Preparation

Qualitative research is only as good as the investigator. It is the researcher who, through skill, patience, and wisdom, obtains the information necessary during data collection and fieldwork to produce a rich qualitative study. Good qualitative researchers must be prepared to learn to be trusted in the setting; they must be patient and wait until they are accepted by informants; they must be flexible and resilient; and, as Wax (1971) notes, they must be prepared to "make fools of themselves."

An important quality that will help ensure success is versatility. Experienced researchers are versatile in research methods and know that there is always a best way to obtain the necessary information. They are persistent, recognizing that good fieldwork is often merely a matter of completing one small task after another. Good researchers are meticulous about their documentation, file methodically, and keep notes up-to-date. They are well prepared in their topic, so they can pick up subtle clues in interviews and latch on to, and follow, leads. The ability to follow leads also means that the researcher is well versed in social science theory. The researcher must be able to recognize remnants of other theorists' work, so that when glimpses of interesting leads are present in an interview, these leads may be pursued and verified, or recognized as new and unique phenomena. The good researcher is familiar enough with social science theory that he or she can recognize an appropriate "framework" or paradigm for the study and still work inductively, letting the qualitative assumptions drive the research. For example, the qualitative researcher will recognize the contribution of symbolic interactionist theory in grounded theory or the theoretical base that culture provides for ethnography, using these paradigms as *perspectives* without permitting them to dominate the data. Mature investigators have confidence in their own interpretations of the data and in their own ideas, and are articulate enough to express and defend them.

Information must be verified and cross-checked constantly, on an ongoing basis, and researchers must be constantly reviewing notes and other data collected. They are not stymied by ambiguity. They are not discouraged when progress is slow, nor are they hasty in jumping to conclusions. Good researchers revel in the intellectual work of making sense of their data; they thrive on living with information, on being haunted by the puzzle of their data. They keep working until the study is published. Although the confidence that comes with experience reinforces some of these qualities, it is important for neophyte researchers to know they are not alone in experiencing conceptual confusion in the midst of a qualitative project.

Creating and Refining the Research Question

The wording of the research question determines the focus and scope of the study. As qualitative inquiry is often tenuous in the early stages (in that the investigator does not have extensive knowledge about the setting), the researcher should make the question as broad as possible rather than prematurely delimit the study with a narrow question. Narrowness distracts the researcher from seeing the whole picture. For example, Norris (1991), when studying the experience of mothers with adolescent daughters undergoing abortion, initially focused on the abortion as a discrete event. Later in the study, however, she realized that the abortion was actually part of a larger process of "monitoring . . . daughters' contraceptive behavior." The researcher should state the question so that he or she can later refine it to make it appropriate to maximize the research effort. The researcher can do this as soon he or she begins to understand "what is going on" in the setting and what is possible given the constraints.

Occasionally, when the researcher enters the setting, it becomes evident that the original question is a poor fit or would be poorly answered in the setting, and the question—and sometimes the topic—must be discarded. When this occurs, it is usually necessary for the researcher to notify the IRB and the agencies involved, including the funding agency, that the focus of the study has changed.

In participant observation, familiarity with the setting dulls the researcher's awareness, and the significance and quality of the data are reduced when the researcher does not view the setting "as a stranger" (Agar, 1980). As the researcher gets to know others in the setting and becomes very familiar with the routine—perhaps even becomes bored, with a feeling of having "seen it all"—data may be considered "saturated" and the observer should withdraw from the setting.

Writing the Proposal

The first principle of grantsmanship is to recognize that a good proposal is an argument—a fair and balanced one, but nevertheless an argument—for the researcher's project. The proposal must make a case to the granting agency that the research question is interesting, that the study is important, and, most important, why it should be funded. Thus the proposal must be written persuasively. (This may seem strange advice for novice researchers, who for many years have been taught to write *objectively,* without emotion.) The proposal must be complete, with all major authors listed. It must be clear, interesting to read, technically neat, and professional in appearance. The final version should be printed out on a laser printer, after the researcher has double-checked the budget and the references, and has made sure he or she has followed the agency's guidelines with utmost care. A sloppily prepared proposal will, at best, send a message to the agency that if it funds the proposal, the research may also be sloppy. At worst, the proposal will not even be considered for funding, but will be returned to the investigator because missing information or missing pieces of the proposal prohibit it from being considered.

Granting agencies must have good reasons for funding a study and must be able to justify that funding to their boards of directors, to the press, and to the public. It is the responsibility of the proposal writer to provide these reasons. Apparently trivial research questions are not awarded grant funds. If the study will have clear cost benefits, the researcher should present those figures as expected annual savings, and so forth. If the expected gains from the research are less tangible, such as "improved staff morale," the researcher would be wise to focus on the cost benefits of "reducing staff turnover." If the proposal is for basic research—that is, research that addresses an interesting question but has no clear-cut benefits—the proposal writer needs to make the interesting question fascinating. He or she needs to entice the reviewers into the proposal, so that by the end of the first page they will also be captivated with the problem. The writer should place the problem in context to show, for instance, that "when we understand this, we will be able to work on that." This strategy makes the significance of the problem clear even to reviewers who are outside the researcher's discipline. And because some of the reviewers will be from other disciplines, the proposal writer should assume nothing and explain everything.

Because qualitative research is unstructured, the results unpredictable, and the outcome uncertain, it is difficult to write a WYSIWYG ("what you see is what you get") proposal. It may not be possible for the researcher to project what he or she will find or to promise exciting results; rather, it is a skill to balance both persuasiveness and realism. This problem makes writing the proposal difficult, but if the researcher does not try to "sell" the idea, the proposal will not be funded.

Before the researcher submits a proposal to a granting agency, he or she should have it reviewed by seasoned experts to ensure that the research design is "tight," that the methods are rigorous, and that the tone is balanced. The proposal should also be reviewed by someone outside the field to ensure that it is interesting, clear, and comprehensive. As most review committees consist primarily of quantitative researchers, some qualitative researchers have their proposals reviewed by quantitative researchers so that any anticipated "flaws" in the methods will be addressed before the proposals go to the review committee. These presubmission reviews take time; researchers should allow at least a month in the proposal-preparation timeline for these reviews and subsequent revisions.

The second principle in writing a successful proposal is that one should think and plan *before* starting to write. The researcher should select a topic, a research question, and mentally walk through the steps in the research process, as earlier described. As most writer's block comes from not knowing what to write, this planning process greatly facilitates the process of writing. It also helps the researcher to identify the advantages and disadvantages of various approaches and designs. For instance, the researcher can plan by identifying the types of data sources available. Incorporating observational data and other data sources into the study affects the complexity of the study, which, in turn, directly affects the cost of data collection, data analysis, and the duration of the project. The options of using more than one site, of using a comparative design, of triangulating other data sources, and of conducting a prospective design or a cross-sectional design all have profound ramifications for budgeting and are so costly that it is not usually possible to add such changes to the study design *after* the budget has been approved (without a supplement). Ideally, such options should be calculated into the budget in the submission, and the design justified in the methods section of the proposal. In addition, selecting—and justifying—the method is an essential step in preparing the proposal; the ways to plan this have been discussed above.

Once decisions have been made regarding the research design and the setting, the actual writing of the proposal can begin. Although the components of a proposal vary from funding agency to funding agency, those listed in Table 13.3 are basic requirements. The researcher should read the agency's guidelines carefully for the order of these components, and for any page-length restrictions. In particular, he or she should look for any limits on budget requests. Some agencies, for example, will not fund equipment or travel, and other sources of funding must be identified if essential items are to be obtained elsewhere.

In addition to the stance of the researcher writing a persuasive document, the qualitative researcher may find him- or herself describing the research methods in terms that may be meaningless to researchers who do not use qualitative methods. In 1983, Downs wrote in an editorial that as long as "qualitative researchers refuse to describe how their theory was derived . . . we have a smile without a cat." Although this strong statement was targeted toward completed articles, it is also true for the proposal. Tripp-Riemer and Cohen (1991) suggest providing examples of data analysis and theory development by placing paragraphs of fictive text in the data analysis section of the proposal and coding this text to demonstrate

Table 13.3 Components of a Qualitative Proposal

Title/signature page
- full title of proposal and running head
- list of investigators (with signature lines), affiliations, phone and fax numbers
- total budget and start and completion dates of project
- names, signature lines, and addresses for the institutional research administration personnel

Abstract page

Body of the proposal
- introduction
- statement of purpose or aims
- review of the literature
  - importance of project
  - research question
- methods
  - description of setting and participants
  - data collection
    - procedure for data collection
  - data analysis
- human subjects protection
- timeline (schedule for plan of work)

References

Appendices
- investigators' vita
  - summary of principal investigator's and other key personnel's vita (limited to two pages per person)
- consent forms
- interview schedules
- publications
  - previous publications by investigator pertinent to this project

how the coding is done. Another suggestion is to select such text carefully so that it provides another piece of information about research in the topic at hand. For instance, although fictive, the text may be used to illustrate the experiences of participants, and thus to help build a case that an important and urgent area for study is addressed in the proposal.

The appendices of the proposal contain the budget pages, IRB approvals, letters of permission from administrators in the agency indicating their support for the project and permission to conduct the study, and letters of agreement to serve from prospective staff. A great deal of attention must be given to the budget to ensure that realistic and adequate funding is requested for the project. Appendix A of this chapter includes suggestions for preparing a budget for a qualitative proposal. IRB clearance must follow the requirements of the researcher's home institution, the host institution, and the funding agency. Federal regulations require that any research that will be conducted on human subjects must be reviewed by a board charged with assessing the risks and benefits of the project. As qualitative research is usually of naturalistic design (i.e., there is no research intervention), and thus the researcher is not disrupting or increasing the risks of *everyday life,* such projects often receive expedited review. However, the researcher should refer to "Protection of Human Subjects," Part 46 of the *Code of Federal Regulations,* Title 45 (revised in 1983) or consult his or her IRB for further information (see Appendix B, which presents the types and levels of human subjects review required for approval of NIH grant applications).

The Stage of Entry

Once the researcher receives funding from the granting agency, the data collection may start. The most difficult part of the entire project is entering the setting for the first time and knowing what to do, or knocking on the first door to solicit the first participant. The researcher may find that practicing explaining the study (in the form of role play) will help him or her overcome this barrier somewhat. Still, the new researcher can expect to feel awkward, useless, uncomfortable, in the way, and a nuisance in the research setting.

During the first period of data collection in an ethnographic study the researcher's observations must remain unfocused. Because feelings of confusion associated with "being new" are extreme, data collection is necessarily unfocused. The researcher should spend the first few days learning who's who; he or she may find it helpful to make an organizational chart of all the participants in the setting and a map of the physical layout. The researcher needs to take this time to learn the routine and the setting's formal and informal rules. He or she should observe for short periods and then retire to record field notes.

Sampling

As the researcher learns the roles and relationships among participants, he or she may identify appropriate informants. A good informant is one who has the knowledge and experience the researcher requires, has the ability to reflect, is articulate, has the time to be interviewed, and is willing to participate in the study (Morse, 1986, 1991b). *Primary selection* of participants describes the opportunity for the researcher to sample informants using these criteria. *Secondary selection* of participants takes place if the researcher cannot select participants according to these criteria and obtains participants by some other means, such as through advertising (Morse, 1991b). In this case, it is possible that the researcher may conduct an interview that is of little use to the project. If this happens, he or she should complete the interview but not waste research time and funds having the interview transcribed. The researcher should simply put such interviews aside (not dispose of or erase them), in case the information becomes important at a later date.

Patton (1990) provides guidelines for sampling and suggests that the logic and power behind purposeful selection of informants is that the sample should be *information rich.* First, *extreme* or *deviant case* sampling is used to select participants who exemplify characteristics of interest. For example, if studying the pain experience, the researcher selects participants who have experienced excruciating pain rather than participants with chronic pain. Extreme cases maximize the factors of interest, thus clarifying factors of importance.

Intensity sampling has less emphasis on extremes. With intensity sampling, one selects participants who are experiential experts and who are authorities about a particular experience. For instance, when studying patient-nurse relationships, the researcher would select participants who have been hospitalized over an extended period of time, who have experience in forming relations with many nurses, and who have observed others in such relationships.

Maximum variety sampling is the process of deliberately selecting a heterogeneous sample and observing commonalities in their experiences. It is a most useful methods of sampling when exploring abstract concepts, such as hope, and selecting, for instance, participants from a variety of backgrounds in which hope is evidently of primary importance. Patton (1990) notes that two types of data are obtained using this technique. The first is high-quality case descriptions, useful for documenting uniqueness; second, significant shared patterns of commonalities existing across participants may be identified.

Critical case sampling is the selection of examples that are significant for the identification of critical incidents that may be generalized to other situations. Again, the analysis focuses on instances, attributes, or key factors that contribute significantly to the example. Once analysis is progressing, data are enriched by the purposeful selection of *confirming cases* and *disconfirming* (negative) *cases.*

Interview Techniques

The primary feature of all these methods of sampling is that the situation of the sample is determined according to the needs of the study, and not according to external criteria, such as random selection. Participants are representative of the same experience or knowledge; they are not selected because of their demographic reflection of the general population.

The researcher should keep the first interviews with participants broad, letting the participants "tell their stories." He or she can then use subsequent interviews to obtain more targeted information and to fill gaps left by the earlier interviews. When the researcher no longer feels uncomfortable in the setting and can relax and focus on what is happening, instead of on him- or herself, then the stage of productive data collection begins.

When participants in the setting eventually begin to understand what the study is about and to recognize the special interests of the researcher, they may facilitate the inquiry by offering information. Finally, the researcher has reciprocal obligations to the participants (Reinharz, 1992). Such courtesies as providing cookies and coffee to facilitate focus group interaction can help to smooth data collection (Carey, 1994).

The Stage of Productive Data Collection

Productive data collection is the most exciting phase of qualitative inquiry; during this phase, out of confusion, order and understanding *emerge.* But the emergence of this understanding does not take place without effort. Only with diligent observation and conceptual work on the part of the researcher do the patterns of relationships become apparent. This takes time, determination, persistence, and perseverance. It takes the ability to withstand frustration and discouragement when pieces of the puzzle apparently do not fit. It requires wisdom and contemplation to understand the relationships of seemingly unrelated facts or "negative cases"—informants or behaviors that do not conform to the apparent patterns.

The analysis of data begins shortly after the data collection commences and continues during data collection and beyond. The concurrent processes of data collection and analysis allow the analysis to guide data collection in a process of theoretical sampling, so that excess and unnecessary data are not collected. Thus research costs are kept to a minimum and researcher confusion is reduced. The outcome is that the researcher maintains control rather than "drowning in data."

The use of data management methods during the study is essential for the efficiency of the study. Transcripts and notes must be easily retrieved, easily cross-referenced, and easily separated from and linked with their original sources. In precomputer days, this was achieved by cutting and pasting—literally by cutting the desired passages from the transcript and taping the segments onto separate pieces of paper (for a detailed description of this procedure, see Field & Morse, 1991, pp. 101-102). Researchers may wish to become acquainted with the various qualitative data analysis software tools, applications for which are discussed by Richards and Richards in Chapter 28 of this volume. Once the researcher appreciates the basics of analysis, he or she will find it worthwhile to master one of the many computer programs designed to facilitate content analysis (Fielding & Lee, 1991; for a comprehensive review of available programs, see Tesch, 1990, 1991).

Qualitative research does not have to be a "lone ranger" endeavor, with a single researcher struggling alone in a basement with piles of data. Researchers have conducted ethnography in teams, and the team approach has many advantages. For instance, it allows for more complete coverage of the setting and a more rapid period of data collection. Further, a research group may have an exponential effect on the analysis, as the insights of one person trigger new perspectives or insights in other team members. Thus leads may be confirmed or refuted more quickly. However, the team must have several characteristics: Team members must be able to brainstorm together frequently, preferably every day; members must have respect for the contributions of others; and relationships among team members must be excellent and egalitarian. If members of the team are from different disciplines, their implicit disciplinary perspectives may weaken—or may enrich—theoretical development of the research as the different perspectives provide paradigmatic tensions within the group. Members of the research team should also be aware from the outset that it may be more difficult to work within a multidisciplinary team than within a unidisciplinary team. One discipline may be more dominant than another, and different disciplines often use different terms for the same phenomena, making communication difficult. But the advantages that come from insights of such theoretically diverse teams are immense, and productivity can be enhanced many fold over the single-investigator model.

As the study progresses, theoretical insights and linkages between categories increase, making the process exciting as "what is going on" finally becomes clearer and more obvious. Data collection and sampling are dictated by and become directed entirely toward the emergent model. The researcher seeks indices of saturation, such as repetition in the information obtained and confirmation of previously collected data. Using theoretical sampling, he or she looks for negative cases to enrich the emergent model and to explain all variations and diverse patterns.

Ensuring Rigor

There are numerous methods of ensuring rigor in qualitative work, some more appropriate than others. The major methods for ensuring rigor are intricately linked with reliability and validity checks. Descriptions of the main methods follow.

Criteria of adequacy and appropriateness of data. In qualitative research, *adequacy* refers to the amount of data collected, rather than to the number of subjects, as in quantitative research. Adequacy is attained when sufficient data have been collected that saturation occurs and variation is both accounted for and understood. *Appropriateness* refers to selection of information according to the theoretical needs of the study and the emerging model. Sampling occurs purposefully, rather than by some form of random selection from a purposefully chosen population, as in quantitative research. In qualitative research, the investigator samples until repetition from multiple sources is obtained. This provides concurring and confirming data, and ensures saturation. The results of the study must be rich, and sampling strategies such as seeking negative cases also contribute to ensuring the adequacy and appropriateness of the data (Morse, 1986).

The audit trail. Careful documentation of the conceptual development of the project should leave an adequate amount of evidence that interested parties can reconstruct the process by which the investigators reached their conclusion. The audit trail consists of six types of documentation: raw data, data reduction and analysis products, data reconstruction and synthesis products, process notes, materials relating to intentions and dispositions, and instrument development information (this list was developed by Halpern, 1983, and reported in Lincoln & Guba, 1985, pp. 319-320).

Verification of the study with secondary informants. The resulting model may be taken back to the informants and presented to them. Often informants will be able to confirm immediately the accuracy and validity of the study, and may even, at that time, offer additional stories to confirm the model further (Glaser, 1978). However, sometimes the results report on findings that are implicit in the setting; then even the participants are not aware of the findings and must themselves "check out" the results. This occurred in a study on childbirth in Fiji in which the results of an ethnography revealed that Fiji-Indian primipara in labor did not have basic knowledge of the mechanics of delivery and in fact did not know how the baby was "going to get out." The Fiji-Indian nurses had learned such "facts of life" during their nursing education, but values of modesty prevented the nurses from sharing their knowledge with their patients, and thus from recognizing the culturally condoned ignorance of the Fiji-Indian mothers. Therefore, the nurses were surprised and shocked to discover this fact, and needed to confirm and reconfirm this lack of knowledge in their patients in order to satisfy their own sense of discovery (see Morse, 1989).

Multiple raters. Occasionally, a qualitative investigator uses a second investigator to read and code a transcript, or checks the "validity" of a category by asking someone else to affirm that, indeed, he or she is "seeing what is there." This process actually violates the process of induction, because the first investigator has a bank of knowledge from conducting other interviews and from observing that the second researcher does not have.

As the process of inductive qualitative inquiry frequently depends on insight and on the process of linking data (both among categories and with established theory), expecting another investigator to have the same insight from a limited data base is unrealistic.

Furthermore, limiting each step of analysis to small bits of data may even impede inquiry and stunt the development of the model. (I argue elsewhere that the process of synthesizing data is similar to the cognitive process of synthesizing others' articles for a literature review. No one takes a second reader to the library to check that indeed he or she is interpreting the original sources correctly, so why does anyone need a reliability checker for his or her data? See Morse, 1994.) Thus the quantitative model of ensuring reliability and validity by using external raters is not recommended for qualitative research.

The Stage of Withdrawal

Unfortunately, the productive period of data collection does not last. The assimilation of the researcher into the setting is a constant process, and eventually a point is reached when the researcher is viewed as a *part of the setting.* The researcher eventually becomes a full member of the group. At this stage, two processes impede data collection. First, the researcher loses sensitivity to the day-to-day activities in the setting. As daily activities become predictable and the researcher becomes bored, his or her ability to see and to record details of events becomes dulled and data collection becomes increasingly difficult. Second, the researcher loses objectivity toward the setting and the members of the group. As a fully indoctrinated member of the group, the researcher develops loyalties, becoming aligned with the group and the institution, and the neutral stance of the researcher-as-a-data-collector is lost.

The major sign that the researcher has reached the point of withdrawal is the tendency to "go native." The researcher may suddenly recognize that he or she is putting other goals ahead of the research. For instance, the researcher may suddenly realize that he or she did not record an event in the field notes because it may reflect poorly on the participants, or because it was "everyday" or not special or interesting enough. When this happens, the researcher must realize that it is necessary to withdraw from the setting. However, analysis is not complete, and as it may be necessary to return to the setting to collect confirming data, to fill in gaps, or to observe special cases or events, it is important that he or she not withdraw completely. In leaving, the researcher should try to say something to participants that will allow him or her to return, if necessary, such as "I *think* I have finished, but may I come back if I find that I need to ask some more questions or observe something else?"

Public statements that the main part of data collection is soon to be completed usually bring out many participants who are suddenly determined to have their say, to tell the researcher "exactly how it is." This is a normal part of withdrawal and one that may put new life into the research. However, if the researcher is not learning anything new, he or she may be reasonably certain that data are saturated.

During this time, data analysis should be intense. The model or theory should becoming more refined and the researcher should be quite excited about the results. Explaining the emerging model to colleagues and having them ask questions will refine the results and move the researcher forward in his or her thinking. The more the researcher presents the theory, the easier it will be to write. Links will become obvious and the researcher will become more articulate.

The Stage of Writing

Qualitative writing is different from quantitative writing. Whereas the latter consists of a concise presentation of the methods and the results of the study, the qualitative report must be a convincing argument systematically presenting data to support the researcher's case and to refute alternative explanations (see Morse, in press). Two main approaches to qualitative articles are (a) to write the article as though the reader is solving the puzzle with the researcher, and (b) to present a summary of the major finding and then present the findings that supports the conclusion. Researchers should use quotations to illustrate their interpretations of the data, rather than in place of descriptive text.

One question that is frequently asked is, How much editing can be done on a quotation? It is important not to edit the essence of the quotation from the passage, but at the same time it is legitimate to remove the "mmms" and the pauses unless the intonation and expression are important for the meaning. The researcher may also remove irrelevant phrases and sentences, replacing them with ellipses. He or she should pay close attention to the punctuation, checking each passage with the audiotape to ensure that commas and periods (indicating pauses and breaks in the speech) are correctly used to maintain the speaker's expression.

At the beginning of the study (when giving informed consent), the participants were promised anonymity for their participation. The researcher must check carefully that none of the quotations used makes a speaker recognizable through some contextual reference. He or she must ensure that demographic data are presented in aggregates, so that identifiers (such as gender, age, and years of experience) are not linked (making individuals recognizable) and are not consistently associated with the same participant throughout the text, even if a code name is used. This prevents those who know all the participants in the setting from determining who participated in the study and who did not. In addition, the text should not identify which informants provided quotes. Tagging quotations with participant numbers may also place participants at risk of being identified.

If the institution's administrators choose to be acknowledged publicly for their contribution to the project, the researcher should allow them to read a draft of the completed document to ensure that they still wish to be listed in the acknowledgments. Administrators forget that they cannot be both publicly thanked for their cooperation and not identified. If they want to be acknowledged, the researcher should request a letter of permission before listing the organization's name in the acknowledgments. One administrator may request such a citation, but someone else, perhaps a board member, may take exception to the citation at a later date.

The organization's and the participants' efforts demand some reciprocal gesture from the researcher. He or she should arrange for the results to be presented to the institution at a future date (before the participants hear about the research at a conference) and prepare a summary of the study to be mailed to all participants and others who are interested. Finally, the researcher should provide the institution with a copy of the completed study and the final report to the funding agency.

Publication is the most important means for disseminating research findings. Qualitative research may not always be "split" into several articles, and many publishers are willing to publish entire studies as monographs. Some studies, however, lend themselves naturally to segmentation, with each portion making a reasonably comprehensive article. Publication in shorter articles has the advantage of increasing citations in serial indexes, which, in turn, lead to speedier dissemination of the work.

Conclusion

In this chapter, I have described techniques for designing and conducting a qualitative project. I have addressed some of the special problems that occur in qualitative research, such as how to present a proposal in a convincing manner—so that the idea will be fundable—while maintaining the flexibility necessary to achieve the qualitative research goals. I have also addressed the issue of how to maintain the freedom necessary to embark on qualitative inquiry without invalidating the study with deductive assumptions and prematurely developed research plans. I have also outlined techniques for preparing a proposal, from idea to submission. Finally, I have described some issues related to the selection of an appropriate methodology and design according to the nature of the research question and the purpose of the study. The remaining chapters in Part III of the *Handbook* address the major qualitative methods used in qualitative inquiry.

Appendix A: Hints for Budgeting

The following list will assist the researcher in preparing a qualitative budget:

1. *Personnel:* A secretary can do much more to facilitate the project than simply transcribe the interviews. He or she can make appointments for interviews, monitor the budget, catalog tapes, and organize consent forms, articles, and transcribed interviews. To calculate the length of time needed for transcribing, a rule of thumb for a fast typist (i.e., more than 65 words per minute) is four times the length of the tape. If the typist replays the tape to check the transcriptions, change this to six times the length of the

recording. Calculate the length of time you expect to complete the work, and then double it. This allows for a more realistic completion of the project, and allows for "disasters" that will inevitably delay the completion of the project. Remember Strauss's (1987) advice that qualitative inquiry cannot be forced or rushed.

2. *Equipment:* Purchase the best tape recorder. Tape recorders wear out, and generally they are not worth repairing. A researcher cannot afford to lose an interview because the tape has tangled. A foot pedal for the tape recorder will be helpful for transcribing or making notes while listening to the tape, as it leaves both hands free. As a clear recording will make for easier transcribing, use an external microphone. A solar-powered microphone is a good investment, as it is not dependent on batteries.
3. *Supplies:* Medium-quality tapes are fine. The cheapest 90-minute tapes should be avoided as they tend to tangle relatively easily. Allow for plenty of photocopying.

Appendix B: Level of Human Subject Review

The types and levels of approval required for NIH grant applications are listed here. Quoted material is from "Protection of Human Subjects" (Part 46 of *Code of Federal Regulations,* Title 45, revised 1983).

Minimal risk in research is defined as "the probability and magnitude of physical or psychological harm that is normally encountered in daily lives, or in the routine medical, dental, or psychological examination of healthy persons" (p. 14). Three levels of approval exist: exempt review, expedited review, and full review. Definitions of these and types of research of interest to qualitative researchers are as follows:

1. *Exempt review:* Research that is exempt from review is research that is conducted in "established or commonly accepted educational settings, involving normal educational practices; research involving survey or interview procedures, except where the human subjects (i) can be identified directly or through identifiers linked to the subject, and (ii) the subject's responses, if they become known outside the research, could reasonably place the subject at risk of criminal or civil liability or be damaging to the subject's financial standing or employability, and (iii) the research deals with sensitive aspects of the subject's own behavior, such as illegal conduct, or use of alcohol" (p. 5). It also includes observational research of public behavior, when the data are recorded anonymously, as well as research involving the collection or study of publicly available existing data, records, pathological specimens, or diagnostic specimens (p. 5).
2. *Expedite review:* Expedite review is the approval of the research by the chairperson of the IRB (or his or her designate), and is used for research that is on the list of research that contains no more than minimal risk. Included in this list are "voice recordings made for research purposes" and "the study of existing data, documents, records, pathological specimens, or diagnostic specimens" (p. 19).
3. *Full review:* This is the review of the research by the IRB, which considers that the risks to the subject are minimized, that the risks to the subject are reasonable in relation to the anticipated benefits, and the importance of the knowledge that may reasonably be expected to result (p. 8).

References

Agar, M. H. (1980). *The professional stranger: An informal introduction to ethnography.* New York: Academic Press.

Anderson, G. L. (1989). Critical theory in education: Origins, current status, and new directions. *Review of Educational Research, 59,* 240-270.

Atkinson, P. (1992). The ethnography of a medical setting: Reading, writing and rhetoric. *Qualitative Health Research, 2,* 451-474.

Benson, D., & Hughes, J. A. (1983). *The perspective of ethnomethodology.* London: Longman.

Bergum, V. (1991). Being a phenomenological researcher. In J. M. Morse (Ed.), *Qualitative nursing research: A contemporary dialogue* (pp. 55-71). Newbury Park, CA: Sage.

Campbell, J. C. (1991). Voices and paradigms: Perspectives on critical and feminist theory. *Advances in Nursing Science, 13*(3), 1-15.

Carey, M. A. (1994). The group effect in focus groups: Planning, implementing, and interpreting focus group research. In J. M. Morse (Ed.), *Critical issues in qualitative research methods* (pp. 225-241). Newbury Park, CA: Sage.

Chenitz, W. C., & Swanson, J. M. (1986). *From practice to grounded theory.* Menlo Park, CA: Addison-Wesley.

Code, L. (1991). *What can she know? Feminist theory and the construction of knowledge.* Ithaca, NY: Cornell University Press.

Denzin, N. K. (1970). Symbolic interactionism and ethnomethodology. In J. Douglas (Ed.), *Understanding everyday life* (pp. 261-286). Chicago: Aldine.

Denzin, N. K. (1989). *Interpretive interactionism.* Newbury Park, CA: Sage.

Devault, M. L. (1990). Talking and listening from women's standpoint: Feminist strategies for interviewing and analysis. *Social Problems, 37,* 96-116.

Douglas, J. (Ed.). (1970). *Understanding everyday life.* Chicago: Aldine.

Downs, F. (1983). "One dark and stormy night" [Editorial]. *Nursing Research, 32,* 259.

Eibl-Eibesfeldt, I. (1989). *Human ethology.* New York: Aldine de Gruyter.

Ellen, R. F. (Ed.). (1984). *Ethnographic research.* London: Academic Press.

Fetterman, D. M. (1989). *Ethnography: Step by step.* Newbury Park, CA: Sage.

Field, P. A., & Morse, J. M. (1991). *Nursing research: The application of qualitative approaches.* London: Chapman & Hall.

Fielding, N. G., & Lee, R. M. (Eds.). (1991). *Using computers in qualitative research.* London: Sage.

Giorgi, A. (1970). *Psychology as a human science: A phenomenologically based approach.* New York: Harper & Row.

Glaser, B. G. (1978). *Theoretical sensitivity.* Mill Valley, CA: Sociology Press.

Glaser, B. G. (1992). *Basics of grounded theory analysis.* Mill Valley, CA: Sociology Press.

Glaser, B. G., & Strauss, A. L. (1967). *The discovery of grounded theory: Strategies for qualitative research.* Chicago: Aldine.

Grant, L., & Fine, G. A. (1992). Sociology unleashed: Creative directions in classical ethnography. In M. D. LeCompte, W. L. Millroy, & J. Preissle (Eds.), *The handbook of qualitative research in education* (pp. 405-446). New York: Academic Press.

Halpern, E. S. (1983). *Auditing naturalistic inquiries: The development and application of a model.* Unpublished doctoral dissertation, Indiana University.

Hammersley, M., & Atkinson, P. (1983). *Ethnography: Principles in practice.* London: Tavistock.

Harding, S. (Ed.). (1987). *Feminism and methodology: Social science issues.* Bloomington: Indiana University Press.

Heritage, J. (1984). *Garfinkel and ethnomethodology.* Cambridge, UK: Polity.

Hughes, C. C. (1992). "Ethnography": What's in a word—Process? Product? Promise? *Qualitative Health Research, 2,* 451-474.

Jorgensen, D. L. (1989). *Participant observation: A methodology for human studies.* Newbury Park, CA: Sage.

Leiter, K. (1980). *A primer on ethnomethodology.* New York: Oxford University Press.

Lincoln, Y. S., & Guba, E. G. (1985). *Naturalistic inquiry.* Beverly Hills, CA: Sage.

Morse, J. M. (1986). Qualitative research: Issues in sampling. In P. L. Chinn (Ed.), *Nursing research methodology: Issues and implementation* (pp. 181-193). Rockville, MD: Aspen.

Morse, J. M. (1989). Cultural variation in behavioral response to parturition: Childbirth in Fiji. *Medical Anthropology, 12*(1), 35-54.

Morse, J. M. (1991a). Approaches to qualitative-quantitative methodological triangulation. *Nursing Research, 40,* 120-123.

Morse, J. M. (1991b). Strategies for sampling. In J. M. Morse (Ed.), *Qualitative nursing research: A contemporary dialogue* (pp. 127-145). Newbury Park, CA: Sage.

Morse, J. M. (1994). "Emerging from the data": The cognitive processes of analysis in qualitative inquiry. In J. M. Morse (Ed.), *Critical issues in qualitative research methods* (pp. 23-43). Newbury Park, CA: Sage.

Morse, J. M. (in press). Disseminating qualitative research. In E. Dunn (Ed.), *Foundations of primary care research: Disseminating research findings.* Newbury Park, CA: Sage.

Morse, J. M., & Bottorff, J. L. (1990). The use of ethology in clinical nursing research. *Advances in Nursing Science, 12*(3), 53-64.

Norris, J. (1991). Mothers' involvement in their adolescent daughters' abortions. In J. M. Morse & J. L. Johnson (Eds.), *The illness experience: Dimensions of suffering* (pp. 201-236). Newbury Park, CA: Sage.

Patton, M. Q. (1990). *Qualitative evaluation and research methods* (2nd ed.). Newbury Park, CA: Sage.

Quantz, R. A. (1992). On critical ethnography (with some postmodern considerations). In M. D. LeCompte, W. L. Millroy, & J. Preissle (Eds.), *The handbook of qualitative research in education* (pp. 447-505). New York: Academic Press.

Reinharz, S. (1992). *Feminist methods in social research.* New York: Oxford University Press.

Rogers, M. F. (1983). *Sociology, ethnomethodology, and experience.* Cambridge, UK: Cambridge University Press.

Sanjek, R. (Ed.). (1990). *Fieldnotes: The makings of anthropology.* Albany: State University of New York Press.

Scherer, K. R., & Ekman, P. (1982). *Handbook of methods in nonverbal behavior research.* Cambridge, UK: Cambridge University Press.

Spradley, J. P. (1979). *The ethnographic interview.* New York: Holt, Rinehart & Winston.
Spradley, J. P. (1980). *Participant observation.* New York: Holt, Rinehart & Winston.
Stern, P. N. (1994). Eroding grounded theory. In J. M. Morse (Ed.), *Critical issues in qualitative research methods* (pp. 212-223). Newbury Park, CA: Sage.
Strauss, A. L. (1987). *Qualitative analysis for social scientists.* New York: Cambridge University Press.
Strauss, A. L., & Corbin, J. (1990). *Basics of qualitative research: Grounded theory procedures and techniques.* Newbury Park, CA: Sage.
Tesch, R. (1990). *Qualitative research: Analysis types and software tools.* New York: Falmer.
Tesch, R. (1991). Computer programs that assist in the analysis of qualitative data: An overview. *Qualitative Health Research, 1,* 309-325.
Tripp-Riemer, T., & Cohen, M. Z. (1991). Funding strategies for qualitative research. In J. M. Morse (Ed.), *Qualitative nursing research: A contemporary dialogue* (pp. 243-256). Newbury Park, CA: Sage.
van Gennep, A. (1992). The research topic: Or, folklore without end. In J. M. Morse (Ed.), *Qualitative health research* (pp. 65-68). Newbury Park, CA: Sage. (Original work published 1967)
van Manen, M. (1984). Practicing phenomenological writing. *Phenomenology + Pedagogy, 2,* 36-69.
van Manen, M. (1990). *Researching the lived experience.* London: University of Western Ontario.
Wax, R. H. (1971). *Doing fieldwork: Warnings and advice.* Chicago: University of Chicago Press.
Werner, O., & Schoepfle, G. M. (1987a). *Systematic fieldwork: Foundations of ethnography and interviewing* (Vol. 1). Newbury Park, CA: Sage.
Werner, O., & Schoepfle, G. M. (1987b). *Systematic fieldwork: Ethnographic analysis and data management* (Vol. 2). Newbury Park, CA: Sage.
Wilson, H., & Hutchinson, S. (1991). Triangulation of qualitative methods: Heideggerian hermeneutics and grounded theory. *Qualitative Health Research, 1,* 263-276.
Wolcott, H. F. (1992). Posturing in qualitative inquiry. In M. D. LeCompte, W. L. Millroy, & J. Preissle (Eds.), *The handbook of qualitative research in education* (pp. 3-52). New York: Academic Press.

14

Case Studies

ROBERT E. STAKE

SOME case studies are qualitative studies, some are not. In this chapter I will concentrate on case studies where qualitative inquiry dominates, with strong naturalistic, holistic, cultural, phenomenological interests. Case study is not a methodological choice, but a choice of object to be studied. We choose to study the case. We could study it in many ways. The physician studies the child because the child is ill. The child's symptoms are both qualitative and quantitative. The physician's record is more quantitative than qualitative. The social worker studies the child because the child is neglected. The symptoms of neglect are both qualitative and quantitative. The formal record the social worker keeps is more qualitative than quantitative.[1] In many professional and practical fields, cases are studied and recorded. As a form of research, case study is defined by interest in individual cases, not by the methods of inquiry used.

Perhaps a majority of researchers doing case studies call their work by some other name. Howard Becker, for example, when asked at the second Cambridge Conference (Simons, 1980) what he calls his own studies, reluctantly said, "Fieldwork," adding that such labels contribute little to the understanding of what researchers do. The name *case study* is emphasized by some of us because it draws attention to the question of what specifically can be learned from the single case. That epistemological question is the driving question of this chapter: What can be learned from the single case? I will emphasize designing the study to optimize understanding of the case rather than generalization beyond.

Identification of the Case

A case may be simple or complex. It may be a child or a classroom of children or a mobilization of professionals to study a childhood condition. It is one among others. In any given study, we will concentrate on the one. The time we may spend concentrating our inquiry on the one may be long or short, but while we so concentrate, we are engaged in case study.

Custom has it that not everything is a case. A child may be a case. A doctor may be a case—but *his doctoring* lacks the specificity, boundedness, to be called a case.[2] An agency may be a case. The reasons for child neglect or the policies of dealing with neglectful parents would seldom be considered a case. Those topics are generalities rather than specificities. The case is a specific. Even more, the case is a functioning specific. The case, in the words of Louis Smith (1978), is a "bounded system." In the social sciences and human services, it has working parts, it probably is purposive, even having a self. It is an integrated system. The parts do not have to be working well, the purposes may be irrational, but it is a system.

Its behavior is patterned. Consistency and sequentialness are prominent. It is common to recognize that certain features are within the system, within the boundaries of the case, and other features outside. Some are significant as context. William Goode and Paul Hatt (1952) have observed that it is not always easy for the case researcher to say where the child ends and where the environment begins. But the boundedness and the behavior patterns of the system are key factors in understanding the case (Stake, 1988).

Ultimately we may be more interested in a phenomenon or a population of cases than in the individual case. We cannot understand this case without knowing about other cases. But while we are studying it, our meager resources are concentrated on trying to understand its complexities. For the while, we probably will not study comparison cases. We may simultaneously carry on more than one case study, but each case study is a concentrated inquiry into a single case.

The concept of *case* remains subject to debate,[3] and the term *study* is ambiguous (Kemmis, 1980). A case study is both the process of learning about the case and the product of our learning. Lawrence Stenhouse (1984) advocates calling the product a "case record," and occasionally we do, but the practice of calling the final report a "case study" is widely established. Custom is not so strong that researchers (other than graduate students) will get into trouble by calling anything they please a case study.[4] But the more the object of study is a specific, unique, bounded system, the greater the usefulness of the epistemological rationale described in this chapter.

Intrinsic and Instrumental Interest in Cases

Different researchers have different purposes for studying cases. To keep such differences in mind, I find it useful to identify three types of study. In what we may call *intrinsic case study,* study is undertaken because one wants better understanding of this particular case. It is not undertaken primarily because the case represents other cases or because it illustrates a particular trait or problem, but because, in all its particularity and ordinariness, this case itself is of interest. The researcher temporarily subordinates other curiosities so that the case may reveal its story. The purpose is not to come to understand some abstract construct or generic phenomenon, such as literacy or teenage drug use or what a school principal does. The purpose is not theory building—though at other times the researcher may do just that. Study is undertaken because of intrinsic interest in, for example, this particular child, clinic, conference, or curriculum. Some books that illustrate intrinsic case study include the following:

- *Akenfield* (Blythe, 1955/1969)
- *Argonauts of the Western Pacific* (Malinowski, 1922/1984)
- *Bread and Dreams: A Case Study of Bilingual Schooling in the U.S.A.* (MacDonald, Adelman, Kushner, & Walker, 1982)
- *God's Choice* (Peshkin, 1986)

In what we may call *instrumental case study,* a particular case is examined to provide insight into an issue or refinement of theory. The case is of secondary interest; it plays a supportive role, facilitating our understanding of something else. The case is often looked at in depth, its contexts scrutinized, its ordinary activities detailed, but because this helps us pursue the external interest. The case may be seen as typical of other cases or not. (I will discuss the small importance of typicality later.) The choice of case is made because it is expected to advance our understanding of that other interest. Because we simultaneously have several interests, often changing, there is no line distinguishing intrinsic case study from instrumental; rather, a zone of combined purpose separates them. The following books illustrate instrumental case study:

- *A Bright and Shining Lie: John Vann and America in Vietnam* (Sheehan, 1988)
- *Boys in White: Student Culture in Medical School* (Becker, Geer, Hughes, & Strauss, 1961)
- *Middletown: A Study in American Culture* (Lynd & Lynd, 1929)
- *La Vida* (Lewis, 1966)

With even less interest in one particular case, researchers may study a number of cases jointly in order to inquire into the phenomenon, population, or general condition. We might call this *collective case study.*[5] It is not the study of a collective but instrumental study extended to several cases. Individual cases in the collection may or may not be known in advance to manifest the common characteristic. They may be similar or dissimilar, redundancy and variety each having voice. They are chosen because it is believed that understanding them will lead to better understanding, perhaps better theorizing, about a still larger collection of cases. Books illustrating collective case study include the following:

- *Children of Crisis* (Coles, 1967)
- *Habits of the Heart: Individualism and Commitment in American Life* (Bellah, Madsen, Sullivan, Swidler, & Tipton, 1985)
- *Innovation Up Close: How School Improvement Works* (Huberman & Miles, 1984)
- *Savage Inequalities* (Kozol, 1991)

Authors and reports seldom fit neatly into such categories, and I see these three as heuristic more than functional. Peshkin responded to my classification of *God's Choice* by saying: "I mean to present my case so that it can be read with interest in the case itself, but I always have another agenda—to learn from the case about some class of things. Some of what that will be remains an emergent matter for a long time." For three years, Peshkin studied a single school, Bethany Baptist Academy. Until the final chapter, he did not tell the reader about the emergent matters of great importance to him and to school people and citizens broadly. The first order of business was to understand the case. The immediate, if not ultimate, interest was intrinsic. The methods Peshkin used centered on the case, not intentionally on his abiding concerns about community, freedom, and survival.

Other types of case study could be acknowledged. There is a common form used in teaching, we could call it the teaching case study. It is used to illustrate a point, a condition, a category, something important for instruction (Kennedy, 1979). For decades, Harvard Law School and School of Business professors have paraded these cases. For staff development and management training, such reports constitute the articles of the *Journal of Case Research,* key publication of the North American Case Research Association. Used for instruction and consultation, they result from instrumental case study.[6]

One could also make a separate category for biography. Louis Smith's contribution to this *Handbook* (Chapter 18) is case centered, noting that biography calls for demanding chronological structures and extra attention to procedures for the protection of human subjects. Similarly, television documentaries, many of them easily classifiable as case studies, require their own methods. In law, the case has a special definition: the practice of law itself could be called case study. The work of ethnographers, critical theorists, institutional demographers, and many others has conceptual and stylistic patterns that not only amplify the taxonomy but extend the foundation for case study research in the social sciences and social services. My purpose in categorization here is more limited: To emphasize variation in the concern for and methodological orientation to the case, I have named three types of study—intrinsic, instrumental, and collective.

Study of the Particular

Case researchers seek out both what is common and what is particular about the case, but the end result regularly presents something unique (Stouffer, 1941). Uniqueness is likely to be pervasive, extending to

1. the nature of the case
2. its historical background
3. the physical setting
4. other contexts, including economic, political, legal, and aesthetic
5. other cases through which this case is recognized
6. those informants through whom the case can be known

To study the case, many researchers will gather data on all the above.

Uniqueness, particularity, diversity is not universally loved. Case study methodology has suffered somewhat because it has sometimes been presented by people who have a lesser regard for study of the particular (Denzin, 1989; Glaser & Strauss, 1967; Herriott & Firestone, 1983; Yin, 1984). Many social scientists have written about case study as if intrinsic study of a particular case is not as important as studies to obtain generalizations pertaining to a population of cases. They have emphasized case study as typification of other cases, as exploration leading up to generalization-producing studies, or as an occasional early step in theory building. Thus, by these respected authorities, case study method has been little honored as the intrinsic study of a valued particular, as it is generally in biography, institutional self-study, program evaluation, therapeutic practice, and many lines of work. But insistence on the ultimacy of theory building appears to be diminishing in qualitative social science.

Case study can usefully be seen as a small step toward grand generalization (Campbell, 1975), but generalization should not be emphasized in all research (Feagin, Orum, & Sjoberg, 1991; Simons, 1980). Damage occurs when the commitment to generalize or create theory runs so strong that the researcher's attention is drawn away from features important for understanding the case itself.[7] The case study researcher faces a strategic choice in deciding how much and how long the complexities of the case should be studied. Not everything about the case can be understood—how much needs to be? Each researcher will make up his or her own mind.

TABLE 14.1 An Example of Issue Development in a Study

1. *Topical issue:* The goals of the music education program.
2. *Foreshadowed problem:* The majority of the community supports the present emphasis on band, chorus, and performances, but a few teachers and community leaders want a more intellectual emphasis, such as history, literature, and critical review of music.
3. *Issue under development:* What is the extent of interest of this teaching staff in teaching music courses required of everyone?
4. *Assertion:* This community would not generate the extra funding necessary for providing intellectual learning of music for all secondary school students.

Uniqueness of Situations

With its own unique history, the case is a complex entity operating within a number of contexts, including the physical, economic, ethical, and aesthetic. The case is singular, but it has subsections (e.g., production, marketing, sales departments), groups (e.g., students, teachers, parents), occasions (e.g., workdays, holidays, days near holidays), a concatenation of domains—many so complex that at best they can only be sampled.

Holistic case study calls for the examination of these complexities. As Egon Guba and Yvonna Lincoln point out in Chapter 6 of this volume, much qualitative research is based on a holistic view that social phenomena, human dilemmas, and the nature of cases are situational and influenced by happenings of many kinds. Qualitative researchers are sometimes disposed toward causal determination of events, but more often tend to perceive, as did Tolstoy in *War and Peace,* events not simply and singly caused. Many find the search for cause of little use, dramatizing, rather, the coincidence of events, seeing some events purposive, some situational, many of them interrelated. They favor inquiry designs seeking data describing diverse operations of the case. To do case studies does not require examination of diverse issues and contexts, but that is the way that most qualitative researchers do them.

Issues

Whether so called or not, the researcher's themes or "abstract dimensions" are often *issues,* problematic circumstances that draw upon the common disciplines of knowledge, such as sociology, economics, ethics, and literary criticism. With broader purview than that of crafters of experiments and testers of hypotheses, qualitative case researchers orient to complexities connecting ordinary practice in natural habitats to the abstractions and concerns of diverse academic disciplines. This broader purview is applied to the single case. Generalization and proof (Becker, 1958) are not without risk.[8]

Even when stated as generalities, the issues are matters for study regarding the specific case. Starting with a topical concern, researchers pose foreshadowed problems,[9] concentrate on issue-related observations, interpret patterns of data that reform the issues as assertions. The transformation I have experienced in my work in program evaluation is illustrated by the sequence in Table 14.1, issues for a hypothetical case study of a music education program.

In choosing issues to organize their study, researchers accentuate one task or another. To treat the case as an exemplar, they ask, Which issues bring out our initial concerns, the dominant theme? To maximize understanding of the case, they ask, Which issues seek out compelling uniquenesses? For an evaluation study, they ask, Which issues help reveal merit and shortcoming? And in general, they ask, Which issues facilitate the planning and activities of inquiry, including inspiring and rehabilitating the researcher? Issues are chosen partly in terms of what can be learned within the opportunities for study. They will be chosen differently depending on the importance of each task, differently by different researchers. One might say a personal contract is drawn between researcher and phenomenon. For all the devotion to science or a client, What is to be learned here that a solitary researcher feels compelled to learn?

The issues used to *organize* the study may or may not be the ones used to report the case to others. Observing is different work from presenting the case report. At the end, it may be the readers' issues that determine what will be said. Some researchers choose to serve the readers, even when quite unsure as to who the eventual readers might be and as to the concerns they have.

Telling the Story

It is not uncommon for qualitative case researchers to call for letting the case "tell its own story" (Carter, 1993; Coles, 1989). We cannot be sure that a case telling its own story will tell all or tell well, but the ethnographic ethos of *interpretive* study, seeking out emic meanings held by the people within the case, is strong. The choices of presentation styles are many; John Van Maanen (1988) identifies seven: realistic, impressionistic, confessional, critical, formal, literary, and jointly told. One cannot know at the outset what the issues, the perceptions, the theory will be. Case researchers enter the scene expecting, even knowing, that certain events, problems, relationships will be important, yet discover that some actually are of little consequence (Parlett & Hamilton, 1976; Smith, Chapter 18, this volume). Case content evolves in the act of writing itself.

Even though committed to empathy and multiple realities, it is the researcher who decides what is the case's own story, or at least what of the case's own story he or she will report. More will be pursued than was volunteered. Less will be reported than was learned. Even though the competent researcher will be guided by what the case may indicate is most important, even though patrons and other researchers will advise, what is necessary for an understanding of the case will be decided by the researcher. It may be the case's own story, but it is the researcher's dressing of the case's own story. This is not to dismiss the aim of finding the story that best represents the case, but to remind that the criteria of representation ultimately are decided by the researcher.

Many a researcher would like to tell the whole story but of course cannot; the whole story exceeds anyone's knowing, anyone's telling. Even those inclined to tell all find strong the obligation to winnow and consolidate. A continuum runs from telling lots to telling nothing. The holistic researcher, like the single-issue researcher, must choose. Criteria for selecting content are many (Van Maanen, 1988). Some are set by funding agencies, prospective readers, rhetorical convention, the researcher's career pattern, the prospect of publication. Some criteria are set by a notion of what represents the case most fully, most appreciably for the hospitality received, most comprehensibly. These are subjective choices not unlike those all researchers make in choosing what to study. Some are made while designing the case study, but some continue to be made through the final hours.

Learning From the Particular Case

The researcher is a teacher using at least two pedagogical methods (Eisner, 1985). Teaching *didactically,* the researcher teaches what he or she has learned. Arranging for what educationists call *discovery learning,* the researcher provides material for readers to learn, on their own, things the teacher does not know as well as those he or she does know. What can one learn from a single case? Donald Campbell (1975), David Hamilton (1980), Stephen Kemmis (1980), Robert Yin (1989), and William Firestone (in press) have considered the epistemology of the particular. How we may learn from the singular case ultimately derives from how the case is like and not like other cases—yet, as I claim later, direct comparison diminishes opportunity to learn from it.

From case reports we learn both propositional and experiential knowledge (Geertz, 1983; Polanyi, 1962; Rumelhart & Ortony, 1977; von Wright, 1971). Certain descriptions and assertions are assimilated by readers into memory. When the researcher's narrative provides opportunity for vicarious experience, readers extend their memories of happenings. Naturalistic, ethnographic case materials, to some extent, parallel actual experience, feeding into the most fundamental processes of awareness and understanding. Deborah Trumbull and I have called these processes *naturalistic generalization* (Stake & Trumbull, 1982). The reader comes to know some things told, as if he or she had experienced them. Enduring meanings come from encounter, and are modified and reinforced by repeated encounter.

In life itself, this occurs seldom to the individual alone but in the presence (if not proximity) of others. In a social process, together they bend, spin, consolidate, and enrich their understandings. We come to know what has happened partly in terms of what others reveal as their experience. The case researcher emerges from one social experience, the observation, to choreograph another, the report. Knowledge is socially constructed—we constructivists believe (see Schwandt, Chapter 7, this volume)—and thus case study researchers assist readers in the construction of knowledge.

Knowledge Transfer From Researcher to Reader

Both researcher and reader need conceptual structures, advanced organizers (Ausubel & Fitzgerald, 1961), schemata (Anderson, 1977), scaffolding (Cazden, 1988), an unfolding of realization (Bohm, 1985). They do not have to be aware of this need. Thought itself, conversation surely, and writing especially draw phrases into paragraphs, append labels onto constructs. Attention focuses. Generalization can be an unconscious process.

In private and personal ways, ideas are structured, highlighted, subordinated, connected, embedded *in* contexts, embedded *with* illustration, laced with favor and doubt. However moved to share ideas, however clever and elaborated their writings, case researchers, as others, pass along to readers some of their personal meanings of events and relationships—and fail to pass along others. They know that the reader too will add and subtract, invent and shape—reconstructing the knowledge in ways that leave it differently connected and more likely to be personally useful.

Knowledge of the case faces hazardous passage from writer to reader. The writer needs ways of safeguarding the trip. Even as reading begins, often much earlier, the case assumes a place in the company of previously known cases. Conceptually for the reader, the new case cannot be but some combination of cases already known. A new case without commonality cannot be understood. Yet a new case without distinction will not be noticed. Researchers cannot know well the already-known cases, the peculiarities of mind, of their readers. They seek ways to protect and validate the transfer of knowledge.

The researcher recognizes the need to accommodate to readers' preexisting knowledge. Though everyone deals with this need every day and draws upon a lifetime of experience, we know precious little about how new experience merges with old. According to Spiro, Vispoel, Schmitz, Samarapungavan, and Boerger (1987), most personal experience is "ill-structured," neither pedagogically nor epistemologically neat; it follows that a well-structured, propositional presentation will often not be the better way to "transfer" experiential knowledge. The reader has a certain "cognitive flexibility," the readiness to assemble a situation-relative schema from the knowledge fragments of a new encounter. Spiro et al. contend that

> the best way to learn and instruct in order to attain the goal of cognitive flexibility in knowledge representation for future application is by a method of case-based presentations which treats a content domain as a landscape that is explored by "criss-crossing" it in many directions, by reexamining each case "site" in the varying contexts of different neighboring cases, and by using a variety of abstract dimensions for comparing cases. (p. 178)

Transfer remains difficult to understand. Even less understood is how a small aspect of the case may be found by many readers to modify an existing understanding about cases in general, even when the case is not typical. In a ghetto school, I observed a teacher with one set of rules for classroom decorum, except that for one nearly expelled, indomitable youngster, a more liberal set had to be continuously invented. Reading my account, teachers from very different schools agreed with both. "Yes, you have to be strict with the rules." "Yes, sometimes you have to bend the rules." They recognized in the report an unusual but generalizable circumstance. People find in case reports certain insights into the human condition, even while they are well aware of the atypicality of the case. They may be too quick to accept the insight. The case researcher needs to provide grounds for validating both the observation and generalization.

Triangulation

With reporting and reading "ill-structured" and within an atmosphere of constructivism, it is not surprising to find tolerance for ambiguity and championing of pluralism. Still, most case researchers are concerned about the validity of their communication. Meanings do not transfer intact, but take on some of the conceptual uniqueness of the reader, but there is expectation that the meanings of situation, observation, reporting, and reading will have a certain correspondence. Joseph Maxwell (1992) has written of the need for thinking of validity separately for descriptions, interpretations, theories, generalizations, and evaluative judgments.

To reduce the likelihood of misinterpretation, we employ various procedures, including redundancy of data gathering and procedural challenges to explanations (Denzin, 1989; Goetz & LeCompte, 1984). For qualitative case work, these procedures generally are called *triangulation.* David Altheide and John Johnson discuss them in Chapter 30 of this volume, and Michael Huberman and Matthew Miles address them in Chapter 27. Triangulation has been generally considered a process of using multiple perceptions to clarify meaning, verifying the repeatability of an observation or interpretation. But, acknowledging that no observations or interpretations are perfectly repeatable, triangulation serves also to clarify meaning by identifying different ways the phenomenon is being seen (Flick, 1992).

Comparisons

Researchers report their cases as cases that will be compared with others. They differ as to how much they will take responsibility for making comparisons, setting up comparative cases for the reader, or acknowledging reference cases different for each reader. Most naturalistic, ethnographic, phenomenological researchers will concentrate on describing the present case in sufficient detail so that the reader can make good comparisons. Sometimes the researcher will point out comparisons that might be made. More quantitative case researchers will try to provide some comparisons, sometimes by presenting one or more reference cases, sometimes providing statistical norms for reference groups from which a hypothetical reference case can be imagined. Both the quantitative and qualitative approaches provide narrow grounds for strict comparison of cases—even though a tradition of grand comparison exists within comparative anthropology and related disciplines (Firestone, in press; Ragin, 1987; Tobin, 1989).

I see comparison as an epistemological function competing with learning about and from the particular case. Comparison is a powerful conceptual mechanism, fixing attention upon the few attributes being compared and obscuring other knowledge about the case. Comparative description is the opposite of what Clifford Geertz (1973) calls "thick description." Thick description of the music program might include the staffing, recent program changes, the charisma of the choral director, the working relationship with the Catholic church organist, a critical vote of the school board, and the lack of student interest in taking up the clarinet. Such identify the vitality, trauma, and uniqueness of the case. Comparison might be made on any of these characteristics but tends to be made on more general variables traditionally noted in the organization of music programs, such as staffing, budget, and tour policy. Even with major attention to the bases for comparison, they will be few, with uniquenesses and complexities glossed over. Designed comparison substitutes (a) the *comparison* for (b) the *case* as the focus of the study.

Regardless of the type of case study—intrinsic, instrumental, or collective—readers learn little from researcher-provided cases as the basis for comparison. When there are multiple cases of intrinsic interest, then of course it can be useful to compare them. But usually, for the researcher, there is but one or none of intrinsic interest. Readers with intrinsic interest in the case learn more of it directly from the description, not ignoring comparisons with other cases but not concentrating on comparisons. Readers examining instrumental case studies are shown how the phenomenon exists within a particular case. Seldom is there interest in how a case without the phenomenon is different because there are too many ways to be different.[10] Generalizations from differences between any two cases are much less to be trusted than generalizations from one. Illustration as to how the phenomenon occurs in the circumstances of the particular exemplar can be valued and trustworthy knowledge.

Many are the ways of conceptualizing cases to maximize learning from the case. The case is expected to be something that functions, that operates; the study is the observation of operations. There is something to be described and interpreted. The conceptions of most naturalistic, holistic, ethnographic, phenomenological case studies emphasize objective description and personalistic interpretation, a respect and curiosity for culturally different perceptions of phenomena, and empathic representation of local settings—all blending (perhaps clumped) within a constructivist epistemology.

Methods of Study

Perhaps the simplest rule for method in qualitative case work is this: Place the best brains available into the thick of what is going on. The brain work ostensibly is observational, but more basically, reflective. (I would prefer to call it *interpretive* to emphasize the production of meanings, but ethnographers have tried to make that term mean "to learn the special views of actors, the local meanings"; see Erickson, 1986; Schwandt, Chapter 7, this volume.) In being ever reflective, the researcher is committed to pondering the impressions, deliberating recollections and records—but not necessarily following the conceptualizations of theorists, actors, or audiences (Carr & Kemmis, 1986). Local meanings are important; foreshadowed meanings are important; and readers' consequential meanings are important. The case researcher teases out meanings of these three kinds and, for whatever reason, works on one kind more than the others. In each case, the work is reflective.[11]

If we typify qualitative casework, we see data sometimes precoded but continuously interpreted, on first sighting and again and again. Records and tabulations are perused not only for classification and pattern recognition but for "crisscrossed" reflection (Spiro et al., 1987). Qualitative case study is characterized by the main researcher spending substantial time, on site, personally in contact with activities and operations of the case, reflecting, revising meanings of what is going on.

Naturalistic, ethnographic, phenomenological caseworkers seek to see what is natural in happenings, in settings, in expressions of value. What the researchers are unable to see for themselves is obtained by interviewing people who did see or by finding documents recording it. The contributions to this volume by Paul Atkinson and Martyn Hammersley (Chapter 15), Andrea Fontana and James Frey (Chapter 22), Patricia and Peter Adler (Chapter 23), Ian Hodder (Chapter 24), Douglas Harper (Chapter 25), and Jean Clandinin and Michael Connelly (Chapter 26) elaborate extensively on the methods of qualitative research. These pertain, of course, to qualitative case study.

Reviewing the literature, I have found case study methods written about largely by people who believe that the research should contribute to scientific generalization. The bulk of case study work, however, is done by people who have *intrinsic* interests in the cases. Their intrinsic case study designs draw the researcher toward understanding of what is important about that case within its own world, not so much the world of researchers and theorists, but developing its issues, contexts, and interpretations. In contrast, the methods of instrumental case study draw the researcher toward illustrating how the concerns of researchers and theorists are manifest in the case. Because the critical issues are more likely to be known in advance and following disciplinary expectations, such a design can take greater advantage of already-developed instruments and preconceived coding schemes.

In intrinsic case study, researchers do not avoid generalization—they cannot. Certainly they generalize to happenings of their cases at times yet to come and in other situations. They expect their readers to comprehend their interpretations but to arrive as well at their own. Thus the methods for casework actually used are to learn enough about the case to encapsulate complex meanings into a finite report but to describe the case in sufficient descriptive narrative so that readers can vicariously experience these happenings, and draw their own conclusions.

Case Selection

Perhaps the most unique aspect of case study in the social sciences and human services is the selection of cases to study. Intrinsic casework regularly begins with cases prespecified. The doctor, the social worker, the program evaluator receive their cases; they do not choose them. The cases are of prominent interest before formal study begins. Instrumental and collective casework regularly require cases to be chosen. Understanding the critical phenomena may depend on choosing the case well (Patton, 1990; Yin, 1989). Suppose we are trying to understand the behavior of people who take hostages, and decide to probe the phenomenon using a case study. Hostage taking does not happen often—in the whole world there are few cases to choose. Current options—let us imagine—boil down to a bank robber, an airline hijacker, an estranged father who kidnapped his own child, and a Shi'ite Muslim group. We want to generalize about hostage-taking behavior, yet realize that each of these cases, this sample of one, weakly *represents* the larger group of interest.

When one designs a study in the manner advocated by Miles and Huberman (1984; see also Chapter 27, this volume), nothing is more important than making a proper selection of cases. It is a sampling problem. The cases will be selected to represent some population of cases. The phenomenon of interest observable in the case represents the phenomenon generally. For Miles and Huberman, Yin, and Malinowski, the main work is science, an enterprise to gain the best possible explanations of phenomena (von Wright, 1971). In the beginning, phenomena are given; the cases are opportunities to study the phenomena.

The phenomenon on the table is hostage taking. We want to improve our understanding of hostage taking, to fit it into what we know about criminology, conflict resolution, human relations—that is, various "abstract dimensions."[12] We recognize a large population of hypothetical cases, a small subpopulation of accessible cases. We want to generalize about hostage taking without special interest in any of those cases available for study. On representational grounds, the epistemological opportunity seems small, but we are optimistic that we can learn some important things from almost any case. We choose one or a small number of exemplars. Hostages usually are strangers who happen to be available. We might rule out studying a father who takes his own child as hostage. Such kidnappings may actually be more common than other kinds, but we rule out the father. We are more interested in hostage-taking accompanying a criminal act, hostage taking in order to gain refuge. The researcher examines various interests in the phenomenon, selecting a case of some typicality, but leaning toward those cases that seem to offer *opportunity to learn.* My choice would be to take that case from which we feel we can learn the most.[13] That may mean taking the one that we can spend the most time with. Potential for learning is a different and sometimes superior criterion to representativeness. Often it is better to learn a lot from an atypical case than a little from a magnificently typical case.

Another illustration: Suppose we are interested in the attractiveness of interactive (the visitor manipulates, gets feedback) displays in children's museums. We have resources to study four museums, to do a collective study of four cases. It is likely that we would set up a typology, perhaps of (a) museum types, namely, art, science, and history; (b) city types, namely, large and very large; and (c) program types, namely, exhibitory and participative; making a 12-cell matrix. Examples probably cannot be found for all 12 cells, but resources do not allow studying 12 anyway. With four to be studied, we are likely to start out thinking we should have one art, one history, and two science museums (because interactive displays are more common in science museums), two located in large and two in very large cities, and two each of the program types. But when we actually look at existing cases, the logistics, the potential reception, the resources, and additional characteristics of relevance, we move toward choosing four museums to study that offer variety (falling short of structured representation) across the attributes, the four that give us the best opportunities to learn about interactive displays.[14] Any best possible selection of four museums from a balanced design would not give us compelling representation of museums as a whole, and certainly not a statistical basis for generalizing about interactions between interactivity and site characteristics. Several desirable types usually have to be omitted.

Even for collective case studies, selection by sampling of attributes should not be the highest priority. Balance and variety are important; opportunity to learn is of primary importance.

Sampling Within the Case

The same process of selection will occur as part of intrinsic case study. Even though the case is decided in advance (usually), there are subsequent choices to make about persons, places, and events to observe. Here again, training and intuition tell us to seek a good sample. Suppose that we are studying a program for placing computers in the homes of fourth graders for scholastic purposes.[15] The cases—that is, the school sites—have already been selected. Although there is a certain coordination of activity, each participating researcher has one case study to develop. A principal issue has to do with impact on the family, because certain expectations of computer use accompany placement in the home. (The computer should be available for word processing, record keeping, and games by family members, but certain time should be set aside for fourth-grade homework.) At one site, 50 homes now have computers. The researcher can get certain information from every home, but observation in the home can occur in only a small number. Which homes should be selected? Just as in the collective case study, the researcher notes attributes of interest: gender of the fourth grader, siblings, family structure, home discipline, previous use of computers and other technology in the homes, and so on. The researcher discusses these characteristics with informants, gets recommendations, visits several homes, and gets attribute data. The choice is made,[16] assuring variety but not necessarily representativeness, without strong argument for typicality, again weighted by considerations of access and even by hospitality, for the time is short and perhaps too little can be learned from inhospitable parents. Here, too, the primary criterion is opportunity to learn.

Ethics

Ethical considerations for qualitative research are discussed by Maurice Punch in Chapter 5 of this volume. Case studies often deal with matters of public interest but for which there is neither public nor scholarly "right to know." Funding, scholarly intent, or a passed preliminary oral does not constitute license to invade the privacy of others. The value of the best research is not likely to outweigh injury to a person exposed. Qualitative researchers are guests in the private spaces of the world. Their manners should be good and their code of ethics strict.

With much qualitative work, case study research shares an intense interest in personal views and circumstances. Those whose lives and expressions are portrayed risk exposure and embarrassment: loss of standing, employment, self-esteem. Issues of observation and reportage should be discussed in advance. Limits of accessibility should be suggested and agreements heeded. It is important but not sufficient for targeted persons to receive drafts of how they are presented, quoted, or interpreted, and for the researcher to listen well for cries of concern. It is imperative that great caution be exercised to minimize the risks. Rules for protection of human subjects should be heeded. The researcher should go beyond those rules, avoiding low-priority probing of sensitive issues, drawing upon others to oversee the protective system.

Summary

As I have discussed above, the major conceptual responsibilities of the qualitative case researcher are as follows:

1. bounding the case, conceptualizing the object of study
2. selecting phenomena, themes, or issues—that is, the research questions—to emphasize
3. seeking patterns of data to develop the issues
4. triangulating key observations and bases for interpretation
5. selecting alternative interpretations to pursue
6. developing assertions or generalizations about the case

Except for the first of these, the steps are similar to those taken by other qualitative researchers. The more the researcher has intrinsic interest in the case, the more the focus of study will usually be on the case's uniqueness, particular context, issues, and story. Some major stylistic options for case researchers include the following:

1. how much to make the report a story
2. how much to compare with other cases
3. how much to formalize generalizations or leave that to readers
4. how much, in the report, to include description of the researcher as participant
5. whether or not and how much to anonymize

Case study is a part of scientific method, but its purpose is not limited to the advance of science. Whereas single or a few cases are poor representation of a population of cases and poor grounds for advancing grand generalization, a single case as negative example can establish limits to grand generalization. For example, we lose confidence in the generalization that a child of separated parents is better off placed with the mother when we find a single instance of resultant injury. Case studies are of value in refining theory and suggesting complexities for further investigation, as well as helping to establish the limits of generalizability.

Case study can also be a disciplined force in public policy setting and reflection on human experience. Vicarious experience is an important basis for refining action options and expectations. Formal epistemology needs further development, but somehow people draw from the description of an individual case implications for other cases, not always correctly, but with a confidence shared by people of dissimilar views.

The purpose of case study is not to represent the world, but to represent the case. Criteria for conducting the kind of research that leads to valid generalization need modification to fit the search for effective particularization. The utility of case research to practitioners and policy makers is in its extension of experience. The methods of qualitative case study are largely the methods of disciplining personal and particularized experience.

Notes

1. Case study can be qualitative or quantitative or a combination of the two. In search of fundamental pursuits common to both qualitative and quantitative research, Robert Yin (1992) analyzed three thoroughly crafted research efforts: a quantitative investigation to resolve disputed authorship of the *Federalist Papers,* a qualitative study of Soviet intent at the time of the Cuban missile crisis, and his own studies of the recognizability of human faces. He found four common commitments: to bring expert knowledge to bear upon the phenomena studied, to round up all the relevant data, to examine rival interpretations, and to ponder and probe the degree to which the findings have implication elsewhere. These commitments are as important in case research as in any other kind of research.

2. The editors have reminded me of the ethnomethodological treatment of topic and method. Ethnomethodologists study methods as topics of inquiry, examining how certain things get done, and so on (Garfinkel, 1967). Coming to understand a case usually requires extensive examining of how things get done, but the prime referent in case study is the case, not the methods by which cases operate.

3. Definition of the case is not independent of interpretive paradigm or methods of inquiry. Seen from different worldviews and in different situations, the "same" case is different. And however we originally define the case, the working definition changes as we study. And the definition of the case changes in different ways under different methods of study. The case of Theodore Roosevelt was not just differently portrayed but differently defined as biographer Edmund Morris (1979) presented him as "the Dude from New York," "the Dear Old Beloved Brother," "the Snake in the Grass," "the Rough Rider," "the Most Famous Man in America," and so on.

4. The history of case study, like the history of curiosity and common sense, is found throughout the library. Useful briefs are included in Bogdan and Biklen (1982), Delamont (1992), Feagin, Orum, and Sjoberg (1991), Stake (1978), and throughout this volume.

5. Collective case study is essentially what Robert Herriott and William Firestone (1983) call "multisite qualitative research." A number of German sociologists, such as Martin Kohli and Fritz Schutze, have used collective case studies with Strauss's grounded theory approach.

6. Historians and political scientists regularly examine a singular episode or relationship, such as Napoleon's siege of Moscow or the Cuban missile crisis. I choose not to call these case studies because the episode or relationship—however complex, impacting, and bounded—does not have its own purpose and self.

7. In 1922, Bronislaw Malinowski said, "One of the first conditions of acceptable Ethnographic work certainly is that it should deal with the totality of all social, cultural and psychological aspects of the community" (1922/1984, p. xvi). Good spirit there, although totalities defy the acuity of the eye and the longevity of the watch.

8. Generalization from collective case study has been discussed by Herriott and Firestone (1983), Lofland and Lofland (1984), Miles and Huberman (1984), and again by Firestone (in press).

9. Malinowski (1922/1984) claims we can distinguish between arriving with closed minds and arriving with an idea of what to look for: "Good training in theory, and acquaintance with its latest results, is not identical with being burdened with 'preconceived ideas.' If a man sets out on an expedition, determined to prove certain hypotheses, if he is incapable of changing his views constantly and casting them off ungrudgingly under the pressure of evidence, needless to say his work will be worthless. But the more problems he brings with him into the field, the more he is in the habit of moulding his theories according to facts, and of seeing facts in their bearing upon theory, the better he is equipped for the work. Preconceived ideas are pernicious in any scientific work, but *foreshadowed problems* are the main endowment of a scientific thinker, and these problems are first revealed to the observer by his theoretical studies" (p. 9).

10. Evaluation studies comparing the innovative program to a control case regularly fail to make the comparison

credible. No matter how well studied, the control case too weakly represents cases already known to the reader. By comprehensively describing the program case, the researcher should help the reader draw naturalistic generalizations.

11. Ethnographic use of the term *reflective* sometimes limits attention to the need for self-challenging the researcher's etic issues, frame of reference, cultural bias (see Atkinson & Hammersley, Chapter 15, this volume). That challenge is important, but, following Donald Schön (1983), I refer to a general frame of mind when I call qualitative casework reflective.

12. As indicated in a previous section, I call them issues or issue areas. Mary Kennedy (1979) calls them "relevant attributes." Spiro et al. (1987) call them "abstract dimensions." Malinowski (1922/1984) calls them "theories." In our research, these will be our working theories more than the grand theories of the disciplines.

13. My emphasis is on learning the most about both the individual case and the phenomenon, especially the latter if the special circumstances may yield unusual insight into an issue.

14. Firestone (in press) advises maximizing diversity and being "as like the population of interest as possible."

15. This in fact happened with the Buddy Project, a component of the Indiana public school reform effort in 1990-1993 (see Quinn & Quinn, 1992).

16. Patton (1990), Strauss and Corbin (1990), and Firestone (in press) have discussed successive selection of cases over time.

References

Anderson, R. C. (1977). The notion of schema and the educational enterprise. In R. C. Anderson, R. J. Spiro, & W. E. Montague (Eds.), *Schooling and the acquisition of knowledge* (pp. 415-431). Hillsdale, NJ: Lawrence Erlbaum.

Ausubel, D. P., & Fitzgerald, D. (1961). Meaningful learning and retention: Interpersonal cognitive variables. *Review of Educational Research, 31,* 500-510.

Becker, H. S. (1958). Problems of interference and proof in participant observation. *American Sociological Review, 23,* 652-660.

Becker, H. S., Geer, B., Hughes, E. C., & Strauss, A. L. (1961). *Boys in white: Student culture in medical school.* Chicago: University of Chicago Press.

Bellah, R. N., Madsen, R., Sullivan, W. M., Swidler, A., & Tipton, S. M. (1985). *Habits of the heart: Individualism and commitment in American life.* Berkeley: University of California Press.

Blythe, R. (1969). *Akenfield.* London: Penguin. (Original work published 1955)

Bogdan, R. C., & Biklen, S. K. (1982). *Qualitative research for education: An introduction to theory and methods.* Boston: Allyn & Bacon.

Bohm, D. (1985). *Unfolding meaning: A weekend of dialogue with David Bohm.* New York: Routledge.

Campbell, D. T. (1975). Degrees of freedom and case study. *Comparative Political Studies, 8,* 178-193.

Carr, W. L., & Kemmis, S. (1986). *Becoming critical: Education, knowledge and action research.* London: Falmer.

Carter, K. (1993). The place of story in the study of teaching and teacher education. *Educational Researcher, 22,* 5-12.

Cazden, C. B. (1988). *Classroom discourse: The language of teaching and learning.* Portsmouth, NH: Heinemann Educational Books.

Coles, R. (1967). *Children of crisis.* Boston: Little, Brown.

Coles, R. (1989). *The call of stories: Teaching and the moral imagination.* Boston: Houghton Mifflin.

Delamont, S. (1992). *Fieldwork in educational settings: Methods, pitfalls and perspectives.* London: Falmer.

Denzin, N. K. (1989). *The research act* (3rd ed.). Englewood Cliffs, NJ: Prentice Hall.

Eisner, E. (Ed.). (1985). *Learning and teaching the ways of knowing* (84th yearbook of the National Society for the Study of Education). Chicago: University of Chicago Press.

Erickson, F. (1986). Qualitative methods in research on teaching. In M. C. Wittrock (Ed.), *Handbook of research on teaching* (3rd ed., pp. 119-161). New York: Macmillan.

Feagin, J. R., Orum, A. M., & Sjoberg, G. (1991). *A case for the case study.* Chapel Hill: University of North Carolina Press.

Firestone, W. A. (in press). Alternative arguments for generalizing from data as applied to qualitative research. *Educational Researcher.*

Flick, U. (1992). Triangulation revisited: Strategy of validation or alternative? *Journal for the Theory of Social Behaviour, 22,* 175-198.

Garfinkel, H. (1967). *Studies in ethnomethodology.* New York: Prentice Hall.

Geertz, C. (1973). Thick description: Toward an interpretive theory of culture. In C. Geertz, *The interpretation of cultures* (pp. 3-30). New York: Basic Books.

Geertz, C. (1983). *Local knowledge: Further essays in interpretive anthropology.* New York: Basic Books.

Glaser, B. G., & Strauss, A. L. (1967). *The discovery of grounded theory: Strategies for qualitative research.* Chicago: Aldine.

Goetz, J. P., & LeCompte, M. D. (1984). *Ethnography and qualitative design in educational research.* New York: Academic Press.

Goode, W. J., & Hatt, P. K. (1952). The case study. In W. J. Goode & P. K. Hatt, *Methods of social research* (pp. 330-340). New York: McGraw-Hill.

Hamilton, D. (1980). Some contrasting assumptions about case study research and survey analysis. In H. Simons (Ed.), *Towards a science of the singular* (pp. 76-92). Norwich: University of East Anglia, Centre for Applied Research in Education.

Herriott, R. E., & Firestone, W. A. (1983). Multisite qualitative policy research: Optimizing description and generalizability. *Educational Researcher, 12*(2), 14-19.

Huberman, A. M., & Miles, M. B. (1984). *Innovation up close: How school improvement works.* New York: Plenum.

Kemmis, S. (1980). The imagination of the case and the invention of the study. In H. Simons (Ed.), *Towards a science of the singular* (pp. 93-142). Norwich: University of East Anglia, Centre for Applied Research in Education.

Kennedy, M. M. (1979). Generalizing from single case studies. *Evaluation Quarterly, 3,* 661-678.

Kozol, J. (1991). *Savage inequalities.* New York: Harper.

Lewis, O. (1966). *La vida.* New York: Random House.

Lofland, J., & Lofland, L. H. (1984). *Analyzing social settings: A guide to qualitative observational research.* Belmont, CA: Wadsworth.

Lynd, R. S., & Lynd, H. M. (1929). *Middletown: A study in American culture.* New York: Harcourt, Brace.

MacDonald, B., Adelman, C., Kushner, S., & Walker, R. (1982). *Bread and dreams: A case study of bilingual schooling in the U.S.A.* Norwich: University of East Anglia, Centre for Applied Research in Education.

Malinowski, B. (1984). *Argonauts of the western Pacific.* Prospect Heights, IL: Waveland. (Original work published 1922)

Maxwell, J. A. (1992). Understanding and validity in qualitative research. *Harvard Educational Review, 63,* 279-300.

Miles, M. B., & Huberman, A. M. (1984). *Qualitative data analysis: A sourcebook of new methods.* Beverly Hills, CA: Sage.

Morris, E. (1979). *The rise of Theodore Roosevelt.* New York: Coward, McCann & Geognegan.

Parlett, M., & Hamilton, D. (1976). Evaluation as illumination: A new approach to the study of innovative programmes. In G. V. Glass (Ed.), *Evaluation studies review annual* (Vol. 1, pp. 141-157). Beverly Hills, CA: Sage.

Patton, M. Q. (1990). *Qualitative evaluation and research methods* (2nd ed.). Newbury Park, CA: Sage.

Peshkin, A. (1986). *God's choice.* Chicago: University of Chicago Press.

Polanyi, M. (1962). *Personal knowledge: Towards a post-critical philosophy.* Chicago: University of Chicago Press.

Quinn, W., & Quinn, N. (1992). *Buddy evaluation.* Oakbrook, IL: North Central Regional Educational Laboratory.

Ragin, C. C. (1987). *The comparative method.* Berkeley: University of California Press.

Rumelhart, D. E., & Ortony, A. (1977). The representation of knowledge in memory. In R. C. Anderson, R. J. Spiro, & W. E. Montague (Eds.), *Schooling and the acquisition of knowledge* (pp. 99-135). Hillsdale, NJ: Lawrence Erlbaum.

Schön, D. (1983). *The reflective practitioner: How professionals think in action.* New York: Basic Books.

Sheehan, N. (1988). *A bright and shining lie: John Vann and America in Vietnam.* New York: Random House.

Simons, H. (Ed.). (1980). *Towards a science of the singular.* Norwich: University of East Anglia, Centre for Applied Research in Education.

Smith, L. M. (1978). An evolving logic of participant observation, educational ethnography and other case studies. In L. Shuman (Ed.), *Review of research in education* (Vol. 6, pp. 316-377). Itasca, IL: Peacock.

Spiro, R. J., Vispoel, W. P., Schmitz, J. G., Samarapungavan, A., & Boerger, A. E. (1987). Knowledge acquisition for application: Cognitive flexibility and transfer in complex content domains. In B. C. Britton (Ed.), *Executive control processes* (pp. 177-199). Hillsdale, NJ: Lawrence Erlbaum.

Stake, R. E. (1978). The case study method of social inquiry. *Educational Researcher 7*(2), 5-8.

Stake, R. E. (1988). Case study methods in educational research: Seeking sweet water. In R. M. Jaeger (Ed.), *Complementary methods for research in education* (pp. 253-278). Washington, DC: American Educational Research Association.

Stake, R. E., & Trumbull, D. J. (1982). Naturalistic generalizations. *Review Journal of Philosophy and Social Science, 7,* 1-12.

Stenhouse, L. (1984). Library access, library use and user education in academic sixth forms: An autobiographical account. In R. G. Burgess (Ed.), *The research process in educational settings: Ten case studies* (pp. 211-234). London: Falmer.

Stouffer, S. A. (1941). Notes on the case-study and the unique case. *Sociometry, 4,* 349-357.

Strauss, A. L., & Corbin, J. (1990). *Basics of qualitative research: Grounded theory procedures and techniques.* Newbury Park, CA: Sage.

Tobin, J. (1989). *Preschool in three cultures.* New Haven, CT: Yale University Press.

Van Maanen, J. (1988). *Tales of the field: On writing ethnography.* Chicago: University of Chicago Press.

von Wright, G. H. (1971). *Explanation and understanding.* London: Routledge & Kegan Paul.

Yin, R. K. (1984). *Case study research: Design and methods.* Beverly Hills, CA: Sage.

Yin, R. K. (1989). *Case study research: Design and methods* (2nd ed.). Newbury Park, CA: Sage.

Yin, R. K. (1992, November). *Evaluation: A singular craft.* Paper presented at the annual meeting of the American Evaluation Association, Seattle.

15

Ethnography and Participant Observation

PAUL ATKINSON
MARTYN HAMMERSLEY

ETHNOGRAPHIC methods, relying substantially or partly on "participant observation," have a long if somewhat checkered career in the social sciences. They have been employed, in various guises, by scholars identified with a variety of disciplines. In this chapter we shall not attempt a comprehensive review of the historical and contemporary methodological literature. Rather, we shall focus on several complementary themes that relate to some of the sources and dimensions of diversity and difference in ethnographic research, the recurrent tensions within the broad ethnographic tradition, and contemporary responses to these.

Definition of the term *ethnography* has been subject to controversy. For some it refers to a philosophical paradigm to which one makes a total commitment, for others it designates a method that one uses as and when appropriate. And, of course, there are positions between these extremes. In practical terms, *ethnography* usually refers to forms of social research having a substantial number of the following features:

- a strong emphasis on exploring the nature of particular social phenomena, rather than setting out to test hypotheses about them
- a tendency to work primarily with "unstructured" data, that is, data that have not been coded at the point of data collection in terms of a closed set of analytic categories
- investigation of a small number of cases, perhaps just one case, in detail
- analysis of data that involves explicit interpretation of the meanings and functions of human actions, the product of which mainly takes the form of verbal descriptions and explanations, with quantification and statistical analysis playing a subordinate role at most

The definition of *participant observation* has been less controversial, but its meaning is no easier to pin down. A distinction is sometimes drawn between participant and nonparticipant observation, the former referring to observation carried out when the researcher is playing an established participant role in the scene studied. However, although it is important to recognize the variation to be found in the roles adopted by observers, this simple dichotomy is not very useful, not least because it seems to imply that the nonparticipant observer plays no recognized role at all. This can be the case, but it need not be. More subtle is the widely used fourfold typology: complete observer, observer as participant, participant as observer, and complete participant (Gold, 1958; Junker, 1960). Even this tends to run together several dimensions of variation, such as the following:

- whether the researcher is known to be a researcher by all those being studied, or only by some, or by none
- how much, and what, is known about the research by whom
- what sorts of activities are and are not engaged in by the researcher in the field, and how this locates her or him in relation to the various conceptions of category and group membership used by participants
- what the orientation of the researcher is; how completely he or she consciously adopts the orientation of insider or outsider[1]

Moreover, it has been argued that in a sense *all* social research is a form of participant observation, because we cannot study the social world without being part of it (Hammersley & Atkinson, 1983). From this point of view participant observation is not a particular research technique but a mode of being-in-the-world characteristic of researchers.

Both ethnography and participant observation have been claimed to represent a uniquely humanistic, interpretive approach, as opposed to supposedly "scientific" and "positivist" positions. At the same time, within the ethnographic tradition there are authors espousing a "scientific" stance, as opposed to those who explicitly reject this in favor of an engaged advocacy and a critical stance. The philosophical, ethical, and methodological strands intertwine. They meet and coalesce to form particular "schools" or subtypes of ethnography; they engage with different theoretical movements and fashions (structural functionalism, symbolic interactionism, cultural and cognitive anthropology, feminism, Marxism, ethnomethodology, critical theory, cultural studies, postmodernism, and so on). There is never an orthodoxy. Rather, there is a constant process of oppositions, of successive heterodoxies and heresies. Just as the ethnographer in the field often cultivates the position of the "marginal native" (Freilich, 1970), so ethnographers collectively seek to distance themselves repeatedly from versions of "mainstream" orthodoxy. These are enshrined in the creation myths of ethnography itself. They are carried through into contemporary debates and differences over methodology. The particular focus for methodological or epistemological controversy changes, of course. Earlier debates concerned the problems of data collection, inference, and topic. In the later sections of this chapter we examine more recent controversies, including those concerning the textual character of ethnography and the problems of representation and authority associated with that. The fashionable preoccupations of post-structuralism and postmodernism have both stimulated interest in these new issues and provided a new slant on older themes. They have given a new critical edge to the recurrent methodological issues: the tensions between disinterested observation and political advocacy, between the "scientific" and the "humane," between the "objective" and the "aesthetic." Ethnography has, perhaps, never been so popular within the social sciences. At the same time, its rationales have never been more subject to critical scrutiny and revision.

A Historical Sketch

The beginnings of modern forms of ethnographic fieldwork are usually identified with the shift by social and cultural anthropologists in the late nineteenth and early twentieth centuries toward collecting data firsthand. Often regarded as of most significance here is Malinowski's (1922) fieldwork in the Trobriand Islands, the distinctiveness of which lay in his concern to document the everyday social life of the islanders (Burgess, 1982, pp. 2-4; Kaberry, 1957; Richards, 1939; Young, 1979). However, there are no simple and uncontroversial beginnings in history, and some commentators have taken a longer view, tracing elements of the ethnographic orientation back to eighteenth- and nineteenth-century German philosophy (Hammersley, 1989), to the Renaissance (Rowe, 1965), and even to the writings of the ancients, for example, Herodotus (Wax, 1971).

Although in its particular style and substance ethnography is a twentieth-century phenomenon, its earlier history can be illuminating. It has certainly been shaped by its association with Western interest in the character of non-Western societies and the various motives underlying that interest (Asad, 1973; Clifford, 1988; Marcus & Fischer, 1986). Equally, however, it reflects the influence of historicism, an orientation stemming in large part from the Renaissance, but developed theoretically in the nineteenth century as hermeneutics, the study of the principles of understanding historical texts. At the heart of this was a recognition that people of the past were different in culture from those of today—indeed, that those who lived in different periods in Western history inhabited different cultural worlds. This is not just a matter of the *recognition* of differences but also the judgment that these differences cannot be properly understood by seeing them in terms of deplorable deviation from the norms of the observer's here and now or as signs of cultural backwardness. And it was not long before this recognition of cultural differences was also applied by Westerners to societies contemporaneous with their own, especially to the newly discovered cultures of South America and the East. Most important of all, historicism posed the methodological problem of whether and how other cultures could be understood, a problem that still lies at the heart of modern ethnography.

Perhaps the most distinctive feature of the twentieth century in this respect is the increasing recognition that the problem of understanding is not restricted to the study of past times and other societies—it applies to the study of one's own social surroundings too. The application of ethnographic method by Western anthropologists and sociologists to the investigation of their own societies has been a central feature of twentieth-century social science (Cole, 1977). Furthermore, this is not just a matter of the discovery of pockets of "traditional" culture on the peripheries of these societies (for example, see Arensberg & Kimball, 1940), it also involves the recognition that diverse cultures are to be found in their metropolitan centers (e.g., Hannerz, 1969; Suttles, 1968; Whyte, 1955, 1981).[2]

Running alongside and influencing these developments was the institutionalization of the social sciences in Western universities, a process displaying recurrent crises, most of which centered on the possibility, character, and desirability of a science of social life. In the nineteenth century the conflict was drawn between those attempting to apply an empiricist conception of natural science method to the study of human behavior and those who saw a different model of scientific scholarship as appropriate to the humanities and social sciences. For those influenced by hermeneutics, social research was distinct from physical science because in seeking to understand human actions and institutions we could draw on our own experience and cultural knowledge, and through that reach understanding based on what we share with other human beings, despite cultural differences. Others placed emphasis on the difference between the concern of the natural sciences with the discovery of universal laws (in other words, a nomothetic orientation) and the task of the human sciences as understanding particular phenomena in their sociohistorical contexts (an idiographic orientation) (for discussion of these positions, see, e.g., Frisby, 1976; Hammersley, 1989; von Wright, 1971).

There has been a tendency for ethnographers and others looking back on this history to see it as the story of a conflict between two sides: the positivist paradigm on the one hand against the interpretive or hermeneutic paradigm on the other, with ethnography assumed to belong to the latter (Filstead, 1970; J. K. Smith, 1989; Smith & Heshusius, 1986). This is a misleading picture, however. What we find when we look more closely is a diversity of ideas about the character of human social life and how it is to be understood, as well as about the nature of method in natural science and its relevance to the study of human behavior. To illustrate this point we shall look briefly at two of the key phases in the development of ethnography in the twentieth century: the work of the founders of modern anthropology and that of the Chicago school of sociology.

It makes little difference for our purposes here whom one takes as the key figure in the founding of modern anthropology. All three of the main candidates—Boas, Malinowski, and Radcliffe-Brown—were committed to anthropology as a science, albeit perhaps as a special sort of science. And ethnography was central to their idea of what was scientific about anthropological work: It involved the collection of information firsthand by the anthropologist and the description of the social and cultural characteristics of existing "primitive" societies—as against attempts to infer their history or to judge them in terms of evolutionary level. In other words, the prime motivation on the part of all three founders was the rejection of speculation in favor of empirical investigation, a theme that has always been a central characteristic of empiricism, though not exclusive to it. Furthermore, they all took the natural sciences as an important model for anthropology, though not one to be followed slavishly. Radcliffe-Brown's (1948) aim of creating a "natural science of society" was not discrepant, in broad terms, with the orientations of Malinowski or Boas (see also Harris, 1969; Leach, 1957). At the same time, all three believed that social and cultural phenomena were different in character from physical phenomena and had to be understood in terms of their distinctive nature, an idea that led some of their followers (notably those of Boas) subsequently to deny the appropriateness of the scientific model (for example, see Radin, 1931/1965; see also the discussion in Harris, 1969). But that model, in some form, was never completely abandoned by the bulk of anthropologists, though it probably is under more pressure today than ever before. The tension within ethnography, between science and the humanities, was present from the start; and, as we shall see, it has never been resolved (Redfield, 1962).

Although Chicago sociology of the 1920s and 1930s does not seem to have been strongly influenced by anthropology, its orientation was similar in many respects. Most striking of all, to us today, there was little questioning of the relevance of natural science as a methodological model for social research. Even the debate between advocates of case study and statistical method that raged in the 1920s and 1930s was framed in terms of conflicting interpretations of science rather than acceptance and rejection of it (Bulmer, 1984; Hammersley, 1989; Harvey, 1987). The most influential figure at Chicago was of course Robert

Park, who wedded a newspaper reporter's concern with the concrete and unique to a neo-Kantian philosophical justification for such a focus in terms of the idiographic character of the cultural sciences. And yet he, like William I. Thomas before him, blended this with a nomothetic interest in the discovery of sociocultural laws (Park & Burgess, 1921, 1969). An important influence on this attempt by many in the Chicago school to fuse scientific and hermeneutic influences was pragmatist philosophy, especially the writings of William James, John Dewey, and George Herbert Mead. All these philosophers sought to combine a scientific orientation to the study of human behavior with the heritage of German idealism and historicism. Indeed, they seem to have regarded a scientific reading of Hegel as providing a means of overcoming divisions such as that between the sciences and the humanities. Once again, however, this attempted synthesis must be judged to have been by no means entirely successful.[3]

The subsequent history of ethnography, both in anthropology and sociology, reflects the continuing tension between attraction to and rejection of the model of the natural sciences; yet with few abandoning one pole wholeheartedly for the other. Furthermore, in recent years ethnography has witnessed great diversification, with somewhat different approaches being adopted in different areas, guided by different concerns (from traditional sociocultural description, through applied work designed to inform policy makers, to a commitment to advocacy and furthering political emancipation). And these different goals are variously associated with different forms of ethnographic practice: traditional, long-term, in-depth investigation sometimes being abandoned for condensed fieldwork or primary reliance on unstructured interviews, or for consultancy work or participation in political struggles.

In the next section we shall look in more detail at the major debates to which the ambivalent history and diverse character of modern ethnography have led: the question of whether ethnography is or can be scientific; questions about the proper relationship between ethnographic research and social and political practice; and, finally, arguments surrounding the textual strategies used by ethnographers to represent the lives of others, and the methodological, aesthetic, ethical, and political issues raised by these. These various themes are, of course, frequently closely interrelated.

Ethnography: Science or Not?

As we noted in the previous section, the question of whether there can be a science of social life has preoccupied social scientists for more than a century, and it has been an especially important element in much methodological thinking about ethnography. However, this question is not one that can usefully be answered simply in the affirmative or negative. There is a wider range of possible answers. There are three dimensions structuring this range of possibilities:

- There can be differences in views about which of the natural sciences is to be taken as paradigmatic for scientific method.
- There can be various interpretations even of any method held to be characteristic of particular sciences at particular times.
- There can be disagreements about what aspects of natural scientific method should and should not be applied to social research.

Much thinking about ethnographic methodology in recent years has been based on a rejection of "positivism," broadly conceived as the view that social research should adopt scientific method, that this method is exemplified in the work of modern physicists, and that it consists of the rigorous testing of hypotheses by means of data that take the form of quantitative measurements. Quantitative sociological research is often seen as exemplifying this positivist viewpoint, and it has been criticized by ethnographers for failing to capture the true nature of human social behavior. This arises because it relies on the study of artificial settings (in the case of experiments) and/or on what people say rather than what they do (in the case of survey research); because it seeks to reduce meanings to what is "observable"; and because it treats social phenomena as more clearly defined and static than they are, and as mechanical products of social and psychological factors. This is not to say that quantitative methods are rejected in toto by ethnographers; indeed, structured forms of data collection and quantitative data analysis are frequently employed to some degree or other in ethnographic work. What is rejected is the idea that these methods are the only legitimate, or even the most important, ones. This implies a rejection not so much of quantitative method or even of natural science as a model, but rather of positivism.[4]

However, in recent years a more radical attitude has appeared that *does* seem often to involve rejection of both quantitative method and the scientific model. Whereas at one time ethnographers questioned the frequently assumed relationship between science and quantification, this is now less common; often, the two are rejected together (see, e.g., Lincoln & Guba, 1985; J. K. Smith, 1989). In part, this reflects a general cultural disillusionment with natural science. It is now widely seen as the source of highly destructive weaponry and of substantial planetary pollution, for example. Indeed, some regard it as an oppressive force that dominates the modern world. Elements of this view are to be found in the writings of critical theorists (see Held, 1981; Wellmer, 1969/1974) and the work of feminists, where science is sometimes associated with male aggression and patriarchy (see, for instance, Harding, 1986). Both of these approaches have become influential among ethnographers and have led many to move away from the model of science toward exploring alternatives that reopen links with the humanities (see, e.g., Eisner, 1985, 1988, 1991).

In part, what is involved here is a questioning of the objectivity of social research, ethnographic research included. For instance, it is argued by feminists that the findings of much social research, including ethnographic work, reflect the masculinist assumptions of researchers. It is not just that they have tended to neglect and occasionally to disparage the activities and experiences of women, but that the whole perspective on the world that they provide is limited by their male point of view. This is not dissimilar in character to earlier Marxist criticisms of the ideological character of bourgeois social science, and analogous criticisms have long been found among advocates of black sociology (for a discussion that draws these parallels, see Hammersley, 1992a).

Increasingly, however, this challenge to the objectivity of ethnographic (and other) research has been developed into a more fundamental questioning of the very possibility of social scientific knowledge. It is pointed out that the accounts produced by researchers are constructions, and as such they reflect the presuppositions and sociohistorical circumstances of their production. This is held to contradict the aspiration of social science (including much ethnography) to produce knowledge that is universally valid, in other words, that captures the *nature* of the social world. In the past, ethnographers very often relied precisely on arguments about the greater capacity of their approach to represent the nature of social reality accurately (see, e.g., Blumer, 1969). Such arguments are rarer these days, under the influence of various forms of antirealism, whether constructivism (Guba, 1990), philosophical hermeneutics (J. K. Smith, 1989), or poststructuralism (Clough, 1992; Denzin, 1990; Lather, 1991).

An interesting illustration of the last of these influences is to be found in commentaries by Denzin and Richardson on a recent dispute about the accuracy of Whyte's (1955) classic ethnographic study of Boston's North End. Whyte's pioneering study was concerned with documenting various aspects of the lives of people in this community, especially the "Corner Boys." The accuracy of Whyte's account is questioned by Boelen (1992) on the basis of some recent interviews, though the original account is defended by a surviving member of the Corner Boys (Orlandella, 1992). Moving off at a tangent, Denzin (1992) and Richardson (1992) effectively dismiss this dispute on the grounds that all accounts are constructions and that the whole issue of which account more accurately represents reality is meaningless.

Also associated with this radical critique has been a tendency to direct some of the criticisms that have long been applied to quantitative research at traditional ethnography itself. It too is now seen by some as reifying social phenomena, as claiming illegitimate expertise over the people studied, as being based on relationships of hierarchy, control, and so on. Indeed, it has been argued that it represents a subtler form of control than quantitative research because it is able to get closer to the people studied, to discover the details of their behavior and the innards of their experience (Finch, 1986; Stacey, 1988).

The epistemological challenge to the credentials of ethnography that is at the root of these criticisms is undoubtedly fruitful in many respects. Some of the arguments used to promote ethnography against quantitative method and to justify its features are open to serious question. To take just one example, the whole notion of what counts as a theory in ethnography is ill defined, and the concept of "theoretical description" that has guided much ethnographic research in sociology is of doubtful value (Hammersley, 1992b, chap. 1). At the same time, there is a tendency for this questioning to lead to skepticism and relativism. It is not always clear how thoroughgoing this relativism and skepticism is. Often it seems to be applied selectively, but without much indication of what principles might underlie the selectivity (Woolgar & Pawluch, 1985, refer to this in another context as "ontological gerrymandering"). Where the attempt is made to embrace skepticism and relativism wholeheartedly, on the other hand, the end point seems likely to be a debilitating nihilism. What is required, it seems to us, is a careful reassessment of the methodological and philosophical arguments surrounding the concept of science and of the relationship of ethnography to this. Above all, we must not be misled into assuming that we are faced merely with a choice between dogmatism and relativism, between a single oppressive conception of science and some uniquely liberating alternative.

Theory and Practice

Another area of disagreement and debate that has become of great salience in recent years is the question of the relationship between ethnographic research and social and political practice. In the past, and probably still today, most ethnography has been directed toward contributing to disciplinary knowledge rather than toward solving practical problems. Although such work may ultimately contribute knowledge of wide public relevance, this contribution has not usually been very immediate or specific. Furthermore, the knowledge produced has often been presented as valuable for its own sake as much as for any instrumental value it has.

Although ethnographers have usually wished to address those beyond the boundaries of their disciplinary communities, very often this has not involved any marked deviation from the sort of research, or even the sort of written presentation, appropriate to academic work. The relationship between research and practice assumed here is what has been called the enlightenment model (Bulmer, 1982; Janowitz, 1971; for a more elaborate conception of the various possible roles of the researcher, see Silverman, 1985, 1989). However, not all ethnographic research has operated on this model. For a long time, the applied anthropology movement in the United States has exemplified a different stance, being specifically concerned with carrying out research that is designed to address and contribute directly to the solution of practical problems. This is a tradition that has flourished and transformed itself in recent years, coming to be applied within mainstream U.S. society, not just outside it (Eddy & Partridge, 1978; van Willigen, 1986). In addition, its practical and political orientation has spread more widely, with the disciplinary model coming under increasing criticism.

Even those anthropologists and sociologists primarily concerned with contributing to disciplinary knowledge have sometimes felt it necessary to engage in advocacy on the part of the people they have studied. Furthermore, there have been calls for this to be developed further—indeed, to be integrated into the research process (Paine, 1985). It is suggested that by its very nature anthropology (and the point can be extended without distortion to ethnographic work in general) involves a "representation" of others even when it does not explicitly claim to speak for or on behalf of them. And it is argued that there are ethical and political responsibilities arising from this fact.

However, neither this argument nor the sort of practice recommended on the basis of it is straightforward. Drawing on their own experience, Hastrup and Elsass (1990) point out that the context in which any advocacy is to take place is a complex one: It is not composed simply of an oppressed and an oppressor group but of a diversity of individuals and groups motivated by various ideals and interests, and pursuing various political strategies. Furthermore, the group to be "represented" is not always internally homogeneous and is rarely democratically organized. Also, there is often genuine uncertainty about what is and is not in the interests of the group and of members of it. In particular, there is the danger of adopting ethnographic myths, such as that Indian groups represent "islands of culture" that must be defended against the apparently cultureless settlers, or that informants speak "cultural truths."

In recent years there has also been a growing application of ethnographic methods, by sociologists, anthropologists, and others, in applied fields such as education, health, and social policy. This reflects, in part, a decline of confidence in quantitative research on the part of funders and a willingness on the part of some of them to finance qualitative research. In Britain, ironically, this trend has been more obvious in the field of commercial market research than in government-funded work, though there are signs of change (Walker, 1985). This change is also evident in the United States, where, for example, federally funded evaluations in education have increasingly involved ethnographic components (see Fetterman, 1988; Fetterman & Pitman, 1986; Rist, 1981). At the same time, there has been some debate about whether, and in what senses, this applied research is ethnographic. Some anthropologists, in particular, see it as abandoning key elements of what they regard as ethnography (Wolcott, 1980). And it is true that in several respects this trend has resulted in significant modification of ethnographic practice. An interesting example is the condensed fieldwork advocated and practiced by some researchers in the field of educational evaluation (see, e.g., Walker, 1978; for an assessment, see Atkinson & Delamont, 1985).

Sometimes associated with the moves toward more applied forms of ethnographic work have been calls for collaborative research. In part, these have arisen out of concern about the lack of impact that ethnographic (and other) research has had on social and political practice. Some believe that its impact would be greater if practitioners were themselves involved in the research process, both because that involvement would be likely to change the research and make it more practically relevant and because they would be more motivated to draw on it as a result of being involved. There have been other important influences pushing in the direction of collaborative research, however, notably Marxist critical theory and feminism. These demand that research contribute to the political struggles of oppressed groups, not merely the working class, but also women, ethnic minorities, the disabled, and so on. And the commitment to collaboration stems from a reconceptualization of the central political goal of the Left as the extension of democracy, and the belief that those committed to that goal must exemplify their commitment to it in the practice of research. From this point of view, traditional ethnographic work has been criticized for embodying a hierarchical and therefore undemocratic relationship between researcher and researched, because it is the former who makes the decisions about what to study and how to study it, and whose voice is represented in the written ethnography (see, for example, Gitlin, Siegel, & Boru, 1989).

There is little doubt of the need for ethnographers to rethink the relationship between their work and social and political practice. However, it would be a mistake in our view to seek to restructure ethnography on the basis of a single conception of that relationship. Above all, it is of considerable importance that we do not lose sight of what has hitherto been the goal of ethnographic research, namely, the production of knowledge. We should not replace this with the pursuit of practical goals that, although sometimes valuable in themselves, are no *more* worthy in general terms of our time and effort than the pursuit of knowledge. This is especially so when these goals are of a kind that we may be much less able to achieve. It is true that conventional research never changes the world at a stroke, and that often it may not have much effect even over the long term. But that does not mean that it is of no value. It is also worth remembering that changing the world can be for the worse as well as for the better. Utopian attempts to do politics by means of research are of no service to anyone.

Rhetoric and Representation

In recent years the literature on ethnography and participant observation has been enriched by a growing corpus of reflections on the rhetoric of ethnographic accounts. Attention has been given, for example, to the aesthetics and ethics of ethnographic texts, including the relationship between authority and authorship, and indeed to the connections among rhetoric, representation, and logic generally. This "rhetorical turn" among ethnographers is part of a much broader movement of scholarship toward an interest in the rhetoric of inquiry that has been manifested in many of the human and social disciplines. It has engaged with various important (if often diffuse) theoretical and methodological tendencies—not least feminism, poststructuralism, and postmodernism. The most significant contributions, and the earliest, from social scientists came from cultural and social anthropologists. More recently, attention has been paid to this issue by sociologists. Although the respective disciplines have slightly different emphases, the broad themes have been similar: the conventionality of ethnographic texts, the representation of "Self" and "Other" in such texts, the character of ethnographies as a textual genre, the nature of ethnographic argumentation and the rhetoric of evidence.

The starting point for this "rediscovery of rhetoric" has been the acknowledgment that there is no perfectly transparent or neutral way to represent the natural or social world. For example, however "impersonal" and formulaic the work of the natural scientist, it stands in no "natural" relationship to the phenomena and events it describes. On the contrary, the textual products of natural science are highly conventional. Their apparent guarantee of authenticity and credibility is dependent on readers' adopting shared strategies of reading and interpretation.

In just the same way, the human sciences draw on common sets of conventional devices to construct and convey their characteristic portrayals of social scenes, actors, and cultural meanings. Thus White's (1973) extensive writing on the writing of historical texts has exerted an influence far beyond historiography. Likewise, McCloskey's (1985) wry and erudite commentaries on the rhetoric of economics have provided important benchmarks and exemplars. Among social and cultural anthropologists, the standard ethnography or monograph was—to a considerable extent—a taken-for-granted format. As Boon (1983) points out, however, the typical framework of anthropological monographs imposed a common pattern on, rather than revealing one in, the vast array of human societies they described. He argues that the "classic" form of the anthropological monograph was a direct, if implicit, embodiment of the domain assumptions of functionalist anthropology.

The watershed of critical awareness of ethnographic textuality was the highly influential collection of papers edited by Clifford and Marcus (1986), *Writing Culture.* The works brought together in that collection all emphasize, in various ways, the nature of the textual imposition that anthropology exerts over its subject matter. They emphasize the complex interplay of literary and rhetorical, historical, and ideological influences on the production and reception of anthropological ethnographies.

Clifford and Marcus's volume is partly, but not perfectly, parallel to that of Geertz (1973), who began to assert that anthropological writings could be regarded as "fiction," in the sense that they are made: They are crafted by their authors and shaped by "literary" conventions and devices. Geertz (1988) went on later to document the distinctive literary styles used by a number of founding figures, British and American. In the same way, several contributors to the Clifford and Marcus volume sought to illuminate the "literary" antecedents and parallels for ethnographic writing. Pratt (1986, 1991), for instance, developed there—and elsewhere—the parallels and self-conscious contrasts between anthropological ethnography and travel writing.

In a similar vein, an early contribution from Atkinson (1982) explored some of the literary origins and parallels for sociological ethnography associated with the Chicago school. In common with many of the anthropological commentaries appearing at that time, Atkinson's work was influenced by aspects of contemporary literary criticism. Structuralist and poststructuralist theory emphasized that the "realism" of realist fictional writing drew on particular conventions of reading and writing. In the same way, it was possible to explore how the authenticity of "factual" accounts, such as ethnographies, was generated through equally (and very similar) conventional means.

Some aspects of the "literary" antecedents and convergences have been sketched in the literature. For anthropology, commentators have drawn attention to literary as well as biographical affinities between the work of Malinowski and Conrad (Clifford, 1988), between surrealism and French ethnography (Clifford, 1988), and in the poetic writing of Benedict and Sapir (Brady, 1991; Prattis, 1985). To a rather lesser extent, sociological traditions have been explored from a similarly literary perspective. Atkinson (1982) makes a preliminary identification of Chicago school urban ethnographies with the naturalistic and realistic novels of American literature. But if the respective intellectual communities wish to pursue these schemes, there is much yet to do. We still have rather few detailed examinations of the general cultural and—in the widest sense—"literary" contexts within which particular ethnographic traditions have been formed. In Britain, for example, the sociological foundations laid by urban investigators such as Booth and Rowntree have major affinities with several literary models. The investigative journalism of more popular writers, and the fictional products of authors such as Dickens, provide rich mixtures of realism, melodrama, and the grotesque that find their parallels in the tone, style, and sensibilities of the sociological tradition. Likewise, the long and rich tradition of "community" studies on both sides of the Atlantic needs careful reading against the kind of literary analyses of the contrast between the urban and the rural furnished by, say, Raymond Williams (1973).

The point of such "literary" analysis is not merely to create "interesting" parallels and contrasts, nor yet to attempt to trace the literary antecedents of particular anthropological or sociological texts. It is, rather, to remove the false distinction between "science" and "rhetoric." The essential dialectic between the aesthetic and humanist, on the one hand, and the logical and scientific, on the other, is thus reaffirmed. A recognition of the conventional quality and literary antecedents of the ethnographic text in turn raises questions about the distinctive characteristics of ethnography as a genre of textual product. It is not enough, in the eyes of many contemporary commentators, simply to note that our texts are (in Geertz's sense) fiction. It is important to map the conventions that are deployed in constructing particular anthropological and sociological styles. It is thus possible to explore relationships among schools of thought, traditions, and individual authorship with repertoires of textual device through which scholarly accounts are constructed.

This identification of style and genre has taken various turns. A group of British anthropologists (Fardon, 1990) has explored how different textual styles have accorded with different regional biases and preoccupations. (They in turn criticize several of the "textual" critics for treating anthropological ethnography as a more or less undifferentiated textual type.) Likewise, Van Maanen's (1988) highly influential contribution explores the characteristics of various modes of ethnographic writing. Most notably, perhaps, he contrasts the styles of "realist" and "confessional" accounts by sociologists and anthropologists, the former style typically being central, the latter traditionally being more marginal, perhaps relegated to a methodological appendix. This contrast, which is built into a great deal of ethnographic output, is itself a textually based convention whereby the tension between the "personal" and the "impersonal" has been managed by successive authors and schools of ethnography.

In the "classic" ethnographies of urban sociology and anthropology, the conventions of textual production were not always apparent. The reason is simple: Their authors and readers drew on textual paradigms and devices that were entirely familiar and "natural." Thus the highly "readable" ethnographies, such as Whyte's *Street Corner Society* (1955), conveyed vivid accounts of social settings by virtue of their "literary" qualities. As Gusfield (1990), among others, has pointed out in an analysis of Liebow's *Tally's Corner* (1967), such a realist ethnography achieves its effects through its narrative structures and its rhetorical and stylistic devices. Similarly, drawing explicitly on models from literary criticism, as well as on the work of previous commentators (e.g., Brown, 1977; Edmondson, 1984), Atkinson (1990) identifies the recurrent textual methods and motifs by which ethnographic texts have been constructed. He looks at several standard elements of literary analysis, and thus examines the use of various major devices and tropes. For example, narrative forms are used to convey accounts of social action and causation. Likewise, the "characters" or actors in the account are assembled out of narrative and descriptive fragments. Hence ethnographers use their "literary" competence to reconstruct social action and social actors. In common with many other critics and commentators, Atkinson traces the use of various figures of speech—tropes—such as metaphor, irony, and synecdoche. The demonstration that the "ethnography" is based on conventional literary resources does not, of course, invalidate their use. It commends a disciplined use of them: The use of ethnographic realism can never be innocent in the future. But there is no reason on that score alone to search out alternative literary forms, although some critics and commentators have advocated and practiced ethnographic writing that departs from the conventional realist text in various ways (for examples, see Crapanzano, 1980; Dwyer, 1982; Krieger, 1983; Shostak, 1981; Woolgar, 1988).

In the hands of many, the textual or rhetorical turn serves not just aesthetic or methodological interests, but has inescapably ethical and political implications. A good deal of anthropological reflection has focused on the textual representation of the Author and of the Other in the ethnography. Here, of course, anthropologists find common interest with more general cultural critics, such as Said's (1978) account of Orientalism, or Spivak (1989) (see Pratt, 1992, for an exemplar that brings the interests together). It is argued that a paradox lies at the heart of the ethnographic endeavor and of "the ethnography" as a textual product. On the one hand is the ethnographer's epistemological, personal, and moral commitment to his or her hosts. The image—often, the reality—of prolonged immersion in "the field" and the emphasis on participant observation commit the ethnographer to a shared social world. He or she has become a "stranger" or "marginal native" in order to embark upon a process of cultural learning that is predicated on a degree of "surrender" to "the Other" (see Wolff, 1964). The epistemology of participant observation rests on the principle of interaction and the "reciprocity of perspectives" between social actors. The rhetoric is thus egalitarian: observer and observed as inhabitants of a shared social and cultural field, their respective cultures different but equal, and capable of mutual recognition by virtue of a shared humanity. The classic texts of ethnography, on the other hand, have (it is claimed) all too often inscribed a radical distinction between the Author and the Other. The "realist" techniques of standard ethnographic reportage may implicitly endow the ethnographer—as the implied Narrator—with a privileged gaze that reproduces the authorial omniscience characteristic of many examples of narrative fiction. The text brings actors and culture together under the auspices of a single, all-encompassing point of view. By contrast, the Other is rendered solely as the object of the ethnographer's gaze. The voice of the ethnographer is privileged, that of the Other is muted. As a consequence, there have been various moves to produce ethnographic texts that replace the "monologic" mode with more "dialogic" forms, in which the text allows for a multiplicity of "voices." This perspective brings together a textual, methodological, and moral commitment. Dwyer's (1982) self-conscious adoption of a dialogic textual format is a benchmark contribution to this style of presentation, although it falls short of a full-fledged dialogic approach.

The moral concerns of commentators on ethnographic rhetoric have been echoed by advocates of feminist points of view (see Stanley & Wise, 1983). The textual practices of a privileged "Western" observer may be compared to the inscription of a privileged masculine discourse. There have, therefore, been attempts to produce feminist texts that subvert the taken-for-granted formats. Krieger's (1983) "stream-of-consciousness" style is offered as an exemplar (see Devault, 1990). The feminist appraisal of ethnographic writing is in turn part of a more general appraisal of social scientific writing and an interest in various genres—most notably biography and autobiography (see Stanley, 1990, 1992; see also D. Smith, 1987, pp. 105ff.). Stanley and Wise, Smith, and others provide an interesting link between a feminist standpoint and a readiness to treat textual forms as problematic. The concern is epistemological and ethical, personal and professional. From the feminist standpoint, of course, they are all implicative of one another.

The rhetorical turn is also intimately related to a "postmodern" tendency in the construction of ethnography. The postmodern ethnography explores the discontinuities, paradoxes, and inconsistencies of culture and action. In contrast with the supposed "modern" ethnography, it does so not in order to resolve or to reconcile those differences. The classic modern ethnography (the postmodernist holds) brought the various fragmentary representations of social life under the auspices of a dominant narrative and a single, privileged point of view. The postmodern author seeks to dissolve that disjuncture between the observer and the observed. The trope of "participant observation," which captures the ambivalence of distance and familiarity, is replaced by one of "dialogue," showing "the cooperative and collaborative nature of the ethnographic situation" (Tyler, 1986, p. 126).

Moreover, the postmodern ethnography is held to adopt a radically alternative attitude toward its textual character. Tyler (1986), for instance, rejects any claim that the ethnography can be said to "represent" the social world. He prefers the terminology and imagery of "evoking" (though he omits consideration of just what is being evoked). A sophisticated discussion of evocation and ethnographic "complexity" is also provided by Strathern (1991). The subject matter of postmodernity and postmodern ethnographic texts are dialectically related. This is aptly illustrated in Dorst's (1989) account of an American town, *Chadd's Ford.* There Dorst describes how this Pennsylvania suburb creates itself through various forms of representation and acts of identification (not least identification with and through the paintings of Andrew Wyeth). Dorst collates various local devices whereby surface appearances of the locality itself are contrived.

Rose (1989) has written an even more extreme version of such a postmodern text. Again, it depends on the collation and juxtaposition of strikingly different collections of materials. It incorporates not just radical shifts of subject matter and perspective but also strikingly different styles of writing. (As has been pointed out, Bateson's ethnography *Naven,* 1936, was an early example of a textually variegated ethnographic account; see Clifford, 1988, p. 146.) Although the "realist" ethnography clearly remains alive and well, it is also clear that—for better or worse—the postmodern turn will encourage some sociologists and anthropologists to experiment with textual styles and formats. In doing so, they will help to focus attention on the conventional character of all ethnographic reportage. It will become part of the craft knowledge of ethnographic authors that textual forms and styles will be self-consciously recognized and explored (see Atkinson, 1990). In this way, a variety of textual styles may become characteristic of the genres of ethnography.

In recent years there has been such a consistent emphasis on the rhetoric or "poetics" of ethnography that there has been some danger of undue attention to these literary and aesthetic issues. Problems of logic and inference have been obscured. Recognition that scholarly texts have conventional and literary aspects seems to have led some practitioners to undue extremes. As we have noted, textual experimentation—sometimes to the point of obscurantism—has now been undertaken, particularly in the name of "postmodernism." This emphasis on textuality is, however, in danger of privileging the rhetorical over the "scientific" or rational. Hammersley (1991, 1993) suggests that we need to pay attention to strategies of reading and writing ethnography, but primarily in order to evaluate the quality of arguments and the use of evidence. Like most of the "textual" commentators, he acknowledges that much of the sociological or anthropological argument proceeds implicitly. It is conveyed in the textual arrangement of narrative, descriptions, and tropes. But he advocates explicit critical attention to those textual elements in order to evaluate the quality of the arguments—however conveyed. He thus reaffirms the more "scientific" aspect of the overall evaluation of the ethnographic enterprise.

Toward a Conclusion: Contemporary Crises and Renewals

Ethnographic approaches to social research have been adopted in numerous disciplines and applied fields: social and cultural anthropology, sociology, human geography, organization studies, educational research, cultural studies. It is noteworthy that in none of these disciplinary areas is there a single philosophical or theoretical orientation that can lay unique claim to a rationale for ethnography and participant observation. Across the spectrum of the social sciences, the use and justification of ethnography is marked by diversity rather than consensus. On that basis, it is arguable that it is futile to try to identify different types of "qualitative research." Rather, one has to recognize different theoretical or epistemological positions, each of which may endorse a version of ethnographic work. It is certainly a mistake to try to elevate "ethnography" (or some equivalent category) to the status of a quasi-paradigm in its own right. There are some common threads, of course, but it is noticeable that many recent or contemporary advocates define their activities in terms of what they are not—in opposition to less preferred perspectives—rather than in a positive way.

Historically, for instance, there has been little in common between the methodological appeals of sociology and anthropology. And those appeals in turn are not very accurately grounded in the actual histories of the respective fields. Many sociologists have claimed an elective affinity (at least) between participant observation and symbolic interactionism (Williams, 1976). One can indeed find many points of contact between the interactionists' view of the social actor, social action, and social order and the practical accomplishment of fieldwork. Both stress the extent to which meanings and understandings emerge through processes and transactions of interaction. In that context, Chicago school sociology is often invoked as the originating inspiration. It is, therefore, ironic that Chicago sociology itself was not especially dominated by ethnographic fieldwork; that early Chicago school urban ethnography was not necessarily very similar to more recent approaches; that earlier Chicago urban sociology was not exclusively predicated on "symbolic interactionism"—which was largely a subsequent codification of presuppositions.

Likewise, others identify an ethnomethodologically informed ethnography. Here the stress is on the investigation of everyday methods for the practical accomplishment of social life. It often involves something of a relaxation of a "pure" version of ethnomethodology. The latter is drawn on, often eclectically and in combination with other perspectives, to illuminate topics and problems of interest to a more conventional, mainstream sociology. Whether or not ethnomethodology can be shown to live up to the claims of some of its practitioners that it is a uniquely fundamental or "foundational" discipline, there is no doubt that it has furnished significant subject matter, and new research questions, for ethnographic orientations. It has, however, introduced some specific limitations. With their emphasis on the detailed analysis of spoken interaction, some versions of ethnomethodology have tended to encourage a rather restricted view of what constitutes "the field." If too great reliance is placed on the analysis of spoken interaction, then the field of investigation may become reduced to those settings and situations for which audio or video recordings can be made. By the same token, the special contribution of participant observation is negated, or reduced to a very minor role in the acquisition of background knowledge of the social context (Atkinson, 1992). The same point may be made about the contribution of discourse analysis (see, for example, Potter & Wetherell, 1987). Close attention to the forms of language and social interaction are undoubtedly important adjuncts to more general, holistic ethnographic approaches. But they cannot fully substitute for ethnographic inquiry.[5]

In other quarters, an emphasis on semiotics or hermeneutics has informed ethnographic data collection and analysis. Here an attention to culture as a system of signs and texts provides the major impetus. In ethnography the textual metaphor of culture has found its major proponent in Geertz, whose formulation of "thick description" stresses the interpretation of cultural meaning. This interpretive perspective in cultural anthropology contrasts clearly with more formal and—according to the interpretivists—reductionist views such as structuralism or ethnoscience. The interpretive approach implies a relativism that eschews a nomothetic approach, while warranting the capacity of the ethnographer to interpret cultures and their local manifestations. Interpretivism in this mode conceives of "culture" in terms of its own poetics—its metaphors, tropes, and other forms of representation. This sense of the "textuality" of social life has in turn been linked to a heightened awareness of the textual character of "the ethnography" itself, as we mentioned earlier.

There are common threads and recurrent motifs running through the entire ethnographic tradition. Yet there is no simple one-to-one relationship between ethnography and any given theoretical perspective. It is not the case that all ethnography has been undertaken under the auspices of one epistemological orthodoxy. Rather, the distinctive characteristics of ethnographic work have been differentially appealed to by different disciplines and tendencies. As we have tried to show, this has produced a highly complex and contentious discursive field.

Notes

1. There are researchers who have intentionally "gone native" for the purposes of research, for example, Jules-Rosette (1978).

2. We should not forget the nineteenth-century precursors of this work, the writings of Engels (1845/1968), Booth (1889-1902), and Webb and Webb (1932), though they were more concerned with documenting living conditions than culture.

3. Its instability is exemplified in the disputes about how their work should be interpreted and what lessons should be drawn from it for sociology. See, for example, Bales (1966), McPhail and Rexroat (1979), Lewis and Smith (1980), Stewart (1981), Blumer (1983), and Fine and Kleinman (1986).

4. Blumer's methodological writings exemplify this (see Blumer, 1969; for discussions, see Baugh, 1990; Hammersley, 1989).

5. Their appeal for some researchers undoubtedly rests on the appearance of greater precision and rigor, analysis being restricted to what can be validated on the basis of the availability of permanent recordings. And, indeed, some ethnomethodological writing has a strongly empiricist streak, see Atkinson (1988).

References

Arensberg, C., & Kimball, S. (1940). *Family and community in Ireland.* Cambridge, MA: Harvard University Press.

Asad, T. (Ed.). (1973). *Anthropology and the colonial encounter.* New York: Humanities Press.

Atkinson, P. A. (1982). Writing ethnography. In H. J. Helle (Ed.), *Kultur und Institution* (pp. 77-105). Berlin: Dunker & Humblot.

Atkinson, P. A. (1988). Ethnomethodology: A critical review. *Annual Review of Sociology, 14,* 441-465.

Atkinson, P. A. (1990). *The ethnographic imagination: Textual constructions of reality.* London: Routledge.

Atkinson, P. A. (1992). *Understanding ethnographic texts.* Newbury Park, CA: Sage.

Atkinson, P. A., & Delamont, S. (1985). Bread and dreams or bread and circuses? In M. Shipman

(Ed.), *Educational research: Principles, policies and practices* (pp. 26-45). London: Falmer.

Bales, R. (1966). Comment on Herbert Blumer's paper. *American Journal of Sociology, 71,* 547-548.

Bateson, G. (1936). *Naven.* Cambridge, UK: Cambridge University Press.

Baugh, K. (1990). *The methodology of Herbert Blumer.* Cambridge, UK: Cambridge University Press.

Blumer, H. (1969). On the methodological status of symbolic interactionism. In H. Blumer, *Symbolic interactionism* (pp. 1-60). Englewood Cliffs, NJ: Prentice Hall.

Blumer, H. (1983). Going astray with a logical scheme. *Symbolic Interaction, 6,* 127-137.

Boelen, W. A. M. (1992). *Street corner society*: Cornerville revisited. In *Street corner society* revisited [Special issue]. *Journal of Contemporary Ethnography, 21,* 11-51.

Boon, J. A. (1983). Functionalists write too: Frazer, Malinowski and the semiotics of the monograph. *Semiotica, 46,* 131-149.

Booth, C. (1889-1902). *Life and labour of the people of London* (17 vols.). London: Macmillan.

Brady, I. (Ed.). (1991). *Anthropological poetics.* Lanham, MD: Rowman & Littlefield.

Brown, R. H. (1977). *A poetic for sociology.* Cambridge, MA: Harvard University Press.

Bulmer, M. (1982). *The uses of social research.* London: Allen & Unwin.

Bulmer, M. (1984). *The Chicago school of sociology.* Chicago: University of Chicago Press.

Burgess, R. G. (Ed.). (1982). *Field research: A source book and field manual.* London: Allen & Unwin.

Clifford, J. (1988). *The predicament of culture: Twentieth-century ethnography, literature, and art.* Cambridge, MA: Harvard University Press.

Clifford, J., & Marcus, G. E. (Eds.). (1986). *Writing culture: The poetics and politics of ethnography.* Berkeley: University of California Press.

Clough, P. T. (1992). *The end(s) of ethnography: From realism to social criticism.* Newbury Park, CA: Sage.

Cole, J. W. (1977). Anthropology comes part way home: Community studies in Europe. *Annual Review of Anthropology, 6,* 349-378.

Crapanzano, V. (1980). *Tuhami: Portrait of a Moroccan.* Chicago: University of Chicago Press.

Denzin, N. K. (1990). The spaces of postmodernism: Reading Plummer on Blumer. *Symbolic Interaction, 13,* 145-154.

Denzin, N. K. (1992). Whose Cornerville is it, anyway? In *Street corner society* revisited [Special issue]. *Journal of Contemporary Ethnography, 21,* 120-132.

Devault, M. L. (1990). Women write sociology: Rhetorical strategies. In A. Hunter (Ed.), *The rhetoric of social research: Understood and believed* (pp. 97-110). New Brunswick, NJ: Rutgers University Press.

Dorst, J. D. (1989). *The written suburb: An ethnographic dilemma.* Philadelphia: University of Pennsylvania Press.

Dwyer, K. (1982). *Moroccan dialogues: Anthropology in question.* Baltimore: Johns Hopkins University Press.

Eddy, E. M., & Partridge, W. L. (Eds.). (1978). *Applied anthropology in America.* New York: Columbia University Press.

Edmondson, R. (1984). *Rhetoric in sociology.* London: Macmillan.

Eisner, E. (1985). On the differences between artistic and scientific approaches to qualitative research. In E. Eisner, *The art of educational evaluation: A personal view.* London: Falmer.

Eisner, E. (1988). The primacy of experience and the politics of method. *Educational Researcher, 17*(5), 15-20.

Eisner, E. (1991). *The enlightened eye: Qualitative inquiry and the enhancement of educational practices.* New York: Macmillan.

Engels, F. (1968). *The condition of the working class in England in 1844.* London: Allen & Unwin. (Original work published 1845)

Fardon, R. (Ed.). (1990). *Localizing strategies: Regional traditions of ethnographic writing.* Edinburgh: Scottish Academic Press.

Fetterman, D. M., & Pitman, M. A. (Eds.). (1986). *Educational evaluation: Ethnography in theory, practice, and politics.* Beverly Hills, CA: Sage.

Fetterman, D. M. (Ed.). (1988). *Qualitative approaches to evaluation in education: The silent scientific revolution.* New York: Praeger.

Filstead, W. J. (1970). Introduction. In W. J. Filstead (Ed.), *Qualitative methodology.* Chicago: Markham.

Finch, J. (1986). *Research and policy.* London: Falmer.

Fine, G., & Kleinman, S. (1986). Interpreting the sociological classics: Can there be a "true" meaning of Mead? *Symbolic Interaction, 9,* 129-146.

Freilich, M. (Ed.). (1970). *Marginal natives: Anthropologists at work.* New York: Harper & Row.

Frisby, D. (1976). Introduction to the English translation. In T. Adorno, H. Albert, R. Dahrendorf, J. Habermas, H. Pilot, & K. Popper, *The positivist dispute in German sociology* (pp. ix-xliv). London: Heinemann.

Geertz, C. (1973). *The interpretation of cultures: Selected essays.* New York: Basic Books.

Geertz, C. (1988). *Works and lives: The anthropologist as author.* Stanford, CA: Stanford University Press.

Gitlin, A., Siegel, M., & Boru, K. (1989). The politics of method: From leftist ethnography to educative research. *Qualitative Studies in Education, 2,* 237-253.

Gold, R. (1958). Roles in sociological field observations. *Social Forces, 36,* 217-223.

Guba, E. (Ed.). (1990). *The paradigm dialog.* Newbury Park, CA: Sage.

Gusfield, J. (1990). Two genres of sociology. In A. Hunter (Ed.), *The rhetoric of social research: Understood and believed* (pp. 62-96). New Brunswick, NJ: Rutgers University Press.

Hammersley, M. (1989). *The dilemma of qualitative method: Herbert Blumer and the Chicago tradition*. London: Routledge.

Hammersley, M. (1991). *Reading ethnographic research: A critical guide*. London: Longman.

Hammersley, M. (1992a). On feminist methodology. *Sociology, 26*, 187-206.

Hammersley, M. (1992b). *What's wrong with ethnography? Methodological explorations*. London: Routledge.

Hammersley, M. (1993). The rhetorical turn in ethnography. *Social Science Information, 32*(1), 23-37.

Hammersley, M., & Atkinson P. (1983). *Ethnography: Principles in practice*. London: Tavistock.

Hannerz, U. (1969). *Soulside*. New York: Columbia University Press.

Harding, S. (1986). *The science question in feminism*. Milton Keynes, UK: Open University Press.

Harris, M. (1969). *The rise of anthropological theory*. London: Routledge & Kegan Paul.

Harvey, L. (1987). *Myths of the Chicago school of sociology*. Aldershot, UK: Gower.

Held, D. (1981). *An introduction to critical theory*. London: Hutchinson.

Hastrup, K., & Elsass, P. (1990). Anthropological advocacy: A contradiction in terms? *Current Anthropology, 31*, 301-311.

Janowitz, M. (1971). *Sociological methods and social policy*. New York: General Learning.

Jules-Rosette, B. (1978). The veil of objectivity: Prophecy, divination and social inquiry. *American Anthropologist, 80*, 549-570.

Junker, B. (1960). *Field work*. Chicago: University of Chicago Press.

Kaberry, P. (1957). Malinowski's contribution to fieldwork methods and the writing of ethnography. In R. Firth (Ed.), *Man and culture: An evaluation of the work of Bronislaw Malinowski* (pp. 71-91). New York: Harper & Row.

Krieger, S. (1983). *The mirror dance: Identity in a women's community*, Philadelphia: Temple University Press.

Lather, P. (1991). *Getting smart: Feminist research and pedagogy with/in the postmodern*. New York: Routledge.

Leach, E. (1957). The epistemological background to Malinowski's empiricism. In R. Firth (Ed.), *Man and culture: An evaluation of the work of Bronislaw Malinowski* (pp. 119-139). New York: Harper & Row.

Lewis, J. D., & Smith, R. L. (1980). *American sociology and pragmatism*. Chicago: University of Chicago Press.

Lincoln, Y. S., & Guba, E. G. (1985). *Naturalistic inquiry*. Beverly Hills, CA: Sage.

Malinowski, B. (1922). *Argonauts of the western Pacific*. London: Routledge & Kegan Paul.

Marcus, G., & Fischer, M. (1986). *Anthropology as cultural critique: An experimental moment in the human sciences*. Chicago: University of Chicago Press.

McCloskey, D. N. (1985). *The rhetoric of economics*. Madison: University of Wisconsin Press.

McPhail, C., & Rexroat, C. (1979). Mead vs. Blumer. *American Sociological Review, 44*, 449-467.

Orlandella, A. R. (1992). Boelen may know Holland, Boelen may know Barzini, but Boelen "doesn't know diddle about the North End!" In *Street corner society* revisited [Special issue]. *Journal of Contemporary Ethnography, 21*, 69-79.

Paine, R. (Ed.). (1985). *Advocacy and anthropology: First encounters*. St. Johns: Memorial University of Newfoundland, Institute of Social and Economic Research.

Park, R., & Burgess, E. (Eds.). (1921). *Introduction to the science of sociology*. Chicago: University of Chicago Press.

Park, R., & Burgess, E. (Eds.). (1969). *Introduction to the science of sociology* (3rd ed.). Chicago: University of Chicago Press.

Potter, J., & Wetherell, M. (1987). *Discourse and social psychology*. London: Sage.

Pratt, M. L. (1986). Fieldwork in common places. In J. Clifford & G. E. Marcus (Eds.), *Writing culture: The poetics and politics of ethnography* (pp. 27-50). Berkeley: University of California Press.

Pratt, M. L. (1992). *Imperial eyes: Travel writing and transculturation*. London: Routledge.

Prattis, J. I. (Ed.). (1985). *Reflections: The anthropological muse*. Washington, DC: American Anthropological Association.

Radcliffe-Brown, A. R. (1948). *A natural science of society*. New York: Free Press.

Radin, P. (1965). *Method and theory of ethnology*. New York: Basic Books. (Original work published 1931)

Redfield, R. (1962). Relation of anthropology to the social sciences and the humanities. In R. Redfield, *Human nature and the study of society* (pp. 107-121). Chicago: University of Chicago Press.

Richards, A. (1939). The development of field work methods in social anthropology. In F. C. Bartlett (Ed.), *The study of society* (pp. 272-316). London: Routledge and Kegan Paul.

Richardson, L. (1992). Trash on the corner: Ethics and technography. In *Street corner society* revisited [Special issue]. *Journal of Contemporary Ethnography, 21*, 103-119.

Rist, R. (1981). On the application of qualitative research to the policy process: An emergent linkage. In L. Barton & S. Walker (Eds.), *Social crisis and educational research* (pp. 153-170). London: Croom Helm.

Rose, D. (1989). *Patterns of American culture: Ethnography and estrangement*. Philadelphia: University of Pennsylvania Press.

Rowe, J. H. (1965). The Renaissance foundation of anthropology. *American Anthropologist, 67*, 1-20.

Said, E. (1978). *Orientalism*. New York: Pantheon.

Shostak, M. (1981). *Nisa: The life and words of a !Kung woman*. Cambridge, MA: Harvard University Press.

Silverman, D. (1985). *Qualitative methodology and sociology*. Aldershot, UK: Gower.

Silverman, D. (1989). The impossible dreams of reformism and romanticism. In J. F. Gubrium & D.

Silverman (Eds.), *The politics of field research: Beyond enlightenment* (pp. 30-48). Newbury Park, CA: Sage.

Smith, D. (1987). *The everyday world as problematic.* Boston: Northeastern University Press.

Smith, J. K. (1989). *The nature of social and educational inquiry.* Norwood, NJ: Ablex.

Smith, J. K., & Heshusius, L. (1986). Closing down the conversation: The end of the quantitative-qualitative debate among educational inquirers. *Educational Researcher, 15,* 4-12.

Spivak, G. C. (1989). *In other worlds.* London: Methuen.

Stacey, J. (1988). Can there be a feminist ethnography? *Women's Studies International Forum, 11,* 21-27.

Stanley, L. (1990). *Feminist praxis.* London: Routledge.

Stanley, L. (1992). *The auto/biographical I: The theory and practice of feminist auto/biography.* Manchester, UK: Manchester University Press.

Stanley, L., & Wise, S. (1983). *Breaking out: Feminist consciousness and feminist research.* London: Routledge & Kegan Paul.

Stewart, R.L. (1981). What George Mead should have said. *Symbolic Interaction, 4,* 157-166.

Strathern, M. (1991). *Partial connections.* Lanham, MD: Rowan & Littlefield.

Suttles, G. (1968). *The social order of the slum: Ethnicity and territory in the inner city.* Chicago: University of Chicago Press.

Tyler, S. A. (1986). Post-modern ethnography: From document of the occult to occult document. In J. Clifford & G. E. Marcus (Eds.), *Writing culture: The poetics and politics of ethnography* (pp. 122-140). Berkeley: University of California Press.

Van Maanen, J. (1988). *Tales of the field: On writing ethnography.* Chicago: University of Chicago Press.

van Willigen, J. (1986). *Applied anthropology: An introduction.* South Hadley, MA: Bergin & Garvey.

von Wright, G. (1971). *Explanation and understanding.* London: Routledge & Kegan Paul.

Walker, R. (1978). The conduct of educational case studies. In B. Dockerill & D. Hamilton (Eds.), *Rethinking educational research* (pp. 30-63). London: Hodder & Stoughton.

Walker, R. (Ed.). (1985). *Applied qualitative research.* Aldershot, UK: Gower.

Wax, R. H. (1971). *Doing fieldwork: Warnings and advice.* Chicago: University of Chicago Press.

Webb, S., & Webb, B. (1932). *Methods of social study.* London: Longmans Green.

Wellmer, A. (1974). *Critical theory of society.* New York: Seabury. (Original work published 1969)

White, H. (1973). *Metahistory: The historical imagination in nineteenth century Europe.* Baltimore: Johns Hopkins University Press.

Whyte, W. F. (1955). *Street corner society: The social structure of an Italian slum* (2nd ed.). Chicago: University of Chicago Press.

Whyte, W. F. (1981). *Street corner society: The social structure of an Italian slum* (3rd ed.). Chicago: University of Chicago Press.

Williams, R. (1973). *The country and the city.* London: Chatto & Windus.

Williams, R. (1976). Symbolic interactionism: Fusion of theory and research. In D. C. Thorns (Ed.), *New directions in sociology* (pp. 115-138). Newton Abbott: David & Charles.

Wolcott, H. F. (1980). How to look like an anthropologist without really being one. *Practicing Anthropology, 3*(2), 56-59.

Wolff, K. H. (1964). Surrender and community study: The study of Loma. In A. J. Vidich, J. Bensman, & M. R. Stein (Eds.), *Reflections on community studies* (pp. 233-263). New York: Harper & Row.

Woolgar, S. (Ed.). (1988). *Knowledge and reflexivity.* London: Sage.

Woolgar, S., & Pawluch, D. (1985). Ontological gerrymandering: The anatomy of social problems explanations. *Social Problems, 32,* 214-227.

Young, M. W. (1979). Introduction. In M. W. Young (Ed.), *The ethnography of Malinowski: The Trobriand Islands 1915-18* (pp. 1-20). London: Routledge & Kegan Paul.

16

Phenomenology, Ethnomethodology, and Interpretive Practice

JAMES A. HOLSTEIN
JABER F. GUBRIUM

FROM the 1960s through the 1970s, a family of qualitative research approaches concerned with reality-constituting interpretive practice hovered at the periphery of sociology, generating almost as much puzzlement—and even hostility—as it did empirical findings (see Atkinson, 1988; Coser, 1975; J. Douglas, 1970; Gouldner, 1970; Mehan & Wood, 1976). Harold Garfinkel's (1967) disruptions of the social order and his description of a transsexual's management of femininity, methodological critiques of conventional sociology (Cicourel, 1964; Garfinkel, 1967; Kitsuse & Cicourel, 1963), and even Peter Berger and Thomas Luckmann's (1966) claim that reality is socially constructed piqued the discipline, spawning both vitriol from the old guard and a rich body of theory and research on a new front. The approaches still seem radical to some, challenging many of the presuppositions of more familiar brands of sociology. Yet recent developments of phenomenologically and ethnomethodologically informed empirical programs have led to an almost grudging acceptance if not appreciation of the approaches as neighbors residing in the "suburbs" of sociology (Pollner, 1991).

This chapter discusses phenomenology, ethnomethodology, and related sociological programs of inquiry concerned with interpretive practice. Although the approaches bear a resemblance, their differences are not mere variations on a single enterprise. Clearly they are all indebted to the phenomenological tradition, but the analytic paths taken from the basic tenets diverge into a rich variety of constructionist, ethnomethodological, conversation-analytic, and interpretive strains. Researchers are now making new attempts to begin to consider interpretive practice for the ways that the objectivity of the world is locally accomplished and managed with reference to broad organizational, social, and cultural resources, thus tying what Garfinkel (1967) called "artfulness" to established interpretive structures. The link between interpretive practice and interpretive structures provides a way of understanding the deprivatization of experience as contemporary life is increasingly conducted in public organizational spheres. We begin our discussion by outlining the phenomenological tenets of the approaches.

Phenomenological Tenets

Approaches to the study of interpretive practice share a set of subjectivist assumptions about the nature of lived experience and social order, derived most directly from Alfred Schutz's attempt to develop a social phenomenology bridging sociology with Edmund Husserl's (1970) more philosophical phenomenology. Concerned with the experiential underpinnings of knowledge, Husserl insisted that the relation between perception and its objects was not passive. He argued that human consciousness actively constitutes the objects of experience. This has become foundational for the qualitative study of reality-constituting practices, but it has been turned in a variety of directions.

Schutz (1962, 1964, 1967, 1970) took up Husserl's interest in the ways in which ordinary members of society constitute and reconstitute the world of everyday life, introducing a set of tenets that provide the basis for subsequent phenomenological, ethnomethodological, and constructionist theorizing and empirical work. Stressing the constitutive nature of consciousness and interaction, Schutz (1964) argued that the social sciences should focus on the ways that the life world—that is, the experiential world every person *takes for granted*—is produced and experienced *by members*: "The safeguarding of the subjective point of view is the only but sufficient guarantee that the world of social reality will not be replaced by a fictional non-existing world constructed by the scientific observer" (p. 8). In this view, subjectivity is paramount as the scientific observer deals with how social objects are made meaningful. The emphasis is on how those concerned with objects of experience apprehend and act upon the objects as "things" set apart from observers.

This is a radical departure from the experiential assumptions of the *natural attitude* (Schutz, 1970)—the everyday interpretive stance that takes the world to be principally "out there," separate and distinct from any act of perception or interpretation. In the natural attitude, persons assume that the life world exists before they are present and will be there after they depart. Schutz's recommendation was to study social action that takes place within the natural attitude by *bracketing* the life world, that is, setting aside one's taken-for-granted orientation to it. All ontological judgments about the nature and essence of things and events are suspended. The observer can then focus on the ways in which members of the life world themselves interpretively produce the recognizable, intelligible forms they treat as real.

The orientation to the subjectivity of the life world led Schutz to examine the commonsense knowledge and practical reasoning members use to "objectify" its social forms. Schutz noted that an individual approaches the life world with a *stock of knowledge* composed of commonsense constructs and categories that are social in origin. These images, theories, ideas, values, and attitudes are applied to aspects of experience, making them meaningful. Stocks of knowledge are resources with which persons interpret experience, grasp the intentions and motivations of others, achieve intersubjective understandings, and coordinate actions.

Stocks of knowledge produce a familiar world, one with which members already seem to be acquainted. In part this is because of the typified manner by which knowledge is articulated. The myriad phenomena of everyday life are subsumed under a more limited number of ostensibly shared constructs and categories, general and flexible guidelines for understanding and interpreting experience. *Typifications* make it possible to account for experience, rendering things and occurrences recognizable as being of a particular type or realm. At the same time, typifications are indeterminate, adaptable, and modifiable. Stocks of knowledge are always essentially incomplete, open-ended. Meaning requires the interpretive application of a category to the concrete particulars of a situation.

If human consciousness necessarily typifies, Schutz (1970) argued, language is the central medium for transmitting typifications and thereby meaning. This provides a methodological orientation for a phenomenology of social life concerned with the relation between language use and the objects of experience. Within the contrasting natural attitude, the meaning of a word is taken to be what it references, corresponds with, or stands for in the real world—following a correspondence theory of meaning. In this framework, the essential task of language is to convey information, to describe reality. Viewed as a system of typifications, however, words can be seen as the constitutive building blocks of everyday reality. Accordingly, social phenomenology rests on the tenet that social interaction constructs as much as conveys meaning.

Finally, Schutz noted that our taken-for-granted use of language and typifications creates a sense that the life world is substantial; it is always there apart from our apprehension of it. The majority of one's experiences confirm and reinforce the notion that individuals who interact with one another do so in a world that is experienced in fundamentally the same fashion by all parties, even though mistakes may be made in its apprehension. In other words, we assume that others experience the world basically in the way we do, and that we can therefore understand one another in our dealings in and with the world. We take our subjectivity for granted, overlooking its constitutive character, presuming that we *intersubjectively* share the same reality. Schutz points out that this intersubjectivity is an ongoing accomplishment, a set of understandings sustained from moment to moment by participants in interaction.

Schutz's social phenomenology aimed for a social science that would "interpret and explain human action and thought" through descriptions of the foundational structures of "the reality which seems self-evident to men remaining within the natural attitude" (Schutz & Luckmann, 1974, p. 3). This was an uncompromising interpretive enterprise focused on everyday subjective meaning and experience, the goal of which was to explicate how objects and experience are meaningfully constituted and communicated in the world of everyday life. The program was to treat subjectivity as a topic for investigation in its own right, not as a methodological taboo.

Ethnomethodological Contours

Although ethnomethodology is indebted to Schutz's social phenomenology, it is not a mere extension of his program. Ethnomethodology addresses the problem of order by combining a "phenomenological sensibility" (Maynard & Clayman, 1991) with a paramount concern for constitutive social practice (Garfinkel, 1967). From an ethnomethodological standpoint, the world of "social facts" is accomplished through members' interpretive work—activity through which actors produce and organize the very circumstances of everyday life.

In part, Garfinkel's (1952, 1967) foundational program for ethnomethodology was a response to his teacher Talcott Parsons's (1968) theory of action (Heritage, 1984). For Parsons, social order was made possible through institutionalized systems of norms, rules, and values. Garfinkel sought an alternative to this approach in which social actors, as Garfinkel wrote, were portrayed as "judgmental dopes" responding to external social forces and motivated by internalized directives and imperatives. Garfinkel's response was a model of social order built through the contingent, embodied, ongoing interpretive work of ordinary members of society. He viewed persons as possessing practical linguistic and interactional competencies through which the observable, accountable, orderly features of everyday reality were produced—"members" whose activity constitutes social order. Ethnomethodology's topic became members' practical everyday procedures—that is, "ethnomethods"—for creating, sustaining, and managing a sense of objective reality.

Empirical investigation of "members' methods" has its point of departure in phenomenological bracketing. Adopting a policy of "ethnomethodological indifference" (Garfinkel & Sacks, 1970), the analyst suspends all commitments to an a priori or privileged version of social structure, focusing instead on how members accomplish, manage, and reproduce a *sense* of social structure. Analysis centers on the properties of practical reasoning and the constitutive work that produces the unchallenged appearance of a stable reality, while resisting judgmental characterizations of the "correctness" of members' activities. Contrary to conventional sociology's tendency to ironicize and criticize members' commonsense formulations in comparison with sociologists' views, ethnomethodologists focus on folk methods and commonsense reasoning, abiding by the maxim "Don't argue with the members" (Pollner, personal communication, 1993).

Ethnomethodologists have examined a variety of aspects of social order. One objective, for example, is the description of how order—say, recognizable structures of observable behavior, systems of motivation, or causal ties between motivations and patterns of behavior—is made visible through members' descriptive and accounting practices (Zimmerman & Wieder, 1970). Whereas conventional sociology focuses on rules, norms, and shared meanings as explanations for patterned behavior, ethnomethodology also makes rules topical, but in a distinctly different way. It sets aside the notion that behavior is rule governed or motivated by shared values and expectations in order to observe how conduct is described and explained with reference to rules, values, motives, and the like. The appearance of behavior as being the consequence of a rule is treated as just that—the appearance of an event as an instance of compliance or noncompliance with a rule. By invoking rules and elaborating their sense for specific cases, members describe their activities as rational, coherent, precedented, and orderly (Zimmerman, 1970).

A juror in the midst of deliberation, for instance, may account for her verdict by saying that the judge's instructions on how to consider the case at hand compelled her to decide in her fashion. A rule—the judge's instruction—is used to make sense of the juror's decision making, giving it the appearance of rationality, legality, and correctness because it was done "according to the rule" (Holstein, 1983). Another juror might account for his verdict by saying it was serving the interest of "justice," in this case citing a moral value or principle to explain the decision (Maynard & Manzo, 1993). From an ethnomethodological standpoint, the legal correctness of these decisions is not at issue; instead, the focus is on the use of rules, values, principles, and the like as sense-making devices. The aim is not to provide causal explanations of patterned behavior, but to describe how members recognize, describe, explain, and account for the order of their everyday lives (Zimmerman & Wieder, 1970).

Ethnomethodology's emphasis on the practical production of a sense of reality forms its specific analytic contours. Rather than assuming that members share meanings and definitions of situations, ethnomethodologists note how members continuously rely upon the interpretive capacities of coparticipants in interaction to assemble and reveal a locally visible sense of order. Social structures are locally produced, sustained, and experienced as normal environments—that is, routine, taken-for-granted states of affairs. Indeed, the notion of a singular, objective reality itself is sustained by everyday practices of mundane reason (Pollner, 1987).

If realities are produced "from within," by way of members' interpretive procedures, members' social circumstances are *self-generating*. This implicates two essential properties of meaning revealed by ethnomethodological analysis. First, meanings are essentially *indexical,* that is, they depend on context. Objects and events have equivocal or indeterminate meanings without a visible context. It is only through their situated use in talk and interaction that objects and events become concretely meaningful. Second, the circumstances that provide the context for meaning are themselves self-generating. Interpretive activities are simultaneously *in* and *about* the settings to which they orient, and that they describe. Socially accomplished realities are thus *reflexive*; descriptive accounts of settings give shape to those settings while simultaneously being shaped by the settings they constitute.

Opposite sides of the same coin, indexicality and reflexivity are unavoidable features of social reality; their manifestations and consequences are central ethnomethodological research topics (for example, see Pollner, 1991; Wieder, 1988). Studies of situated interpretive practice necessarily require close attention to the fine details of talk and interaction. Ethnomethodological analysis focuses on the interactionally unfolding features of social settings, treating talk and interaction as topics for analysis rather than as mere communications about more sociologically important underlying phenomena.

Whereas much ethnomethodological research has been ethnographic (e.g., Emerson, 1969; see Maynard & Clayman, 1991, for a review of other studies), it pays especially close attention to the interactional, particularly discursive aspects of the settings studied. Traditional ethnographies generally assume that language is a neutral conduit for description; words represent or tell about culturally circumscribed realities (Atkinson, 1990; Clifford & Marcus, 1986; Clough, 1992; Geertz, 1988; Gubrium & Silverman, 1989). In contrast, an ethnomethodological approach treats objective reality as an interactional and discursive accomplishment; descriptions, accounts, or reports are not merely about some social world as much as they are constitutive of that world. The approach does not attempt to generate information about interaction or discourse through interviews or questionnaires, but relies upon naturally occurring talk to reveal the ways ordinary interaction produces social order in the settings where the talk occurs. When subjects or informants talk, their utterances are not taken as more or less accurate or authentic reports about circumstances, conduct, states of mind, or other reportables. Instead, the talk is considered as the very action through which local realities are accomplished.

From a procedural standpoint, ethnomethodological research must be keenly attuned to naturally occurring discourse and interaction as constitutive elements of the settings studied (see Atkinson & Drew, 1979; Maynard, 1984, 1989; Mehan & Wood, 1975; Sacks, 1972). The point of departure, however, may vary. Although always concerned with the domain of talk and interaction, more ethnographically oriented studies emphasize discourse-in-context, looking more to the situated content of talk as constitutive of local meaning. At the other end of the continuum, the analyst may be more inclined to emphasize the sequential structuring of talk as a means of building context and meaning. Although particular aspects of the domain may be highlighted, structure, context, and content all remain central ethnomethodological concerns.

The emphasis on talk-in-interaction (rather than talk and interaction) has been developed into what some claim is a distinct variant of ethnomethodology—conversation analysis (see Heritage, 1984; Sacks, Schegloff, & Jefferson, 1974; Zimmerman, 1988). Although some contend that its connection to ethnomethodology is tenuous (Atkinson, 1988; Lynch & Bogen, in press; for counterarguments, see Maynard & Clayman, 1991; ten Have, 1990), conversation analysis may be linked to ethnomethodology by their common interest in the local, embodied, methodical construction of intelligible and analyzable social action (Maynard & Clayman, 1991).

Focusing on the competencies that underlie ordinary social activities, conversation analysis attempts to describe and explicate the collaborative practices speakers use and rely upon when they engage in intelligible interaction. Both the production of conduct and its interpretation are seen as the accountable products of a common set of methods or procedures (Heritage, 1984). It is through these procedures that the intelligibility of the social world is made evident. As Emanuel Schegloff and Harvey Sacks (1973) argue regarding the patterned conversations they observed: "Insofar as the [conversational] materials we worked with exhibited orderliness, they did so not only to us . . . but for the co-participants who produced them. If the materials were . . . orderly, they were so because they had been methodically produced by the members of society for one another" (p. 290).

John Heritage (1984) summarizes the fundamentals of conversation analysis in three premises.

First, interaction is structurally organized, and this may be observed in the regularities of ordinary conversation. All aspects of interaction can be found to exhibit organized patterns of stable, identifiable structural features. They stand independent of the psychological or other characteristics of particular speakers, representing ubiquitous features of talk-in-interaction itself to which participants orient. Second, all interaction is contextually oriented in that talk is both productive of and reflects the circumstances of its production. Third, these two properties characterize all interaction so that no order of detail can be dismissed as disorderly, accidental, or irrelevant to the ongoing interaction.

This focus on the real-time, sequential details of ordinary conversation requires naturalistic methods of study. Naturally occurring talk is tape-recorded (increasingly, videotaping is encouraged) and transcribed to reproduce the fine-grained detail of speech exchanges (see Atkinson & Heritage, 1984). Analysis then centers on the collaborative, constantly emerging structure of conversation itself, identifying principles that underpin the sequential organization of talk, the local management of turn taking, and practices relating to opening, sustaining, and closing orderly sequences. In brief, talk is systematically examined for the methodical, structured ways that the orderliness of interaction is recurrently accomplished.

Another strain of contemporary ethnomethodology has proceeded in a significantly different direction, concentrating more on detailed descriptions of the features of practical actions through which order is accomplished. In contrast to what some have labeled the "enriched positivism" of conversation analysis (Lynch & Bogen, in press) as it has been promoted by Sacks and his circle, Garfinkel (1988) and others have begun to elaborate a "post-analytic" (Lynch & Bogen, in press) ethnomethodology that is less inclined to universalistic generalizations regarding the enduring structures or machineries of ordinary interaction. This work concentrates on the highly localized competencies that constitute various domains of "work"—most notably the work of the sciences, for example, astronomy (Garfinkel, Lynch, & Livingston, 1981), biology and neurology (Lynch, 1985), and mathematics (Livingston, 1986). The goal is to specify the "quiddity" or "just whatness" of social practices within tightly circumscribed, specialized domains of knowledge and action (Heritage, 1987). These studies focus on the embodied conceptualizations and practices that practitioners within a particular domain of work recognize as belonging to that domain (Heritage, 1987). The emphasis is antitheoretical (Fish, 1989) in that it discourages the formulation of comprehensive frameworks for investigating the myriad practices that constitute social order. Instead, the program advocates studies of specific interactional practices through which order is manifested and rendered accountable in highly specific social, historical, and practical circumstances (Bogen & Lynch, 1993).

Expanding the Scope

The ethnomethodological emphasis on practice is shared by several newly developing variations of the approach. The following subsections describe some adaptations, elaborations, and reformulations of ethnomethodological themes that are expanding the theoretical and empirical scope of Garfinkel's original program.

Local Interpretive Resources

The agent at the center of one variation remains that of the practitioner of everyday life who works at discerning and designating the recognizable and orderly parameters of everyday life in order to get on with the business at hand. Although the work is seen as practical and "artful" in the ethnomethodological sense of the term, the practitioner is not viewed as building reality "from scratch"—from the ground up, as it were—on each and every interpretive occasion. Rather, interpretive work is conditioned by arrays of local interpretive resources—recognizable categories, familiar vocabularies, organizational missions, professional orientations, group cultures, and other existing frameworks for assigning meaning to matters under consideration. At the same time, these contexts of interpretation are themselves ongoing accomplishments, reflexively supplying meaning to actions and objects as those meanings maintain, elaborate, or alter the circumstances in which they occur (Garfinkel, 1967; Heritage, 1984).

The use of local interpretive resources is typically astute; resources are crafted to the demands of the occasion. Meaning is never completely predetermined; it must always be convincingly and accountably articulated with concrete particulars. At the same time, interpretive practice engages institutional frameworks, formal and informal categories, and long-standing cultural patterns—socially established structures of meaning (Geertz, 1973, 1983). Description and interpretation often seem quite familiar; they must make sense. Not only must adequate descriptions be recognizable (Sacks, 1974), but they are accountable in that they must convince socially defined competent agents that the circumstances in question warrant the attributions that are attached. Thus, although social reality is situationally and artfully constructed, this is accomplished in relation to concrete interpretive parameters. Social order is assembled from "cultural particulars" (Silverman, 1985) that may be widely available yet contingently asserted.

The combined concern for interpretive resources and artful practice offers a perspective that has been applied to a wide variety of topics, including family (Gubrium & Holstein, 1990, 1993a, 1993b; Holstein & Gubrium, 1993), the life course (Gubrium, Holstein, & Buckholdt, 1994), human service work (G. Miller, 1991a, 1991b), domestic violence and battered women's shelters (Loseke, 1992), mental illness and involuntary commitment (Holstein, 1993), family therapy (Gubrium, 1992), social problems (Holstein & Miller, 1993; Miller & Holstein, 1989; L. J. Miller, 1993), and trouble and deviance (Emerson & Messinger, 1977).

The linkage between interpretive practice and resource is facilitated by reference to some well-known disciplinary concerns, in particular, aspects of Durkheim's (1961) reflections on collective representation and various formulations of the role of culture, institutional context, and discourse structures.

Collective Representations

Contemporary positivist sociology traces some of its roots to Emile Durkheim's (1964) call for the scientific study of social facts. Read interpretively, aspects of Durkheim's work also provide a basis for studying how meaning is attached to objects of everyday life (Pfohl, 1992; Silverman, 1985). Durkheim (1961) referred to widely available categories of meaning and understanding—social forms such as religion, community, family, and home—as collective representations. By this he meant that social objects and categories can be viewed as abstractly representing the organization of persons' lives. As Mary Douglas (1986) notes, Durkheim considered collective representations to be "publicly standardized ideas [that] constitute social order" (p. 96). Durkheim paid little attention to the interactive processes through which social order is achieved, but this reading of his framework is useful for orienting to meaning as socially, not individually, accomplished.

Interpretive practice can be understood to involve the articulation of publicly recognized structures, categories, or images with aspects of experience in ways that accountably produce broadly recognizable instances of the objects or events so categorized (Gubrium, 1988; Holstein, 1993). David Silverman (1985) sees this practical linkage of interpretive structure and "artfulness" as a way of establishing a middle ground between such polar sociological extremes as so-called macro and micro forms of analysis.

Collective representations enter into the interpretive process in a manner similar to Schutz's (1970) "schemes of interpretation," as widely available, experientially acquired frameworks for organizing and making sense of everyday life. The schemes collectively represent the social forms or structures of our lives, such as the popular stage models of human development that are taken to reflect personal experience in relation to time (Gubrium, Holstein, & Buckholdt, 1994). The schemes mediate individual biography and interpersonal relations, reflecting and perpetuating culturally promoted understandings of, and orientations to, everyday experience. Interpretation is shaped by the resources that are locally available, recognized, and accepted, making meaningful experience—its perception, representation, and authenticity—a socially rather than privately constructed phenomenon (Silverman, 1987).

Rhetorics of Everyday Life

One way of analyzing interpretive structures is to explicate the rhetorics of collective representation. Cultural studies of various types provide insight into the array of interpretive resources and categories available for use in constituting everyday realities. Studies of social movements and their role in the formation of public issues and promulgation of interpretive categories for personal troubles also have this aim.

The constructionist approach to social problems is a prominent instance of this line of research in sociology. Spector and Kitsuse (1987), for example, outline a program for studying social problems as "the activities of individuals or groups making assertions of grievances and claims with respect to some putative condition" (p. 75). The study of social problems from this perspective requires descriptions of the emergence, nature, and maintenance of claims-making and responding activity that constitutes "condition categories" (Ibarra & Kitsuse, 1993) used to identify social problems. Center stage is the large-scale and mass-media rhetoric or "publicity" (Gubrium, 1993) that promotes "images of issues" (Best, 1989) that may be applied to categorize experience.

Accenting the artful, other studies in this vein focus on the activities through which collective representations are locally applied to personal troubles (see Mills, 1959). Jaber Gubrium (1986) shows how the Alzheimer's disease movement provides a medical rhetoric for interpreting the cognitive ravages of aging. Such personal troubles as the stress of caregiving and the fear of institutionalization collectively represent a disease experience. Similarly, Gale Miller (1991a) documents how the rhetoric of labor market conditions and job applicant attitudes collectively constitute social relations in a work incentive program. Donileen Loseke (1992) deconstructs the claims forming the collective representations of wife abuse and battered women, then explicates the organizational practices through which shelter workers attach the images to actual persons and events. Concrete instances of battered women and wife abuse, Loseke explains, are the interpretive result of a newly recognized public category for viewing individual cases.

Local Culture, Discourse Structures, and Organizational Embeddedness

Meaning structures are public, but they are also locally circumscribed. In a sense, Clifford Geertz (1983) recognized this when he argued that knowledge is "always ineluctably local" (p. 4). As the corpus of local knowledge coalesces into a local culture—that is, a set of more or less regularized ways of assigning meaning and responding to things (Gubrium, 1989)—interpretive practice reflects local circumstances and resources.

Local culture comes in various guises. Small groups, formal organizations, and other domains of everyday life condition what we encounter and how we make sense of it. Mary Douglas (1986) goes so far as to suggest that human reason is organized and expressed through processes of "institutional thinking." Applying the phrase metaphorically, she argues that socially organized circumstances provide models of social order through which experience is assimilated and organized. She states, for example, that "an answer is only seen to be the right one if it sustains the institutional thinking that is already in the minds of individuals as they try to decide" (p. 4).

According to Douglas, institutions are organized social conventions involving typical and routine ways of representing social reality. As she formulates them, these representational conventions are similar to what Michel Foucault (1972) calls "discursive formations." Contextually grounded discourses, vocabularies, and categories form local interpretive resources or cultures for defining and classifying aspects of everyday life. Parenthetically, as Sacks (1974) notes, "a culture . . . does not, so to speak, merely fill brains in roughly the same way, it fills them so that they are alike in fine detail" as well, providing an ethnomethodological contour (p. 218).

Interpretive practice also is *organizationally embedded* (Gubrium, 1988; Gubrium & Holstein, 1990). This is a shorthand way of saying that interpretation reflects publicly recognized contexts, that social objects are constituted within discernibly organized circumstances. We use the term *organizational* in its most general sense—any socially organized circumstance—while recognizing that interpretation is increasingly conditioned by the more strictly defined parameters of formal organizations (see Gubrium & Holstein, 1990). As everyday life is more and more conducted within formally organized settings, the formulation of meaning becomes decidedly public—deprivatized—as it is conditioned by organizationally promoted ways of making sense of experience. Indeed, the organizational embeddedness of experience has so diversified the meanings of self and our social relations as to transform modern institutional life into a postmodern form (Gubrium, 1992; Gubrium, Holstein, & Buckholdt, 1994).

Although organized settings provide accountable modes of representation, the settings do not determine interpretive practice. Concertedly local, interpretation relies upon delimited cultural categories that are diversely and artfully articulated with, and attached to, experience. Whether the local culture under consideration is characteristic of a particular organization, profession, ethnic or gender group, or another collectivity or setting, the culture supplies *resources* for interpretation, not injunctions or absolute directives. Experience constituted in a particular organization or setting may take on the general qualities that the organization or setting promotes, but interpretation also is practical, artfully maneuvering what is locally available and circumstantial. Practitioners of everyday life are not "organizational dopes," mere extensions of organizational thinking. They exercise interpretive discretion, mediated by complex layerings of interpretive influence. They also carry with them the biographical basis for resistance, personal and interpersonal histories that compete with organizational categories as means for interpreting experience (Gubrium & Holstein, 1993a).

Prevailing interpretations thus emerge as provisional adaptations of diverse local resources and conditions, serving the practical needs at hand, until further notice. Culture orients and equips the process, but interpretive inventiveness and serendipity intervene. The process repeatedly and reflexively turns back on itself, as substance, structure, and practice are enmeshed in the ongoing production, reproduction, and redesignation of meaning and order.

Emerging Classic Themes

Some recent developments in ethnomethodology and related approaches have turned to classic sociological themes. This represents a further broadening of the enterprise, one that also bridges what have been conceived as incompatible micro- and macro-level concerns. Richard Hilbert (1992), for example, argues that many of ethnomethodology's central considerations also reside in the theoretical writings of Max Weber and Durkheim. Hilbert suggests that modern interpreters—most notably Talcott Parsons—have obscured or suppressed many of the radical themes of the classics. Ethnomethodology, he claims, has rediscovered and reinvigorated theoretical arguments that Durkheim and Weber initiated, and thus addresses problems at the very core of the discipline.

Although ethnomethodology has generally been considered a microsociological orientation, Dorothy Smith combines ethnomethodological, Marxist, and feminist insights to develop a different set of classic themes. Taking her point of departure from women's experience, Smith argues that what she calls "textually mediated" activity and "relations of ruling" combine in practice to articulate the meanings of being female—especially the meaning of motherhood. Her studies of women's work as mothers (Griffith & Smith, 1990; Smith, 1989; Smith & Griffith, 1990) show how the working discourse of mothers' institutional linkages with home, work, and school articulates an everyday world for mothers that reproduces their subordination to a system of patriarchy.

Smith extends her critique to the "relations of ruling" operating in social science research practices that virtually "rule" women because typical research designs are insensitive to women's lived experience. For example, Smith takes exception to William J. Wilson's (1987) taken-for-granted distinction between "intact" families and those that are not intact (Smith, 1993). She argues that Wilson's view of family life is "SNAF-mediated," meaning that the view is a kind of text based on an idealized image of the "standard North American family." Wilson's reliance on this view leads his research to "overrule" women's diverse and legitimate familial experiences.

Closer to more traditional ethnomethodological concerns, David Silverman's (1987) research on communication and medical practice focuses on the role of context in interpretation, but with a decided social policy orientation. His studies of doctor-patient interactions in various medical settings show that although talk and interaction constitute the meaning of patienthood, the family, and the illness experience, the working medical vocabularies of particular settings mediate understandings of illnesses, intervention, progress, and recovery. Silverman's work not only examines the organizational embeddedness of discourse, but also provides directives for refashioning social relations, especially when he asks such questions as, "What can social science contribute?" (Silverman, 1985, chap. 9).

A new set of conversation-analytic studies has also turned to "institutional talk" (Drew & Heritage, 1993). Although the point of departure remains the transsituational regularities of conversational structure, more emphasis is being given to the ways that institutional or organizational context conditions interactional practice. Drew and Heritage (1993), for example, note that institutional talk is normally informed by the goal orientations of relatively restricted, organizationally conventional forms. Institutional location also tends to constrain the ways that members participate in interaction, and presents inferential frameworks and procedures to which they may orient. Although they rely less upon the analytic apparatus of conversation analysis, studies such as Robert Dingwall and Phil Strong's (1985) examination of the role of language and practical reasoning in the production of organizational realities elaborate the theme of talk and organizational context.

Gubrium's (1992) comparative ethnography of clinical discourse in two family therapy programs also underscores institutional groundings, linking broader issues of rationalization with more ethnomethodological concerns. Gubrium shows how organizational communication constructs domestic disorder, making it visible in locally understandable terms. Contrasting images of home life in the two therapeutic settings—one viewing domestic order as a system of authority, the other seeing it as a configuration of emotional bonds—serve to articulate different senses of family troubles, of being "out of control." The idea that the reality of home life and domestic troubles are embedded in organizational activities and mediated by institutional images provides a basis for arguing that domestic life is both socially constructed and manifoldly rationalized—that is, constituted under the auspices of the many organizations that suffuse contemporary life. Gubrium argues that as everyday reality is increasingly grounded in diverse public settings, its rationalization is more artful and local—less total—than in Weber's (1947) conceptualization.

Conclusion

All told, the range of qualitative research approaches manifesting "phenomenological sensibilities" has grown considerably. Indeed, although Maynard and Clayman (1991) celebrate the "diversity of ethnomethodology," proclaiming the "enormous range of ethnomethodological research" over the past three decades, their assessment seems too modest, perhaps even parochial. More broadly, studies of interpretive practice evincing an "ethnomethodological sensibility" but moving beyond the traditional purview are flourishing. New analytic resources are being mobilized, as, for example, Durkheimian and Foucauldian insights into overarching collective representations and discourse structures are linked to local interpretive procedures. New issues are being raised regarding linkages between classic and contemporary questions of social order, between ostensibly micro- and macro-level concerns. New analytic resources are developing to explicate more fully the roles of discourse, conversational structure, and the content and context of interactional exchanges.

With the new connections, interpretation is being thrust into the context of the postmodern and beyond. It might be argued that ethnomethodology represents something of a deconstructionist (Derrida, 1977) turn in sociology, with its concern for the reflexivity of social interaction and context paralleling in some ways Derrida's attention to the continuous "play of difference"—the constant swirl of reality-constituting activity—that produces perennially new realities in literary texts. Highlighting both interpretive resources and interpretive practice, however, provides a means of linking the play of difference to the *in situ* activities that produce, manage, and contain social order. The focus on broader interpretive contexts at least partially binds the play of difference to the relatively circumscribed resources of organizational and institutional settings as contexts.

This moves the analytic enterprise in a post-Derridian direction (Gubrium, 1992; Gubrium & Holstein, 1990; Holstein, 1993). The interpretation of lived experience (compared with, say, literary text) is shaped by contexts that may be relatively fixed, that mediate reality production accordingly. The accomplishment of order and meaning is highly localized, artful yet contextually conditioned. The focus on interpretive resources reappropriates classic sociological themes—rationalization and collective representation, for example—to the enactment of meaningful reality, blurring the distinction between macro and micro. Practice remains the common thread as some of the recent occupants of sociological "suburbs" are rediscovering the analytic verve of older cities.

References

Atkinson, J. M., & Drew, P. (1979). *Order in court.* Atlantic Highlands, NJ: Humanities Press.

Atkinson, J. M., & Heritage, J. (Eds.). (1984). *Structures of social action.* Cambridge, UK: Cambridge University Press.

Atkinson, P. A. (1988). Ethnomethodology: A critical review. *Annual Review of Sociology, 14,* 441-465.

Atkinson, P. A. (1990). *The ethnographic imagination: Textual constructions of reality.* London: Routledge.

Berger, P. L., & Luckmann, T. (1966). *The social construction of reality.* Garden City, NY: Doubleday.

Best, J. (1989). *Images of issues.* Hawthorne, NY: Aldine de Gruyter.

Bogen, D., & Lynch, M. (1993). Do we need a general theory of social problems? In J. A. Holstein & G. Miller (Eds.), *Reconsidering social constructionism: Debates in social problems theory* (pp. 213-237). Hawthorne, NY: Aldine de Gruyter.

Cicourel, A. V. (1964). *Method and measurement in sociology.* New York: Free Press.

Clifford, J., & Marcus, G. E. (Eds.). (1986). *Writing culture: The poetics and politics of ethnography.* Berkeley: University of California Press.

Clough, P. T. (1992). *The end(s) of ethnography: From realism to social criticism.* Newbury Park, CA: Sage.

Coser, L. (1975). Two methods in search of a substance. *American Sociological Review, 40,* 691-700.

Derrida, J. (1977). *Of grammatology.* Baltimore: Johns Hopkins University Press.

Dingwall, R., & Strong, P. M. (1985). The interactional study of organizations. *Urban Life, 14,* 205-232.

Drew, P., & Heritage, J. (Eds.). (1993). *Talk at work.* Cambridge, UK: Cambridge University Press.

Douglas, J. (Ed.). (1970). *Understanding everyday life.* Chicago: Aldine.

Douglas, M. (1986). *How institutions think.* Syracuse, NY: Syracuse University Press.

Durkheim, E. (1961). *The elementary forms of the religious life.* New York: Collier-Macmillan.

Durkheim, E. (1964). *The rules of sociological method.* New York: Free Press.

Emerson, R. M. (1969). *Judging delinquents.* Chicago: Aldine.

Emerson, R. M., & Messinger, S. (1977). The micro-politics of trouble. *Social Problems, 25,* 121-134.

Fish, S. (1989). *Doing what comes naturally: Change, rhetoric, and the practice of theory in literary and legal studies.* Durham, NC: Duke University Press.

Foucault, M. (1972). *The archaeology of knowledge.* New York: Pantheon.

Garfinkel, H. (1952). *The perception of the other: A study in social order.* Unpublished doctoral dissertation, Harvard University.

Garfinkel, H. (1967). *Studies in ethnomethodology.* Englewood Cliffs, NJ: Prentice Hall.

Garfinkel, H. (1988). Evidence for locally produced, naturally accountable phenomena of order, logic, reason, meaning, method, etc. in and as of the essential quiddity of immortal ordinary society (I of IV): An announcement of studies. *Sociological Theory, 6,* 103-109.

Garfinkel, H., Lynch, M., & Livingston, E. (1981). The work of a discovering science construed with materials from the optically discovered pulsar. *Philosophy of the Social Sciences, 11,* 131-158.

Garfinkel, H., & Sacks, H. (1970). On the formal structures of practical actions. In J. C. McKinney & E. A. Tiryakian (Eds.), *Theoretical sociology* (pp. 338-366). New York: Appleton-Century-Crofts.

Geertz, C. (1973). *The interpretation of cultures: Selected essays.* New York: Basic Books.

Geertz, C. (1983). *Local knowledge: Further essays in interpretive anthropology.* New York: Basic Book.

Geertz, C. (1988). *Works and lives: The anthropologist as author.* Stanford, CA: Stanford University Press.

Gouldner, A. W. (1970). *The coming crisis of Western sociology.* New York: Avon.

Griffith, A. I., & Smith, D. E. (1990). "What did you do in school today?": Mothering, schooling, and social class. In G. Miller & J. A. Holstein (Eds.), *Perspectives on social problems* (Vol. 2, pp. 3-24). Greenwich, CT: JAI.

Gubrium, J. F. (1986). *Oldtimers and Alzheimer's: The descriptive organization of senility.* Greenwich, CT: JAI.

Gubrium, J. F. (1988). *Analyzing field reality.* Newbury Park, CA: Sage.

Gubrium, J. F. (1989). Local cultures and service policy. In J. F. Gubrium & D. Silverman (Eds.), *The politics of field research: Beyond enlightenment* (pp. 94-112). Newbury Park, CA: Sage.

Gubrium, J. F. (1992). *Out of control: Family therapy and domestic disorder.* Newbury Park, CA: Sage.

Gubrium, J. F. (1993). For a cautious naturalism. In J. A. Holstein & G. Miller (Eds.), *Reconsidering social constructionism: Debates in social problems theory* (pp. 89-101). Hawthorne, NY: Aldine de Gruyter.

Gubrium, J. F., & Holstein, J. A. (1990). *What is family?* Mountain View, CA: Mayfield.

Gubrium, J. F., & Holstein, J. A. (1993a). Family discourse, organizational embeddedness, and local enactment. *Journal of Family Issues, 14,* 66-81.

Gubrium, J. F., & Holstein, J. A. (1993b). Phenomenology, ethnomethodology, and family discourse. In P. Boss, W. Doherty, R. LaRossa, W. Schum, & S. Steinmetz (Eds.), *Sourcebook of family theory and methods* (pp. 649-670). New York: Plenum.

Gubrium, J. F., Holstein, J. A., & Buckholdt, D. R. (1994). *Constructing the life course.* Dix Hills, NY: General Hall.

Gubrium, J. F., & Silverman, D. (Eds.). (1989). *The politics of field research: Beyond enlightenment.* Newbury Park, CA: Sage.

Heritage, J. (1984). *Garfinkel and ethnomethodology.* Cambridge: Polity.

Heritage, J. (1987). Ethnomethodology. In A. Giddens & J. Turner (Eds.), *Sociological theory today* (pp. 224-271). Stanford, CA: Stanford University Press.

Hilbert, R. A. (1992). *The classical roots of ethnomethodology.* Chapel Hill: University of North Carolina Press.

Holstein, J. A. (1983). Jurors' use of judges' instructions. *Sociological Methods and Research, 11,* 501-518.

Holstein, J. A. (1993). *Court-ordered insanity: Interpretive practice and involuntary commitment.* Hawthorne, NY: Aldine de Gruyter.

Holstein, J. A., & Gubrium, J. F. (1993). Constructing family: Descriptive practice and domestic order. In T. Sarbin & J. Kitsuse (Eds.), *Constructing the social* (pp. 232-250). London: Sage.

Holstein, J. A., & Miller, G. (1993). Social constructionism and social problems work. In J. A. Holstein & G. Miller (Eds.), *Reconsidering social constructionism: Debates in social problems theory.* Hawthorne, NY: Aldine de Gruyter.

Husserl, E. (1970). *Logical investigation.* New York: Humanities Press.

Ibarra, P. R., & Kitsuse, J. I. (1993). Vernacular constituents of moral discourse: An interactionist proposal for the study of social problems. In J. A. Holstein & G. Miller (Eds.), *Reconsidering social constructionism: Debates in social problems theory* (pp. 25-58). Hawthorne, NY: Aldine de Gruyter.

Kitsuse, J. I., & Cicourel, A. V. (1963). A note on the uses of official statistics. *Social Problems, 11,* 131-139.

Livingston, E. (1986). *The ethnomethodological foundations of mathematics.* London: Routledge & Kegan Paul.

Loseke, D. R. (1992). *The battered woman and shelters: The social construction of wife abuse.* Albany: State University of New York Press.

Lynch, M. (1985). *Art and artifact in laboratory science.* London: Routledge & Kegan Paul.

Lynch, M., & Bogen, D. (in press). Harvey Sacks' primitive natural science. *Theory, Culture & Society.*

Maynard, D. W. (1984). *Inside plea bargaining: The language of negotiation.* New York: Plenum.

Maynard, D. W. (1989). On the ethnography and analysis of discourse in institutional settings. In J. A. Holstein & G. Miller (Eds.), *Perspectives on social problems* (Vol. 1, pp. 127-146). Greenwich, CT: JAI.

Maynard, D. W., & Clayman, S. E. (1991). The diversity of ethnomethodology. *Annual Review of Sociology, 17,* 385-418.

Maynard, D. W., & Manzo, J. (1993). On the sociology of justice. *Sociological Theory, 11,* 171-193.

Mehan, H., & Wood, H. (1975). *The reality of ethnomethodology.* New York: John Wiley.

Mehan, H., & Wood, H. (1976). De-secting ethnomethodology. *American Sociologist, 11,* 13-31.

Miller, G. (1991a). *Enforcing the work ethic: Rhetoric and everyday life in a work incentive program.* Albany: State University of New York Press.

Miller, G. (1991b). Family as excuse and extenuating circumstance: Social organization and use of family rhetoric in a work incentive program. *Journal of Marriage and the Family, 53,* 609-621.

Miller, G., & Holstein, J. A. (1989). On the sociology of social problems. In J. A. Holstein & G. Miller (Eds.), *Perspectives on social problems* (Vol. 1, pp. 1-18). Greenwich, CT: JAI.

Miller, L. J. (1993). Claims-making from the underside: Marginalization and social problems analysis. In J. A. Holstein & G. Miller (Eds.), *Reconsidering social constructionism: Debates in social problems theory* (pp. 349-376). Hawthorne, NY: Aldine de Gruyter.

Mills, C. W. (1959). *The sociological imagination.* New York: Oxford University Press.

Parsons, T. (1968). *The structure of social action.* New York: Free Press.

Pfohl, S. (1992). *Death at the Parasite Cafe.* New York: St. Martin's.

Pollner, M. (1987). *Mundane reason: Reality in everyday and sociological discourse.* Cambridge, UK: Cambridge University Press.

Pollner, M. (1991). Left of ethnomethodology: The rise and decline of radical reflexivity. *American Sociological Review, 56,* 370-380.

Sacks, H. (1972). An initial investigation of the usability of conversational data for doing sociology. In D. Sudnow (Ed.), *Studies in social interaction* (pp. 31-74). New York: Free Press.

Sacks, H. (1974). On the analyzability of stories by children. In R. Turner (Ed.), *Ethnomethodology* (pp. 216-232). Harmondsworth: Penguin.

Sacks, H., Schegloff, E., & Jefferson, G. (1974). A simplest systematics for the organization of turn-taking for conversation. *Language, 50,* 696-735.

Schegloff, E. A., & Sacks, H. (1973). Opening up closings. *Semiotica, 7,* 289-327.

Schutz, A. (1962). *The problem of social reality.* The Hague: Martinus Nijhoff.

Schutz, A. (1964). *Studies in social theory.* The Hague: Martinus Nijhoff.

Schutz, A. (1967). *The phenomenology of the social world.* Evanston, IL: Northwestern University Press.

Schutz, A. (1970). *On phenomenology and social relations.* Chicago: University of Chicago Press.

Schutz, A., & Luckmann, T. (1974). *The structures of the life world.* London: Heinemann.

Silverman, D. (1985). *Qualitative methodology and sociology.* Aldershot: Gower.

Silverman, D. (1987). *Communication and medical practice.* London: Sage.

Smith, D. E. (1993). The standard North American family: SNAF as an ideological model. *Journal of Family Issues, 14,* 50-65.

Smith, D. E. (1989). Women's work as mothers: A new look at the relation of class, family, and school achievement. In J. A. Holstein & G. Miller (Eds.), *Perspectives on social problems* (Vol. 1, pp. 109-127). Greenwich, CT: JAI.

Smith, D. E., & Griffith, A. I. (1990). Coordinating the uncoordinated: Mothering, schooling, and the family wage. In G. Miller & J. A. Holstein (Eds.), *Perspectives on social problems* (Vol. 2, pp. 25-44). Greenwich, CT: JAI.

Spector, M., & Kitsuse, J. (1987). *Constructing social problems.* Hawthorne, NY: Aldine de Gruyter.

ten Have, P. (1990). Methodological issues in conversation analysis. *Bulletin de Methodologie Sociologique, 27,* 23-51.

Weber, M. (1947). *Theory of social and economic organization.* New York: Free Press.

Wieder, D. L. (1988). *Language and social reality.* Washington, DC: University Press of America.

Wilson, W. J. (1987). *The truly disadvantaged: The inner city, the underclass, and public policy.* Chicago: University of Chicago Press.

Zimmerman, D. H. (1970). The practicalities of rule use. In J. Douglas (Ed.), *Understanding everyday life* (pp. 221-238). Chicago: Aldine.

Zimmerman, D. H. (1988). On conversation: The conversation-analytic perspective. In J. A. Anderson (Ed.), *Communication yearbook 11* (pp. 406-432). Newbury Park, CA: Sage.

Zimmerman, D. H., & Wieder, D. L. (1970). Ethnomethodology and the problem of order. In J. Douglas (Ed.), *Understanding everyday life* (pp. 285-295). Chicago: Aldine.

17

■

Grounded Theory Methodology

An Overview

ANSELM STRAUSS
JULIET CORBIN

THE purpose of this chapter is to give an overview of the origins, purposes, uses, and contributions of grounded theory methodology. We will not address the methodology's suggested procedures or much of the logic lying behind them, as these have been discussed extensively elsewhere (see, e.g., Corbin & Strauss, 1990; Glaser, 1978; Glaser & Strauss, 1967; Strauss, 1987; Strauss & Corbin, 1990; see also Charmaz, 1983, 1990). We will assume here that readers either are acquainted with some of those writings or, if sufficiently interested in this chapter, will turn to those sources.

Grounded theory is a *general methodology* for developing theory that is grounded in data systematically gathered and analyzed. Theory evolves during actual research, and it does this through continuous interplay between analysis and data collection. A central feature of this analytic approach is "a general method of [constant] comparative analysis" (Glaser & Strauss, 1967, p. vii); hence the approach is often referred to as the *constant comparative method* (for the original formulation, see Glaser, 1965/1967). Since its introduction 25 years ago, a number of guidelines and procedures have evolved through the research experience of its users; these are designed to enhance the effectiveness of this methodology *in* research. The suggested guidelines and procedures allow much latitude for ingenuity and are an aid to creativity (see below for further discussion).

In this methodology, theory may be *generated* initially from the data, or, if existing (grounded) theories seem appropriate to the area of investigation, then these may be *elaborated* and modified as incoming data are meticulously played against them. (For this second point, see Strauss, 1987; see also a similar approach by a sociologist influenced by Glaser & Strauss's *The Discovery of Grounded Theory,* 1967—Diane Vaughan, 1992; she terms it "theoretical elaboration.") Researchers can also usefully carry into current studies any theory based on their *previous research,* providing it seems relevant to these—but again the matching of theory against data must be rigorously carried out.

Grounded theory methodology explicitly involves "generating theory and doing social research [as] two parts of the same process" (Glaser, 1978,

AUTHORS' NOTE: This summary statement represents the authors' views as participants in, contributors to, and observers of grounded theory's evolution. Others who have been part of this intellectual movement will differ in their views of some points made here and the relative importance we give to them. We thank Leonard Schatzman for his careful reading of the manuscript and some very useful comments.

p. 2). In proposing this approach to the development of theories, Glaser and Strauss were fully cognizant that alternative approaches to creating and elaborating theory—without explicit linkage to actual research—were popular, or assumed, or vigorously argued for (at the time, these included those of Parsons, Merton, and Blau); they still are (see Laumann, Habermas, or Alexander). In that sense, but also in its inclusion of both general guidelines and, over the years, more specific procedures for producing grounded theories, this approach is still unique. Impressed by this radical *research* approach to theory development, Baszanger (1992, pp. 52-53), a French sociologist, has recently commented on the concerted and detailed "hard work" entailed in generating the resultant concepts and tracing their relationships.

Some Similarities and Differences With Other Modes

Similarities

Grounded theory studies share some similarities with other modes of carrying out qualitative research. Sources of data are the same: interviews and field observations, as well as documents of all kinds (including diaries, letters, autobiographies, biographies, historical accounts, and newspaper and other media materials). Videotapes may also be used. Like other qualitative researchers, grounded theorists can utilize quantitative data or combine qualitative and quantitative techniques of analysis (see the discussion below, but also see Glaser & Strauss, 1967, pp. 185-220). Advocates of this methodology assume, as do many other researchers, that some form of social science is possible and desirable. Also, as have others, grounded theorists have redefined the usual scientific canons for the purposes of studying human behavior (see explicit discussions in Glaser & Strauss, 1967, pp. viii, 224; Strauss & Corbin, 1990). As Glaser and Strauss (1967) assert:

> In this book we have raised doubts about the applicability of these [the usual] canons of rigor as proper criteria for judging the credibility of theory based on the use of this methodology. We have suggested that criteria of judgment be based instead on the detailed elements of the actual strategies used for collecting, coding, analyzing, and presenting data when generating theory, and on the way in which people read the theory. (p. 224)

Involved in this commonly shared redefining is an insistence that ours is interpretive work and, as described below, that interpretations *must* include the perspectives and voices of the people whom we study. Interpretations are sought for understanding the actions of individual or collective actors being studied. Yet, those who use grounded theory procedures share with many other qualitative researchers a distinctive position. They accept responsibility for their interpretive roles. They do not believe it sufficient merely to report or give voice to the viewpoints of the people, groups, or organizations studied. Researchers assume the further responsibility of interpreting what is observed, heard, or read (we comment further on this later in the chapter).

Differences

The major difference between this methodology and other approaches to qualitative research is its emphasis upon theory development. Researchers can aim at various levels of theory when using grounded theory procedures. However, most grounded theory studies have been directed at developing substantive theory. This is because of the overwhelming substantive interests of grounded theory researchers rather than the nature of their methodology. As will be discussed later, higher-level "general" theory is also possible, but when grounded this differs from more deductive types of general theory because of its generation and development through interplay with data collected in actual research (for an example, see Glaser & Strauss, 1970). Regardless of level of theory, there is built into this style of extensive interrelated data collection and theoretical analysis an explicit mandate to strive toward *verification* of its resulting hypotheses (statements of relationships between concepts). This is done *throughout the course* of a research project, rather than assuming that verification is possible only through follow-up quantitative research. Enhanced also by its procedures is the possibility of developing theory of great conceptual density and with considerable meaningful variation. *Conceptual density* refers to richness of concept development and relationships—which rest on great familiarity with associated data and are checked out systematically with these data. (This is different from Geertz's "thick descriptions," where the emphasis is on description rather than conceptualization.)

Other Distinguishing Characteristics: Procedures

Certain other general procedures have made this methodology effective and influential. Besides the constant making of comparisons, these include the systematic asking of generative and concept-relating questions, theoretical sampling, systematic coding procedures, suggested guidelines for attaining conceptual (not merely descriptive) "density," variation, and conceptual integration. More recently, the conceptualization and diagramming of a "conditional matrix" (Corbin & Strauss, 1988; Strauss & Corbin, 1990) helps toward specifying conditions and consequences, at every level of scale from the most "macro" to the "micro," and integrating them into the resulting theory.

As we shall refer to the conditional matrix below, a few words about this analytic tool should be useful. This matrix can be visualized "as a set of circles, one inside the other, each [level] corresponding to different aspects of the world. . . . In the outer rings stand those conditional features *most distant* to action/interaction; while the inner rings pertain to those conditional features bearing *most closely* upon an action/interaction sequence" (Strauss & Corbin, 1990, p. 161). Levels include conditions running from international through national, community, organizational and institutional, suborganizational and subinstitutional, group, individual, and collective to action pertaining to a phenomenon. In any given study, the conditions at all levels have relevance, but just how needs to be traced. "The researcher needs to fill in the specific conditional features for each level that pertain to the chosen area of investigation," regardless of which particular level *it* is (Strauss & Corbin, 1990, p. 161).[1]

Evolution in the Use of the Methodology

Early History

Grounded theory was presented initially by Glaser and Strauss in *The Discovery of Grounded Theory* (1967). This book had three avowed purposes. The first was to offer the rationale for theory that was *grounded*—generated and developed through interplay with data collected during research projects. This type of theory, Glaser and Strauss argued, would contribute toward "closing the embarrassing gap between theory and empirical research" (p. vii). Grounded theories and their possibilities were posed against dominant functionalist and structuralist theories (represented by those of such theorists as Parsons, Merton, and Blau), which Glaser and Strauss regarded as inordinately speculative and deductive in nature. The second purpose was to suggest the logic for and specifics of grounded theories. The third aim was to legitimate careful qualitative research, as by the 1960s this had sunk to a low status among an increasing number of sociologists because it was not believed capable of adequate verification.

Ironically, *Discovery* soon achieved its third aim, becoming an early instance of today's strong rationale that underpins qualitative modes of research. It took about two decades, however, before American sociologists, especially those doing qualitative research, showed much appreciation for the more explicit and systematic conceptualization that constitutes theory. It was then that this aspect of the methodology began to become more widely appreciated, probably in conjunction with increasing numbers of books and papers using this methodology and its suggested procedures. The publication of additional methodological writings—as cited above—by grounded theorists also made it more visible and available.

The simultaneous publication of *Discovery* in the United States and England made "grounded theory" well known, at least among qualitatively inclined researchers and their graduate students in those countries. In the years after its publication, first Glaser and then Strauss taught a continuing seminar in qualitative analysis, grounded theory-style, to graduate students in the Department of Social and Behavioral Sciences at the University of California in San Francisco. Many graduates have published monographs and papers using grounded theory methodology about a variety of phenomena. These writings have undoubtedly contributed to making qualitative researchers increasingly aware of this mode of analysis. This has been true especially for medical sociologists, because the first two grounded theory monographs were about dying in hospitals (Glaser & Strauss, 1964, 1968).

Because grounded theory is a general methodology, a *way of thinking about and conceptualizing data,* it was easily adapted by its originators and their students to studies of diverse phenomena. To name only a few, these included professional socialization (Broadhead, 1983), policy arenas (Wiener, 1981), remarriage after divorce (Cauhape, 1983), interaction between builders and a would-be homeowner (Glaser, 1972), homecoming (Hall, 1992), the management of a hazardous pregnancy (Corbin, 1992), ovarian egg donation between sisters (Lessor, 1993), spousal abuse (Lempert, 1992), experiences with chronic illness (Charmaz, 1980), and the work of scientists (Clarke, 1990a, 1990b; Fujimura, 1987; Star, 1989a, 1989b), as well as the development of general theory about status passages (Glaser & Strauss, 1970), negotiation (Strauss, 1978), and the control of information ("awareness contexts") (Strauss, 1987, 1991; for more studies, see the appendix to this chapter). Meanwhile, additional books explicating this style of analysis were also published, contributing to a wider international awareness of the methodology and its procedures (Glaser, 1978; Strauss, 1987; Strauss & Corbin, 1990; see also Charmaz, 1983, 1990).

Developments in Use of Grounded Theory

Although much of the original research using grounded theory procedures was done by sociologists, probably the use of these procedures has never been entirely restricted to this group. Researchers in psychology and anthropology are increasingly using grounded theory procedures. Researchers in practitioner fields such as education, social work, and nursing have increasingly used grounded theory procedures alone or in conjunction with other methodologies. These include phenomenology, in its various social science versions (see Benner, 1989), particular techniques (scales and other instruments), and in combination also with quantitative methods. That practitioners would find grounded theory methodology of use in their studies was signaled as an anticipated possibility in *Discovery,* where Glaser and Strauss (1967) asserted, in a chapter titled "Applying Grounded Theory," that an important feature of a grounded theory is its "fitness":

> A grounded theory that is faithful to the everyday realities of a substantive area is one that has been carefully *induced* from diverse data. . . . Only in this way will the theory be closely related to the daily realities (what is actually going on) of substantive areas, and so be highly applicable to dealing with them. (pp. 238-239)

As with any general methodology, grounded theory's actual use in practice has varied with the specifics of the area under study, the purpose and focus of the research, the contingencies faced during the project, and perhaps also the temperament and particular gifts or weaknesses of the researcher. For instance, Adele Clarke (1990a, 1990b) and S. Leigh Star (1989a) each utilized historical data in conjunction with fieldwork and interview data because their research purposes included gaining an understanding of historical origins and historical continuities in the scientific disciplines they studied. Carolyn Wiener (1981), in her study of the national alcohol arena and its many participants and issues, largely relied on published contemporary documents supplemented by intensive interviews and observations at conferences. Individual researchers invent different specific procedures. Almost always too, in handling the difficult problem of conceptual integration, they learn that advice given in the methodological writings and/or the grounded theory seminar requires adaptation to the circumstances of their own thought processes. Personal histories of dealing with particular bodies of data also affect adaptation of the general methodology.

Researchers utilizing grounded theory have undoubtedly been much influenced by contemporary intellectual trends and movements, including ethnomethodology, feminism, political economy, and varieties of postmodernism. Thus the specific uses and views of grounded theory have been either directly influenced or indirectly affected, in terms of thinking through the different assumptions and emphases of alternative modes of analysis (for an instance, see the thoughtful paper by Joan Fujimura, 1991). Our interpretation of this development in the use and conceptualization of grounded theory is not that its central elements—especially constant comparison—are altering, but that additional ideas and concepts suggested by contemporary social and intellectual movements are entering analytically as *conditions* into the studies of grounded theory researchers.

This methodology's stance on such matters is one of openness, including, as we now interpret that openness, in conditional matrix terms. One of the methodology's central features is that its practitioners can respond to and change with the times—in other words, as conditions that affect behavior change, they can be handled analytically, whether the conditions are in the form of ideas, ideologies, technologies, or new uses of space. The general procedure is to ask, What is the influence of gender (for instance), or power, or social class on the phenomena under study?—then to trace this influence as precisely as possible, as well as its influence flowing in reverse direction. Grounded theory procedures force us to ask, for example: What is power in this situation and under specified conditions? How is it manifested, by whom, when, where, how, with what consequences (and for whom or what)? Not to remain open to such a range of questions is to obstruct the discovery of important features of power *in situ* and to preclude developing its further conceptualization. Knowledge is, after all, linked closely with time and place. When we carefully and specifically build conditions into our theories, we eschew claims to idealistic versions of knowledge, leaving the way open for further development of our theories.

Diffusion of the Methodology

In reflecting about the increasing numbers and kinds of research in which grounded theory has been utilized, we have been struck by certain features of its diffusion. Ordinarily, an intellectual trend spreads out from an inventive group or institution largely through face-to-face teaching. In the instance of this methodology, the diffusion appears largely to have taken place—and is today occurring—through its literature, including foreign-language translations and computer software (e.g., NUD•IST—see Richards, Richards, McGalliard, & Sharrock, 1992; and ATLAS/ti—see Mühr, 1992; see also Tesch, 1990) that claims relationships to grounded theory methods.

The diffusion of this methodology seems recently to be increasing exponentially in numbers of studies, types of phenomena studied, geographical spread, and disciplines (education, nursing, psychology, and sociology, for example). The diffusion of grounded theory procedures has now also reached subspecialties of disciplines in which we would not have anticipated their use—and does not always appear in ways that other grounded theorists would recognize as "grounded theory." For instance, there are studies of business management, communication studies concerning such areas as the use of computers by the physically disabled, and "grounded theory" applied to the building of a theoretical model of the epistemology of knowledge production. (We say more about the extension of the methodology later in this chapter.)

Risks Attending Diffusion

This methodology now runs the risk of becoming fashionable. Part of the risk is that users do not understand important aspects of the methodology (as indicated earlier), yet claim to be using it in their research. For instance, they discover a basic process but fail to develop it conceptually, because they overlook or do not understand that variation gives a grounded theory analysis its conceptual richness. People who think they are doing grounded theory studies often seem to concentrate on coding as this methodology's chief and almost exclusive feature, but do not do *theoretical* coding. ("Theoretical codes conceptualize how the substantive codes may relate to each other as hypotheses to be integrated into a theory"; Glaser, 1978, p. 72.) Also, even theoretical coding, unless done in conjunction with the making of constant comparisons, is unlikely to produce conceptually rich theory. Another part of the risk attending grounded theory's rapid diffusion is that some researchers deliberately do not aim at developing theories. Therefore, they ignore this central feature of the methodology, often using its procedures inappropriately or overlooking alternative methodologies that could serve their purposes better.

Also, researchers are still claiming to use "grounded theory methods" because their studies are "inductive." Certainly, thoughtful reaction against restrictive prior theories and theoretical models can be salutary, but too rigid a conception of induction can lead to sterile or boring studies. Alas, grounded theory has been used as a justification for such studies. This has occurred as a result of the initial presentation of grounded theory in *Discovery* that has led to a persistent and unfortunate misunderstanding about what was being advocated. Because of the partly rhetorical purpose of that book and the authors' emphasis on the need for *grounded* theories, Glaser and Strauss overplayed the inductive aspects. Correspondingly, they greatly underplayed both the potential role of extant (grounded) theories and the unquestionable fact (and advantage) that trained researchers are theoretically sensitized. Researchers carry into their research the sensitizing possibilities of their training, reading, and research experience, as well as explicit theories that might be useful if played against systematically gathered data, in conjunction with theories emerging from analysis of these data (Corbin & Strauss, 1990; Glaser, 1978; Strauss, 1987). Many people still get their conceptions of grounded theory from the original book, and have missed the later more realistic and balanced modifications of that book's purposeful rhetoric.

Quantitative Methods and Grounded Theory

Here is an observation about the historic relationship—or, better, lack of relationship—between quantitative researchers and grounded theory, and what may currently be happening to this relationship. As mentioned earlier, *Discovery* made clear that grounded theory was a general methodology, applicable to quantitative as well as qualitative studies. ("We believe that *each form of data is useful for both verification and generation of theory,* whatever the primacy of emphasis. Primacy depends only on the circumstances of research, on the interests and training of the researcher, and on the kinds of material [needed for] theory. . . . *In many instances, both forms of data are necessary*"; Glaser & Strauss, 1967, pp. 17-18.) However, the emphasis and the subtitle of *Discovery* (*Strategies for Qualitative Research*), perhaps combined with the dominance of quantitative methods in sociology and elsewhere for the two decades following its publication, seemingly ensured that only qualitative researchers would pay attention to its messages. Glaser's later publication, *Theoretical Sensitivity* (1978), has had its impact almost wholly on qualitative researchers. We ourselves wrote specifically for qualitative researchers, as the titles of our books signaled (see, e.g., Strauss & Corbin, 1990; but also Strauss, 1987). Increasingly, quantitative researchers seem dissatisfied with purely quantified results and are turning toward supplementary qualitative analyses, while qualitative researchers have become less defensive about their modes of analysis and more open to working with quantitative researchers on research projects. Sometimes they combine quantitative methods with their qualitative ones. Grounded theory research will undoubtedly be affected by these trends.

Theory and Interpretation

This methodology is designed to further the development of effective theory. Why theory? After all, the entire conception of a social "science" is under attack today, especially by some postmodernist and feminist scholars. This is not the appropriate place to counter that attack (and anyhow, a number of defenders of the scientific faith have reexplained and defended the rationale for science). One certainly does not have to adopt a positivistic position or the procedures and specific methods of the physical and biological sciences to argue for the desirability of a social science.

On the other hand, neither does one have to insist that all social inquiry, or even qualitative research, must lead to the development or utilization of theory. Qualitative modes of interpretation run the gamut from "Let the informant speak and don't get in the way," on through theme analysis, and to the elucidation of patterns (biographical, societal, and so on), theoretical frameworks or models (sometimes only loosely developed), and theory formulated at various levels of abstraction (Tesch, 1990). All of these modes certainly are useful for some purposes and not so useful for others. So we do *not* argue that creating theory is more important than any other mode of interpretation, or that it produces more useful or significant results; we argue only that theory should be grounded in the sense described earlier—in interplay with data and developed through the course of actual research.

That said, we turn next to some very brief remarks directed toward the following questions insofar as they pertain to grounded theories. What does theory *consist* of? What does it look like when presented? What is its relation to "*reality*" and "*truth*?" How does it relate to actors' perspectives? Of what use is it, and what responsibilities do researchers/theorists have for producing it?

What Does Theory Consist Of?

Theory consists of *plausible* relationships proposed among *concepts* and *sets of concepts.*[2] (Though only plausible, its plausibility is to be strengthened through continued research.) Without concepts, there can be no propositions, and thus no cumulative scientific (systematically theoretical) knowledge based on these plausible but testable propositions. (On this point, we recommend Herbert Blumer's ironically titled paper "Science Without Concepts," 1934/1969, in which he clearly outlines the necessity of concepts and conceptual relationships for scientific understanding.)

Grounded theory methodology is designed to guide researchers in producing theory that is "conceptually dense"—that is, with many conceptual relationships. These relationships, stated as propositions, are, as in virtually all other qualitative research, presented in discursive form: They are embedded in a thick context of descriptive and conceptual writing (Glaser & Strauss, 1967, pp. 31-32; Strauss, 1987, pp. 263-264). Discursive presentation captures the conceptual density and conveys descriptively also the substantive content of a study far better than does the natural science form of propositional presentation (typically couched as "if-then").

Theoretical conceptualization means that grounded theory researchers are interested in *patterns* of action and interaction between and among various types of social units (i.e., "actors"). So they are not especially interested in creating theory about individual actors as such (unless perhaps they are psychologists or psychiatrists). They are also much concerned with discovering *process*—not necessarily in the sense of stages or phases, but of reciprocal changes in patterns of action/interaction and in relationship with changes of conditions either internal or external to the process itself.[3] When stages or phases are distinguished for analytic purposes by the researcher, this signifies a conceptualization of what occurs under certain conditions: with movement forward, downward, up and down, going one way then another—all depending on analytically specified conditions. Insofar as theory that is developed through this methodology is able to specify consequences and their related conditions, the theorist can claim predictability for it, in the limited sense that *if* elsewhere approximately similar conditions obtain, *then* approximately similar consequences should occur.

Perhaps a few words should be added to counter possible reactions that this version of theory is overly austere and formal in nature, even if not so in presentation. Earlier we alluded to the relevance ("fit") of substantive grounded theories in terms of what the researcher has actually seen and/or heard, and later more will be said about the relevance of theory in its application. Here we would only note two additional features of grounded theories, regardless of what their levels of abstraction may be. First, theories are always traceable to the data that gave rise to them—within the interactive context of data collecting and data analyzing, in which the analyst is also a crucially significant interactant. Second, grounded theories are very "fluid" (this is the adjective used to characterize them by Joan Fujimura in a personal communication). Because they embrace the interaction of multiple actors, and because they emphasize temporality and process, they indeed have a striking fluidity. They call for exploration of each new situation to see *if* they fit, *how* they might fit, and how they *might not* fit. They demand an openness of the researcher, based on the "forever" provisional character of every theory. For all that, grounded theories are not just another set of phrases; rather, they are systematic statements of plausible relationships.

What Grounded Theory Writing Looks Like

One reviewer of an earlier version of this chapter suggested that readers might profit from one or two extended quotations illustrating what a grounded theory looks like. In turn, we suggest they might sample from the list of substantive writings by us, our working colleagues, and our ex-students contained in the references as well as the appendix to this chapter. Short of that, we quote from a chapter about "closed awareness context" that is probably quite well known:

> There are at least five important structural conditions which contribute to the existence and maintenance of the closed awareness context. [These are then discussed in detail for two and a half pages. Then types of interaction that occur under closed awareness conditions are presented both descriptively (with quotations) and with analytic sensitivity. Then, since process is important, the authors write:] Inherently, this closed awareness context tends toward instability, as the patient moves either to suspicion or full awareness of . . . terminality. The principal reasons for the instability . . . require only brief notation, as they have already been adumbrated. First, any breakdown in the structural conditions that make for the closed awareness context may lead to its disappearance. Those conditions include [examples are given]. . . . Some unanticipated disclosures or tip-offs, stemming from organizational conditions, can also occur. [More examples are given, including variations by ward.] New symptoms understandably are likely to perplex and alarm the patient; and the longer his retrogressive course, the more difficult it becomes to give him plausible explanations, though a very complicated misrepresentational drama can be played for his benefit. Even so, it becomes somewhat more difficult to retain . . . trust over a long time. [More comparisons and variations are given.] . . . Another threat to closed awareness . . . is that some treatments make little sense to a patient who does not recognize that he is dying. . . . At times, moreover, a patient may be unable to cope with his immensely deteriorating physical condition, unless nurses interpret that condition and its symptoms to him. To do this, nurses may feel forced to talk of his dying. Not to disclose . . . can torture and isolate the patient, which runs counter to a central value of nursing care, namely to make the patient as comfortable as possible. . . . The danger that staff members will give the show away . . . also increases as the patient nears death, especially when the dying takes place slowly. . . . This last set of conditions brings us to the question of whether, and how, personnel actually may engineer a change of the closed awareness context. [Examples are given of observations of how this is done.] Indeed, when the family actually knows the truth, the hazards to maintaining closed awareness probably are much increased, if only because kin are more strongly tempted to signal the truth. [There follows then a systematic detailing of consequences: for patients, nurses, physicians, kin, ward, and hospital.] (Glaser & Strauss, 1964, pp. 29-46)

Relationship of Theory to Reality and Truth?

Nowadays there is much debate about these two questions. We follow closely here the American pragmatist position (Dewey, 1937; Mead, 1917): A theory is not the formulation of some discovered aspect of a preexisting reality "out there." [4] To think otherwise is to take a positivistic position that, as we have said above, we reject, as do most other qualitative researchers. Our position is that truth is enacted (Addelson, 1990): Theories are interpretations made from given perspectives as adopted or researched by researchers. To say that a given theory is an interpretation—and therefore fallible—is not at all to deny that judgments can be made about the soundness or probable usefulness of it.

All interpretations, whether or not they have the features or status of theory, are temporally limited—in a dual sense. First, they are always provisional, they are never established forever; their very nature allows for endless elaboration and partial negation (qualification). Second, like many other kinds of knowledge, theories are limited in time: Researchers and theorists are not gods, but men and women living in certain eras, immersed in certain societies, subject to current ideas and ideologies, and so forth. Hence as conditions change at any level of the conditional matrix, this affects the validity of theories—that is, their relation to contemporary social reality. Theories are constantly becoming outdated or in need of qualification because, as one of us once wrote:

> We are confronting a universe marked by tremendous fluidity; it won't and can't stand still. It is a universe where fragmentation, splintering, and disappearance are the mirror images of appearance, emergence, and coalescence. This is a universe where nothing is strictly determined. Its phenomena should be partly determinable via naturalistic analysis, including the phenomenon of men [and women] participating in the construction of the structures which shape their lives. (Strauss, 1978, p. 123)

In short, theories are embedded "in history"—historical epochs, eras, and moments are to be taken into account in the creation, judgment, revision, and reformulation of theories.

The interpretive nature of grounded theories means that such conceptualizing is an intellectual process that extends throughout the entire course of a given research project. This is a very complex process, and the next pages will in some sense elaborate its complexity.

Multiple Actors' Perspectives and Analytic Interpretations

Grounded theory methodology incorporates the assumption, shared with other, but not all, social science positions concerning the *human* status of actors whom we study. They have perspectives on and interpretations of their own and other actors' actions. As researchers, we are required to learn what we can of their interpretations and perspectives. Beyond that, grounded theory requires, because it mandates the development of theory, that those interpretations and perspectives become incorporated into our own interpretations (conceptualizations).

Grounded theory procedures enhance this possibility, directing attention, for instance, to *in vivo* concepts that reflect actors' own deep concerns; or its procedures force researchers to question and skeptically review their own interpretations at every step of the inquiry itself. A major argument of this methodology is that *multiple perspectives* must be systematically sought during the research inquiry. This tenet contributes to building theory inclusive of lay conceptions and helps to prevent getting captured by those. Perhaps not every actor's perspectives can be discovered, or need be, but those of actors who sooner or later are judged to be significantly relevant must be incorporated into the emerging theory. (In the language of our contemporaries, multiple "voices" are attended to, but note that these are *also* interpreted conceptually by the researcher who follows our methodology.) Coding procedures—including the important procedures of constant comparison, theoretical questioning, theoretical sampling, concept development, and their relationships—help to protect the researcher from accepting any of those voices on their own terms, and to some extent forces the researcher's own voice to be questioning, questioned, and provisional.

In grounded theory, concepts are formulated and analytically developed, conceptual relationships are posited—but we are emphasizing here that they are inclusive of the multiple perspectives of the actors. Thus grounded theories, which are abstractions quite like any other theories, are nevertheless grounded directly and indirectly on perspectives of the diverse actors toward the phenomena studied by us. Grounded theories connect this multiplicity of perspective with patterns and processes of action/interaction that in turn are linked with carefully specified conditions and consequences.

Effective theoretical coding is also greatly enhanced by theoretical sensitivity (Glaser, 1978; Strauss & Corbin, 1990). This consists of disciplinary or professional knowledge, as well as both research and personal experiences, that the researcher brings to his or her inquiry. This point links with previous discussion of the conditional matrix, because the more theoretically sensitive researchers are to issues of class, gender, race, power, and the like, the more attentive they will be to these matters. The procedures of theoretical sampling and constant comparison are allied with theoretical sensitivity.

Apropos of theoretical sensitivity, we should add that in all modes of qualitative research the interplay between researcher and the actors studied—if the research is intensive—is likely to result in some degree of reciprocal shaping. This is because researcher and data (words and phrases, actions, videotapes) speak to each other. In grounded theory studies, the conversation is centered on theoretical analysis, so the shaping is also related to the process of becoming increasingly theoretically sensitive. During or at the end of the study, the researcher may give information back to the actors, in the form of a final theoretical analysis or framework or, more frequently, through observations informed by an evolving theory. In turn, the theorist, over the course of the research project, may be much affected by the experience of analysis itself (contributed to in some sense by the respondents). Also, the theorist is affected by experiences *with* the respondents, who may not incidentally be contributing ideas, concepts (including *in vivo* concepts), and enduring perspectives to the analysis. In short, the researcher-theorist is becoming increasingly theoretically sensitized, including, as noted earlier, scrutinizing the literature for received theories that might possibly be relevant to the emerging theory developed largely through the continuing conversation with "the data." [5]

Theorists' Responsibilities
and Uses of Theory

Emphasizing as it does the theoretical aspects of social research, grounded theory pushes its practitioners toward theoretical interpretations. Thereby they have obligations to contribute to the knowledge of their respective disciplines or professions. However, we who aim at grounded theories also believe (as do many other researchers) that we have obligations to the actors we have studied: obligations to "tell their stories" to them and to others—to give them voice—albeit in the context of their own inevitable interpretations. We owe it to our "subjects" to tell them verbally or in print what we have learned, and to give clear indications of why we have interpreted them as we have. Furthermore, as noted in *Discovery,* a grounded theory "must correspond closely to the data if it is to be applied in daily situations" (Glaser & Strauss, 1967, p. 238). And this faithfulness to the substantive data, this "fit" to a substantive area, is a powerful condition for usefulness in the practical life of the theory. Its usefulness can be a matter of "understanding" as well as of direct application.

Certainly, this does not mean every grounded theory must have immediate or direct application, yet we do have an obligation also toward "society," at least to those social worlds toward which we have commitments. These commitments carry responsibilities to develop or use theory that will have at least some practical applications, that can be of service to wider audiences than are strictly constituted by our disciplinary or professional colleagues or even the *specific* groups, organizations, or social worlds that we have studied. Translation of even well-grounded substantive theory is not necessarily immediate, and ultimately the responsibility may rest on educators or actual practitioners "in the field." One example of a successful application through combined efforts of two researchers/theorists (a sociologist and a researcher/nurse educator) and clinical nurses/educators is the extension of the concept of "trajectory" into a model fairly directly applicable to the giving of nursing care and to research on nursing care (Woog, 1992).

Grounded theories can also be relevant and possibly influential either to the "understanding" of policy makers or to their direct action. As an instance of the former, we point to a policy book on health care (Strauss & Corbin, 1990) that offers a critique of the present health care system and a blueprint for a rather different one that has typically been rejected by practical-minded policy readers but has opened horizons of understanding to those not so committed to current arrangements.

Our stand on this third obligation, to the wider society, seems at variance with others taken by those who would confine actions, or reform activities, only to improving the lot of the people actually studied. Because all theory carries implications for action, we would not so confine its applicability. Careful grounded theory is likely to be used, and used in ways other than any dreamed of by us researchers/theorists—far beyond our commitments and desires. Hence we bear the special responsibility of attempting to reach at least the audiences that we ourselves wish to reach.

Higher-Order Grounded Theories

In *Discovery,* a chapter titled "From Substantive to Formal Theory" (1967) begins with a very important set of ideas; indeed, they seem even more important now. Their significance lies both in the continued predominance of substantive theory (or substantive studies *sans* theorizing) and the paucity of higher-level social theories that are *grounded in specific research inquiries.* Here is the quotation:

> Since substantive theory is grounded in research on one particular substantive area (work, juvenile delinquency, medical education, mental health) it might be taken to apply only to that specific area. A theory at such a conceptual level, however, may have important general implications and relevance, and become almost automatically a springboard or stepping stone to the development of a grounded formal [or as is more usually said, "general"] theory. . . . Substantive theory is a strategic link in the formulation and generation of grounded formal theory. We believe that although formal theory can be generated directly from data, it is more desirable, and usually necessary, to start the formal theory from a substantive one. The latter not only provides a stimulus to a "good idea" but it also gives an initial direction in developing relevant categories and properties and in choosing possible modes of integration. Indeed it is difficult to find a grounded formal theory that was not in some way stimulated by a substantive theory. Often the substantive and formal theories are formulated by different authors. Sometimes in formal theory the substantive theory is implicit, having been developed previously by the author or another writer. (Glaser & Strauss, 1967, p. 79)

In the pages that followed this statement, Glaser and Strauss noted the drawbacks of formulating formal theory on the basis of data from only one rather than several substantive areas. In a book published three years later (1970), those authors presented a formal theory about status passages that was both a development of previous conceptualizations and based on data amassed from a multitude of substantive areas. A later book offered a theory of negotiation (Strauss, 1978), taking off from a theoretical formulation known as "negotiated order" (Strauss, Bucher, Ehrlich, Sabshin, & Schatzman, 1963, 1964), and from an examination of data drawn both from various substantive areas and several monographs or social and political theorists' writings. Earlier, Strauss (in a 1970 work reprinted in 1987, pp. 306-311) published a paper titled "Discovering New Theory From Previous Theory" that suggested in detail how a grounded substantive theory could be greatly extended, leading either to a more elaborated substantive theory or to formal theories developed in conjunction with multiarea data. (For similar discussions of substantive and formal theories, see Glaser, 1978, pp. 143-157; Strauss, 1987, pp. 241-248.)

As mentioned earlier, Diane Vaughan (1992), a thoughtful theorist and excellent researcher, has written about an alternative but related approach to producing general theory. She advocates "theory elaboration," which consists of taking off from extant theories and developing them further in conjunction with "qualitative case analysis." By *theory,* she means "theoretical tools in general," including (formulated) theory, models, and concepts. By *elaboration,* she means "the process of refining the theory, model or concept in order to specify more carefully the circumstances in which it does or does not offer potential for explanation" (p. 175). (Her examples, however, are mostly of her own grounded theories and research, but she also utilizes some existing substantive grounded ones.) From reading her, we have gained an appreciation of further techniques for attaining theories that are more general, that embrace but transcend the substantive while at the same time linking those with previous theories (see also Gerson, 1991). It is apparent that we will face complexities in developing theories at different levels or degrees of abstraction. These complexities have not yet been clarified in the literature. (The terms *general* and *formal* are too crude to catch those degrees or levels of theory.)

So here is a challenge that should be faced by anyone who believes theory should be grounded! We should not settle only for substantive theories, no matter how stimulating or useful they are—for furthering theory development, for understanding phenomena, for *Verstehen* of people and actions, or for their practical use in guiding behavior or policy. General theory also has its place as a powerful tool for all those same purposes. The danger of such theorizing is not that it is abstract—for that can be a great advantage—but that it can be speculatively remote from the phenomena it purports to explain. Grounded theory methodology insists that no matter how general—how broad in scope or abstract—the theory, it should be developed in that back-and-forth interplay with data that is so central to this methodology.

Yet whether general or substantive theory is sought, there is a potential danger in using this methodology if a researcher is overly familiar with and attached to the concepts and conceptual frameworks presented in previous grounded theory studies. The danger is that these may be used without genuine grounding in the current study. They too must be grounded in the interplay with data, just as are those taken from other sources.

Social and Intellectual Trends and Grounded Theory

To round off this chapter, the editors of this volume have requested that we make a guess at what the future might hold for grounded theory. Crystal gazing is not our forte, but we can at least anticipate the following. First, consider certain strong social and intellectual trends that are likely to affect greatly the awareness, rejection, and varied uses of this methodology:

1. the continued fragmentation of traditional social and behavioral science disciplines into subdisciplines, each with its currently distinctive issues, types of data, and often specific research procedures
2. an increasing interest in and the presumed necessity for social research within various professions and their subunits, and directed toward an increasing or at least changing set of issues
3. a continued reliance on qualitative methods alone or in conjunction with quantitative ones, by increasing numbers of professional and disciplinary researchers
4. an increasing interest in theoretical interpretations of data, along with divergent definitions of theory believed to fit the nature of one's materials
5. a continuation of the current trend of antagonism toward anything that goes by the name of science and especially toward its canons
6. the spread of postmodernism, but a variegated spread, given that there are many and sometimes divergent directions within this general intellectual movement

7. a continued trend toward the use of computer programs to order and interpret data, perhaps with visual and oral accompaniments
8. in the world at large, probably a continued and even greater emphasis on individual and collective identity (nationalism, for instance), requiring improved methods for understanding the meanings and symbolization of actors

All of these trends should profoundly affect the use and evaluation of grounded theory. Think, if you will, of this general methodology as in early stages of the comparable development of survey research circa 1940. What researchers did with survey methodology, once aware of it, was to reject it for one reason or another, or over the years to use it in its original formulation, elaborate it, or adapt it in various ways, including combining it with other methodologies. The fate of grounded theory methodology should not be appreciably different.

So at least it can be safely predicted, keeping the previously noted social-intellectual conditions in mind, that the following *processes* will occur:

1. Researchers in additional substantive and professional areas and countries will experiment with and use or adapt the methodology.
2. Adaption will include combining it with other methodologies (hermeneutical, phenomenological, for instance). It will also be combined with quantitative methods on predominantly quantitative or predominantly qualitative projects, or on projects of equal emphasis.
3. Particular fields will combine the methodology with other methodologies rather than consider them to be competing. (For instance, researchers in nursing use various combinations of ethnography, phenomenology, and grounded theory; presumably psychologists will combine or are combining the latter with more traditional or emerging research methods.)
4. An increasing number of computer programs will include the possibility of utilizing the methodology, and these programs will become more sophisticated and will be used increasingly for this purpose.
5. The procedures suggested or used in the current grounded theory literature will become elaborated *and* specific adaptations will be made by researchers for a greater range of phenomena. This elaboration and adaption will include also multisite studies in a variety of settings, including cross-cultural work.
6. Varieties of theory (or "interpretation") will be developed by different researchers and in different areas, all of whom will use one or another adapted/elaborated version of the methodology.

Recently, an astute sociologist asked us to say something about the outer limits of research that *we* would or could continue to call "grounded theory." The features of this methodology that we consider so central that their abandonment would signify a great departure are the grounding of theory upon data through data-theory interplay, the making of constant comparisons, the asking of theoretically oriented questions, theoretical coding, and the development of theory. Yet, no inventor has permanent possession of the invention—certainly not even of its name—and furthermore we would not wish to do so. No doubt we will always prefer the later versions of grounded theory that are closest to or elaborate our own, but a child once launched is very much subject to a combination of its origins and the evolving contingencies of life. Can it be otherwise with a methodology?

Appendix: A Sampling of Substantive Writings by UCSF Researchers

Biernacki, P. (1986). *Pathways from heroin addiction.* Philadelphia: Temple University Press.

Charmaz, K. (1987). Struggling for a self: Identity levels of the chronically ill. In P. Conrad & J. Roth (Eds.), *The experience of chronic illness.* Greenwich, CT: JAI.

Corbin, J., & Strauss, A. (1991). Comeback: Overcoming disability. In G. Albrecht & J. Levy (Eds.), *Advances in medical sociology* (Vol. 2). Greenwich, CT: JAI.

Fagerhaugh, S., & Strauss, A. (1977). *The politics of pain management.* Menlo Park, CA: Addison-Wesley.

Fagerhaugh, S., Strauss, A., Suczek, B., & Wiener, C. (1987). *Hazards in hospital care.* San Francisco: Jossey-Bass.

Rosenbaum, M. (1981). *Women on heroin.* New Brunswick, NJ: Rutgers University Press.

Strauss, A., Fagerhaugh, S., Suczek, B., & Wiener, C. (1985). *The organization of medical work.* Chicago: University of Chicago Press.

Strauss, A., & Glaser, B. (1970). *Anguish: A case history of a dying trajectory.* San Francisco: Sociology Press.

Wiener, C., Strauss, A., Fagerhaugh, F., & Suczek, B. (1979). Trajectories, biographies, and the evolving medical scene: Labor and delivery and the intensive care nursery. *Sociology of Health and Illness, 1,* 261-283.

Notes

1. Here is a nice illustration of tracing effects of conditions, or in the authors' (ex-students of Strauss's) words, "things, attributes, elements are *in the situation itself*. . . . For example, Fujimura (1987) noted that stockholders in biotechnology companies are very present elements in the laboratory (though rarely in person), and not merely contextual. Stockholders routinely constrained decision making in the construction of doable problems and what the next step in a project might be. The claims and other products that emerge from the situation embody all the elements within it, human and nonhuman alike. Therefore specifying the elements is a highly significant task" (Clarke & Fujimura, 1992, pp. 17-18).

2. "A coherent group of general propositions used [provisionally] as principles of explanation for a class of phenomena" (Stein & Urdang, 1981, p. 1471).

3. "*To capture process analytically,* one must show the evolving nature of events by noting why and how action/interaction—in the form of events, doings or happenings—will change, stay the same . . . ; why there is progression of events or what enables continuity of a line of action/interaction, in the face of changing conditions, and with what consequences" (Strauss & Corbin (1990, p. 144; but see discussion, pp. 143-157).

4. The pragmatists emphasized consequences and the antecedent conditions that precipitated them, and urged abandonment of the impossible quest for Truth. Grounded theory advocates follow this general position. Reading an earlier version of this chapter, one reviewer asked about our position on the relationships of ideology and power to truth. In brief: Power certainly affects the ability to convince audiences, including probably oneself, if one takes one's power seriously. Ideologies we all have—we all have political and other positions—but unquestioning allegiance to those, with little or no attempt to challenge or "test" them, leads sociologists like Irving Horowitz, quite correctly, we believe, into battle with sociological ideologues. Grounded theory has procedures that help one to challenge one's own ideologies and implicit positions. The feminist critique of the objective biases of traditional science seems to us correct insofar as some scientists may assume they are just human instruments reporting on nature (it used to be God's nature) "out there." Contemporary physical and biological scientists seem to understand quite well the naïveté of such a position, although they also, sometimes, individually display awesome hubris.

A related point, raised by another reviewer, is that "researchers often *write* as though order were implicit . . . and inhered in the data, when what they really meant was that order emerged from interaction between the researcher, his/her data, and some theoretical sensitivity suggested by the original research question." That is exactly the point!

5. A reviewer of an earlier version of this chapter suggested that our statement about theoretical sensitivity is an overstatement because naive researchers "may be even more likely to see things that don't make sense, and therefore asks questions why? or may be more likely to ask why don't you think about it (do it) this way?" He has a point, given that new perspectives can precipitate significant and even radical issues. Personal experiences are also immensely vital to theoretical sensitivity (Corbin & Strauss, 1990; Glaser, 1978).

References

Addelson, K. (1990). Why philosophers should become sociologists (and vice versa). In H. Becker & M. McCall (Eds.), *Symbolic interaction and cultural studies* (pp. 119-147). Chicago: University of Chicago Press.

Baszanger, I. (1992). Introduction. In *La Trame de la Negociation: Sociologie Qualitative et Interactionnisme* (pp. 11-63). Paris: L'Harmattan.

Benner, P. (1989). *The primacy of caring: Stress and coping in health and illness.* Menlo Park, CA: Addison-Wesley.

Blumer, H. (1969). Science without concepts. In H. Blumer, *Symbolic interactionism: Perspective and method* (pp. 153-170). Englewood Cliffs, NJ: Prentice Hall. (Reprinted from *American Journal of Sociology,* 1934, *36,* 515-533)

Broadhead, R. (1983). *Private lives and professional identity of medical students.* New Brunswick, NJ: Transaction.

Cauhape, E. (1983). *Fresh starts: Men and women after divorce.* New York: Basic Books.

Charmaz, K. (1980). The construction of self-pity in the chronically ill. *Studies in Symbolic Interaction, 3,* 123-145.

Charmaz, K. (1983). The grounded theory method: An explication and interpretation. In R. Emerson (Ed.), *Contemporary field research* (pp. 109-126). Boston: Little, Brown.

Charmaz, K. (1990). "Discovering" chronic illness: Using grounded theory. *Sociology of Health and Illness, 30,* 1161-1172.

Clarke, A. (1990a). Controversy and the development of reproductive sciences. *Social Problems, 27,* 18-37.

Clarke, A. (1990b). A social worlds research adventure: The case of reproductive sciences. In S. Cozzens & T. Gieryn (Eds.), *Theories of science in society* (pp. 23-50). Bloomington: Indiana University Press.

Clarke, A., & Fujimura, J. (Eds.). (1992). *The right tools for the job: At work in twentieth-century life sciences.* Princeton, NJ: Princeton University Press.

Corbin, J. (1992). Caregiving. *Revue Internationale d'Action Communautaire, 28,* 39-49.

Corbin, J., & Strauss, A. (1988). *Unending work and care: Managing chronic illness at home.* San Francisco: Jossey-Bass.

Corbin, J., & Strauss, A. (1990). Grounded theory method: Procedures, canons, and evaluative criteria. *Qualitative Sociology, 13,* 3-21.

Dewey, J. (1937). *Logic: The theory of inquiry.* New York: Holt.

Fujimura, J. (1987). Constructing doable problems in cancer research: Articulating alignment. *Social Studies of Science, 17,* 257-293.

Fujimura, J. (1991). On methods, ontologies, and representation in the sociology of science: Where do we stand? In D. Maines (Ed.), *Social organization and social process* (pp. 207-248). New York: Aldine de Gruyter.

Gerson, E. (1991). Supplementing grounded theory. In D. Maines (Ed.), *Social organization and social process* (pp. 285-301). New York: Aldine de Gruyter.

Glaser, B. (1967). The constant comparative method of qualitative analysis. In B. Glaser & A. Strauss, *The discovery of grounded theory: Strategies for qualitative research* (pp. 101-116). Chicago: Aldine. (Reprinted from *Social Problems,* 1965, *12,* 436-445)

Glaser, B. (1972). *Experts versus laymen: A study of the patsy and the subcontractor.* New Brunswick, NJ: Transaction.

Glaser, B. (1978). *Theoretical sensitivity.* Mill Valley, CA: Sociological Press.

Glaser, B., & Strauss, A. (1964). *Awareness of dying.* Chicago: Aldine.

Glaser, B., & Strauss, A. L. (1967). *The discovery of grounded theory: Strategies for qualitative research.* Chicago: Aldine.

Glaser, B., & Strauss, A. (1968). *Time for dying.* Chicago: Aldine.

Glaser, B., & Strauss, A. (1970). *Status passages.* Chicago: Aldine.

Hall, C. (1992). *Homecoming: The self at home.* Unpublished doctoral thesis, University of California, San Francisco, Department of Social and Behavioral Sciences.

Lempert, L. (1992). *The crucible: Violence, help seeking, and abused women's transformations of self.* Unpublished doctoral thesis, University of California, San Francisco, Department of Social and Behavioral Sciences.

Lessor, R. (1993). All in the family: Social processes in ovarian egg donation between sisters. *Sociology of Health and Illness, 15,* 393-413.

Mead, G. (1917). Scientific method and the individual thinker. In J. Dewey (Ed.), *Creative intelligence* (pp. 167-227). New York: Holt.

Mühr, T. (1992). *ATLAS/ti user manual: Beta version 0.94c.* Berlin: Berlin Technical University.

Richards, T., Richards, L., McGalliard, J., & Sharrock, B. (1992). *NUD•*IST 2.3: Users manual. La Trobe, Australia: Replee Pty/La Trobe University.

Star, S. L. (1989a). *Regions of the mind: Brain research and the quest for scientific certainty.* Stanford, CA: Stanford University Press.

Star, S. L. (1989b). The structure of ill-structured solutions: Boundary objects and heterogeneous distributed problem solving. In M. Huhns & L. Gasser (Eds.), *Distributed artificial intelligence* (Vol. 3, pp. 37-54). Menlo Park, CA: Morgan Kauffmann.

Stein, J., & Urdang, L. (1981). *The Random House dictionary of the English language.* New York: Random House.

Strauss, A. (1978). *Negotiations: Varieties, contexts, processes and social order.* San Francisco: Jossey-Bass.

Strauss, A. (1987). *Qualitative analysis for social scientists.* New York: Cambridge University Press.

Strauss, A. (1991). *Creating sociological awareness.* New Brunswick, NJ: Transaction.

Strauss, A., Bucher, R., Ehrlich, D., Sabshin, M., & Schatzman, L. (1963). The hospital and its negotiated order. In E. Freidson (Ed.), *The hospital in modern society* (pp. 147-169). New York: Free Press.

Strauss, A., Bucher, R., Ehrlich, D., Sabshin, M., & Schatzman, L. (1964). *Psychiatric ideologies and institutions.* New York: Free Press.

Strauss, A., & Corbin, J. (1990). *Basics of qualitative research: Grounded theory procedures and techniques.* Newbury Park, CA: Sage.

Tesch, R, (1990). *Qualitative research: Analysis types and software tools.* New York: Falmer.

Vaughan, D. (1992). Theory elaboration: The heuristics of case analysis. In H. Becker & C. Ragin (Eds.), *What is a case?* (pp. 173-202). New York: Cambridge University Press.

Wiener, C. (1981). *The politics of alcoholism.* New Brunswick, NJ: Transaction.

Woog, P. (Ed.). (1992). *The chronic illness trajectory framework: The Corbin and Strauss nursing model.* New York: Springer.

18

■

Biographical Method

LOUIS M. SMITH

A Perspective on Biography: Domain, Variety, and Complexity

Biographers write lives.

Leon Edel, *Writing Lives,* 1984

This statement, "Biographers write lives," is not so simple as it sounds. It is the first line in Leon Edel's (1984) "manifesto" on doing biography. "Writing lives" carries connotations that seem more than a bit broader than biography per se. Handbooks and handbook chapters, such as this, are codifications, statements of rules of practice useful to practitioners—in this instance, practitioners of qualitative research methods. When one writes lives, so I would argue, one finds that every rule, even when so simply stated as a "rule of thumb," always plays through some individual person and becomes his or her interpretation as the rule is thought about or put into practice. And when one writes a handbook chapter, giving form to an idea, such as "biographical method," the individual author expresses a personal point of view. In an unusual sense, I would argue, every text that is created is a self-statement, a bit of autobiography, a statement that carries an individual signature. Such reasoning suggests that all writing should be in the first person, reflecting that individual voice, even when one writes a chapter in a handbook. At an extreme, paraphrasing Saroyan, I almost want to make the case that it's autobiography, all down the line.

In this essay I will speak in the first person, in spite of some conventional wisdom that suggests "handbooks" are more detached summaries of general knowledge. My audience is students and scholars of qualitative methods who are interested in adding biographical method and life writing to their inquiry repertory. My outline is fairly simple. First is a brief overview of domain or "turf." Second, I present a process account of "doing biography," the problems one encounters, the alternatives available, the trade-offs, and the decisions one tries to live with. The third section is a too-brief excursion into the place of biography in the several intellectual disciplines that make use of life writing. Finally, I offer a few tentative generalizations to integrate the overall perspective.

The Domain of Biography: General and Personal

Formally, biography is "the written history of a person's life"—so says *Webster's Dictionary.*

AUTHOR'S NOTE: As usual, I want to thank my colleagues and students in the Department of Education at Washington University. In particular, the members of my recent seminars have been most helpful.

The *Oxford English Dictionary* nearly agrees, but not quite. "A written record of the life of an individual" is that volume's second usage. The word *life* appears in both definitions. *Person* and *individual* seem close synonyms, although some might argue that a person, a human being, is only one kind of individual within the larger category of individuals. And some might argue that *record* is different from *history,* perhaps less interpretive. Finally, *written* defines oral traditions as outside the genre. A too-limiting constraint for contemporary students and scholars? Obviously, yes! But the major point of this personal perspective and more formal definitional introduction lies in the domain or turf to be encompassed in any discussion of biography. The *OED,* in its first definition, confounds further the domain of biography as it states, "the history of the lives of individual men, as a branch of literature." Women are excluded. The social sciences of anthropology, psychology, and sociology are excluded. From this point on, the concept of biography, and the activity it signifies, becomes contentious—some would argue "political." And that is an important generalization.

Finally, part of what I want to say in this chapter draws upon several vivid personal professional experiences I have had in qualitative research. Three decades ago, I spent a long semester in an elementary classroom taught by a man named William Geoffrey. We wrote a book about that experience, *The Complexities of an Urban Classroom* (Smith & Geoffrey, 1968). It was cast as a "microethnography" of the classroom, a study of a small social system. In another sense the book was a piece of a biography, the story of one semester of Geoffrey and his teaching. In a further sense, it became part of my autobiography, the most important professional learning experience of my life, an "epiphany" or "turning point," in Denzin's (1989) interpretive theory of biography. The text carried, in a subdued way, both of those personal stories. At the time, neither of us thought about the experience or the book as his or my biography or autobiography. But, I would say now, it can be reconstrued in this alternative way.

The second personal experience that is very pertinent was a follow-up study, the "life histories" of the teachers and administrators of the Kensington Elementary School and the Milford School District. We called that *Educational Innovators: Then and Now* (Smith, Kleine, Prunty, & Dwyer, 1986). Life histories, at least as we developed them in this instance from long, two- to seven-hour, interviews, are briefer, more focused biographies, mostly told from the teachers' own perspectives. One of the major personal outcomes of that work was the realization that at some point I wanted to do what I came to call "a real biography." I am now in the middle, actually toward the end, of that experience, a biography that carries the title *Nora Barlow and the Darwin Legacy* (Smith, in press). That effort, as process and product, will flow in and out of this essay. Each of these experiences has led to considerable reflection on "how we did what we did," what we have called "miniature theories of methodology," often written as "methodological appendices." For me, writing this chapter on "biographical method" is not a simple, detached, impersonal exercise. And that may be good or bad, as we shall see.

Variants of Biography

Life writing comes with many labels—portrayals, portraits, profiles, memoirs, life stories, life histories, case studies, autobiographies, journals, diaries, and on and on—each suggesting a slightly different perspective under consideration. Most of these can be tracked through dictionary definitions, illustrations in this text, and various sources listed in the references. Noting variety in biography is perhaps too simple a point. But the world seems full of true believers, individuals who want to restrict options to one or just a few alternatives in creating or criticizing biography. Further, one of the points I want to make is that life writing is in serious contention among readers, critics, and practitioners of biography. For instance, one of the most investigated individuals in the Western world is Charles Darwin.[1] A brief glance at him, his interpreters, and the written records involving him suggests the range of possibilities in doing life writing and the difficulties of interpretation for anyone contemplating biography.

Darwin's first major publication—life writing, if you will—was his journal (1839) of the five-year voyage of HMS *Beagle* as it circumnavigated the world between 1831 and 1836. Also in 1839, FitzRoy, captain of the *Beagle,* published his journal, a companion volume about the voyage. In 1845, Darwin revised, with significant additions and abridgments, his journal. New, but only slightly different, editions appeared in 1860 and 1870. Some hundred years after the voyage, in 1933, Nora Barlow published *Charles Darwin's Diary of the Voyage of the H.M.S. Beagle.* Approximately one-fourth of the material in that publication was new, previously unpublished. Barlow included a number of footnotes, a list of *dramatis personae* with brief identifying biographical information, maps, six pages of "bibliography," of Darwin publications from the *Beagle* period, and other related material.

In his late 60s, Darwin wrote an autobiography for the "amusement" of his family. Darwin's son Francis published the autobiography in 1888 as part of the three-volume *Life and Letters of Charles Darwin.* But the autobiography had been expurgated. In

1958, Nora Barlow published a "de-edited" version of the autobiography, restoring some 6,000 words. In recent years, additions to a long list of major biographies continue to appear. Bowlby (1990) and Desmond and Moore (1991) have contributed at great length (500 and 800 pages) major new views. The list continues,[2] but the major point here is that biography, "life writing," comes in multiple forms, lengths, focuses, and perspectives. A related point is the importance of insight and creativity on the part of the biographer in the studying, constructing, and writing of lives or parts of lives.

The Special Instance of Autobiography

Autobiography is a special case of life writing. Writing autobiographies and critiques of autobiography is one of the most rapidly developing and, recently, one of the most controversial forms (Lejeune, 1989; Olney, 1980; Stanley, 1992). Autobiography suggests the power of agency in social and literary affairs. It gives voice to people long denied access. By example, it usually, but not always, eulogizes the subjective, the "important part of human existence" over the objective, "less significant parts of life." It blurs the borders of fiction and nonfiction. And, by example, it is a sharp critique of positivistic social science. In short, from my perspective, autobiography in its changing forms is at the core of late twentieth-century paradigmatic shifts in the structures of thought. And that is quite an agenda. Even as I state these tentative generalizations, I have to pull back, at least to a degree, for the eminent and consummate behavioristic psychologist B. F. Skinner (1977, 1979, 1983) has written a three-volume autobiography that denies every one of the points. The simple lesson is, Don't generalize or evaluate too quickly about life writing!

With tantalizing good humor, Pritchett (1977), in his presidential address to the English Association, pushed some of the limits of "autobiography." In his opening paragraph he posed one controversial version of the difficulties this variant of life writing creates for the scholar as reader: "It is common among knowing reviewers to lump autobiography and the novel together as examples of two different ways of telling agreeable lies." For anyone with "scientific" leanings, doing "fiction" is anathema. *Caveat emptor* is an immediate response. The paragraph continues:

> But, of course, you have only to start writing your autobiography to know how crucial the distinction is. The novelist distributes himself in disguise among the characters in his work. It is easy for him to pretend he's a man, woman, or child and, if he likes, in the first person. The autobiographer on the other hand comes forward as the hero or the anti-hero of his story and draws other people into himself.

But Pritchett can't quite let the audience off so easily as he concludes the paragraph with the bon mot:

> In a sense he is sort of stripper: the suspense of his story lies in guessing how far he will undress. Or, of course—if he is writing about his career—we see him putting more and more important clothes on. (p. 3)

In a penetrating essay, Gusdorf (1980) makes a similar point more pithily, that autobiography is "a sort of posthumous propaganda for posterity" (p. 36).

For the reader, determining what one learns from an autobiography becomes an exercise in critical judgment. Few would argue that they have not learned something of importance from reading an autobiography. But here as well, readers must do their own constructing, reconstructing, and evaluating. Reading Eakin (1989) reinforces such a conclusion.

The larger theory of knowledge issues and dilemmas—What do we know? How confident can we be in our knowledge?—becomes clearly visible in assaying this kind of scholarly inquiry. Olney (1980), in his historical and critical overview, does a kind of analysis on the label per se:

auto	bios	graphy
self	life	writing

As his argument proceeds, Olney sees the self in a never-ending transition, ending only in death. And that self will see the life from a different point of view at different points in the life. Finally, and this point is made even more strongly in Gusdorf's (1980) essay from the same volume, the very act of writing forces a self-examination that changes both the self and quite possibly the life as well. In a sense, three open-ended systems are in constant flux, flow, and interchange. From my point of view, positive knowledge about anything in the human condition is a misconstrual. At the same time, one knows more than "nothing." Knowledge has a quality of a balancing act. The problems are both more subtle and more complex than Pritchett's metaphor of robing and disrobing and Eakin's analysis of Lejeune's definitional problems, although these are important parts of the dilemma.

In related disciplines, the historian Hexter (1971) speaks of the first and second records in historical inquiry. The first is the something "out there" that has happened over time in the past. The "second record" is what each historian brings to the first record—the questions, the values, the beliefs, and the idiosyncratic life experiences, some professional and some personal. If his distinction is credible, history has a quality of being "autohistory." The anthropologist Malinowski (1922) makes a similar point, that the anthropologist should bring along the best of contemporary theory when he or she goes into the field setting. In this personal intellectual baggage, Malinowski makes an oft-quoted distinction between "foreshadowed problems" and "preconceived solutions," a distinction often hard to define in the particular situation. And those foreshadowed problems do not remain static but take on a life of their own in the field and in the writing of ethnographic reports, monographs, and books. The autobiographical, if not autobiography in the formal sense—that is, the personal—enters into any creative intellectual construction. Other students, especially the feminists and minority members of our culture, see larger political and ethical issues within the genre. Liberation, oppression, and multicultural themes get writ large in much autobiography, a point I shall raise later in this essay. Conceptual labels such as "auto/biographical" (Stanley, 1992) attempt to reflect and redirect inquiry in life writing.[3]

What Life Writers Do: The Craft of Biography

Writing lives is the devil.

Virginia Woolf
(quoted in Edel, 1984, p. 17)

Several years ago, Donald Schön (1983, 1987) introduced the concept of the "reflective practitioner" into the professional literature. In one sense, his argument is simple. Professional practitioners, be they physicians, architects, or teachers—or, one might add, craftspersons or artists—face "situations of practice" characterized by complexity, uncertainty, instability, uniqueness, and value conflict. In my view, that is a formidable set of dimensions. In Schön's view, the problems professionals face cannot be solved by the formulas of "technical rationality." I would extend his view to social scientists in general and those doing qualitative case studies in particular. The problems and dilemmas confronting life writers as they practice some aspect or form of the craft of biography have the same quality. The decisions biographers make are constituted by ambiguity, and that is part of the excitement and the agony of doing biography (Smith, 1990, 1992).

Among a number of life writers illustrating the particulars of the processes involved in the craft of biography, none surpasses the insights of Catherine Drinker Bowen (1959, 1968), James Clifford (1970), and Leon Edel (1984). Each of their books is an autobiographical statement of its author's perspective on biography: Edel—"all my writings on biography which I wish to preserve" (p. 248); Bowen—"the biographer's way of life, which to my mind is a pleasant way" (p. ix); and Clifford—"the operative concerns of a writer who decides to recreate the career of another person" (p. vii). It is to them, and a few others, I turn for an outline of understandings and generalizations in the practice of the biographical craft.

Selecting a Subject and First Inquiries

The obvious first task of biography is the decision concerning a person to write about. One must select a hero or heroine, be he or she recognized as such or not by the population at large. The autobiographer solves this first problem simply, although questions arise immediately as to why an individual would think his or her life worth telling—for example, has a kind of self-deception already begun? In contrast, the biographer needs to think carefully and analytically, to perceive intuitively an anomaly, or to be serendipitous, that is, just plain lucky. The literature is full of examples of each variant of what social scientists call "problem finding," a major element in creativity. And if one wants to complicate these simple interpretations, and perhaps make oneself a bit uneasy, follow Leon Edel (1984) as he reflects: "In a world full of subjects—centuries crowded with notables and dunces—we may indeed ask why a modern biographer fixes his attention on certain faces and turns his back on others" (p. 60). The biographer's personality—motives, fears, unconscious conflicts, and yearnings—reaches out to responsive, if not similar, territory in the person to be subject. The dance of Boswell and Johnson, of Strachey and his eminent Victorians, and of more recent American biographers and their choices is analyzed vividly by Edel. In a compelling short preface to *Young Man Luther,* Erik Erikson (1962) poses the issues this way:

> I have attempted in this preface to give a brief rationale for writing this book; I doubt, though, that the impetus for writing anything but a textbook can ever be rationalized. My choice of subject forces me to deal with problems of faith and problems of Germany, two enigmas which I could have avoided by writing about some other young great man. *But it seems that I did not wish to avoid them.* (p. 9; emphasis added)

What meets the eye is never quite what it seems—so Edel and others show and tell us.

Often the problem finding is mixed with discovering an important new pool of data. Derek Hudson (1972) commented in the introduction to his biography of A. J. Munby, the "hero" of the Hannah Cullwick story:

> I first became aware of A. J. Munby in the autumn of 1968. I was looking through *The Oxford Companion to English Literature* and came to the heading: MUNBY, ARTHUR JOSEPH (1828-1910). After mentioning various books of his verse, the brief entry concluded: "Munby was secretly and happily married to his servant, who refused to quit her station. The fact explains some of the allusions in his poems." (p. 1)

Then began his chase to find the manuscripts. That exciting adventure of biographer Derek Hudson is told briefly in the introduction and epilogue to the biography *Munby: Man of Two Worlds.* Later, others picked up on Hudson's efforts (Hiley, 1979; Stanley, 1984) and Hannah Cullwick, maid-of-all-work, became a nineteenth-century heroine. Photographic records would illuminate her life, Munby's life, and the nether side of women's work, women's lives, and social class in the Victorian era in England. One finds one improbable biographical story after another.

And, if you want to laugh and cry, and sometimes get angry, read Catherine Drinker Bowen's *Adventures of a Biographer* (1959). Her stories of being denied the role of authorized biographer of Chief Justice Holmes, of being made to feel an outsider at the American Historical Association, and of being snubbed at a display of John Adams's artifacts will make at least some of you want to become biographers. Some of the hellishness of life writing becomes clearer here, as well.

These exploratory activities and experiences, finding the pieces of the jigsaw puzzle, Clifford labels "outside research."[4] Clifford contrasts these with "inside research," the utilizing of library resources. He is content to tell a half dozen of these fascinating and improbable stories of his own adventures and those of others. He does not reach for patterns or conceptualizations of the activities. In contrast, in telling some of my own stories (Smith, 1990, 1992), I initially labeled the outside activity "anthropological biography"; later, I called it "ethnographic biography." The broader and compelling insight, for me, was the similarity between aspects of doing biography and ethnography, the latter having its own well-developed modes of inquiry. What a windfall it would seem if the ethnographic ideas of Bronislaw Malinowski, William Foote Whyte, and Clifford Geertz, among others, could be brought to bear on the craft of biography! The possibilities of intellectual integration and synthesis become readily apparent. One hopes that such possibilities will spill over into practice.

But my central point is the vagaries involved in selecting an individual to be the subject of one's biography and in beginning the inquiries into the life. A further corollary is caution in criticizing or judging too quickly anyone's motivation and selection of a subject for his or her life writing. Major personal issues may be involved.

Creating and/or Using an Archive

Life writing as an empirical exercise feeds on data: letters, documents, interviews. In these days of high intellectual specialization, many biographers miss the joys and the frustrations of creating an archive. But in the doing of archival creation, one runs into a number of interesting difficulties.

In general, part of my personal problem-solving strategy is to have several "tentative models" in my head whenever I approach new problems. As I began on the Nora Barlow task, I had heard that the Margaret Mead archive was housed in the Library of Congress. I already knew that Barlow and Mead were friends. I telephoned the Library of Congress to find out if any of the Barlow letters were in the Mead collection. I was told, "Yes, we have a number of her letters." During an American Educational Research Association meeting in Washington I stole away for a couple of half days and photocopied some 80 letters. Substantively, I learned that in her letters Barlow rarely discussed her Darwin work with either Mead or Gregory Bateson. Even as she was working on the HMS *Beagle* materials, Darwin's time "in the field," Mead and Bateson were getting married and were researching in Bali and elsewhere—that is, doing their own creative ethnographic work. And somehow no connections were ever drawn. I was amazed at that. That experience led to one of the most significant driving questions in the biography: Who did Nora Barlow talk to about her intellectual work? From a symbolic interactionist perspective, one's immediate social intellectual world is important in what one does. The thematic question is both relevant and important. I have spent several years answering that question; it is a large part of the structure of the biography per se. And it arose as I was building an archive of Nora Barlow's letters.

My wife and I spent parts of three summers creating the Nora Barlow archives—more than 1,000 A-4 envelopes in 38 R-Kive 725 Bankers Boxes and a small catalogue as well. In very practical terms, we have separate boxes for letters: immediate family, extended family, and friends and colleagues. They are arranged alphabetically and chronologically. Similarly, we have boxes of published and unpublished manuscripts, also ordered chronologically. There are also photos and books and more photos and books. All are now stored in the large temperature- and humidity-controlled wing adjacent to the Manuscripts Room of the Cambridge University Library. It makes one feel almost a "real" archivist. As Edel (1984) says, in his usual pithy style, "Biography, like history, is the organization of human memory. Assembled and hoarded papers are bits and pieces of that memory" (p. 93).

In addition, a major outcome of the archival activity is an overview of the life—original materials over nine or ten decades of her life span of 103 years. The archival work begins the construction of the life. "Becoming an archivist" (Smith, 1992) carries its own stories and theoretical implications. Other biographers "just" confront someone else's archival efforts. But what would one, you or I, do with Margaret Mead and 600 feet of data? But then, I have never been in a presidential library—Truman, Kennedy, Johnson, Nixon. What does one do with that kind of archival wealth? McCullough (1992) hints at all that in the acknowledgments at the end of his recent *Truman*.

Finally, no one library or home study, even one as full as Nora Barlow's, contains all of the papers that are important for the life story. "Pools of data" exist in all sorts of likely and unlikely places. Finding those is another story in doing biography, as my discussion has already indicated. The intellectual and social process turns back upon itself, in spite of attempts at analytic clarity. The general point is clear: One either finds or builds a data file, an archive, as one step in the process of doing biography. Resourcefulness and imagination can and should occur here as elsewhere in the process.

Finding and Developing One's Theme

One of the most difficult decisions facing the biographer as he or she practices the craft of biography resides in the slant, perspective, or theme that is needed to guide the development of the life to be written. Sometimes the theme comes early, based on an insight from preliminary knowledge and an overview of the subject's life. In two previous essays I have recounted in some detail knowing early that "the Darwin legacy" was the theme to integrate the life of Nora Barlow (Smith, 1987, 1990). The perception was grounded in the knowledge of her four books, written late in life, the first as she turned 50, and then one each in her 60s, 70s, and 80s. But sometimes also, reconstruals vie with the original decision as new data enter, new facets of the life begin to form, new views of the significance of the story arise, and new audiences appear or become salient. The biographer's agony is caught with what might be called "the restless theme" (Smith, 1992). In the biography of Nora Barlow, the "intellectual aristocracy" became a major competing theme. I agonized over that during much of my spring 1990 sabbatical in Cambridge. Which theme is superordinate and which is subordinate? Which will carry better the burden of the evidence of the life? And for which audience? The biographer's internal argument over which theme is the more powerful eventually is entangled in the question of "audience" and publisher. To whom does one want to speak, and who wants to produce the book?

The decisions regarding theme are both part of, and followed closely by, what Bowen (1968) calls "plotting the biography." "Conflict," "suspense," "humor," and "humanity" are some of the terms she uses to highlight issues and decisions regarding plot. Chronology is always important, but a simple chronology of birth, education, marriage, career, and death won't do—for her. What is the book to say about the hero or heroine? Is it a happy or tragic life? And what of the times the central figure lived through? And what scenes and incidents give the life a fullness and a richness? And who are the friends and acquaintances who breathe vitality into the existence? And how do they come and go over the years? In Bowen's view the life writer must have all this finding, settling on, and developing the theme in mind as he or she starts to put words linearly onto sheets of paper. And then, at least in some instances, the writing takes over and transforms things—such as a theme—once again.

"The Figure Under the Carpet"

In the flow of interrelated problems and decisions—picking a subject, developing a theme, becoming aware of the multilayered contexts of lives—none is more difficult than insight into "the figure under the carpet," as Leon Edel (1979) phrases the problem of coming to know the essence of one's subject. The metaphor is mixed but vivid. From one perspective, the view can make one pause, if not forget that "essences" are in high debate these days, and the best one can do is construct a pattern that fits well the data one has of the life of the person being studied and written about. The figure under the carpet is not so much found as constructed. The "mask of life"—the appearance, the facade, the overt behavior one sees (or finds in letters, diaries, and other documents)—and the underlying "life myth"—the major inferences into the character and personality of the person being written about—are like a tapestry, which shows images on its front side and displays the underlying construction on the back. In three pages, Edel dissects Ernest Hemingway—the macho, warring, champion of all he undertook tapestry and "the troubled, uncertain, insecure figure, who works terribly hard to give himself eternal assurance," the figure under the carpet (p. 27). Great biographers look for that figure, construct it carefully, and paint it convincingly; lessor ones never do. Edel, thinking and acting like a composite of Sherlock Holmes and Sigmund Freud, hunts among slips of the tongue, anomalies in everyday behavior, the significant gestures, and the moving and poignant statement in a letter, essay, or novel for clues to that elusive figure.

Bowen, denied the letters of Justice Holmes, which were reserved for the official, the definitive, the authorized biography, talked to, so it seems, nearly everyone who had known Holmes. Eleven of his twelve law secretaries agreed to be interviewed by her. And often she sought out the places where Holmes had lived and worked. Through small detail she pursued the figure under the carpet. Even here, however, subtleties occur. As Bowen (1959) notes, "But the subject of a biography cannot remain at one age—at fifty, at twenty-five, at forty. He must grow old and the reader must see and feel the process" (p. 65). And what, we might ask, of the life myth? How does it evolve, change, grow, and decline—if it does?

Each biographer carries his or her own conception of personality, or character, as it is called by literary biographers. To Virginia Woolf (1927/1960), biography was about the truthful transmission of personality. The truth is like "granite," and personality, at least in the selection of which truths to present, is like a "rainbow." In Woolf's view, truth and personality make one of the biographer's perennial dilemmas. Present-day scholars often see truth as less than granite. As I will argue shortly, sometimes the implicit personality theories can be helpful as sensitizing concepts, and at other times they can be blinders. Once again, Edel (1984) suggests imaginative—and perhaps impractical—ways of coming to terms with such problems—reading psychoanalytic literature, being psychoanalyzed, or even entering into collaborative relationships with an analyst in doing biography. From my perspective, and in a not so simple manner, the biographer brings all of his or her own personality, understandings, and experience to the task of creating a view of the individual under study. If that be true, it poses severe problems for traditional social science, for the sources and implementation of creativity can only be bolstered by technocratic procedures, not carried by them. That raises a long and tortuous argument for those of us working in that tradition.

Form and Shape

Even as one comprehends databases, themes, and underlying patterns or figures in the biography, other dilemmas and choices remain. One of the biographer's major decisions lies in the form or type of biography to be attempted. Clifford (1970) presents a taxonomy of types and a discussion of the factors to be considered in the decision. The underlying dimension of the classification is the degree of objectivity to subjectivity, perhaps better labeled the degree of intrusion of the author into the manuscript. He suggests five points on the continuum.

The "objective biography" is impossible in an absolute sense, but some biographies tend toward a factual collation, usually held together by chronology, with minimal biographer interpretation. In terms of an earlier perspective, if not cliché, "the facts speak for themselves." This type of biography shades into the "scholarly-historical," a form retaining heavy factual emphasis and a strong chronological organization, but with increasing historical background and attempts to develop the underlying character of the subject as defining features. The intruding author is beginning to construct a form with context. This is perhaps the most prevalent type among academic biographers.

The "artistic-scholarly" form involves some of the same exhaustive research, but the biographer takes the role "of an imaginative creative artist, presenting the details in the liveliest and most interesting manner possible" (p. 85). The rainbow is coming to dominate the granite. According to Clifford, most of Catherine Drinker Bowen's biographies fall here. And these efforts are damned by some as "popular." In this regard, I find Bowen's (1959) comment as she attended a frustrating-to-her meeting of the American Historical Association particularly instructive: "There are ways to come at history, I thought, pursuing my way down the hotel corridor. Let us say the professors come at it from the northeast and I from the southwest. Either way will serve, provided the wind blows clean and the fog lifts" (p. 102). Domains of intolerance and true belief infuriated her, and sometimes the wind does not blow clean and the fog does not lift.

"Narrative biography" involves a fictionalizing of scenes and conversations, based on letters and documents, that make the writing both factual and highly imaginative at the same time. The end of the continuum is the fifth form, the "fictional biography," almost a historical novel, with minimal attention to original research and primary resources. The difficulty in putting biographies into these categories appears when one names Irving Stone as an instance of an author whose work falls into the fifth category. For example, correspondence in the Nora Barlow archives contains questions from him to her about items such as the nature of the china used in the Darwin household, asked as Stone wrote his biography of Darwin, *The Origin.*

The continuum is helpful for biographers as they think about the kind of book they want to write or feel they are able to write. And that, the special talents and skills the biographer brings to the task, is an undertreated issue in my view.[5]

Context and Writing

Heroes and heroines do not exist in isolation. Contexts exist in lives and context exists in writing lives. In a vivid illustration, Bowen suggests the problems in beginning and ending the written biography per se. In *Yankee From Olympus,* Oliver Wendell Holmes, Jr., does not appear in the first 80 pages (seven chapters) of the biography, for to understand Holmes, Bowen argues, one must understand New England, Yankee traditions, and Holmes's father, the senior Oliver, who was poet, physician, professor, and storytelling author of "Autocrat of the Breakfast Table." Other biographies begin alternatively. If the subject is well known, the "opening scene" can be of his or her birth; if the subject is unknown, it might be better to present "some scene to catch the reader's attention, show that the hero and his doings are important and exciting and perhaps have a bearing upon history" (Bowen, 1968, p. 21). So Bowen contributes to a reflective conversation with her fellow biographers on a particular dilemma of the craft.

Bowen (1968) also addresses the issue of how the biographer thinks through the "end scene." Most striking perhaps is her account of her book *John Adams and the American Revolution.* Adams's last words were "Thomas Jefferson survives"; he was unaware that Jefferson had died the same day. As Bowen notes, "This double departure of the heroes was epic, tremendous, and needed only to be set down in its bare facts. How could a biographer miss, I asked myself, and looked forward with relish from the day Adams was chosen as subject" (p. 38). But she lost her plot, the proportions of the life, and the original shape of the book, and she had a manuscript already book length with some 50 years to go before 1826. She ended the story in 1776, not a bad eventful moment, but still not the grander ending scene she really wanted. Along the way in her essay, Bowen raises important ideas, such as the "burden of the whole," the keeping of the totality in mind as one writes, the fact that "sometimes luck favors the biographer," the joy in finding a key note lost for years; she notes that "history came at least to a partial rescue" in her case, in the form of what would become Independence Day, July 4. And that provided a significant way of ending the biography, even if less than the possibilities of 1823.

Following upon Bowen, a neophyte biographer can be sensitized and begin thinking through his or her specific subject and situation. Critical judgment, reflective practice, is never right or wrong in some absolute or technical rule-application sense. Nonetheless, some decisions work out better than others, and helping with all this is what a theory of biographical method should be about.

A Brief Conclusion on Craft

Virginia Woolf was half right: Writing lives *is* the devil. But a strand of intellectual excitement, approaching ecstasy, also exists. If one is fortunate to find a heroine or hero from another time, place, and culture, the biographical activity takes on a strong cast of ethnography. Earlier craft skills come into play, even though always with a bit different flavor. The intellectual problems seem to demand more of creativity than of technical or rule-governed problem solving. And that is a challenge to the practice of traditional social science. Some of my students and colleagues suggest that the integration might occur in "metacognition," self-directed thinking about thinking. My own tentative choice of guiding labels is "reflective practice," caught vividly by Donald Schön (1987): "Clearly, it is one thing to be able to reflect-in-action and quite another to be able to reflect on our reflection in action so as to produce a good verbal description of it; and it is still another thing to be able to reflect on the resulting description" (p. 31). The problems of the craft of biography are "messy," not "well-formed." The problems contain elements of ambiguity, complexity, uncertainty, value conflict, and uniqueness.

In too-brief fashion I have presented some of the dilemmas and some of the several taxonomies of resolutions used by such master biographical practitioners as Catherine Drinker Bowen, James Clifford, and Leon Edel. Thinking along with them creates images and metaphors for handling one's own devils. Doing biography is a great way to live.

Disciplinary Strands: Alternative Interpretations

There is no theory that is not a fragment, carefully prepared, of some autobiography.

Paul Valéry
(quoted in Olney, 1980, preface)

Biographical method can be viewed in alternative, and perhaps more abstract, ways than as a craft or process. For better and worse—that is, the benefits of focused vision and the limits of sometimes narrowed vision—much intellectual activity is organized as academic disciplines. Several of the disciplines have claims on biography and biographical method. Even though they can be clustered into literature, history, social science, education, and feminist and minority perspectives, each of these can be differentiated further. Even a cursory scanning of references and illustrations indicates that these disciplinary points of view often run relatively independent of each other.[6] That independence seems limiting, if not tragic, for students and scholars who want diverse images and models of how life writing might be conceived and carried out, to enhance their own intellectual creativity. And lurking behind, almost hauntingly so, is the idea of autobiography, undermining many of the claims of detachment and specialization from the disciplines. Are our theories, as Valéry suggests, "simple" extensions of our autobiographies? If so, what then becomes of social science?

Literary Biography

Reading literary biographies and accompanying statements of biographical method is exciting, especially if one is partial to competition, conflict, and sharp jousting. The contentiousness is neither superficial nor limited to domains and turf, but spills over into style and substance of the biography. Note the strongly stated positions of two eminent English intellectuals and biographers. In his preface to *Eminent Victorians,* Strachey (1918) reoriented English biography with his critique of traditional biographies: "Those two fat volumes with which it is our custom to commemorate the dead—who does not know them, with their ill-digested masses of material, their slipshod style, their tone of tedious panegyric, their lamentable lack of selection, of detachment, of design?" (p. viii). In his view, "it is perhaps as difficult to write a good life as it is to live one."

In 1932, G. M. Trevelyan, in a new preface to an older biography (1876) seemed to write almost in rebuttal and in elaboration to Strachey. He comments regarding the "life and letters" biography:

> My father [G. O. Trevelyan] certainly chose the form of biography most suitable to his uncle [Lord Macaulay]. He had not Boswell's rare gift of reproducing the essence of conversation, nor did Macaulay's real strength lie, like Dr. Johnson's in his tongue, but rather in his pen. His letters would reveal him and amuse the reader. It would have been equally beside the mark to treat Macaulay in a subjective, psychological character sketch, such as "the new biography" prefers, with the documents and letters omitted. Macaulay was not subtle enough for such subtleties, and his letters are much too good to miss. His description of his interview with the clergyman who thought Napoleon was the Beast in Revelations (p. 342) both amuses us more and tells us more about Macaulay than a page of psychological analysis. In this book the man lives and speaks for himself. (pp. v-vi)

In this short paragraph, Trevelyan raises a much more complex set of events facing the biographer: the special talents of the biographer, the special strengths of the subject, the importance of an interpretive character sketch versus letting the individual speak for him- or herself, and the need for or desirability of a psychological analysis.

The debate continues to the present. Other perspectives are possible as well. More recently, Horner (1987), in her brief introduction to the Radcliffe Biography Series, has noted that "fine biographies give us both a glimpse of ourselves and a reflection of the human spirit. Biography illuminates history, inspires by example, and fires the imagination to life's possibilities. Good biography can create lifelong models for us" (p. ix). That position opens further doors insofar as it is reminiscent of Kluckhohn's (1949) powerful statement of anthropology being a "mirror of man." Concepts and metaphors of biography run in many directions.

Earlier transformations occurred as well. Boswell's *Life of Johnson* dominated the English scene after its publication in 1791. Rogers, in an introduction to the 1980 Oxford University Press edition, comments on the book with phrases such as "lonely eminence," "towered over lesser works," and "dominated the skyline" of biography. In my view, Boswell's own eight-page introduction is a marvelous and strikingly modern essay in its own right. He presents a view of his relationship to Johnson—in my words, that of "humble servant." He was a friend of some 20 years; had the biography in mind from the start; cleared his "rights of human subjects," in that Johnson knew what he was about; kept voluminous records of activities, conversations, and events; cautioned against "panegyrick"; urged the importance of chronology; argued the method of conversation as the method to "best display his character"; cited Plutarch on the importance of an action of small note, a short saying, or a jest as the door to an individual's "real" character; quoted Johnson about how to study and understand Johnson; and staked his territory vis-à-vis other biographers who knew Johnson less well. Boswell read widely and knew about biography; he reflected well upon the process, and he wrote a memorable biography.

Illuminating Boswell's eight pages is Edel's (1984) brilliant essay on Boswell. Here we find Boswell arranging meetings, setting scenes, and determining the course of conversations—shades of Monet arranging and planting his gardens at Giverny to enhance his paintings of the bridge and lily ponds! Who and what is to be believed about anything in biography? It seems that one pits one's own intelligence against the world and others' views of the world, if they be two phenomena, gathers data and evidence from whatever simple and esoteric sources one can find, and does the best one can. And that can be exciting, frustrating, and terrifying—if one has high need of certainty.

So change and contentiousness exist, and have existed for centuries, in and around literary biography. Further implications for the life writer seem to follow on this generalization. In situations of intellectual conflict considerable room exists for multiple alternatives, choices, reflection, and creativity, that is, individual agency. Artistry as well as factual representation and reality, in varying proportions, vie with each other. Granite and rainbows again! That seems another important generalization for individuals who want to write lives.

History

History lies somewhere between the humanities and the social sciences. However, construed in a disciplinary sense, history has claims on biography, as our introductory definitions indicate. In a series of three major essays, Lawrence Stone (1981) has addressed the relationship of history to the social sciences, the nature and place of prosopography in historical thinking, and the changing emphasis on narration in history. But it is the "prosopography" essay that is most germane here. In resurrecting the classical label for "group biography," Stone argues for its contemporary importance.

The collective study of lives, Stone asserts, leads to insight into two of the most basic problems in history. The roots of political actions lie in the motives, personalities, and characters of key individual actors in any set of important historical events. Private events and papers relate a different facet of politics than do public events and speeches. And it is not only the great men and women who are important, but also the other people who surround them in complex social events. Stone argues that not only is biography important, but group biography, that is, prosopography, adds a further dimension. The social and symbolic interactionists from other social sciences would strongly agree.[7] Second, the study of group biography gives insight into the larger problems of social structure and social mobility. Networks, overlapping boards, connections, and family relationships are built on individual people interacting together for their own interests. Mapping those careers and linkages is an important means of understanding.

In a small way, we found this kind of approach, what we called life histories of a group of educational administrators and teachers who had created the innovative Kensington Elementary School, to be a powerful way of understanding the rise and fall of the school and the complexities of educational innovation and reform (Smith et al., 1986; Smith, Dwyer, Prunty, & Kleine, 1988; Smith, Prunty, Dwyer, & Kleine, 1987). Overall we blended history, ethnography, and life history as inquiry methods. Part of our rationale concerned the idea of a case study, a bounded system, in our view. The individual life history pieces or brief biographies were interlinked because of the time the staff taught and administered together in the Kensington Elementary School and the Milford School District. That linkage presented possibilities of understanding beyond any one individual biography. Powerful group patterns emerged in their lives.

One of Stone's conclusions is that group biography can link together "constitutional and institutional history" and "personal biography," two of the oldest and best developed parts of the historian's craft, but ones that have run too independent of each other. Biography becomes not an end in itself, but a helpful element in the pursuit of other ends.[8] In addition, the rise of oral history, investigative journalism in the political domain, and the making of archives into presidential libraries offers an array of possibilities to the historian as life writer. Old ideas and methods take on a fresh look and open up imaginative possibilities in new contexts.

Social Science Perspectives

Although variation exists among social scientists, most argue that biography should move beyond narration and storytelling of the particular into more abstract conceptualizations, interpretations, and explanations. Writing lives can serve multiple purposes. In general, "scientists" seek patterns in the forms of concepts, hypotheses, theories, and metaphors. These patterns are both the fruits of scientific inquiry and practice and the stimulus for further inquiry and improved practice. For convenience, I divide the social scientists by discipline—anthropologists, psychologists, and sociologists. Some might argue that a trichotomy of conservative, liberal, and radical is a more powerful split. And others see the paradigmatic assumptions—positivism, neopositivism, interpretivism, and critical theory as more powerful organizing conceptions. Finding the joints at which to cut "nature" seems more and more difficult. Some would argue that Plato was wrong—at least for social science and the humanities.

Anthropologists. Anthropologists have had a long relationship with biography, mostly under the rubrics of "life histories" and "culture and personality." Langness (1965: Langness & Frank, 1981) presents an overview of this history and the multiple approaches being used. To pick only one strand, Oscar Lewis and Robert Redfield illustrate some of the excitement in the field. Both did ethnographies of Tepoztlan, attempts at a total view, Redfield's (1930) in the 1920s and Lewis's (1951) "restudy" two decades later. But the views were different: the positive side, bright view of Redfield contrasted with the dark side, nether view of Lewis. And that posed a severe intellectual problem for holistic anthropologists. Redfield (1955) responded with *The Little Community,* one of the most provocative and, I would maintain, underappreciated methodological books in social science. Essentially, he argued for a half dozen approaches for studying the small community. Three chapters are particularly important for the interpretations here—"A Typical Biography," "A Kind of Person," and "An Outlook on Life." The sequence of events as an individual passes through a culture during the course of a life is one view of that culture. And the resulting kind of person and his or her outlook on life are related additional ways of viewing a culture. These views play off against ecological, social structural, and historical perspectives. Cultures can be written through lives. And that is part of some of the best of Lewis's later work, life stories of individuals and families who moved from rural Tepoztlan to urban Mexico City. In *Five Families* (1959) and *The Children of Sanchez* (1961), Lewis tape-recorded individual life stories and, with only minor editing, presented them as documents of lives, "multiple autobiographies," to use his label. Out of this work came the controversial conception of the "culture of poverty." Valentine (1968) raised a "critique and counterproposals" of Lewis's use of the long autobiographical life story data for the kind of theoretical interpretations lying within the conception of the "culture of poverty."

After writing one of the most autobiographically laden accounts of fieldwork ever presented in his "Deep Play: Notes on the Balinese Cockfight" (in Geertz, 1973), Geertz, in a more recent book, *Works and Lives: The Anthropologist as Author* (1988), faces directly the issue of the dual role of the anthropological investigator between the horns of the "other," the individual or the culture being studied, and the "text," the narrative written about the world "out there." With his usual persuasive style, he makes the point that the reader's acceptance of the text occurs not because of its factual weight or the theoretical places being created, but rather because of its narrative strength, based on rhetorical devices, convincing the reader that he, the anthropologist, was really there. "Vas you dere Sharlie?" is his paraphrase of an earlier literary statement. And what better, in his earlier "Deep Play," than the scramble by Geertz and his wife to escape the police breaking up the cockfight and the charade of having tea with a local dignitary when all the postfight commotion was occurring. Geertz's "host" had not only been at the cockfight but had helped organize it. Geertz's more recent analysis, without reference to the early piece, is a vivid exposition of that earlier writing strategy. For Geertz the incident was a major breakthrough in community acceptance of his fieldwork. For the reader, it authenticated everything substantive he had to say about Bali. I was left with the feeling, "After that episode, how could he have gotten anything wrong?" But Geertz in 1988 writes not only of the relationship between the investigator and the community or individual being studied, but mainly of the relationship between the investigator and the kind of text he or she has written. Although not intended as biography, the narrative of his argument is carried by the intellectual and professional lives of four major anthropologists—Lévi-Strauss, Evans-Pritchard, Malinowski, and Benedict. The writing of lives can and does serve many purposes.

Recently, Rabinow (1977) and Crapanzano (1980), both writing Moroccan culture and biography, suggest difficulties and creative possibilities in understanding and blending life writing and cultural analysis. The identities of literature and science are lost and recreated brilliantly.

Psychologists. Psychologists have trouble with biography. On the one hand, psychoanalytic literature has influenced countless life writers; Leon Edel is one of the more noteworthy. With a psychoanalytic perspective, almost as a wand, he probes problems, issues, and interpretations with ease and facility as he writes biographies, critiques biographies, and surveys the tremendous volume of literature on biography. But academic psychologists have never lived easily with psychoanalysis. On the other hand, too, psychologists have a passion for truth, and a particular kind of truth at that, exemplified in experimentation, quantification, and tested propositions. Some see psychology as physics writ large. Garraty (1954, 1957), citing varied attempts at quantification of life documents, such as graphology, content analysis, and discomfort-relief quotients, turns his hand to issues of personality in biography. Though raised in that tradition, I now find it chilling to the creativity involved in the writing of lives.

A kind of middle ground is found in the work of Gordon Allport and Henry Murray. Allport, an out-of-step third-force psychologist, produced a fascinating set of books relevant to biography. His well-received *Personality* (1937) was followed by his classic *The Use of Personal Documents in Psychological Science* (1942), and the brilliant *Letters from Jenny* (1965). In the last, he presented and then explored a large collection of letters written by a woman named Jenny, mostly to her son and daughter-in-law. They are vivid, troubling, introspective accounts of both her life as a working woman and mother and her accompanying mental states. The exploration involved Allport in a consideration of several competing theories for understanding and explaining the letters. Existential psychology and Freudian psychoanalysis vied with his own structural-dynamic approach. He concluded with an estimate of Jenny's mental health. The life story, told mostly in the letters, with minimal commentary, was in the service of general theory. Allport also took up the challenge of Stefan Zweig in his infamous quote regarding writers such as Proust and Flaubert: "Writers like these are giants in observation and literature, whereas in psychology the field of personality is worked by lesser men, mere flies, who have the safe anchorage of a frame of science in which to place their petty platitudes and minor heresies" (quoted in Allport, 1960, p. 6). Allport (1960) makes the case for both literature and psychology in his "Personality: A Problem for Science or a Problem for Art?"

Henry Murray's contribution to biography also lies in his explorations in personality, and in a book by the same title (Murray et al., 1938); in his invention of the TAT, the thematic apperception test; and in his collaboration with a remarkable group of colleagues and students who have pursued problems in the nature of lives. With the anthropologist Clyde Kluckhohn he edited the well-recognized *Personality in Nature, Society, and Culture* (Kluckhohn & Murray, 1953). Concepts such as needs, presses, proceedings, serials, plans, schedules, ego strength, and proactive systems guided the work of several generations of American psychologists interested in lives and life writing. *Lives in Progress* (White, 1952) is a major illustration of the post-Murray approach. The eclectic emphasis on biology, family, social circumstances, and the individuals themselves appears and reappears. Erikson, another former Murray colleague, in his *Childhood and Society* (1963) and his *Young Man Luther* (1962) brought the "eight ages of man," "identity crises," and other conceptualizations to life writing. The ideas of Murray and others in the psychobiography and psychohistory traditions are extended in McAdams and Ochberg (1989) and Runyan (1982, 1988).

In the more recent *Seasons of a Man's Life,* Levinson (1978) accents the stages in adult life and the difficult transitions—most noteworthy, the midlife crisis—as a framework for the consideration of a life. The dilemma of the general and the particular appears once again. Academic psychologists tend to pursue the former with greater zeal. Although major disagreements exist here, Coles, in a series of books that includes *Women of Crisis II* (Coles & Coles, 1980), attacks vigorously the social scientists and the theorists, even while developing and presenting, mostly implicitly, his own more subtle theoretical point of view (Smith et al., 1986, pp. 21-23). It is an exciting world; the granite and rainbow dichotomy does not rest easily within psychology.

As much as any disciplinary group, psychologists have used biography in the service of other ends. One illustration must suffice. In his very stimulating *Contrary Imaginations,* Liam Hudson (1966) collected short, open-ended autobiographical statements of clever English schoolboys. "Just describe those aspects of your life which seem to you interesting or important" provoked responses useful in clarifying major hypotheses in his study. More far-reaching was his turning the autobiographical perspective on himself and his career shifts from experimental psychology to a more humanistic kind of psychology in his *The Cult of the Fact* (1972). He sets his authorial position with a powerful initial sentence: "The story begins in Cambridge, in the spring of 1968; my eleventh year in Cambridge, and my third in the superlative if stagey ambiance of King's College" (p. 15). For anyone who has spent any time in Cambridge, the invitation is irresistible. Insights and personal help come in strange ways! I have now a major lead toward revising and extending my *Doing Ethnographic Biography: A Reflective Practitioner at Work During a Spring in Cambridge* (1992). Serendipity once again! Psychologists really should have less trouble with biography.

Sociologists. Like psychologists and anthropologists, sociologists have been ambivalent toward biography. But writing lives, in the form of life histories, became part of the world of the Chicago school with the publication of Clifford Shaw's *The Jack-Roller* in 1930. And life history was only one of the broader category of qualitative inquiries, labeled better as "case studies." From the Gold Coast to the Ghetto, they were to have a permanent impact on sociological thought and method. And out of such work, and the seminal thought of George Herbert Mead, was to come the very influential symbolic interactionism as a social science point of view. In two short introductions, one to a republication of Shaw's book and the other to his own collected essays, Howard Becker (1966, 1970) makes the case for both this kind of "close-up" sociology and the place of biographical and autobiographical life histories in sociology.

I can remember reading several of the Chicago case study books in a general sociology course when I was an undergraduate, being absorbed in them and the four wishes of Thomas as discussed in Waller (1932), but not being able to integrate all that into the kind of "scientific" psychology I was to learn in graduate school. Now, several decades later, as a latter-day practitioner of case studies of schools, curricula, and school districts, and life histories of teachers, and now of more formal biography, I find the power of the Chicago perspective awesome.

Becker makes the argument for life histories as part of a "mosaic" of community and institutional investigations, as important "touchstones" for considering any abstract theory of person and community, and the testing of implicit assumptions about human beings in the larger sociological studies. Biography has an overriding dimension, the chronology between birth and death. In a social science that often makes pleas for "process" interpretations, the clash between the synchronic and the diachronic usually ends in the victory of the more structural synchronic. Biography, and history as well, opens the theorist to data organized on a diachronic timeline. In addition, biography with a concern for the way a specific individual perceives and construes the world also moves the sociological interpreter toward the subject's perspective rather than the observer's point of view, a major issue labeled by the anthropologist Clifford Geertz as "experience near" versus "experience distant" conceptualizations.

Following in these same traditions, Denzin (1989) raises his sociological perspective as "interpretive biography," the creating of literary and narrative accounts and stories of lived experience. He pursues in great analytic detail the development of taxonomies and concepts; the multiple ways lives can be studied, construed, and written; and the implications of taking one perspective or another. "Turning points," the never-ending construction and reconstruction of lives, and obituaries as documents (that is, brief life statements), the cultural categories we use in describing lives, and the ethical responsibilities in studying lives, suggest the creative range of ideas his brand of sociology brings to the biographical task. In much the same tradition, with some stronger overtones of radicalism as well, Bertaux (1981) edited an international collection of essays, *Biography and Society: The Life History Approach in the Social Sciences*. Sociology is reclaiming one of its important roots. C. Wright Mills (1959) would be pleased as history, biography, and social structure have moved a step closer to productive syntheses.

Taking the sociological position just a shade more toward journalism are life writers such as Studs Terkel (1970, 1972), who describes his study *Hard Times* as an "oral history." In a page or two to a half dozen pages he presents brief vignettes of the lives of individuals who lived through the Depression years of the 1930s in the United States. One might see it as a collection of "episodes" in autobiographical life stories, with some biographical editing by Terkel from his tape-recorded interviews. In his introduction, labeled "A Personal Memoir," he classifies the effort this way:

> This is a memory book, rather than one of hard fact and precise statistic. In recalling an epoch, some thirty, forty, years ago, my colleagues experienced pain, in some instances; exhilaration, in others. Often it was a fusing of both. A hesitancy, at first, was followed by a flow of memories: long-ago hurts and small triumphs. Honors and humiliations. There was laughter, too. (Terkel, 1970, p. 17)

Inner perspectives, experience near phrasings and conceptualizations, and tidal waves of feeling and emotion present individuals and their lives. These coalesce into larger images and patterns. Whether journalism, or oral history, or a kind of sociology, the labels seem less relevant than the power Terkel brings to the reporting and evoking of images. Most social scientists would envy his ability to capture his focus in *Working*:

> It is about search, too, for daily meaning as well as daily bread, for recognition as well as cash, for astonishment rather than torpor; in short, for a sort of life rather than a Monday through Friday sort of dying. Perhaps immortality, too, is part of the quest. To be remembered was the wish, spoken and unspoken, of the heroes and heroines of this book. (Terkel, 1972, p. xiii)

Creativity and insight come in varied forms. Honoring them is high on my list of life-writing priorities.

Feminist and Minority Perspectives

Anyone who has ever felt left out, ignored, or powerless has the beginnings of an understanding of the feminist and minority perspectives that have arisen in recent decades with great vigor and anger in the field of biography and autobiography. From the *Oxford English Dictionary*'s early limiting definitions of who is included and excluded to the more personal reports of experience, the argument grows. In a small but poignant and potent personal experience, while walking through the corridors of the Cambridge University Library, actually from the Manuscripts Room on the third floor to the Tea Room in the basement, while working on the biography of Nora Barlow, I noted an exhibition of books from the seventeenth century focusing on the "Worthies of England" (Smith, 1992). Though "worthies" was a label new to me, it seems to say it all. In that era it was clear who was important and who decided on the criteria of importance. That human experience is gendered is the fundamental truth underlying the feminist perspective. Race and class as categories of individuals echo, follow quickly upon, similar assumptions.

Examining issues in equity, power, social structure, agency, self-definition, and their interrelations, so it is argued by feminists, will be enhanced by the writing of all kinds of personal narratives of all kinds of lives of all kinds of women. Images, models, and insights for change exist in the life-writing narratives and critical reflections upon those stories. A gripping particularistic account of these issues appears in the "Origins" chapter of the Personal Narratives Group (1989) book, *Interpreting Women's Lives.* Variations in lifestyles, with their attendant satisfactions and deep dissatisfactions, appear along with an array of conceptual attempts to broaden the meaning of the experiences recounted. This broadening occurs with counternarratives as illustrations and arguments for women who are not thinking or feeling or behaving as they are "supposed to," constructing and negotiating new alternatives, and the troubling constraints posed by one's disciplinary training in the humanities versus the social sciences.

Ultimately, the Personal Narratives Group structured its book around four major sensitizing concepts: context, narrative form, narrator-interpreter relations, and truths. Each of these "lenses" or "pieces of madras cloth" illuminates the meanings of women's life stories. *Context* refers to the particular conditions that prevail in any society at any moment in time. *Narrative forms,* the fluid shapes into which one's creative constructions of lives flow, are rich with alternatives. The *narrator-interpreter* relations conception addresses the multiple people involved in living, narrating, writing, critiquing, and meaning making in biography, and also the complex interrelationships of the individuals themselves. *Truths* refers to "the multiplicity of ways in which a woman's life story reveals and reflects important features of her conscious experience and social landscape, creating from both her essential reality" (p. 14).

If those abstractions, retold here for brevity, lose their concrete meaning, the reader has only to go to any of the individual essays for the particulars. For instance, Swindells's essay reinterprets Stanley (1984) on the Hannah Cullwick diaries. The diaries were written by a Victorian maidservant, a "maid-of-all-work," at the urging of A. J. Munby, "man of two worlds," her male exploiter and later husband (if these be different). Recently they were published by a feminist press and interpreted by the editor (Stanley, 1984). More recently, the diaries have been reinterpreted by Swindells, and given additional interpretation by the Personal Narratives Group editors. Now each reader, with the help of Derek Hudson's (1972) biography of Munby and Hiley's (1979) book of photographs (mostly Munby's) *Victorian Working Women: Portraits From Life,* can make his or her own interpretation. It is an incredible story—or set of interrelated stories. The exciting complexities of "auto/biographical" methods, to use Stanley's phrasing, in the late twentieth century are readily apparent.

Alternative, more conventional if not more tempered, accounts appear in such highly discussed books as Mary Catherine Bateson's (1990) *Composing a Life* and Carolyn Heilbrun's (1988) *Writing a Woman's Life.* Bateson's five biographical stories of lives raise conceptualizations such as "unfolding stories," "improvisation" versus "a vision already defined," "patchwork quilt" as a metaphor for a life, and "a rethinking of the concept of achievement." I was reminded of an earlier and personally influential book by Gruenberg and Krech (1952), *The Many Lives of Modern Woman,* which provided a metaphor and guided the decisions of some of us a generation or two ago.

Heilbrun's opening sentence gives pause to anyone contemplating any aspect of the topic "biography and women." She begins:

> There are four ways to write a woman's life: the woman herself may tell it, in what she chooses to call an autobiography; she may tell it in what she chooses to call fiction; a biographer, woman or man, may write the woman's life in what is called a biography; or the woman may write her own life in advance of living it, unconsciously, and without recognizing or naming the process. (p. 11)

"Nostalgia," "anger," and "taking control of their own lives" are concepts that appear early and throughout her analysis. Early autobiographies by women, and many of the more recent as well, read "flat" to Heilbrun, especially as she contrasts the autobiographies with the more emotional books of letters. Perhaps it is my contentiousness, but I find some of her interpretations open to further exploration. She cites the differences between two of May Sarton's autobiographical books: *Plant Dreaming Deep* (1968) tends toward a positive, upbeat flavor, whereas *Journal of a Solitude* (1973) tends to probe the nether side of life, but, in my view, tragedy as well as anger. And for reasons not clear to me as reader, Heilbrun does not mention the earlier *I Knew a Phoenix: Sketches for an Autobiography* (1959), in which Sarton draws portraits of her parents: George Sarton, the historian of science, and Mabel Elwes Sarton, painter, interior decorator, and artisan, and the joys and despair of Europe in the World War I era. Her own youth is caught in a series of sketches, "The Education of a Poet." May Sarton, as person, writer, and text, seems much more complex than

Heilbrun's brief comments and interpretations indicate.

And Heilbrun is very complex as well. I encountered her first as writer of the introductory essays to two of Vera Brittain's *Testament* books, a kind of "documentary" history through autobiography (see, e.g., Heilbrun, 1981). Much of *Writing a Woman's Life* appears there. Vera Brittain and Winifred Holtby seem, to me as a bit more than casual observer, to have influenced Heilbrun mightily. More recently I have started reading the Amanda Cross mystery novels. Picture this: Heilbrun writes under the pseudonym of Amanda Cross (mystery writers don't get tenure in literature at Columbia, she says); the heroine of the novels is Kate Fansler, a detective and university literary critic, and in one of the more recent novels, *The Players Come Again* (1990), heroine Fansler is writing a biography of a woman who is allegedly the author of her husband's world-famous stream-of-consciousness novel. Perhaps all this life writing will be clearer when I have read the rest of Heilbrun's long series of books and essays. For the moment—what a provocative set of ambiguous interpretive possibilities!

Further, what Heilbrun calls "the claim of achievement, the admission of ambition, the recognition that accomplishment" was earned appeared in the letters of some writers but not in their formal autobiographies. In her view, scripts, other than reflecting men's stories, for telling life stories seldom existed in the lives of eminent women. In my view, Healey's (1986) *Wives of Fame* gives the beginning of a kind of redressing of the comment "I didn't know he had a wife" regarding Jenny—and Marx; and Mary—and Livingstone; and Emma—and Darwin. Heilbrun's own anecdotes and stories continue excitedly, culminating in statements about aging, courage, freedom, and endings. She argues that being 50 years old is an important transition time. To a social scientist, many of these interpretations are empirically testable propositions. Another agenda?

The life-writing literature by minority and ethnic groups is immense and growing as well. From the early autobiographies of Booker T. Washington and Frederick Douglass to the more recent ones by Malcolm X and Maya Angelou, the multiple definitions of the black experience have continued to cumulate. Butterfield's *Black Autobiography in America* (1974) presents a vivid historical picture of major transitions from the early slave narrative period, to one of search, and now to the period of rebirth, to use his phrases. The first sentence of the introduction presages the overall perspective of the book:

> George Orwell's image of the future in *1984* was of a boot stamping on the human face forever. He could have used the same image to represent the Negro past in America, fitting the boot easily to the foot of a slavetrader, overseer, master, policeman, soldier, vigilante, capitalist, and politician. (p. 1)

Overall, his interpretation of autobiography is a mix of history and literature and an attempt to integrate "objective fact and subjective awareness." In his later, more interpretive chapters, Butterfield analyzes issues of constructing black identity in terms of politics, separatism, and revolution among many young black writers. In his essay "The Language of Black Satire" he cites powerful short excerpts from Cleaver, Seale, and others, most of whom spent time in prison. Butterfield's "history as subjective experience" is an exercise in a set of propositions linking personal experience to individuality, an awakening of a "truer and better self," and the birth of a new world. Example follows example.

As I read Haley's epilogue at the end of *The Autobiography of Malcolm X,* multiple "biographical method" questions arose. In what sense is the book Malcolm X's autobiography and in what sense is it Haley's biography of him? Is Stanley's phrasing "auto/biography" the more viable alternative? And what should we make of the point in time in which the book was narrated and written? While the book was in process, Malcolm X parted company with Elijah Muhammad. The climax of the book was now different. Should the early materials be rewritten? Malcolm said no. What problems were created for Haley, the writer of the auto/biography? The questions run on insistently.

As I reread Anne Moody's *Coming of Age in Mississippi* (1968), a larger essay loomed in my mind. Life stories can be a powerful influence on creativity, and that is no mean accomplishment. I believe it was her four-part table of contents—"Childhood," "High School," "College," and "The Movement"—and the vivid vignettes and brief stories from the text per se that seemed so simply similar to many of my interests and perspectives. I saw the possibilities of comparisons and contrasts between her book and the very different but equally powerful *Period Piece: A Cambridge Childhood,* Gwen Raverat's (1952) auto/biography of the Darwin family at the turn of the century. In addition, our multiple ethnographic case studies of pupils, teachers, and schools in and around the metropolitan area of St. Louis and the central Midwest in the United States, all of which have biographical and autobiographical strands, would provide a large further comparison and contrast. Bridging some of these differences is Wilma Wells, my colleague and coauthor of *"Difficult to Reach, Maintain, and Help" Urban Families in PAT: Issues, Dilemmas, Strategies, and Resolutions in Parent Education* (Smith & Wells, 1990). This was very heavily an auto/biographical account of struggles to educate poor urban mothers in child-rearing practices. As I think about such work, family, schooling, class, and caste cut across gender, generations, and continents. Now, the larger essay and this paragraph seem like a promissory note for a new, autobiographical book that will bring together numerous loose ends, nagging unsolved problems, from a professional lifetime. At this point I feel I am co-opting someone else's narrative. But Anne Moody is alive, and not so well, in St. Louis's urban ghetto in 1993.

The influential life-writing literature from the feminist and minority perspectives reflects back on some of the intellectual cynicism regarding autobiography. Some believe that autobiography is impossible, as noted earlier in this essay. Criticism has its own complexities and power.

Professional Education

Much of recent life writing in professional education carries the same intellectual flavor of the feminist and minority perspective, finding voice among the disenfranchised, the powerless, or those with alternative visions. Marilyn Cohn and Robert Kottkamp (1992) gave their book *Teachers* the subtitle *The Missing Voice in Education.*

Several strands seem especially important. Representative of a first strand are collections of essays such as Ball and Goodson's (1985) *Teachers' Lives and Careers* and Goodson's (1992) *Studying Teachers' Lives.* Conceptually the major thrust lies in the accenting of "agency," of teachers in the daily give and take of teaching in classrooms and schools. This is particularly important in a domain that experiences fads of curriculum reform and school innovation under the control of central office administrators, university educationists, and subject matter specialists. Perhaps the most telling illustration was the development of "teacher-proof" curricula in the 1960s by disciplinary specialists. The new materials were supposed to be so powerful and well done that even incompetent teachers, like you and me, could not spoil them in the transmission from text to students. Similarly, the field of school innovation and change, exemplified by the "RD&D" (research, development, and diffusion) model, placed the classroom teacher as one technocratic spot in the conveyor belt of school change. Images of Charlie Chaplin on the assembly line in *Modern Times* suggest the frenetic, but not so hilarious, life of the teacher. Teacher life stories attempt to change both the teachers themselves and the educational system of which they are a part. Another minority group is seeking a voice.

A second strand with both distant roots and recent flowering is made up of those teachers with alternative visions. A. S. Neill is best known for his *Summerhill* (1960), but even more impressive is his *A Dominie's Log* and the other two dominie books (see Neill, 1975). The *Log* contains all the significant material that he was not permitted to include in the official records he had to keep for the inspectorate. Sylvia Ashton-Warner's *Teacher* (1963) brings a personal view of New Zealand, multiculturalism, and a more organic way of teaching. And the "romantics" of the 1960s and 1970s, such as Hentoff (1966), Hernden (1966, 1971), and Holt (1964), present powerful life-writing statements. Nonmainstream voices entered into the dialogue about schooling.

A third strand that seldom is described as life writing is the growing interest in "action research." As described by Elliott (1991) and others, action research involves teachers studying their own teaching. In a cycle that involves proposing, planning, implementing, observing, recording (through diaries and journals), reflecting, and writing, teachers have begun to talk about their teaching, their hopes and desires, the immediate context of a particular group of pupils, a particular set of curriculum materials, and a particular school with its particular principal and staff of colleagues. Although the focus is usually on an innovative teaching strategy or piece of curriculum, I would argue that a more powerful way of thinking about action research is to construe the activity as "really" a piece of teacher autobiography. And if this be true, then action researchers should be including more personal context, larger chunks of autobiography, in their research statements. For educationists, the epigraph from Valéry with which I began this section needs to be extended beyond "theory" to "practice" as well.

Conclusions

No foundation. All the way down the line.

William Saroyan,
The Time of Your Life, 1939

Several conclusions, not quite foundations, in the form of patterns, tentative generalizations, or lessons seem to follow reasonably closely upon the arguments presented in this chapter. In wrestling with the theme and audience of this chapter I found I wanted to say something of the multiple and conflicting definitions and perspectives of life writing; I wanted to address the process or craft aspects of doing biography; and finally I wanted to acquaint any one disciplinarian with images of life writing from other disciplines. Eventually, integration or talking across boundaries was on my agenda. My focal audiences, as frequently is the case, are my graduate students interested in doing one form or another of qualitative inquiry. They seem not too far from a larger population of students and scholars.

Underlying this essay is an image of an ideal. For reasons I understand only partially, I am drawn to those scholars who write interesting and important biographies, who seem to know huge amounts of the relevant literature on life writing, and who reflect insightfully upon the craft, the process of doing biography—an awesome and nearly unattainable ideal! In attempting to actualize such an ideal, I have raised a few of the older, more classical biographers and their perspectives as well as the more contemporary. In addition, and as part of a perspective on the importance of the individual as agent, I have written in the first person and about some of my own efforts, even though the chapter is part of a "handbook," which usually assumes a more detached perspective.

For the educational and social science researcher interested in qualitative methods, biography—and its variants, autobiography, life history, and life story—seems a rich and only partially exploited form of inquiry for reaching multiple intellectual goals and purposes. In her recent book, Stanley (1992) makes a strong case for the label "auto/biographical." In an important summary, Lancey (1993) suggests "personal accounts." *Life writing* might be the more apt generic label.

Although this discussion has not been organized explicitly on a historical or chronological basis, it is clear that the nature, purpose, form, and function of life writing have evolved over recent years and decades, as well as centuries. For scholars with even a bit of an innovative or experimentalist set of values, current biographical forms and formats should be seen as only tentative guidelines toward their own creative inquiry endeavors. Any constraining formalistic definitions and rules about the nature and function of biography seem out of keeping with the vigor of intellectual activity under way.

Almost as a corollary of the prior generalizations, biographical inquiry is in high contention among scholars within and among different disciplines—literature, history, sociology, psychology, and anthropology. Each of these traditions has evolved its own standards and perspectives on life writing. Conflict seems everywhere. Each discipline, and subgroups within disciplines, vents its anger and displeasure upon other groups and traditions. Ecumenical approaches often are not seen as desirable. Large personal, professional, and disciplinary issues and interests are at stake. The best counsel seems to be, Realize that this is happening, come to know as much of the variety as time permits, and integrate the differences in ways that contribute to one's own creativity in life writing.

The kind of data drawn upon by different researchers—letters, interviews, documents, self-statements, and so on—as they construct their biographies will vary in amount, quality, relevance, and perceived significance. Autobiographies—sometimes as statements in their own right and sometimes as data for other statements—seem to draw disdain from several quarters and high support from others. Critics and evaluators will need to use their own judgment, just as the biographer per se must do, to assess the meaning and the quality of the effort. In my view, building a rationale for any particular form of life writing as legitimate inquiry seems possible in the diversity of orientations presented here. The important test case for an academic might well be: What variants are permissible as Ph.D. dissertations? Clearly, formal biographies of eminent white males qualify. But what of a Moody or a latter-day Cullwick? Would their autobiographies or diaries count? I would argue yes, but others might disagree. And the debate would continue: Purposes? Limits? Criteria?

In my view, doing biography is an active constructionist activity, from the picking of a hero or heroine to the seeking of data pools, to the selection of issues and themes, and to the final image or portrait that is drawn. The importance of serendipity in selecting a subject for a biography, in determining a particular theme and perspective, and in working one's way through the doing of the biography needs to be noted as a significant possibility in both purpose and strategy. While searching for one solution, life writers seem to find other things. Serendipity needs to be contrasted with more formal intellectual approaches, which are often, in my view, an illustration of reconstructed logic rather than logic in use. Theories of biography remain partial and limited in scope.

One of my major aspirations in this essay has been the presentation of ideas and people who espouse the ideas, that is, the perspectives that will "move along" the inquiries of the readers. At a minimum, if I have intrigued any of you who have never done life histories or biographies, or those of you who have never read Bowen, Clifford, or Edel, among others, to begin those journeys, this essay will have been a success.

Finally, many social scientists who worry about the relationships among inquiry, theory, and practice speak of the importance of "sensitizing concepts," "models," and "metaphors" as aids to thinking about and doing practical activity. Engaging in life-writing inquiry is, in part, a craft, an instance of practice. In my interpretation of these views, I believe an essentially pragmatic perspective arises. I believe that the stories and ideas that one creates should be useful for solving further problems in one's professional life. Autobiography is writ large, at least implicitly. Reflective practice is another of the broader and more significant conceptions. This essay on "biographical method" is intended to fall within these traditions.

Notes

1. A similar extended illustration could be drawn using the multiple life writings by and about a figure such as Virginia Woolf (1929, 1938, 1940). Bell's (1972) two-volume biography of Woolf contrasts sharply with the more recent biography by DeSalvo (1989), who accents a sexual abuse theme.

2. The Darwin illustration can be pursued further with such variants as Kohn (1985), Barrett (1977), Gruber (1981), Healey (1986), Marks (1991), Darwin and Seward (1903), F. Darwin (1909), and Barlow (1946, 1967).

3. My current views presented here are in transformation once again as I participate in a Washington University faculty seminar on "autobiography." The stimulating discussion ranges across the humanities—comparative literature, performing arts, romance languages—and occasionally the social sciences.

4. Clifford (1970) tells a similar set of fascinating stories under the heading "the vague footnote," which sent him off to Wales in the 1930s.

5. Bowen (1968, p. 11) suggests an alternative typology: narrative, topical, or essay for forming and shaping the biography. See, for example, Sarton's (1959) *I Knew a Phoenix,* which carries the subtitle *Sketches for an Autobiography.*

6. Even as this essay is being revised, my Washington University colleagues in the faculty seminar have inundated me with literally dozens (hundreds?) of references, especially from comparative literature, that I have never seen. It is a humbling experience.

7. A number of sources exist in the symbolic interactionist tradition; classically, Blumer's (1969) "Chicago school" of sociology's extension of George Herbert Mead is critical. Recently, Hargreaves (1986) has presented, especially for the educationist, a potent summary perspective with the title "Whatever Happened to Symbolic Interactionism?" Dexter's (1970) methodological book *Elite and Specialized Interviewing* is grounded in a similar view (see, e.g., p. 5).

8. The relationship of shorter biographical studies in the service of other inquiry approaches is a major intellectual and practical issue in itself. I have touched on it only briefly and in passing.

References

Allport, G. W. (1937). *Personality.* New York: Holt.

Allport, G. W. (1942). *The use of personal documents in psychological science.* New York: Social Science Research Council.

Allport, G. W. (1960). Personality: A problem for science or a problem for art? In G. W. Allport, *Personality and social encounter* (pp. 3-15). Boston: Beacon.

Allport, G. W. (1965). *Letters from Jenny.* New York: Harcourt, Brace & World.

Ashton-Warner, S. (1963). *Teacher.* New York: Simon & Schuster.

Ball, S., & Goodson, I. (Eds.). (1985). *Teachers' lives and careers.* London: Falmer.

Barlow, N. (Ed.). (1933). *Charles Darwin's diary of the voyage of the H.M.S. Beagle.* Cambridge, UK: Cambridge University Press.

Barlow, N. (Ed.). (1946). *Charles Darwin and the voyage of the Beagle.* New York: Philosophical Library.

Barlow, N. (Ed.). (1958). *The autobiography of Charles Darwin 1809-1882.* London: Collins.

Barlow, N. (Ed.). (1967). *Darwin and Henslow: The growth of an idea. Letters 1831-1860.* Berkeley: University of California Press.

Barrett, P. (Ed.). (1977). *The collected papers of Charles Darwin* (Vols. 1-2). Chicago: University of Chicago Press.

Bateson, M. C. (1990). *Composing a life.* New York: Plume/Penguin.

Becker, H. S. (1966). Introduction. In C. Shaw (Ed.), *The jack-roller: A delinquent boy's own story* (pp. v-xviii). Chicago: University of Chicago Press.

Becker, H. S. (1970). *Sociological work.* Chicago: Aldine.

Bell, Q. (1972). *Virginia Woolf: A biography* (Vols. 1-2). New York: Harcourt Brace Jovanovich.

Bertaux, D. (Ed.). (1981). *Biography and society: The life history approach in the social sciences.* Beverly Hills, CA: Sage.

Blumer, H. (1969). *Symbolic interactionism.* Englewood Cliffs, NJ: Prentice Hall.

Bowen, C. D. (1959). *Adventures of a biographer.* Boston: Little, Brown.

Bowen, C. D. (1968). *Biography: The craft and the calling.* Boston: Little, Brown.

Bowlby, J. (1990). *Charles Darwin: A new life.* New York: W. W. Norton.

Butterfield, S. (1974). *Black autobiography in America.* Amherst: University of Massachusetts Press.

Clifford, J. L. (1970). *From puzzles to portraits: Problems of a literary biographer.* Chapel Hill: University of North Carolina Press.

Cohn, M., & Kottkamp, R. (1992). *Teachers: The missing voice in education.* Albany: State University of New York Press.

Coles, R., & Coles, J. H. (1980). *Women of crisis II: Lives of work and dreams.* New York: Delacorte.

Crapanzano, V. (1980). *Tuhami: Portrait of a Moroccan.* Chicago: University of Chicago Press.

Cross, A. (1990). *The players come again.* New York: Random House.

Darwin, C. (1839). *Journal of researches into the geology and natural history of the various countries visited by H.M.S. Beagle, under the command of Captain Fitzroy, R.N., from 1832-1836.* London: Henry Colburn.

Darwin, F. (Ed.). (1888). *Life and letters of Charles Darwin* (Vols. 1-3). London: Murray.

Darwin, F. (Ed.). (1909). *The foundations of the* Origin of Species*: Two essays written in 1842 and 1844 by Charles Darwin.* Cambridge, UK: Cambridge University Press.

Darwin, F., & Seward, A. (Eds.). (1903). *More letters of Charles Darwin* (Vols. 1-2). London: J. Murray.

Denzin, N. (1989). *Interpretive biography.* Newbury Park, CA: Sage.

DeSalvo, L. (1989). *Virginia Woolf: The impact of childhood sexual abuse on her life and work.* New York: Ballantine.

Desmond, A., & Moore, J. (1991). *Darwin.* London: Michael Joseph.

Dexter, L. A. (1970). *Elite and specialized interviewing.* Evanston: Northwestern University Press.

Eakin, P. J. (1989). Foreword. In P. Lejeune, *On autobiography* (pp. vii-xxviii). Minneapolis: University of Minnesota Press.

Edel, L. (1979). The figure under the carpet. In M. Pachter (Ed.), *Telling lives: The biographer's art* (pp. 16-34). Washington, DC: New Republic Books.

Edel, L. (1984). *Writing lives: Principia biographica.* New York: W. W. Norton.

Elliott, J. (1991). *Action research for educational change.* Milton Keynes, UK: Open University Press.

Erikson, E. H. (1963). *Childhood and society* (2nd ed.). New York: W. W. Norton.

Erikson, E. H. (1962). *Young man Luther: A study in psychoanalysis and history.* New York: W. W. Norton.

FitzRoy, R. (1839). *Proceedings of the second expedition, 1831-1836.* London: Henry Colburn.

Garraty, J. (1954). The interrelations of psychology and biography. *Psychological Bulletin, 51,* 569-582.

Garraty, J. (1957). *The nature of biography.* New York: Alfred A. Knopf.

Geertz, C. (1973). *The interpretation of cultures: Selected essays.* New York: Basic Books.

Geertz, C. (1988). *Works and lives: The anthropologist as author.* Stanford, CA: Stanford University Press.

Goodson, I. (Ed.). (1992). *Studying teachers' lives.* London: Routledge.

Gruber, H. E. (1981). *Darwin on man: A psychological study of scientific creativity* (2nd ed.). Chicago: University of Chicago Press.

Gruenberg, S., & Krech, H. (1952). *The many lives of modern woman.* Garden City, NY: Doubleday.

Gusdorf, G. (1980). Conditions and limits of autobiography. In J. Olney (Ed.), *Autobiography: Essays theoretical and critical* (pp. 28-48). Princeton, NJ: Princeton University Press.

Hargreaves, D. (1986). Whatever happened to symbolic interactionism? In M. Hammersley (Ed.), *Controversies in classroom research.* Milton Keynes, UK: Open University Press.

Healey, E. (1986). *Wives of fame: Mary Livingstone, Jenny Marx, Emma Darwin.* London: New English Library, Hodder & Stoughton.

Heilbrun, C. (1981). Introduction. In V. Brittain, *Testament of a friendship* (pp. xv-xxxii). New York: Wideview.

Heilbrun, C. (1988). *Writing a woman's life.* New York: W. W. Norton.

Hentoff, N. (1966). *Our children are dying.* New York: Viking.

Hernden, J. (1966). *The way its spozed to be.* New York: Bantam.

Hernden, J. (1971). *How to survive in your native land.* New York: Bantam.

Hexter, J. (1971). *The history primer.* New York: Basic Books.

Hiley, M. (1979). *Victorian working women: Portraits from life.* London: Gordon Fraser.

Holt, J. (1964). *How children fail.* New York: Pitman.

Horner, M. S. (1987). The Radcliffe Biography Series. In R. Coles (Ed.), *Simone Weil: A modern pilgrimage* (pp. ix-x). Reading, MA: Addison-Wesley.

Hudson, D. (1972). *Munby: Man of two worlds.* London: Murray.

Hudson, L. (1966). *Contrary imaginations: A psychological study of the English schoolboy.* Harmondsworth: Penguin.

Hudson, L. (1972). *The cult of the fact.* London: Jonathan Cape.

Kluckhohn, C. (1949). *Mirror for man: The relation of anthropology to modern life.* New York: McGraw-Hill.

Kluckhohn, C., & Murray, H. A. (1953). *Personality in nature, society, and culture.* New York: Alfred A. Knopf.

Kohn, D. (Ed.). (1985). *The Darwin heritage.* Princeton, NJ: Princeton University Press.

Lancey, D. (1993). *Qualitative research in education.* New York: Longman.

Langness, L. L. (1965). *The life history in anthropological science.* New York: Holt, Rinehart & Winston.

Langness, L. L., & Frank, G. (1981). *Lives: An anthropological approach to biography.* Novato, CA: Chandler & Sharp.

Lejeune, P. (1989). *On autobiography.* Minneapolis: University of Minnesota Press.

Levinson, D., with Darrow, C. N., Klein, E. B., Levinson, M. H., & McKee, B. (1978). *The seasons of a man's life.* New York: Alfred A. Knopf.

Lewis, O. (1951). *Life in a Mexican village: Tepoztlan restudied.* Urbana: University of Illinois Press.

Lewis, O. (1959). *Five families.* New York: Basic Books.

Lewis, O. (1961). *The children of Sanchez.* New York: Random House.

Malinowski, B. (1922). *Argonauts of the western Pacific.* London: Routledge & Kegan Paul.

Marks, R. (1991). *Three men of the Beagle.* New York: Alfred A. Knopf.

McAdams, D., & Ochberg, R. (Eds.). (1980). *Psychobiography and life narratives.* Durham, NC: Duke University Press.

McCullough, D. (1992). *Truman.* New York: Simon & Schuster.

Mills, C. W. (1959). *The sociological imagination.* London: Oxford University Press.

Moody, A. (1968). *Coming of age in Mississippi.* New York: Dell.

Murray, H. A., et al. (1938). *Explorations in personality: A clinical and experimental study of fifty men of college age.* New York: Oxford University Press.

Neill, A. S. (1960). *Summerhill: A radical approach to child rearing.* New York: Hart.

Neill, A. S. (1975). *The dominie books of A. S. Neill: A dominie's log; A dominie in doubt; A dominie dismissed.* New York: Hart.

Olney, J. (Ed.). (1980). *Autobiography: Essays theoretical and critical.* Princeton, NJ: Princeton University Press.

Personal Narratives Group. (1989). *Interpreting women's lives: Feminist theory and personal narratives.* Bloomington: Indiana University Press.

Pritchett, V. S. (1977). *On autobiography.* London: English Association.

Rabinow, P. (1977). *Reflections on fieldwork in Morocco.* Berkeley: University of California Press.

Raverat, G. (1952). *Period piece: A Cambridge childhood.* London: Faber & Faber.

Redfield, R. (1930). *Tepoztlan: A Mexican village.* Chicago: University of Chicago Press.

Redfield, R. (1955). *The little community.* Chicago: University of Chicago Press.

Rogers, P. (1980). Introduction. In J. Boswell, *Life of Johnson* (pp. v-xxxvi). Oxford: Oxford University Press.

Runyan, W. (1982). *Life histories and psychobiography.* New York: Oxford University Press.

Runyan, W. (Ed.). (1988). *Psychology and historical interpretation.* New York: Oxford University Press.

Sarton, M. (1959). *I knew a phoenix: Sketches for an autobiography.* New York: W. W. Norton.

Sarton, M. (1968). *Plant dreaming deep.* New York: W. W. Norton.

Sarton, M. (1973). *Journal of a solitude.* New York: W. W. Norton.

Schön, D. (1983). *The reflective practitioner: How professionals think in action.* New York: Basic Books.

Schön, D. (1987). *Educating the reflective practitioner: Toward a new design for teaching and learning in the professions.* San Francisco: Jossey-Bass.

Shaw, C. (1930). *The jack-roller: A delinquent boy's own story.* Chicago: University of Chicago Press.

Skinner, B. F. (1977). *Particulars of my life.* New York: Alfred A. Knopf.

Skinner, B. F. (1979). *The shaping of a behaviorist: Part two of an autobiography.* New York: Alfred A. Knopf.

Skinner, B. F. (1983). *A matter of consequences: Part three of an autobiography.* New York: Alfred A. Knopf.

Smith, L. M. (1987). The voyage of the *Beagle*: Fieldwork lessons from Charles Darwin. *Educational Administration Quarterly, 23,* 5-30.

Smith, L. M. (1990). One road to historical inquiry: Extending one's repertory of qualitative methods. In W. Eaton (Ed.), *History, politics, and methodology in American education: Collected essays* (pp. 79-109). New York: Teachers College Press.

Smith, L. M. (1992). *Doing ethnographic biography: A reflective practitioner at work during a spring in Cambridge.* Manuscript submitted for publication.

Smith, L. M. (in press). *Nora Barlow and the Darwin legacy.* Ames: Iowa State University Press.

Smith, L. M., Dwyer, D. C., Prunty, J. J., & Kleine, P. F. (1988). *Innovation and change in schooling: History, politics, and agency.* London: Falmer.

Smith, L. M., & Geoffrey, W. (1968). *The complexities of an urban classroom.* New York: Holt, Rinehart & Winston.

Smith, L. M., Kleine, P. F., Prunty, J. J., & Dwyer, D. C. (1986). *Educational innovators: Then and now.* London: Falmer.

Smith, L. M., Prunty, J. J., Dwyer, D. C., & Kleine, P. F. (1987). *The fate of an innovative school: The history and present status of the Kensington School.* London: Falmer.

Smith, L. M., & Wells, W. (1990). *"Difficult to reach, maintain, and help" urban families in PAT: Issues, dilemmas, strategies, and resolutions in parent education* (Final report to the Smith-Richardson Foundation). St. Louis, MO: Washington University.

Stanley, L. (Ed.). (1984). *The diaries of Hannah Cullwick, Victorian maidservant.* New Brunswick, NJ: Rutgers University Press.

Stanley, L. (Ed.). (1992). *The autobiographical I: The theory and practice of feminist auto/biography.* Manchester, UK: Manchester University Press.

Stone, L. (1981). *The past and the present.* Boston: Routledge & Kegan Paul.

Strachey, L. (1918). *Eminent Victorians.* New York: Harcourt, Brace.

Terkel, S. (1970). *Hard times: An oral history of the Great Depression.* New York: Avon.

Terkel, S. (1972). *Working.* New York: Avon.

Trevelyan, G. M. (1932). Preface. In G. O. Trevelyan, *The life and letters of Lord Macaulay* (pp. v-vii). London: Oxford University Press.

Valentine, C. (1968). *Culture and poverty: Critique and counterproposals.* Chicago: University of Chicago Press.

Waller, W. (1932). *The sociology of teaching.* New York: John Wiley.

White, R. W. (1952). *Lives in progress.* New York: Dryden.

Woolf, V. (1929). *A room of one's own.* New York: Harcourt, Brace.

Woolf, V. (1938). *Three guineas.* New York: Harcourt, Brace.

Woolf, V. (1940). *Roger Fry: A biography.* New York: Harcourt, Brace.

Woolf, V. (1960). *Granite and rainbow.* London: Hogarth. (Original work published 1927)

19

■

Historical Social Science

Methodologies, Methods, and Meanings

GAYE TUCHMAN

ONE question logically precedes any advice about the use of historical methods in social science research: What do social scientists mean by *historical research*? Articles distinguishing between historical sociology and sociological history tend to develop ideal-typical portraits of each endeavor.[1] Rather than presenting ideal types, this essay will unfold as much qualitative research does—by inference. Nonetheless, this essay has an implicit theme: Whether done by social scientists or by historians, historical work requires a point of view. A point of view necessarily includes an interpretive framework that implicitly contains some notion of the "meaning of history."

The theoretical use of historical data also implies a methodology. I do not use the term *methodology* in its current sense of "application of a specific method," such as analysis of documents or participant observation. Rather, I use *methodology* in its classic sense: the study of the epistemological assumptions implicit in specific methods. I thus assume that a methodology includes a way of looking at phenomena that specifies how a method "captures" the "object" of study.

I have placed the terms *captures* and *object* in quotation marks in the preceding statement because they are problematic. Not all methodologies imply that the researcher should "capture" the "object" of study. Feminist methodologies oppose these terms, because they imply that a researcher is trying to dominate the phenomenon under consideration (see Keller, 1985). Other chapters in this volume review some of the implications of current methodologies. This essay necessarily adopts a methodology; to wit, adequate social science includes a theoretical use of historical information. Any social phenomenon must be understood in its historical context. To grasp historical information, one must have a point of view, including an interpretive framework that includes some notion of the "meaning" of history.

However, just as the nature of social science is widely debated, so too what history "means" is problematic. Indeed, that "meaning" is precisely what historians debate. Sometimes they debate the relevance of theories shared with the social sciences: Does a Marxist or a Weberian interpretation of a specific phenomenon best capture its "essence"? How, if at all, is geography central to grasping the development of specific regions, such as the development of the Mediterranean area (Braudel, 1972)? Which social group should historians study and why: elites, the poor, intellectuals? What are the consequences of studying which

AUTHOR'S NOTE: I am grateful to librarian Scott Kennedy for showing me how to locate research tools in a computerized library. I profited from readings of a very early draft by Douglas Heckathorn and Myra Marx Ferree, and Norman Denzin and Yvonna Lincoln provided marvelous suggestions for improving subsequent drafts.

group? What picture of the past does the historian create by her or his choice?[2] Sometimes historians debate periodization, or how the division of history into periods influences generalizations (Kelly, 1977). Sometimes they debate the nature of historical narratives: Is there a "grand narrative" that can tell the story of, say, European development? Can the history of other continents (or minority peoples) be incorporated in a grand narrative? Or even, Is the historian's task the development of a grand narrative (Coontz, 1992; Himmelfarb, 1987)?

There are no simple answers to questions about the "meaning of history," just as there are no ready answers to the "meaning" of social science or—to draw an admittedly foolish comparison—to the meaning of life. Given that I do not believe there are a series of correct answers, I will ask such questions as the following: How have empirically minded sociologists grappled with distinctions between the historical and sociological enterprises? How has historical information figured in social science classics? Within the past few decades, how have historians seemingly modified the nature of the historical enterprise? How are those modifications relevant to social scientific research?

Defining Social Science as Different From History

To establish their legitimacy, early American sociologists tried to identify how their field differed from more traditional fields of study. In 1921, Robert Park and Ernest Burgess reflected on the nature of history and sociology. Both, they wrote, "are concerned with man as a person, as a 'political animal,' participating with his fellows in a common fund of social traditions and cultural ideals" (p. 10). According to these early qualitative American sociologists:

> History . . . seeks to reproduce and interpret concrete events as they actually occurred in time and space. Sociology . . . seeks to arrive at natural laws and generalizations in regard to human nature and society, irrespective of time and place. . . . History seeks to find out what actually happened and how it all came about. Sociology . . . seeks to explain, on the basis of a study of other instances, the nature of the process involved. (p. 11)

However, today many European and North American historians and sociologists reject Park and Burgess's formulation. Since the publication of Park and Burgess's classic *Introduction to the Science of Sociology* (1921), historians have increasingly "compared instances" and have frequently adopted quantitative methods to do so. Sociologists have come to recognize that the great nineteenth-century European sociologists, now canonized as classic theorists, were not writing theory that "reject[s] the application of theoretical statement to the empirical world, declaring empirical evidence to be irrelevant for . . . theorizing" (Scheuch, 1992, p. 769). Rather, they were writing "theory of . . . "—theory relevant to empirical issues. Their questions were as broad as, What is the meaning of capitalism for contemporary societies? To glean answers, they had to "do history." To address the historical processes relevant to their questions, they examined cross-national data. Some of these data were quantitative.

Classical Theory and Historical Data

I will discuss the canonized work of Karl Marx and Max Weber as prototypical examples because their work has been so central to social science. Because books by these men are often assigned in undergraduate and graduate courses, my discussion assumes that the reader has passing familiarity with these classic texts. In each of the texts considered, historical knowledge is essential to interpretation of the argument. To read the works of Marx and Weber, one must also understand how nineteenth-century historians interpreted the past.

Marx

To understand Marx and Engels's "political pamphlet" *The Communist Manifesto,* one must understand the social relationships and processes associated with feudalism, including both the interdependence of the church and state and the economic interdependence of families. Otherwise it seems incomprehensible that more serfs did not flee the land. Similarly, unless one knows of the existence of dress codes in medieval cities (not discussed in Marx), one cannot comprehend the failure of many urban servants to flee their masters.

I chose these two examples because of an incident in one of my classes: A Kenyan graduate student had not realized the full impact of feudalism as a system of peonage that forced serfs to give a large share of their agricultural produce to the feudal aristocracy, supported extensive landholdings of the church, which also bound serfs to their land, and encouraged familial ties between the aristocracy and the church hierarchy. When this student grasped how severe the oppression of serfs had been, he could not understand why they did not flee. Having little appreciation of the flora available in, say, France, he supposed fleeing serfs could find food and shelter in forests in winter and could freely kill animals without fear of laws against poaching. The Kenyan student accepted the assurance of a French student that one could not easily survive in many European forests. But then the Kenyan faced another problem: He supposed that serfs in one region would gladly take in a fleeing refugee. He did not appreciate the degree of interdependence among serfs—how in traditional European societies an individual could not hope to survive outside of the local collectivity because these traditional societies did not embrace strangers. (This "mechanical solidarity," to use Durkheim's phrase, is captured by the very term *outlaw,* a person sentenced to be "out"side of the protective "law" for a year, a fate that endangered survival.) Lacking this historical background, the student could not comprehend why Marx discussed the dire exploitation afflicting the early nineteenth-century proletariat as "progress" over medieval oppression. In sum, without the appropriate historical background, the Kenyan found the argument of the *Communist Manifesto* difficult to grasp.

Weber

Some appreciation of past realities is also necessary to grasp the thrust of Max Weber's classic *The Protestant Ethic and the Spirit of Capitalism* (1904-1905/1976): Early modern European capitalism was different in kind than earlier forms of capitalism, and its character was influenced by ideas associated with Protestantism, as well as by other factors. I start with a minor example, Weber's footnote 8. It concerns the association between religion and education and is part of Weber's attempt to argue against objections to his historical interpretation. The footnote includes the table reproduced here as Table 19.1. It also includes a translator's note, for translator Talcott Parsons felt he had to provide definitions of terms in the table for the data to be meaningful.

The passage in the text reads: "It may be, as has been claimed, that the greater participation of Protestants in the positions of ownership and management in modern economic life may to-day be understood, in part at least, simply as a result of the greater material wealth they have inherited. But there are other phenomena which cannot be explained in the same way" (p. 37). Next comes Weber's example: the association between religion and the percentage of students and graduates of higher-education institutions relative to the proportion of individuals of specified religions in the population of Baden. The paragraph ends:

TABLE 19.1 The Association Between Education and Religion

	Protestant (%)	*Catholic* (%)	*Jews* (%)
Gymnasium	43	46	9.5
Realgymnasium	69	31	9
Oberrealschulen	52	41	7
Realschulen	49	40	11
Höhere Bürgerschulen	51	37	12
Average	48	42	10
Percentage in population	37	61.3	1.5

SOURCE: Weber (1904-1905/1976, pp. 188-189); last line added from the text of Weber's footnote 8.
NOTE: All rows do not add to 100%.

> But among the Catholic graduates themselves the percentage of those graduating from the institutions preparing, in particular, for technical studies and industrial and commercial occupations, but in general from those preparing for middle-class business-life, lags still farther behind the percentage of Protestants. On the other hand, Catholics prefer the sort of training which the humanistic Gymnasium affords. That is a circumstance to which the above explanation does not apply, but which, on the contrary is one reason why so few Catholics are engaged in capitalistic enterprise. (p. 38)

Footnote 8 (pp. 188-189) presents the percentage of Protestants, Catholics, and Jews in Baden in 1895 and what percentage of each of five types of schools was composed of Protestants, Catholics, and Jews. Parsons's translator's note then explains, "In the *Gymnasium* the main emphasis is on the classics. In the *Realgymnasium* Greek is dropped and Latin is reduced in favour of modern languages, mathematics and science. The *Realschule* and *Oberrealschule* are similar to the latter except that Latin is dropped entirely in favour of modern languages." I have added a line to the table; it gives the percentage of each religious group in the population of Baden in 1895.

Parsons has not told the reader what was taught in the *Höhere Bürgerschulen,* higher city schools, nor why Jews are so overrepresented in these schools. But, for now, merely note that Parsons recognized that the meaning of the table—its relevance to the text—is incomprehensible if one does not know what each school taught. (Later I will use this table to discuss the relevance of chasing down byways to interpret the frame of an argument.)[3]

Although the data in the previous example concern education and religion at roughly the time Weber was writing *The Protestant Ethic and the*

Spirit of Capitalism (1904-1905/1976) today commentators agree that Weber used historical data to rebut Herbert Spenser and Karl Marx, even as he offered his own "theory of" the development of capitalism. Though Weber does not provide direct citation to Spenser and Marx, his language is redolent of theirs. For instance:

> Thus the capitalism of to-day, which has come to dominate economic life, educates and selects the economic subjects which it needs through a process of economic survival of the fittest. But here one can easily see the limits of the concept of selection as a means of historical explanation. In order that a manner of life so well adapted to the peculiarities of capitalism could be selected at all, i.e. should come to dominate others, it had to originate somewhere, and not in isolated individuals alone, but as a way of life common to whole groups of men. This origin is what needs explanation. (p. 55)

Weber continues, "Concerning the doctrine of the more naive historical materialism, that such ideas originate as a reflection or superstructure of economic situations, we shall speak of more in detail below. At this point it will suffice for our purposes to call attention to the fact that without doubt . . . the spirit of capitalism . . . was present before the capitalistic order" (p. 55).[4]

To go beyond the argument over antecedents (and so causality), one must have some historical sophistication. Pertinent questions include the following: How did capitalism change from its mercantile beginnings? Was the process of change "uniform" across various countries? Without being able to assess how and why Weber disagreed with Spenser and Marx, one may suspect that Weber is merely offering a refutation to earlier theories. But, although in *Protestant Ethic* Weber seems to feel that historical materialism is naive, his conclusion—that "the cloak of [Protestant] ascetic rationalism" had developed into an "iron cage"—is as bitter a condemnation of the social organization of advanced capitalism as anything Marx wrote. And Weber is certainly more pessimistic about attempts to ameliorate capitalism than is Marx. Historical knowledge—some grasp of the differences between English capitalism in the 1840s and German capitalism at the turn of the century—helps one to interpret Weber's attitude, although aspects of his biography are germane as well. By the beginning of the twentieth century, the advent of bureaucratic organization, emerging management techniques, and the ability of capitalism to withstand revolutionary attack in Western societies made it clear that capitalism was not about to dissolve.

Historical knowledge is also necessary if one is to interpret what Weber identifies as the nub of his argument. Toward the end of a four-page footnote, Weber writes:

> The essential point of the difference is . . . that an ethic based on religion places certain psychological sanctions (not of an economic character) on the maintenance of the attitude prescribed by it, sanctions which, so long as the religious belief remains alive, are highly effective, and which mere worldly wisdom . . . does not have at its disposal. Only in so far as these sanctions work, and above all, in the direction in which they work, which is *often different from the doctrine of the theologians*, does such an ethic gain an independent influence on the *conduct of life* and thus on the economic order. This is, to speak frankly, the point of this whole essay, which I had not expected to find so completely overlooked. (p. 197; emphasis added)

Although Weber seems determined to make his intent clear, this footnote still permits conflicting interrogations. Each scrutiny is truly a "cross"-examination, for each implies a different interpretation of past practices (and so a different interpretation of the text) and simultaneously a different interpretation of the text (and so a different interpretation of past practices). Does Weber offer a social psychological interpretation of capitalism, as the functionalists taught? Is the essence of this argument that the spirit of capitalism arose from the psychological loneliness experienced by Protestants who yearned for assurance that they belonged to God's Elect? Does it arise from the social organization of Protestant life, exemplified by the New England Puritans? Is Weber engaging in a cultural analysis based in a humanistic sociology of knowledge[5] that stresses daily practice? Is Weber most interested in how a phenomenon—the spirit of capitalism—became transformed over time?

I do not wish to offer my own interpretation of Weber's classic, or to delve into historians' refutations of Weber. (Those refutations concern the validity of Weber's evidence.) Rather, I note that the theoretical use of historical data implies methodological issues. The term *methodological* affirms the late nineteenth-century German insight that any empirical study, including any historical study, requires an interpretive approach—a philosophy of method, an epistemology—that guides the identification of appropriate data. Given that it is clear that Weber's use of specific historical data was intentional, one must ask of Weber much the same questions one would ask of any essay or monograph: Why these data? Why does the argument of *The Protestant Ethic and the Spirit of Capitalism* turn on Benjamin Franklin's maxims, Puritan daily practices, and, less heavily, theology?

In sum, Marx and Weber wrote as though one must come to grips with historical realities to explore the *meaning* of contemporary practices and processes. To interpret their theoretical work, one must appreciate what they took for granted as characteristic of *their* time *and* their interpretations of the past. For instance, Weber's refutation of Marx draws on the late nineteenth- and early twentieth-century assumption that Marx's writings were crude, unidimensional materialism. But both these classic theorists realized that contemporary practices are historically embedded. To use today's theoretical concepts: Social meanings are recursive (Giddens, 1984). The past continues to speak to the present. All that we take for granted as "natural" is a product of both historical and contemporary processes. Our task as social scientists is to interpret those multifaceted meanings, including their interactions with one another.[6] How to choose a point of view that serves as an interpretive frame is quite another matter.

Contemporary Cliometrics and Point of View

As do other academic specialists, historians argue about the point of view appropriate to their research. For the past 20 years, they have argued about whether what we call history—the story of people and societies across time—concerns the perceptions and activities of elites or of "ordinary" folk (social history). To some extent, the research practices of different types of historians have involved different sorts of data. For instance, in the 1970s social historians saw themselves as young Turks battling against more traditional historians, whom they accused of an atheoretical acceptance of the version of events promulgated by members of the elites whose activities the more traditional historians studied. The social historians wanted to demonstrate that those past elites (and so present historians) had misinterpreted "concrete events as they actually occurred in time and space" (Park & Burgess, 1921, p. 11). And so many social historians turned to statistics (named *cliometrics* to honor Clio, the ancient Greek muse of history).

Cliometrics can be used to study any phenomenon for which there are reliable and valid data.[7] Such data may concern the wages of factory workers, patterns of literacy, or the education of elites. I offer two examples of cliometrics. The first juxtaposes two views of the participation of women in the English labor force during the Industrial Revolution. One is a statement made in 1838 by a member of the British Parliament; the other, a summary of tables about the distribution of women and men in the paid labor force in Great Britain (in 1851) and France (in 1866). The second case involves the literary activities of the middle and upper classes.

Example 1: The Participation of Women in the Nineteenth-Century Workforce

The member of Parliament expressed "one of the enduring images of industrialization, created by contemporaries and transmitted by historians"—"the female factory worker" as "prototype of the wage-earning woman . . . a young 'mill girl' or a married 'operative,' turned from her family by the need to earn wages" (Tilly & Scott, 1978, p. 63). His words:

> Amongst other things I saw a cotton mill—a sight that froze my blood. The place was full of women, young, all of them, some large with child, and obliged to stand twelve hours each day. . . . The heat was excessive in some of the rooms, the stink pestiferous, and in all an atmosphere of cotton flue. I nearly fainted. The young women were all pale, sallow, thin, yet generally fairly grown, all with bare feet—a strange sight to English eyes. (quoted in Tilly & Scott, 1978, p. 64)

Interpreting quantitative data, Tilly and Scott (1978) announce that this depiction is misleading:

> Industrialization did mean that many more women had to help their families earn wages. Instead of contributing their labor to household production, they had to sell their labor power and bring in cash. Textile factories did create jobs for women. But these factories were neither the only nor the predominant form of female wage-earning activity during the nineteenth century in England. . . . *The impact of industrialization on women's employment was more varied and far less dramatic than the standard image of the mill girl implies.* (p. 64; emphasis added)

Their reasoning continues, although England and France had quite different economies in the nineteenth century, "in both countries, women tended to be concentrated in unmechanized, 'traditional' sectors of the economy, except for the textile industry. The mechanized textile industry's growth in these countries marked the entry of women into wage labor in factory settings. Nevertheless it was only part of the picture."

Tilly and Scott then use the language of statistics: "In the economy outside of textiles, the smaller the scale of organization, the larger the size of the female work force" (p. 68). Even in the more industrialized England, most women workers were not in manufacturing: "Overall, textile workers represented 22 percent of the female labor force. In contrast, domestic service claimed 40 percent"

(p. 68). Thus "*domestic service was the typical form of female employment outside of agriculture before industrialization. In England, it apparently expanded as an occupation as the country industrialized*" (p. 68). Tilly and Scott's cliometrics rebut past understandings of the role of women in industrialization as surely as Weber intended his analysis of a cultural phenomenon—the spirit of Protestantism—to rebut what he understood to be "crude historical materialism."

But Tilly and Scott's cliometrics cannot refute aspects of standard historical interpretations: The elite clearly identified female employment with the textile industry, and elites behaved as though their interpretation were accurate. Their interpretation had consequences; to paraphrase W. I. Thomas's classic insight: If people believe that a phenomenon is real, it is real in its consequences. By debating women's employment *as though* work in the textile industry were ideal-typical, the early nineteenth-century British elite constructed and acted on a version of reality that did not correspond to the conditions of working-class women.

Thus Tilly and Scott's cliometrics raise two different issues. One may be phrased as a research question: How did elites' "fictive" definition of the situation affect their actions and so influence the life conditions experienced by nineteenth-century British working-class women? The other related issue is more philosophical: How does the deconstruction of the past influence one's story of the past? Tilly and Scott proclaim that historians have misinterpreted the situation of working women. They present what they believe to be the "true" story. Can this "true" story be accepted at face value, or do the conflicting stories present a more complex task? Again, I phrase the relevant issues as questions: How are we to adjudicate between the two stories as constructions of historians? Can we hope to achieve some adjudication without coming to grips with the sociohistorical meanings of power? In my use, the phrase *sociohistorical meanings of power* has several referents: (a) nineteenth-century interpretations and contestation of power between the elite and the working class and, within social classes, between women and men; and (b) differential distributions of professional power among twentieth-century historians, who contest the quality of one another's scholarship and so credibility and who also contest the "proper" subjects of historical scholarship.

The contrast between social history and what I have termed *traditional history* raises other issues as well, namely, the *reliability* of informants and the discernment of *patterns*. Presumably, the member of Parliament quoted above commented on characteristics of female factory workers after he had toured many factories. He could claim to be what a participant observer might call a "reliable informant" about women operatives and about factory conditions, but *not* about the pattern of women's employment. To be a reliable informant about the general pattern (in this case, the distribution of women workers), he would have had to have noticed a phenomenon he appears to have taken for granted: the pervasiveness of women domestics in upper-middle-class homes, including presumably his own. We can assume that the M.P. took this form of employment for granted because it was so fundamental to Victorian life—so beyond notice. I infer from such novels as Mrs. Gaskell's *Cranford* and George Eliot's *Middlemarch* that one can classify a family's economic status by the number and kind of servants it employed.[8] Thus I conclude that the M.P.'s observations are reliable about some things, but not others: A highly placed government official was in a position to report about phenomena in which he participated. We might trust his reflections, including his description of patterns, if we felt he was an astute observer whose impartiality or biases we could independently assess. But simultaneously we must also realize that *often people cannot see patterns, precisely because those patterns are so central to their lives that they take the patterns for granted.*

Cliometrics can provide information about historical patterns that may not have been obvious (or even discernible) to people living when those patterns existed. If one accepts the positivist assumption that information can be accurately transformed into quantitative data, and if one accepts the reliability of the sources from which Tilly and Scott gleaned these data, then one can accept as "accurate" the patterns they present. But patterns are just that: *merely patterns.* Attributing *meaning* to patterns is quite another matter. Sometimes one can discern meanings—or make historical generalizations—only with the help of a knowledgeable informant, a historical figure who has been in a position to gather reliable information. Let me be more concrete.

Example 2: The Literary Activity of Victorian Women

When starting the research that became *Edging Women Out: Victorian Novelists, Publishers, and Social Change* (Tuchman with Fortin, 1989), I had a simple hypothesis: When the British novel was a relatively unimportant genre, women wrote it; as, for a variety of reasons, the novel became more important, men redefined it as "high culture" and as an enterprise best undertaken by males. The methods appropriate to test this hypothesis included development of quantified data that could be analyzed statistically.[9] After reading literary histories to determine periodization,

Nina Fortin and I found the hypothesized patterns concerning the acceptance or rejection of fiction and nonfiction manuscripts submitted to Macmillan and Company (London) from November 1866 through December 1917. But we needed reliable informants to attribute *meaning*. Our "informants" were nineteenth-century writers whom we needed to interview retrospectively.

We needed to learn whether "informants"—the "referees" who had served as editorial consultants and analyzed the merits of submissions—were reliable.[10] We had to know not merely what they had said about which manuscript (available through archives), but what they had published, how their own work had been received, and how their contemporaries had assessed their literary and editorial competence. We had to learn whether the reports written by Macmillan's editorial consultants used the same criteria and were penned in the same style as reports submitted to other publishing houses. We also had to know the historical context, including information about the production and distribution of Victorian books over time, economic factors influencing sales, shifts in the business cycle, and shifts in literary tastes among both the elite and what literary critics have called "the common reader." Such information enabled us to flesh out our description of three periods.

The following fleshed-out interpretation is still rather bare: Until roughly 1840, most British novelists were women. Then, as women novelists in England and on the Continent achieved both glory and, in some instances, considerable income, some men realized that writing novels might bring them fame and fortune. Nonetheless, through roughly 1880, women were more likely than men to submit fiction manuscripts to Macmillan. Women were also more likely than men to have their novels accepted—although Macmillan's editorial consultants often denigrated rejected women's fiction, whereas they identified the rejected novels of men as the work of youth.

From roughly 1880 through 1900, both male critics and their female compatriots who had accepted male standards as universal standards worked to define the realistic novel as the high-culture novel. At Macmillan and Company, fiction submissions grew significantly relative to submissions of nonfiction. Submissions by men account for this increase. They were at least as likely to be accepted as those of women. And Macmillan's editorial consultants identified rejected novels by women as "old-fashioned romances," noted that the talented women novelists of the 1840s had virtually disappeared, and continued to find masculine virtues in the rejected novels of men.

At the beginning of the twentieth century, the situation shifted once again. In part because of changes in the system used to distribute the novel, mainly the collapse of the hegemony previously enjoyed by Charles Mudie's Select (Circulating) Library, in part because of the new vogue for theater, in part because of the strictures the Great War placed on both women and men, fiction submissions to Macmillan decreased—both in raw numbers and relative to nonfiction. Nonetheless, men's hegemony over the esteemed novel had been institutionalized: although through 1917 women submitted more fiction than did men, novels by men were more likely to be accepted than were those proffered by women. At Macmillan, an elite Victorian publishing house—still celebrated as one of the seven major fiction houses of the Victorian era—men had edged women out.

But even though Macmillan's editorial consultants were lauded "English *Men* of Letters," questions remained. Were the rejected manuscripts any good? Were their authors serious writers or ninnies? We would have liked to use qualitative data: to read accepted and rejected manuscripts. Often it is more difficult to discern patterns in qualitative than in quantitative data, but qualitative data are richer: They are more likely to be meaning-ful(l)—more likely to let a researcher see *how* a social world seemed and felt to a variety of its members. They are more likely to reveal process. Some scientists believe that the key scientific question is *how,* not *why.* For instance, evolutionary biologists believe that *why* tends to devolve into a search for origins, whereas *how* enables comments about process. Unfortunately, we could not locate qualitative data and had to make do with such quantitative data as the reconstructed publishing careers of rejected male and female authors. These data enabled us to infer that men did not edge women out of the occupation of novelist. They edged women out of being high-culture novelists.

Such statements provide only a preliminary grounding of observed patterns in historical reality. They cannot tell what it meant to be a male or female novelist in Victorian England: what it felt like, how women novelists were treated, how their works were read. I cannot provide here the historical context we used to place these issues in the context of a changing literature system. But one idea does bear repetition: Without a historical context, even quantitative patterns are meaningless.

Another idea is implicit in this summary of the process of doing this research. It bears formal introduction: *In historical research, as in all other kinds of research, the data to be used depend upon the question the researcher wishes to answer and the information the researcher can find to answer the question.* Let me return to the classics. Weber made it clear that he examined Benjamin Franklin's aphorisms because (a) he wanted to look at the "*ethos*" of capitalism as it appeared in daily life; (b) others had identified those aphorisms as "the supposed confession of faith of the

Yankee," a creature who seemed to be the apotheosis of bourgeois capitalism; and (c) Western capitalism differs from the "greed of the Chinese Mandarin, the old Roman aristocrat, or the modern peasant" (p. 56)—all of whom cared about money. Weber's question about the origin of capitalism, including his desire to develop a multicausal argument, required him to establish the historical antecedents of conceptual artifacts—"ideal types"—across societies with different economies and cultures. He wished, among other things, to establish differences in kind. So, too, Marx and Engels had to demonstrate differences in kind—the feudal modes of production versus the capitalist mode of production; the feudal class system versus the capitalism class system; oppression versus exploitation—to posit "laws" or patterns of historical development.[11]

The problem, of course, is that to understand one's question one needs some background in the relevant historical period. Unfortunately, most American-educated researchers do *not* have historical knowledge at hand. American academic training has taken place in a national culture firmly dominated by "anti-intellectualism, pragmatism, materialism, [and] populism" (Lamont & Wuthnow, 1990, p. 302), so that the American social sciences tend to be "ahistorical, pragmatic, and scientistic" (see Wolff, 1981, on American studies of culture), as is also true of most American sociology. Furthermore, the American intellectual tradition tends to define power more narrowly than does its European counterparts (Lamont & Wuthnow, 1990, p. 298), who view power in a historical scope. For instance, British considerations of power relations (in media, including advertising) "can be read as refining Marx and Engels' dominant ideology thesis which centers on the role of ideology in cementing relations of domination by camouflaging exploitation and differences in class interest" (Lamont & Wuthnow, 1990, p. 298).

History as the Story of Lived Experience

But how are Americans to gain the required historical sophistication? One answer is that social scientists need to grasp (a) that history is more than the passage of events whose sequence may be memorized and (b) that the past has continuing relevance for the present.[12] Most simply, we all live history, and not merely in the grand sense of wars, recessions, and political transformation. Rather, we live out the assumptions of our *époque* in the most mundane aspects of our daily lives. Sometimes we are conscious of how our activities articulate with our times: When the member of Parliament reported his horror of the experiences of mill girls, he was doing so for a reason—presumably to eradicate this evil. Why else could he have spoken as he did in this public forum? Sometimes, we are not conscious of how history pervades our activities. What Raymond Williams (1977) has called the "structure of feeling" of an era guides the minutiae of everyday life. But we often take for granted that structure of feeling.

Gravestones provide a good example of how history is a living story that speaks both the tension between past and present and an era's structure of feelings. When a family member tells a stone carver what to inscribe on the tombstone of a relative, the words chosen are meaningful.[13] They express groups norms about the information and sentiments appropriate for a tombstone, such as how to sum up a life and the attitude to be taken toward death.[14] A late eighteenth-century tombstone inside a church in lower Manhattan bears the following description of a man who died in his mid-20s: "He lived a useful life." Similar sentiments do not grace Victorian gravestones. These "remember" the deceased with "love." The contrast between the gravestones of the two periods bespeaks the very different attitudes toward life and death of people living a mere 100 years apart.[15]

A gravestone may also consciously deviate from norms; it may hide some "facts" about a person's life to highlight others. Sometimes one may infer group norms from just such deviations. An example from my own family reveals how past (European) family norms influenced a mid-twentieth-century (American) gravestone. This example illustrates another principle as well: the need for corroborative data in oral history as in all historical research.

In the 1920s, one of my European-born great-uncles married his European-born niece. Their marriage followed Eastern European, but not American, custom. It seemed shameful to their American-born children and nieces and nephews. At least, so I infer. Several pieces of evidence support my inference. Gravestones in my family's plot report individuals' English names and Hebrew names. Hebrew names take the form "first and middle name, daughter (or son) of first and middle name of father." Rather than declaring her "real Hebrew name" (Tova, daughter of Maier), this woman's gravestone declares in Yiddish "Tova, daughter of a good man." [16] When in 1986 I asked relatives then in their 70s the name of Tova's father, no one would say. I inferred the truth when my mother's first cousin became befuddled during a conversation and explained that my great-grandparents had given two of their daughters the identical name. I knew her explanation went against traditional naming practices and inferred Tova's parentage. When confronted, my mother confirmed my surmise and swore me to secrecy lest I hurt the feelings of other members of our family. Tova's own niece (then in her 60s) had never been told that Tova was her mother's sister. The intricacies of my own family are of little consequence, but the example illustrates how one may reason with information to learn how deviations from the norm highlight potential conflicts between past and present practices.

Not only do "documentary" history and oral history require corroborative data from several reliable informants (or sources), they also require both inductive and deductive methods. One of the first people I had asked about Tova's parentage was indeed the woman whose feelings my mother wanted to protect: Tova's sister's 60-year-old daughter. A good informant on our mutual relatives in their 50s and 60s, she was not reliable about older relatives.[17] Had I spoken only with her, I would not have solved the riddle of the gravestone, nor could I have solved the riddle without some knowledge of the naming practices of European Jews who immigrated to the United States at the turn of nineteenth century. This knowledge, part of the "stock of knowledge at hand" with which I grew up, helped to provide a point of view.

Learning History

But how can a novice acquire a historical point of view, especially if she or he is dealing with unfamiliar materials? Let us suppose for the moment that a young researcher has a question that has a historical dimension, appreciates that history is more than a laundry list of names, events, and dates, but is not schooled in the relevant periods. That lack of formal knowledge may impede serious research precisely because historians bring their own points of view to their arguments about the past. Without some familiarity with the issues about which historians argue, one has difficulty reading their texts in a meaningful way. One needs knowledge of the main lines of dispute to grasp why they chose to present some data, but not others. Accordingly, the researcher's first task is to acquire the necessary background—not only to learn the dates, names, and key events, but also to master controversies among historians about whether, how, and why those dates, names, and events matter.

There are several ways to learn about a specific period or topic. The easiest is to take a good history course that covers the material (and arguments) one needs to know. As academic schedules often make additional course work impossible, there are other alternatives. One may ask friends, colleagues, and historians for help in locating an expert who can compile a reading list. Lacking access to an expert (or a required reading list), one can go to the reference section of a research library and construct a reading list from specialized bibliographies, handbooks, and dictionaries. A reference librarian can help to locate the relevant books; so can the favorite tool of many reference librarians—*The Guide to Reference Books* (Sheehy, 1986) and its supplements. One can check the utility of the reading list one has compiled by consulting the *Social Science Citation Index* to learn whether many researchers have used the items on a "homemade" reading list in their own work. The second alternative borders on self-instruction; the third alternative requires self-instruction.

Autodidacticism, even quasi-autodidacticism, takes longer: It may take a researcher six months to a year to figure out what questions the historians are asking, especially because historians' texts do not use the conventions associated with publication in the social sciences. Historians tend to write narrative, not theory. Generally, they do not begin their work with an introductory theoretical section (or chapter) and end it with a concluding section (or chapter). Judged by the authorial conventions of the social sciences, most books by historians "just end." As historians tend to weave their ideas into their stories, one must read carefully enough to know what the stories are about. Sometimes one must read very carefully indeed even to know with whom historians are taking issue and why. Without some guidance, one may simply miss the point.[18]

Another warning is in order. Supposedly, the social scientist has come to a historical question because of the nature of his or her own research problem. That question was probably inspired by questions in his or her own field, not by the issues historians debate. Possible exceptions include problems currently stimulating interdisciplinary research, such as issues in women's studies. But even when a question has been inspired by interdisciplinary reading, chances are that a historian would frame the question differently than would a member of another discipline. It is tempting, but dangerous, to confuse historians' disputes with one's own theoretical aim. Their disputes best serve as sensitizing devices: ways of interpreting their data, of approaching what went on in the past and of understanding how, in the past, different people in different life situations saw their world.

Let me return to a previous example, footnote 8 of Weber's *The Protestant Ethic and the Spirit of Capitalism.* Recall that it concerned the association between religion and education. Weber reproduced this table from a contemporary source, but the presentation is nonetheless incorrect. One row adds to 109%. Weber "percentaged" in the wrong direction: The table uses school as an independent variable to predict religion, not religion as an independent variable to predict type of schooling.

Weber made a common error. Such errors are good for a chuckle, but may be irrelevant to a theory. Weber's mistake does *not* invalidate his argument. The data in footnote 8 concern religion and schools in 1895. Weber's argument concerns the advent of modern capitalism during the Reformation. To be sure, Weber also presents arguments about the character of late nineteenth-century capitalism. But Weber never claimed that the Protestant ethic caused "ascetic rationalism" to become an "iron cage." Rather, he believed that "religious asceticism" had "escaped from the cage" of contemporary capitalism and that early twentieth-century capitalism "needs its support no longer" (pp. 181-183).

Just as squabbles about the correct presentation of quantitative data may be irrelevant to the nub of a theory, so too historians' disputes may be irrelevant to a social scientist. Again, an example: Suppose one wishes to learn about the meaning of television commercials in contemporary life. The problem clearly has a historical dimension: Advertisements predate television. Because cultural practices are recursive, we may wish to learn more about the first ads, but historians disagree about when the first ads appeared. Some trace advertising to the early Greeks. Others point to eighteenth-century English practices. One could travel the byways to decide which historian gives the "right" date, but the "right" date is irrelevant to the meaning of television ads in contemporary life. As Williams (1980) explains, it would be more fruitful to explore a historical issue germane to communication theory, namely, the changing articulation among ads, production and distribution systems, and consumption patterns. As always, the researcher must decide which aspects of these relationships are relevant to the problem.

Historiography

One must also learn how to find data. Ideally, one would take a course in historiography (historical methods). Such courses come in at least two variations: philosophy of method (or narrative) and the hands-on approach (nuts and bolts). The appendix to this chapter presents information on the second approach; it stresses that even "nuts and bolts" raise interpretive issues.

Interpretive issues are at the core of today's debates about philosophy of method and narrative. Many contemporary historians extend the interpretive issues implicit in data collection to the construction of a historical narrative. But just as one cannot speak about sociological theory as though it were a unified endeavor, so too one cannot write of historians' views of their enterprise as though they share a common view. The most pertinent example is debate about the construction of narrative.

History as Text

Just as the debate about the utility of cliometrics tended to be associated with social history, so too many of the current debates in historiography arose with the advent of cultural history, a relatively new field practiced by the (momentarily) "newest young Turks." There are several ways to interpret the term *cultural history*. It can refer to (a) the history of culture, narrated according to standard practice (i.e., the division of culture into periods or the influence of such changing technologies as the electronic media on cultural phenomena); (b) an exploration of the meanings of cultural practices (e.g., how the first books were rendered part of "oral cultures" and used by some Catholics in supposedly "Protestant ways"; Davis, 1975); (c) a historical explication of cultural texts to learn about social relationships (e.g., how a story about an incident in a printer's Paris shop reveals tensions between guild members and apprentices that, in turn, contravene assumptions about guilds as corporate actors; Darnton, 1984); or (d) an analysis of cultural myths and practices as "representations."[19]

The term *representation* invokes specific theories. It means much more than depiction, illustration, image, or portrayal. Rather, it serves as a referent to postmodernist theories, which see both written documents and mundane activities as "texts." Initially based in the ideas of linguist Ferdinand de Saussure, these theories argue that the assumptions of an era (an *époque*) are both inscribed and embedded in (documentary or lived) texts. Texts are to be analyzed as parts of webs or systems of signification that may be viewed as "a set of language systems." Because language systems are characteristic of an era (place, class, or situation), one can analyze any particular text in relationship to other texts; that is, as part of a *structure* of meaning. Indeed, the analyst's (researcher's) task is to elucidate that structure. Hence these theories are called "structuralist."

Poststructuralist notions of representation follow this idea to its logical conclusions. Mukerji and Schudson (1991) explain: "If no one is the author, perhaps everyone is the author. Probably the central tenet of post-structuralist analyses is that texts are multivocal. Texts are seen as having a variety of potential meanings, none of which is the real meaning to be derived by some superior reader" (p. 46). They continue:

> Poststructuralists have generally been more interested in the variability of readings than in the perfectibility of the reading process. They claim not only that different interpretations are a necessary part of reading because different readers approach texts with different assumptions about writing and reading, but also that texts themselves are . . . riddled with contradictions. All texts . . . , subtly or openly, intentionally or unconsciously, allude to or incorporate other texts, so they make themselves inevitably open to multiple readings. (pp. 46, 47)

This poststructuralist tenet about texts has several implications. One is that there is no "true," "objective" reading of history as text. The potential multiplicity of meanings do not mean that any one interpretation is incorrect; rather, any one reading of a historical datum may coexist with other readings that are also "true."

Historian's Account as Text

These theories also imply that the historian's account is an assembled text. It, too, is multivocal and bespeaks the context of its production. It, too, is an assemblage that bespeaks the historian's *époque* rather than the voice of the historian-author. How, then, should we read the accounts of historians? Again the answers vary.

Some historians are wed to the idea of the "grand narrative," the all-encompassing story that relates the march of humanity through civilization(s) or some corner of time and place. Indeed, through much of the twentieth century, historians have interpreted their task as the production of grand narratives, which include either implicit or de facto explanations of the relationships among phenomena across time and place. These historians view poststructuralisms and postmodernisms as anathema, for these new theories obviously subvert the very notion of *the* grand narrative (see Himmelfarb, 1987).

Historians who pledge allegiance to positivism also find postmodernisms antithetical to their basic methodological tenets. They use the word *speak* quite differently than do those influenced by linguistic structuralism. If the facts speak for themselves, the facts cannot be "multivocal." "Speaking facts" do not require the historian as interpreter: If and when facts seem to contradict one another, one should gather more facts to deduce "the truth." In this view, "facts" guide explanation (or what I have described as the interpretive enterprise). For these historians, basic historiographic rules about the reliability and validity of facts and sources (see the appendix to this chapter) themselves guide the acceptance of a phenomenon as a fact. Their text is not an assemblage.

Still other historians speak for eclecticism and refuse to adopt any one philosophy of history. Instead, they recognize the potential utility of many approaches and note, as does Joan Scott (1988, 1989), that a plurality of approaches can be useful, especially within specialty areas. This pluralistic view embraces "historical texts as montage." So-called women's history provides an apt series of examples. For instance, some historical work easily classified as women's history uses cliometrics. Other historians of women detest cliometrics and view it as a positivistic endeavor. (As used here, the word *positivism* is not a compliment.) Yet others would say that they are "merely" trying to make sense of a specific historical phenomenon from the point of view of women—to be "gynocentric."[20] Still other historians of women identify themselves as practitioners of "cultural studies," an interdisciplinary approach that draws on European Marxisms, postmodernisms, and a concern with how cultural phenomena influence social arrangements. Although no one of these approaches may document "the truth," together they present a revealing montage.

I have borrowed the word *montage* from art. It is also used in cinema. However, *montage* is not part of a historian's professional vocabulary. The word is useful precisely because it suggests that artistry is necessarily implicated in the historian's endeavor. But even the most accomplished art historian might blanch if asked to explain how he or she distinguishes a "good" montage from a "poor" one.

The problem of distinction affects the social sciences as well. For instance, social scientists, whose work involves the generation of "meaningful" accounts from qualitative data, find it difficult to agree upon how one should construct an ethnography. Is one's task to reproduce or to interpret?[21] Is the task of the ethnographer (or historian) to assemble data so skillfully that a sophisticated reader would learn "how to be" the resident of a small village in Taiwan or of an eighteenth-century New England hamlet? The monographs of some ethnographers and historians read *as though* their authors were trying to "reproduce"—to explain "how to." For others, "how to" does not suffice. Rorty explains:

> The anthropologist is not doing his job if he merely offers to teach us how to bicker with his favorite tribe, how to be initiated into their rituals, etc. What we want to be told is whether that tribe has anything interesting to tell us—interesting to *our* light, answering to *our* concerns, informative about what *we* know to exist. Any anthropologist who rejects this assignment on the grounds that

filtering and paraphrase would distort and betray the integrity of the tribe's culture would no longer be an anthropologist, but a sort of cultist. He is, after all, working for *us,* not *them.*

The passage continues, "Similarly, the historian of X, where X is something we feel to be real and important, is working for those of us who share that knowledge, not for our unfortunate ancestors, who did not" (Rorty, quoted in Harlan, 1989a, p. 608; emphasis in Harlan; but see Hollinger, 1989; Rorty, Schneewind, & Skinner, 1984). But some historians would demur. They find a topic interesting precisely because it was important to our "unfortunate" ancestors, even though it may not seem germane to us.

Harlan's distinction is unfortunate. Whether an ethnographer or historian is working for *us* or *them,* that person still faces the task of assembling a credible story, of creating a montage that *speaks.* It may speak what the author wants to tell, or the author may identify his or her text as multivocal—a text that speaks itself. As previously indicated, how or what the historian's text speaks is yet another issue of historiographic debate. Harlan (1989a, 1989b) argues that historians should decry the new postmodernisms introduced to American scholarship by literary theorists. He talks of the implications of postmodernisms for history as the "return of literature" to historical discourse after a century's absence. He feels many historians "are afraid that if they once let themselves be distracted by theory they will spend their days wandering in a cognitive labyrinth from which they will find no way to depart. Literary criticism is clearly the worst of these labyrinths, especially its postmodern version" (Harlan, 1989a, p. 583). For others, those labyrinths may be important sensitizing devices, insisting—as they do—that both the historian and the qualitative social scientist are engaged in interpretive endeavors.

Ultimately, of course, these arguments about how to do historical research and how to write history are debates about the nature of history. Joan Scott (1989) has explained that the contemporary debate about historiography is an argument about both power *among* historians and power *in* history. She deserves the last substantive word:

By "history," I mean not what happened, not what "truth" is "out there" to be discovered and transmitted, but what we *know* about the past, what the rules and conventions are that govern the production and acceptance of the knowledge we designate as history. My first premise is that history is not purely referential but is rather constructed by historians. Written history both reflects and creates relations of power. Its standards of inclusion and exclusion, measure of importance, and rules of evaluation are not objective criteria but politically produced conventions. What we know as history is, then, the result of past politics; today's contests are about how history will be constituted for the present.

Scott continues:

History is inherently political. There is no single standard by which we can identify "true" historical knowledge. . . . Rather, there are contests, more and less conflictual, more and less explicit, about the substance, uses, and meanings of the knowledge that we call history. . . . This process is about the establishment [and challenge] and protection [and contestation] of hegemonic definitions of history.

Conclusion

At the start of this essay, I stated that early twentieth-century sociologists distinguished between history and sociology. The utility of Park and Burgess's 1921 contrast has virtually disappeared. What remains in both fields is recognition that research is an interpretive enterprise. The debates about interpretation abound. I have not attempted to find a theoretical pattern underlying how historians argue these issues. Rather, their disagreements are meaningful precisely because they raise the very epistemological issues that qualitative social scientists are confronting. They are familiar, if contested, terrain. The historical debates matter to social scientists because, reading "new" histories and experimenting with historical methods, we must be able to call on our training in theoretical literatures to interpret our encounters with the historians. To use some of the jargon that besets historians (as it besets social scientists), the crisis in historiography speaks the general crisis of meaning and knowing that afflicts our own episteme.

Appendix: Nuts and Bolts

The hands-on approach to historiography asks, How does one find information and how does one assess it? The classic text is Barzun and Graff's *The Modern Researcher* (1957). This book is still useful as a guide to the sort of reasoning one would use to find data and to judge reliability, but many of its suggestions are simply out of date. Most research libraries have introduced electronic tools since the publication of *The Modern Researcher.*

Some work once done by an assiduous search of reference books may now be done through "hard copy" (books), CD-ROM, or electronic rental of a database, such as *Historical Abstracts, American History and Life,* or *Sociological Abstracts.* Many research libraries have these databases on line.

Perhaps the distinction most pertinent to a novice is that between secondary and primary sources. Like all attempts to draw a line, the demarcation is more easily stated than accomplished. To wit, secondary sources are books and articles written by historians and social scientists about a topic. Primary sources are most often the historical data (documents or practices) of the period one is trying to explain. But the distinction is fuzzy. For instance, should one consider an acclaimed nineteenth-century article about eighteenth-century literature a primary or a secondary document? Does it make sense to say that an individual doing research about nineteenth-century culture should view the article as a primary source, but one doing research about the eighteenth century should view it as a secondary source? The discussion below assumes that secondary sources are books and articles written by historians, social scientists, or critics within the past 50 years.

Secondary Sources

Once one has read enough history to have some familiarity with a period, one may change the kind of material one is reading. What one reads next depends on one's research question. For instance, if one's question pertains to nineteenth-century women's magazines, four bodies of literature are relevant: those by (a) communications specialists, (b) literary critics, (c) historians, and (d) scholars in women's studies. If one already knows of a particularly good monograph relevant to the topic, one may check its references. For instance, on this topic one might check what such historians as Barbara Welter (1976) have written about the "cult of true womanhood," for part of her argument is based on nineteenth-century women's magazines. To learn more, one might check her sources or use the *Social Science Citation Index* and the *Arts and Humanities Citation Index* to see who has cited them and how.

There are also alternative procedures for locating examples of the relevant literatures. One might turn to "Homer," the most common computerized index to a library. Experimentation would reveal whether a library has holdings relevant to women's magazines. Here is the logic of such a computerized search. At the University of Connecticut's Homer Babidge Library (currently classifying its collection), 5,000 titles are now classified under "literature." The subclassification "literature-periodicals" includes item 1437, *The Literary Index to American Magazines, 1815-1865* (Wells, 1980). An additional search of the 793 items classified under "feminism" locates the subcategory "feminist periodicals, 1855-1984." Following the computer's categories, one might then check for relevant material under "women's studies" (95 entries) or "women's periodicals" (22 entries). Indeed, these subcategories lead to *American Women's Magazines: An Annotated Historical Guide* (Humphreys, 1989).

Other searches might follow a slightly variant logic. If one wants to know about the regulation of the newspaper industry at the turn of the nineteenth century, one might start a search either by using Homer or by checking in such a useful source as *The International Encyclopedia of Communications* (Barnouw, 1989). If one's question pertains to the regulation of television or radio, books and articles by communications scholars, economists, and historians are probably relevant and can be located through Homer, the *International Encyclopedia of Communications,* or *Mass Media Bibliography: An Annotated Guide to Books and Journals for Research and Reference* (Blum & Wilhoit, 1990), and even the OCLC (On-line Computer Library Center), which has replaced the hard-copy *Union Catalogue* and lists which library owns which books.

Unfortunately, locating secondary sources does not end one's task. One must discover whether the scholarship meets acceptable standards. One way to check on sources is to see whether they are frequently cited. Reference books facilitate this task. For instance, one may look up an article or book in either the *Social Science Citation Index* or the *Arts and Humanities Citation Index.* In theory, the more an article or book is cited, the greater its contribution to the literature and so the greater its utility in your attempt to learn what you want to know. However, two caveats are in order. First, some books and articles may be cited because other authors believe they are wrong. One might find a frequently cited article only to discover subsequently (through further reading) that it is used as the classic example of, say, a common misinterpretation. Second, some articles or books that have made major contributions may not be cited very much, because they are in a very specialized area. Even the best work in an arcane area may receive few citations.

Whatever the route one chooses to locate relevant secondary sources and to check their utility, one must ask of these texts the same questions one asks of other texts: Why is this author making this argument? Do other scholars dispute this argument? Why these particular materials, but not others? Do the author's questions suggest other issues relevant to the project at hand?

Lacking a good answer, one can check book reviews in the scholarly journals of the time to see how the material under consideration was received. Let me take an immodest example, my own book *Making News* (Tuchman, 1978). To learn about its reception, one might use the *Social Science Citation Index* to locate reviews. Discovering that Todd Gitlin reviewed *Making News* in *Contemporary Sociology,* one would read the review and use a citation index to learn about Gitlin. A reference to Gitlin's *The Whole World Is Watching* (1980) might suggest checking his book to learn his perspective and to discover other useful references. Indeed, because one is trying to locate materials and assessments of materials, one must pay assiduous attention to footnotes. If necessary, one may use OCLC to locate a library that owns the material one needs and then borrow it through interlibrary loan.

Primary Sources

Finding and assessing primary historical data is an exercise in detective work. It involves logic, intuition, persistence, and common sense—the same logic, intuition, persistence, and common sense that one would use to locate contemporary data or information pertinent to one's daily life. For instance, if one needed a part for a refrigerator whose manufacturer had gone out of business, one would contact a specialist—an appliance service—to learn whether that firm has the part. If it does not, one might contact a series of appliance services. One will either find the part or learn that it is no longer available. Specialists know things that nonspecialists do not know.

Academic are specialists, too. For instance, virtually any researcher who studies news knows of the existence of the Vanderbilt University Television News Archives. (It has tapes of television nightly news broadcasts from August 1968 through the present and publishes an index and abstracts available through many university libraries.)[22] Similarly, the existence of such compendia as *Facts on File* and the *Index to the New York Times* is common knowledge. Most researchers also realize the utility of legal records, often available through the Freedom of Information Act. Because legal disputes and government hearings are arguments, they revolve around what different parties believe to be the implications of regulations and taken-for-granted norms.

Frequently, however, common knowledge does not cross academic specialties. During their graduate school education, twentieth-century historians learn how to use the Freedom of Information Act to obtain American documents.[23] Historians also accumulate information about the location of specific archives in much the same way sociologists accumulate information about the variables included in some standard quantitative data sets.[24] One may discover whether there is an archive to mine by asking an accomplished historian. Another way is to consult annotated lists of archives available in the libraries of research universities or other major libraries. One useful source is the *National Inventory of Documentary Sources in the United States* (NIDS) (Agee, Bertelsen, Holland, & Wivel, 1985). It includes information about federal documents and libraries. Another is the *Directory of Archives and Manuscript Repositories in the United States* (National Historical Publications and Records Commission, 1988). One can also use OCLC to locate other commercial bibliographies that might provide the names of useful collections. But again, simply locating an archive is not the end of one's task. Archives are often less convenient to use than are data sets. One may order a data set in a computer-mountable tape or even in CD-ROM and so use it through a

PC. Frequently, one must go to an archive. There are exceptions; some archives are being issued in microfiche or on film, as one can discover through assiduous use of such appropriate reference books as NIDS, but many are not.

If one cannot afford to travel to the appropriate archive (or get a grant to do so), one can try to imagine what data appropriate to one's question would look like. If one is working in, say, the early twentieth century, one may check sociological journals to learn whether anyone has written articles related to the problem under study. If the author is still alive, he or she may have saved the data. If the person is dead, he or she, or his or her descendants, may have deposited the relevant data in the library of an institution where the author taught. For instance, the University of Chicago has a collection of Robert Park's work; the Pennsylvania State University houses the papers of L. L. Bernard.

Quantitative historical data contain all of the problems associated with contemporary quantitative data—and then some. Quantitative data are collected and coded with particular questions in mind. Additionally, ideologies of the era in which the data were collected are frequently embedded in the coding categories.

Official censuses serve as a useful example of how ideologies are captured in coding categories. Bose (1987) explains, "The international debate among census statisticians at the end of the 19th century . . . confirms that the methods of reporting female and child labor were subject to political ideology and social influences" (p. 101). Britain wanted to portray itself as a "community of workers and a strong nation." It classified unpaid domestic workers and the female relatives of farmers and small businessmen in their own separate category. Two Australian colonies demurred from this approach; each tried another method. One classified these women under their fathers' and husbands' occupations; the others did not assume that the women participated in the family enterprises. In 1890, the Australian colonies called a conference to resolve their conflict. Its participants agreed to classify the whole population into "breadwinners" and "dependents," for the Australians wanted to create an image of a country where women did not need to work.[25]

Qualitative data present problems too. Let us assume that women's letters and diaries are pertinent to one's research question and that one can locate pertinent examples. One cannot simply read them. As in the previous examples about gravestones, one must read enough examples to infer the norms for what could be written and how it could be expressed. For instance, in the early nineteenth century, some (primarily female) schoolteachers instructed girls in journal writing and read their journals to do so. How would such instruction have influenced the journals kept by these girls as adults? Delving into the diary writer's psychology will not necessarily answer this question. Rather, it is useful to view the nineteenth-century journal writer as an informant. Just as one tries to understand how a contemporary informant speaks from a specific social location, so too one would want to establish the social location of a historical figure. One might ask of these and other diaries: What is characteristic of middle-class female diary writers? What is characteristic of this informant? How should one view what this informant writes? These same questions are germane to correspondence.

Archival data present other problems as well. Who saved them and why? Who sorted them and how? These inferential tasks have a contemporary analogy. Let me create its scenario: An academic department has a head clerk who has devised an idiosyncratic filing system. You have to find a form in order to receive your pay and the clerk is not available. If the form is not under "forms," maybe it's under "pay." Maybe it's under "salaries." Maybe it's under "incoming students." Maybe it's under "personnel." What categories might an idiosyncratic person have used to construct those files? Unless the files are random (unlikely, because then the clerk would not be able to find anything either), there are limited possibilities. One must discover them and check the possibilities in order of likelihood. The option selected depends on which alternatives looks as though it will yield the result most quickly. As in any other kind of research, one must decide how much time or money one is willing to expend to get what one needs.

If one cannot locate the data one needs, there are alternative ways to proceed. One can ask the archivist the most likely location. One can sample the archive by requesting documents in different categories to discover what each category means. By understanding the system used to identify main categories, one may narrow the search among subcategories. Again, locating documents is not the end of the process. A social scientist wants to infer patterns. That process resembles how one makes inferences from any qualitative data. Detecting a pattern requires being open to the material (just as one must be open to hearing what one's informants say in an interview) and having some imagination. Now, however, one must have both a social science and a historical imagination. By *historical imagination,* I mean some grasp of how a document would have been interpreted in its time.

Any researcher has at hand material that might help in the process of reconstructing meaning. Because the researcher started this project by reading the work of historians, he or she may have some sense of the period and some "feel" for the materials under investigation—a grasp of "structures of feeling" (Williams, 1977). But other materials help too. Let us consider again a very common historical document, a letter. One needs to understand it—not just what it says explicitly, but what it means. To understand meaning, one must understand the literary form.[26] Some eighteenth- and nineteenth-century letters have been included in memoirs (see Roberts, 1834); others have been collected in books (Johnson, 1925). Suppose the improbable: One cannot find examples of eighteenth-century letters. As usual, there is an alternative. If one is working in the eighteenth century, one can read an epistolary novel (such as Fanny Burney's *Evelina*) to infer letter-writing conventions. But one would want to realize the implications of using any alternative. Because Burney was writing a novel, she used her fictive letters to draw character. Does another late eighteenth-century novel use the same epistolary conventions?

Using different types of data, such as newspapers, one would ask slightly different questions, but they too would involve trying to grasp contemporary conventions.[27] The communication literature is replete with information about how news was gathered and processed. But if the research produced since 1940 does not help one to understand how newspapers work, one may check legal records, especially libel suits against the news media. Particularly in the past 15 years, libel suits have included information about the routines of news coverage. Indeed, it is possible that the court records and supporting documents of a significant libel suit, such as *Westmoreland v. CBS,* may make television news coverage of the Vietnam War more open to some kinds of theoretical interpretation than a content analysis would.

If one could summarize these "nuts and bolts," the moral of this appendix would be: Ask questions of all data, primary and secondary sources. Do not assume that anything about data is "natural," inevitable, or even true. To be sure, a datum has a physical presence: One may touch the page, picture, tombstone, or microfiche one has located. But that physical truth may be radically different from the interpretive truth needed to assess the application or test a theory.

Notes

1. These articles ask, How does *sociological history* differ from *historical sociology*? (These are but two of the terms invoked in the debate.) Some authors stress that sociologists use historical data to test sociological concepts and theories, whereas historians use sociological ideas to understand historical data (Bonnell, 1980). Others object that "the divergent practices of sociologically oriented historians and historically oriented sociologists have helped to reinforce the sense that the aims of historians are divergent from those of theory constructors" (Megill, 1989, p. 635). Meanwhile, theorists inspired by what I shall be discussing as "postmodernisms" seek to identify the different narrative practices used by historians and sociologists to clarify the ideal-typical distinctions of their endeavors (Hall, 1992). I believe such discussions are more useful to people who wish to draw boundaries between sociology and history than they are to people who have questions they wish to answer.

2. For a debate on these issues, see the June 1989 issue of the *American Historical Review.*

3. Later I will discuss a quantitative error in this table that the translator did not mention.

4. Some commentators also suggest that Weber adopted the interpretation of Marx dominant at the beginning of the twentieth century. That interpretation defined Marx as an economic determinist. Some late twentieth-century commentators reject this view of Marx. Others criticize Parsons's translation of *The Protestant Ethic and the Spirit of Capitalism.* They say that Parsons

rendered some meanings so as to make Weber's ideas more compatible with Parsons's own theories.

5. The German term used to classify Weber's enterprise—*Geisteswissenschaft*—may be translated as either "the sociology of knowledge" or "the study of the humanities."

6. This sentence obviously implies that one can know "what actually happened." Some contemporary historiographers do not accept this assumption, but see historical texts as constructed accounts. Assessments of the reliability and validity of those accounts may themselves be determined by the systems of meanings fostered and accepted by our own historical era.

7. I am assuming that when one discusses quantitative patterns, one applies standard definitions of validity and reliability.

8. One obvious implication is that one may read novels as historical documents about social practices, as done by a group of literary critics and historians called the "New Historicists" (see, e.g., Greenblatt, 1988; Hunt, 1992).

9. I write as though this were a simple task. It took roughly seven people-years to gather, code, and transform the relevant data into computerized data sets.

10. Our consultants were reliable observers. One was a major Victorian critic whose works are still in print. We learned about them through literary histories, contemporary literary criticism, biographies, and obituaries.

11. The term *laws* implies a positivist orientation.

12. Historically constructed meanings become the raw materials for new cultural creation. However, longstanding cultural meanings also set limits on what groups can use to construct new collective activities and forms of identity (see Tuchman & Levine, 1993).

13. Note the cultural supposition that a family member selects the gravestone and decides what is to be written on it.

14. Indeed, Western groups assume that gravestones provide the opportunity for a commentary on life and death.

15. Ann Douglas uses gravestones to trace the development of Victorian attitudes toward the deaths of children.

16. None of the other gravestones uses Yiddish, although I suppose that language might have been used for such inscriptions when the family lived in Europe.

17. I first called Tova's niece because of another research priority, conservation of funds. I could reach her with a local phone call.

18. Narrative is also the virtue of historical writing. Historians sometimes tell deceptively simple stories. Much prose in the social sciences would be improved if the authors could construct narratives as elegant as those required of historians.

19. See, for example, the journal *Representations*.

20. Joan Kelly's (1977) article "Did Women Have a Renaissance?" is an apt example. She argues that what for men was a "rebirth" was for women a loss of the power to define the sort of knowledge they needed and to teach it one another.

21. I assume that all description involves interpretation.

22. A telephone call to the archives placed November 5, 1992, produced the unhappy information that this nonprofit source may close for lack of funds.

23. A telephone call to the general recording at the Library of Congress produced the telephone number for the National Reference Service. Its information expert kindly produced the names of two possible sources: *How to Use the Freedom of Information Act* (Sherick, 1978) and *The Citizen's Guide on How to Use the Freedom of Information Act and the Privacy Act in Requesting Government Documents* (U.S. House of Representatives, 1977). The latter is a periodical. The information expert also noted that almost all federal agencies maintain Freedom of Information Act offices and that one should check with an agency to see exactly what it requires before submitting a written request for information.

24. Historians also record their data differently than do social scientists. When using archives, they record bin, drawer, and call numbers, as well as date and publisher. There are good reasons to follow the historians' example. Suppose you need to double-check a datum, but you are in Texas and the datum is in New York. If you have recorded everything needed to find the information, a friend of a friend can copy it for you. Also, if you eventually wish to publish your work with a house that favors the style of historical references, you will need to know bin and drawer numbers.

25. Bose (1987) also explains how ideology may be embedded in instruction to coders who must classify a woman as belonging to one or another paid occupation.

26. Letters to friends were a "female literary form" in the eighteenth and nineteenth centuries.

27. Even such sources as the *Congressional Record* have built-in biases (see Leonard, 1986). Representatives and senators may enter materials, including speeches, that they never introduced on the floor of the House or Senate.

References

Agee, V., Bertelsen, J., Holland, R. J., & Wivel, C. (Comps.). (1985). *National inventory of documentary sources in the United States* (compiled for the National Historical Publications and Records Commission). Teaneck, NJ: Chadwyck-Healey.

Barnouw, E. (Ed.). (1989). *The international encyclopedia of communications.* New York: Oxford University Press.

Barzun, J., & Graff, H. (1957). *The modern researcher.* New York: Harcourt, Brace.

Blum, E., & Wilhoit, F. G. (1990). *Mass media bibliography: An annotated guide to books and journal for research and reference* (3rd ed.). Urbana: University of Illinois Press.

Bonnell, V. (1980). The use of theory, concepts and comparison in historical sociology. *Comparative Studies in Society and History, 22,* 156-173.

Bose, C. (1987). Devaluing women's work: The undercount of women's employment in 1900 and 1980. In C. Bose, R. Feldberg, & N. Sokoloff (Eds.), *Hidden aspects of women's work* (pp. 95-115). New York: Praeger.

Braudel, F. (1972). *The Mediterranean and the Mediterranean world in the age of Philip II.* New York: Harper & Row.

Coontz, S. (1992). *The way we never were: Families and the nostalgia trap.* New York: Basic Books.

Darnton, R. (1984). *The great cat massacre and other episodes in French cultural history.* New York: Basic Books.

Davis, N. Z. (1975). *Society and culture in early modern France.* Stanford, CA: Stanford University Press.

Giddens, A. (1984). *The constitution of society.* Berkeley: University of California Press.

Gitlin, T. (1980). *The whole world is watching: The role of the media in the making and unmaking of the New Left.* Berkeley: University of California Press.

Greenblatt, S. J. (1988). *Shakespearean negotiations: The circulation of social energy in Renaissance England.* Berkeley: University of California Press.

Hall, J. R. (1992). Where history and sociology meet: Forms of discourse and socio-historical inquiry. *Sociological Theory, 10,* 164-193.

Harlan, D. (1989a). Intellectual history and the return of literature. *American Historical Review, 94,* 581-609.

Harlan, D. (1989b). Reply to David Hollinger. *American Historical Review, 94,* 622-626.

Himmelfarb, G. (1987). *The new history and the old.* Cambridge, MA: Harvard University Press.

Hollinger, D. A. (1989). The return of the prodigal: The persistence of historical knowing. *American Historical Review, 94,* 610-621.

Humphreys, N. K. (1989). *American women's magazines: An annotated historical guide.* New York: Garland.

Hunt, L. (1992). *The family romance of the French Revolution.* Berkeley: University of California Press.

Johnson, R. B. (1925). *Letters of Hannah More.* London: John Lane.

Keller, E. F. (1985). *Reflections on gender and science.* New Haven, CT: Yale University Press.

Kelly, J. (1977). Did women have a Renaissance? In R. Bridenthal & C. Koontz (Eds.), *Becoming visible: Women in European history.* Boston: Houghton Mifflin.

Lamont, M., & Wuthnow, R. (1990). Betwixt and between: Recent cultural sociology in Europe and the United States. In G. Ritzer (Ed.), *Frontiers of social theory* (pp. 287-315). New York: Columbia University Press.

Leonard, T. C. (1986). *The power of the press: The birth of American political reporting.* New York: Oxford University Press.

Megill, A. (1989). Recounting the past: Description, explanation, and narrative in historiography. *American Historical Review, 94,* 627-653.

Mukerji, C., & Schudson, M. (1991). Introduction. In C. Mukerji & M. Schudson (Eds.), *Rethinking popular culture: Contemporary perspectives in cultural studies.* Berkeley: University of California Press.

National Historical Publications and Records Commission. (1988). *Directory of archives and manuscript repositories in the United States.* Phoenix: Oryx.

Park, R., & Burgess, E. (Eds.). (1921). *Introduction to the science of sociology.* Chicago: University of Chicago Press.

Roberts, W. (1834). *Memoirs of the life and correspondence of Mrs. Hannah More.* London: R. B. Seeley & W. Burnside.

Rorty, R., Schneewind, J. B., & Skinner, Q. (Eds.). (1984). *Philosophy in history.* New York: Cambridge University Press.

Scheuch, E. K. (1992). German sociology. In E. F. Borgatta & M. L. Borgatta (Eds.), *Encyclopedia of sociology* (Vol. 2, pp. 762-772). New York: Macmillan.

Scott, J. W. (1988). *Gender and the politics of history.* New York: Columbia University Press.

Scott, J. W. (1989). History in crisis? The others' side of the story. *American Historical Review, 94,* 680-692.

Sheehy, E. P., with the assistance of Keckeissen, R. G. (1986). *The guide to reference books* (10th ed.). Chicago: American Library Association.

Sherick, L. G. (1978). *How to use the Freedom of Information Act.* New York: Arco.

Tilly, L., & Scott, J. W. (1978). *Women, work and family.* New York: Holt, Rinehart & Winston.

Tuchman, G. (1978). *Making news: A study in the construction of reality.* New York: Free Press.

Tuchman, G., with Fortin, N. E. (1989). *Edging women out: Victorian novelists, publishers, and social change.* New Haven, CT: Yale University Press.

Tuchman, G., & Levine, H. G. (1993). New York Jews and Chinese food: The social construction of an ethnic pattern. *Journal of Contemporary Ethnography, 22*(3).

U.S. House of Representatives, Committee on Government Operations. (1977). *The citizen's guide on how to use the Freedom of Information Act and the Privacy Act in requesting government documents.* Washington, DC: House Committee Periodicals.

Weber, M. (1976). *The Protestant ethic and the spirit of capitalism* (T. Parsons, Trans.). New York: Charles Scribner. (Original work published 1904-1905)

Wells, D. A. (1980). *The literary index to American magazines, 1815-1865.* Metuchen, NJ: Scarecrow.

Welter, B. (1976). *Dimity convictions: The American woman in the nineteenth century.* Athens: Ohio University Press.

Williams, R. (1977). *Marxism and literature.* New York: Oxford University Press.

Williams, R. (1980). Advertising: The magic system. In R. Williams, *Problems in materialism and culture* (pp. 170-195). London: Verso.

Wolff, J. (1981). *The social production of art.* New York: St. Martin's.

20

Three Approaches to Participative Inquiry

PETER REASON

FROM one perspective, the orthodox scientific worldview is the product of the Enlightenment and represents a liberating step for human society in releasing itself from the bonds of superstition and Scholasticism. From another perspective, it is a movement to narrow our view of our world and to monopolize knowing in the hands of an elite few, and is fueled by patriarchy, alienation, and materialism; it is the product of a society committed to the domination of nature and of other peoples, of a society committed to a transcendental theology that sees man (*sic*) in the image of God and thus outside His creation (Baring & Cashford, 1991). So whereas on the one hand the scientific perspective has taught us the value of critical public testing of what is taken as knowledge, another consequence has been to place the researcher firmly outside and separate from the subject of his or her research, reaching for an objective knowledge and for one separate truth (Bateson, 1972b).

I believe and hope that there is an emerging worldview, more holistic, pluralist, and egalitarian, that is essentially participative. It is fueled by holistic and systemic thinking (Bateson, 1972b; Maturana & Varela, 1986; Skolimowski, 1992), feminism (Lichtenstein, 1988; Plant, 1989; Reinharz, 1992), liberationist education (Freire, 1970; Rogers, 1969), an extended epistemology (Habermas, 1972), new visions of spirituality and theology (Fox, 1991), deep ecology (Naess, 1989), and the metaphors of "new" physics, mathematics, and biology (Schwartz & Ogilvy, 1980). This worldview sees human beings as cocreating their reality through participation: through their experience, their imagination and intuition, their thinking and their action (Heron, 1992). As Skolimowski (1992) puts it, "We always partake of what we describe" (p. 20), so our "reality" is a product of the dance between our individual and collective mind and "what is there," the amorphous primordial givenness of the universe. This participative worldview is at the heart of inquiry methodologies that emphasize participation as a core strategy.

Let me be clear that my personal and professional commitment is to contribute to the emergence of this more participative worldview; that I write this chapter as an advocate of the methods presented rather than as an outside reviewer. I

AUTHOR'S NOTE: My colleague Judi Marshall has been a constant source of comment, encouragement, and challenge throughout the writing of this chapter. Our graduate research students' stimulating questions invited us to address the similarities and differences of different participative approaches. Dave Brown, John Clark, John Gaventa, Davydd Greenwood, Budd Hall, Marja Liisa Swantz, Rajesh Tandon, and Gary Woodhill all made helpful suggestions along the way. John Heron, Iain Mangham, David Sims, and Bill Torbert critically read early drafts. The official reviewers, Professors Giroux, Kuzel, and Whyte, provided helpful feedback on earlier drafts. Finally, Yvonna Lincoln and Norman Denzin were both supportive and challenging in their role as editors of the volume.

have devoted the past 15 years of my professional life to the development and application of co-operative inquiry in which the emphasis is on working with groups as co-researchers. As I look at the practice of action inquiry I am excited and awed by the challenge of developing the kind of self-reflexive critical awareness-in-action it demands. As I read about the work of practitioners of participatory action research, whose emphasis is on establishing liberating dialogue with impoverished and oppressed peoples, I understand the link between power and knowledge and realize the privileged position that I am in as a white male European academic. It seems to me to be urgent for the planet and for all its creatures that we discover ways of living in more collaborative relation with each other and with the wider ecology. I see these participative approaches to inquiry and the worldview they foster as part of this quest.

I have chosen three approaches to research as participation as the focus of my discussion: co-operative inquiry, participatory action research, and action inquiry. These three seem to me to be well articulated in both theory and practice and to stand together in quite radical contrast to orthodox scientific method; at the same time, all start from quite different premises and emphasize different aspects of the participative inquiry process. I acknowledge that in making my choices I have left out other approaches: appreciative inquiry (Cooperrider & Srivastva 1987), "emerging varieties" of action research (Elden & Chisholm, 1993), applied anthropology (Stull & Schensul, 1987), critical ethnography (Quantz, 1992), research partnerships (Whitaker, Archer, & Greve, 1990), and others.

In this chapter I take each approach separately and set out what I see as its underlying assumptions and practice. I attempt to give a flavor of the language and perspective of each, to do justice to the three as separate traditions. Then, in later sections of the chapter, I explore some of the similarities and differences among the three approaches and make critical comparisons. I attempt to show how the three approaches complement each other, so that together they stand as the beginnings of a robust "paradigm" of research with people.

Before proceeding further, let me acknowledge the paradox of writing "about" research with people, for I cannot really do it alone. In its complete version, participation belongs to the people who participate, and thus to all those who have joined in this kind of research, who include disadvantaged people in Asia, Africa, and South America; factory workers in the United States and Scandinavia; medical and nursing practitioners in England; and aboriginal people in Australia. In some ways to write (and to read) "about" these people's experience in coming to understand their own worlds is to repossess it as an academic subject that can be studied from outside. These approaches to inquiry through participation need to be seen as living processes of coming to know rather than as formal academic method. And, as we shall see, one of the key questions about research is the political one: Who owns the knowledge, and thus who can define the reality?

One final word of caution: Although I attempt to provide the flavor of each of three approaches, I am not able to provide an exhaustive review of each, nor can I explore some of the subtleties of theory and practice. I have the feeling that those who are closely identified with any of these methods may find my presentation biased and inadequate, whereas some of those coming from more traditional research strategies may be put off by the language, which is often passionate and committed, and will want a more formal definition of each approach. So I have the strange feeling that I am not merely entering a lion's den, but that I am entering several lions' dens simultaneously. So be it.

Co-Operative Inquiry

Co-operative inquiry has its roots in humanistic psychology, in the idea that persons can with help choose how they live their lives, free from the distress of early conditioning and restrictive social custom (e.g., Heron, 1977; Maslow, 1968; Rogers, 1961; Rowan, 1976), and that working together in a group with norms of open authentic communication will facilitate this (see, e.g., Randall & Southgate, 1980; Srivastva, Obert, & Neilson, 1977).

The proposal for cooperative experiential inquiry was first made by John Heron (1971; see also Heron, 1981a, 1981b, 1992; Reason, 1988, in press; Reason & Heron, 1986). At the heart of his critique of orthodox inquiry is the idea that its methods are neither adequate nor appropriate for the study of *persons,* for persons are to some significant degree self-determining. Orthodox social science inquiry methods, as part of their rationale, exclude the human subjects from all the thinking and decision making that generates, designs, manages, and draws conclusions from the research. Such exclusion treats the subjects as less than self-determining persons, alienates them from the inquiry process and from the knowledge that is its outcome, and thus invalidates any claim the methods have to be a science of persons.

To say that persons are self-determining is to say that they are the authors of their own actions—to some degree actually, and to a greater degree potentially. In other words, their intentions and purposes, their intelligent choices, are causes of their behavior. One can do research on persons in the full and proper sense of the term only if one addresses them as self-determining, which means that what they do and what they experience as part of the research must be to some significant degree determined by them. So in cooperative inquiry all those involved in the research are both co-researchers, whose thinking and decision making contribute to generating ideas, designing and managing the project, and drawing conclusions from the experience, and *also* co-subjects, participating in the activity being researched.

Ideally, there is full reciprocity, so that each person's agency is fundamentally honored in both the exchange of ideas and the action. This does not necessarily mean that all those involved in the inquiry enterprise contribute in identical ways. An inquiry group, like any human group, has to struggle with the problems of inclusion, influence, and intimacy; people will take different roles, and there will be differences in both the quality and quantity of members' contributions. In particular, one or more members may have initiated the inquiry as part of their organizational role or more informally; these members or others may act as facilitators of the inquiry process. How the group manages these potential differences in power will affect the quality of its work. Thus, although ideally full consensus will be reached on all decisions, this is rarely practical; at a minimum, everyone involved needs to be initiated into the inquiry process and needs to give free and informed assent to all decisions about process and outcome. (For discussion of these pragmatic issues in establishing an inquiry group, see Reason, 1988, in press.)

Heron (1981b) also suggests an extended epistemology that includes at least three kinds of knowledge: (a) *Experiential knowledge* is gained through direct encounter face-to-face with persons, places, or things; (b) *practical knowledge* concerns "how to" do something—it is knowledge demonstrated in a skill or competence; and (c) *propositional knowledge* is knowledge "about" something, and is expressed in statements and theories. In research on persons, the propositional knowledge stated in the research conclusions needs to be rooted in and derived from the experiential and practical knowledge of the subjects in the inquiry. If the propositions are generated exclusively by a researcher who is not involved in the experience being researched, and are imposed without consultation on the practical and experiential knowledge of the subjects, we have findings that directly reflect neither the experience of the researcher nor that of the subjects.

Recently, Heron (1992) has clarified the additional notion of *presentational knowledge* as the process by which we first order our tacit experiential knowledge into patterns, and that is expressed in images, dream, story, creative imagination. The development of presentational knowledge is an important (and often neglected) bridge between experiential knowledge and propositional knowledge.

Methodology

Co-operative inquiry can be described as taking place in four phases of action and reflection.

Phase 1. Co-researchers agree on an area for inquiry and identify some initial research propositions. They may choose to explore some aspect of their experience, agree to try out in practice some particular skills, or seek to change some aspect of their world. They also agree to some set of procedures by which they will observe and record their own and each other's experience. This phase involves primarily *propositional* knowing.

For example, health visitors in southwest England were invited by one of their colleagues to form an inquiry group to explore the sources of stress in their work. After much resistance to the idea that they could be "researchers," the members of the group decided to explore the stress that comes from the "hidden agendas" in their work—the suspicions they had about problems such as depression, child abuse, and drug taking in the families they visit that are unexpressed and unexplored (Traylen, 1989, in press).

Phase 2. The group then applies these ideas and procedures in their everyday life and work: They initiate the agreed actions and observe and record the outcomes of their own and each other's behavior. At this stage they need to be particularly alert for the subtleties and nuances of experience, and to ways in which their original ideas do and do not accord with experience. This phase involves primarily *practical* knowing.

Thus the health visitors first explored among themselves their feelings about these "hidden agendas" and decided to experiment with confronting them. They practiced the skills they thought they would need through role play, and then agreed to try raising their concerns directly with their client families.

Phase 3. The co-researchers will in all probability become fully immersed in this activity and experience. They may be excited or bored, engaged or alienated; they may sometimes forget they are involved in an inquiry project; they may forget or otherwise fail to carry out and record the agreed-upon procedures; or they may stumble on unexpected and unpredicted experiences and develop creative new insights. This stage of full immersion is fundamental to the whole process:

It is here that the co-researchers, fully engaged with their experience, may develop an openness to what is going on for them and their environment that allows them to bracket off their prior beliefs and preconceptions and so see their experience in a new way. This phase involves mainly *experiential* knowing.

The health visitors' experience of trying out these new behavior strategies was both terrifying and liberating in ways none of them had expected. On the one hand, they felt they were really doing their job; on the other hand, they were concerned about the depth of the problems they would uncover and whether they had adequate skills to cope with them. The initiator in particular was anxious and had disturbing dreams.

Phase 4. After an appropriate period engaged in Phases 2 and 3, the co-researchers return to consider their original research propositions and hypotheses in the light of experience, modifying, reformulating, and rejecting them, adopting new hypotheses, and so on. They may also amend and develop their research procedures more fully to record their experience. Thus this phase involves a critical return to *propositional* knowing.

The health visitors met periodically to review and make sense of their experiences. One outcome of their work was changes they made in their own professional practice; another was the report they wrote in their own language about their experiences that was made available to their colleagues and managers; a third was the master's dissertation written by the initiator (Traylen, 1989).

Validity in Co-Operative Inquiry

Co-operative inquiry claims to be a valid approach to research with persons because it "rests on a collaborative encounter with experience" (Reason & Rowan, 1981). This is the touchstone of the approach in that any practical skills or theoretical propositions that arise from the inquiry can be said to derive from and be congruent with this experience. The validity of this encounter with experience in turn rests on the high-quality, critical, self-aware, discriminating, and informed judgments of the co-researchers, which may be called "critical subjectivity" (Reason & Rowan, 1981, chap. 10).

Critical subjectivity is a state of consciousness different from either the naive subjectivity of "primary process" awareness and the attempted objectivity of egoic "secondary process" awareness. Critical subjectivity means that we do not suppress our primary subjective experience, that we accept that our knowing is from a perspective; it also means that we are *aware of* that perspective and of its bias, and we *articulate* it in our communications. Critical subjectivity involves a self-reflexive attention to the ground on which one is standing and thus is very close to what Bateson (1972a) describes as Learning III. (The notion of critical subjectivity also appears close to Keller's [1985] notion of "dynamic objectivity.")

This notion of critical subjectivity means that there will be many versions of "reality" to which people may hold with a self-reflexive passion. It also means that the method is open to all the ways in which human beings fool themselves and each other in their perceptions of the world, through faulty epistemology, cultural bias, character defense, political partisanship, spiritual impoverishment, and so on. In particular, co-operative inquiry is threatened by unaware projection and consensus collusion.

Unaware projection means that we deceive ourselves. We do this because inquiring carefully and critically into those things we care about is an anxiety-provoking business that stirs up our psychological defenses. We then project our anxieties onto the world we are supposed to be studying (Devereaux, 1967), giving rise to a whole variety of self-deceptions in the course of the inquiry. *Consensus collusion* means that the co-researchers may band together as a group in defense of their anxieties, so that areas of their experience that challenge their worldview are ignored or not properly explored.

It is important to find ways to explore and counteract these defensive tendencies, as the health visitors challenged themselves to look at aspects of their work that caused profound anxiety. A comprehensive set of procedures has been developed that serve to engage with and explore (but not eliminate) these threats to validity. These include cycling and recycling between action and reflection so that issues are examined several times in different ways, exploring the authenticity of participation within the group, using self-development methods to look at the impact of unacknowledged anxiety, and establishing norms whereby group members can challenge unwarranted assumptions (Heron, 1988; Reason & Rowan, 1981; Tiernan et al., in press).

These validity procedures are useful for systematically reviewing the quality of inquiry work. Their application does not mean that the experiential, practical, or propositional knowing that comes out of the research is valid in any absolute sense of the term, but rather that it is possible to see more clearly and communicate to others the perspective from which that knowing is derived, and to illuminate the distortions that may have occurred.

Participatory Action Research

Participatory action research (PAR) is probably the most widely practiced participative research approach; it is important because it emphasizes the political aspects of knowledge production. There are several different communities of PAR practitioners who represent their work in different ways; what follows is necessarily a generalized account in which I have drawn strongly on Fals-Borda and Rahman's recent book *Action and Knowledge* (1991), and to a lesser extent on other discussions of PAR: Fernandes and Tandon (1981); Hall, Gillette, and Tandon (1982); Tandon (1989); Cancian and Armstead (1992); Hall (1993). For a comprehensive bibliography, see Cancian and Armstead (1993).

Fals-Borda and Rahman (1991) place PAR firmly within the long tradition of liberationist movements: "Those who adopted PAR have tried to practice with a radical commitment that has gone beyond usual institutional boundaries, reminiscent of the challenging tradition of Chartists, utopians, and other social movements of the nineteenth century" (p. vii). Similarly, the brochure for PRIA (n.d.), the Society for Participatory Research in Asia, states, "Participatory Research implies an effort on the part of the people to understand the role of knowledge as a significant instrument of power and control."

Thus the primary task of PAR is the "enlightenment and awakening of common peoples" (Fals-Borda & Rahman, 1991, p. vi). Given this orientation, the PAR tradition starts with concerns for power and powerlessness, and aims to confront the way in which the established and power-holding elements of societies worldwide are favored because they hold a monopoly on the definition and employment of knowledge. Concerns for epistemology and methodology appear secondary to this primary concern.

A second important starting point is the lived experience of people, and the idea that through the actual experience of something we may "intuitively apprehend its essence; we feel, enjoy, and understand it as reality" (Fals-Borda & Rahman, 1991, p. 4). Thus in PAR the knowledge and experience of people—often oppressed groups—is directly honored and valued.

So the PAR strategy has a double objective. One aim is to produce knowledge and action directly useful to a group of people—through research, adult education, and sociopolitical action. The second aim is to empower people at a second and deeper level through the process of constructing and using their own knowledge: They "see through" the ways in which the establishment monopolizes the production and use of knowledge for the benefit of its members. This is the meaning of consciousness-raising or *conscientization,* a term popularized by Paulo Freire (1970) for a "process of self-awareness through collective self-inquiry and reflection" (Fals-Borda & Rahman, 1991, p. 16).

A third important starting point for PAR is authentic commitment. PAR values the processes of genuine collaboration, which it sees as "rooted in cultural traditions of the common people . . . which are resplendent with feelings and attitudes of an altruistic, cooperative and communal nature and which are genuinely democratic" (Fals-Borda & Rahman, 1991, p. 5). Those agents of change who initiate PAR processes among oppressed peoples must embrace a genuine commitment to work with these democratic values and to honor the wisdom of the people. A key notion here is dialogue, because it is through dialogue that the subject-object relationship of traditional science gives way to a subject-subject one, in which the academic knowledge of formally educated people works in a dialectical tension with the popular knowledge of the people to produce a more profound understanding of the situation.

Some practitioners (e.g., Hall, 1992) claim that the term *participatory action research* was originally used to describe this form of liberationist inquiry in the underprivileged parts of both the "Third World" and the developed West (Gaventa, 1991). Other practitioners have applied the term to their work in Western organizations (Cohen, Greenwood, & Harkavay, 1992; Greenwood, Whyte, & Harkavay, 1993; Whyte, 1991), borrowing, it is argued, the terminology of the "original" version. Many PAR practitioners object to this: It is offensive, first, because it is seen as a way in which the rich establishment is once again co-opting and colonizing the world of the underprivileged; second, because this approach is based on a liberal rather than a radical ideology and holds quite different assumptions about the relationship between popular knowledge and "scientific knowledge"; and third, because to use the same term for significantly different processes confuses the necessary debate between the variety of collaborative inquiry approaches (Brown, 1993; but see also Whyte, 1992).

Critique of Orthodox Research

Practitioners of PAR work mainly in communities that are vulnerable to colonization by the dominant culture. The primary critique of nonparticipatory research is that it serves this dominant culture through monopolizing the development and use of knowledge to the disadvantage of the communities in which the research takes place, and is thus exploitive.

Tandon (1982) offers four points in his critique of monopolistic research. The *absolutist* critique argues that pure knowledge generation cannot be the aim of social research because the assumption that there can be one pure truth in social research is erroneous. The *purist* critique attacks the social science crusade for objectivity: When strict separation is maintained between researcher and subject in the guise of maintaining rigor, all control of the research is retained in the hands of the researcher. The *rationalist* critique points out that the classical research paradigm has, in the interests of maintaining objectivity, overemphasized thinking as the means of knowing, neglecting feeling and acting. And the *elitist* critique points out that as the dominant research paradigm is available only to a body of professionals who enjoy elite status, the research they conduct is most likely to enhance the economic and ideological advantage of their class.

Tandon (1989) has developed this critique to argue that, in contrast, PAR values the people's knowledge, sharpens their capacity to conduct their own research in their own interests, helps them appropriate knowledge produced by the dominant knowledge industry for their own interests and purposes, allows problems to be explored from their perspective, and, maybe most important, liberates their minds for critical reflection, questioning, and the continuous pursuit of inquiry, thus contributing to the liberation of their minds and the development of freedom and democracy.

Methods in Participatory Action Research

In reading the literature on PAR it is easier to discover the ideology of the approach than a detailed description of what actually takes place. As Tandon (1989) points out, PAR is a *methodology* for an alternate system of knowledge production based on the people's role in setting the agendas, participating in the data gathering and analysis, and controlling the use of the outcomes. The PAR methodology may use diverse *methods,* both quantitative and qualitative, to further these ends, many of which will derive from vernacular (often oral) traditions of communication and dissemination of knowledge (Hall, 1993). The preferred way to communicate the practice of PAR seems to be through the description of actual cases. A criticism from outside is that many of these lack the kind of detail that would enable a reader to comprehend fully and learn about the approach taken.

Further, in keeping with the emphasis on PAR as inquiry as empowerment, the actual methodologies that in orthodox research would be called research design, data gathering, data analysis, and so on take second place to the emergent processes of collaboration and dialogue that empower, motivate, increase self-esteem, and develop community solidarity. As de Roux (1991) puts it, the methodologies employed must at

> the rational level . . . be capable of releasing the people's pent-up knowledge, and in doing so liberate their hitherto stifled thoughts and voices, stimulating creativity and developing their analytical and critical capabilities. . . . [And] at the emotional level, the process [must] be capable of releasing feelings, of tearing down the participants' internal walls in order to free up energy for action. (p. 44)

Community meetings and events of various kinds are an important part of PAR, serving to identify issues, to reclaim a sense of community and emphasize the potential for liberation, to make sense of information collected, to reflect on progress of the project, and to develop the ability of the community to continue the PAR and developmental process. These meetings engage in a variety of activities that are in keeping with the culture of the community and might look out of place in an orthodox research project. Thus storytelling, sociodrama, plays and skits, puppets, song, drawing and painting, and other engaging activities encourage a social validation of "objective" data that cannot be obtained through the orthodox processes of survey and fieldwork. It is important for an oppressed group, which may be part of a culture of silence based on centuries of oppression, to find ways to tell and thus reclaim their own story (Salazar, 1991).

The process of participation and dialogue often starts with an intervention that has a formal objective of adult literacy or development of health care. Thus in a tribal village in India funds were originally provided for an adult education project. Despite many difficulties, not least of which was dealing with the "culture of silence" of the village, the educators were able to develop these classes as "a forum for open discussion on the socio-economic position of the village and a place for beginning action to change it" (Singh, 1981, p. 164). The outcome of this was not only improved economic conditions (the villagers decided to build a road to the village, where no proper link with the wider world had existed), but also an enhanced sense of community self-determination and a social structure in which future development decisions might be made.

PAR may also use methodology that looks more "orthodox": The systematic gathering of information, for example, through survey techniques, and then making sense of it from the perspective of the community is often an important source of people's knowledge and empowerment (de Roux, 1991; Gaventa & Horton, 1981; Rahman, 1991; Tandon & Brown, 1981).

Action Science and Action Inquiry

In his early work on action inquiry, Torbert (1981b) argued that

> research and action, even though analytically distinguishable, are inextricably intertwined in practice. . . . Knowledge is always gained in action and for action. . . . From this starting point, to question the validity of social science is to question, not how to develop a *reflective* science *about* action, but how to develop genuinely well-informed action—how to conduct an *action science*. (p. 145)

Action science and action inquiry are forms of inquiry into practice; they are concerned with the development of effective action that may contribute to the transformation of organizations and communities toward greater effectiveness and greater justice (Torbert, 1991a). Action science is a body of work developed over the past two decades primarily by Argyris and Schön (1974, 1978; Argyris, Putnam, & Smith, 1985; Schön, 1983). Starting in part from this work, Torbert has emphasized some contrasting issues in his development of action inquiry, particularly with regard to power and leadership.

Theories of Action

Central to the action science perspective is the identification of the theories that actors use to guide their behavior; the claim is that it is possible to identify such theories and in broad terms to predict their consequences. A key distinction here is between espoused theories, which are those an individual claims to follow, and theories-in-use that can be inferred from action; these two may be consistent or inconsistent, and the actor may or may not be aware of any inconsistency. Theories-in-use may be made explicit by reflection on action (Argyris et al., 1985, pp. 81-83).

One of the major difficulties of action science rests in the defensiveness of human beings, their ability to produce self-fulfilling and self-sealing systems of action and justification, often with patterns of escalating error (Argyris et al., 1985, p. 61). These difficulties are compounded by the requirement to reflect not only on the action strategy being employed, but also on the "governing variables" (Argyris et al., 1985, p. 84), the assumptions that lie behind and inform the action strategy. Thus the critical distinction also made by Argyris and Schön (1974) between single-loop and double-loop learning, *double-loop learning* referring to the capacity of individuals to reflect on and amend not only their action strategies, but also the governing variables behind those strategies.

Argyris and his colleagues have identified two theories of action that illustrate these issues. Model I is a defensive theory that limits action science, commonplace in Western institutions; Model II is a normative theory that promotes a spirit of open inquiry.

The governing variables of Model I are (a) to achieve the purpose as the actor defines it; (b) to win, not to lose; (c) to suppress negative feelings; and (d) to emphasize rationality. This theory of action gives rise to defensive and controlling behavior that limits and cuts short possibilities for inquiry and learning. There is little public testing of ideas, and behavior is fixed in a self-sealing conventional pattern leading to decreased effectiveness.

In contrast to Model I, the "normative perspective that guides the action scientist" is found in Model II, the governing variables of which include (a) valid information, (b) free and informed choice, and (c) internal commitment. These are "the features of the alternative worlds that action science seeks to create" (Argyris et al., 1985, p. 98). These very different governing variables lead to behavioral strategies that actively seek information and increased participation from others, and thus lead to greater effectiveness.

Torbert's articulation of action inquiry builds on the work of Argyris and his colleagues, but also departs from it in significant ways. Action *science* focuses on the implicit cognitive models of practitioners and on their actual verbal actions. Action *inquiry,* although it addresses these, in addition addresses outcomes (measured empirically) and the quality of one's own attention (monitored by meditative exercises as one acts). Further, action inquiry addresses the question of how to transform organizations and communities into collaborative, self-reflective communities of inquiry.

Torbert argues that for an individual, community, or organization to practice action inquiry, that person, community, or organization requires valid knowledge of four "territories" of human experience: first, knowledge about the system's own *purposes*—an intuitive or spiritual knowledge of what goals are worthy of pursuit and what demands attention at any point in time (and thus also the knowledge of when another purpose becomes more important); second, knowledge about its *strategy,* an intellectual or cognitive knowledge of the theories underlying its choices; third, a knowledge of the *behavioral* choices open to it—essentially a practical knowledge, resting on an awareness of oneself and on interpersonal skill; and finally, knowledge of the *outside world,* in particular an empirical knowledge of the consequences of its behavior. Thus:

> The vision of action inquiry is an attention that spans and integrates the four territories of human experience. This attention is what sees, embraces, and corrects incongruities among mission, strategy, operations, and outcomes. It is the source of the "true sanity of natural awareness of the whole." (Torbert, 1991a, p. 219)

For Torbert (1991a), action inquiry is "a kind of scientific inquiry that is conducted in everyday

TABLE 20.1 Governing Frames at Successive Developmental Stages

Stage	*Torbert*	*Kegan*	*Loevinger*	*Governing Frame*	*Focus of Awareness*
1	impulsive	impulsive	impulsive	impulse rules reflexes	
2	opportunist	imperial	opportunistic	needs, interests rule impulses	outside world, effects
3	diplomat	interpersonal	conformist	expectations rule interests	socially expected behavior
4	technician	(transition)	(transition)	internal craft logic rules expectations	internal logic, thought
5	achiever	institutional	conscientious	system success in environment rules craft logics	interplay of plan, practice, and effect
6	strategist	(transition)	autonomous	principle rules system	synthetic theory of system environment development over time
7	magician	(transition)	(transition)	process (interplay of principle/action) awareness rules principle	interplay of awareness, thought, action, and outside world in eternal now
8	ironist	interindividual	integrated	intersystem development awareness rules process	interplay of self and other systems in Kairatic history

SOURCE: Torbert (1989, 1991a).

life." Action inquiry differs from orthodox science in that it is concerned with "primary" data encountered "on-line" and "in the midst of perception and action" and only secondarily with recorded information. Action inquiry is "consciousness in the midst of action" (p. 221).

Now, as Torbert (1976) points out, "the discipline and rigor involved in this sort of research is formidable"; he suggests that a person must undergo what appears to be an unimaginable scale of self-development before becoming capable of relationally valid action (p. 167). In exploring this issue of personal development further, Torbert draws on the ancient tradition of search for an integrative quality of awareness and on modern theories of ego development, particularly the work of Loevinger (1976) and Kegan (1980) (see Table 20.1).

From these theories we can see that only toward the *later* stages of development is the person "aware that there are alternative frames, that perceptions, including one's own, are always framed by assumptions, and that such assumptions can be tested and transformed" (Torbert, 1989, p. 86). Thus it is not until the stage Torbert calls the *strategist* does behavior that can be characterized as collaborative inquiry appear: Earlier stages are characterized by what he calls "mystery-mastery" behavior, which is similar to Argyris's Model I. Collaborative inquiry involves the individual practitioner in continually reflecting on his or her own behavior-in-action while simultaneously behaving in a fashion that invites other members of the community to do the same (and is thus similar to Argyris's Model II).

For the organization or community, collaborative inquiry involves explicit shared reflection about the collective dream and mission, open rather than masked interpersonal relations, systematic evaluation and feedback of collective and individual performance, and direct facing and creative resolution of those paradoxes that otherwise become polarized conflicts (Torbert, 1987, p. 128).

In his later writing, Torbert (1991a, n.d.) emphasizes that transformational leadership and the exercise of transforming power are essential if organizational cultures characterized by mystery-mastery or Model I processes are to change into communities of inquiry characterized by collaborative inquiry or Model II. He suggests there are four types of social power: unilateral power, diplomatic power, rational power, and transforming power. These are based on discussions of Hobbes, Rousseau, Kant, and Rawls, respectively. Organizations will not change through the exercise of unilateral leadership or through abdication of leadership. Rather, they require the power of balance, a subtle, ironic, at times diabolical, certainly paradoxical, exercise of all four types of power. Torbert uses Gandhi as one example of a transformational leader quite willing to act unilaterally and to break all codes of acceptable behavior when he viewed it to be in the service of his people.

But even when using power unilaterally, transforming leadership invites cooperation and mutuality from others. It is based on an effort to be aware of the present moment in all its fullness, recognizing that such an effort can never be completely successful. Transforming power is not just open to feedback, but is actively vulnerable in seeking challenge and contradiction, seeking out ways in which its exercise is blind and unaware. Transforming power is particularly sensitive to the timeliness of behavior, and to the analogical, metaphorical quality of action. And the intent of transforming power is to empower all those who come within its reach, including those who oppose its influence. Torbert's (1991a, n.d.) recent work provides many examples of the quest for the exercise of such transforming power.

The Practice of Action Science and Action Inquiry

The purpose of both practices is to engage with one's own action and with others in a self-reflective way, so that all become more aware of their behavior and of its underlying theories. Both practices base their work on the "raw" data of accounts and recordings of practice (usually in the form of "talk") gathered by the actors themselves, and both encourage public testing of one's own perceptions and the use of action experiments to test new theories of action and to develop new skills. One of the key skills in this process is to find ways of sidestepping one's own and others' defensive responses to the painful process of self-reflection.

Both Argyris and his colleagues and Torbert explore in detail the behavioral skills needed for this. Argyris, pointing to the extreme difficulties of discovering mistakes in action, suggests seven heuristic rules for the action scientist (Argyris et al., 1985, pp. 258-261). Similarly, Torbert identifies four dimensions of conversation—framing, advocacy, illustration, and inquiry—that correspond to the four territories of experience—purpose, strategy, behavior, and the outside world. In *framing,* the speaker names assumptions that bound the conversation, the "name of the game," the purpose of speaking; in *advocacy,* a particular path of action is argued for explicitly; in *illustration,* the advocacy is grounded in a concrete example or colorful story; and in *inquiry,* the listeners are explicitly invited to respond.

Torbert argues that confusion and the misuse of power result when these four parts of speech are left tacit, and asserts that a person practicing action inquiry will, as well as developing a span of attention across the four territories of consciousness, cultivate a form of speech that explicitly includes these four aspects of conversation. The process of self-study in action is a way of cultivating this span of awareness and behavioral flexibility (Torbert, 1991a, 1991b; Torbert & Fisher, 1992).

Co-Operative Inquiry, Participatory Action Research, and Action Inquiry: A Comparison

These three approaches to participative research start from different ideological perspectives, draw on different intellectual traditions, and emphasize different aspects of practice. Yet together they stand in marked contrast to orthodox social research. To date they have to a very large extent been self-contained traditions, with little constructive interchange of ideas and practice, so a comparison can be expected to show what they might learn from each other and ways in which they may be complementary in practice. (I have resisted the temptation to compare the three in a chart or diagram because I feel that this might lead the reader to see comparisons in a more robust way than intended.)

Ontology

The ontological position of all participative approaches to inquiry is well expressed by Paulo Freire (1982):

> The concrete reality for many social scientists is a list of particular facts that they would like to capture; for example, the presence or absence of water, problems concerning erosion in the area. For me, the concrete reality is something more than isolated facts. In my view, thinking dialectically, the concrete reality consists not only of concrete facts and (physical) things, but also includes the ways in which the people involved with these facts perceive them. Thus in the last analysis, for me, the concrete reality is the connection between subjectivity and objectivity, never objectivity isolated from subjectivity. (p. 30)

This is close to a relativist ontology (Guba, 1990). In some important senses we choose our reality and our knowing of it—individually and collectively; therefore, valid human inquiry essentially requires full participation in the creation of personal and social knowings:

> We have to learn to think dialectically, to view reality as a process, always emerging through a self-contradictory development, always becoming; knowing this reality is neither subjective nor objective, it is both wholly independent of me and wholly dependent on me. (Reason & Rowan, 1981, p. 241)

As methods of *action* inquiry, practitioners of all three would emphasize that these constructions of reality become manifest not just through the "mind," but through the *reflective action* of persons and communities. They draw on many sources: on Dewey's (1929) criticism of the traditional separation of knowledge and action, on MacMurray's (1957) argument for the primacy of action over reflection, on Habermas's (1972) articulation of a critical science serving emancipatory interests, on Maxwell's (1984) proposal for a philosophy of wisdom based on offering solutions to practical human concerns, on Skolimowski's (1992) argument that the process of living is a process of knowing. PAR would emphasize the collective aspect of this, pointing to ways in which the reality of oppressed people is colonized by an alien reality, whereas Torbert (1991a) would emphasize the intensely personal in his quest for living inquiry.

Knowledge arises in and for action. The interest, as Argyris and his colleagues point out, is not in developing an applied science, but in a genuine science of action. All three forms of inquiry emphasize the systematic testing of theory in live-action contexts.

The implication of this epistemology of action is that the primary outcome of all these forms of inquiry is a change in the lived experience of those involved in the inquiry. Participants are empowered to define their world in the service of what they see as worthwhile interests, and as a consequence they change their world in significant ways, through action—building a road to their village, developing a new form of holistic medical practice—and through experience—developing a sense of empowerment and competence. The articulation of the new forms of knowledge in lectures, articles, and books is a secondary outcome.

Epistemology

The three approaches unite to emphasize the fundamental importance of experiential knowing. Thus for co-operative inquiry experience is the "touchstone" of the method, involving a "fundamental phenomenological discrimination of persons in relation to their world" (Heron, 1981a, p. 158; 1992); for PAR it is "through the actual experience of something that we intuitively apprehend its essence; we feel, enjoy and understand it as reality" (Fals-Borda & Rahman, 1991, p. 4); and the vision of action inquiry is of an interpenetrating consciousness of living inquiry (Torbert, 1991a, p. 258). Thus all three approaches hold strongly the vision that people can learn to be self-reflexive about their world and their action within it. The notions of praxis, critical subjectivity, double-loop learning, and interpenetrating consciousness are very close.

All three approaches articulate an extended epistemology: For the co-operative inquiry this involves an interplay of experiential, presentational, propositional, and practical knowledge; for PAR it involves the reclaiming of three broad ways of knowing—thinking, feeling, and acting (Tandon, 1989); and for action inquiry it is an attention that interpenetrates the territories of intuitive purposes, intellectual strategy, behavioral expression, and the outside world. All three perspectives embrace the idea that experiential knowing arises through participation with others.

With this emphasis on experiential knowing comes the need to explore the question of subjectivity. The co-operative inquiry perspective is that research is always personal, political, and spiritual; knowledge is always from a perspective and for a purpose. The co-operative inquiry method—the cycling and recycling through phases of action and reflection, and the application of validity procedures—is the discipline through which the co-inquirers are able to *critically see through* their subjectivity. They are able to articulate the perspective they are taking and begin to see through the distortions that arise through the bias of their personal and class position. Thus the process of inquiry must also always involve the personal development of the co-inquirers as they move from being relatively unreflexively subjective toward a position of critical subjectivity (Reason & Marshall, 1987; Reason & Rowan, 1981, chap. 10).

The PAR perspective provides us in addition with understanding of how ideology and epistemology, knowledge and power, are bound up together. If an inquiry is primarily engaged in service of a dominant class it will not need to dialogue with people: it is not interested in their reality, but rather in imposing on them a dominant reality. On the other hand, if an inquiry is engaged in the service of the development of people, it will necessarily engage with them in dialogue. This points us in the direction of the possibility of a "real popular science" (Fals-Borda, 1981, 1982).

I have been asked by the editors of this volume to comment on the relationship between the epistemology of participative approaches to inquiry and postmodern and poststructural perspectives. These, as I understand them, argue that we cannot sensibly speak of raw, lived experience because experience can be accessed only through the discourse or text through which it is expressed, and that there are multiple shifting discourses, all determined through the social context. Thus any attempt at an experiential knowing is impossible from the start because we can do no more than interpret our experience through existing categories of thought, all of which lie open to radical deconstruction.

I have two problems with this perspective. First, the argument for experiential knowing is that of a radical phenomenology: Our primal experience of the world, if we will only open ourselves to it, is present prior to culture (Heron, 1992). To be sure, our experience is deeply influenced by our discourse, but we can learn to bracket off that discourse and approach experience more directly. We can do this through mindfulness disciplines (meditation, T'ai Chi, Gurdjief work [Torbert, n.d.], Alexander Technique, and so on), through consciousness-raising, and through systematic engagement with the cycles of action and reflection that are a central part of participative and action inquiry methods.

My second problem is that the poststructural perspective, certainly in its extreme form, is overintellectualized and thus both nihilistic and oppressive. Voices are just voices; they have no claim to truth, so the search for voice is seen as being the search for any old voice. And given current power relations on the planet, the first voices likely to be "deconstructed" are those of people already oppressed, the voices of the poor, of women, but also the voices of the body and of the earth itself. Spretnak (1992) argues that the excesses of philosophical deconstructionism are as life denying as scientism, and points out that the erasure of the body is first and foremost the erasure of the female body.

Participative, action-oriented approaches to inquiry work to move beyond this overintellectualized approach and to ground knowing and action literally in the body of experience—"coming to our senses," as Berman (1989) puts it.

Data

It is interesting to note that the three approaches place different emphases on what is to be taken as "data," the recording of experience for the purpose of reflection. At the more conservative end, Argyris's version of action science relies almost entirely on formally recorded reports of conversations. Torbert's version of action inquiry includes as data a whole range of personal experience and idiosyncratic expression, and, although primarily verbal, reaches toward what he terms the "meditatively postverbal" (personal communication, 1992). Co-operative inquiry relies primarily on rational verbal reports of experience, but is branching out into imaginative storytelling (Reason & Hawkins, 1988) and metaphor (Cunningham, 1984).

Toward the other end of the spectrum, PAR wholeheartedly embraces a whole range of expressive forms, including song, dance, and theater, as well as more orthodox forms of data. This expressive activity in PAR not only enriches the inquiry, but provides a means through which ordinary people may experience and validate the data being used. If we take Heron's admonition to take expressive forms of knowing seriously and learn from the example of PAR, we may see much richer, more colorful, and more intense forms of inquiry in the future.

Attitudes Toward Leadership

In celebrating the common people's knowledge, and in emphasizing the role of participation and self-direction in development, the perspective of PAR is radically egalitarian. Rahman (1991, p. 20) argues that movements for social change are normally led by intellectuals who are in a position to provide leadership not because of any particular aptitude but because they are privileged by their economic and social status. He points to the many dangers of relying on an elite leadership for social transformation: the dangers of inflated egos; the fragility of commitment in the face of attractive temptations; the problems of the growth in size of the elite class as a movement grows and the danger of attracting new adherents holding altogether different commitments; and, finally, the self-perpetuating character of the institutions created to provide leadership. He argues that "democracy . . . is a necessity for revolutionary development" because it gives "freedom to take initiatives" (p. 22).

Yet, paradoxically, many PAR projects would not occur without the initiative of someone with time, skill, and commitment, someone who will almost inevitably be a member of a privileged and educated group. PAR appears to sit uneasily with this. Salazar (1991) points out how both participatory researchers and those with whom they aspire to work are in Colombian society part of a "long chain of transmission of authoritarian traits," and that outsiders are prone to "see what should be done" and maybe rush in without full participation. Thus "authoritarian attitudes (even unconsciously) may lead to actions which reproduce current domination patterns" (p. 56). On the other hand, Brown (1993) and his colleagues have established training programs for leaders of nongovernmental organizations doing innovative work in developing countries.

It is interesting to contrast this wary attitude toward leadership with Torbert's (1991a) argument that transformational leadership and the skilled exercise of the power of balance is *essential* for the development of social systems toward greater justice and effectiveness. Heron (1989) similarly argues for what he terms "distress-free charismatic authority" in group facilitation, which he sees as involving an ever-changing balance among three modes: hierarchy and the exercise of legitimate authority; the peer principle and the sharing of power with a group; and the autonomy principle, which respects the freedom of each person to exercise his or her own judgment.

Although we may accept that persons are fundamentally self-directing and celebrate the common people's altruism and ability to cooperate, we must also recognize that in Northern and Southern societies alike many of the groups who might benefit from participative inquiry are alienated from the processes of knowledge creation and may be part of a "culture of silence" (Singh, 1981; Whitmore, in press). It is arguable that a practice that emphasizes participation demands an understanding of enlightened leadership. Thus co-operative inquiry is an emergent process that participants are first led through, amend and develop in the light of their experience, and finally embrace as their own. Action inquiry includes the construction of "liberating structures" (Torbert, 1991a, chap. 5) that paradoxically demand the exercise of freedom. PAR requires sustained authentic dialogue between intellectuals and the people they wish to serve.

In all this there is a tension between the ideal—and the rhetoric—of participation and the practical demands for effective leadership. This tension, this living paradox, we have to live with, to find creative resolution moment to moment.

These questions of leadership draw our attention to the process of training—both the training of initiating facilitators and "animators" and the training of participants. There is a whole range of skills required for participative research, skills that are very different from those of orthodox research, and that include personal skills of self-awareness and self-reflexiveness, facilitative skills in interpersonal and group settings, political skills, intellectual skills, and data management skills. For discussions on training for leadership in PAR, see de Oliveira (1982); D'Abreo (1981); PRIA (1982, 1987a, 1987b); Bobo, Kendall, and Max (1991); Highlander Center (1989); Brown (1993); and Fals-Borda (1988). For work addressing training for leadership in action sciences and action inquiry, see Argyris et al. (1985, chaps. 9-12), Schön (1983), Torbert (1981a, 1991a, 1991b), and Krim (1988); for co-operative inquiry, see especially Heron (1989).

A Mutual Critique of the Three Approaches

While accepting that the three methodologies are in some sense cousins in a family of participative research, it is useful to look from one to the others in a friendly and supportive critique. Thus co-operative inquiry appears from the perspective of PAR to overemphasize the psychological at the expense of the political, the microprocesses of small group behavior at the expense of the wider political processes that define reality. And from the perspective of action inquiry it can be seen as lacking a robust theory of action and of the exercise of power.

From the perspective of co-operative inquiry the writings on PAR appear to romanticize the goodness and democratic tendencies of the common people, and to ignore the ways in which all groups may be destructive and distort their experience. Reports on PAR projects often appear to be long on ideology and short on systematic practice. From the perspective of action inquiry, PAR, in emphasizing the importance of sharing power, fails to consider seriously the ways in which leaders of democratic movements must develop personally and learn to exercise transforming power.

Finally, action inquiry may appear from the other two perspectives to be advocating an updated version of a Western and masculine "rugged individualism," to be elitist in its emphasis on the later stages of ego development, and to ignore the contribution of common people in both the small group and the wider collective.

A Possible Integration

What, then, are the major strengths of each approach and how might they be integrated? The PAR strategy of developing knowledge through empowering dialogue initially between an animator and a community of people appears to be most appropriate when the inquiry involves a relatively large number of people who are initially disempowered. PAR also draws our attention to the political issues concerning ownership of knowledge, and to the need to create communities of people who are capable of continuing the PAR process. We see this process at work in the underprivileged rural and urban settings in Southern countries, and as Gaventa (1991) points out, it is also appropriate in Northern countries, particularly as the gap between rich and poor grows wider.

Co-operative inquiry is a strategy more likely to be successful with a group of people who experience themselves as relatively empowered and who wish to explore and develop their practice together. Thus it is a form of inquiry appropriate for smaller groups of professionals—for example, doctors, teachers, or managers—who wish to explore and develop their practice systematically. It is also a process through which a group of disempowered people may join together to explore their world, although initially such a group may be more dependent on an initiating facilitator in the manner of PAR.

Action inquiry draws our attention to the particular individual skills required for valid inquiry with others. It confronts us with the need to cultivate a wide-ranging and subtle attention; it suggests that we can develop such an attention only as we move toward the later stages of ego development; and it offers methods for the detailed examination of our purposes, theories, and behavior, and the consequences of these for our world. Torbert suggests that, in a sense, action inquiry is a discipline relevant to those most deeply committed to participative approaches to inquiry, persons who wish to play leadership roles in cultivating this process with others and who wish to inquire about their actual effects as they do so (personal communication, 1992).

One might say that PAR serves the community, cooperative inquiry the group, and action inquiry the individual practitioner. But this is clearly a gross oversimplification, because each of the triad is fully dependent on the others. It would seem that a PAR project would be strengthened if the animators met together as a co-operative inquiry group to reflect on their practice; a co-operative inquiry would be helped if the members cultivated the interpenetrating attention advocated by action inquiry.

Let me then speculate about how these three processes might come together in one project. Imagine a group of people concerned with changing some aspect of their world—it might be a group of PAR animators engaged in developmental work in rural villages, or a group of teachers exploring education as liberation in London or New York, or a group of health care professionals wishing to work in a more holistic and person-centered fashion. Members of such a group would meet together as a co-operative inquiry group, defining their common area of interest and moving through cycles of action and reflection, meeting regularly to review progress.

In their work with a wider group of people—the villagers, the students, the patients—they would engage in the developmental dialogue of PAR. They would work to gain entry and trust in a community, help that community define its needs, and engage in all the processes of PAR discussed above. This might mean that a particular project becomes the focus of this aspect of their work—a developmental process in a village, a self-help or healing group with patients.

At the same time, they would scrutinize their individual practices through action inquiry, keeping comprehensive records of their experiences and behaviors, reviewing these in detail, engaging in experiments in action, and so on. Of course, these PAR and action inquiry processes would also become the subjects for mutual reflection in the co-operative inquiry group, which would probably lead to creative new ways of engaging in the wider group involved in PAR, so the whole process would knit together as one whole.

In view of the complementarity of these three approaches to research with people, it is curious that so far they have developed in separate communities with little cross-fertilization of ideas. It is my hope that this chapter will provide a stimulus for some future dialogue.

References

Argyris, C., Putnam, R., & Smith, M. C. (1985). *Action science: Concepts, methods, and skills for research and intervention.* San Francisco: Jossey-Bass.

Argyris, C., & Schön, D. (1974). *Theory in practice: Increasing professional effectiveness.* San Francisco: Jossey-Bass.

Argyris, C., & Schön, D. (1978). *Organizational learning.* Reading, MA: Addison-Wesley.

Baring, A., & Cashford, J. (1991). *The myth of the goddess: Evolution of an image.* London: Viking.

Bateson, G. (1972a). The logical categories of learning and communication. In G. Bateson, *Steps to an ecology of mind.* San Francisco: Chandler.

Bateson, G. (1972b). *Steps to an ecology of mind.* San Francisco: Chandler.

Berman, M. (1989). *Coming to our senses: Body and spirit in the hidden history of the West.* New York: Simon & Schuster.

Bobo, K., Kendall, J., & Max, S. (1991). *Organizing for social change.* New Market, TN: Highlander Center.

Brown, L. D. (1993). Participatory action research for social change: Collective reflections with Asian nongovernmental development organizations. In M. Elden & R. Chisholm (Eds.), Varieties of action research [Special issue]. *Human Relations, 46,* 249-273.

Cancian, F. M., & Armstead, C. (1992). Participatory research. In E. F. Borgatta & M. Borgatta (Eds.), *Encyclopedia of sociology* (Vol. 3). New York: Macmillan.

Cancian, F. M., & Armstead, C. (1993). Bibliography on participatory research. *Collaborative Inquiry, 9.*

Cohen, A. B., Greenwood, D. J., & Harkavay, I. (1992). Social research for social change: Varieties of participatory action research. *Collaborative Inquiry, 7,* 2-8.

Cooperrider, D. L., & Srivastva, S. (1987). Appreciative inquiry in organizational life. In W. Pasmore & R. Woodman (Eds.), *Research in organizational change and development* (Vol. 1, pp. 129-169). Greenwich, CT: JAI.

Cunningham, I. (1984). *Teaching styles in learner centred management development programmes.* Unpublished doctoral dissertation, Lancaster University.

D'Abreo, D. A. (1981). Training for participatory evaluation. In W. Fernandes & R. Tandon (Eds.), *Participatory research and evaluation: Experiments in research as a process of liberation.* New Delhi: Indian Social Institute.

de Oliveira, R. D. (1982). The militant observer: A sociological alternative. In B. Hall, A. Gillette, & R. Tandon (Eds.), *Creating knowledge: A monopoly? Participatory research in development.* New Delhi: Society for Participatory Research in Asia.

de Roux, G. I. (1991). Together against the computer. In O. Fals-Borda & M. A. Rahman (Eds.), *Action and knowledge: Breaking the monopoly with participatory action research.* New York: Intermediate Technology/Apex.

Devereaux, G. (1967). *From anxiety to method in the behavioural sciences.* The Hague: Mouton.

Dewey, J. (1929). *The quest for certainty.* New York: Minton, Balch.

Elden, M., & Chisholm, R. (Eds.). (1993). Varieties of action research [Special issue]. *Human Relations, 46*(2).

Fals-Borda, O. (1981). Science and the common people. *Journal of Social Studies, 11,* 1-21.

Fals-Borda, O. (1982). Participatory research and rural social change. *Journal of Rural Cooperation, 10,* 25-40.

Fals-Borda, O. (1988). *Knowledge and people's power: Lessons with peasants in Nicaragua, Mexico and Colombia.* New Delhi: Indian Social Institute.

Fals-Borda, O. & Rahman, M. A. (Eds.). (1991). *Action and knowledge: Breaking the monopoly with participatory action research.* New York: Intermediate Technology/Apex.

Fernandes, W., & Tandon, R. (Eds.). (1981). *Participatory research and evaluation: Experiments in research as a process of liberation.* New Delhi: Indian Social Institute.

Fox, M. (1991). *Creation spirituality: Liberating gifts for the peoples of the earth.* New York: HarperCollins.

Freire, P. (1970). *Pedagogy of the oppressed.* New York: Herder & Herder.

Freire, P. (1982). Creating alternative research methods: Learning to do it by doing it. In B. Hall, A. Gillette, & R. Tandon (Eds.), *Creating knowledge: A monopoly? Participatory research in development.* New Delhi: Society for Participatory Research in Asia.

Gaventa, J. (1991). Toward a knowledge democracy. In O. Fals-Borda & M. A. Rahman (Eds.), *Action and knowledge: Breaking the monopoly with participatory action research.* New York: Intermediate Technology/Apex.

Gaventa, J., & Horton, B. (1981). A citizen's research project in Appalachia. *Convergence, 14,* 30-40.

Greenwood, D. J., Whyte, W. F., & Harkavay I. (1993). Participatory action research as process and as goal. In M. Elden & R. Chisholm (Eds.), Varieties of action research. *Human Relations, 46,* 175-192.

Guba, E. G. (Ed.). (1990). *The paradigm dialog.* Newbury Park, CA: Sage.

Habermas, J. (1972). *Knowledge and human interests; Theory and practice; Communication and the evolution of society* (J. J. Shapiro, Trans.). London: Heinemann.

Hall, B., Gillette., A., & Tandon, R. (Eds.). (1982). *Creating knowledge: A monopoly? Participatory research in development.* New Delhi: Society for Participatory Research in Asia.

Hall, B. (1992, December). Letter to the editor. *Collaborative Inquiry, 8.*

Hall, B. (1993). Participatory research. In *International encyclopedia of education.* London: Pergamon.

Heron, J. (1971). *Experience and method: An inquiry into the concept of experiential research.* Surrey, UK: University of Surrey, Human Potential Research Project.

Heron, J. (1977). *Catharsis in human development.* Surrey, UK: University of Surrey, Human Potential Research Project.

Heron, J. (1981a). Experiential research methodology. In P. Reason & J. Rowan (Eds.), *Human inquiry: A sourcebook of new paradigm research.* Chichester, UK: John Wiley.

Heron, J. (1981b). Philosophical basis for a new paradigm. In P. Reason & J. Rowan (Eds.), *Human inquiry: A sourcebook of new paradigm research.* Chichester, UK: John Wiley.

Heron, J. (1988). Validity in co-operative inquiry. In P. Reason (Ed.), *Human inquiry in action.* London: Sage.

Heron, J. (1989). *The facilitator's handbook.* London: Kogan Page.

Heron, J. (1992). *Feeling and personhood: Psychology in another key.* London: Sage.

Highlander Center. (1989). *Highlander: An approach to education presented through a collection of writings.* New Market, TN: Author. (Available from Highlander Center, 159 Highlander Way, New Market, TN 37820, USA)

Kegan, R. (1980). *The evolving self.* Cambridge, MA: Harvard University Press.

Keller, E. F. (1985). *Reflections on gender and science.* New Haven, CT: Yale University Press.

Krim, R. (1988). Managing to learn: Action inquiry in city hall. In P. Reason (Ed.), *Human inquiry in action.* London: Sage.

Lichtenstein, B. M. (1988). Feminist epistemology: A thematic review. *Thesis Eleven, 21,* 140-151.

Loevinger, J. (1976). *Ego development.* San Francisco: Jossey-Bass.

MacMurray, J. (1957). *The self as agent.* London: Faber & Faber.

Maslow, A. (1968). *Toward a psychology of being.* New York: Van Nostrand.

Maturana, H., & Varela, F. (1986). *The tree of knowledge: A new look at the biological roots of human understanding.* Boston: New Science Library.

Maxwell, N. (1984). *From knowledge to wisdom: A revolution in the aims and methods of science.* Oxford: Basil Blackwell.

Naess, A. (1989). *Ecology, community and lifestyle.* Cambridge: Cambridge University Press.

Plant, J. (Ed.). (1989). *Healing the wounds: The promise of ecofeminism.* Philadelphia: New Society.

PRIA. (1982). *Participatory training for rural development.* New Delhi: Society for Participatory Research in Asia.

PRIA. (1987a). *Participatory training for adult educators.* New Delhi: Society for Participatory Research in Asia.

PRIA. (1987b). *Training of trainers: A manual for participatory training methodology in development.* New Delhi: Society for Participatory Research in Asia.

PRIA. (n.d.). [Brochure]. (Available from the Society for Participatory Research in Asia, 42 Tughlakabad Institutional Area, New Delhi-62, India)

Quantz, R. A. (1992). On critical ethnography (with some postmodern considerations). In M. D. LeCompte, W. L. Millroy, & J. Preissle (Eds.), *The handbook of qualitative research in education* (pp. 447-505). New York: Academic Press.

Rahman, M. A. (1991). Glimpses of the "other Africa." In O. Fals-Borda & M. A. Rahman (Eds.), *Action and knowledge: Breaking the monopoly with participatory action research.* New York: Intermediate Technology/Apex.

Randall, R., & Southgate, J. (1980). *Co-operative and community group dynamics . . . or your meetings needn't be so appalling.* London: Barefoot.

Reason, P. (Ed.). (1988). *Human inquiry in action.* London: Sage.

Reason, P. (Ed.). (in press). *Participation in human inquiry.* London: Sage.

Reason, P., & Hawkins, P. (1988). Inquiry through storytelling. In P. Reason (Ed.), *Human inquiry in action.* London: Sage.

Reason, P., & Heron, J. (1986). Research with people: The paradigm of co-operative experiential inquiry. *Person Centred Review, 1,* 456-475.

Reason, P., & Marshall, J. (1987). Research as personal process. In D. Boud & V. Griffin (Eds.), *Appreciating adults learning: From the learner's perspective.* London: Kogan Page.

Reason, P., & Rowan, J. (Eds.). (1981). *Human inquiry: A sourcebook of new paradigm research.* Chichester, UK: John Wiley.

Reinharz, S. (1992). *Feminist methods in social research.* New York: Oxford University Press.

Rogers, C. (1961). *On becoming a person.* London: Constable.

Rogers, C. (1969). *Freedom to learn.* New York: Charles Merrill

Rowan, J. (1976). *Ordinary ecstasy: Humanistic psychology in action.* London: Routledge & Kegan Paul.

Salazar, M. C. (1991). Young laborers in Bogota: Breaking authoritarian ramparts. In O. Fals-Borda & M. A. Rahman (Eds.), *Action and knowledge: Breaking the monopoly with participatory action research.* New York: Intermediate Technology/Apex.

Schön, D. A. (1983). *The reflective practitioner: How professionals think in action.* New York: Basic Books.

Schwartz, P., & Ogilvy, J. (1980). *The emergent paradigm: Changing patterns of thought and belief* (Analytical Report No. 7, Values and Lifestyles Program). Menlo Park, CA: SRI International.

Singh, M. (1981). Literacy to development: The growth of a tribal village. In W. Fernandes & R. Tandon (Eds.), *Participatory research and evaluation: Experiments in research as a process of liberation.* New Delhi: Indian Social Institute.

Skolimowski, H. (1992). *Living philosophy: Eco-philosophy as a tree of life.* London: Arkana.

Spretnak, C. (1992). *States of grace: The recovery of meaning in the postmodern age.* New York: Harper.

Srivastva, S., Obert, S. L., & Neilson, E. (1977). Organizational analysis through group processes: A theoretical perspective. In C. L. Cooper (Ed.), *Organizational development in the UK and USA.* London: Macmillan.

Stull, D. D., & Schensul, J. (1987). *Collaborative research and social change: Applied anthropology in action.* Boulder, CO: Westview.

Tandon, R. (1982). A critique of monopolistic research. In B. Hall, A. Gillette, & R. Tandon (Eds.), *Creating knowledge: A monopoly? Participatory research in development.* New Delhi: Society for Participatory Research in Asia.

Tandon, R. (1989). Participatory research and social transformation. *Convergence, 21*(2/3), 5-15.

Tandon, R., & Brown, L. D. (1981). Organization building for rural development: An experiment in India. *Journal of Applied Behavioural Science, 17,* 172-189.

Tiernan, M. de V., et al. (in press). Issues of power in collaborative experiential inquiry. In P. Reason (Ed.), *Participation in human inquiry.* London: Sage.

Torbert, W. R. (1976). *Creating a community of inquiry: Conflict, collaboration, transformation.* New York: John Wiley.

Torbert, W. R. (1981a). Empirical, behavioural, theoretical and attentional skills necessary for collaborative inquiry. In P. Reason & J. Rowan (Eds.), *Human inquiry: A sourcebook of new paradigm research.* Chichester, UK: John Wiley.

Torbert, W. R. (1981b). Why educational research has been so uneducational: The case for a new model of social science based on collaborative inquiry. In P. Reason & J. Rowan (Eds.), *Human inquiry: A sourcebook of new paradigm research.* Chichester, UK: John Wiley.

Torbert, W. R. (1987). *Managing the corporate dream: Restructuring for long-term success.* Homewood, IL: Dow Jones-Irwin.

Torbert, W. R. (1989). Leading organizational transformation. In W. Pasmore & R. Woodman (Eds.), *Research in organizational change and development* (Vol. 3, pp. 83-116). Greenwich, CT: JAI.

Torbert, W. R. (1991a). *The power of balance: Transforming self, society, and scientific inquiry.* Newbury Park, CA: Sage.

Torbert, W. R. (1991b). Teaching action inquiry. *Collaborative Inquiry, 5.*

Torbert, W. R. (n.d.). *Leadership and the spirit of inquiry.* Unpublished manuscript.

Torbert, W. R., & Fisher, D. (1992). Autobiographical awareness as a catalyst for managerial and organizational development. *Journal of Management Education and Development, 23*(3), 184-198.

Traylen, H. (1989). *Health visiting practice: An exploration into the nature of the health visitor's relationship with their clients.* Unpublished master's dissertation, University of Bath, School of Management.

Traylen, H. (in press). Health visiting practice: A cooperative inquiry. In P. Reason (Ed.), *Participation in human inquiry.* London: Sage.

Whitaker, D., Archer, L., & Greve, S. (1990). *Research, practice and service delivery: The contribution of research by practitioners.* London: Central Council for Education and Training in Social Work.

Whitmore, E. (in press). To tell the truth. In P. Reason (Ed.), *Participation in human inquiry.* London: Sage.

Whyte, W. F. (Ed.). (1991). *Participatory action research.* Newbury Park, CA: Sage.

Whyte, W. F. (1992). Note on concept clarification in research methodology. *Collaborative Inquiry, 8,* 5-6.

21

Clinical Research

WILLIAM L. MILLER
BENJAMIN F. CRABTREE

Conversing at the Wall

MELISSA belongs to the clan of one-breasted women (T. T. Williams, 1991) and lives amidst a Yankee New England landscape of walls. Poor, frightened, and 32 years old, she knows the breast cancer is spreading. Her life, composed of memories, children, career, lovers, and anticipated hopes, appears shredded; she fears no one is listening. Her doctors hide their fears and lose their empathy behind liver enzyme tests and offers of experimental chemotherapy clinical trial protocols. They feel tired, overregulated, and inadequate in the face of death but conceal their emotions behind a wall of professional arrogance. Melissa is administered a survey, which measures social support, locus of control, and risk exposure, by epidemiologists who fear loss of funding to the richly endowed laboratory across the street. There, experimental work on gene transfer techniques continues even as the investigators grouse about the annoying scratches of soft data epidemiologists, politicians, and feminists. Both groups of researchers hide behind their walls of objectivity and measurement. Meanwhile, a local social scientist listens to Melissa's story, observes the landscape of separation and domination, and then retreats behind an academic wall of jargon and disciplinary tradition. Terrified, angry, and confused, Melissa suffers more losses behind her own private wall.

This is the clinical research space we have witnessed—many conversations behind walls, but increased suffering in the clinical world. In this chapter, we imagine a clinical research space where Melissa, her doctors, and the researchers meet and seek transformation. We imagine a conversation at the walls (Brueggemann, 1991)—at the place where the walls meet clinical reality. This volume celebrates the qualitative research community's conversation behind the wall—the internal discourse about who we are and what we do, and about the faith and hope for our own transformation that is engendered there. Clinical biomedical research is currently dominated by positivism and a patriarchal bias that has ignored the qualitative and critical conversation. Fortunately, calls have begun for a shift away from a strictly positivist position, opening the way for greater methodological diversity, including the use of qualitative research methods (e.g., Freymann, 1989; McWhinney, 1986, 1989; Waitzkin, 1991). Patients and clinicians have usually been left out of all research conversations.[1] This chapter is about translation—about conversation at the walls. At the walls separating clinician from patient, qualitative from quantitative, academy from practice, very different ways or cultures of knowing can meet and converse. The clinical questions are the common ground (Taylor, 1993). It is at the walls where, in a language understandable by the existing clinical world, a space for more expansive imagination is created, tools for listening and seeing are shared, and transforming stories are enacted.

The understanding of clinical research presented in this chapter arises from the nexus of applied anthropology and the practice of primary health care. Both authors have joint appointments in family medicine and anthropology; we are on both sides of several walls. Our social science roots were fed by the development of clinically applied anthropology (Chrisman, 1977; Chrisman & Maretzki, 1982; Fabrega, 1976, 1979; Foster, 1974; Foster & Anderson, 1978; Polgar, 1962) in the 1970s, nurtured by the later work of Kleinman (1988, 1992; Kleinman, Eisenberg, & Good, 1978), Good and Good (1981), Lock (1982, 1986), Pelto and Pelto (1990), and Young (1982a, 1982b), and currently challenged by the poststructuralist debate (Burawoy et al., 1991; Clifford & Marcus, 1986; Jackson, 1989). One of us (WLM) has a busy urban family practice, and both of us actively participate in the politics and discourse of academic biomedicine and academic social science. The biomedical influence, with its perceived therapeutic imperative, steers toward pragmatic interventions and the desire for explicitness in information gathering and decision making and highlights the appeal of positivism and technology. The actual practice of patient care reveals the uncertainty and particularity (McWhinney, 1989) of clinical praxis and turns one toward storytelling, relationship, and interpretation. Trying to publish storied knowledge in biomedical journals exposes the realities of power and domination. The juxtapositions of seeing patients and teaching anthropology graduate students, medical students, and family practice residents focus the need to integrate teaching, practice, and research and locates a common ground for conversation—the clinical experience and the questions that arise there.

The guiding premise of this chapter is that the questions emerging from clinical experience frame conversation and determine research design (Brewer & Hunter, 1989; Diers, 1979; Miller & Crabtree, 1992). Clinical researchers have at least six discernible research styles available: experimental, survey, documentary-historical, field (qualitative), philosophical, and action/participatory (Lather, 1991; see also Reason, Chapter 20, this volume). The clinical research space needs to be open to all of these possible sources and types of knowledge. Thus this chapter is structured around the following three goals: creating an open research space that celebrates qualitative and critical approaches to the clinical world; providing the tools necessary for discovering and confirming clinical stories and knowledge within this space; and identifying and describing the means for sharing the stories and knowledge. The emphasis is on the clinical text of Western biomedicine and the particular subtext of the patient-physician clinical encounter, because of our own location in that place, but the discussion is easily transferred to other clinical contexts, such as nursing care, education, and organizational management (see also Berg & Smith, 1988; Sapsford & Abbott, 1992; Schein, 1987).

Creating a Space

The clinic is a public sanctuary for the voicing of trouble and dispensation of relief.[2] Each clinic participant crafts meaning out of the "facts" and "feelings" inherent in each clinical encounter and seeks to weave a comforting cloth of *support*. Clinical participants rarely study themselves in their clinical context and thus fail to challenge their own situated knowledge(s) and empower their own transformation. This requires bringing qualitative methods to the clinical experience, an experience where people appear unhappy.

"My back! I can't go on this way!" exclaims Liz, 34, single, high school educated, Hispanic, and mother of two preschool children, when Dr. George Ford, a primary care physician, enters the clinical space. He immediately pursues diagnosing the "disease" producing her pain. Unable to identify pathology, he concludes it is "only a strain" and hurriedly recommends bed rest, moist heat, and analgesics. Liz, unable to stay bed bound in an apartment with a 1-year-old and a 3-year-old, experiences worsening pain. Over the next year, the pain remains and finally results in surgery, chronic pain, disability, and permanent loss of employment. Elizabeth Ramirez's self-concept as Hispanic, woman, parent, employee, and citizen is hopelessly bedridden. George, confused and unhappy, continues seeing his patients.

This is the real world of clinical practice, involving intentions, meanings, intersubjectivity, values, personal knowledge, and ethics. Yet, most published clinical research consists of observational epidemiology (Feinstein, 1985; Kelsey, Thompson, & Evans, 1986; Kleinbaum, Kupper, & Morgenstern, 1982; Sackett, 1991) and clinical trial designs (Meinert, 1986; Pocock, 1983). These studies involve separating the variables of interest from their local, everyday milieus, entering them into a controlled research environment, and then trying to fit the results back into the original context. For example, Dr. Ford is aware of randomized trials demonstrating clinical efficacy for short-term bed rest in patients with back pain (Deyo, Diehl, & Rosenthal, 1986; Wiesel, Cuckler, DeLuca, et al., 1980), but he encounters difficulty when applying this information to the particular back pain and disability experienced by Ms. Ramirez.

Qualitative researchers have seen and heard the story and suffering of Liz and George, but it has been retold in a language that patients and clinicians do not understand (e.g., Fisher, 1986; Fisher & Todd, 1983; Lazarus, 1988; Mishler, 1984; West, 1984; G. Williams, 1984). Neither clinicians nor patients know the language of "ethnomethodology," "hermeneutics," "phenomenology," "semiotics," or "interpretive interactionism." Most qualitative clinical research is published in a language and in places that benefit researchers and not the patients and practitioners. Qualitative researchers have asked that clinicians join, listen to, and speak the "voice of the lifeworld" (Mishler, 1984). We ask clinical qualitative researchers to do the same.

The dominant biomedical world and the small qualitative research community both tend to maintain methodological and academic rigidity. Bringing clinical researchers to their walls is not easy. The strategy we advocate for creating a space assumes that change is more experience based than rational and that clinical participants must actively try methods if they are to adopt them. Thus we emphasize clinical participants' answering their own questions, using methods appropriate for those questions.

The dominant biomedical paradigm is rooted in a patriarchal positivism; *control through rationality* is the overriding theme. Deborah Gordon (1988) identifies the following seven basic premises of the biomedical model:

1. scientific rationality
2. emphasis on individual autonomy, rather than on family or community
3. the body as a biochemical machine, with emphasis on physiochemical data and objective, numerical measurement
4. mind/body dualism
5. diseases as entities
6. emphasis on the "visual"
7. reductionism and the seeking of universals

The characteristics of the clinical medical world that follow from this model include the following:

1. male centeredness
2. physician centeredness
3. specialist orientation
4. emphasis on credentials
5. high value on memory
6. a process orientation, with emphasis on technology, ritual, and therapeutic activism
7. division of the clinical space into "front" (receptionists, billing clerks, and office managers) and "back" (doctors, nurses, and phlebotomists)
8. the definition, importance, and sanctity of "medical time"
9. emphasis on patient satisfaction
10. reverence for the privacy of the doctor-patient relationship (Helman, 1990; Pfifferling, 1981; Stein, 1990)

These are the assumptions, values, and beliefs that characterize the dominant voice of the medical clinic and that currently define the boundaries of clinical research.

We propose that clinical researchers investigate questions emerging from the clinical experience, pay attention to and reveal any underlying values and assumptions, and direct the results toward clinical participants. This refocuses the gaze of clinical research onto the clinical experience and redefines its boundaries as the answer to three questions: Whose question is it? Are hidden assumptions of the clinical world revealed? For whom are the research results intended (i.e., who is the stakeholder or audience)? Patients and providers are invited to explore their own and/or each other's questions and concerns with whatever methods are necessary. Clinical researchers share ownership of the research with clinical participants, thus undermining the patriarchal bias of the dominant paradigm and opening its assumptions to investigation. This is the situated knowledge, the "somewhere in particular" (Haraway, 1991, p. 196), where space is created to find a larger, more inclusive vision of clinical research.

What are some of the clinically grounded questions that can serve as windows for opening imagination at the walls? Clinicians and patients seeking *support* in the health care setting confront three fundamental questions of clinical praxis: What is going on with my *body*? What is happening with my *life*? Who has what *power*? Each of these questions has *physical/behavioral, cultural/historical, social/emotional,* and *spiritual* ramifications. For example, from the story of Dr. Ford and Ms. Ramirez, there are body questions about support. Are anti-inflammatory medications more effective than simple analgesics? How many patients perceive side effects from anti-inflammatory medications? What is the lived experience and meaning of back pain for patients and clinicians? There are questions concerning the support of one's life or biography. Do explanatory models of back pain relate to rehabilitation outcome? How does one's self-concept relate to back pain? What are patients' and clinicians' hopes, despairs, fears, and insecurities concerning back pain? How does past experience connect to the immediate experience of back pain? There are questions of power about how people are supported. What is happening when patients with back pain present to clinicians in different organizational contexts of care? What patterns exist in these different settings? Who influences whom? How is the patient or clinician's power undermined or enhanced? Many of these questions are adequately addressed only if qualitative methods enter into the clinical research space.

Providing the Tools for Multimethod Clinical Research

Research Design

Design decisions begin with the question. A fundamental tenet of the proposed vision of clinical research is that *the question and clinical context are primary; methods must adjust to the clinical setting and the clinical question.* Clinical researchers should remain free to mix and match methods as driven by particular clinically based questions. Interpretive social science has traditionally feared mixed methods because this usually has meant treating qualitative as only a method subservient to the positivist paradigm or materialistic inquiry. We not only imagine a clinical research space where qualitative methods are empowered and constructivist and critical paradigms accepted, but note that it already exists (see the examples to follow).

If the question about one's body, one's life, or power concerns "how many," "how much," "how often," "what size," or numerically measurable associations among phenomena, then a survey research style using the designs and methods of observational epidemiology is appropriate. If the question asks "if _, then _," or "is _ more effective than _," then an experimental style is reasonable. Many questions about body, life, and power, however, concern experience, meaning, patterns, relationships, and values; these questions refer to knowledge as story. Who will support Liz and George? How are treatments embodied by Ms. Ramirez into her life story (see Johnson, 1987; Kirmayer, 1992; Martin, 1987)? How do insurance practices and workers' compensation laws constrain the possibilities of Liz and George's lived story? These questions weave the concerns of body, life, and power into a holistic narrative and call for the designs and methods of the qualitative clinical researcher.

In attempting to evaluate the physical/behavioral, conceptual/historical, social/emotional, and spiritual features relevant to a particular clinical question, multiple paradigms (see the chapters in Part II of this volume) and methods are necessary. In some studies, the aims of the research and the research question can be clearly addressed using a single research method. This *single method design* may be either qualitative or quantitative. For example, an important question for helping Dr. Ford and Ms. Ramirez get past their misunderstandings is, How do patients and physicians understand pain? As this question asks for qualitative description (What meanings/practices occur in lived experience?), a field study using open-ended in-depth interviews is an appropriate approach. Such a clinical study was done and reported by a family physician/psychologist research team who observed and interviewed 28 family practice residents using a grounded interpretive investigation to facilitate understanding what happens when residents encounter dying patients (Dozor & Addison, 1992).

The research design often requires both qualitative and quantitative approaches (Stange & Zyzanski, 1989). There are at least four different formats in which qualitative and quantitative methods are integrated within a multimethod approach: concurrent design, nested design, sequential design, and combination design. Each of these is illustrated with examples from the story of Ms. Ramirez and Dr. Ford and from the clinical research literature. We have found these formats helpful in explaining qualitative research to traditional, more quantitatively oriented, clinical researchers.

Concurrent design. In some circumstances it is helpful if two independent studies are conducted concurrently on the same study population and the results then converged (e.g., Chesla, 1992; Fielding & Fielding, 1986). For example, clinical trials are enhanced if the researchers simultaneously conduct interpretive studies to help them understand the clinical trial process and to help explain why an intervention does or does not work. Dr. Ford might want to know, Is an anti-inflammatory medication more effective than a simple analgesic in hastening patients' return to work? This prescription-testing question suggests a randomized clinical trial. But Dr. Ford also wants to know about the context and process of the trial (What is going on here? How does it work?) so he can better understand how to apply the results to Ms. Ramirez's particular situation. A concurrent field study can address these additional concerns. As an illustration, Willms (1991) has reported on the qualitative portion of a "concurrent design" based on a clinical trial of a smoking intervention (Wilson, Taylor, Gilbert, et al., 1988).

Nested design. Qualitative and quantitative methods can also be directly integrated within a single research study. In order to avoid Type III error (i.e., solving the wrong problem), quantitative studies need to incorporate qualitative methods to help identify and operationalize key variables. Dr. Ford may puzzle, Do themes in patients' back pain narratives serve as prognostic indicators for predicting rehabilitation outcomes? The overall question seeks statistical explanation generation (Does variable x relate to other variables?), but the key variable, "themes in patient narratives," requires identification (What is important here?). Dr. Ford can answer both questions by simultaneously collecting and analyzing pain narratives to measure the key independent variables within the context of a prospective epidemiological study design, thus nesting field methods within a survey style. For example, Borkan, Quirk, and Sullivan (1991) used a "nested design" in which the injury narratives from elderly hip fracture patients became key measurements for an epidemiological study looking at hip fracture rehabilitation outcome.

Sequential design. For many research questions, it is useful for the results of one study to inform another. This is the context in which epidemiologists most easily grasp the significance of qualitative methods. They recognize the importance of using field methods for identifying and describing key variables before developing measurement instruments for hypothesis testing. The reverse can also be true. Dr. Ford theorizes there is a relationship between low self-esteem and the likelihood of back pain becoming chronic. Then he wonders, What is the experience of back pain in patients with reported feelings of low self-esteem? This theory-testing question requires that a survey method be used to identify a sampling frame of patients with back pain and low self-esteem for subsequent qualitative investigation. Snadden and Brown (1991) used such a "sequential design," in which a questionnaire measuring attitudes concerning asthma was used to identify respondents reporting high levels of stigma, who were then interviewed using interpretive research methods.

Combination design. Some questions seek to grasp the rich complexity of context and thus require some combination of the above design options. Ethnographers and evaluation researchers commonly use such case study design (Lincoln & Guba, 1985; Merriam, 1988; Patton, 1990; Pelto & Pelto, 1978; Yin, 1989). Dr. Ford overhears Dr. Anne Jefferson commenting on how much she enjoys caring for patients with back pain. Dr. Ford asks himself, How is the experience of clinicians and patients around the presentation of back pain shaped by the organizational context of care? In order to answer this question, he designs a comparative ethnographic study of his and Dr. Jefferson's practices. The study includes sequential design using field methods to identify patterns followed by survey techniques to confirm the findings, and the study uses a single-method design involving record review. Using a "combination design" within a heuristic framework, Miller (1992) included semistructured ethnoscience interviews, key informant interviews, and participant observation to understand how practicing family physicians manage their daily practices.

The clinical research space, created by focusing on the questions arising from the clinical experience, opens many possibilities for using the full range of qualitative methods. The challenge is to translate qualitative collection and analysis methods into clear, jargon-free language without sacrificing the methods' integrity rooted in the disciplinary conversations behind the wall. The next two subsections, on collection and analysis, present one translation for discussing qualitative methods at the wall of clinical research.

Collection Strategies

A full range of qualitative data collection approaches is presented in the chapters in Part IV of this volume. The research questions uncovered by Dr. Ford and Ms. Ramirez highlight the diversity of designs and methods required of the multimethod clinical researcher. To address questions about individual pain experience and the important themes in a person's pain stories, the investigators are best served by an open-ended, individual in-depth interview collection strategy. Data for addressing the question about the group of patients with low self-esteem and back pain, however, are more efficiently collected using focus group interviews. Participant observation, on the other hand, is preferred for exploring the process and behavior occurring during the clinical trial investigating the efficacy of anti-inflammatory medication.

Clinical researchers need a full inventory of qualitative collection methods so they can choose a culturally and developmentally appropriate communication tool for the topic of interest (Briggs, 1986). This often-overlooked guideline for choosing collection strategies is especially important in the clinical setting, where it can help avoid doing harm to research participants. For example, if Ms. Ramirez prefers sharing her personal experience of battering and back pain as a third-person, "this friend I know" story in small, informal groups, then becoming a participant in those groups is more sensitive and appropriate than using probing individual in-depth interviews. The latter can have profound effects on participants by exposing intense pain and shame without the social and cultural resources readily available for support. This concern is all the more imperative given that institutional review boards at most medical institutions do not see qualitative designs as "real" research and thus almost automatically give them expedited approval.

Qualitative clinical researchers must carefully consider sampling strategies before beginning data collection. Traditional clinical investigators assume this means some type of randomization protocol. The notion of small size, purposeful, or information-rich sampling strikes them as anecdotal and not trustworthy. How can one make any generalizations? they ask. The conversation is continued by distinguishing among clinicians' different ways of knowing and by staying focused on the question. Clinicians readily admit to using clinical experience, the notion of "typicality," and intuition along with probability-based studies in their clinical work. Which of these ways of knowing they use predominantly depends on the question and the quality and richness of their knowledge. Information-rich sampling options are more easily grasped when explained in this context. Kuzel (1992) and Patton (1990) have written excellent summaries of the many sampling strategies available to help qualitative clinical researchers decide what, how, and how many.

Analysis Strategies

Qualitative analysis is much more complex and potentially confusing than data collection and has not been well translated for clinical audiences. Fortunately, Renata Tesch (1990) has recently presented one of the first systematic and explicit overviews of qualitative analysis with a focus on computer applications. She identifies the following three core steps common to nearly all qualitative analysis methods: developing an organizing system, segmenting the data, and making connections. In earlier work, we have identified "four idealized analytic styles" based on these core steps: immersion/crystallization, editing, template, and quasi-statistical (see Figure 21.1) (Miller & Crabtree, 1992). Lumping the many diverse qualitative analysis traditions into these four categories simplifies the language without losing the core meaning; qualitative analysis is made more accessible to biomedical clinicians and patients.

In immersion/crystallization, the three core steps are collapsed into an extended period of intuition-rich immersion within the text (Moustakas, 1990; Stein, 1990). It is the interpreter, as an editor, who serves as the organizing system in the editing style (Addison, 1992; Crabtree & Miller, 1992a; McCracken, 1988; Strauss & Corbin, 1990; Willms, Best, Taylor, et al., 1990), whereas an open-ended template or codebook is the organizing system for template analysis (Crabtree & Miller, 1992b; Miles & Huberman, 1984; Spradley, 1979, 1980). A more detailed codebook is used in quasi-statistical analysis (Weber, 1985). Each style represents a different relationship between the analyst and the text.

How does one pick which analysis style to use for a particular research topic? Figure 21.2 presents an analysis space that includes a horizontal continuum of the four analysis styles representing the distance the analyst is from the actual text. This continuum reflects the structural rigidity of the organizing system. The vertical continuum represents the use of a specific analysis filter through which the text material is perceived. Some of these filters are very specific and explicitly limit what can be perceived in the text given the particular style used, whereas other filters are very porous and leave the analyst open to much more of the text-as-it-is. For example, traditional ethnography (TE), which uses the outline of cultural materials (Murdock, Ford, Hudson, et al., 1950) as its perceptual filter and thus has a carefully defined screen, is low in the space but within the editing style (see Crabtree & Miller, 1991, 1992a), which is on the more open spectrum of distance from text. Hermeneutics (H), through the process of bracketing, seeks to open the analyst to maximum experience within an editing-style relationship, and thus uses a more open perceptual filter (Addison, 1992; Allen & Jenson, 1990).

The analysis space, similar to the understanding of naturalistic inquiry presented by Willems and Rausch (1969), is used to design the analysis approach. First, the researcher must examine the question and aims of the research. If the goal is exploration, discovery, or seeking to understand the experience of others, the analyst must use an analytic method that keeps him or her more open and intimate with the text. If the goal is theory testing, however, an approach involving more structure and distance from the text is desirable. A second consideration is the amount of knowledge already in hand about the subject or question of interest. If there is much existing literature, especially qualitative literature, then more structure and distance is beneficial. If theory is very explicit and well established in the area of inquiry, then using an approach with a more defined filter is helpful. A third consideration is design coherence with the data collection technique. For example, observational data, already filtered by a note taker, might be analyzed better using methods with a more defined perceptual filter, whereas analysis methods with a less defined filter are preferable with in-depth interview data.

Finally, the operating paradigm affects the researcher's approach to analysis. Materialistic inquiry calls for a more structured relationship with the text and a more clearly defined perceptual filter, because control, prediction, and consistency are valued. Constructivist inquiry, on the

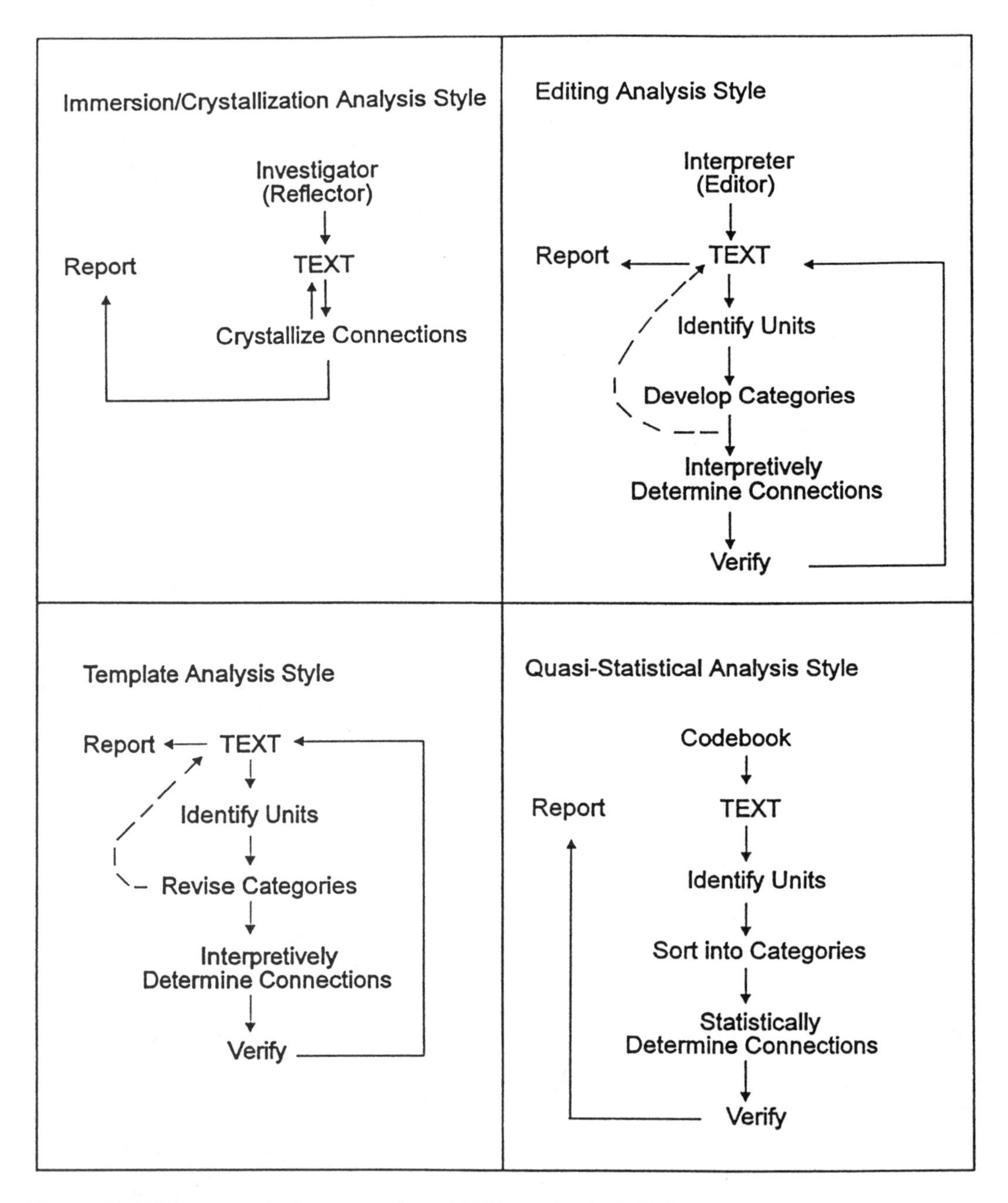

Figure 21.1. Diagrammatic Representation of Different Analysis Styles
SOURCE: Crabtree and Miller (1992b).

other hand, is iterative, and the analysis approach often changes through the collection/analysis cycles and needs to remain open to emergent experience and design.

The analytic approach chosen is usually a compromise among the factors noted above. One of the research examples from the story of Dr. Ford and Ms. Ramirez helps illustrate this choice process. Dr. Ford used a survey to identify patients with low self-esteem and back pain and then conducted focus group interviews with these patients, seeking to answer the question, What is the experience of back pain in patients reporting feelings of low self-esteem? As the question explores what

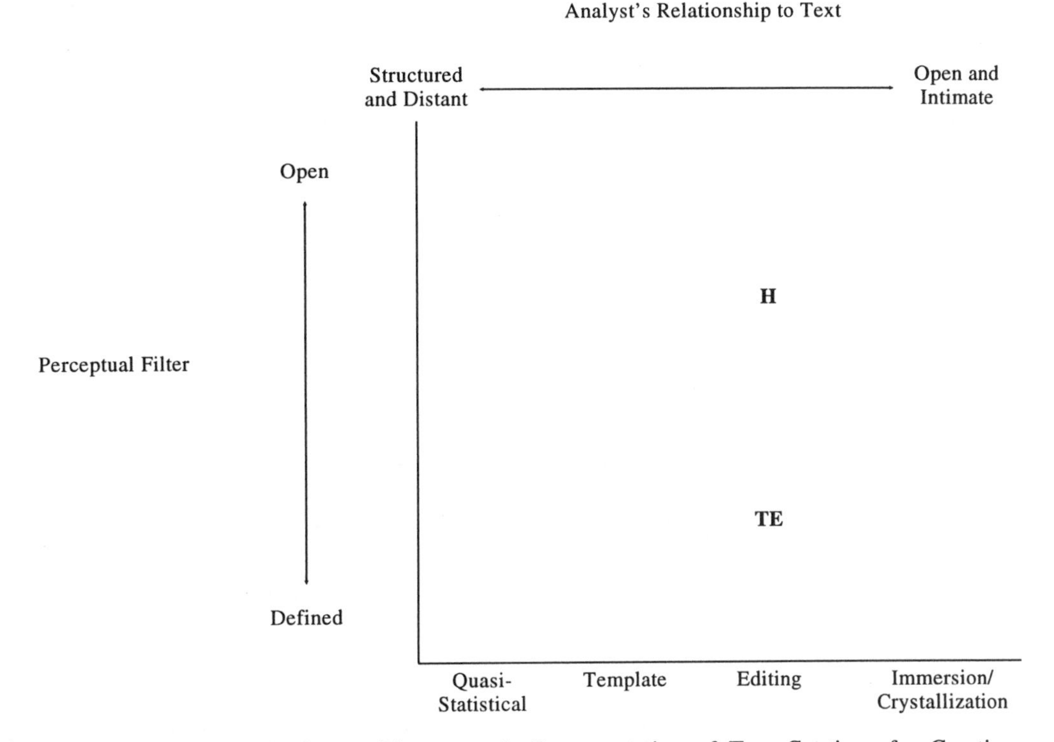

Figure 21.2. The Analytic Space: Diagrammatic Representation of Two Continua for Creating a Qualitative Analysis Strategy

is happening in patients' narrative lives, the operating paradigm is constructivist inquiry. Collection and analysis are done iteratively. The goal of exploration, the absence of significant literature about the question, and the use of interviews argue for a style that is unstructured, fosters intimate contact with the text, and minimizes perceptual filtering in the initial analysis of the first focus group transcripts and field notes. An immersion/crystallization style or a very open editing style (such as hermeneutics) with no explicit perceptual screen is thus appropriate. The analysis of subsequent focus group transcripts may shift to a more explicit editing or template style depending on the specifics of the emerging understanding. When the analysis nears completion, the research process shifts to decisions about telling the story.

Telling the Stories

Where to Tell the Stories

Qualitative clinical research is now being discussed and tried within primary care internal medicine and family medicine because specific efforts were made to translate and introduce qualitative research in workshops within professional meetings, through newsletters, and through methods publications emphasizing clinical usefulness.[3] Developing networks with leaders in primary care research was prioritized. This was facilitated by qualitative researchers demonstrating skill in dominant paradigm methods (e.g., Crabtree, Gelfand, Miller, et al., 1992), and by a multimethod or mixed-method emphasis arguing for the additive and not exclusionary value of qualitative approaches to questions (e.g., Miller, Crabtree, & Yanoshik, 1991).

Qualitative clinical research is now appearing in clinical journals, especially in the field of primary care. *Qualitative Health Research* and *Culture, Medicine, and Psychiatry* are bridge-building publications with an almost exclusive emphasis on qualitative clinical research. All of the primary care journals now have reviewers trained in qualitative research, and all have published examples of qualitative studies. *Family Medicine* focuses on methodology and education-related studies. The *Archives of Family Practice, Family Practice, Journal of the American Board of Family Practice, Journal of Family Practice, Journal of General Internal Medicine,* and *Nurse Practitioner* all emphasize research of direct clinical relevance. The *Family Practice Research Journal* is specifically targeted for the novice researcher. The next step is to establish means of communicating results with the patient population.

How to Tell the Stories

There are some specific writing strategies that will facilitate communication of and receptivity to qualitative clinical research (Richardson, 1990; Wolcott, 1990). The most important is avoiding jargon and keeping language simple and concrete. The use of typologies and continua as rhetorical frames is helpful because these initially appear rational and measurable, qualities valued by traditional clinical researchers. Interpretive aspects can be maintained through the emphasis of cultural/historical and/or inductive construction and grounding in lived clinical experience. It is also useful for researchers to communicate either in the biomedically dominant visual mode—through tables, charts, diagrams, and data matrices—or in the clinically familiar narrative mode of case reports.

The dominant audience for clinical research perceives the issues of "validity," "reliability," and "generalizability" as scientific fundamentalist dogma resulting in heightened concerns about *bias*. Daly and McDonald (1992) recently published an account of a collaborative, multimethod study of the impact of echocardiography on patients' perceptions of self. Their story describes how difficult it can be to have a conversation at the wall: "The biggest problem was that physicians saw qualitative research methods as . . . prone to bias. Highly structured methods of analyzing qualitative data were effectively used . . . and are probably necessary for 'covering one's back' in multidisciplinary teams" (p. 416). The strategies Daly and McDonald present affirm a need for qualitative researchers to translate their wisdom from behind the wall and engage in conversations at the wall. But we believe it is *not* necessary to "cover one's back" and possibly sacrifice the integrity of qualitative approaches.

Developing a common language does not need to mean being co-opted by the dominant frames of discourse and having to use a language of analogy, such as *transferability* is analogous to *generalizability*. We are seeking a conversation at the wall where the unique strengths of each can be applied to the many questions arising out of the clinical experience. The prevailing mode of discourse for qualitative clinical researchers no longer needs to be one of justification (Kahn, 1993). Perception and subjectivity or "bias" are essential data and a crucial part of the knowledge generated by qualitative research. Local context and the human story, of which each individual and community story is a reflection, are primary goals of qualitative research, and not "generalizability." The methodological guidelines for quantitative methods are not relevant for qualitative clinical researchers. The rules of evidence for qualitative clinical research are addressed by Richardson in Chapter 32 of this volume, but can be translated for clinical audiences in the form of telling methodologically, rhetorically, and clinically convincing stories.

Methodologically convincing stories answer the question, How was the research designed and done? It is important to make explicit how and why the research design, sampling strategies, and data collection and analysis techniques fit the question and research context, as discussed earlier. It is helpful to mention when the research design is cross-sectional, prospective, case control, or similar to some other one from observational epidemiology (Ward, 1993). Specific techniques, such as triangulation, member checking, and searching for disconfirming evidence (Kuzel & Like, 1991), should also be addressed when applicable.

Relationship is essential to the clinical experience. Kahn (1993) has proposed that a language of relationship be used to judge the methodological adequacy of clinical qualitative research. A methodologically convincing story addresses three different relationships. The investigator's *relationship with informants* is noted, with emphasis on how each influenced the other during the research process. The *relationship with the data* is described, in a way that is certain to comment on the circularity or iterative aspects of the research experience. Finally, the *relationship with the readers* is defined, such that the researcher's authorial intent is clear.

A *rhetorically convincing story* answers the question, How believable is this text? The audience is drawn into the story and begins imagining that the story is about them. When this occurs, the conclusions make more sense for the reader. The language and style of writing need to be familiar to the audience. Some of the quotations and observations selected to illustrate interpretations also need to reflect the readers' experiences and/or values. A rhetorically convincing story assures the reader that the author has walked in their shoes. Bunge (1961) reviews some of the features that characterize a believable story.

A *clinically convincing story* answers the question, Does this study make clinical sense? A story is clinically convincing if it successfully answers the three questions defining the clinical research space. The *question* must matter to clinical participants and the results specifically address that question. This usually means attention is directed to the pragmatic intervention and policy focus of the clinical world. The *audience* or stakeholder is also a clinical participant for whom the results matter, and this is obvious in the text. Finally, the manuscript reveals *assumptions* about the physical/behavioral, social/emotional, cultural/historical, or spiritual aspects of clinical participants' bodies, lives, and/or power.

Qualitative clinical research is convincing if the methods are appropriate for the question and the investigator's relationships with informants, data, and audience are clearly addressed; if the audience recognizes itself in the findings; and if the question and results matter to clinical participants. All of these criteria are more easily satisfied if a collaborative team does the research. When this team includes clinical participants, a community of discourse is created where conversations at the walls can begin (see Denz-Penhey & Murdoch, 1993).

Summary

There are many clinical worlds. Each of them is a place where support is sought and power invoked. The clinical world and people's need for support occur in nursing, primary health care, specialized medical care, administration and management, education, social work, family therapy, mental health, public health, engineering, and law. In each of these worlds there are questions emerging from practice. These are the questions, the settings, and the participants for doing qualitative clinical research. This is where the conversation starts. The research is judged by the clinical difference it makes.

People continue to meet in clinics hoping to weave a comforting cloth of support, but the created relationships and patterns are now more varied, more confusing, and often too expensive. Concerns about access and cost do matter, but they are not adequately addressed without facing the abusive and dismembering experience of being a woman in the medical clinic, the pervasive delegitimation of patient experience, the clinicians' increasing sense of helpless imprisonment, and the mounting problems, discontinuities, and cultural conflicts within local communities. Knowing the probabilities is not enough and is often inappropriate. The stories' uniqueness and context are also essential threads in the fabric. Without them our bodies and lives remain fragmented and power is imposed. Melissa remains isolated within the clan of one-breasted women. She, and we, need the breadth of qualitative research. Qualitative clinical researchers must move from behind their walls, engage the clinical experience and its questions, and practice humility and fidelity within a community of discourse at the walls. This is a dangerous, but exciting, conversation, because it promises that no one can stay the same. Clinical research can heal by transforming into praxis. A recently published qualitative clinical study concludes, "The response of the general practitioner to the results was the recognition that he and his patients were operating on different levels of knowledge concerning their problem. As one who regarded himself as a champion of these patients and the legitimacy of their illness, this came as something of a shock" (Denz-Penhey & Murdoch, 1993, p. 17). As he was changed, so can we all be changed. In time, all walls crumble, power shifts, and healing begins.

Notes

1. The word *patient* derives from the Latin word *patiens,* meaning "to suffer," and from the Latin words *paene,* "almost," and *penuria,* "need." People seek clinicians because they have need and are suffering. They are no longer complete; they lack adequate support. People come to clinicians because they do not perceive themselves as equal and/or whole. They are "patients" in need of movement toward wholeness.

2. The word *clinic* derives from the Greek words *klinikos,* meaning "of a bed," and *klinein,* "to lean, recline." From this sense, *a clinic is a physical and social place for those in need of support* (this support can be medical, managerial, educational, legal, economic, religious, nursing, social, psychological, or some combination of these). This understanding defines clinic as a bounded text for research.

3. The professional meetings include those of the Primary Care Research Methods and Statistics Conference, the North American Primary Care Research Group, the Society of General Internal Medicine, and the Society for the Teachers of Family Medicine. The newsletters are the *Interpreter* and *Medical Encounter,* and the methods publications are represented by the Sage Publications book series, *Research Methods for Primary Care.*

References

Addison, R. B. (1992). Grounded hermeneutic research. In B. F. Crabtree & W. L. Miller (Eds.), *Doing qualitative research* (pp. 110-124). Newbury Park, CA: Sage.

Allen, M. N., & Jenson, L. (1990). Hermeneutical inquiry: Meaning and scope. *Western Journal of Nursing Research, 12,* 241-253.

Berg, D. N., & Smith, K. K. (Eds.). (1988). *The self in social inquiry: Researching methods.* Newbury Park, CA: Sage.

Borkan, J. M., Quirk, M., & Sullivan, M. (1991). Finding meaning after the fall: Injury narratives from elderly hip fracture patients. *Social Science and Medicine, 33,* 947-957.

Brewer, J., & Hunter, A. (1989). *Multimethod research: A synthesis of styles.* Newbury Park, CA: Sage.

Briggs, C. (1986). *Learning to ask.* Cambridge, UK: Cambridge University Press.

Brueggemann, W. (1991). *Interpretation and obedience: From faithful reading to faithful living.* Minneapolis: Fortress.

Bunge, M. (1961). The weight of simplicity in the construction and assaying of scientific theories. *Philosophy of Science, 28,* 120-149.

Burawoy, M., Burton, A., Ferguson, A. A., Fox, K. J., Gamson, J., Gartrell, N., Hurst, L., Kurzman, C., Salzinger, L., Schiffman, J., & Ui, S. (Eds.). (1991). *Ethnography unbound: Power and resistance in the modern metropolis.* Berkeley: University of California Press.

Chesla, C. A. (1992). When qualitative and quantitative findings do not converge. *Western Journal of Nursing Research, 14,* 681-685.

Chrisman, N. J. (1977). The health seeking process: An approach to the natural history of illness. *Culture, Medicine, and Psychiatry, 1,* 351-377.

Chrisman, N. J., & Maretzki, T. W. (Eds.). (1982). *Clinically applied anthropology: Anthropologists in health science settings.* Boston: D. Reidel.

Clifford, J., & Marcus, G. E. (Eds.). (1986). *Writing culture: The poetics and politics of ethnography.* Berkeley: University of California Press.

Crabtree, B. F., Gelfand, A. E., Miller, W. L., et al. (1992). Categorical data analysis in primary care research: Log-linear models. *Family Medicine, 24,* 145-151.

Crabtree, B. F., & Miller, W. L. (1991). A qualitative approach to primary care research: The long interview. *Family Medicine, 23,* 145-151.

Crabtree, B. F., & Miller, W. L. (1992a). The analysis of narratives from a long interview. In M. Stewart, F. Tudiver, M. Bass, et al. (Eds.), *Tools for primary care research* (pp. 209-220). Newbury Park, CA: Sage.

Crabtree, B. F., & Miller, W. L. (1992b). A template approach to text analysis: Developing and using codebooks. In B. F. Crabtree & W. L. Miller (Eds.), *Doing qualitative research* (pp. 93-109). Newbury Park, CA: Sage.

Daly, J., & McDonald, I. (1992). Covering your back: Strategies for qualitative research in clinical settings. *Qualitative Health Research, 2,* 416-438.

Denz-Penhey, H., & Murdoch, J. C. (1993). Service delivery for people with chronic fatigue syndrome: A pilot action research study. *Family Practice, 10,* 14-18.

Deyo, R. A., Diehl, A. K., & Rosenthal, M. (1986). How many days of bedrest for acute low back pain? A randomized clinical trial. *New England Journal of Medicine, 315,* 1064-1070.

Diers, D. (1979). *Research in nursing practice.* Philadelphia: J. B. Lippincott.

Dozor, R. B., & Addison, R. B. (1992). Toward a good death: An interpretive investigation of family practice residents' practices with dying patients. *Family Medicine, 24,* 538-543.

Fabrega, H., Jr. (1976). The function of medical care systems: A logical analysis. *Perspectives in Biology and Medicine, 20,* 108-119.

Fabrega, H., Jr. (1979). The ethnography of illness. *Social Science and Medicine, 13,* 565-575.

Feinstein, A. R. (1985). *Clinical epidemiology: The architecture of clinical research.* Philadelphia: W. B. Saunders.

Fielding, N. G., & Fielding, J. L. (1986). *Linking data.* Beverly Hills, CA: Sage.

Fisher, S. (1986). *In the patient's best interest: Women and the politics of medical decisions.* New Brunswick, NJ: Rutgers University Press.

Fisher, S., & Todd, A. D. (Eds.). (1983). *The social organization of doctor-patient communication.* Washington, DC: Center for Applied Linguistics.

Foster, G. M. (1974). Medical anthropology: Some contrasts with medical sociology. *Medical Anthropology Newsletter, 6,* 1-6.

Foster, G. M., & Anderson, B. G. (1978). *Medical anthropology.* New York: John Wiley.

Freymann, J. G. (1989). The public's health care paradigm is shifting: Medicine must swing with it. *Journal of General Internal Medicine, 4,* 313-319.

Good, B. J., & Good, M. D. (1981). The meaning of symptoms: A cultural hermeneutic model for clinical practice. In L. Eisenberg & A. M. Kleinman (Eds.), *The relevance of social science for medicine* (pp. 165-196). Boston: D. Reidel.

Gordon, D. (1988). Tenacious assumptions in Western medicine. In M. Lock & D. Gordon (Eds.), *Biomedicine examined* (pp. 19-56). Boston: D. Reidel.

Haraway, D. J. (1991). *Simians, cyborgs and women: The reinvention of nature.* London: Routledge.

Helman, C. G. (1990). *Culture, health and illness.* Boston: Butterworth-Heinemann.

Jackson, M. (1989). *Paths toward a clearing: Radical empiricism and ethnographic inquiry.* Bloomington: Indiana University Press.

Johnson, M. (1987). *The body in the mind.* Chicago: University of Chicago Press.

Kahn, D. L. (1993). Ways of discussing validity in qualitative nursing research. *Western Journal of Nursing Research, 15,* 122-126.

Kelsey, J. L., Thompson, W. D., & Evans, A. S. (1986). *Methods in observational epidemiology.* New York: Oxford University Press.

Kirmayer, L. J. (1992). The body's insistence on meaning: Metaphor as presentation and representation in illness experience. *Medical Anthropology Quarterly, 6,* 323-346.

Kleinbaum, D. G., Kupper, L. L., & Morgenstern, H. (1982). *Epidemiologic research: Principles and quantitative methods.* Belmont, CA: Lifetime Learning.

Kleinman, A. M. (1992). Local worlds of suffering: An interpersonal focus for ethnographies of illness experience. *Qualitative Health Research, 2,* 127-134.

Kleinman, A. M. (1988). *The illness narratives: Suffering, healing, and the human condition.* New York: Basic Books.

Kleinman, A. M., Eisenberg, L., & Good, B. (1978). Culture, illness, and care: Clinical lessons from anthropologic and cross-cultural research. *Annals of Internal Medicine, 88,* 251-258.

Kuzel, A. J. (1992). Sampling in qualitative inquiry. In B. F. Crabtree & W. L. Miller (Eds.), *Doing qualitative research* (pp. 31-44). Newbury Park, CA: Sage.

Kuzel, A. J., & Like, R. C. (1991). Standards of trustworthiness for qualitative studies in primary care. In P. G. Norton, M. Stewart, F. Tudiver, M. J. Bass, & E. V. Dunn (Eds.), *Primary care research: Traditional and innovative approaches* (pp. 138-158). Newbury Park, CA: Sage.

Lather, P. (1991). *Getting smart: Feminist research and pedagogy with/in the postmodern.* New York: Routledge.

Lazarus, E. S. (1988). Theoretical considerations for the study of the doctor-patient relationship: Implications of a perinatal study. *Medical Anthropology Quarterly, 2,* 34-58.

Lincoln, Y. S., & Guba, E. G. (1985). *Naturalistic inquiry.* Newbury Park, CA: Sage.

Lock, M. (1982). On revealing the hidden curriculum. *Medical Anthropology Quarterly, 14,* 19-21.

Lock, M. (1986). The anthropological study of the American medical system: Center and periphery. *Social Science and Medicine, 22,* 931-932.

Martin, E. (1987). *The woman in the body: A cultural analysis of reproduction.* Boston: Beacon.

McCracken, G. (1988). *The long interview.* Newbury Park, CA: Sage.

McWhinney, I. R. (1986). Are we on the brink of a major transformation of clinical method? *Canadian Medical Association Journal,. 135,* 873-878.

McWhinney, I. R. (1989). An acquaintance with particulars. *Family Medicine, 21,* 296-298.

Meinert, C. L. (1986). *Clinical trials: Design, conduct, and analysis.* New York: Oxford University Press.

Merriam, S. B. (1988). *Case study research in education.* San Francisco: Jossey-Bass.

Miles, M. B., & Huberman, A. M. (1984). *Qualitative data analysis: A sourcebook of new methods.* Beverly Hills, CA: Sage.

Miller, W. L. (1992). Routine, ceremony, or drama: An exploratory field study of the primary care clinical encounter. *Journal of Family Practice, 34,* 289-296.

Miller, W. L., & Crabtree, B. F. (1992). Primary care research: A multimethod typology and qualitative roadmap. In B. F. Crabtree & W. L. Miller (Eds.), *Doing qualitative research* (pp. 3-28). Newbury Park, CA: Sage.

Miller, W. L., Crabtree, B. F., & Yanoshik, M. K. (1991). Expanding the boundaries of family medicine research. *Family Medicine, 23,* 425-426.

Mishler, E. G. (1984). *The discourse of medicine: Dialectics of medical interviews.* Norwood, NJ: Ablex.

Moustakas, C. (1990). *Heuristic research: Design, methodology, and applications.* Newbury Park, CA: Sage.

Murdock, G. P., Ford, C. S., Hudson, A. E., et al. (1950). *Outline of cultural materials* (3rd ed.). New Haven, CT: Human Relations Area Files.

Patton, M. Q. (1990). *Qualitative evaluation and research methods* (2nd ed.). Newbury Park, CA: Sage.

Pelto, P. J., & Pelto, G. H. (1978). *Anthropological research: The structure of inquiry* (2nd ed). New York: Cambridge University Press.

Pelto, P. J., & Pelto, G. H. (1990). Field methods in medical anthropology. In T. M. Johnson & C. F. Sargent (Eds.), *Medical anthropology: Contemporary theory and method* (pp. 269-297). New York: Praeger.

Pfifferling, J. H. (1981). A cultural prescription for medicocentrism. In L. Eisenberg & A. M. Kleinman (Eds.), *The relevance of social science for medicine* (pp. 197-222). Boston: D. Reidel.

Pocock, S. J. (1983). *Clinical trials: A practical approach.* New York: John Wiley.

Polgar, S. (1962). Health and human behavior: Areas of interest common to the social and medical sciences. *Current Anthropology, 3,* 159-205.

Richardson, L. (1990). *Writing strategies: Reaching diverse audiences.* Newbury Park, CA: Sage.

Sackett, D. L. (1991). *Clinical epidemiology: A basic science for clinical medicine* (2nd ed.). Boston: Little, Brown.

Sapsford, R., & Abbott, P. (1992). *Research methods for nurses and the caring professions.* Bristol, PA: Open University Press.

Schein, E. H. (1987). *The clinical perspective in fieldwork.* Newbury Park, CA: Sage.

Snadden, D., & Brown, J. B. (1991). Asthma and stigma. *Family Practice, 8,* 329-335.

Spradley, J. P. (1979). *The ethnographic interview.* New York: Holt, Rinehart & Winston.

Spradley, J. P. (1980). *Participant observation.* New York: Holt, Rinehart & Winston.

Stange, K. C., & Zyzanski, S. J. (1989). Integrating qualitative and quantitative research methods. *Family Medicine, 21,* 448-451.

Stein, H. F. (1990). *American medicine as culture.* Boulder, CO: Westview.

Strauss, A. L., & Corbin, J. (1990). *Basics of qualitative research: Grounded theory procedures and techniques.* Newbury Park, CA: Sage.

Taylor B. (1993). Phenomenology: One way to understand nursing practice. *International Journal of Nursing Studies, 30,* 171-179.

Tesch, R. (1990). *Qualitative research: Analysis types and software tools.* New York: Falmer.

Waitzkin, H. (1991). *The politics of medical encounters: How patients and doctors deal with social problems.* New Haven, CT: Yale University Press.

Ward, M. M. (1993). Study design in qualitative research: A guide to assessing quality. *Journal of General Internal Medicine, 8,* 107-109.

Weber, R. P. (1985). *Basic content analysis.* Beverly Hills, CA: Sage.

West, C. (1984). *Routine complications: Troubles with talk between doctors and patients.* Bloomington: Indiana University Press.

Wiesel, S. W., Cuckler, J. M., DeLuca, F., et al. (1980). Acute low back pain: An objective analysis of conservative therapy. *Spine, 5,* 324-330.

Willems, E. P., & Rausch, H. L. (1969). *Naturalistic viewpoints in psychological research.* New York: Holt, Rinehart & Winston.

Williams, G. (1984). The genesis of chronic illness: Narrative re-construction. *Sociology of Health and Illness, 6,* 175-200.

Williams, T. T. (1991). *Refuge: An unnatural history of family and place.* New York: Pantheon.

Willms, D. G. (1991). A new stage, a new life: Individual success in quitting smoking. *Social Science and Medicine, 33,* 1365-1371.

Willms, D. G., Best, J. A., Taylor, D. W., et al. (1990). A systematic approach for using qualitative methods in primary prevention research. *Medical Anthropology Quarterly, 4,* 391-409.

Wilson, D. M. C., Taylor, D. W., Gilbert, J. R., et al. (1988). A randomized trial of a family physician intervention for smoking cessation. *Journal of the American Medical Association, 260,* 1570-1574.

Wolcott, H. F. (1990). *Writing up qualitative research.* Newbury Park, CA: Sage.

Yin, R. K. (1989). *Case studies research* (rev. ed.). Newbury Park, CA: Sage.

Young, A. (1982a). The anthropologies of illness and sickness. In B. Siegel, A. Beals, & S. Tyler (Eds.), *Annual review of anthropology* (Vol. 11, pp. 257-285). Palo Alto, CA: Annual Reviews.

Young, A. (1982b). When rational men fall sick: An inquiry into some assumptions made by medical anthropologists. *Culture, Medicine, and Psychiatry, 5,* 317-335.

PART IV
METHODS OF COLLECTING AND ANALYZING EMPIRICAL MATERIALS

The constructionist (and constructivist) position tells us that the socially situated researcher creates, through interaction, the realities that constitute the places where empirical materials are collected and analyzed. In such sites, the interpretive practices of qualitative research are implemented. These practices are methods and techniques for producing empirical materials as well as theoretical interpretations of the world. Part IV examines the multiple practices and methods of analysis qualitative researchers-as-*bricoleurs* now employ.

The Interview

The interview is the favorite methodological tool of the qualitative researcher. In Chapter 22, Andrea Fontana and James Frey review the history of the interview in the social sciences, noting its three major forms—structured, unstructured, and open-ended—while showing how the tool is modified and changed during use.

The interview is a conversation, the art of asking questions and listening. It is not a neutral tool, for the interviewer creates the reality of the interview situation. In this situation answers are given. Thus the interview produces situated understandings grounded in specific interactional episodes. This method is influenced by the personal characteristics of the interviewer, including race, class, ethnicity, and gender.

Fontana and Frey review the important work of feminist scholars on the interview, especially the arguments of British sociologist Ann Oakley (1981), who has identified a major contradiction between scientific, positivistic research, which requires objectivity and detachment, and feminist-based interviewing, which requires openness, emotional engagement, and the development of a potentially long-term, trusting relationship between the interviewer and the subject. Guiding Oakley's highly influential model is a proposed "feminist ethic of commitment and egalitarianism in contrast with the scientific ethic of detachment and role differentiation between researcher and subject" (Reinharz, 1992, p. 27).

A feminist interviewing ethic, as Fontana and Frey suggest, redefines the interview situation. It directs attention to the fact that research is activity "fundamentally grounded in talk . . . and that language itself reflects male experiences, and that its categories are often incongruent with women's lives" (Devault, 1990, pp. 96-97). This ethic transforms interviewers and respondents into coequals who are carrying on a conversation about mutually relevant, often biographically critical, issues. This personalization of the interview method makes it a potential agent of social change, where new identities and new definitions of problematic situations are created, discussed, and experimented with. This ethic changes the interview into an important tool for the types of clinical and applied action research discussed by Reason (Chapter 20) and Miller and Crabtree (Chapter 21) in Part III.

Observational Methods

Naturalistic observation, going to a social situation and looking, is another favorite way of gathering material about the social world. Noting that observation methods remain a stepchild to their more widely recognized offshoot, participant observation, Patricia and Peter Adler, in Chapter 23, take up the history, forms, stages and some of the ethical problems involved with this technique.[1]

From the postpositivist perspective as developed by the Adlers, the problems of observation are legion, involving questions of validity and reliability, observer and setting bias, observer effects, and the absence of member checks. Adler and Adler discuss traditional, multimethod strategies for addressing these issues, and also show how the method has been put to excellent use by formal sociologists of the "new" Iowa school, as well as scholars working in the traditions of dramaturgical and introspective sociology and ethnomethodology.

Adler and Adler outline the ethical problems involved with this method (see also Punch, Chapter 5, this volume), especially those involving invasions of privacy and disguised research. They note that the hidden or disguised voyeur has been one of the many identities social science observers have utilized. Their chapter can be read as suggesting that it is time to rethink the warrant and high value the social sciences have given to voyeurism and the voyeuristic activities of the detached, watchful observer who invades the personal, sacred spaces of others. Indeed, although they do not develop this point, a feminist ethic of caring and commitment seems to undercut the pure observational project, for it requires the formation of a long-term trusting relationship between the observer and those studied.

Finally, the Adlers confront an obdurate fact of contemporary academic life, the institutional review board (IRB). They challenge the right of IRBs to limit, or prohibit, disguised observation. Yet, as many have argued, these boards are not likely to go away. The issue, in our view, is learning how to live with them.

This may well involve the institutional development of the implications of a consequentialist-feminist ethics committed to caring, trust, and long-term relationships. Under such an ethical model the surveillance ethics of review boards become muted, if not moot.

Reading Material Culture and Its Records

Mute evidence—that is, written texts and cultural artifacts—endures physically and leaves its traces on the past. It is impossible to talk to these materials. They must be interpreted, for in them are found important meanings about the past and the human shape of lived cultures. Archaeologists study these materials. In a chapter that moves with ease across and within the postpositivist and postmodern sensibilities, Ian Hodder shows how this is done in Chapter 24. Central to his position is the constructionist (and constructivist) argument that researchers create, through a set of interpretive practices, the materials and evidence they then theoretically analyze. Material culture is a social and political construction, and, as Gaye Tuchman argues in Chapter 18 of this volume, how the past is reconstructed very much determines how it will be constituted in the present.

Visual Methods

Visual sociologists and anthropologists use film, video, and photography as means of recording and documenting social life. Often called the mirror with a memory, photography takes the researcher into the subject's world, where the issues of observer identity, the subject's point of view, and what to photograph become problematic. In Chapter 25, Douglas Harper presents a history of this method and brings it up against postmodern developments in ethnography.

Historically, visual sociology began within the postpositivist tradition, providing visual information for the realist tales of traditional ethnography. However, like ethnography, visual sociology is in a period of deep questioning and great change. Visual sociology, Harper contends, must find a place in this new ethnography. He engages this new turn, discussing the ideological aspects of representation, the social construction of images, the authority of visual knowledge, and the ethics of a new visual sociology. He articulates his new perspective by showing how visual sociologists resolve particular problems in their research, including using the mechanical capabilities of the camera, framing (point of view), printing techniques, image sequencing, and the influences of the photographer on the lives of the people studied.

It is clear that visual methods will soon have a place of increased importance and centrality in the qualitative research project. Visual ethnographies, documentaries, and the reading of film as social texts are important strategies and resources for this project. Visual literacy, which is replacing print literacy, and visual texts, which are replacing print texts, define this historical moment. The new visual sociology will lead the way in reading, constructing, and interpreting these texts. These are further reasons for qualitative researchers to pay more attention to these alternative forms of representing and collecting empirical materials.

Personal Experience Methods

Personal experience, like the biographical experiences analyzed by Louis Smith in Chapter 17, reflects the flow of thoughts and meanings persons bring to their immediate situations. These experiences can be routine or problematic. They occur within the life of a person. When they are related, they assume the shape of a story, or a narrative. It is very difficult to study direct, lived experience, because language, speech, and thought mediate and define the very experience one attempts to describe. Accordingly, researchers study the stories people tell one another about the experiences they have had. These stories may be personal experience narratives or self-stories, accounts made up as the person goes along. In Chapter 26, Jean Clandinin and Michael Connelly review these methods of studying personal experience, anchoring their use in the discourses of poststructuralism and postmodernism.

Clandinin and Connelly outline three methodological questions, or issues, that confront the researcher who uses personal experience methods; these begin with the field experience, then involve the texts written about the experience, and conclude with the research accounts of the experience. These three issues lead to a consideration of field notes, photographs, field texts, oral histories, research interviews, and autobiographical writing. The research texts that are produced out of such material implicate the investigator in a feminist, caring, committed ethic with those who have been studied. These texts are also shaped by the use of voice, signature, and the imagined presence of a reading audience. Thus do Clandinin and Connelly show how personal experience becomes part of the postmodern project.

Data Management and Analysis Methods

The management, analysis, and interpretation of qualitative empirical materials is a complex process. In Chapter 27, Michael Huberman and Matthew Miles advance a sophisticated and comprehensive model of this process. Their framework model distinguishes within- from between-case analysis while emphasizing the necessary connection between a theory and its concepts and the empirical indicators that reflect back through the concepts to the theory. Drawing on the grounded theory approach, they show how codes, memos, and diagrams can help a researcher work from field notes to some conceptual understanding of the processes being studied. This model stresses variables and causal links between variables while focusing on an iterative approach that is fully open to discovery and the treatment of negative cases. This framework is very compatible with computer-assisted methods of analysis.

This is an elegant and systematic postpositivist approach to the problem. Huberman and Miles are transcendental realists (i.e., they believe that social phenomena exist in the objective world and there are lawful relationships among them), and their model argues for rigor in the collection, production, analysis, and presentation of qualitative empirical materials. They use analytic induction and grounded theory, and they believe in studies that can be replicated and judged against the canons of good science. The reflexive turn organizing their concluding arguments is a reflexivity contained within the postpositivist paradigm.

As deployed by Huberman and Miles, this model satisfies the positivist critics of qualitative research, hence its enormous appeal and widespread use. Yet we believe the framework remains basically unresponsive to the more poststructural, constructionist, cultural studies, feminist, and critical theory perspectives. These models argue against a transcendental realism. They see the world of data (empirical materials) as one that is created in and through the interactions that occur between the observer and the observed. Still, many of the guidelines Huberman and Miles set forth in their chapter would be useful to, and could easily be used by, these other approaches, especially those versions still attached to the postpositivist paradigm. They are, after all, tools for building qualitative interpretations. Thus the tools are not at issue, only what is done with them.

Computer-Assisted Qualitative Analysis

Many qualitative researchers now work with computers. In the past decade, multiple software programs have appeared that assist in the analysis of qualitative materials. Field research, as Clandinin and Connelly note, leads to the production of large amounts of textual material, notes, journal entries, recorded conversations, descriptions of the field setting, memos, thoughts on coding schemes, emotional experiences, and so on. These materials all take the form of texts, the analysis of which can be very time-consuming.

In Chapter 28, Thomas Richards and Lyn Richards analyze the most influential programs in this field. These programs have multiple text management uses, including coding, locating, and retrieving key materials, phrases, and words; building conceptual models; sorting categories; attaching key words and codes to text segments; isolating negative or deviant cases; and creating indices. Team research is also facilitated through the use of computers: Files can be shared, mailed back and forth, or transmitted electronically. Computer programs can also be used for theory construction. Some implement the logic and structure of the grounded theory model of Glaser, Strauss, and Corbin.[2] Richards and Richards review all of these uses.

In using any of these models, Richards and Richards note, it is important not to let the computer (or the software package) determine the form and content of interpretive activity. The emphasis on codes and categories can produce endless variable analyses that fail to take account of important situational and contextual factors.[3] There is a frequent tendency to reduce field materials to only codable data. There is also the danger that the transcription of field notes may be turned over to persons who lack intimate familiarity with the field setting and the processes being studied (Lee & Fielding, 1991, p. 12).

Seidel (1991) speaks of a form of analytic madness that can accompany the use of these methods. This madness can create several problems. It can lead to an infatuation with the large volume of data one can deal with. In addition, researchers may develop understandings based on misunderstandings; that is, patterns identified in the data may be "artifacts of a relationship we have with the data" (p. 114). Further, the researcher may focus only on those aspects of the research that can be helped by computer methods (Agar, 1991, p. 193). The researcher selects software and readies it for use on the study materials. A problem arises when the researcher limits him- or herself to conducting only research that fits available software.

Finally, there are possible ethical problems. Akeroyd (1991) isolates the crux of the matter: the potential loss of personal privacy that can occur when a personal, confidential database is developed on an individual or group. When such materials are entered into a computer database, the problem of security is immediately created. In multiuser systems, privacy cannot be guaranteed (Akeroyd, 1991, p. 100): Nothing is any longer completely private and completely secure.

This cautionary discussion needs to be balanced with a treatment of the positive features and uses of these methods, which are thoroughly developed by Richards and Richards.[4] Their text sketches the history of software programs in this field, stressing those that are most user friendly. They emphasize the need for interactional programs that allow the researcher to learn from and build on the analysis as it is occurring.

Narrative, Content, and Semiotic Analysis

Qualitative researchers study spoken and written records of human experience, including transcribed talk, films, novels, and photographs. Historically, these have been the three major social science approaches to textual-discourse analysis. Each is associated with a long theoretical and research tradition: content analysis with the quantitative approach to media studies, semiotics with the structural tradition in literary criticism, and narrative or discourse analysis with the recent poststructural development in interpretive theory.

Documents of experience can be content analyzed; that is, themes, issues, and recurring motifs within them can be isolated, counted, and interpreted. Alternatively, such documents can be read as narratives, or stories, wherein the researcher analyzes the narrative, temporal, and dramatic structures of a text, forsaking the rigor of counting, for a close, interpretive reading of the subject matter at hand. This reading can be supplemented by the semiotic method, which searches for oppositions, categories, and linguistic structures in the text. Peter Manning and Betsy Cullum-Swan examine these three strategies of interpretation in Chapter 29.

Traditional, classic content analysis is marked by Bernard Berelson's classic *Content Analysis in Communication Research* (1952). This text and its influences are still felt today. In it, Berelson offered a rigorous quantitative approach to the content analysis of media messages. This work was immediately challenged by Siegfried Kracauer (1953), a German critical theorist, who called for qualitative content analysis techniques drawing on hermeneutical, textual procedures. Kracauer argued that the "inadequacy of quantitative analyses stems from the methods themselves: when trying to establish the meaning of texts by breaking them down into quantifiable units (words, expressions), analysts in fact destroy the very object they are supposed to be studying" (quoted in Larsen, 1991, p. 123). Kracauer advocated an approach that examined the content of a text as a totality. The task of the analyst is to bring out the hidden meanings in the text.

The structuralist project elaborated Kracauer's arguments by developing a more consistent theory of the text and its constituent elements. The science of signs, called semiotics, was the key to this project. From it emerged the more contemporary poststructural methods, previously discussed in this volume by Fiske (Chapter 11), and addressed in Part IV by Clandinin and Connelly (Chapter 26). Manning and Cullum-Swan extend and expose the limits of each of these perspectives. Their powerful reading of the menus at McDonald's reveals how semiotics and fieldwork can be combined in a semiotic discourse analysis. The postmodern world can be read as a giant text. An understanding of this world requires the use of the narrative methods discussed by Manning and Cullum-Swan.

Conclusion

The researcher-as-*bricoleur* should have a working familiarity with all of the methods of collecting and analyzing empirical materials presented in this section. This familiarity should include an understanding of the history of each method and technique as well as hands-on experience with it. Only in this way can a researcher fully appreciate the limitations and strengths of each. At the same time, he or she will more clearly see how each, as a set of practices, creates its own subject matter.

In addition, it must be understood that each paradigm and perspective, as presented in Part II, has a distinct history with these methods of research. Although the methods-as-tools are somewhat universal in application, they are not uniformly used by researchers from all paradigms, or, if they are used, they are fitted to the particularities of the paradigm in question.

Of the five specific methods presented in this section (interviews, observation, cultural artifacts, visual methods, and personal experience methods), positivists and postpositivists are most likely to make use of structured interviews and those cultural artifacts that lend themselves to formal analysis. Constructionists and critical theorists also have histories of using all of the five methods, as do feminists, ethnic researchers, and cultural studies investigators. Similarly, researchers from all paradigms and perspectives can profitably make use of the data management and analysis methods and the computer-assisted models discussed by Huberman and Miles and Richards and Richards.

Notes

1. Of course, psychologists and educators in the ecological tradition (such as Barker and Wright) have long used observational methods, yet these rigorous methods have seldom been employed by sociologists.

2. Tesch (1991, pp. 18-20) has enumerated a variety of interpretive traditions and text-based forms of analysis that now use computer-assisted methods: classic and ethnographic content analysis, discourse and ethnographic analyses of conversations, document analysis of historical materials, event structure analysis, and grounded theory construction.

3. The potential shift to variable analysis moves computer-assisted methods firmly in the direction of positivist and postpositivist models of interpretation.

4. In this regard, Tesch's (1993) discussion of personal computers in qualitative research should be examined.

References

Agar, M. (1991). The right brain strikes back. In N. G. Fielding & R. M. Lee (Eds.), *Using computers in qualitative research* (pp. 181-194). Newbury Park, CA: Sage.

Akeroyd, A. V. (1991). Personal information and qualitative research data: Some practical and ethical problems arising from data protection legislation. In N. G. Fielding & R. M. Lee (Eds.), *Using computers in qualitative research* (pp. 89-106). Newbury Park, CA: Sage.

Berelson, B. (1952). *Content analysis in communication research.* Glencoe, IL: Free Press.

Devault, M. L. (1990). Talking and listening from women's standpoint: Feminist strategies for interviewing and analysis. *Social Problems, 37,* 96-116.

Kracauer, S. (1953). The challenge to qualitative content analysis. *Public Opinion Quarterly, 16,* 631-642.

Larsen, P. (1991). Textual analysis of fictional media content. In K. B. Jensen & N. W. Janowski (Eds.), *A handbook of qualitative methodologies for mass communication research* (pp. 121-134). New York: Routledge.

Lee, R. M., & Fielding, N. G. (1991). Computing for qualitative research: Options, problems, and potential. In N. G. Fielding & R. M. Lee (Eds.), *Using computers in qualitative research* (pp. 1-13). Newbury Park, CA: Sage.

Oakley, A. (1981). Interviewing women: A contradiction in terms. In H. Roberts (Ed.), *Doing feminist research* (pp. 30-61). London: Routledge.

Reinharz, S. (1992). *Feminist methods in social research.* New York: Oxford University Press.

Seidel, J. (1991). Method and madness in the application of computer technology to qualitative data analysis. In N. G. Fielding & R. M. Lee (Eds.), *Using computers in qualitative research* (pp. 107-116). Newbury Park, CA: Sage.

Tesch, R. (1991). Software for qualitative researchers: Analysis needs and program capabilities. In N. G. Fielding & R. M. Lee (Eds.), *Using computers in qualitative research* (pp. 16-37). Newbury Park, CA: Sage.

Tesch, R. (1993). Personal computers in qualitative research. In M. D. LeCompte & J. Preissle, with R. Tesch (Eds.), *Ethnography and qualitative design in educational research* (2nd ed., pp. 279-314). New York: Academic Press.

22

Interviewing

The Art of Science

ANDREA FONTANA
JAMES H. FREY

> *If all the problems of question wording could be traced to a single source, their common origin would probably prove to be in taking too much for granted.*
>
> S. Payne, *The Art of Asking Questions,* 1951

ASKING questions and getting answers is a much harder task than it may seem at first. The spoken or written word has always a residue of ambiguity, no matter how carefully we word the questions and report or code the answers. Yet, interviewing is one of the most common and most powerful ways we use to try to understand our fellow human beings. Interviewing is a paramount part of sociology, because interviewing is interaction and sociology is the study of interaction (see Benney & Hughes, 1956). Thus the interview becomes both the tool and the object, the art of sociological sociability, an encounter in which "both parties behave as though they are of equal status for its duration, whether or not this is actually so" (Benney & Hughes, 1956, p. 142).

Interviewing has a wide variety of forms and a multiplicity of uses. The most common type of interviewing is individual, face-to-face verbal interchange, but it can also take the form of face-to-face group interviewing, mailed or self-administered questionnaires, and telephone surveys. Interviewing can be structured, semistructured, or unstructured. It can be used for marketing purposes, to gather political opinions, for therapeutic reasons, or to produce data for academic analysis. It can be used for the purpose of measurement or its scope can be the understanding of an individual or a group perspective. An interview can be a one-time, brief exchange, say five minutes over the telephone, or it can take place over multiple, lengthy sessions, sometimes spanning days, as in life-history interviewing.

In this chapter we briefly outline the history of interviewing before turning to a discussion of the academic uses of interviewing. Although the focus of this volume is qualitative methodology, in order to illustrate the full import of interviewing we need to discuss the major types of interviewing—structured, group, and unstructured—as well as

AUTHORS' NOTE: We wish to thank, for insightful comments and wonderfully encouraging suggestions, Norman Denzin, Yvonna Lincoln, Arlene Daniels, and David Silverman. We followed their suggestions and their ideas.

other ways to conduct interviews. Next, we address in detail the various elements of qualitative interviewing. We then discuss some problems of gender as it relates to interviewing, as well as issues of interpretation and reporting. Finally, we broach some considerations related to ethical issues.

The History of Interviewing

Some form or another of interviewing has been with us for a very long time, as even ancient Egyptians conducted censuses of their population (Babbie, 1992). In recent times, the tradition of interviewing has been twofold. Interviewing found great popularity and widespread use in clinical diagnosis and counseling, where the concern was on the quality of the response, and later, during World War I, interviewing came to be widely employed in psychological testing, with an emphasis on measurement (Maccoby & Maccoby, 1954).

The individual generally credited with being the first to develop a social survey relying on interviewing was Charles Booth (see Converse, 1987). In 1886, Booth embarked on a comprehensive survey of the economic and social conditions of the people of London; this survey was later published as *Life and Labour of the People in London* (1902-1903). In this early study, Booth embodied what were to become separate interviewing methods; he not only implemented survey research but triangulated his work by relying on unstructured interviews and ethnographic observations:

> The data were checked and supplemented by visits to many neighborhoods, streets and homes, and by conferences with various welfare and community leaders. From time to time Booth lived as a lodger in districts where he was not known, so that he could become more intimately acquainted with the lives and habits of the poorer classes. (Parten, 1950, pp. 6-7)

Many other surveys of London and other English cities followed, patterned after Booth's example. In the United States similar work ensued. Among others, an 1885 study attempted to do in Chicago what Booth had done in London (see Converse, 1987) and, in 1896, admittedly following Booth's lead, the American sociologist W. E. B. Du Bois studied the black population of Philadelphia (see Du Bois, 1899). Surveys of cities and small towns followed; most notable among them were R. S. Lynd and H. M. Lynd's *Middletown* (1929) and *Middletown in Transition* (1937).

Opinion polling was another early form of interviewing. Some took place well before the turn of the century, but this form really came into its own in 1935 with the founding of the American Institute of Public Opinion by George Gallup. Preceding Gallup, both in psychology and in sociology, in the 1920s there was a movement toward the study (and usually measurement) of attitudes. W. I. Thomas and Florian Znaniecki used the documentary method to introduce the study of attitudes in social psychology. Thomas's influence, along with that of Robert Park, sparked a number of community studies at the University of Chicago that came to be known collectively as the works of the Chicago school. Although researchers from the Chicago school are reputed to have used the ethnographic method in their inquiries, some scholars disagree and have noted that many of the Chicago school studies lacked the analytic component of modern-day ethnography and thus are, at best, "first hand descriptive studies" (Harvey, 1987, p. 50). Regardless of the correct label for the Chicagoans' fieldwork, they clearly relied on a combination of observation, personal documents, and informal interviews in their studies. Interviews were especially in evidence in the work of Thrasher (1927), who, in his study of gang members, relied primarily on about 130 qualitative interviews, and in that of Nels Anderson (1923), whose classic study of hoboes relied on informal, in-depth conversations.

While it was left to Howard Becker and Everett Hughes to formalize and give impetus to sociological ethnography in the 1950s and 1960s, interviewing began to lose both the eclectic flavor given to it by Charles Booth and the qualitative accent of the Chicagoans. Understanding gang members or hoboes through interviews lost importance; what became relevant was the use of interviewing in survey research as a tool to quantify data. This was not new; opinion polls and market research had been doing it for years. But during World War II there was a tremendous increase in survey research, as the U.S. armed forces hired great numbers of sociologists as survey researchers. More than half a million American soldiers were interviewed in one manner or another (Young, 1966), and their mental and emotional lives were reported in a four-volume survey, *Studies in Social Psychology in World War II*. The research for the first two volumes of this study, titled *The American Soldier*, was directed by Samuel Stouffer. This work had tremendous impact and led the way to a widespread use of systematic survey research.

What was new, however, was that quantitative survey research was to move into academia and come to dominate sociology for the next three decades. An Austrian immigrant, Paul Lazarsfeld, spearheaded this move. He welcomed *The*

American Soldier with great enthusiasm. In fact, Robert Merton and Lazarsfeld (1950) edited a book of reflections on *The American Soldier.* Lazarsfeld moved to Columbia in 1940, taking with him his market research and other applied grants, and became instrumental in the directing of the Bureau of Applied Social Research. Two other "survey organizations" were also formed: In 1941, Harry Field began the National Opinion Research Center, first at Denver and then at Chicago; and in 1946, Likert and his group founded the Survey Research Center at Michigan.

Academia at the time was dominated by theoretical concerns, and there was some resistance to this applied, numerically based, kind of sociology. Sociologists and other humanists were critical of Lazarsfeld and the other survey researchers. Herbert Blumer, C. Wright Mills, Arthur Schlesinger, Jr., and Pitirin Sorokin, among others, voiced their displeasure, as reported by Converse (1987):

- Sorokin: "The new emphasis on quantitative work was obsessive, and he called the new practitioners 'quantophrenics'—with special reference to Stouffer and Lazarsfeld" (p. 253).
- Mills: "Those in the grip of the methodological inhibition often refuse to say anything about modern society unless it has been through the fine little mill of the Statistical Ritual" (p. 252).
- Schlesinger: "[They are] social relations hucksters" (p. 253).

But the survey researchers had powerful allies also, such as Merton, who joined the Survey Center at Columbia in 1943, and government monies were becoming increasing available for survey research. The 1950s saw the growth of survey research in the universities and a proliferation of survey research texts. Gradually, survey research increased its domain over sociology, culminating in 1960 with the election of Lazarsfeld to the presidency of the American Sociological Association. The methodological dominance of survey research continued unabated through the 1970s and 1980s and into the 1990s, although other methods began to erode the prominence of survey research.

Qualitative interviewing continued to be practiced, hand in hand with participant observation methods, but it too assumed some of the quantifiable scientific rigor that so preoccupied survey research. This was especially visible in grounded theory (Glaser & Strauss, 1967), with its painstaking emphasis on coding data, and in ethnomethodology, with its quest for invariant properties of social action (Cicourel, 1970), albeit ethnomethodology was critical of interviewing and its assumptions, especially the fact that interactants act "as if" they understand each other, while instead relying on glosses to "fill gaps" in understanding (Cicourel, 1964; Garfinkel, 1967). Other qualitative researchers suggested variations. John Lofland (1971) criticized grounded theory for paying little attention to data gathering techniques; Jack Douglas (1985) suggested lengthy, existential one-on-one interviews lasting one or more days; and James Spradley (1980) stressed the importance of sequencing in both ethnographic observation and ethnographic interviewing.

Recently, postmodernist ethnographers have concerned themselves with some of the assumptions and moral problems present in interviewing and with the controlling role of the interviewer. These concerns have led to new directions in qualitative interviewing, focusing on increased attention to the voices and feelings of the respondents (Marcus & Fischer, 1986) and the interviewer-respondent relation (Crapanzano, 1980). The importance of the researcher's gender in interviewing (Gluck & Patai, 1991) has also come to the fore in feminist/postmodernist studies, as has the issue of race (Stanfield, 1985). Both have further problematized concerns about membership and understanding in interviewing. On a less positive note, it must be mentioned that the interview has become a commodity in popular culture (and sports). Thus celebrities such as Bob Dylan and John Lennon (Wenner, 1992) or Charles Barkley (Montville, 1993) become objectified, living (or dead but nostalgic) commodities in a media market.

Structured Interviewing

Structured interviewing refers to a situation in which an interviewer asks each respondent a series of preestablished questions with a limited set of response categories. There is generally little room for variation in response except where an infrequent open-ended question may be used. The responses are also recorded by the interviewer according to a coding scheme that has already been established by the project director or research supervisor. The interviewer controls the pace of the interview by treating the questionnaire as if it were a theatrical script to be followed in a standardized and straightforward manner. Thus all respondents receive the same set of questions, asked in the same order or sequence, by an interviewer who has been trained to treat every interview situation in a like manner. There is very little flexibility in the way questions are asked or answered in the structured interview setting. Instructions to interviewers often include some of the following guidelines:

- Never get involved in long explanations of the study; use standard explanation provided by supervisor.
- Never deviate from the study introduction, sequence of questions, or question wording.
- Never let another person interrupt the interview; do not let another person answer for the respondent or offer his or her opinions on the question.
- Never suggest an answer or agree or disagree with an answer. Do not give the respondent any idea of your personal views on the topic of the question or survey.
- Never interpret the meaning of a question; just repeat the question and give instructions or clarifications that are provided in training or by supervisors.
- Never improvise, such as by adding answer categories, or make wording changes.

Interviews by telephone, face-to-face interviews in households, intercept interviews in shopping malls and parks, or the interviews generally associated with survey research are most likely to be included in this category.

This interview context calls for the interviewer to play a neutral role, never interjecting his or her opinions of the respondent's answers. The interviewer is to establish what has been called "balanced rapport"; he or she must be, on the one hand, casual and friendly but, on the other hand, directive and impersonal. The interviewer must perfect a style of "interested listening" that rewards the respondent's participation but does not evaluate the responses (Converse & Schuman, 1974).

The guidelines set forth above are intended to produce an ideal interview, but in practice this does not happen. Errors occur, and they commonly evolve from three sources: (a) respondent behavior, as when the respondent gives a "socially desirable" response to please the interviewer or omits relevant information to hide something from the interviewer (Bradburn, 1983); (b) the type of questionnaire (face-to-face or telephone) or the wording of the questions; and (c) an interviewer with flawed questioning techniques, or who changes the wording of the interview (Bradburn, Sudman, & Associates, 1979; Frey, 1989; Peneff, 1988).

The predetermined nature of structured interviewing is aimed at minimizing errors. However, structured interviewers are aware that interviews take place in a social interaction context, and they are influenced by that context. As Converse and Schuman (1974) observe, "There is no single interview style that fits every occasion or all respondents" (p. 53). This means that interviewers must be aware of respondent differences and must be flexible enough to make proper adjustments for unanticipated developments.

It is not enough to understand the mechanics of interviewing; it is also important to understand the respondent's world and forces that might stimulate or retard response (Kahn & Cannell, 1957). Still, the structured interview proceeds under a stimulus-response format, assuming that if questions (previously determined to elicit adequate indicators of the variable under examination) are phrased correctly, the respondent will answer them truthfully. Such an interviewing style often elicits rational responses, but it overlooks or inadequately assesses the emotional dimension.

Group Interviews

There is a developing form of interviewing that can be implemented in structured, semistructured, or unstructured format and that is gaining some popularity among social scientists. It is the group interview, or the systematic questioning of several individuals simultaneously in formal or informal settings (Frey & Fontana, in press). The use of the group interview is not meant to replace individual interviewing, but it is an option that deserves consideration because it can provide another level of data gathering or a perspective on the research problem not available through individual interviews.

Group interviewing has ordinarily been associated with marketing research, where the "focus group" has been used for some time to gather consumer opinions on product characteristics, advertising themes, and service delivery. This format has also been used to a considerable extent by political parties and candidates who are interested in voter reactions to issues and policies. The group interview has also been used in sociological research. Bogardus (1926) used groups to test his social distance scale, Zuckerman (1972) interviewed Nobel laureates, Thompson and Demerath (1952) looked at management problems in the military, Morgan and Spanish (1984) studied health issues, and Merton and his associates studied the impact of propaganda using group interviews. In fact, Merton, Fiske, and Kendall (1956) coined the term "focus group" to apply to a situation in which the interviewer asks group members very specific questions about a topic after considerable research has already been completed. There is some evidence that established anthropologists such as Malinowski used this technique, even though it was not reported (Frey & Fontana, 1991). Blumer (1969) also notes the importance of inter-

TABLE 22.1 Type of Group Interviews and Dimensions

Type	*Setting*	*Role of Interviewer*	*Question Format*	*Purpose*
Focus group	formal-preset	directive	structured	exploratory pretest
Brainstorming	formal or informal	nondirective	very unstructured	exploratory
Nominal/Delphi	formal	directive	structured	pretest exploratory
Field, natural	informal spontaneous	moderately nondirective	very unstructured	exploratory phenomenological
Field, formal	preset, but in field	somewhat directive	semistructured	phenomenological

SOURCE: Frey and Fontana (in press).

viewing a select group; he mentions "seeking participants . . . who are acute observers and who are well informed. . . . A small number of such individuals brought together as a discussion and resource group, is more valuable many times over than any representative sample" (p. 41). Blumer (1967) used this method in the Oakland drug study. Today, group interviews in general are generically designated "focus group" interviews, even though there is considerable variation in the natures and types of group interviews.

The group interview is essentially a qualitative data gathering technique that finds the interviewer/moderator directing the interaction and inquiry in a very structured or very unstructured manner, depending on the interview's purpose. For instance, the purpose may be exploratory; the researcher may bring several persons together to test a methodological technique, to try out a definition of a research problem, or to identify key informants. An extension of the exploratory intent is the use of the group interview for the purpose of pretesting questionnaire wording, measurement scales, or other elements of a survey design. This is now quite common in survey research (Desvousges & Frey, 1989). Group interviews can also be used for triangulation (Denzin, 1989b) purposes or employed in conjunction with other data gathering techniques. Finally, phenomenological purposes are served where group interviews are conducted in an unstructured way in the field. Table 22.1 compares the types of group interviews on various dimensions.

The skills required of a group interviewer are not significantly different from those needed by an interviewer of individuals. The interviewer must be flexible, objective, empathic, persuasive, a good listener, and so on. But the group does present some unusual problems. Merton et al. (1956) note three specific skills needed by the group interviewer: First, the interviewer must keep one person or a small coalition of persons from dominating the group; second, he or she must encourage recalcitrant respondents to participate; and third, he or she must obtain responses from the entire group to ensure the fullest possible coverage of the topic. In addition, the interviewer must balance the directive interviewer role with the role of moderator, which calls for the management of the dynamics of the group being interviewed: "The group interviewer must simultaneously worry about the script of questions and be sensitive to the evolving patterns of group interaction" (Frey & Fontana, in press).

The group interview has the advantages of being inexpensive, data rich, flexible, stimulating to respondents, recall aiding, and cumulative and elaborative, over and above individual responses. This type of interview is not, however, without problems. The emerging group culture may interfere with individual expression, the group may be dominated by one person, the group format makes it difficult to research sensitive topics, "groupthink" is a possible outcome, and the requirements for interviewer skills are greater because of group dynamics. Nevertheless, the group interview is a viable option for both qualitative and quantitative research.

Unstructured Interviewing

Unstructured interviewing provides a greater breadth than the other types, given its qualitative nature. In this section we will discuss the traditional type of unstructured interview: the open-ended ethnographic (in-depth) interview. Many qualitative researchers differentiate between in-depth (or ethnographic) interviewing and participant observation. Yet, as Lofland (1971) points out, the two go hand in hand, and many of the data gathered in participant observation come from informal interviewing in the field. Consider the following report, from Malinowski's (1989) diary:

> Saturday 8 [December 1917]. Got up late, felt rotten, took enema. At about 1 I went out; I heard cries; [people from] Kapwapu were bringing *uri*

> to Teyava. I sat with the natives, talked, took pictures. Went back. Billy corrected and supplemented my notes about *wasi.* At Teyava, an old man talked a great deal about fishes, but I did not understand him too well. Then we moved to his *bwayama.* Talked about *lili'u.* They kept questioning me about the war—In the evening I talked to the policeman about *bwaga'u, lili'u* and *yoyova.* I was irritated by their laughing. Billy again told me a number of interesting things. Took quinine and calomel. (p. 145)

Malinowski's "day in the field" shows how very important unstructured interviewing is in conducting fieldwork and clearly illustrates the difference between structured and unstructured interviewing. Malinowski has some general topics he wishes to know about, but he does not use closed-ended questions or a formal approach to interviewing. What's more, he commits (as most field-workers do) what structured interviewers would see as two "capital offenses": (a) He answers questions asked by the respondents, and (b) he lets his personal feelings influence him (as all field-workers do), and thus deviates from the "ideal" of a cool, distant, and rational interviewer.

Malinowski's example captures the differences between structured and unstructured interviewing. The former aims at capturing precise data of a codable nature in order to explain behavior within preestablished categories, whereas the latter is used in an attempt to understand the complex behavior of members of society without imposing any a priori categorization that may limit the field of inquiry. Indeed, Malinowski goes beyond any form of interviewing; he "immerses" himself in the native culture, letting it soak in by his mere interacting with the natives and "being there."

Spradley (1979) describes the following interviewer-respondent interaction, which would be unthinkable in traditional sociological circles yet is the very essence of unstructured interviewing—the establishment of a human-to-human relation with the respondent and the desire to *understand* rather than to *explain*:

> Presently she smiled, pressed her hand to her chest, and said: "Tsetchwe." It was her name. "Elizabeth," I said, pointing to myself. "Nisabe," she answered. . . . Then, having surely suspected that I was a woman, she put her hand on my breast gravely, and, finding out that I was, she touched her own breast. Many Bushmen do this; to them all Europeans look alike. "Tasu si" (women), she said. Then after a moment's pause Tsetchwe began to teach me. (pp. 3-4)

Spradley goes on to discuss all the things an interviewer learns from the natives about them, their culture, their language, their ways of life. Although each and every study is different, these are some of the basic elements of unstructured interviewing. These elements have been discussed in detail elsewhere, and we need not elaborate upon them too much (for detailed accounts of unstructured interviewing, see, among others, Adams & Preiss, 1960; Denzin, 1989b; Lofland, 1971; Spradley, 1979). Here we provide brief synopses; please remember that they are presented as heuristic devices, as every study uses slightly different elements and often in different combinations.

Accessing the Setting

How do we "get in"? This of course varies with the group one is attempting to study. One may have to disrobe and casually stroll in the nude if doing a study of nude beaches (Douglas & Rasmussen, 1977), or one may have to buy a huge motorcycle and frequent seedy bars in certain locations if attempting to befriend and study the Hell's Angels (Thompson, 1985). The different ways and attempts to "get in" vary tremendously, but they all share the common goal of gaining access to the setting. Sometimes there is no setting per se, as when one of the authors (Fontana, 1977) attempted to study poor elderly on the streets and had to gain access anew with each interviewee.

Understanding the Language and Culture of the Respondents

Irwin Deutscher (1968) wrote a seminal article on problems of language (lexicon, syntax, and phoneme) and meaning. To emphasize and clarify some of the problematics of language, Deutscher addressed the difficult task of asking questions cross-culturally.

Rosalie Wax (1960) gives perhaps the most poignant description available of learning the language and culture of the respondents in her study of "disloyal" Japanese in concentration camps in the United States between 1943 and 1945. She had to overcome a number of language and cultural problems in her study. Respondents may be fluent in the language of the interviewer, but there are different ways of saying things, and, indeed, certain things should not be said at all, linking language and cultural manifestations. Wax (1960) makes this point:

> I remarked that I would like to see the letter. The silence that fell on the chatting group was almost palpable, and the embarrassment of the hosts was painful to see. The *faux pas* was not asking to see a letter, for letters were passed about rather freely.

It rested on the fact that one did not give a Caucasian a letter in which the "disloyal" statement of a friend might be expressed. (p. 172)

Some researchers, especially in anthropological interviews, tend to rely on interpreters, and thus become vulnerable to an added layer of meanings, biases, and interpretations that may lead to disastrous misunderstanding (Freeman, 1983). At times, a specific jargon, such as the medical metalanguage of physicians, may be a code that is hard for nonmembers to understand.

Deciding on How to Present Oneself

Do we present ourselves as representatives from academia studying medical students (Becker, 1956)? Do we approach an interview as a woman-to-woman discussion (Spradley, 1979)? Do we "dress down" to look like the respondents (Fontana, 1977; Thompson, 1985)? Do we represent the colonial culture (Malinowski, 1922) or do we humbly present ourselves as "learners" (Wax, 1960)? The decision of how to present oneself is very important, because after one's presentational self is "cast" it leaves a profound impression on the respondents and has great influence on the success (or failure) of the study. Sometimes, inadvertently, the researcher's presentational self may be misrepresented, as John Johnson (1976) discovered in studying a welfare office, when some of the employees assumed he was a "spy" for management despite his best efforts to convince them of the contrary.

Locating an Informant

The researcher must find an insider, a member of the group studied, willing to be an informant and to act as a guide to and translator of cultural mores and, at times, jargon or language. Although interviews can be conducted without an informant, a researcher can save much time and avoid many mistakes if a good informant becomes available. The "classic" sociological informant is Doc in William Foote Whyte's *Street Corner Society* (1943). Without Doc's help and guidance, it is doubtful that Whyte would have been able to learn about his subjects to the level he did. Very instructive is Paul Rabinow's (1977) discussion of his relation with his main informant, Abd al-Malik ben Lahcen. Malik acted as a translator but also provided Rabinow with access to the cultural ways of the subjects, and by his actions provided insights for Rabinow to the vast differences between a University of Chicago researcher and a native Moroccan.

Gaining Trust

Survey researchers asking respondents whether or not they would favor the establishment of a nuclear dump in their state (Frey, 1993) do not have too much work to do in the way of gaining trust; respondents have opinions about nuclear dumps and are very willing to express them, sometimes forcefully. But what about asking respondents about their frequency of sexual intercourse or their preferred birth-control practices? That is clearly a different story, and one needs to establish some trust with such respondents (Cicourel, 1974). Paul Rasmussen (1989) had to spend months as a "wallflower" in the waiting room of a massage parlor before any of the masseuses gained enough trust in him to divulge to him, in unstructured interviews, the nature of their "massage" relations with clients. Gaining trust is essential to an interviewer's success, and even once it is gained trust can be very fragile indeed; any *faux pas* by the researcher may destroy days, weeks, or months of painstakingly gained trust.

Establishing Rapport

Because the goal of unstructured interviewing is *understanding,* it becomes paramount for the researcher to establish rapport. He or she must be able to put him- or herself in the role of the respondents and attempt to see the situation from their perspective, rather than impose the world of academia and preconceptions upon them. Close rapport with respondents opens doors to more informed research, but it may also create problems, as the researcher may become a spokesperson for the group studied, losing his or her distance and objectivity, or may "go native" and become a member of the group and forgo the academic role. At times, what the researcher may feel is good rapport turns out not to be, as Thompson (1985) found out in a nightmarish way when he was subjected to a brutal beating by the Hell's Angels just as his study of them was coming to a close. At the other end of the spectrum, some researchers may never feel they have good rapport with subjects; for example, Malinowski (1989) always mistrusted the motives of the natives and at times was troubled by what he saw as their brutish sensuality or angered by their outright lying or deception: "After lunch I [carried] yellow calico and spoke about the *baloma.* I made a small *sagali,* Navavile. I was *fed up* with the *niggers*" (p. 154).

Collecting Empirical Materials

Being out in the field does not afford one the luxury of videotapes, soundproof rooms, and high-quality recording equipment. Lofland (1971) provides detailed information on doing and writing up interviews and on the types of field notes one ought to take and how to organize them. Yet often one must make do; the "tales" of field-workers' attempts to make field notes range from holding a miniature tape recorder as inconspicuously as possible to taking mental notes and then rushing to the privacy of a bathroom to jot them down, on toilet paper at times. We agree with Lofland (1971) that regardless of the circumstances one ought to (a) take notes regularly and promptly; (b) write everything down, no matter how unimportant it may seem at the time; (c) try to be as inconspicuous as possible in note taking; and (d) analyze one's notes frequently.

Other Types of Unstructured Interviewing

We will consider the issue of interpreting and reporting empirical materials later in this chapter. Now we will briefly outline some different types of unstructured interviews.

Oral History

The oral history does not differ from the unstructured interview methodologically, but in purpose. Oral collection of historical material goes back to ancient days, although its modern formal organization can be traced to 1948, when Allan Nevins began the Oral History Project at Columbia University (Starr, 1984, p. 4). Oral history captures a variety of people's lives, from common folks talking about their jobs, as in Studs Terkel's *Working* (1975), to historical recollections of famous people, such as President Harry Truman in Merle Miller's *Plain Speaking* (see Starr, 1984). Often, oral history transcripts are not published but may be found in libraries, silent memoirs awaiting someone to rummage through them and bring their testimony to life.

Often oral history is a way to reach groups and individuals who have been ignored, oppressed, and/or forgotten. A classic example is the work of Lomax and Lomax (1934/1966), who used ballads and folk songs as verbal expressions and cultural commentaries on "the cowboy, the miner, the tramp, the lumberjack, the Forty-niner, the soldier, the sailor, the Plantation Negro" (p. xxvii). Also, the forgotten people involved in the Vietnam War—blacks (Terry, 1984) and women (Fontana & Collins, 1993; Marshall, 1987)—have been brought to the fore through their personal accounts.

Recently, oral history has found popularity among feminists (Gluck & Patai, 1991) as a way to understand and bring forth the history of women in a culture that has traditionally relied on a masculine interpretation: "Refusing to be rendered historically voiceless any longer, women are creating a new history—using our own voices and experiences" (Gluck, 1984, p. 222). The attempt continues, through the use of oral history to reconnect to the women missing in history and the women who are missing in their own histories, to capture the work of women, the lives and experiences of women, and the social and personal meanings of women (Gluck & Patai, 1991; Reinharz, 1992).

Creative Interviewing

Close to oral history but used more conventionally as a sociological tool is Jack Douglas's (1985) "creative interviewing." Douglas argues against the "how-to" ways to conduct interviews because unstructured interviews take place in the largely situational everyday world of members of society. Thus interviewing and interviewers must necessarily be creative, forget "how-to" rules, and adapt themselves to the ever-changing situations they face. Like oral historians, Douglas sees interviewing as collecting oral reports from the members of society. These reports go well beyond the length of conventional unstructured interviews and may become "life histories," taking multiple sessions over many days with the subject(s). "Forgetting the rules" in creative interviewing allows research subjects to express themselves more freely, and thus to have a greater voice both in the research process and in the research report.

Postmodern Interviewing

Douglas's concern with the important role played by the interviewer *qua* human being, which is also shared by the feminist oral historians, became a paramount element of postmodern anthropologists and sociologists in the mid-1980s. Marcus and Fischer (1986) address ethnography at large, but their discussion is very germane to unstructured interviewing because, as we have seen, it constitutes the major way of collecting data in fieldwork. Marcus and Fischer voice reflexive concerns about the ways in which the researcher influences the study, in both the methods of data collection and the techniques of reporting findings; this concern leads to new ways to conduct interviews in the hope of minimizing the interviewer's influence. This influence, of course, cannot be eliminated, but it can be neutralized if its assumptions and premises are made as clear as possible.

One way to do this is through *polyphonic* interviewing, in which the voices of the subjects are recorded with minimal influence from the researcher and are not collapsed together and reported as one, through the interpretation of the researcher. Instead, the multiple perspectives of the various subjects are reported and differences and problems encountered are discussed, rather than glossed over (see Krieger, 1983). *Interpretive* interactionism follows in the footsteps of creative and polyphonic interviewing, but, borrowing from James Joyce, adds a new element, that of epiphanies, described as "those interactional moments that leave marks on people's lives [and] have the potential for creating transformational experiences for the person" (Denzin, 1989a, p. 15). Thus the topic of inquiry becomes dramatized by the focus on existential moments in people's lives, producing richer and more meaningful data. *Critical ethnography* (and interviewing) (Giroux, 1992; Lincoln & Guba, 1985) relies on critical theory; it is ethnography that accounts for the historical, social, and economical situations. Critical ethnographers realize the strictures caused by these situations and their value-laden agendas. Critical ethnographers see themselves as blue-collar "cultural workers" (Giroux, 1992) attempting to broaden the political dimensions of cultural work while undermining existing oppressive systems. Finally, as postmodernists seek new ways of understanding and reporting data, some are combining visual and written modes of communication. Ulmer (1989) introduces the concept of *oralysis,* "referring to the ways in which oral forms, derived from everyday life, are, with the recording powers of video, applied to the analytical tasks associated with literate forms" (p. xi). In oralysis, the traditional product of interviewing, talk, is coupled with the visual, providing, according to Ulmer, a product more consonant with a society that is dominated by the medium of television. Becker (1981) also engages in visual/written sociological commentaries, as does Douglas Harper (1982). The journal *Visual Sociology* is devoted to such commentaries.

Gendered Interviews

> The housewife goes into a well-stocked store to look for a frying pan. Her thinking probably does not proceed exactly this way, but it is helpful to think of the many possible two-way choices she might make: Cast iron or aluminum? Thick or thin? Metal or wooden handle? Covered or not? Deep or shallow? Large or small? This brand or that? Reasonable or too high in price? To buy or not? Cash or charge? Have it delivered or carry it. . . . The two-way question is simplicity itself when it comes to recording answers and tabulating them. (Payne, 1951, pp. 55-56)

This quote represents the prevalent paternalistic attitude toward women in interviewing (see Oakley, 1981, p. 39) as well as the paradigmatic concern with coding answers and therefore presenting limited, dichotomous choices. Apart from a tendency to be condescending toward women, the traditional interview paradigm does not account for gendered differences. In fact, Babbie's classic text *The Practice of Social Research* (1992) briefly references gender only three times and says nothing about the influence of gender on interviews. As Ann Oakley (1981) cogently points out, both the interviewers and the respondents are considered faceless and invisible, and they must be if the paradigmatic assumption of gathering value-free data is to be maintained. Yet, as Denzin (1989a, p. 116) tells us, "gender filters knowledge"; that is, the sex of the interviewer and of the respondent does make a difference, as the interview takes place within the cultural boundaries of a paternalistic social system in which masculine identities are differentiated from feminine ones.

In typical interviews there exists a hierarchical relation, with the respondent being in the subordinate position. The interviewer is instructed to be courteous, friendly, and pleasant:

> The interviewer's manner should be friendly, courteous, conversational and unbiased. He should be neither too grim nor too effusive; neither too talkative nor too timid. The idea should be to put the respondent at ease, *so that he will talk freely and fully.* (Selltiz, Jahoda, Deutsch, & Cook, 1965, p. 576; emphasis added)

Yet, as the last above-quoted line shows, this demeanor is a ruse to gain the trust and confidence of the respondent without reciprocating in any way. Interviewers are not to give their own opinions and are to evade direct questions. What seems to be a conversation is really a one-way pseudo-conversation, raising the ethical dilemma (Fine, 1983-1984) of studying people for opportunistic reasons. When the respondent is female the interview presents added problems, because the preestablished format directed at information relevant for the study tends both to ignore the respondent's own concerns and to curtail any attempts to digress and elaborate. This format also stymies any revelation of personal feelings and emotions.

Warren (1988) discusses problems of gender in both anthropological and sociological fieldwork, and many of them apply to the ethnographic interview. Some of these problems are the traditional ones of entrée and trust, which may be heightened by the sex of the interviewer, especially in highly sex-segregated societies: "I never witnessed any ceremonies that were barred to women. Whenever I visited compounds I sat with the women while the men gathered in the parlors or in front of the compound. . . . I never entered any of the places where men sat around to drink beer or palm wine and to chat" (Sudarkasa, 1986; quoted in Warren, 1988, p. 16).

Solutions to the problem have been to view the female anthropologist as androgyne or to grant her honorary male status for the duration of her research. Warren (1988) points to some advantages of being female and therefore seen as harmless or invisible; Hanna Papanek (1964) addresses the greater role flexibility of women interviewers in countries where women are secluded. Other problems concern the researcher's status or race and the context of the interview; again, these problems are magnified for female researchers in a paternalistic world. Female interviewers at times face the added burden of sexual overtures or covert sexual hassle (Warren, 1988, p. 33), or are considered low-status strangers (Daniels, 1967).

Feminist researchers have suggested ways to circumvent the traditional interviewing paradigm. It has been suggested that interviewing is a masculine paradigm (Oakley, 1981), embedded in a masculine culture and stressing masculine traits while at the same time excluding from interviewing traits such as sensitivity, emotionality, and others that are culturally viewed as feminine.

There is a growing reluctance, especially among female researchers (Oakley, 1981; Reinharz, 1992; Smith, 1987), to continue interviewing women as "objects," with little or no regard for them as individuals. Whereas this reluctance stems from moral and ethical issues, it is also very relevant methodologically. As Oakley (1981) points out, in interviewing there is "no intimacy without reciprocity" (p. 49). Thus the emphasis is shifting to allow the development of a closer relation between interviewer and respondent, attempting to minimize status differences and doing away with the traditional hierarchical situation in interviewing. Interviewers can show their human side and answer questions and express feelings. Methodologically, this new approach provides a greater spectrum of responses and a greater insight into respondents—or "participants," to avoid the hierarchical pitfall (Reinharz, 1992, p. 22)—because it encourages them to control the sequencing and the language of the interview and also allows them the freedom of open-ended responses (Oakley, 1981; Reinharz, 1992; Smith, 1987). Thus: "Women were always . . . encouraged to 'digress' into details of their personal histories and to recount anecdotes of their working lives. Much important information was gathered in this way" (Yeandle, 1984; quoted in Rienharz, 1992, p. 25).

This commitment to maintaining the integrity of the phenomena and preserving the viewpoint of the subjects as expressed in their everyday language is akin to phenomenological and existential sociologies (Douglas & Johnson, 1977; Kotarba & Fontana, 1984) and also reflects the concern of postmodern ethnographers (Marcus & Fischer, 1986). The differences are (a) the heightened moral concern for subjects/participants; (b) the attempt to redress the male-female hierarchy and existing paternalistic power structure; (c) the paramount importance placed upon membership, as the effectiveness of male researchers in interviewing female subjects has been largely discredited; and (d) the realization that the old "distanced" style of interviewing cuts the subjects' involvement drastically and, thus, rather than giving us an "objective" interview, gives us a one-sided and therefore inaccurate picture.

Some feminist sociologists have gone beyond the concern with interviewing or fieldwork in itself. Laurel Richardson (1992) is striving for new forms of expression to report findings and has presented some of her fieldwork in the form of poetry. Patricia Clough (1992) questions the whole enterprise of fieldwork under the current paradigm and calls for a reassessment of the whole sociological enterprise and for a rereading of existing sociological texts in a light that is not marred by paternalistic bias. These researchers' voices echo the concern of Dorothy Smith (1987), who eloquently states:

> The problem [of a research project] and its particular solution are analogous to those by which fresco painters solved the problems of representing the different temporal moments of a story in the singular space of the wall. The problem is to produce in a two-dimensional space framed as a wall a world of action and movement in time. (p. 281)

Framing and Interpreting Interviews

Besides the problem of framing real-life events in a two-dimensional space, we face the added problems of how the framing is being done and who is doing the framing. In sociological terms this means that the type of interviewing selected, the techniques used, the ways of recording information, all come to bear on the results of the study. Additionally, data must be interpreted and the researcher has a great deal of influence on what part of the data will be reported and how it will be reported.

Framing Interviews

There have been numerous volumes published on the techniques of structured interviewing (see, among others, Babbie, 1992; Bradburn et al., 1979; Gorden, 1980; Kahn & Cannell, 1957). There is also a voluminous literature on group interviewing, especially in marketing and survey research (for an up-to-date review of literature in this area, see Stewart & Shamdasani, 1990). Recently, the uses of group interviewing have been linked to qualitative sociology also (Frey & Fontana, in press; Morgan, 1988). Unstructured interviewing techniques have been covered abundantly (Denzin, 1989b; Lofland, 1971; Lofland & Lofland, 1984; Spradley, 1979). Also noteworthy is Kuhn's article "The Interview and the Professional Relationship" (1962), in which he considers interview as a "performance" and warns against "mystification," or loss of sincerity in the interview by attempting to overmanage it.

As we have noted, unstructured interviews vary widely, given their informal nature and the nature of the setting, and some eschew any preestablished set of techniques (Douglas, 1985). Yet, there are techniques involved in interviewing, whether one is just being "a nice person" or is following a format. Techniques can be varied to meet various situations, and varying one's techniques is known as employing tactics. Traditional techniques tell us that the researcher is involved in an informal conversation with the respondent, thus he or she must maintain a tone of "friendly" chat while trying to remain close to the guidelines of the topics of inquiry he or she has in mind. The researcher begins by "breaking the ice" with general questions and gradually moves on to more specific ones, while also, as inconspicuously as possible, asking questions intended to check the veracity of statements made by the respondent. The researcher, again according to traditional techniques, should avoid getting involved in a "real" conversation in which he or she answers questions asked by the respondent or provides personal opinions on the matters discussed. One avoids "getting trapped" by shrugging off the relevance of one's opinions (e.g., "It doesn't matter how I feel, it's your opinion that's important") or by feigning ignorance (e.g., "I really don't know enough about this to say anything—you're the expert"). Of course, as noted in the above discussion on gendered interviewing, the researcher may reject these outdated techniques and "come down" to the level of the respondent and engage in a "real" conversation with "give and take" and empathic understanding (see Daniels, 1983). This makes the interview more honest, morally sound, and reliable, because it treats the respondent as an equal, allows him or her to express personal feelings, and therefore presents a more "realistic" picture than can be uncovered using traditional interview methods.

The use of language and specific terms is very important for creating a "sharedness of meanings" in which both interviewer and respondent understand the contextual nature of the interview. For instance, in studying nude beaches, Douglas and Rasmussen (1977) discovered that the term "nude beach virgin" had nothing to do with chastity, but referred to the fact that a person's buttocks were white, thus indicating to others that he or she was a newcomer to the nude beach. Language is also important in delineating the type of question (broad, narrow, leading, instructive, and so on). Unstructured conversation, mere chitchat, listening to others without taking notes or trying to direct the conversation is also important to establish rapport and immerse oneself in the situation, while gathering a store of "tacit knowledge" about the people and the culture being studied (see our discussion of Malinowski above).

Nonverbal elements are also important in interviewing. There are basically four kinds of nonverbal technique:

> *Proxemic* communication is the use of interpersonal space to communicate attitudes, *chronemics* communication is the use of pacing of speech and length of silence in conversation, *kinesic* communication includes any body movements or postures, and *paralinguistic* communication includes all the variations in volume, pitch and quality of voice. (Gorden, 1980, p. 335)

All of these are very important for the researcher and the researched alike, because nonverbal communication both informs and sets the tone for the interview. Looks, body postures, long silences, the way one dresses—all are significant in the interactional interview situation. Goffman (1959, 1971) has explored in detail the importance of nonverbal features in interaction as well as the consonance between verbal and nonverbal features. An amusing example of the wrong use of nonverbal communication is provided by Thompson (1985). Because he was attempting to be allowed to study the Hell's Angels as a participant observer, he began to frequent their hangouts, dress the part, and speak the proper jargon. He even bought a motorcycle—however, he got into trouble by buying a British model; he had failed to realize that for true-blue Angels, only a Harley-Davidson will do.

Finally, techniques vary with the group being interviewed. One will need a different approach for interviewing children (Fine & Sandstrom, 1988) from that required for interviewing widows (Lopata, 1980); drug dealers will not wish to be interviewed at all (Adler, 1985). The researcher must adapt to the world of the individuals studied and try to share their concerns and outlooks. Only by doing so can he or she learn anything at all. As Patricia Adler (1985) slowly and painfully discovered, it is not easy to gain the trust of drug dealers so that they will allow you to interview them.

Interpreting Interviews

Many studies using unstructured interviews are not reflexive enough about the interpreting process; common platitudes proclaim that data speak for themselves, that the researcher is neutral, unbiased, and "invisible." Data reported tend to flow nicely, there are no contradictory data and no mention of what data were excluded and/or why. Improprieties never happen and the main concern seems to be the proper, if unreflexive, filing, analyzing, and reporting of events. But anyone who has engaged in fieldwork knows better; no matter how organized the researcher may be, he or she slowly becomes buried under a growing mountain of field notes, transcripts, newspaper clippings, and tape recordings. Traditionally, readers were presented with the researcher's interpretation of the data, cleaned and streamlined and collapsed in rational, noncontradictory accounts. More recently, sociologists have come to grips with the reflexive, problematic, and, at times, contradictory nature of data and with the tremendous, if unspoken, influence of the researcher as an author (see Dickens & Fontana, 1994; Geertz, 1988). What Van Maanen (1988) calls "confessional style" began in earnest in the 1970s (see Johnson, 1976) and has continued unabated to the present day, in a soul cleansing by researchers of problematic feelings and sticky situations in the field. Although perhaps somewhat overdone at times, these "confessions" are very valuable, as they make readers aware of the complex and cumbersome nature of interviewing people in their natural settings and lend a tone of realism and veracity to studies: "Yesterday I slept very late. Got up around 10. The day before I had engaged Omaga, Koupa, and a few others. They didn't come. Again I fell into a rage" (Malinowski, 1967/1989, p. 67).

Showing the human side of the researcher and the problems of unstructured interviewing has taken new forms in deconstructionism (Derrida, 1976), where the influence of the author is brought under scrutiny. The text created by the rendition of events by the researcher is "deconstructed," as his or her biases and taken-for-granted notions are exposed and, at times, alternative ways to look at the data are introduced (Clough, 1992).

Postmodern social researchers, as we have seen, attempt to expose and openly acknowledge the role of the researcher *qua* field-worker and *qua* author. Thus, for instance, Crapanzano (1980) reports Tuhami's accounts, whether they be sociohistorical renditions, dreams, or outright lies, because they all constitute parts of his Morrocan Arab subject's sense of self and personal history. In interviewing Tuhami, Crapanzano learns not only about his subject but about himself:

> As Tuhami's interlocutor, I became an active participant in his life history, even though I rarely appear directly in his recitations. Not only did my presence, and my questions, prepare him for the text he was to produce, but they produced what I read as a change of consciousness in him. They produced a change of consciousness in me too. We were both jostled from our assumptions about the nature of the everyday world and ourselves and groped for common reference points within this limbo of interchange. (p. 11)

No longer pretending to be faceless subject and invisible researcher, Tuhami and Crapanzano are portrayed as individual human beings with their own personal histories and idiosyncrasies, and we, the readers, learn about two people and two cultures.

Ethical Considerations

Because the objects of inquiry in interviewing are human beings, extreme care must be taken to avoid any harm to them. Traditional ethical concerns have revolved around the topics of *informed consent* (consent received from the subject after he or she has been carefully and truthfully informed about the research), *right to privacy* (protecting the identity of the subject) and *protection from harm* (physical, emotional, or any other kind). Whereas no sociologist or other social scientist would dismiss these three concerns as trivial, there are other ethical concerns that are less unanimously upheld. The controversy over overt/covert fieldwork is more germane to participant observation, but could include the surreptitious use of tape-recording devices. Warwick and Douglas, for instance, argue for the use of covert methods because they mirror the deceitfulness of everyday-life reality, whereas others, such as Kai Erikson, are vehemently opposed to the study of uninformed subjects (see Punch, 1986).

Another problematic issue stems from the degree of involvement on the part of the researcher with the group under study. Whyte was asked to vote illegally (to vote more than once) during local elections by the members of the group he had gained access to and befriended, gaining their trust. He used "situational ethics," and judged the legal infraction to be minor in comparison to the loss of his fieldwork if he refused to vote as he was asked. Thompson was faced with a more serious possible legal breach. He was terrified of having to witness one of the alleged rapes for which the Hell's Angels have become notorious, but, as he reports, none took place during his research. The most famous, and probably most widely discussed, case of questionable ethics in qualitative sociology is Laud Humphreys's research for *Tearoom Trade* (1970). Humphreys studied homosexual encounters in public restrooms in parks ("tearooms") by acting as a lookout ("watchqueen"). This fact in itself may be seen as ethically incorrect, but it is the following one that has raised many academic eyebrows. Unable to interview the men in the "tearooms," Humphreys recorded their car license plate numbers, which he used to trace the men to their residences. He then changed his appearance and interviewed many of the men in their homes, without being recognized.

Another ethical problem is raised by those who question the veracity of reports made by researchers. For example, Whyte's (1943) famous study of Italian men in Boston has recently come under severe scrutiny (Boelen, 1992), as some have alleged that he portrayed the "Corner Boys" in demeaning ways that did not reflect their visions of themselves. Whyte's case is still unresolved, but it does illustrate the delicate issue of ethical decisions in the field and in reporting field notes, even some 50-odd years later!

A growing number of scholars, as we have seen (Oakley, 1981), feel that most of traditional in-depth interviewing is unethical, whether wittingly or unwittingly, and we agree wholeheartedly. The techniques and tactics of interviewing are really ways of manipulating respondents while treating them as objects or numbers rather than individual human beings. Should the quest for objectivity supersede the human side of those whom we study? Consider the following experience that one of us had:

> One day while doing research at the convalescent center, I was talking to one of the aides while she was beginning to change the bedding of one of the patients who had urinated and soaked the bed. He was the old, blind, ex-wrestler confined in the emergency room. Suddenly, the wrestler decided he was not going to cooperate with the aide and began striking violently at the air about him, fortunately missing the aide. Since nobody else was around, I had no choice but to hold the patient pinned down to the bed while the aide proceeded to change the bedding. It was not pleasant: The patient was squirming and yelling horrible threats at the top of his voice; the acid smell of urine was nauseating; I was slowly losing my grip on the much stronger patient, while all along feeling horribly like Chief Bromden when he suffocates the lobotomized Mac Murphy in Ken Kesey's novel. *But there was no choice, one just could not sit back and take notes while the patient tore apart the aide.* (Fontana, 1977, p. 187; emphasis added)

Clearly, as we move forward with sociology, we cannot, to paraphrase what Herbert Blumer said so many years ago, let the methods dictate our images of human beings. As Punch (1986) suggests, as field-workers we need to exercise common sense and moral responsibility, and, we would like to add, to our subjects first, to the study next, and to ourselves last.

Conclusion

In this chapter we have outlined the history of interviewing, with its qualitative and quantitative origins. We have looked at structured, group, and various types of unstructured interviewing. We have examined the importance of gender in interviewing and the ways in which framing and interpreting affect interviews. Finally, we have examined the importance of ethics in interviewing.

Clearly, different types of interviewing are suited to different situations. If we wish to find out how many people oppose a nuclear repository, survey research is our best tool, and we can quantify and code the responses and use mathematical models to explain our findings (Frey, 1993). If we are interested in opinions about a given product, a focus group interview will provide us with the most efficient results; if we wish to know and understand about the lives of Palestinian women in the resistance (Gluck, 1991), we need to interview them at length and in depth in an unstructured way.

Many scholars are now realizing that to pit one type of interviewing against another is a futile effort, a leftover from the paradigmatic quantitative/qualitative hostility of past generations. Thus an increasing number of researchers are using multimethod approaches to achieve broader and often better results. This is referred to as *triangulation* (Denzin, 1989b). In triangulating, a researcher may use several methods in different combinations. For instance, group interviewing has long been used to complement survey research and is now being used to complement participant observation (Morgan, 1988).

Interviewing is currently undergoing not only a methodological change but a much deeper one, related to self and other (see Fine, Chapter 4, this volume). The "other" is no longer a distant, aseptic, quantified, sterilized, measured, categorized, and cataloged faceless respondent, but has become a living human being, usually a forgotten or an oppressed one—a black combatant in a Vietnam camp or myriad women, up to now sociologically invisible, finally blossoming to full living color and coming into focus as real persons, as the interviewer recognizes them as such. Also, in learning about the other we learn about the self (Crapanzano, 1980). That is, as we treat the other as a human being, we can no longer remain objective, faceless interviewers, but become human beings and must disclose ourselves, learning about ourselves as we try to learn about the other.

The brief journey we have taken through the world of interviewing should allow us to be better informed and perhaps more sensitized to the problematics of asking questions for sociological reasons. We must remember that each individual has his or her own social history and an individual perspective on the world. Thus we cannot take our task for granted. As Oakley (1981) notes, "Interviewing is rather like a marriage: everybody knows what it is, an awful lot of people do it, and yet behind each closed front door there is a world of secrets" (p. 41). She is quite correct—we all think we know how to ask questions and talk to people, from common, everyday folks to highly qualified quantophrenic experts. Yet, to learn about people we must remember to treat them as people, and they will uncover their lives to us. As long as many researchers continue to treat respondents as unimportant, faceless individuals whose only contribution is to fill one more boxed response, the answers we, as researchers, will get will be commensurable with the questions we ask and with the way we ask them. We are no different from Gertrude Stein, who, on her deathbed, asked her lifelong companion, Alice B. Toklas, "What is the answer?" And when Alice could not bring herself to speak, Gertrude asked, "Then what is the question?" The question must be asked person-to-person if we want it to be answered fully.

References

Adams, R. N., & Preiss, J. J. (1960). *Human organizational research: Field relations and techniques.* Homewood, IL: Dorsey.

Adler, P. (1985). *Wheeling and dealing.* New York: Columbia University Press.

Anderson, N. (1923). *The hobo: The sociology of the homeless man.* Chicago: University of Chicago Press.

Babbie, E. (1992). *The practice of social research* (6th ed.). Belmont, CA: Wadsworth.

Becker, H. S. (1956). Interviewing medical students. *American Journal of Sociology, 62,* 199-201.

Becker, H. S. (1981). *Exploring society photographically.* Evanston, IL: Northwestern University, Mary and Leigh Block Gallery.

Benney, M., & Hughes, E. (1956). Of sociology and the interview: Editorial preface. *American Journal of Sociology, 62,* 137-142.

Blumer, H. (1969). *Symbolic interactionism: Perspective and method.* Englewood Cliffs, NJ: Prentice Hall.

Blumer, H., with Sutter, A., Smith, R., & Ahmed, S. (1967). *The world of youthful drug use.* Berkeley: University of California Press.

Boelen, W. A. M. (1992). *Street corner society*: Cornerville revisited. *Journal of Contemporary Ethnography, 21,* 11-51.

Bogardus, E. S. (1926). The group interview. *Journal of Applied Sociology, 10,* 372-382.

Booth, C. (1902-1903). *Life and labour of the people in London.* London: Macmillan.

Bradburn, N. M. (1983). Response effects. In P. H. Rossi, J. D. Wright, & A. B. Anderson (Eds.), *Handbook of survey research* (pp. 289-328). New York: Academic Press.

Bradburn, N. M., Sudman, S., & Associates. (1979). *Improving interview method and questionnaire design.* San Francisco: Jossey-Bass.

Cicourel, A. (1964). *Method and measurement in sociology.* New York: Free Press.

Cicourel, A. (1970). The acquisition of social structure: Toward a developmental sociology of language and meaning. In J. D. Douglas (Ed.), *Understanding everyday life: Toward a reconstruction of social knowledge* (pp. 136-168). Chicago: Aldine.

Cicourel, A. (1974). *Theory and method in a study of Argentine fertility.* New York: John Wiley.

Clough, P. T. (1992). *The end(s) of ethnography: From realism to social criticism.* Newbury Park, CA: Sage.

Converse, J. M. (1987). *Survey research in the United States: Roots and emergence 1890-1960.* Berkeley: University of California Press.

Converse, J. M., & Schuman, H. (1974). *Conversations at random: Survey research as interviewers see it.* New York: John Wiley.

Crapanzano, V. (1980). *Tuhami: Portrait of a Moroccan.* Chicago: University of Chicago Press.

Daniels, A. K. (1967). The low-caste stranger in social research. In G. Sjoberg (Ed.), *Ethics, politics, and social research* (pp. 267-296). Cambridge, MA: Schenkman.

Daniels, A. K. (1983). Self-deception and self-discovery in field work. *Qualitative Sociology, 6,* 195-214.

Denzin, N. K. (1989a). *Interpretive interactionism.* Newbury Park, CA: Sage.

Denzin, N. K. (1989b). *The research act* (3rd ed.). Englewood Cliffs, NJ: Prentice Hall.

Desvousges, W. H., & Frey, J. H. (1989). Integrating focus groups and surveys: Examples from environmental risk surveys. *Journal of Official Statistics, 5,* 349-363.

Deutscher, I. (1968). Asking questions cross-culturally: Some problems of linguistic comparability. In H. S. Becker, B. Geer, D. Riesman, & R. Weiss (Eds.), *Institutions and the person* (pp. 318-341). Chicago: Aldine.

Derrida, J. (1976). *Of grammatology* (G. C. Spivak, Trans.). Baltimore: Johns Hopkins University Press.

Dickens, D., & Fontana, A. (Eds.). (1994). *Postmodernism and social inquiry.* New York: Guilford.

Douglas, J. D. (1985). *Creative interviewing.* Beverly Hills, CA: Sage.

Douglas, J. D., & Johnson, J. M. (1977). *Existential sociology.* Cambridge, UK: Cambridge University Press.

Douglas, J. D., & Rasmussen, P., with Flanagan, C. A. (1977). *The nude beach.* Beverly Hills, CA: Sage.

Du Bois, W. E. B. 1899). *The Philadelphia Negro: A social study.* Philadelphia: Ginn.

Fine, G. A., & Sandstrom, K. (1988). *Knowing children: Participant observation with minors.* Newbury Park, CA: Sage.

Fine, M. (1983-1984). Coping with rape: Critical perspectives on consciousness. *Imagination, Cognition and Personality, 3,* 249-267.

Fontana, A. (1977). *The last frontier: The social meaning of growing old.* Beverly Hills, CA: Sage.

Fontana, A., & Collins, C. (1993). *The forgotten self: Women in Vietnam.* Paper presented at the annual meeting of the Society for the Study of Symbolic Interaction, Miami, FL.

Freeman, D. (1983). *Margaret Mead and Samoa: The making and unmaking of an anthropological myth.* Cambridge, MA: Harvard University Press.

Frey, J. H. (1989). *Survey research by telephone* (2nd ed.). Newbury Park, CA: Sage.

Frey, J. H. (1993). Risk perception associated with a high-level nuclear waste repository. *Sociological Spectrum.*

Frey, J. H., & Fontana, A. (1991). The group interview in social research. *Social Science Journal, 28,* 175-187.

Frey, J. H., & Fontana, A. (in press). *The group interview.* Newbury Park, CA: Sage.

Garfinkel, H. (1967). *Studies in ethnomethodology.* Englewood Cliffs, NJ: Prentice Hall.

Geertz, C. (1988). *Works and lives: The anthropologist as author.* Stanford, CA: Stanford University Press.

Giroux, H. (1992). *Border crossings: Cultural workers and the politics of education.* New York: Routledge.

Glaser, B. G., & Strauss, A. L. (1967). *The discovery of grounded theory: Strategies for qualitative research.* Chicago: Aldine.

Gluck, S. B. (1984). What's so special about women: Women's oral history. In D. Dunaway & W. K. Baum (Eds.), *Oral history: An interdisciplinary anthology* (pp. 221-237). Nashville, TN: American Association for State and Local History.

Gluck, S. B. (1991). Advocacy oral history: Palestinian women in resistance. In S. B. Gluck & D. Patai (Eds.), *Women's words: The feminist practice of oral history* (pp. 205-220). London: Routledge.

Gluck, S. B., & Patai, D. (Eds.). (1991). *Women's words: The feminist practice of oral history.* London: Routledge.

Goffman, E. (1959). *The presentation of self in everyday life.* Garden City, NY: Anchor.

Goffman, E. (1971). *Relations in public.* New York: Harper & Row.

Gorden, R. L. (1980). *Interviewing: Strategy, techniques, and tactics.* Homewood, IL: Dorsey.

Harper, D. (1982). *Good company.* Chicago: University of Chicago Press.

Harvey, L. (1987). *Myths of the Chicago school of sociology.* Aldershot, England: Avebury.

Humphreys, L. (1970). *Tearoom trade: Impersonal sex in public places.* Chicago: Aldine.

Johnson, J. (1976). *Doing field research.* New York: Free Press.

Kahn, R., & Cannell, C. F. (1957). *The dynamics of interviewing.* New York: John Wiley.

Kotarba, J. A., & Fontana, A. (Eds.). (1984). *The existential self in society.* Chicago: University of Chicago Press.

Krieger, S. (1983). *The mirror dance: Identity in a women's community.* Philadelphia: Temple University Press.

Kuhn, M. (1962). The interview and the professional relationship. In A. Rose (Ed.), *Human behavior and social processes: An interactionist approach* (pp. 193-206). Boston: Houghton Mifflin.

Lincoln, Y. S., & Guba, E. G. (1985). *Naturalistic inquiry.* Beverly Hills, CA: Sage.

Lofland, J. (1971). *Analyzing social settings.* Belmont, CA: Wadsworth.

Lofland, J., & Lofland, L. (1984). *Analyzing social settings: A guide to qualitative observation and analysis* (2nd ed.). Belmont, CA: Wadsworth.

Lomax, J., & Lomax, A. (1966). *American ballads and folk songs.* New York: Macmillan. (Original work published 1934)

Lopata, H. Z. (1980). Interviewing American widows. In W. Shaffir, R. Stebbins, & A. Turowetz (Eds.), *Fieldwork experience: Qualitative approaches to social research* (pp. 68-81). New York: St. Martin's.

Lynd, R. S., & Lynd, H. M. (1929). *Middletown: A study in contemporary American culture.* New York: Harcourt, Brace.

Lynd, R. S., & Lynd, H. M. (1937). *Middletown in transition: A study in cultural conflicts.* New York: Harcourt, Brace.

Maccoby, E. E., & Maccoby, N. (1954). The interview: A tool of social science. In G. Lindzey (Ed.), *Handbook of social psychology: Vol. 1. Theory and method* (pp. 449-487). Reading, MA: Addison-Wesley.

Malinowski, B. (1922). *Argonauts of the western Pacific.* London: Routledge & Kegan Paul.

Malinowski, B. (1989). *A diary in the strict sense of the term.* Stanford, CA: Stanford University Press. (Original work published 1967)

Marcus, G. E., & Fischer, M. (1986). *Anthropology as cultural critique: An experimental moment in the human sciences.* Chicago: University of Chicago Press.

Marshall, K. (1987). *In the combat zone.* New York: Penguin.

Merton, R. K., Fiske, M., & Kendall, P. L. (1956). *The focused interview.* Glencoe, IL: Free Press.

Merton, R. K., & Lazarsfeld, P. F. (Eds.). (1950). *Continuities in social research: Studies in the scope and method of "The American soldier."* Glencoe, IL: Free Press.

Montville, L. (1993). He's everywhere. *Sports Illustrated, 78*(17), 78-90.

Morgan, D. (1988). *Focus groups as qualitative research.* Newbury Park, CA: Sage.

Morgan, D., & Spanish, M. T. (1984). Focus groups: A new tool for qualtiative research. *Qualitative Sociology, 7,* 253-270.

Oakley, A. (1981). Interviewing women: A contradiction in terms. In H. Roberts (Ed.), *Doing feminist research* (pp. 30-61). London: Routledge & Kegan Paul.

Papanek, H. (1964). The woman field worker in a purdah society. *Human Organization, 22,* 160-163.

Parten, M. (1950). *Surveys, polls, and samples.* New York: Harper.

Payne, S. L. (1951). *The art of asking questions.* Princeton, NJ: Princeton University Press.

Peneff, J. (1988). The observers observed: French survey researchers at work. *Social Problems, 35,* 520-535.

Punch, M. (1986). *The politics and ethics of fieldwork.* Newbury Park, CA: Sage.

Rabinow, P. (1977). *Reflections on fieldwork in Morocco.* Berkeley: University of California Press.

Rasmussen, P. (1989). *Massage parlor prostitution.* New York: Irvington.

Reinharz, S. (1992). *Feminist methods in social research.* New York: Oxford University Press.

Richardson, L. (1992). The poetic representation of lives: Writing a postmodern sociology. In N. K. Denzin (Ed.), *Studies in symbolic interaction* (Vol. 13, pp. 19-28). Greenwich, CT: JAI.

Selltiz, C., Jahoda, M., Deutsch, M., & Cook, S. W. (1965). *Research methods in social relations.* London: Methuen.

Smith, D. E. (1987). *The everyday world as problematic: A feminist sociology.* Boston: Northeastern University Press.

Spradley, J. P. (1979). *The ethnographic interview.* New York: Holt, Rinehart & Winston.

Spradley, J. P. (1980). *Participant observation.* New York: Holt, Rinehart & Winston.

Starr, L. (1984). Oral history. In D. Dunaway & W. K. Baum (Eds.), *Oral history: An interdisciplinary anthology* (pp. 3-26). Nashville, TN: American Association for State and Local History.

Stanfield, J. (1985). *Philanthropy and Jim Crow in American social sciences.* Westport, CT: Greenwood.

Stewart, D., & Shamdasani, P. (1990). *Focus groups: Theory and practice.* Newbury Park, CA: Sage.

Sudarkasa, N. (1986). In a world of women: Field work in a Yoruba community. In P. Golde (Ed.), *Women in the field: Anthropological experiences* (pp. 167-191). Berkeley: University of California Press.

Terkel, S. (1975). *Working.* New York: Avon.

Terry, W. (1984). *Bloods: An oral history of the Vietnam War by black veterans.* New York: Random House.

Thompson, H. (1985). *Hell's Angels.* New York: Ballantine.

Thompson, J., & Demerath, M. J. (1952). Some experiences with the group interview. *Social Forces, 31,* 148-154.

Thrasher, F. M. (1927). *The gang: A study of 1,313 gangs in Chicago.* Chicago: University of Chicago Press.

Ulmer, G. (1989). *Teletheory: Grammatology in an age of video.* New York: Routledge.

Van Maanen, J. (1988). *Tales of the field: On writing ethnography.* Chicago: University of Chicago Press.

Warren, C. A. B. (1988). *Gender issues in field research.* Newbury Park, CA: Sage.

Wax, R. (1960). Twelve years later: An analysis of field experiences. In R. N. Adams & J. J. Preiss (Eds.), *Human organization research* (pp. 166-178). Homewood, IL: Dorsey.

Wenner, J. (1992, October 15). A letter from the editor. *Rolling Stone.*

Whyte, W. F. (1943). *Street corner society: The social structure of an Italian slum.* Chicago: University of Chicago Press.

Yeandle, S. (1984). *Women's working lives: Patterns and strategies.* New York: Tavistock.

Young, P. (1966). *Scientific social surveys and research* (4th ed.). Englewood Cliffs, NJ: Prentice Hall.

Zuckerman, H. (1972). Interviewing an ultra-elite. *Public Opinion, 36,* 159-175.

23

■

Observational Techniques

PATRICIA A. ADLER
PETER ADLER

THIS chapter builds upon the previous abstract and theoretical discussions of qualitative methods to focus on one specific mode of qualitative data gathering: naturalistic observation. In the following pages we examine some of the essential features of naturalistic observation, discussing methodological issues, strengths, and weaknesses in its practice. We then consider several theoretical traditions underlying observation, showing how exemplary individuals and their works in these paradigms enact the conceptual and epistemological themes. We then bring select themes into sharper focus in a discussion of ethical issues related to observational research and the influence of scholarly and political forces in shaping these. We conclude by extrapolating from the present into the future, speculating on how these forces will play out against the tide of shifting epistemological currents.

For as long as people have been interested in studying the social and natural world around them, observation has served as the bedrock source of human knowledge. Early classicists rooted their understandings of the world, from Aristotle's botanical observations on the island of Lesbos to Herodotus's chronicled observations of the Greco-Persian wars, in their own visions, travels, and direct experiences. Comte, the founder of sociology, elucidated observation as one of the four core research methods (along with comparison, historical analysis, and experimentation) appropriate to his fledgling science of society. Not only is observation one of the earliest and most basic forms of research, but it is the most likely to be used in conjunction with others, such as participant observation, experimental design, and interviewing.

As members of society, we also make observations of the everyday world. These guide us in forging paths of action and interpreting the actions and reactions of others. They also generate the kind of "common sense" or "cultural knowledge" that Johnson (1975, p. 21) has argued lies at the base of all knowledge and theory, from that amassed by the layperson to that conducted by the survey, experimental, participant, or simple observational methodologist. What differentiates the observations of social scientists from those of everyday-life actors is the former's systematic and purposive nature. Social science researchers study their surroundings regularly and repeatedly, with a curiosity spurred by theoretical questions about the nature of human action, interaction, and society.

AUTHORS' NOTE: We would like to acknowledge gratefully the assistance of Spencer Cahill, Carol Brooks Gardner, Lyn Lofland, Jeff Nash, and Carol Warren, who shared ideas with us and permitted us a glimpse into their methodological worlds.

Morris (1973) offers a broad explanation of observation that defines it as "the act of noting a phenomenon, often with instruments, and recording it for scientific or other purposes" (p. 906). Although we sometimes think of observation as involving only visual data gathering, this is far from true; all of the senses can also be fully engaged in this endeavor, from smell to hearing, touch, and taste. Observation thus consists of gathering impressions of the surrounding world through all relevant human faculties. This generally necessitates direct contact with the subject(s) of observation, although remote observation can be carried out by recording the data with photography, audiotape, or videotape and studying it either concurrently or later.[1] In either case, researchers must actively witness the phenomena they are studying in action.

One of the hallmarks of observation has traditionally been its noninterventionism. Observers neither manipulate nor stimulate their subjects. They do not ask the subjects research questions, pose tasks for them, or deliberately create new provocations. This stands in marked contrast to researchers using interview questionnaires, who direct the interaction and introduce potentially new ideas into the arena, and to experimental researchers, who often set up structured situations where they can alter certain conditions to measure the covariance of others. Simple observers follow the flow of events. Behavior and interaction continue as they would without the presence of a researcher, uninterrupted by intrusion.

Yet often when we think of the social scientist as observer, we conjure up an image of a laboratory scientist in a white coat, jotting notes on a clipboard while observing people from behind a one-way mirror. This detached and sterile view of observation is rooted in the quantitative observational paradigm, one enhanced by the prestige accorded science since the birth of the Enlightenment. Quantitative observational research has forged a stronghold in experimental psychology and sociological small group research through careful attention to the precise operationalization and measurement of dependent variables.

Quantitative observations, conducted in situations deliberately designed to ensure standardization and control, differ markedly from observations framed by the qualitative paradigm. Qualitative observation is fundamentally naturalistic in essence; it occurs in the natural context of occurrence, among the actors who would naturally be participating in the interaction, and follows the natural stream of everyday life. As such, it enjoys the advantage of drawing the observer into the phenomenological complexity of the world, where connections, correlations, and causes can be witnessed as and how they unfold. Qualitative observers are not bound, thus, by predetermined categories of measurement or response, but are free to search for concepts or categories that appear meaningful to subjects. As Carol Brooks Gardner (personal communication, 1993) told us in describing her recognition of significant findings: "I look for the 'Click!' experience—something of a sudden, though minor, epiphany as to the emotional depth or importance of an event or a phenomenon." Naturalistic observers thus often differ from quantitative observers in the scope of their observations: Whereas the latter focus on minute particles of the world that can be agglomerated into a variable, the former look for much larger trends, patterns, and styles of behavior. These differences are rooted not only in variations between the ways the two groups observe, but in the types of questions they pose.

Qualitative observation has remained underaddressed in the methodological literature. It has been elaborated for the student audience in some general methods texts that treat observation as one research strategy in a broad consideration of all data gathering techniques (e.g., Kidder, 1981; Phillips, 1985). Other exemplary works that have more specifically addressed qualitative observational methods include Webb, Campbell, Schwartz, and Sechrest's (1966) early work on unobtrusive measures; Gold's (1958) classic typology of observational roles; Schatzman and Strauss's (1973) interpretive guide to naturalistic research; Spradley's (1980) more formal handbook, which focuses on the stages of observation; and Denzin's (1989) comprehensive description of research methods for studying social interaction.

Yet observation by itself has remained a stepchild to its more widely recognized offshoot: participant observation. Most of the major research treatments of qualitative methods (Berg, 1989; Douglas, 1976; Glesne & Peshkin, 1992; Hammersley & Atkinson, 1983; Jorgensen, 1989; Lofland & Lofland, 1984) focus on participant observation to the virtual exclusion of observation as a method in its own right. This may be traced to the strong theoretical roots of participant observation in the symbolic interaction perspective; interactionist researchers usually want to gather data from their subjects while interacting with them. Although pure observation is somewhat propelled by the symbolic interactionist perspective, the questions it answers make it more compatible with the scope of the dramaturgical perspective and, to a secondary extent, ethnomethodology. Yet dramaturgy has failed to inspire methodological discussions and expositions comparable to those of symbolic interactionism. In fact, few of the dramaturgical perspective's major exponents, Goffman included, have discussed their methodology explicitly. This may be because it is seen as subjective and, hence, difficult to legitimate. Ethnomethodology, and especially its late twentieth-century incarnation, conversation analysis, suffers from no such reticence, however, and is well explicated methodologically in such works as Handel (1982), Heritage (1984), and Jefferson (1989).

Yet what is missing in all of these treatments is a comprehensive elaboration of the theory, methods, and epistemology grounding naturalistic observation. Our aim, in this chapter, is to provide such a comprehensive treatment by integrating more general comments about observational methods with a discussion of its theoretical roots and current major practitioners. We discuss these features of naturalistic observation and describe and analyze its role as both an independent and an integrated research technique.

Methodological Issues

Observational research can vary considerably in its character among different practitioners, through the stages of a research project, in various settings, and depending on the relationship of researchers to their subjects.

Researchers may choose to focus on a group where they intentionally place themselves in a particular location to observe subjects' behavior, or they may observe the behavior of those falling naturally around them. For example, Carpenter, Glassner, Johnson, and Loughlin (1988) observed adolescents in junior and senior high schools during their lunch and recess periods to learn about how these young people structured their leisure time. In addition to observing them at school before, after, and during lunch break from classes, they followed their subjects into recreational activities around town, to parks, skating rinks, video arcades, bars, movie theaters, people's homes, and various other places. These observations involved subjects with whom the researchers were not previously familiar and foreign locations. Others who study more generic populations, behavior, or spaces may not have to travel to make their observations. In describing her research on public space, Lyn Lofland (personal communication, 1993) has noted:

> For the past twenty years the "vantage point" when I'm doing direct observation has continued to be [constant]. Since I'm "passing" as someone who is simply hanging about in public, I get engaged by others in interaction, though I have rarely initiated it myself.... A lot of my data have come from situations in which I was out in public for nonresearch purposes. That is, I watch myself acting in public and note what I do and what others do vis-à-vis me, just as if I were someone else. So, I guess you could say that I move from being the largely uninvolved observer to the fully involved participant observer. . . . Obviously I don't take myself as a stand-in for "everywoman," but neither do I think my reactions are likely to be that peculiar.

In contrast, Lofland's studies of public space show the observer in a familiar location, observing people like herself, and drawing on her own background familiarity with the setting and behavior. These projects show some of the differences observers encounter between subjects who are demographically different from themselves, in having to travel intentionally to research settings, and in the types of research relationships that may occur. Yet they also show some of the constancy: Observers are likely to employ all their faculties in data gathering and are also likely to draw on their broad cultural or commonsense knowledge, what Douglas (1976) has called "general cultural understanding."

Research Roles

As Lofland has also noted, the role of the researcher in the setting may vary in involvement. In Gold's (1958) classic typology of naturalistic research roles, he outlined four modes through which observers may gather data: the complete participant, the participant-as-observer, the observer-as-participant, and the complete observer. The midpoint of these roles sought to balance involvement with detachment, familiarity with strangeness, closeness with distance, based on the classical Chicago school conceptualization of research (see Adler & Adler, 1987). New conceptions of qualitative research have evolved since these were first proposed, with practitioners' attitudes shifting toward greater involvement, even membership roles, as we have previously outlined, in their settings (Adler & Adler, 1987). Three membership roles appear to predominate: the complete-member-researcher, the active-member-researcher, and the peripheral-member-researcher. The current span of observational research roles includes some combination of these two groups of typologies.

Gold's complete observer role describes researchers who are fundamentally removed from their settings. Their observations may occur from the outside, with observers being neither seen nor noticed. Contemporary varieties of this role might include the videotaping, audiotaping, or photographing noninteractive observer. This role most closely approximates the traditional ideal of the "objective" observer. The observer-as-participant role describes researchers primarily observing their subjects for extremely brief periods as they attempt to conduct structured interviews. In Gold's conceptualization, this role did not have much use for the naturalistic observer. It has assumed a more useful meaning for contemporary researchers, however, depicting those who enter settings for the purpose of data gathering, yet who interact only casually and nondirectively with subjects while engaged in their observational pursuits (e.g., the Carpenter et al. study mentioned above). This is clearly an overt role, as the observer's identity remains strongly research oriented and does not cross into the friendship domain. Neither of these roles is currently as popular with qualitative researchers as it was at mid-century.

Instead, naturalistic social scientists have moved into a variety of membership roles in their settings. Researchers in peripheral membership roles feel that an insider's perspective is vital to forming an accurate appraisal of human group life, so they observe and interact closely enough with members to establish an insider's identity without participating in those activities constituting the core of group membership. Both covert and overt stances are possible here, sometimes in concert. For example, we took peripheral membership roles in our research on upper-level drug dealers and smugglers (reported in P. A. Adler, 1985), where we established ourselves as members of the social crowd, accepted as "wise" and trustworthy individuals who refrained from participating in the actual trafficking. We also took peripheral membership roles in our observations of the peer culture of elementary school children (Adler, Kless, & Adler, 1992), studying them while we circulated as adult parents, coaches, car pool drivers, and so on in their lives.

The active membership role describes researchers who become more involved in the setting's central activities, assuming responsibilities that advance the group, but without fully committing themselves to members' values and goals. Peter Adler assumed such a posture in our research on college athletes (Adler & Adler, 1991a) by becoming an assistant coach on the basketball team, supervising the academic progress of team members and counseling them informally on career options. Observers in this role often take an overt stance as they forge close and meaningful bonds with setting members.

Finally, researchers in the complete membership role are those who study scenes where they are already members or those who become converted to genuine membership during the course of their research. This stance draws either on the burgeoning tradition of opportunistic research (Riemer, 1977) and "auto-ethnography" (Hayano, 1979), including Hayano's (1982) observations of fellow denizens of California's all-night card rooms, or on the early ethnomethodological stricture to "become the phenomenon" (Mehan & Wood, 1975) in order to immerse oneself and grasp the complete depth of the subjectively lived experience.

Observers can thus take roles that range anywhere from the hidden or disguised voyeur, who watches from outside or with a passive (even electronic) presence, to the active participant, involved in the setting, who acts as a member and not as a researcher so as not to alter the flow of the interaction unnaturally.

Stages of Observation

The observational research process evolves through a series of different activities as it progresses from start to finish. The observer's first task is to select a setting. This can be done for one of several reasons: The observer may have a theoretical interest in a particular type of scene or behavior, or may have potential access to a particular setting; the observer may be already ensconced in a setting and may "opportunistically" decide to study it (Riemer, 1977), or he or she may be commissioned to study it. For an observer not already in the setting, the next task is to gain entrée. Depending on the setting, its accessibility to outsiders, and its degree of organization (see Adler & Adler, 1991b), the observer may be able to pass freely through the setting at will, may be able to scope out the people and customs informally prior to committing him- or herself to a research role or identity, or may have to apply to official gatekeepers for formal entrée. The unobtrusiveness of observational research, compared with other means of data gathering, makes the first two possibilities more likely.

If the researcher is working alone, he or she may begin observing immediately. Researchers working in teams may have to train members on how and what to observe. In Nash's work with student observers, for example, he has often used students from his course on dramaturgical sociology, who are knowledgeable about the conceptual issues driving their observational frame (personal communication, 1993). The concrete products of observations may vary; some observers record written text that follows a free-association form, whereas others incorporate more structure. In his "tearoom" observations, Humphreys (1975) used sheets that he designed specifically for the project, featuring divided pages: On one part of the page the layout of the tearoom was depicted, and he used that to draw simple diagrams of the interaction; the rest of the page was devoted to explicit descriptions of participants' appearance, clothing, modes of transportation, roles, interactions, and exits. Denzin (1989) has suggested that all observation notational records should contain explicit reference to participants, interactions, routines, rituals, temporal elements, interpretations, and social organization. Most observational notes incorporate some combination of these features.

The nature of researchers' observations inevitably shifts in range and character from the early to later stages of an observational project. Spradley (1980), and Jorgensen (1989) following him, has discussed initial observations as primarily "descriptive" in nature. Unfocused and general in scope, they are usually based on broad questions, providing a base for the researcher to branch out in myriad future directions. After observers become more familiar with their settings and grasp the key social groups and processes in operation, they may distinguish features of the scenes that most interest them. At this point they are likely to shift to more "focused observations," directing their attention to a deeper and narrower portion of the people, behaviors, times, spaces, feelings, structures, and/or processes. Research questions or problems may emerge that shape future observations and begin the formation of typologies. This stage of observation generates clearer research questions and concepts that then require "selected observations." At this point, researchers focus on establishing and refining the characteristics of and relations among the elements they have previously selected as objects of study. Specific questions arise that must be answered in constructing models about the categories within and among things in the setting. Overall, as Spradley has noted, the stages of observation form a funnel, progressively narrowing and directing researchers' attention deeper into the elements of the setting that have emerged as theoretically and/or empirically essential.

Observational data gathering continues until researchers achieve theoretical saturation (Glaser & Strauss, 1967)—that is, when the generic features of their new findings consistently replicate earlier ones. Researchers' analysis of the data, begun from earliest conceptualization, is related to existing models in relevant literature. Depending on the observers' styles of data analysis, they may engage in more casual theorization or more formal theory building. In pursuing this deepening and restriction of concentration, observers may move through the stages of research from open-ended search, to hypothesis formation, to theory conceptualization. Although greater emphasis has traditionally been placed on the context of discovery, observation can yield findings consonant with the context of verification as well, through systematic attention to regular patterns of occurrences and their conditions.

Problems of Observation

One of the chief criticisms leveled against observational research lies in the area of *validity.* Without the benefit of members' analyses, observers are forced to rely more exclusively on their own perceptions. They are therefore more susceptible to bias from their subjective interpretations of situations (Denzin, 1989; Schatzman & Strauss, 1973; Webb et al., 1966). Without subjects' quotes to enrich and confirm researchers' analyses, or interobserver cross-checking to lend greater credence to their representations, some observers have had difficulty legitimating their work to a scholarly audience. This may explain why so few articles based *solely* on observational research are published, even in qualitative journals.

Yet there are measures observers can take to overcome this problem and enhance the validity of their research. First, using multiple observers or teams, especially if they are diverse in age and gender, can enhance the validity of observations, as researchers can cross-check each others' findings and eliminate inaccurate interpretations (Adler & Adler, 1987; Denzin, 1989; Phillips, 1985). Second, following an analytic inductive methodology by testing emergent propositions in the search for negative cases generates assertions that are more likely to be perceived as grounded and universal (Schatzman & Strauss, 1973). Third, in presenting their data, observers can use *verisimilitude,* or *vraisemblance,* a style of writing that draws the reader so closely into subjects' worlds that these can be palpably felt. When such written accounts contain a high degree of internal coherence, plausibility, and correspondence to what readers recognize from their own experiences and from other realistic and factual texts, they accord the work (and the research on which it is based) a sense of "authenticity" (Atkinson, 1990). Thus observational research derives validity from the *vraisemblance* of its textual renderings.

A second main criticism of observational research suggests that it lacks *reliability*; without statistical analysis to confirm the significance of observed patterns or trends, researchers cannot ensure that their findings are real and not merely the effects of chance (Denzin, 1989; Kidder, 1981). Like many qualitative methods, naturalistic observation yields insights that are more likely to be accurate for the group under study and unverified for extension to a larger population. Yet there are measures observers can follow that will enhance the generalizability of their findings. Observations conducted systematically and repeatedly over varying conditions that yield the same findings are more credible than those gathered according to personal patterns (Denzin, 1989). The two variables that particularly warrant varying are time (for what Kidder, 1981, calls test-retest comparisons) and place (Lofland, in press), in order to ensure the widest range of observational consistency. Lofland (in press) has particularly noted variations and contradictions that have arisen in observations of the public realm at different times (day, night), under different climates (winter, summer), and by researchers of different gender. These concerns over validity and reliability derive from a postpositivist paradigm (see Richardson, Chapter 32, this volume) and lose salience as issues in the postmodern framework.

Rigors of Observation

One great strength of the observational method lies in the ease through which researchers can gain *entrée* to settings. Because it is unobtrusive and does not require direct interaction with participants, observation can be conducted inconspicuously (Webb et al., 1966). In fact, there are entire settings and types of behavior, as Humphreys (1975) has shown, that could not be studied through other, more blatant, methods.

Relatedly, observational methods embody the least potential for generating *observer effects.* There are many ways researchers can affect their subjects, from the self-fulfilling to the self-negating prophesy (Kidder, 1981). Many people believe that entirely avoiding researcher influence on subjects is an idealistic improbability (Adler & Adler, 1987; Jarvie, 1969; Johnson, 1975), yet there are ways that such effects can be diminished. The naturalness of the observer role, coupled with its nondirection, makes it the least noticeably intrusive of all research techniques (Phillips, 1985).

Another of the strengths associated with observational research lies in its *emergence.* Although not the only such method, observation, like participant observation and unstructured depth interviewing, draws both strength and weakness from its potential for creativity. Instead of working with predetermined categories, observers construct theories that generate categories and posit the linkages among them. At any point in the process, observers are free to alter the problems and questions they are pursuing as they gain greater knowledge of their subjects. Compared with more structured methods, then, observation has the flexibility to yield insight into new realities or new ways of looking at old realities (Kidder, 1981). This is particularly exemplified in Goffman's work (e.g., Goffman, 1961, 1963).

Finally, observation produces especially great rigor *when combined with other methods.* In contrast to experiments conducted in the laboratory that lack a natural setting and context of occurrence, and interviews with subjects that are constructions of subjects' recollection and (sometimes self-serving) perceptions, researchers' observations of their settings and subjects can be considered hard evidence. These are especially valuable as an alternate source of data for enhancing cross-checking (Douglas, 1976) or triangulation (Denzin, 1989) against information gathered through other means. Although direct observation may be marred by researcher biases, at least these are consistent and known. Direct observation, when added onto other research yielding depth and/or breadth, enhances consistency and validity.

Observational Paradigms

A number of theoretical and/or research traditions are closely associated with observational methods. Looking back from the classical period of sociology into more contemporary movements, in this section we discuss some of the concerns, beliefs, and research questions that have driven observational research. For each field we present some of the core concerns and the work of exemplary researchers to show not only the common base of observational research, but its flexibility in service to diverse purposes.

Formal Sociology

The formal approach to sociology was advocated by Georg Simmel, one of the classical progenitors of the discipline. Rather than focusing exclusively on the content of social interactions and relations, Simmel argued that we should study the forms, or structures, according to which these are patterned. What especially fascinated Simmel, and what he saw as the base of social order, was "sociation," the crystallized interactions among people. This intricate web of multiple relations between individuals in constant interaction with one another constituted society. Some of the major forms of sociation Simmel analyzed include superordination and subordination, marital and martial conflict, and dyads and triads. Such relationships, whether fleeting and ephemeral or institutionalized, formed his unit of analysis.

Simmel also directed his attention to relationships in his study of social types. These types generally had two features in common: (a) They were defined by their relationship to others, such as "the stranger," who was among the people but not one of them, and "the poor," whose definition resided in their being regarded as deserving assistance; and (b) they were marginal. Whereas the relational feature is central to Simmel's theoretical perspective, the marginality is tied to his method.

Like many other theorists, Simmel based his ideas about society on his own direct observations. Simmel's position in society placed him in an excellent vantage point from which to observe; throughout his life he himself was a marginal man. Although a brilliant scholar, he was held back from the kind of academic appointment he deserved by anti-Semitism and his wide-ranging, interdisciplinary interests. Simmel's marginality highlights a common feature of the observer role: It may integrate participation with nonparticipation in such a way that both total detachment and full membership are precluded. Observers need close access to their settings and subjects to enhance direct insight and understanding, but their failure to be admitted to the center of action gives them a role that fosters scrutiny of those in the center as well as those on the outside. Frisby (1981) has suggested that Simmel represents a sort of "sociological *flaneur*," a stroller through life who makes observations in a detached manner, usually from a safe distance (Smith, 1992). As we will see, the marginal vantage emerges as one that often calls forth observation as a methodology.

Contemporary practitioners of formal sociology include members of the "new" Iowa school (see Buban, 1986; Couch, Saxton, & Katovich, 1986). Following the original direction of Manford Kuhn and the more recent inspiration of Carl Couch, these symbolic interactionists focus on the structuredness of human interaction. They see social reality and social process as jointly constructed by self and other through the forms of sociation residing in the interconnections developed among people. The dyad, not the individual, is their unit of analysis.

Methodologically, they follow Kuhn's propensity toward data gathered in a controlled, systematic fashion. Eschewing the limiting Twenty Statements Test, they prefer to videotape interactions, thereby creating complete records of social events (Saxton & Couch, 1975). Videotaping the data offers the advantages of being able to freeze interactions to reexamine them repeatedly, to subject them to rescrutiny by multiple observers, and to capture behavioral nuances precisely (Couch, 1984; Katovich, Weiland, & Couch, 1978). To ensure a greater degree of control over behavior, and hence over concepts and hypotheses to be developed and later tested as well, new Iowa school proponents prefer to bring their data to their videotape equipment, rather than to carry their equipment into the field. They thus situate their subjects in laboratories. Although aware of the possible drawbacks inherent in this unnatural environment and the necessary simplification of the social acts performed there, they see a greater payoff in the control gained. Research from this perspective has focused on how people develop solidary relationships (Miller, Hintz, & Couch, 1975), how they operate giant bureaucracies (Katovich, Weiland, & Couch, 1981), and how they turn others into stutterers.

Dramaturgical Sociology

Often regarded as the intellectual successor to Simmel, Erving Goffman focused his gaze on the interaction order. By studying how people act, interact, and form relationships, he sought to understand how they accomplish meaning in their lives. He was particularly interested in how people construct their self-presentations and carry them off in front of others. His dramaturgy suggested that there was an intentionality behind the planning and execution of these performances, that they were accomplished with an eye toward people's achieving the best impression of themselves in the view of others. In so doing, they go beyond the simple role making envisioned by Mead (1934) to more manipulative role playing. Goffman's view of the self was based on its empirical manifestations. His writings were conceptually oriented but empirically grounded, more persuasive in their appeal to the commonalities of people's joint experiences than empirically rigorous. Yet he was fundamentally an observer of social life. As Brissett and Edgley (1990) have described his perspective: "The theater of performances is not in people's heads, it is in their public acts. People encounter each other's minds only by interacting, and the quality and character of these interactions come to constitute the consequential reality of everyday life" (p. 37). To grasp that reality, Goffman studied the interaction rituals of public behavior.

Goffman's vantage on the field came from a position of self-imposed marginality. Unlike Simmel, who could not find acceptance, Goffman would not seek it. He preferred social distance, from which he could observe the actions of those around him, even those closest to himself, with cynical detachment. He also took an aloof stance toward the academy, eschewing the normative forums of presenting scholarly ideas, preferring instead to write essays (Brissett & Edgley, 1990). Like Simmel, he took the role of the *flaneur* (Smith, 1992).

Goffman seldom remarked on his own methodology. Generally, he preferred to let his conceptualizations validate his methods if they proved to be insightful. In a rare comment, however, he characterized his methodological approach: "The method that is often resorted to here—unsystematic, naturalistic observation—has very serious limitations. I claim as a defense that the traditional research designs thus far employed have considerable limitations of their own" (Goffman, 1971, p. xv).

Observation is well suited to the dramaturgical perspective because it enables researchers to capture the range of acts, from the minimovements to the grand gestures, of people in all ranks of life. Although Goffman established a precedent for being inattentive to methodology, this tradition has been carried on by others following his interests in the dramaturgical construction of the interaction order. Notable among these successors is the work of Spencer Cahill and Carol Brooks Gardner. Cahill is best known for his studies of children in the public order, especially their role in public life. He suggests that, contrary to others' assertions, the boundaries between children and adults are strong, and can be recognized in the way children are treated in public (Cahill, 1990). In a study of children's socialization into the "religion of civility" forming contemporary American culture, he describes the means by which adults treat instances of children's public deviant behavior, using these as means to teach their offspring appropriate behavioral comportment (Cahill, 1987).

In these and other studies, Cahill employed teams of student observers who went to public arenas such as city streets, shopping malls, parks, restaurants, and laundromats to make observations. Commenting on his methodology, he noted:

> We visited these settings at different times of the day and week for the explicit purpose of observing children's behavior and treatment in public places. We recorded observed episodes of interaction in field notes either while the interactions were occurring or immediately thereafter. In addition, we also occasionally recorded episodes of interaction in field notes that we observed in the course of our daily rounds. Although we typically wrote our field notes in full view of those whom we were observing, they were apparently unaware that we were recording their behavior. (Cahill, 1987, p. 314)

Gardner's work has focused on gender and stigma in public space. Her studies of the disabled examine how they deal with stigma and the reactions of others who both assist and ignore them when they attempt to navigate the physical difficulties of the outside world. In some of her work on gender she has examined the differences between men's and women's openness to others in public. Drawing on observations conducted in public and semipublic places such as bars, restaurants, stores, streets, rodeos, operas, and movie theaters, she noticed that women employ several strategies to restrict their "access information," maintaining closure and withholding knowledge of their names and addresses as well as being guarded about whom they allow themselves to trust for public conversation, in order to protect themselves from becoming crime victims (Gardner, 1988). Like her subjects, Gardner (personal communication, 1993) noted an awareness about her own safety in public while conducting observations that influenced where she went and how she positioned herself in relation to her subjects. Yet in discussing the traditional marginal role of the observer, Gardner (personal communication, 1993) notes a certain feeling of marginality herself: "I often think of myself as something of a marginal person in every milieu I find myself in: a Jew among Christians; a converted Jew among born Jews; an observational sociologist among number-worshipers; a hyper-aware person in a land of mellowed-out satisfaction."

Gardner's and Cahill's research highlights several dimensions of the observational method through both differences and similarities. Whereas Gardner worked alone, Cahill used an observational team. Both used unstructured recording techniques, jotting immediate notes about what they saw, to be analyzed later. Both went to public and semipublic locations for research and nonresearch purposes, blending the observer-as-participant with the participant-as-observer roles. They also discovered that taking notes about others' behavior in public aroused little notice, and found it unnecessary and unproblematic to disclose their research intentions.

Studies of the Public Realm

Building off the dramaturgical tradition are a range of observational studies focusing on behavior in public space. This was Goffman's preferred location of study, and through his inspiration it has blossomed into a research arena in its own right. Studies of the public realm address issues of moral order, interpersonal relations, forms of functioning, and norms of relating to strange individuals and different categories of individuals. The public realm represents an arena particularly characteristic of modern, urban society, with its density, heterogeneity, and danger. Observational techniques are particularly suited to studying this phenomenon because they enable researchers to gather data on large groups of people at a time, and to isolate patterns of group behavior.

Two major progenitors of this field are Lyn Lofland and Jeff Nash. Lofland's (1973) early work on cities examined the nature of existence in an arena filled with strangers. She suggests that people work to reduce the anonymity and alienation of an urban living situation by creating enclaves of private and semiprivate space around themselves. When they venture out from beyond these, they must be sufficiently knowledgeable about the potential range of social types they might encounter to know how to interpret people's actions.

Lofland employed a mixture of intentional and serendipitous research strategies, going into the field to make observations and remaining four and five hours at a time as well as being attentive to public behavior while she was engaged in her regular everyday pursuits. She made immediate notations of her impressions, often writing voluminously for hours. At all times she assumed the role of the covert observer, which was particularly natural as there were no gatekeepers in the public and semipublic settings she frequented (bus depots, airports, restaurants, theaters, libraries, university residence halls, and parks). In reflecting on her methodology, one thing Lofland (personal communication, 1993) highlights is the safety issue:

> I have put limits on myself. I never tried to test boundaries—that is, I was never interested in going to places where I was pretty sure I'd be unwelcome or in danger. That is, I generally played it safe in terms of possible psychic and physical threats. But just being out in public a lot means that one is going to be exposed to at least mild threat at least occasionally, and my researcher self, at least, welcomed these occasions. I might add that I've always paid pretty close attention to those situations in which I felt uncomfortable or frightened—that is, I have always made extensive notes (or in some instances photographs) of the social and/or physical character of the setting in which such feelings emerged.

Some of Nash's research on public order includes studies of bus ridership (1975), outdoor behavior in frozen places (1981), and indoor behavior in public skyways (Nash & Nash, in press). In these works, respectively, he draws on observations made during three years of his own bus riding to describe a mobile urban community, he describes the breakdown of public norms that occurs under conditions of unusual thermal hardship, and he analyzes a series of skyways designed to replace the frigid outdoor space of the Minneapolis-St. Paul area. In the last of these studies, Jeff Nash and Anedith Nash assembled a research team of students to make observations in these connected plazas, buildings, and passageways. Their joint analysis looks at the influence of structural conditions on the relative vitality and population diversity of these locales, as well as the techniques by which people develop environmental mastery of the system.

Although Nash's transit observations were collected routinely (with the exception that he made no field notes while riding), his discussion of leading observational teams offers insight. Students were gathered from intersession courses on public life and later from courses on data analysis, where they read Goffman's *Relations in Public* (1971) and discussed conceptual analysis. Although the students' observations reflected inexperience, their field notes could be distilled at the end of the observational sessions to identify overlaps, similarities, and correlations. This resembles Cahill's (1987) role with his team, where he "continually reorganized and reviewed [their] field notes in order to discover common patterns, uncover general themes, and evaluate emerging hypotheses" (p. 314).

Another notable observational work falling within the public realm is Laud Humphreys's *Tearoom Trade* (1975). Like the others previously discussed, Humphreys assumed a covert observer-as-participant role in his setting (the "watchqueen"), observing men engage in impersonal homosexual activities at a bathroom in a public park. His observations were rigorous, as after each encounter he meticulously filled out a "systematic observation sheet" on which he recorded the date, place, description of the activity and its participants, license plate numbers of the participants' automobiles, and a sketch of the participants' placements. Although public and private restrooms have elsewhere been studied by observational teams as backstage regions (Cahill, 1985), this research focused on a highly deviant and hitherto unresearched behavior. Humphreys described the various roles in the setting (waiter, voyeur, masturbator, insertor, insertee) as well as the means by which potential members nonverbally conducted the negotiations for the deviant transaction. He described the characteristics of participants and their relations both among themselves and vis-à-vis potentially dangerous outsiders.

Although the book received widespread scholarly acclaim, it also set off waves of concern, as Humphreys tracked down his subjects through their license plate numbers and interviewed them anonymously one year later, looking totally different, as part of a large public health survey. This enabled him to gather demographic information about the characteristics of his population he would not otherwise have been able to obtain. The stigma associated with his topic and the unorthodox nature of his mixed methodology resulted in scrutiny of his observational methods they might not otherwise have encountered. We discuss these issues below.

What we see in these observational studies are variations in researcher involvement, researcher openness, use of teams, and gender issues. Observers have successfully taken roles ranging from total participation to studied detachment and have been both open and secretive about their research intent. Teams have been used as successfully as lone observation, and have yielded the benefit of greater diversity, energy, and scope. One aspect of observational research raised by both female but none of the male researchers we have examined is the safety issue. Women in the public domain find themselves sensitive to concerns men might not ever consider. This highlights the gendered nature of fieldwork and suggests that more mixed-gender observational teamwork might be fruitful.

Auto-Observation

Thus far we have discussed observations that focus on the group level, studying strangers and friends, often in public or semipublic places. But observation is also a powerful research tool when focused on more intimate levels of analysis. Social scientists have applied observational techniques with great success to studying themselves and their companions. The use of the self as a research tool for understanding society is rooted in the early origins of sociology. It was Dilthey (1961) who first proposed that we seek *Verstehen* (understanding) of human beings by empathizing with them. Incorporated by Weber into his methodological stance, *Verstehen* became a cornerstone of neoidealist and, subsequently, contemporary interpretive epistemology. Its strongest embodiment has been realized within existential sociology (see Douglas & Johnson, 1977), the proponents of which argue that "one must immerse oneself in everyday reality—feel it, touch it, hear it, and see it—in order to understand it" (Kotarba & Fontana, 1984, p. 6). This approach draws somewhat upon Schutz's (1971) notion of "reciprocity of perspective," that people can see the world from the eyes of others, in assuming that people experience similar feelings and emotions in reacting to the world around them. Observers who place themselves in the same situations as their subjects will thereby gain a deeper existential understanding of the world as the members see and feel it. This notion fosters a research role that is very close to the members, and augments researchers' observations of these others with observations of their own thoughts and feelings.

One such auto-observational study was conducted by Kretzmann (1992) in a blood plasma center. Assuming an active membership role, he took a covert stance and observed, eavesdropped on, and casually interacted with participants. From his vantage point he was able to experience the disdain and distrust staff members directed toward donors, and to describe and analyze the negative identity work they visited upon their clientele.

In contrast to Kretzmann's study, where he entered a setting and assumed the behavior of participants in order to acquire these self-observations, others opportunistically turn settings in which they are members or experiences they are having into topics of auto-observation. Ellis's (1993) recent book documents her relationship with her partner and his subsequent demise to emphysema over a grueling eight-year period. In the book, Ellis relies on systematic sociological introspection (Ellis, 1991) to plumb and record the depths of the emotional feelings she experienced throughout this time. Her text chronicles in narrative, often diarylike, form the events of those years and her emotional reactions to them. She then analyzes how this emotional journey took her through a renegotiation of meaning and identity common to many who suffer such loss or significant change in their life circumstances.

Ellis's auto-observation, like that of others, led her to become both subject and object of inquiry. She notes, "Taking the observer role gives me distance from the experience" (1993, pp. 1-2). This is a vital component of naturalistic observation via membership roles and shows once again the marginal role of observers, even in settings where they naturally belong. The detachment formerly lodged in researchers' objectivity and uninvolvement with their subjects is relocated in the withdrawal from what Schutz (1967) has called the "natural stance" of the everyday-life member to what Douglas (1976) has called the "theoretic stance" of the social scientific analyst. It is here that the conceptual optic scans and interprets the reams of raw, unprocessed data.

This observational approach offers the advantage of great depth, yielding insights about core meanings and experiences. It complements the more formal observational concerns that emphasize structure over content. Other notable works in which researchers have openly acknowledged using self-observation as a legitimate and insightful source of data include Johnson's (1975) study of social workers, Krieger's (1985) study of a lesbian community, Crapanzano's (1970) study of Morocco, Hayano's (1982) study of card rooms, and our study of a college basketball team (see particularly P. Adler, 1984).

Ethnomethodology

Whereas auto-observers and existential sociologists focus on the depth of meaningful experience, ethnomethodologists are concerned with how people accomplish their everyday lives (for a fuller discussion, see Holstein & Gubrium, Chapter 16, this volume). They take as their goal the elucidation of how everyday life is forged, hence socially constructed, by members. Much of their interest lies with processes that are below the surface of conscious awareness, at the taken-for-granted level. Such researchers thus eschew interview data, even from depth interviews, as mere "accounts," valueless for their purpose because of the problems of subject bias, self-deception, lack of insight, and dishonesty. Instead, they prefer to use observational techniques that focus on very micro exchanges, from the "adjacency pairs" that occur during the first seven seconds of a telephone call (Schegloff, 1968) to the means through which people yield and seize the floor during turn taking in conversations (McHoul, 1978). Ethnomethodologists gather data that can be analyzed later in minute detail, such as through audio- and videotaping. These tapes are often transcribed and analyzed via an intricate notational system that allows readers to view the conversational overlaps, pauses, and intonations to within one-tenth of a second. Researchers are less concerned with the vicissitudes of their role in the setting than they are with making (or obtaining) recordings of mundane, everyday life that illustrate people operating naturally, in their native contexts of occurrence.

Contemporary ethnomethodologists have directed a particular emphasis toward conversation analysis (Heritage, 1984). They regard language as the fundamental base of communication, the base of social order. Yet Sacks (1963) asserts that language should not be part of an analytic apparatus until it is described. Conversation analysts have thus aimed to describe and analyze language use. Their end goal has been to build upward from a base of language and communication to understand the nature of roles, relationships, and social norms in settings and thereby discern the underlying structure of social reality.

A major study of the language of courtroom negotiation was conducted by Douglas Maynard (1984), in which he observed the negotiations occurring in a single courtroom and judges' chambers among participants in 54 misdemeanor cases. He audiotaped as many situations as he could and supplemented these with handwritten notes on conversations and situations he could not record. His role, he notes, was somewhere between the known and unknown observer: He had been granted entrée by the presiding judge and formally introduced to the most regular courtroom members, but there were many others (defendants, members of the public, attorneys who visited the courtroom less frequently) who were unaware of his research role. His analysis of his recordings offered him several benefits: He could reproduce as much detail from the conversations as possible; he could use this detail to build rigor and enhance the replicability of the research for others examining the same data; and he could obtain a record that did not rely on what the researcher thought was interesting or important before analyzing the data.

This research shows the differences that can be obtained through observational research conducted under different theoretical auspices. Compared with observations made from within the interpretive perspective, ethnomethodological observation yields a product that is more structural and objective, less mediated by the subjective perspective of the researcher. The detailed transcriptions produced of the speech, pauses, overlaps, and intonations of everyday conversations can also be reexamined repeatedly by multiple observers. This approach also entails a different role for the researcher, who is less likely to interact with setting participants than to operate recording equipment.

Maynard took notes and ran his tape recorder as he was present in the setting, but others may be either more or less intrusive. In studying the Watergate tapes, for example, Molotch and Boden (1985) analyzed the videotapes of the Watergate hearings. More common is the use of videotape recording to capture such things as the hesitations, restarts, pauses, and gaze behavior of participants (e.g., Goodwin, 1981). With their intrusive camera lenses, videotaping observers are more likely to produce unnatural influences on their subjects. These types of observations are also more focused than those made by interactionist researchers, as they are fixed in their location and restricted to the immediate communicative features of situations.

Ethical Issues

Several features of observational research make it vulnerable to questions of ethical malpractice. Of all social science data gathering techniques, it is the least obtrusive. Although this is one of its great strengths, it also renders it liable to abuse in the invasion of privacy. Invasion of privacy can take two forms: venturing into private places, and misrepresenting oneself as a member. In this section we draw on the example of Humphreys's (1975) tearoom research to facilitate our discussion of these two issues.

By the nature of their inconspicuousness, observers can venture into places to gather data that are inaccessible to the general public. Deviant behavior often takes place in such private locales, away from the prying eyes of moral entrepreneurs. Some sociologists, in discussing ethical guidelines, have suggested that private locales ought to remain protected from the prying eyes of sociologists as well (Erikson, 1967). Summarizing the comments of others, Humphreys (1975) noted:

> Are there, perhaps, some areas of human behavior that are not fit for social scientific study at all? Should sex, religion, suicide or other socially sensitive concerns be omitted from the catalogue of possible fields of sociological research? At first glance, few would answer yes to this question. Nevertheless, several have suggested to me that I should have avoided this research subject altogether. Their contention has been that in an area of such sensitivity it would be best to "let sleeping dogs lie." (pp. 167-168)

Responding to this ethical contention, Humphreys laid out his rationale for such research:

> You do walk a really perilous tightrope in regard to ethical matters in studies like this, but unless

> someone will walk it, the only source of information will be the police department, and that's dangerous for a society. The methods I used were the least obtrusive possible. Oh, I could have hidden in the ceiling as the police do, but then I would have been an accomplice in what they were doing. (pp. 179-180)

The debate following publication of Humphreys's work drew enough attention to be noticed outside of academic circles. Reacting for the press, columnist Nicholas von Hoffman (1975) of the *Washington Post* presented another view:

> This newspaper could probably learn a lot of things that the public has a right and need to know if its reporters were to use disguises and the gimmickry of modern, transistorized, domestic espionage, but there is a policy against it. No information is valuable enough to obtain by nipping away at personal liberty, and that is true no matter who's doing the gnawing, John Mitchell and the conservatives over at the Justice Department or Laud Humphreys and the liberals over at the Sociology Department. (p. 181)

Yet even if observers forgo observation in private places, they cannot easily escape this dilemma. Much observational research, as we have seen from the examples discussed, takes place in public or semipublic settings; the theoretical traditions guiding them foster an interest in social order and the forms of social structure. However, as Lofland (1973) noted in her study of urban living, even public spaces can be transformed, through their use, into private enclaves. Carol Warren (personal communication, 1993) describes such an invasion of her privacy while out in public:

> I was sitting with a friend in a coffee shop chatting. A man wandered in, scoped the place out, and sat down at a table in front of ours. He did not go buy any food or drink at the counter. After a short while he moved from the table to a bench directly next to our table. I observed all this peripherally, and did not think much about it. After a while, he got out a pen and started writing on this pad he was carrying. It occurred to me then that he was an ethnographer taking notes on this public setting. As soon as I had this thought I became furiously indignant, and felt invaded. I was very surprised at my own reactions, since the arguments about not observing in public space had made no sense to me. Later I thought that although this was a public space it was also a privatized one, in which each separate unit in that space had their own focus of attention and interaction.

What we learn from these potentially similar reactions to observational research is that the definitions of public and private may be inadequate for describing the public realm. Lofland (1989) has suggested a third form of social territory in the public realm, the parochial, which is characterized by a sense of commonality among acquaintances and neighbors who are involved in interpersonal networks that are located within "communities." Humphreys's tearooms could fall either into this parochial category or could be viewed as a private realm "bubble" within the public realm (Lofland, in press). Second, situational factors affect nearly all absolute issues; an unobtrusive observer in a more private setting offended no members, whereas an obtrusive observer in a public setting offended his subjects. In choosing between these two polar positions, researchers might temper their decisions by considering the relative harm and benefits to both private persons in society and the advancement of scientific knowledge. Their own needs must then be fettered by a sensitivity to the rights of unknowing others.

The related ethical issue concerns disguised research. Humphreys purposely disguised himself as the "watchqueen," or lookout, in his tearooms, after unsuccessfully trying out the roles of straight person and waiter. The former had met with a disruption of activity followed by the general exodus of participants from the scene, and the latter, which he tried next, with invitations to join the action. A cooperating respondent suggested the watchqueen role to Humphreys as a membership role that was not overtly sexual. By serving as the voyeur-lookout he was able to move around the room freely, observe all the action, and avoid pressures into more active participation.

Disguised or covert research has come under significant moral attack from social scientists. These calls have echoed forcefully in the hallways of the federal government, with momentous effects subsequently ensuing in the funding, sponsoring, and outlawing of research. Erikson (1967) has proposed two rules regarding misrepresentation in research:

> It is unethical for a sociologist to deliberately misrepresent his identity for the purpose of entering a private domain to which he is not otherwise eligible.
>
> It is unethical for a sociologist to deliberately misrepresent the character of the research in which he is engaged. (p. 373)

Several of the reactions to Humphreys's work suggested that he had no right to misrepresent himself deliberately as a member to gain access to the scene (von Hoffman, 1975), that he was overly concerned with the needs of the researcher and not enough with the freedom of the subjects

(Warwick, 1973), that he inadequately considered the potential costs to his subjects should their activity be exposed (Warwick, 1973), and that he underestimated the power of the government to compel him to surrender evidence about his subjects should it become interested in this illegal activity (Glazer, 1975).

Others reacted in defense of Humphreys's work, arguing that the crucial issue is the need for research to cast light on social science areas otherwise blanketed by "ignorance and darkness." They praised the scrupulous attention Humphreys gave to protecting the identities of his subjects and argued that the goal of social scientists, unlike those of journalists and police, who sensationalize and expose, is to generalize from their subjects' actions to generic understandings of human behavior (Horowitz & Rainwater, 1975). *Tearoom Trade* was praised for its meticulous and sophisticated attention to social science research procedure (Glazer, 1975) and was granted the prestigious C. Wright Mills Award from the Society for the Study of Social Problems for its contribution to the study of critical social issues.

The Humphreys research offers a vivid illustration of disguised research, but the overt versus covert nature of most observers' roles is often more ambiguous. Maynard reflected on how he and his research were unknown to many in the courtroom, and Lofland noted that she generally passed as a member while doing her observation. Observers of public space usually find themselves in the same situation, as do many who make social science observations while engaged in their normal public or private activities. In guiding researchers to think about this issue, there are those who feel that we have enough legal and moral strictures guiding us to provide us with sensible and sensitive frameworks (Douglas, 1979), whereas others believe that people should be bound by firmer policies and restrictions rather than left to their own judgment (Reiman, 1979). At the present time, the policies and restrictions established by institutional review boards guiding research on human subjects, which exist at every university receiving government funding, have outlawed disguised research. It is up to each university to interpret how broadly it wants to apply this mandate to nonfunded research. Once again, researchers are reminded that they must take into account subjects' rights to freedom from manipulation when weighing the potential benefits of the research role against the harms that could accrue.

The Future of Observation

Forecasting the wax and wane of social science research methods is always uncertain, but it is possible to extrapolate on existing trends. Editors of scholarly journals have found it difficult to accept the legitimacy of solely observational research, and they probably will continue to do so. Problems of subjectivity and excessive reliance on observer articulation still hamper this technique, and the theoretical traditions driving it are not that actively populated. Thus observation is unlikely to disappear, but it is also unlikely to ascend swiftly in acclaim.

The recent vast incursion of institutional review boards, importing with them government regulation of research, may alter the data gathering landscape, however. According to these standards, all observation (including observation by participants) of public behavior must be submitted for committee approval. Any such research where (a) human subjects could potentially be identified (either directly or through identifiers linked to the subjects), (b) the recorded observations could reasonably place the subjects at risk of criminal or civil liability or be damaging to the subjects' financial standing or employability, or (c) the research deals with sensitive aspects of the subjects' own behavior, such as illegal conduct, drug use, sexual behavior, or use of alcohol, is subject to potential censure (University of Colorado, Informed Consent Packet, Human Research Committee).

According to these guidelines, Humphreys never could have researched or written *Tearoom Trade*. In fact, these criteria fundamentally outlaw data gathered through direct experience or observation on nearly all aspects of deviant behavior. The implications for the future of this field of sociology are large. And as long as universities remain in dire financial straits and continue to be propelled by a fear of lawsuits from disgruntled subjects, administrators of higher education will never stand up for the needs or rights of scholarship against the flow of government grant funding.

Where the future of observation shines more brightly is in the use of this technique as an integrated rather than a primary method. When employed as part of a methodological spectrum that includes member-articulated data gathering strategies such as depth interviewing or participant observation, it is the most powerful source of validation. Freed from subjects' whimsical shifts in opinion, self-evaluation, self-deception, manipulation of self-presentation, embarrassment, and outright dishonesty, observation rests on something researchers can find constant: their own direct knowledge and their own judgment. It thus stands as the fundamental base of all research methods. With the dwindling of federal money for large survey research and the rise of public health problems lodged among hidden populations, researcher-gathered data has received an increase of support. This has already begun and will continue to generate more grant money, more research interest, and more scholarly legitimation of integrated field research techniques resting on a base of direct observation.

Note

1. Some exceedingly interesting work is being done in the realm of visual sociology via photography. For more detailed information than is possible to include in this treatment, see Becker (1981, 1986), the journal *Visual Sociology* (sponsored by the International Visual Sociology Association), and Douglas Harper's contribution to this volume (Chapter 25).

References

Adler, P. (1984). The sociologist as celebrity: The role of the media in field research. *Qualitative Sociology, 7,* 319-326.

Adler, P. A. (1985). *Wheeling and dealing.* New York: Columbia University Press.

Adler, P. A., & Adler, P. (1987). *Membership roles in field research.* Newbury Park, CA: Sage.

Adler, P. A., & Adler, P. (1991a). *Backboards and blackboards.* New York: Columbia University Press.

Adler, P. A., & Adler, P. (1991b). Stability and flexibility: Maintaining relations within organized and unorganized groups. In W. Shaffir & R. Stebbins (Eds.), *Experiencing fieldwork* (pp. 173-183). Newbury Park, CA: Sage.

Adler, P. A., Kless, S. J., & Adler, P. (1992). Socialization to gender roles: Images of popularity among elementary school boys and girls. *Sociology of Education, 65,* 169-187.

Atkinson, P. A. (1990). *The ethnographic imagination: Textual constructions of reality.* London: Routledge.

Becker, H. S. (1981). *Exploring society photographically.* Evanston, IL: Northwestern University, Mary and Leigh Block Gallery.

Becker, H. S. (1986). *Doing things together: Selected papers.* Evanston, IL: Northwestern University Press.

Berg, B. (1989). *Qualitative research methods for the social sciences.* Boston: Allyn & Bacon.

Brissett, D., & Edgley, C. (1990). *Life as theater* (2nd ed.). New York: Aldine de Gruyter.

Buban, S. L. (1986). Studying social process: The Chicago and Iowa schools revisited. In C. J. Couch, S. Saxton, & M. A. Katovich (Eds.), *Studies in symbolic interaction: Supplement 2. The Iowa school* (Part A) (pp. 25-38). Greenwich, CT: JAI.

Cahill, S. (1987). Children and civility: Ceremonial deviance and the acquisition of ritual competence. *Social Psychology Quarterly, 50,* 312-321.

Cahill, S. (1990). Childhood and public life: Reaffirming biographical divisions. *Social Problems, 37,* 390-402.

Cahill, S., with Distler, W., Lachowetz, C., Meaney, A., Tarallo, R., & Willard, T. (1985). Meanwhile backstage: Public bathrooms and the interaction order. *Urban Life, 14,* 33-58.

Carpenter, C., Glassner, B., Johnson, B., & Loughlin, J. (1988). *Kids, drugs, and crime.* Lexington, MA: Lexington.

Couch, C. J. (1984). *Constructing civilizations.* Greenwich, CT: JAI.

Couch, C. J., Saxton, S., & Katovich, M. A. (Eds.). (1986). *Studies in symbolic interaction: Supplement 2. The Iowa school* (Part A). Greenwich, CT: JAI.

Crapanzano, V. (1970). The writing of ethnography. *Dialectical Anthropology, 2,* 69-73.

Denzin, N. K. (1989). *The research act* (3rd ed.). Englewood Cliffs, NJ: Prentice Hall.

Dilthey, W. (1961). *Patterns and meanings in history* (H. P. Rickman, Trans.). New York: Harper & Row.

Douglas, J. D. (1976). *Investigative social research.* Beverly Hills, CA: Sage.

Douglas, J. D. (1979). Living morality versus bureaucratic fiat. In C. Klockars & F. O'Connor (Eds.), *Deviance and decency: The ethics of research with human subjects* (pp. 13-34). Beverly Hills, CA: Sage.

Douglas, J. D., & Johnson, J. (1977). *Existential sociology.* Cambridge: Cambridge University Press.

Ellis, C. (1991). Sociological introspection and emotional experience. *Symbolic Interaction, 14,* 23-50.

Ellis, C. (1993). *Final negotiations.* Manuscript submitted for publication.

Erikson, K. T. (1967). A comment on disguised observation in sociology. *Social Problems, 14,* 366-373.

Frisby, D. (1981). *Sociological impressionism: A reassessment of the social theory of Georg Simmel.* London: Heinemann.

Gardner, C. B. (1988). Access information: Public lies and private peril. *Social Problems, 35,* 384-397.

Glaser, B. G., & Strauss, A. L. (1967). *The discovery of grounded theory: Strategies for qualitative research.* Chicago: Aldine.

Glazer, M. (1975). Impersonal sex. In L. Humphreys, *Tearoom trade: Impersonal sex in public places* (enlarged ed., pp. 213-222). New York: Aldine.

Glesne, C., & Peshkin, A. (1992). *Becoming qualitative researchers.* White Plains, NY: Longman.

Goffman, E. (1961). *Asylums.* Garden City, NY: Doubleday.

Goffman, E. (1963). *Stigma: Notes on the management of spoiled identity.* Englewood Cliffs, NJ: Prentice Hall.

Goffman, E. (1971). *Relations in public.* New York: Basic Books.

Gold, R. L. (1958). Roles in sociological field observations. *Social Forces, 36,* 217-223.

Goodwin, C. (1981). *Conversational organization: Interaction between speakers and hearers.* New York: Academic Press.

Hammersley, M., & Atkinson, P. (1983). *Ethnography: Principles in practice.* London: Tavistock.

Handel, W. (1982). *Ethnomethodology.* Englewood Cliffs, NJ: Prentice Hall.

Hayano, D. (1979). Auto-ethnography: Paradigms, problems, and prospects. *Human Organization, 38,* 99-104.

Hayano, D. (1982). *Poker faces.* Berkeley: University of California Press.

Heritage, J. (1984). *Garfinkel and ethnomethodology.* Cambridge: Polity.

Horowitz, I. L., & Rainwater, L. (1975). On journalistic moralizers. In L. Humphreys, *Tearoom trade: Impersonal sex in public places* (enlarged ed., pp. 181-190). New York: Aldine.

Humphreys, L. (1975). *Tearoom trade: Impersonal sex in public places* (enlarged edition). New York: Aldine.

Jarvie, I. C. (1969). The problem of ethical integrity in participant-observation. *Current Anthropology, 10,* 505-508.

Jefferson, G. (Ed.). (1989). *Harvey Sacks lectures 1964-65.* Dordrecht, Netherlands: Kluwer Academic Publishers.

Johnson, J. (1975). *Doing field research.* New York: Free Press.

Jorgensen, D. L. (1989). *Participant observation.* Newbury Park, CA: Sage.

Katovich, M. A., Weiland, M. W., & Couch, C. J. (1978). *The impact of news on representative-constituent relationships: Toward a theory of representative democracy.* Unpublished manuscript.

Katovich, M. A., Weiland, M. W., & Couch, C. J. (1981). Access to information and internal structures of partisan groups: Some notes on the iron law of oligarchy. *Sociological Quarterly, 22,* 431-446.

Kidder, L. H. (1981). *Selltiz, Wrightsman and Cook's research methods in social relations* (4th ed.). New York: Holt, Rinehart & Winston.

Kotarba, J. A., & Fontana, A. (Eds.). (1984). *The existential self in society.* Chicago: University of Chicago Press.

Kretzmann, M. J. (1992). Bad blood: The moral stigmatization of paid plasma donors. *Journal of Contemporary Ethnography, 20,* 416-441.

Krieger, S. (1985). Beyond subjectivity: The use of the self in social science. *Qualitative Sociology, 8,* 309-324.

Lofland, J., & Lofland, L. (1984). *Analyzing social settings: A guide to qualitative observation and analysis* (2nd ed.). Belmont, CA: Wadsworth.

Lofland, L. (1973). *A world of strangers.* New York: Basic Books.

Lofland, L. (1989). Social life in the public realm: A review. *Journal of Contemporary Ethnography, 17,* 453-482.

Lofland, L. (in press). Observations and observers in conflict: Field research in the public realm. In S. Cahill & L. Lofland (Eds.), *The community of the streets.* Greenwich, CT: JAI.

Maynard, D. W. (1984). *Inside plea bargaining: The language of negotiation.* New York: Plenum.

McHoul, A. (1978). The organization of turns at formal talk in the classroom. *Language in Society, 7,* 183-213.

Mead, G. H. (1934). *Mind, self and society: From the standpoint of a social behaviorist.* Chicago: University of Chicago Press.

Mehan, H., & Wood, H. (1975). *The reality of ethnomethodology.* New York: John Wiley.

Miller, D. E., Hintz, R. A., Jr., & Couch, C. J. (1975). The elements and structure of openings. In C. J. Couch & R. A. Hintz, Jr. (Eds.), *Constructing social life* (pp. 1-24). Champaign, IL: Stipes.

Molotch, H. L., & Boden, D. (1985). Talking social structure. *American Sociological Review, 50,* 273-287.

Morris, W. (Ed.). (1973). *The American Heritage dictionary of the English language.* Boston: Houghton Mifflin.

Nash, J. (1975). Bus riding: Community on wheels. *Urban Life, 4,* 99-124.

Nash, J. (1981). Relations in frozen places: Observations on winter public order. *Qualitative Sociology, 4,* 229-243.

Nash, J., & Nash, A. (in press). The skyway system and urban space: Vitality in enclosed public places. In S. Cahill & L. Lofland (Eds.), *The community of the streets.* Greenwich, CT: JAI.

Phillips, B. (1985). *Sociological research methods.* Homewood, IL: Dorsey.

Reiman, J. (1979). Research subjects, human subjects, and political subjects. In C. Klockars & F. O'Connor (Eds.), *Deviance and decency: The ethics of research with human subjects* (pp. 35-57). Beverly Hills, CA: Sage.

Riemer, J. (1977). Varieties of opportunistic research. *Urban Life, 5,* 467-477.

Sacks, H. (1963). On sociological description. *Berkeley Journal of Sociology, 8,* 1-16.

Saxton, S. L., & Couch, C. J. (1975). Recording social interaction. In C. J. Couch & R. A. Hintz, Jr. (Eds.), *Constructing social life* (pp. 255-262). Champaign, IL: Stipes.

Schatzman, L., & Strauss, A. L. (1973). *Field research: Strategies for a natural sociology.* Englewood Cliffs, NJ: Prentice Hall.

Schegloff, E. A. (1968). Sequencing in conversational openings. *American Anthropologist, 70,* 1075-1095.

Schutz, A. (1967). *The phenomenology of the social world* (G. Walsh & F. Lehnert, Trans.). Evanston, IL: Northwestern University Press.

Schutz, A. (1971). *Collected papers* (Vol. 1) (M. Natanson, Ed.). The Hague: Martinus Nijhoff.

Smith, G. (1992, October 13). *A Simmelian reading of Goffman's rhetoric.* Guest lecture presented at the University of Colorado.

Spradley, J. P. (1980). *Participant observation.* New York: Holt, Rinehart & Winston.

von Hoffman, N. (1975). Sociological snoopers. In L. Humphreys, *Tearoom trade: Impersonal sex in public places* (enlarged ed., pp. 177-181). New York: Aldine.

Warwick, D. P. (1973). Tearoom trade: Means and ends in social research. *Hastings Center Studies, 1,* 27-38.

Webb, E. J., Campbell, D. T., Schwartz, R. C., & Sechrest, L. (1966). *Unobtrusive measures: Nonreactive research in the social sciences.* Chicago: University of Chicago Press.

24

■

The Interpretation of Documents and Material Culture

IAN HODDER

THIS chapter is concerned with the interpretation of mute evidence—that is, with written texts and artifacts. Such evidence, unlike the spoken word, endures physically and thus can be separated across space and time from its author, producer, or user. Material traces thus often have to be interpreted without the benefit of indigenous commentary. There is often no possibility of interaction with spoken emic "insider" as opposed to etic "outsider" perspectives. Even when such interaction is possible, actors often seem curiously inarticulate about the reasons they dress in particular ways, choose particular pottery designs, or discard dung in particular locations. Material traces and residues thus pose special problems for qualitative research. The main disciplines that have tried to develop appropriate theory and method are history, art history, archaeology, anthropology, sociology, cognitive psychology, technology, and modern material culture studies, and it is from this range of disciplines that my account is drawn.

Written Documents and Records

Lincoln and Guba (1985, p. 277) distinguish documents and records on the basis of whether the text was prepared to attest to some formal transaction. Thus records include marriage certificates, driving licenses, building contracts, and banking statements. Documents, on the other hand, are prepared for personal rather than official reasons and include diaries, memos, letters, field notes, and so on. In fact, the two terms are often used interchangeably, although the distinction is an important one and has some parallels with the distinction between writing and speech, to be discussed below. Documents, closer to speech, require more contextualized interpretation. Records, on the other hand, may have local uses that become very distant from officially sanctioned meanings. Documents involve a personal technology, and records a full state technology of power. The distinction is also relevant for qualitative research, in that researchers may often be able to get access to documents, whereas access to records may be restricted by laws regarding privacy, confidentiality, and anonymity.

Despite the utility of the distinction between documents and records, my concern here is more the problems of interpretation of written texts of all kinds. Such texts are of importance for qualitative research because, in general terms, access can be easy and low cost, because the information provided may differ from and may not be available in spoken form, and because texts endure and thus give historical insight.

It has often been assumed, for example, in the archaeology of historical periods, that written texts provide a "truer" indication of original meanings than do other types of evidence (to be considered below). Indeed, Western social science has long privileged the spoken over the written and the written over the nonverbal (Derrida, 1978). Somehow it is assumed that words get us closer to minds. But as Derrida has shown, meaning does not reside in a text but in the writing and reading of it. As the text is reread in different contexts it is given new meanings, often contradictory and always socially embedded. Thus there is no "original" or "true" meaning of a text outside specific historical contexts. Historical archaeologists have come to accept that historical documents and records give not a better but simply a different picture from that provided by artifacts and architecture. Texts can be used alongside other forms of evidence so that the particular biases of each can be understood and compared.

Equally, different types of text have to be understood in the contexts of their conditions of production and reading. For example, the analyst will be concerned with whether a text was written as result of firsthand experience or from secondary sources, whether it was solicited or unsolicited, edited or unedited, anonymous or signed, and so on (Webb, Campbell, Schwartz, & Sechrest, 1966). As Ricoeur (1971) demonstrates, concrete texts differ from the abstract structures of language in that they are written to do something. They can be understood only as what they are—a form of artifact produced under certain material conditions (not everyone can write, or write in a certain way, or have access to relevant technologies of reproduction) embedded within social and ideological systems.

Words are, of course, spoken to do things as well as to say things—they have practical and social impact as well as communication function. Once transformed into a written text the gap between the "author" and the "reader" widens and the possibility of multiple reinterpretations increases. The text can "say" many different things in different contexts. But also the written text is an artifact, capable of transmission, manipulation, and alteration, used and discarded, reused and recycled—"doing" different things contextually through time. The writing down of words often allows language and meanings to be controlled more effectively, and to be linked to strategies of centralization and codification. The word, concretized or "made flesh" in the artifact, can transcend context and gather through time extended symbolic connotations. The word made enduring in artifacts has an important role to play in both secular and religious processes of the legitimation of power. Yet there is often a tension between the concrete nature of the written word, its enduring nature, and the continuous potential for rereading meanings in new contexts, undermining the authority of the word. Text and context are in a continual state of tension, each defining and redefining the other, saying and doing things differently through time.

In a related way, the written texts of anthropologists and archaeologists are increasingly coming under scrutiny as employing rhetorical strategies in order to establish positions of authority (e.g., Tilley, 1989). Archaeologists are used to the idea that their scientific activities leave traces and transform the worlds they study. Excavations cannot be repeated, and the residues of trenches, spoil tips, and old beer cans remain as specific expressions of a particular way of looking at the world. The past has been transformed into a present product, including the field notes and site reports. Ethnographic field notes (Sanjek, 1990) also transform the object of study into a historically situated product, "capturing" the "other" within a familiar routine. The field text has to be contextualized within specific historical moments.

I shall in this chapter treat written texts as special cases of artifacts, subject to similar interpretive procedures. In both texts and artifacts the problem is one of situating material culture within varying contexts while at the same time entering into a dialectic relationship between those contexts and the context of the analyst. This hermeneutical exercise, in which the lived experience surrounding the material culture is translated into a different context of interpretation, is common for both texts and other forms of material culture. I will note various differences between language and material culture in what follows, but the interpretive parallels have been widely discussed in the consideration of material culture as text (e.g., Hodder, 1991; Moore, 1986; Tilley, 1990).

Artifact Analysis and Its Importance for the Interpretation of Social Experience

Ancient and modern buildings and artifacts, the intended and unintended residues of human activity, give alternative insights into the ways in which people perceived and fashioned their lives. Shortcuts across lawns indicate preferred traffic patterns, foreign-language signs indicate the degree of integration of a neighborhood, the number of cigarettes in an ashtray betrays a nervous tension, and the amount of paperwork in an "in" tray is a measure of workload or of work efficiency and priority (Lincoln & Guba, 1985, p. 280). Despite the inferential problems surrounding such evidence, I wish to establish at the outset that material traces of behavior give an important and different insight from that provided by any number of questionnaires.

"What people say" is often very different from "what people do." This point has perhaps been most successfully established over recent years by research stemming from the work of Bill Rathje (Rathje & Murphy, 1992; Rathje & Thompson, 1981). In studies in Tucson, Arizona, and elsewhere, Rathje and his colleagues collected domestic garbage bags and itemized the contents. It became clear that, for example, people's estimates about the amounts of garbage they produced were wildly incorrect, that discarded beer cans indicated a higher level of alcohol consumption than was admitted to, and that in times of meat shortage people threw away more meat than usual as a result of overhoarding. Thus a full sociological analysis cannot be restricted to interview data. It must also consider the material traces.

In another series of studies, the decoration of rooms as well as pots and other containers has been interpreted as a form of silent discourse conducted by women, whose voice has been silenced by dominant male interests. Decoration may be used to mark out, silently, and to draw attention to, tacitly, areas of female control, such as female areas of houses and the preparation and provision of food in containers. The decoration may at one level provide protection from female pollution, but at another level it expresses female power (Braithwaite, 1982; Donley, 1982; Hodder, 1991).

The study of material culture is thus of importance for qualitative researchers who wish to explore multiple and conflicting voices, differing and interacting interpretations. Many areas of experience are hidden from language, particularly subordinate experience. Ferguson (1991) has shown how study of the material traces of food and pots can provide insight into how slaves on plantations in the American South made sense of and reacted to their domination. The members of this normally silenced group expressed their own perspective in the mundane activities of everyday life.

Analysis of such traces is not a trivial pursuit, as the mundane and the everyday, because unimportant to dominant interests, may be of great importance for the expression of alternative perspectives. The material expression of power (parades, regalia, tombs, and art) can be set against the expression of resistance. The importance of such analysis is increased by the realization that material culture is not simply a passive by-product of other areas of life. Rather, material culture is active (Hodder, 1982). By this I mean that artifacts are produced so as to transform, materially, socially, and ideologically. It is the exchange of artifacts themselves that constructs social relationships; it is the style of spear that creates a feeling of common identity; it is the badge of authority that itself confers authority. Material culture is thus *necessary for* most social constructs. An adequate study of social interaction thus depends on the incorporation of mute material evidence.

Toward a Theory of Material Culture

Having established that the study of material culture can be an important tool for sociological and anthropological analysis, it is necessary to attempt to build a theory on which the interpretation of material culture can be based. A difficulty here has been the diversity of the category "material culture," ranging from written texts to material symbols surrounding death, drama, and ritual, to shopping behavior and to the construction of roads and airplanes. As a result, theoretical directions have often taken rather different paths, as one can see by comparing attempts to build a comprehensive theory for technological behavior (Lemonnier, 1986) and attempts to consider material culture as text (Tilley, 1990).

Ultimately, material culture always has to be interpreted in relation to a situated context of production, use, discard, and reuse. In working toward that contextual interpretation, it may be helpful to distinguish some general characteristics and analogies for the different types of material culture. In this attempt to build a general theory, recent research in a range of disciplines has begun to separate two areas of material meaning.

Some material culture is designed specifically to be communicative and representational. The clearest example is a written text, but this category extends, for example, to the badge and uniform of certain professions, to red and green stop and go traffic lights, to smoke signals, to the images of Christ on the cross. Because this category includes written texts, it is to be expected that meaning in this category might be organized in ways similar to language. Thus, as with words in a language, the material symbols are, outside a historical context, often arbitrary. For example, any design on a flag could be used as long as it differs from the designs on other flags and is recognizable with its own identity. Thus the system of meanings in the case of flags is constructed through similarities and differences in a semiotic code. Miller (1982) has shown how dress is organized both syntagmatically and paradigmatically. The choice of hat, tie, shirt, trousers, shoes, and so on for a particular occasion is informed by a syntax that allows a particular set of clothes to be put together. On the other hand, the distinctions among different types of hats (bowler, straw, cloth, baseball) or jackets constitute paradigmatic choices.

The three broad areas of theory that have been applied to this first type of material meaning derive from information technology, Marxism, and structuralism. In the first, the aim has been to account for the ways in which material symboling can provide adaptive advantage to social groups. Thus the development of complex symboling systems allows more information to be processed more efficiently (e.g., Wobst, 1977). This type of approach is of limited value to qualitative research because it is not concerned with the interpretation and experience of meaningful symbols. In the second, the ideological component of symbols is identified within relations of power and domination (Leone, 1984; Miller & Tilley, 1984) and increasingly power and systems of value and prestige are seen as multiple and dialectical (Miller, Rowlands, & Tilley, 1989; Shanks & Tilley, 1987). The aim of structuralist analysis has been to examine design (e.g., Washburn, 1983) or spatial relationships (e.g., Glassie, 1975; McGhee, 1977) in terms of underlying codes, although here too the tendency has been on emphasizing multiple meanings contested within active social contexts as the various directions of poststructuralist thought have been debated (Tilley, 1990).

In much of this work the metaphor of language has been applied to material culture relatively unproblematically. The pot appears to "mean" in the same way as the word *pot.* Recent work has begun to draw attention to the limitations of this analogy between material culture and language, as will become clear in my consideration of the second type of material culture meaning. One can begin to explore the limitations of the analogy by considering that many examples of material culture are not produced to "mean" at all. In other words, they are not produced with symbolic functions as primary. Thus the madeleine cookie discussed in Proust's *A la recherche du temps perdu* (*Swann's Way*) was produced as an enticing food, made in a shape representing a fluted scallop. But Proust describes its meaning as quite different from this symbolic representation. Rather, the meaning was the evocation of a whole series of childhood memories, sounds, tastes, smells surrounding having tea with his mother in winter.

Many if not most material symbols do not work through rules of representation, using a language-like syntax. Rather, they work through the evocation of sets of practices within individual experience. It would be relatively difficult to construct a grammar or dictionary of material symbols except in the case of deliberately representational or symbolic items, such as flags and road signs. This is because most material symbols do not mean in the same way as language. Rather, they come to have abstract meaning through association and practice. Insofar as members of society experience common practices, material symbols can come to have common evocations and common meanings. Thus, for example, the ways in which certain types of food, drink, music, and sport are experienced are embedded within social convention and thus come to have common meaning. A garlic crusher may not be used overtly in Britain to represent or symbolize class, but through a complex set of practices surrounding food and its preparation the crusher has come to mean class through evocation.

Because objects endure, have their own traces, their own grain, individual objects with unique evocations can be recognized. The specific memory traces associated with any particular object (a particular garlic crusher) will vary from individual to individual. The particularity of material experience and meaning derives not only from the diversity of human life but also from the identifiability of material objects. The identifiable particularity of material experience always has the potential to work against and transform society-wide conventions through practice. Because of this dialectic between structure and practice, and because of the multiple local meanings that can be given to things, it would be difficult to construct dictionaries and grammars for most material culture meanings.

Another reason for the inability to produce dictionaries of material culture returns us to the difficulty with which people give discursive accounts of material symbolism. The meanings often remain tacit and implicit. A smell or taste of a madeleine cookie may awake strong feelings, but it is notoriously difficult to describe a taste or a feel or to pin down the emotions evoked. We may know that in practice this or that item of clothing "looks good," "works well," or "is stylish," but we would be at a loss to say what it "means" because the item does not mean—rather, it is embedded in a set of practices that include class, status, goals, aesthetics. We may not know much about art, but we know what we like. On the basis of a set of practical associations, we build up an implicit knowledge about the associations and evocations of particular artifacts or styles. This type of embedded, practical experience seems to be different from the manipulation of rules of representation and from conscious analytic thought. Material symbolic meanings may get us close to lived experience, but they cannot easily be articulated.

The importance of practice for the social and symbolic meanings of artifacts has been emphasized in recent work on technology (Schlanger, 1990). Each technical operation is linked to others in operational chains (Leroi-Gourhan, 1964) involving materials, energy, and gestures. For example, some clays are better for throwing than others, so that type of clay constrains whether a manufacturer can make thrown pots or hand-built statuettes. Quality of clay is related to types of temper that should be used. All such operational chains are nondeterministic, and some degree of social choice is involved (Lemonnier, 1986; Miller, 1985). All operational chains involve aspects of production, exchange, and consumption, and so are part of a network of relations incorporating the material, the economic, the social, and the conceptual.

The practical operational chains often have implications that extend into not only social but also moral realms. For example, Latour (1988) discusses hydraulic door closers, devices that automatically close a door after someone has opened it. The material door closer thus takes the place of, or delegates, the role of a porter, someone who stands there and makes sure that the door stays shut after people have gone through. But use of this particular delegate has various implications, one of which is that very young or infirm people have difficulty getting through the door. A social distinction is unwittingly implied by this technology. In another example, Latour discusses a key used by some inhabitants of Berlin. This double-ended key forces the user to lock the door in order to get the key out. The key delegates for staff or signs that might order a person to "relock the door behind you." Staff or signs would be unreliable—they could be outwitted or ignored. The key enforces a morality. In the same way "sleeping policemen" (speed bumps) force the driver of a car to be moral and to slow down in front of a school, but this morality is not socially encoded. That would be too unreliable. The morality is embedded within the practical consequences of breaking up one's car by driving too fast over the bumps. The social and moral meanings of the door closer, the Berlin key, or the speed bump are thoroughly embedded in the implications of material practices.

I have suggested that in developing a theory of material culture, the first task is to distinguish at least two different ways in which material culture has abstract meaning beyond primary utilitarian concerns. The first is through rules of representation. The second is through practice and evocation—through the networking, interconnection, and mutual implication of material and nonmaterial. Whereas it may be the case that written language is the prime example of the first category and tools the prime example of the second, language also has to be worked out in practices from which it derives much of its meaning. Equally, we have seen that material items can be placed within language-like codes. But there is some support from cognitive psychology for a general difference between the two types of knowledge. For example, Bechtel (1990, p. 264) argues that rule-based models of cognition are naturally good at quite different types of activity from connectionist models. Where the first is appropriate for problem solving, the second is best at tasks such as pattern recognition and motor control. It seems likely then that the skills involved in material practice and the social, symbolic, and moral meanings that are implicated in such practices might involve different cognitive systems than involved in rules and representations.

Bloch (1991) argues that practical knowledge is fundamentally different from linguistic knowledge in the way it is organized in the mind. Practical knowledge is "chunked" into highly contextualized information about how to "get on" in specific domains of action. Much cultural knowledge is nonlinear and purpose dedicated, formed through the practice of closely related activities. I have argued here that even the practical world involves social and symbolic meanings that are not organized representational codes but that are chunked or contextually organized realms of activity in which emotions, desires, morals, and social relations are involved at the level of implicit taken-for-granted skill or know-how.

It should perhaps be emphasized that the two types of material symbolism—the representational and the evocative or implicative—often work in close relation to each other. Thus a set of practices may associate men and women with different parts of houses or times of day, but in certain social contexts these associations might be built upon to construct symbolic rules of separation and exclusion and to build an abstract representational scheme in which mythology and cosmology play a part (e.g., Yates, 1989). Such schemes also have ideological components that feed back to constrain the practices. Thus practice, evocation, and representation interpenetrate and feed off each other in many if not all areas of life. Structure and practice are recursively related in the "structuration" of material life (Giddens, 1979; see also Bourdieu, 1977).

Material Meanings in Time

It appears that people both experience and "read" material culture meanings. There is much more that could be said about how material culture works in the social context. For instance, some examples work by direct and explicit metaphor, where similarities in form refer to historical antecedents, whereas others work by being ambiguous and abstract, by using spectacle or dramatic effect, by controlling the approach of the onlooker, by controlling perspective. Although there is not space here to explore the full range of material strategies, it is important to establish the temporal dimension of lived experience.

As already noted, material culture is durable and can be given new meanings as it is separated from its primary producer. This temporal variation in meaning is often related to changes in meaning across space and culture. Archaeological or ethnographic artifacts are continually being taken out of their contexts and reinterpreted within museums within different social and cultural contexts. The Elgin Marbles housed in the British Museum take on new meanings that are in turn reinterpreted antagonistically in some circles in Greece. American Indian human and artifact remains may have a scientific meaning for archaeologists and biological anthropologists, but they have important emotive and identity meanings for indigenous peoples.

Material items are continually being reinterpreted in new contexts. Also, material culture can be added to or removed from, leaving the traces of reuses and reinterpretations. In some cases, the sequence of use can give insight into the thought processes of an individual, as when flint flakes that have been struck off a core in early prehistory are refitted by archaeologists today (e.g., Pelegrin, 1990) in order to rebuild the flint core and to follow the decisions made by the original flint knapper in producing flakes and tools. In other cases, longer frames of time are involved, as when a monument such as Stonehenge is adapted, rebuilt, and reused for divergent purposes over millennia up to the present day (Chippindale, 1983). In such an example, the narrative held within traces on the artifact has an overall form that has been produced by multiple individuals and groups, often unaware of earlier intentions and meanings. Few people today, although knowledgeable about Christmas practices, are aware of the historical reasons behind the choice of Christmas tree, Santa Claus, red coats, and flying reindeer.

There are many trajectories that material items can take through shifting meanings. For example, many are made initially to refer to or evoke metaphorically, whereas through time the original meaning becomes lost or the item becomes a cliché, having lost its novelty. An artifact may start as a focus but become simply a frame, part of an appropriate background. In the skeuomorphic process a functional component becomes decorative, as when a gas fire depicts burning wood or coal. In other cases the load of meaning invested in an artifact increases through time, as in the case of a talisman or holy relic. Material items are often central in the backward-looking invention of tradition, as when the Italian fascist movement elevated the Roman symbol of authority—a bundle of rods—to provide authority for a new form of centralized power.

This brief discussion of the temporal dimension emphasizes the contextuality of material culture meaning. As is clear from some of the examples given, changing meanings through time are often involved in antagonistic relations between groups. Past and present meanings are continually being contested and reinterpreted as part of social and political strategies. Such conflict over material meanings is of particular interest to qualitative research in that it expresses and focuses alternative views and interests. The reburial of American Indian and Australian aboriginal remains is an issue that has expressed, but perhaps also helped to construct, a new sense of indigenous rights in North America and Australia. As "ethnic cleansing" reappears in Europe, so too do attempts to reinterpret documents, monuments, and artifacts in ethnic terms. But past artifacts can also be used to help local communities in productive and practical ways. One example of the active use of the past in the present is provided by the work of Erickson (1988) in the area around Lake Titicaca in Peru. Information from the archaeological study of raised fields was used to reconstruct agricultural systems on the ancient model, with the participation and to the benefit of local farmers.

Method

The interpretation of mute material evidence puts the interactionist view under pressure. How can an approach that gives considerable importance to interaction with speaking subjects (e.g., Denzin, 1989) deal with material traces for which informants are long dead or about which informants are not articulate?

I have already noted the importance of material evidence in providing insight into other components of lived experience. The methodological issues that are raised are not, however, unique. In all types of interactive research the analyst has to decide whether or not to take commentary at face value and how to evaluate spoken or unspoken responses. How does what is said fit into more general understanding? Analysts of material culture may not have much spoken commentary to work with, but they do have patterned evidence that has to be evaluated in relation to the full range of available information. They too have to fit different aspects of the evidence into a hermeneutical whole (Hodder, 1992; Shanks & Tilley, 1987). They ask, How does what is done fit into more general understanding?

In general terms, the interpreter of material culture works between past and present or between different examples of material culture, making analogies between them. The material evidence always has the potential to be patterned in unexpected ways. Thus it provides an "other" against which the analyst's own experience of the world has to be evaluated and can be enlarged. Although the evidence cannot "speak back," it can confront the interpreter in ways that enforce self-reappraisal. At least when a researcher is dealing with prehistoric remains, there are no "member checks" because the artifacts are themselves mute. On the other hand, material culture is the product of and is embedded in "internal" experience. Indeed, it could be argued that some material culture, precisely because it is not overt, self-conscious speech, may give deeper insights into the internal meanings according to which people lived their lives. I noted above some examples of material culture being used to express covert meanings. Thus the lack of spoken member checks is counteracted by the checks provided by unspoken material patterning that remain able to confront and undermine interpretation.

An important initial assumption made by those interpreting material culture is that belief, idea, and intention are important to action and practice (see above). It follows that the conceptual has some impact on the patterning of material remains. The ideational component of material patterning is not opposed to but is integrated with its material functioning. It is possible therefore to infer both utilitarian and conceptual meaning from the patterning of material evidence.

The interpreter is faced with material data that are patterned along a number of different dimensions simultaneously. Minimally, archaeologists distinguish technology, function, and style, and they use such attributes to form typologies and to seek spatial and temporal patterning. In practice, however, as the discussion above has shown, it has become increasingly difficult to separate technology from style or to separate types from their spatial and temporal contexts. In other words, the analytic or pattern-recognition stage has itself been identified as interpretive.

Thus at all stages, from the identification of classes and attributes to the understanding of high-level social processes, the interpreter has to deal simultaneously with three areas of evaluation. First, the interpreter has to identify the contexts within which things had similar meaning. The boundaries of the context are never "given"; they have to be interpreted. Of course, physical traces and separations might assist the definition of contextual boundaries, such as the boundaries around a village or the separation in time between sets of events. Ritual contexts might be more formalized than or may invert mundane contexts. But despite such clues there is an infinity of possible contexts that might have been constructed by indigenous actors. The notion of context is always relevant when different sets of data are being compared and where a primary question is whether the different examples are comparable, whether the apparent similarities are real.

Second, in conjunction with and inseparable from the identification of context is the recognition of similarities and differences. The interpreter argues for a context by showing that things are done similarly, that people respond similarly to similar situations, within its boundaries. The assumption is made that within the context similar events or things had similar meaning. But this is true only if the boundaries of the context have been correctly identified. Many artifacts initially identified as ritual or cultic have later been shown to come from entirely utilitarian contexts. Equally, claimed cross-cultural similarities always have to be evaluated to see if their contexts are comparable. Thus the interpretations of context and of meaningful similarities and differences are mutually dependent.

The identification of contexts, similarities, and differences within patterned materials depends on the application of appropriate social and material culture theories. The third evaluation that has to be made by the interpreter is of the relevance of general or specific historical theories to the data at hand. Observation and interpretation are theory laden, although theories can be changed in confrontation with material evidence in a dialectical fashion. Some of the appropriate types of general theory for material culture have been identified above. The more specific theories include the intentions and social goals of participants, or the nature of ritual or cultic as opposed to secular or utilitarian behavior.

In terms of the two types of material meaning identified earlier, rules of representation are built up from patterns of association and exclusion. For example, if a pin type is exclusively associated with women in a wide variety of contexts, then it might be interpreted as representing women in all situations. The aspect of womanhood that is represented by this association with pins is derived from other associations of the pins—perhaps with foreign, nonlocal artifacts (Sorensen, 1987). The more richly networked the associations that can be followed by the interpreter, and the thicker the description (Denzin, 1989) that can be produced, the subtler the interpretations that can be made.

For the other type of material meaning, grounded in practice, the initial task of the interpreter is to understand all the social and material implications of particular practices. This is greatly enhanced by studies of modern material culture, including ethnoarchaeology (Orme, 1981). Experimental archaeologists (Coles, 1979) are now well experienced in reconstructing past practices, from storage of cereals in pits to flaking flint tools. Such reconstructions, always unavoidably artificial to some degree, allow some direct insight into another lived experience. On the basis of such knowledge the implications of material practices, extending into the social and the moral, can be theorized. But again it is detailed thick description of associations and contexts that allows the material practices to be set within specific historical situations and the particular evocations to be understood.

An example of the application of these methods is provided by Merriman's (1987) interpretation of the intentions behind the building of a wall around the elite settlement of Heuneberg, Germany, in the sixth century B.C. (an example similar to that provided by Collingwood, 1956). In cultural terms, the Hallstatt context in central Europe, including Germany, can be separated from other cultural areas such as the Aegean at this time. And yet the walls are made of mud brick and they have bastions, both of which have parallels only in the Aegean. In practice, mud brick would not have been an effective long-term form of defense in the German climate. Thus some purpose other than defense is supposed. The walls are different from other contemporary walls in Germany and yet they are similar to walls found in the Aegean context. Other similarities and differences that seem relevant are the examples of prestige exchange—valuable objects such as wine flagons traded from the Aegean to Germany. This trade seems relevant because of a theory that elites in central Europe based their power on the control of prestige exchange with the Mediterranean. It seems likely, in the context of such prestige exchange, that the walls built in a Mediterranean form were also designed to confer prestige on the elites who organized their construction. In this example the intention of the wall building is interpreted as being for prestige rather than for defense. The interpretation is based on the simultaneous evaluation of similarities and differences, context and theory. Both representational symbolism (conferring prestige) and practical meanings (the building of walls by elites in a non-Mediterranean climate) are considered. For other examples of the method applied to modern material culture, see Hodder (1991) and Moore (1986).

Confirmation

How is it possible to confirm such hypotheses about the meanings of mute material and written culture? Why are some interpretations more plausible than others? The answers to such questions are unlikely to differ radically from the procedures followed in other areas of interpretation, and so I will discuss them relatively briefly here (see Denzin, 1989; Lincoln & Guba, 1985). However, there are some differences in confirming hypotheses regarding material objects. Perhaps the major difficulty is that material culture, by its very nature, straddles the divide between a universal, natural science approach to materials and a historical, interpretive approach to culture. There is thus a particularly marked lack of agreement in the scientific community about the appropriate basis for confirmation procedures. In my view, an interpretive position can and should accommodate scientific information about, for example, natural processes of transformation and decay of artifacts. It is thus an interpretive position that I describe here.

The twin struts of confirmation are coherence and correspondence. Coherence is produced if the parts of the argument do not contradict each other and if the conclusions follow from the premises. There is a partial autonomy of different types of theory, from the observational to the global, and a coherent interpretation is one in which these different levels do not produce contradictory results. The partial autonomy of different types of theory is especially clear in relation to material culture. Because material evidence endures, it can continually be reobserved, reanalyzed, and reinterpreted. The observations made in earlier excavations are continually being reconsidered within new interpretive frameworks. It is clear from these reconsiderations of earlier work that earlier observations can be used to allow different interpretations—the different levels of theory are partially autonomous. The internal coherence between different levels of theory is continually being renegotiated.

As well as internal coherence there is external coherence—the degree to which the interpretation fits theories accepted in and outside the discipline. Of course, the evaluation of a coherent argument itself depends on the application of theoretical criteria, and I have already noted the lack of agreement in studies of material culture about foundational issues such as the importance of a natural science or humanistic approach. But whatever their views on such issues, most of those working with material culture seem to accept implicitly the importance of simplicity and elegance. An argument in which too much special pleading is required in order to claim coherence is less likely to be adopted than is a simple or elegant theory. The notion of coherence could also be extended to social and political issues within and beyond disciplines, but I shall here treat these questions separately.

The notion of correspondence between theory and data does not imply absolute objectivity and independence, but rather embeds the fit of data and theory within coherence. The data are made to cohere by being linked within theoretical arguments. Similarly, the coherence of the arguments is supported by the fit to data. On the other hand, data can confront theory, as already noted. Correspondence with the data is thus an essential part of arguments of coherence. There are many aspects of correspondence arguments that might be used. One is the exactness of fit, perhaps measured in statistical terms, between theoretical expectation and data, and this is a particularly important aspect of arguments exploiting the mute aspects of material culture. Other arguments of correspondence include the number of cases that are accounted for, their range in space and time, and the variety of different classes of data that are explained. However, such numerical indications of correspondence always have to be evaluated against contextual relevance and thick description to determine whether the different examples of fit are relevant to each other. In ethnographic and historical contexts correspondence with indigenous accounts can be part of the argument that supports contextual relevance.

Other criteria that affect the success of theories about material culture meaning include fruitfulness—how many new directions, new lines of inquiry, new perspectives are opened up. Reproducibility concerns whether other people, perhaps with different perspectives, come to similar results. Perhaps different arguments, based on different starting points, produce similar results. I have already noted that one of the advantages of material evidence is that it can continually be returned to, unexcavated parts of sites excavated and old trenches dug out and reexamined. Intersubjective agreement is of considerable importance although of particular difficulty in an area that so completely bridges the science-humanity divide. The success of interpretations depends on peer review (either informal or formally in journals) and on the number of people who believe, cite, and build on them.

But much depends too on the trustworthiness, professional credentials, and status of the author and supporters of an interpretation. Issues here include how long the interpreter spent in the field and how well she or he knows the data: their biases, problems, and unusual examples. Has the author obtained appropriate degrees and been admitted into professional societies? Is the individual an established and consistent writer, or has he or she yet to prove her- or himself? Does the author keep changing her or his mind?

In fact, the audience does not respond directly to an interpretation but to an interpretation written or staged as an article or presentation. The audience thus responds to and reinterprets a material artifact or event. The persuasiveness of the argument is closely tied to the rhetoric within which it is couched (Gero, 1991; Hodder, 1989; Spector, 1991; Tilley, 1989). The rhetoric determines how the different components of the discipline talk about and define problems and their solutions.

Conclusion

Material culture, including written texts, poses a challenge for interpretive approaches that often stress the importance of dialogue with and spoken critical comment from participants. Material culture evidence, on the other hand, may have no living participants who can respond to its interpretation. Even if such participants do exist, they may often be unable to be articulate about material culture meanings. In any case, material culture endures, and so the original makers and users may be able to give only a partial picture of the full history of meanings given to an object as it is used and reinterpreted through time.

The challenge posed by material culture is important for anthropological and sociological analysis because material culture is often a medium in which alternative and often muted voices can be expressed. But the "reader" of material culture must recognize that only some aspects of material culture meaning are language-like. The meaning of much material culture comes about through use, and material culture knowledge is often highly chunked and contextualized. Technical operations implicate a wide network of material, social, and symbolic resources and the abstract meanings that result are closely tied in with the material.

The methods of interpretation of material culture center on the simultaneous hermeneutical procedures of context definition, the construction of patterned similarities and differences, and the use of relevant social and material culture theory. The material culture may not be able directly to "speak back," but if appropriate procedures are followed there is room for the data and for different levels of theory to confront interpretations. The interpreter learns from the experience of material remains—the data and the interpreter bring each other into existence in dialectical fashion. The interpretations can be confirmed or made more or less plausible than others using a fairly standard range of internal and external (social) criteria.

References

Bechtel, W. (1990). Connectionism and the philosophy of mind: An overview. In W. G. Lycan (Ed.), *Mind and cognition: A reader.* Oxford: Basil Blackwell.

Bloch, M. (1991). Language, anthropology and cognitive science. *Man, 26,* 183-198.

Bourdieu, P. (1977). *Outline of a theory of practice.* Cambridge, UK: Cambridge University Press.

Braithwaite, M. (1982). Decoration as ritual symbol. In I. Hodder (Ed.), *Symbolic and structural archaeology* (pp. 80-88). Cambridge, UK: Cambridge University Press.

Chippindale, C. (1983). *Stonehenge complete.* London: Thames & Hudson.

Coles, J. M. (1979). *Experimental archaeology.* London: Academic Press.

Collingwood, R. (1956). *The idea of history.* Oxford, UK: Oxford University Press.

Denzin, N. K. (1989). *Interpretive interactionism.* Newbury Park, CA: Sage.

Derrida, J. (1978). *Writing and difference.* London: Routledge & Kegan Paul.

Donley, L. (1982). House power: Swahili space and symbolic markers. In I. Hodder (Ed.), *Symbolic and structural archaeology* (pp. 63-73). Cambridge, UK: Cambridge University Press.

Erickson, C. L. (1988). Raised field agriculture in the Lake Titicaca Basin: Putting ancient agriculture back to work. *Expedition, 30*(3), 8-16.

Ferguson, L. (1991). Struggling with pots in Colonial South Carolina. In R. McGuire & R. Paynter (Eds.), *The archaeology of inequality* (pp. 28-39). Oxford: Basil Blackwell.

Gero, J. (1991). Who experienced what in prehistory? A narrative explanation from Queyash, Peru. In R. Preucel (Ed.), *Processual and postprocessual archaeologies* (pp. 126-189). Carbondale: Southern Illinois University.

Giddens, A. (1979). *Central problems in social theory.* London: Macmillan.

Glassie, H. (1975). *Folk housing in middle Virginia.* Knoxville: University of Tennessee Press.

Hodder, I. (1982). *Symbols in action.* Cambridge, UK: Cambridge University Press.

Hodder, I. (1989). Writing archaeology: Site reports in context. *Antiquity, 63,* 268-274.

Hodder, I. (1991). *Reading the past.* Cambridge, UK: Cambridge University Press.

Hodder, I. (1992). *Theory and practice in archaeology.* London: Routledge.

Latour, B. (1988). Mixing humans and nonhumans together: The sociology of a door closer. *Social Problems, 35,* 298-310.

Lemonnier, P. (1986). The study of material culture today: Towards an anthropology of technical systems. *Journal of Anthropological Archaeology, 5,* 147-186.

Leone, M. (1984). Interpreting ideology in historical archaeology. In D. Miller & C. Tilley (Eds.), *Ideology, power and prehistory* (pp. 25-36). Cambridge, UK: Cambridge University Press.

Leroi-Gourhan, A. (1964). *Le geste et la parole.* Paris: Michel.

Lincoln, Y. S., & Guba, E. G. (1985). *Naturalistic inquiry.* Beverly Hills, CA: Sage.

McGhee, R. (1977). Ivory for the sea woman. *Canadian Journal of Archaeology, 1,* 141-159.

Merriman, N. (1987). Value and motivation in prehistory: The evidence for "Celtic spirit." In I. Hodder (Ed.), *The archaeology of contextual meanings* (pp. 111-116). London: Unwin Hyman.

Miller, D. (1982). Artifacts as products of human categorisation processes. In I. Hodder (Ed.), *Symbolic and structural archaeology* (pp. 89-98). Cambridge, UK: Cambridge University Press.

Miller, D. (1985). *Artifacts as categories.* Cambridge, UK: Cambridge University Press.

Miller, D., Rowlands, M., & Tilley, C. (1989). *Domination and resistance.* London: Unwin Hyman.

Miller, D., & Tilley, C. (1984). *Ideology, power and prehistory.* Cambridge: Cambridge University Press.

Moore, H. (1986). *Space, text and gender.* Cambridge, UK: Cambridge University Press.

Orme, B. (1981). *Anthropology for archaeologists.* London: Duckworth.

Pelegrin, J. (1990). Prehistoric lithic technology. *Archaeological Review from Cambridge, 9,* 116-125.

Rathje, W., & Murphy, C. (1992). *Rubbish! The archaeology of garbage.* New York: HarperCollins.

Rathje, W., & Thompson, B. (1981). *The Milwaukee Garbage Project.* Washington, DC: American Paper Institute, Solid Waste Council of the Paper Industry.

Ricoeur, P. (1971). The model of the text: Meaningful action considered as text. *Social Research, 38,* 529-562.

Sanjek, R. (Ed.). (1990). *Fieldnotes: The makings of anthropology.* Albany: State University of New York Press.

Schlanger, N. (1990). Techniques as human action: Two perspectives. *Archaeological Review from Cambridge, 9,* 18-26.

Shanks, M., & Tilley, C. (1987). *Reconstructing archaeology.* Cambridge: Cambridge University Press.

Sorensen, M.-L. (1987). Material order and cultural classification. In I. Hodder (Ed.), *The archaeology of contextual meanings* (pp. 90-101). Cambridge, UK: Cambridge University Press.

Spector, J. (1991). What this awl means: Toward a feminist archaeology. In J. M. Gero & M. W. Conkey (Eds.), *Engendering archaeology* (pp. 388-406). Oxford: Basil Blackwell.

Tilley, C. (1989). Discourse and power: The genre of the Cambridge inaugural. In D. Miller, M. Rowlands, & C. Tilley (Eds.), *Domination and resistance* (pp. 41-62). London: Unwin Hyman.

Tilley, C. (Ed.). (1990). *Reading material culture.* Oxford: Basil Blackwell.

Washburn, D. (1983). *Structure and cognition in art.* Cambridge, UK: Cambridge University Press.

Webb, E. J., Campbell, D. T., Schwartz, R. C., & Sechrest, L. (1966). *Unobtrusive measures: Nonreactive research in the social sciences.* Chicago: University of Chicago Press.

Wobst, M. (1977). Stylistic behavior and information exchange. *University of Michigan Museum of Anthropology, Anthropological Paper, 61,* 317-342.

Yates, T. (1989). Habitus and social space. In I. Hodder (Ed.), *The meanings of things* (pp. 248-262). London: Unwin Hyman.

25

■

On the Authority of the Image

Visual Methods at the Crossroads

DOUGLAS HARPER

VISUAL sociology is primarily a subfield of qualitative sociology—the recording, analysis, and communication of social life through photographs, film, and video. Visual sociology is related to visual ethnography as it developed in anthropology, and to documentary photography, which has existed largely outside the university. At the present time, ethnography and documentary photography, the two sources for visual sociology, are being questioned and fundamentally recast. Thus visual sociology has one foot in a set of traditional approaches (visual ethnography and documentary photography) and the other in the experiments of the new ethnography and postmodern versions of documentary photography. It is a tricky position. Visual sociology must trace its roots to this shifting ground, holding on to what is valuable in the traditional while adopting elements of the new. In this chapter I will trace the origins and developments of visual sociology, discuss the current debates among the postmodern critics, and suggest an integrated approach for the future.

Visual Ethnography and the "Realist Tale"

Anthropology came into existence in the late decades of the nineteenth century and was first thought of as closely related to biology, at that time primarily a science of classification. Photography was useful in providing visual information for the classification of races used to support theories of social evolution, the main preoccupation of early anthropology. The story of photography's role in this early history is well told in a recent volume edited by Elizabeth Edwards (1992), who suggests that photography was first thought of "as a simple . . . truth-revealing mechanism" (p. 4) utilized throughout anthropology's worldwide research arena. By about 1920 photography had largely lost its importance in anthropology because research interests shifted to social organization, which was thought to be less visual, and because photography itself had begun to lose its mystique. By 1920, Edwards suggests, "photography had become just another ancillary tool in the fieldworker's arsenal. Photographs became . . . marginal to the process of explanation rather than becoming part of a centrally conceived resource . . . a technique perceived as recording surface rather than depth, which was the business of the anthropologist" (p. 4).

From this rather unpromising situation, Bateson and Mead, working in the 1930s, largely reinvigorated the use of visual methods in anthropology. But although their book, *Balinese Character* (Bateson & Mead, 1942), showed the potential of visual ethnography for a wide-ranging study of culture, it did not inspire a revolution in ethnographic methods. The importance of *Balinese Character* remains, however, for those seeking a current practice; I will examine it here in some detail.

Bateson and Mead had each studied and written about Balinese culture for nearly a decade when they turned to photographs:

> We were separately engaged in efforts to translate aspects of culture never successfully recorded by the scientist, although often caught by the artist, into some form of communication sufficiently clear and sufficiently unequivocal to satisfy the requirements of scientific enquiry . . . [our several monographs on the Bali] all attempted to communicate those intangible aspects of culture which had been vaguely referred as its *ethos.* As no precise scientific vocabulary was available, the ordinary English words were used, with all their weight of culturally limited connotations, in an attempt to describe the way in which the emotional life of these various South Sea people was organized in culturally standardized forms. (p. xi)

Finding words inadequate, they turned to a method whereby text and images mutually inform:

> We are attempting a new method of stating the intangible relationships among different types of culturally standardized behavior by placing side by side mutually relevant photographs. . . . By the use of photographs, the wholeness of each piece of behavior can be preserved, while the special cross-referencing desired can be obtained by placing the series of photographs on the same page. (p. xii)

The authors worked as a team, Bateson photographing as Mead directed. They made more than 25,000 photographs over a two-year field experience, from which they selected 759 for *Balinese Character.* These photographs were sorted into Balinese cultural categories: "spatial orientation and levels," "learning," "integration and disintegration of the body," "orifices of the body," "autocosmic play," "parents and children," "siblings," "stages of child development," and "rites of passage." Their book offered a new model for integrating images and text. For example, in the chapter on rites of passage, photographic plates (pages with between 6 and 10 photographs each) visualize subtopics such as tooth filing, marriage, funerals, exhumation, and other rituals. The photographs are in numbered sequence and face pages of detailed explanation, image by image. The analysis moves from the level of concept to detailed study of specific events, elements, or moments.

The significance of the Bateson and Mead project is that the photographs are regarded as a part of culturally informed observation. Bateson writes: "In general we found that any attempt to select for special details was fatal, and that the best results were obtained when the photography was most rapid and almost random" (Bateson & Mead, 1942, p. 50). The mass of visual data—25,000 images—were catalogued, studied, distilled, and sorted into themes that derived from the cultural knowledge of the anthropologists. The images were arranged in groups that allowed several perspectives on a single subject to be presented simultaneously, or in sequences that showed how a social event evolved through time. Single images are important primarily in how they become a part of more elaborate visual statements. Finally, the anthropologists explained the cultural meaning of the photographs in lengthy descriptions that they placed on facing pages, presenting a model for image/text balance and organization.

There have been no visual ethnographies that equal *Balinese Character* in depth or comprehensiveness. Several visual monographs have applied some of Bateson and Mead's working methods and presentational styles. These include Danforth and Tsiaras's (1982) study of death rituals of rural Greece, which follows the format of *Balinese Character* but concentrates on a single ritual; Cancian's (1974) visual ethnography of Mexican peasant culture, which studies deviance and social disorganization; and Gardner and Heider's (1968) visual ethnography of the largely ritualistic war of Dani of New Guinea. These and a small number of other visual ethnographies are at the more experimental end of what John Van Maanen (1988) calls the "realist tale" of ethnography.

The conventions of the "realist tale"—taken-for-granted aspects of traditional ethnography—obscure the problems inherent in the anthropologist's claims for scientific legitimacy. These conventions, according to Van Maanen (1988, pp. 46-49), define the author as scientific expert who, of course, uses technical language to communicate his or her findings. Thus the experiences or emotions of the author are as inappropriate in the conventional ethnography as they would be in a report of a genetics experiment. In the realist tale, the subject matter is a documentary accounting interpreted by theoretical concepts of anthropology. The point of view of the subjects is offered in quotes, separated from the rest of the text, keeping the voice of the author in control.

Photography had a natural place in these reports, regarded primarily as a *reflection* rather than as an *interpretation* of what was photographed. George and Louise Spindler (1967) in their foreword to John Collier's classic text on visual anthropology, comment:

> Usually an anthropologist takes a photograph to illustrate a finding that he has already decided is significant. . . . He waits until whatever it is happens, then points his camera at it. His camera then

> is incidental to his research activity and comes into use late in the fieldwork period. He uses the camera not as a research technique, but as a highly selective confirmation that certain things are so, or as a very selective sample of "reality." (p. x)

Spindler and Spindler later comment that Collier has argued for a more inductive photographic ethnography (particularly in the use of photographs to elicit interviews, which I will discuss later), but the table of contents of Collier's text shows photography in the service of the traditional ethnography. Collier argues that visual ethnography is an efficient way to survey and map material culture or social interaction, leading to techniques such as sociometric analysis.

Still photography in ethnography has not developed much beyond the handful of experiments cited here, which logically developed from the standard photographically illustrated ethnographic monograph. Visual anthropology has become mostly a discipline of film and video, as even a quick reading of the journals *Visual Anthropology* and *Visual Anthropology Review* attest. To the extent that anthropologists use photographs, they generally relegate them to record keeping or cataloguing.

Documentary Photography and the Development of Visual Sociology

Visual sociology began during the 1960s. The visual anthropology movement, centered in the Third World and increasingly concerned with film and video, had a minor impact on the parallel movement in sociology. Rather, the first visual sociologists tended to be inspired by documentary photographers working on many of the issues that sociologists felt ought to be on the sociological agenda. These included photographic studies of drugs and drug culture (Clark, 1971), black ghetto life (Davidson, 1970), small-town southern poverty and racism (Adelman, 1972), the southern civil rights movement (Hansberry, 1964), institutionalization (Jackson, 1977; Lyon, 1971), social class (Estrin, 1979; Owens, 1973), the unionization of migrant farmworkers (Fusco & Horowitz, 1970), the countercultural life (Simon & Mungo, 1972), the antiwar movement (Kerry, 1971), the free speech movement (Copeland, 1969), and the social irresponsibility of corporate capitalism (Smith & Smith, 1975). Aspiring visual sociologists drew inspiration from the liberal humanist tradition of documentary photography, which dated to Jacob Riis's (1890/1971) examination of the poverty of the urban immigrant, the Farm Security Administration photographic documentation of poverty during the 1930s (Agee & Evans, 1939; Stryker & Wood, 1973), and, more indirectly, Robert Frank's (1959/1969) photographic portrait of an alienated, materialistic American culture in the 1950s. These books were made up mostly of photographs, sometimes with a well-developed text (for example, in Smith & Smith, 1975) that generally provided background for the photos. The documentary photographers were not sociologists, and although their books lacked sociological frames or theories, the documentarians did have a great deal to offer sociologists seeking a more direct and critical sociology. Sociologists looking for a visual method recognized that the documentary photographers often had deep involvement with their subjects, and thus an insider's knowledge, much as would a sociological field-worker. Adelman's (1972) study of southern poverty and racism, for example, emerged from his experiences as a VISTA worker; Eugene and Aileen Smith (1975), while writing *Minamata,* lived for several years in the Japanese village poisoned by corporate mercury dumping. Some of these studies were autobiographical and showed the importance of subtle, cultural knowledge; Estrin (1979) photographed her upper-class family and friends, and Owens (1973) photographed his own suburban community. Others, like Robert Frank, a Swiss photographer, simply traveled around the United States making photographs, but his images (1959/1969) resonated with widely held sociological ideas. In the documentary movement there was very little, if any, discussion of the issues of representation, ideology, or how the relationships with subjects influenced these largely photographic studies. As mentioned, these studies were characterized by the sense that the photographer should expose social problems in order to educate the public in order to change society. This idea, we shall see later, has lost a great deal of its currency.

From this beginning Howard S. Becker's (1974) lead article in Volume 1, Number 1, of the first journal devoted to the study of visual communication defined the basis for a visual sociology. Becker noted that photography and sociology had about the same birth date and that they had both been concerned with, among other things, the exploration of society. Early issues of the *American Journal of Sociology* routinely used photographs; Lewis Hine's early twentieth-century photographic surveys of social problems such as child labor were supported by the Russell Sage Foundation. From the beginning of photography, however, there was a split between those who saw photography as description ("documentary" photography) and those who saw it as art. As sociology has become more like science, Becker points out, photography has become more like art. Thus sociology and photography had ceased, by the time of the writing of the article, to have much to do with each other; his article was intended to begin dialogue and cross-fertilization between the two. Sociologists should study photography, Becker suggests, because photographers have studied many of the same topics sociologists routinely study: communities, social problems, work, social class, the "ambience of urban life," and more abstract themes such as social types or modal personalities.

An important theme raised by Becker concerns the role of theory in photographic representation. Although photographs are potentially packed with information, photographers "tend to restrict themselves to a few reiterated simple statements. Rhetorically important as a strategy of proof, the repetition leads to work that is intellectually and analytically thin" (Becker, 1974, p. 11). To make the photographs "intellectually denser," Becker suggests that the photographer must become conscious of the theory that guides his or her photography. That theory may be "lay theory"—taken-for-granted assumptions about how the world is organized—or it may be "deep, differentiated and sophisticated knowledge of the people and activities they investigate . . . for photographic projects concerned with exploring society it means learning to understand society better" (p. 11). Recall that Bateson and Mead, both professional anthropologists, had spent several years in the field and had completed ethnographic studies of several aspects of the culture they then turned to with their cameras. Their theories of the group they photographed were correspondingly complex, and grounded in anthropological knowledge. Becker reminds us that photographs, often thought of as "truth," are more precisely reflections of the photographer's point of view, biases, and knowledge (or lack of knowledge). Thus the integration of photography and sociology must begin with the understanding of just how much *un*sociological photography we are accustomed to seeing. Sociological photography may be guided by sociological concepts, which grow inductively as one's theories are revised.

Becker addresses how issues of validity, reliability, and sampling are treated by the visual sociologist. In simple terms, these are the questions: Has the ethnographer reported accurately what she or he has seen? Is the event reported on repeated enough times so that the single event can be understood to stand for a regularly repeating class of events? Do the events reported characterize the behavior of the group?

The issue begins with the recognition that the photographic image is "true" in the sense (physical or electronic manipulation aside) that it holds the visual trace of the reality at which the camera was pointed. But the more fundamental issue is to recognize that all images, despite their relationship to the world, are socially and technically constructed. The credibility of an image should be based on commonsense reasoning and evidence, rather than on debates about the essential quality of the photograph. The more we know about how the photograph came into existence, the more we can judge its validity. Thus to the question of whether the photograph represents the *only* truth of a particular setting, the answer lies in "distinguishing between the statement that X is true about something and the statement that X is all that is true about something" (Becker, 1986, p. 252). The problem of validity and reliability is related to access: whether the photographer has been able to observe and photograph a full range of activities that explore the particular question he or she is interested in. The camera makes access more difficult; in some circumstances it makes it impossible. Because photographing is much more active than observing, it certainly influences how the field-worker is received in the field.

Because the camera portrays people clearly, the issue of fieldwork ethics has a special place in visual sociology. There is no formula that works in all situations, but the issue should be framed morally. Steven Gold (1989) suggests that for the visual ethnographer,

> sensitivity is rooted in a covenantal rather than contractual relationship between researcher and host. Unlike a contract that simply specifies rights and duties, a covenant requires the researcher to consider his or her relationship with subjects on a much wider level, accepting the obligations that develop between involved, interdependent persons. . . . For visual sociology, the concepts of sensitivity and covenantal ethics are clearly related. A researcher cannot engage in the reciprocal relationship required by the covenant without making efforts to understand his or her hosts' beliefs, values, and views of the world. Similarly, the covenantal ethnic reminds the researcher to consider his other subjects' needs when researching and publishing. (pp. 104-105)

Each project must be considered individually, and the researcher must apply all he or she knows from his or her own understanding of fieldwork methods to the visual project. Because the camera intrudes and reveals, it must be used with the wants, needs, and cultural perspectives of the subjects at the forefront of one's consciousness. Beyond that, each solution must be made individually.

Thus visual sociology draws on traditions of ethnographers using cameras to record what were thought to be exotic cultures and of concerned people photographing society for some of the same reasons sociologists study it, as well as from fieldwork practices in sociology. It has been said by many that the camera is a telling symbol of modernism: a machine that advances the purposes of an empirical science, of which sociology has traditionally been a part, a science whose existence itself is the result of the liberal agenda of social reform. But the assumptions that underlie sociology, documentary photography, and ethnography have shifted since Becker wrote what was a clarion call for sociologists to take up cameras. The larger mandate of science itself is questioned, as is sociology's status as a science; liberalism, for many, has lost its potency; photographs are seen as problematic and tentative statements rather than reflections of truth. Thus, although visual sociology must recognize its roots in the traditions of ethnography and documentary, it must acknowledge and integrate the insights of the new critical comment in these areas as well. I shall now introduce the critical takes on ethnography and photography.

New Ethnography

The idea of ethnography as "partial truth" rather than complete document lies at the basis of the new ethnography. The book or film (or other mode of communication) that represents culture is partial, or incomplete, because culture itself is not precisely boundaried and continually evolves. For example, Dorinne Kondo (1990), an American of Japanese descent who wrote an ethnography of a Japanese workplace through an analysis of her own complex, partially cross-cultural, experience, writes:

> Culture . . . is no reified thing or system, but a meaningful way of being in the world, inseparable from the "deepest" aspects of one's "self"—the trope of depth and interior space itself a product of our own cultural conventions. These cultural meanings are themselves multiple and contradictory, and though they cannot be understood without reference to historical, political and economic discourses, the experience of culture cannot be reduced to these nor related to them in any simple, isomorphic way. (pp. 300-301)

Kondo constructs cultural description through her own negotiation of a liminal status and thus teaches us as much by looking inward as through her interaction with her cultural others.

Ethnographic knowledge traditionally derives from the interaction between the subject and the researcher. The postmodern critique questions the normal assumptions surrounding this interaction. Stephen Tyler (1986), for example, suggests an ethnographic model consisting of "a cooperatively evolved text consisting of fragments of discourse intended to evoke in the minds of both reader and writer an emergent fantasy of a possible world of commonsense reality" (p. 125). Paul Stoller's account of his apprenticeship among sorcerers in western Niger (Stoller & Olkes, 1987) emerged from cultural collaboration of the deepest type imaginable, that of becoming a culturally alien spiritual being; the author's ethnographic presentation is novelistic—narrative, conversational, and personally probing. Other experiments are written in a way that intends to bring the reader to the cultural world, rather than to report on it from a distance. To communicate the essentially cyclical nature of the tramp experience, I describe six weeks on the road in the company of tramp workers (Harper, 1982). The book examines work and migration, elements of a repeating pattern in a migrant lifestyle, much as the experience itself unfolded. The center of the book is the relationship on the move between the writer and the tramp—a variation of a typical momentary but culturally organized social bond.

Finally, the new ethnography challenges the very idea of abstracted analysis: "Post-modern ethnography . . . does not move toward abstraction, away from life, but back to experience. It aims not to foster the growth of knowledge but to restructure experience; not to understand objective reality, for that is already established by common sense, nor to explain how we understand, for that is impossible, but to reassimilate, to reintegrate the self in society and to restructure the conduct of everyday life" (Tyler, 1986, p. 135). For example, David Sudnow's (1978) study of the organization of improvised conduct attempts to communicate what the hand feels or thinks as one plays keyboard jazz or types one's ideas. The language violates taken-for-granted assumptions about action and motive, and the description ventures into areas that had not been described before. Whether the inquiry is successful by the standards of traditional ethnography (speaking of demonstrable truth) is beside the point. We know a truth about the accomplishment of jazz through Sudnow's research, but this knowledge is more an empathic understanding than a basis for prediction.

From the vantage point of the new critique, then, ethnography is most usefully thought of as a created tale that comes a lot closer to describing reality if it is done without trying to fulfill the impossible and undesirable (for ethnography) standards of science. Ethnography should draw upon narrative; include the point of view, voice, and experience of the author; and experiment with ways of telling. Similar themes (with their own twists, of course) are found in critiques of photo documentary, which leaves visual ethnography in the position of drawing upon critical commentary from two very different locations, each suggesting change in a similar direction.

The Postmodernist Critique of Documentary Photography

The postmodern critique of documentary photography begins with the idea that the meaning of the photograph is constructed by the maker and the viewer, both of whom carry their social positions and interests to the photographic act. We are often reminded that the powerful, the established, the male, the colonizer typically portray the less powerful, less established, female, and colonized. Even exceptions such as Hubbard's (1991) collection of photographs by homeless children or Ewald's (1985) portraits and stories by Appalachian children are still, one can argue, part of this configuration in that the money, support, and editorial control of these books remain in the established publishing world.

The postmodern critique reminds us that the meaning of the photograph changes in different viewing contexts. The history of photography shifts from a history of the images of great photographers to a history of the uses of photographs, and whole photographic traditions. Excellent contemporary examples are case studies in the above-cited history of anthropological photography (Edwards, 1992). These case studies are not interesting to the extent that they tell us the size, shape, and material culture of long-disappeared Third World peoples, but they are interesting because they tell us how the colonials portrayed the colonized.

These insights confront the idea that photographs carry documentary truthfulness in the manner taken for granted in early anthropological or documentary photography. They also challenge the oft-stated notion that documentary photographs show the human condition—something we all supposedly recognize but cannot define.

The second overarching concern in the postmodern critique of documentary is the assertion that even if documentary was once a part of liberal humanism, liberal humanism is now thought of as a failed program based on naive assumptions. In Martha Rosler's (1989) words:

> In the liberal documentary, poverty and oppression are almost invariably equated with misfortunes caused by natural disasters: causality is vague, blame is not assigned, fate cannot be overcome. . . . Like photos of children in pleas for donations to international charity organizations, liberal documentary implores us to look in the face of deprivation and to weep (and maybe to send money). (p. 307)

Documentary photography advances the causes of a liberal system because it does not see the ideological aspects of its own patterns of representation. As noted above, documentary typically focuses on the specific and thus hides or mutes the critiques of the system; social problems are seen as personal stories and social ugliness is made beautiful or provocative. All of these characteristics of documentary photography, says the postmodern critic, obscure the very social realities the documentarian wishes to portray. These critical themes may be uncomfortable for many, but they cannot be ignored.

Building a Visual Sociology

What can we say about a visual approach for today's and tomorrow's sociology? The following will be relevant for sociologists who want to do research and/or to teach visually, often separate groups with related but slightly different orientations and goals. I will look at the contributions of the four elements discussed thus far: traditional visual ethnography, documentary photography, and postmodern critiques directed to both practices.

Although an emerging visual sociology cannot treat business as usual, there are many elements in traditional ways of doing things that remain useful. First is the realization that to accomplish in-depth understanding one must undertake long and intense periods of field research. In fact, in our own first experiences in the field we think and photograph from our own cultural lenses. We must learn to see through the lenses of the cultural Other—in the ways field-workers always have gained cultural knowledge. The irony for visual sociology is that one can take an extraordinary number of photographs in a very short time (*National Geographic* photographers, for example, routinely expose a hundred rolls of film—3,600 separate images—*per day*), and creating so much *information* tricks one into thinking one has created *knowledge*. I experienced this phenomenon when photographing the work of a backwoods mechanic (Harper, 1987b). The transition from images that communicated poverty and disorder to those that showed community and creative intelligence was made only with the spirited involvement of my subject/friend. Thus the first step to a vital visual ethnography is the same level of commitment that is necessary for all field research.

The second principle of traditional ethnography that must be retained is the indispensable role of theory in our work. This means simply that our photographic work should be guided by ideas that, directly or indirectly, relate to sociology. There is probably no better example than *Balinese Character,* discussed above. I assign visual sociology students the task of photographing sociological ideas—often a simple idea such as social interaction—and the discussions that emerge from the class viewing of the images have been the richest I have had as a teacher. It is disarmingly difficult to answer the question, as the group gazes at a student's photos: What sociological idea are you exploring with these photographs? How might you have better explored these ideas? The discussions typically lead from a very simple idea to several levels of complexity. Student interaction is intense as students learn from each other's experiments and seek their own solutions. Sociological thinking becomes a kind of problem solving that makes the world increasingly intelligible.

The point must be carried into our own work. We must continually remember that while we are photographing we are, indeed, gathering information; but that information must be created, organized, and presented in terms of ideas that we can verbalize. If we do not work from such a perspective, we will create visual information that will unconsciously reflect our personal taken-for-granted assumptions—the very thing that sociologists should suspend as they enter and try to understand the worlds of others.

It may be that photography works better with microtheory than with macrotheory, but just because photography does not easily facilitate such standard procedures as variable analysis (images could be sorted, compared, or otherwise analyzed statistically, but it probably would not be the best use of photographic information), that does not mean that photography cannot confront critical questions about social structure or social organization. Photographers such as El Lissitzky and Alexander Rodchenko used photomontage in the 1920s in the Soviet Union to describe the evolving sensibilities of the revolution; John Heartfield, working in Germany in the years before World War II, used photomontage to debunk and unmask Nazism (Ades, 1976). Leo Frankenberger (1991), a contemporary student of visual sociology, built photomontages from documentary photographs of a neighborhood to be demolished, onto which he fastened images of the people who live and lived in the neighborhood. His photomontage takes us inside the exteriors of the soon to be destroyed buildings to understand the lives lived there. These kinds of projects may work mostly as metaphor; rather than making the kind of statement sociologists expect from statistical studies, they are suggestive, empathic, descriptive.

I am suggesting in these comments that visual sociology begin with traditional assumptions and practices of sociological fieldwork and sociological analysis. The photograph can be thought of as data; in fact, the unique character of photographic images forces us to rethink many of our assumptions about how we move from observation to analysis in all forms of sociological research. But note that I suggest that image making and analysis *begins* with these and other traditional assumptions and practices. It does not end there.

Visual sociology has probably the least connection to the traditional practice of documentary photography, partly because traditional photo documentary has lost much of the cultural influence it asserted through much of the twentieth century. Documentary projects have evolved more experimental, personal, or abstracted forms, which sometimes provide models for a visual sociology. Jacob Holdt's (1985) decades-long voyage through the American underclass, for example, radically confronts the practice of making social problems beautiful or artful—Holdt used a cheap pocket camera and drugstore developing and did not frame images with an artist's eye. The visual confrontation with the subject is intensely direct and is mated to a text that forcefully tells the story of the ongoing journey and the human dramas that unfold along the way. Nick Waplington (1991) takes us to the mundane events of British working-class weekends; his photographs document the energetic, chaotic, person-filled "back stage" of life—people lying around, bodies askew on rough and serviceable furniture; kids playing a hundred games of their own invention; families drinking beer and pinching each other; men fixing old cars on the streets in front of their flats; women shopping, laden with their kids. The emphasis on the mundane, for Waplington, vitalizes a documentary practice that has tended to emphasize the spectacular. The result is visual ethnography of daily life that directly explores concepts of front stage/back stage familiar to all students of social interaction.

In general, however, documentary practice has moved closer to fine arts photography—relying on more subtle and abstract forms of photographic expression—at the same time that much fine arts photography has evolved to a kind of diffused social criticism, much more suggestive than evidential or literal, emerging more from the photographer's *view* of society than from a sustained analysis. It is difficult to imagine that visual sociology borrows directly from these forms aside from experiments, as suggested above.

We turn next to insights and contributions from critiques of documentary and ethnography.

Crafting Tales

We begin with the traditional sociology report—the use of third person, the pretense of "objectivity," the language of analysis—qualified, dispassionate, precise, and arid. The new ethnography embraces diametric oppositions to these forms: the first person, the understanding that all presentation is subjective, the language of narrative—vibrant, suggestive, engaged, and passionate. Photographs can, of course, serve either function. The photo on one's driver's license, for example, objectively and dispassionately documents one's identity. And, as developed above, photography in the service of traditional ethnography has worked largely in this spirit. Our understanding of photography as constructed, embodying, in fact, the essence of our point of view, however, leads us to see photography as a natural part of a new ethnography. Tales can easily be visual; we are accustomed to the idea of images-through-time in film. Images can organized in sequences that explore sociological ideas; these visual narratives might explore cycles in a cultural life (Harper, 1987a)—the migration, work, and drinking sprees of migrant workers, or the peasant pilgrimages of Europe (Bot, 1985). Emmet (1989) uses a photo narrative to describe nearly 10 years in the lives of a family of migrant farmworkers. These experiments in visual narrative scratch the surface of a potential method in a new ethnography.

Photo Elicitation

The new ethnography seeks to redefine the relationship between the researcher and the subject. The ideal model suggests collaboration rather than the traditional sense of research as a one-way flow of information, from subject to researcher, on terms and in terms of the researcher. The technique of photo elicitation promises a particularly apt alternative: a model for collaboration in research. Photo elicitation, first described by Collier (1967), is a very simple variation on the theme of open-ended interviewing. The open-ended interview is an exchange initiated and guided by the researcher in which the subject, one hopes, provides in-depth responses to complex questions. The open-ended interview rests on the assumption that the researcher will ask questions that are culturally meaningful to the subject. As most people who have done this kind of research know, it is more easily described than accomplished. In the photo-elicitation interview, interview/discussion is stimulated and guided by images. Typically these are photographs that the researcher has made of the subject's world (Gold, 1991; Harper, 1987b). A shocking thing happens in this interview format; the photographer, who knows his or her photograph as its maker (often having slaved over its creation in the darkroom) suddenly confronts the realization that he or she knows little or nothing about the cultural information contained in the image. As the individual pictured (or the individual from the pictured world) interprets the image, a dialogue is created in which the typical research roles are reversed. The researcher becomes a listener and one who encourages the dialogue to continue. The individual who describes the images must be convinced that his or her taken-for-granted understanding of the images is not shared by the researcher, often a startling realization for the subject as well.

This method has yet to catch on as a frontline sociological method, yet its potential is nearly endless. The photo interview may take place with photographs people have in their home collections, as many of my students have done. The photos may come from a historical archive, and may be used to re-create a historical understanding, a method I am using in an ongoing study of a dairy farm community. Or the method may stretch the collaborative bond to the end that the subjects direct the making of photographs before interpreting them in interviews, as done in a study of a Dutch neighborhood by a group of Dutch students (van der Does, Edelaar, Gooskens, Liefting, & van Mierlo, 1992). The well-achieved photo-elicitation interview really redefines the essential relationships of research, and the natural form for presenting this research is that of evenly constructed conversations.

These sensibilities from the new ethnography open the door for a creative and engaged visual ethnography. Given the expressive potential of photography and the intellectual ferment surrounding experiments in ethnography, the marriage of visual methods and ethnography seems natural.

Postmodern Critique of Documentary

It is in the postmodern critique of documentary where perhaps the greatest challenges to and, at the same time, some of the most useful contributions to a developing visual sociology lie. At its extreme, this critique calls for the end of photography, linking the photographic gaze to politically reactionary voyeurism. As noted above, this critique has characterized traditional documentary as linked to the prevailing power centers, thus reinforcing existing social arrangements even when it attempts to criticize. Part of this comes from the fact that photography typically focuses on discernible individuals or events; the power arrangements of the society are visually abstract, perhaps invisible. A response is to create photographic/textual statements that are critiques of documentary—demasking how prevailing forms of documentary communicate (Rosler, 1989). These acts of deconstruction are defined as Marxist because they suggest how social groups gain and maintain control through cultural manipulation, and are informed by a Freudian critique that asserts that our own act of seeing in the traditional documentary is fueled by voyeuristic pleasure (Clough, 1992).

So the postmodern critic/"photographer" more typically appropriates images from the culture, usually from mass media, and juxtaposes these images (or parts of images) to other scraps from the culture; words, phrases from mass culture or other sources (at times, photographs by the critic, such as in the work of Burgin, 1986) that serve as metaphor rather than as analysis. These comments about the culture are seen as an act of deconstruction, much as were the collages of John Heartfield and other artists from eras in which art was a more progressive cultural force. Although some of the statements that emerge from these practices lead us to see class and gender relations and oppression in new and provocative ways, they are hardly revolutionary. The artist/critic has all too often withdrawn from society to offer a commentary on the nature of social life. If visual sociology follows this path, it will become the expression of artistic opinion rather than the study of social life.

Where, then, lies the contribution of the postmodern criticism of the documentary? First is the important shift from concern with the "great artists of the documentary" to the study of the history of the uses of photography. Here visual sociology becomes a form of critical history, well demonstrated by Edwards (1992), cited above. With this understanding comes a certain loss of naïveté and what has to be considered sociological understanding.

Second, and relatedly, the new criticism allows us to confront the problem of ideology, the manner in which unequal relationships are hidden or ignored in the practice of photography. Traditionally this has meant that photography has been implicated as part of the power and domination that lie behind the relationship of the colonized or the native (the subject of the ethnography) and the colonizing culture, that of the ethnographer, but it includes issues of gender and class. Noteworthy examples are Solomon-Godeau's (1991) several studies of gendered photography, including her deconstruction and reconsideration of erotic photography, her development of Jean Clair's characterization of "the gaze as erection of the eye" in order to "better understand—in order to combat effectively—the complex network of relations that meshes power, patriarchy, and representation" (p. 237), and her several essays that begin to define a feminist photographic aesthetic and practice.

The new ethnographers must understand power relationships outside of the small social units they study, and they need to see their own work in the context of larger frames of power. To these ends, the visual sociologist working in the area of social criticism has much to gain from the sensibilities of those working in what has come to be known as the postmodern left.

I take a practical attitude toward the future of visual sociology. Although visual sociology has not exactly become a mass movement, changes in sociology itself (including a growing criticism of traditional empiricism and the experimental movements in ethnography cited above) are taking place; there is a growing body of visual work (including a professional journal, *Visual Sociology*) and a sponsoring organization, the International Visual Sociology Association, which has held conferences on visual sociology for more than a decade and is doing quite well indeed. Those who have used and taught visual methods share an excitement of discovery and creation. It is clear that visual representations help us learn ourselves; they help us communicate to others; they help us teach our students to see and struggle through their own attempts at recording, analyzing, and communicating. Most fundamentally, images allow us to make kinds of statements that cannot be made by words; thus images enlarge our consciousness and the possibilities for our sociology. Click!

References

Adelman, B. (1972). *Down home.* New York: McGraw-Hill.

Ades, D. (1976). *Photomontage.* New York: Pantheon.

Agee, J., & Evans, W. (1939). *Let us now praise famous men.* Cambridge, MA: Houghton Mifflin.

Bateson, G., & Mead, M. (1942). *Balinese character: A photographic analysis.* New York: New York Academy of Sciences.

Becker, H. S. (1974). Photography and sociology. *Studies in the Anthropology of Visual Communication, 1*(1), 3-26.

Becker, H. S. (1986). *Doing things together.* Evanston: Northwestern University Press.

Bot, M. (1985). *Misere: The great pilgrimages of penance in Europe.* Rotterdam, Netherlands: Marrie Bot.

Burgin, V. (1986). *Between.* London: Basil Blackwell.

Cancian, F. (1974). *Another place.* San Francisco: Scrimshaw.

Clark, L. (1971). *Tulsa.* New York: Lunstrum.

Clifford, J., & Marcus, G. E. (Eds.). (1986). *Writing culture: The poetics and politics of ethnography.* Berkeley: University of California Press.

Clough, P. T. (1992). *The end(s) of ethnography: From realism to social criticism.* Newbury Park, CA: Sage.

Collier, J., Jr. (1967). *Visual anthropology: Photography as a research method.* New York: Holt, Rinehart & Winston.

Copeland, A. (Ed.). (1969). *People's park.* New York: Ballantine.

Danforth, L., & Tsiaras, A. (1982). *Death rituals of rural Greece.* Princeton, NJ: Princeton University Press.

Davidson, B. (1970). *E100 Street.* Cambridge, MA: Harvard University Press.

Edwards, E. (Ed.). (1992). *Anthropology and photography 1860-1920.* New Haven, CT: Yale University Press.

Emmet, H. L. (1989). *Fruit tramps: A family of migrant farmworkers.* Albuquerque: University of New Mexico Press.

Estrin, M. L. (1979). *To the manor born.* Boston: Little, Brown.

Ewald, W. (1985). *Portraits and dreams.* New York: Writers & Readers.

Frank, R. (1969). *The Americans.* New York: Aperture. (Original work published 1959)

Frankenberger, L. (1991). Going out of business in Highland Park. *Visual Sociology Review, 6*(1), 24-32.

Fusco, P., & Horowitz, G. D. (1970). *La causa.* New York: Collier.

Gardner, R., & Heider, K. (1968). *Gardens of war: Life and death in the New Guinea stone age.* New York: Random House.

Gold, S. J. (1989). Ethical issues in visual field work. In G. Blank, J. McCarthy, & E. Brent (Eds.), *New technology in sociology: Practical applications in research and work* (pp. 99-112). New Brunswick, NJ: Transaction.

Gold, S. J. (1991). Ethnic boundaries and ethnic entrepreneurship: A photo-elicitation study. *Visual Sociology, 6*(2), 9-23.

Hansberry, L. (1964). *The movement.* New York: Simon & Schuster.

Harper, D. (1982). *Good company.* Chicago: University of Chicago Press.

Harper, D. (1987a). The visual ethnographic narrative. *Visual Anthropology, 1*(1), 1-19.

Harper, D. (1987b). *Working knowledge: Skill and community in a small shop.* Chicago: University of Chicago Press.

Holdt, J. (1985). *American pictures.* Copenhagen: American Pictures Foundation.

Hubbard, J. (1991). *Shooting back: A photographic view of life by homeless children.* San Francisco: Chronicle.

Jackson, B. (1977). *Killing time.* Ithaca, NY: Cornell University Press.

Kerry, J. (1971). *The new soldier.* New York: Macmillan.

Kondo, D. (1990). *Crafting selves.* Chicago: University of Chicago Press.

Lyon, D. (1971). *Conversations with the dead.* New York: Holt, Rinehart & Winston.

Owens, B. (1973). *Suburbia.* San Francisco: Straight Arrow.

Riis, J. A. (1971). *How the other half lives.* New York: Dover. (Original work published 1890)

Rosler, M. (1989). In, around and afterthoughts (on documentary photography). In R. Bolton (Ed.), *The contest of meaning: Critical histories of photography.* Cambridge: MIT Press.

Simon, P., & Mungo, R. (1972). *Moving on standing still.* New York: Grossman.

Smith, W. E., & Smith, A. (1975). *Minamata.* New York: Holt, Rinehart & Winston.

Solomon-Godeau, A. (1991). *Photography at the dock: Essays on photographic history, institutions and practices.* Minneapolis: University of Minnesota Press.

Spindler, G., & Spindler, L. (1967). Foreword. In J. Collier, Jr., *Visual anthropology: Photography as a research method.* New York: Holt, Rinehart & Winston.

Stoller, P., & Olkes, C. (1987). *In sorcery's shadow.* Chicago: University of Chicago Press.

Stryker, R., & Wood, N. (1973). *In this proud land.* Greenwich: New York Graphic Society.

Sudnow, D. (1978). *Ways of the hand: The organization of improvised conduct.* Cambridge, MA: Harvard University Press.

Tyler, S. A. (1986). Post-modern ethnography: From document of the occult to occult document. In J. Clifford & G. E. Marcus (Eds.), *Writing culture: The poetics and politics of ethnography* (pp. 122-140). Berkeley: University of California Press.

van der Does, S., Edelaar, S., Gooskens, I., Liefting, M., & van Mierlo, M. (1992). Reading images: A study of a Dutch neighborhood. *Visual Sociology, 7*(1), 4-68.

Van Maanen, J. (1988). *Tales of the field: On writing ethnography.* Chicago: University of Chicago Press.

Waplington, N. (1991). *Living room.* New York: Aperture.

26

Personal Experience Methods

D. JEAN CLANDININ
F. MICHAEL CONNELLY

It will be hard to put into words but here goes . . . you and I were sitting on opposite sides of a huge room, it seemed like a loft or something huge like that . . . and all that was left around us were the rafters and beams and some of the boards on the wall. . . . we were calling across this long distance to each other, surrounded by this building that was coming down. . . . there seemed to be a sense of urgency for us and we were shouting, not angrily. . . . Somehow there was a sense that soon something was going to crash and we would have to leave or something . . . anyway a sense of the time running out. . . . When I woke up I was telling you that we should sit beside each other and talk rather than shout at each other across this huge room, at least for as long as we could still talk. . . . I don't know what it all means but I do think that perhaps if we sat beside each other we could go on talking until whatever was going to happen happened . . . and so I wonder if you would come and sit beside me (metaphorically speaking) so we could talk. . . . Do you think you could do that? . . . or would you like me to walk across the room to sit beside you. . . . I am walking now and saying that I wish we could spend whatever time we have left talking and working with each other. . . . I want to spend the time until the huge barn or whatever it was is gone. . . . I want to spend the time sitting next to you on the floor talking and working together.

Suppose we were to ask you as reader to tell us the meaning of this passage. What would you say? Chances are you would either speak freely, treating the passage as a kind of inkblot test, or you would refuse to comment, not knowing the context. Either way, the status of the passage as representing experience would be minimal and the emphasis in your response would be on presenting your own experience. The situation is controlled by us because we have brought the passage forward, and its experiential status depends upon what we choose to convey contextually. Is the passage an excerpt from a work of fiction? A likely possibility, given its content. Is it derived from a study? A likely possibility, as this is a chapter on method. Or is it an artifact created by us to introduce the chapter? Still another likely possibility. You have no way of knowing, and the choice of whether to leave the statement ambiguous or clarify its context is ours, depending on our purpose.

The passage is a verbatim transcript taken from a letter from one of our research participants to another. Knowing this, the status of the passage is clarified in important ways. You know that it is a passage written by a person to another person and witnessed, though the timing is not clear, by two researchers. The fact that it is a participant's experience and not a researcher's interpretation or reconstruction of it makes a difference to your understanding of the passage. Still, our experience as researchers is clearly intermingled here, if not for the participants, at least for you as reader because you know only what we have chosen to tell and that is a highly selective constructive act on our part, depending on the stories we wish to convey about our participants, ourselves as researchers, and ourselves as methodologists writing to other researchers.

Let us back the inquiry up one step, and instead of asking you the reader to respond to our question, let us tackle it ourselves. You become an observer of the intertwined experience of researcher and participant. Before providing any further context, we feel there are several experiential features of the passage worth noting. First, the opening content of the passage is a dream. We shall not get into validity and reliability questions over the relationship of written dream text, dreams, and life experience. There is a clear-cut context assumed by the author, who speaks in two voices, both as dreamer and as dream narrator to the colleague. Both voices speak as directly as human beings can of experience and both texts spoken by each voice are shaped as a story. Though there is no indication of temporal location, there is a temporal quality to both stories. In the dream the characters are waiting not quite passively as the room around them disassembles, and it is implied that in due course the building will be gone and that this will influence the relationship. There is an implicit plot line that takes place over time. Likewise, the narrator imagines the dream somehow to parallel events in the ongoing life of the participants, and the narrator's story closely parallels the dream story. The two are so intimately linked that a reader has to watch closely for the transition from dream to waking life; indeed, both stories are part of the participant's life experience.

Though two stories are clearly visible in the passage, and though it is possible to create a researcher story of the meaning of each of the stories in isolation and in relation to one another, the larger life story context from which both of these stories derive their meaning is missing for readers, but not, of course, for the participants. To return the interpretive task to our readers for the moment, it is unclear, for you, whether we, as researchers, are mere voyeurs of a life drama that we have been privileged to record or whether the drama takes place within the context of our own story, whether as researchers who have created a research setting in which the text was generated or whether the story takes place within the context of our own larger life story, in which case we, as researchers, are observing ourselves in participation with participants. It is even possible that we are the participants and that the study in question is an autobiographical one, a possibility that especially sharpens Rose's (1990) ethnographic question, "What are we doing here?" in which he is concerned not merely with the prosaic matter of researchers writing for status, postgraduate degrees, promotion, and tenure, but in the broader sense of building links between experiential inquiry and life experience more generally. What is entailed in "experiencing the experience" is the question highlighted.

We hope that this passage, and our account of it so far, will serve to whet your imagination of what it means to study experience. From time to time throughout this chapter we will return to this passage.

Our imagination as educators has been captured by the possibility of studying experience rather than using experience as a contextual given for educational discourse. We have been impressed with how universal the word *experience* is in education. The word *experience* is found in homes, schools, higher education, and adult learning institutions. It is found in the most practical discussions of education, and it is found in the most revered theoretical texts. It is owned by no subject field and is found in virtually any community of educational discourse. But, to use Adler and Van Doren's (1972) distinction, it tends to function as a word, not a term. It is mostly used with no special meaning and functions as the ultimate explanatory context: Why do teachers, students, and others do what they do? Because of their experience.

When experience becomes more central to theorizing and to understanding practice, it is often criticized as providing inappropriate data. Others offer more ideological objection that, in the end, comes down to arguments over the appropriate form of educational reasoning. These criticisms are not, of course, ad hoc; they constitute the politics of epistemology. From Kuhn (1970) in the sciences to Schwab (1964) in educational studies to Crews (1992) in literary criticism to Taylor (1989, 1992) in moral theory and multiculturalism, we see the shifting frames of reference that define acceptable knowledge and inquiry.

The social sciences are concerned with humans and their relations with themselves and their environments, and, as such, the social sciences are founded on the study of experience. Experience is, therefore, the starting point and key term for all social science inquiry. But scientific, social, and philosophical conditions conspire to create frames of reference that shift the definitions of what is acceptable in the study of experience. One of the current frames is the epistemological notion that meaning is contained in texts and that the study of texts, particularly their deconstruction, is the primary focus for education, anthropology, sociology, linguistic studies, and so forth. Watts (1992) points out that the current conjunction of poststructuralism with "remnants of the new left" has created what he calls a "linguistic left that has moved to center stage in contemporary academic life." This is reflected in a current disposition toward studying texts rather than people and their experience as well as in researchers' explicit and implicit imposition of text forms on experience. In effect, text forms represented by experience rather than the reverse are what are under study. These dispositions are based on the argument that experience cannot speak for itself and the focus needs to be on the meaning contained in texts and the forms by which they are constructed. One such line of thinking is essentially sociological and critical in origin and, roughly speaking, comes from the view that social organization and structure rather than people and experience are the appropriate starting points for social science inquiry. Rose (1990), for instance, writes about "the social forms such as the incorporated university that literally, textually, and legally frame the way we do the business of ethnography today" (p. 10). Another, contrasting, epistemological frame of reference argues that experience is too comprehensive, too holistic, and, therefore, an insufficiently analytic term to permit useful inquiry. This argument tends to be given by those whom Schön (1983, 1991) and Oakshott (1962) call "technical rationalists."

Following Schwab (1964), we call the arguments expressed in these frames of reference, respectively, formalistic and reductionistic. In the light of these objections to the study of experience, the problem of studying experience is to lay claim to the integrity of experience itself and to fend off either its formalistic denial through abstraction and the hegemonies of social organization and structure or its reduction into skills, techniques, and tactics. To do so is partly a matter of participating in the politics of method (Eisner, 1988), a process both Eisner and Pinar (1988) claim "is gaining a foothold for the study of experience."

These various objections, of course, all contain elements of truth important to the study of experience. On the one hand, raw sensory experience is, if not meaningless, next to it. Likewise, the extremes of formalism remove the particulars of experience. For example, E. M. Bruner (1986) writes that "experience structures expressions . . . but expressions also structure experience" (p. 6). In our effort to find a middle ground—a place where we can both say that we are involved in the study of experience and recognize the truths and epistemological values of reductionism and formalism—we have come to the study of narrative and storytelling. We make the assumption that experience is both temporal (D. Carr, 1986; Ricoeur, 1984) and storied (D. Carr, 1986; Crites, 1971; Heilbrun, 1988).

For us, keeping experience in the foreground comes about by periodic returns to the works of Dewey (1916, 1934, 1938). For Dewey, education, experience, and life are inextricably intertwined. In its most general sense, when one asks what it means to study education, the answer is to study experience. Following Dewey, the study of experience is the study of life, for example, the study of epiphanies, rituals, routines, metaphors, and everyday actions. One learns about education from thinking about life, and one learns about life from thinking about education. Sarason's (1988) autobiography makes the point that his life as psychologist and his life at large are intertwined. It is not that he fails to make a distinction between his job as a psychologist and the rest of his life. Rather, it is impossible to separate them in practice: He is a human being as a psychologist and he is a psychologist as a human being. Keeping this sense of the experiential whole is part of the study of narrative.

Broadly speaking, we follow D. Carr's (1986) middle-ground argument, in which the case is made that when persons note something of their experience, either to themselves or to others, they do so not by the mere recording of experience over time, but in storied form. Story is, therefore, neither raw sensation nor cultural form; it is both and neither. In effect, stories are the closest we can come to experience as we and others tell of our experience. A story has a sense of being full, a sense of coming out of a personal and social history.

With this as our standpoint we have a point of reference, a life and ground to stand on, for both imagining what experience is and imagining how it might be studied and represented in researchers' texts. Experience, in this view, is the stories people live. People live stories, and in the telling of them reaffirm them, modify them, and create new ones. For example, in our opening scenario, stories are told by an individual struggling to live a collaborative story with another. Her telling of the stories is an attempt to reaffirm her life story and to modify its living. Stories such as these, lived and told, educate the self and others, including the young and those, such as researchers, who are new to their communities.

A Note on Narrative

There is not space in this chapter to give a full account of narrative terms. We and others have provided extensive elaborations elsewhere (J. Bruner, 1990; Connelly & Clandinin, 1990; Denzin, 1989; Mishler, 1986; Polkinghorne, 1988). It is equally as correct to say *inquiry into narrative* as it is to say *narrative inquiry*. By this we mean that narrative is both phenomenon and method. Narrative names the structured quality of experience to be studied, and it names the patterns of inquiry for its study. To preserve this distinction, we use the reasonably well-established device of calling the phenomenon *story* and the inquiry *narrative*. Thus we say that people by nature lead storied lives and tell stories of those lives, whereas narrative researchers describe such lives, collect and tell stories of them, and write narratives of experience.

Some narrative terms important in our work are *temporality, scene, plot, multiple researcher "I's,"* and *character*. For us, time and place, plot and scene, work together to create the experiential quality of narrative. Scene or place is where the action occurs, where characters are formed and live out their stories and where cultural and social context play constraining and enabling roles. Time is essential to plot. From the point of view of plot, the central structure of time is past-present-future. D. Carr (1986) relates this three-part structure of time to three critical dimensions of human experience—significance, value, intention—and, therefore, of narrative writing. We have dealt with issues of author/researcher's voice as an issue of multiple "I's," drawing attention to the "I" who speaks as researcher, teacher, man or woman, commentator, research participant, narrative critic, and theory builder. Denzin (1989) outlines a similar set of narrative terms, such as *emplotment, text, plot, point of view, personal and impersonal narration,* and *author's voice*.

Levels of Experience

Some terms and distinctions have the quality of repeating themselves by generating the distinction time and again in each of the classes created by the distinctions. Dewey's theory of experience has this quality. An organism, for Dewey, is both individual and social. An individual's experience simultaneously has what he calls internal and existential conditions. For Dewey, a person does not have social experience: An individual is social—no sociality, no person; and vice versa. This quality shows up again in Dewey's thought where community is conceived of as an organism. Thus a community has individual and social qualities. This quality repeats itself as the focus of research attention shifts, say, from individual child, to classroom, to school, to community, to local government, and so on. Whatever is taken to be the individual—for example, a school—defines the existential level of social experience.

The foregoing is important to our purpose because it reveals the conceptual, and constructive, complexity of experience. What is taken to be experience is a function of the observer's interest. At any level there are internal and existential dimensions to be thought through. Furthermore, these dimensions are separable only in thought. In the process of trying to understand and make meaning of the experiential situation, it is the internal and existential whole that is ultimately of interest. In our dream scenario, for example, we might focus our attention on the dream, its telling, the life experience of the dream characters, our research experience of the dreamer's experience, or you, our reader's experience of the scenario and our account of it. Focusing on the dream narrator's experience raises questions of how this person feels in the telling, the moral tone both of the telling and of the dream, specific events in the narrator's life to which it is imagined the dream attaches, and so on. Existentially, questions arise about the person to whom the dream is told, what it is in the two people's relationship that makes the telling worthwhile, who they are and what kind of life they lead, the difference this makes to the telling, and so on. If we were, instead, to focus on our readers' experience, questions arise internally of your emotional, moral, and aesthetic reaction to the dream scenario, to the specific events that come to your mind as you read it, of why and what meaning it has for you, and so on. Existentially, questions arise about what you were doing reading this material, for what purpose, what sense it will make to whatever endeavors you are engaged in, and so on.

In the study of experience it is the researcher's intentionality that defines the starting and stopping points. One of the common laments of those who focus on experience in all its messy complexity is that they lose track of the forest for the trees and find it hard to draw closure to a study. There are no easy ways to sort this out beyond constantly attending to the researcher's purpose from beginning to end of the study. Constant attention to the why of the work goes beyond the simple matter of keeping the researcher's eye on matters of relevance. At least as important is the almost inevitable redefinition of purpose that occurs in experiential studies as new, unexpected, and interesting events and stories are revealed. This matter is often made painfully clear in collaborative work, where the shifting interests and intentions of more than one participant need to be kept in rhythmic balance if the study is to proceed. Suppose, for instance, that the dream scenario was revealed to one of us who thought it was important to our collaborative research story and, therefore, brought it forward for our research discussion. Suppose further that the other person saw little significance in it. In sorting out the matter, our collaborative intentions would be preeminent as we worked together to make sense of the dream scenario.

Situation, the central term in Dewey's theory of experience, is specified by two criteria, interaction and continuity. *Interaction* refers to the intersection of internal and existential conditions as recounted above. *Continuity* refers to the temporal positioning of every situation. Situations do not just happen; they are historical and temporally directional according to the intentionality of the organism undergoing experience. Thus to talk about experience is to talk temporally. D. Carr (1986), drawing on Husserl (1970) and other phenomenologists, lodges a situation in a past horizon called "retention" and a future horizon called "protention." Phenomenologically, according to this view, there is a sense of history even before there is a history. There are, of course, objections to the view that all experience has a temporal quality. Contemplation, for instance, is ordinarily thought of as nontemporal, and, of course, quite apart from theorizing on the matter, much research is concerned with generalizations and principles that are thought to be time independent. For our purposes, however, an adequate study of experience makes time subject to inquiry. Suppose, for example, a study is conducted of elementary school teachers' beliefs about language learning. One way of interpreting the results is to claim certain generalizations about elementary school teachers' beliefs. A narrative interpretation would understand the beliefs not so much as generalizations but as experiential artifacts: monuments constructed out of the internal and existential histories of the teachers involved. Following the first interpretation, the beliefs constitute a structure of generalizations normatively useful for school planners and reformers. On the second, experiential, interpretation the teachers' beliefs are a sign of personal and social historical conditions that convey meaning in the present and that point in different directions than did the first interpretation for school reform.

To summarize, methods for the study of personal experience are simultaneously focused in four directions: inward and outward, backward and forward. By *inward* we mean the internal conditions of feelings, hopes, aesthetic reactions, moral dispositions, and so on. By *outward* we mean existential conditions, that is, the environment or what E. M. Bruner (1986) calls reality. By *backward* and *forward* we are referring to temporality, past, present, and future. To experience an experience is to experience it simultaneously in these four ways and to ask questions pointing each way. The dream text raises questions about, for example, the dreamer's feelings (internal), the person to whom she is speaking and in what setting (external), their histories (backward), and where they are going (forward). Furthermore, each of the levels for possible stories (the dream, the dream text, the participants, their life experience, the researchers, the audience) can be experienced through the asking of questions in the four directions. In this way the experience of the experience, for example, the researchers' experience of the dream text experience, is multifaceted.

The stories that make meaning of the experience at any one of these levels are interrelated. This can be illustrated through a consideration of the duration of time appropriate to each possible inquiry into our dream scenario. (Time duration is only one among a variety of matters that a more comprehensive study of experience would consider.) The time of dreaming is unknown, possibly a few moments. The time it takes to read the dream text is, likewise, a matter of minutes. But the time to write the text is unknown and may have been no longer than the time it took to write or may have involved days or weeks as the dreamer deliberated on the meaning of the dream and whether or not to tell it to her colleague. Temporal duration is significant to the meaning we might make of this event, and the inquiry would need to pursue these temporal matters. Likewise, the time interval between the dream's telling and the colleague's response, as well as the time it took to respond, would provide important material for telling the colleague's story and the participants' relationship generally. Even supposing that the dreaming, telling, and responding took place rapidly, over a short time span, the life context that gave meaning to the dreaming, telling, and responding might be years long. The duration of the life experience called up by the dream and by the participants' discussion would be significant to understanding what is happening here. The same line of thinking applies to us as researchers trying to make sense of the dream scenario, because we, too, need personal experiential referents to understand what is happening. Why are you (the reader) reading the dream text? The dreamer's story invokes experiential memories as we read the text and these memories, and their temporal duration relative to the life history of the participants, makes a difference to the research story we tell of the scenario. It is important, therefore, for us to understand the autobiographical quality of our own experience, the events and their temporal duration called up as we read and make meaning of the event. The same is true for you, our reader.

We have worked our way through the dream scenario and made use of Dewey's theory of inquiry because we believe it is important for those who study personal experience to be open to a rich and sometimes seemingly endless range of possible events and stories and to be prepared to follow leads in many directions and to hold them all in inquiry context as the work proceeds. Experience is messy, and so is experiential research. We shall now offer a structural simplification that should be of some help to those researchers who find themselves in a forest of events and stories pointing inward and outward, and backward and forward.

There are three sets of methodological questions that confront the researcher in finding his or her way through the forest. One set of questions has to do with the field of research experience, the second set with the texts told and written about the field experience, and the third set with the research account. Field, text, research account, and the relations among them, name primary kinds of decisions undertaken by those who study experience. The relations between researcher and field range from being a neutral observer to fully becoming part of the life of participants; the relations between researcher and text based on the field experience involve complex questions of the representation of experience, the interpretation and reconstruction of experience, and appropriate text forms. Questions of telling, that is, of the research account, come down to matters of autobiographical presence and the significance of this presence for the text and for the field. Matters of signature (Geertz, 1988) and voice are important.

We can ask all of these methodological questions of the dream text. The dream text, for example, stands between the field of experience of the participants and the texts that we researchers might write about it. For example, this chapter in which the dream text is now embedded raises questions about who we are within all three sets of questions: who we are in relation to the dream narrator and her colleague, who we are in relation to their text, and who we are as we interpret their text in our research accounts. These three sets of methodological questions serve as a structure for the remainder of this chapter.

Experiencing the Experience

As we begin work on a research project, we often talk about beginning a new story, a story of inquiry. Thinking about an inquiry in narrative terms allows us to conceptualize the inquiry experience as a storied one on several levels. Following Dewey, our principal interest in experience is the growth and transformation in the life stories we, our students, and research participants author. Therefore, difficult as it may be to tell a story, the more difficult but important task in narrative is the retelling of stories that allow for growth and change. We imagine, therefore, that in the construction of narratives of experience, there is a reflexive relationship between living a life story, telling a life story, retelling a life story, and reliving a life story. As researchers, we are always engaged in living, telling, reliving, and retelling our own stories. Our narratives of experience as Jean and Michael are always ongoing ones. We live out stories in our experiences, tell stories of those experiences, and modify them through retelling and reliving them. The research participants with whom we engage also live, tell, relive, and retell their own stories.

As researchers and participants come together, we are all already engaged in these narrative processes. The preconditions for any inquiry are set by prior inquiries. What this means is that there are narratives of inquiry out of which any particular inquiry grows and takes on meaning. These conditioning inquiries also have their own internal and existential conditions. All inquiry may, therefore, be seen as interactions of experiences of participants in a field and researchers' experiences as they come to that field. When we begin experiencing the experience, we need to be sensitive to the stories already being lived, told, relived, and retold. For example, the research participant whose dream text we shared on the first page of this chapter may have been engaged in conversations about her collaborative relationship with the other participant whether or not they were engaged in a research project with us. Our relationship as researchers with them may or may not have changed their ongoing conversation.

It is clear, however, that when we come together in research projects, all of us begin to live and tell a new story of our collaborative work together. For example, we might imagine that because of our research focus on collaboration, the two participants in the conversation about the dream are more aware of living a collaborative story and more intent on trying to figure out how to tell one. These new collaborative stories being lived and told as we work together in a research study also influence our other stories.

As researchers, we also tell another kind of story; that is, we try to tell or represent the story of the research project. We say more about writing the research story in a subsequent section on the transition from field texts to research texts. This consideration of the end of the research process brings us full circle to the beginnings of the inquiry, because in personal experience methods we must acknowledge the centrality of the researchers' own experience: their own tellings, livings, relivings, and retellings. Therefore, one of the starting points is the researchers' own narratives of experience. We try to gain experience of our experience through constructing narratives of that experience. It is here that we deal with questions of who we are in the field and who we are in the texts we write on our experience of the field experience. What becomes apparent here is that many of the ways we come in touch with our own experience, come to know what we know of our experience, is through stories. The methods we use in telling our stories of experience are similar to the ones we use with other research participants. We will discuss several methods here. Story is, however, central to each.

From Field to Field Texts

What are normally called data—journal entries, field notes, photographs, and so on—are, for us, better thought of as field texts. They are texts created by participants and researchers to represent aspects of field experience. Some documents that eventually became field texts may have been created prior to the inquiry, or even during the inquiry but for a different purpose. Such documents became field texts when they became relevant to the inquiry. The dream text is a case in point. How we get from field to field texts is a critical matter in personal experience methods. Central to the creation of field texts is the relationship of researcher to participant. We take for granted that all field texts are selectively chosen from field experience and thereby embody an interpretive process. Even audio and visual recordings are interpretive texts shaped by the recorder. What we want to add to this understanding is the importance of the relationship.

Researcher relationships to ongoing participant stories shape the nature of field texts and establish the epistemological status of them. We assume that a relationship embeds meaning in the text and imposes form on the research texts ultimately developed. A field note is not simply a field note; a photograph is not simply a photograph; an oral history is not simply an oral history. What is told, as well as the meaning of what is told, is shaped by the relationship. The field text created may be more or less collaboratively constructed, may be more or less interpretive, and may be more or less researcher influenced. It depends. For example, the dream text was earlier presented as if it were not collaboratively constructed, not highly interpretive, and without researcher influence. Without knowing the relationship between us as researchers and the participants, you, our reader, have no way of knowing any of these things. If the situation was as implied, then the dream text would be a "realistic" representation of an aspect of the dreamer's life. In effect, the text would be comparatively close to, and representative of, an aspect of the participant's ongoing life. On the other hand, if the text was collaboratively constructed with the researchers, then it would be representative of the research and not of ongoing life without the research. Furthermore, we do not know if the dream text was a faithful record of a dream as it occurred or if it was, instead, an imaginative reconstruction of the emotional quality of the colleagues' relationship. In the latter case, the dream is less a descriptive account than an interpretive, semitheoretical expression. The epistemological status of the stories in the dream text is, therefore, unclear. They may have a "life as it is without influence by the researcher" quality or they may have the quality of stories self-consciously told for consumption by a research audience. Under these two circumstances the status of the stories as representing the field is entirely different. Not to be sensitive to the centrality of relationship in research can, therefore, lead to serious deceptions (Crites, 1979). We may deceive ourselves and others into thinking we know more about the participants' ongoing lives than is epistemologically warranted by our relationship to the participants. There are also interpretive deceptions possible on the side of theoretical understanding of field events in that we may think we have constructed more generalizable categories than warranted. These comments apply to each one of the methods described below for moving from field experience to field text. This is not an all-inclusive list of methods. Readers should also note that each of the methods described has its own body of literature and could take up a chapter on its own.

Oral History

One method for creating field texts is oral history. There is a range of strategies for obtaining an oral history, ranging from the use of a structured set of questions, in which the researchers' intentions are uppermost (Thompson, 1978), to asking a person to tell his or her own story in his or her own way (Anderson & Jack, 1991), in which the participant's intentions are uppermost. In commenting on their own work, Anderson and Jack (1991) write that shifting attention "from information gathering where the focus is on the right questions, to interaction, where the focus is on the process" (p. 23), illustrates the dynamic potential of collaboratively constructed oral history field texts. Depending on the character of the research relationship, the oral history will vary in focus in detailed ways, such as in the particular events narrated and in the emotional quality that appears in the field text. Oral history as a method of getting in touch with another's experience is closely connected with the methods of annals and chronicles.

Annals and Chronicles

Another method for creating field texts is to have participants construct annals of their lives or parts of their lives. An annal, for us, is a line schematic of an individual's life divided into moments or segments by events, years, places, or significant memories. The construction of an annal allows researchers and participants to gain a sense of the whole of an individual's life from his or her point of view. Annals often allow individuals to represent visually something of the topography of their life experiences, the highs and lows, the rhythms they construct around their life cycles. We know, of course, that the way a person constructs an annal is only one representation of his or her life. The way each individual tells his or her own story not only depends upon the purposes and intentions he or she has at the time, but is also dependent upon how the individual is making sense of the researcher's intentions and purposes. Once again, the relationship between researcher and participant makes a difference to the annal constructed.

After a participant has constructed an annal, we ask him or her to tell stories, to construct chronicles around the points marked on the annal. To return for a moment to the opening sequence of this chapter, we might imagine that the research participant who narrated her dream would, if asked to construct an annal, mark the significant moments of what is clearly an important collaborative relationship on her annal. Further, if asked to tell stories, to chronicle these moments, she may tell of meeting her collaborator, of beginning to work collaboratively, of times of tension, and so on.

Frequently we involve participants in creating annals and chronicles as a way to scaffold their oral histories, of beginning the process of having them re-collect their experiences. Annals and chronicles are also a way to begin to hear a person's family stories.

Family Stories

A related method of creating field texts is the telling or writing of family stories. Family stories are stories handed down across generations about family members and family events. Through family stories, people learn self-identity. Phrases such as "You're just like your grandfather" evoke grandfather stories and identify the person with the storied grandfather. The experience of family stories has existential and internal conditions; as Stone (1988) notes:

> The family's first concern is itself, but its second realm of concern is its relation to the world. Family stories about the world are usually teaching stories, telling members still at home the ways of the world according to the experiences its elders have had. . . . Family stories seem to persist in importance even when people think of themselves individually, without regard to their familial roles. The particular human chain we're part of is central to our individual identity. (p. 7)

Photographs, Memory Boxes, Other Personal/Family Artifacts

Many of us collect a variety of materials as we compose our lives. We may collect and save photographs of people remarkable to our lives in some way, of special events, of places. Each photograph marks a special memory in our time, a memory around which we construct stories. Other things find their way into what are sometimes called memory boxes. For instance, the first author's memory "box," not really a box at all, contains old ticket stubs, gifts and trinkets from friends, items made by her son in school, bits of jewelry, and so on. Each item marks a time, a person, an event. She constructs stories around the items. Other items belong more to her family and mark family moments and events. Her great-grandmother's worn quilt, handed down from daughter to daughter and now used to cover her son, the plates her grandmother gave to her mother, her grandfather's watch—all are items around which family stories are composed and told.

All of these items become triggers to our memories, to recollecting the "little fragments that have no beginning and no end" (O'Brien, 1991, p. 39) and around which we tell and retell stories. It is these artifacts collected in our lives that provide a rich source of memories.

Research Interviews

One widely used method of creating field texts is through interview (Mishler, 1986). Interviews can be turned into written field texts through transcription, note taking, and/or the selective use of interview segments. The way an interviewer acts, questions, and responds in an interview shapes the relationship and, therefore, the ways participants respond and give accounts of their experience. This point is illustrated in Anderson and Jack's (1991) commentary on an interview study, in which they write, "Interviewers had either ignored these more subjective dimensions of women's lives or had accepted comments at face value when a pause, a word, or an expression might have invited the narrator to continue" (p. 12). Furthermore, the kinds of questions asked and the ways they are structured provide a frame within which participants shape their accounts of their experience. For example, Belenky, Clinchy, Goldberger, and Tarule's (1986) question, "Looking back over your life, what relationships have been really important to you? Why?" (p. 232) creates a different frame from Mikel Brown's (1989) sequence of questions, "Could you describe to me a situation where you had to make a decision and you weren't sure what was the right thing to do? . . . When you were trying to decide what to do, what was the conflict in this situation?" (pp. 88-89).

In our work with research interviews, we have become aware that there are gender and culture differences in the way individuals experience research interviews. Minister (1991) makes the point that "topic selection determined by interviewer questions, one person talking at a time, the narrator 'taking the floor' with referential language that keeps within the boundaries of selected topics" (p. 35) makes a difference to the content of field texts. In our work, particularly with children and with individuals from other cultures, we have noticed similar effects.

Journals

A powerful way for individuals to give accounts of their experience is through journal writing. May Sarton (1982), poet, novelist, and writer of journals, notes that "journals are a way of finding out where I really am. . . . They have to do with encounters with people who come here, who talk to me, or friends whom I see, or the garden. They sort of make me feel that the fabric of my life has a meaning" (p. 25). E. Carr (1966), another writer of journals, notes that her journals seem to be "made up of scraps of nothing" (p. v). She likens her journal entries to the small English candies called Hundreds and Thousands, which are "so small that separately they are not worth eating" (p. v). However, she writes that "it was these tiny things that, collectively, taught me how to live. Too insignificant to have been considered individually, but like the Hundreds and Thousands lapped up and sticking to our moist tongues, the little scraps and nothingnesses of my life have made a definite pattern" (p. v).

Journals, mostly unpublished, are another method of creating field texts. Many individuals write journals in which they try to keep "ongoing records of practices and reflections on those practices" (Connelly & Clandinin, 1988, p. 34). Children and adolescents often write journals of their thoughts, activities, and stories in attempts to make sense of their experiences. We have also found many journal writers among the teachers with whom we work. In their journals they weave together their accounts of the private and the professional, capturing fragments of experience in attempts to sort themselves out.

Autobiographical Writing

Closely linked to journal writing is autobiographical writing (Grumet, 1988; Olney, 1980; Pinar, 1981). Our journals become a kind of autobiographical writing, but, as Carr and Sarton point out, journals capture the small fragments of experience and not so much a sense of the whole. Autobiographical writing is a way to write of the whole context of life. Molloy (1991) notes that autobiography "is always a re-presentation, that is, a retelling, since the life to which it supposedly refers is already a kind of narrative construct. Life is always, necessarily, a tale" (p. 5). The retelling of a life through autobiographical writing is another method of creating field texts that capture "a tension between self and others, of generating a reflection on the fluctuating place of the subject within its community" (p. 9).

As researchers of personal experience, we recognize that any piece of autobiographical writing is "a particular reconstruction of an individual's narrative, and there could be other reconstructions" (Connelly & Clandinin, 1988, p. 39). There can always be a rich array of possible field texts created as we write autobiographically. For us, however, when autobiographical writing is shaped into an autobiography or memoir (Hampl, 1991), it is a research text.

Letters

We find letters a particularly interesting field text (White & Epston, 1990). Letters, unlike journals, are written to another person with the expectation of a response. In letters we try to give an account of ourselves, make meaning of our experiences, and attempt to establish and maintain relationships among ourselves, our experience, and the experience of another. For example, we opened this chapter with an excerpt from a letter. As presented, the letter is a fragment. There is no salutation and no closure to frame the letter. The salutation and closure of a letter often define the relationship—that is, in Sarton's (1984) words, they "give the reader the sense of a whole moment in time and place" (p. 289). Excerpts, writes Sarton, "lack continuity and appear to take place in some literary limbo" (p. 289). The dream text has this character. In order for us to understand the meaning embedded in the dream text, we need, in addition to the contextual matters described earlier in the chapter, the salutation and the closure that would give some sense of the ongoing relationship as the other is addressed.

In personal experience research, letters, as a research method, may be used among participants, among research collaborators, or among researchers and participants. In each case one of their merits is the equality established, the give and take of conversation.

Conversations

Conversation is a generic term covering many kinds of activities. For example, letter writing is a kind of written conversation. However, the more common kind is oral conversation, between pairs or among groups of individuals. As researchers become aware of the ways research interviews have constrained participants' texts of their experience, some have started to set up more conversational forms as a personal experience method (Oakley, 1981). As with letter writing, conversations are marked by equality among participants and by flexibility to allow group participants to establish the form and topics important to their inquiry. Conversation entails listening. The listener's response may constitute a probe into experience that takes the representation of experience far beyond what is possible in an interview. Indeed, there is probing in conversation, in-depth probing, but it is done in a situation of mutual trust, listening, and caring for the experience described by the other. Once again, we see the centrality of relationship among researchers and participants.

Field Notes and Other Stories From the Field

A great deal has been written about field notes, the mainstay ethnographic data collection method (Sanjek, 1990; Van Maanen, 1988). Field notes may be written by researchers or by participants, and they may be written in more or less detail with more or less interpretive content. In each of the choices, there are consequences for the kind of field text created. Researchers need to be self-conscious about the kind of field record created. Field notes become an important field text in personal experience methods when we acknowledge the relationships we have as researchers with our participants. The nature of these relationships shape the construction of the records. It makes a great deal of difference if we distance ourselves from events in order to record notes or if we actively participate in events as a partner. Similarly, it makes a difference as we create field notes if we see ourselves as recorders of events "over there" or if we see ourselves as characters in the events.

In our opinion, researchers are often more reluctant than necessary to use field records. They worry that field notes will be insufficient to capture field experience adequately. When this happens, tape recorders and videotape tend to be overused, with severe transcription penalties later as field notes are made on the basis of the transcripts. In any event, it is the fear that somehow experience will be lost that drives researchers to try to record or tape all of experience. What we fail to acknowledge clearly enough is that all field texts are constructed representations of experience.

A Note on Ethics

In personal experience methods the ethical dimensions of researcher-participant relationships are highlighted. When we enter into a research relationship with participants and ask them to share their stories with us, there is the potential to shape their lived, told, relived, and retold stories as well as our own. These intensive relationships require serious consideration of who we are as researchers in the stories of participants, for when we become characters in their stories, we change their stories. In other places we have written that personal experience methods have the potential to generate new shared stories for participants and researchers in relationships that are akin to friendships (e.g., Clandinin & Connelly, 1988). As researchers we are also changed, but because we enter the relationships with certain intentions and purposes and, as the ones most often initiating the research relationship, our care and our responsibility is first directed toward participants. Autobiographical studies pose a somewhat unique case within this general point. In autobiographical studies, we must consider issues of care for those field texts and research texts we create about ourselves.

As we move from field texts to research texts, ethical issues remain of great importance. Because personal experience methods involve "real" people, and not just texts, we need to pay the closest attention to the aftermath of the research (Lightfoot, 1983). As personal experience researchers, we owe our care, our responsibility, to the research participants and how our research texts shape their lives. We all can find ourselves in the eventually constructed research texts. If as participants we are portrayed in an unexpected (for us) story, the research text may raise questions about the retelling and reliving of our stories. For researchers these issues of responsibility are always foregrounded as we construct research texts. Anonymity and other ways of fictionalizing research texts are important ethical concerns in personal experience methods. Even in an autobiographical work such as Oakley's (1992) *Taking It Like a Woman,* she cares for herself and other characters in her research text by fictionalizing sections of the work. In the dream text that opened this chapter, we too considered the aftermath of the research text by carefully fictionalizing the field text.

From Field Texts to Research Texts

Sometimes our field texts are so compelling that as researchers we want to stop and let them speak for themselves. Field texts may consist of inviting, captivating family stories, conversations, and even dream texts. But researchers cannot stop there, because the task is to discover and construct meaning in those texts. Field texts need to be reconstructed as research texts. To return to the dream text, for example, the stories told there, along with an array of associated field texts, might seem sufficient because of the coherence of their story lines and their interest to readers. But those texts with their various story lines, though interesting, tend only to define and set the terms for an inquiry. They are the texts of which one asks questions of meaning and social significance. What is the meaning(s) of the dream text and why does it make a difference to figure it out? These are the general questions that drive the transition from field texts to research texts. Responses to these inquiries ultimately shape the research text. Field texts are not, in general, constructed with a reflective intent; rather, they are close to experience, tend to be descriptive, and are shaped around particular events. They have a recording quality to them, whether auditory or visual. Research texts are at a distance from field texts and grow out of the repeated asking of questions concerning meaning and significance. Like Carr's (1966) *Hundreds and Thousands*, a research account looks for the patterns, narrative threads, tensions, and themes either within or across individuals' personal experience. It would be tempting to view this overall process as a series of steps. However, because collaboration occurs from beginning to end, plot outlines are continually revised as consultation takes place over written materials and as further field texts are collected to develop points of importance in the revised story.

The search for these patterns, narrative threads, tensions, and themes that constitutes the inquiry that shapes field texts into research texts is created by the writer's experience. And the researcher's experience, like experience generally, has internal and existential conditions. Just as the researcher's relationship to participants shaped the field text, the researcher's relationship to the inquiry and to the participants shapes the research text. It makes a difference whether the researcher imagines her- or himself as having an emotional and ethical relationship to the participant and to the inquiry. If the researcher cares about the ongoing relationship to the participants as well as to the ways the research account is read and for what purpose, it will make a difference to the way the research account is written. For instance, our collaborative relationships with teachers are carefully negotiated with an eye both to present relationships and to the ways the proposed collaboration will affect our future relations. As noted above, these concerns play out in the emotional and ethical aspects of living as well as in the research text.

Though researchers' internal conditions of experience have tended not to play an important role in research and have often been consciously silenced through such conventional writing expressions as "this research" or "the researcher," researcher voice and signature are now recognized terms in personal experience methods. Who the researchers are makes a difference at all levels of the research, and the signature they put on their work comes out of the stories they live and tell. Existential conditions have been much more acknowledged in research, although we find them played out somewhat differently in personal experience methods. The conditions of most interest to us for this chapter are the inquiry purposes, available forms for expression of the research text, and the audience and the researcher's imagined relations to the audience. Let us turn first to a discussion of the internal conditions of voice and signature.

Internal Conditions

Voice

There is a rich, developing literature on voice. In personal experience methods where there is a relationship between researcher and participants, there are issues of voice that arise for both. For many, especially for women being educated as researchers, voice is an acknowledgment that they have something to say. The methods of writing in liberal arts and science programs tend to emphasize accurate, summative readings of the works of others. But in research it is what the writer has to say, independently and not by way of summary, that matters. We think of this as the development of voice after silence. It is, perhaps, one of the most difficult transitions budding researchers need to make. Without a sense of voice, a researcher is bound to the ever-refined writing and rewriting of field texts at a time that calls for research texts.

But even when one has gained the confidence to inquire, rather than merely to summarize and interpret others, there is still, even for experienced researchers, a dilemma of voice in moving from field texts to research texts. This struggle for research voice is captured by the analogy of living on a knife edge as one struggles to express one's own voice in the midst of an inquiry designed to capture the participants' experience and represent their voices, all the while attempting to create a research text that will speak to, and reflect upon, the audience's voices. This sense of voice, and the dilemma that creates it, can never be sorted out except judicially. The researcher is always speaking partially naked and is genuinely open to legitimate criticism from participants and from audience. Some researchers are silenced by the invitation to criticism contained in the expression of voice.

There are other issues around voice. As we write our research texts, we need to consider the voice that is heard and the voice that is not heard. We may, for example, include the voice of a participant in such a way that she speaks her stories of teaching but not include her voice when she speaks her stories of being abused. Or, to look at the issue of voice in another way, we may include the voice of a participant in such a way that the context of the research text obscures or silences important parts of that participant's voice. There are multiple questions about voice, both our voices as researchers and the voices of participants as we construct our research texts. As researchers, we too struggle to speak our research texts in our multiple voices. Our silences, both those we choose and those of which we are unaware, are also issues of voice in our research texts.

Temporality is linked to voice. The question of who speaks in a text becomes important as we, and the stories we tell of our experience, change over time. An adult person speaking of her experience as a child raises the who speaks question. Is it the adult interpreting the childhood experience, in which case it is the adult speaking? Or is it the adult expressing the child's story as the child would have told the experience, in which case it is the child speaking? Field texts play a key role in sorting this out. Memory, unaided by field texts—for instance, a child's journal; parents', friends', and others' remembrances; photographs of the child—has an uncertain status and, for the most part, expresses a current voice rather than a historical voice.

Signature

Voice and signature are closely connected in the writing that transforms field texts into research texts. When a veil of silence is lifted and the writer knows he or she has something to say and feels the power of voice, that person still must find a way of saying what he or she wishes to speak. There is, says Geertz (1988), no more difficult dilemma for a writer than sorting out how to be in the text. "Being there in the text," he says, is even more difficult than "being there in the field." For Geertz, there are multiple forms for being there in the field as well as multiple forms for being there in the text. "Being there" in the special way that marks each of us as writers constitutes our research signature. The dilemma to which Geertz refers is the dilemma of how lively our signature should be: Too vivid a signature runs the risk of obscuring the field and its participants; too subtle a signature runs the risk of the deception that the research text speaks from the point of view of the participant.

The risks of an overly vivid signature are well known in the literature and come under the heading of the abuses of subjectivity. The risks of too flimsy a signature are not as well thought through, and it is here that modern-day researchers of personal experience need to pay close attention to their writing. The signature can be too thin because other texts and other theories, rather than the writer, sign the work. Equally, the signature can be too thin because the researcher imagines that the participants and their field texts author the work. Both ways of thinning the signature need to be guarded against. In gaining a voice and a signature for it, the researcher puts his or her own stamp on the work.

The text that follows from the signature has rhythm, cadence, and expression that marks the signature and makes the work readily identifiable as the work of a certain author or set of collaborators. This expression of the signature is called "discourse" by Geertz. The signature and its expression in discourse creates an author identity.

Existential Conditions

Three existential conditions of importance to personal experience methods in the movement from field texts to research texts are inquiry purposes, narrative forms, and audience and the researcher's imagined relations to them. We discuss each of these in turn.

Inquiry Purposes

The question raised earlier—What are we doing here?—comes to the forefront in the construction of research texts. Some argue that the act of working with participants in aid of their, and our, growth and transformation is sufficient justification for research work. But in research our responsibility goes beyond those with whom we work to a larger field and research community. Field texts will not adequately influence the discourse or the practices of those beyond the immediate research field. The research text performs this function. The temptation to conclude an inquiry at the stage of field texts combined with productive ongoing relationships with participants is vividly seen in autobiographical works where the construction of stories and their endless refinement into themes of control, power, expression, and so on are often felt to be so meaningful for the author that the question of who cares or who would want to read the autobiographical stories tends to be dismissed. Even in an autobiographical work it is crucial to write not only for the self but also for others. Writing for others takes place in the research text. In a fortuitous twist of fortune, the expressions of meaning contained in research texts are often profound for the self. Just as serving the self serves the community, so too serving the community in research texts also serves the self.

One of the special powers of personal experience methods is that their connection goes beyond theories, researchers, and practitioners, to the life community within which these traditional parties to inquiry relate. Personal experience research is a form of public inquiry that has the potential for transcending the specialties of research in particular subject fields. It does this because personal experience methods connect with fundamentally human qualities of human experience. Personal experience methods are human methods. For this reason the narrative form of the research texts is crucial to the texts' finding a place in public discourse.

Narrative Form

This book is being written at an important time in the development of personal experience methods. Marcus and Fischer (1986) call this time an "experimental moment." There is a willingness to experiment with narrative form. Literary (Bakhtin, 1981), visual (Chatman, 1980), poetic (Rose, 1990), dramatic (Turner, 1980), and other modes of expression are evident. These, and other, forms have recently been set out by Eisner (1991). Without going into detail, it is, perhaps, worth noting that just as painters learn to paint by adopting a painter's style so, too, one of the ways a person may experiment with narrative form is by adopting the signature of a favorite author. A writer might, for instance, experiment with research texts written in Virginia Woolf's or James Joyce's signature. Just as painters often develop their own styles as an outgrowth of experimentation with the signatures of well-known, accomplished painters, so, too, this experimentation eventually may lead to an individual's own research signature as narrative form is adapted to who he or she is. In this process of adaptation and the creation of signature, we are well advised to listen to the remnants of narrative form handed down to us by our own personal narrative histories.

Audience

Everything so far said here bears on the audience and our relationship to it. It makes a great deal of difference how we intend to interact with our audience through the research text. Following Chatman (1990), texts may be descriptive, expositional, argumentative, or narrative. All of these kinds of texts can be used in the service of others. For example, our narrative dream text could be used in a research text to "explain" to an audience how a collaborative relationship and the tensions within it function in inquiry. The dream text could also be part of a larger narrative research text that would invite members of the public to share in a collaborative inquiry relating communities of research and public communities. In the creation of research texts, researchers need to imagine themselves in conversation with an audience. What voice and signature mark the imagined audience? What voice and signature shall we adopt? What kind of conversation do we imagine will ensue?

Relationships Across the Boundaries

Our task in this chapter has been to set forth a discussion of personal experience methods. Inevitably, in doing so, we have transcended our task. What first appears as methods of collecting data turns out to involve an inquiry into the field, field texts, research texts, audience, and the larger community beyond the world of theory and practice defined in any particular study. Earlier we noted that the whole of the social sciences are founded on the study of experience. In our view, experience is the starting point and key term for all social science inquiry. We see personal experience methods as a way to permit researchers to enter into and participate with the social world in ways that allow the possibility of transformations and growth. Personal experience methods offer all of us, not only we as chapter authors, but you as reader, the opportunity to create a middle ground where there is a conversation among people with different life experiences. Personal experience methods inevitably are relationship methods. As researchers, we cannot work with participants without sensing the fundamental human connection among us; nor can we create research texts without imagining a relationship to you, our audience. Voice and signature make it possible for there to be conversations through the texts among participants, researchers, and audiences. It is in the research relationships among participants and researchers, and among researchers and audiences, through research texts that we see the possibility for individual and social change.

References

Adler, M., & Van Doren, C. (1972). *How to read a book.* New York: Simon & Schuster.

Anderson, K., & Jack, D. (1991). Learning to listen: Interview techniques and analyses. In S. Gluck & D. Patai (Eds.), *Women's words: The feminist practice of oral history* (pp. 11-26). New York: Routledge.

Bakhtin, M. M. (1981). *The dialogic imagination.* Austin: University of Texas Press.

Belenky, M., Clinchy, B., Goldberger, N., & Tarule, J. (1986). *Women's ways of knowing: The development of self, voice, and mind.* New York: Basic Books.

Bruner, E. M. (1986). Experience and its expressions. In V. Turner & E. Bruner (Eds.), *The anthropology of experience* (pp. 3-30). Chicago: University of Illinois Press.

Bruner, J. (1990). *Acts of meaning.* Cambridge, MA: Harvard University Press.

Carr, D. (1986). *Time, narrative, and history.* Bloomington: Indiana University Press.

Carr, E. (1966). *Hundreds and thousands: Journal of an artist.* Toronto: Irwin.

Chatman, S. (1980). What novels can do that films can't (and vice versa). In W. J. T. Mitchell (Ed.), *On narrative* (pp. 117-136). Chicago: University of Chicago Press.

Chatman, S. (1990). *Coming to terms: The rhetoric of narrative in fiction and film.* Ithaca, NY: Cornell University Press.

Clandinin, D. J., & Connelly, F. M. (1988). Studying teachers' knowledge of classrooms: Collaborative research, ethics, and the negotiation of narrative. *Journal of Educational Thought, 22,* 269-282.

Connelly, F. M., & Clandinin, D. J. (1988). *Teachers as curriculum planners: Narratives of experience.* New York: Teachers College Press.

Connelly, F. M., & Clandinin, D. J. (1990). Stories of experience and narrative inquiry. *Educational Researcher, 19*(5), 2-14.

Crews, F. (1992). *The critics bear it away: American fiction and the academy.* New York: Random House.

Crites, S. (1971). The narrative quality of experience. *Journal of the American Academy of Religion, 39,* 391-411.

Crites, S. (1979). The aesthetics of self-deception. *Soundings, 62,* 107-129.

Denzin, N. (1989). *Interpretive biography.* Newbury Park, CA: Sage.

Dewey, J. (1916). *Democracy and education.* New York: Macmillan.

Dewey, J. (1934). *Art as experience.* New York: Capricorn.

Dewey, J. (1938). *Experience and education.* New York: Collier.

Eisner, E. (1988). The primacy of experience and the politics of method. *Educational Researcher, 17*(5), 15-20.

Eisner, E. (1991). *The enlightened eye: Qualitative inquiry and the enhancement of educational practices.* New York: Macmillan.

Geertz, C. (1988). *Works and lives: The anthropologist as author.* Stanford, CA: Stanford University Press.

Grumet, M. (1988). *Bitter milk.* Amherst: University of Massachusetts Press.

Hampl, P. (1991). The need to say it. In J. Sternberg (Ed.), *The writer on her work* (Vol. 2). New York: W. W. Norton.

Heilbrun, C. (1988). *Writing a woman's life.* New York: W. W. Norton.

Husserl, E. (1970). *The crisis of European sciences and transcendental phenomenology* (D. Carr, Trans.). Evanston: Northwestern University Press.

Kuhn, T. S. (1970). *The structure of scientific revolutions* (2nd ed.). Chicago: University of Chicago Press.

Lightfoot, S. (1983). *The good high school.* New York: Basic Books.

Marcus, G. E., & Fischer, M. J. M. (1986). *Anthropology as cultural critique: An experimental moment in the human sciences.* Chicago: University of Chicago Press.

Mikel Brown, L. (1989). When is a moral problem not a moral problem? In C. Gilligan, N. Lyons, & T. Hanmer (Eds.), *Making connections: The relational worlds of adolescent girls at Emma Willard School.* Cambridge, MA: Harvard University Press.

Minister, K. A. (1991). A feminist frame for the oral history interview. In S. Gluck & D. Patai (Eds.), *Women's words: The feminist practice of oral history* (pp. 27-44). New York: Routledge.

Mishler, E. (1986). *Research interviewing: Context and narrative.* Cambridge, MA: Harvard University Press.

Molloy, S. (1991). *At face value: Autobiographical writing in Spanish America.* New York: Cambridge University Press.

Oakley, A. (1981). Interviewing women: A contradiction in terms. In H. Roberts (Ed.), *Doing feminist research* (pp. 30-61). London: Routledge & Kegan Paul.

Oakley, A. (1992). *Taking it like a woman.* London: Flamingo.

Oakshott, M. (1962). *Rationalism in politics.* London: Methuen.

O'Brien, T. (1991). *The things they carried.* Toronto: McClelland & Stewart.

Olney, J. (1980). *Autobiography: Essays theoretical and practical.* Princeton, NJ: Princeton University Press.

Pinar, W. F. (1981). Whole, bright, deep with understanding. *Journal of Curriculum Studies, 13*(3), 173-188.

Pinar, W. F. (1988). Preface. In W. F. Pinar (Ed.), *Contemporary curriculum discourse* (pp. v-vii). Scottsdale, AZ: Gorsuch Scarsdale.

Polkinghorne, D. E. (1988). *Narrative knowing and the human sciences.* Albany: State University of New York Press.

Ricoeur, P. (1984). *Time and narrative* (Vol. 1). Chicago: University of Chicago Press.

Rose, D. (1990). *Living the ethnographic life.* Newbury Park, CA: Sage.

Sanjek, R. (Ed.). (1990). *Fieldnotes: The makings of anthropology.* Albany: State University of New York Press.
Sarason, S. B. (1988). *The making of an American psychologist.* San Francisco: Jossey-Bass.
Sarton, M. (1982). *May Sarton: A self-portrait* (M. Simpson & M. Wheelock, Eds.). New York: W. W. Norton.
Sarton, M. (1984). *At seventy: A journal.* New York: W. W. Norton.
Schön, D. A. (1983). *The reflective practitioner: How professionals think in action.* New York: Basic Books.
Schön, D. A. (1991). *The reflective turn: Case studies in reflective practice.* New York: Teachers College Press.
Schwab, J. J. (1964). The structure of the disciplines: Meanings and significances. In G. W. Ford & L. Pugo (Eds.), *The structure of knowledge and the curriculum* (pp. 1-30). Chicago: Rand McNally.
Stone, E. (1988). *Black sheep and kissing cousins: How our family stories shape us.* New York: Times Books.
Taylor, C. (1989). *Sources of the self: The making of the modern identity.* Cambridge, MA: Harvard University Press.
Taylor, C. (1992). *Multiculturalism and "the politics of recognition."* Princeton, NJ: Princeton University Press.
Thompson, P. (1978). *The voice of the past: Oral history.* Oxford: Oxford University Press.
Turner, V. (1980). Social dramas and stories about them. In W. J. T. Mitchell (Ed.), *On narrative* (pp. 137-154). Chicago: University of Chicago Press.
Watts, S. (1992, April 29). Academic leftists are something of a fraud. *Chronicle of Higher Education,* pp. A40-A43.
White, M., & Epston, D. (1990). *Narrative means to therapeutic ends.* New York: W. W. Norton.
Van Maanen, J. (1988). *Tales of the field: On writing ethnography.* Chicago: University of Chicago Press.

27

■

Data Management and Analysis Methods

A. MICHAEL HUBERMAN
MATTHEW B. MILES

Definitions and Assumptions

DISCUSSIONS of qualitative data management and analysis have become more differentiated and integrated over the past decade. In 1976, Sieber's review of seven well-respected texts on field methods found that less than 5-10% of their pages were devoted to analysis as such; in 1979, Miles noted that the qualitative analyst had few guidelines for protection against self-delusion, let alone against unreliable or invalid conclusions more generally. We also commented that analysis methods were rarely reported in enough detail for readers to follow how a researcher got from 3,600 pages of field notes to the final conclusions (Miles & Huberman, 1984).

Today we have come far from that state of affairs. The database we consulted in the preparation of the 1994 edition of *Qualitative Data Analysis: An Expanded Sourcebook* had more than tripled since publication of the first edition (Miles & Huberman, 1984, 1994). There are new journals, several handbooks, innumerable conferences on qualitative issues, special interest groups, and new software packages. It is a growth industry. As a result, many new texts, including the present one, have by now made Sieber's finding obsolete. Gradually, the craft of data management and analysis is becoming explicitly shared. Still, much remains to be done. Competing, polemical arguments are rampant. It is still unlikely that a researcher could write a case study from a colleague's field notes that would be plausibly similar to the original.

In this chapter we focus on data management and analysis methods, aiming to point to useful work as well as to unsolved issues. In turn, we will outline some basic assumptions and definitions, discuss systematic data collection and management issues, and then turn to data analysis concerns—those occurring before and early during data collection, as well as later on, both within and across cases. We conclude with some general issues in analysis: the importance of data displays, threats to analytic validity, and the importance of "transparency"—shareability—of management and analysis procedures themselves.

Working Definitions

In this chapter, we define *data management* pragmatically as the operations needed for a systematic, coherent process of data collection, storage, and retrieval. These operations are aimed at ensuring (a) high-quality, accessible data; (b) documentation of just what analyses have been carried out; and (c) retention of data and associated analyses after the study is complete.

Our definition of *data analysis* contains three linked subprocesses (Miles & Huberman, 1984,

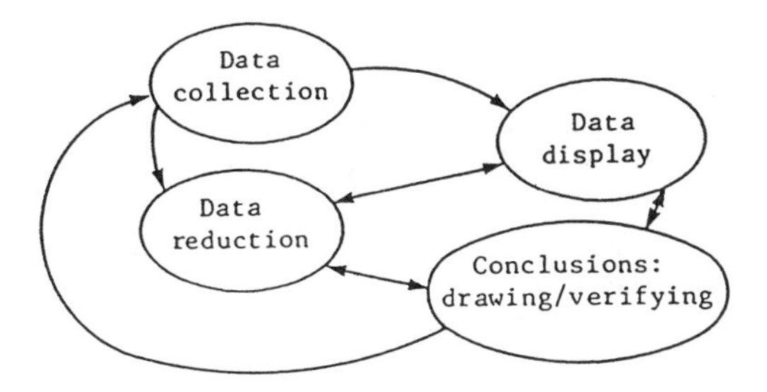

Figure 27.1. Components of Data Analysis: Interactive Model

1994): data reduction, data display, and conclusion drawing/verification (see Figure 27.1). These processes occur *before* data collection, during study design and planning; *during* data collection as interim and early analyses are carried out; and *after* data collection as final products are approached and completed.

With *data reduction,* the potential universe of data is reduced in an anticipatory way as the researcher chooses a conceptual framework, research questions, cases, and instruments. Once actual field notes, interviews, tapes, or other data are available, data summaries, coding, finding themes, clustering, and writing stories are all instances of further data selection and condensation.

Data display, defined as an organized, compressed assembly of information that permits conclusion drawing and/or action taking, is a second, inevitable, part of analysis. The researcher typically needs to see a reduced set of data as a basis for thinking about its meanings. More focused displays may include structured summaries, synopses (Fischer & Wertz, 1975), vignettes (Erickson, 1986), networklike or other diagrams (Carney, 1990; Gladwin, 1989; Strauss, 1987; Werner & Schoepfle, 1987a, 1987b), and matrices with text rather than numbers in the cells (Eisenhardt, 1989a, 1989b; Miles & Huberman, 1984, 1994).

Conclusion drawing and verification involve the researcher in interpretation: drawing meaning from displayed data. The range of tactics used appears to be large, ranging from the typical and wide use of comparison/contrast, noting of patterns and themes, clustering, and use of metaphors to confirmatory tactics such as triangulation, looking for negative cases, following up surprises, and checking results with respondents (Miles & Huberman, 1994). Many accounts of this aspect of analysis demonstrate that there is a multiple, iterative set of tactics in play (Chesler, 1987; Fischer & Wertz, 1975; Schillemans et al., n.d.) rather than one or two central ones. In this sense we can speak of "data transformation," as information is condensed, clustered, sorted, and linked over time (Gherardi & Turner, 1987).

Some Epistemological Assumptions

It is healthy medicine for researchers to make their preferences clear. To know how researchers construe the shape of the social world and how they mean to give us a credible account of it is to know just who we have on the other side of the table. When, for example, a realist, a critical theorist, and a social phenomenologist are competing for our attention, it matters a good deal to know where each is coming from. They will have diverse views of what is real, what can be known, and how these social facts can be rendered faithfully (Guba, 1990; Phillips, 1990; Ratcliffe, 1983).

In our case, we have advertised as "realists" (Huberman & Miles, 1985), but more precisely as "transcendental realists" (Bhaskar, 1978, 1989; Harré & Secord, 1973; Manicas & Secord, 1982). Fundamentally, we think that social phenomena exist not only in the mind, but in the objective world as well, and that there are some lawful, reasonably stable relationships to be found among them. The lawfulness comes from the sequences and the regularities that link phenomena together; it is from these that we derive the constructs that account for individual and social life.

This stance acknowledges the historical and social nature of knowledge, along with the meaning making at the center of phenomenogical experience (Packer & Addison, 1989; Polkinghorne, 1988). Our aim is to "transcend" these processes by carefully constructing explanations that can account for them in plausible ways. Thus transcendental realism calls both for causal explanation and for the evidence to show that each entity or event is an instance of that explanation. So there is a need not only for an explanatory structure, but also for a careful descriptive account of each particular configuration. This is one reason we and others have tilted toward more descriptive yet also more inductive methods of study.

Data Management

Qualitative studies—especially those done by inexperienced or lone-wolf researchers—are vulnerable when it comes to data management. Kvale (1988) provides a wry analysis of the naive question, "How shall I find a method to analyze the 1,000 pages of interview transcripts I have collected?" His first answer is, "Never conduct interview research in such a way that you arrive at a situation where you [have to] ask such a question" (p. 90).

What sort of data are we talking about? Abstractly, qualitative data refer to essences of people, objects, and situations (Berg, 1989). Essentially, a raw experience is converted into words, typically compiled into extended text.

A portion of the raw experience may also be captured as still or moving images; these images can be used in a variety of ways, most of them also involving conversion or linkage to words. See especially Harper (1989) on diverse modes of image analysis. Ball and Smith (1992) also help us see that images are not more "realistic" than words, and are as subject as language to interpretation and captioning, are context dependent, can be faked, and so on.

The words involved are typically based on *observations, interviews,* or *documents* (as Wolcott, 1992, notes, "watching, asking or examining") and carried out close to a local setting for a sustained period. These modes of collecting data may be largely open, unstructured, and event driven, or more tightly defined, structured, and researcher driven.

Normally, the immediately collected information is not immediately available for analysis, but requires some *processing*; raw field notes can be indecipherable scribbles to anyone but the researcher, and must be corrected, extended, edited, and typed up. Audiotapes need to be transcribed, corrected, edited. Similar processing may be required for videotapes.

The "quality" of qualitative data aside, the quantity can be daunting, if not overwhelming. Depending on the level of detail, a day's processed field notes of, say, six interviews may easily run 50-100 single-spaced pages. And as needed site visits pile up, and multiple sites may be involved, the researcher is soon confronted with far more than Kvale's "1,000 pages."

Finally, we need to note here that unless a reasonably coherent system is in place for collecting information from a range of informants, across a potential range of sites, in a roughly comparable format, the researcher will be in data management limbo very quickly. This brings us to issues of storage and retrieval.

Storage and Retrieval

How data are stored and retrieved is the heart of data management; without a clear working scheme, data can easily be "miscoded, mislabeled, mislinked and mislaid" (Wolfe, 1992, p. 293). A good storage and retrieval system is critical for keeping track of what data are available; for permitting easy, flexible, reliable use of data—often by several members of a research team—at different points in time over a project's life; and for documenting the analyses made so that the study can, in principle, be verified or replicated.

There have actually been few detailed discussions of storage and retrieval systems for qualitative data. One is provided by Werner and Schoepfle (1987b), who correctly note that a system needs to be designed far prior to actual data collection. They distinguish among the raw field notes (journals), transcriptions, documents, and interpretive/analytic materials produced by the researcher, and stress the importance of a clear indexing system.

Levine (1985) proposes five general storage and retrieval functions: formatting (how materials are laid out, physically embodied, and structured into types of files), cross-referral (linkage across different files), indexing (defining codes, organizing them into a structure, and pairing codes with specific parts of the database), abstracting (condensed summaries of longer material, such as documents or extended field notes), and pagination (numbers and letters locating specific material in field notes—for example, B J K 1 22 locates for Brookside Hospital the first interview with Dr. Jameson by researcher Kennedy, page 22).

These functions, historically accomplished with notebooks, index cards, file folders, and edge-punch cards, can be carried out far more easily and quickly with computer software (for many specific suggestions, see Weitzman & Miles, 1993; see also Richards & Richards, Chapter 28, this volume). Even so, a physical filing system is also needed for raw field notes, hard copies of transcriptions, audiotapes, memos, and the like. We have proposed a checklist of what information needs to be stored, retrieved, and, usually, retained for a number of years afterward for a qualitative study (Miles & Huberman, 1994; see Table 27.1).

A final remark: A data management system and its effective revision and use over time do not occur in a social vacuum, but in the context of a real project staff, working over a projected and actual total of person-days (which typically amounts to 5-10 times as much time as in the field), and connected by a set of working agreements with study participants (informants, respondents) about the time, energy, information flow, and products that will be involved. (Specific suggestions on these topics appear in Miles & Huberman, 1994.)

Analysis

Analysis via Study Design

Because this material is covered elsewhere in this volume (see Janesick, Chapter 12), we will be brief. First, the design of qualitative studies can in a real sense be seen as analytic. Choices of conceptual framework, of research questions, of samples, of the "case" definition itself, and of instrumentation all involve anticipatory data reduction—which, as we have noted, is an essential aspect of data analysis. These choices have a focusing and bounding function, ruling out certain variables, relationships,

TABLE 27.1 What to Store, Retrieve From, and Retain

1. *Raw material:* field notes, tapes, site documents.
2. *Partially processed data:* write-ups, transcriptions. Ideally, these should appear in their initial version, and in subsequent corrected, "cleaned," "commented-on" versions. Write-ups may profitably include marginal or reflective remarks made by the researcher during or after data collection.
3. *Coded data:* write-ups with specific codes attached.
4. *The coding scheme or thesaurus,* in its successive iterations.
5. *Memos or other analytic material:* the researcher's reflections on the conceptual meaning of the data.
6. *Search and retrieval records:* information showing which coded chunks or data segments the researcher looked for during analysis, and the retrieved material; records of links made among segments.
7. *Data displays:* matrices, charts, or networks used to display retrieved information in a more compressed, organized form, along with the associated analytic text. Typically, there are several revised versions of these.
8. *Analysis episodes:* documentation of what you did, step by step, to assemble the displays and write the analytic text.
9. *Report text:* successive drafts of what is written on the design, methods, and findings of the study.
10. *General chronological log or documentation* of data collection and analysis work.
11. *Index* of all the above material.

and associated data, and selecting others for attention. They also call for creative work. In effect, qualitative designs are not copyable, off-the-shelf patterns, but normally have to be custom-built, revised, and "choreographed" (Preissle, 1991).

Second, there is merit in both "loose," inductively oriented designs, and "tight," more deductively approached ones. The former work well when the terrain is unfamiliar and/or excessively complex, a single case is involved, and the intent is exploratory and descriptive. Tighter designs are indicated when the researcher has good prior acquaintance with the setting, has a good bank of applicable, well-delineated concepts, and takes a more explanatory and/or confirmatory stance involving multiple, comparable cases.

Qualitative studies ultimately aim to describe and explain (at some level) a pattern of relationships, which can be done only with a set of conceptually specified analytic categories (Mishler, 1990). Starting with them (deductively) or getting gradually to them (inductively) are both legitimate and useful paths. The components of such designs are described in the appendix to this chapter.

Interim Analysis

Unlike survey and experimental research, qualitative studies tend to have a peculiar life cycle, one that spreads collection and analysis throughout a study, but that calls for different modes of inquiry at different moments. This has some advantages. For one thing, errors in the field can be undone the next time out; there is always a second chance. Second, instrumentation can be adjusted and added to. In fact, unlike experimental studies, changes in observational protocols or interview schedules in a field study usually reflect a better understanding of the setting, thereby heightening the internal validity of the study.

But there are also some disadvantages. For example, the researcher is faced with the task of trying to reduce the amount of data taken in while still gathering more. The idea here is to focus much of the data collection on emergent themes or constructs (see below) yet still collect additional data. Ongoing analysis is inflationary. Typically, too, the more one investigates, the more layers of the setting one discovers.

Iterative Research

Most of these procedures call for the use of analytic induction. At the heart of analytic induction is the thesis that there are regularities to be found in the physical and social worlds. The theories or constructs that we derive express these regularities as precisely as possible. To uncover these constructs, we use an iterative procedure—a succession of question-and-answer cycles—that entails examining a given set of cases and then refining or modifying those cases on the basis of subsequent ones. Traditionally, the resulting inferences are deemed "valid," in the relaxed sense that they are probable, reasonable, or likely to be true (Robinson, 1951; Znaniecki, 1934).

In qualitative research, these procedures correspond to the "grounded theory" approach (Glaser & Strauss, 1967), which itself shares important features with other approaches to interim analysis (generative analysis, constructive analysis, "illuminative" analysis). In all these cases, however, inductive and deductive analyses are mixed. When a theme, hypothesis, or pattern is identified inductively, the researcher then moves into a verification mode, trying to confirm or qualify the finding. This then keys off a new inductive cycle.

Grounded theory acknowledges one important point: Analysis will be undifferentiated and disjointed until the researcher has some local acquaintance with the setting. This is also the case for theory-driven approaches (e.g., Miles & Huberman, 1994). Seeing how a construct works in the field takes time, especially because its instances are often fleeting, masked by other features, or take shapes different from those found in the research literature or in the lab.

In the typical inductive approach, analysis is set into motion with the first site visits. *Margin notes* are made on the field notes, more *reflective passages* are reviewed carefully, and some kind of *summary sheet* is drafted. At the next level are *coding* and *memo writing,* both handled elsewhere in this volume (see Strauss & Corbin, Chapter 17).

With these caveats in mind, we have derived a set of "tactics" for generating meaning (Miles & Huberman, 1994). Numbered 1 to 13, they are roughly arranged from the descriptive to the explanatory, and from the concrete to the more abstract: *Noting patterns and themes* (1), *seeing plausibility*—making initial, intuitive sense (2)—and *clustering* by conceptual grouping (3) help one to see connections. *Making metaphors,* a kind of figurative grouping of data (4), is also a tactic for achieving more integration among diverse pieces of data. *Counting* (5) is a familiar way to see "what's there"—and to keep oneself honest.

Making contrasts and comparisons (6) is a classic tactic meant to sharpen understanding by clustering and distinguishing observations. Differentiation is also needed, as in *partitioning variables,* unbundling variables that have been prematurely grouped, or simply taking a less monolithic look (7).

More abstract tactics include *subsuming particulars into the general, shuttling back and forth between first-level data and more general categories* (8); *factoring* (9), an analogue of a familiar quantitative technique, allowing the analyst to move from a large number of measured variables to a smaller set of unobserved, usually hypothetical, variables; *noting relations between variables* (10); and *finding intervening variables* (11). Finally, assembling a coherent understanding of a data set is helped through *building a logical chain of evidence* (12) and *making conceptual/theoretical coherence,* typically through comparison with the referent constructs in the literature (13).

Within-Case Analysis: General Issues

There are no fixed boundaries separating "interim" analysis, later analysis, or indeed final analysis. A series of issues appear, however, as particular cases are examined—and prior to the work of cross-case analysis (see the next section). These include the distinction between description and explanation, the general logic of analysis, the importance of data displays, the role of theory, and a workable view of causality.

Description and Explanation

Within-case analysis will invariably come to grips with two levels of understanding. The first is descriptive. The primitive questions of *what* is going on and *how* things are proceeding call for a reasonable accounting of the phenomena observed. This is description; as Bernard (1988) puts it, such analyses "make complicated things understandable by reducing them to their component parts" (p. 317). In effect, as Rein and Schön (1977) suggest, one vehicle for description of local actors, events, and settings is to tell a story (what happened, and then what happened next). Storytelling—a sense-making construction of a "scenario"—seems deeply pervasive in human thought (Goleman, 1992; Read, Druian, & Miller, 1989), but it is also shot through with interpretive shortcomings.

One of the more frequent queries in daily life, and one that invariably gets an answer, is, Why? But that familiar process masks the fact, as Draper (1988) points out, that "explaining" may also include providing requested information, justifying an action, giving reasons, supporting a claim, or making a causal statement. "Scientific" explanation falls in a narrow band of "why" questions, notably the last two. As Kaplan (1964) suggests, an explanation—whether cast in "purposive" or straightforwardly historical terms—is in effect a "concatenated description" that puts one fact or law in relation to others, making the description intelligible. Kaplan also helpfully points out that explanations are always condition and context dependent, partial, inconclusive, and indeterminately applicable—features that are not limited to qualitative studies.

The Importance of Displays in Analysis

To reiterate: Valid analysis is immensely aided by data displays that are focused enough to permit viewing of a full data set in one location and are systematically arranged to answer the research questions at hand. The "full" data set is at hand, albeit in a condensed mode, and can be interrogated. These are not selectively drawn "stacks" or "insights" or "key incidents." The analogue is to the output of statistical packages, which (a) permit analysis to be conducted in close conjunction with the displayed data, (b) allow the analyst to

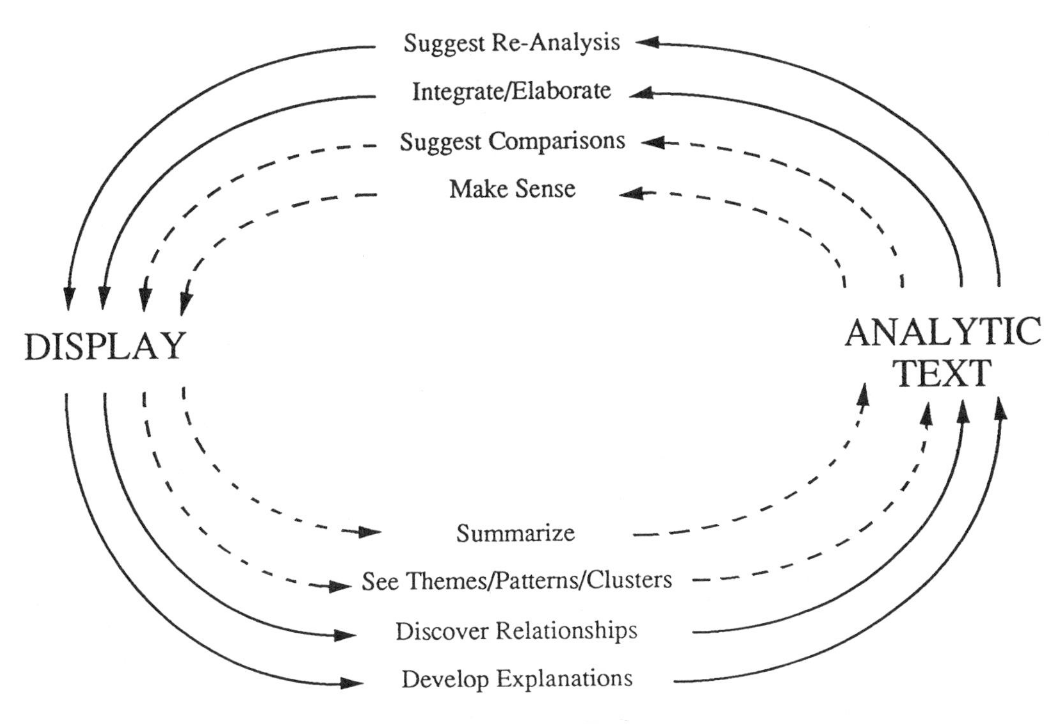

Figure 27.2. Interaction Between Display and Analytic Text

see what further analyses are called for, (c) make for easy comparability across data sets, and (d) heighten credibility in the research report, where data displays normally accompany conclusions.

Here, too, analysis is sequential and interactive. Displayed data and the emerging written text of the researcher's conclusions influence each other. The display helps the writer see patterns; the first text makes sense of the display and suggests new analytic moves in the displayed data; a revised or extended display points to new relationships and explanations, leading to more differentiated and integrated text, and so on. Displays beget analyses, which then beget more powerful, suggestive displays (see Figure 27.2).

The Role of Theory in Within-Case Analysis

Virtuous claims about conclusions are usually supported by three metaclaims: (a) that the researcher has evolved, or has tested, a theory; (b) that all of the relevant data have been examined, and irrelevant data have not sneaked in; and (c) that there has been a steady and explicit "dialogue" (Ragin, 1987) between ideas and evidence.

Good theory, Glaser (1978) suggests, has categories that fit (or have come to fit) the data; is relevant to the core of what is going on; can be used to explain, predict, and interpret what is going on; and is modifiable. So much for the classical view. In practice, theory has a darker side that crops up during analysis. A good exhibit is the comparison between Everhart's (1985a, 1985b) and Cusick's (1985a, 1985b) studies on the meaning of schooling, as analyzed by Noblit (1988). Though both studied American high schools, Noblit shows that their interpretations varied widely. Everhart's critical theory assumptions led him to focus on students, and on schooling as a way to "proletarianize" students and reproduce the structures of capitalism through hierarchy and the passing out of reified information to students as "empty vessels." Cusick's structural-functional assumptions led him to focus on the school as created by staff, and on schooling as driven by an "egalitarian ideal," compromised by racial animosity, with "unappealing knowledge" taking second place to "friendly relations" with students. Each researcher, not surprisingly, saw the other's formulations as "ideological." Allegiance to preexisting "grand theory" led each to drastically different conclusions about very similar phenomena.

Furthermore, the theory-data boundary is permeable. As Van Maanen (1979) notes, there are actually only first-order concepts—the so-called facts of a study, which never "speak for themselves"—and second-order concepts—the "notions used by the researcher to explain the patterning of the first-order concepts" (pp. 39-40). Thus the "facts" one discovers are already the products of many levels of interpretation (Van Maanen, 1988).

At the least, qualitative researchers need to understand just how they are construing "theory" as analysis proceeds, because that construction will—consciously or not—inevitably influence and constrain data collection, data reduction, data display, and the drawing and verification of conclusions. Some alternate constructions include the following:

- "grand theory," as above: a congeries of a few major, well-articulated constructs
- a "map" aiming to generalize the story (or stories) told about a case (Rein & Schön, 1977)
- a predicted pattern of events, to be compared with what is actually observed (Yin, 1991)
- a model, with a series of connected propositions that specify relations, often hierarchical, among components (Reed & Furman, 1992)
- a network of nonhierarchical relationships, expressed through statements defining linkages among concepts (Carley, 1991)

Being clear about such constructions is also important because of the growing use of qualitative analysis software to accomplish the core functions noted above. They too have built-in assumptions about "theory" (see Weitzman & Miles, 1993). For example, programs such as Ethnograph (Qualis Research Associates, 1990) and NUD•IST (Richards & Richards, 1989) help the user develop theory through hierarchically related codes (*A* is an instance of a higher-level concept *B*, which in turn is subsumed in a more general *C*), whereas others, such as ATLAS/ti (Mühr, 1991), HyperRESEARCH (Hesse-Biber, Dupuis, & Kinder, 1990), and MECA (Carley, 1991), focus on theory as a connected network of links among entities (*A* promotes *B*, is part of *C*, hinders *D*, precedes *E* [which is also part of *B*], and so on).

A View of Causality

Finally, within-case analysis frequently confronts the question of understanding causality. Can qualitative studies establish causal relationships at all? That possibility is often attacked from both the right ("Only controlled quantitative experiments can do that") and the left ("Causality is an unworkable concept in human behavior—people are not billiard balls"). In line with our epistemological stance, mentioned at the outset, the position we take here is that qualitative studies (see Van Maanen, 1979, 1983) are especially well suited to finding causal relationships; they can look directly and longitudinally at the local processes underlying a temporal series of events and states, showing how these led to specific outcomes, and ruling out rival hypotheses. In effect, we get inside the black box; we can understand not just that a particular thing happened, but how and why it happened.

The credibility of such claims depends on how one views causality. Herewith we provide a brief summary of ours. First, causality necessarily brings in the question of time as part of an explanation; prior events are assumed to have a connection, more or less clear, with later events. Temporality is crucial (Faulconer & Williams, 1985); assessing causality requires us to understand the "plot"—events arranged in a loose order (Abbott, 1992). Though a variable-oriented viewpoint will always show a looping back of assorted effects onto causes that produce new effects (Eden, Jones, & Sims, 1983; Weick, 1979), the "plots" still unfold over time and must be understood that way at the case level. This is where the more narrative versions of causal analysis find their place (Abbott, 1992).

It is worth pointing out here that we confront one of the most likely threats to conventional causality: that, looked at closely, or "deconstructed," much causal analysis is generated rhetorically, as a series of textual devices, genres, tropes, figures of speech. Narrative accounts, for example, are made up almost exclusively of these figurative devices (Atkinson, 1992; Clough, 1992). Should we assess them in conventional terms? Or should we have specific canons for rhetorical causality that can, in some way, be separated from the logic of evidence we use for analytic explanations? Geertz (1983) has put the problem well in noting the slow movement in explanatory devices from social laws to metaphors of theater and games: "What the lever did for physics, the chess move promises to do for sociology" (p. 22).

Another key characteristic: Causality is local; distant and abstract forces such as "gravity" pale beside the immediate events and processes that occur when one deliberately drops a pencil (the friction between the fingers and the pencil, the decision to open one's fingers, the outward movement of the fingers). The immediate causal nexus is always in front of us, in a particular setting and at a particular time.

Third, a determination of causality cannot be precisely rule bound: to Hume's classical criteria of temporal precedence (*A* before *B*), constant conjunction (when *A*, always *B*), and contiguity of influence (a plausible mechanism links *A* and

B) we have to add others, such as some of those proposed by Hill (1965) in epidemiology: strength of association (much more *B* with *A* than with other possible causes), biological gradient (if more *A*, then more *B*), coherence (the *A-B* relationship fits with what else we know about *A* and *B*), and analogy (*A* and *B* resemble the well-established pattern noted in *C* and *D*).

Fourth, there is always causal multiplexity: Causes are always multiple and "conjunctural," combining and affecting each other as well as the supposed effects (Ragin, 1987). Causes and effects must be seen as configured in networks—themselves deeply influenced by the local context.

Finally, assessing causality is of necessity a retrospective matter, requiring us to note how "some event has occurred in a particular case" (House, 1991). Thus we need the historian's method of "followability" (Abbott, 1992), and will typically be making "a retrospective gathering of events into an account that makes the ending reasonable and believable . . . configur[ing] the events in such a way that their part in the whole story becomes clear" (Polkinghorne, 1988, p. 171; compare Scriven's [1974] discussion of the "modus operandi" approach).

The commonsense causal questions derived here are largely those posed by Lofland and Lofland (1984): What are the conditions under which [X] appears? What facilitates its occurrence? What are circumstances in which it is likely to occur? In the presence of what conditions is it likely to become an outcome? Upon what factors does variation in it depend? Under what conditions is it present and under what conditions is it absent?

Of course, a useful causal explanation should necessarily apply to more than one case. Through analytic induction (Manning, 1982; Miller, 1982) a causal account obtained in one case can be tested elsewhere, be it supported, qualified, or subjected to revision. We now turn to the question of approaches to cross-case analysis.

Cross-Case Analysis

The traditional mode of qualitative analysis has been the single-case study. In most ethnographic research, for example, "cases" are individuals or more molar units meant to share several common characteristics—a family, a tribe, a small business, a neighborhood, a community. Cases can also be instances of a larger phenomenon (e.g., "cases" of bribery, "cases" of learning to fight fires), usually of an important social process.

Such molar units are essentially multiples of individuals: firefighters, teachers, criminals, and so on. Whereas these individuals have typically been aggregated within their settings (e.g., firehouses, schools, particular neighborhoods), we are now seeing studies that focus on sets of individuals within several settings (schools, special programs, businesses), and doing this work with multiple methods (Firestone & Herriott, 1983; Louis, 1982; Schofield, 1990).

One objective here is to extend external validity. For example, looking at multiple actors in multiple settings enhances generalizability; the key processes, constructs, and explanations in play can be tested in several different configurations. And each configuration can be considered a replication of the process or question under study. Multiple cases also identify configurations (of actors, of working arrangements, of causal influences) that hold in some settings but not in others. We thus come out with distinct "clusters" or "families" of cases.

But cross-site analytic work is not so simple. As it turns out, Alcoholic A has a very different profile from Alcoholic B, as Denzin (1989) has pointed out, and the two cannot readily be compared unless we choose to focus on more abstract common characteristics. Thus there is a danger that multiple cases will be analyzed at high levels of inference, aggregating out the local webs of causality and ending with a smoothed set of generalizations that may not apply to any single case. This happens more often than we care to remember.

The tension here is that of reconciling the particular and the universal: reconciling an individual case's uniqueness with the need to understand generic processes at work across cases (Silverstein, 1988). Silverstein argues that each individual has a specific history—which we discard at our peril—but it is a history contained within the general principles that influence its development. Similarly, Noblit and Hare (1983) make a strong case for preserving uniqueness, yet also making comparisons. More recently, they have also cautioned against aggregating or averaging results across cases, in order to avoid misinterpretation and superficiality (Noblit & Hare, 1988).

A Crucial Distinction: Variables and Cases

Consider a typical study, one trying to predict the decision to attend college, with a sample of 300 adolescents and the following set of predictors: gender, socioeconomic status, parental expectations, school performance, peer support, and decision to attend college.

In a variable-oriented analysis, the predictor variables are intercorrelated and the key dependent variable, "decision to attend college," is regressed on the six others. This might show us that deciding to attend college is mainly influenced by school performance, with additional influences from parents' expectations and SES. We see how the variables as concepts are related, but we do not know the profile of any one individual.

In a case-oriented analysis, we would look more closely into a particular case, say, Case 005, who is female, middle-class, has parents with high expectations, and so on. These are, however, "thin" measures. To do a genuine case analysis, we need to look at a full history of Case 005: Nynke van der Molen, whose mother trained as a social worker but is bitter over the fact that she never worked outside the home, and whose father wants Nynke to work in the family florist shop. Chronology is also important: two years ago, Nynke's closest friend decided to go to college, just before Nynke began work in a stable and just before Nynke's mother showed her a scrapbook from social work school. Nynke then decided to enroll in veterinary studies.

These and other data can be displayed in matrix form (see Miles & Huberman, 1994), where the flow and configuration of events and reactions leading to Nynke's decision would come clear. It would also help to "incarnate" what the five predictors look like singly and how they interact collectively. That, in turn, would surface recurrent patterns, "families" or "clusters" of cases with characteristic configurations.

As Ragin (1987) notes, such a case-oriented approach looks at each entity, then teases out configurations *within* each case and subjects them to comparative analysis. In these comparisons (of a smaller number of cases), underlying similarities and systematic associations are sought out with regard to the main outcome variable. From there, a more explanatory model can be explicated, at least for the cases under study.

Each approach has its pluses and minuses. Variable-oriented analysis is good for finding probabilistic relationships among variables in a large population, but has difficulties with causal complexities, or dealing with subsamples. Case-oriented analysis is good at finding specific, concrete, historically grounded patterns common to small sets of cases, but its findings remain particularistic, although several case writers speciously claim greater generality.[1]

Strategies for Cross-Case Analysis

There are many ways to proceed with multiple-case data, or data coming from several sources. Below is a brief sampler, building on the case versus variable orientation we have just reviewed.

Case-oriented strategies. Yin (1984) advocates a *replication* strategy. A conceptual framework oversees the first case study, then successive cases are examined to see whether the new pattern matches the one found earlier. The "grounded theory" approach (e.g., Glaser, 1978) uses the same principle, but builds up the framework inductively, then tests and refines it with recourse to multiple comparison groups.

Denzin (1989) approaches the problem through multiple exemplars. After deconstructing prior conceptions of a particular phenomenon (such as "the alcoholic self"), multiple instances (cases) are collected, then "bracketed," in a phenomenological sense, and are then inspected for essential elements or components. The elements are then rebuilt into a reordered whole and put back into the natural social context.

Many researchers approach cross-case comparison by forming "types" or "families." Cases in a set are inspected to see if they fall into clusters that share certain patterns or configurations. Sometimes the clusters can be arrayed along some dimension (low to high conformity, vague to specific career ambitions, and so on).

Variable-oriented strategies. An often-used approach is *finding themes* that cut across cases. For example, Pearsol (1985) looked at interviews about sex equity programs with 25 teachers. After careful inductive coding, he found recurring themes such as "concern for students," "activist view of change," and "barriers to innovation." (Later he turned to a case-oriented approach, sorting the teachers into six types based on the initial configuration of themes.)

Often a key variable comes clear only during cross-site analysis. The strategy here might be called *pattern clarification.* For example, Eisenhardt (1989a) found evidence for the construct of "power centralization" by looking at data on CEO behavior in 10 microcomputer firms. Her matrix display included adjectives describing decision style, quantitative measures, organizational functions performed by the CEO, and some cameo descriptors (e.g., "[He] depends on picking good people and letting them operate").

Mixed Strategies

A more phenomenological approach, described by Fischer and Wertz (1975), might be called *interactive synthesis.* In studying the meaning of being a crime victim, these authors first wrote individual case synopses, then wrote a cross-case narrative based on a series of themes. They then composed a "general condensation" depicting the essential personal meanings, then cycled back to the case synopses to see how the condensation was exemplified there. Finally, they wrote a "general psychological structure" describing what seems essential in the temporal process of victimization.

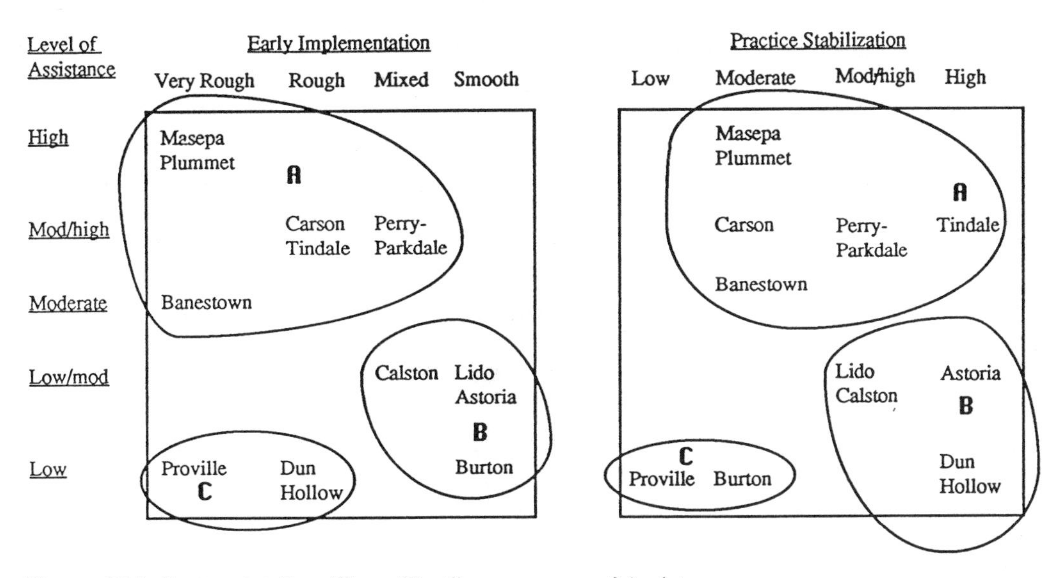

Figure 27.3. Scatterplot Over Time: The Consequences of Assistance

The sequence is carefully assembled. In particular, it includes an analytic mixture that *combines* methods, rather than relying on one and adding others essentially as appendages. Other examples of mixed strategies can be found in the work of Abbott (1992), Gladwin (1989), and Huberman (1991).

Technically, cross-case analyses are most easily made with "displays": matrix or other arrays of the data that allow the researcher to analyze, in a condensed form, the full data set, in order to see literally what is there. From there, several things can happen: The researcher may go back out in the field to retrieve missing data; other arrays may be made for a better look; or columns or rows, or all entries, within the arrays may be reconfigured.

Typically, the researcher begins with *a partially ordered metamatrix,* which brings the basic information from several cases into one big chart. Then come *descriptive or conceptually ordered displays, time-ordered matrices, effects matrices,* and *composite sequence analyses,* showing the flux of different cases through a generally framed flow of events and conditions.

Let us look at the scatterplot display matrix for 12 cases (school districts) shown in Figure 27.3. Note that this is simply a contingency table, crossing two variables ("early implementation" and "practice stabilization") with a third ("level of assistance"). In addition, each of the variables in play is scaled, so that the cases can be arrayed and examined in a roughly comparable way.

Typically, this kind of chart, which *follows* careful case-oriented work, constitutes a variable-oriented analytic sortie. With this display in hand, the researcher usually goes back again to the case-level data. What does "rough" early implementation correspond to at Masepa and Plummet, and are the two cases comparable? Did "assistance" actually seem to have little effect on "early implementation," and, if so, why? And what about the countervailing cases in cluster B? What was the pattern of assistance, the flow over time, the relationship between assistance and stabilization as perceived by informants? This examination then leads to another display, typically in a different form, that arrays the cases according to the forms in which these questions have been posed. In other words, displays come typically in a sequence: unordered, ordered by case on one or several dimensions of interest, regrouped by families of cases that share some characteristics, and displayed again as an interlocking set of more explanatory variables, ones that undergird the clusters of cases that have been identified.

Verifying Conclusions and Threats to Analytic Validity

The "Cohabitation" of Realist and Interpretivist Canons

As we have noted, until recently there were virtually no canons, decision rules, algorithms, or even any agreed-upon heuristics for the conduct of qualitative research. This is less a developmental problem than an absence of consensus in deciding the grounds upon which findings are considered plausible or convincing and procedures are viewed as legitimate ones.

There do appear, however, to be some *procedural* commonalities, in the sequential process of analyzing, concluding, and confirming findings in a field study format. In both cases, the researcher shifts between cycles of inductive data collection and analysis to deductive cycles of testing and verification. As noted, exploratory and confirmatory sampling drive the collection of data that, once analyzed, lead to decisions on which data to collect next. Gradually, these data assemblies become more "conclusive." Roughly put, most "naturalistic" researchers subscribe to this basic analytic cycle.

Verification

Verification entails checking for the most common or most insidious biases that can steal into the process of drawing conclusions. Some of the most frequent shortcomings include the following (Douglas, 1976; Krathwohl, 1993; Miles & Huberman, 1984; Nisbett & Ross, 1980):

- data overload in the field, leading to the analysts thus missing important information, overweighting some findings, skewing the analysis
- salience of first impressions or of observations of highly concrete or dramatic incidents
- selectivity, overconfidence in some data, especially when trying to confirm a key finding
- co-occurrences taken as correlations, or even as causal relationships
- false base-rate proportions: extrapolation of the number of total instances from those observed
- unreliability of information from some sources
- overaccommodation to information that questions outright a tentative hypothesis

The term most often used in connection with analysis and confirmation issues is *triangulation*—a term with multiple meanings. The origin of the term is probably "multiple operationalism" (Campbell & Fiske, 1959): multiple measures that ensure that the variance reflected is that of the trait or treatment and not that associated with the measures. This is best done, for example, by multiplying independent measures and sources of the same phenomenon—for example, informants make the same claim independently, and the researcher observes the phenomenon; test scores back up work samples and observations. "Grounded" theorists have long contended that theory generated from one data source works less well than "slices of data" from different sources (Glaser, 1978).

But triangulation has also come to mean convergence among researchers (agreement between field notes of one investigator and observations of another) and convergence among theories. A general prescription has been to pick triangulation sources that have different biases, different strengths, so they can complement one another.

In the disorderly world of empirical research, however, independent measures never converge fully. Observations do not jibe completely with interview data, nor surveys with written records. In other words, sources can be inconsistent or even conflicting, with no easy means of resolution. In such cases, in fact, we may need to initiate a new way of thinking about the data at hand (Rossman & Wilson, 1985).

Beyond this, triangulation is less a tactic than a mode of inquiry. By self-consciously setting out to collect and double-check findings, using multiple sources and modes of evidence, the researcher will build the triangulation process into ongoing data collection. It will be the way he or she got to the finding in the first place—by seeing or hearing multiple instances of it from different sources, using different methods, and by squaring the finding with others with which it should coincide.

With this logic in mind, we have generated a list of "tactics" for testing or confirming conclusions (Miles & Huberman, 1984, 1994). The tactics meant to ward off the most obvious biases are the following: checking for representativeness, checking for researcher effects (reactivity), and triangulating and weighing the evidence (relying on more robust measures). Tactics for testing the viability of patterns turn around the active search for contrasts, comparisons, outliers, and extreme cases. More elaborate tests of conclusions call for attempts to rule out spurious conclusions, to replicate key findings, to check out rival explanations, and to look for negative evidence. Finally, feedback from informants can be used at any point in the cycle.

A more general and comprehensive approach to the verification of findings and conclusions is "auditing" (see the next section; see also Schwandt & Halpern, 1988). Applied to empirical research, auditing is an accounting metaphor for the systematic review of a given study on the part of an external examiner. Its main interest may be less the quality of an external review than the possibility for qualitative researchers to have a list of analytic bases to touch, so that interested and rigorous peers can determine whether the sampling, measurement, and analyses leading to the main conclusions and explanations stand up to the most common sources of bias and error.

On "Transparency" of Method

The conventions of quantitative research require clear, explicit reporting of data and procedures. That is expected so that (a) the reader will be confident of, and can verify, reported conclusions; (b) secondary analysis of the data is possible; (c) the study could in principle be replicated; and (d) fraud or misconduct, if it exists, will be more trackable. There is an added, internal need: keeping analytic strategies coherent, manageable, and repeatable as the study proceeds. That is, the reporting requirement encourages running documentation from the beginning. In our view, the same needs are present for qualitative studies, even if one takes a more interpretive stance (note, for example, the ideas about "confirmability" and "dependability" proposed by Lincoln & Guba, 1985). As we have written in previous work:

> We have the unappealing double bind whereby qualitative studies can't be verified because researchers don't report on their methodology, and they don't report on their methodology because there are no established canons or conventions for doing so. (Miles & Huberman, 1984, p. 244)

Solutions

The most basic solution has already been discussed (see Table 27.1): careful retention, in easily retrievable form, of all study materials, from raw field notes through data displays and final report text. That solution, however, rests on another: a reflexive stance to the conduct of the study that assumes regular, ongoing, self-conscious documentation—of successive versions of coding schemes, of conceptual arguments among project staff, of analysis episodes—both successful ones and dead ends. We have reported a detailed documentation form for tracking data reduction, data display, and conclusion-drawing operations (Miles & Huberman, 1984), but we are not aware of instances of its use by other researchers. Carney (1990) advocates a "reflexivity journal" for the same purposes.

Recently, however, there has been movement toward more explicit, complete accounts. Some examples include the methodological accounts of phenomenological studies by Bartlett (1990) and Melnick and Beaudry (1990), the "data analysis chronology" in a hermeneutic study by Pearsol (1985), the detailed diary of ethnographic biographical research by L. M. Smith (1992), the careful reporting of case study research methods by Merryfield (1990), the account of "constant comparative" methods by Hodson (1991), and the details of data displays by Eisenhardt (1989a, 1989b). Still, not a few studies restrict their "methods" sections to statements such as "The study employed the constant comparative method," with no further explanation.

Part of the difficulty is that, given the diversity of approaches to qualitative work, there is no standard set of expectations for what a qualitative methods section should look like. As a minimum set, we would propose the following:

- sampling decisions made, both within and across cases
- instrumentation and data collection operations
- database summary: size, how produced
- software used, if any
- overview of analytic strategies followed
- inclusion of key data displays supporting main conclusions

A fourth solution is that of preparing for, and/or actually carrying out, an "audit" of the entire study being conducted. The first feasibility applications were by Halpern (1983); since then, Schwandt and Halpern (1988) have extended the audit idea, applying it to the review of evaluation studies. They suggest six levels of required attention:

- Are findings grounded in the data? (Is sampling appropriate? Are data weighted correctly?)
- Are inferences logical? (Are analytic strategies applied correctly? Are alternative explanations accounted for?)
- Is the category structure appropriate?
- Can inquiry decisions and methodological shifts be justified? (Were sampling decisions linked to working hypotheses?)
- What is the degree of researcher bias (premature closure, unexplored data in field notes, lack of search for negative cases, feelings of empathy)?
- What strategies were used for increasing credibility (second readers, feedback to informants, peer review, adequate time in the field)?

Such audits do not seem to be widely used, but when they are (e.g., Merryfield, 1990), they seem to have decidedly salutary effects, notably the encouragement of systematic record keeping and reflexivity.

Some Problems

The time and energy costs for adequate methodological documentation and/or auditing are not small. We have estimated a 20% increment in analysis time in the use of our documentation log (Miles & Huberman, 1984). Schwandt and Halpern (1988) give no cost figures, but the researcher's work in preparing an "audit trail" and the auditor's analysis, with its very detailed procedures, are at least as expensive. Careful computerization of a study will help, of course, but this carries its own costs. We should probably expect that detailed documentation and auditing will continue to be restricted to high-stakes studies, or to those in which the researcher has a special interest in documentation or auditing as such.

Study documentation and full reportage may also encourage a mechanistic, obsessive approach (see Marshall, 1990, and Noblit, 1988, who worry about the "bureaucratization" of data analysis). Or it may lead to abstract formulations of method that do not quite speak to the realities of qualitative research (see, for example, Constas, 1992, on the documentation of category development procedures). In any case, we need to be realistic about "reproducibility"; even in the field of synthetic chemistry, Bergman (1989) reports that nearly half of studies could not be reproduced, even by the original researchers. So we need a reasonable standard, not an abstractly demanding one.

Finally, we must remember that "transparency" has its risks. For example, maintaining detailed field notes in computer files, and making them available for reanalysis, even with supposed deidentification, raises questions about invasion of privacy and about potential harm to informants (see the very thoughtful discussion by Akeroyd, 1991). Any reasonable approach to methodological transparency must deal with ethical, not just technical, issues.

On balance, these problems do not seem insuperable, and the basic need for transparency remains. We see no reason not to keep advancing the state of the art—probably incrementally—through routinization of running documentation, the evolution of clearer reporting standards, and—now and then, when it matters—the in-depth analysis of method that a strong audit can bring. Given the care and scrupulousness with which qualitative research is meant to be conducted, as much in the ethnographic tradition as in the interpretive tradition, it should be possible to negotiate a minimal set of conventions for the conduct of qualitative research. Given that these traditions do have different frames for ensuring validity and dependability of study findings, there might well be a shared set of conventions along with specific rules for researchers working in different areas. We are getting there. Still, transparency does not come easily when it brings in its wake an added burden and a greater exposure to the judgments of one's professional peers.

Appendix: The Main Conceptual and Analytic Aspects of Design

Conceptual framework. This lays out the key factors, constructs, or variables, and the presumed relationships among them. We have argued that graphic displays of "bins" (main variables) connected by directional arrows specifying intervariable relationships are useful in making researchers' frameworks clear (Miles & Huberman, 1994). Conceptual frameworks, even in a "tight" design, are normally iterated over the life of the study.

Research questions. A set of defined questions (not necessarily "hypotheses") represents the facets of an empirical domain the researcher wants to explore, setting priorities and foci of attention and implicitly excluding a range of unstudied topics. They may be defined causally or noncausally, and deal with research, policy, evaluation, or management issues (N. L. Smith, 1981, 1987; see also Dillon's [1984] application of alternative schemata to a sample of more than 900 research questions). They usually represent a more detailed operationalization of the study's conceptual framework.

Case definition. Essentially, a "case" is a phenomenon of some sort occurring in a bounded context—the unit of analysis, in effect. Normally, there is a focus of attention and a more or less vaguely defined temporal, social, and/or physical boundary involved (e.g., a bypass surgery patient, before, during, and six months after surgery, in the family and hospital context). Foci and boundaries can be defined by social unit size (an individual, a role, a small group, an organization, community, nation), by spatial location, or temporally (an episode, an event, a day). Cases may have subcases embedded within them (Yin, 1984). As with the other conceptual aspects of study design, the definition of the "case" is a strongly analytic, data-selective choice, whether single or multiple cases are involved.

Sampling. Sampling choices within and across cases are powerfully determinative of just which data will be considered and used in analysis. Quantitative researchers often think randomly, statistically, and in terms of context-stripped case selections. Qualitative researchers must characteristically think purposively and conceptually about sampling (see Miles & Huberman, 1994, for specific suggestions).

In addition, within each case (even when the case is an individual), the researcher needs to sample an intricately nested range of activities, processes, events, locations, and times (Bogdan & Biklen, 1982; Lofland & Lofland, 1984; Schwartzman & Werner, 1990; Woods, 1979); such choices are theory driven (Glaser & Strauss, 1967), not driven by a concern with "representativeness." Sampling choices also typically evolve through successive waves of data collection. This is also true of cross-case sampling. Here again, the issue is not so much the quest for conventional generalizability, but rather an understanding of the conditions under which a particular finding appears and operates: how, where, when, and why it carries on as it does. Multiple cases are especially important as "comparison groups" (Glaser & Strauss, 1970); they also permit a "replication" strategy (Yin, 1991), where single-case findings are successively tested in a following series of cases. When multiple cases are carefully ordered along a key dimension, powerful explanations are more likely (see Eisenhardt, 1989b, for a compelling example).

Instrumentation. Other chapters in this volume deal explicitly with this theme, but a few remarks, in keeping with our approach, are in order. The general issue, as put by Warner (1991), is this: How can we maximize construct and descriptive-contextual validity, assure ourselves that our interpretations connect with people's lived experience, and minimize researcher impact? The answers, we think, usually lie in the direction of minimally predesigned instrumentation.

Similarly, how can we enhance internal validity, generalizability to other cases and settings, not to mention sheer manageability of data collection? Here, too, the answers lead us toward more fully predesigned instrumentation.

Note

1. This is a crucial distinction, and it has been handled in several ways. For recent treatments, see Maxwell and Miller (1992) and Runkel (1990).

References

Abbott, A. (1992). From causes to events: Notes on narrative positivism. *Sociological Methods and Research, 20,* 428-455.

Akeroyd, A. V. (1991). Personal information and qualitative research data: Some practical and ethical problems arising from data protection legislation. In N. G. Fielding & R. M. Lee (Eds.), *Using computers in qualitative research* (pp. 88-106). London: Sage.

Atkinson, P. (1992). *Understanding ethnographic texts.* Newbury Park, CA: Sage.

Ball, M. S., & Smith, G. W. H. (1992). *Analyzing visual data.* Newbury Park, CA: Sage.

Bartlett, L. (1990). *The dialectic between theory and method in critical interpretive research.* Queensland, Australia: University of Queensland.

Berg, B. L. (1989). *Qualitative research methods for the social sciences.* Boston: Allyn & Bacon.

Bergman, R. G. (1989). Irreproducibility in the scientific literature: How often do scientists tell the whole truth and nothing but the truth? *Ethical and Policy Perspectives on the Professions, 8*(2), 2-3.

Bernard, H. R. (1988). *Research methods in cultural anthropology.* Newbury Park, CA: Sage.

Bhaskar, R. (1978). *A realist theory of science.* Leeds, UK: Leeds.

Bhaskar, R. (1989). *Reclaiming reality: A critical introduction to contemporary philosophy.* London: Verso.

Bogdan, R. C., & Biklen, S. K. (1982). *Qualitative research for education: An introduction to theory and methods.* Boston: Allyn & Bacon.

Campbell, D., & Fiske, D. (1959). Convergent and discriminant validation by the multitrait-multimethod matrix. *Psychological Bulletin, 56,* 81-105.

Carley, K. (1991). *Textual analysis using maps.* Pittsburgh, PA: Carnegie Mellon University, Department of Social and Decision Sciences.

Carney, T. F. (1990). *Collaborative inquiry methodology.* Windsor, Ontario: University of Windsor, Division for Instructional Development.

Chesler, M. (1987). *Professionals' views of the "dangers" of self-help groups* (CRSO Paper 345). Ann Arbor, MI: Center for Research on Social Organization.

Clough, P. T. (1992). *The end(s) of ethnography: From realism to social criticism.* Newbury Park, CA: Sage.

Constas, M. A. (1992). Qualitative analysis as a public event: The documentation of category development procedures. *American Educational Research Journal, 29,* 253-266

Cusick, P. (1985a). Review of *Reading, writing and resistance. Anthropology Quarterly, 16,* 69-72.

Cusick, P. (1985b). Commentary on the Everhart/Cusick reviews. *Anthropology and Education Quarterly, 16,* 246-247.

Denzin, N. K. (1989). *Interpretive interactionism.* Newbury Park, CA: Sage.

Dillon, J. T. (1984). The classification of research questions. *Review of Educational Research, 54,* 327-361.

Douglas, J. (1976). *Investigative social research.* Beverly Hills, CA: Sage.

Draper, S. W. (1988). What's going on in everyday explanation? In C. Antaki (Ed.), *Analyzing everyday explanations: A casebook of methods* (pp. 15-31). Newbury Park, CA: Sage.

Eden, C., Jones, S., & Sims, D. (1983). *Messing about in problems: An informal structured approach to their identification and management.* Oxford: Pergamon.

Eisenhardt, K. M. (1989a). Building theories from case study research. *Academy of Management Review, 14,* 532-550.

Eisenhardt, K. M. (1989b). Making fast strategic decisions in high-velocity environments. *Academy of Management Journal, 32,* 543-576.

Erickson, F. (1986). Qualitative methods in research on teaching. In M. C. Wittrock (Ed.), *Handbook of research on teaching* (3rd ed., pp. 119-161). New York: Macmillan.

Everhart, R. (1985a). Review of *The egalitarian ideal and the American high school. Anthropology and Education Quarterly, 16,* 73-77.

Everhart, R. (1985b). Comment on the Everhart/Cusick reviews. *Anthropology and Education Quarterly, 16,* 247-248.

Faulconer, J. E., & Williams, R. N. (1985). Temporality in human action: An alternative to positivism and historicism. *American Psychologist, 40,* 1179-1188.

Firestone, W. A., & Herriott, R. E. (1983). The formalization of qualitative research: An adaptation of "soft" science to the policy world. *Evaluation Review, 7,* 437-466.

Fischer, C., & Wertz, F. (1975). Empirical phenomenological analyses of being criminally victimized. In A. Giorgi (Ed.), *Phenomenology and psychological research* (pp. 135-158). Pittsburgh, PA: Duquesne University Press.

Geertz, C. (1983). *Local knowledge: Further essays in interpretive anthropology.* New York: Basic Book.

Gherardi, S., & Turner, B. (1987). *Real men don't collect soft data.* Trento, Italy: Universita di Trento, Dipartimento di Politica Sociale.

Gladwin, C. H. (1989). *Ethnographic decision tree modeling.* Newbury Park, CA: Sage.

Glaser, B. G. (1978). *Theoretical sensitivity: Advances in the methodology of grounded theory.* Mill Valley, CA: Sociology Press.

Glaser, B. G., & Strauss, A. L. (1967). *The discovery of grounded theory: Strategies for qualitative research.* Chicago: Aldine.

Glaser, B. G., & Strauss, A. L. (1970). Discovery of substantive theory: A basic strategy underlying qualitative research. In W. Filstead (Ed.), *Qualitative methodology* (pp. 288-297). Chicago: Rand McNally.

Goleman, D. (1992, May 12). Jurors hear evidence and turn it into stories. *New York Times,* pp. C1, C11.

Guba, E. G. (1990). Carrying on the dialog. In E. G. Guba (Ed.), *The paradigm dialog* (pp. 368-378). Newbury Park, CA: Sage.

Halpern, E. S. (1983). *Auditing naturalistic inquiries, some preliminary applications. Part 1: Development of the process. Part 2: Case study application.* Paper presented at the meeting of the American Educational Research Association.

Harper, D. (1989). Visual sociology: Expanding sociological vision. In G. Blank et al. (Eds.), *New technology in sociology: Practical applications in research and work* (pp. 81-97). New Brunswick, NJ: Transaction.

Harré, R., & Secord, P. (1973). *The explanation of social behavior.* Totowa, NJ: Littlefield, Adams.

Hesse-Biber, S., Dupuis, P., & Kinder, T. S. (1990). *HyperRESEARCH.* Paper presented at the annual meeting of the American Sociological Association, Washington, DC.

Hill, A. B. (1965). The environment and disease: Association or causation? *Proceedings of the Royal Society of Medicine, 58,* 295-300.

Hodson, R. (1991). The active worker: Compliance and autonomy at the workplace. *Journal of Contemporary Ethnography, 20,* 47-78.

House, E. R. (1991). Realism in research. *Educational Researcher, 20*(6), 2-9.

Huberman, A. M. (1991). The professional life cycle of teachers. *Teachers College Record, 91*(1), 31-57.

Huberman, A. M., & Miles, M. B. (1985). Assessing local causality in qualitative research. In D. N. Berg & K. K. Smith (Eds.), *Exploring clinical methods for social research* (pp. 351-381). Newbury Park, CA: Sage.

Kaplan, A. (1964). *The conduct of inquiry.* Scranton, PA: Chandler.

Krathwohl, D. R. (1993). *Methods of educational and social science research: An integrated approach.* White Plains, NY: Longman.

Kvale, S. (1988). The 1000-page question. *Phenomenology and Pedagogy, 6*(2), 90-106.

Levine, H. G. (1985). Principles of data storage and retrieval for use in qualitative evaluations. *Educational Evaluation and Policy Analysis, 7*(2), 169-186.

Lincoln, Y. S., & Guba, E. G. (1985). *Naturalistic inquiry.* Newbury Park, CA: Sage.

Lofland, J., & Lofland, L. H. (1984). *Analyzing social settings: A guide to qualitative observation and analysis* (2nd ed.). Belmont, CA: Wadsworth.

Louis, K. S. (1982). Multisite/multimethod studies. *American Behavioral Scientist, 26*(1), 6-22.

Manicas, P. T., & Secord, P. F. (1982). Implications for psychology of the new philosophy of science. *American Psychologist, 38,* 390-413.

Manning, P. K. (1982). Analytic induction. In R. B. Smith & P. K. Manning, *A handbook of social science methods: Vol. 2. Qualitative methods* (pp. 273-302). Cambridge, MA: Ballinger.

Marshall, C. (1990). Goodness criteria: Are they objective or judgment calls? In E. G. Guba (Ed.), *The paradigm dialog* (pp. 188-197). Newbury Park, CA: Sage.

Maxwell, J. A., & Miller, B. A. (1992). *Two aspects of thought and two components of qualitative data analysis.* Cambridge, MA: Harvard University, Graduate School of Education.

Melnick, C. R., & Beaudry, J. S. (1990, April). *A qualitative research perspective: Theory, practice, essence.* Paper presented at the annual meeting of the American Educational Research Association, Boston.

Merryfield, M. M. (1990, April). *Integrating interpretation and description in case study reporting: Constructing dialogues and scenes.* Paper presented at the annual meeting of the American Educational Research Association, Boston.

Miles, M. B. (1979). Qualitative data as an attractive nuisance: The problem of analysis. *Administrative Science Quarterly, 24,* 590-601.

Miles, M. B., & Huberman, A. M. (1984). *Qualitative data analysis: A sourcebook of new methods.* Newbury Park, CA: Sage.

Miles, M. B., & Huberman, A. M. (1994). *Qualitative data analysis: An expanded sourcebook* (2nd ed.). Newbury Park, CA: Sage.

Miller, S. I. (1982). Quality and quantity: Another view of analytic induction as a research technique. *Quality and Quantity, 16,* 281-295.

Mishler, E. G. (1990). Validation in inquiry-guided research: The role of exemplars in narrative studies. *Harvard Educational Review, 60,* 415-441.

Mühr, T. (1991). ATLAS/ti: A prototype for the support of text interpretation. *Qualitative Sociology, 14,* 349-371.

Nisbett, R. E., & Ross, L. (1980). *Human inference: Strategies and shortcomings of social judgment.* Englewood Cliffs, NJ: Prentice Hall.

Noblit, G. W. (1988, February). *A sense of interpretation.* Paper presented at the Ethnography in Education Research Forum, Philadelphia.

Noblit, G. W., & Hare, R. D. (1983, April). *Meta-ethnography: Issues in the synthesis and replication of qualitative research.* Paper presented at the meeting of the American Educational Research Association.

Noblit, G. W., & Hare, R. D. (1988). *Meta-ethnography: Synthesizing qualitative studies.* Newbury Park, CA: Sage.

Packer, M. J., & Addison, R. B. (1989). Evaluating an interpretive account. In M. J. Packer & R. B. Addison (Eds.), *Entering the circle: Hermeneutic investigation in psychology* (pp. 275-292). Albany: State University of New York Press.

Pearsol, J. A. (1985). *Controlling qualitative data: Understanding teachers' value perspectives on a sex equity education project.* Paper presented at the annual meeting of the American Educational Research Association, Chicago.

Phillips, D. C. (1990). Subjectivity and objectivity: An objective inquiry. In E. W. Eisner & A. Peshkin (Eds.), *Qualitative inquiry in education: The continuing debate* (pp. 19-37). New York: Teachers College Press.

Polkinghorne, D. E. (1988). *Narrative knowing and the human sciences.* Albany: State University of New York Press.

Preissle, J. (1991). *The choreography of design: A personal view of what design means in qualitative research.* Paper presented at the Qualitative Research Conference, University of Georgia, Athens.

Qualis Research Associates. (1990). *The Ethnograph: A program for the computer-assisted analysis of text-based data.* Corvallis, OR: Author.

Ragin, C. C. (1987). *The comparative method: Moving beyond qualitative and quantitative strategies.* Berkeley: University of California Press.

Ratcliffe, J. W. (1983). Notions of validity in qualitative research methodology. *Knowledge: Creation, Diffusion, Utilization, 5,* 147-167.

Read, S. J., Druian, P. R., & Miller, L. C. (1989). The role of causal sequence in the meaning of actions. *British Journal of Social Psychology, 28,* 341-351.

Reed, D. B., & Furman, G. C. (1992). *The* 2 × 2 matrix in qualitative data analysis and theory generation. Paper presented at the annual meeting of the American Educational Research Association, San Francisco.

Rein, M., & Schön, D. (1977). Problem setting in policy research. In C. Weiss (Ed.), *Using social policy research in public policy making.* Lexington, MA: D. C. Heath.

Richards, L., & Richards, T. (1989). *Old goals, new goals: Toward the next generation of qualitative analysis programs.* Bundoora, Victoria, Australia: La Trobe University.

Robinson, W. S. (1951). The logical structure of analytic induction. *American Sociological Review, 16,* 812-818.

Rossman, G. B., & Wilson, B. L. (1985). Numbers and words: Combining quantitative and qualitative methods in a single large-scale evaluation study. *Evaluation Review, 9,* 627-643.

Runkel, P. J. (1990). *Casting nets and testing specimens: Two grand methods of psychology.* New York: Praeger.

Schillemans, L., et al. (n.d.). *Treating victims of incest.* Antwerp, Belgium: Flemish Institute for General Practice and University of Antwerp, Department of Family Medicine.

Schofield, J. W. (1990). Increasing the generalizability of qualitative research. In E. Eisner & A. Peshkin (Eds.), *Qualitative inquiry in education: The continuing debate* (pp. 201-232). New York: Teachers College Press.

Schwandt, T. A., & Halpern, E. S. (1988). *Linking auditing and metaevaluation: Enhancing quality in applied research.* Newbury Park, CA: Sage.

Schwartzman, H., & Werner, O. (1990). Census, taxonomies, and the partition of ethnographic tasks. *Cultural Anthropology Methods Newsletter, 2*(3), 8-9.

Scriven, M. (1974). Maximizing the power of causal investigations: The modus operandi method. In W. J. Popham (Ed.), *Evaluation in education: Current perspectives* (pp. 68-84). Berkeley, CA: McCutchan.

Sieber, S. D. (1976). *A synopsis and critique of guidelines for qualitative analysis contained in selected textbooks.* New York: Center for Policy Research, Project on Social Architecture in Education.

Silverstein, A. (1988). An Aristotelian resolution of the ideographic versus nomothetic tension. *American Psychologist, 43,* 425-430.

Smith, L. M. (1992). Ethnography. In M. C. Alkin (Ed.), *Encyclopedia of educational research* (Vol. 2, 6th ed., pp. 458-462). New York: Macmillan.

Smith, N. L. (1981). Noncausal inquiry in education. *Educational Researcher, 10*(3), 23.

Smith, N. L. (1987). Toward the justification of claims in evaluation research. *Evaluation and Program Planning, 10,* 309-314.

Strauss, A. L. (1987). *Qualitative analysis for social scientists.* Cambridge, UK: Cambridge University Press.

Van Maanen, J. (Ed.). (1979). *Qualitative methodology.* Beverly Hills, CA: Sage.

Van Maanen, J. (Ed.). (1983). *Qualitative methodology* (updated reprint). Beverly Hills, CA: Sage.

Van Maanen, J. (1988). *Tales of the field: On writing ethnography.* Chicago: University of Chicago Press.

Warner, W. (1991). *Improving interpretive validity of camera-based qualitative research.* Paper presented at the Qualitative Health Research Conference, Edmonton, Alberta.

Weick, K. (1979). *The social psychology of organizing.* Reading, MA: Addison-Wesley.

Weitzman, E., & Miles, M. B. (1993). *Computer-aided qualitative data analysis: A review of selected software.* New York: Center for Policy Research.

Werner, O., & Schoepfle, G. M. (1987a). *Systematic fieldwork: Vol. 1. Foundations of ethnography and interviewing.* Newbury Park, CA: Sage.

Werner, O., & Schoepfle, G. M. (1987b). *Systematic fieldwork: Vol. 2. Ethnographic analysis and data management.* Newbury Park, CA: Sage.

Wolcott, H. F. (1992). Posturing in qualitative inquiry. In M. D. LeCompte, W. L. Millroy, & J. Preissle (Eds.), *The handbook of qualitative research in education* (pp. 3-52). New York: Academic Press.

Wolfe, R. (1992). Data management. In M. C. Alkin (Ed.), *Encyclopedia of educational research* (6th ed., pp. 293-299). New York: Macmillan.

Woods, P. (1979). *The divided school.* London: Routledge & Kegan Paul.

Yin, R. K. (1984). *Case study research: Design and methods.* Beverly Hills, CA: Sage.

Yin, R. K. (1991). *Applications of case study research.* Washington, DC: Cosmos Corporation.

Znaniecki, R. (1934). *The method of sociology.* New York: Farrar & Rinehart.

28

■

Using Computers in Qualitative Research

THOMAS J. RICHARDS
LYN RICHARDS

MOST qualitative researchers now work with computers, but relatively few use software designed for qualitative analysis. This is not because they see no need for help in handling rich, complex, or messy data. Rather, computers offer no instant solutions to the problems faced by qualitative researchers, because the data they handle are particularly resistant to tidy processing methods and the methods they use are very unlike the techniques computers easily support. The past decade has produced a plethora of software packages that seem as though they should help, but these are packages designed for executives, librarians, and banks. There is now a much smaller group of programs designed for particular approaches to qualitative research, but they are less accessible and less professionally presented. Thus the researcher is offered a bewildering range of ways of handling textual data on computers, and many of these are quite different from the methods found in qualitative texts. The computer method can have dramatic implications for the research process and outcomes, from unacceptable restrictions on analysis to unexpected opening out of possibilities.

Our purposes in this chapter are to look at methodological features of qualitative data analysis (QDA) to consider how, and how much, and how well, it can be computerized; to give an overview of general-purpose packages that can be used in QDA, and some types of special-purpose QDA packages; to discuss how they can be used and how well they work; to provide some pointers to future software developments; and to stimulate methodological debate on computational QDA. We have written elsewhere of our concerns about the impacts of computing techniques on method and the real dangers of software constraining and distorting research (Richards & Richards, 1991a, 1991b), and of our experiences as researchers making the transition to computers (Richards & Richards, in press). The first remains a background theme in this chapter.

Most reports on software options are accounts of particular programs, usually by their developers and/or marketers. We ourselves are, *inter alia,* developers. (NUD•IST, the software we developed in our research, is now marketed by a company at our university.) Like literary critics who are also novelists, we have a methodological position and a commitment to its products. The reader, thus informed, can evaluate our arguments.

Both as researchers and as software designers, we started from the research processes involved in relating data and theory in qualitative data analysis and the different ways software might support or distort them. This chapter starts there. We then describe and critique a series of types of software in terms of purposes and design, examining the implications of the method supported by each. Thus we offer a methodological map, and, like all maps, it selects the features to be presented.

Our goal is to emphasize the new frontiers, rather than to offer a list of product descriptions.

Product descriptions are readily available from developers (to counter our standpoint): For a special journal issue on this topic, see the November 1991 issue of *Qualitative Sociology*; for conference papers, see Fielding and Lee (1991). Most contributions to those collections (including ours) are arguments for particular software approaches. For penetrating comparative reviews by a nondeveloper and nonmarketer, see Miles and Huberman (1994, Appendix A) and, for more depth, Weitzman and Miles (1994). For earlier partial surveys, compare Tesch (1990) with Pfaffenberger (1988) on sociological approaches, and both with Bailey (1982), Hockey (1980), and Miall (1990) on related software for humanities.

Here instead we offer the researcher a comparative account of software architectures and of the directions of developments. We encourage readers to evaluate software packages in terms of what they propose to do (Did you *want* to do that?) and what new techniques might or might not enhance analysis or restrict method. Having chosen a software approach, the best way to get up-to-date information on software is to send for current product descriptions and demonstration disks and read the survey literature. A list of addresses for the developers of the programs discussed here is included in the appendix to this chapter.

Theory and Data

Working "up" from data is often presented as what qualitative research is especially about. It is done in many ways: building new understandings from "thick descriptions"; reflecting on and exploring data records; discovering patterns and constructing and exploring impressions, summaries, pen portraits. All such efforts have theoretical results. They produce new ideas and new concepts, which are sometimes linked and presented more formally as new theories. Most approaches to qualitative research also work "down" from theory. They incorporate, explore, and build on prior theoretical input, on hunches or ideas or sometimes formal hypotheses. Many also stress the testing of theory derived from the project's data.

Computers easily offer assistance in the management of complex data. They also, with more difficulty, can be used in the discovery and management of unrecognized ideas and concepts, and the construction and exploration of explanatory links between the data and emergent ideas, to make fabrics of argument and understanding around them.

Managing Data

Ideas are produced in qualitative research in heterogeneous ways, many of which are not given the august title of "theorizing." It is not our purpose to survey the range of those methods; rather, we simply note that there is a range and that these methods are supported by software. As other chapters in this volume indicate, different researchers have different methods (and terms) for the exploration and understanding of rich data; production of "thick descriptions" (Geertz, 1973, p. 26); discovery and uses of patterns; construction of new concepts and testing of old; linking of these into theoretical frameworks, explanations, and models; and validating of impressions and conclusions. Nor are these unchanging. Theory testing is emphasized increasingly even in recent writings in the "grounded theory" tradition (Glaser & Strauss, 1967; see also Strauss & Corbin, 1990), which is often, in our view mistakenly, presented as the dominant approach to theorizing in qualitative research.

All these processes involve the recognition of categories *in the data,* generation of ideas about them, and exploration of meanings *in the data.* Because the categories and meanings are found in the text or data records, this process demands data management methods that support insight and discovery, encourage recognition and development of categories, and store them and their links with data. Ease of access to data is important to support recognition of the surprising and unexpected, construction of coherent stories, and exploration of sought patterns, as well as construction and testing of hypotheses (Bogdan & Taylor, 1975). But those methods also must not get in the way, by distorting rich records, diluting "thick descriptions," or demanding routines that destroy insight.

When these theorizing processes were done using manual data-handling methods, researchers often (though by no means always) managed their data by coding for retrieval. The *code-and-retrieve* process consists of labeling passages of the data according to what they are about or other content of interest in them (*coding* or *indexing*), then providing a way of collecting identically labeled passages (*retrieving*). Collecting photocopied segments into labeled hang files and writing text references onto labeled index cards are two obvious noncomputational code-and-retrieve techniques. The technique of annotating passages in page margins is code only.

Before computers, many researchers did not code segments of text. Rather, they felt through, explored, read and reread, "worked and reworked the particulars of ethnographic inquiry" (Kirk & Miller, 1986, p. 32). This required a simpler and more complex form of data management, as researchers compared and systematically built upon data records, keeping growing memo records about the accruing evidence and their exploration of its narrative and convincing body. Theory was arrived at and tested not through the retrieval of text chunks but through complex processes of evidence analysis, including consideration of knowledge about the site or story that is not in the text. For an eloquent account of why code-and-retrieve methods can fail the ethnographer, and of how computing technology rather than the research subject can determine ethnographic method, see Agar (1991)—an autobiography that is the more important because Agar himself is a user of computers and "select-and-sort" techniques.

Many researchers still do not use the code-and-retrieve method. Possibly fewer would use the method now if the software they bought did not support it. But it is certainly the most widely recommended technique for management of rich and complex records. (For different approaches, see, e.g., Hammersley & Atkinson, 1983; Lofland & Lofland, 1984; Lincoln & Guba, 1985; Miles & Huberman, 1984.) However, despite its popularity, the code-and-retrieve method has rarely been examined as a *method.* The literature contains many lucid descriptions of how data records were handled, but reveals little serious debate over what that method of data handling does to data or how it contributes to analysis.

This taken-for-granted method was easily supported by computers and became the basis of most specialist QDA software. Computers, moreover, offered the possibility of addressing its limitations and adapting the code-and-retrieve mode of organization to assist with other theorizing activities. The method was thus subjected to debate in the new context of computing. An odd result of these developments was that the code-and-retrieve method for the first time was treated as in some way atheoretical, merely "descriptive-analytical" (Tesch, 1990). The creation of this dichotomy both underestimates the method and skews critiques of software based on it. One of our arguments below is that all of the specialized software we describe is so based. All of these software packages can be used just for coding and retrieval. And far from merely supporting description, techniques of coding for retrieval strongly support some ways of making ideas, and of constructing and testing theories.

First, the generation of categories, even the simplest descriptors, whether arrived at prior to data reading or by discovery of recurrent topics (Bogdan & Taylor, 1975) or *in vivo* categories in text (Strauss, 1987), is a contribution to theory. Decisions are being made about what is a category of significance to the study, what questions are being asked, what concepts developed, what ideas explored, and whether these categories should be altered, redefined, or deleted during analysis. Second, decisions about what text segments are relevant to a category are never merely clerical decisions; they always involve some theoretical consideration. Third, the viewing of segments from many documents on one topic or selected topics always offers a new way of seeing data. This is the major claim of the method to support analysis, and researchers using it clearly engage in the building up of theories. Moreover, the method supports pursuit of patterns by comparison of text segments on that topic from different sources (e.g., Did the young women have different ideas about domestic duties from women of other age groups?). Such questions may be crucial for locating patterns and are sometimes formally portrayed by presentation of data in qualitative matrices (Miles & Huberman, 1984).

So it is misleading to label the code-and-retrieve method as not theory building. But the challenge remains to adapt it to ways of recording, linking, exploring, testing, and building cumulatively on the insights derived from data. To draw on a distinction first made by Turner (1981), theory *emergence* in qualitative research is interlinked with processes of theory *construction.* Ideas, concepts, and categories discovered in the data are woven by researchers into fabrics of theory. These processes offer greater challenges to software designers.

Theory Construction

Theory *construction* in qualitative research (the exploration and linking of theoretical and other organizing and explanatory concepts and statements) is creative, not merely mechanical. The data-handling tasks associated are thus highly complex. And theory *testing* is usually part of theory construction, not a subsequent stage. Concepts are captured; links are explored, created, and tested; ideas are documented and systematically reworked, in textual memos, models, and diagrams expressing the specification, explication, exploration, and elaboration of theories. How can computers support this?

The code-and-retrieve method, we have argued, supports theory emergence. It also expresses theories that can be represented by codes and then tested by looking for codes in text and studying the relationships of codes. Computer-based code-and-retrieve will do this better, because computers are good at working with structure, not content. In a code-and-retrieve system, we express or define content by coding the text.

Suppose, for example, you have a hypothesis that people of a certain type and in a certain situation will behave in a certain way, and you have comprehensive interviews with individuals that check in each case for the types and conditions and the behavior, and the interview transcripts are coded for these. An example is "Young mothers who are reluctant to return to work explain it in terms of a woman's duty to stay at home." Then a simple study of coding patterns in the interview texts can be used to confirm the theory's *correctness* (check if there are any interviews coded for all the types and conditions but not for the behavior) and *completeness*—"*Only* young mothers . . . "—(check if there are any interviews coded for the behavior but not for all the types and conditions).[1] Note that what we are doing here is successfully using co-occurrences of codes within interview documents as evidence for features of theories: *Textual structure* as delineated by code-and-retrieve methods can be related to *theoretical content* (including information about the world). If this were not so, we would not use code-and-retrieve methods.

But this is not always so. Most social science theories find their support in the *content of the data,* not the *structure of textual records.* Management of records by use of code-and-retrieve in such cases offers help, but that help is limited to retrieving all passages coded with something relevant to the theory in question, so that the researcher can reflect on them all together.

This is not an insignificant contribution. The ability to retrieve all the text about a certain topic or topics strongly supports the development of new insights. The computer can do this quickly and efficiently. Sophisticated programs offer a wide range of ways of selecting retrievals according to co-occurrence or non-co-occurrence of codes in text, allowing the researcher to "fracture" the data (Strauss, 1987) and see it anew. But this contribution to the researcher's ability to access data should not obscure an important distinction: that between the *textual level* of work, which is where code-and-retrieve methods operate, where we code for talk-about-return-to-work and talk-about-mothering, and the *conceptual level* of work, where theories about people and the world are expressed, where evidence and argument are brought to bear, and where returning to work and mothering are explored.

The code-and-retrieve method we have described applies only to text. That which is coded and retrieved is the document. Literally, one codes talk-about-mothering (the text passages), not mothering (the concept). But no researcher stops there. What one would *also* like to do with software is to support directly conceptual-level work, not just textual-level work—that is, to have software that could directly represent the concept of equality and how it gets related to the concept of parenting.

So the dichotomy that matters is not descriptive-analytic versus theoretical: All data management methods involve theorizing. Rather, in assessing what computers contribute we need to distinguish textual-level operations from conceptual-level operations. Whereas code-and-retrieve as we have described it is a textual-level operation, one's codings and retrievals are guided by theoretical interests, are used to shape and test theory, and (inevitably) put theoretical blinkers on one's access to the text. Textual-level operations are theoretically relevant, but they do not construct or operate on theories.

Finding ways of supporting theoretical-level operations in qualitative research offers a major challenge to software designers. Consider, for example, how we work when developing theory from the text. We often get going by finding little things that relate in some meaningful way—perhaps, if our interest is in stress, that certain topics get discussed in anxious ways (and that is something that good coding and retrieval can find for us). So then we start looking for components in those topics that might cause anxiety, often by studying the text, finding or guessing the components and coding for them, recalling situational facts not in the text, and looking for suggestive co-occurrences of codes. We might on a hunch start looking at text passages on people's personal security and how they arrange it (research on background theory here, and lots of coding again), to see if there is some possible connection between components occurring in the anxiety topics and security arrangements. If we find one, the theory is still thin, so we embark on a search for others, and thereby look for a pattern. The result of this is a little group of chunked-together coded text, ideas and hypotheses that, provided they can be kept and accessed as a chunk, can become an ingredient in further more abstracted or wide-ranging explorations. This chunk is said to be of larger "grain size" than its component codings, and it may in turn become an ingredient of a later theorizing of larger grain size still that is built out of existing chunks. (Big fleas are made out of smaller fleas.)

And so the web—of code, explore, relate, study the text—grows, resulting in little explorations, little tests, little ideas hardly worth calling theories but that need to be hung onto as wholes, to be further data for further study. Together they link together with other theories and make the story, the understanding of the text. The strength of this growing interpretation lies to a considerable extent in the fine grain size and tight interknittedness of all these steps; and the job of qualitative data handling (and software) is to help in the development of such growing interpretations.

This network of concepts, evidence, relations of concepts, coordinations of data, of hierarchies of grain size where the theory/data/explanation chunks of one grain size are the data for the work of the next grain size up, is a good fractal-like model of people's explanatory belief systems (belief systems are explanation systems). This is how a person (e.g., a social scientist) reflectively constructs an explanation, a story, for and from data.

The process is not all bottom-up, however. The researcher uses at each stage expectations, prior theories, hunches, experience, and a good education (as with the theoretical determination of textual codes). The network builds up from the bottom, guided by a vision of the structure of a larger-scale network into which these small empirical gleanings must fit. When one gets there, the larger-scale structure is likely to be different in many ways from the early ghostly vision; were it not so, the constructed theory would be quite unempirical, quite unconditioned by one's data. And if one's prior ideas are wildly out, then that will show up in the increasingly procrustean strains of trying to build the anticipated larger structures from the small, heavily data-conditioned ones. Here is where one's critics will show one a more amenable approach to interpreting the data, fewer exceptions requiring fewer ad hoc justifications, more meaningful relationships binding cases and patterns together, more elegance.

We will call this description of building relations between data and theory *data-theory bootstrapping*. Providing direct conceptual-level support for this process puts some interesting demands on software design. Coding for retrieval seems to be basic to such procedures, but researchers also want to hold their growing nets or hierarchies of concepts, evidence links, groupings of ideas, and so on that make up the explanatory structure in an accessible way that will help them see where they have been and give access to the fine grains out of which we build the larger grains. The software system that would help with this would hold not just the data and tools for manipulating it, but also in some sense the growing analysis and explanation system.

And because, in that recursive fractal-like way we have described, the partial results and little theories become part of the data for the next move in the analysis, that software would treat the analysis/explanation material added to the database as more data alongside the original textual material. The very analytic structures, the explanations, become more data. Indeed, the very processes of analysis (the computations) should be fed back in as data. That is, we want to save as data the theory/data/explanation chunks of one grain size so they can be explored as data for explanations at the next level up. Methodologically, this is known as *system closure*: Results obtained about the system, analytic techniques used on the system, become part of the system. A hallmark of qualitative social science research (but not of physics) is that the data being researched in a project are closed over its own techniques and results. System closure is the software feature needed to support directly the conceptual process of data-theory bootstrapping. (Needed, yes, but not sufficient—system closure will not necessarily give you a leg up on direct conceptual-level software operations.)

Qualitative researchers also need to jump from one code to a *conceptually* related one (to explore theory) or to a *factually* related one (to explore patterns in the world the research is about). So the database should maintain and exploit theoretical links between concepts, and the real-world facts about and links among people, places, actions, and so on, not just explore *textual* links between codes representing those concepts, people, and so on. If, for example, we store that John is married to Mary, that John is a blue-collar worker, and that John has been out of work (note that these are facts that might not be expressed in the text at all), we should then be able to ask for all the remarks of women married to out-of-work blue-collar people on some coded topic and *automatically* get Mary's remarks.

The procedures of theory construction described here require above all a very flexible, very easy-to-modify database, that will shift, reorganize, undo, and backtrack to earlier states. This is because the process of constructing an understanding is tentative, involving the exploration and testing of hunches at all grain size levels, hanging onto them if they look good for now, throwing them away when they no longer fit, while maintaining the rest of the growing structure.

Can computers assist with, even improve on, the ways we construct and test theory? Can they go further, and support the *explicit formulation of theory*? What of the explicit *finding and recording of knowledge* about the situation being studied, the putting of data to theory?

Current Situation in Qualitative Software

In the following sections we explore the architecture and purposes of available software. We start with types aimed at a broad class of users, but that can offer advantages not available in specialist packages. This provides a basis for understanding why special-purpose packages arose and what they try to do. We then deal with those, considering first software that adapts the traditional code-and-retrieve method, and then approaches that combine that method with new ways of constructing the links among theories, knowledge, and text, testing them and modeling them.

General-Purpose Software Packages

Word Processors

Apart from the obvious and familiar advantages (such as ability to inspect an entire document, collate and explore selected extracts in a new document, print it out, line number it, edit it), the modern word processor (WP) offers some features unmatched in most specialist QDA software. If the data are textual (e.g., interviews) and in WP document form, these features include the following:

- The ability to handle multiple documents on-screen in separate windows at the same time, which facilitates comparing thematically similar passages in different documents and copying segments of one document to another.
- The ability to handle formatted files (using the WP program's own format conventions) so that tables, diagrams, and the like can be included. Most special-purpose QDA packages work only with text-only ASCII files.
- The ability to include static pictures, charts, tables, and so on as illustrations or as editable models of the emerging ideas and diagrams of the theories. These need not be computer generated, but can be documents of any sort read into a disk file by use of a scanner, and may be in color.
- The ability to include video and audio data, accessible via icons in the WP text.
- Generally good text-search facilities, which in some WP programs support the use of patterns in text search.
- A *publish-and-subscribe* facility, in which a passage from one document is marked as available for inclusion in others (published). When included in another (subscribed to) it is not copied; rather, it is as if the published portion of the first document is visible directly in the second document. In this way, if the published passage is edited at any future time in the first document, those changes show up in the subscribing document.
- A *linking* or *hypertext* facility by which the user can select the subscribed passage and so open a new window into the publishing document at the published text, for inspection and editing. An elegant application of linking, for QDA purposes, is to mark passages in a (publishing) document with keywords or icons, and link the keywords through to the subscribing documents. Selecting the keywords in the subscribing documents will then open a window into the publishing document at the position of the keyword, so the user can see the keyed passage. In this way groups of related passages, in the same or different documents, can get linked together and the user can jump from one to the other.
- An *annotation* facility, in which an icon is inserted in the text and clicking on it opens a text window in which one can read and write memos. The annotations can optionally be printed with the WP file at the point they annotate.

These relatively recent features, such as publish/subscribe, linking, incorporation of video/audio data, and annotations, powerfully extend the more traditional WP features such as text search. For the qualitative analyst they provide imaginative ways of linking data, combining different media appropriately, and relating commentary and theoretical memos.

The main problem with WPs is what they do not do, or support badly. They do not automate the grouping of similarly coded passages—one must copy and paste, or link, them oneself (or at best write a macro). They become very clumsy if one tries to use them to handle large numbers of codes or many references from codes to text. They will not provide text searches for co-occurrences of codes (more on these in later sections). And they will not provide clerical and management tools (e.g., What codes have I used? What do they mean?). In WP programs, clerical data must be stored separately to prevent it getting lost in the data documents, whereas good special-purpose QDA software will hold and retrieve clerical data where and when wanted, to facilitate database exploration.

Nevertheless, smaller projects in particular may welcome the modern word processor as a flexible and full-featured tool for document exploration and the construction of analysis documents that relate themselves neatly to source documents and other media, which can be only a mouse click away. And specialist software packages too often lag way behind in these features.

Text Search Packages

Text search, long ignored by qualitative researchers, offers much more than useful tools for linguistic or protocol analysis. It can find themes in the text, gain instant access to occurrences of a newly discovered theme in text already coded, and locate topic markers such as question numbers.

The principles of most text search tools are much the same, and extend the text search facilities found in WPs. The simplest will search for a string (sequence of characters) in files of text and report each find in some way, such as displaying it in context and outputting its character or line position in the file. A more sophisticated type will support search for Boolean co-occurrences of strings (*and, or,* and *not* searches) within some stated unit of text, such as a line or paragraph, or even allow one to express complex *patterns* in the search, and will report and save every string in the text that matches the pattern. The common grammar used to express patterns is called *regular expression syntax* and is embodied in the famous Unix utility called grep (global regular expression printer), which is usually available as freeware for other types of computers, and is more powerful than most proprietary text search packages.

Text search packages search files (they do not need to be open in a window) and sometimes have special facilities for fast searching for user-supplied keywords in documents and then providing statistically useful results of various sorts on keyword co-occurrences and correlations.

Text search alone is not a sufficient tool for most qualitative researchers, because they also want, among other things, to store finds at a code (a system closure feature). But it is a necessary tool for gaining direct access to data records, rather than accessing them only through codes expressing the researcher's interpretation. When words of the text matter, or codes fail, text search is essential, and the computer searches text much faster than one can code it. Hence software supporting other QDA methods is greatly strengthened if it includes text search facilities.

In addition to general text search packages such as GOfer™ and ZyINDEX™, a number of concordance and similar content-analysis programs have been developed, primarily for literary studies, that will carry out word frequency counts, provide listings of chosen words embedded in a line of context and with a references to where they occur (KWIC—keyword in context—indexes), spot grammatical styles, and usually provide statistics on their finds. Some of these packages are extremely sophisticated (for further details, see Bailey, 1982; Hockey, 1980; Miall, 1990).

Relational Database Management Systems

Relational database management systems (RDBMSs) can undoubtedly be very useful in a social science project, for both management of project information and analysis of research data. However, their powers are often misunderstood and misapplied in the QDA context.

Suppose you have a card file of your interviewees, each card containing name, address, gender, birth date, and date of interview. These cards can be easily replaced in an RDBMS by a two-dimensional table, with one row per card and columns for name, address, and so on. The rows are called *records,* corresponding to each card in the original stack. The columns are called *fields.* You define the fields for each table, then create as many records with those fields as you need. Typically, fields can be defined as *numeric* (holding a number), *Boolean* (holding *true* or *false*), *character* (holding a few words of text, such as a name), *date,* and *memos* (holding your notes on the record). You have to specify how many characters each character field occupies (except memos, which is usually set to some upper limit, such as 800 characters). Whether or not a field is filled in for a given record, it will still occupy that number of characters in disk storage (except for memos, which can grow up to the limit).

The power of database systems comes from tools to *sort* records on any numeric, Boolean, or text field, or combinations thereof, and to *filter* records, extracting certain ones with desired values in various fields. If you think of other fields you want after you have created your database, it is usually easy to add them in. Some RDBMSs also specialize in handling text rather than fixed-size numeric or character fields; these can be of advantage for QDA purposes. Facilities are often provided for text search on text or character fields, but note that text sectors of these fields cannot be coded for retrieval of the coded segments.

In your interview project, having created the database table described above to manage biographical data about interviewees, you could then create further ones to handle data about what they said in the interviews. If the interview comprises a number of questions, with free text answers to each question, a common procedure is to create a database table for each question, one record per interviewee, with a field for the interviewee's name, another containing the entire text of his or her response, and further ones labeled with topic codes containing the portions of the response germane to each topic code.

These database systems are called *relational* because the researcher can relate one such table to another. All he or she needs is to have a field in common. Any of the tables above can be related if they all have the interviewee name field in common. Similarly, tables with a topic field in common can be related through the common topic field, allowing the easy extraction of what an interviewee, or selected interviewees, said on that topic in answer to different questions. The result is that the researcher can use tables jointly to extract interesting data. One could, for example, list all married female interviewees who have a certain attitude toward alcoholism. This enables numerical and comparative studies—What fraction of all married female interviewees are they? Are unmarried females rather different in their attitudes?

So how useful are these systems to a qualitative researcher? They work best for discrete structured data, rather than for long, unstructured textual data requiring close study of content and data-theory bootstrapping. The attempt to create fields corresponding to topic codes, and putting text in those fields, is extremely expensive of storage. Moreover, if one uses many codes, more code fields per record tend to be empty, leading to sparsely filled tables that are hard to work with. RDBMSs work well for such purposes as analyzing the results of structured questionnaires that get discrete data as answers—names, places, and so on—or for analyzing social systems that can be described in discrete terms (participants, objects, transactions between, and so on). After all, RDBMSs have grown up to handle the discrete data of businesses—employee data, inventory, sales transactions, and the like—for purposes of analysis of business trends.

Like many general-purpose tools, however, they can be ingeniously extended. One such extension is a powerful technique for the construction of comprehensive relational databases known as the entity-relationship approach (ERA) (Chen, 1976). This approach comes into its own when the subject of the research project can be characterized as a system whose operation is to be studied, such as a classroom situation, a workplace, or a household. The user draws up a network diagram in which the *nodes* (the "knots" in the network that the lines join) are the various entities under study, such as the personnel and departments and functions in the company, the means of communication used in the company. Any relations among these entities are drawn as labeled lines (*arcs*) linking the nodes, for example, "reports to," "communicates with," "uses."

In this way the network diagram will specify and relate the major activities and entities in the system, such as the people involved, their tools, their goals within the system, their choices among tools, their actions. If the qualitative data about each of these features (nodes and arcs in the net) tend to be discrete rather than narrative (e.g., for an activity: type of activity, date and time of its occurrence, tools used, participants, its goals), then a whole database table can be set up for that node, whose records hold data about each item of that type that is observed in the study. Observation of the system (studying classroom activities, observing the shuffling of information around the office, and so on) then provides the data that go into the records.

The links in the network diagram show how to relate the database tables in the linked nodes to each other (the *relational* aspect of an RDBMS), and then the very powerful browsing features of a good RDBMS package can be applied to study and find patterns in the operation of the system under study. Winer and Carrière (1991) provide a very instructive and lucid account of a highly innovative system using RDBMSs in this way.

Where data are often discrete and the subject of study can be thought of as a system, the ERA diagrams provide a powerful discipline for creating semantically clear and precise network diagrams describing the system. No meaningless arrows or confused categories here. Then, using the ERA to create a relational database for the data provides a powerful data analysis system for the researcher. But a word of warning: You will want on your research team a computer scientist trained in *data modeling* (construction of ERA diagrams that can be turned neatly into an RDBMS system); the task of system analysis necessary to set up the database system is a skilled professional process. A better idea might be to start teaching data modeling in sociological methods courses—that might help to critique the current often meaningless use of diagrams in sociological literature, and to develop powerful skills in representing social systems and modeling theories.

HyperCard® and Hypermedia

The popular Apple® product HyperCard is a nonrelational database management system with an appealing user interface. A table of records is represented as a "stack" of file cards, only the top one of which (i.e., one record) is visible at a time. One can easily design the visual appearance of card stacks using HyperCard's simple drawing and design facilities. Typically, this is done by designing "fields" to hold the desired data on each card. "Buttons" can be added to the cards that, when selected by mouse click, carry out some predefined actions, such as displaying the next card in the stack. A simple and rather weak programming language allows "stackware authors" (don't call them programmers) to program the behavior of cards, especially button actions.

This simple software metaphor lends itself to some clever applications for QDA. You can tell the products by their Hyper-names, but don't assume they all do the same thing. Hyperqual is a simple code-and-retrieve program (Tesch, 1990). A sophisticated Scottish newcomer, HyperSoft, ingeniously addresses modeling tasks. HyperRESEARCH, discussed below, takes a specific approach to hypothesis testing. These all have in common the restriction of displaying only one record at a time, and none can act as a *relational* database, because there is no simple way in HyperCard of relationally linking stacks by common data fields.

HyperCard is very good at storing text, as one can add scrolling text fields to cards. These fields can support text code-and-retrieve facilities, with the advantage of "one-step" coding (no need to code paper records and then input coding data). Moreover, by positioning buttons over words or phrases and programming the button action to go to other cards with the same words or phrases, one can provide a sort of *hypertext* facility—a way of linking similar text passages so that one can move from one to the other. (Where the links are not just with text, but, for example, with audio and video media, we call this facility *hypermedia.*) The hypermedia facilities of HyperCard can be exploited to link field data text to the researcher's memos about it, or to records of associated factual data, or to link the passages of the research report to evidence material relevant to each passage. Other packages, such as StorySpace™, are designed to support these facilities directly, and should be taken seriously as tools for imaginative exploration (and creation) of text. For an example of such work using another such package, NoteCards™, see Halasz, Moran, and Trigg (1987). For a general survey of hypertext principles and software, see Conklin (1987).

Conclusion

Software not designed for QDA can be useful for certain purposes, but it can also constrain researchers who need flexibility and multiple methods. However, a study of how these systems work is essential if researchers are to know what they might expect of specialist software. From these general-purpose approaches, specialist qualitative research software should now gain such features as the following:

- publish-and-subscribe facility as a way of maintaining segmentation (coding) of text that changes; for example, as one adds commentary directly into the field notes
- pattern-based text search, *plus* the ability to code the finds automatically
- the way RDBMS packages organize discrete qualitative data; sort, filter, and make reports on it; and can be used to find patterns in the data
- hypermedia features that support "commenting" on segmented text and other media data directly, associating database material and audio/video playback with text, and storing memos linked to text, then moving easily among memos, data, and text

Special-Purpose Software for QDA

The 1980s delivered a collection of QDA software tools designed to address the peculiar needs of QDA work. Recent software systems build on the techniques developed by the pioneer programs, and incorporate both their ability to do the tasks of coding for retrieval and, we would argue, the disadvantages of that method. We distinguish five types of specialist software, each identified by its information representation and processing methods. The first, code-and-retrieve, is a form of information processing that is incorporated in each of the other four. All of the later types provide other ways of storing and accessing knowledge and constructing, exploring, and testing data and theory. In each case we describe one (sometimes the only) software example.

Code-and-Retrieve Software

This type of software was the first development for QDA, created by social scientists attempting to replicate the code-and-retrieve techniques that they had used manually. It has been around long enough for studies by or of its users to appear (e.g., Tallerico, 1991), and the range and operation of packages then available has been fully described by Tesch (1990).

Code-and-retrieve packages, all in different ways, allow one to enter (and change) coding of specified text segments of documents into a database, then collect and display all text segments marked by the same code. Some have enhancements that improve considerably on manual methods. The first available and best-known example of this type of software is the Ethnograph (Seidel & Clark, 1984). In its forthcoming version 4, the Ethnograph will do the following:

- retrieve on presence or absence of two (or more) codes; that is, report and optionally display all text portions indexed by all of the nominated codes, or by one but not the second—doing so-called Boolean searches using logical *and* and relative *not* or searches for sequences or proximity of codes
- support the collection of documents into sets, called *catalogues*; retrieval operations can then be restricted to a chosen catalogue
- do text search
- store memos

- display the occurrences of codes in files or specified text portions
- display subheaders to identify speakers or context
- display statistics about the number of retrievals
- hold factual information about each document as codes applying to the whole document (called *face-sheet variables*) or to individuals (in a *speaker sheet,* recording religion, gender, age group, and so on) (These codes can be used in multicode retrieval. Note that a face-sheet variable, though conveniently indexing a whole document, is actually coding a *fact,* and so operates at the conceptual level as well as the textual level. Imaginatively used in retrievals, this provides a powerful way of relating conceptual-level operations to textual-level ones.)

The method thus offers much assistance in managing data, and also, as we argued above, in building and using theoretical categories. But it also has major problems, and software developments have sought to address these. First, the method "decontextualizes" (Seidel's term, used in Tesch, 1990, p. 115). Stripping the segment out of context is necessary and desirable if it is to be "recontextualized" in the new category context. But the context of data is essential to any "holistic" interpretation. Second, the method always threatens with rigidity. All code-and-retrieve software permits introduction and deletion of codes at any time, but this leaves problems in constructing new categories after the coding of many records without those categories; for example, how to return to the passages previously missed? And third, this method tends to impose on qualitative research a chronology more like that of survey research: sequential stages of data collection, data coding, then data analysis. Analysis is postponed if researchers find difficulty in keeping the ideas and insights emerging while clerically coding (and computers will do much more coding, so the task can become more dominating).

Developers of software supporting code-and-retrieve usually and rightly deplore these effects, particularly the last, and attribute them, particularly the last, to bad habits in the user rather than the software. Each of these problems is accessible to computer solution, but, like most manual systems, software systems do not easily support the integration of the process of coding (often perceived as dreary and clerical) with the (tentative, exciting) processes of discovery and surprise, or recording of new ideas and exploration of links between emerging categories. Developers make no claim that code-and-retrieve software supports anything like the entire qualitative research process, but minimally that it speeds up and extends the common clerical business of document coding, and makes the clerical business of retrieval guaranteed complete relative to the coding (unlike flicking through pages of transcript looking for marginal annotations). It is probably this perception of code-and-retrieve software that has led to the mistaken view that it has no theory-finding, theory-building, or theory-testing ramifications.

Software is certainly responding to these challenges. "Decontextualized" text collected at a code was always easy to chase back to the original context via information about the location of segments; but software using multiple window interfaces will allow the original documents to be viewed alongside the grouped retrievals. Limits on the number of codes available and/or the number of times a given rich passage can be coded are being extended or even removed. Considerable effort has gone into making the codes and their contents flexible, so data segments can be easily recoded and inconsistencies in coding discovered, and codes viewed, redefined, amalgamated, deleted, and duplicated *safely.* Retrieval styles are now more flexible and include exploration of context by sequencing or proximity of codes in the text. Questioning is no longer limited to the *intersection* of codes at particular text segments. (*In document co-occurrence* is often more important, to find documents coded somewhere with specified codes, though the segments coded do not intersect.) Storing *knowledge* about the situations or people or behaviors studied is often supported, even if that knowledge does not refer to whole documents. And recent software assists researchers, as filing cabinets never did, in managing codes and in the storage of ideas *about* codes and data, in memos, related both to the codes and to the data, as well as in checking reliability and consistency of coding and coders. Some systems combining code-and-retrieve with text search allow automatic indexing of text finds, and a few offer pattern-based text search, essential if the text does not conveniently always offer exactly the characters sought.

Coding for retrieval is one procedure incorporated, increasingly with extra facilities, in virtually all sophisticated QDA software, because it is one very major type of software support that most forms of QDA need, and that general-purpose software cannot provide easily if at all. But the method retains the limitation we stressed in the early sections, that the code-and-retrieve method directs analysis to occurrence or not of specified codes at selected portions of text.

Rule-Based Theory-Building Systems

One direction has been to seek ways of more explicitly specifying, developing, and, especially, testing theory. In commercial expert system software, this is often done using the idea of a *production-rule system.* An example of this genre is HyperRESEARCH, a tool that shows what HyperCard can do if you really work at it (Hesse-Biber, Dupuis, & Kinder, 1991). In its fundamentals this is a code-and-retrieve system, but it exploits the Macintosh™ computer and HyperCard to include pictures and audio- and videotapes among the documents it can index. It also contains many of the desirable enhancements to code-and-retrieve technology we nominated above. It will do text search with "autocoding" of the finds. It will do Boolean searches for in-document co-occurrences of codes, not just for places in the documents where codes intersect. But, significantly, it allows one to retain retrievals in the system. Like autocoding of text search finds, this is a significant system closure feature.

It does this through the use of *production rules.* A production rule is an if-then rule of the form "If conditions C_1 to C_n hold for some data, then perform action A on the data." In HyperRESEARCH, the form is "If a case is coded as C_1 . . . and C_n, then code it also as A." (HyperRESEARCH looks at its data in terms of *cases,* rather than documents, and tries to find theories that explain all the cases studied. Textual data for the cases could be split across different documents.) The new code A (called the *goal*) is then added to the database, referencing the cases coded with *all* of C_1 to C_n. Once the conclusion code A is in the database, it can be used as a condition for another rule, which the user can then begin constructing.

Alternatively, one can build up rule sets "backward," beginning with a rule expressing one's overall hypothesis, then trying to find rules whose conclusions are the conditions of the hypothesis. This process is repeated until one arrives at rules whose conditions are all codes in the textual database. Running the rules forward then enables one to find cases where, by virtue of having all the right initial conditions in their text, the conclusion of the ultimate (initial) hypothesis also holds, even though it is not coded in the text. In the example given by the developers (Hesse-Biber et al., 1991), the overall hypothesis is that if a mother has a negative influence on her daughter's self-image (C_1) and the daughter dislikes her appearance (C_2), then the mother has damaged the daughter's self-image (A, the goal of the research). Then if this C_1 and C_2 are not codes used in the research, they may be defined as goals of further rules, such as, if the mother is critical of the daughter's body image and the mother-daughter relationship is strained, and the daughter is experiencing weight loss, then add that the mother has negatively influenced the daughter's self-image (C_1). In this way one creates "chains" of rules backward from the goal until one is using only conditions that are already codes in the case documents. At that stage the rule set can be "run" to find how many of the cases end up with the goal statement added to them.

This sounds rather like a knowledge-based expert system in artificial intelligence, in that it contains qualitative production rules. But taking the rules together, it amounts to a search for the cases that have coded *somewhere in them* all the conditions of all the rules that are actual indexing codes (i.e., in-case co-occurrences). If (continuing the example of the previous paragraph) the initial codes in the documents used in the rule set are K_1 to K_m, we are doing an in-case co-occurrence search for these codes, nothing more. Cases where the search succeeds are treated as confirming the final hypothesis "If C_1 and C_2, then A," and those where it fails as (presumably) disconfirming it.

But be careful of the methodology here! The *disconfirming* instances of a hypothesis "If C_1 to C_n hold, then A holds" are cases where *all* the conditions hold and the goal, A, *does not* hold. Cases where not all the conditions hold are not disconfirming instances at all. Typically, C_1 to C_n are a mixture of theoretical statements and specific conditions that hold for a given case, and A is an *observable* feature of the case. In other words, *it must be possible* to evaluate whether the goal holds in a case *independent* of whether the conditions all hold. But given that there is no independent coding of cases for A (rather, A is added whenever C_1 to C_n hold), we can never find a case in which C_1 to C_n hold but A does not—the hypothesis is a tautology. What we *can* find is cases where not all of C_1 to C_n hold, but that proves nothing about the hypothesis. In fact, what the running of the whole rule set boils down to is simply looking for cases where the original codes K_1 to K_m occur!

What, then, is the value of production-rule systems for QDA? These rules are certainly an intuitive way of articulating at least some sorts of theory. They do provide a way of bridging the gap between textual-level analysis and the representation and analysis of facts and theories to which we have drawn attention. Starting at the textual level, the production rules allow the definition of increasingly abstract and theoretical concepts in terms initially of the textual codings (K_1 to K_m in the above example) and ultimately whole theories as the later production rules. This conforms closely to the model of data-theory bootstrapping, and provides an elegant way of relating textual-level and conceptual-level operations. But for the process to be of any value in theory testing, as distinct from theory construction, the cases must *independently* be coded with all the rule goals, and the rules run as a search procedure for cases where all conditions of a rule hold but the goal does not.

A methodological difficulty with this is that production rules are supposed to bridge the textual/conceptual divide by making their goals (A's) be more theoretical concepts defined in terms of less theoretical existing ones (the C's). Now we are saying the A's must be observable features already coded into the text.

Note carefully that this argument is not so much critical of HyperRESEARCH, which provides powerful additions to code-and-retrieve and the incorporation of production rules, as it is of thoughtless ways of employing the production-rule facility. In qualitative research, such misuses could contradict the central goals of building up understanding from data by forever returning to it. This is not easily achieved by getting a machine to insert new codes when it finds others, without care to see if the insertion of the new code is justified by the text. There are also dangers of building, in any software, an edifice of sophisticated reasoning on textual-structure coding. A weak link will always be the adequacy of the coding process, and this caution applies to all the following sections.

Logic-Based Systems

Discussion of production-rule systems leads naturally to logic-based systems. These use if-then rules for their representation of hypotheses, as the production-rule systems do, but the type of rule and the way it works is very different and more sophisticated. The rules are those of *clausal form logic,* a computationally useful way of expressing and computing with the standard calculus of formal logic (Richards, 1989). A useful fragment of clausal form logic lends itself well to computer implementation, both to represent data in a way that is an alternative to RDBMSs and to compute with those data using logical deduction. This computational paradigm is known as *logic programming* and is realized in the computer language Prolog (Clocksin & Mellish, 1984). The best-known examples of its employment for QDA purposes are in AQUAD for IBM-PC computers (Huber & Garcia, 1991) and QUALOG for mainframes (Shelly & Sibert, 1985), on which AQUAD was based. AQUAD is not only written in Prolog, but makes Prolog available to users to express hypotheses and compute with them. QUALOG uses a different logic programming language, LogLISP. We will discuss only AQUAD here as our exemplar of this genre.

Like nearly all QDA systems, AQUAD supports code-and-retrieve. However, it provides a sophisticated set of retrieval patterns, called hypothesis structures, used in *linkage analysis.* Although some of these retrieval patterns are Boolean, such as looking for one code or another in a text, many are more interesting, such as searching for positive *and negative* cases of one code occurring *within a certain distance* of another in the text. The output of such searches is typically numerical tables showing cases where the searched-for linkage did hold and, for instance, the textual distance between the codes. This is why the linkage analyses are seen as hypothesislike, and not just bare retrievals of text. The flavor of linkage analysis is not "Show me all text of codes A and B within textual distance d," but "To what extent do codes A and B occur within textual distance d—is it a significant association?" This is a very powerful feature that helps link qualitative and quantitative analysis in one research project.

Where the 12 provided hypothesis patterns are insufficient, the user can access the Prolog language and program the hypothesis structure he or she wishes to use, as a Prolog procedure, then run it to get the desired retrieval. This facility is challenging for nonprogrammers, and even for programmers unfamiliar with Prolog, as is plain from the user manual examples (at least to one of us, TJR, who has been teaching Prolog for more than a decade). This is where the logic-based nature of AQUAD shows up—hypotheses simply are statements of clausal form logic embedded in Prolog procedures, along with control structures, print control statements, string search commands, and the other paraphernalia of a program; and these are what the user must write to extend the power and expressiveness of AQUAD.

Two other built-in features of AQUAD should be mentioned for their general utility in QDA work. The first is the support of qualitative matrices. The user nominates two sets of related codes, such as a range of emotions and a range of personal data on the interviewees (e.g., age group), as columns and rows. Each cell in the resulting table contains the text segments indexed by both the column and row codes for the cell, that is, the result of a Boolean intersection or AND retrieval. Inspection of the resulting matrix is a powerful heuristic in QDA.

The second feature is the *configuration analysis.* This derives from a powerful technique in formal logic, the Quine-McClusky algorithm (McDermott, 1985), which was introduced to QDA by Ragin (1987). Suppose you guess that the presence or absence of conditions C_1 to C_n may be causally relevant to the occurrence of outcome A. Then, where C_1 to C_n and A are codes that can be found in a case (e.g., interview) in AQUAD, you can use configuration analysis to see which of the C's really are relevant to the occurrence or prevention of A, whether by their presence or absence, and what those combinations of the C's are. As a simple example, hypothesize that whenever C_1, C_2, and C_3 occur in a case, so does A. And suppose your data show this is perfectly correct, but *also* show that whenever C_1 and C_2

occur but C_3 does not, A still occurs. Then in the presence of C_1 and C_2, C_3 is irrelevant to the occurrence of A. Configuration analysis detects all such cases automatically. Note how powerfully this method extends the easy code-and-retrieve ability to check the correctness and consistency of hypotheses, discussed earlier. This is an elegant example of how computerization can enhance precomputational techniques. In AQUAD, the C's and the A can be not just codes, but any of the linkage structures expressible in the system or constructible in Prolog by the user.

Configuration analysis is one of several types of *induction* techniques used in artificial intelligence to find necessary or sufficient conditions of outcomes or, equivalently, to find the simplest set of if-then rules predicting a given outcome. These induction techniques deserve far more exploitation in computational QDA than they have received, because (a) they are almost impossible to use manually; (b) they are of great power and reliability in finding and simplifying associations of codes; (c) they are qualitative in nature, relying on presence/absence of codes, Occam's razor, and Popperian falsification of hypotheses by single counterinstances (rather than the relativistic quantification of acceptability of hypotheses that occurs in statistical analyses); and (d) they are a powerful way of making textual-level code-and-retrieve methods highly relevant to theorizing.

So how does logic fare as a tool in computational QDA? We have said that induction techniques deserve much development. Logic programming, on the other hand, although highly expressive, is at least currently a tool of such complexity that many users will be unwilling to learn it. Moreover, it is used entirely, at present, to express textual relations between codes (this code following that one in the text, and so on), and not the conceptual relations between the coded entities (person C_1 knows person C_2, the greeting protocol C_3 is a functional component of establishing social relationship C_4, and so on). Undoubtedly one of the research directions of the coming decade is the idea of writing and testing hypotheses based on codes at the conceptual-relation and not the textual-relation level, and using formal logic to do it, and making the logic available in a way that is habitable by the average user of QDA software. In the section below on conceptual networks we will see one partial approach to this.

An Index-Based Approach

We turn now with some trepidation to describing a design approach used in our own rather hybrid software system, NUD•IST™ version 3.0. This system combines and relates many of the features in other specialized designs described here. Like them, it is based on a code-and-retrieve facility and endeavors to go beyond simply retrieving text according to how it was coded. It can be thought of as having two major components for managing not only documents but also ideas. The first, a *document system,* holds textual-level data about documents, which may be on-line disk files or off-line documents such as books or anything else that can be sequentially segmented for coding (videotapes are supported directly via a link to the CVideo™ system). These documents may be indexed by typing in codes or by text search and autoindexing. On-line documents can be edited at any time, even after indexing. Use of multiple windows allows views into many documents or their indexing at once. Retrievals can be done by a wide range of Boolean, context, proximity, and sequencing searches, and grouped into qualitative matrices. Results of retrievals can be stored as index codes, as can the results of text searches, which can be regular expression pattern based. All NUD•IST operations can be executed in batch mode if desired, to automate repetitive work. Thus far NUD•IST is a code-and-retrieve system, and many users, we find, use it only in this way.

But the codes and references are kept in an *index system* designed also to allow the user to create and manipulate concepts and store and explore emerging ideas. The *nodes* of the index system, where indexing is kept, are optionally organized into hierarchies, or *trees,* to represent the organization of concepts into categories and subcategories, a taxonomy of concepts and index codes. Trees, of which there may be any number, are visually represented on the screen. The user can select a node, explore or change it, or move it elsewhere in the tree system. The trees and the nodes in them can represent anything the user wishes, such as people, objects, emotions, or ideas. They can store factual data (about cases, data types, settings, and so on), if nodes represent values of variables. Links between ideas, such as *causes, talked about, married,* can be represented in further nodes or in the node linkages in the trees. In this way the nodes in the index system can be treated as both textual level (coding documents) and conceptual level (recording things about the world and storing theory). This duality is made possible by the tree structure, which can represent conceptual relations, hence permitting nodes to be treated as concepts, not just as index codes into text. This is aided by being able to give nodes definitions and textual memos that the user can write and edit. (Documents can have memos too.) Document and node memos can also be treated as data documents and indexed like any other documents, so the index searching tools can be applied to them like any other documents, to explore the interrelationships of ideas being created.

Thus the index system approach builds on and extends the code-and-retrieve technique, emphasizing system closure. The user can explore the document and index systems and the relations between the two provided by the coding of documents. As theoretical-level structures change, the user can alter the index system without losing the references to documents supporting analysis at the textual level (groupings of text references by subjects). When such operations are carried out, NUD•IST adds to the node memo a log of what was done. Thus each node has a documented history, helping the user in auditing the research process as well as aiding interpretation of the index system as a structure of theoretical-level concepts and assertions. Where the index trees are used taxonomically, higher nodes automatically represent meaningful groupings of the textual data indexed at lower-level nodes, thus assembling and retrieving textual references for the generic concepts out of references for more specific ones. Techniques exploiting the tree structuring of the index system allow theory testing as well as the representation of facts and hypotheses.

As its authors, we find it easy and necessary to criticize NUD•IST: Criticisms feed back as future design features. First, NUD•IST appears, compared with the other systems described here, as a rather awkward hybrid, containing features of code-and-retrieve, ways of handling production-rule and other types of conceptual-level reasoning, conceptual representations alternative to conceptual network systems, and database storage facilities, all interacting through interlocking tools. NUD•IST was designed originally for provision of a range of software tools, from which users could choose according to their theoretical and methodological needs. We have learned that merely providing such varied tools can be confusing; tool sets must be integrated and easily accessible if they are to be used skillfully by the very wide range of researchers seeking QDA software.

Second, the system removes so many constraints, of size and variety of records and indexes, that a sort of methodological anomie can result. We have learned too that novice researchers, who may find their own rich and messy records to be alarming in their diversity, may be further alarmed by software that seems designed to celebrate diversity. User reports make it clear that the full implications of system closure are not easily grasped early. And, perhaps most important, the software offers many ways for a researcher never to finish a study. Novices too are often stalled by anxiety about creating a perfect index system up front, not trusting the promise that they can create and recreate the index system as they develop theories and discover patterns.

Third, the approach lacks visual display of conceptual-level diagrams and models, such as conceptual networks, that researchers may need in order to see their emerging theories before they can confidently continue with theory construction. They can see and manipulate visual models of their index systems, but not models of their emerging theories. They have to go to graphics programs (or even pencil and paper) to do that. Or, if their theories are of the right type, they can use conceptual network systems instead.

Conceptual Network Systems

Concept diagrams, conceptual graphs, semantic nets, and *conceptual networks* are all (roughly) different names given to the same idea, of representing conceptual information in a graphic manner, as opposed to production rules or the symbolic approach of formal logic. They appeal initially to researchers who have worked pictorially, by doodling diagrams on blackboards, or more formally in an attempt to give graphic representation to emerging theory and thereby draw out discovered linkages.

The objects in one's conceptual system (people, groupings of people, properties such as age or being a vegetarian, places, emotions—essentially anything one might code for a QDA project) are represented by little boxes on a sheet of paper. (Put them in alphabetical order and one has one's code list.) Now one joins various boxes with labeled arrows to indicate relationships between them; for instance, a *loves* arrow from the *John* box to the *Mary* box to indicate that John loves Mary, a *causes* arrow from the *anger* box to the *violence* box, and so on. Technically, the boxes are called *nodes,* the arrows joining them are *directed arcs,* and the whole resulting network is a *directed graph.* The arrows represent relationships and the boxes represent objects, properties, and concepts. An introduction to semantic nets, which also discusses their limitations compared with logic, may be found in Richards (1989, chap. 1); Sowa (1991) provides a full treatment. Semantic nets have also been discussed above, as the *entity-relationship approach* to designing an RDBMS.

Commonly occurring arcs are *isa* ("is a") and *ako* ("a kind of"); for example, [Mary]—isa→[Protestant]—ako→[Christian]—ako→[religious believer]. Others are *belongs-to* (class membership) and *case-of,* such as [Mary]—belongs- to→[20s]—case-of→[age group]. These often have useful logical properties that can be exploited to do reasoning about the knowledge in the graph. Ako for example is *transitive,* that is, if A ako B, and B ako C, then A ako C. Thus, above, we infer [Protestant]—ako→[religious believer]. Rather similarly, we can infer [Mary]—isa→[religious believer].

Semantic nets make for intuitive and logically rich representation systems that have, like production rules and formal logic, been widely exploited in artificial intelligence work. If one wants to see all the relationships an object in one's system has, for instance, one need only look at its node in the graph and follow the arcs to and from it. But semantic nets have their limits. One cannot use an arc to represent a three-place relation or greater, such as Reverend A married Miss B to Mr. C, or person A sold item B to person C for $D. And if one wishes to represent the fundamental logical ideas of *not, or* and *all, some,* the tricks one needs to get up to can make the graphs quite unintuitive.

Semantic nets are meant to be used with some semantic rigor, like any precise language. When a node is drawn, it is meant to be clear what that node represents (Is it a concept, the objects falling under the concept, the common property of those objects, or the collection of those objects?); when an arrow is drawn, the relationship the arrow represents is meant to be clear (What does it mean? Does it relate the two node categories as a whole or the objects categorized in the two nodes?), as is the reason for the sense of the arrow (Why not double-headed? Why not the other way? Why have it at all?).

Several researchers have recommended the use of commercial computer drawing packages for qualitative model building (e.g., Padilla, 1991), and many use such diagrams as pictorial props in their publications. But what computing, and the literature on conceptual graphs, offers is the chance to be systematic and rigorous in the construction of these graphs so that they represent knowledge that can be searched for, extracted, and reasoned with.

One systematic and advanced approach to conceptual graphs is ATLAS/ti (Mühr, 1991). Again, the basis is code-and-retrieve functions in text, and these are reasonably sophisticated, with interesting ideas, particularly the idea of being able to group codes into "families." To code-and-retrieve is added an admirable memoing facility, and codes can apply to memos as well as to the original documentary text—a system closure feature. A particularly useful retrieval idea is ordering codes by date of last use, number of references, and the like. There is a good pattern-based text search facility, the finds of which can be coded—as in HyperRESEARCH and NUD•IST, this is another system closure feature.

Conceptual graphs are supported by an on-screen "intelligent" editing facility (i.e., the system makes the drawing of nodes, arcs, and their labels trivially easy, and also makes an internal logical representation of the graph one is drawing—it is not just a picture). Nodes can be codes (and hence have associated text). Arcs can be given one of a built-in set of relation names, such as *causes, isa, part-of, contradicts,* so that when such a relation is set up, its built-in logic, such as transitivity, becomes available for the system's reasoning about the network. Alternatively, a user can choose a name of his or her own for an arc (e.g., *supports position*) and provide a logic for that relation in a simple way. ATLAS will redraw a graph if it becomes too tangled.

These graphs operate at a conceptual level, not at the textual level. That is, the relationships between the nodes (codes) relate what the nodes represent (e.g., [anger]—causes→[violence]) rather than the nodes' textual references (e.g., passages about violence follow passages about anger). Thus, like NUD•IST but in a different and more visually direct way, ATLAS represents theory and factual knowledge, not relying on its indirect representation through textual relations that might be held relevant to a conceptual linkage.

What is the value of a conceptual graph representation of a project and its information? Networks are best seen as a tremendous generalization of the rather primitive information representation available in a code-and-retrieve system, which comprises simply an unstructured set of codes plus support for exploring their textual relations. Here we have a rich representation system for using nodes not just as textual codes, but as parts of graphs modeling systems in the world being studied, theories, and so on. Allied with ATLAS's sophisticated text retrieval system, the graphs support subtle exploration of text via a visually immediate interface that relates the text to the systems or theories in the world being studied. In cases such as evidence analysis, for example, facts gleaned about the historical situation under study can be represented directly into the network, for example, [Macbeth]—killed→[Duncan], and the study of the text coded at [Macbeth] and [Duncan] provides evidence for the claim. Standard semantic network techniques (which the ATLAS system will support, although it does not seem to exploit them) even permit the relations, such as killing, to be treated as nodes and so have associated text, which adds to the richness of the representation and subtlety of the exploration.

So, how useful are semantic networks? They are certainly, in ATLAS, very easy to construct and rich to explore. They lack the "intelligence" of production rules or formal logic as being "runnable" theories whose execution has some definite useful result, and they (at least in the ATLAS form) lack the power to represent crucial logical concepts that a logic system has, such as expressing generality, negation or absence, and alternativeness. It is very hard to see, for example, how configuration analysis, such as in AQUAD, could be represented, let alone executed, via ATLAS semantic nets.

The type of qualitative research project involved tends to dictate whether a semantic network approach such as ATLAS will be useful. It would be much better than code-and-retrieve at data-theory bootstrapping work. Its main value is where the subject of investigation can be seen as comprising a number of topics with some major characteristics of note and relationships to each other (a system). Then it can be of considerable heuristic value to draw that up in a semantic net and use the resulting nodes and arc labels as the basis for text segmentation or other data organization. (See our remarks above about the types of projects for which the entity-relationship approach to RDBMSs applies.)

For researchers wishing to organize concepts, the tree structures of an index system approach and the semantic net modeling of theories offer related but different advantages. Trees have the advantage that their structure is uniform and easily comprehensible. But that can also be a disadvantage, as the real world is often neither uniform nor comprehensible. Semantic nets directly and visually offer more forms of concept organization. Both methods support the most common form, the taxonomic tree, in which the children of any node can be treated as specializations, in some sense, of their parent concept: a kind of, a part of, is a, member of a group, case of, and so on. These are the main types of link used in semantic nets to convey logical properties of concept relations such as transitivity, and hence to support reasoning. But semantic nets represent relations between concepts that go beyond a thesauruslike taxonomy. The trees of NUD•IST are more restricted, but NUD•IST uses index system search plus the saving of search results as nodes as an alternative to semantic nets (worse for some things—it is less visual—and better for others—the system, not the user, looks for the links, and it is flexible).

As taxonomy structures, both have limitations. Semantic nets encourage researchers to keep the number of nodes small: (a) Computer screens cannot display more than a few tens, (b) the number of links (and hence the complexity) increases with the square of the number of nodes, and (c) big networks just look confusing. ATLAS offers a number of techniques for managing that sort of growing complexity, and future research in this field must concentrate on this issue. Index trees offer a different limitation for taxonomies, given that they impose hierarchy. Some concepts can be treated as specializations of several more general ones, not just one. Allowing a node to have multiple parents could handle this, but may prove confusing. Moreover, although trees offer the user the ability to structure data and ideas about data, they do not allow him or her to name links. One purpose of naming links is to associate logical properties with the links of a given name, for example, transitivity for *a kind of.* In an index structure approach, links are recorded and explored not by dragging and naming arrows but by creating and shifting nodes, a less visual and immediate process.

Conclusions

Artificial intelligence research has thus contributed to qualitative analysis powerful techniques for managing not only documents but also concepts, and for constructing and expressing theories. Many researchers may of course never want these features, and will use computers for enhanced code-and-retrieve for collecting related passages for their contemplation. One needs indeed to avoid the danger that the style of the software one uses can coerce a project along a particular direction.

However, coercion is not a function of sophistication—the simpler code-and-retrieve packages can coerce a project into particular directions just because of their lack of support of various analyses that can be done on retrieved codes, such as co-occurrence patterns. And it is very hard to see how features such as configuration analysis, or organization of concepts into hierarchies or nets, or indeed the very provision of conceptual-level tools, can be other than powerful heuristics for qualitative researchers—if well used. The secret is, of course, not to force a feature onto a researcher if it is not appropriate for a particular task—and to provide flexibility and a "light touch" in the more powerful features so that they do not run away with their users.

In terms of research directions, look for developments in the logic programming approach, to make its power more accessible to the nonprogrammer and to extend its rules to express more directly conceptual-level structures and knowledge about the world under study. Look for wider deployment of configuration analysis and ways of generalizing that technique, and other methods of supporting inductive searches. The entity-relationship approach needs cross-breeding with good solid code-and-retrieve facilities, to provide relational database systems more attuned to text-based QDA work. Look too for ways of supporting project management, in particular (given the tentative, cut-and-try nature of a lot of QDA exploration), support for forking research work at a point in time into several future paths, pruning the unpromising ones, backtracking to earlier forks, and pursuing more alternatives within the promising paths. The growing bridges between qualitative and quantitative research are demanding software support, so look for innovative research on how to support that computationally.

Above all, look for ways of developing computer support of conceptual-level work in text-based research, not just textual-level work. That is the very hard research, for, as we hope this chapter makes clear, although software designs imported from artificial intelligence and database research are providing the breakthroughs, none of them is exactly what QDA needs. The problem and the excitement is that QDA is probably the most subtle and intuitive of human epistemological enterprises, and therefore likely to be the last to achieve satisfactory computerization.

Appendix: Software Developers

AQUAD. G. L. Huber, Universität Tübingen, Institut für Erziehungswissenschaft I, Münzgasse 2230, 7400 Tübingen 1, Germany.

ATLAS/ti. Thomas Mühr, Technische Universität Berlin, Project Public Health A4, Hardenbergstrasse 4-5, 10623 Berlin, Germany.

CVideo. Knowledge Revolution, 15 Brush Place, San Francisco, CA 94103, USA.

The Ethnograph. Qualis Research Associates, P.O. Box 2070, Amherst, MA 01004, USA.

HyperCard 2.0. Manufactured by Apple® Corp., available from any Apple retail outlet.

HyperRESEARCH. S. Hesse-Biber, Department of Sociology, Boston College, Chestnut Hill, Boston, MA 02167, USA.

NoteCards. Xerox Palo Alto Research Center, 3333 Coyote Hill Road, Palo Alto, CA 94304, USA.

NUD•IST. Qualitative Solutions and Research, Box 171, La Trobe University Post Office, Vic 3083, Australia. Fax (+61-3) 479-1441.

StorySpace. Central Services, 1703 East Michigan Avenue, Jackson, MI 49202, USA.

Note

1. Formally, if you have an if-then hypothesis of the form "If C_1 and C_2 and . . . hold, then A holds," then it is shown to be *correct* if no case is found of all the C's occurring without the A occurring; and it is shown to be *complete* if in every case where A occurs, all the C's occur too. A correct hypothesis shows that A always occurs under these conditions, whereas a complete one shows there is no other set of conditions under which A occurs—both relative to the data, of course. Plainly, code-and-retrieve methods can easily test correctness and completeness of if-then statements.

References

Agar, M. (1991). The right brain strikes back. In N. G. Fielding & R. M. Lee (Eds.), *Using computers in qualitative research* (pp. 181-194). Newbury Park, CA: Sage.

Bailey, R. W. (Ed.). (1982). *Computing in the humanities.* Amsterdam: North-Holland.

Bogdan, R. C., & Taylor, S. J. (1975). *Introduction to qualitative research methods: A phenomenological approach to the social sciences.* New York: John Wiley.

Chen, P. (1976). The entity-relationship model: Toward a unified view of data. *ACM Transactions on Database Systems, 1,* 19-36.

Clocksin, W. F., & Mellish, C. S. (1984). *Programming in Prolog* (2nd ed.). Berlin: Springer.

Conklin, J. (1987). Hypertext: An introduction and survey. *IEEE Computer, 20,* 17-41.

Fielding, N. G., & Lee, R. M. (Eds.). (1991). *Using computers in qualitative research.* Newbury Park, CA: Sage.

Geertz, C. (1973). *The interpretation of cultures: Selected essays.* New York: Basic Books.

Glaser, B. G., & Strauss, A. L. (1967). *The discovery of grounded theory: Strategies for qualitative research.* Chicago: Aldine.

Halasz, F. G., Moran, T. P., & Trigg, R. H. (1987). *NoteCards in a nutshell.* Paper presented at the ACM Conference on Human Factors in Computing Systems, Toronto.

Hammersley, M., & Atkinson, P. (1983). *Ethnography: Principles in practice.* London: Tavistock.

Hesse-Biber, S., Dupuis, P., & Kinder, T. S. (1991). HyperRESEARCH: A computer program for the analysis of qualitative data with an emphasis on hypothesis testing and multimedia analysis. *Qualitative Sociology, 14,* 289-306.

Hockey, S. (1980). *A guide to computer applications in the humanities.* London: Duckworth.

Huber, G. L., & Garcia, C. M. (1991). Computer assistance for testing hypotheses about qualitative data: The software package AQUAD 3.0. *Qualitative Sociology, 14,* 325-348.

Kirk, J., & Miller, M. L. (1986). *Reliability and validity in qualitative research.* Newbury Park, CA: Sage.

Lincoln, Y. S., & Guba, E. G. (1985). *Naturalistic inquiry.* Beverly Hills, CA: Sage.

Lofland, J., & Lofland, L. (1984). *Analyzing social settings* (2nd ed.). Belmont, CA: Wadsworth.

McDermott, R. M. (1985). *Computer-aided logic design.* Indianapolis: Sams.

Miall, D. S. (Ed.). (1990). *Humanities and the computer: New directions.* Oxford: Clarendon.

Miles, M. B., & Huberman, A. M. (1984). *Qualitative data analysis: A sourcebook of new methods.* Beverly Hills, CA: Sage.

Miles, M. B., & Huberman, A. M. (1994). *Qualitative data analysis: A new sourcebook of methods* (2nd ed.). Newbury Park, CA: Sage.

Mühr, T. (1991). ATLAS/ti: A prototype for the support of text interpretation. *Qualitative Sociology, 14,* 349-371.

Padilla, R. (1991). Using computers to develop concept models of social situations. *Qualitative Sociology, 14,* 263-274.

Pfaffenberger, B. (1988). *Microcomputer applications in qualitative research.* Beverly Hills, CA: Sage.

Ragin, C. C. (1987). *The comparative method: Moving beyond qualitative and quantitative strategies.* Berkeley: University of California Press.

Richards, L., & Richards, T. J. (1991a). Computing in qualitative analysis: A healthy development? *Qualitative Health Research, 1,* 234-262.

Richards, L., & Richards, T. J. (1991b). The transformation of qualitative method: Computational paradigms and research processes. In N. G. Fielding & R. M. Lee (Eds.), *Using computers in qualitative research* (pp. 38-53). Newbury Park, CA: Sage.

Richards, L., & Richards, T. J. (in press). From filing cabinet to computer. In R. W. Burgess & A. Bryman (Eds.), *Analyzing qualitative data.* London: Routledge.

Richards, T. J. (1989). *Clausal form logic: The elements of computer reasoning systems.* London: Addison-Wesley.

Seidel, J. V., & Clark, J. A. (1984). The Ethnograph: A computer program for the analysis of qualitative data. *Qualitative Sociology, 7,* 110-125.

Shelly, A., & Sibert, G. (1985). *The QUALOG users' manual.* Syracuse, NY: Syracuse University, School of Computer and Information Science.

Sowa, J. F. (Ed.). (1991). *Principles of semantic networks: Explorations in the representation of knowledge.* San Mateo, CA: Morgan Kaufmann.

Strauss, A. L. (1987). *Qualitative analysis for social scientists.* New York: Cambridge University Press.

Strauss, A. L., & Corbin, J. (1990). *Basics of qualitative research: Grounded theory procedures and techniques.* Newbury Park, CA: Sage.

Tallerico, M. (1991). Applications of qualitative analysis software: A view from the field. *Qualitative Sociology, 14,* 275-285.

Tesch, R (1990). *Qualitative research: Analysis types and software tools.* London: Falmer.

Turner, B. A. (1981). Some practical aspects of qualitative data analysis. *Quality and Quantity, 15,* 225-247.

Weitzman, E., & Miles, M. B. (1994). *Computer programs for qualitative data analysis.* Newbury Park, CA: Sage.

Winer, L. R., & Carrière, M. (1991). A qualitative information system for data management. *Qualitative Sociology, 14,* 245-262.

29

Narrative, Content, and Semiotic Analysis

PETER K. MANNING
BETSY CULLUM-SWAN

DOCUMENTARY data have always been central to social science, but modes of analyzing them vary, and the centrality of documentary evidence also varies within the social sciences and in subfields within them.[1] Some of these shifts are the topic of this chapter. We intend to chart the relationships among narrative, content, and semiotic analysis, illustrating the changing meanings of texts (written documents) and their role in social research and theorizing.

In the early part of this century, social scientists studied people, trying to extract from written materials the patterns, orders, senses, and meanings of their life experiences. Documents, almost from the beginning of empirical work in sociology, have been controversial (Blumer, 1939; Gottschalk, Kluckhohn, & Angell, 1945). The first major American empirical study, the classic by W. I. Thomas and Florian Znaniecki, *The Polish Peasant* (1918), relied upon diaries, letters, and other personal documents to characterize the impact of immigration to the United States upon Polish immigrants. However, since Emile Durkheim's *Suicide* (1951) established sociology as a discipline, sociology and other social sciences have been wedded to positivistic methods (methods that take the external world as extant and reproducible through scientific or logical means) and associated concepts of validity, reliability, generalization, prediction, and control (Denzin, 1989). They combine these methodological and often technical concerns (based on the canons of statistical measurement) somewhat uneasily with often subtle interpretive theoretical frameworks.

In many respects, the debate over the use of documents in social science concerns validity, reliability, representativeness, and generalizability of findings drawn from textual evidence. Ironically, the question of which methodology is superior for interpreting words, rather than numbers, has not been debated. The social sciences, with the possible exception of content analysis, have not developed systematic evaluative techniques for documentary analysis (see Berelson, 1952; Holsti, 1969). The dominance of quantitative methods has resulted in an underdeveloped theory of qualitative textual analysis and heavy reliance on literary criticism, linguistics, computer science, and cognitive psychology for models for assessing the quality of documents.

This Chapter's Focus

We begin with a brief history of documentary or textual analysis, outlining the changing paradigms within which these research approaches are used, including documentary research and narrative, discourse, and content analysis. We then introduce semiotics, which brings us to examples of the varieties of structuralist and semiotic analysis. Structuralists assume that content is a function of form and code and meaning is a product of a system of relationships. Documents are "products," like speech itself, of a system within which they are defined and made meaningful. Documents so defined are converted into "texts" to be read and interpreted (Foucault, 1973, p. 47).

This radical redefinition of documents, we argue in the penultimate section of the chapter, changes methodological stances. The impact of independent and "exogenous variables" on the meaning, content, or structure of documents, and their validity or reliability, becomes a background, whereas the foreground is the relationship between the "text" as a social construction and its form or its imputed audience-derived meanings. In the final section of the chapter we address selected consequences of the radical relativism produced by structuralism and semiotics. We illustrate these consequences with examples of ethnographic, or culturally descriptive, semiotic research. We end the chapter with two forms of semiotic analysis of McDonald's.

Content and Narrative Analysis

Content Analysis

After World War II, sociologists and students of mass communications refined content analysis. Content analysis is a quantitatively oriented technique by which standardized measurements are applied to metrically defined units and these are used to characterize and compare documents (Berelson, 1952; Kracauer, 1993). Content analysis has been used to characterize the content of popular magazines (Lowenthal, 1962) and other documents. Content analysis was massively facilitated by the electronic computer and computer-based programs such as the General Enquirer (Stone, Dunphy, & Kirsch, 1967). Recently, its use has been most popular in cultural studies and mass communications research.

Aside from the methodological problems associated with any quantitative technique (sampling, generalization, validity, especially external validity, and reliability), content analysis has been unable to capture the *context* within which a written text has meaning. Context has been variously defined, in terms of an ongoing narrative ("plot"), the immediate semantic environment, the literary tropes operating, and connections between the text and experience or knowledge (Eco, 1979). Ethnomethodological approaches (see Holstein & Gubrium, Chapter 16, this volume) attempt to understand context as the taken-for-granted knowledge brought to the experience and displayed in the talk. Levinson (1983) defines context as a matter of pragmatics, "what the reader brings to" the utterance or, in this case, the text. The microinteractional aspect of content analysis has never been fully solved. That is, what is brought to a reading by a reader can be estimated using panels or samples of readers or coders, or by literary or social science experts who define meaning authoritatively. Barthes (1975b), in urging consideration of the "readerly text," highlights the subtle interactions among reading, the text, and the reader. This remains an open or moot point.

Narrative Analysis

Narrative analysis takes a number of analytic forms. We discuss them here in declining level of formality, that is, the degree to which the internal coherence of the text is defined in advance with reference to codes, syntax, grammar, or forms.

Russian formalism, associated with the works of R. Jakobson, V. Sklovskij, M. Bakhtin, B. Uspensky, and V. Propp, and the Rumanian-French writer Tzvetan Todorov, emphasizes the role of form in conveying meaning in a narrative (see Jameson, 1972). Perhaps the most famous example of formalist-structuralism is Propp's (1968) elegant propositional quasi-algebraic analysis of the Russian fairy tale. Propp claims the Russian fairy tale can be understood using only four principles: The functions of characters are stable elements in a tale; the functions known in a fairy tale are limited; the sequence of functions is always identical; and fairy tales are of one type with regard to structure (our paraphrase from Propp, 1968, chap. 2). Lévi-Strauss's (1963) analysis of myth (based in Roman Jakobson's structural linguistics) uses binary oppositions, a closed system of relations, a synchronic model, and standardized units. Lévi-Strauss, unlike Propp, argues that a story ("myth") unfolds paradigmatically in terms of oppositions, rather than linearly in terms of functions. Other variants on structuralist semiotics are found in the works of Lotman (1990) and Griemas (1966), which can be summarized by the semiotic square that combines opposition and contradiction to analyze the structure of social systems (e.g., law; see Jackson, 1986).

Systematic forms of narrative analysis, "top-down" or "bottom-up" approaches, make quite different assumptions about the organization of cognitive meaning. Top-down versions have had considerable influence in education and cognitive psychology (Rumelhart, 1977; Rumelhart & Norman, 1981). The investigator begins with a set of rules and principles and seeks to exhaust the meaning of a text using the rules and principles (see Boje, 1991; Heise, 1992). In using the Ethnograph, a program for narrative analysis, an event such as the Russian Revolution is first reduced to a series of propositions. Events require prerequisites (preconditions such as those leading to the Russian Revolution—hunger); events must exhaust the conditions that the prerequisites created (all conditions must be related to an outcome—hunger leads to riots); events' prerequisites must be subsequently exhausted before they can be repeated. Thus what is "tested" is the preconceived closed and logically constrained binary model (events either happened or they did not) of the researcher. This approach is influenced by cognitive psychology and artificial intelligence, and such analyses are made possible by the memory capacity and flexibility of computers and software. Bottom-up versions, found in most ethnographic work, on the other hand, derive context-dependent units to produce an infrastructure that explains the tale's effect. Dwyer (1982), for example, presents his material as a dialogue between himself and the other, a Faquir, whereas Crapanzano (1980) interpolates and comments on Moroccan culture. Often such reports rely on personal interviews or documents, and the translation of these materials into parts of a coherent argument remains fuzzy (Atkinson, 1992; Riessman, 1993).

Some studies contrast narratives, self-formatted stories, with formal, externally formatted narratives, such as medical interviews. Cicourel (1973, 1982, 1985, 1986) demonstrates that neither approach adequately captures human information processing and sense making. Furthermore, he questions the assumption of both of these models that views human reasoning as algorithmic and linear. The basic distinction between a preformatted interaction with an instrumental purpose, such as a medical or survey research interview, and a personal story, with its wandering, complex, sensate, and expressive forms, is a primary contrast in the literature on narratives. Whereas the life situation of the person, the embodied here-and-now reality, is looked at from the body's perspective, the medical interview looks at the body as an objective, functioning machine.

Medical writing on stories is revealing. Diverse writers, many of them medically trained, such as Kleinman (1988), Brody (1987), Coles (1989), Mishler (1984), and Paget (1988) in medical social science, argue for the utility of narrative analysis but share no common definition, purpose, method or technique, or mode of analysis. They assert that stories reflect human feelings and lived experience, and that healing necessarily involves the telling, hearing, and unraveling of stories. However, each presents a unique, appealing, aesthetic, and humanistic rationale for his or her approach and weaves it into the logic of the medical interview.

The concern with lives and lived experience resurfaced relatively late in narrative analysis. The emphasis in contemporary anthropology and feminism is upon the study of lives from the narrator's experience, as a shared production with social scientists. These stories are seen as real, yet with a tenuous grip on a consensually defined social reality that can be validly and reliably reproduced by social scientists. Emphasizing the role of these narratives in empowering persons through more subtle understandings of their life situations stands the structuralist concern with the power of codes, rules, and social functions of texts on its head.[2]

To a striking extent, narrative analysis is rather loosely formulated, almost intuitive, using terms defined by the analyst (see Riessman, 1993). Narrative analysis typically takes the perspective of the teller, rather than that of the society, as in Propp's and Lévi-Strauss's models. If one defines narrative as a story with a beginning, middle, and end that reveals someone's experiences, narratives take many forms, are told in many settings, before many audiences, and with various degrees of connection to actual events or persons. Thus themes, principal metaphors, definitions of narrative, defining structures of stories (beginning, middle, and end), and conclusions are often defined poetically and artistically and are quite context bound (Atkinson, 1990; see also Potter & Wetherell, 1987). For example, using a small number of stories, or even one, organizational analysts assert the importance of stories in organizations (Martin, 1990; Martin, Feldman, Hatch, & Sitkin, 1983). These approaches are little shaped by the traditions of content analysis or the coding used in quantitative sociological work, and are used to contrast the "human" or "cultural" dimension of organizations rather than to illuminate personal lives.

At the extreme, macrotextual analysis sees the verbalization and representation of society and groups through words. These representations are seen as marking, dramatizing, and constructing often complex social relations. Macrotextual work draws on the ideas of Kenneth Burke—dramaturgy (1966; Gusfield, 1989), Hugh D. Duncan—dramatism (1962, 1968, 1969), and Murray Edelman—symbolic analyses of politics (1966, 1977, 1992; Merelman, 1984, 1992). This approach views texts as symbolic action, or means to frame a situation, define it, grant it meaning, and mobilize appropriate responses to it. Burke, for example, uses five basic terms of dramatism for analysis of any discourse: act, scene, agent, agency, and purpose (these ideas are paralleled in Goffman's early work; see Perinbanayagam, 1991). This scheme has been well applied to the assessment of the effectiveness of court stories (Bennett & Feldman, 1986). Societal-level analysis of discourse, such as of anti-drunken driving messages (Gusfield, 1966, 1986; Jacobs, 1989), tourism (MacCannell,

1976/1989), and comparative societal representation (Lincoln, 1992), works by identifying broad themes, audiences, and symbols used to persuade and mobilize groups. In this sense, macrotextual or narrative analysis sees society as a "speaker" and social signs, including words, as texts (Brown, 1987, 1989, 1992).

Semiotics

Semiotics, or the science of signs, provides a set of assumptions and concepts that permit systematic analysis of symbolic systems. The Swiss linguist Ferdinand de Saussure (1857-1913) founded semiotics (Culler, 1977). Saussure's (1915/1966) work and writings of the American pragmatist Charles Peirce (1931) and Charles Morris are the primary sources of the theory underlying semiotics. Although semiotics is based on language, language is but one among many sign systems of varying degrees of unity, applicability, and complexity. Morse code, etiquette, mathematics, music, and even highway signs are examples of semiotic systems. Sign systems can be loosely or tightly connected or articulated, and the relations within them can be various: homological, analogical, even metaphoric. Social semioticians see social life, group structure, beliefs, practices, and the content of social relations as functionally analogous to the units that structure language. By extension of this semiotic position, all human communication is a display of signs, something of a text to be "read." Disagreement remains about the utility of semiotics and the relevance of the linguistic conceit or analogy to social analysis (see, for example, Noth, 1990).

A *sign* is something that represents or stands for something else in the mind of someone. A sign is composed in the first instance of an *expression,* such as a word, sound, or symbol, and a *content,* or something that is seen as completing the meaning of the expression (Hjemslev, 1961). For example, a lily is an expression linked conventionally with death, Easter, and resurrection as a content. Smoke is linked to cigarettes and to cancer, and Marilyn Monroe to sex. Each of these connections is social and arbitrary, so that many kinds of links exist between expression and content.[3]

The process of linking or connecting expression and content is social and depends upon the perspective of the observer. A sign is essentially incomplete because it requires an *interpretant,* or context. That which links the expression and the content is brought to the signifying event. When the interpretant changes, signs change meaning. Behind any idea or feature of the social world is yet another interpretant. This the basis for the radical claim that no reality lies under or behind a sign, and no "real world" exists. Semiotics, in short, studies whatever can be taken to be a sign, or against which any sign can be checked. The interpretant of a sign is another sign, and that sign is validated as it were by yet another sign, and so on without end (Eco, 1979, p. 7).

The connections made between expression and content and among signs are mental. Thus semiotics depends upon a "primitive phenomenology"; that is, meaningful connections between the expression and content are socially created and maintained (Culler, 1975). Typically, these connections are shared and collective, and provide an important source of the ideas, rules, practices, codes, and recipe knowledge called "culture" (Barley, 1983; Culler, 1975). Culture is a reference point—a means by which one comes to believe in the reality of the expression (Eco, 1979, pp. 71-72). These connections between clusters of signs are sometimes called *paradigms.* Several paradigms or domains of meaning, when collected, constitute a *field* (Bourdieu, 1977, p. 47). A field may be created or constituted by discourse, as for example in an artistic or scientific field, by practices, or by material objects. Of particular interest here are discourse fields that can be mapped onto larger social structures of signs. Organizations, for example, can be characterized by logic that is constituted of fields of argumentation. That which provides the social connection among the components of a sign, a set of signs clustered as texts, and even assembled as discourse, is a *code.*

Sign functions are important in social analysis because signs, and signs about signs, that represent social differentiation mark and reinforce social relations (Guiraud, 1975). To some degree, the potentially volatile contextual nature of meaning is reduced by shared knowledge, rules and codes employed within a culture to make sense of fields of signs. More often, the understandings are a function of "knowledgeability" (Giddens, 1984) or tacit, nonverbal meanings, taken for granted and unrecognized even by participants. Nevertheless, these are powerful constraints upon meaning.

The connections among signs are variable, and the resultant meanings are variable as well. It has been conventional to restrict the range of meanings of expression content to three levels: denotative, connotative, and mythological or allegorical. Denotative meaning is seen in connections between a grade and a level of school performance. We read one as the other: 4.0 = excellent; 3.5.= very good, and so on. A connotation is created when "honors" are conferred on those scoring above a given GPA level. This status becomes "mythical" if the label "honors" is taken to indicate "knowledge." The connotative and mythical level of interpretation, as Barthes (1967, 1972, pp. 115ff.) illustrates, results from the unexamined nonempirical or belief-based connections drawn between denotative and connotative meanings. Signs, whatever the context, can also produce or express emotions as well as cognitions or logical formulations.

As meanings collect under an ideological canopy, unpacking them becomes more complex and problematic, and knowing the culture becomes essential. Culture is sedimented in institutions that "pin down" and stabilize the links between expression and content and contain the codes that anchor the potentially migratory expression (Bourdieu, 1977). Thus, within a given cultural system, power and authority stabilize floating and arbitrary expressions to establish and generate structurally dictated sign concreteness.

As a result of semiotics, theoretic influences now flow from structural linguistics, pragmatics, phenomenological sociology, and, most notably, varieties of "structuralism," poststructuralism, and postmodernism (Borgmann, 1992; Culler, 1975; Denzin, 1986; Guiraud, 1975; Hawkes, 1977; Kurzweil, 1980; Rose, 1992; Rosenau, 1992; Sturrock, 1979). Let us review them.

Structuralism

Structuralism, both a theoretical perspective and methodological approach in contemporary social sciences, combines a formal model of explanation found in math, economics, and psychology, and an analytic approach derived from semiotics. Structuralism, a formal mode of analysis derived from Saussurian linguistics, sees social reality as constructed largely by language, and language forms as the material from which social research is fashioned. A major shift in social theory resulted in the 1960s from popularization of structuralism in social science initiated by the anthropologist Claude Lévi-Strauss (1963, 1966). Structuralism produced the "linguistic turn" in social theory, reshaping American social thought. Structuralism sees "documents," once viewed as actual physical or concretely assessable objects, as "texts," analytic phenomena produced by definitions and theoretical operations (Barthes, 1975b; Foucault, 1973, p. 47). Texts, previously considered self-writings for others' readings, become real and decipherable through a set of institutionally generated codes, or interpretive frames.

Structuralism seeks to identify the elements of a whole through systematic procedures "the method of analysis is structuralist when meaning, in the object analyzed, is taken to be dependent on the arrangement of its parts" (Descombes, 1980, p. 84). Structuralism is essentially a comparative method, because it seeks isomorphism in two or more contents. Once these units, parts, or elements are analytically sorted out, they can be combined, recombined, and transformed to create new models.

Structural explanation seeks to identify and array the units in a system to discover the "deeper" relationships or pattern(s) underlying an event or series of events. The explanation sought for observed phenomena is in terms of underlying rules, principles, or conventions that produce surface meanings. Structuralism relies on tautology, not causal explanations, synchronic analyses that obviate history (except as a signified representation). In theory, structuralism works with a closed system of meanings in which elements can be derived and sorted according to some principles or rules, and some calculus of possibilities can be derived (Ricoeur, as quoted in Culler, 1975, p. 26). Explanation is "a semantic process that generates a certain type of statement: namely, one that *meaningfully* encodes already encoded . . . values" (Lemert, 1979a, p. 944).

Structuralism is called "dehumanizing" in its drift and implications. It rejects the "homocentric" subjectivism and metaphysics of theories such as existentialism and pragmatism: Persons are not seen as bundles of sentiments or investigated "with reference to inner subjective and cultural meanings" (Lemert, 1979b, p. 100). Experience is secondary to systems of order, such as kinship, or law, or education. The person is merely the "speaking object," a user of codes and symbols who selects among preconstituted options, voices, and programs. Structures exist as the organizing centers of social action; persons are in every sense not only the creations of such structures, but manifestations of elements and rules created by social structures.

Poststructuralism

Poststructuralism, illustrated in the works of Lacan, Kristeva, Barthes, Foucault, Bourdieu, Touraine, Ricouer, and Guattari and Deleuze, contains modifications of structuralist themes. The philosopher Jacques Derrida, who developed Heidegger's notion of deconstruction, is "poststructuralist" in chronological terms, but in many respects he interpolates between the varieties of structuralism (Lemert, 1981, 1990). Poststructuralism contains some elements of the original Saussurian model and elaborates others that emerged after the decline in interest in the rigid program of Lévi-Strauss.

The "undecidable" or the uncertainty in meaning that arises from changes in context is an irreducible and a given in all texts. One must accept the difficulty of reading intentions from speech acts or texts and eschew final answers through philosophical analysis. Formal models of meaning

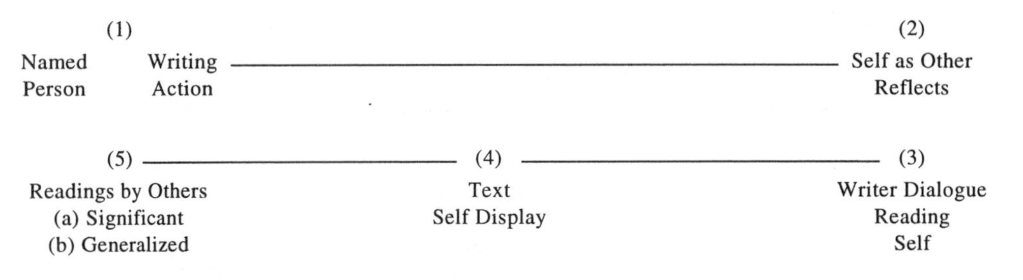

Figure 29.1. An Interactionist Model of Document Production

cannot be forced into simple matrices based on a series of binary oppositions. Barthes has sought to elevate the importance of pleasure, sexuality, and the emotions. The "irrational" has a new place in analyses of political myth (Barthes, 1972) and sexuality (Barthes, 1975a; Foucault, 1978). The decentered subject reemerges (Lemert, 1979b) now as an empty, noncontrolling *object* of actions, something merely acted upon (Milovanovic, 1993). This theme of passivity and objectification is central in Baudrillard's work, although it is also emergent in Derrida's and Foucault's.

Poststructuralists urge careful reconsideration of written texts and their formulation, constitution, and conventional interpretation. To some extent, because the conventional canons of interpretation reflect dominant values (and writers), they obscure the virtues of writers, ideas, perspectives, and values deemed "marginal." In this sense, poststructuralism turns attention to the margins and reverses the usual adherence to dominant cultural values. The literature of the Third World, of people of color, of writers from non-European countries, is to be read and understood within the given cultural context, rather than from the perspective of Western European or Greco-Roman traditions. A text, in poststructuralist terms, is not an object or thing, but an occasion for the interplay of multiple codes and perspectives. One must seek to extract and examine the operations or means by which meaning is conveyed (see Derrida, 1976; Kristeva, 1980, p. 37). Reading a novel is an occasion for semiotic practice in which the synthesized patterns of several utterances can be read (our paraphrase of Kristeva, 1980, p. 37). Any writing contains multiple codes and times, and may even frame other writing within it (see Barthes, 1975b).

Once the field is a text itself, the previous anchoring of anthropology and sociology in "facts" and "data" vanishes, and authors speculate about fundamental issues of epistemology (Tyler, 1987), literary forms, and genres (Atkinson, 1990, 1992; Geertz, 1988); the senses arise as themes (Stoller, 1992), and individual speakers disappear into discourse patterns (Moerman, 1988).

Some Analytic Consequences of the Semiotic/Linguistic Turn

A classic interactionist interpretation of the artistic process imagines it as a linear, "production line" process in which persons write documents for readers (see Clifford, 1988; Clifford & Marcus, 1986). Semiotics, and the structuralist model of social relations based upon it, is significant with respect to documentary analysis because the imagery or model differs from the interactionist model. Figure 29.1 outlines the interactionist model.

The Interactionist Model

In the classic interactionist model of documentary analysis, a solitary internalized reflexivity takes place. An embodied person (1) (with a name, personal identity, and location in time and space) performs an action, "writing" (2). This action, reflecting a "self," including both an "I" and a "me," is reflected upon by the self as other. The writer (3) reflects upon the self writing and reads the product as an activity reflecting upon the role, or "writer." Writing represents an aspect of a writer's self. The writer's self is displayed in the text (4). The products of self-conscious writing activity, "texts" (diaries, stories, autobiographies, biographies, letters, novels, confessionals, depositions, and research) are read (5). These "readings" are re-presentations of the writer's documentary presentation of self.

Let us elaborate this model so as to contrast it better with a structuralist semiotic model. Reading entails an audience, some members of which are significant others for the writer, and for whom the person writes. Reading is done by scholars, critics, other writers, reviewers, historians, and related intellectuals. The serious critic intends to reconstruct the process of writing, reading, and reflection and to ruminate upon, according to the conventional canons of taste and the genre, the quality of the writing. The critic's task is to place the writing, the text, and its readings into alternative contexts or fields, or to recode the text. Adequate criticism should enable others to "penetrate" the author's intent and the tenor of the times within which the text existed, to strip away lies and stylistic obfuscations, and to discover therefore the deeper or "real" meaning of a written product. Various levels of social reality can be explored, much as an archaeological expedition penetrates ever more deeply into a site.

A Structuralist Model

Structuralists modify Figure 29.1 (a model of artistic "production" generally, if one substitutes "plastic form" or "representation" for "text" in the figure). They make several radical disjunctive moves that alter many of the assumptions of objectivist/positivist social sciences as well as literary criticism. Fundamentally, the assumed-to-be-intimate and indivisible connections among persons, bodies, selves, lives, experiences, and stories are made problematic (see Denzin, 1989, chap. 2). Reality is socially constructed, as are the signs that convey, indicate, or represent it. Structuralists assume the relativity of the expression (including the possibility of nonreferential expressions). Meaning is context dependent, a function of coding (Barthes, 1975b). Loose relationships exist between the surface features of a narrative and underlying code(s) for decoding or translating a text. Although, ironically, stories always have this loose connection to the world—that is, they are not always referential to actual events—the elision of forms in the narrative model makes judgments of the meaning of a "story" problematic. A text can always be rendered in another code, another voice can be heard, a new standpoint illuminated (Clifford, 1988; Tyler, 1987; Van Maanen, 1988).

All texts metaphorically speak with many voices and contain within them many potential alternative readings. Within any story, the narrative line can be distinguished from the subject of the story. Reading as an activity creates another representation and shifts the field of the text. The unity of embodied self-writer-text-audience is analytically strewn asunder. Even the modes of discourse of science and history are seen as problematic (H. White, 1978).

But this repositioning of meaning as a function of codes has even more radical variants. A "crisis in representation" is precipitated by structuralism and semiotics. Consider these examples.

Frequently seen now is the journalistic conceit of wholly fabricating quotes, persons, scenes, long dialogues, and even events as a means of dramatizing and integrating "truth" and "fiction." Popularized by Tom Wolfe, and displayed in *The Right Stuff* (1979), the "new journalism" stylishly integrates the discretion to create lives found in fiction with the appeal of characters who are real people making real decisions in real life (see Agar, 1990). The consequences of these modes of fabrication are seen in the recent Masson-Malcolm trial (in May 1993), in which damaging quotes alleged to be from Masson and used by Malcolm were contested by Masson.

Media logic suffuses all media forms and confounds experienced reality with the artifices of the media. Fiction, news, and current events are collapsed in TV programs such as *Top Cops, Cops,* and *Rescue 911.* All produce versions of reality. Altheide (1993) notes that the elision of social control through the media with entertainment is rapidly escalating. A current television show, *Case Closed,* employs private investigators to hunt clues and pursue cases abandoned by the police. Further, the integration of advertising, news, and drama is now proceeding. Real-life events (e.g., the invasion and fire at the Branch Davidian compound in Waco, Texas; the explosion of a Pan Am jet over Lockerbie, Scotland) are "news" and "advertisements" for forthcoming television films (Altheide, 1993).

The media influence the diffusion of rapid-fire collage, atemporal, surreal, vividly colored, and fragmented imagery, almost a visual explosion, associated with many music videos, into television news, melodrama, and advertising. The model is MTV (Kaplan, 1987). These sound fragments and geometric distortions of faces and figures have largely displaced films with a logical progression, a story line, and a narrative structure (beginning, middle, and end, or opening, crisis, resolution, and closing).

These manifestations of structuralism's influence move a considerable distance from the classic interactionist model of reading and meaning. These changes in form result because social relations produce similar modes of experiencing and analysis of such experiencing for media, the public, and scholars. Highly reflexive societies reflect on and analyze that preoccupation with reflection.

Two Semiotic Approaches to McDonald's

Structuralist semiotics is not without weaknesses. It has limited capacity to explain change, the interaction of self and group, the history of an individual or group experience with a symbol system, or changes in sign systems themselves. Change in the meaning of signs over time, semiosis, is best revealed through in-depth interviewing and systematic observation. The interpretant, perspective, or standpoint of the observer from which the system is constructed must be identified in social and cultural context. In this sense, a social semiotics requires (or assumes) a rich ethnographic texture within which the semiotic analysis can be socially embedded. To analyze a menu, for example, semiotically and out of ethnographic context is sensible only if a reader is a sophisticated and experienced observer of the same "facts."

We contend that a *semiotic discourse analytic* (Cullum-Swan, 1989) provides a history and context for understanding meaning that is congruent with a symbolic interactionist perspective. Meaning is derived or accomplished from an understanding of cultural knowledge and social forms rather than from personal knowledge gained through reflexive communication with others (Mead, 1934). The purpose of such an analysis is to place signs in context with the relevant interpretants over time. This permits analysis of differential meaning by demographic features, such as gender, race, and class, and by personal elements, such as self, role relations, and group membership (Blumer, 1969). Our examples illustrate the utility of both a semiotic method (an analysis of the codes that organize the menu) and semiotic discourse analysis. We believe they are complementary methods that together provide a more complete understanding of how personal experience and cultural milieus contribute to sign interpretation.

A Menu: The Structuralist View

McDonald's is perhaps the world's best-known business, and among the most successful (Peters & Waterman, 1982). Its success is related to its fit with many contemporary urban lifestyles: it is fast, efficient, predictable, standardized, routinized, and bureaucratically organized (Ritzer, 1993). Its logic is apparent and seems to tap into basic understandings of categories, classifications, boundaries and frames, associations, and meaningful divisions among foods and drinks. Perhaps two generations have been socialized to the McDonald's experience, and the menu needs little explanation for the typical American child (who can connect the pictures to the physical objects to which they refer). The conventions connecting expression and content are known; the McDonald's sign system is known and well embedded in the culture. With the exception of a few local variations, the menu is standardized to facilitate rapid decisions at any McDonald's. Below, we attempt to show *how* these signs convey meaning in a particular context.[4]

The first task is to discover the political and social *field,* the set of objective and subjective pressures giving meaning to the structure and codes to be studied. We call this the "fast food" field.[5] The signs and sign vehicles (which carry the abstract sign) speak to rapidity of transaction (the cash registers are built into the counters). The modes of service available to the customer—drive through, take out, or eat in—range from fast to faster.

Taking the menu, a central symbol or collective representation, as primary data, we ask: What principles organize it? How does it convey constraint and order choice? The menu is divided into colored panels. These are devoted to types of items, some of which are clustered into "meals." This suggests that a color and meal-based *code,* or principle for assembling meaning and constituting messages (Eco, 1979), orders the menu. Shown above and in front of the customer and extending from left to right are 13 plastic boxes: 8 panels list food or drink items and 5 show pictures. Pictures contrast with, mark, and dramatize the information-laden panels. The panels, from left to right, show the following:

1. picture (Egg McMuffin)
2. breakfast items—7
3. Extra Value (breakfast) Meals—5 (side items underneath)
4. picture (McChicken sandwich)
5. sandwiches (beef)—6
6. sandwiches (chicken and fish)—3 (french fries listed underneath)
7. picture (Extra Value Meals)
8. Extra Value (lunch or dinner) Meals
9. beverages—11 with size variations
10. picture (McDonald's Value Pack Meals and children's meals that include toys)
11. Happy Meals (children's) (salads listed underneath)
12. desserts (gift certificate listed underneath)
13. picture (ice cream sundae)

What do the colors on the panels mean? Above the colored panels are labels: over panels 1-3, "breakfast" (yellow); over 5, 6, and 8, "sandwiches," "french fries," and "Extra Value Meals" (red); over 9, "beverages" (blue); over 11, "Happy Meals" and "salads" (brown); and over 12, "desserts" (purple). Primary colors (yellow, red, and blue), divide and mark core items, whereas subdued colors (brown and purple) mark peripheral items (drinks and desserts are not included in combination meals). In addition to marking core and periphery items, the colors indicate courses, if one considers salads and desserts as such in an Anglo-American meal. The color-coded panels mark a basic division in the United States between breakfast and lunch or dinner. The color code divides breakfast (yellow) from lunch and dinner (red) for adults. No such distinction is made for children (brown—Happy Meals are served for either lunch or dinner).

The horizontal panels are also coded by individual (à la carte items) and three combination "meals": "Happy Meals" for children and "Extra Value" breakfast and lunch/dinner combinations. Meals include base items plus a core item. For example, breakfast value meals include hash browns, a large coffee or an orange juice, and one of the five (sausage or egg, biscuit or muffin) breakfast core items. Extra Value Meals include a medium drink, large fries, and a sandwich or Chicken McNuggets. Combinations not only increase per person spending, but speed and simplify ordering and billing.

Having seen that colors and space are used to divide items and distinguish meals by time of day and age of consumer, we can look inside each panel to ask what orders the items (expressions) within it. Each panel is an *associative context* (paradigm) listing similar foods. The panels contain metonymic (part/whole) contrasts between substitutable items (e.g., panel 5 shows six types of beef sandwich: Big Mac, Quarter Pounder with Cheese, McLean burger, hamburger and cheeseburger [listed on the same line], and double cheeseburger). Is there a rationale for the vertical arrangement of the items, one on top of the other? What is it? What things does the menu not reflect? Price is not primary, but a secondary or tertiary code. The price is shown to the right of each sandwich in panels 5, 6, and 9, but is not the basis for their order. Nor are sandwiches listed in order of complexity (layers, sauces) or size. The menu is an advertisement. The most commonly ordered items are high on the list. Similarly, Coke, Diet Coke, and Sprite, followed by H-C Orange (all Coca-Cola products), are the first two lines, and decaffeinated coffee and orange juice are the bottom two.

Having seen the codes, what can one discover about the associations across items of the menu? Do they cohere as a sign system? Both connotative and denotative meanings are shared. The primary denotations of each item, as noted, are courses, prices, single and combination "meals," core and periphery of given meals, and adult/child. Adding the "Mc" prefix creates connotative unity: "Egg McMuffin," "McLean," "Big Mac," "Chicken McNuggets." These "Mcs" are institutional markers, or signs about signs, that collect disparate items into a unifying institutional theme. The links between these signs are analogical, or based on similarity.

In short, the semiotics of the McDonald's menu are well chosen for effect. They reflect knowledge of the content and timing of American meals as well as age and lifestyle distinctions, and employ spatial and visual organization that facilitates visibility, simplicity, and utilitarian orientation to the message (Jakobson, 1960). To summarize the coding of the McDonald's menu, the most important code is color/meal, followed by core/periphery (of meal items), adult/child, and individual/combination meals. A secondary code is vertical placement *within* a panel, a metonymic list of items. These placements reflect marketing aims and the popularity of items—that is, the higher, the more popular.[6]

This analysis suggests that the purpose of the sign system is to convey messages that enable fast decisions and increase turnover, and clusters that raise per person expenditure and minimize complex, ad hoc item selection. Colors, panels, clusterings of signs, and the simple, brief, evocative, and terse names coded into the menu and the cash register for billing and collection ease all bespeak efficient, routinized, fast-transaction-based food service.

A Semiotic Discourse Approach to McDonald's Experiences

We draw on focused, in-depth interviews to draw out the meaning of the McDonald's experience. Such interviews provide the best tool for eliciting data for a semiotic discourse analysis because they reveal the circumstances subjects recall in going to McDonald's and their associations with the visits. Selves, developed over time and reflecting the sedimentation of experience, are intertwined with McDonald's. These selves are linked to significant others lodged in the "me" and are part of the replaying of joint actions. Self, other, and experience are inextricably interwoven in a biographical and physical context. These associations are personal and historical but also organizationally generated; they explore the experiential meanings attached to individual visits to McDonald's rather than cultural knowledge displayed in a skillful order.

Biographical Associations

Any McDonald's visit may call up past visits with family, a team, friends, and personal associations. The following scenario typifies individual associations and experiences at McDonald's and suggest how two are woven together.

One example comes from a colleague. As a child, she had chronic health problems calling for regular and painful treatments at a doctor's office. A trip to McDonald's was the reward for being a "good girl." As an adult, she has extremely negative associations about McDonald's; she rarely enters its dreaded portals, and has been there only twice in the past 25 years. On the first of those two visits, she was sold a still-frozen "filet of fish" sandwich. On that visit, she was in line with a "regular" who was firmly entrenched in his customer role. It was clear from his affect and conversation that he was mentally retarded. He genuinely enjoyed his visits—they were the high point of his day! He came every day for dinner and systematically ate his way through the menu, eating one particular sandwich according to the day of the week. He knew all the employees by name, and they knew and could predict his order by the day of the week—for instance, fish on Friday, Big Mac on Sunday. This specific setting and employees were his home in symbolic terms, providing a routine in an otherwise empty life. On the second of her two visits, our colleague wisely purchased only coffee. The greasy smell of a McDonald's is firmly lodged in her memory and is sufficient to make her ill. Other negative associations arise in spite of the cheerful externalities of McDonald's.[7]

Organizationally Produced Meanings

Many people have negative or at least ambivalent associations with McDonald's. People choose it when they are disorganized, hurried, harassed or distracted, uncomfortably hungry, lonely and alone, and short of cash. Only children with no negative associations (going happily with friends or family) and disenfranchised, marginal adults—such as the homeless or the mentally ill or retarded—remain entirely positive, and anticipate, McDonald's. The corporation, through charitable activities and gaudy, enthusiastic, loud, family-focused ads, simulates happiness, togetherness, and "giving Mom a break" ("You deserve a break today, so get up and get away to McDonald's" was a recent ad jingle).

These are systematic attempts to replace or displace attention from the potentially ambivalent or negative significance of a McDonald's trip. The symbolization serves to defer focus from the reality of a visit. Organizational processes are linked to the creation of a consumer culture, marketing the positive experience of going to McDonald's, such as "happy" meals, clowns, playgrounds, golden arches—reminiscent of rainbows and heaven. Further organizational attempts to create a pseudo-gemeinschaft (Merton, 1961) environment are manifest in the physical and spatial attributes of the place and the "professional education" given to employees.

Many themes of American society—fast, cheap food, served by strangers with a minimal of interaction, obligation, and reciprocity—are displayed in the social organization of serving as well as in the well-recognized building (Ritzer, 1993). The rhetoric of space, spoken by convenient and capacious parking lots, broad, glass-enclosed buildings, semiopen kitchens, and abundant seating, is welcoming to Americans.

As in a Las Vegas casino, time is suspended in McDonald's. It is always daytime, and light and ambiance are not softened to romanticize the experience. Inside, one's gaze falls upon the huge, sunlike, lighted menu. The yellow brightness is almost overwhelming to burned-out, tired, and jaded "evening diners." The building conveys antiseptic cleanliness. The early original buildings were constructed of white, tilelike materials and resembled operating rooms. The severe simplicity of architecture and the interior decor do not connote any particular class or culture, except that of postindustrial society. There are no personal menus, maitre d's, waiters to tip, or preferred seating areas. All are treated equally, and "what you want is what you get." The only requirements are shoes, shirt, and a couple of bucks. One is not encouraged to eat at a leisurely pace. (In a London McDonald's near Marylebone Road, the molded plastic seats are slanted downward, so that one rests against them, but cannot really occupy them.)

The organization works efficiently and effectively to present a front-stage set of simulacra that communicate a fun and friendly, family-oriented, accessible, convenient setting for eating staffed by pleasant and tidy people. This is the public, advertised front. There is a systematic attempt to connote "home" as well. One can see backstage into the kitchen, which is the hub and heart of a home, and see and hear the cooking and compiling of food orders ("I need another Big Mac, please").

Public presentation and private reality differ. Supposedly, as at home, one can dash in and "grab something" or spend some time eating and relaxing. However, it is not a relaxing atmosphere: People rush in and out, babies cry, employees wash tables as one eats, and lonely diners sit silently, not participating in leisurely conversation with significant others. McDonald's confuses in other ways, claiming to be the world's biggest recycler of paper and waste, but not mentioning that it is also the world's biggest producer of trash. It displays pamphlets emphasizing nutrition, yet most of the entrées have dangerously high levels of fat and calories. "Environment-friendly" pamphlets written in 1990 project unfulfilled levels of recycling for 1991, and function ritually to show the organization's concern for health and the environment. Despite these apparent conflicts, the obvious appeal of McDonald's to many is that it offers cheap food, quick service, and instrumental modes of obtaining it.

McDonald's tries to ritualize the experience. A key ritual is the greeting, "Welcome to McDonald's. How may I serve you?" as if it were a home, not a restaurant. Ironically, choice and "having it your way" are extremely limited. Have you ever attempted to order a Big Mac without sauce? You wait—perhaps as punishment for interrupting the system. Or you may be informed that you must accept it as is. This does not mimic the indulgent mother who cooks for 10 years without onions to please a family member. The identification of food with mother, comfort, and love is implicit, even though the meals are not served by motherly people, but by a diverse lot of mostly young teenagers.

McDonald's efficient and democratic servers learn their trade at "Hamburger U." They learn the theory and practice of standardized food production, including such elements as the size of bag required for a given number of items, the ritual greeting, proper hygiene and attire, and the execution of snappy service. The best learners are inculcated with management skills and will acquire the nuances of supervising production. McDonald's promotes from within.

However, this apparent egalitarianism does not always work. Sometimes, the interactive effects among race, sex, age, and ethnicity of the servers, management, and customers can result in frustration and passive aggressive behaviors. Waiting 20 minutes for a Big Mac is considerably more annoying than a similar wait for cherries jubilee. One informant of ours recounted a McDonald's visit on an Ohio turnpike. The "management" was a Caucasian female; most of the employees were young Afro-American males. The entire crew claimed to be "on break," and was totally unresponsive to the manager's instructions and virtually ignored the milling and irritated customers.

McDonald's as a Dramatic Production

Impression management is essential to modern business success. Erving Goffman (1959) has alerted us to the importance of fronts, strategies, and impression management with reference to individuals, but organizations also manage impressions. The costumes and props of McDonald's have become more complex, elaborated, and expensive over time. The original "restaurant" was a small, boxy "drive-in" with two or three employees and no seating. This differed from the typical drive-in, which offered personalized curb service and delivery at the car. The primary innovation was the speed of service. This change in service, in reality extremely depersonalizing, required the customer to wait in line at a window with a tray, carry his or her own food to a table, and neatly clean the table and dispose of all trash at the completion of the meal. This was touted as an advance because it was *fast* (or faster).

As the organizational chart became more elaborate, so did the dramatic production of the McDonald's Corporation. Cast and setting were dramatically transformed! Indoor seating, increased menu items, fancy and colorful uniforms, drive-through windows, buildings with historical themes, children's accoutrements (highchairs, bibs, diaper changing areas), the cast of Ronald McDonald and Friends, attached indoor and outdoor playgrounds, and large, gleaming restrooms symbolized the new meaning attached to a McDonald's visit. These simple and powerful organizational signifieds become unconsciously combined with complex and sometimes conflicting personal associations.

These changes are indicative of semiosis, the changing meaning of the McDonald's sign production apparatus over time. Transformations in menu items, building form, seating arrangements, bathroom facilities, and the standardized cheerful affect of the employees are reactive to societal shifts as well as to changes in individual "taste." The continued worldwide growth and profitability of the organization testify to management's ability to "read" and manipulate the audience.

In this semiotic discourse analysis, ethnographic materials illuminate the signification process. A theme here is the complex interplay of private, experiential, and personal signifieds with public and organizationally constructed signifieds. This symbolic "struggle" is a function of the organizationally generated meanings, the elaborate and methodical cultural production of McDonald's, as well as personal meanings.

McDonald's is an example of an organizational culture that strategically facilitates management's aims: making profits and pleasing customers (Peters & Waterman, 1982). As we have attempted to show here, McDonald's is a brilliantly conceived dramatic production well designed to confuse. It manipulates people's sense of front- and backstage areas, public and private spaces, home and business, and instrumental and expressive aspects of food and eating, and subtly markets the creation and consumption of experience. As in the case of Disneyland, the fundamental purpose is to market experience at a profit (Van Maanen, 1992). The symbolizations employed by McDonald's serve to suppress and delay personal and group meanings contrary to the business purposes of the corporation and to elevate the connotations of "fun eating."

Conclusion

We have argued that although documents have long occupied an important role in the social sciences, the perspectives within which they are viewed as data have changed significantly. The quest changed from the reconstruction of personal experience to the epistemology and production of a text. Content and narrative analysis struggle continuously with the problem of context or the embeddedness of a text or story within personal or group experience. Semiotics seizes on signs and how they mean, obviating the question of experience, the self, and much of the Western attitude toward literature and the social sciences. Emphasis shifts to codes, paradigms, and explanations for the ordered meaning of a text, rather than the character, biography, or intent of the writer or subject of the writing. We have also provided a brief example of semiotic discourse analysis, using the McDonald's menu and the McDonald's experience as topics.

It would appear that these points are consistent with the drift of postmodernist thinking. McDonald's exemplifies the postmodern idea of "floating signifiers," contents arbitrarily linked to expressions, and the generation of desire by sign manipulation (Baudrillard, 1979). Once the aim is selling experience, even the connotation or suggestion of desirability produced by associations with a signifier is a powerful tool. McDonald's is a vast enactment of commodified experience, and it is a "text to be read." Thus the humanistic concerns of the social sciences return, awkwardly, in the analysis of the structural sources of the production of experience and the simulation of culture.

Notes

1. In psychology, for example, texts were analyzed with a combination of projective tests, clinical analyses, and more precise modes of assessing the content of written documents. Psychology essentially abandoned what Robert White (1963), following Henry A. Murray, called "the study of lives," autobiographical materials, history, and even the self as a fundamental concept (Gergen, 1991; Potter & Wetherell, 1987).

2. Some of these ideas are modified from Green (1993, p. 3, Table 1.1). *Semiotics* takes as its fundamental unit the sign and studies the types of coherence among signs and sign systems. Its pragmatic dimensions concern how signs are used and what they mean in context. Related areas of study (see Eco, 1979) are sign production (how new signs are developed), a theory of codes (how signs are understood as messages and the underlying principles organizing a given sign system), and signification and communication (the structure of information conveying systems and S-codes, or a system of elements that can be linked to others to communicate, e.g., information theory, physics, mathematics). *Speech act theory,* which is not discussed here, as it is not a textual analysis or production methodology, uses the "utterance" or speech act as a key unit, and studies language performance, the social organization of speech acts, and meaning as related to the cultural and social context in which they are uttered. *Textual analysis* uses sentences and larger fragments of texts as units of analysis, and studies the interaction between textual forms and genres and audience reactions or responses produced. Although heavily influenced by computer-generated content analysis, the original purpose was interpretation of the hermeneutics of texts. *Discourse analysis* takes as its unit longer segments of texts or rhetoric, oscillating between the structure of the argument to the impact or meaning of it.

3. All of our examples are "arbitrary," or based on cultural knowledge. C. S. Peirce (1931) argues that what we call sign-referent links are of three kinds: (a) iconic, based on the mode of representation; (b) indexical, based on natural or causal relations between expression and content; and (c) arbitrary, based on cultural knowledge. Eco (1979, p. 178) argues, and we agree, that Peirce's tripartite distinctions are based on the assumption that the "real" character of content can be known.

4. Our fieldwork was done previously. We refined our analytic focus and modes of data gathering and reduction. The fieldwork reported here, substantiated by some 40 years of McDonald's dining, was executed in two McDonald's in East Lansing, Michigan, on May 29-June 1, 1993.

5. Among the national organizations in this field are Arby's, Burger King, McDonald's, and Wendy's (see Feinstein, 1989). The "fast-food" field contrasts with other forms of restaurant dining. It is indicated by a brief, limited public menu, shown above the server as an overhead lighted display at the front of every store, uncomfortable seats, food dispensed at a counter (no table service), optional take-out service, and preprepared standardized food. The server, cashier, and cleaner roles are interchangeable. Customers dispose of their rubbish when finished, sharing the task with young workers.

6. Space does not permit a more detailed analysis of the coding of particular food and drink items using two oppositions to organize them (Lévi-Strauss, 1969): the raw versus the cooked, and hot and cold.

7. Another friend has a terrible fear of clowns and had recurrent childhood nightmares involving villainous clowns. As Ronald McDonald, a clown, is the personal representative of the corporation, and his frightening visage is omnipresent in the media and at the restaurant, our friend fears McDonald's. The prospect of a combination of a circus and a trip to McDonald's is enough to send him off the deep end. Similarly, many children of divorced families are taken to McDonald's because of chaos during the breakup of the household and subsequently by their fathers during visitation. These children might also have very negative feelings about fast-food chains.

References

Agar, M. (1990). Text and fieldwork: Exploring the excluded middle. In J. Van Maanen (Ed.), The presentation of ethnographic research [Special issue]. *Journal of Contemporary Ethnography, 19,* 73-88.

Altheide, D. L. (1993). *News as advertisement.* Unpublished manuscript, Arizona State University.

Atkinson, P. A. (1990). *The ethnographic imagination: Textual constructions of reality.* London: Routledge.

Atkinson, P. A. (1992). *Understanding ethnographic texts.* Newbury Park, CA: Sage.

Barley, S. (1983). Semiotics and the study of occupational and organizational cultures. *Administrative Science Quarterly, 28,* 393-413.

Barthes, R. (1967). *Elements of semiology and writing degree zero.* Boston: Beacon.

Barthes, R. (1972). *Mythologies* (A. Lavers, Trans.). New York: Hill & Wang.

Barthes, R. (1975a). *The pleasure of the text* (R. Miller, Trans.). New York: Hill & Wang.

Barthes, R. (1975b). *S/Z.* London: Jonathan Cape.

Baudrillard, J. (1979). *Seduction.* New York: St. Martin's.

Bennett, W. L., & Feldman, M. (1986). *Reconstructing reality in the courtroom.* New Brunswick, NJ: Rutgers University Press.

Berelson, B. (1952). *Content analysis in communication research.* Glencoe, IL: Free Press.

Blumer, H. (1939). *Critiques of research in the social sciences* (Vol. 1) (Bulletin 44). New York: Social Science Research Council.

Blumer, H. (1969). *Symbolic interactionism: Perspective and method.* Englewood Cliffs, NJ: Prentice Hall.

Boje, D. (1991). The story telling organization: A study of story performance in an office supply firm. *Administrative Science Quarterly, 36,* 106-126.

Borgmann, A. (1992). *Crossing the postmodern divide.* Chicago: University of Chicago Press.

Bourdieu, P. (1977). *Outline of a theory of practice.* Cambridge: Cambridge University Press.

Brody, H. (1987). *Stories of sickness.* New Haven, CT: Yale University Press.

Brown, R. H. (1987). *Society as text.* Chicago: University of Chicago Press.

Brown, R. H. (1989). *Social science as civic discourse.* Chicago: University of Chicago Press.

Brown, R. H. (1992). *Writing the social text.* Hawthorne, NY: Aldine.

Burke, K. (1966). *A rhetoric of motives and a grammar of motives.* Cleveland: World.

Cicourel, A. (1973). *Cognitive sociology.* New York: Free Press.

Cicourel, A. (1982). Language and belief in a medical setting. In H. Brynes (Ed.), *Contemporary perceptions of language: Interdisciplinary dimensions* (pp. 48-78). Washington, DC: Georgetown University Press.

Cicourel, A. (1985). Text and discourse. *Annual Review of Anthropology, 14,* 159-185.

Cicourel, A. (1986). Social measurement as the creation of expert systems. In D. Fiske & R. A. Schweder (Eds.), *Metatheory in social science* (pp. 246-270). Chicago: University of Chicago Press.

Clifford, J. (1988). *The predicament of culture: Twentieth-century ethnography, literature, and art.* Cambridge, MA: Harvard University Press.

Clifford, J., & Marcus, G. E. (Eds.). (1986). *Writing culture: The poetics and politics of ethnography.* Berkeley: University of California Press.

Crapanzano, V. (1980). *Tuhami: Portrait of a Moroccan.* Chicago: University of Chicago Press.

Coles, R. (1989). *The call of stories.* Boston: Houghton Mifflin.

Culler, J. (1975). *Structuralist poetics.* Ithaca, NY: Cornell University Press.

Culler, J. (1977). *Ferdinand de Saussure.* Harmondsworth: Penguin.

Cullum-Swan, B. (1989). *Behavior in pubic places: A frame analysis of gynecological exams.* Unpublished master's thesis, Michigan State University, Department of Sociology.

Denzin, N. K. (1986). Postmodern social theory. *Sociological Theory, 4,* 194-204.

Denzin, N. K. (1989). *The research act* (3rd ed.). Englewood Cliffs, NJ: Prentice Hall.

Derrida, J. (1976). *On grammatology* (G. C. Spivak, Trans.). Baltimore: Johns Hopkins University Press.

Descombes, V. (1980). *Modern French philosophy.* Cambridge, UK: Cambridge University Press.

Duncan, H. D. (1962). *Communication and social order.* Totowa, NJ: Bedminster.

Duncan, H. D. (1968). *Symbols in society.* New York: Oxford University Press.

Duncan, H. D. (1969). *Symbols and social theory.* New York: Oxford University Press.

Durkheim, E. (1951). *Suicide.* Glencoe, IL: Free Press.

Dwyer, K. (1982). *Moroccan dialogue: Anthropology in question.* Baltimore: Johns Hopkins University Press.

Eco, U. (1979). *A theory of semiotics.* Bloomington: Indiana University Press.

Edelman, M. (1966). *The symbolic uses of politics.* Urbana: University of Illinois Press.

Edelman, M. (1977). *Political language.* New York: Academic Press.

Edelman, M. (1992). *Constructing the political spectacle.* Chicago: University of Chicago Press.

Feinstein, J. (1989). *Dining out.* New York: New York University Press.

Foucault, M. (1973). *The order of things: An archaeology of the human sciences.* New York: Vintage.

Foucault, M. (1978). *A history of sexuality.* New York: Pantheon.

Geertz, C. (1988). *Works and lives: The anthropologist as author.* Stanford, CA: Stanford University Press.

Gergen, K. J. (1991). *The saturated self: Dilemmas of identity in contemporary life.* New York: Basic Books.

Giddens, A. (1984). *The constitution of society.* Berkeley: University of California Press.

Goffman, E. (1959). *The presentation of self in everyday life.* Garden City, NY: Doubleday.

Gottschalk, L., Kluckhohn, C., & Angell, R. C. (1945). *The use of personal documents in history, anthropology and sociology* (Bulletin 53). New York: Social Science Research Council.

Green, B. S. (1993). *Gerontology and the construction of old age.* Hawthorne, NY: Aldine.

Griemas, A. J. (1966). *Structural semiotics.* Lincoln: University of Nebraska Press.

Guiraud, P. (1975). *Semiology.* London: Routledge & Kegan Paul.

Gusfield, J. (1966). *Symbolic crusade.* Urbana: University of Illinois Press.

Gusfield, J. (1986). *The culture of public problems.* Chicago: University of Chicago Press.

Gusfield, J. (1989). (Ed.). *Kenneth Burke on symbols and society.* Chicago: University of Chicago Press.

Hawkes, T. (1977). *Semiotics and structuralism.* Berkeley: University of California Press.

Heise, D. (1992). *Ethnograph* (2nd ed.). Chapel Hill: University of North Carolina Press.

Hjemslev, L. (1961). *Prolegomena to a theory of language* (rev. ed.). Madison: University of Wisconsin Press.

Holsti, O. (1969). *Content analysis for social sciences.* Reading, MA: Addison-Wesley.

Jackson, B. (1986). *Semiotics and legal theory.* London: Routledge & Kegan Paul.

Jacobs, J. (1989). *Drunk driving.* Chicago: University of Chicago Press.

Jakobson, R. (1960). Closing statement. In T. Seboek (Ed.), *The uses of language* (pp. 330-377). Cambridge: MIT Press.

Jameson, F. (1972). *The prison house of language.* Princeton, NJ: Princeton University Press.

Kaplan, E. A. (1987). *Rocking around the clock.* London: Methuen.

Kleinman, A. (1988). *The illness narratives.* New York: Basic Books.

Kracauer, S. (1993). The challenge to qualitative content analysis. *Public Opinion Quarterly, 16,* 631-642.

Kristeva, J. (1980). *Desire in language.* New York: Columbia University Press.

Kurzweil, E. (1980). *The age of structuralism.* New York: Columbia University Press.

Lemert, C. (1979a). Language, structure and measurement. *American Journal of Sociology, 84,* 929-957.

Lemert, C. (1979b). Structuralist semiotics. In S. McNall (Ed.), *Theoretical perspectives in sociology* (pp. 96-111). New York: St. Martin's.

Lemert, C. (1981). Reading French sociology. In C. Lemert (Ed.), *French sociology* (pp. 4-32). New York: Columbia University Press.

Lemert, C. (1990). Varieties of French structuralism. In G. Ritzer (Ed.), *Theoretical sociology* (pp. 230-254). New York: Columbia University Press.

Levinson, S. (1983). *Pragmatics.* Cambridge, UK: Cambridge University Press.

Lévi-Strauss, C. (1963). *Structural anthropology.* New York: Basic Books.

Lévi-Strauss, C. (1966). *The savage mind* (2nd ed.). Chicago: University of Chicago Press.

Lévi-Strauss, C. (1969). *The raw and the cooked.* New York: Harper & Row.

Lincoln, B. (1992). *Discourse and the construction of society.* New York: Oxford University Press.

Lotman, Y. (1990). *Universe of the mind: A semiotic theory of culture.* Bloomington: Indiana University Press.

Lowenthal, L. (1962). *Literature, culture and society.* Englewood Cliffs, NJ: Prentice Hall.

MacCannell, D. (1989). *The tourist.* Boston: Schocken. (Original work published 1976)

Martin, J. (1990). Deconstructing organizational taboos. *Organization Science, 1,* 339-359.

Martin, J., Feldman, M. S., Hatch, M. J., & Sitkin, S. (1983). The uniqueness paradox in stories. *Administrative Science Quarterly, 28,* 438-453.

Mead, G. H. (1934). *Mind, self and society: From the standpoint of a social behaviorist.* Chicago: University of Chicago Press.

Merelman, R. (1984). *Making something of ourselves.* Berkeley: University of California Press.

Merelman, R. (1992). *Language, symbols and politics.* Boulder, CO: Westview.

Merton, R. K. (1961). *Social theory and social structure.* New York: Free Press.

Milovanovic, D. (1993). *Postmodern law and discourse.* Liverpool: Deborah Charles.

Mishler, E. (1984). *The discourse of medicine.* Norwood, NJ: Ablex.

Moerman, M. (1988). *Talking culture.* Philadelphia: University of Pennsylvania Press.

Noth, W. (1990). *Handbook of semiotics.* Bloomington: Indiana University Press.

Paget, M. (1988). *The unity of mistakes.* Philadelphia: Temple University Press.

Peirce, C. S. (1931). *Collected papers.* Cambridge, MA: Harvard University Press.

Perinbanayagam, R. (1991). *Discursive acts.* Hawthorne, NY: Aldine.

Peters, T. J., & Waterman, R. H., Jr. (1982). *In search of excellence.* New York: Harper & Row.

Potter, J., & Wetherell, M. (1987). *Discourse and social psychology.* London: Sage.

Propp, V. (1968). *The morphology of the folktale* (2nd ed., rev.). Austin: University of Texas Press.

Riessman, C. (1993). *Narrative analysis.* Newbury Park, CA: Sage.

Ritzer, G. (1993). *The McDonaldization of society.* Newbury Park, CA: Pine Forge.

Rose, M. (1990). *The post-modern and the post-industrial.* Cambridge, UK: Cambridge University Press.

Rosenau, P. M. (1992). *Postmodernism and the social sciences.* Princeton, NJ: Princeton University Press.

Rumelhart, D. (1977). Understanding and summarizing brief stories. In D. LaBerge & J. Samuels (Eds.), *Basic processes in reading perception and comprehension* (pp. 265-303). Norwood, NJ: Ablex.

Rumelhart, D., & Norman, D. A. (1981). Analogical processes in learning. In J. R. Anderson (Ed.), *Cognitive skills and their acquisition* (pp. 335-359). Hillsdale, NJ: Lawrence Erlbaum.

Saussure, F. de. (1966). *Course in general linguistics* (C. Bally & A. Sechehaye, Eds.; W. Baskin, Trans.). New York: McGraw-Hill. (Original work published 1915)

Stoller, P. (1992). *The taste of ethnographic things.* Philadelphia: University of Pennsylvania Press.

Stone, P. J., Dunphy, D., & Kirsch, J. (1967). *The General Enquirer.* Cambridge: Harvard University Press.

Sturrock, J. (1979). *Structuralism and since.* London: Open University Press.

Thomas, W. I., & Znaniecki, F. (1918). *The Polish peasant* (Vols. 1-2). Chicago: University of Chicago Press.

Tyler, S. A. (1987). *The unspeakable: Discourse, dialogue, and rhetoric in the postmodern world.* Madison: University of Wisconsin Press.

Van Maanen, J. (1988). *Tales of the field: On writing ethnography.* Chicago: University of Chicago Press.

Van Maanen, J. (1992). Displacing Disney: Some notes on the flow of culture. *Qualitative Sociology, 15,* 31-45.

White, H. (1978). *Topics of discourse.* Baltimore: Johns Hopkins University Press.

White, R. (1963). *The study of lives.* New York: Atherton.

Wolfe, T. (1979). *The right stuff.* New York: Farrar, Strauss & Giroux.

PART V
THE ART OF INTERPRETATION, EVALUATION, AND PRESENTATION

In conventional terms, the following section of the *Handbook* signals the terminal phase of qualitative inquiry. The researcher and evaluator now assesses, analyses, and interprets the empirical materials that have been collected. This process, conventionally conceived, implements a set of analytic procedures that produces interpretations, which are then integrated into a theory, or put forward as a set of policy recommendations. The resulting interpretations are assessed in terms of a set of criteria from the positivist or postpositivist tradition, including validity, reliability, and objectivity. Those that stand up to scrutiny are put forward as the findings of the study.

Part V explores the art and politics of interpretation and evaluation, arguing that the processes of analysis, evaluation, and interpretation are neither terminal nor mechanical. They are always ongoing, emergent, unpredictable, and unfinished. They are done through the process of writing, itself an interpretive, personal, and political act. They are like a dance, to invoke the metaphor used by Valerie Janesick in Chapter 12 of this volume.

We begin by assessing a number of criteria that have been traditionally (as well as recently) used to judge the adequacy of qualitative research. These criteria flow from the major paradigms now operating in this field (in Chapter 31, Norman Denzin explores these criteria in depth).

Criteria for Evaluating Qualitative Research

There is considerable debate over what constitutes good interpretation in qualitative research (Hammersley, 1992, p. 57; see also Altheide & Johnson, Chapter 30, this volume). Modifying Hammersley (1992, p. 57), there are four basic positions on this issue. First, there are those who apply the same criteria to qualitative research as are employed in quantitative inquiry. Here there is the belief that one set of criteria should be applied to all scientific research, that is there is nothing special about qualitative research that demands a special set of criteria. As we argued in our introduction to Part II, the positivist and postpositivist paradigms apply four standard criteria to disciplined inquiry: internal validity, external validity, reliability, and objectivity. The use of these criteria, or their variants, is consistent with this first position, which we label *positivist.*

The second position, *postpositivist,* argues that a set of criteria unique to qualitative research needs to be developed. This is so because it represents "an alternative paradigm to quantitative social research" (Hammersley, 1992, p. 57). Although there is considerable disagreement over what these criteria should be, there is agreement that they should be different (see Lincoln & Guba, 1985). In practice, this position has often led to the development of criteria that are in agreement with the postpositivist criteria; they are merely fitted to a naturalistic research context (see, for example, Kirk & Miller, 1986). Hammersley (1992, p. 64) summarizes postpositivist criteria in the following way. Such researchers assess a work in terms of its ability to (a) generate generic/formal theory; (b) be empirically grounded and scientifically credible; (c) produce findings that can be generalized, or transferred to other settings; and (d) be internally reflexive in terms of taking account of the effects of the researcher and the research strategy on the findings that have been produced.[1]

The *constructivists* offer an important departure from postpositivism. They argue for quality criteria that translate internal and external validity, reliability, and objectivity into trustworthiness and authenticity. These criteria are different from those employed by *critical theorists,* who stress action, praxis, and the historical situatedness of findings. In contrast, *feminist scholarship,* in the three traditions outlined by Olesen (empiricist, standpoint, cultural studies), works, respectively, within the traditional positivist, postpositivist, and postmodern (and poststructural; see below) models of evaluation. Ethnic, critical theory, and cultural studies models of inquiry are similarly so aligned. As one moves from the postpositivist to the postmodern and poststructural positions, increased importance is attached to such antifoundational criteria as emotionality, caring, subjective understanding, dialogic texts, and the formation of long-term, trusting relationships with those studied.

The third position, *postmodernism,* argues that "the character of qualitative research implies that there can be no criteria for judging its products" (Hammersley, 1992, p. 58). This argument contends that the very idea of assessing qualitative research is antithetical to the nature of this research and the world it attempts to study (see Smith, 1984, p. 383). This position doubts all criteria and privileges none, although those who work within it favor criteria like those adopted by some poststructuralists (see below; see also Richardson's discussion of the crystal in Chapter 32).

The fourth position, *poststructuralism,* contends that an entirely new set of criteria, divorced from the positivist and postpositivist traditions, needs to be constructed. Such criteria would flow from the qualitative project, stressing subjectivity, emotionality, feeling, and other antifoundational factors (see Ellis & Flaherty, 1992, pp. 5-6; Richardson, 1991; Seidman, 1991).

Reflective, Reflexive Ethnography

The above discussion frames the first chapter in this section. Reflective, reflexive ethnography examines the criteria it uses when interpretive, explanatory statements are made. In Chapter 30, David Altheide and John Johnson review the recent literature on this topic, including the nonpositivist search for validity. They identify several different perspectives on validity, including validity as culture, ideology, gender, language, relevance, standards, and reflexive accounting. As their referents indicate, these seven positions read validity through lenses that are no longer confined to pure knowledge, or truth claims. Thus validity is seen as a process shaped by culture, ideology, gender, language, and so on.

Altheide and Johnson prefer to conceive of validity as reflexive accounting. They connect this position to a framework they call "analytic realism." This perspective assumes the researcher interprets the world, and this interpretive process rests on an ethnographic ethic. This ethic directs attention to the situated, relational, and textual structures of the ethnographic experience. Researchers are obliged to delineate clearly the interactions that have occurred among themselves, their methodologies, and the settings and actors studied.

Validity-as-reflexive-accounting works from the postpositivist position, as presented by Hammersley. Altheide and Johnson believe that a set of criteria unique to qualitative research needs to be developed. The reflexive spirit of their ethnographic ethic implements the call for internal reflexivity that Hammersley associates with the postpositivist paradigm.

The Art and Politics of Interpretation

Working from the poststructural and postmodern positions, Norman Denzin, in Chapter 31, argues that interpretation is an artful political process. There is no single interpretive truth. Interpretations are narrative, or storied, accounts. Interpretation-as-storytelling may privilege any of a number of different narrative positions. These positions refer back to the major paradigms and interpretive positions discussed above (positivism, postpositivism, constructionism, critical theory, feminism, cultural studies, ethnic models of inquiry). Separate interpretive styles are associated with these traditions, including the theoretical form of the text (substantive, formal, critical) and its narrative structure (essay, experimental, and so on).

Denzin predicts the continued production of more elaborate interpretive epistemologies based on race, class, gender, and ethnicity. Such moves will continue to privilege the personal and the political in the qualitative text. This will increase the importance of such work for social change.

Writing as Inquiry

Writers interpret as they write, so writing is a form of inquiry. In Chapter 32, Laurel Richardson explores new writing and interpretive styles that flow from what she calls the contemporary or postmodern sensibility. These new forms include narratives of the self, fiction, poetry, drama, performance science, polyvocal texts, responsive readings, aphorisms, comedy and satire, visual presentations, and mixed genres. Richardson then discusses in detail one class of experimental genre, which she calls "evocative representations." Work in this genre includes narratives of the self and ethnographic fictional representations.

A central image in her text is the crystal, which she contrasts to the triangle. Traditional postpositivist research has relied upon triangulation, including the use of multiple methods, as a method of validation. This model implies a fixed point of reference that can be triangulated. Postmodernist, mixed-genre texts do not triangulate. The central image is the crystal, which "combines symmetry and substance with an infinite variety of shapes, substances, transmutations, . . . and angles of approach." Crystals are prisms that reflect and refract, creating ever-changing images and pictures of reality. Crystallization deconstructs the traditional idea of validity, for now there can be no single, or triangulated, truth.

The Practice and Promise of Qualitative Program Evaluation

Program evaluation is, of course, a major site of qualitative research. (Earlier *Handbook* chapters by Hamilton, Stake, Reason, and Miller and Crabtree have established this fact.) Evaluators are interpreters. Their texts tell stories. These stories, Jennifer Greene argues in Chapter 33, are inherently political. Greene examines this political process in terms of the postpositivist, pragmatic, interpretivist, and critical paradigms. She reviews the work of the major figures in this area, including Guba and Lincoln, Patton, Stake, and Eisner. In her conclusion she calls for more morally engaged evaluation practices that are responsive to the feminist, emancipatory, and critical inquiry traditions. She seeks an explicit political agenda for program evaluation, and finds the means for that agenda in the qualitative research tradition.

Influencing Policy With Qualitative Research

Qualitative researchers can influence social policy, and Ray Rist shows how they do this in Chapter 34. He shows how qualitative research has pivotal relevance in each stage of the policy cycle, from problem formulation to the implementation and accountability stages. Qualitative researchers can isolate target populations, show the immediate effects of certain programs on such groups, and isolate the constraints that operate against policy changes in such settings. Unlike others, who relegate qualitative research to a secondary position in this process, Rist's model gives it a central part in the shaping of social policy.

The Greene and Rist texts connect back to the applied research traditions identified by Hamilton (Chapter 3) and Reason (Chapter 20). They show how the interpretive, qualitative text can morally empower citizens and shape government policies. At the same time, they chart new lines of action for evaluators who are themselves part of the ruling apparatuses of society (Ryan, 1993). Rist and Greene reclaim a new moral authority for the evaluator. This claim can also empower the qualitative researcher who does not engage in direct program evaluation.

Conclusion

The readings in Part V affirm our position that qualitative research has come of age. Multiple discourses now surround topics that in earlier historical moments where contained within the broad grasp of the positivist and postpositivist perspectives. There are now many ways to write, read, assess, evaluate, and apply qualitative research texts. This complex field invites reflexive appraisal, which is the topic of Part VI.

Note

1. Hammersley's own criteria, as discussed in the introduction to Part III, collapse this list into two dimensions: credibility and relevance.

References

Ellis, C., & Flaherty, M. G. (1992). An agenda for the interpretation of lived experience. In C. Ellis & M. G. Flaherty (Eds.), *Investigating subjectivity: Research on lived experience* (pp. 1-16). Newbury Park, CA: Sage.

Hammersley, M. (1992). *What's wrong with ethnography? Methodological explorations.* London: Routledge.

Kirk, J., & Miller, M. L. (1986). *Reliability and validity in qualitative research.* Beverly Hills, CA: Sage.

Lincoln, Y. S., & Guba, E. G. (1985). *Naturalistic inquiry.* Beverly Hills, CA: Sage.

Richardson, L. (1991). Postmodern social theory: Representational practices. *Sociological Theory, 9,* 173-179.

Ryan, K. E. (1993, November 5). *Evaluation ethics: Contributions from forms of feminine moral thinking.* Paper presented at the annual meeting of the American Evaluation Association, Dallas.

Seidman, S. (1991). Postmodern anxiety: The politics of epistemology. *Sociological Theory, 9,* 180-190.

Smith, J. K. (1984). The problem of criteria for judging interpretive inquiry. *Educational Evaluation and Policy Analysis, 6,* 379-391.

30

■

Criteria for Assessing Interpretive Validity in Qualitative Research

DAVID L. ALTHEIDE
JOHN M. JOHNSON

POGO could have had students of ethnography in mind when he stated, "We has met the enemy, and it is us." After decades of academic and paradigmatic politics, ethnographic and qualitative research finds itself in an astonishing position. This is unanticipated by all, especially by those closest to it, who were for so many decades accustomed to its devalued, unappreciated, marginal status. There is a remarkable new interest in ethnographic and qualitative research. It occurs even in disciplines (such as education, justice studies, clinical work, legal studies, policy analysis) where the practice is underdeveloped. This growing interest has been observed by others. Evidence for the trend can be gleaned from many sources. Yet, as Pogo suggests, students of ethnography have become their own worst critics, often resurrecting epistemological issues about the problematics of "objectivity," "purpose of knowledge," and filtering through new insights about communication contexts, logic, and formats.

Unprecedented criticism of ethnographic or qualitative method, substance, style, practice, and relevance has emerged. The criticism emerges not from the traditional enemies, the positivists who fault qualitative research for its failure to meet some or all of the usual positivistic criteria of truth, but from the insiders to the ethnographic movement. This trend is consistent with a newer and more extreme "reflexive turn" by ethnographic practice about 20-25 years ago. This reflexive turn has added much to our understanding of how qualitative research is actually done, but has additionally raised hitherto unanticipated dilemmas about representation and legitimation (standpoint or voice). More specifically, important questions have been raised about the role of the ethnographer in the reports produced, the basis for knowledge claims, and how a relativistic perspective in ethnography can produce solid findings.

Our purpose in this chapter is to address some of these dilemmas as we have encountered them in our work, and to offer suggestions for judging ethnographic products. Our purpose of clarifying the domain of meaningful existence poses special problems, as we have abandoned the positivists' formula for objective knowledge. A critical question is, How should interpretive methodologies be judged by readers who share the perspective that *how* knowledge is acquired, organized, and interpreted is relevant to *what* the claims are? Our position is this: As long as we strive to base our claims and interpretations of social life on data of any kind, we must have a logic for assessing and communicating the interactive process through which the investigator acquired the research experience and information. If we are to understand the "detailed means through which human beings engage in meaningful action and create a world of their own or one that is shared with others" (Morgan, 1983, p. 397), we must acknowledge that "insufficient attention has as yet been devoted to evolving criteria for assessing the general quality and rigor of interpretive research" (Morgan, 1983, p. 399).

Our main conceptual vehicle is "validity" and related issues. We set forth a perspective for assessing qualitative research, but our main interest is in establishing some working boundaries for approaching the problem. We examine points raised by a number of thoughtful critiques, particularly some of the more recent writings of "postmodernist" scholars. Following an overview of some alternative views about validity offered by these critics, we set forth a different position on the issue of validity. We suggest some general guidelines for assessing ethnographic research and examine a key issue for grounding alternative plans for this classical approach to social science, establishing a goal/purpose/grounding for an *ethnographic ethic* that can be located within an ecology of knowledge. We then focus on a model of ethnography, *analytic realism,* based on the view that the social world is an interpreted world, not a literal world.

Ethnography in Perspective

For as long as scholars have conducted qualitative or ethnographic research, they have studied the research process. At the turn of the century and in the decades immediately following it, knowledge and insights about the processes and problems of qualitative research were published, but were also communicated orally. In anthropology, Franz Boas and his students orally communicated their vigorous and vibrant ethnographic traditions. Indeed, anthropologists and sociologists, although differing historically in their respective preferences for "exotic/foreign" peoples or "the urban underclass," nevertheless were quite similar in their approaches. In sociology, Robert Park and the many qualitative researchers of the Chicago school communicated their insights and reflections to insiders and neophytes. During the 1960s and 1970s, there was a more pointed critique and analysis of ethnography, *a reflexive turn in qualitative research.*

One meaning of *reflexivity* is that the scientific observer is part and parcel of the setting, context, and culture he or she is trying to understand and represent. After the reflexive turn, increasing numbers of qualitative researchers began to appreciate what this meant for the validity of ethnographic or qualitative research. There was a new appreciation of the older problems and issues in ethnography, as more and more scholars began to realize that the traditional problems of entrée or access to a setting, personal relations with the members in a setting, how field research data were conceived and recorded, and a host of other pragmatic issues had important implications for what a particular observer reported as the "findings" of the research. This growing recognition contributed to a vibrant and creative period of self-criticism and self-reflection among ethnographers.

For the contemporary qualitative researcher who is sensitive to the research process, the past 25 years, in particular, have included many publications that seek to analyze the intimate relationship between the research process and the findings it produces. There are numerous reports dealing with research processes, from "membership roles in fieldwork" (see Adler & Adler, 1987) to "leaving" a research setting (Altheide, 1980). Many ethnographers have addressed these problems of validity and verisimilitude with straightforward honesty and integrity. As a result, we now understand much more about the complexities and nuances of the qualitative research process, and how the resolution of pragmatic research questions bears upon the important issues of validity and field research (see Clifford & Marcus, 1986; Geertz, 1973). John Van Maanen's contribution *Tales of the Field* (1988) reflects an effort to do for sociological ethnographies what the Clifford and Marcus collection *Writing Culture* (1986) has done for anthropological ethnography.

These works and others have led to heated debates about the nature of ethnography, particularly as they are read by younger scholars and others unfamiliar with many of the groundbreaking analyses of reflexivity that were published by symbolic interactionists, ethnomethodologists, and phenomenologists in the 1970s (see Jorgensen, 1989). Included among the more recent issues concerning ethnographic research are *representation,* or the problems of showing the realities of the lived experiences of the observed settings, and *reporting,* or how the language used by a social scientist may necessarily include rhetorical features. Cutting through both are related issues of *interpretation* and *voice,* or whose point of view is taken to report the findings (Snow & Morrill, 1993, p. 8). From this vantage point, ethnographies represent "stories" or narrative "tales" that are told, in part, to fit the genre of storytelling. The problem, then, is that if a different style or genre is selected in giving an ethnographic account, we have a different view or story presented. What, in short, ethnographers are claimed to be doing in such cases is providing a "text," which in turn is read and interpreted by readers or audiences, who, because of their own interpretive and sense-making capacities, will derive their own unique meanings or "readings" of the text.

Taken as a whole, we can say with confidence that these more recent writings have sensitized us to the fact that there is more to ethnography than "what happens in the field." Another important part of it is what takes place "back in the office" when the observer or researcher is "writing it up."

The Quest for an Interpretive Validity

The traditional criteria of methodological adequacy and validity were formulated and essentially "owned" by positivism, the philosophical, theoretical, and methodological perspective that has justified the use of quantitative methods in the social sciences for most of the twentieth century. Promoting the nineteenth-century model of science-as-the-physical-sciences, positivism seeks the development of universalistic laws, whereby actual or real events in the world are explained in a deductive fashion by universal laws that assert definite and unproblematic relationships. Through the use of techniques that produce the numerical data presumed to reflect true measures of objective categories, the positivist opts for sense-directed data, giving the "empirical science" its meaning. The perspective includes the common assertion that "reliability," or the stability of methods and findings, is an indicator of "validity," or the accuracy and truthfulness of the findings.

Ethnographers usually took a different approach. Few doubted that there was a reality that could be known. Most ethnographers focus on the processes that members used in constructing or creating their activities, and how they found or established order in their activities. This focus on what some have termed the "definition of the situation" was oriented to meanings and interpretations of members who lived in specific historical, social, and cultural contexts, and faced numerous practical challenges and limitations. It was on descriptions—including descriptions of language, nuances, and, of course, routines—that ethnographers based their reports. As the anthropologist Laura Nader (1993) comments about a collection of field studies:

> The concept "ethnography" has been gradually reduced in meaning in recent years and in proportion to its popularity. . . . Ethnographic is not ethnography. . . . Anthropologists are less preoccupied with being scientific than are their social science colleagues, more intent on recording and interpreting another people's way of life—ethnography we call it. Ethnography entails deep immersion and is seldom accomplished in short periods of time. It is a special kind of description, not to be confused with qualitative and descriptive studies of another kind. The goal of ethnography, as Malinowski put it, is "to grasp the native's point of view, his relation to life, to realize his vision of his world." Anthropology *is* a feat of empathy and analysis. (p. 7)

A key part of the method, then, is to see firsthand what occurs; failing that, ethnographers would ask informants and others for their recollections, points of view, and interpretations. Although the predictability sought by positivists was not the issue, ethnographers argued that their approach provided knowledge as understanding, rather than control. Even though ethnographers realized that the contextual and often emergent nature of their work made precision beyond a reasonable expectation impractical, they wrote—and spoke—authoritatively about their accounts before sympathetic audiences.

The nature of these contexts, goals, and perspectives, and the nature of relevant audiences have been questioned in recent years. The social fact of ethnography is that it is conducted by human beings who witness numerous contexts, layered one upon—and through—the other. Time, purpose, approach, language, styles, and loyalties are all implicated. A small but growing number of critics argue, therefore, that the essential reflexive character of all ethnographic accounts renders them not only "nonobjective" but partisan, partial, incomplete, and inextricably bound to the contexts and rationales of the researcher, contexts he or she may represent (albeit unknowingly) and the rhetorical genres through which the flawed ethnographic reports are manifested and held forth.

Positivism answered the validity question in terms of reliability: Reliable (repeatable, generalizable) methods and findings were valid ones. The current widespread awareness of the social construction of reality, the confusion in coming to grips with "reflexivity," has ironically led to a radical antifunctionalist position. This stance claims that knowledge, even the knowledge process, is without grounding, without authority, and therefore, many things "go." That is, "knowledge" itself is no loner the criterion, because all "knowledge claims" are based on various assumptions. Most critics would agree that an "assumptionless" science is not possible, while they would also maintain that research and inquiry are desirable. What has changed is the purpose of research, and what those standards for assessing the purpose might be. Research is no longer coupled with knowledge, but has been given multiple choices (such as liberation, emancipation, programmatic politics, expressive "art"). Depending on one's choice, research is defined accordingly. For many scientific ethnographers, however, Hammersley's (1992) view remains cogent: "An account is valid or true if it represents accurately those features of the phenomena that it is intended to describe, explain or theorize" (p. 69). For many others, however, this vision of "realism" is no longer compelling.

All knowledge and claims to knowledge are reflexive of the process, assumptions, location, history, and context of knowing and the knower. From this point of view, validity depends on the "interpretive communities," or the audiences—who may be other than researchers and academics—and the goals of the research. Validity will be quite different for different audiences. From another point of view, the one we suggest, a narrower conception of validity is tied more to the researcher/design/academic audience(s).

Different moments in the validity quest/critique have been examined by observers stressing *power,* including culture, ideology, gender, language/text, relevance/advocacy. Numerous writings by students of culture, including those associated with ideologies, including feminism, have sought to identify the unstated grounding and assumptions of validity/knowledge claims. Sharing in more ways than they differ, these points of departure often converge. Central to many of these arguments is that validity should be either abandoned altogether as a viable concept or radically qualified, or "hyphenated." Many of the following depictions have been cast in such phrases as *successor validity, catalytic validity, interrogated validity, transgressive validity, imperial validity, simulacra/ironic validity, situated validity,* and *voluptuous validity* (see Atkinson, 1990, 1992; Eisner & Peshkin, 1990; Guba, 1990; Hammersley, 1990, 1992; Lather, 1993; Wolcott, 1991). The main positions on validity are depicted below.

Validity-as-culture (VAC) is well known to social science students. A basic claim is that the ethnographer reflects, imposes, reproduces, writes, and then reads his or her cultural point of view for the "others." Point of view is the culprit in validity. The solution entails efforts to include more points of view, including reassessing how researchers view the research mission and the research topic. Atkinson (1992) suggests that ethnographies can be mythologized, "but the sense of class continuities is hardly surprisingly stronger in the British genre than in the American which is more preoccupied with a sense of place" (p. 34).

Validity-as-ideology (VAI) is very similar to VAC, except the focus is on the certain specific cultural features involving social power, legitimacy, and assumptions about social structure, such as subordinate/superordinate.

Validity-as-gender (VAG), like VAC and VAI, focuses on taken-for-granted assumptions made by "competent" researchers in carrying out their conceptual and data collection tasks, including some issues about power and domination in social interaction. One concern is that these asymmetrical aspects of social power may be normalized and further legitimated.

Validity-as-language/text (VAL) resonates with all the validities described above, particularly how cultural categories and views of the world, as implicated in language and, more broadly, "discourse," restrict decisions and choices through how things are framed.

Validity-as-relevance/advocacy (VAR) stresses the utility and "empowerment" of research to benefit and uplift those groups often studied—relatively powerless people, such as the poor, or peasants.

Validity-as-standards (VAS) asserts that the expectation about a distinctive authority for science, or the researchers legitimated by this "mantle of respectability," is itself suspect, and that truth claims are so multiple as to evade single authority or procedure. In the extreme case, science ceases to operate as a desirable model of knowledge, because it is, after all, understanding rather than codified, theoretically integrated information—as knowledge—that is to be preferred.

The hyphenated validities described above are offered as illustrations of the range of attention the "problem of validity" has received. Common to most formulations is an abandonment of any pretense of linkage or adequacy of representations of a life world within a broader context. Rather, the general model seems to be that validity should be relevant and serviceable for some application of knowledge: Is knowledge useful? Does it, for example, liberate, or empower? These, in our view, are useful arguments to clarify issues and to caution researchers, subjects, and readers (audiences) alike. Insofar as they enable audience members to engage in the dialogue of evaluating and reflecting on research reports, this is good. However, there will be no satisfactory view about quality ethnography without a clear statement about validity that goes beyond the researcher's purpose or ideology.

Qualitative research, as many of the chapters in this volume make clear, is carried out in ways that are sensitive to the nature of human and cultural social contexts, and is commonly guided by the ethic to remain loyal or true to the phenomena under study, rather than to any particular set of methodological techniques or principles. Although the positivists' experience is now widely acknowledged even by its practitioners to have serious shortcomings in being unable to produce valid results through their quantitatively driven methods, it has been the notion of validity (especially external validity) that has contributed to current "major reconsiderations" by its staunchest supporters. Hammersley (1992) notes some of these relationships in ethnographic research:

> For me, research is a process of inquiry which is collective not individual; and it is geared towards

> the production of valid and relevant knowledge, rather than to the solution of practical problems. . . . The great value of research on this model is that it produces knowledge that, on the average, is likely to contain fewer errors than knowledge from any other source. This arises from the role of the research community in checking the results of particular studies, and the fact that it deploys, or should deploy, a more skeptical form of assessment than is typical elsewhere. The orientation to routinely skeptical colleagues is the main distinguishing characteristic of research, as compared with other sorts of inquiry including the sorts of everyday inquiry that we all occasionally engage in as practitioners of one sort or another. (p. 131)

Any attempt to set forth meaningful criteria for assessing the adequacy of qualitative research must begin with a sense of the goals of ethnography. What is ethnography committed to, and what forms might this take? The frame we choose to delineate our perspective on these important topics is an ethical and humanistic one, rather than conventional scientific parameters of idealism or realism. In short, before setting forth "how to assess" ethnography, we prefer to set forth "what we intend by ethnography."

Principles of an Ethnographic Ethic

An ethnographic ethic calls for retaining many long-standing and taken-for-granted canons of ethical ethnography, including the critical commitment to search for the members' understandings, contexts, and so on, of the settings studied. *Validity-as-reflexive-accounting* (VARA) is an alternative perspective to those noted above. It places the researcher, the topic, and the sense-making process in interaction. Works and criteria suggested by Dingwall (1992), Hammersley (1990), Athens (1984), Lincoln and Guba (1985), and Guba (1990) have been particularly helpful. In keeping with the position of analytic realism, based on the view that the social world is an interpreted world, not a literal world, always under symbolic construction (even deconstruction!), the basic idea is that the focus is on the process of the ethnographic work (see Athens, 1984; Dingwall, 1992):

1. the relationship between what is observed (behaviors, rituals, meanings) and the larger cultural, historical, and organizational contexts within which the observations are made (the substance);
2. the relationships among the observer, the observed, and the setting (the observer);
3. the issue of perspective (or point of view), whether the observer's or the members', used to render an interpretation of the ethnographic data (the interpretation);
4. the role of the reader in the final product (the audience); and
5. the issue of representational, rhetorical, or authorial style used by the author(s) to render the description and/or interpretation (the style).

These five dimensions of qualitative research include problematic issues pertaining to validity. Each of these areas includes questions or issues that must be addressed and pragmatically resolved by any particular observer in the course of his or her research. The ethnographic ethic calls for ethnographers to substantiate their interpretations and findings with a reflexive account of themselves and the processes of their research.

Analytic realism is an approach to qualitative data analysis and writing. It is founded on the view that the social world is an interpreted world. It is interpreted by the subjects we study. It is interpreted by the qualitative researcher. It is based on the value of trying to represent faithfully and accurately the social worlds or phenomena studied. Analytic realism rejects the dichotomy of realism/idealism, and other conceptual dualisms, as being incompatible with the nature of lived experience and its interpretation. Like pragmatism, it cuts across conventional questions about ontology, truth, and method, and instead redirects such concerns to the empirical world of lived experience. Analytic realism assumes that the meanings and definitions brought to actual situations are produced through a communication process. As researchers and observers become increasingly aware that the categories and ideas used to describe the empirical (socially constructed) world are also symbols from specific contexts, this too becomes part of the phenomena studied empirically, and incorporated into the research report(s).

Our general approach to evaluating ethnographic work can be stated as follows: The process by which the ethnography occurred must be clearly delineated, including accounts of the interactions among context, researcher, methods, setting, and actors.[1] Hammersley's (1992) notion of "subtle realism" is akin to our analytic realism in terms of the stronger emphasis we put on verifiable knowledge about the interpretive process as a way of knowing:

> This subtle realism retains from naive realism the idea that research investigates independent,

> knowable phenomena. But it breaks with it in denying that we have direct access to those phenomena, in accepting that we must always rely on cultural assumptions, and in denying that our aim is to reproduce social phenomena in some way that is uniquely appropriate to them. Obversely, subtle realism shares with skepticism and relativism a recognition that all knowledge is based on assumptions and purposes and is a human construction, but it rejects these positions' abandonment of the regulative idea of independent and knowable phenomena. Perhaps most important of all, subtle realism is distinct from both naive realism and relativism in its rejection of the notion that knowledge must be defined as beliefs whose validity is known with certainty. (p. 52)

This approach, tied to naturalism, identifies four general criteria of ethnographic quality: plausibility, credibility, relevance, and importance of the topic. Hammersley (1992, p. 62) appears to be more comfortable with the first two, committed to the third as a way of justifying our public response, and quite ambivalent about the fourth, importance. Notwithstanding the political contextuality of each, his explication of scientific—that is, disciplined—research as distinctive from everyday thinking and observing is noteworthy.[2]

Within the province of analytic realism, an ethnographic ethic encompasses these dimensions. Distinct from "ethical ethnography," an ethnographic ethic integrates many of the traditional concerns and perspectives of ethnography with more recent insights gleaned from the reflexive turn noted above, as well as tacit knowledge and reflexive accountability, which we will examine below. Throughout, an ethnographer's commitment is to obtain the members' perspectives on the social reality of the observed setting. Of course, we now know that many settings in modern life have many perspectives and voices, which means that ethnographers should faithfully report this multivocality (or cacophony) and, if possible, show where the author's voice is located in relation to these.

Central to this ethic is the renewed realization that all knowledge is perspectival, so the ethical practice of ethnography demands that the author's perspective be specified. Ever since the Enlightenment, there has been a long-standing ambivalence and tension between "scientific" and "historicist" perspectives (Diamond, 1964; Maquet, 1964), which essentially involves where a given observer puts the decisive weight or emphasis on the contextually particular or more general patterns of a particular observed setting. Many of our most famous ethnographers (including Kroeber, Sapir, Benedict, Mead, and Tyler) have decidedly straddled the fence on this issue, wanting to have both substantive particularity and processual abstraction, and usually concluding with neither. The perspectival nature of knowledge is an obdurate fact of ethnography. The approach of the ethnographic ethic acknowledges this, and provides the reader with an explicit statement about "where the author is coming from," which is the ethnographic version of truth in advertising, an ethical responsibility for those who elect to exercise the social science power and authorial voice. The tension inherent in this problem is useful, inevitable, and provides floating stepping-stones for the creative investigator, not unlike the "science/art" tension celebrated by theoretical physicists.

> In my view, the immediate audience for research must be the research community, even though the ultimate aim is to produce knowledge that is of value to others. Therefore, communications to policy-makers from researchers should draw on multiple studies and on the necessarily always provisional conclusions of the research community about their validity, rather than reporting the outcome of a particular piece of research. (Hammersley, 1992, p. 132)

This audience has special interests, including the necessity of distinguishing data from analysis, a capacity to promote theoretical sampling (e.g., comparisons and contrasts) as well as an accounting of its research design (see Dingwall, 1992).

The classical ethic in ethnography begins and ends with commonsense members of the settings studied, with real persons (not "Man/Woman" in the abstract), which is why many ethnographies are so commonsensically appealing to laypersons and nonethnographic social scientists alike. The goal of an ethnography is understanding, and a corollary assumption is that understanding is ultimately useful, even in some unknown or unknowable sense. But this classical ethic is no longer shared, as the ethical pluralism so evident in the larger society now characterizes scientific practice as well, embodied in the theoretical and paradigmatic specialization of the latter. With the newly legitimated agendas of theory-driven and action-driven ethnography, ethical practice asks a specification of these purposes so that readers and audiences (who no doubt approach such works at this moment in historical time with assumptions and expectations of descriptive realism and externality) will have a more truthful introduction to what they are about to buy.

Research Design, Methods, and Problems

How a researcher accounts for his or her approach to certain aspects of research, including the routine sources of problems, is key for evaluating the work substantively and methodologically. The existing methods literature shows that certain problems are inevitable and unavoidable in the conduct of ethnographic research, problems that inevitably influence the observations, findings, and analyses (see Hammersley & Atkinson, 1983). Any particular observer must achieve some pragmatic resolution of these dilemmas, and his or her research observations and field experiences are thereby influenced in some unknown manner by whatever practical resolution is achieved. Given that the society we seek to study and understand is so complex, pluralistic, and changing, and as so few of us have any personal experience in the wide range of settings we read about in ethnographic reports, one criterion of verisimilitude useful in assessing ethnographic reports is learning about how a given observer resolved the inevitable field problems.

For example, reflexive ethnographies illustrate that each and every setting, without exception, is socially stratified. The stratified hierarchies vary from one setting to another, and the stratification has different consequences in one setting compared with others, but all settings are stratified in some manner, and commonly on the basis of gender, age, race, and/or ethnicity, or social class/education/occupation. Because a setting's stratification will be related to its categories and classification of membership groups and alliances, the personal qualities of a given ethnographer will "fit" or "not fit" somewhere in this schema. The quality and validity of the information thus obtained from ethnographic research will be related to how a given observer met and resolved these issues for the particular setting studied. The problem is, in some manner, inevitable and unavoidable, and cannot be transcended by the ethnographer's heroic diligence or empathic virtue. As we discuss more fully below, claims of full membership or "becoming the phenomenon" do not adequately resolve this dilemma, except perhaps in the most narrowly homogeneous social groups, as in small cults, for example, which are highly exceptional rather than commonplace in contemporary society. Most of the settings of our ethnographic interest are very complex and stratified, with differing and shifting member perspectives, allegiances, and loyalties. For this reason we continue with some criteria for accounting for ourselves, which will then be followed by some notes about accounting for the substantive findings.

Reflexive Accounting for Substance

As we learn more about other significant and essentially invariable dimensions of settings, such as hierarchical organization, these are added. In order to satisfy the basic elements of the ethnographic ethic, the following "generic" topics should be included in ethnographic reports:

- the contexts: history, physical setting, and environment
- number of participants, key individuals
- activities
- schedules, temporal order
- division of labor, hierarchies
- routines and variations
- significant events and their origins and consequences
- members' perspectives and meanings
- social rules and basic patterns of order

These dimensions provide a template for the investigator as well as framework in which a prospective reader of the report can understand what contributes to the *definition of the situation,* its nature, character, origin, and consequences.

Our experience suggests that the subjects of ethnographic studies are invariably temporally and spatially bounded. That the range of activities under investigation occurs in time and space (which becomes a "place" when given a meaning) provides one anchorage, among many others, for penetrating the hermeneutic circle. A key feature of this knowledge, of course, is its incompleteness, its implicit and tacit dimensions. Our subjects always know more than they can tell us, usually even more than they allow us to see; likewise, we often know far more than we can articulate. Even the most ardent social science wordsmiths are at a loss to transform nuances, subtleties, and the sense of the sublime into symbols! For this reason we acknowledge the realm of *tacit knowledge,* the ineffable truths, unutterable partly because they are between meanings and actions, the glue that joins human intentionality to more concretely focused symbols of practice. As we will discuss further below, the key issue is not to capture the informant's voice, but to elucidate the experience that is implicated by the subjects in the context of their activities as they perform them, and as they are understood by the ethnographer. Harper's (1987) explanation of how he used a photographer in a study of a local craftsman illustrates this intersection of meaning:

> The key, I think, is a simple idea that is the base of all ethnography. I want to explain the way Willie has explained to me. I hope to show a small social world that most people would not look at very closely. In the process I want to tell about

some of the times between Willie and me, thinking that at the root of all sociology there are people making connections, many like ours. (p. 14)

The ethnographer, of course, would add that what one sees and directly experiences is also important.

Tacit Knowledge and an Ecology of Understanding

Good ethnographies display tacit knowledge. With apologies to William James, Alfred Schutz, and others, we focus on the dimensions of "an ecology of knowing." Contextual, taken-for-granted, tacit knowledge plays a constitutive role in providing meaning. Social life is spatially and temporally ordered through experiences that cannot be reduced to spatial boundaries as numerous forms of communication attempt to do, especially those based on textual and linear metaphors. More specifically, experience is different from words and symbols about those experiences. Words are always poor representations of the temporal and evocative life world. Words and texts are not the primary stuff of the existential moments of most actors in what Schutz (1967) terms the "natural attitude." They are very significant for intellectuals and wordsmiths who claim to represent such experiences. Yet, as those word workers have come to rely on and represent words and other texts for the actual experiences, their procedures of analysis have been reified to stand for the actual experience. Therein lies much of the problem that some have termed the "crisis in representation."

Capturing members' words alone is not enough for ethnography. If it were, ethnographies would be replaced by interviews. Good ethnographies reflect tacit knowledge, the largely unarticulated, contextual understanding that is often manifested in nods, silences, humor, and naughty nuances. This is the most challenging dimension of ethnography, and gets to the core of the members' perspective or, for that matter, the subtleties of membership itself. This is the stuff of ethnography referred to above in the quote from Laura Nader (1993): "Anthropology is a feat of empathy and analysis" (p. 7). But, without doubting the wisdom of Professor Nader, it is necessary to give an accounting of how we know things, what we regard and treat as empirical materials—the experiences—from which we produce our second (or third) accounts of "what was happening." [3]

One approach to making ourselves more accountable, and thereby sharing our experience and insights more fully with readers, is to locate inquiry within the process and context of actual human experience. Our experience suggests that researchers should accept the inevitability that all statements are reflexive, and that the research act is a social act. Indeed, that is the essential rationale for research approaches grounded in the contexts of experience of the people who are actually involved in their settings and arenas.

The context of experience is our domain. Tacit knowledge exists in that time when action is taken that is not understood, when understanding is offered without articulation, and when conclusions are apprehended without an argument. The nature of meaning and its unfortunate location between language and experience produces an imperfect fit. The issue was cast by William James (and by others, in different terms) as the interplay between the "kernel" of an idea or experience and its "fringe," or the symbolic awareness that helped define borders of an experience as part of others. Thunder, James wrote, is recognized as "contrasting-with-silence." We do not apprehend anything without connecting it to something else, and that "else" turns out to be everything in our life world and its appropriate zones of relevance.

The array of contextual understanding and information is always simultaneously too much and too little for optimum intersubjective understanding. As Schutz argued, we rely on certain routines to connect various finite provinces of meaning to a situation, and mine may not be commensurate with yours. Over time, however, we concede the differences for the purpose at hand, a project of action, and we draw on recipes, typifications, and taken-for-granted understandings and assumptions. These, Schutz taught, constitute the world of the natural attitude, the basic wide-awake orientation of how we engage the world and others.

The Implications of Tacit Knowledge

Words are like weapons that can be used to produce discontinuities in our experience. The equation of meaning and text destroys the ineffable linkages between our raw experiences and their poetic interpretations (see Bauman, 1988). Tacit knowledge includes what actors know, take for granted, and leave unexplicated in specific situations, things that may have been "learned" in some formal or semiformal sense at some earlier time, both substantively and procedurally. Tacit knowledge may also include deep structures from the *emotional memory* of past generations, enabling responses and actions deeply ingrained in human emotional and physical survival. Social scientists share with societal members some or all of these features of tacit knowledge, those aspects of *common sense* that provide the deep rules and deep substantive or cultural background critical for understanding any specific utterance or act. Social scientific analyses not only make use of these commonsense resources, but often analyze them as topics, too.

There are varieties of tacit knowledge, of course. Two general distinctions can be offered between general cultural knowledge and more specific situational and experiential knowledge. Our intent is not simply to list a variety of examples, but rather to suggest some analytic elements of tacit knowledge that may be useful in the current debate about the nature of our subject matter as social observers, or the "knowers," on the one hand, and the subject matter, or the "known," on the other. It is our contention that any claim to treat the subject matter of social science as merely "discursive" or "textual" materials overlooks the subtle and significant role of tacit knowledge. Indeed, we would further suggest that often such errors of omission are made because the observer takes for granted the central role of tacit knowledge that joins him or her to the subject matter. As it is not regarded as problematic, its constitutive role is not considered, and therefore remains outside of the central discourse of analysis, despite its significance for the subject and topic under investigation.

The most critical component of tacit knowledge is what it contributes to the definition of a situation. The temporal and spatial components are clear. For example, is this a new or different situation from the one I was in a moment ago, or is it quite similar? Has this changed? This largely nondiscursive knowledge is employed in an instant and shapes the discourse about a topic or situation that will follow. For example, bureaucratic settings have numerous occasions for what could be termed "bureaucratic tacit knowledge." This includes understandings about written and verbal communications, different accounting schemes and language. Any experienced bureaucratic worker recognizes, for example, that control is communicated in various ways, including the amount of talk one performs in certain settings, such as meetings. Moreover, anyone recognizes that there is a directory of legitimate and illegitimate terminology. For example, within social science departments today, any discussion regarding hiring someone almost never includes an explicit statement that "hiring this person will make us look good to the central administration," or "I will support this hiring decision in order to gain points with my colleagues, whose support I will need soon on another matter." In short, the language is always one of quality and excellence, even though, in numerous instances, faculty members and others who publicly postured one way will admit that the "discussion" was a ruse for another purpose. It is this sense of "other purposes" that directs our sociological gaze to tacit knowledge.

An issue related to tacit knowledge is the problem of communication. By and large, tacit knowledge is nondiscursive, whereas textual and many other symbolic forms of communication are discursive. The problem, then, is how to talk about what is seldom spoken about, and, indeed, one of its features is that it is beyond words, seemingly more basic and pervasive than the spatial configuration of spoken words, and especially written words, allows. More is involved here than simply positing that "to speak of something changes it"; we believe that, but this is a different issue. The issue, again, is how something that operates in existential moments and has a distinctive temporal form can be adequately communicated.

The difficulty with tacit knowledge is that it is not easily compatible with what we term the *bias of communication.* We refer to the more public and shareable communication form and logic. In general, this means that time is replaced by spatial assignment of symbols; space and place come to supersede temporal dimensions of the subject matter. More specifically, communication permits—indeed, demands—that shareable and nonidiosyncratic understandings and meanings be constructed through rules of grammar, syntax, and orderly formats of expression. The communication form, like all formats of communication, makes the invisible visible, reproducible, and memorable. The mechanisms and procedures have their own logic, and press content into its shape. Make no mistake, this process has such an impact on subsequent behavior and communication that it has been heralded as the foundation of the symbolic interaction process, with which we are so familiar. This has implications for how we might assess the appropriateness of the reporting style and approach of an ethnography.

It is the nature of different kinds of experience in everyday affairs that is important for current debates about the relationship between the knower and the known. This nexus between what we know and how we know it forges a critical linkage for the analytic realist seeking to fulfill the ethnographic ethic to turn his or her attention to the nature and criteria for assessing the adequacy of the research process itself. Accordingly, we approach the researcher's activities and perspectives.

Accounting for Ourselves

A key part of the ethnographic ethic is how we account for ourselves. Good ethnographies show the hand of the ethnographer. The effort may not always be successful, but there should be clear "tracks" indicating the attempt has been made. We are in the midst of a rediscovery that social reality is constructed by human agents—even social scientists!—using cultural categories and language in specific situations or contexts of meaning. This interest is indeed welcome, because it gives us license to do yet another elucidation of the "concept of knowing."

There is a distinction to be drawn between interesting, provocative, and insightful accounts of ethnographic research and high-quality ethnographic work. Given our emphasis on the reflexive nature of social life, it will not surprise the reader that we prefer those studies that enable the ethnographic audience to engage the researcher symbolically, and enter through the research window of clarity (and opportunity). Although no one is suggesting a "literal" accounting, our work and that of many others suggests that the more a reader (audience member) can engage in a symbolic dialogue with the author about a host of routinely encountered problems that compromise ethnographic work, the more our confidence increases. Good ethnographies increase our confidence in the findings, interpretations, and accounts offered.

Our collective experience in reading a literature spanning more than 50 years, along with our own work on numerous topics and projects, suggests that there is a minimal set of problem areas likely to be encountered in most studies. We do not offer solutions to the problems we discuss below, but only suggest that these can provide a focus for a broader and more complete account of the reflexive process through which something is understood (Altheide, 1976; Denzin, 1992; Douglas, 1976; Johnson, 1975). Such information enables the reader to engage the study in an interactive process that includes seeking more information, contextualizing findings, and reliving the report as the playing out of the interactions among the researcher, the subjects, and the topic in question.

Suggested items for locating and informing the role of the researcher vis-à-vis the phenomenon include a statement about topics previously delineated in other work (Altheide, 1976, pp. 197ff.):

- entrée—organizational and individual
- approach and self-presentation
- trust and rapport
- the researcher's role and way of fitting in
- mistakes, misconceptions, surprises
- types and varieties of data
- data collection and recording
- data coding and organization
- data demonstration and analytic use
- narrative report

More detailed accounts could be offered as a subset of several of the above. Consider problems of communication with informants: misinformation, evasions, lies, fronts, taken-for-granted meanings, problematic meanings, self-deceptions. We do not claim that attending to the relevance of these issues in a study makes the study more truthful, but only that the truth claims of the researcher can be more systematically assessed by readers who share a concern with the relationship between *what* was observed and *how* it was accomplished.

The idea for the critical reader of an ethnography is to ask whether or not any of the above were likely to have been relevant problems, whether they were explicitly treated as problematic by the researcher, and, if so, how they were addressed, resolved, compromised, avoided, and so forth. Because these dimensions of ethnographic research are so pervasive and important for obtaining truthful accounts, they should be implicitly or explicitly addressed in the report. Drawing on such criteria enables the ethnographic reader to approach the ethnography interactively and critically, and to ask, What was done, and how was it done? What are the likely and foreseen consequences of the particular research issue, and how were they handled by the researcher? These dimensions represent one range of potential problems likely to be encountered by an ethnographer.

No study avoids all of these problems, although few researchers give reflexive accounts of their research problems and experiences. One major problem is that the phenomenon of interest is commonly multiperspectival; there is usually a multiplicity of modes of meanings, perspectives, and activities, even in one setting. Indeed, this multiplicity is often unknown to many of the official members of the setting. Thus one does not easily "become the phenomenon" in contemporary life. As we strive to make ourselves, our activities, and our claims more accountable, a critical step is to acknowledge our awareness of a process that may actually impede and prevent our adequate understanding of all relevant dimensions of an activity.

Ethnographic Writing

Ethnographic reports reflect some of the criteria the researcher had in mind when the research began. One of our aims in this chapter has been to set forth one distinction based on an ethnographic ethic and grounded in what we term analytic realism. One of the points stressed above is the narrative account, or style, of the report. In a sense, the "type of story" told, as Van Maanen (1988) and others have noted, can essentially "frame" the work and take it over; the content of the ethnographic report may be racing to keep up with the story structure. As Fine and Martin's (1990) analysis of Erving Goffman's classic *Asylums* suggests, humor as a form can show the horrific sadness of everyday routines:

> We read *Asylums* as a political tract, aimed, in part, as unmasking the "fraud" of mental hospitals and psychiatric practice. It does not aim to demean individuals, but it does take on this system and those elements of the outside world that are being convenienced by the existence of the system. The mental institution is functional like the institution of slavery is functional, it makes life easier for some at the expense of others. (p. 110)

Underlying analytic realism is the assertion that the perspectival nature of knowledge is an obdurate fact of all ethnography, and thus an ethical approach acknowledges this and provides the audience with explicit statements about "where the author is coming from." For those who choose to exercise the social science power and authorial voice, this is one of the moral imperatives of ethnographic reportage.

Ethnography as Text: Interpretive Validity

Within the ecology of knowledge, analytic realism acknowledges that how findings are represented is very important for claims making and assessment. The broad issue is "representation" and in what form or genre the ethnographic report is presented—for example, in a "realist" tale, "confessional" tale, or "impressionist" tale (Van Maanen, 1988). It is also important to note, as Dingwall (1992) advises, that there is a clear distinction apparent in the text between the data or materials and the analysis. The nature and process by which communication is organized is central to how ethnography is produced as a document. Fortunately, previous work (see Altheide, 1985; Altheide & Snow, 1979, 1991) in the area of *media logic* and especially the nature and use of *formats,* or how experience is defined, recognized, organized, selected, and presented, helps us anticipate many of the problems that have been noticed in recent years by postmodern writers and others.

Postmodern critics, apparently in agreement with some of the literature noted above, observe that the most critical feature of representations (e.g., reports, data) are their logics, metanarratives by which they are presented as though derived independent of a researcher's context, rhetoric, discipline, and narrative style. This, of course, is an issue of format. What many of the changes in representation essentially amount to are different formats. One of the recent students of ethnographic writing to notice this is Paul Atkinson, whose *Understanding Ethnographic Texts* (1992) cleverly applies many of the arguments presented above about formats of ethnographic writing. After noting that "society is not a kind of text" and that "textual formats make the social world reliable" (p. 11), Atkinson writes about how postmodern ethnographic accounts challenge conventional formats for order, representation, and integration:

> The standard literary formats of academic monographs (chapters, sub-headings, titles, indexes, etc.) are also arbitrary forms of classification and codification. . . . Postmodern tendencies replace the familiar formats of realist writing with a range of different types. (p. 14)

After noting that some ethnographic accounts, such as M. J. Mulkay's *The Word and the World: Explorations in the Form of Sociological Analysis* (1985), are presented through one-act plays and giving the book its own "voice," Atkinson nevertheless urges caution, advising researchers not to go to extremes. Implicit in his insights is the critical point that we can say something narratively only through metanarratives, and these are, essentially, formats. Even though postmodern writers often aspire to be "evocative," they do so by implicitly being representational (e.g., people have to have some idea about a common referent to participate in irony): "From the point of view of the extreme 'textualist,' ethnographic writing refers to itself and to other texts. It does not report a social world that is independent of its textual representations" (p. 51). Atkinson (1992) then adds, "But we should not and need not therefore assume that they have no capacity to represent and reveal aspects of the social world."

For Atkinson and others, then, formats as metanarratives are important to identify in our efforts to "unpack" ethnography, but it is neither intellectually cogent nor practical to suggest that "all is text."

> It would therefore be quite wrong for a reader of this book to leave it with the view that there is "nothing beyond the text." Such a view capitulates the mistaken separation of Science and Rhetoric. It was wrong to celebrate science and ignore rhetoric. It is equally wrong simply to reverse the emphasis. Scholarship is rhetorical in the sense that its arguments are shaped, illustrated, and explained to audiences of readers. Its practitioners must use the methods of representation that are to hand. But that is not a dispensation for irresponsibility. On

> the contrary, just as the researcher must take responsibility for theoretical and methodological decisions, so textual or representational decisions must be made responsibly. We do not have perfect theoretical and epistemological foundations; we do not have perfect methods for data collection; we do not have perfect or transparent modes of representation. We work in the knowledge of our limited resources. But we do not have to abandon the attempt to produce the disciplined accounts of the world that are coherent, methodical, and sensible. (Atkinson, 1992, p. 51)

Analytic realism acknowledges that the anticipation of reporting (and even narrative frameworks) can inform what it is one "grasps" in a setting, and "how" that is to be done. The ethnographer is not committed to "any old story," but wants to provide an account that communicates with the reader the truth about the setting and situation, as the ethnographer has come to understand it. For the ethnographer, the notion of validity does count, although it is acknowledged that other researchers at different times may come away with different interpretations. However, not all observations and interpretations will be equally problematic; any ethnographer will be able to identify those features of the setting that became a conceptual grounding for the work, such as perhaps some physical settings, demographic foundations, or scheduling of particular activities. Given these considerations, and prior to more detailed discussion about the problem areas of ethnographic work, some discussion about related dimensions of validity may be helpful, particularly sorting out the relationship between what we find and how we report it.

Another important problem has less to do with avowed similarities and differences between social science and literature, and that is the distinction between the writer and the audience. All accounts are produced with some audience in mind. (A writer cannot neatly be separated from "the audience" because he or she was an audience member before becoming a writer.) Thus, in a sense, every writer presumes some version of a "generalized other" for whom the account is intended. However, elementary social psychological research has confirmed what the Scottish moralists and others have argued quite eloquently: Because perception is active and thereby contributes to any experience, everyone may see and interpret things a bit differently. In terms of reading, this means that each reader will bring a context of meaning and interpretation to an account, or text, and will interpret it accordingly. This interpretation or "reading" may or may not be commensurate with what the writer intended. In this regard, the social scientist is no different from the novelist. Both produce texts for others to interpret and re-create. The upshot is that social scientists are also claims makers and "tellers of stories," albeit of a different sort. We insist that what separates ethnographers from the others is not so much the objective truth of what is being stated as it is the *process* or *way of knowing*. We should continue to be concerned with producing texts that explicate *how* we claim to know *what* we know. It is precisely the difficulty of intersubjective understanding that demands that social scientists as claims makers be clear and precise in delineating the basis for their claims.

Cultural messages are made meaningful within situations of use. A valid interpretation of text without a context is impossible. Symbols and their meanings are interpretive and relational. Although few would deny this claim, there does seem to be some clear disagreement about the notion of relational, in terms of what, extent, and significance. For example, any account of the "meaning of *Dallas*" or some other cultural product, whether a TV show, an icon, a commercial advertisement, or something else, without some general location of a point of reference is interesting, but always incorrect. If any such interpretation strikes a chord in us it is because we can locate it within our own experience. To make general claims without knowing how the message was produced or, probably more significantly, how the audience member was situated to interpret it, is to make a gross, but interesting and often provocative, error.

It is the context that provides for interpretive meaning. Good sociological accounts point out the multiplicity of meanings and perspectives, and the rationality of these perspectives, by setting forth the context(s). This is not obvious, particularly when more and more scholars are taking it for granted—indeed, insisting—that text can be "read" through a set of interpretive procedures and decoding books, usually produced in the confines of academic offices or libraries. But we do not want to imply that one cannot generalize beyond situations. Rather, there is a more fundamental point that should not be misunderstood: Meaning is put together and packaged, as it were, through nonverbal, usually nonlinear, and "invisible" features of context, often commonsensically referred to as tone, emotion, history, or experience.

Understanding context is important for intelligibility and comprehension. The significance of context for interpretation and understanding, and the inevitability of reflexivity for all sense making, offers ethnography an additional resource for its authority. Field-workers place themselves in the contexts of experience in order to permit the reflexivity process to work. Experienced ethnographers, then, do not avoid reflexivity; they embrace it. A good example is Manning's (1987) study of police call codes. Although Manning does a sophisticated analysis of what certain codes reflexively index, it is only his in-depth awareness of the police and organizational culture that provides the knowledge for the meaning of the message. He knows the work, the language, and the situations, typical, routine, and unique. As he clearly acknowledges, he could not have rendered a valid sociological account without this awareness.

The general impact of the bias of communication is to disqualify anything that does not meet the requirements of the communication logic. There are numerous other communication logics that are less discursive, more private, and encoded as symbols within symbols. As Schutz and others have argued, intimates, especially lovers, have this unspeakable, nonpublic, and seemingly "electric" awareness of feeling and mood—all without a spoken word, even without a noticeable symbolic body-language shift. We would simply reiterate that the meanings of things are not always contained in what is communicated in a text, but rather, the context, awareness, and experience as tacit knowledge sets the tone.

The claim that we are all "telling stories" has led many analysts to move away from sociological analyses of topics in favor of looking at how we tell the stories, which, by implication, is more invariant and therefore more significant than the sociological experience of sense making. Moreover, the status of sociology, science, and any sense-making effort comes to stand or fall on the rising epistemic status of storytelling as a form of truth seeking. Although we certainly should reflect on how we make sense of our research experiences, and how we may transform them—indeed, constitute them—through the process of "telling" or "reporting" these experiences, we should not become trapped by sociological logic. For example, although we can analyze sociological accounts through story and narrative forms, it is equally true that we have for years analyzed narrative accounts—stories—through a sociological perspective.

We would like to offer a different slant on the problem of storytelling in order to improve our awareness of tacit knowledge. Our perspective is that we are not compelled to tell stories, but to give accounts of our research experiences and ideas. All accounts are not stories, unless we define them circularly as such. We can, of course, tell stories, realizing that the structure of such accounts may be analyzed through the logic of particular genres that are deemed to encompass our particular "stories." But we can also settle for clear, coherent accounts (reports, vignettes, findings, essays, or the like) that may be open to ambiguity and uncertainty while still making a claim. We should not, in other words, privilege a cultural format of communication—"the story" with capturing and misrepresenting other claims, including those of tacit knowledge.

Conclusion

Reflexive ethnography has taught us much in two decades, and the next decade will undoubtedly offer more. But the lessons to be drawn from its teachings are not unambiguously clear. We have attempted to present some of the key issues and most engaging critiques of ethnography, along with a framework for reformulating validity, interpretive validity, as well as some general principles or rules of thumb for assessing qualitative and particularly ethnographic research. The literature points out, illustrates, and documents the wide range of personal, interpersonal, political, ethical, practical, economic, occupational, and rhetorical influences on scientific problems, research, and products. It is clear that individuals draw different conclusions from all of this, and make different commitments as a result. This is a chaotic but exciting and creative time for ethnography and all of its newly emergent forms. On the one hand, we wish to celebrate this period of creative endeavor and say, "Let a thousand blossoms bloom." On the other hand, our growing wisdom tells us that the new era requires a new skepticism in the reading of ethnographic research. As we have stressed, one is not logically driven to accept solipsism simply because research and reason indicate that "bedrock objectivity" is untenable when human beings driven by meanings and perspective—science—attempt to study systematically the activities and meanings of fellow humans! Nor do we accept the contention of some that the "problem of reflexivity," which has been seriously investigated by social scientists for at least 30 years (and quite longer by philosophers) denies the researcher superior authority over all knowers, even when specific criteria and questions direct inquiry.

Among the key problems to be discussed by ethnographers and all qualitative researchers are issues about ethnographic loyalty and commitment, whether this is to the people/settings we study or the audiences we seek to influence with our reports (e.g., policy makers) or an ideological commitment to "higher goals" ("liberation" of "oppressed" groups, relevance, and so forth). We anticipate additional discussion about issues involving the utility of "discourse analysis," "semiotics," deconstruction, and other methods for analyzing cultural symbols and markers of social life. Perhaps most challenging during the next decade will be careful analyses of the role of new formats for defining, selecting, organizing, and presenting information, as well as their relevance for communicating issues about validity. Will social science audiences, for example, extend poetic readings, one-act plays, and dramatic presentations the same legitimacy as "conventional" formats? These issues and many more now define the ongoing dialogue about ethnography.

The challenge remains to think about the work and how we do it, but, above all, still to do the work of understanding and presenting various life worlds and their important participants. Just as surely as everyday-life participants negotiate and resolve their uncertainties about their own knowledge and criteria of knowing, so, too, can ethnographers reflect on our purpose at hand and celebrate one of our meaningful activities, that of clarifying the nature, context, process, significance, and consequences of the ways in which human beings define their situations.

Notes

1. This position is similar to formulations by other researchers who have pondered the criteria of good ethnography. A few whose insights we have found helpful include Hammersley (1990, 1992), Atkinson (1990, 1992), Dingwall (1992), Athens (1984), and Silverman (1989). However, our position differs in important ways from at least some of the criteria offered by others, such as Guba (1990), who calls for the reports to be meaningful ("demystifying") to the subjects themselves, for the researcher's prior theoretical understandings to be modified, and for the research to start with a realist ontology. Our elements also do not include a criterion of relevance or "importance" because we concur with Hammersley (1992, pp. 119, 124ff.) that the "policy criterion of validity for ethnography" is fraught with problems.

2. This is more significant in view of the claims of many postmodern detractors that all grounds of authority—expert and layperson—are plausible and, in the face of the problematics of validity, equally tenable.

> The key difference [between science and everyday claim checking] . . . is that researchers specialise in inquiry, whereas in everyday life inquiry is a minor and subordinate element of other activities. And the other side of this is that the publication of research findings involves a claim to authority; and such publications are often accorded more authority than the judgements of nonresearchers. The justifications seem to me to lie in a form of social organisation that subjects claims to a more severe level of routine validity checking than is common in most other spheres of life and involves sustained attempts to resolve disagreements by debate and further inquiry, rather than by other means. (Hammersley, 1992, p. 62)

Hammersley then adds that all findings must be subject to communal assessment in an effort to resolve disagreements by seeking common grounds of agreement, that scientists must be willing to change their views, and that the scientific community must be inclusive, and open to anyone to participate who is able and willing to operate on the basis of these principles.

3. To do it well may be a gift, but to be able to account for how we did it, and to provide a broken line for others—such as students—to follow, is part of our challenge, and we must attend to the issue. In this sense, we think Snow and Morrill (1993) are correct, that sociologists have been more careful about some of our ethnographic claims, and have done better at "debriefing" our approaches—at least insofar as we put ourselves on the line—than have anthropologists. And it does matter. We need not assume our methods will be completely transparent, but we can at least take steps to cut through the professorial and perspectival haze that can choke future analyses and generations of fieldworkers as surely as Southern California smog can distort a Pacific vista.

References

Adler, P. A., & Adler, P. (1987). *Membership roles in field research.* Newbury Park, CA: Sage.

Altheide, D. L. (1976). *Creating reality: How TV news distorts events.* Beverly Hills, CA: Sage.

Altheide, D. L. (1980). Leaving the newsroom. In W. B. Shaffir, R. A. Stebbins, & A. Turowetz (Eds.), *Fieldwork experience: Qualitative approaches to social research* (pp. 301-310). New York: St. Martin's.

Altheide, D. L. (1985). *Media power.* Beverly Hills, CA: Sage.

Altheide, D. L., & Snow, R. P. (1979). *Media logic.* Beverly Hills, CA: Sage.

Altheide, D. L., & Snow, R. P. (1991). *Media worlds in the postjournalism era.* Hawthorne, NY: Aldine de Gruyter.

Athens, L. (1984). Scientific criteria for evaluating qualitative studies. In N. K. Denzin (Ed.), *Studies in symbolic interaction* (Vol. 5). Greenwich, CT: JAI.

Atkinson, P. A. (1990). *The ethnographic imagination: Textual constructions of reality.* London: Routledge.

Atkinson, P. A. (1992). *Understanding ethnographic texts.* Newbury Park, CA: Sage.

Bauman, Z. (1988). Is there a postmodern sociology? *Theory, Culture & Society, 5,* 217-238.

Clifford, J., & Marcus, G. E. (Eds.). (1986). *Writing culture: The poetics and politics of ethnography.* Berkeley: University of California Press.

Denzin, N. K. (1992). Whose Cornerville is it, anyway? *Journal of Contemporary Ethnography, 21,* 120-132.

Diamond, S. (1964). The search for the primitive. In S. Diamond, *Man's image in medicine and anthropology* (pp. 27-66). New York: International Universities Press.

Dingwall, R. (1992). "Don't mind him—he's from Barcelona": Qualitative methods in health studies. In J. Daly, I. McDonald, & E. Willis (Eds.), *Researching health care* (pp. 161-174). London: Routledge.

Douglas, J. D. (1976). *Investigative social research.* Beverly Hills, CA: Sage.

Eisner, E. W., & Peshkin, A. (Eds.). (1990). *Qualitative inquiry in education: The continuing debate.* New York: Teachers College Press.

Fine, G. A., & Martin, D. D. (1990). A partisan view: Sarcasm, satire, and irony as voices in Erving Goffman's *Asylums. Journal of Contemporary Ethnography, 19,* 89-115.

Geertz, C. (1973). *The interpretation of cultures: Selected essays.* New York: Basic Books.

Guba, E. G. (1990). Subjectivity and objectivity, In E. W. Eisner & A. Peshkin (Eds.), *Qualitative inquiry in education: The continuing debate* (pp. 74-91). New York: Teachers College Press

Hammersley, M. (1990). *Reading ethnographic research: A critical guide.* London: Longman.

Hammersley, M. (1992). *What's wrong with ethnography? Methodological explorations.* London: Routledge.

Hammersley, M., & Atkinson, P. (1983). *Ethnography: Principles in practice.* London: Tavistock.

Harper, D. (1987). *Working knowledge: Skill and community in a small shop.* Berkeley: University of California Press.

Johnson, J. M. (1975). *Doing field research.* New York: Free Press.

Jorgensen, D. L. (1989). *Participant observation: A methodology for human studies.* Newbury Park, CA: Sage.

Lather, P. (1993). Fertile obsession: Validity after poststructuralism. *Sociological Quarterly, 35.*

Lincoln, Y. S., & Guba, E. G. (1985). *Naturalistic inquiry.* Beverly Hills, CA: Sage.

Manning, P. (1987). *Semiotics and fieldwork.* Newbury Park, CA: Sage.

Maquet, J. J. (1964). Objectivity in anthropology. *Current Anthropology, 5,* 47-55.

Morgan, G. (Ed.). (1983). *Beyond method.* Beverly Hills, CA: Sage.

Mulkay, M. J. (1985). *The word and the world: Explorations in the form of sociological analysis.* London: George Allen & Unwin.

Nader, L. (1993). Paradigm busting and vertical linkage. *Contemporary Sociology, 33,* 6-7.

Richardson, L. (1990). Narrative and sociology. *Journal of Contemporary Ethnography, 19,* 116-135.

Schutz, A. (1967). *The phenomenology of the social world.* Evanston, IL: Northwestern University Press.

Silverman, D. (1989). Six rules of qualitative research: A post-romantic argument. *Symbolic Interaction, 12,* 215-230.

Snow, D. A., & Morill, C. (1993). Reflections on anthropology's ethnographic crisis of faith. *Contemporary Sociology, 22,* 8-11.

Van Maanen, J. (1988). *Tales of the field: On writing ethnography.* Chicago: University of Chicago Press.

Wolcott, H. F. (1990). On seeking—and rejecting—validity in qualitative research. In E. W. Eisner & A. Peshkin (Eds.), *Qualitative inquiry in education: The continuing debate* (pp. 121-152). New York: Teachers College Press.

31

■

The Art and Politics of Interpretation

NORMAN K. DENZIN

Once upon a time, the Lone Ethnographer rode off into the sunset in search of his "native." After undergoing a series of trials, he encountered the object of his quest in a distant land. There he underwent his rite of passage by enduring the ultimate ordeal of "fieldwork." After collecting "the data," the Lone Ethnographer returned home and wrote a "true" account of "the culture."

Renato Rosaldo, *Culture and Truth,* 1989

I have been working to change the way I speak and write.

bell hooks, *Yearning,* 1990

IN the social sciences there is only interpretation. Nothing speaks for itself. Confronted with a mountain of impressions, documents, and field notes, the qualitative researcher faces the difficult and challenging task of making sense of what has been learned. I call making sense of what has been learned *the art of interpretation.* This may also be described as moving from the field to the text to the reader. The practice of this art allows the field-worker-as-*bricoleur* (Lévi-Strauss, 1966, p. 17) to translate what has been learned into a body of textual work that communicates these understandings to the reader.

These texts, borrowing from John Van Maanen (1988), constitute tales of the field. They are the stories we tell one another. This is so because interpretation requires the telling of a story, or a narrative that states "things happen this way because" or "this happened, after this happened, because this happened first." Interpreters as storytellers tell narrative tales with beginnings, middles, and ends. These tales always embody implicit and explicit theories

AUTHOR'S NOTE: I would like to thank Mitch Allen, Kenneth Gergen, Meaghan Morris, Laurel Richardson, Katherine E. Ryan, and Yvonna Lincoln for their comments on earlier versions of this chapter.

of causality, where narrative or textual causality is presumed to map the actual goings-on in the real world (Ricoeur, 1985, p. 4). How this complex art of interpretation and storytelling is practiced is the topic of this chapter.

The history of qualitative research in the social sciences reveals continual attempts to wrestle with this process and its methods. In this chapter I review several of these methods, or traditions, paying special attention to those that have been employed in the most recent past, including the constructivist,[1] grounded theory, feminist, Marxist, cultural studies, and poststructural perspectives.[2] I examine problems generic to this process, and briefly allude to my own perspective, interpretive interactionism (Denzin, 1989). I conclude with predictions concerning where the art and politics of interpretation will be 10 years from now.

The Interpretive Crisis in the Social Sciences

The following assumptions organize my analysis. First, the social sciences today face a crisis of interpretation, for previously agreed-upon criteria from the positivist and postpositivist traditions are now being challenged (Guba, 1990b, p. 371; Rosaldo, 1989, p. 45). This crisis has been described as poststructural and postmodern, a new sensibility regarding the social text and its claims to authority. Describing this new situation, Richardson (1991) observes, "The core of [this] sensibility is doubt that any discourse has a privileged place, any method or theory a universal and general claim to authoritative knowledge" (p. 173).

Second, each social science community (Fish, 1980) has its own criteria for judging the adequacy of any given interpretive statement. These criteria will be grounded in the canonical texts the community takes to be central to its mission. What works in one community may not work in another. Patricia Hill Collins (1990) contends, for example, that the Eurocentric, masculine positivist epistemology asks African American women to "objectify themselves, devalue their emotional life, displace their motivations for furthering knowledge about Black women, and confront in an adversarial relationship those with more social, economic and professional power" (p. 205).

Third, this crisis can be resolved only from *within* social science communities. It is doubtful that a new set of criteria shared by all points of view will, can, or should be developed. This means that "once the privileged veil of truth is lifted, feminism, Afro-American, gay, and other disparaged discourses rise to the same epistemological status as the dominant discourse" (Richardson, 1991, p. 173).

Fourth, increasingly, the criteria of evaluation will turn, as Richardson notes, on moral, practical, aesthetic, political, and personal issues—the production, that is, of texts that articulate an emancipatory, participative perspective on the human condition and its betterment.

Fifth, as Clough (1992, p. 136) argues, the problems of writing are not different from the problems of method or fieldwork. It is not the case, as some may contend, that the above problems can be answered only through new forms of writing. As Yvonna Lincoln and I argue in Chapter 1 of this volume, these new writing forms function primarily as sources of validation for a reinvigorated empirical science. They direct attention away from the ways in which the experimental text can perpetuate new forms and technologies of knowledge and power that align qualitative research with the state. The insistence that writing and fieldwork are different cannot be allowed (Clough, 1992, p. 136).

The age of a putative value-free social science appears to be over. Accordingly, sixth, any discussion of this process must become political, personal, and experiential. Following John Dewey, I believe that the methods for making sense of experience are always personal. Life and method, as Clandinin and Connelly argue in Chapter 26 of this volume, are inextricably intertwined. One learns about method by thinking about how one makes sense of one's own life. The researcher, as a writer, is a *bricoleur.* He or she fashions meaning and interpretation out of ongoing experience. As a *bricoleur,* the researcher uses any tool or method that is readily at hand. I discuss, then, the politics, craft, and art of experience and interpretation.

From Field to Text to Reader

Moving from the field to the text[3] to the reader is a complex, reflexive process. The researcher creates a field text consisting of field notes and documents from the field. From this text he or she creates a research text, notes and interpretations based on the field text, what David Plath (1990) calls "filed notes." The researcher then re-creates the research text as a working interpretive document. This working document contains the writer's initial attempts to make sense out of what has been learned, what Clandinin and Connelly (Chapter 26, this volume) term "experiencing experience." The writer next produces a quasi-public text, one that is shared with colleagues, whose comments and suggestions the writer seeks. The writer than transforms this statement into a public document, which embodies the writer's self-understandings, which are now inscribed in the experiences of those studied.[4] This statement, in turn, furnishes the context for the understandings the reader brings to the experiences being described by the writer. Reading and writing, then, are central to interpretation, for, as Geertz (1973, p. 18) argues, interpretation involves the construction of a reading of an event, both by the writer and by the reader. To paraphrase Geertz, a good interpretation takes us into the center of the experiences being described.

Such interpretations, however, may not take us to the heart of the matter, as these matters are understood in the everyday world. Here is Rosaldo (1989) describing, in anthropological terms, the daily family breakfast at the home of his prospective parents-in-law: "Every morning the reigning patriarch, as if just in from the hunt, shouts from the kitchen, 'How many people would like a poached egg?' Women and children take turns saying yes or no. In the meantime the women talk among themselves and designate one among them the toast maker" (pp. 46-47).

Rosaldo (1989) says of this account, "My rendition of a family breakfast in the ethnographic present transformed a relatively spontaneous event into a generic cultural form. It became a caricatured analysis . . . the reader will probably not be surprised to hear that my potential in-laws laughed and laughed as they listened to the microethnography . . . about their family breakfast" (p. 48). Rosaldo employs terms that Geertz (1983) would call experience-distant, or second order. Terms and phrases such as *reigning patriarch* and *in from the hunt* may work for the anthropologist talking to another anthropologist, but they lack relevance and meaning for Rosaldo's prospective new family.

Interpretation is an art; it is not formulaic or mechanical.[5] It can be learned, like any form of storytelling, only through doing. Indeed, as Laurel Richardson argues in Chapter 32 of this volume, writing is interpretation, or storytelling. Fieldworkers can neither make sense of nor understand what has been learned until they sit down and write the interpretive text, telling the story first to themselves and then to their significant others, and then to the public.

A situated, writing self structures the interactions that take place among the writer, the text, and the reader. The writer presents a particular and unique self in the text, a self that claims to have some authority over the subject matter that is being interpreted. However, the rules for presenting this self are no longer clear. Krieger (1991) comments: "The challenge lies in what each of us chooses to do when we represent our experiences. Whose rules do we follow? Will we make our own? Do we . . . have the guts to say, 'You may not like it, but here I am'?" (p. 244).

Interpretation as Storytelling

The storytelling self (see Manning & Cullum-Swan, Chapter 29, this volume) that is presented is always one attached to an interpretive perspective, an "espoused theory" (Argyris & Schön, 1974, p. viii) that gives the writer a public persona. Four major paradigms (positivist and postpositivist, constructivist, critical) and three major perspectives (feminist, ethnic models, cultural studies) now structure qualitative writing. The stories qualitative researchers tell one another come from one or another of these paradigms and perspectives.

These paradigms and perspectives serve several functions for the writer. They are masks that are hidden behind, put on, and taken off as writers write their particular storied and self-versions of a feminist, gay-lesbian, Afro-American, Hispanic, Marxist, constructionist, grounded theory, phenomenological, or interactionist text. They give the writer a public identity. These masks direct the writer into specific theoretical and research traditions, what Argyris and Schön (1974) call "theories-in-use" (p. viii). Each tradition has its own taken-for-granted and problematic writing style.

These masks offer scenarios that lead writers to impose a particular order on the world studied. For example, if the paradigm is positivist or postpositivist, the writer will present a text that stresses variables, hypotheses, and propositions derived from a particular theory that sees the world in terms of causes and effects (see Guba & Lincoln, 1989, p. 84). Strauss and Corbin (1990) offer a simple example: "Conditions of intense pain will be followed by measures taken to relieve pain" (p. 111). Here antecedent conditions (intense pain) produce subsequent actions (measures to relieve the pain).

If the paradigm is constructivist, the writer will present a text that stresses emergent designs and emergent understandings. An interpretive, or phenomenologically based, text would emphasize socially constructed realities, local generalizations, interpretive resources, stocks of knowledge, intersubjectivity, practical reasoning, and ordinary talk (Holstein & Gubrium, Chapter 16, this volume).

A writer working from a feminist standpoint paradigm (see Olesen, Chapter 9, this volume) will attempt to tell a situated story stressing gender, reflexivity, emotion, and an action orientation (Fonow & Cook, 1991, p. 2), examining, for example, how "the ideology of the 'single parent' [organizes] multiple sites (parent-teaching contact) in education" (Smith, 1992, p. 97). Similarly, a Marxist or emancipatory text will stress the importance of terms such as *action, structure, culture,* and *power,* which are then fitted into a general model of society (Carspecken & Apple, 1992, p. 513; see also, in this volume, Kincheloe

& McLaren, Chapter 8; Fiske, Chapter 11; Reason, Chapter 20).

Writing Issues: Sense Making, Representation, Legitimation, Desire

Any discussion of how the researcher moves from the field to the text must address a host of issues or problems closely related to storytelling traditions. These issues group into four areas. (Each problem works its effects on the field, research, and interpretive texts that lay the foundation for the writer's final, public document.) These problems may be conceptualized as phases, each turning on a different issue, and each turning back on the others, as in Dilthey's (1900/1976) hermeneutic circle. They may be named and called the interpretation, or sense-making, representation, legitimation, and desiring phases of moving from field to text to reader. They interact with each other as the writer wrestles with them in the field, research, interpretive, and public phases of textual construction.

Sense Making

The first issue concerns how the writer moves from and through field notes into the actual writing process (into the research and interpretive texts), making decisions about what will be written about, what will be included, how it will be represented, and so on. A considerable literature surrounds this process (see Wolcott, 1990, for a review; see also Sanjek, 1990). For example, Strauss and Corbin (1990, p. 197) direct investigators in this field and research text phase to write memos, as well as theoretical, operational, and code notes concerning conceptual labels, paradigm features, emerging theoretical understandings, and visual representations of relationships between concepts and analytic terms. Richardson (Chapter 32, this volume) discusses other forms of anticipatory interpretive writing, including observation, methodological, theoretical, and personal notes that are kept in an ongoing journal.

Representation

The second area speaks to such topics as voice, audience, the "Other," and the author's place in the reflexive texts that are produced (see Geertz, 1988; Krieger, 1991; Richardson, 1990, 1992; Rose, 1990; Van Maanen, 1988; see also Richardson, Chapter 32, this volume). To paraphrase Brady (1991, p. 5), there is more than one way to do representation. Representation, of course, is always self-presentation. That is, the Other's presence is directly connected to the writers' self-presence in the text. The Other who is presented in the text is always a version of the researcher's self. Krieger (1991) argues: "When we discuss others, we are always talking about ourselves. Our images of 'them' are images of 'us' " (p. 5). This can occur poetically, as in Laurel Richardson's (1992) poem "Louisa May's Story of Her Life." Richardson has Louisa May say of herself:

> I grew up poor in a rented house
> in a very normal sort of way
> on a very normal sort of street
> with some very nice middle-class friends.
> (p. 127)

Here Richardson's poetic self poetically presents Louisa May's truncated life story.

Representation turns on voice and the use of pronouns, including first-person statements. Patricia Hill Collins (1990) describes her use of pronouns:

> I often use the pronoun "our" instead of "their" when referring to African-American women, a choice that embeds me in the group I am studying instead of distancing me from it. In addition, I occasionally place my own concrete experience in the text. To support my analysis, I cite few statistics and instead rely on the voices of Black women from all walks of life. (p. 202)

Frequently writers are positioned outside, yet alongside, those Others they write about, never making clear where they stand in these hyphenated relationships (see Fine, Chapter 4, this volume) that connect the Other to them. When Others are not allowed to speak, they remain "an absent presence without voice" (hooks, 1990, p. 126). There are major problems with this approach to "Othering," and it has been extensively criticized (Denzin, 1990; see also Fine, Chapter 4, this volume). In such situations it is best to let Others do their own talking. However, even when "we" allow the Other to speak, when we talk about or for them, we are taking over their voice. A multivoiced as opposed to single-voiced text can partially overcome this issue (see Bakhtin, 1986; also Collins, 1990).

Legitimation

The third problem centers on matters of epistemology, including how a public text legitimates itself, or makes claims for its own authority. Traditional foundationalist topics such as reliability, validity, and generalizability may be encountered here (see Hammersley, 1992; Lather, 1993; see also, in this volume, Stake, Chapter 14; Altheide

& Johnson, Chapter 30; Lincoln & Denzin, Chapter 36). The postmodern sensibility doubts foundational arguments that seek to anchor a text's authority in such terms. A more local, personal, and political turn is taken. On this, Seidman (1991) is informative: "Instead of appealing to absolutist justifications, instead of constructing theoretical logics and epistemic casuistries to justify a conceptual strategy . . . I propose that we be satisfied with local, pragmatic rationales for our conceptual [interpretive] approaches" (p. 136; see also Lather, 1993).

Desire

There is still a fourth problem, or phase, in this project, given in the subtitle to Howard S. Becker's influential 1986 book, *Writing for Social Scientists: How to Start and Finish Your Thesis, Book, or Article.* This problem circles back on the first, making decisions about what will be written. But it goes deeper and refers to the writing practices that field-workers deploy: how one moves from a blank page (or screen) to a written text, one sentence after another, building an emergent, reflexive interpretation of the subject matter at hand (see Richardson, Chapter 32, this volume; also see Becker, 1986; for an interpretation of Becker's strategies, see Clough, 1992, chap. 5). The topic, to borrow Roland Barthes's (1975) phrase, is the pleasure of the text. Or, as Laurel Richardson (Chapter 32, this volume) says, "Can we create texts that are vital?"

A vital text is not boring. It grips the reader (and the writer). A vital text invites readers to engage the author's subject matter. Many qualitative research texts are boring. Writers have been taught to write in a particular style, a style that takes the "omniscient voice of science, the view from everywhere" (Richardson, Chapter 32, this volume). The postmodern sensibility encourages writers to put themselves into their texts, to engage writing as a creative act of discovery and inquiry. However, engaging or boring writing has more to do with the writer than with the paradigm or perspective that is employed.

I turn now to the problems generic to the sense-making, representation, legitimation, and desiring phases of writing. This will involve additional consideration of the relationship between the writer and the text.

Two Models of the Writer

The foregoing discussion has separated, or isolated, four phases of writing. Although analytically useful, this formulation conveys a sometimes heroic, romantic picture of the writer and the text. It presumes a writer with the guts to tell it like it is, to put him- or herself on the line, so to speak. It presumes a socially situated (and isolated), unique writer who has the courage and authenticity to write a bold new text. This writer first experiences, feels, and thinks. Having had the experience, this bold writer then writes, deploying one or more narrative traditions in the story he or she tells.[6]

This model makes writing an expressive, and not a productive, process. It romanticizes the writer and his or her experiences. It distances experience from its expressions. Sense making, interpretation, representation, and claims for legitimacy are all part of the same process. They can be separated only artificially.

Interpretation is a productive process that sets forth the multiple meanings of an event, object, experience, or text. Interpretation is transformative. It illuminates, throws light on experience. It brings out, and refines, as when butter is clarified, the meanings that can be sifted from a text, an object, or a slice of experience. So conceived, meaning is not in a text, nor does interpretation precede experience, or its representation. Meaning, interpretation, and representation are deeply intertwined in one another.

Raymond Carver (1989), the short story writer, describes it this way. Writing is an "act of discovery" (p. 25). The writer deals with moments of experience. The writer brings all of his or her powers, "intelligence and literary skill" (p. 27) to bear on these moments to show how "things out there really are and how he [or she] sees those things—like no one else sees them" (p. 27). This is done "through the use of clear and specific language; language that will bring to life the details that will light up the story for the reader . . . the language must be accurately and precisely given" (p. 27).

Experimental writing, Carver argues, is "original." "The real experimenters have to Make It New . . . and in the process have to find things out for themselves. . . . writers want to carry news from their world to ours" (p. 24). This means that "absolutely everything is important" (p. 38), including where the writer puts the "commas and periods" (p. 38). The writer invests experience with meaning, showing how everything has suddenly become clear. What was unclear before has "just now become clear" (p. 23). Such understandings emerge in moments of sudden awakening. The writer brings this sense of discovery and awakening to the reader.

Writing, then, relives and reinscribes experience, bringing newly discovered meanings to the reader. No cheap tricks, Carver (1989, p. 23) says, no gimmicks. Writing must bring news of the world to the reader. In writing, the writer creates this world. He or she fills it with real and fictional people. Their problems and their crises are brought to life. Their lives gone out of control are vividly described. Their lives, suddenly illuminated with new meanings and new transformation of self, are depicted.

What is given in the text, what is written, is made up and fashioned out of memory and field notes. Writing of this order, writing that powerfully reinscribes and re-creates experience, invests itself with its own power and authority. No one else but this writer could have brought this new corner of the world alive in this way for the reader.

Thus are expressive (romantic) and productive views of writing mutually complementary. The field-worker must be a committed writer, but the stories that are boldly told are those that flow from a commitment not to shock, or brutalize, or alienate the reader (Carver, 1989, p. 24). Experimentation is not an excuse or a "license to be careless, silly or imitative" (p. 24).

The Writing Process

Understanding and mystery are central to the writing project. Carver's writer unravels a mystery, discovering and then understanding what was previously hidden and unclear. He or she cuts to the heart of an experience, disclosing its immediate, as well as deep, symbolic and long-lasting meanings for the people involved. This suggests that the writer accurately describes a hidden or submerged reality that the text brings to light. So conceived, a text establishes its own verisimilitude. It tells the truth. But there are complicated relations among truth, reality, and the text (see also Lincoln & Denzin, Chapter 36, this volume). Every writing genre has its own laws of verisimilitude.

For example, verisimilitude is the theme of the murder mystery. "Its law is the antagonism between truth and verisimilitude" (Todorov, 1977, p. 86). In a murder mystery, the murderer must appear to be innocent and the innocent person must be made to appear guilty. "The truth has no verisimilitude, and the verisimilitude has no truth" (Todorov, 1977, p. 86). The end of the narrative must, of course, resolve this tension or contradiction. It must show the apparently innocent person to be guilty, and the apparently guilty party to be innocent. Only in the conclusion to the mystery, as Todorov (1977) notes, do truth and verisimilitude coincide. Thus is truth only and always a "distanced and postponed verisimilitude" (p. 88). Truth is a textual production.

So in the end, clear description, as defined by a genre, provides the basis for interpretation, understanding, and verisimilitude. That is, an event or process can be neither interpreted nor understood until it has been well described. However, the age of "objective" description is over. We are, as Lather (1991, p. 91) argues, in the age of inscription. Writers create their own situated, inscribed versions of the realities they describe.

There is more than one way to do a description-as-an-inscription. Thin description simply states a set of facts (Geertz, 1973, pp. 9-10; Ryle, 1968, pp. 8-9), for example:

> X drank a cup of coffee at 9:30 a.m. on Wednesday February 3 as he e-mailed a message to his editor and co-editor.

Here is a thick description, taken from a Carver short story, "So Much Water So Close to Home" (1989). The action described in this passage sets the context for the nervous breakdown of the woman who narrates the story. Four men have gone to the mountains on a fishing trip.

> They parked the car in the mountains and hiked several miles to where they wanted to fish. They carried their bedrolls, food and cooking utensils, their cards, their whisky. The first evening at the river, even before they could set up camp, Mel Dorn found the girl floating face down in the river; nude, lodged near the shore in some branches. He called the other men and they all came to look at her. They talked about what to do . . . one of them thought they should start back to the car at once. The others stirred the sand with their shoes and said they felt inclined to stay. They pleaded fatigue, the late hour, the fact that the girl 'wasn't going anywhere.' In the end they all decided to stay. (pp. 186-187)

A thin description simply reports facts, independent of intentions or circumstances. A thick description, in contrast, gives the context of an experience, states the intentions and meanings that organized the experience, and reveals the experience as a process. Out of this process arises a text's claims for truth, or its verisimilitude.

Ethnography, Geertz (1973, p. 10) suggests, is thick description, a "written representation of a culture" (Van Maanen, 1988, p. 1). Field-workers inscribe social discourse. They write it down, turning a passing event into something that now exists in its inscriptions (Geertz, 1973, p. 19). What is written down is itself interpretive, for the researcher interprets while writing, attempting in the process to rescue the " 'said' I of such discourse from its perishing occasions and fix it in perusable terms" (Geertz, 1973, p. 20). The intent is to create the conditions that will allow the reader, through the writer, to converse with (and observe) those who have been studied.

Building on what has been described and inscribed, interpretation creates the conditions for authentic, or deep, emotional understanding. Authentic understanding is created when readers are able to live their way into an experience that has been described and interpreted. Return to Rosaldo's (1989) Ilongot headhunters. Early in his research, Rosaldo explained the headhunting ritual with exchange theory. He presented his theory to an older Ilongot man named Insan:

> What did he think, I asked, of the idea that headhunting resulted from the way that one death (the beheaded victim's) canceled another (the next of kin). He looked puzzled, so I went on to say that a victim of a beheading was exchanged for the death of one's own kin. . . . Insan reflected a moment, and replied that he imagined somebody could think such a thing . . . but that he and other Ilongots did not think any such thing. (pp. 3-4)

Fifteen months after his wife Michelle's tragic death in the field, Rosaldo returned to his headhunting materials. There, attempting to deal with his own rage, he found the meaning of the Ilongot ritual, and the rage that headhunting addressed. He states, "Either you understand it or you don't" (pp. 1-2). Unless you have had the experience, you cannot understand it.

Interpretation is done, of course, by an interpreter, or storyteller. There are two types of interpreters: people who have actually experienced what has been described, and those who are often ethnographers, or field-workers, so-called well-informed experts. These two types (local and scientific) of interpreters often give different meanings to the same set of thickly described/inscribed experiences. Local interpreters use experience-near concepts—words and meanings that actually operate in the worlds studied (Geertz, 1983, p. 57). These individuals seek emic, or contextual, situated understandings. Scientific interpreters frequently use experience-distant terms—words whose meanings lie in the observer's theory (Geertz, 1983, p. 57). They produce etic, or abstract, noncontextualized interpretations.

Geertz (1973) clarifies the goal in this situation:

> [We] set down the meaning particular social actions have for the actors whose actions they are . . . stating as explicitly as we can manage, what the knowledge thus attained demonstrates about the society in which it is found. . . . Our double task is to uncover the conceptual structures that inform our subject's acts, the "said" of social discourse, and to construct a system of analysis . . . [which reveals] what is generic to those structures. (p. 27)

Thick descriptions and inscriptions create thick interpretations.[7] Thick interpretations interpret thick descriptions, in terms of the local theories that are structuring people's experiences.

In nearly all situations, individuals are able to articulate interpretive stories, or working theories, about their conduct and their experiences. These theories-as-stories are contained in the oral and cultural texts of the group and are based on local knowledge—that is, what works for them (Geertz, 1983). These pragmatic theories give meaning to problematic experiences. The interpreter attempts to uncover these theories, showing how they work in the lives of the individuals studied.

The Text, Its Authority, and Style

A text and an author's authority can always be challenged. This is so for three reasons. First, stories can always be told (inscribed) in different ways, and the Others who are spoken for may offer different tellings of their story. Second, all texts are biased productions. Many reflect patriarchal, male, interpretive biases (Collins, 1990, pp. 203-206). Third, the interpretive criteria that an author employs may be questioned, and the logic of the text that is assembled may be called into doubt. I will briefly discuss each of these points.

Different Tellings

In a recent article, W. A. Marianne Boelen (1992) criticizes William Foote Whyte's classic study *Street Corner Society* (1943) on several grounds. She notes that Whyte did not know Italian, was not an insider to the group studied, did not understand the importance of the family in Italian group life, and, as a consequence, seriously misrepresented many of the facts in "Cornerville" society. Whyte (1992) has disputed Boelen's charges, but they linger, especially in light of Doc's (Whyte's key informant) estrangement from Whyte. But unnoticed in the Whyte-Boelen exchange is the fact that no permanent telling of a story can be given. There are only always different versions of different, not the same, stories, even when the same site is studied.[8]

Writing Styles

There are several styles of qualitative writing, several different ways of describing, inscribing, and interpreting reality. Each style creates the conditions for its own criticism. Some version of the realist tale, or style, however, predominates. The realist tale attempts to make the subject's world transparent, to bring it alive, to make it visible (Clough, 1992, p. 132). There are three prevailing realist styles: mainstream, interpretive, and descriptive.

Mainstream realist writing presents thick and thin descriptions of the worlds studied, giving accounts of events, persons, and experiences. These texts assume the author can give an objective accounting, or portrayal, of the realities of a group or an individual. Such texts often utilize experience-distance concepts, such as kinship structure, to explain a group's way of life. Mainstream realism leads to the production of analytic, interpretive texts that are often single voiced.

Interpretive realism describes those texts where authors insert their personal interpretations into the life situations of the individuals studied. Clifford Geertz's (1973) study of the Balinese (which uses thick description) frequently privileges Geertz's interpretations. For example, he states: "In the cockfight, man and beast, good and evil, ego and ideology . . . fuse in a bloody drama of hatred, cruelty, violence and death" (p. 442). Here experience and its meanings are filtered through the researcher's, not the subject's, eyes.

In descriptive realism the writer attempts to stay out of the way and to allow the world being described to speak for itself. Of course, this is impossible, for all writing is interpretive. However, the impulse is to tell a multivoiced story (see, for example, Bruner & Gorfain, 1991; Ulmer, 1989). The excerpt from the Carver story quoted above is an example of this form of storytelling.[9]

Bias

Viewing the world through the male voice and gaze, too many writers equate masculinity with objectivity and femininity with subjectivity. In general, as Reinharz (1992) observes, "quantitative research defines itself as hard, firm, real . . . and strong . . . [and] defines qualitative research as soft, mushy, fuzzy, and weak" (p. 295). (This point is explored extensively in this volume by Fine, Chapter 4; Olesen, Chapter 9; Richardson, Chapter 32). But all texts are biased, reflecting the play of class, gender, race, ethnicity, and culture, suggesting that so-called objective interpretations are impossible.

The Logic of the Text

Any social text as a story can be analyzed in terms of its treatment of five paired terms:

1. the real world of lived experience and its representation in the text;
2. the text itself and the author, including the author's voice (first person, third person);
3. lived experience and its representation in the text (transcriptions from interviews and so on); and
4. subjects and their intentional meanings
5. the reader and the text (see Van Maanen, 1988, p. 6).

In telling a story, the author attempts to weave a text that re-creates for the reader the real world that was studied. Subjects, including their actions, experiences, words, intentions, and meanings, are then anchored inside this world as the author presents experience-near, experience-distant, local, and scientific theories of it. Readers take hold of this text and read their way into it, perhaps making it one of the stories they will tell about themselves. They develop their own naturalistic generalizations and impressions, based on the tacit knowledge and emotional feelings the text creates for them (see Stake, 1983, p. 282; see also Chapter 14, this volume).

As a narrative production, interpretive writing is like fiction. It is created out of the facts of experience (things that did occur, might have occurred, or could occur). The story that is told often turns the researcher into a masculinized hero who confronts and makes sense of the subject's life situation. This situation is frequently conceptualized as a struggle that locates the subject's experiences within the primordial contexts of work, family, kinship, and marriage. This struggle is given meaning by the writer of the text, who becomes the only person authorized to represent the subject's story. The story that is finally told becomes the researcher's accomplishment, his or her self-fashioned narration of the subject's story (Clough, 1992, p. 17).

An Analysis of Interpretive Practices

To summarize: The art of interpretation produces understandings that are shaped by genre, narrative, stylistic, personal, cultural, and paradigmatic conventions. I turn next to a review of the major paradigms and perspectives that now structure qualitative research writing practices: positivist and postpositivist, constructivist, critical (Marxist, emancipatory), and poststructuralist—including ethnic, feminist, and cultural studies—models. I select an exemplar from each tradition.[10] As Yvonna Lincoln and I argue in Chapter 1 of this volume, qualitative research is now in its "fifth moment," writing its way out of writing culture.

Grounded Theory as an Interpretive Style (Postpositivism)

The grounded theory perspective reflects a naturalistic approach to ethnography and interpretation, stressing naturalistic observations, open-ended interviewing, the sensitizing use of concepts, and a grounded (inductive) approach to theorizing, which can be both formal and substantive. Strauss and Corbin (1990; see also Chapter 17, this volume) outline the criteria for judging a grounded theory study. They preface their discussion thus: "The usual canons of 'good science' should be retained, but require redefinition in order to fit the realities of qualitative research" (p. 250). These usual canons of good science are significance, theory-observation compatibility, generalizability, consistency, reproducibility, precision, and verification. Strauss and Corbin argue, for example, that if a similar set of conditions exists, and if the same theoretical perspective and the same rules for data gathering and analysis are followed, two researchers should be able to reproduce the same theoretical explanations of a given phenomenon.

Investigators should be able to provide information on the sample (including theoretical variations), core categories, key events and incidents, hypotheses, and negative cases that emerged and were pursued during the research process. The empirical grounding of a study (its grounded theory) should be judged by the range, density, linkages between, and systematic relatedness of its theoretical concepts, as well as by the theory's specificity and generality. Strauss and Corbin (1990) urge that these criteria be followed so that readers can "judge the credibility of [the] theory" (p. 258).

The grounded theory perspective is the most widely used qualitative interpretive framework in the social sciences today.[11] Its appeals are broad, for it provides a set of clearly defined steps any researcher can follow (see also Prus, 1991). Its dangers and criticisms, which arise when it is not fully understood, are multiple. There may be a flood of concepts unattached to the empirical world, and the analyst may get lost in coding and category schemes. Just exactly what a theory is, is also not clear (see Woods, 1992, p. 391). Some suggest that because the facts of a theory are always theory laden, a theory can only ever discover and hence ground itself (Lincoln & Guba, 1985, p. 207). The overemphasis on theory has also been criticized, including the use of previous theory as a guide to research and the attempts to make previous theory more dense (but see Gerson, 1991, p. 285). This preoccupation with prior theory can stand in the way of the researcher's attempts to hear and listen to the interpretive theories that operate in the situations studied. The perspective's affinities with positivism have also been criticized (Roman, 1992, p. 571). There is also a textual style that frequently subordinates lived experience and its interpretations to the grounded theorist's reading of the situation.

At the same time, grounded theory answers to a need to attach the qualitative research project to the "good science" model. Yet the perspective (see Strauss & Corbin, Chapter 17, this volume) continues to fit itself to feminist and other post-structural, postmodern interpretive styles (Star, 1991).

Constructivism as an Interpretive Style

The constructivist program of Lincoln, Guba, and others represents a break with the postpositivist tradition, while retaining (at one level) a commitment to the grounded theory approach of Strauss and associates.[12] A good constructionist interpretation (text) is based on purposive (theoretical) sampling, a grounded theory, inductive data analysis, and idiographic (contextual) interpretations. The foundation for interpretation rests on triangulated empirical materials that are trustworthy. Trustworthiness consists of four components: credibility, transferability, dependability, and confirmability (these are the constructionist equivalents of internal and external validity, reliability, and objectivity; Lincoln & Guba, 1985, p. 300).[13]

Trustworthy materials are subjected to the constant comparative method of analysis that grounded theory deploys, that is, comparing incidents applicable to categories, integrating categories and their properties, delimiting and writing the theory. These materials are then developed into a case report that is again subjected to a comprehensive member check and an external audit. This done, the study is ready for public release (Lincoln & Guba, 1985, p. 381).

These constructivist interpretive strategies address many of the perceived problems in grounded theory, including the theory- and value-laden nature of facts, ambiguities in incidence, and category analysis. The paradigm, while disavowing the ontology, epistemology, and methodologies of postpositivism (Guba, 1990a, p. 27), sustains, at one level, Strauss and Corbin's commitment to the canons of good science. Hence the enormous commitment to methods and procedures that will increase a text's credibility, transferability, dependability, and confirmability.

Feminists, liberation theologists, Freirian critical theorists, and neo-Marxists may criticize the paradigm for not being ideological enough (Lincoln, 1990, p. 83). However, it is moving in these directions, as the authors seek a language and a set of practices that more fully celebrate and implement the moral, ethical, and political dimensions of social research (Lincoln, 1990, p. 86). Still, some would contend that it (like grounded theory) has yet to engage fully the new sensibilities flowing from the poststructural and postmodern perspectives.

Critical Theory as an Interpretive Style

There are multiple critical theory and participatory action frameworks (Guba, 1990a, p. 25; see also the works in this volume by Kincheloe & McLaren, Chapter 8; Fiske, Chapter 11; Reason, Chapter 20). All share a critical realist ontology, a subjectivist epistemology, and a dialogic, transformative, ethnographic methodology (Guba, 1990a, p. 25). This often produces a criticism of traditional, naturalistic ethnographies (Roman, 1992, p. 558).

There are two distinct traditions within the cultural studies, critical theory model. One school, following Paulo Freire (1982, p. 30), regards concrete reality, dialectically conceived, as the starting point for analysis that examines how people live their facts of life into existence. The other school reads social texts (popular literature, cinema, popular music) as empirical materials that articulate complex arguments about race, class, and gender in contemporary life. Some scholars merge the ethnographic and textual approaches (see Fiske, Chapter 11, this volume), examining how cultural interpretations are acted on and given meaning in concrete local cultural communities. Such work moves back and forth between concrete ethnographic texts and the content, semiotic, and narrative analysis of systems of discourse—for example, a particular television show or a film (see Manning & Cullum-Swan, Chapter 29, this volume).

Critical inquiry is theory driven by neo-Marxist and cultural studies models of the raced, classed, and gendered structures of contemporary societies (Carspecken & Apple, 1992, pp. 541-542). An emancipatory principle drives such research, which is committed to engaging oppressed groups in collective, democratic theorizing about "what is common and different in their experiences of oppression and privilege" (Roman, 1992, p. 557). A constant focus is given to the material and cultural practices that create structures of oppression.

A critical text is judged by its ability to reveal reflexively these structures of oppression as they operate in the worlds of lived experience. A critical text thus creates a space for multiple voices to speak; those who are oppressed are asked to articulate their definitions of their situations. For some, critical theory must be testable, falsifiable, dialogic, and collaborative (Carspecken & Apple, 1992, pp. 547-548). Others reject the more positivist features of this formulation (Roman, 1992, p. 558). Dorothy Smith (1992, p. 96), for example, evaluates a text by its ability to reveal the invisible structures of oppression in women's worlds.

Thus a good critical, emancipatory text is one that is multivocal, collaborative, naturalistically grounded in the worlds of lived experience, and organized by a critical, interpretive theory. Such formulations have been criticized for their tendency to impose their voices and values on the groups studied (Quantz, 1992, p. 471), for not being reflexive enough, and for being too theoretical (top-down theory), too preoccupied with theory verification (Roman, 1992, p. 571), and not sufficiently aware of postmodern sensibilities concerning the text and its social construction (Clough, 1992, p. 137).

These approaches, with their action criteria, politicize qualitative research. They foreground praxis, yet leave unclear the methodological side of the interpretive process that is so central to the grounded theory and constructionist approaches.

Poststructural Interpretive Styles

I will discuss three poststructural interpretive styles, those connected to the standpoint and cultural studies perspectives (Clough, 1992; Denzin, 1989; Lather, 1991, 1993; Smith, 1992; see also Olesen, Chapter 9, this volume), those articulated by women of color (Collins, 1990; hooks, 1990), and my own approach, interpretive interactionism. Each of these perspectives is intimately connected to the critical and emancipatory styles of interpretation.

Style 1: Women of Color

Collins (1990, pp. 206-219) offers four criteria of interpretation, which are contrasted to the positivist approaches to research. Derived from an Afrocentric standpoint, her criteria focus on the primacy of concrete lived experience, the use of dialogue in assessing knowledge claims, the ethic of caring, and the ethic of personal accountability.

Experience as a criterion of meaning directs attention to black sisterhood, to the stories, narratives and Bible principles embodied in black church and community life. Concrete black feminine wisdom is contrasted to knowledge without wisdom: "A heap see, but a few know" (Collins, 1990, p. 208). Wisdom is experiential, cultural, and shared in the black feminine community. Dialogue, bell hooks argues, is humanizing speech. Black feminists assess knowledge claims through discourse, storytelling, connected dialogue in a group context. This emphasis on dialogue is directly translated into the black feminist text. Zora Neale Hurston, for example, located herself inside the folktales she collected, and carried on extensive dialogues with them, thus creating a multivocal text (Collins, 1990, p. 214).

Dialogue extends to the ethic of caring, which suggests that "personal expressiveness, emotions and empathy are central to the knowledge validation process" (Collins, 1990, p. 215). This ethic values individual uniqueness and the expression of emotionality in the text, and seeks writers who can create emotional texts that others can enter into. The ethic of personal accountability makes individuals accountable for their values and the political consequences of their actions.

These four criteria embody a "self-defined Black women's standpoint using an Afrocentric epistemology" (Collins, 1990, p. 219). They call into question much of what now passes for truth in methodological discourse. They articulate criteria that stand in vivid contrast to those criteria contained in the grounded theory, constructionist, critical, and emancipatory traditions.

Style 2: Poststructural Feminist Interpretive Styles

Fonow and Cook (1991, pp. 2-13) suggest that four interpretive themes structure feminist research: an emphasis on researcher and textual reflexivity; an action and praxis orientation; an attention to the affective, emotional components of research; and concrete grounding in immediate situations. Lather (1991) extends this discussion. Her argument is threefold. First, feminist research challenges narrative realism, and the traditional naturalistic ethnography, because there is now an "uncertainty about what constitutes an adequate depiction of reality" (p. 91). As noted above, Lather argues that the age of description has ended. We are, as we have always been, in the moment of inscription, wherein writers create their own situated versions of the worlds studied. Accordingly, the social text becomes a stage, or a site where power and knowledge are presented. This means, third, we must explore alternative ways of presenting and authorizing our texts.

Lather (1993) then turns to a discussion of five new forms of validity, different ways of authorizing a text. These new forms are called reflexive, ironic, neopragmatic, rhizomatic, and situated validity. Each enacts a multivoiced, reflexive, open-ended, emotionally based text that is action, or praxis, based. For Lather and others in this tradition, theory is interpretation. There is no break between empirical activity (gathering empirical materials, reading social texts) and theorizing. Theory as interpretation is always anchored in the texts that it analyzes and reads. Conceptualizing theory-as-interpretation or theory-as-criticism means that the writer employs a style that immediately connects a theoretical term to its referent. For example, ideology is given in a popular culture text, or desire is present in a Madonna pose. Rosaldo (1989) provides an example; here the text merges with its subject matter—criticism and interpretation are not separated:

> My anger at recent films that portray imperialism with nostalgia informs this chapter. Consider the enthusiastic reception of *Heat and Dust, A Passage to India, Out of Africa,* and *The Gods Must Be Crazy.* The white colonial societies portrayed in these films appear decorous and orderly, as if constructed in accord with the norms of classic ethnography. . . . Evidently a mood of nostalgia makes racial domination appear innocent and pure. (p. 68)

Style 3: Interpretive Interactionism

I turn now to a brief exposition of another interpretive style, what I have elsewhere termed *interpretive interactionism* (Denzin, 1989). Interpretive research begins and ends with the biography and the self of the researcher. The events and troubles that are written about are ones the writer has already experienced and witnessed firsthand. The task is to produce "richly detailed" inscriptions and accounts of such experiences.

The focus of the research is on those life experiences (epiphanies) that radically alter and shape the meanings persons give to themselves and their life projects. In epiphanies, personal character is manifested and made apparent. By recording these experiences in detail, and by listening to the stories people tell about them, the researcher is able to illuminate the moments of crisis that occur in a person's life. Having had such experiences, the individual is often never quite the same again. (Examples of epiphanies include religious conversions, divorces, incidents of family violence, rape, incest, murder, and loss of a job.)

Sartre's (1963, pp. 85-166) progressive-regressive method of analysis organizes the interpretive process. The investigator situates a subject, or class of subjects, within a given historical moment. Progressively, the method looks forward to the conclusion of a set of acts or experiences undertaken by the subject. Regressively, the method works back in time to the historical, gender, class, race, cultural, biographical, and emotional conditions that moved the subject forward into the experience that is being studied.

Interpretive materials are evaluated by their ability to illuminate phenomena as lived experience. Such materials should be based on thickly contextualized materials that are historical, relational, and processual. The core of these materials will be the personal experience stories subjects tell one another. These stories should be connected to larger institutional, group, and cultural contexts, including written texts and other systems of discourse (cinema, music, folklore). The understandings that are put forth should engulf all that has been learned about the phenomenon. The moral biases that organize the research should be made evident to the reader. The competing models of truth and interpretation (rationality and emotionality) that operate in the subject's situations should be revealed. The stories that are presented to readers should be given in the language, feelings, emotions, and actions of those studied.[14]

Criticisms of Poststructuralism

Poststructural, postmodern, feminist texts have been criticized because of their interpretive criteria. Critics complain that there is no way to evaluate such work because traditional, external standards of evaluation (internal and external validity, reliability, objectivity) are not followed. This means, the argument goes, that there is no way to evaluate a good or bad poststructural, feminist text. Others argue that the feminist and poststructural text imposes an interpretive framework on the world, and does not allow subjects to speak. These criticisms come, of course, from the positivist and postpositivist traditions.

These criticisms are rejected on several grounds. First, they are seen as not reflecting an understanding of the new postmodern sensibility, which doubts and challenges any attempt to legitimate a text in terms of positivist or postpositivist criteria. Such criteria represent attempts to bring legitimacy and authority to the scientific project. Science, in its traditional forms, is the problem. Knowledge produced under the guise of objective science is too often used for purposes of social control (Clough, 1992, p. 134). The criteria of evaluation that poststructuralists employ answer to a different set of problems and to a different project. They seek a morally informed social criticism, a sacred version of science that is humane, caring, holistic, and action based (see Reason, 1993; see also Lincoln & Denzin, Chapter 36, this volume).

Poststructuralists celebrate uncertainty and attempt to construct texts that do not impose theoretical frameworks on the world. They seek to let the prose of the world speak for itself, while they remain mindful of all the difficulties involved in such a commitment. They, more than their postpositivist counterparts, are sensitive to voice and to multiple perspectives.

Multiple Interpretive Communities

There are many ways to move from the field to the text, many ways to inscribe and describe experience. There are multiple interpretive communities that now circulate within the many terrains of qualitative research. These communities take different stances on the topics treated above, including the matters of writing, description, inscription, interpretation, understanding, representation, legitimation, textual desire, and the logic and politics of the text.

A simplistic approach to the many paradigm dialogues that are now occurring (Guba, 1990a) might use the old-fashioned distinctions between humanists and scientists, between the "tender-minded" and the "tough-minded," to borrow William James's (1908/1978, pp. 10-13) terms. Such distinctions are displayed in Table 31.1. But critical analysis soon makes this pretty picture messy. On the surface, critical, emancipatory, feminist, interactional, poststructural, and postmodern researchers belong to the tender-minded interpretive community. Following James, they are more intuitive, emotional, and open-ended in their interpretive work. Some are quite dogmatic about this. But many critical theorists write realist texts, are hard-nosed empiricists, work within closed theoretical systems, and follow the canons of good science.

In the same vein, positivists, postpositivists, grounded theorists, and constructivists appear to belong to the tough-minded interpretive community. They are hard-nosed empiricists, system builders, often pluralistic in their use of theory, and skeptical of nonsystematic theory and empirical work. But there are feminists who use grounded

TABLE 31.1 Two Interpretive Communities

Tender-Minded	*Tough-Minded*
Intuitive	Hard-nosed empiricists
Emotional	Rational, cognitive
Open-ended texts	Closed texts, systems
Interpretation as art	Interpretation as method
Personal biases	Neutrality
Experimental texts	Traditional texts
Antirealism	Realist texts
Antifoundational	Foundational
Criticism	Substantive theory
Science-as-power	Good science canons
Multivoiced texts	Single-voiced texts

theory methods and produce traditional-looking texts, based on foundational criteria. There are tough-minded constructivists who are antirealist and antifoundational, and who regard interpretation as more art than method.

Clearly, simplistic classifications do not work. Any given qualitative researcher-as-*bricoleur* can be more than one thing at the same time, can be fitted into both the tender- and the tough-minded categories. It is clear that in the fifth (and sixth) moments of qualitative research, the concerns from each of James's two communities work alongside and inform one another. Accordingly, it can be argued that the following contradictory understandings operate in this broad field we have called qualitative research.

Interpretation is an art that cannot be formalized. Scholars are increasingly concerned with the logic of the text, especially the problems involved in presenting lived experience and the point of view of the Other. Many are preoccupied with the biases in the emotional stories they tell and are drawn to experimental forms of writing; some reject mainstream narrative realism. It is common for texts now to be grounded in antifoundational systems of discourse (local knowledge, local emotions). These texts tell emancipatory stories grounded in race, class, and gender. Personal experience is a major source of empirical material for many, as are cultural texts and materials gathered via the ethnographic method. More than a few researchers expose their writerly selves in first-person accounts, and many are attempting to produce reader-friendly, multivoiced texts that speak to the worlds of lived experience. It is becoming commonplace for qualitative researchers to be advocates of the moral communities they represent, while attempting to participate directly in social change.

At the same time, there are those who remain committed to mainstream realism. They write texts that adhere to complex sets of methodological principles connected to postpositivist foundational systems of meaning ("good science"). Their texts are grounded in concrete empirical materials (case studies) and are inductively interpreted through the methods of grounded theory or variations thereof. Existing theories, both substantive and formal, structure inquiry, which is organized in a rigorous, stepwise manner.

Finally, there are conflicting views and disagreements on the very topic of interpretation itself. The immediate, local, personal, emotional biases of many lead them to tell stories that work outward from the self to society. These writers are writing to make sense of their own lives. Others write to make sense of "another's" life. In the end it is a matter of storytelling and the stories we tell each other.

Into the Future

Of course, persons who do interpretations feel uncomfortable doing predictions. But where the field of interpretation, the art and politics of telling stories, will be in 10 years should be addressed. If the past predicts the future, and if the decade of the 1980s and the first half of the 1990s are to be taken seriously, then interpretation is moving more and more deeply into the regions of the postmodern sensibility. A new postconstructivist paradigm may emerge. This framework may attach itself to a new and less foundational postpositivism and a more expansive critical theory framework built on modified grounded theory principles.

Epistemologies of color will proliferate, building on Afrocentric (Collins), Chicana (Rosaldo, Chabram-Daernersesian, Anzaldua), Native American, Asian (Trinh T. Minh-ha), Third World (Spivak), and other minority group perspectives. More elaborated epistemologies of gender (and class) will appear, including "queer theory" (Seidman, 1993), and feminisms of color. These interpretive communities will draw on their minority group experiences as the basis of the texts they write, and they will seek texts that speak to the logic and cultures of these communities.

These race-, ethnicity-, and gender-specific interpretive communities will fashion interpretive criteria out of their interactions with the postpositivist, constructivist, critical theory, and poststructural sensibilities. These criteria will be emic, existential, political, and emotional. They will push the personal to the forefront of the political, where the social text becomes the vehicle for the expression of politics.

This projected proliferation of interpretive communities does not mean that the field of qualitative research will splinter into warring factions, or into groups that cannot speak to one another. Underneath the complexities and contradictions that define this field rest three common commitments. The first reflects the belief that the world of human experience must be studied from the point of view of the historically and culturally situated individual. Second, qualitative researchers will persist in working outward from their own biographies to the worlds of experience that surround them. Third, scholars will continue to value and seek to produce works that speak clearly and powerfully about these worlds. To echo Raymond Carver (1989, p. 24), the real experimenters will always be those who Make it New, who find things out for themselves, and who want to carry this News from their world to ours.

And so the stories we tell one another will change and the criteria for reading stories will also change. And this is how it should be. The good stories are always told by those who have learned well the stories of the past, but who are unable to tell them any longer because those stories no longer speak to them, or to us.

Notes

1. Here I deal with the constructivism of Guba and Lincoln, not the social constructionism of Gergen. Schwandt (Chapter 7, this volume) compares and contrasts these two frameworks.

2. See the relevant chapters in this volume that take up each of these traditions, including those by Fine (Chapter 4), Guba and Lincoln (Chapter 6), Schwandt (Chapter 7), Kincheloe and McLaren (Chapter 8), Olesen (Chapter 9), Fiske (Chapter 11), Atkinson and Hammersley (Chapter 15), Holstein and Gubrium (Chapter 16), Strauss and Corbin (Chapter 17), Altheide and Johnson (Chapter 30), Richardson (Chapter 32), and Marcus (Chapter 35).

3. Rosaldo (1989) argues that anthropological doctrine presents this as a three-step process, involving preparation, knowledge, and sensibility, but cautions that "one should work to undermine the false comfort it can convey. At what point can people say that they have completed their learning or life experience?" (p. 8).

4. Mitch Allen and Yvonna Lincoln clarified these steps for me.

5. Yvonna Lincoln suggests that this may have been less the case in earlier historical moments, when realist tales were organized in terms of well-understood conventions.

6. I am deeply indebted to Meaghan Morris for her help in clarifying the meanings in this section.

7. Elsewhere I have offered a typology of descriptions and interpretations, including descriptions that are primarily micro, macro, biographical, situational, interactional-relational, incomplete, glossed, pure, and interpretive, and interpretations that are thin, thick, native, observer based, analytic, descriptive-contextual, and relational-interactive (Denzin, 1989, pp. 99, 111-120).

8. The Whyte-Boelen exchange is similar, in these respects, to earlier controversies in this area, including the famous Redfield-Sanchez and Mead-Freeman debates over who got it right—the original, classic study or the reinvestigation of the same site by a later researcher.

9. Mainstream, interpretive, and descriptive realist stories may be supplemented by more traditional and experimental formats, including confessional ("the problems I encountered doing my study") and impressionistic ("dramatic and vivid pictures from the field") tales of the field (Van Maanen, 1988), as well as personal memoirs of the field experience (Stoller & Olkes, 1987), narratives of the self (see Ellis & Bochner, 1992; Ellis & Flaherty, 1992; Ronai, 1992), fiction texts (Stewart, 1989), and ethnographic dramas and performance texts (McCall & Becker, 1990; Richardson & Lockridge, 1991; for a review, see Richardson, Chapter 32, this volume).

10. These, of course, are my interpretations of these interpretive styles. The reader should also consult the presentation of these paradigms in Chapter 6 of this volume, by Guba and Lincoln, as well as Chapter 1.

11. The presence is greatest, perhaps, in education, the health sciences, and communication, but also in sociology, less so in anthropology. When one peels back the layers of discourse embedded in any of the numerous qualitative guides to interpretation and theory construction, the core features of the Strauss approach are present, even when Strauss and associates are not directly named.

12. It argues that the facts for any theory are always interpreted and value laden, that no theory can ever be fully tested (or grounded), and an interactive relationship always exists between the observer and the observed. A dialectical, dialogic hermeneutic posture organizes inquiry that is based on thick descriptions of action and subjective experience in natural situations.

13. Specific strategies and criteria are attached to each of these components. Credibility is increased through prolonged field engagement, persistent observation, triangulation, peer debriefing, negative case analysis, referential analysis (Eisner's term for cinematic methods that provide a record of social life), and member checks (talking to people in the field). Thick description provides for transferability, whereas dependability can be enhanced through the use of overlapping methods, stepwise replications, and inquiry (dependability) audits (the use of well-informed subjects) (Lincoln & Guba, 1985, p. 316). Confirmability builds on audit trails (a "residue of records stemming from inquiry"; p. 319) and involves the use of written field notes, memos, a field diary, process and personal notes, and a reflexive journal.

14. The five steps to interpretation (Denzin, 1989, p. 27) should be followed: deconstruction, capture, bracketing, construction, contextualization.

References

Argyris, C., & Schön, D. A. (1974). *Theory in practice.* San Francisco: Jossey-Bass.

Bakhtin, M. M. (1986). *Speech genres and other essays.* Austin: University of Texas Press.

Barthes, R. (1975). *The pleasure of the text.* New York: Hill & Wang.

Becker, H. S. (1986). *Writing for social scientists: How to start and finish your thesis, book, or article.* Chicago: University of Chicago Press.

Boelen, W. A. M. (1992). *Street Corner Society*: Cornerville revisited. *Journal of Contemporary Ethnography, 21,* 11-51.

Brady, I. (Ed.). (1991). Introduction. In I. Brady (Ed.), *Anthropological poetics* (pp. 3-36). Savage, MD: Rowman & Littlefield.

Bruner, E. M., & Gorfain, P. (1991). Dialogic narration and the paradoxes of Masada. In I. Brady (Ed.), *Anthropological poetics* (pp. 177-206). Savage, MD: Rowman & Littlefield.

Carspecken, P. F., & Apple, M. (1992). Critical research: Theory, methodology, and practice. In M. D. LeCompte, W. L. Millroy, & J. Preissle (Eds.), *The handbook of qualitative research in education* (pp. 507-554). New York: Academic Press.

Carver, R. (1989). *Fires.* New York: Vantage.

Clough, P. T. (1992). *The end(s) of ethnography: From realism to social criticism.* Newbury Park, CA: Sage.

Collins, P. H. (1990). *Black feminist thought: Knowledge, consciousness and the politics of empowerment.* New York: Routledge.

Denzin, N. K. (1989). *Interpretive interactionism.* Newbury Park, CA: Sage.

Denzin, N. K. (1990). Harold and Agnes: A feminist narrative undoing. *Sociological Theory, 8,* 198-216.

Dilthey, W. L. (1976). *Selected writings.* Cambridge, UK: Cambridge University Press. (Original work published 1900)

Ellis, C., & Flaherty, M. G. (Eds.). (1992). *Investigating subjectivity: Research on lived experience.* Newbury Park, CA: Sage.

Ellis, C., & Bochner, A. P. (1992). Telling and performing personal stories: The constraints of choice in abortion. In C. Ellis & M. G. Flaherty (Eds.), *Investigating subjectivity: Research on lived experience* (pp. 79-101). Newbury Park, CA: Sage.

Fish, S. (1980). *Is there a text in this class? The authority of interpretive communities.* Cambridge, MA: Harvard University Press.

Freire, P. (1982). *Pedagogy of the oppressed.* New York: Continuum.

Fonow, M. M., & Cook, J. A. (1991). Back to the future: A look at the second wave of feminist epistemology and methodology. In M. M. Fonow & J. A. Cook (Eds.), *Beyond methodology: Feminist scholarship as lived research* (pp. 1-15). Bloomington: Indiana University Press.

Geertz, C. (1973). *The interpretation of cultures: Selected essays.* New York: Basic Books.

Geertz, C. (1983). *Local knowledge: Further essays in interpretive anthropology.* New York: Basic Book.

Geertz, C. (1988). *Works and lives: The anthropologist as author.* Stanford, CA: Stanford University Press.

Gerson, E. M. (1991). Supplementing grounded theory. In D. R. Maines (Ed.), *Social organization and social process: Essays in honor of Anselm Strauss* (pp. 285-302). New York: Aldine de Gruyter.

Guba, E. G. (1990a). The alternative paradigm dialog. In E. G. Guba (Ed.), *The paradigm dialog* (pp. 17-30). Newbury Park, CA: Sage.

Guba, E. G. (1990b). Carrying on the dialog. In E. G. Guba (Ed.), *The paradigm dialog* (pp. 368-378). Newbury Park, CA: Sage.

Guba, E. G., & Lincoln, Y. S. (1989). *Fourth generation evaluation.* Newbury Park, CA: Sage.

Hammersley, M. (1992). *What's wrong with ethnography? Methodological explorations.* London: Routledge.

hooks, b. (1990). *Yearning: Race, gender, and cultural politics.* Boston: South End.

James, W. (1978). *Pragmatism and the meaning of truth.* Cambridge, MA: Harvard University Press. (Original work published 1908)

Krieger, S. (1991). *Social science and the self: Personal essays as an art form.* New Brunswick, NJ: Rutgers University Press.

Lather, P. (1991). *Getting smart: Feminist research and pedagogy with/in the postmodern.* New York: Routledge.

Lather, P. (1993). Fertile obsession: Validity after poststructuralism. *Sociological Quarterly, 35.*

Lincoln, Y. S. (1990). The making of a constructivist: A remembrance of transformations past. In E. G. Guba (Ed.), *The paradigm dialog* (pp. 67-87). Newbury Park, CA: Sage.

Lincoln, Y. S., & Guba, E. G. (1985). *Naturalistic inquiry.* Beverly Hills, CA: Sage.

Lévi-Strauss, C. (1966). *The savage mind* (2nd ed.). Chicago: University of Chicago Press.

McCall, M., & Becker, H. S. (1990). Performance science. *Social Problems, 32,* 117-132.

Plath, D. (1990). Fieldnotes, filed notes, and the conferring of note. In R. Sanjek (Ed.), *Fieldnotes: The makings of anthropology* (pp. 371-384). Albany: State University of New York Press.

Prus, R. C. (1991). *Road hustler* (exp. ed.). New York: Steranko.

Quantz, R. A. (1992). On critical ethnography (with some postmodern considerations). In M. D. LeCompte, W. L. Millroy, & J. Preissle (Eds.), *The handbook of qualitative research in education* (pp. 447-505). New York: Academic Press.

Reason, P. (1993). Sacred experience and sacred science. *Journal of Management Inquiry, 2,* 10-27.

Reinharz, S. (1992). *Feminist methods in social research.* New York: Oxford University Press.

Richardson, L. (1990). *Writing strategies.* Newbury Park, CA: Sage.

Richardson, L. (1991). Postmodern social theory: Representational practices. *Sociological Theory, 9,* 173-179.

Richardson, L. (1992). The consequences of poetic representation: Writing the other, rewriting the self. In C. Ellis & M. G. Flaherty (Eds.), *Investigating subjectivity: Research on lived experience* (pp. 125-137). Newbury Park, CA: Sage.

Richardson, L., & Lockridge, E. (1991). The sea monster: An ethnographic drama. *Symbolic Interaction, 14,* 335-340.

Ricoeur, P. (1985). *Time and narrative* (Vol. 2). Chicago: University of Chicago Press.

Roman, L. G. (1992). The political significance of other ways of narrating ethnography: A feminist materialist approach. In M. D. LeCompte, W. L. Millroy, & J. Preissle (Eds.), *The handbook of qualitative research in education* (pp. 555-594). New York: Academic Press.

Ronai, C. R. (1992). The reflexive self through narrative: A night in the life of an erotic dancer/researcher. In C. Ellis & M. G. Flaherty (Eds.), *Investigating subjectivity: Research on lived experience* (pp. 102-124). Newbury Park, CA: Sage.

Rosaldo, R. (1989). *Culture and truth: The remaking of social analysis.* Boston: Beacon.

Rose, D. (1990). *Living the ethnographic life.* Newbury Park, CA: Sage.

Ryle, G. (1968). *The thinking of thoughts* (University Lectures, No. 18). Saskatoon: University of Saskatchewan.

Sanjek, R. (1990). *Fieldnotes: The makings of anthropology.* Albany: State University of New York Press.

Sartre, J.-P. (1963). *Search for a method.* New York: Alfred A. Knopf.

Seidman, S. (1991). The end of sociological theory: The postmodern hope. *Sociological Theory, 9,* 131-146.

Seidman, S. (1993). *Embattled Eros: Sexual politics and ethics in contemporary America.* New York: Routledge.

Smith, D. (1992). Sociology from women's perspective: A reaffirmation. *Sociological Theory, 10,* 88-97.

Stake, R. (1983). The case study method in social inquiry. In G. Madaus, M. Scriven, & D. Stufflebeam (Eds.), *Evaluation models* (pp. 279-286). Boston: Kluwer-Nijhoff.

Star, S. L. (1991). The sociology of the invisible: The primacy of work in the writings of Anselm Strauss. In D. R. Maines (Ed.), *Social organization and social process: Essays in honor of Anselm Strauss* (pp. 265-284). New York: Aldine de Gruyter.

Stewart, J. (1989). *Drinkers, drummers and decent folk: Ethnographic narratives of Village Trinidad.* Albany: State University of New York Press.

Stoller, P., & Olkes, C. (1987). *In sorcery's shadow.* Chicago: University of Chicago Press.

Strauss, A. L., & Corbin, J. (1990). *Basics of qualitative research: Grounded theory procedures and techniques.* Newbury Park, CA: Sage.

Todorov, T. (1977). *The poetics of prose.* Ithaca, NY: Cornell University Press.

Ulmer, G. (1989). *Teletheory.* New York: Routledge.

Van Maanen, J. (1988). *Tales of the field: On writing ethnography.* Chicago: University of Chicago Press.

Whyte, W. F. (1943). *Street corner society: The social structure of an Italian slum.* Chicago: University of Chicago Press.

Whyte, W. F. (1992). In defense of *Street Corner Society. Journal of Contemporary Ethnography, 21,* 52-68.

Wolcott, H. F. (1990). *Writing up qualitative research.* Newbury Park, CA: Sage.

Woods, P. (1992). Symbolic interactionism: Theory and method. In M. D. LeCompte, W. L. Millroy, & J. Preissle (Eds.), *The handbook of qualitative research in education* (pp. 336-404). New York: Academic Press.

32

■

Writing
A Method of Inquiry

LAUREL RICHARDSON

> *The writer's object is—or should be—to hold the reader's attention. . . .*
> *I want the reader to turn the page and keep on turning to the end.*
> Barbara Tuchman, *New York Times,* February 2, 1989

IN the spirit of affectionate irreverence toward qualitative research, I consider writing as a *method of inquiry,* a way of finding out about yourself and your topic. Although we usually think about writing as a mode of "telling" about the social world, writing is not just a mopping-up activity at the end of a research project. Writing is also a way of "knowing"—a method of discovery and analysis. By writing in different ways, we discover new aspects of our topic and our relationship to it. Form and content are inseparable.

I have composed this chapter into two *equally* important, but differently formatted, sections. I emphasize the *equally* because the first section, an essay, has rhetorical advantages over its later-born sibling. In the first section, "Writing in Contexts," I position myself as a reader/writer of qualitative research. Then, I discuss (a) the historical roots of social scientific writing, including its dependence upon metaphor and prescribed formats, and (b) the postmodernist possibilities for qualitative writing, including experimental representation. In the second section, "Writing Practices," I offer a compendium of writing suggestions and exercises organized around topics in the text.

Necessarily, the chapter reflects my own process and preferences. I encourage researchers to explore their own processes and preferences through writing—and rewriting and rewriting. Writing from our Selves should strengthen the community of qualitative researchers and the individual voices within it, because we will be more fully present in our work, more honest, more engaged.

Writing in Contexts

I have a confession to make. For 30 years, I have yawned my way through numerous supposedly exemplary qualitative studies. Countless numbers of texts have I abandoned half read, half

AUTHOR'S NOTE: I thank Ernest Lockridge for reading this chapter multiple times. I also thank Arthur Bochner, Norman Denzin, Carolyn Ellis, Michelle Fine, Yvonna Lincoln, Meaghan Morris, and John Van Maanen for their readings of earlier versions of this chapter and Barrie Thorne for her suggestions.

scanned. I'll order a new book with great anticipation—the topic is one I'm interested in, the author is someone I want to read—only to find the text boring. Recently, I have been "coming out" to colleagues and students about my secret displeasure with much of qualitative writing, only to find a community of like-minded discontents. Undergraduates are disappointed that sociology is not more interesting; graduate students confess that they do not finish reading what has been assigned because it is boring; and colleagues express relief to be at long last discussing qualitative research's own dirty little secret: Our empire is (partially) unclothed.

Speaking of this, and in this way, risks identifying my thoughts with that dreadful genre, *putdownism.* But that is not the emotional core or intention of my remarks. Rather, I want to raise a serious problem. Although our topics often are riveting and our research carefully executed, our books are underread. Unlike quantitative work, which can carry its meaning in its tables and summaries, qualitative work depends upon people's reading it. Just as a piece of literature is not equivalent to its "plot summary," qualitative research is not contained in its abstracts. Qualitative research has to be read, not scanned; its meaning is in the reading.

Qualitative work could be reaching wide and diverse audiences, not just devotees of the topic or the author. It seems foolish at best, and narcissistic and wholly self-absorbed at worst, to spend months or years doing research that ends up not being read and not making a difference to anything but the author's career. Can something be done? That is the question that drives this chapter: How do we create texts that are vital? That are attended to? That make a difference? One way to create those texts is to turn our attention to writing as a method of inquiry.

I write because I want to find something out. I write in order to learn something that I didn't know before I wrote it. I was taught, however, as perhaps you were, too, not to write until I knew what I wanted to say, until my points were organized and outlined. No surprise, this static writing model coheres with mechanistic scientism and quantitative research. But, I will argue, the model is itself a sociohistorical invention that reifies the static social world imagined by our nineteenth-century foreparents. The model has serious problems: It ignores the role of writing as a dynamic, creative process; it undermines the confidence of beginning qualitative researchers because their experience of research is inconsistent with the writing model; and it contributes to the flotilla of qualitative writing that is simply not interesting to read because adherence to the model requires writers to silence their own voices and to view themselves as contaminants.

Qualitative researchers commonly speak of the importance of the individual researcher's skills and aptitudes. The researcher—rather than the survey, the questionnaire, or the census tape—is the "instrument." The more honed the researcher, the greater the possibility of "good" research. Students are trained to observe, listen, question, and participate. Yet they are trained to conceptualize writing as "writing up" the research, rather than as a method of discovery. Almost unthinkingly, qualitative research training validates the mechanistic model of writing, even though that model shuts down the creativity and sensibilities of the individual researcher.

One reason, then, that our texts are boring is that our sense of self is diminished as we are homogenized through professional socialization, through rewards and punishments. Homogenization occurs through the suppression of individual voices. We have been encouraged to take on the omniscient voice of science, the view from everywhere. How do we put ourselves in our own texts, and with what consequences? How do we nurture our own individuality and at the same time lay claim to "knowing" something? These are both philosophically and practically difficult problems.

Postmodernist Context

We are fortunate, now, to be working in a postmodernist climate (see, e.g., Agger, 1990; Lehman, 1991; Lyotard, 1979). Postmodernism has affected all the disciplines and has gained ascendancy in the humanities, arts, philosophy, and the natural sciences. Disciplinary boundaries are regularly broken. Literary studies are about sociological questions; social scientists write fiction; sculptors do performance art; choreographers do sociology; and so on. (See, for literary criticism, Eagleton, 1983; Morris, 1988. For philosophy, see Hutcheon, 1988; Rorty, 1979; Nicholson, 1990. For physics, Gleick, 1984. For mathematics, Kline, 1980. For arts, Trinh, 1989. For communications, Carey, 1989. For social sciences, Clifford & Marcus, 1986; Clough, 1992; Denzin, 1986, 1991; Fiske & Schweder, 1986; Geertz, 1983; Marcus & Fischer, 1986; Richardson, 1991; Seidman & Wagner, 1991; Turner & Bruner, 1986. For education, Lather, 1991.)

The core of postmodernism is the *doubt* that any method or theory, discourse or genre, tradition or novelty, has a universal and general claim as the "right" or the privileged form of authoritative knowledge. Postmodernism *suspects* all truth claims of masking and serving particular interests in local, cultural, and political struggles. But postmodernism does not automatically reject conventional methods of knowing and telling as false or archaic. Rather, it opens those standard methods to inquiry and introduces new methods, which are also, then, subject to critique.

The postmodernist context of doubt distrusts all methods equally. No method has a privileged status. The superiority of "science" over "literature"—or, from another vantage point, "literature" over "science"—is challenged. But a postmodernist position does allow us to know "something" without claiming to know everything. Having a partial, local, historical knowledge is still knowing. In some ways, "knowing" is easier, however, because postmodernism recognizes the situational limitations of the knower. Qualitative writers are off the hook, so to speak. They don't have to try to play God, writing as disembodied omniscient narrators claiming universal, atemporal general knowledge; they can eschew the questionable metanarrative of scientific objectivity and still have plenty to say as situated speakers, subjectivities engaged in knowing/telling about the world as they perceive it.

A particular kind of postmodernist thinking that I have found especially helpful is *poststructuralism* (for an overview, see Weedon, 1987). Poststructuralism links language, subjectivity, social organization, and power. The centerpiece is language. Language does not "reflect" social reality, but produces meaning, creates social reality. Different languages and different discourses within a given language divide up the world and give it meaning in ways that are not reducible to one another. Language is how social organization and power are defined and contested and the place where our sense of selves, our *subjectivity,* is constructed. Understanding language as competing discourses, competing ways of giving meaning and of organizing the world, makes language a site of exploration, struggle.

Language is not the result of one's individuality; rather, language constructs the individual's subjectivity in ways that are historically and locally specific. What something means to individuals is dependent on the discourses available to them. For example, being hit by one's spouse is experienced differently if it is thought of within the discourse of "normal marriage," "husband's rights," or "wife battering." If a woman sees male violence as "normal" or a "husband's right," then she is unlikely to see it as "wife battering," an illegitimate use of power that should not be tolerated. Experience is thus open to contradictory interpretations governed by social interests rather than objective truth. The individual is both site and subject of discursive struggles for identity. Because the individual is subject to multiple and competing discourses in many realms, one's subjectivity is shifting and contradictory, not stable, fixed, rigid.

Poststructuralism thus points to the *continual cocreation of Self and social science*; they are known through each other. Knowing the Self and knowing "about" the subject are intertwined, partial, historical, local knowledges. Poststructuralism, then, permits—nay, invites—no, incites us to reflect upon our method and explore new ways of knowing.

Specifically, poststructuralism suggests two important things to qualitative writers: First, it directs us to understand ourselves reflexively as persons writing from particular positions at specific times; and second, it frees us from trying to write a single text in which everything is said to everyone. Nurturing our own voices releases the censorious hold of "science writing" on our consciousness, as well as the arrogance it fosters in our psyche. Writing is validated as a method of knowing.

Historical Contexts: Writing Conventions

Language, then, is a constitutive force, creating a particular view of reality and of the Self. Producing "things" always involves value—what to produce, what to name the productions, and what the relationship between the producers and the named things will be. Writing "things" is no exception. No textual staging is ever innocent (including this one). Styles of writing are neither fixed nor neutral but reflect the historically shifting domination of particular schools or paradigms.

Having some sense of the history of our writing practices helps us to demystify standard practices and loosen their hold on our psyches. Social scientific writing, like all other forms of writing, is a sociohistorical construction and, therefore, mutable.

Since the seventeenth century, the world of writing has been divided into two separate kinds: literary and scientific. Literature, from the seventeenth century onward, was associated with fiction, rhetoric, and subjectivity, whereas science was associated with fact, "plain language," and objectivity (Clifford, 1986, p. 5). Fiction was "false" because it invented reality, unlike science, which was "true," because it simply "reported" "objective" reality in a single, unambiguous voice.

During the eighteenth century, assaults upon literature intensified. John Locke cautioned adults to forgo figurative language lest the "conduit" between "things" and "thought" be obstructed. David Hume depicted poets as professional liars. Jeremy Bentham proposed that the ideal language would be one without words, only unambiguous symbols. Samuel Johnson's dictionary sought to fix "univocal meanings in perpetuity, much like the univocal meanings of standard arithmetic terms" (Levine, 1985, p. 4).

Into this linguistic world the Marquis de Condorcet introduced the term *social science.* He contended that "knowledge of the truth" would be "easy and error almost impossible" if one adopted precise language about moral and social issues (quoted in Levine, 1985, p. 6). By the nineteenth century, literature and science stood as two separate domains. Literature was aligned with "art" and "culture"; it contained the values of "taste, aesthetics, ethics, humanity, and morality" (Clifford, 1986, p. 6), and the rights to metaphoric and ambiguous language. Given to science was the belief that its words were objective, precise, unambiguous, noncontextual, nonmetaphoric.

But because literary writing was taking a second seat in importance, status, impact, and truth value to science, some literary writers attempted to make literature a part of science. By the late nineteenth century, "realism" dominated both science and fiction writing (Clough, 1992). Honoré de Balzac spearheaded the realism movement in literature. He viewed society as a "historical organism" with "social species" akin to "zoological species." Writers deserving of praise, he contended, must investigate "the reasons or causes" of "social effects"—the "first principles" upon which society is based (Balzac, 1842/1965, pp. 247-249). For Balzac, the novel was an "instrument of scientific inquiry" (Crawford, 1951, p. 7). Following Balzac's lead, Emile Zola argued for "naturalism" in literature. In his famous essay "The Novel as Social Science," he argued that the "return to nature, the naturalistic evolution which marks the century, drives little by little all the manifestation of human intelligence into the same scientific path." Literature is to be "governed by science" (Zola, 1880/1965, p. 271).

Throughout the twentieth century, crossovers—uneasy and easy, denied and acknowledged—have characterized the relationship between science and literary writing. Today, scholars in a host of disciplines are involved in tracing these relationships and in deconstructing scientific and literary writing (see Agger, 1989; Atkinson, 1990; Brodkey, 1987; Brown, 1977; Clough, 1992; Edmondson, 1984; Nelson, Megill, & McCloskey, 1987; Simons, 1990). Their deconstructive analyses concretely show how all disciplines have their own set of literary devices and rhetorical appeals, such as probability tables, archival records, and first-person accounts.

Each writing convention could be discussed at length, but I will discuss only two of them—metaphor and writing formats. I choose these because I believe they are good sites for experimenting with writing as a method of inquiry (see the section "Writing Practices," below). Thinking critically about social science's metaphors and writing formats helps break their brake on our pens and word processors.

Metaphor

A literary device, *metaphor,* is the backbone of social science writing. Like the spine, it bears weight, permits movement, is buried beneath the surface, and links parts together into a functional, coherent whole. As this metaphor about metaphor suggests, the essence of metaphor is the experiencing and understanding of one thing in terms of another. This is accomplished through comparison (e.g., "My love is like a green, green toad") or analogy (e.g., "the evening of life").

Social scientific writing uses metaphors at every "level." Social science depends upon a deep epistemic code regarding the way "that knowledge and understanding in general are figured" (Shapiro, 1985-1986, p. 198). Metaphors external to the particular piece of research prefigure the analysis with a "truth-value" code belonging to another domain (Jameson, 1981). For example, the use of *enlighten* to indicate imparting or gaining knowledge is a light-based metaphor, what Derrida (1982) refers to as the "heliocentric" view of knowledge, the passive receipt of rays. Immanent in these metaphors are philosophical and value commitments so entrenched and familiar that they can do their partisan work in the guise of neutrality, passing as literal.

Consider the following statements about theory (examples inspired by Lakoff & Johnson, 1980, p. 46):

- What is the *foundation* of your theory?
- Your theory needs *support.*
- Your position is *shaky.*
- Your argument is *falling apart.*
- Let's *construct* an argument.
- The *form* of your argument needs buttressing.
- Given your *framework,* no wonder your argument *fell apart.*

The italicized words express our customary, unconscious use of the metaphor, "Theory is a building." The metaphor, moreover, structures the actions we take in theorizing and what we believe constitutes theory. We try to build a theoretical structure, which we then experience as a structure, which has a form and a foundation, which we then experience as an edifice, sometimes quite grand, sometimes in need of shoring up, and sometimes in need of dismantling or, more recently, deconstructing.

Metaphors are everywhere. Consider *functionalism, role* theory, *game* theory, *dramaturgical analogy, organicism, social evolutionism,* the social *system, ecology, labeling* theory, *equilibrium, human capital,* the *power elite, resource mobilization,* ethnic *insurgency, developing* countries, *stratification,* and *significance* tests. Metaphors organize sociological work and affect the interpretations of the "facts"; indeed, facts are interpretable ("make sense") only in terms of their place within a metaphoric structure. The "sense making" is always value constituting—making sense in a particular way, privileging one ordering of the "facts" over others.

Writing Formats

In addition to the metaphoric basis of social scientific writing, there are prescribed writing formats: How we are expected to write affects what we can write about. The referencing system in the social sciences, for example, discourages the use of footnotes, a place for secondary arguments, novel conjectures, and related ideas. Knowledge is constituted as "focused," "problem" (hypothesis) centered, "linear," straightforward. Other thoughts are extraneous. Inductively accomplished research is to be reported deductively; the argument is to be abstracted in 150 words or less; and researchers are to identify explicitly with a theoretical label. Each of these conventions favors—creates and sustains—a particular vision of what constitutes sociological knowledge. The conventions hold tremendous material and symbolic power over social scientists. Using them increases the probability of one's work being accepted into "core" social science journals, but is not *prima facie* evidence of greater—or lesser—truth value or significance than social science writing using other conventions.

Additional social science writing conventions have shaped ethnographies. Needful of distinguishing their work from travelers' and missionaries' reports as well as from imaginative writing, ethnographers adopted an impersonal, third-person voice to explain an "observed phenomenon" and trumpet the authenticity of their representations. John Van Maanen (1988) identifies four conventions used in traditional ethnographies, or what he calls "realist tales." First, there is *experiential author(ity).* The author as an "I" is mostly absent from the text, which talks about the people studied; the author exists only in the preface, establishing "I was there" and "I'm a researcher" credentials. Second, there is *documentary style,* with a plethora of concrete, particular details that presume to represent the typical activity, pattern, or culture member. Third, *the culture members' point of view* is claimed to be presented through their accounts, quotations, explanations, language, cultural clichés, and so on. And fourth, the author claims *interpretive omnipotence.* The ethnographer's "no-nonsense" interpretations of the culture are claimed as valid. Many of the classic books in the social sciences are realist tales. These include Kai Erikson's *Everything in Its Path* (1976), William Foote Whyte's *Street Corner Society* (1943), Elliot Liebow's *Tally's Corner* (1967), and Carol Stack's *All Our Kin* (1974).

Other genres of qualitative writing—such as texts based on life histories or in-depth interviews—have their own sets of traditional conventions (see Mischler, 1991; Richardson, 1990). In these traditional texts, the researcher proves his or her credentials in the introductory or methods section, and writes the body of the text as though the quotations and document snippets are naturally there, genuine evidence for the case being made, rather than selected, pruned, and spruced up for their textual appearance. Like ethnography, the assumption of *scientific authority* is rhetorically displayed in these qualitative texts. Examples of traditional "life-story" texts include Lillian Rubin's *Worlds of Pain* (1976), Sharon Kaufman's *The Ageless Self* (1986), and my own *The New Other Woman* (Richardson, 1985).

Experimental Writing

In the wake of feminist and postmodernist critiques of traditional qualitative writing practices, qualitative work has been appearing in new forms; genres are blurred, jumbled. I think of them as *experimental representations.* Because experiments are experimental, it is difficult to specify their conventions. One practice these experiments have in common, however, is the *violation of prescribed conventions*; they transgress the boundaries of social science writing genres.

Experimental representation is an emergent and transgressive phenomenon. Although some people are uncomfortable with it both as an idea and as a practice, I highly recommend experimental writing as a method of knowing. Because experimentation is taking place in (because of?) the postmodernist context, experimentation can be thought about within that frame. Working within the "ideology of doubt," experimental writers raise and display postmodernist issues. Chief among these are questions of how the author positions the Self as a knower and teller. For the experimental writer, these lead to the intertwined problems of subjectivity/authority/authorship/reflexivity, on the one hand, and representational form, on the other.

Postmodernism claims that writing is always partial, local, and situational, and that our Self is always present, no matter how much we try to suppress it—but only partially present, for in our writing we repress parts of ourselves, too. Working from that premise, we are freed to write material in a variety of ways: to tell and retell. There is no such thing as "getting it right," only "getting it" differently contoured and nuanced. When experimenting with form, ethnographers learn about the topic and about themselves what is unknowable, unimaginable, using prescribed writing formats. So, even if one chooses to write a final paper in a conventional form, experimenting with format is a practical and powerful way to expand one's interpretive skills and to make one's "old" materials "new."

We can deploy different forms for different audiences and different occasions. Some experimentation can be accomplished simply by writing the same piece of research for an academic audience, a trade book audience, and the popular press (see Richardson, 1990). The potential for alternative forms of representation, however, go way beyond those stagings.

Social scientists are now writing "narratives of the self" (e.g., Ellis, 1992, 1993; Geertz, 1988; Kondo, 1990; Krieger, 1991; Ronai, 1992; Steedman, 1986; I. K. Zola, 1983), fiction (see Frohock, 1992; Stewart, 1989; Wolf, 1992), poetry (e.g., Brady, 1991; Diamond, 1981; Patai, 1988; Prattis, 1985; Richardson, 1992a), drama (Ellis & Bochner, 1992; Paget, 1990; Richardson, 1993; Richardson & Lockridge, 1991), "performance science" (McCall & Becker, 1990), "polyvocal texts" (e.g., Butler & Rosenblum, 1991; Krieger, 1983; Schneider, 1991), "responsive readings" (see Richardson, 1992b), "aphorisms" (E. Rose, 1992), comedy and satire (e.g., Barley, 1986, 1988), visual presentations (e.g., Harper, 1987), mixed genres (e.g., Dorst, 1989; Fine, 1992; hooks, 1990; Lather, 1991; Linden, 1992; Pfohl, 1992; D. Rose, 1989; Stoller, 1989; Trinh, 1989; Ulmer, 1989; Walkerdine, 1990; Williams, 1991; Wolf, 1992), and more. It is beyond the scope of this chapter to outline or comment on each of these experimental forms. Instead, I will address a class of experimental genres that deploy literary devices to re-create lived experience and evoke emotional responses. I call these *evocative representations.* I resist providing the reader with snippets from these forms because snippets will not do them justice and because I hope readers will read and experiment for themselves. I do describe some texts, but I have no desire to valorize a new canon. Again, *process* rather than product is the purpose of this chapter.

Evocative experimental forms display interpretive frameworks that demand analysis of themselves as cultural products and as methods for rendering the sociological. Evocative representations are a striking way of seeing through and beyond sociological naturalisms. They are powerful tools in the "writing as analysis" tool chest. Casting sociology into evocative forms reveals the underlying labor of sociological production and its rhetoric, as well as its potential as a human endeavor, because evocative writing touches us where we live, in our bodies. Through it we can experience the self-reflexive and transformational process of self-creation. Trying out evocative forms, we relate differently to our material; we know it differently. We find ourselves attending to feelings, ambiguities, temporal sequences, blurred experiences, and so on; we struggle to find a textual place for ourselves and our doubts and uncertainties.

One form of evocative writing is the *narrative of the self.* This is a highly personalized, revealing text in which an author tells stories about his or her own lived experience. Using dramatic recall, strong metaphors, images, characters, unusual phrasings, puns, subtexts, and allusions, the writer constructs a sequence of events, a "plot," holding back on interpretation, asking the reader to "relive" the events emotionally with the writer. Narratives of the self do not read like traditional ethnography because they use the writing techniques of fiction. They are specific stories of particular events. Accuracy is not the issue; rather, narratives of the self seek to meet literary criteria of coherence, verisimilitude, and interest. Because narratives of the self are staged as imaginative renderings, they allow the field-worker to exaggerate, swagger, entertain, make a point without tedious documentation, relive the experience, and say what might be unsayable in other circumstances. Writing these frankly subjective narratives, ethnographers are somewhat relieved of the problems of speaking for the "Other," because they are the Other in their texts.

In *ethnographic fictional representations,* another evocative form, writers define their work as fiction, as products of the imagination. The writers are seeking a format in which to tell a "good story"; that story might be about the self, but more likely it is about the group or culture studied. In addition to the techniques used by self-narrators, ethnographic fiction writers draw upon other devices, such as flashback, flashforward, alternative points of view, deep characterization, tone shifts, synecdoche, dialogue, interior monologue, and, sometimes, even the omniscient narrator. The ethnographic setting encases the story, the cultural norms are seen through the characters, but the work is understood as fiction. Although writing up qualitative research as fiction frees the author from the constraints of science, competing with "real" fiction writers is chancy. And if the author wants the work to have an impact for social change, fiction may be a rhetorically poor way to stage the research. But it may just be a good way for the writer to see the material from different points of view.

A third evocative form is *poetic representation.* A poem, as Robert Frost articulates it, is "the shortest emotional distance between two points"—the speaker and the reader. Writing sociological interviews as poetry displays the role of the *prose trope* in constituting knowledge. When we read or hear poetry, we are continually nudged into recognizing that the text has been constructed. But all texts are constructed—prose ones, too; therefore, poetry helps problematize reliability, validity, and "truth."

When people talk, whether as conversants, storytellers, informants, or interviewees, their speech is closer to poetry than it is to sociological prose (Tedlock, 1983). Writing up interviews as poems honors the speaker's pauses, repetitions, alliterations, narrative strategies, rhythms, and so on. Poetry may actually better represent the speaker than the practice of quoting snippets in prose. Further, poetry's rhythms, silences, spaces, breath points, alliterations, meter, cadence, assonance, rhyme, and off-rhyme engage the listener's body, even when the mind resists and denies it. "Poetry is above all a concentration of the power of language which is the power of our ultimate relationship to everything in the universe. It is as if forces we can lay claim to in no other way become present to us in sensuous form" (DeShazer, 1986, p. 138). Settling words together in new configurations lets us hear, see, and feel the world in new dimensions. Poetry is thus a *practical* and *powerful* method for analyzing social worlds.

Ethnographic drama is a fourth evocative genre. Drama is a way of shaping an experience without losing the experience; it can blend realist, fictional, and poetic techniques; it can reconstruct the "sense" of an event from multiple "as-lived" perspectives; and it can give voice to what is unspoken, but present, such as "cancer," as portrayed in Paget's (1990) ethnographic drama, or abortion, as in Ellis and Bochner's (1992) drama. When the material to be displayed is intractable, unruly, multisited, and emotionally laden, drama is more likely to recapture the experience than is standard writing.

Constructing drama raises the postmodern debate about "oral" and "written" texts. Which comes first? Which one should be (is) privileged, and with what consequences? Why the bifurcation between "oral" and "written"? Originating in the lived experience, encoded as field notes, transformed into an ethnographic play, performed, tape-recorded, and then reedited for publication, the printed script might well be fancied the definitive or "valid" version, particularly by those who privilege the published over the "original" or the performance over the lived experience. What happens if we accept this validity claim? Dramatic construction provides multiple sites of invention and potential contestation for validity, the blurring of oral and written texts, rhetorical moves, ethical dilemmas, and authority/authorship. It doesn't just "talk about" these issues, it *is* these issues.

A last evocative form to consider is *mixed genres*. The scholar draws freely in his or her productions from literary, artistic, and scientific genres, often breaking the boundaries of each of those as well. In these productions, the scholar might have different "takes" on the same topic, what I think of as a postmodernist deconstruction of triangulation.

In traditionally staged research we valorize "triangulation" (for discussion of triangulation as method, see Denzin, 1978; for an example, see Statham, Richardson, & Cook, 1991). In that process, a researcher deploys "different methods"—such as interviews, exploration of census data, and document checking—to "validate" findings. These methods, however, carry the *same domain* assumptions, including the assumption that there is a "fixed point" or "object" that can be triangulated. But in postmodernist mixed-genre texts, we do not triangulate; we *crystallize*. We recognize that there are far more than "three sides" from which to approach the world.

I propose that the central image for "validity" for postmodernist texts is not the triangle—a rigid, fixed, two-dimensional object. Rather, the central image is the crystal, which combines symmetry and substance with an infinite variety of shapes, substances, transmutations, multidimensionalities, and angles of approach. Crystals grow, change, alter, but are not amorphous.

Crystals are prisms that reflect externalities and refract within themselves, creating different colors, patterns, arrays, casting off in different directions. What we see depends upon our angle of repose. Not triangulation, crystallization. In postmodernist mixed-genre texts, we have moved from plane geometry to light theory, where light can be both waves and particles.

Crystallization, without losing structure, deconstructs the traditional idea of "validity" (we feel how there is no single truth, we see how texts validate themselves); and crystallization provides us with a deepened, complex, thoroughly partial, understanding of the topic. Paradoxically, we know more and doubt what we know.

We see this crystallization process in several recent books. Margery Wolf, in *A Thrice-Told Tale* (1992), takes the same event and tells it as fictional story, field notes, and a social scientific paper. John Stewart, in *Drinkers, Drummers and Decent Folk* (1989), writes poetry, fiction, ethnographic accounts, and field notes about Village Trinidad. Valerie Walkerdine's *Schoolgirl Fictions* (1990) develops/displays the theme that "masculinity and femininity are fictions which take on the status of fact" (p. xiii) by incorporating into the book journal entries, poems, essays, photographs of herself, drawings, cartoons, and annotated transcripts. Ruth Linden's *Making Stories, Making Selves: Feminist Reflections on the Holocaust* (1992) intertwines autobiography, academic writing, and survivors' stories in a Helen Hooven Santmyer Prize in Women's Studies book, which was her dissertation. Patti Lather's *Getting Smart: Feminist Research and Pedagogy with/in the Postmodern* (1991), a winner of the American Educational Studies Critics Choice book award, displays high theory and transcript, pedagogue and students. John Dorst's *The Written Suburb* (1989) presents a geographic site as site, image, idea, discourse, and an assemblage of texts.

In some mixed-genre productions, the writer/artist roams freely around topics, breaking our sense of the externality of topics, developing our sense of how topic and self are twin constructs. With the artful self in display, the issues of constructedness and authorial responsibility are profiled. Susan Krieger's *Social Science and the Self: Personal Essays on an Art Form* (1991) is a superb example. The book is "design oriented," reflecting Krieger's attachment to Pueblo potters and Georgia O'Keefe, and, as she says, it "looks more like a pot or a painting than a hypothesis" (p. 120). Trinh T. Minh-ha's *Woman, Native, Other* (1989) breaks down writing conventions within each of the essays that constitute the book, mixing poetry, self-reflection, feminist criticism, photographs, and quotations that help readers experience postcoloniality. John Van Maanen's *Tales of the Field* (1988) analyzes examples of realist, confessional, and impressionist narratives. Stephen Pfohl's *Death at the Parasite Cafe* (1992) employs collage strategies and synchronic juxtapositions, blurring critical theory and militant art forms. Anthologies also reflect these mixed genres. Carolyn Ellis and Michael Flaherty's *Investigating Subjectivity: Research on Lived Experience* (1992) is one example, and the series, *Studies in Symbolic Interaction,* is another.

Whither and Whence?

The contemporary postmodernist context in which we work as qualitative researchers is a propitious one. It provides an opportunity for us to review, critique, and re-vision writing. Although we are freer to present our texts in a variety of forms to diverse audiences, we have different constraints arising from self-consciousness about claims to authorship, authority, truth, validity, and reliability. Self-reflexivity unmasks complex political/ideological agendas hidden in our writing. Truth claims are less easily validated now; desires to speak "for" others are suspect. The greater freedom to experiment with textual form, however, does not guarantee a better product. The opportunities for writing worthy texts—books and articles that are "good reads"—are multiple, exciting, and demanding. But the work is harder. The guarantees are fewer. There is a lot more for us to think about.

One thing for us to think about is whether writing experimentally for publication is a luxury open only to those who have academic sinecure. Can/should only the already tenured write in experimental modes? Are the tenured doing a disservice to students by introducing them to alternative forms of writing? Will teaching them hereticisms "deskill" them? Alienate them from their discipline? These are heady ethical, pedagogical, and practical questions. I struggle with them in my teaching, writing, and collegial discussions. I have no definitive answers, but I do have some thoughts on the issues.

First, there are many different avenues open for the sociological writer (see Denzin, in press; Richardson, 1990). There is no single way—much less "right" way—of staging a text. The same material can be written for different audiences—positivists, interactionists, postmodernists, feminists, humanities professors, cultural studies scholars, policy makers, and so on. That is why it is called *material.* Like wet clay, it is there for us to shape. What are our purposes? What are our goals? Who do we want to reach? What do we want to accomplish? If you are a graduate student, your likely purpose is the approval of your Ph.D. dissertation by your committee; if you are an untenured academic, your concern is probably the acceptance of an article by a mainline journal. Writing for those purposes is one way of knowing the material and one way of communicating with one kind of reader. Writing in standard ways does not prevent us from writing in other ways. We cannot write every way, for every purpose, at the same time. Most important, once we understand how to stage a dissertation or journal article rhetorically, we are more likely to get it accepted, get tenured, or the like. Even liberatory and radical messages can be published in conservative journals, if the writer follows the rules (Agger, 1990). Consequently, deconstructing traditional writing practices is a way of making writers more conscious of writing conventions, and, therefore, more competently able to meet them and to get their messages into mainstream social science.

Second, writing is a process of discovery. My purpose is not to turn us into poets, novelists, or dramatists—few of us will write well enough to succeed in those competitive fields. Most of us, like Poe, will be at best only almost poets. Rather, my intention is to encourage individuals to accept and nurture their own voices. The researcher's self-knowledge and knowledge of the topic develops through experimentation with point of view, tone, texture, sequencing, metaphor, and so on. The whole enterprise is demystified. Even the analysis paralysis that afflicts some readers of postmodernism is attenuated when writers view their work as process rather than as definitive representation.

Third, writing practices can improve traditional texts because writers relate more deeply and complexly to their materials. The writer understands the material in different ways. The deepened understanding of a Self deepens the text. The text will be less boring because the writer will be more consciously engaged in its production, more present to self and others.

Finally, contemporary experimental writing is a harbinger; qualitative research has been and will continue to be changed by and through it. High-grade journals—such as *The Sociological Quarterly, Symbolic Interaction, Journal of Contemporary Ethnography,* and *Qualitative Sociology*—already publish experimental pieces. The annual, *Studies in Symbolic Interaction,* showcases evocative writing. Presses such as Routledge, University of Chicago, University of Michigan, University of Indiana, University of Pennsylvania, Rutgers University Press, and Sage Publications regularly publish experimental work by both well-known and lesser-known authors. Traditional ethnographers write more reflexively and self-consciously (see Thorne, 1993). Even those opposed to postmodernism legitimate it through dialogue (Whyte, 1992). Throughout the social sciences, convention papers include transgressive presentations. Entire conferences are devoted to experimentation, such as the "Redesigning Ethnography" conference at the University of Colorado, which featured speakers from different disciplines. At least two well-respected interpretive programs—at the University of Illinois (under Norman Denzin) and at the University of South Florida (under Arthur Bochner and Carolyn Ellis)—are teaching about representational issues. All of these changes in academic practices are signs of *paradigm changes.*

In the 1950s, the sociology of science was a new, reflexively critical area. Today, the sociology of science undergirds theory, methods, and interdisciplinary "science studies." In the 1960s, "gender" emerged as a theoretical perspective. Today, gender studies is one of the largest (if not the largest) subfield in social sciences. In part, science studies and gender studies thrived because they identified normative assumptions of social science that falsely limited knowledge. They spoke "truly" to the everyday experiences of social scientists. The new areas hit us where we lived—in our work and in our bodies. They offered alternative perspectives for understanding the experienced world.

Today, the postmodernist critique is having the same impact on social sciences that science studies and gender have had, and for similar reasons. Postmodernism identifies unspecified assumptions that hinder us in our search for understanding "truly," and it offers alternative practices that work. We feel its "truth"—its moral, intellectual, aesthetic, emotional, intuitive, embodied, playful pull. Each researcher is likely to respond to that pull differently, which should lead to writing that is more diverse, more author centered, less boring, and humbler. This is a time of transition, a propitious moment. Where this experimentation will eventually take us, I do not know, but I do know that we cannot go back to where we were.

Writing Practices

> Writing, the creative effort, should come first—at least for some part of every day of your life. It is a wonderful blessing if you will use it. You will become happier, more enlightened, alive, impassioned, light hearted and generous to everybody else. Even your health will improve. Colds will disappear and all the other ailments of discouragement and boredom. (Ueland, 1938/1987)

In what follows, I suggest some ways of using writing as a method of knowing. I have chosen exercises that have been productive for me and my students because they demystify writing, nurture the researcher's voice, and serve the process of discovery. I wish I could guarantee them to bring good health as well! The practices are organized around topics discussed in the text.

Metaphor

Using old, wornout metaphors, although easy and comfortable, after a while invites stodginess and stiffness. The stiffer you get, the less flexible you are. You invite being ignored. In less metaphoric terms, if your writing is clichéd, you will not stretch your own imagination (ouch! hear the cliché! hear the cliché of me pointing out the cliché!) and you will bore people.

1. In standard social scientific writing, the metaphor for theory is that it is a "building" (structure, foundation, construction, deconstruction, framework, form, and so on). Consider a different metaphor for theory, such as "theory as a tapestry" or "theory as an illness." Write a paragraph about theory using your metaphor. (See above for examples of "theory as building.") Do you "see" differently and "feel" differently about theorizing when you use an unusual metaphor?
2. Consider alternative sensory metaphors for "knowledge" other than the heliocentric one men-

tioned above. What happens when you rethink/resense "knowledge" as situated in "voice"? In touch?

3. What metaphors do you use in your writing? Take a look at one of your papers and highlight your metaphors and images. What are you saying through metaphors that you did not realize you were saying? What are you reinscribing? Do you want to? Can you find different metaphors that change how you "see" ("feel"?) the material? Your relationship to it? Are your mixed metaphors pointing to confusion in yourself or to social science's glossing over of ideas?

4. Take a look at George Lakoff and Mark Johnson's *Metaphors We Live By* (1980). It is a wonderful book, a compendium of examples of metaphors in everyday life and how they affect our ways of perceiving, thinking, and acting. What everyday metaphors are shaping your knowing/writing? What alternative ones can you find?

Writing Formats

1. Choose a journal article that you think exemplifies the writing conventions of the mainstream of your discipline. Then write a two- to four-page analysis of that article. How is the argument staged? Who is the presumed audience? How does the paper inscribe ideology? How does the author claim "authority" over the material? Where is the author? Where are "you" in this paper? Who are the subjects and who are the objects of research here?

2. Choose a journal article that exemplifies excellence in qualitative research, and write a two- to four-page analysis of that article. How has the article built upon normative social science writing? How is authority claimed? Where is the author? Where are "you" in the article? Who are the subjects and who are the objects of research here?

3. Choose a paper you have written for a class or that you have published that you think is pretty good. How did you follow the norms of your discipline? Were you conscious of doing so? How did you stage your paper? What parts did your professor/reviewer laud? How did you depend upon those norms to carry your argument? Did you elide over some difficult areas through vagueness, jargon, calls to authorities, or other rhetorical devices? What voices did you exclude in your writing? Who is the audience? Where are the subjects in the paper? Where are you? How do you feel about the paper now? About your process of constructing it?

Experimental Writing

An excellent way to open yourself up to experimental writing is to learn from creative writers. They have much to teach us about writing, and about ourselves. Even if you chose to write a fairly traditional text, the creative writing experience will enrich that text.

1. Join or start a writing group. This could be a writing support group, a creative writing group, a poetry group, a dissertation group, or another kind. (For dissertation and article writing, see Becker, 1986; Fox, 1985; Richardson, 1990; Wolcott, 1990.)

2. Work through a creative writing guidebook. Natalie Goldberg (1986, 1990), Rust Hills (1987), Brenda Ueland (1938/1987), and Deena Metzger (1993) all provide excellent guides.

3. Enroll in a creative writing workshop. This experience is valuable for both beginning and experienced researchers. Here is testimony from Barrie Thorne (personal communication, September 2, 1992), an experienced, compelling, and traditionally inclined ethnography writer: "Taking a weekly creative writing class from Deena Metzger has been an important part of this quest. She encourages connecting with the unconscious, reaching for unusual verbs and evocative concrete detail, and exploring the emotional side of writing."

4. Use "writing up" field notes as an opportunity to expand your writing vocabulary, habits of thought, and attentiveness to your senses, and as a bulwark against the censorious voice of science. Where better to develop your sense of self, your voice, than in the process of doing your research? Apply creative writing skills to your field notes. I turn again to Barrie Thorne's description and testimony, not only because it is instructive, but because she writes within mainstream ethnographic tradition:

> Field notes . . . have a private and intimate character; one can innovate, make false starts, flare up with emotions without feeling an anonymous audience at one's shoulder. . . . As I write field notes, I push for full description, avoiding sociological jargon, staying close to what I saw, while letting my imagination roam around the event, searching for patterns and larger chains of significance (as they occur to me, I write these analytic hunches in capital letters in parentheses).

5. Some of us are more "choked" than Barrie Thorne in our field note writing, and we may need other devices to free our writing. For some it may mean rethinking what we have been taught about objectivity, science, and the ethnographic project. What works for me is to give different labels to different content. Building upon Glaser and Strauss's (1967) work, I use four categories, which you may find of value:

- *Observation notes* (ON): These are as concrete and detailed as I am able to make them. I want to think of them as fairly accurate renditions of what I see, hear, feel, taste, and so on.
- *Methodological notes* (MN): These are messages to myself regarding how to collect "data,"—who to talk to, what to wear, when to phone, and so on. I write a lot of these because I like methods, and I like to keep a process diary of my work.
- *Theoretical notes* (TN): These are hunches, hypotheses, poststructuralist connections, critiques of what I am doing/thinking/seeing. I like writing these because they open up my text—my field note text—to alternative interpretations and a critical epistemological stance. It is a way of keeping me from being hooked on my "take" on reality.
- *Personal notes* (PN): These are feelings statements about the research, the people I am talking to, myself doing the process, my doubts, my anxieties, my pleasures. I do no censoring here at all. I want all my feelings out on paper because I like them and because I know they are there anyway, affecting what/how I lay claim to knowing. Writing personal notes is a way for me to know myself better, a way of using writing as a method of inquiry into the self.

6. Keep a journal. In it, write about your feelings about your work. This not only frees up your writing, it becomes the "historical record" for writing a narrative of the self.

7. If you wish to experiment with evocative writing, a good place to begin is by transforming your field notes into drama. See what ethnographic rules you are using (such as fidelity to the speech of the participants, fidelity in the order of the speakers and events) and what literary ones you are invoking (such as limits on how long a speaker speaks, keeping the "plot" moving along, developing character through actions). Writing dramatic presentations accentuates ethical considerations. If you doubt that, contrast writing up an ethnographic event as a "typical" event with writing it as a play, with you and your hosts cast in roles that will be performed before others. Who has ownership of spoken words? How is authorship attributed? What if people don't like how they are characterized? Are courtesy norms being violated? Experiment here with both oral and written versions of your drama.

8. Experiment with transforming an in-depth interview into a poetic representation. Try using only the words, rhythms, figures of speech, breath points, pauses, syntax, and diction of the speaker. Where do you figure in the poem? What do you know about the interviewee and about yourself that you did not know before you wrote the poem? What poetic devices have you sacrificed in the name of science?

9. Experiment with writing narratives of the self. Keep in mind Barbara Tuchman's warning: "The writer's object is—or should be—to hold the reader's attention. . . . I want the reader to turn the page and keep on turning to the end. This is accomplished only when the narrative moves steadily ahead, not when it comes to a weary standstill, overlaced with every item uncovered in the research" (in *New York Times,* February 2, 1989).

10. Consider a fieldwork setting. Consider the various subject positions you have or have had within it. For example, in a store you might be a salesclerk, customer, manager, feminist, capitalist, parent, child, and so on. Write about the setting (or an event in the setting) from several different subject positions. What do you "know" from the different positions? Next, let the different points of view dialogue with each other. What do you discover through these dialogues?

11. Consider a paper you have written (or your field notes). What has been left out? Who is not present in this text? Who has been repressed? Who has been marginalized? Rewrite the text from that point of view.

12. Write a story about the "self" from your point of view (such as something that happened in your family or in your seminar). Then, interview another participant (such as a family or seminar member) and have that person tell you his or her story of the event. See yourself as part of the other individual's story in the same way he or she is part of your story. How do you rewrite your story from the other person's point of view? (This is an exercise used by Carolyn Ellis.)

13. Collaborative writing is a way to see beyond one's own naturalisms of style and attitude. This is an exercise that I have used in my teaching, but it would be appropriate for a writing group as well. Each member writes a story of his or her life. It could be a feminist story, success story, quest story, cultural story, professional socialization story, realist tale, confessional tale, or whatever. All persons' stories are photocopied for the group. The group is then broken into subgroups (I prefer groups of three), and each subgroup collaborates on writing a new story, the collective story of its members. The collaboration can take any form: drama, poetry, fiction, narrative of the selves, realism, whatever the subgroup chooses. The collaboration is shared with the entire group. All members then write about their

feelings about the collaboration and what happened to their stories, their lives, in the process.

14. A variant on exercise 13 is for each member to tape-record his or her own story and for other members to create a written text out of the oral one (a technique used by Art Bochner). The "originator" of the story then comments upon the others' telling. This is a good way to break down oral and written codes.

I hope these exercises are helpful. I hope you find new ways to experiment. I hope we all do.

> Willing is doing something you know already—there is no new imaginative understanding in it. And presently your soul gets frightfully sterile and dry because you are so quick, snappy, and efficient about doing one thing after another that you have no time for your own ideas to come in and develop and gently shine. (Ueland, 1938/1987, p. 29)

Happy writing and rewriting!

References

Agger, B. (1989). *Reading science: A literary, political and sociological analysis.* Dix Hills, NY: General Hall.

Agger, B. (1990). *The decline of discourse: Reading, writing and resistance in postmodern capitalism.* Bristol, PA: Falmer.

Atkinson, P. A. (1990). *The ethnographic imagination: Textual constructions of reality.* London: Routledge.

Balzac, H. de. (1965). Preface to *The human comedy,* from *At the sign of the cat and racket* (C. Bell, Trans., 1897; original work published 1842). In R. Ellman & C. Feidelson, Jr. (Eds.), *The modern tradition: Backgrounds of modern literature* (pp. 246-254). New York: Oxford University Press.

Barley, N. (1986). *Ceremony: An anthropologist's misadventures in the African bush.* New York: Henry Holt.

Barley, N. (1988). *Not a pleasant sport.* New York: Henry Holt.

Becker, H. S. (1986). *Writing for social scientists: How to finish your thesis, book, or article.* Chicago: University of Chicago Press.

Brady, I. (Ed.). (1991). *Anthropological poetics.* Savage, MD: Rowman & Littlefield.

Brodkey, L. (1987). *Academic writing as social practice.* Philadelphia: Temple University Press.

Brown, R. H. (1977). *A poetic for sociology.* Cambridge, UK: Cambridge University Press.

Butler, S., & Rosenblum, B. (1991). *Cancer in two voices.* San Francisco: Spinsters.

Carey, J. W. (1989). *Communication as culture: Essays on media and society.* Cambridge, UK: Cambridge University Press.

Clifford, J. (1986). Introduction: Partial truths. In J. Clifford & G. E. Marcus (Eds.), *Writing culture: The poetics and politics of ethnography* (pp. 1-26). Berkeley: University of California Press.

Clifford, J., & Marcus, G. E. (Eds.). (1986). *Writing culture: The poetics and politics of ethnography.* Berkeley: University of California Press.

Clough, P. T. (1992). *The end(s) of ethnography: From realism to social criticism.* Newbury Park, CA: Sage.

Crawford, M. A. (1951). Introduction. In H. de Balzac, *Old Goriot.* New York: Penguin.

Denzin, N. K. (1978). *The research act.* New York: McGraw-Hill.

Denzin, N. K. (1986). A postmodern social theory. *Sociological Theory, 4,* 194-204.

Denzin, N. K. (1991). *Images of postmodern society.* Newbury Park, CA: Sage.

Denzin, N. K. (in press). The lessons James Joyce teaches us. *Qualitative Studies in Education.*

Derrida, J. (1982). *The margins of philosophy* (A. Bass, Trans.). Chicago: University of Chicago Press.

DeShazer, M. K. (1986). *Inspiring women: Reimagining the muse.* New York: Pergamon.

Diamond, S. (1981). *Totems.* Barrytown, NY: Open Book.

Dorst, J. D. (1989). *The written suburb: An American site, an ethnographic dilemma.* Philadelphia: University of Pennsylvania Press.

Eagleton, T. (1983). *Literary theory: An introduction.* Minneapolis: University of Minnesota Press.

Edmondson, R. (1984). *Rhetoric in sociology.* London: Macmillan.

Ellis, C. (forthcoming). *Final negotiations.* Philadelphia: Temple University Press.

Ellis, C. (1993). Telling a story of sudden death. *Sociological Quarterly, 34,* 711-730.

Ellis, C., & Bochner, A. P. (1992). Telling and performing personal stories: The constraints of choice in abortion. In C. Ellis & M. G. Flaherty (Eds.), *Investigating subjectivity: Research on lived experience* (pp. 79-101). Newbury Park, CA: Sage.

Erikson, K. T. (1976). *Everything in its path: Destruction of the community in the Buffalo Creek flood.* New York: Simon & Schuster.

Fine, M. (1992). *Disruptive voices: The possibility of feminist research.* Ann Arbor: University of Michigan Press.

Fiske, D. W., & Schweder, R. A. (Eds.). (1986). *Metatheory in social science: Pluralisms and subjectivities.* Chicago: University of Chicago Press.

Fox, M. F. (Ed.). (1985). *Scholarly writing and publishing: Issues, problems, and solutions.* Boulder, CO: Westview.

Frohock, F. (1992). *Healing powers.* Chicago: University of Chicago Press.

Geertz, C. (1983). *Local knowledge: Further essays in interpretive anthropology.* New York: Basic Books.

Geertz, C. (1988). *Works and lives: The anthropologist as author.* Stanford, CA: Stanford University Press.

Glaser, B. G., & Strauss, A. L. (1967). *The discovery of grounded theory: Strategies for qualitative research.* Chicago: Aldine.

Gleick, J. (1984, June 10). Solving the mathematical riddle of chaos. *New York Times Magazine,* pp. 30-32.

Goldberg, N. (1986). *Writing down the bones: Freeing the writer within.* Boston: Shambala.

Goldberg, N. (1990). *Wild mind: Living the writer's life.* New York: Bantam.

Harper, D. (1987). *Working knowledge: Skill and community in a small shop.* Chicago: University of Chicago Press.

Hills, R. (1987). *Writing in general and the short story in particular.* Boston: Houghton Mifflin.

hooks, b. (1990). *Yearning: Race, gender, and cultural politics.* Boston: South End.

Hutcheon, L. (1988). *A poetics of postmodernism: History, theory and fiction.* New York: Routledge.

Jameson, F. (1981). *The political unconscious.* Ithaca, NY: Cornell University Press.

Kaufman, S. (1986). *The ageless self: Sources of meaning in later life.* Madison: University of Wisconsin Press.

Kline, M. (1980). *Mathematics: The loss of certainty.* New York: Oxford University Press.

Kondo, D. (1990). *Crafting selves.* Chicago: University of Chicago Press.

Krieger, S. (1983). *The mirror dance: Identity in a women's community.* Philadelphia: Temple University Press.

Krieger, S. (1991). *Social science and the self: Personal essays on an art form.* New Brunswick, NJ: Rutgers University Press.

Lakoff, G., & Johnson, M. (1980). *Metaphors we live by.* Chicago: University of Chicago Press.

Lather, P. (1991). *Getting smart: Feminist research and pedagogy with/in the postmodern.* New York: Routledge.

Lehman, D. (1991). *Signs of the times: Deconstruction and the fall of Paul de Man.* New York: Poseidon.

Levine, D. N. (1985). *The flight from ambiguity: Essays in social and cultural theory.* Chicago: University of Chicago Press.

Liebow, E. (1967). *Tally's corner: A study of Negro street corner men.* Boston: Little, Brown.

Linden, R. R. (1992). *Making stories, making selves: Feminist reflections on the Holocaust.* Columbus: Ohio State University.

Lyotard, J.-F. (1979). *The postmodern condition: A report on knowledge* (G. Bennington & G. Masumi, Trans.). Minneapolis: University of Minnesota Press.

Marcus, G. E., & Fischer, M. J. M. (1986). *Anthropology as cultural critique: An experimental moment in the human sciences.* Chicago: University of Chicago Press.

McCall, M., & Becker, H. S. (1990). Performance science. *Social Problems, 32,* 117-132.

Metzger, D. (1993). *Writing for your life: A guide and companion to the inner worlds.* New York: HarperCollins.

Mischler, E. G. (1991). *Research interviewing: Context and narrative.* Cambridge, MA: Harvard University Press.

Morris, M. (1988). *The pirate's fiancee: Feminism, reading, and postmodernism.* New York: Verso.

Nelson, J. S., Megill, A., & McCloskey, D. N. (Eds.). (1987). *The rhetoric of the human sciences: Language and argument in scholarship and human affairs.* Madison: University of Wisconsin Press.

Nicholson, L. J. (Ed.). (1990). *Feminism/postmodernism.* New York: Routledge.

Paget, M. (1990). Performing the text. *Journal of Contemporary Ethnography, 19,* 136-155.

Patai, D. (1988). Constructing a self: A Brazilian life story. *Feminist Studies, 14,* 142-163.

Pfohl, S. J. (1992). *Death at the Parasite Cafe: Social science (fictions) and the postmodern.* New York: St. Martin's.

Prattis, I. (Ed.). (1985). *Reflections: The anthropological muse.* Washington, DC: American Anthropological Association.

Richardson, L. (1985). *The new other woman: Contemporary single women in affairs with married men.* New York: Free Press.

Richardson, L. (1990). *Writing strategies: Reaching diverse audiences.* Newbury Park, CA: Sage.

Richardson, L. (1991). Postmodern social theory: Representational practices. *Sociological Theory, 9,* 173-180.

Richardson, L. (1992a). The consequences of poetic representation: Writing the other, rewriting the self. In C. Ellis & M. G. Flaherty (Eds.), *Investigating subjectivity: Research on lived experience* (pp. 125-140). Newbury Park, CA: Sage.

Richardson, L. (1992b). Resisting resistance narratives: A representation for communication. *Studies in Symbolic Interaction, 13,* 77-83.

Richardson, L. (1993). The case of the skipped line: Poetics, dramatics and transgressive validity. *Sociological Quarterly, 34,* 695-710.

Richardson, L., & Lockridge, E. (1991). The sea monster: An "ethnographic drama." *Symbolic Interaction, 14,* 335-340.

Ronai, C. R. (1992). The reflexive self through narrative: A night in the life of an erotic dancer/researcher. In C. Ellis & M. G. Flaherty (Eds.), *Investigating subjectivity: Research on lived experience* (pp. 102-124). Newbury Park, CA: Sage.

Rorty, R. (1979). *Philosophy and the mirror of man.* Princeton, NJ: Princeton University Press.

Rose, D. (1989). *Patterns of American culture: Ethnography and estrangement.* Philadelphia: University of Pennsylvania Press.

Rose, E. (1992). *The werald.* Boulder, CO: Waiting Room.

Rubin, L. B. (1976). *Worlds of pain: Life in the working-class family.* New York: Basic Books.

Schneider, J. (1991). Troubles with textual authority in sociology. *Symbolic Interaction, 14,* 295-320.
Seidman, S., & Wagner, D. (Eds.). (1991). *Postmodernism and social theory.* New York: Basil Blackwell.
Shapiro, M. (1985-1986). Metaphor in the philosophy of the social sciences. *Cultural Critique, 2,* 191-214.
Simons, H. W. (1990). *Rhetoric in the human sciences.* London: Sage.
Stack, C. B. (1974). *All our kin: Strategies for survival in a black community.* New York: Harper & Row.
Statham, A., Richardson, L., & Cook, J. A. (1991). *Gender and university teaching: A negotiated difference.* Albany: State University of New York Press.
Steedman, K. (1986). *Landscape for a good woman: A story of two lives.* New Brunswick, NJ: Rutgers University Press.
Stewart, J. (1989). *Drinkers, drummers and decent folk: Ethnographic narratives of Village Trinidad.* Albany: State University of New York.
Stoller, P. (1989). *Taste of ethnographic things: The senses in anthropology.* Philadelphia: University of Pennsylvania Press.
Tedlock, D. (1983). *The spoken word and the work of interpretation.* Philadelphia: University of Pennsylvania Press.
Thorne, B. (1993). *Gender play.* New Brunswick, NJ: Rutgers University Press.
Trinh, M. T. T. (1989). *Woman, native, other: Writing postcoloniality and feminism.* Bloomington: Indiana University Press.
Turner, V., & Bruner, E. M. (Eds.). (1986). *The anthropology of experience.* Champagne-Urbana: University of Illinois Press.
Ueland, B. (1987). *If you want to write: A book about art, independence and spirit.* Saint Paul, MN: Graywolf. (Original work published 1938)
Ulmer, G. (1989). *Teletheory: Grammatology in the age of video.* New York: Routledge.
Van Maanen, J. (1988). *Tales of the field: On writing ethnography.* Chicago: University of Chicago Press.
Walkerdine, V. (1990). *Schoolgirl fictions.* London: Verso.
Weedon, C. (1987). *Feminist practice and poststructuralist theory.* New York: Basil Blackwell.
Whyte, W. F. (1943). *Street corner society: The social structure of an Italian slum.* Chicago: University of Chicago Press.
Whyte, W. F. (1992). In defense of *Street corner society. Journal of Contemporary Ethnography, 21,* 52-68.
Williams, P. J. (1991). *The alchemy of race and rights: Diary of a law professor.* Cambridge, MA: Harvard University Press.
Wolf, M. (1992). *A thrice-told tale: Feminism, postmodernism, and ethnographic responsibility.* Stanford, CA: Stanford University Press.
Wolcott, H. F. (1990). *Writing up qualitative research.* Newbury Park, CA: Sage.
Zola, E. (1965). The novel as social science. In R. Ellman & C. Feidelson, Jr. (Eds.), *The modern tradition: Backgrounds of modern literature* (pp. 270-289). New York: Oxford University Press. (Original work published 1880)
Zola, I. K. (1983). *Missing pieces: A chronicle of living with a disability.* Philadelphia: Temple University Press.

33

■

Qualitative Program Evaluation

Practice and Promise

JENNIFER C. GREENE

Sylvia Winslow, chair of a state legislative committee on health, is concerned about the effectiveness of the state's prenatal care services. Recent reports from varied sources—most dramatically in the media—have underscored the difficulties that rural women especially have in finding prenatal care and the tragedies that result from inadequate care. Sylvia asks the staff of her health committee for a comprehensive update on the state's prenatal care program, with special focus on issues of access and quality.

Albert Peters enrolls his son in a new program at the local high school that claims to be offering a different vision of secondary education. Critical elements of this vision for Albert and his son include heterogeneous grouping, a curriculum infused with multicultural ideas and values, and a strong mentoring system in which faculty guide each youth's program and progress. Albert genuinely believes that a program, such as this one might be, in which all kids are respected and assumed to have unique and valuable gifts is the only way his son will make it through high school. It is October already, and Albert wants some information on the nature and quality of this educational experience for his son. Albert calls the high school principal to request such information.

Chapter 1, the U.S. federal government's long-term compensatory education program, is up for reauthorization in two years. In anticipation of the probable debate, the chair of the Senate Education and Labor Committee asks the U.S. General Accounting Office to provide a summary assessment of Chapter 1 success over the past five years.

Evan Gonzalez, the human resource director at IVM, a major electronics corporation, is alarmed at the increasing number of employees utilizing the company's counseling and psychological services. Evan's concern is both for the employees—What is going on in the company or in specific communities to invoke such a demand for mental health services?—and for the company, as these services are extremely costly. Evan raises his questions at the next management meeting.

Sam Brown has been advocating for the homeless in his county for five years now, and he is weary. He needs some kind of catalyst to mobilize his constituents and to energize concerned supporters toward concrete action by the county board. If he could have current information on the numbers of homeless in the county, on their personal tragedies, and on the social costs of homelessness, well, that might just do the trick.

AUTHOR'S NOTE: My sincere thanks to the reviewers and the editors for their constructive contributions to this chapter.

Contexts of Program Evaluation

The above are examples of some of the many scenarios of social program evaluation. They vary in the nature of the social issues involved, in the perspectives taken on the issues, in the geographic scope of services to be reviewed, in the kinds of information sought, and in the stated purposes for which the information will be used. Underlying these differences, however, are some fundamental commonalities that demarcate evaluation contexts, and that thereby distinguish program evaluation as a unique form of social inquiry.

Perhaps most distinctive about program evaluation is its political inherency (Patton, 1987), the "recognition that politics and science are both integral aspects of evaluation" (Cronbach & Associates, 1980, p. 35), and that "the evaluator has political influence even when he does not aspire to it" (Cronbach & Associates, 1980, p. 3). Evaluations are conducted on social programs—most important, on social programs in the public domain.[1] Social programs are manifest responses to priority individual and community needs and are themselves "the creatures of political decisions. They [are] proposed, defined, debated, enacted, and funded through political processes, and in implementation they remain subject to [political] pressures—both supportive and hostile" (Weiss, 1987, p. 47). So program evaluation is integrally intertwined with political decision making about societal priorities, resource allocation, and power. "By its very nature [evaluation] makes implicit political statements about such issues as the problematic nature of some programs and the unchallengeability of others" (Weiss, 1987, p. 48).

Moreover, the work of social program evaluators is framed by the concerns and interests of selected members of the setting being evaluated. Evaluation questions about the significance of program goals or about the quality and effectiveness of program strategies reflect not inquirer autonomy or theoretical predictions, but rather a politicized process of priority setting. In all evaluation contexts there are multiple, often competing, potential audiences—groups and individuals who have vested interests in the program being evaluated, called *stakeholders* in evaluation jargon. These range from policy makers and funders like Sylvia Winslow and the U.S. Congress, to program administrators and staff like Evan Gonzalez of IVM, to intended beneficiaries like parent Albert Peters and homeless advocate Sam Brown, and to the citizenry at large. And so, unlike most other social scientists, who assume an audience of peers/scholars, evaluators must negotiate whose questions will be addressed and whose interests will be served by their work.

Evaluation results then enter the political arena of social program and policy decision making not as decontextualized, abstract, or theoretical knowledge claims, but rather as practical knowledge claims, as empirically justified value judgments about the merit or worth of the program evaluated. Evaluators describe and infer about practical matters, about the significance of concrete program experiences for various stakeholders. But evaluators do more than describe and infer. At root, evaluation is about valuing (Scriven, 1967) and judging (Stake, 1967). Hence evaluators also infuse directly into the political strands of social policy making the standards or criteria used for rendering judgments. Like the selection of evaluation questions and audiences, determining the standards against which a program will be judged is a contested task. Increasingly, particularly in qualitative evaluations, these valuing standards are identified and offered pluralistically, as multiple sets. Program effectiveness, for example, has many hues, depending on one's vantage point in both space and time. Administrators might well understand effectiveness as efficiency, beneficiaries as significant relief from life's daily struggles, and funders as the long-term realization of tax dollars saved.

Evaluation Methodologies

Yet neither these diverse criteria for program effectiveness nor different stakeholders' widely divergent evaluation questions can be equally well addressed by the same evaluation methodology. In this respect, it is the fundamental political nature of program evaluation contexts, intertwined with the predispositions and beliefs of the evaluator, that shape the contours of evaluation methodologies and guide the selection of a specific evaluation approach for a given context. Different evaluation methodologies are expressly oriented around the information needs of different audiences—from the macro program- and cost-effectiveness questions of policy makers to the micro questions of meaning for individual participants. These varied audience orientations further represent, explicitly or implicitly, the promotion of different values and political stances. Evaluation methodologies hence constitute coordinated frameworks of philosophical assumptions (about the world, human nature, knowledge, ethics), integrated with ideological views about the role and purpose of social inquiry in social policy and program decision making, with accompanying value stances regarding the desired ends of programs and of inquiry, and finally—last as well as least—with complementary methods preferences. Again, it is because evaluation is politically contextualized that constitutive differences in evaluation

TABLE 33.1 Major Approaches to Program Evaluation

Philosophical Framework	*Ideological Framework/ Key Values Promoted*	*Key Audiences*	*Preferred Methods*	*Typical Evaluation Questions*
Postpositivism	Systems theory/ efficiency, accountability, theoretical causal knowledge	High-level policy and decision makers	Quantitative: experiments and quasi-experiments, systems analysis, causal modeling, cost-benefit analysis	Are desired outcomes attained and attributable to the program? Is this program the most efficient alternative?
Pragmatism	Management/ practicality, quality control, utility	Mid-level program managers, administrators, and other decision makers	Eclectic, mixed: structured and unstructured surveys, questionnaires, interviews, observations	Which parts of the program work well and which need improvement? How effective is the program with respect to the organization's goals? With respect to beneficiaries' needs?
Interpretivism	Pluralism/ understanding, diversity, solidarity	Program directors, staff, and beneficiaries	Qualitative: case studies, interviews, observations, document review	How is the program experienced by various stakeholders?
Critical, normative science	Emancipation/ empowerment, social change	Program beneficiaries, their communities, other "powerless" groups	Participatory: stakeholder participation in varied structured and unstructured, quantitative and qualitative designs and methods; historical analysis, social criticism	In what ways are the premises, goals, or activities of the program serving to maintain power and resources inequities in the society?

methodologies extend well beyond alternative methods and also beyond alternative philosophies of science (see Guba, 1990) to incorporate alternative ideologies (Scriven, 1983) and alternative philosophies of ethics, democracy, and justice (House, 1980).

Table 33.1 offers a descriptive categorization of four major genres of evaluation methodologies. The first, which represents the historically dominant tradition in program evaluation, is oriented around the macro policy issues of program effectiveness and cost efficiency. Sylvia Winslow's questions about the quality of her state's prenatal health care services and the U.S. Senate's questions about Chapter 1 success illustrate the broad program effectiveness issues this evaluation genre is designed to address. In this genre primary emphasis is placed on program effectiveness as outcomes and, concomitantly, on the social value of accountability. Early postpositivist evaluation was typified by large-scale studies of Great Society programs, such as the Head Start evaluation (Cicirelli & Associates, 1969) and, later, the New Jersey Negative Income Tax Experiment (Rossi & Lyall, 1978). These studies demonstrated well the failure of experimental logic to meet the demands of evaluation settings. Even so, with "old certainties unthroned, but not abolished" (Cook, 1985, p. 37) and new efforts to reclaim the primacy of science, and hence of scientists, in social programming—as best represented by theory-driven evaluation (Chen & Rossi, 1983)—postpositivist evaluators retain a strong position amidst theorists and methodologists and a still-dominant position among evaluation practitioners and, perhaps most notably, evaluation audiences. *How can this be an evaluation if it doesn't have a control group?* remains a familiar lament from the field.

The second genre of evaluation methodologies arose largely in response to the failure of experimental science to provide timely and useful information for program decision making. Characteristic of these methodologies are their orientation to decision making and hence to management, their primary emphasis on producing useful information, their practical and pragmatic value base, and their eclectic methodological stance. Evaluators in this genre pragmatically select their methods to match the practical problem at hand, rather than as dictated by some abstract set of philosophical tenets (Howe, 1988; Patton, 1988). For example, in order to decide what action if any to take in the face of IVM employees' increasing use of psychological services, Evan Gonzalez and other IVM managers are likely to need a variety of qualitative, quantitative, and perhaps even historical information related to the experiences and contexts of the workplace. Decision- and utilization-oriented evaluators focus on providing support for efficient and effective program management. As an unwavering champion of practical, utilization-focused evaluation, Michael Patton's (1990) approach to qualitative evaluation clearly falls within this genre.

Yet it is in the third cluster that more traditionally qualitative approaches to evaluation have found their home. Part of the interpretive turn in social science, these approaches share a common grounding in a basically interpretive philosophy of science (Smith, 1989; Soltis, 1990), a value orientation that characteristically promotes pluralism in evaluation contexts, and a case study methodological orientation with an accompanying reliance on qualitative methods. Part of the responsive tradition in program evaluation, these approaches seek to enhance contextualized program understanding for stakeholders closest to the program (like Albert Peters and his son), and thereby promote values of pluralism as well as forge direct channels to program improvement. Robert Stake's (1975) and Egon Guba and Yvonna Lincoln's (1981) responsive approaches to evaluation, and, though not as good a fit, Elliot Eisner's (1976) connoisseurship evaluation are major exemplars of qualitative evaluation approaches in this genre.

Finally, the fourth cluster represents the more recent *normative turn* in social science. The feminist, neo-Marxist, critical, and other theorists in this genre promote "openly ideological" forms of inquiry that seek to illuminate the historical, structural, and value bases of social phenomena and, in doing so, to catalyze political and social change toward greater justice, equity, and democracy. A normative evaluation stance well matches homeless advocate Sam Brown's need for information that would help catalyze action toward greater justice for homeless people. Although many proponents of a normative approach to evaluation are long on rhetoric and short on guidelines for the field, some work on the practice of normative evaluation is being done (Greene, 1991; McTaggart, 1990; Sirotnik & Oakes, 1990). For the present discussion, the democratic evaluation approach championed by British and Australian practitioners (MacDonald, 1976) is an important exemplar. As well, Guba and Lincoln's (1989) more recent development of fourth-generation evaluation bears examination as it promotes an activist ideology while maintaining a grounding in an essentially interpretivist philosophy.

Explicit recognition of the ideological contours of program evaluation did not always exist. Rather, both inside and outside the field, a methods orientation has predominated. One continuing legacy of this orientation is the naming of different evaluation approaches by their primary methods, no more common than in the label of "qualitative evaluation" for any approach that utilizes primarily qualitative methods. Yet, as just argued, what importantly distinguishes one evaluation methodology from another is not methods, but rather whose questions are addressed and which values are promoted. Among the major extant evaluation approaches that rely on qualitative methods, there is only some consensus on these political and value dimensions. Patton, Stake, MacDonald, and Guba and Lincoln represent distinct, even competing, positions on these dimensions. Qualitative research traditions show similar variability (Atkinson, Delamont, & Hammersley, 1988; Jacob, 1987).

In my discussion in this chapter I will emphasize distinctions among significant evaluation approaches that incorporate qualitative methods. And that's progress! Not long ago, interpretivist philosophies and qualitative methods were just gaining a toehold in the evaluation community, amidst considerable, often acrimonious, debate. In the next section, I offer a brief historical perspective on the ascendance and acceptance of qualitative methods in program evaluation methodologies. This is followed by an elaboration of the philosophical bases of qualitative evaluations, and then an examination of qualitative evaluations in practice. I conclude the chapter by noting the continuing challenges for program evaluators and providing a summary assessment regarding the future promise of qualitative evaluations. I will argue that because of their inherent paradigmatic relativity, many qualitative evaluation approaches can effectively respond to or be shaped to fit diverse and emergent inquiry forms and functions. Yet, absent a coherent value orientation or vision (such as the social activism that frames fourth-generation evaluation), qualitative evaluations cannot move beyond responsiveness to become proactive players in the social policy-making arena.

From Whence Came Qualitative Evaluations

In the mid-1960s, evaluators were urged to use one preferred set of methodological principles and

> procedures—those of the experimental model—to assess the extent to which programs had attained their goals. In keeping with the tenets of experimental science, evaluators of this era adopted stances of objectivity and believed that the results of their work would anchor social planning and policy making in a politically neutral and scientific rationality. (Greene & McClintock, 1991, p. 13)

This portrait of the early days of contemporary program evaluation is distinctive for its narrow vision and naive arrogance. What has happened in the last quarter century to so dramatically transform the theory and, to a lesser but still substantial degree, the practice of social program evaluation? Developments in two aspects of evaluation methodology stand out as major forces for change: (a) evaluation's contextual, political aspect, and (b) evaluation's philosophical, methodological aspect (Greene & McClintock, 1991). The intertwined process of reciprocal change and influence in these two aspects tells much of the story of contemporary evaluation's evolution.[2]

Taking Off the White Lab Coat

The failures of experimental program evaluations to contribute to the enthusiasm and innovation of the Great Society era are legendary. They include recognition of the lack of fit between the requirements of the experimental model and the exigencies of social program contexts. For example, there were serious questions raised about the ethics of denying a purportedly beneficial program to some people in order to fulfill the randomization requirement of experimental design. Moreover, as prescribed by the experimental model, early program evaluators distanced themselves from the political dimensions of their work, intentionally seeking the objective stance of "politically neutral and scientific rationality." Carol Weiss (1970, 1972, 1977) most influentially critiqued this distanced stance, arguing that it substantially underlay the marginal potency of evaluations of this era. Weiss maintained that social policy and program decision making were not rational processes to which data-based enterprises such as program evaluation could contribute the definitive piece of information. Rather, "the politics of program survival and the politics of higher policymaking accord evaluative evidence relatively minor weight in the decisional calculus" (Weiss, 1987, p. 62). In short, neither distanced objectivity nor neutral rationality was going to earn program evaluators a seat at the decision-making table.

There were other influential disjunctures between the framework of experimental science and the contexts of program evaluation. As early as 1963, Lee Cronbach questioned the dominant focus of evaluative efforts on the stated goals and objectives of social programs, arguing that evaluation could more usefully contribute to program improvement through a focus on program planning and implementation. Over the years, Cronbach has continued to argue for a pragmatic, contextually useful role for program evaluation (see, e.g., Cronbach, 1982; Cronbach & Associates, 1980), in contrast to a scientistic or theory-oriented role. As a highly respected and influential theorist, Cronbach provided arguments that were important in easing the later entry and acceptance of qualitative evaluation approaches. Cronbach's views are tellingly and engagingly represented in his now-famous debate with Donald Campbell over the relative importance in evaluation studies of external validity and contextual meaningfulness (championed by Cronbach) versus internal validity and causal claims (promoted by Campbell) (for a summary of this debate, see Mark, 1986).

Michael Scriven (1967) has also challenged the goal orientation of experimental evaluation, arguing not against a focus on program outcomes or effects, but rather against an exemption of stated program goals and objectives from evaluative scrutiny. Social programs, that is, should be evaluated according to the merit and worth of their actual effects, independent of their intended effects. Adopting this explicitly value-oriented framework for evaluation, Scriven argues, renders existing social policy and program goals themselves contestable. *In what ways does this program effectively meet an important need among the designated beneficiaries?* is a Scrivenesque evaluation question, later popularized, in theory though far less in practice, in his goal-free approach to program evaluation (Scriven, 1973).

Additionally, Ernest House (1976, 1977, 1980) has contributed a distinctive and important voice to the argument that the white-coated experimental scientist is not an appropriate role model for program evaluators. House's views blend several different strands of logic and argumentation, including the fundamental grounding of evaluative work in political considerations of social and distributive justice, and developments in the philosophy of science (outlined in the next section). House (1980) argues that experimental science as a model for program evaluation fails because "it focuses on the truth aspect of validity to the exclusion of the credibility and normative aspects" (p. 251). Yet, by essence of his or her social function, "the evaluator is engaged with the world. His [or her] work directly affects who gets what" (pp. 254-255). Further, as an inherently political activity, evaluation "is intimately implicated in the distribution of basic goods in society . . . [So] evaluation should not only be true; it should also be just" (p. 121).

Challenging (Especially Cartesian) Foundations

A significant force for change in the form and function of program evaluation, then, were contextual challenges to the meaningfulness of experimental logic for evaluation—challenges that arose largely from within the evaluation community. Interwoven with these challenges were major fractures in the philosophical justification for experimental inquiry that permeated the evaluation community from the outside domains of the philosophy of science. In particular, the Cartesian foundationalism of positivistic science—and the concomitant premiums placed on objectivity, the proper methods, detached neutrality, and grand theory—were dethroned. Many philosophers of science came to agree that there is no place or time outside the observer from which he or she can objectively view and judge the validity of knowledge claims. Rather, all observations are imbued with the historical, theoretical, and value predispositions of the observer. Hence knowledge claims are not separable from, but rather interlocked with values; are not universal, but rather time and place bound; are not certain, but rather probabilistic and contestable (see Bernstein, 1983, for an outstanding example of these philosophical projects).

Endeavoring to be participants and not just bystanders in this Kuhnian challenge to *normal science,* program evaluators read philosophy, educated themselves about long-standing philosophical issues such as the fact/value distinction, and argued with each other at conferences and in other public forums about the intrinsic sensibility of varied philosophical developments and about their relevance to the essentially practical work of evaluation. It was in this context that interpretivist philosophies and qualitative methods entered evaluative discourse. Evaluation methodologies rooted in interpretivist philosophies and incorporating qualitative methods were developed as alternatives to a rejected positivist philosophy and experimentalist methodology (Guba & Lincoln, 1981; House, 1980; Parlett & Hamilton, 1976; Stake, 1975, 1978). In fact, within the evaluation and some other applied social science communities, much of this discourse was familiarly named the *quantitative-qualitative paradigm debate.* Although qualitative evaluations were initially contested on both practical and methodological grounds, the debate eventually evolved to a detente (Cook & Reichardt, 1979; Smith & Heshusius, 1986), signaling the important acceptance of these alternative evaluation methodologies, at least among many evaluation theorists and methodologists.[3] Coming both from long-standing inquiry traditions such as ethnography, symbolic interactionism, and phenomenology and from the more recent critiques of established social science, the arguments favoring the legitimacy and potential usefulness of qualitative approaches to applied social inquiry quite simply overwhelmed, or in some cases co-opted (Gage 1989), the opposition.

Accepting Diversity in Approaches to Evaluation

It was actually the combined force of the political-contextual and the methodological-philosophical arguments that catalyzed the development and later acceptance of a diverse range of alternative approaches to program evaluation, including practical, decision-oriented approaches and approaches framed around qualitative methodologies. This diversity is now being extended, with increasing calls to recenter social program evaluation around normative concerns (Schwandt, 1989; Sirotnik, 1990), as addressed in ensuing sections of this chapter.

The current accepted legitimacy of diverse evaluation approaches is well illustrated by the *Standards for Evaluation of Educational Programs, Projects, and Materials,* originally developed in 1981 by the Joint Committee on Standards for Educational Evaluation, representing 12 professional associations, and in the process of being updated. Reflecting the importance of contextual sensitivity and methodological diversity in the evaluation field, the 30 standards developed are clustered within four critical attributes of program evaluation: utility, feasibility, propriety, and accuracy. Moreover, the standards "do not exclusively endorse any one approach to evaluation. Instead, the Joint Committee has written standards that encourage the sound use of a variety of evaluation methods. . . . Usually, it is desireable to employ multiple methods, qualitative as well as quantitative" (Stufflebeam, 1991, p. 257). In other words, "merit lies not in form of inquiry, but in relevance of information" (Cronbach & Associates, 1980, p. 7). Although praised for their openness to alternative methods, the standards have also been criticized for their decision-oriented bias, for their reliance to some degree on the conceptual vocabulary of conventional science, and hence for their only partial embracement of alternative evaluation methodologies (e.g., Linn, 1981).

With these historical notes as important context, the next two sections of this chapter more closely examine qualitative approaches to evaluation, first in their philosophical form and then in their practical form.

The Logic of Justification for Qualitative Evaluations

Just as there is no one form of qualitative evaluation practice, there is no single philosophical logic of justification universally embraced by qualitative evaluators. Yet, there is a dominant set of philosophical tenets and stances guiding qualitative evaluation fieldwork, one with both a historical legacy and a strong contemporary presence in other domains of applied social science. This philosophical inquiry framework—variously called qualitative, ethnographic, and naturalistic—is most aptly called interpretivist (Smith, 1989). This label directly connotes one of its central premises, namely, that "in the world of human experience, there is only interpretation" (Denzin, 1989, p. 8). The dominance of an interpretivist logic of justification for qualitative evaluations can be traced primarily to the highly influential work of Yvonna Lincoln and Egon Guba (1985; Guba & Lincoln, 1981, 1989). These authors have been leading advocates of alternative paradigm inquiry, particularly within the evaluation field. Consistently grounded in detailed explications of philosophical debates and developments, their work has been influential in making the philosophical premises of inquiry both visible and accessible to many in the evaluation community. Although Guba and Lincoln's own philosophical thinking and naming have evolved over the years, core elements of their philosophical worldview have remained essentially the same. Drawing on their work and that of others, notably John Smith (1989), I will now provide an overview of the interpretivist paradigm, as generally understood and utilized by qualitative program evaluators.

The Interpretivist Paradigm in Evaluation

At root, interpretivism is about *contextualized meaning*. Interpretivist logic rejects the primacy of scientific realism, in either its traditional or more contemporary forms (House, 1991), along with its accompanying correspondence theory of truth. Rather, in interpretivism, social reality is viewed as significantly socially constructed, "based on a constant process of interpretation and reinterpretation of the intentional, meaningful behavior of people—including researchers" (Smith, 1989, p. 85), and "truth is ultimately a matter of socially and historically conditioned agreement" (p. 73). "'Reality' resides neither with an objective external world nor with the subjective mind of the knower, but within dynamic transactions between the two" (Barone, 1992b, p. 31). Social inquiry therefore is mind dependent; inquiry descriptions and interpretations are themselves constructions and (re)interpretations; and there can be no separation of the investigator from the investigated (Smith, 1989, chap. 4). Interpretivist inquiry is unabashedly and unapologetically subjectivist. It is also dialectic, for the process of meaning construction transforms the constructors.

Moreover, what is important to know, what constitutes an appropriate and legitimate focus for social inquiry, is the phenomenological meaningfulness of lived experience—people's interpretations and sense makings of their experiences in a given context. As Smith (1989) notes, this process is inevitably hermeneutical because "investigators, like everyone else, are part of the circle of interpretation" (p. 136). So understanding meaning as the goal of interpretivist inquiry "is not a matter of manipulation and control, particularly via method, but rather it is a question of openness and dialogue" (p. 137).

Meanings thus understood, or knowledge claims in interpretivist inquiry, take the form of working hypotheses or contextualized, temporary knowledge. Interpretivist knowledge claims are contestable precisely because they are contextualized and multiplistic, and also because they represent an intertwinement of facts and values. There are "no facts without values, and different values can actually lead to different facts" (Smith, 1989, p. 111). In this respect, interpretivism is value laden while it is simultaneously value relative or equally malleable by inquirers with quite different value stances (Greene, 1990, 1992). That is, interpretivist practice intentionally reveals the value dimensions of lived experience (because there are no facts without values), but the dimensionality revealed is importantly connected to, even constitutive of, the value orientations and stances of the inquirer (because different values can lead to different facts). Interpretivism as a philosophical logic of justification for inquiry acknowledges, even celebrates, the permeation of values throughout the inquiry process and results, but does not advocate or prescribe any one particular set of values for social inquiry. These are thus brought by the inquirer and, in this way, the values promoted by interpretivist inquiry practice are inherently varied and diverse.

Methodologically, interpretivism is most consonant with natural settings, with the human inquirer as the primary gatherer and interpreter of meaning, with qualitative methods, with emergent and expansionist inquiry designs, and with hermeneutic understanding, in contrast to interventionist prediction and control, as the overall goal of inquiry (Guba & Lincoln, 1989; Lincoln, 1990).

Yet, perhaps more significantly, the interpretive logic of justification represents a decentering of inquiry theory and practice from questions of method (Greene, 1992). In the field of program evaluation, which has long been characterized as, if not faulted for being, method driven, this is a substantial change. Like other interpretive inquirers, interpretivist evaluators reject the conventional stance that proper methods can insulate against bias and thereby ensure objectivity and truth. Yet, unlike some of their more radical peers, who disclaim the existence of any privileged methods that will enhance the acceptability of an inquirer's interpretations (Smith, 1989, p. 160), most interpretivist evaluators seek some procedural guidelines and support for their work. In particular, interpretivist evaluators seek to authenticate their interpretations as empirically based representations of program experiences and meanings, rather than as biased inquirer opinion. Time-honored procedures such as triangulation and negative case analysis (Denzin, 1978) and newer procedures such as member checks, peer debriefers, and audits (Lincoln & Guba, 1985) are all utilized by interpretivist evaluators to enhance the credibility of their inferences. Evaluators sense particular pressure to invoke such procedures because the contexts of program evaluation continue to demand assurances of methodological quality and data integrity in evaluative work. This work can make no contributions to social policy and program decision making unless it is perceived as credible and trustworthy.

So, although methods may not occupy center stage in interpretive evaluation approaches, questions of procedure in these approaches remain. And these questions are problematic because "to argue that certain procedures are required would simply pose a contradiction—the attempt to provide a methodological foundation for knowledge based on nonfoundational assumptions" (Smith, 1989, p. 159). On the one hand, interpretivist evaluators need methodological quality assurances for their audiences. On the other hand, the very idea of prescriptions for quality or any other methodological concern is philosophically inconsistent with the basic tenets of interpretivism. In response to this dilemma, interpretivist evaluators have generally accepted Smith's (1989, 1990) recasting of methodological concerns as choices, procedural guidelines as heuristics, and quality criteria as ever-evolving, open-ended lists.

Paradigms and Practice

Of course, not all qualitative evaluators find Smith's perspective sensible. Patton (1990), for example, offers a highly interpretivist frame for his qualitative evaluation approach in the form of "strategic themes," and simultaneously—without a single pang of philosophical conscience—promotes conventional measurement validity and reliability as key quality dimensions of qualitative data (p. 461). This is because Patton (1988, 1990) eschews the idea that inquiry paradigms frame or delimit methodological choices:

> Rather than believing that one must choose to align with one paradigm or another, I advocate a paradigm of choices. A paradigm of choices rejects methodological orthodoxy in favor of *methodological appropriateness* as the primary criterion for judging methodological quality. The issue then becomes . . . whether one has made sensible methods decisions given the purpose of the inquiry, the questions being investigated, and the resources available. (Patton, 1990, pp. 38-39)

For Patton, the selection, design, and implementation of evaluation methods should be flexibly based on practical need and situational responsiveness, rather than on the consonance of a set of methods with any particular philosophical paradigm. And so, "objectivist" and "subjectivist" methods can be used together unproblematically. This *practical pragmatic* stand is strongly supported by other applied social inquirers (e.g., Bryman, 1988; Firestone, 1990; Pitman & Maxwell, 1992), as well as by arguments from a position of *philosophical pragmatism* (e.g., Howe, 1988).

Although clearly supporting multiplistic mixes of qualitative and quantitative methods at the methodological level, Guba and Lincoln strongly contest the mixing of inquiry approaches at the paradigm level. They argue, for example, that one cannot simultaneously adhere to the objectivist detachment of conventional science and the subjectivist involvement of interpretivism. There are others who agree that paradigms are irreconcilable, yet still seek not accommodation but dialectically enhanced inquiry benefits through a pluralistic acceptance of multiple ways of knowing. To illustrate, Salomon (1991) maintains that social issues are vastly complex and thus require both an "analytic" and a "systemic" approach to inquiry, used in a complementary fashion across studies toward more complete understanding. This essential tension between philosophical paradigms and practice is likely to remain contested. It matters to evaluators because it has important effects on how we envision and do our work, as elaborated in the next section.

The Practice of Qualitative Evaluations

There are several critical dimensions of qualitative evaluation practice. Most qualitative evaluators (a) use case studies to frame their work and hence emphasize context, but not generalizability, as an essential element of meaning; (b) rely heavily but not exclusively on qualitative methods for meaning construction; (c) acknowledge if not celebrate the influential presence of their own selves in the inquiry process; and (d) seek in their work primarily to augment practical program understanding. The ensuing discussion will elaborate these dimensions, as well as connect them to prominent qualitative evaluation theories. In this way, salient features of each theory are highlighted, allocating more comprehensive portrayals of the theories to the works referenced.

Cases and Contexts

Some years ago, Robert Stake (1978) began encouraging evaluators to direct their energies toward the practical program concerns of stakeholders in the immediate context, rather than toward the more abstract questions of remote decision makers. Stake argued that by responsively focusing on the priority issues of practitioners within a given program or bounded case, evaluators can construct rich experiential understandings of that case. Such understandings, in turn, not only provide powerful information for program improvement, but also constitute a basis for *naturalistic generalizations,* which are grounded in the vicarious experience and tacit knowledge of the case reader. "Naturalistic generalizations develop within a person as a product of experience. They derive from the tacit knowledge of how things are . . . they seldom take the form of predictions but lead regularly to expectations. They guide action, in fact they are inseparable from action" (Stake, 1983, p. 282). Eisner (1991) makes a similar argument regarding the thematics of evaluative connoisseurship. Thematics represent the concrete universals of the case evaluated, the lessons learned, the moral of the story, and, as such, are of likely interest to others outside the case evaluated.

However, developing generalizable knowledge—even in such nonpropositional forms—is not the primary justification for embracing a case study framework for qualitative evaluations. Quite the contrary—the case for case studies in qualitative evaluations rests on a confluence of their responsive political-value stance and their underlying interpretivist assumptions. *Responsive* evaluation, first championed by Stake (1975; see also Stake, 1991), seeks expressly to uncover and then address the concerns of program stakeholders in the setting being evaluated toward the improvement of practice in that setting. From this responsive perspective, program improvement is more likely if local rather than remote concerns are addressed in the evaluation and if local rather than remote values are explicated and used to make program judgments. Although not all qualitative evaluators maintain an exclusive focus on program practitioners, most remain within evaluation's responsive tradition. In large part, this is because this tradition is philosophically buttressed by interpretivism's view of knowledge as contextualized meaning. As an essential part of meaning, context must be described and its contributions understood.

Qualitative evaluations thus characteristically take the form of case studies, with respectful attention to context, and rarely, if ever, resemble surveys, quasi-experiments, or other inquiry formats. Deciding just what constitutes a case, however, usually requires considered judgment, involving a balancing of desired results with available resources. Rarely do evaluation resources enable an in-depth assessment of all possible cases in a program setting. In an educational program evaluation, for example, considering the whole school district as a case is unlikely to be as feasible or as useful as considering schools, or grade levels within schools, or social groups within neighborhoods as possible cases. The latter are more likely to offer differentiated understandings of such key evaluation foci as peer group norms and influences.

A Preference for Qualitative Methods

All qualitative approaches to program evaluation are distinguished by their preference for qualitative methods, including open-ended interviews, on-site observation, participant observation, and document review. For many theorists and practitioners, these methods offer the greatest consonance with the interpretivist perspective that frames and guides their work. Qualitative methods rely on the interactional, adaptive, and judgmental abilities of the human inquirer; the interpretivist challenge of understanding and interpreting meaning demands no less.

Methods choices in evaluation studies are not only influenced by philosophical assumptions and frameworks. As important, or even more important, methods choices must match the information needs of the identified evaluation audiences. For this reason, surveys, client record analysis, and other quantitative methods are commonly incorporated into interpretivist evaluations. Representing an extreme position on this matter, the influential evaluation theorist Michael Patton (1990) advocates qualitative methods when they represent the best match to the intended evaluation user's information needs, rather than because they are consonant with interpretivism. That is, Patton contends that methods choices should devolve not primarily from some abstract philosophical paradigm, but rather substantially from the concrete information needs of identified evaluation users.

When these information needs comprise multiple perspectives, contextualized meanings, or the experience of program participation, for example, then qualitative methods should be employed. This aphilosophical stance on the justification for methods choices sets Patton somewhat apart from most other qualitative evaluation theorists, including Stake, Guba and Lincoln, and Eisner.

The Acknowledged Self in Inquiry

> Perception of the world is perception influenced by skill, point of view, focus, language, and framework. The eye, after all, is not only a part of the brain, it is a part of tradition. . . . [So what] we know is a function of a *transaction* between the qualities of the world we cannot know in their pure, nonmediated form, and the frames of reference, personal skills, and individual histories we bring to them. . . . [Knowledge or] experience thus conceived is a form of human achievement; it is not simply had, it is made. (Eisner, 1992, pp. 11-13)

> Evaluators are subjective partners with stakeholders in the literal creation of evaluation data. (Guba & Lincoln, 1989, p. 110)

Although Eisner and Guba and Lincoln differ in significant aspects of their theories, they share the premise that human knowledge is literally constructed during inquiry and hence is inevitably entwined with the perceptual frames, histories, and values of the inquirer. Qualitative evaluation à la Eisner or Guba and Lincoln is unabashedly subjective, unapologetically imbued with the individual perspectives and frames of the inquirer. No apologies are offered here, for two main reasons. First, along with many others in and outside of interpretivism, these theorists maintain that objectivity—understood as distanced detachment and neutrality intended to guard against bias and thereby to ensure the attainment of truth—is not possible and therefore should be rejected as a regulative ideal for social inquiry. Second, from an interpretivist perspective, it is precisely the individual qualities of the human inquirer that are valued as indispensable to meaning construction. In fact, Eisner's evaluation theory directly calls upon the substantive expertise of the individual connoisseur or expert. With a conjoint grounding in the arts, this theory highlights the enlightened eye and the seasoned judgment of the inquirer, along with his or her expertise in representation or in making public what has been seen. Eisner's evaluation connoisseur is an expert in the program to be assessed. Relying heavily on qualitative methods, the connoisseur collects information and then uses his or her expert frames and insights to integrate, interpret, and judge.

Thus the self of the qualitative evaluator is acknowledged to be present in the inquiry, a presence that permeates all methodological decisions and penetrates the very fabric of meaning constructed. Yet, just how much influence is acceptable and just how such influence can be monitored or detected, as needed, are issues of little consensus within the qualitative evaluation community. Eisner would contend, for example, that as the connoisseur, the qualitative evaluator carries authority that is supreme, and his or her influence in all aspects of the inquiry is expressly valued. In contrast with his view of the evaluator as a technical consultant, Patton would allocate more substantive authority to evaluation users. And he would rely on the proper application of qualitative methods to minimize the evaluator's presence in the program experiences and meanings investigated and understood. Given their vision of the evaluator as a negotiator, Guba and Lincoln would take a middle position, arguing that the meanings created and the interpretation and use of those meanings are responsibilities shared among the evaluator and program stakeholders. This range of views on the desired presence of self in qualitative evaluation is reflected in varied views on its primary purpose, as discussed next.

The Envisioned Inquiry in Society

Some vision of purpose is, at root, what guides all evaluation practice. In the responsive tradition in evaluation, inquirers have sought to augment local program understanding with the hope of moving toward program improvement. And the primary audiences for responsive evaluation have been program practitioners and participants. This vision of evaluation as the generation of local contextualized insights, as the reflective sharing of new program perspectives, as the telling of diverse program stories, is highly congruent with an interpretivist philosophy and a qualitative methodology. For example, participant observation is ideally suited for constructing the emic meaning of program participation for varied participants in that particular context.

For some within the evaluation community, however, understanding emic meaning and relating diverse program stories is not enough. Rather, as social inquirers in the public domain, we are morally and ethically compelled to assume greater responsibility for and a more active role in the social policy arena. Because our work can affect who gets what (House, 1980), we must be actively engaged with the consequences of our work. Yet, because of its inherent value relativity, interpretivism—while permitting alternative visions of evaluation purpose—does not in and of itself provide sufficient guidance or warrant for any particular alternative vision. Such guidance and warrant must come from somewhere outside the interpretivist logic of justification.

One important, long-standing exemplar of such politically engaged evaluation is the democratic evaluation tradition promoted by MacDonald (1976), Simons (1987), McTaggart (1990), and others. This evaluation model most centrally seeks to balance the public's right to know with the individual's right to privacy and to be discrete. The balance is sought via prescribed procedures for accessing, reviewing, negotiating, and releasing evaluation data. The concept of democratic evaluation is derived from the tradition of liberal democracy, and is thus politically and morally acceptable to existing power holders in democratic societies. At the same time, democratic evaluation seeks within its own boundaries to forge power-equalizing interactions and to establish a flow of information that is independent of hierarchical interests. Hence, in a democratic evaluation context, all relevant perspectives can be represented, information can be fairly and equitably exchanged, and open deliberation can be encouraged (Simons, 1987).

Guba and Lincoln's (1989) more recent fourth-generation evaluation approach represents a purposeful blending of an essentially interpretivist philosophy with an outside warrant for social action into what they call a *constructivist* framework for evaluation. Moving beyond the telling of stories, constructivism requires that evaluation catalyze social action. Yet, in consonance with interpretivism, the specific contours and facets of that action are not prescribed but rather emerge from the setting. In this way, constructivism differs from the more prescriptive empowerment, equity, and social justice agendas of critical, feminist, and other normative inquiry approaches. With this infusion of an outside warrant, fourth-generation evaluation seeks not so much program understanding as social change-oriented action, and the fourth-generation evaluator's role is not so much one of describer and consultant as one of negotiator and social change catalyst. More significantly, Guba and Lincoln's fourth-generation departures from the responsive tradition in evaluation well illustrate the critical vulnerabilities of qualitative evaluation today. These vulnerabilities are primarily in the areas of purpose and audience, in the envisioned role of inquiry in society. Interpretivism envisions no particular role, although an increasing clamor of contemporary voices is insisting otherwise. A sampling of these voices and what they portend for qualitative evaluation in the years ahead conclude this chapter.

Continuing Challenges

> Given the inescapable incursion of values into human activity, Freire's . . . dictum that there can be no neutral education is extended to practices of social inquiry. The inescapable political content of theories and methodologies becomes increasingly apparent. (Lather, 1992, p. 4)

> Social justice is among the most important values we should hope to secure in evaluation studies. . . . Public evaluation should be an institution for democratizing public decision making. . . . As a social practice, evaluation entails an inescapable ethic of public responsibility . . . [serving] the interests of the larger society and of various groups within society, particularly those most affected by the program under review. (House, 1990, pp. 23-24)

Of pivotal significance to the dizzying pluralism of social inquiry in the present era is the recognition that values permeate all observations, and hence all methods that are used to gather the observations, and hence all methodologies that frame and guide implementation of the methods. A critical question of the era is, thus, What values or whose? And in the public contexts of social program evaluation, the question becomes, What societal values or what visions of community constitute warranted frames for evaluation methodology?

Ernest House offers a vision rooted in conceptions of social justice (see also Sirotnik, 1990). Thomas Schwandt (1989, 1991) argues for a morally engaged evaluation practice that "aims at achieving insight and awareness into what it means to live a human life" (1991, p. 70). Schwandt's ideas incorporate recent challenges to the liberalist political tradition and concomitant arguments to replace our failed representative democracy with a genuinely participatory one (Barber, 1984) or with a communitarian ethic rooted in human interdependence and solidarity (Sullivan, 1986). An additional emancipatory vision for applied social inquiry is broadly represented by critical social scientists (e.g., Fay, 1987) and, more tellingly, by practicing participatory evaluators (Brunner & Guzman, 1989; Whitmore, 1990). In this vision, evaluation is viewed primarily as a process for promoting empowerment and requisite structural change. All of these visions offer an explicit political agenda for program evaluation, thereby not only recognizing the presence of values in inquiry, but specifically promoting one particular normative frame.

Of key relevance to the present discussion are questions of the intersection between this "inescapable" normative turn in social inquiry and qualitative approaches to program evaluation. In response, I would argue that qualitative approaches are highly compatible with and hence have much to offer more openly ideological approaches to program evaluation at the level of method or technique. Qualitative methods, for example, can effectively give voice to the normally silenced and can poignantly illuminate what is typically masked. Qualitative methods and approaches are already being employed in such ideologically oriented inquiry frameworks as critical ethnography (Anderson, 1989), narrative inquiry (Barone, 1992a; Bruner, 1986), and feminist social science (Lather, 1992). To illustrate, Fine (Chapter 4, this volume), notes, "More interestingly, qualitative researchers have begun to interrupt Othering by forcing subjugated voices in context to the front of our texts and by exploiting privileged voices to scrutinize the technologies of Othering." And Lather (1992) states:

> Feminist methodologies and epistemologies, [Harding] suggests, require new feminist uses of these familiar research methods . . . [of] listening to informants, observing behavior, [and] examining historical records. . . . Studying women from the perspective of their own experiences so that they/we can better understand our situations in the world is research designed for women instead of simply research *about* women. (p. 6)

At the broader level of methodology or paradigm, however, the interpretivist framework does not provide sufficient warrant or guidance for any given normative agenda. Interpretivism justifies values in inquiry, but does not justify any particular ones. As participants in the social policy arena, program evaluators are increasingly being called upon to get involved, to be a part of the action, to become public scientists. With their acknowledgment of values, qualitative approaches can help evaluators illuminate alternative paths or courses of action. Such approaches can be molded to fit varied and emerging inquiry shapes, from technical reports to dramatic dialogue. And they can adaptively respond to varied and evolving inquiry functions, including shifting social action agendas. For these reasons, qualitative approaches are likely to continue to be a significant and useful alternative in the methodological repertoire of program evaluators. Yet, also for these reasons, qualitative evaluations as a genre are destined to remain within evaluation's responsive tradition—beautifully responsive but, in being so, unable to assume a more proactive role in the social policy sphere. And so, because the evaluator as public scientist must be proactive, must him- or herself become an active and accountable player in the policy arena, qualitative evaluations will not be enough.

Notes

1. Evaluations are also conducted on objects (product evaluation) and on people (personnel evaluation), as well as on programs that few would consider social (e.g., executive professional development via outdoor experiences). Although Scriven (1991) and others would argue that the logic of evaluation is the same across different forms and objects of evaluation, I believe they constitute radically different tasks requiring qualitatively and politically different responses. This chapter, therefore, is restricted to social program evaluation, predominantly in the public domain.

2. Most major evaluation texts also have chapters on evaluation's history. See, for example, Guba and Lincoln (1981, 1989); Madaus, Scriven, and Stufflebeam (1983); Patton (1986); Rossi and Freeman (1985); and Shadish, Cook, and Leviton (1991).

3. That this debate runs deep and long is attested to by the recent sequence of Presidential Addresses by the 1990 and 1991 presidents of the American Evaluation Association, an exchange of quantitative and qualitative views that rekindled emotional layers of this debate (Lincoln, 1991; Sechrest, 1992). Moreover, as noted previously, important sectors of the evaluation community, including many practitioners and audiences, missed the qualitative-quantitative debate entirely. Admittedly, this debate can certainly be viewed as a rarefied intellectual exchange of no relevance to daily life. Nonetheless, there remains a gap between evaluation theory and practice, with much of the latter based on discarded epistemologies and paradigms. This gap remains troublesome to evaluators concerned about both defensible theory and meaningful practice.

References

Anderson, G. L. (1989). Critical ethnography in education: Origins, current status, and new directions. *Review of Educational Research, 59,* 249-270.

Atkinson, P., Delamont, S., & Hammersley, M. (1988). Qualitative research traditions: A British response to Jacob. *Review of Educational Research, 58,* 231-250.

Barber, B. (1984). *Strong democracy: Participatory politics for a new age.* Berkeley: University of California Press.

Barone, T. E. (1992a). Beyond theory and method: A case of critical storytelling. *Theory Into Practice, 31*(2), 142-146.

Barone, T. E. (1992b). On the demise of subjectivity in educational inquiry. *Curriculum Inquiry, 22,* 25-38.

Bernstein, R. J. (1983). *Beyond objectivism and relativism.* Philadelphia: University of Pennsylvania Press.

Bruner, J. (1986). *Actual minds, possible worlds.* Cambridge, MA: Harvard University Press.

Brunner, I., & Guzman, A. (1989). Participatory evaluation: A tool to assess projects and empower people. In R. F. Conner & M. Hendricks (Eds.), *International innovations in evaluation methodology* (pp. 9-18). San Francisco: Jossey-Bass.

Bryman, A. (1988). *Quantity and quality in social research.* London: Unwin Hyman.

Chen, H., & Rossi, P. H. (1983). Evaluating with sense: The theory-driven approach. *Evaluation Review, 7,* 283-302.

Cicirelli, V. G., & Associates. (1969). *The impact of Head Start: An evaluation of the effects of Head Start on children's cognitive and affective development* (Report to the Office of Economic Opportunity). Athens, OH: Ohio University/Westinghouse Learning Corporation.

Cook, T. D. (1985). Postpositivist critical multiplism. In L. Shotland & M. M. Mark (Eds.), *Social science and social policy* (pp. 21-62). Beverly Hills, CA: Sage.

Cook, T. D., & Reichardt, C. S. (Eds.). (1979). *Qualitative and quantitative methods in evaluation research.* Beverly Hills, CA: Sage.

Cronbach, L. J. (1963). Course improvement through evaluation. *Teachers College Record, 64,* 672-683.

Cronbach, L. J. (1982). *Designing evaluations of educational and social programs.* San Francisco: Jossey-Bass.

Cronbach, L. J., & Associates. (1980). *Toward reform of program evaluation.* San Francisco: Jossey-Bass.

Denzin, N. K. (1978). *The research act: An introduction to sociological methods.* New York: McGraw-Hill.

Denzin, N. K. (1989). *Interpretive interactionism.* Newbury Park, CA: Sage.

Eisner, E. W. (1976). Educational connoisseurship and criticism: Their forms and functions in educational evaluation. *Journal of Aesthetic Education, 10,* 135-150.

Eisner, E. W. (1991). Taking a second look: Educational connoisseurship revisited. In M. W. McLaughlin & D. C. Phillips (Eds.), *Evaluation and education: At quarter century* (pp. 169-187). Chicago: University of Chicago Press.

Eisner, E. W. (1992). Objectivity in educational research. *Curriculum Inquiry, 22,* 9-15.

Fay, B. (1987). *Critical social science.* Ithaca, NY: Cornell University Press.

Firestone, W. A. (1990). Accommodation: Toward a paradigm-praxis dialectic. In E. G. Guba (Ed.), *The paradigm dialog* (pp. 105-124). Newbury Park, CA: Sage.

Gage, N. L. (1989). The paradigm wars and their aftermath: A "historical" sketch of research on teaching since 1989. *Educational Researcher, 18*(7), 4-10.

Greene, J. C. (1990). Three views on the nature and role of knowledge in social science. In E. G. Guba (Ed.), *The paradigm dialog* (pp. 227-245). Newbury Park, CA: Sage.

Greene, J. C. (1991). *Responding to evaluation's moral challenge.* Paper presented at the annual meeting of the American Educational Research Association, Chicago.

Greene, J. C. (1992). The practitioner's perspective. *Curriculum Inquiry, 22*(1), 39-45.

Greene, J. C., & McClintock, C. (1991). The evolution of evaluation methodology. *Theory Into Practice, 30*(1), 13-21.

Guba, E. G. (Ed.). (1990). *The paradigm dialog.* Newbury Park, CA: Sage.

Guba, E. G., & Lincoln, Y. S. (1981). *Effective evaluation.* San Francisco: Jossey-Bass.

Guba, E. G., & Lincoln, Y. S. (1989). *Fourth generation evaluation.* Newbury Park, CA: Sage.

House, E. R. (1976). Justice in evaluation. In G. V Glass (Ed.), *Evaluation studies review annual* (Vol. 1). Beverly Hills, CA: Sage.

House, E. R. (1977). *The logic of evaluative argument.* Los Angeles: University of California, Center for the Study of Evaluation.

House, E. R. (1980). *Evaluating with validity.* Beverly Hills, CA: Sage.

House, E. R. (1990). Methodology and justice. In K. A. Sirotnik (Ed.), *Evaluation and social justice* (pp. 23-36). San Francisco: Jossey-Bass.

House, E. R. (1991). Realism in research. *Educational Researcher, 20*(6), 2-9.

Howe, K. R. (1988). Against the quantitative-qualitative incompatibility thesis or dogmas die hard. *Educational Researcher, 17*(8), 10-16.

Jacob, E. (1987). Qualitative research traditions: A review. *Review of Educational Research, 57,* 1-50.

Joint Committee on Standards for Educational Evaluation. (1981). *Standards for evaluations of educational programs, projects, and materials.* New York: McGraw-Hill.

Lather, P. (1992). Critical frames in educational research: Feminist and poststructural perspectives. *Theory Into Practice, 31*(2), 1-13.

Lincoln, Y. S. (1990). The making of a constructivist: A remembrance of transformations past. In E. G. Guba (Ed.), *The paradigm dialog* (pp. 67-87). Newbury Park, CA: Sage.

Lincoln, Y. S. (1991). The arts and sciences of program evaluation (AEA 1991 Presidential Address). *Evaluation Practice, 12*(1), 1-7.

Lincoln, Y. S., & Guba, E. G. (1985). *Naturalistic inquiry.* Beverly Hills, CA: Sage.

Linn, M. (1981). Standards for evaluating out-of-school learning. *Evaluation News, 2*(2), 171-176.

MacDonald, B. (1976). Evaluation and the control of education. In D. A. Tawney (Ed.), *Curriculum evaluation today: Trends and implications.* London: Falmer.

Madaus, G. F., Scriven, M., & Stufflebeam, D. L. (Eds.). (1983). *Evaluation models: Viewpoints on educa-*

tional and human services evaluation. Boston: Kluwer-Nijhoff.

Mark, M. M. (1986). Validity typologies and the logic and practice of quasi-experimentation. In W. M. K. Trochim (Ed.), *Advances in quasi-experimental design and analysis.* San Francisco: Jossey-Bass.

McTaggart, R. (1990, April). *Dilemmas in democratic evaluation: Politics and validation.* Paper presented at the annual meeting of the American Educational Research Association, Boston.

Parlett, M., & Hamilton, D. (1976). Evaluation as illumination: A new approach to the study of innovative programs. In G. V Glass (Ed.), *Evaluation studies review annual* (Vol. 1). Beverly Hills, CA: Sage.

Patton, M. Q. (1986). *Utilization-focused evaluation* (2nd ed.). Beverly Hills, CA: Sage.

Patton, M. Q. (1987). Evaluation's political inherency: Practical implications for design and use. In D. J. Palumbo (Ed.), *The politics of program evaluation* (pp. 100-145). Newbury Park, CA: Sage.

Patton, M. Q. (1988). Paradigms and pragmatism. In D. M. Fetterman (Ed.), *Qualitative approaches to evaluation in education: The silent scientific revolution* (pp. 116-137). New York: Praeger.

Patton, M. Q. (1990). *Qualitative evaluation and research methods* (2nd ed.). Newbury Park, CA: Sage.

Pitman, M. A., & Maxwell, J. A. (1992). Qualitative approaches to evaluation: Models and methods. In M. D. LeCompte, W. L. Millroy, & J. Preissle (Eds.), *The handbook of qualitative research in education* (pp. 729-770). New York: Academic Press.

Rossi, P. H., & Freeman, H. E. (1985). *Evaluation: A systematic approach* (3rd ed.). Beverly Hills, CA: Sage.

Rossi, P. H., & Lyall, K. C. (1978). An overview of the NIT experiment. In T. D. Cook, M. L. DelRosario, K. M. Hernigan, M. M. Mark, & W. M. K. Trochim (Eds.), *Evaluation studies review annual* (Vol. 3, pp. 412-428). Beverly Hills, CA: Sage.

Salomon, G. (1991). Transcending the qualitative-quantitative debate: The analytic and systemic approaches to educational research. *Educational Researcher, 20*(6), 10-18.

Schwandt, T. A. (1989). Recapturing moral discourse in evaluation. *Educational Researcher, 18*(8), 11-16, 34.

Schwandt, T. A. (1991). Evaluation as moral critique. In C. L. Larson & H. Preskill (Eds.), *Organizations in transition: Opportunities and challenges for evaluation* (pp. 63-72). San Francisco: Jossey-Bass.

Scriven, M. (1967). The methodology of evaluation. *AERA Monograph Series in Curriculum Evaluation, 1,* 39-83.

Scriven, M. (1973). Goal-free evaluation. In E. R. House (Ed.), *School evaluation: The politics and process* (pp. 319-328). Berkeley, CA: McCutchan.

Scriven, M. (1983). Evaluation ideologies. In G. F. Madaus, M. Scriven, & D. L. Stufflebeam (Eds.), *Evaluation models: Viewpoints on educational and human services evaluation* (pp. 229-260). Boston: Kluwer-Nijhoff.

Scriven, M. (1991). Beyond formative and summative evaluation. In M. W. McLaughlin & D. C. Phillips (Eds.), *Evaluation and education: At quarter century* (pp. 19-64). Chicago: University of Chicago Press.

Sechrest, L. (1992). Roots: Back to our first generations (AEA 1991 Presidential Address). *Evaluation Practice, 13*(1), 1-7.

Shadish, W. R., Cook, T. D., & Leviton, L. C. (1991). *Foundations of program evaluation: Theories of practice.* Newbury Park, CA: Sage.

Simons, H. (1987). *Getting to know schools in a democracy: The politics and process of evaluation.* London: Falmer.

Sirotnik, K. A. (Ed.). (1990). *Evaluation and social justice.* San Francisco: Jossey-Bass.

Sirotnik, K. A., & Oakes, J. (1990). Evaluation as critical inquiry: School improvement as a case in point. In K. A. Sirotnik (Ed.), *Evaluation and social justice* (pp. 37-53). San Francisco: Jossey-Bass.

Smith, J. K. (1989). *The nature of social and educational inquiry: Empiricism versus interpretation.* Norwood, NJ: Ablex.

Smith, J. K. (1990). Alternative research paradigms and the problem of criteria. In E. G. Guba (Ed.), *The paradigm dialog* (pp. 167-187). Newbury Park, CA: Sage.

Smith, J. K., & Heshusius, L. (1986). Closing down the conversation: The end of the quantitative-qualitative debate. *Educational Researcher, 15*(1), 4-12.

Soltis, J. F. (1990, April). *The hermeneutics/interpretive tradition and its virtues.* Paper presented at the annual meeting of the American Educational Research Association, Boston.

Stake, R. E. (1967). The countenance of educational evaluation. *Teachers College Record, 68,* 523-540.

Stake, R. E. (1975). *Evaluating the arts in education: A responsive approach.* Columbus, OH: Merrill.

Stake, R. E. (1978). The case study method in social inquiry. *Educational Researcher, 7*(1), 5-8.

Stake, R. E. (1983). The case study method in social inquiry. In G. F. Madaus, M. Scriven, & D. L. Stufflebeam (Eds.), *Evaluation models: Viewpoints on educational and human services evaluation* (pp. 279-286). Boston: Kluwer-Nijhoff.

Stake, R. E. (1991). Retrospective on "The countenance of educational evaluation." In M. W. McLaughlin & D. C. Phillips (Eds.), *Evaluation and education: At quarter century* (pp. 67-88). Chicago: University of Chicago Press.

Stufflebeam, D. L. (1991). Professional standards and ethics for evaluators. In M. W. McLaughlin & D. C. Phillips (Eds.), *Evaluation and education: At quarter century* (pp. 249-282). Chicago: University of Chicago Press.

Sullivan, W. M. (1986). *Reconstructing public philosophy*. Berkeley: University of California Press.

Weiss, C. H. (1970). The politicization of evaluation research. *Journal of Social Issues, 26*, 57-68.

Weiss, C. H. (Ed.). (1972). *Evaluating action programs: Readings in social action and education*. Boston: Allyn & Bacon.

Weiss, C. H. (Ed.). (1977). *Using social research in public policy making*. Lexington, MA: Lexington.

Weiss, C. H. (1987). Where politics and evaluation research meet. In D. J. Palumbo (Ed.), *The politics of program evaluation* (pp. 47-70). Newbury Park, CA: Sage.

Whitmore, E. (1990). *Focusing on the process in evaluation: It's the "how" that counts*. Paper presented at the annual meeting of the American Evaluation Association, Washington, DC.

34

Influencing the Policy Process With Qualitative Research

RAY C. RIST

MORE than 20 years ago, James Coleman wrote, "There is no body of methods; no comprehensive methodology for the study of the impact of public policy as an aid to future policy." This now-famous quote still rings true. Indeed, one can argue that in the intervening decades, the tendency in policy research and analysis has become ever more centrifugal, spinning off more methodologies and variations on methodologies, more conceptual frameworks, and more disarray among those who call themselves policy analysts or see themselves working in the area of policy studies. A number of critics of the current scene of policy studies and the attendant applications of so many different methodologies have argued that any improvements in the techniques of policy research have not led to greater clarity about what to think or what to do. More charitably, it could be said that the multiplicity of approaches to policy research should be welcomed, as they bring different skills and strengths to what are admittedly difficult and complex issues.

Regardless of whether one supports or challenges the contention that policy research has had a centrifugal impact on the knowledge base relevant to policy making, the bottom line remains much the same: What policy researchers tend to consider as improvements in their craft have not significantly enhanced the role of research in policy making. Instead, the proliferation of persons, institutes, and centers conducting policy-related work has led to more variation in the manner by which problems are defined, more divergence in the ways in which studies are designed and conducted, and more disagreement and controversy over the ways in which data are analyzed and findings reported. The policy maker now confronts a veritable glut of differing (if not conflicting) research information.

A sobering but provocative counterintuitive logic is at work here: Increased personnel, greater allocation of resources, and growing sophistication of methods have not had the anticipated or demonstrated effect of greater clarity and understanding of the policy issues before the country. Rather, current efforts have led to a more complex, complicated, and partial view of the issues and their solutions. Further, as Smith (1991) would argue, this tendency to greater complexity has left both the policy makers and the citizens less able to understand the issues and to see how their actions might affect the present condition.

Whereas one may grant that early analyses, for example, in the areas of education or social welfare, were frequently simplistic and not especially sophisticated in either the design or application of

AUTHOR'S NOTE: The views expressed here are those of the author, and no endorsement by the U.S. General Accounting Office is intended or should be inferred.

policy methods, the inverse does not, in and of itself, work to the advantage of the policy maker. Stated differently, to receive a report resplendent with "state-of-the-art" methodologies and complex analyses that tease out every nuance and shade of meaning on an issue may provide just as little guidance for effective decision making as did the former circumstances. The present fixation on the technical adequacy of policy research without a commensurate concern for its utilization is to relegate that work to quick obscurity (Chelimsky, 1982).

If this admittedly brief description of the current state of policy research approximates the reality, then a fundamental question arises: Is the presumption correct that research cannot be conducted that is relevant to the policy process? It is my view that the presumption is not correct. Research can contribute to informed decision making, but the manner in which this is done needs to be reformulated. We are well past the time when it is possible to argue that good research will, because it is good, influence the policy process. That kind of linear relation of research to action simply is not a viable way in which to think about how knowledge can inform decision making. The relation is both more subtle and more tenuous. Still, there is a relation. It is my intent in this chapter to address how some of the linkages of knowledge and action are formed, particularly for the kinds of knowledge generated through qualitative research.[1]

The Nature of Policy Decision Making

Policy making is multidimensional and multifaceted. Research is but one (and often minor at that) among the number of frequently contradictory and competing sources that seek to influence what is an ongoing and constantly evolving process. The emphasis here on policy making being a *process* is deliberate. It is a process that evolves through cycles, with each cycle more or less bounded, more or less constrained by time, funds, political support, and other events. It is also a process that circles back on itself, iterates the same decision issue time and again, and often does not come to closure. Choosing not to decide is a frequent outcome.

Such a description of the policy process suggests the need for a modification, if not a fundamental reframing, of the traditional understanding of policy making. In this latter, more traditional approach, decision making in the policy arena is understood as a discrete event, undertaken by a defined set of actors working in "real time" and moving to their decision on the basis of an analysis of their alternatives. Weiss (1982) has nicely summarized this notion of "decision making as an event":

> Both the popular and the academic literature picture decision making as an event; a group of authorized decision makers assemble at particular times and places, review a problem (or opportunity), consider a number of alternative courses of action with more or less explicit calculation of the advantages and disadvantages of each option, weigh the alternatives against their goals or preferences, and then select an alternative that seems well suited for achieving their purposes. The result is a decision. (p. 23)

She also nicely demolishes this view when she writes:

> Given the fragmentation of authority across multiple bureaus, departments, and legislative committees, and the disjointed stages by which actions coalesce into decisions, the traditional model of decision making is a highly stylized rendition of reality. Identification of any clear-cut group of decision makers can be difficult. (Sometimes a middle-level bureaucrat has taken the key action, although he or she may be unaware that his or her action was going to be—or was—decisive.) The goals of policy are often equally diffuse, except in terms of "taking care of" some undesirable situation. Which opinions are considered, and what set of advantages or disadvantages are assessed, may be impossible to tell in the interactive, multiparticipant, diffuse process of formulating policy. The complexity of governmental decision making often defies neat compartmentalization. (p. 26)

Of particular relevance here is that the focus on decision making as an ongoing set of adjustments, or midcourse corrections, eliminates the bind of having to pinpoint the event—that is, the exact time, place, and manner—in which research has been influential on policy. Parenthetically, because the specifics can seldom be supplied, the notion that research *should* have an impact on decision making seems to have become more and more an article of faith. That researchers have so persistently misunderstood decision making, and yet have constantly sought to be of influence, is a situation deserving of considerably more analysis than it receives. So long as researchers presume that research findings must be brought to bear upon a single event, a discrete act of decision making, they will be missing those circumstances and processes where, in fact, research can be useful. However, the reorientation away from "event decision making" and to "process decision making" necessitates looking at research as serving an "enlightenment function" in contrast to an "engineering function" (see Janowitz, 1971; Patton, 1988; Weiss, 1988).

Viewing policy research as serving an enlightenment function suggests that policy researchers work with policy makers and their staffs over time to create a contextual understanding about an issue, build linkages that will exist over time, and strive constantly to educate about new developments and research findings in the area. This is in contrast to the engineering perspective, where it is presumed that sufficient data can be brought to bear to determine the direction and intensity of the intended policy initiative, much as one can develop the specifications for the building of a bridge. If the policy direction is sufficiently explicit, then the necessary information relevant to the development of the policy can be collected, so this view would contend, and the policy actions can be deliberate, directed, and successful.

These comments should not be taken as a diatribe against research or an argument that knowledge counts for naught. Quite the contrary. Systematic knowledge generated by research is an important and necessary component in the decision-making process. Further, it is fair to note that there is seldom enough research-based information available in the policy arena. William Ruckelshaus once noted that although he was the administrator of the Environmental Protection Agency, he made many decisions when there was less than 10% of the necessary research information available to him and his staff. The relevance and usefulness of policy research will not become apparent, however, unless there is a reconsideration of what is understood by decision making in the policy process. A redefinition is needed of the context in which to look for a linkage between knowledge and action. Unpacking the nature of the policy cycle is the strategy employed here to address this redefinition of policy decision making.

The Policy Cycle and Qualitative Research

There are two levels of decision making in the policy arena. The first involves the establishment of the broad parameters of government action, such as providing national health insurance, establishing a national energy policy, restructuring the national immigration laws, or reexamining the criteria for determining the safety and soundness of the country's financial institutions. At this level and in these instances, policy research input is likely to be quite small, if not nil. The setting of these national priorities is a political event, a coming together of a critical mass of politicians, special interest groups, and persons in the media who are able among them to generate the attention and focus necessary for the items to reach the national agenda.

"Iron triangles" built by the informal linking of supporters in each of these three arenas are not created by the presence or absence of policy research. One or another research study might be quoted in support of the contention that the issue deserves national attention, but it is incidental to the more basic task of first working to place the issue on the national agenda. If one wishes to influence any of the players during this phase of the policy process, it is much more likely to be done through personal contact, by organizations taking positions, or through the creation of sufficient static in the policy system (for example, lining up special interest groups in opposition to a proposal, even as there are groups in favor). This works to the benefit of the opposition in that media coverage will have to be seen to be "balanced" and coverage of the opposition can create the impression that there is not the strong unified support for a position that otherwise would seem to be the case.

Once the issue is on the agenda of key actors or organizations within the policy establishment, there are possibilities for the introduction and utilization of policy research. It is here at this second level of policy making—the level where there are concerns about translating policy intentions into policy and programmatic realities—that I will focus in this chapter.

The framework in which the contributions of policy research in general and qualitative research in particular can best be understood is that of the policy cycle, a concept that has been addressed for more than a decade (see, e.g., Chelimsky, 1985; Guba, 1984; Nakamura & Smallwood, 1980; Rist, 1989, 1990, 1993). I will develop my discussion of the policy cycle here according to its three phases—policy formulation, policy implementation, and policy accountability. Each of these three phases has its own order and logic, its own information requirements, and its own policy actors. Further, there is only some degree of overlap among the three phases, suggesting that they do merit individual analysis and understanding.

The opportunities for qualitative research within the policy cycle are thus defined and differentiated by the information requirements at each phase. The questions asked at each phase are distinct, and the information generated in response to these same questions is used to different ends. It is to a detailed examination of these three phases of the policy cycle and the manner in which qualitative research can inform each phase that I now turn.

Policy Formulation

Nakamura and Smallwood (1980) define a policy as follows: "A policy can be thought of as a set of instructions from policy makers to policy implementers that spell out both goals and the means for achieving those goals" (p. 31). How is it that these instructions are crafted, by whom, and with what relevant policy information and analysis? The answers can provide important insights into the process of policy formulation. Nakamura and Smallwood offer a relevant departure point with their description of the actors involved in policy formulation:

> In general, the principal actors in policy formulation are the "legitimate" or formal policy makers: people who occupy positions in the governmental arena that entitle them to authoritatively assign priorities and commit resources. These people include elected officials, legislators, and high-level administrative appointees, each of whom must follow prescribed paths to make policy. . . . Since these formal policy makers represent diverse constituencies—electoral, administrative, and bureaucratic—the policy making process offers many points of access through which interest groups and others from arenas outside government can exercise influence. Thus policy making usually involves a diverse set of authoritative, or formal, policy makers, who operate within the governmental arena, plus a diverse set of special interest and other constituency groups from outside arenas, who press their demands on these formal leaders. (pp. 31-32)

As the formulation process begins, there are a number of pressing questions. Answering each question necessitates the compiling of whatever information is currently available plus the development of additional information when the gaps are too great in what is currently known. The information needs can generally be clustered around three broad sets of questions. Each of these clusters is highly relevant to policy formulation; in each there are important opportunities for the presentation and utilization of qualitative research.

The first set of information needs revolves around an understanding of the policy issue at hand. What are the contours of this issue? Is the problem or condition one that is larger now than before, about the same, or smaller? Is anything known about whether the nature of the condition has changed? Do the same target populations, areas, or institutions experience this condition now as earlier? How well can the condition be defined? How well can the condition be measured? What are the different interpretations and understandings about the condition, its causes and its effects? The issue here, stated differently, is one of the ability of policy makers to define clearly and understand the problem or condition that they are facing and for which they are expected to develop a response.

Charles Lindblom (1968) has nicely captured some of the conceptual complexity facing policy makers as they try to cope with the definition of a policy problem or condition:

> Policy makers are not faced with a given problem. Instead they have to identify and formulate their problem. Rioting breaks out in dozens of American cities. What is the problem? Maintaining law and order? Racial discrimination? Incipient revolution? Black power? Low income? Lawlessness at the fringe of an otherwise relatively peaceful reform movement? Urban disorganization? Alienation? (p. 13)

The second cluster of questions focuses on what has taken place previously in response to this condition or problem. What programs or projects have previously been initiated? How long did they last? How successful were they? What level of funding was required? How many staff members were required? How receptive were the populations or institutions to these initiatives? Did they request help or did they resist the interventions? Did the previous efforts address the same condition or problem as currently exists, or was it different? If it was different, how so? If it was the same, why are yet additional efforts necessary? Are the same interest groups involved? What may explain any changes in the present interest group coalition?

The third cluster of questions relevant to the policy formulation stage of the cycle focuses on what is known of the previous efforts and their impacts that would help one choose among present-day options. Considering trade-offs among various levels of effort in comparison to different levels of cost is but one among several kinds of data relevant to considering the policy options. There may also be data on the time frames necessary before one could hope to see impacts. Trade-offs between the length of the developmental stage of the program and the eventual impacts are relevant, particularly if there are considerable pressures for short-term solutions. The tendency to go to "weak thrust, weak effect" strategies is well understood in these circumstances. Alternatively, if previous efforts did necessitate a considerable period of time for measurable outcomes to appear, how did the policy makers in those circumstances hold on to the public support and keep the coalitions intact long enough for the results to emerge?

Qualitative research is highly relevant to the information needs at this stage in the policy cycle.

Studies on the social construction of problems, on the differing interpretations of social conditions, on the building and sustaining of coalitions for change, on previous program initiatives and their impacts, on community and organizational receptivity to programs, on organizational stability and cohesion during the formulation stage, and on the changing nature of social conditions are all germane to the questions posed here.

There is an additional contribution that qualitative work can make at this stage of the policy process, and it is that of studying the intended and unintended consequences of the various policy instruments or tools that might be selected as the means to implement the policy (Salamon, 1989). There is a present need within the policy community to ascertain what tools work best in which circumstances and for which target populations. Very little systematic work has been done in this area—which frequently leaves policy makers essentially to guess as to the trade-offs between the choice of one tool and another.

Information of the kind provided by qualitative research can be of significant help in making decisions, for example, about whether to provide direct services in health, housing, and education or provide vouchers to recipients, whether to provide direct cash subsidies or tax credits to employers who will hire unemployed youth, and whether to increase funding for information campaigns or to increase taxes as strategies to discourage smoking. These are but three examples where different policy tools are available and where choices will have to be made among them.

Key among the activities in the policy formulation stage is the selection of the most appropriate policy strategy to achieve the desired objective. Central to the design of this strategy is the selection of one or more tools available to the government as the means to carry out its intentions. Qualitative studies of how different tools are understood and responded to by target populations is of immense importance at this stage of the policy process.

Unfortunately, although the demand for analysis of this type is great, the supply is extremely limited. The qualitative study of policy tools is an area that is yet to be even modestly explored within the research community.

Although qualitative research can be relevant at this stage, it is also the case that its applications are problematic. The basic reason is that seldom is there enough time to both commission and complete new qualitative research within the existing window of opportunity during policy formulation. Thus the applications have to rely on existing qualitative research—and that may or may not exist. Here is one key means by which good, well-crafted qualitative work on topical social issues can find its way into the policy arena. As policy makers start on the formulation effort, their need to draw quickly on existing work puts a premium on those research studies that have worked through matters of problem definition, the social construction of problems, community studies, retrospective assessments of prior initiatives, and so on.

The problematic nature of the applications of qualitative research at this stage is further reinforced by the fact that seldom are research funds available for studies that address the kinds of questions noted above in the three clusters. If the problem or condition is not seen to be above the horizon and thus on the policy screen, there is little incentive for a policy maker or program manager to use scarce funds for what would appear to be nonpragmatic, "theoretical" studies. And by the time the condition has sufficiently changed or become highly visible as a social issue for the policy community, qualitative work is hard-pressed to be sufficiently time sensitive and responsive. The window for policy formulation is frequently very small and open only a short time. The information that can be passed through has to be ready and in a form that enhances quick understanding.

The above constraints on the use of qualitative research at this stage of the policy cycle should not be taken as negative judgments on either the utility or the relevance of such information. Rather, it is only realistic to acknowledge that having the relevant qualitative research available when it is needed for policy formulation is not always possible. As noted earlier, this is an area where there are potentially significant uses for qualitative studies. But the uses are likely to come because of scholars and researchers who have taken on an area of study for their own interest and to inform basic understandings in the research community, rather than presuming before they begin that they would influence the formulation process. It is only the infrequent instance where there is sufficient time during the formulation stage for new qualitative work to be conducted.

It should be stressed here that the restrictions on the use of qualitative work during the formulation phase of the policy cycle come much more from the nature of the policy process than from the nature of qualitative work. The realities of the legislative calendar, the short lives of most senior political appointees in any one position, the mad scramble among competing special interest groups for their proposals to be addressed and acted upon, and the lack of concentration by the media on any issue for very long all inhibit the development of research agendas that address the underlying issues. This is ironic because it is clear that the country will face well into the foreseeable future the issues of health care allocation and quality, immigration controls and border security, educational retraining of dislocated workers, and youth unemployment, to name but four areas that have heretofore persistently stayed near or at the top of the national policy agenda. Basic, in-depth qualitative work in these and other key areas could inform the policy formulation process for years to come. But the pressures and structural incentives in the policy system all go in the other direction. To wit: Develop short-term proposals with quick impacts to show responsiveness and accommodate all the vested interests in the iron triangle.

In sum, with respect to this first phase of the policy cycle, qualitative research can be highly influential. This is particularly so with respect to problem definition, understanding of prior initiatives, community and organizational receptivity to particular programmatic approaches, and the kinds of impacts (both anticipated and unanticipated) that might emerge from different intervention strategies. This information would be invaluable to policy makers. But, as noted, the use of the material can be hindered by such factors as whether or not the information exists, is known to the policy community, and is available in a form that makes it quickly accessible. Overcoming these obstacles does not guarantee the use of qualitative research in the formulation process, but one can be strongly assured that if these obstacles are present, the likelihood of the use of qualitative material drastically diminishes.

Policy Implementation

The second phase of the policy cycle is that of policy implementation. It is in this stage that the policy initiatives and goals established during policy formulation are to be transformed into programs, procedures, and regulations. The knowledge base that policy makers need to be effective in this phase necessitates the collection and analysis of different information from that found in policy formulation. With the transformation of policies into programs, the concern moves to the operational activities of the policy tool and the allocation of resources. The concern becomes one of how to use the available resources in the most efficient and effective manner in order to have the most robust impact on the program or condition at hand. As Pressman and Wildavsky (1984) have written in this regard:

> Policies imply theories. Whether stated explicitly or not, policies point to a chain of causation between initial conditions and future consequences. If X, then Y. Policies become programs when, by authoritative action, the initial conditions are created. X now exists. Programs make the theories operational by forging the first link in the causal chain connecting actions to objectives. Given X, we act to obtain Y. Implementation, then, is the ability to forge subsequent links in the causal chain so as to obtain the desired results. (p. xxii)

The research literature on policy and program implementation indicates that that is a particularly difficult task to accomplish (see, e.g., Hargrove, 1985; Pressman & Wildavsky, 1984; Yin, 1985). Again, quoting Pressman and Wildavsky:

> Our normal expectations should be that new programs will fail to get off the ground and that, at best, they will take considerable time to get started. The cards in this world are stacked against things happening, as so much effort is required to make them work. The remarkable thing is that new programs work at all. (p. 109)

It is in this context of struggling to find ways of making programs work that the data and analyses from qualitative research can come into play. The information needs from qualitative research at this stage of the policy cycle cluster into several areas. First, there is a pressing need for information on the implementation process per se. Qualitative researchers, through case studies, program monitoring, and process evaluations, can inform program managers responsible for the implementation of the policy initiative.

Qualitative work can focus on such questions as the degree to which the program is reaching the intended target audience, the similarities and contrasts in implementation strategies across sites, the aspects of the program that are or are not operational, whether the services slated to be delivered are in fact the ones delivered, and the operational burdens placed on the institution or organization responsible for implementation (i.e., Is there the institutional capacity to respond effectively to the new policy initiative?). The focus is on the day-to-day realities of bringing a new program or policy into existence. This "ground-level" view of implementation is best done through qualitative research. The study of the rollout of an implementation effort is an area where qualitative work is at a clear advantage over other data collection strategies.

A second cluster of research questions amenable to qualitative work in the implementation arena focuses on the problem or condition that prompted the policy or program response in the first place. No problem or condition stands still, simply because the policy community has decided to take action on what was known at the time the decision was made. Problems and conditions change—both before and after a policy response is decided upon. Thus the challenge for qualitative researchers is to continue to track the condition, even as the implementation effort swings into action. Qualitative work can provide ongoing monitoring of the situation—whether the condition has improved, worsened, remained static; whether the same target population is involved as earlier; whether the condition has spread or contracted; and whether the aims of the program still match the assumptions and previous understandings of the condition. Qualitative work can provide an important reality check for program managers as to whether the program is or is not appropriate to the current condition. Qualitative work that monitors the condition in real time can play a key role in the continuous efforts of program managers to match their services or interventions to the present circumstances.

The third cluster of necessary policy questions during this implementation phase of the policy cycle focuses on the efforts made by the organization or institution to respond to the initiative. Here, for example, qualitative data would be relevant for learning how the organizational response to the condition or problem has been conceptualized. Are the social constructions of the problem that were accepted at the policy formulation stage by federal policy makers accepted during implementation by the program managers and staff months later and perhaps thousands of miles away? What has been the transformation of the understandings that have taken place when the policy or program is actually being implemented? Do the policy makers and the program implementation folks accept the same understandings as to the intent of the policy—let alone the same understandings of the problem that the policy is suppose to address?

Another aspect of this need for qualitative data concerns the organizational response. Here questions would be asked that address the expertise and qualifications of those responsible for the implementation effort, the interest shown by management and staff, the controls in place regarding the allocation of resources, the organizational structure and whether it adequately reflects the demands on the organization to respond to this initiative, what means exist in the organization for deciding among competing demands, the strategies the organization uses to clarify misunderstandings or ambiguities in how it defines its role in implementation, and, finally, what kinds of interactive information or feedback loops are in place to assist managers in their ongoing efforts to move the program toward the stated objectives of the policy. It is information of precisely this type on the implementation process that Robert Behn (1988) notes is so critical to managers as they struggle to "grope along" and move toward organizational goals.

Policy Accountability

The third stage in the policy cycle comes when the policy or program is sufficiently mature that one can address questions of accountability, impacts, or outcomes. Here again, the information needs are different from those in the two previous stages of the policy cycle. The contributions of qualitative research can be pivotal in assessing the consequences of the policy and program initiative. Just as the questions change from one part of the policy cycle to another, so too does the focus of the qualitative research necessary to answer these same questions.

First there is the matter of what the program or policy did or did not accomplish: Were the objectives for the program met? Qualitative research can specifically help in this regard by addressing, for example, whether the community and police were actively working together in a neighborhood "crime watch" program, whether the appropriate target audience of homeless persons in another program received the health services they were promised, and whether in a third program youth were given the type and quantity of on-the-job training that resulted in successful placements in permanent positions.

When a program reaches the stage that it is appropriate to discuss and assess impacts, qualitative research provides a window on the program that is simply not available in any other way. Qualitative research allows for the study of both anticipated and unanticipated outcomes, changes in understandings and perceptions as a result of the efforts of the program or policy, the direction and intensity of any social change that results from the program, and the strengths and weaknesses of the administrative/organizational structure that was used to operationalize the program. Policy makers have no equally grounded means of learning about program impacts and outcomes as they do with qualitative research findings.

These grounded means of knowing also carry over into what one might traditionally think of as quantitative assessments of policy. Qualitative work can provide to program managers and policy makers information on how confident they can or should be in the measures being used to determine program influence. Although the intent may be that of a highly reliable and replicable instrument that allows for sophisticated quantification, it is the qualitative work that can address the issue of validity.

The issues of reliability and validity are well known in the research literature and need not be reviewed here. Suffice it to say that policy makers and program managers have been misled more than once by investing a great deal of time and effort on their instrumentation without equal emphasis on answering the question of whether their measures were the appropriate ones to the problem or condition at hand. Studies of school desegregation and busing or health care in nursing homes are but two areas where a heavy emphasis on quantifying outcomes and processes have left key aspects of the condition undocumented and thus unattended to by those who should have been paying attention.

There is an additional aspect of this first cluster of information needs that merits special attention vis-à-vis qualitative research. This has to do with whether the original objectives and goals of the policy stayed in place through implementation. One message has come back to policy makers time and again: Do not take for granted that what was intended to be established or put in place through a policy initiative will be what one finds after the implementation process is complete. Programs and policies make countless midcourse corrections, tacking constantly, making changes in funding levels, staff stability, target population movements, political support, community acceptance, and the like.

It is through the longitudinal perspective of qualitative work that such issues can be directly addressed. Blitzkrieg assessments of programs are simply unable to pick up the backstage issues and conflicts that will inevitably be present and that may directly influence the direction and success of the program (Rist, 1980). To ignore staff turnover in a program that is highly staff-intensive in the provision of services, for instance, is to miss what may be the key ingredient in any study of implementation. But recognizing that it may be an issue in the first place is one of the ways in which qualitative work distinguishes itself from other research strategies.

The second cluster of information needs that emerge when a program is being assessed for impacts and outcomes is that of addressing whether and what changes may have occurred in the problem or condition. Central to any study of outcomes is the determination of whether in fact the condition itself has changed or not and what relevance the program or policy did or did not have to the present circumstances.

Although it is rudimentary to say so, it is worth stating explicitly that problems can change or not, totally independently of any policy or program initiative. Conceptually what we have is a situation in which impacts could or could not have occurred, and the consequence would be change or no change in a program or condition.

For example, a positive outcome of a policy could be no worsening of a condition, that is, no change in the original status that first prompted the policy response. Developing local intervention programs that stalled any growth in the number of child abuse cases could be considered a positive outcome. The key question is, of course, whether the evidence of no growth can be attributed to the intervention program or some other factor that was affecting the community independent of the intervention program itself, such as broad media coverage of a particularly savage beating of a child and, in the aftermath, considerable additional media coverage of how parents can cope with their urges to injure their children.

Qualitative work in this instance could focus on such impacts as the outreach efforts of the program to attract parents who had previously abused their children; efforts to reach parents who are seeking help to build better skills in working with their children; patterns and trends in child abuse as discussed by schoolteachers, day-care providers, and others who have ongoing and consistent contact with children; and whether and how parents are now coping with the stresses that might cause them to abuse their children.

The above discussion also generates an additional area in which qualitative work can assist at this stage of the policy cycle. It is the close-in and intensive familiarity with the problem or condition that comes from conducting qualitative work that would allow the researcher to make judgments on whether the situation is of a magnitude and nature that further action is necessary. If the study indicates that the problem or condition is diminishing in severity and prevalence, then further funding of a programmatic response may not be necessary. As a contrary example, the data from qualitative work may suggest that the condition has changed directions—that is, moved to a new target population—and a refocusing of the program is necessary if it is to be responsive.

Social conditions do not remain static, and the realization that the characteristics of a condition can change necessitates periodic reexamination of the original policy intent (policy formulation). Qualitative researchers can position themselves so that they can closely monitor the ongoing characteristics of a condition. With this firsthand and close-in information, they are well suited to suggest any necessary changes to both the policy formulation and implementation strategies for subsequent intervention efforts.

The third information need at this stage of the policy cycle where qualitative work can be of direct use comes with the focus on accountability. Here qualitative work can address concerns of management supervision, leadership of the organization with clear goals in mind, the attention to processes and procedures that would strengthen the capacity of the organization to implement the policy initiative effectively, the use of data-based decision making, and the degree of alignment or congruence between the leadership and the staff. All of these issues speak directly to the capacity of an organization to mobilize itself to provide effective service to its customers. If the organization is not positioned to do so, then there are clear issues of accountability that rest with the leadership.

Qualitative researchers who come to know an organization thoroughly and from the inside will be in a unique position from which to address the treatment and training of staff, reasons for attrition and low morale, the service-oriented philosophy (or lack of it) among the staff and leadership, the beliefs of the staff in the viability and worthiness of the program to address the problem, the quality and quantity of information used within the program for decision making, and the like. These are true qualitative dimensions of organizational life. It is essential that these be studied if judgments are to be made on the efficiency and effectiveness of any particular programmatic strategy. These judgments become central to subsequent decisions on the potential selection of a policy tool that would require a similar program intervention.

There are clear concerns of management accountability that must be discussed and assessed whenever programs are to be funded anew or redirected. Some of these concerns deal directly with impacts on the problem or condition, whereas others focus on the internal order and logic of the organization itself. Stated differently, it is important during the accountability phase to determine the degree to which any changes in the condition or problem can be directly attributed to the program and whether the program optimized or suboptimized the impact it had. Likewise, it is important to ascertain whether the presence (or absence) of any documented impacts is the result of the coherence of the policy formulation or the nature of program implementation. Finding that instance where coherent and robust policy initiatives are operationalized within a well-managed organization necessitates the complex assessment of what impacts can be attributed to the policy and what to its successful implementation. Qualitative research has a perspective on how to undertake this kind of assessment that other research approaches do not and for which the other approaches would have to rely heavily on proxy measures.

Policy Tools

The analysis thus far has focused on the nature of the policy cycle and how each phase of the cycle has different information requirements for policy makers and program managers. The effort has been to document how qualitative research can play an active and positive role in answering the information needs at each of these phases and for both the policy makers and the program managers. In this section, the attention shifts to a focus on what are termed *policy tools.*

Such an emphasis is important because a deeper understanding of the tools available to government and how each can be more or less effectively used to achieve policy objectives can clearly inform all three stages of the policy cycle. Key to the efforts in policy formulation is the selection of an appropriate tool—be it a grant, a subsidy, a tax credit, a loan, a new regulation, the creation of a government-sponsored enterprise, or the provision of direct services, to name but 7 of the more than 30 tools currently used by government.

The selection of one tool rather than another is a policy choice for which few guiding data are available. Further, research to help policy makers in this regard is extremely sparse. Policy makers decide either based on past experience with a tool ("We used tax credits before, let's use tax credits again") or because they have a clear proclivity for or against a particular tool (conservatives would resist direct government services and seek instead a tool that locates the activity in the private sector, e.g., grants for the construction of public housing or the privatization of all concessions in national parks). It is safe to assert that neither qualitative nor quantitative researchers have shown much interest in this area. Beyond the works of Linder (1988), Linder and Peters (1984, 1989), May (1981), and Salamon (1981, 1989), there is not much research, either theoretical or empirical, to be cited.

What follows is an effort to identify four areas where qualitative work could be highly valuable to discussions regarding policy tools. For each of these areas, there is at present a nearly complete research void. It should be stressed that the short discussion to follow is not meant to be a definitive statement on how qualitative work can address the information needs of policy makers as they choose among tools, nor is it the definitive research agenda on the strengths and weaknesses of different tools.

It needs to be restated that few researchers of any persuasion have moved into this difficult but highly policy-relevant area. The reasons for this hesitancy are outside the bounds of this discussion, but it is clear that the policy analysis and research communities have, with few exceptions, steered wide of this port of inquiry. Building primarily on the works of Linder, Peters, and Salamon, what follows is offered as a modest agenda for those qualitative researchers who are interested in exploring new and untested ways of involving qualitative work within the policy arena. A more elaborate and detailed research agenda in this area is still well over the horizon.

As noted, four areas amenable to qualitative study will be briefly discussed. These are resource intensiveness, targeting, institutional constraints, and political risks. The tentativeness of this proposal has to be stressed yet again. There may well be multiple other ways in which to frame the qualitative study of policy tools. What follows here is predicated on the previous discussion regarding the policy cycle. The framework for the qualitative study of policy tools is essentially a matrix analysis, whereby each of these four areas can be studied in each of the three phases of the policy cycle. All 12 combinations will not be individually addressed here; rather, the focus will be on the four broad areas that can help to clarify the trade-offs among tools.

Resource intensiveness refers to the constellation of concerns involving the complexity of the operations, the relative costliness of different options, and the degree of administrative burden that different tools place on organizations. Tools vary widely in their complexity, their demands on organizations for technical expertise to administer and manage, their direct and indirect costs by sector, and the degree to which they are direct or indirect in their intent. And just to complicate matters more, the mix of these concerns for any given tool will shift as one moves from one phase of the policy cycle to another. Keeping the financial costs low and federal involvement to a minimum, for example, may be high priorities in Washington during the policy formulation stage, but these will also have the consequences during the policy implementation stage of serving few of the eligible target population, adding complexity through mandated state administration, and reducing direct impacts. Managing toxic waste cleanups is but one example that is somewhat parallel to this brief scenario.

For qualitative researchers, the challenges here are multiple, not the least because they would necessitate more direct attention to organizational analysis. But there is also the clear opportunity to ask questions within organizations and to assess organizational capacity in ways that have not traditionally been done. Administrative burden has not been a topic of much (if any) qualitative research, but it is a very real consideration in the policy arena. Learning more of how to conceptualize this concern, how it is understood at various levels of government and within the private sector, and how different tools vary in this regard would be of considerable interest to policy makers in departments as well as those responsible for regulator and administrative oversight in organizations such as the Office of Management and Budget in the White House.

At present, a concept such as administrative burden is ill defined and subject to widely varying interpretations. In the absence of any systematic research, one person's definition and experience with "administrative burden" is as good as any other person's—and maybe better if he or she has more institutional or organizational influence. Additional examples concerning such concepts as "operational complexity" and "institutional capacity" are readily apparent.

Targeting refers to the capacity of the policy tool to be aimed at particular populations, problems, or institutions for whom the tool is primarily intended. A tool that, for example, seeks to help homeless persons who are mentally ill and also veterans would be highly targeted. Such a tool would be differentiated from a tool that is either diffuse or low in target specificity, for example, a tax credit for the interest earned in individual retirement accounts.

There are several key aspects of the targeting issue for a policy tool that qualitative researchers could address. First, there is the matter of the precision of the targeting. Qualitative researchers, in reference to the example just given, could help policy makers work through the strategies and definitional problems inherent in determining who is or is not homeless, who has or has not been diagnosed as mentally ill, and how to screen homeless veterans for service when documentation, service records, and so on are all likely to be lost or when persons simply cannot remember their own names.

A second aspect of targeting in selecting a policy tool is that of the amenability of the tool to adjustment and fine tuning. If the characteristics of the target population start to change, can the tool be adjusted to respond to this change? Flexibility in some instances would be highly desirable, whereas in others it may be irrelevant. For example, it would be beneficial to choose a policy instrument that responds to fluctuations and variations in the refugee populations coming into the United States, whereas it would be unnecessary in the instance of an entitlement program for which age is the only criterion for access to services.

Qualitative studies of different populations targeted by tools and the need (or lack thereof) of specificity in the targeting would be highly useful in policy formulation. There is also the opportunity in this area to explore whether those who have been targeted by a program believe this to be the case. Establishing community mental health centers could have some in the target population coming because of the "community health" emphasis, others coming for the "mental health" emphasis, and still others not showing up at all because they are not certain whose community is being referred or because they would never want anyone in their own neighborhood to know they have mental health problems. Linking services to target populations in the absence of such qualitative information suggests immediately the vulnerability and precariousness of presuming to establish service centers without the detailed knowledge of the populations for whom the effort is intended.

The example of community mental health centers leads to a third consideration in the targeting area—that of adaptability across uses. Can community mental health centers also serve other needs of the designated population, for example, nutrition and education, as well as serve as centers for entirely other target populations who are in the same residential vicinity? Can they serve as centers for the elderly, for latchkey children, for infant nutrition programs, and so on? The issue is one of flexibility and acceptance as well as neutrality in the perceptions of the other target groups. There may be groups who would not want to come to a mental health center, but who would be quite pleased to meet in a church or at a school. Gaining insight on these matters is clearly important as decisions are made on the location and mix of community services to be offered at any one location. Qualitative studies on these issues can inform policy makers and program managers in ways that will clearly affect the success or failure of different strategies.

Institutional capacity refers to the ability of the institution to deliver on the tasks that have been delegated to it. When a policy option clearly relies on a single institution to achieve certain objectives—for example, using the public schools as the vehicle to teach English to non-English-speaking children—there has to be some degree of certainty that the institution has the capacity to do so. Countless experiences with different policy initiatives have shown time and again that some institutions simply did not have, at the time, the capacity to do what was expected of them.

Further, there can be constraints placed on the institution that make it difficult if not impossible for the objective to be achieved. In addition to the more readily anticipated constraints of funding, staff availability, quality of facilities, and low political support, there are also constraints associated with the degree of intrusiveness the institution can exercise as well as the level of coerciveness allowed. The hesitancy of policy makers to allow intrusive efforts by the Internal Revenue Service to collect unpaid taxes has a clear impact on the ability of the organization to do so. The same can be said with respect to the IRS on the matter of coerciveness. Policy makers have simply decided to keep some organizations more constrained than others in carrying out their functions, for fear of abuse. Policy tools that have to rely on voluntary compliance or are framed to have an indirect effect face constraints different from those where these do not apply.

Qualitative research into the domain of institutional constraints and how it is that these constraints play out in the relation of the organization to the fulfillment of its mission is not, to my knowledge, now being done. It may be argued that it is not necessary, as the constraint dimension for any policy tool is too removed from research influence. That is, any constraints on an organization are more philosophical and ideological than operational. Yet the issue of institutional capacity and what does or does not hinder the ability of the organization to achieve its stated objectives is important to understand explicitly. If policy makers establish the parameters around an organization to the degree that it can never clearly achieve its goal (e.g., the IRS and unpaid back taxes), then there is a built-in level of failure that ought not be ignored and for which the institution should not be held accountable.

Political risk is the fourth dimension of the study of policy tools where qualitative research can directly contribute. Here the issues cluster around concerns of unanticipated risk, chances of failure, and timing. The selection of a policy tool is made with some outcome in mind—either direct or indirect. Yet there is always the possibility of unanticipated outcomes—again either direct or indirect. The selection of a tool necessarily has to take into account the risk of unknown outcomes and how these might affect the success of the policy.

Qualitative research, by the nature of its being longitudinal, done in naturalistic settings, and focused on the constructions of meaning developed by participants, is in a unique position from which to assess the possibility of tools having the impacts intended by policy makers. Low risk of unknown outcomes—for example, in increasing the security at U.S. federal courthouses—eliminates some level of uncertainty from the decision that does not happen when the risk of unknown outcomes is quite high, such as moving to year-round school schedules or as was learned when the movement to deinstitutionalize the mentally ill resulted in tens of thousands of mentally ill persons being left on their own with no means of support or treatment.

One other aspect of the political risk factor that qualitative research can address is the sustainability of the policy initiative. Close-in studies of the operational life of a policy initiative can gain a perspective on the commitment of those involved, their belief in the worthiness of the effort, the amount of political support they are or are not engendering, and the receptivity of the target population to the effort. If all these indicators are decidedly negative, then the sustainability of the initiative is surely low.

It is difficult to achieve success in policy efforts in the best of circumstances; it is that much harder when all the indicators point in the opposite direction. Qualitative research should have a distinct window from which to judge matters of political risk. Understanding of the participants, willingness to assume the causal linkage posited in the policy itself, and the degree of risk of unknown outcomes all influence the likelihood that any policy tool will achieve its intended results.

Concluding Observations

In reviewing this assessment of the contributions of qualitative work to the policy process, it is apparent that the contributions are more in the realm of the potential than the actual. There is no broad-based and sustained tradition within contemporary social science of focusing qualitative work specifically on policy issues, especially given the real time constraints that the policy process necessitates. Yet it is also clear that the opportunities are multiple for such contributions to be made. The issue is chiefly one of how to link those in the research and academic communities who are knowledgeable in conducting qualitative research studies to those in the policy arena who can commission such work and who will make use of the findings. The analysis of different strategies for building these linkages would require a separate paper; suffice it to say here that much hard thinking and numerous exploratory efforts will be required for the potential to become the actual. The issues of institutional cultures, academic reward systems, publication requirements, funding sources, and methodological limitations are but five among many that will have to be addressed if the linkages are to be built. And even beyond the resolution of (or at least the careful thinking about) these issues is the fundamental question of whether there is the will to bring qualitative work directly into the policy arena. Much of what has been written here will remain speculative unless and until there is some consensus among the practitioners of qualitative research that making this transition is worthwhile. The policy community is, I believe, ready for and would be receptive to anything those in the qualitative research community could offer, should they choose to make the effort to do so.

Note

1. I want to stress early on that in this chapter I will not seek to develop distinctions among various conventionally used terms for qualitative research. Thus, in the pages that follow, terms such as *qualitative work, qualitative research,* and *qualitative methods* will all be used to denote the same frame of reference. I most frequently use the term that appears in the title of this handbook, *qualitative research.* I leave it to other authors in this volume to develop those distinctions as appropriate. I would also note, in defense of not trying to specify in much detail just exactly what the meaning is behind the use of any one of these terms, that early reviewers of this chapter suggested at least four other terms I might use in lieu of those I have. These terms included *naturalistic, constructionist, interpretive,* and *ethnographies.* I am sure that the delineation of distinctions has an important place in this book; it is just not my intent to do so here.

I also want to note early on that I am not going to try to differentiate among various qualitative data collection strategies, or means of analysis, as to their particular spheres of potential influence. Thus in this chapter I will not try to indicate what policy relevance or influence one might expect from case studies (and there are multiple variations in this single area alone) in contrast, for example, to multimethod studies. My intent is to place qualitative work broadly within the policy arena, not to develop a prescriptive set of categories about which methods or modes of analysis are likely to lead to what types of influence.

References

Behn, R. D. (1988). Managing by groping along. *Journal of Policy Analysis and Management, 7*(4).

Chelimsky, E. (1982). Making evaluations relevant to congressional needs. *GAO Review, 17*(1).

Chelimsky, E. (1985). Old patterns and new directions in program evaluation. In E. Chelimsky (Ed.), *Program evaluation: Patterns and directions.* Washington, DC: American Society For Public Administration.

Guba, E. G. (1984). The effect of definitions of policy on the nature and outcomes of policy analysis. *Educational Leadership, 42*(2).

Hargrove, E. (1985). *The missing link: The study of the implementation of social policy.* Washington, DC: Urban Institute Press.

Janowitz, M. (1971). *Sociological methods and social policy.* New York: General Learning Press.

Lindblom, C. E. (1968). *The policy making process.* Englewood Cliffs, NJ: Prentice Hall.

Linder, S. H. (1988). Managing support for social research and development: Research goals, risk, and policy instruments. *Journal of Policy Analysis and Management, 7*(4).

Linder, S. H., & Peters, B. G. (1984). From social theory to policy design. *Journal of Public Policy, 4*(3).

Linder, S. H., & Peters, B. G. (1989). Instruments of government: Perceptions and contexts. *Journal of Public Policy, 9*(1).

May, P. J. (1981). Hints for crafting alternative policies. *Policy Analysis, 7*(2).

Nakamura, R. T., & Smallwood, F. (1980). *The politics of policy implementation.* New York: St. Martin's.

Patton, M. Q. (1988). *Qualitative evaluation and research methods* (2nd ed.). Newbury Park, CA: Sage.

Pressman, J. L., & Wildavsky, A. (1984). *Implementation* (3rd ed.). Berkeley: University of California Press.

Rist, R. C. (1980). Blitzkrieg ethnography: On the transformation of a method into a movement. *Educational Researcher, 9*(2).

Rist, R. C. (1989). Management accountability: The signals sent by auditing and evaluation. *Journal of Public Policy, 9*(3).

Rist, R. C. (Ed.). (1990). *Program evaluation and the management of government: Patterns and prospects across eight nations.* New Brunswick, NJ: Transaction.

Rist, R. C. (1993). Program evaluation in the United States General Accounting Office: Reflections on question formulation and utilization. In R. Conner et al. (Eds.), *Advancing public policy evaluation: Learning from international experiences.* Amsterdam: Elsevier.

Salamon, L. M. (1981). Rethinking public management: Third-party government and the changing forms of government action. *Public Policy, 29*(3).

Salamon, L. M. (1989). *Beyond privatization: The tools of government action.* Washington, DC: Urban Institute Press.

Smith, J. A. (1991). *The idea brokers: Think tanks and the rise of the new policy elite.* New York: Free Press.

Weiss, C. H. (1982). Policy research in the context of diffuse decision making. In R. C. Rist (Ed.), *Policy studies review annual.* Beverly Hills, CA: Sage.

Weiss, C. H. (1988). Evaluations for decisions: Is anybody there? Does anybody care? *Evaluation Practice, 9*(1).

Yin, R. K. (1985). Studying the implementation of public programs. In W. Williams (Ed.), *Studying implementation.* Chatham, NJ: Chatham House.

PART VI
THE FUTURE OF QUALITATIVE RESEARCH

And so we come to the end, which is only the starting point for a new beginning. We opened this handbook with the argument that the field of qualitative research is defined by a series of tensions and contradictions. These tensions have been felt in every chapter in this volume. Here we list many of them, for purposes of summary only. They take the form of questions:

1. Whose history and which applied and theoretical traditions do we follow into the future?
2. How do we study the "Other" without studying ourselves?
3. What ethical codes must be formulated to fit the contemporary period?
4. Will a new interpretive paradigm emerge out of the conflicts that exist between the many paradigms and perspectives we have presented in this volume?
5. How will ethnic and feminist paradigms be fitted to this new synthesis, if it comes?
6. What will the cultural studies paradigm bring to qualitative research?
7. What new methods and strategies of inquiry will emerge?
8. How will the next generation of qualitative researchers react to data management methods and computer-assisted models of analysis?
9. Will the postmodern sensibility begin to form its own foundational criteria for evaluating the written text?
10. What place does positivism and its successor, postpositivism, have in a research endeavor that devalues universals to local interpretation, questions the existence of a guiding "truth," and emphasizes subjectivity in the research process?
11. What part can "fifth moment" qualitative research, including program evaluation and analysis, play in the understanding and improvement of programs and policy?

12. When all universals are gone, including the postmodern worldview, in favor of local interpretations, how can we continue to talk and learn from one another?

There are no definitive answers to any of these questions. Here we can only suggest, in the barest of detail, our responses to them. In our concluding chapter we elaborate these responses, grouping them around six basic themes, or issues: positivism and postpositivism, the crises of representation and legitimation, the treatment of the Other and the Other's voice, conflicts between science and religion, and the implications of new technologies for qualitative research. Examined from another angle, the questions listed above focus on the social text, history, politics, ethics, the Other, and interpretive paradigms.

The Social Text

George Marcus, in Chapter 35, tells us that we are in a new historical moment, where simplistic, ethnographic cultural translations will cease to be accepted. The age of final authoritative readings of any cultural situation seems to be over. Reflexive, experimental texts that are messy, subjective, open-ended, conflictual, and feminist influenced will become the norm.

We agree with Marcus, and predict that three dominant forms of textuality will emerge in the sixth moment. The first form will be the classic, realist ethnographic text, redefined in postpositivist terms. The second form will be Marcus's messy, experimental text. The third textual form will mold the classic realist text with experimental variations, defined by poststructural considerations. (A fourth form, a legacy from the modernist moment, will be the qualitative text defined by traditional, positivist criteria.)

These four forms correspond, of course, to the four basic positions on evaluating the qualitative text that we outlined in our introduction to Part V. In the sixth moment these forms will inform and interact with one another. At the same time, there will be a merging of evaluative criteria that cross-cut these four forms. Positivist and postpositivist texts will be criticized from the poststructural and postmodern perspectives, especially in their treatment and representation of the Other. In turn, postmodern and poststructural texts will be held accountable to the kinds of issues raised by Altheide and Johnson (Chapter 30), including features from an ethnographic ethic that are sensitive to the situated, relational, and textual aspects of the research process.

Computer-assisted methods for managing empirical materials will shape each of these textual forms. Writers-as-field-workers will learn new ways of conversing with themselves as they represent their field experiences textually.

History, Paradigms, Politics, Ethics, and the Other

Many things are changing as we write our way out of writing culture and move into the sixth moment of qualitative research. Multiple histories and theoretical frameworks, where before there were just a few, now circulate in this field. Today positivism and postpositivism are challenged and supplemented by constructivist, critical theory, feminist, ethnic, and cultural studies paradigms and perspectives. Many different applied action and participatory research agendas inform program evaluation and analysis.

We now understand that we study the other to learn about ourselves, and many of the lessons we have learned have not been pleasant. We seek a new body of ethical directives fitted to postmodernism. The old ethical codes failed to examine research as a morally engaged project. They never seriously located the researcher within the ruling apparatuses of society. A contextual-consequentialist ethical system will continue to evolve, informed at every point by the feminist, ethnic, and cultural studies sensibilities. Blatant voyeurism will continue to be challenged.

The cultural studies and critical theory perspectives, with their emphases on moral criticism, will shape the traditional empiricist foundations of qualitative research. The dividing line between science and morality will continue to be erased. A postmodern, poststructural science will move closer to a sacred science of the moral universe.

As we draw near to the end of the twentieth century, we see more clearly the iron cage, to use Weber's phrase, that has trapped us. Like a bird in a cage, for too long we have been unable to see the pattern that we have been caught up in. Coparticipants in a secular science of the social world, we became part of the problem. Entangled in the ruling apparatuses we wished to undo, we perpetuated systems of knowledge and power that we found, underneath, to be all too oppressive. It is not too late to get out of the cage. Like birds set free, we are now able to move about, to fly into the sixth moment.

And so we enter, or leave, the fifth moment. In our concluding chapter, we elaborate our thoughts about the next generation of qualitative research.

35

■

What Comes (Just) After "Post"?

The Case of Ethnography

GEORGE E. MARCUS

IN an important sense, we are already in a post-"post" period—post-poststructuralism, post-postmodernism, and so on. At a recent conference, Clifford Geertz observed, in response to a question about the impact of postmodern influences upon the interpretive mode of qualitative social science, that the storm seems to have blown over, but its effects will be enduring and far-reaching. Indeed, as a half-serious ethnographer of the many academic conferences I have attended over the past several years, but particularly over the past year or so, I have noted a widespread "reaction formation" to the years of postmodern debate that might best be characterized as ambivalent rejection. Most, who have undoubtedly been influenced by it in their own thinking, ironically now hold postmodernism apart as an object or referent, applying to some unspecified others—definitely not to themselves—and view the term with ambivalence and suspicion, but as a fatal attraction nonetheless.

Discussions of the contemporary world of immense social and cultural changes in terms of postmodernism may thus be showing distinct signs of exhaustion. Indeed, at conferences and seminars I have noted several scholars carefully avoiding reference to the term in their own work; it has become the unmentionable "P word," often referred to as such. Yet, the substantive influences of whatever it was that was discussed in these seminal debates, apparently in the process of being exorcized as a fashion that has gone on for too long, have had profound, transformative effects on how all varieties of qualitative social science are now conducted. Thus, absent or receding as a riveting controversy of academic discussion, postmodernism is still very much present in its specific effects on particular disciplinary traditions and interdisciplinary efforts such as "cultural studies." (*Cultural studies* seems to be a successor identity for the space occupied by earlier postmodern debates, but with the aim of giving these debates both institutional presence and a political, ethical relevance to academic work concerning contemporary global social movements and events; see Grossberg, Nelson, & Treichler, 1992.)

We now have the opportunity—perhaps for the first time—to examine what this controversy has meant for the practices and debates of academic and disciplinary projects it has touched (some would say infected). The remainder of this chapter is intended as a contribution to this opportunistic re-vision of disciplines in the immediate wake of the "post" debates as fashionable moments of controversy—in this case, of ethnography in anthropology and cultural studies generally, which has become, along with "reading texts," one of the most favored and prestigious forms of conceiving the style in which scholars do qualitative research.

In anthropology, the intervention of postmodernism has centered on the critique of ethnography, as both mode of inquiry and writing. The emerging presence of various styles of reflexivity in ethnographic writing has stood, accurately or not, for the influence of (or, for some, infection by) postmodernism. In much of this chapter I will consider the kinds of interests at stake in positions taken on reflexivity in the writing of ethnography.

In the United States, discussions of postmodernism have grown over the past decade and a half from their specific references to aesthetic styles in art, architecture, and literature to a general sign of radical critique concerning styles of discourse and research in all the disciplines of the humanities and social sciences. Postmodernism has been given theoretical substance by the works of the French poststructuralists (who themselves had little use for the term, save, momentarily, Lyotard), which only became available through frequent translation in the early 1980s. Existentially, it has been powered by the widespread feeling that the conditions of social life (especially in the West, and especially in the frame of American postwar hegemony) were in fundamental transformation, a breakup of a world order, systemically conceived, into fragments that have not yet taken new configurations that can be easily identified. This world of established, but unstable, institutions rapidly generating emergent forms of diversity has defined the social conditions of a *postmodernity* for which the ethos, at least, of *postmodernism* as a style of knowledge production is particularly appropriate. Both in *revealing* conditions of postmodernity as well as in *enacting* them, postmodernist writing has been seductively attractive in defining the radical form of contemporary cultural criticism.

Yet it is important to understand that the critiques of disciplinary traditions (especially the traditions' post-World War II penchant for privileging and desiring to reproduce the perceived achievements of the natural sciences) were already well under way before the specter of postmodernism arose in general awareness in the early 1980s. Postmodernism merely intersected with the developing internal critiques of fields such as literature, history, sociology, law, philosophy, and anthropology, and both radicalized and consolidated them. As suggested, postmodernism has been sustained as an "alien other" by the internal critics of disciplinary traditions who assimilated its powerful and radical aspects for their own purposes while holding postmodernism itself at arm's length as an object of suspicion and ambivalence. All the while, its seductive example of extremity has radicalized, consolidated, and pushed forward alternatives for practice in the ongoing internal critiques of disciplinary traditions.

In anthropology, the ethos of postmodernism has intersected specifically with the strong critique of ethnographic rhetoric and writing that powerfully brought together and rearticulated three separate strands of critique that had been developing in Anglo-American anthropology since the 1960s and even before. The first strand was the exposure of the "messiness" of fieldwork as a method of social science through an outpouring of "trial-and-tribulation," "confessional" accounts (for a partial review of this literature, see Marcus & Fischer, 1986; Van Maanen, 1988). The second strand involved the contextualization of anthropology in the history of colonialism, particularly during the period of decolonization for the British and of the Vietnam War for the Americans (see Asad, 1973; Hymes, 1969). The final strand encompasses the not-yet-pointed critique from hermeneutics of anthropological styles of interpreting language, culture, and symbols (see Geertz, 1973a, 1973b). Influenced by literary theory (in turn influenced by poststructuralists), by the kind of rhetorical critique developed of history by Hayden White (e.g., 1973, 1978), and by a renewed interest in the history of anthropology itself, a group of anthropologists, historians, and theorists of literature and language, with whom I and members of my department have been associated, produced work from the mid-1980s on (including most prominently *Writing Culture* [Clifford & Marcus, 1986], but also *Anthropology as Cultural Critique* [Marcus & Fischer, 1986]; *The Predicament of Culture* [Clifford, 1988]; and *The Unspeakable* [Tyler, 1987], among others) that brought to the surface in an articulate way profound discontents with the state of anthropology. The power of this intervention was in critique rather than in defining a new paradigm or setting a new agenda.[1] The critique has legitimated new objects, new styles of research and writing, and a shift in the historic purpose of anthropological research toward its long-standing, but underdeveloped, project of cultural critique. It has also tended to reorient the relevant interdisciplinary interests of anthropologists toward the humanities, especially as it became obvious that the most energetic thinking about culture, especially in cross-cultural and transcultural frameworks, had been coming from among literary scholars such as Edward Said, Gayatri Spivak, and Homi Bhabha.

The frame of postmodernism, by this time an interdisciplinary focus or sign of radical critique, has merely enhanced and consolidated the radical critical tendencies within anthropology, which were once again powerfully brought to the surface in the mid-1980s through attention to the language, conventions, and rhetoric by which anthropological knowledge through ethnography has been produced. The specter of postmodernism has held anthropology accountable, then, for its own radical critical possibility, which it had submerged in its legitimation as an academic field. How, and to what degree, alternative possibilities of work within the ethnographic tradition might emerge from the specific practices and responses that the critique of the mid-1980s, now labeled (justly or not) postmodern, are questions I want to take up. But before doing so, I want to make certain observations, in the form of a set of listed points, about how postmodernism has posed predicaments for the writing practices of anthropologists, what new tendencies it has encouraged, and what old ones it has radicalized.

1. Regardless of stated commitments to interdisciplinary work through the devaluing of disciplinary traditions, or to postmodern nonconformity in the way research is conceived, I have not seen any works by anthropologists that have not validated the practice of ethnography (this is *not* the same thing as validating ethnographic authority; rather, ethnography is validated as the central identity of the discipline in its new interdisciplinary, postmodern milieu). Thus, although old forms of ethnography may have been called into question, ethnography itself, in its possibilities beyond its disciplinary uses so far, has not been. In fact, different conceptions of ethnography (and the fieldwork it entails) define the limits within which postmodern reimaginings in anthropology occur. Outside anthropology, the practice of ethnography (especially among exotic others) continues to define its mystique, appeal, and identity for its interdisciplinary partners in history, feminism, film studies, comparative literature, and the like (see the prestigious place that ethnography occupies in the recent collection *Cultural Studies* [Grossberg et al., 1992]).

2. What postmodernism has meant specifically for anthropology is a license to create an interesting traffic between the cognitive techniques of now classic aesthetic, avant-garde modernisms (such as early twentieth-century literary modernism, or Russian formalism, or, especially, the later avant-gardes of the 1920s and 1930s such as the surrealists; for a thorough review of these movements, see Bradbury & McFarlane, 1976). There are no innovative moves in so-called experimental ethnography so far that do not have previous histories in modernism. What *is* new (and perhaps shocking) is the open use of modernist sensibilities and techniques having to do with reflexivity, collage, montage, and dialogism within an empiricist genre with a strong, scientific claim to construct reliable knowledge about other forms of life. The struggle in contemporary works of so-called postmodern anthropology is between the currently liberating techniques and cognitions of a modernist sensibility and the continuing desire to report objectively on a reality other than the anthropologist's own. Maybe it is the conditions of postmodernity in the cultural situations that anthropologists encounter that make this belated migration from the sphere of art to the sphere of aspirant science, at least, feasible. In this heady enterprise, there is a responsibility on the part of experimental ethnographers (or theorists of ethnography) to understand the fate of certain techniques of radical critical aestheticism (such as montage, negative dialectics, and Brechtian theater; again see Bradbury & McFarlane, 1976) in their earlier appearances, and to ensure that their application now does not represent a nostalgia for aesthetics against a villainized positivism.

3. Again, I want to raise here the question of the anthropologist's explicit relation to a postmodernist identity. As I have noted, in discussions about postmodernism that I have read, it is rare that anyone will claim for him- or herself a postmodernist personal intellectual style—will indeed say, "I am a postmodernist." Rather, for those who have written most cogently about postmodernism (e.g., David Harvey, in *The Condition of Postmodernity,* 1989; or John Rajchman, in his excellent short essay, "Postmodernism in a Nominalist Frame: The Emergence and Diffusion of a Cultural Category," 1987, in which he writes with ironic amazement that such a "motley and elastic range of things" could become such an object of fascination), the term has a phantom, indefinite referent, but certainly not oneself. One takes a critical attitude toward others' practice of it, but rarely in fact do the features attributed to this intellectual style not rub off on the critic (e.g., by the end of his book, Harvey has assimilated the sensible dimensions of postmodernism, while isolating its extremism; through such critical engagement, he ends up infected by it, assuming postmodernist characteristics in spite of himself). So in anthropology, the label "postmodern anthropology" attributed usually hostilely to the critics of ethnography fails to find any (save Tyler, see below) who will own up to it, and one finds that those making the attribution end by claiming postmodernist innovations for themselves, save for its excesses. In effect, by the logic of academic fashions, everyone seems to want to be "with it," more than ever, but at the least cost to the orientations in which they have previously vested themselves. Postmodernism—like anthropology itself—being a *bricoleur*'s art, can, of course, tolerate this ambivalence in individual scholars' ways of absorbing it.

4. The very few cases in which individuals identify themselves as postmodernist or enact postmodernism in their writing are instructive. Stephen Tyler is the only one among the group associated with articulating the critique of ethnography who explicitly champions postmodernism and enacts it in his writing. This entails a radical and endlessly parodic mode of writing. With brilliant consistency and resolution, Tyler creates a thoroughly parodic discourse about parody. Although

full of powerful insights about language, writing, orality, and especially ethnographic representation, his bold experiment seems, finally, limiting. He develops some nearly unbearable truths that would make it difficult to lend special importance or justification to any practice of ethnography.

Yet, short of Tyler's bold attempt at endless self-parody, championing postmodernism while making the claim that one is practicing it runs into serious contradictions. One can see this, for instance, in a recent paper by Rosemary Coombe (1991), where she states, "As a postmodernist, I believe that form has implications for the issues that we address and that conventional forms of discourse limit and shape the realities we recognize" (p. 1857). Indeed, in what follows, Coombe's paper looks and reads pretty much like a law journal paper, and submits to most of its conventions (careful citations, long footnotes, and so on) perhaps in spite of Coombe herself. Subverting standard conventions of discourse does seem to be a sign of experiments in ethnographic writing, as we will see in the discussion of "messy" texts below. But subversion is more an indication of tensions in the "messiness" of a text in which a new kind of study is struggling to be born within an older framework, rather than a self-conscious claim or conceit of being postmodernist by doing "it" in one's writing, as fails in the case of Coombe and succeeds in the case of Tyler—neither one being likely replacements for dealing with postmodernism as an infectious object held at arm's length.

5. The following paragraphs address three of the most important effects on current anthropological practices that key features associated with postmodernism would have.

Cultural translation, which is what ethnography is, never fully assimilates difference (see Talal Asad's [1986] keenly critical discussion of this in *Writing Culture*). In any attempt to interpret or explain another cultural subject, a surplus of difference always remains, partly created by the process of ethnographic communication itself. Thus radical, intractable difference, as in Lyotard's (1988) notion of the differend, confronts the idea of difference in the liberal concept of culture that has dominated in Anglo-American anthropology, and that historically triumphed (in parallel with the pervasiveness of consumer culture of late capitalism) over the concept of culture within an earlier evolutionary frame of social thought. Culture as the object of ethnography is predicated on the notion that the difference of others can be fully *consumed,* assimilated to theory and description by cracking codes of structure, through better translation, and so on. The postmodern idea of radical or surplus difference counters the liberal concept with the idea that difference can never be fully consumed, conquered, or experienced, and thus any interpretive framework must remain partly unresolved in a more serious sense than is usually stipulated as a matter of "good manners" in doing interpretive work. Radical, surplus difference is a fundamental challenge and stimulus to remake the language and forms of ethnographic writing.

Associated with the above, the postmodern premise that there is no possibility of fixed, final, or monologically authoritative meaning has radicalized the critique within anthropology of its own forms of representation by challenging the authority on which they have been based. This impossibility also undermines the practice of a kind of interpretation from which authoritative meanings can be derived (the kind of interpretive practice that Geertz earlier promoted in anthropology that constituted cultures through the metaphor of text, and the practice of interpretation through the metaphor of reading; for example, see his seminal essay on the Balinese cockfight included in his 1973 collection).

The postmodern notion of juxtapositions (that is, blocking together incommensurables, as advocated by Lyotard; see Readings, 1991) serves to renew the practice of comparison in anthropology, long neglected, but in altered ways. Juxtapositions do not have the obvious metalogic of older styles of comparisons in anthropology (e.g., controlled comparison within a culture area or "natural" geographic region), but emerge from putting questions to an emergent object of study, whose contours, sites, and relationships are not known beforehand, but that themselves are a contribution of making an account that has different, complexly connected real-world sites of investigation. The postmodern object of study is ultimately mobile and multiply situated, so that any ethnography of such an object has a comparative dimension integral to it, in the form of juxtapositions of seeming incommensurables or phenomena that might conventionally have appeared "worlds apart." Comparison reenters the very act of ethnographic specificity. It does so through a postmodern vision of seemingly improbable juxtapositions, the global collapsed into and made an integral part of parallel, related local situations, rather than being something monolithic and external to them. This move toward comparison as juxtaposition firmly deterritorializes culture in ethnographic writing. It also stimulates accounts of cultures composed in a landscape for which there is as yet no developed theoretical conception.

These three challenges to the conventional ways and premises by which ethnography has been conceived lead to the "messy text" as manifestly the most complex and interesting form of experimentation with ethnographic writing now being produced.

Messy Texts, or Worlds Apart Cultural Criticism

While many in anthropology have at least acknowledged the therapeutic value of the 1980s' critique of ethnographic writing, there has also been a widespread nervousness that this has gone on too long, and as such is leading in unproductive directions, that innovations in the form of ethnography cannot possibly carry the burden that abstract theoretical discourse and clear distinctions between arguments and supporting data once did. Contrary to those who want to move quickly beyond the notion of experimentalism, I remain convinced that the form that ethnographies might take remains a key concern in generating theoretical and research design discussions that especially confront issues of postmodernist styles of knowledge production and of real social conditions of postmodernity among our subjects.

To me, the most interesting experiments, sometimes in spite of themselves, confront the problem that ethnography, which is centrally interested in the creativity of social action through imagination, narrativity, and performance, has usually been produced through an analytic imagination that in contrast is impoverished, and is far too restrictive especially under contemporary conditions of postmodernity. For example, once we know, or analytically fix by naming, that we are writing about violence, migration, the body, memory, or whatever, we have already circumscribed the space and dimensions of the object of study—we know what we are talking about prematurely. But you can be sure that the object of study always exceeds its analytic circumscription, and especially under conditions of postmodernity. That is, there remains the surplus of difference beyond, and perhaps because of, our circumscription.

The mark of experimental, critical work is its resistance to this too-easy assimilation of the phenomenon of interest by given analytic, ready-made concepts. Such resistance is manifested in a work's messy, many-"sited"ness, its contingent openness as to the boundaries of the object of study (which emerge in the space of the work, whose connections by juxtaposition are themselves *the* argument), its concern with position, and its derivation/negotiation of its analytic framework from indigenous discourse, from mappings within the sites in which the object of study is defined and among which it circulates. Contemporary works I have in mind, by no means all of them within the ethnographic tradition, but all of which have worked well for me in teaching, are *Primate Visions: Gender, Race, and Nature in the World of Modern Science,* by Donna Haraway (1989); *Debating Muslims: Cultural Dialogues in Postmodernity and Tradition,* by Michael M. J. Fischer and Mehdi Abedi (1990); *Shamanism, Colonialism, and the Wild Man: A Study of Terror and Healing,* by Michael Taussig (1987); and *Lives in Trust: The Fortunes of Dynastic Families in Late Twentieth Century America,* by myself with Peter Dobkin Hall (1992).

Although the authors of these texts are often conscious of themselves as engaged in experimental work, there is much more to these texts, struggling with conventional form to provide new cognitive mappings, than special pleading, self-indulgence, avant-gardism, or a genius act. They refuse to assimilate too easily or by foreclosure the object of study, thus committing a kind of academic colonialism whereby the deep assumption seeps into a work that the interests of the ethnographer and those of his or her subjects are somehow aligned.

There are several other reasons for constructing messy texts. I have identified three additional rationales, and mention them only briefly here. First, they arise simply from confronting the remarkable space/time compression that defines the conditions of peoples and culture globally (this is of course the defining empirical feature of the condition of postmodernity for theorists such as David Harvey and Anthony Giddens). This raises the problem of how an account is to be given of everyday life in which what was formerly incommensurable is brought into relationship or at least contact; the global, or aspects of global process, is now encompassed by the local, and purely local meanings are no longer a sufficient object of study.

Second, they wrestle with the loss of a credible holism, so important in previous ethnographic writing, and especially functionalist accounts (see Thornton, 1988). In messy texts there is a sense of a whole, without evoking totality, that emerges from the research process itself. The territory that defines the object of study is mapped by the ethnographer who is within its landscape, moving and acting within it, rather than drawn from a transcendent, detached point.

Third, messy texts are messy because they insist on an open-endedness, an incompleteness, and an uncertainty about how to draw a text/analysis to a close. Such open-endedness often marks a concern with an ethics of dialogue and partial knowledge that a work is incomplete without critical, and differently positioned, responses to it by its (one hopes) varied readers.

Thus the important questions to pose about messy texts concern how they end (openly, with utopian hope, pragmatic resolution, and so on), what space they lay out, and how the conceptual apparatus (and the *naming* of its object) emerges as a function of the hesitation to establish conceptual or analytic authority by fiat. However, it should be clear that messy texts, aside from the features that I have listed, are by no means uniform in their sensibilities or theoretical influences, nor are they models for a new genre of critical work. I find them interesting as *symptoms* of struggle within given formats and practices of analytic writing to produce unexpected connections and thus new descriptions of old realities. In so doing they critically displace sets of representations that seem no longer to account for worlds that we thought we knew, or could at least name.

Indeed, most ethnographers are not writing messy texts, but the specter of postmodernism (and postmodernity) with which the appearance of such unusual writing is associated has been a subject of widespread discussion, and at the level of what most anthropologists might or might not do differently than before, postmodernism comes down to the "sign" of reflexivity—how much of it (if any) and in what form it should appear in one's ethnographic work.[2]

Ideological Strategies of Reflexivity

It is now time to back up and consider what sorts of discussions of postmodernism in contemporary anthropology and other fields that share a strong identification with and valorization of the practice of ethnography lead to the opening of possibility of "messy text" experimentation. The crucial turn, it seems to me, has been the position taken toward self-critical reflexivity in ethnographic writing. The sometimes heated discussions about the desirability of reflexivity mark the opening of the ethnographic tradition to new possibility; a departure from the ideology of objectivity, distance, and the transparency of reality to concepts; and the need to explore the ethical, political, and epistemological dimensions of ethnographic research as an integral part of producing knowledge about others. Rather than being interested here in the theory and philosophy of reflexive practice itself, I am concerned with the complex politics of theory (the different positions taken, interests implied, and stakes defined) that the discussion of postmodernism in the specific terms of reflexivity in ethnography has engendered.

I do not choose reflexivity arbitrarily as the loaded sign of these politics, but from the point of view of an (amateur) ethnographer of these politics. I have noted that reflexivity is the label in common currency used to stand for as-yet unrealized alternative possibility in the production of ethnography. For me, then, reflexivity is not so much a methodological matter as an ideological one that in turn masks anxiety about a broader, but less conceivable, postmodernism. In this regard, Graham Watson, in his paper "Make Me Reflexive—But Not Yet: Strategies for Managing Essential Reflexivity in Ethnographic Discourse" (1987), makes an important distinction between *essential* reflexivity and a *derived* or, as I call it, ideological reflexivity. Essential reflexivity is an integral feature of all discourse (as in the indexical function of speech acts); one cannot choose to be reflexive or not in an essential sense—it is always a part of language use. What remains is how to deal with the fact of reflexivity, how to strategize about it for certain theoretical and intellectual interests. And this is the ideological dimension of reflexivity in which I am interested here. In the current polemics about the use of reflexivity, one encounters, for example, a frequent bad-faith, flippant dismissal of reflexivity, or, among those who favor it, one often encounters competitive, "more reflexive than thou" positions (see, e.g., in Clifford & Marcus, 1986, Paul Rabinow's critique of the arch critic of ethnography, James Clifford, for not being sufficiently self-critical, and the charge of insufficient critical reflexivity that has been a main line of attack by feminists on the mostly male critics of ethnography, for being *mostly* male).

Finally, it might be noted that perhaps the most intense polemics about reflexivity nowadays occurs in academic departments among dissertation committees over graduate student projects—is reflexivity a self-indulgence or an aspect of method? Graduate students most of all want to know pragmatically how to deal with reflexivity in the writing that will give them a credential within a disciplinary tradition. How much reflexivity? Where in a text and what forms can it take? Finally, why?

Four Styles of Reflexivity

Reflexivity is an immense area of comment and interest. Thus the following discussion needs a controlling frame, the most appropriate of which involves the fields for which ethnography as a practice has had a special value, has been regenerative over the past decade of revitalization in the humanities and related fields in the United States, often powered by a fascination with defining postmodern(ism/ity), but also institutionalized in interdisciplinary centers across American academia (most often known as humanities or "cultural studies" centers). These fields include the following:

- sociology of the sort theorized by Pierre Bourdieu and Anthony Giddens (but also the sociology practiced in British cultural studies, and now in American cultural studies, for which ethnography has had a special appeal; see Grossberg et al., 1992)

- anthropology, for which ethnography has been a signature practice
- feminism, for which ethnography has been one among related genres through which theory and research have been produced

Before examining the stake in reflexivity in each of these fields, I want to discuss a baseline form of reflexivity with which the term is usually associated.

1. The baseline form of reflexivity is associated with the self-critique and personal quest, playing on the subjective, the experiential, and the idea of empathy. It is this sort of reflexivity that most leads to nervous response and dismissals as dead-end self-indulgence, narcissism, and solipsism. Typical is Marshall Sahlins's report of an apocryphal exchange, quoted by Judy Stacey (1990): "But as the Fijian said to the New Ethnographer, 'that's enough talking about you; let's talk about me' " (p. 232). But feminists have shown us why we must be prepared to take this kind of reflexivity much more seriously (see especially Clough, 1992).

In anthropology, elaborate subjectivist accounts of fieldwork experience became the prime means of unfixing the notion that fieldwork could be a method on a par with, say, surveys. Such reflexivity, previously limited to confessional framings of functionalist ethnography, exposed the epistemological and ethical grounds of anthropological knowledge to full critical discussion and opened the way for a critical hermeneutics (as in the debate between Gadamer and Habermas, as lucidly summarized in Holub, 1991), to become a major influence on anthropological theory and research practice. But this is where the main contribution of this kind of reflexivity has rested, and once its critical function has been well absorbed, it loses its power and falls prey to those who would nervously dismiss reflexivity altogether. At most, such reflexivity opens the possibility for the so-called polyphonous text or the completely collaborative project, but often as not, it ends by reinforcing the perspective and voice of the lone, introspective field-worker without challenging the paradigm of ethnographic research at all—to the contrary.

In feminism, this very subjectivist kind of reflexivity has had much more weight. It is indeed the signature of a distinctively feminist cognition that runs through many genres of feminist writing. As such, reflexivity is a performed politics, and the means of overcoming the gendered character of supposedly value-free objectivist discourse. In feminism, this kind of reflexivity was pioneered in the form of autobiography, and its appearance as a style of ethnography is simply a carryover. As such, ethnography is fully integrated into an arena of discourse in which subjectivist reflexivity is not only fully legitimated, but has a special power, function, and politics.

The situation in anthropology is of course quite different. There, subjectivist reflexivity challenged the sacred boundaries of identity, differentiating scientific ethnography from travel accounts, memoirs, missionary reports, and so on. It had nothing like the preexisting legitimacy or purpose in anthropology that it had in feminism. Whereas subjectivist reflexivity in anthropological ethnography dead-ends, as I have suggested, in feminist writing, and ethnography, it leads to the practice of positioning that manifests itself either as a doctrinal kind of identity politics or as an ambitious and comprehensive means of reenvisioning the frameworks and practices of ethnographic research and writing (for a superb example, see Stacey, 1990).

2. Beyond the baseline forms of subjectivist reflexivity is the position on reflexivity in Pierre Bourdieu's sociology, which can also stand here in a general way for the kind of reflexivity in ethnography that has had appeal for British (and, by derivation, American) cultural studies. For instance, the use of reflexivity in Paul Willis's *Learning to Labour* (1977/1981) is tied to the commitment to sustain objectivity, the distance and abstraction of theoretical discourse, and empiricism as distinctive historical contributions of sociology (and a related social theory) as a discipline. With such a commitment, ethnography retains its identity as a method, and reflexivity is valuable only in methodological terms as a research tool. As we have seen, Bourdieu is hostile to reflexivity as touching on the subjective. The following quotations from the preface to *The Logic of Practice* (Bourdieu, 1990a) are revealing:

> In opposition to intuitionism, which fictitiously denies the distance between the observer and the observed, I kept on the side of the objectivism that is concerned to understand the logic of practices, at the cost of a methodical break with primary experience; but I never ceased to think that it was also necessary to understand the specific logic of that form of "understanding" without experience that comes from mastery of the principles of experience—that what had to be done was not to sweep away the distance magically through spurious primitivist participation, but *to objectify the objectifying distance and the social conditions*

> *that make it possible, such as the externality of the observer, the objectifying techniques that he uses etc.* Perhaps because I had a less abstract idea than some people of what it is to be a mountain peasant, I was also, and precisely to that extent, more aware that the distance is insurmountable, irremovable, except through self-deception. Because theory—the word itself says so—is a spectacle, which can only be understood from a viewpoint away from the stage on which the action is played out, the distance lies perhaps not so much where it is usually looked for, in the gap between cultural traditions, as in the gulf between two relations to the world, one theoretical, the other practical. (p. 14; emphasis added)

> Distance is not abolished by bringing the outsider fictitiously closer to an imaginary native, as is generally attempted; it is by distancing, through objectification, the native who is in every outside observer, that the native is brought closer to the outsider. . . . In contrast to the personalist denial which refuses scientific objectification and can only construct a fantasized person, sociological analysis, particularly when it places itself in the anthropological tradition of exploration of forms of classification, makes a self-reappropriation possible, by objectifying the objectivity that runs through the supposed site of subjectivity, such as the social categories of thought, perception, and appreciation which are the unthought principles of all representation of the "objective" world. By forcing one to discover externality at the heart of internality, banality in the illusion of rarity, the common in the pursuit of the unique, sociology does more than denounce all the impostures of egoistic narcissism; it offers perhaps the only means of contributing, if only through awareness of determinations, to the construction, otherwise abandoned to the forces of the world, of something like a subject. (pp. 20-21)

In absolutely opposing any sort of identity between the worlds of the observer (the academic social scientist) and the observed (the peasant, for instance), while at the same time privileging, perhaps as the manifestation of reason, the domain of distanced "theory," Bourdieu is outside postmodern sensibilities that find value in various strategies (e.g., through dialogism) for collapsing high and low culture, the theoretical and the practical, and the identities of the narrator and those narrated. As such, reflexivity, which Bourdieu *does* valorize, has a very restrictive function. Self-critical reflexivity is for Bourdieu a renewed and more powerful form of the old project of the sociology of knowledge, but this time, fully integrated as a dimension of sociological method.

In his fervent desire to assert the absolute priority of objectivity/objectivizing in the sociologist's work, even in being reflexive, Bourdieu presents an account that is tone deaf to the inevitable moments of *subjective* self-criticism that have always been a part of even the most scientific ethnography. In denying or ignoring this integral dimension of the most objectifying methods, Bourdieu misses the sort of tensions that propel the ethnographer toward reflexivity in the first place, whatever eventual ideological form it may take in writing (subjective, an aspect of method, and so on). Personal reflexivity is present in several of his own works (he even appeals to it ironically in the above quotes), but in the conventional way, it is pushed to the margins.

Indeed, the great virtue of Bourdieu's cultural critique is in the personal motivations that led him out of ethnography, which he eventually came to see in a politicized context of decolonizing Algeria, back toward the major educational and class institutions of France that shape "the scholastic point of view" (Bourdieu, 1990b). This move from apolitical structural anthropology in Algeria during the revolution to the critical sociology of his home institutions, especially those that engendered him intellectually as an ethnologist/sociologist, is the process of producing an objectified form of reflexivity, making an object of that which shapes your own knowledge, never giving into a romantic subjectivist fantasy. The objective, critical treatment of the contexts that produce objectifying modes of thought (reason) is indeed a valuable form of reflexivity with many possibilities regarding how to expand/reconstruct the ethnographic research project. But more's the pity, then, to constrain this possibility severely by assimilating this kind of critique as a method that does not seriously alter the forms that past sociological (and ethnographic) practice within it have taken.

3. The most interesting form of self-critical reflexivity in anthropology, beyond its null form discussed above, is one that emphasizes the intertextual or diverse field of representation that any contemporary project of ethnography enters and crosses in order to establish its own subject and define its own voice. This is reflexivity as a politics of location, as Fred Myers (1988) has termed it.

This revision of ethnography changes the understanding of the general character of what ethnography is about. In the past, ethnography has been associated with discovery, that is, with describing specific groups of people who had not been treated before. Restudies have been oddities in anthropology, and the full matrix of existing representations (missionaries, travelers, journalists, the people's own, for instance) in which an ethnographer produces his or her own text has always been downplayed. "One tribe, one ethnographer" is the persisting romantic ethic of the way research is organized long after the European age of exploration and discovery has ended. And there is a careful and sensitive etiquette in force about not working on another anthropologist's people or, at least, group. Against this, modernist (or postmodernist) ethnography is supremely aware that it operates in a complex matrix of already existing alternative representations, and indeed derives its critical power and insight from this awareness (or form of reflexivity). Of a deconstructive bent, modernist ethnography counts on not being first, on not discovering. It remakes, re-presents, other representations.

Experimental ethnography thus depends on preexisting, more conventional narrative treatments and is parasitic on them. Such ethnography is a comment, a remaking of a more standard realist account. Therefore, the best subjects of contemporary ethnography are those that have been heavily represented, narrated, and made mythic by the conventions of previous discourse. Marcus and Hall (1992), for example, show how knowledge of the structure of great American fortunes and the cultural influence they have exercised depends on the displacement of the perennial, pervasive, and mythic "family dynasty" genre in terms of which Americans have written about and comprehended these otherwise overshadowed, or even buried, stories of money "with a cultural face."

Part of the experimentation is in revealing the intertextual nature of any contemporary ethnography; it works through already constituted representations by both the observed and previous observers. There is no sense of discovery in the classic sense in contemporary ethnography. It forgoes the nostalgic idea that there are literally completely unknown worlds to be discovered. Rather, in full, reflexive awareness of the historical connections that already link it to its subject matter, contemporary ethnography makes historically sensitive revisions of the ethnographic archive with eyes fully open to the complex ways that diverse representations have constituted its subject matter. Such representations become an integral part of one's fieldwork.

The field of representations is by no means a mere supplement to fieldwork. Representations are social facts, and define not only the discourse of the ethnographer, but his or her literal position in relation to subjects. Fred Myers shows this well in his paper, "Locating Ethnographic Practice: Romance, Reality, and Politics in the Outback" (1988). Called to mediate the appearance of a "lost tribe" of aborigines (from a group with whom Myers had worked for years) who had made contact with the domain of white Australian society, Myers found himself involved in a complex set of interests and characterizations of the event (the government's, the media's, the people's own) for which existing anthropological modes of representing aborigines did not prepare him. He had to think his way through various interests and associated representations in order to locate himself and his discipline's discourse in relation to them. As Myers observes:

> For many practicing anthropologists, the literariness of rhetorical self-awareness gives it a rather self-absorbed, intellectualist, elitist, or apolitical quality removed from the nitty-gritty of social life. It can be, on the contrary, quite sensitive to relations of power, conflict, and implicit judgments. The question raised may be appropriate to an anthropology that is less centralized, that has many masters—or many different sorts of audience. . . . so-called postmodern anthropology is . . . asking questions similar to those generated increasingly by work under local auspices, that is, of a decentered and less Eurocentric anthropology. (p. 611)
>
> The value of rhetorical self-awareness is in drawing our attention to the constructions through which, as professionals, we have learned partly to read but which still mask many difficult and misleading assumptions about the purpose and politics of our work. (p. 622)

Myers in this episode of advocacy fieldwork literally had to renegotiate the meaning of "aborigines" in Australian anthropological discourse through critical self-awareness of the overlapping alternative representations with different valences of social power and influence behind them. In his work, the primary focus is upon a group of aborigines, and as an actor, his commitment remains with them also. Although his concern was not with furthering anthropology through experimental ethnography (which might have led him to a "messy" text), at least he draws attention to the key importance of a kind of reflexivity that locates the ethnographer through a keen sensitivity to the complex overlay of related, but different, accounts of almost any object of ethnographic interest.

4. The feminist version of the highly valued, powerfully evoked baseline form of subjectivist, experiential reflexivity has more recently been discussed and theorized as the practice of *positioning,* which is not that different from the politics of location that gives shape to reflexivity in critical ethnography within anthropology as described above. Positioning (of standpoint epistemologies) as a practice in feminism is most committed to the situatedness and partiality of all claims to knowledge, and hence contests the sort

of essentialist rhetoric and binarism (male/female, culture/nature) as a cognitive mode that has so biased toward rigidity and inflexibility questions of gender or "otherness" in language use. The *ethic* and practice of positioning defeats these rigidities of language and opens possibilities for different sorts of identities and concepts of race, culture, and gender to emerge.

On the one hand, the practice of positioning envisions a satisfying ethics of research practice (one that is a major motivation in the production of messy texts): any positioned or situated argument is an invitation to critical response to its partiality. Positioning assumes all work is incomplete, and requires response (and thus engagement) from others positioned differently. This ethical concern of positioning carries with it the antiessentialism so central to feminist thought.

On the other hand, the limitation of positioning is that it is often focused as a deeply reflexive meditation upon a relationship that produces ethnography (e.g., see Judy Stacey's "Can There Be a Feminist Ethnography?" 1988). As such, it yields the map, the totality, the social whole in which it is embedded, or it uses a "canned" monolithic construction to stand for this whole beyond the intimacy of ethnography, such as "patriarchal, corporate, and/or late consumer capitalism." To yield the larger landscape in which it operates out of concern for not "totalizing" only lets this landscape be constructed in reception—by readers who will give the framework of the ethnography a larger context, and not of course necessarily in the way that the feminist ethnographer might want. As noted, one goal of "messy" texts is to reclaim this larger framing "whole" of ethnography without being totalizing.

As we will see in a moment, it is Donna Haraway's specific formulation of the positioning practice out of feminism that most pushes it in the direction of ambitious, messy experimentation. Yet the practice of positioning can easily get stuck in a sterile form of identity politics, in which it is reduced to a formulaic incantation at the beginning of ethnographic papers in which one boldly "comes clean" and pronounces a positioned identity (e.g., "I am a white, Jewish, middle-class, heterosexual female"). This kind of reflexive location of oneself, while potentially a practice of key importance, all too often becomes a gesture that is enforced by politically correct convention. (The locating of one's position by parsing it into components of identity is most powerful, in my readings, when it is done as a critique of a writer's monologic authority; e.g., see the brilliant conclusion of Aijaz Ahmad's 1987 critique of a paper by Fredric Jameson, "Third-World Literature in the Era of Multinational Capital," published in *Social Text,* in which he deconstructs Jameson's identity into its unacknowledged gendered, racial, and cultural components.)

In her 1988 paper "Situated Knowledges: The Science Question in Feminism and the Privilege of Partial Perspective," Donna Haraway builds the feminist version of reflexivity as positioning into a reimagining of the dimensions of fine-grained, interpretive research (in her case coming out of the feminist study of science, but also fully congenial to anthropology's ethnographic study of forms of life as cultures). The following manifestolike quotations give a sense of her scheme:

> So, I think my problem, and "our" problem, is how to have *simultaneously* an account of radical historical contingency for all knowledge claims and knowing subjects, a critical practice for which recognizing our own "semiotic technologies" for making meanings, *and* a no-nonsense commitment to faithful accounts of a "real" world, one that can be partially shared and that is friendly to earthwide projects of finite freedom, adequate material abundance, modest meaning in suffering, and limited happiness. (p. 579)

> Not so perversely, objectivity turns out to be about particular and specific embodiment and definitely not about the false vision promising transcendence of all limits and responsibility. The moral is simple: only partial perspective promises objective vision. All Western cultural narratives about objectivity are allegories of the ideologies governing the relations of what we call mind and body, distance and responsibility. Feminist objectivity is about limited location and situated knowledge, not about transcendence and splitting of subject and object. It allows us to become answerable for what we learn how to see. (pp. 582-583)

> Situated knowledges are about communities, not about isolated individuals. The only way to find a larger vision is to be somewhere in particular. The science question in feminism is about objectivity as positioned rationality. Its images are not the products of escape and transcendence of limits (the view from above) but the joining of partial views and halting voices into a collective subject position that promises a vision of the means of ongoing finite embodiment, of living within limits and contradictions—of views from somewhere. (p. 590)

As with Bourdieu, in Haraway's essay we have a committed return to objective knowledge, but what a difference in how Haraway's notion of objectivity is constituted, and what a difference in the practice of reflexivity she defines in order to constitute it! Haraway's visionary program defines a space of juxtapositions and unexpected associations formed by a nomadic, embedded analytic vision constantly monitoring its location and partiality of perspective in relation to others. Whether or not one appreciates fully Haraway's "gonzo" idiom and rhetoric, she has taken the locational and positioning conception of reflexivity (shared by both feminism and anthropology) and expanded it into a field of experimentation of both open possibility and an open-ended ethics. As such, we have come full circle to my identification of "messy" texts as the most interesting current form that postmodernism specifically takes in ethnographic writing, and the way that certain strategies for practicing reflexivity might lead to such experimentation. In so doing, Haraway's program within the frame of feminism parallels and expresses more completely the implication of the sort of study encouraged by the locational politics of reflexivity in anthropology.

A Closing Note

I believe the major fear in the general reception to the now decade-long radicalization of tendencies (and possibilities) that have been present from the very inception of qualitative social science is that of transgression, of excessive skepticism, and of a paralyzing relativism—of a crossing of limits beyond which "anything goes" (the form in which one often hears such a fear voiced) and where even the possibility of communitas—of a shared discourse—among scholars has become imperiled. By having taken advantage of what seems to be a current exhaustion with the explicit rhetoric of the postmodern debates themselves in order to assess what they have specifically meant for at least one important domain of qualitative social science—that of ethnography in its appeal across various disciplinary and protodisciplinary boundaries—I hope I have provided in this chapter a contribution to undercutting this fear and its repressive implication. After all, though there may be differing opinions on the ultimate value of the postmodern debates for research traditions, there is little disagreement about the widespread sense of the need for a distinctive set of changes in the ways contemporary societies and cultures are studied.

Messy texts are neither models to follow nor the much-awaited products of a new paradigm, nor empty conformity with radicalizing fashion. Rather, they represent the substantive, deep effects of postmodern debates on personal styles of thought and work in established disciplines. They are the testing ground—always a mix of strong engagement by authors with "what goes on" among particular subjects of study and of an equally strong reflexive engagement with their own self-making as scholars— in which qualitative social science is being remade in the absence of authoritative models, paradigms, or methods. The concerns of such texts, far from being predictable and narrow, are as broad and diverse as the concerns that have shaped traditions of qualitative social science itself. In this immediate post-"post" moment, the only long-range forecast that one could make is that there is no sign of an end to change.

Notes

1. The critical, rather than paradigmatic, character of recent debates cannot be emphasized enough, as well as the difference that full recognition of this should make in the way such debates are received. Most social scientists are in the habit of expecting innovation to come in the form of systematic paradigms from which emerge distinctive models of research practice and product to be tested and shared. No less powerful in its effects, innovation by critique requires a different set of expectations in reception. I have employed the label *experimentation,* for better or worse, to refer to the output from critique (Marcus & Fischer, 1986). A key concern for many social scientists, both pro and con recent trends, is how long critique/experimentation can go on before the return of paradigmatic styles of work. Usually, moments of critique/experimentation tend to be unstable ruptures that fall relatively quickly to the pejorative charge of fashion, however important their residues may be. To the pleasure of some and the despair of others, the postmodern debates have had a remarkable capacity for mutation and development, making the current trend of research and thought in a variety of disciplines unusually enduring.

2. As a sort of ethnohistorian of present trends, I am especially fascinated by those messy texts that register within themselves the larger ongoing transformations of older traditions of qualitative social science on the personal styles of their authors' research and writing. My favorite examples are Renato Rosaldo's influential *Ilongot Headhunting, 1883-1974* (1980) and Dorinne Kondo's more recent, and equally influential, *Crafting Selves* (1990). Rosaldo's work includes a creative analysis of feuding in Ilongot society, very much within the tradition of the ethnographic analysis of these peoples and perhaps his homage to the tradition in which he was raised academically. However, his work is framed and eventually dominated by questions concerning the nature of indigenous history that set a new agenda entirely for work on peoples such as the Ilongot. Significantly, this new agenda is established by writing in the reflexive mode—by no means self-indulgent—in which Rosaldo precisely defines through personal experience the points at which he was motivated to change his thinking about the Ilongot. Though ten years later, and with a different set of concerns and positioning in relation to her object of study, Kondo develops similar transformations in her ethnography. Once a structural analyst of Japanese

society, now an interpreter of Japanese selfhood, with a critical edge established by her opening inquiry into her complex personal relationship to the Japanese in the framework of ethnographic research, Kondo delivers the goods, so to speak, in her analysis of labor-management relations in the sort of small firms on which large corporations in Japan strategically depend. The volume ends poignantly with a statement about the stakes of this kind of anthropology for issues of feminism and ethnic identity that gained stronger definition in Kondo's thinking following her dissertation research.

References

Ahmad, A. (1987). Jameson's rhetoric of otherness and the "national allegory." *Social Text, 6*(2), 3-25.

Asad, T. (Ed.). (1973). *Anthropology and the colonial encounter.* New York: Humanities Press.

Asad, T. (1986). The concept of cultural translation in British social anthropology. In J. Clifford & G. E. Marcus (Eds.), *Writing culture: The poetics and politics of ethnography* (pp. 141-164). Berkeley: University of California Press.

Bourdieu, P. (1990a). *The logic of practice.* Stanford, CA: Stanford University Press.

Bourdieu, P. (1990b). The scholastic point of view. *Cultural Anthropology, 5,* 380-391.

Bradbury, M., & McFarlane, J. (Eds.). (1976). *Modernism, 1890-1930.* New York: Penguin.

Clifford, J. (1988). *The predicament of culture: Twentieth-century ethnography, literature, and art.* Cambridge, MA: Harvard University Press.

Clifford, J., & Marcus, G. E. (Eds.). (1986). *Writing culture: The poetics and politics of ethnography.* Berkeley: University of California Press.

Clough, P. T. (1992). *The end(s) of ethnography: From realism to social criticism.* Newbury Park, CA: Sage.

Coombe, R. J. (1991). Objects of property and subjects of politics: Intellectual property laws and democratic dialogue. *Texas Law Review, 69,* 1853-1880.

Fischer, M. M. J., & Abedi, M. (1990). *Debating Muslims: Cultural dialogues in postmodernity and tradition.* Madison: University of Wisconsin Press.

Geertz, C. (1973a). *The interpretation of cultures: Selected essays.* New York: Basic Books.

Geertz, C. (1973b). Deep play: Notes on the Balinese cockfight. In C. Geertz, *The Interpretation of cultures: Selected essays.* New York: Basic Books.

Grossberg, L., Nelson, C., & Treichler, P. A. (Eds.). (1992). *Cultural studies.* New York: Routledge.

Haraway, D. J. (1988). Situated knowledges: The science question in feminism and the privilege of partial perspective. *Feminist Studies, 14,* 75-99.

Haraway, D. J. (1989). *Primate visions: Gender, race, and nature in the world of modern science.* New York: Routledge.

Harvey, D. (1989). *The condition of postmodernity: An enquiry into the origins of cultural change.* Oxford: Basil Blackwell.

Holub, R. C. (1991). *Jürgen Habermas: Critic in the public sphere.* New York: Routledge.

Hymes, D. (Ed.). (1969). *Reinventing anthropology.* New York: Pantheon.

Kondo, D. (1990). *Crafting selves: Power, gender, and discourses of identity in a Japanese workplace.* Chicago: University of Chicago Press.

Lyotard, J.-F. (1988). *The differend: Phrases in dispute* (2nd ed.). Minneapolis: University of Minnesota Press.

Marcus, G. E., with Hall, P. D. (1992). *Lives in trust: The fortunes of dynastic families in late twentieth century America.* Boulder, CO: Westview.

Marcus, G. E., & Fischer, M. J. M. (1986). *Anthropology as cultural critique: An experimental moment in the human sciences.* Chicago: University of Chicago Press.

Myers, F. (1988). Locating ethnographic practice: Romance, reality, and politics in the outback. *American Ethnologist, 15,* 609-624.

Rajchman, J. (1987). Postmodernism in a nominalist frame: The emergence and diffusion of a cultural category. *Flash Art, 137,* 49-51.

Readings, B. (1991). *Introducing Lyotard: Art and politics.* New York: Routledge.

Rosaldo, R. (1980). *Ilongot headhunting, 1883-1974: A study in society and history.* Stanford, CA: Stanford University Press.

Stacey, J. (1988). Can there be a feminist ethnography? *Women's Studies International Forum, 11*(1), 21-27.

Stacey, J. (1990). *Brave new families: Stories of domestic upheaval in late twentieth century America.* New York: Basic Books.

Taussig, M. (1987). *Shamanism, colonialism, and the wild man: A study in terror and healing.* Chicago: University of Chicago Press.

Thornton, R. (1988). The rhetoric of ethnographic holism. *Cultural Anthropology, 3,* 285-303.

Tyler, S. A. (1987). *The unspeakable: Discourse, dialogue, and rhetoric in the postmodern world.* Madison: University of Wisconsin Press.

Van Maanen, J. (1988). *Tales of the field: On writing ethnography.* Chicago: University of Chicago Press.

Watson, G. (1987). Make me reflexive—but not yet: Strategies for managing essential reflexivity in ethnographic discourse. *Journal of Anthropological Research, 43,* 29-41.

White, H. (1973). *Metahistory.* Baltimore: Johns Hopkins University Press.

White, H. (1978). *Tropics of discourse.* Baltimore: Johns Hopkins University Press.

Willis, P. (1981). *Learning to labour: How working class kids get working class jobs.* New York: Columbia University Press. (Original work published 1977)

36

The Fifth Moment

YVONNA S. LINCOLN
NORMAN K. DENZIN

WRITING the present is always dangerous, a biased project conditioned by distorted readings of the past and utopian hopes for the future. In what follows we sketch our utopian vision of the future of qualitative research. This vision is based on our reading of the fifth moment. We begin by delineating the central characteristics of this moment and the problems that define it. We then discuss how researchers are coping with these problems. We conclude with predictions about the sixth moment, based on our readings of the present.

Two theses organize our discussion. First, the history of qualitative research is defined more by breaks and ruptures than by a clear evolutionary, progressive movement from one stage to the next. These breaks and ruptures move in cycles and phases, so that what is passé today may be in vogue a decade from now. Just as the postmodern, for example, reacts to the modern, some day there may well be a neomodern phase that extols Malinowski and the Chicago school and finds the current poststructural, postmodern moment abhorrent.

Our second assumption builds on the tensions that now define qualitative research. There is an illusive center to this contradictory, tension-riddled enterprise that seems to be moving further and further away from grand narratives and single, overarching ontological, epistemological, and methodological paradigms. This center lies in the humanistic commitment of the qualitative researcher to study the world always from the perspective of the interacting individual. From this simple commitment flow the liberal and radical politics of qualitative research. Action, feminist, clinical, constructivist, ethnic, critical, and cultural studies researchers are all united on this point. They all share the belief that a politics of liberation must always begin with the perspectives, desires, and dreams of those individuals and groups who have been oppressed by the larger ideological, economic, and political forces of a society, or a historical moment.

This commitment defines an ever-present but always shifting center in the discourses of qualitative research. The center shifts and moves as new, previously oppressed or silenced voices enter the discourse. Thus, for example, feminists and ethnic researchers have articulated their own relationship to the postpositivist and critical paradigms. These new articulations then refocus and redefine previous ontologies, epistemologies, and methodologies, including positivism and postpositivism. These two theses suggest that only the broad outlines of the future, the sixth moment, can be predicted.

Defining the Present

Recall our definition of this sprawling field. Slightly rephrased, it reads as follows:

> Qualitative research is an interdisciplinary, transdisciplinary, and sometimes counterdisciplinary field. It cross-cuts the humanities, the social sciences, and the physical sciences. Qualitative research is many things at the same time. It is multiparadigmatic in focus. Its practitioners are sensitive to the value of the multimethod approach. They are committed to the naturalistic perspective and to the interpretive understanding of human experience. At the same time, the field is inherently political and shaped by multiple ethical and political positions.
>
> Qualitative research embraces two tensions at the same time. On the one hand, it is drawn to a broad, interpretive, postmodern, feminist, and critical sensibility. On the other hand, it can also be drawn to more narrowly defined positivist, postpositivist, humanistic, and naturalistic conceptions of human experience and its analysis.

In the fifth moment all of these tensions will continue to operate as the field confronts and continues to define itself in the face of six fundamental issues embedded in these tensions. The first issue involves positivism and postpositivism. The present moment is characterized, in part, by a continuing critique of positivism and postpositivism that is coupled with ongoing self-critique and self-appraisal. Every contributor to this volume has reflectively wrestled with the location of his or her topic in the present moment, discussing its relationship to previous positivist and postpositivist formulations.

The second and third issues are what we have called the *crises of representation and legitimation.* These two crises speak, respectively, to the Other and its representation in our texts and to the authority we claim for our texts. The fourth issue is the continued emergence of a cacophony of voices speaking with varying agendas from specific gender, race, class, ethnic, and Third World perspectives.

Fifth, throughout its history, qualitative research has been defined in terms of shifting scientific, moral, sacred, and religious discourses. Vidich and Lyman clearly establish this fact in their history of colonial ethnography in Chapter 2 of this volume. Since the Enlightenment, science and religion have been separated, but only at the ideological level, for in practice religion has constantly informed science and the scientific project (Rosaldo, 1989, p. 74). The borders between these two systems of meaning are becoming more and more blurred. Critics increasing see science from within a magical, shamanistic framework (Rosaldo, 1989, p. 219). Others are moving science away from its empiricist foundations and closer to a critical, interpretive project that stresses morals and moral standards of evaluation (Clough, 1992, pp. 136-137).

The sixth issue crucial to qualitative research in the fifth moment is that of the influence of technology. As we shall argue below, technology will continue to mediate, define, and shape qualitative research practices.

The tensions that surround the six issues described here and the strategies developed to address them will continue to define the center and the margins of qualitative research.

Coping With the Present

Our challenge here is not to produce yet another critique of qualitative research. The salient features of that critique are well known, and have been discussed throughout the various chapters and section introductions of this handbook. They mark the central controversies that define this field of discourse. Postmodernists take these issues for granted, whereas they are sites of contention for postpositivists:

- The qualitative researcher is not an objective, authoritative, politically neutral observer standing outside and above the text (Bruner, 1993, p. 1).
- The qualitative researcher is "historically positioned and locally situated [as] an all-too-human [observer] of the human condition" (Bruner, 1993, p. 1).
- Meaning is "radically plural, always open, and . . . there is politics in every account" (Bruner, 1993, p. 1).

These controversies shape the questions we listed in our introduction to Part VI. Clearly, the problems in the fifth moment are multiple.

Correcting Excesses and Revisiting the Past

The fifth moment addresses these problems in three ways. First, it continues to sharpen the above critique while, second, attempting to correct its excesses. Qualitative research, like other scholarly domains, displays a tendency to move from one intellectual fashion to another, from positivism to postpositivism, semiotics and structuralism, poststructuralism and postmodernism, and so on (see Bruner, 1993, p. 24; Ortner, 1984). In such moves there is often a tendency to reject wholesale an entire theoretical perspective, or paradigm, as if postpositivism were passé, for example. It should not work this way. There is a real need to return, as Bruner (1993) argues, to "the originals of out-of-fashion texts" (p. 24). Such a return is necessary for two reasons: First, we need to relearn these texts, to see if standard criticisms still hold today; second, we need to study the best works from these traditions, so as to understand how the masters in a given "passé" perspective in fact did their work.

It must be noted that revisiting works from earlier historical moments operates at different levels of abstraction. Although colonialist, positivist ethnography may be passé, the basic strategies and techniques of case studies, ethnographies, observation, interviewing, and textual analysis still form the basis for research in the fifth and sixth moments. In a parallel vein, although certain of the postpositivist assumptions of the grounded theory approach may be criticized, the generic method of building interpretations up out of observations and interactions with the world will not change.

Third, it is time to get on with the multidisciplinary project called qualitative research. Too much critique will stifle this project. This critique, it must be noted, assumes two forms, and both can be counterproductive. Endless self-referential criticisms by poststructuralists can produce mountains of texts with few referents to concrete human experience. Such are not needed. The same conclusion holds for positivist and postpositivist criticisms of poststructuralism (and the responses to these criticisms). These criticisms and exchanges can operate at a level of abstraction that does little to help the people who just go out and do research.

The basic issue is simple: how best to describe and interpret the experiences of other peoples and cultures. The problems of representation and legitimation flow from this commitment.

The Crisis of Representation

As indicated above, this crisis asks the questions, Who is the Other? Can we ever hope to speak authentically of the experience of the Other, or an Other? And if not, how do we create a social science that includes the Other? The short answer to these questions is that we move to including the Other in the larger research processes that we have developed. For some, this means participatory, or collaborative, research and evaluation efforts (see, in this volume, Reason, Chapter 20; Miller & Crabtree, Chapter 21). These activities can occur in a variety of institutional sites, including clinical, educational, and social welfare settings.

For still others, it means a form of liberatory investigation wherein Others are trained to engage in their own social and historical interrogative efforts, and then are assisted in devising answers to questions of historical and contemporary oppression that are rooted in the values and cultural artifacts that characterize their communities. In this volume, Hamilton (Chapter 3), Reason (Chapter 20), and Greene (Chapter 33) discuss the various strategies that can be used when such inquiries are undertaken, including the major different forms of participatory action and evaluation research.

For yet other social scientists, including the Other means becoming coauthors in narrative adventures. And for still others, it means constructing what are called "experimental," or "messy," texts, where multiple voices speak (see, in this volume, Richardson, Chapter 32; Marcus, Chapter 35), often in conflict, and where the reader is left to sort out which experiences speak to his or her personal life. For still others, it means presenting to the inquiry and policy community a series of autohistories, personal narratives, lived experiences, poetic representations, and sometimes fictive and/or fictional texts (see, in this volume, Clandinin & Connelly, Chapter 26; Richardson, Chapter 32) that allow the Other to speak for him- or herself. The inquirer or evaluator becomes merely the connection between the field text, the research text, and the consuming community in making certain that such voices are heard. Sometimes, increasingly, it is the institutionalized Other who speaks, especially as the Other gains access to the knowledge-producing corridors of power and achieves entrée into the particular group of elites known as intellectuals and academics or faculty. John Stanfield, in Chapter 10 of this volume, elaborates the issues that are involved when this happens.

The point is that both the Other and more mainstream social scientists recognize that there is no such thing as unadulterated truth, that speaking from a faculty, an institution of higher education, or a corporate perspective automatically means that one speaks from a privileged and powerful vantage point—and that this vantage point is one to which many do not have access, whether because of social station or level of education.

Judith Stacey (1988) speaks of the difficulties involved in representing the experiences of the Other about whom texts are written. Writing from a feminist perspective, she argues that a major contradiction exists in this project, despite the desire to engage in egalitarian research characterized by authenticity, reciprocity, and trust. This is so because actual differences of power, knowledge, and structural mobility still exist in the researcher-subject relationship. The subject is always at grave risk of manipulation and betrayal by the ethnographer. In addition, there is the crucial fact that the final product is too often that of the researcher, no matter how much it has been modified or influenced by the subject.

Thus, even when research is written from the perspective of the Other—for example, women writing about women—the women doing the writing may "unwittingly preserve the dominant power relations that they explicitly aim to overcome" (Bruner, 1993, p. 23; see also Mascia-Lees, Sharpe, & Cohen, 1993, p. 245). The feminist solution requires a merger of scholarship "with a clear politics to work against the forces of oppression" (Mascia-Lees et al., 1993, p. 246).

The recent libel trial of Janet Malcolm and *New Yorker* magazine is instructive on these points (Gross, 1993). Malcolm was accused by Jeffrey N. Masson of fabricating five quotations in her two-part 48,500-word *New Yorker* profile of him. The federal jury ruled for Masson, concluding that Malcolm had fabricated the five quotations, and that two of them met all of the criteria for libel, as defined by the Supreme Court: They were made up, or materially altered, Malcolm knew they were defamatory and acted with "reckless disregard" for their accuracy, and Masson had been damaged by them (Gross, 1993).

This case is important for several reasons. As ethnographers move more deeply into the production of fictional texts, they must take steps to ensure that the words they put in subjects' mouths were in fact spoken by those subjects. The ethics of textual production argue for the meticulous checking of verifiable facts; that is, one must be certain that statements depicted as quotes were in fact made. But more important, the ethnographer must take care when changing contexts and reordering events for dramatic purposes. No one wants to libel another individual. The ethnographer must walk a fine line in those situations where he or she wishes to uncover wrongdoing, illegal acts, or morally offensive conduct.

The Author's Place in the Text

The feminist solution clarifies the issue of the author's place in the interpretations that are written. This problem is directly connected to the problem of representation. It is often phrased in terms of a false dichotomy, that is, "the extent to which the personal self should have a place in the scientific scholarly text" (Bruner, 1993, p. 2). This false division between the personal and the ethnographic self rests on the assumption that it is possible to write a text that does not bear the traces of its author. Of course, this is not possible. All texts are personal statements.

The correct phrasing of this issue turns on the amount of the personal, subjective, poetic self that is in fact openly given in the text. Bruner (1993) phrases the problem this way: "The danger is putting the personal self so deeply back into the text that it completely dominates, so that the work becomes narcissistic and egotistical. No one is advocating ethnographic self-indulgence" (p. 6). The goal is to return the author to the text openly, in a way that does "not squeeze out the object of study" (p. 6).

There are many ways to return the author openly to the qualitative research text. Authors may write fictional narratives of the self (see Richardson, Chapter 32, this volume), or produce performance texts. Authors can give dramatic readings, or transform their field interviews into poetic texts, or poetry, or short stories and plays (Rose, 1993). Authors can engage in dialogue with those studied. Authors may write through narrators, "directly as a character . . . or through multiple characters, or one character may speak in many voices, or the writer may come in and then go out of the [text]" (Bruner, 1993, p. 6; see also Ellis, 1991, 1994; Ellis & Bochner, 1992).

The Crisis of Legitimation

It is clear that postmodern and poststructural arguments are moving further and further away from postpositivist models of validity and textual authority. This is the *crisis of legitimation.* This so-called crisis arose when anthropologists and other social scientists addressed the authority of the text. By *the authority of the text* we reference the claim any text makes to being accurate, true, and complete. Is a text, that is, faithful to the context and the individuals it is supposed to represent? Does the text have the right to assert that it is a report to the larger world that addresses not only the researcher's interests, but also the interests of those studied?

This is not an illegitimate set of questions, and it affects all of us and the work that we do. And although different social scientists might approach the questions from different angles, these twin crises are confronted by everyone.

A poststructural interpretive social science challenges postpositivist arguments concerning the text and its validity. It interprets validity as a text's call to authority and truth, and calls this version of validity *epistemological.* That is, a text's authority is established through recourse to a set of rules concerning knowledge, its production, and representation. These rules, as Scheurich (1992, p. 1) notes, if properly followed, establish validity. Without validity there is no truth, and without truth there can be no trust in a text's claims to validity. With validity comes power (Cherryholmes, 1988), and validity becomes a boundary line that "divides good research from bad, separates acceptable (to a particular research community) research from unacceptable research . . . it is the name for inclusion and exclusion" (Scheurich, 1992, p. 5).

Poststructuralism reads the discussions of logical, construct, internal, ethnographic, and external validity, text-based data, triangulation, trustworthiness, credibility, grounding, naturalistic indicators, fit, coherence, comprehensiveness (see Eisenhart & Howe, 1992, pp. 657-669), plausibility, truth, and relevance (Atkinson, 1990, pp. 68-72) as attempts to reauthorize a text's authority in the postpositivist moment. Altheide and Johnson (Chapter 30, this volume) review extensively the assumptions that organize this project.

These words, and the methodological strategies that lie behind them, represent attempts to thicken and contextualize a work's grounding in the external, empirical world. They represent efforts to develop a set of transcendent rules and procedures that lie outside any specific research project. These rules, if successfully followed, allow a text to bear witness to its own validity. Hence a text is valid if it is sufficiently grounded, triangulated, based on naturalistic indicators, carefully fitted to a theory (and its concepts), comprehensive in scope, credible in terms of member checks, logical, and truthful in terms of its reflection of the phenomenon in question. The text's author then announces these validity claims to the reader. Such claims now become the text's warrant to its own authoritative re-presentation of the experience and social world under inspection.

Epistemological validity can now be interpreted as a text's desire to assert its own power over the reader. Validity represents the always just out of reach, but answerable, claim a text makes for its own authority. (After all, the research could have always been better grounded, the subjects more representative, the researcher more knowledgeable, the research instruments better formulated, and so on.) A fertile obsession, validity is the researcher's mask of authority (Lather, 1993), which allows a particular regime of truth within a particular text (and community of scholars) to work its way on the world and the reader.

It is now necessary to ask, What do we do with validity once we have met poststructuralism? Several answers are suggested. They all turn back on the crisis of representation, and involve, in one form or another, the problem of how the Other's perspective and experience are expressed in a text.

The first answer is political. If there is a center to poststructural thought it lies in the recurring attempt to strip a text, any text, of its external claims to authority. Every text must be taken on its own terms. Furthermore, the desire to produce an authoritative (valid) text is renounced, for any text can be undone in terms of its internal structural logic.

The unmasking of validity-as-authority now exposes the heart of the argument. If validity is gone, values and politics, not objective epistemology, govern science. This is familiar territory, and the answer is equally familiar. It is given in Foucault's concept of a subversive genealogy, a strategy that refuses to accept those "systems of discourse (economic, political, scientific, narrative)" (Denzin, 1991, p. 32) that "ignore who we are collectively and individually" (Racevskis, 1983, p. 20).

A poststructural social science project seeks its external grounding not in science, in any of its revisionist forms, but rather in a commitment to a post-Marxism and a feminism with hope, but no guarantees (Hall, 1986, p. 58). It seeks to understand how power and ideology operate through systems of discourse, asking always how words and texts and their meanings play a pivotal part in "those decisive performances of race, class, gender . . . [that] shape the emergent political conditions . . . we refer to as the postmodern world" (Downing, 1987, p. 80). A good text is one that invokes these commitments. A good text exposes how race, class, and gender work their ways in the concrete lives of interacting individuals. Lather (1986, p. 67) calls this catalytic validity, the degree to which a given research project empowers and emancipates a research community.

Verisimilitude

The second solution dispenses with the quest for validity and seeks to examine critically, instead, a text's verisimilitude, or ability to reproduce (simulate) and map the real. There are two essential levels of verisimilitude—as a set of laws set by convention, and as a mask that presents these laws as a text's submission to the rules of a particular genre (Todorov, 1977, p. 84). In its most naive form, verisimilitude describes a text's relationship to reality. It asks, Are the representations in a text consistent with the real? Is the text telling the truth? Certain actions, for example, are said to lack verisimilitude "when they seem unable to occur in reality" (Todorov, 1977, p. 82). A second meaning of verisimilitude refers to the relationship of a particular text to some agreed-upon opinion, for example, epistemological validity, or what Mishler (1990, p. 417) calls valid exemplars accepted by a relevant community of scientists. Here it is understood that separate interpretive communities (Fish, 1980) have distinctively unique standards or versions of verisimilitude as proof, truth, or validity.

As Todorov (1977, p. 83) notes, there are as many verisimilitudes as there are genres (comedy, detective fiction, tragedy, and so on). In the social sciences there are multiple genres, or writing forms: book reviews, presidential addresses to scholarly societies, research notes, critical essays, grant proposals, research reports, committee reports, and so on (see Agger, 1989; see also Richardson, Chapter 32, this volume). Each form has its own laws of genre. The validity of a statistical table is different from the so-called validity of thick description in an ethnographer's report (Geertz, 1973). Two separate verisimilitudes are operating in these two contexts.

Verisimilitude can be described as the mask a text assumes as it convinces the reader it has conformed to the laws of its genre; in so doing, it has reproduced reality in accordance with those rules. Every text enters into a relationship with verisimilitude and its laws, including taking verisimilitude, or validity, as its theme, in which case the text must establish an *antiverisimilitude,* that is, a text that appears to lack truth, validity, or verisimilitude. Such moves allow a text to make a separation between truth and verisimilitude, for what appears to be true is false, and what appears to be false is true.

Two questions now emerge. The first doubles back on itself: Can a text have verisimilitude and not be true, and, conversely, can a text be true, but lack verisimilitude? The recent controversy surrounding William Foote Whyte's classic work *Street Corner Society* (1943, 1955, 1981), as discussed in a special issue of the *Journal of Contemporary Ethnography* (April 1992), illuminates this question, which turns on the status of a text's grounding in the real world. Whyte's work, historically accepted as a truthful text with high verisimilitude, is challenged by Boelen (1992, p. 49), another researcher, who claims Whyte's study, while having some degree of verisimilitude, lacks truth. Whyte, Boelen argues, misrepresented the real structure of Italian street-corner life, and perpetuated false truths about that life. Whyte (1992) replies that his study was based on member checks and hence had both verisimilitude and truth. His critic, he asserts, has misunderstood his original text and has not penetrated the real fabrics of street-corner life in the Italian community.

The implications of this exchange are clear.[1] The truth of a text cannot be established by its verisimilitude. Verisimilitude can always be challenged. Hence a text can be believed to be true even as it lacks verisimilitude. (The opposite case holds as well.) Challenges to verisimilitude in qualitative research rest on the simple observation that a text is always a site of political struggle over the real and its meanings. Truth is political, and verisimilitude is textual.

The second question following from this discussion of verisimilitude becomes, Whose verisimilitude? It is the researcher's goal to contest multiple verisimilitudes, multiple versions of reality, and the perceived truths that structure these realities. A text's verisimilitude is given in its ability to reproduce and deconstruct the reproductions and simulations that structure the real. This is *deconstructive verisimilitude.*[2]

The Crisis of Vocality: New and Old Voices Coping With the Present

A variety of new and old voices—such as critical theory, feminist, and ethnic scholars—have also entered the present situation, offering solutions to the crises and problems that have been identified above. The move is toward pluralism, and many social scientists now recognize that no picture is ever complete, that what is needed is many perspectives, many voices, before we can achieve deep understandings of social phenomena, and before we can assert that a narrative is complete.

The modernist dream of a grand or master narrative is now a dead project; the recognition of the futility and oppression of such a project is the postmodern condition. The postmodern project challenges the modernist belief (and desire) that it is possible to develop a progressive program for incorporating all the cultures of the world under a single umbrella. The postmodern era is defined, in part, by the belief that there is no single umbrella in the history of the world that might incorporate and represent fairly the dreams, aspirations, and experiences of all peoples.

Critical Theorists

The critical theorists, from the Frankfurt, to the Annales, world-system, and participatory action research schools, continue to be a major presence in qualitative research, as Kincheloe and McLaren observe in Chapter 8 of this volume. The critique and concern of the critical theorists has been an effort to design a pedagogy of resistance. The pedagogy of resistance, of taking back "voice," of reclaiming narrative for one's own rather than adapting to the narratives of a dominant majority, has been most explicitly laid out by one working with adults, Paolo Freire in Brazil. Freire's work is echoed most faithfully by a group of activist priests and scholars who are exploring what is called "liberation theology"—the joining of the Catholic church to egalitarian ends for the purposes of overturning oppression and achieving social justice through empowerment of the marginalized, the poor, the nameless, the voiceless. Their project is nothing less than the radical restructuring of society toward the ends of reclaiming historic cultural legacies, social justice, the redistribution of power, and the achievement of truly democratic societies.

Feminist Researchers

The feminists have argued that there is a missing voice, and a missing picture, in the history of the sciences, religion, and the arts. Three different groups—feminist philosophers, scientists, and theologians—are represented in this discourse. Each has had an unsettling—if not unnerving—effect on arguments about how we "do" qualitative research.

The first two groups—the philosophers and the scientists—have mounted two separate, but related, arguments. The first is that traditional science has acted to maintain the Enlightenment dualism, with its major premise that there is a separate and distinct "social reality" "out there" somewhere, separated from those who experience it, and that it is the scientists' job to uncover this separate reality, and report on it, for that is the essence of "Truth."

Poststructural feminists urge the abandonment of any distinction between empirical science and social criticism. That is, they seek a morally informed social criticism that is not committed to the traditional concerns of empirical science. This traditional science, they argue, rests a considerable amount of its authority on the ability to make public what has traditionally been understood to be private (Clough, 1992, p. 137). Feminists dispute this distinction. They urge a social criticism that takes back from science the traditional authority to inscribe and create subjects within the boundaries and frameworks of an objective social science. This social criticism "gives up on data collection and instead offers rereadings of representations in every form of information processing, empirical science, literature, film, television, and computer simulation" (Clough, 1992, p. 137).

A second set of feminist philosophers notes distinct problems with several of the scientific method's most basic premises: the idea that scientific objectivity is possible, the effect that the mandate for objectivity has on the subjects of research, and the possibility of conducting an unbiased science at all. Olesen reviews these arguments in Chapter 9 of this volume, explicating the disastrous consequences of objectifying the targets, subjects, and participants of our research.

Liberation and feminist theologians are central to this new discourse. They ask hard questions, such as, Where and what are the places of women, persons of color, the poor, the homeless, and the hungry in the church, in science, in art, and in literature?

Ethnic Scholars

There is yet another group of concerned scholars determining the course of qualitative research: the ethnic/racial/cultural studies experts who examine the question of whether history has deliberately omitted some cultures from speaking. This new generation of scholars, many of them persons of color, challenges both historical and contemporary social scientists on the accuracy, veracity, and authenticity of the latter's work, contending that no picture can be considered final when the perspectives and narratives of so many are missing, distorted, or subordinated to self-serving dominant majority interests. The result of such challenges has been twofold; they have brought about a reconsideration of the Western canon, and they have contributed to an increase in the number of historical and scientific works that recognize and reconstruct the perspectives of those whose perspectives and constructions have been missing for so long. In Chapter 10 of this volume John Stanfield outlines this literature and its major moments, figures, and arguments.

Thus have we written the present. A messy moment, multiple voices, experimental texts, breaks, ruptures, crises of legitimation and representation, self-critique, new moral discourses, and technologies. We venture now into the future, attempting to describe the possibilities of the sixth moment. Several themes emerge, or will not go away: the voice and presence of the Other, historically called *the native*; the social text; and the sacred, the humanistic, and the technological.

Back to the Future

We cannot predict the future, but we can speculate about it, because the future never represents a clean break with the past.

The Other's Voice

Throughout its twentieth-century history, up to a scant quarter century ago, qualitative researchers were still talking seriously about the problems of "going native," using the word that previously inscribed the Other in qualitative discourse. Who today can even use the word! After-hours tales, over drinks, mostly white, male, middle-class North American ethnographic researchers whispered of those of their colleagues who had engaged that final perdition, overidentification with those he (seldom she) had studied. Today, no one takes seriously talk of "going native." In fact, its disappearance as a category of concern among sociologists and anthropologists is scarcely remarked, but, like the silences between lovers, it is all the more significant for its absence. In its place looms the Other, whose voice researchers now struggle to hear.

The disappearance of the word *native* is significant; its silence, deafening. In the postmodern world we are executing as our own heirs, in the legacy we have left ourselves and the students who come after us, "going native" is a category that speaks volumes to both our distorted senses of scientific objectivity and our colonial past. We struggle to find ways to make our texts meaningful beyond the artificial structures of conventional objectivity. We try to come to terms with our own "critical subjectivities." All the while, we have also admitted our guilt and complicity in the colonizing aspects of our work, pointedly subsumed by the term *native* itself. Even using the term is offensive.

But worse than politically incorrect, it stands as witness to our conceits as field-workers. How could we have considered ourselves civilized and objective alongside another class of individuals clearly not "civilized," or well below us on a presumed continuum of becoming civilized? Vidich and Lyman, in Chapter 2 of this volume, trace the history of those ideas that undergirded and supported the very concepts that gave rise to the professional tragedy of "going native." Key to this was the Enlightenment legacy that led us to believe we could, indeed, prepare texts that purported to be whole and truthful accounts, objective accounts, of those "natives"/Others.

So we are not likely to hear much about "going native" again. That world has passed. Few mourn its passing—in fact, quite the opposite. Today we are trying to live ever closer to the lives about which we write. Many examples are available. Others are forthcoming that try to show not that we can live those lives, but that we have lived close enough to them to begin to understand how their worlds have been constructed (see, for instance, the May 5, 1993, issue of the *Chronicle of Higher Education,* pp. A6-A7, A12).

The Social Text: Telling Stories From the Field

We are becoming extremely conscious of how our "tales of the field" can be categorized. We now understand at least the flaws that accompany "realist" and "confessional" tales, if not other kinds (Van Maanen, 1988). And many are trying to move toward extended understandings, extended vicariousness, in their texts. Many now are experimenting with form, format, voice, shape, style. Laurel Richardson, in her excellent and moving chapter in this handbook, shares with us some of the more powerful literary narrative styles that are being utilized.

This experimentation with text grows from several sources: our concern with representation of the Other; our willingness to all but abandon, or at least drastically modify, the realist text; and our growing sophistication surrounding the problems of situatedness in texts. We know that our texts have specific locations. We know that they represent—whether in some hidden way or openly—our baggage as individual social scientists. We care less about our "objectivity" as scientists than we do about providing our readers with some powerful propositional, tacit, intuitive, emotional, historical, poetic, and empathic experience of the Other via the texts we write.

The problem of representation will not go away. Indeed, at its heart lies an inner tension, an ongoing dialectic, a contradiction, that will never be resolved. On the one hand there is the concern for validity, or certainty in the text as a form of isomorphism and authenticity. On the other hand there is the sure and certain knowledge that all texts are socially, historically, politically, and culturally located. We, like the texts we write, can never be transcendent.

So the experiments will continue, proliferate, grow both more "ironic" (see, e.g., Marcus, Chapter 35, this volume) and simultaneously less self-mocking. There will also be an expansion of the genres of literature from which they borrow. The tension of this dialectic will continue to be felt throughout the ethnographic community, but resolved publicly and privately in many more ways than we have yet seen.

The Sacred, the Humanistic, and the Technological

The West has become increasingly aware of the ecological disasters that massive industrialization and consumption have wrought. We have slowly begun to reconnect with the sense of conjoint destiny with Planet Earth. As these understandings increase, we are likely to see a reconsideration of whether science and religion are truly separate entities.

The modernist idea of separation of religion and science overturned centuries of marriage between the two. The modernist project ignored the deeply spiritual search for meaning and prophecy thought to be hidden in the whole of the universe. It read through the stars (astrology), or the search for the "philosopher's stone," an element thought to have the power to bring spiritual wisdom and riches to the alchemist who discovered it. No one would argue that we need to return to the days of astrologers or alchemists. But it is true that many, including scientists, are searching to find some spiritual core in themselves, a way of reconnecting to meaning, purpose, and the sense of wholeness and holiness that once, in another age, permeated the everyday lives of ordinary men and women.

Peter Reason (1993) writes about the return of spirituality to science. He talks about "sacred experience and sacred science." He—and perhaps others—is beginning to think deeply about how we use science, and what kinds of science we might have. Can there be a sacred science? Such a science would link all its practitioners and participants in bonds that are respectful of our humanity. A sacred science would be supportive of our struggle for dignity. It would lead us to understand how we can throw off oppression and help others to do likewise.

Since the turn of the century, the human disciplines have been moving on a spiritual journey that would join science and the sacred. This can be seen in the writings of many, from Durkheim, Weber, James, Freud, Jung, Fromm, Horney, and Gregory Bateson through Carlos Castañeda, Mary Daly, Renato Rosaldo, Bennetta Jules-Rosette, Mary Douglas, and many others. Indeed, anthropological writers from Rosalie Wax onward have spoken, in their "confessional" tales, of the changes in themselves that resulted from their engaging particular questions to study.

Peter Reason (1993) would have us consider the more elemental spiritualities of these inquiry processes. The connections among spirituality, shamanism, magic, the world of the spirit (for instance, in studies of Santeria), the world of the sorcerer (as in Castañeda's or Lévi-Strauss's work)—all relate in some way to the larger questions of how we use science not only to "know," to "understand," but also to grow spiritually (see also Taussig, 1987).

And so we will likely see a reemergence of deliberation about how science and the sacred fit together. There will be a gradual denial of the Enlightenment wrench that separated the soul from secular concerns. This process is already in motion. It can be seen everywhere: the interest in vision quests in North America, the curiosity about magical rituals from around the world, the search for objects that have spiritual and healing powers that even the most secular of us collects (the crystal that sits on the computer of one of us; the earthy Indian artifacts that line the study of the other), the dance rituals of some researchers that allow them to "center" with their participants, the growing concern with global ecological issues, the dinner-table conversation around appropriate technology and ideas of how small is beautiful.

All of these happenings and rituals point to the tingling, edgy mindfulness that science and technology have not provided the answers we expected or hoped for. And they suggest that concerns of the spirit are already returning to the human disciplines, and will be more important in the future. A sacred science is certain to make its effects felt within the emerging discourses of qualitative research.

Mediating Technologies

At the everyday, practical level, technology, as it has always done, will continue to mediate the fieldwork and analysis phases of qualitative research. However, in the fifth and sixth moments electronic and video technologies, including interactive computers and interactive video, will radically transform every phase and form of qualitative research. Laptop computers will be taken into the field. Modems will connect researchers to their offices and laser printers. Electronically transmitted texts will replace the printed page. New methods for processing text-based materials, as Richards and Richards argue in Chapter 28, will be developed. New research topics (e.g., self and identity in cyberspace) grounded in the new media technologies (e.g., digitized video data) are also likely to emerge.

Electronic mail systems have already created new communities of qualitative researchers, and these communities will continue to grow. These new electronic social worlds change the concept of community. They shift its locus away from face-to-face interaction to text-mediated communication contexts. New writing selves interact in this cyberspace, selves lodged and created in the virtual reality of the electronic text. These faceless, electronic selves find themselves located in simulated communities. These communities have their own interactional norms concerning the public, the private, the sacred, the secular, and the rational.

New forms of the text, building on hypertext, will also appear. This will change the traditional relationship between the reader and the writer. In the electronic spaces of hypertext, readers become writers, *bricoleurs* who construct the text out of the bits and pieces and chunks of materials left for them by the writer. The writer now disappears, receding into the background, his or her traces found only in the new hypertext that has been created by the reader (see Foden, 1993, p. 5).

And so we are at, or in, the brink of a moment. Because we cannot see clearly where we are, we have no idea of how far we have come, or when we will get to wherever it is we are going.

Coda

In Chapter 35 of this volume, George Marcus argues that we are already in the post-"post" period—post-poststructuralism, post-postmodernism. What this means for interpretive ethnographic practices is still not clear, but it is certain that things will never again be the same. We are in a new age where messy, uncertain multivoiced texts, cultural criticism, and new experimental works will become more common, as will more reflexive forms of fieldwork, analysis, and intertextual representation.

Another way, then, of describing this moment in time and space is to paraphrase Thomas Berry, who has noted that we are between stories. The Old Story will no longer do, and we know that it is inadequate. But the New Story is not yet in place. And so we look for the pieces of the Story, the ways of telling it, and the elements that will make it whole, but it hasn't come to us yet. So we are now the ultimate *bricoleurs,* trying to cobble together a story that we are beginning to suspect will never enjoy the unity, the smoothness, the wholeness that the Old Story had. As we assemble different pieces of the Story, our *bricolage* begins to take not one, but many shapes.

Slowly it dawns on us that there may not be one future, one "moment," but rather many; not one "voice," but polyvocality; not one story, but many tales, dramas, pieces of fiction, fables, memories, histories, autobiographies, poems, and other texts to inform our sense of lifeways, to extend our understandings of the Other, to provide us with the material for what Marcus and Fischer (1986) label "cultural critique." The modernist project has bent and is breaking under the weight of postmodern resistance to its narratives, to what Berry calls "the Old Story."

The answer to the question, Where have we come to? is unclear, as is the answer to the question, What are the many futures that lie ahead for qualitative research? We are not wandering, for that implies that we have no direction. But likewise, as is plain from the several ontologies and many epistemologies that inform and contradict each other, we are not marching in a column toward a common future. Instead, we seem to be charting different terrain, the geography of which is not clear to us. Like the *bricoleurs* of Lévi-Strauss, we are creating solutions to our problems with makeshift equipment, spare parts, and assemblage. But like Mad Max the Road Warrior, a postnuclear survivor, we have something that runs, and we can indeed weave meaning from even a stark emotional and social landscape.

But *bricoleurs* are more than simply jacks-of-all-trades; they are also inventors, in the best sense of the word. *Bricoleurs* know that they have few tools, and little by way of appropriate parts, and so become inventors. They invent ways of repairing; they recycle used fabric into beautiful quilts; they, like Pirsig's hero in *Zen and the Art of Motorcycle Maintenance,* know that for a particular repair, nothing is better than a strip of a Coors beer aluminum can; having no art lessons, they become Grandma Moses. In the *bricoleur*'s world, invention is not only the child of necessity, it is the demand of a restless art.

The methods of qualitative research thereby become the "invention," and the telling of the tales—the representation—become the art, even though, as *bricoleurs,* we all know we are not working with standard-issue parts, and we have come to suspect that there are no longer any such parts made (if ever there were). And so we cobble. We cobble together stories that we may tell each other, some to share our profoundest links with those whom we studied; some to help us see how we can right a wrong or relieve oppression; some to help us and others to understand how and why we did what we did, and how it all went very wrong; and some simply to sing of difference.

And perhaps it is the case that the *Handbook* itself is the fifth moment. Perhaps it is the particular time in our history to take stock of where we are, to think about where we are going, to try to imagine a new future. Perhaps what we have asked our authors to do is to define this fifth moment, and speculate about what the sixth moment might be like—whether it will be a time when the Story is once again in place, or whether it will continue to be a time when fields and disciplines appear to be in disarray. This book, this effort, might well become, to historians who come long after us, a moment unto itself, a chapter in an evolution that we ourselves are not able to bound, to frame, or to capture for its essence.

Whatever the moment is, we hope that this handbook will be a prompt for new tales, for improvisations, for experiments, for interpolations and additional interpretations. The Story is by no means in place yet, although we await the visit of yet another blind Homer to piece together not only what we know of this fabulous land, but a new set of chapters for us. And as we wait, we remember that our most powerful effects as storytellers come when we expose the cultural plots and practices that guide our writing hands. These practices and plots lead us to see coherence where there is none, or to create meaning without an understanding of the broader structures that tell us to tell things in a particular way. Erasing the boundaries of self, Other, and history, we seek to learn how to tell new stories, stories no longer contained within or confined to the tales of the past. And so we embark together on a new project, a project with its own as yet not fully understood cultural plots and cultural practices.

And what remains, throughout, will be the steady, but always changing, commitment of all qualitative researchers—the commitment to study human experience from the ground up, from the point of interacting individuals who, together and alone, make and live histories that have been handed down from the ghosts of the past.

Notes

1. There have been other exchanges of this order in the history of anthropology, including the one between M. Mead and D. Freeman over Mead's early research.

2. A third answer entertains alternative forms of validity, poststructurally conceived. Lather (1993) suggests five new forms of validity (reflexive, ironic, neopragmatic, rhizomatic, situated), which can be noted only briefly here. *Reflexive validity* describes a text's attempt to challenge its own validity claims. *Ironic validity,* like deconstructive verisimilitude, proliferates multiple representations and simulations of the real, showing the strengths and limitations of each, arguing that no single representation is superior to another. *Neopragmatic validity* foregrounds dissensus, heterogeneity, and multiple discourses that destabilize the researcher's position as the master of truth and knowledge. *Rhizomatic validity* represents attempts to present nonlinear texts with multiple centers where multiple voices speak and articulate their definitions of the situation. *Situated validity* imagines a feminist validity opposed to the dominant male voice, which excludes women in their multiplicities—their bodies, their emotions, the maternal world (see Lather, 1993).

References

Agger, B. (1989). *Reading science: A literary, political and sociological analysis.* Dix Hills, NY: General Hall.

Atkinson, P. A. (1990). *The ethnographic imagination: Textual constructions of reality.* London: Routledge.

Boelen, W. A. M. (1992). *Street corner society*: Cornerville revisited. *Journal of Contemporary Ethnography, 21,* 11-51.

Bruner, E. M. (1993). Introduction: The ethnographic self and the personal self. In P. Benson (Ed.), *Anthropology and literature* (pp. 1-26). Urbana: University of Illinois Press.

Cherryholmes, C. H. (1988). *Power and criticism: Poststructural investigations in education.* New York: Teacher's College Press.

Clough, P. T. (1992). *The end(s) of ethnography: From realism to social criticism.* Newbury Park, CA: Sage.

Denzin, N. K. (1991). Empiricist cultural studies in America: A deconstructive reading. *Current Perspectives in Social Theory, 2,* 17-39.

Downing, D. B. (1987). Deconstruction's scruples: The politics of enlightened critique. *Diacritics, 17,* 66-81.

Eisenhart, M. A., & Howe, K. R. (1992). Validity in educational research. In M. D. LeCompte, W. L. Millroy, & J. Preissle (Eds.), *The handbook of qualitative research in education* (pp. 643-680). New York: Academic Press.

Ellis, C. (1991). Emotional sociology. *Studies in Symbolic Interaction, 12,* 123-145.

Ellis, C. (1994). Telling a story of sudden death. *Sociological Quarterly, 35.*

Ellis, C., & Bochner, A. P. (1992). Telling and performing personal stories: The constraints of choice in abortion. In C. Ellis & M. G. Flaherty (Eds.), *Investigating subjectivity: Research on lived experience* (pp. 79-101). Newbury Park, CA: Sage.

Ellis, C., & Flaherty, M. G. (Eds.). (1992). *Investigating subjectivity: Research on lived experience.* Newbury Park, CA: Sage.

Fish, S. (1980). *Is there a text in this class? The authority of interpretive communities.* Cambridge, MA: Harvard University Press.

Geertz, C. (1973). *The interpretation of cultures: Selected essays.* New York: Basic Books.

Gross, J. (1993, June 4). Impasse over damages in New Yorker libel case. *New York Times,* p. A1.

Hall, S. (1986). On postmodernism and articulation: An interview with Stuart Hall (edited by Lawrence Grossberg). *Journal of Communication Inquiry, 10,* 45-60.

Lather, P. (1986). Issues of validity in openly ideological research: Between a rock and a soft place. *Interchange, 17,* 63-84.

Lather, P. (1993). Fertile obsession: Validity after poststructuralism. *Sociological Quarterly, 35.*

Marcus, G. E., & Fischer, M. J. M. (1986). *Anthropology as cultural critique: An experimental moment in the human sciences.* Chicago: University of Chicago Press.

Mascia-Lees, F. E., Sharpe, P., & Cohen, C. B. (1993). The postmodernist turn in anthropology: Cautions from a feminist perspective. In P. Benson (Ed.), *Anthropology and literature* (pp. 225-248). Urbana: University of Illinois Press.

Mishler, E. G. (1990). Validation in inquiry-guided research: The role of exemplars in narrative studies. *Harvard Educational Review, 60,* 415-441.

Ortner, S. B. (1984). Theory in anthropology since the sixties. *Society for Comparative Study of Society and History, 26,* 126-166.

Reason, P. (1993). Sacred experience and sacred science. *Journal of Management Inquiry, 2,* 10-27.

Racevskis, K. (1983). *Michel Foucault and the subversion of intellect.* Ithaca, NY: Cornell University Press.

Rosaldo, R. (1989). *Culture and truth: The remaking of social analysis.* Boston: Beacon.

Rose, D. (1993). Ethnography as a form of life: The written word and the work of the world. In P. Benson (Ed.), *Anthropology and literature* (pp. 192-224). Urbana: University of Illinois Press.

Scheurich, J. J. (1992). *The paradigmatic transgressions of validity.* Unpublished manuscript.

Stacey, J. (1988). Can there be a feminist ethnography? *Women's Studies International Forum, 11,* 21-27.

Taussig, M. (1987). *Shamanism, colonialism, and the wild man: A study in terror and healing.* Chicago: University of Chicago Press.

Todorov, T. (1977). *The poetics of prose.* Ithaca, NY: Cornell University Press.

Van Maanen, J. (1988). *Tales of the field: On writing ethnography.* Chicago: University of Chicago Press.
Whyte, W. F. (1943). *Street corner society: The social structure of an Italian slum.* Chicago: University of Chicago Press.
Whyte, W. F. (1955). *Street corner society: The social structure of an Italian slum* (2nd ed.). Chicago: University of Chicago Press.
Whyte, W. F. (1981). *Street corner society: The social structure of an Italian slum* (3rd ed.). Chicago: University of Chicago Press.
Whyte, W. F. (1992). In defense of *Street corner society. Journal of Contemporary Ethnography, 21,* 52-68.

Name Index

Subject Index

About the Authors

Patricia A. Adler (Ph.D., University of California, San Diego) is Associate Professor of Sociology at the University of Colorado. She has written and taught in the areas of deviance, drugs in society, social theory, and the sociology of children. A second edition of her book, *Wheeling and Dealing* (Columbia University Press), was released in 1993. Her other recent publications include "The 'Post' Phase of Deviant Careers: Reintegrating Drug Traffickers" (in *Deviant Behavior*), "Socialization to Gender Roles: Popularity Among Elementary School Boys and Girls" (in *Sociology of Education*), and "Personalizing Mass Education" (in *Teaching Sociology*). With Peter Adler, she is coeditor of the *Journal of Contemporary Ethnography* and *Sociological Studies of Children*. Their most recent book together, *Backboards and Blackboards,* based on a five-year participant observation study of college athletes, was published by Columbia University Press in 1991. Currently, they are studying the culture of elementary school children.

Peter Adler (Ph.D., University of California, San Diego) is Professor and Chair of Sociology at the University of Denver. His research interests include social psychology, qualitative methods, and the sociology of sport and leisure. His recent publications include *Membership Roles in Field Research* (Sage) and articles in *Administrative Science Quarterly* and *Social Psychology Quarterly.* With Patricia A. Adler, he is coeditor of the *Journal of Contemporary Ethnography* and *Sociological Studies of Children.* Their most recent book together, *Backboards and Blackboards,* based on a five-year participant observation study of college athletes, was published by Columbia University Press in 1991. Currently, they are studying the culture of elementary school children.

David L. Altheide (Ph.D., University of California, San Diego) is a Regents' Professor in the School of Justice Studies at Arizona State University. His research interests in mass media, social control, and qualitative research methods are recorded in several books, including *Creating Reality: How TV News Distorts Events* (1976) and *Media Power* (1985). He is the 1986 Winner of the Charles Horton Cooley Award of the Society for the Study of Symbolic Interaction. He is also coauthor, with John M. Johnson, of *Bureaucratic Propaganda* and, with Robert P. Snow, *Media Worlds in the Postjournalism Era* (1991). His most recent book is *An Ecology of Communication: Cultural Formats of Control* (1994).

Paul Atkinson is Professor of Sociology and Head of the School of Social and Administrative Studies in the University of Wales, Cardiff. His past research has included ethnographic work on medical education, industrial training for unemployed school leavers, and the everyday work of hematologists. He is currently directing research on the work of discovery among a group of medical geneticists and, with Sara Delamont and Odette Parry, on the academic socialization of doctoral students in the natural and social sciences. He took his B.A. in social anthropology at Cambridge and his Ph.D. at Edinburgh. His current methodological interests include work on the rhetoric of ethnography and the use of various computing strategies for qualitative data analysis. His books include *The Clinical Experience* (1981), *Language, Structure and Reproduction* (1985), *The Ethnographic Imagination* (1990), *Understanding Ethnographic Texts* (1992), and, with Martyn Hammersley, *Ethnography: Principles in Practice* (1983). A second edition of the last of these is currently in preparation. A monograph on medical talk and medical work, based on fieldwork with hematologists, is also forthcoming.

D. Jean Clandinin is Associate Professor and Director of the Centre for Research for Teacher Education and Development at the University of Alberta, Edmonton, Canada. She is a former teacher, counselor, and school psychologist and has worked in educational research in teaching and teacher education for the past 15 years. She is author or coauthor of several books, including *Teachers as Curriculum Planners: Narratives of Experience* (with F. Michael Connelly, 1988) and *Learning to Teach: Teaching to Learn. Stories of Collaboration in Teacher Education* (with Pat Hogan, Annie Davies, and Barbara Kennard, 1993). She is currently working on two new books with F. Michael Connelly titled *Narrative and Education* and *Teachers' Professional Knowledge Landscapes.* She is the 1993 winner of the American Educational Research Association Raymond B. Cattell Early Career Award.

F. Michael Connelly studied at the University of Alberta, Columbia University, and the University of Chicago. He is Professor and Director, Joint Centre for Teacher Development, Ontario Institute for Studies in Education, and the Faculty of Education, University of Toronto. He previously taught secondary school in Alberta and has held teaching positions at the Universities of Alberta, Illinois, and Chicago. He coordinated the Canadian component of the Second International Science Study, serves as editor of *Curriculum Inquiry,* and is a former member of the board of directors of the John Dewey Society for Study of Education and Culture. He is codirector, with D. Jean Clandinin, of a long-term study of teachers' personal practical knowledge and teachers' professional knowledge landscapes. He has published numerous articles and chapters in contributed volumes and is coauthor, with D. Jean Clandinin, of *Teachers as Curriculum Planners: Narratives of Experience* (1988). He was the recipient of the 1987 Outstanding Canadian Curriculum Scholar Award of the Canadian Society for the Study of Education and of the 1991 Canadian Education Association/Whitworth Award for Educational Research.

Juliet Corbin is a Lecturer at the School of Nursing, San Jose State University, San Jose, California, and Research Associate, Department of Social and Behavioral Sciences, University of California, San Francisco. She is coauthor, with Anselm Strauss, of *Basics of Qualitative Research* (1990), as well as coauthor of the research monograph *Unending Work and Care* (1988) and of the policy book *Shaping a New Health Care System* (1988). She has also authored or coauthored a number of research and methodological papers, including an important theoretical work titled "A Trajectory Model for Reorganizing the Health Care System." She is currently researching the role of the body in action and writing up a fieldwork study about the flow of work in hospitals.

Benjamin F. Crabtree, Ph.D., is a medical anthropologist and Associate Professor and Director of Research in the Department of Family Practice, University of Nebraska Medical Center. He has published numerous articles and chapters on both qualitative and quantitative methods, covering topics ranging from time-series analysis and log-linear models to in-depth interviews and qualitative analysis strategies. He is coeditor of *Doing Qualitative Research* and his work has appeared in such journals as the *Journal of Clinical Epidemiology, Public Health Reports,* and *Family Medicine.*

Betsy Cullum-Swan (M.A., Michigan State University, 1987) is an Instructor in the Department of Sociology at Michigan State University. She has published several chapters in books, and her reviews and articles have appeared in such journals as *Semiotica* and *Symbolic Interaction.* Her research interests are in the areas of social psychology (sex and gender roles) and medical semiotics. She has been the recipient of the Excellence in Teaching Award of Michigan State University. She is currently researching, using semiotic discourse analysis, the meanings and consequences of invasive trauma. She will receive her Ph.D. in 1994.

Norman K. Denzin is Professor of Sociology, Communications, and Humanities at the University of Illinois, Urbana-Champaign. He is the author of numerous books, including *Sociological Methods, The Research Act, Interpretive Interactionism, The Recovering Alcoholic,* and *The Alcoholic Self,* which won the Cooley Award from the Society for the Study of Symbolic Interaction in 1988. He is the editor of *Studies in Symbolic Interaction: A Research Journal* and *The Sociological Quarterly.*

Michelle Fine is Professor of Psychology at the City University of New York Graduate Center and Senior Consultant at the Philadelphia Schools Collaborative. Her recent publications include *Beyond Silenced Voices: Class, Race and Gender in American Schools* (1992), *Disruptive Voices: The Transgressive Possibilities of Feminist Research* (1992), and *Framing Dropouts: Notes on the Politics of an Urban High School* (1991).

John Fiske is Professor of Communication Arts at the University of Wisconsin—Madison, before which he taught in Australia and the United Kingdom. His books on television and popular culture include *Reading Television* (with John Hartley; 1978), *Television Culture* (1987), *Understanding Popular Culture* (1989), *Reading the Popular* (1989), and *Power Plays Power Works* (1993).

Andrea Fontana is Professor of Sociology at the University of Nevada, Las Vegas. He received his Ph.D. from the University of California, San Diego, in 1976. He has published articles on aging, leisure, theory, and postmodernism. He is the author of *The Last Frontier,* coauthor of *Social Problems* and *Sociologies of Everyday Life,* and coeditor of *The Existential Self in Society* and *Postmodernism and Social Inquiry.* He and James H. Frey have just finished coauthoring a monograph titled *The Group Interview.*

James H. Frey is Professor of Sociology and Director of the Center for Survey Research at the University of Nevada, Las Vegas. He is the author of *Survey Research by Telephone* and *An Organizational Analysis of University-Environment Relations* in addition to several papers on survey methods, sport sociology, work in the leisure industry, and deviance. He is coauthor of *The Group Interview* and *Government and Sport: The Public Policy Issues.*

Jennifer C. Greene is an Associate Professor in the field of human service studies at Cornell University. As an applied methodologist, she works primarily within a graduate-level program in human service program evaluation and planning. Her responsibilities include both teaching and research in the broad domain of applied social inquiry methodology. She has also been a practicing evaluator for 15 years. Her research interests focus on the social-political dimensions of applied social inquiry, specifically on enhancing the potential of social research to contribute to democratic principles and practices. Methodologically, these interests encompass qualitative, participatory, action-oriented, and mixed-methods approaches to social inquiry.

Egon G. Guba is Professor Emeritus of Education, Indiana University. He received his Ph.D. degree from the University of Chicago in quantitative inquiry (education) in 1952, and thereafter served on the faculties of the University of Chicago, the University of Kansas City, the Ohio State University, and Indiana University. For the past 15 years, he has studied paradigms alternative to the received view and has formed a personal commitment to one of these: constructivism. He is coauthor of *Effective Evaluation* (1981), *Naturalistic Inquiry* (1985), and *Fourth Generation Evaluation* (1989), all with Yvonna S. Lincoln, and editor of *The Paradigm Dialog* (1990), which explores the implications of alternative paradigms for social inquiry.

Jaber F. Gubrium is Professor in the Department of Sociology at the University of Florida. He has conducted research on the social organization of care in diverse treatment settings, from nursing homes and physical rehabilitation to counseling centers and family therapy. His continuing fieldwork on the organizational embeddedness of social forms serves as a basis for the formulation of a sociology of description. He is the editor of the *Journal of Aging Studies* and author of *Living and Dying at Murray Manor* (1975), *Oldtimers and Alzheimer's* (1986), *Analyzing Field Reality* (1988), *The Mosaic of Care* (1991), *Out of Control* (1992), and *Speaking of Life* (1993). He is also coauthor, with James Holstein, of *What Is Family?* (1990) and *Constructing the Life Course* (1994).

David Hamilton is the Sydney Jones Professor of Education at the University of Liverpool. Since completing postgraduate studies at the University of Edinburgh, he has held positions at the Scottish Council for Educational Research and at the Universities of East Anglia, Illinois, and Glasgow. His recent publications include *Towards a Theory of Schooling* (1989) and *Learning About Education: An Unfinished Curriculum* (1990). His long-standing interest in the conduct and rationality of educational research has often taken a historical and international slant. As head of an education department that has a strong interest in teacher education, he is also interested in teaching as a practical science and in the relationship of practical training to the current fortunes of higher education.

Martyn Hammersley is Reader in Educational and Social Research, School of Education, The Open University, Milton Keynes, United Kingdom. He was educated in sociology at the London School of Economics and the University of Manchester. His main areas of research have been in the sociology of education and social research methodology. He has written many articles in these fields, and his books include *Ethnography: Principles in Practice* (with Paul Atkinson; 1983), *The Dilemma of Qualitative Method* (1989), *Reading Ethnographic Research* (1991), and *What's Wrong With Ethnography?* (1992).

Douglas Harper is Professor and Chair of the Department of Sociology, University of South Florida. He is founding editor of *Visual Sociology* and past Vice President of the International Visual Sociology Association. He has published two ethnographies with the University of Chicago Press: *Good Company,* which documents the work, drink, and freight-train migrations experienced by American tramps; and *Working Knowledge,* a sociological biography of a rural mechanic. He was also codirector of the documentary film *Ernie's Sawmill.* He has taught at the State University of New York at Potsdam and the University of Amsterdam in addition to the University of South Florida. His current research interests include agricultural communities, cultures of rural poverty, and visual ethnography.

Ian Hodder is Reader in Prehistory in the Department of Archaeology, Cambridge; a fellow of Darwin College, Cambridge; and

Director of the Cambridge Archaeological Unit. He obtained his B.A. in archaeology in the University of London in 1971 and his Ph.D. in the University of Cambridge in 1975, the latter on the topic of spatial analysis in archaeology. From 1974 to 1977 he was a Lecturer in the Department of Archaeology, University of Leeds, before returning to Cambridge. He has also been a Visiting Professor at the University of Amsterdam and Paris 1/Sorbonne, the State University of New York, Binghamton, and the University of Minnesota, and a Fellow at the Center for Advanced Studies in the Behavioral Sciences, Stanford. His books include *Spatial Analysis in Archaeology* (with C. Orton, 1976), *Symbols in Action* (1982); *The Present Past* (Batsford, 1982), *Reading the Past* (1986), *The Domestication of Europe* (1990), and *Theory and Practice in Archaeology* (1992).

James A. Holstein is Professor of Sociology at Marquette University. His research brings an ethnomethodologically informed constructionist perspective to a variety of topics, including mental illness, social problems, family, the life course, and dispute processing. His recent publications include *Court-Ordered Insanity* (1993) and *What Is Family?* (1990) and *Constructing the Life Course* (1993), coauthored with Jaber Gubrium. He and Gale Miller have recently coedited *Reconsidering Social Constructionism* and *Constructionist Controversies,* and they also coedit the research annual *Perspectives on Social Problems.*

A. Michael Huberman, an educational psychologist, is Visiting Professor at the Harvard University Graduate School of Education and Senior Research Associate at the New England Laboratory for School Improvement. Previously, for some 20 years, he was Professor of Education at the University of Geneva in Switzerland. His objective in coming to the United States has been to harmonize work in the field with teaching and research in a university setting. His main fields of interest are teachers' life cycles, program implementation, and qualitative methodologies. His most recent books are *The Lives of Teachers* (1993), a translation from the French, and *Qualitative Data Analysis* (2nd edition, 1994), coauthored with Matthew Miles.

Valerie J. Janesick is Associate Professor of Curriculum and Instruction at the University of Kansas, Lawrence. She teaches classes in qualitative research methods, curriculum theory, curriculum planning and evaluation, and developing intercultural awareness in education. She holds a courtesy appointment in the Department of Russian and East European Studies, which allows her to organize numerous faculty and student exchanges between Moscow, St. Petersburg, and Izhevsk, Russia, and Lawrence. Her research interests include qualitative research methods, ethics in research, and comparative curriculum issues in Russian, Japanese, and Chinese schools. As a dancer, arts educator, and researcher on teaching, she has focused on international perspectives and cultural use of languages in the educational setting. Her writings have been published in *Curriculum Inquiry, Anthropology and Education Quarterly,* and various education journals. She is currently working on a text on understanding ethical issues in fieldwork through qualitative case studies. Her hobbies include photography and documentary filmmaking. She is currently planning to do a documentary on Japanese arts education programs as a result of her recent Fulbright study in Japan.

John M. Johnson (Ph.D., University of California, San Diego) is a Professor in the School of Justice Studies at Arizona State University. He has published numerous books and articles on field research, including his pathbreaking *Doing Field Research* (1975) and *Existential Sociology* (1977), coedited with Jack Douglas. He is a former President of the Society for the Study of Symbolic Interaction and serves as editor of the journal *Symbolic Interaction*. His current research interests include the sociology of emotions, domestic violence, and deviance.

Joe L. Kincheloe is Professor of Education at Florida International University, Miami, Florida. He is the author of *Teachers as Researchers: Qualitative Paths to Empowerment, Toward a Critical Politics of Teacher Thinking: Mapping the Postmodern,* and *Toil and Trouble: Good Work, Smart Workers, and the Integration of Academic and Vocational Education.* He is also coauthor of *The Stigma of Genius: Einstein and Beyond Modern Education* (with Shirley Steinberg and Deborah Tippins). He has published 100 articles in social foundations of education, social theory, and education and qualitative research.

Yvonna S. Lincoln is Professor of Higher Education and Head of the Department of Educational Administration at Texas A&M University. She has an Ed.D. from Indiana University and previously taught at the University of Kansas and Vanderbilt University. She is a specialist in higher education research, organizational analysis, program evaluation, and alternative paradigm research. Her work has been published in such well-received books as *Fourth Generation Evaluation, Naturalistic Inquiry, Effective Evaluation* (all coauthored with Egon Guba), and *Organizational Theory and Inquiry,* as well as in a host of published papers and conference presentations. She has been honored with awards for her research from the American Evaluation Association, Division J (Post-Secondary and Higher Education) of the American Educational Research Association, and the Association for Institutional Research. She has served as President of the American Evaluation Association and as Vice President of Division J of the American Educational Research Association, and has been keynote speaker at more than a dozen conferences.

Stanford M. Lyman is Robert J. Morrow Eminent Scholar and Professor of Social Science, Florida Atlantic University. In addition to holding posts at major universities in the United States, he has served as Fulbright Lecturer in Japan (1981), Visiting Foreign Expert at Beijing Foreign Studies University, China (1986), and U.S. Information Agency Lecturer in Singapore, Taiwan, Hong Kong, Ghana, Liberia, Nigeria, and former Yugoslavia. In 1976, he was elected to a lifetime honorary appointment as Senior Lecturer, Linacre College, Oxford. He is author or coauthor of 18 books, including *Civilization: Contents, Discontents, Malcontents, and Other Essays in Social Theory* (University of Arkansas Press, 1990), *The Seven Deadly Sins: Society and Evil* (revised and expanded edition, General Hall, 1989), *A Sociology of the Absurd* (with Marvin B. Scott; 2nd edition, General Hall, 1989), and *Social Order and the Public Philosophy: An Analysis and Interpretation of the Work of Herbert Blumer* (with Arthur J. Vidich; University of Arkansas Press, 1988). In 1994, the University of Illinois Press will publish *Color, Culture, Civilization: Race and Minority Issues in American Society.*

Peter K. Manning (Ph.D., Duke University, 1966) is Professor of Sociology and Criminal Justice at Michigan State University. He has been a Visiting Professor at the State University of New York, Albany, MIT, and the University of London, Goldsmiths' College, and was a Fellow at the U.S. Justice Department and of Balliol and Wolfson Colleges, Oxford. During 1983-1986, he held a senior research position in the Centre of Socio-Legal Studies, Oxford. He is the author of many articles, chapters, and books, including *Police Work* (1977), *Narcs' Game* (1980), *Symbolic Communication* (1990), and *Organizational Communication* (1992). He is listed in *Who's Who in the World* and *Who's Who in America,* and has been awarded the Beto Lecturership at Sam Houston State University, a Special Recognition Award from the Society for Symbolic Interaction, and in 1993, the Bruce Smith Sr. Award of the Academy of Criminal Justice Sciences for "outstanding contributions to criminal justice."

George E. Marcus is Chair of the Department of Anthropology at Rice University. He is coeditor, with James Clifford, of *Writing*

Culture: The Poetics and Politics of Ethnography (1986) and coauthor, with Michael M. J. Fischer, of *Anthropology as Cultural Critique: An Experimental Moment in the Human Sciences* (1986). He was inaugural editor of the journal *Cultural Anthropology* and currently produces a series of annuals for the University of Chicago Press called *Late Editions: Cultural Studies for the End of the Century.*

Peter L. McLaren is formerly Renowned Scholar-in-Residence and Director of the Center for Education and Cultural Studies, Miami University of Ohio. He has recently assumed the position of Associate Professor, Graduate School of Education, University of California, Los Angeles. He is the author of numerous publications, and his most recent works include *Paulo Freire: A Critical Encounter* (coedited with Peter Leonard), *Politics of Liberation* and *Critical Literacy* (both coedited with Colin Lankshear), and *Between Borders* (coedited with Henry A. Giroux). He is also the author of *Life in Schools* and the recently reissued *Schooling as a Ritual Performance.*

Matthew B. Miles, a social psychologist, has been Senior Research Associate at the Center for Policy Research, New York, since 1970. Before that he was Professor of Psychology and Education at Teachers College, where he worked from 1953 onward. He has had long-term interest in planned educational change, leading studies of leadership and intensive group training, school organizational renewal, educational innovation, program implementation, design of new schools, and the work of "change agents." Recent books he has coauthored include *Assisting Change in Education* (1990), *Improving the Urban High School: What Works and Why* (1990), *How Schools Improve: International Report* (1992), *Qualitative Data Analysis* (2nd edition, 1994), and *Computer Programs for Qualitative Data Analysis* (1994). His current research focuses on cognitive mapping of school restructuring, and on advances in qualitative data analysis.

William L. Miller, M.D., M.A., a family physician anthropologist in the Department of Family Medicine at the University of Connecticut, is active in an effort to make qualitative research more accessible to health care researchers. He has contributed book chapters and articles detailing step-by-step applications of qualitative methods, including the book *Doing Qualitative Research,* which he coedited. His research interests center on the role of the patient-physician relationship in health care, on physician and patient understanding of pain and pain management, and on hypertension.

Janice M. Morse, R.N., Ph.D., is Professor of Nursing, Department of Nursing and Behavioral Sciences, College of Health and Human Development, at the Pennsylvania State University. With doctorates in both nursing and anthropology, she conducts research into patient care, in particular into patient comfort, patient falls, and patient restraints; into women's health issues, such as menarche, childbirth, and breast-feeding; and cross-cultural health. She has published more than 100 articles and several books. Recently, she edited *Critical Issues in Qualitative Research Methods* (1994) and *Qualitative Nursing Research: A Contemporary Dialogue* (revised edition, 1991) and coedited, with Joy Johnson, *The Illness Experience: Dimensions of Suffering* (1991). She is also the editor of an international multidisciplinary journal, *Qualitative Health Research.*

Virginia Olesen recalls that her history as a feminist started in her childhood, when voter registration officials in Lovelock, Nevada, tried to prevent her mother, a lifelong Democrat, from voting that party because they assumed her mother, like her father, was a registered Republican. During her career in the Department of Social and Behavioral Sciences, School of Nursing, University of California, San Francisco, she started one of the country's first feminist courses in the sociology of women's health and later founded the Women Health and Healing Program, a feminist specialty for graduate students in nursing and sociology. She has written on estrogen replacement therapy, toxic shock, professional socialization, and qualitative methods, particularly fieldwork. She recently took advantage of the University of California's early retirement program to gain more time for feminist qualitative research, writing, and activism in the area of women's health.

Maurice Punch studied at the universities of Exeter, London, Cambridge, and Essex (M.A., 1966, and Ph.D., 1972). He has taught at Essex University; State University of Utrecht; State University of New York, Albany; and Nijenrode, the Netherlands Business School. Since joining Nijenrode in 1977, he has held many academic and administrative positions; currently he is Research Professor and Director of Faculty and Doctoral Research within the Faculty Management Committee. Fellowships from Nuffield and Leverhulme enabled him to visit the University of Amsterdam in 1973 and 1974, and he was Visiting Professor at SUNY, Albany, School of Criminal Justice, for fall semester 1981. In England he specialized in the sociology of education, and in the Netherlands (where he has lived since 1975) he has researched the management of the police organization (including corruption) and is now concerned with corporate crime, deviant behavior, and regulation and control in business. He has published in English, Dutch, and American journals and has written several books.

Peter Reason is affiliated with the School of Management, University of Bath. Following undergraduate studies at Cambridge University, he worked as a personnel officer before completing a doctorate in organizational behavior at Case Western Reserve University in 1973. He is coeditor of *Human Inquiry: A Sourcebook of New Paradigm Research* (with John Rowan, 1981) and editor of *Human Inquiry in Action* (1988) and has written book chapters and journal articles on cooperative inquiry and its application to management and holistic medicine. He is founder and editor of *Collaborative Inquiry,* an international newsletter. His substantive research has been in the fields of holistic and complementary medicine. He is also trained as a humanistic psychology practitioner and has facilitated training groups in humanistic group work.

Lyn Richards is a Reader in Sociology at La Trobe University. She has an honors degree in politics from the University of Adelaide and an M.A. in sociology from La Trobe University, and she teaches family sociology and qualitative research at graduate, undergraduate, and professional advanced training levels. Her research projects are all about change and nonchange in family life, the ways family lives are shaped, the ideologies that govern them, and how these change and fail to change. Her most recent book, *Nobody's Home* (1990), is the result of a five-year study of a new suburb and the choices and constraints of those who live their suburban dreams there. With Tom Richards, she developed the NUD•IST software to support that five-year longitudinal qualitative and quantitative project. Before this study, she wrote *Having Families* and, with Jan Harper, *Mothers and Working Mothers,* dealing with issues of motherhood and its demands, and the choice of workforce participation for mothers of young infants. Both books are now in second editions (1985, 1986).

Thomas J. Richards is Associate Professor and Reader in Computer Science at La Trobe University, Melbourne, Australia. He did his undergraduate work at Victoria University of Wellington and his D.Phil. at University College, Oxford, and has since held posts at the University of Auckland and La Trobe University. He is a Fellow of the Royal Astronomical Society, London. He comes to computer science from a research and teaching background in mathematical logic, philosophy and methodology of science, and formal theory of languages and knowledge. His current areas of research and teaching are artificial intelligence and software science. He has a long history of international publications in these fields, including two books on mathematical logic. His current research, with his wife, Lyn Richards, is on the application of software science, artificial intelligence, and logical theory to the analysis of unstructured qualitative data.

Laurel Richardson is a Professor of Sociology at the Ohio State University, where she teaches qualitative sociology, theory, and gender. She has published extensively in sociology journals, and her most recent books include *Writing Strategies: Reaching Diverse Audiences* (1990), *Feminist Frontiers III* (1993), and *Gender and University Teaching* (1991). Her research interest is in representational issues. She is currently applying her feminist-poststructuralist sensibilities to the writing of a monograph about the production and reception of alternative forms of staging sociological knowledge.

Ray C. Rist is currently the Director of the Case Studies Program at the U.S. General Accounting Office, Washington, DC. He has been with the GAO since 1981 and has held a range of positions, including Deputy Director of the Program Evaluation and Methodology Division and Director of Operations in the General Government Division. He served as Associate Director of the National Institute of Education from 1974 through 1976, and has also held a number of academic appointments, including at Cornell University, George Washington University, and, most recently, as the first holder of the Leon Sachs Chair in Public Policy at the Johns Hopkins University. He has authored or edited 18 books and has published more than 100 articles. He has also lectured in more than 30 countries and has served as the Senior Fulbright Fellow at the Max Planck Institute in Berlin, Germany.

Thomas A. Schwandt is an Associate Professor in the School of Education at Indiana University, where he teaches courses in qualitative methodology, philosophy of social science, and program evaluation. In addition to being an apologist for interpretive traditions, he writes about reuniting cognitive and moral concerns in social inquiry. His current work focuses on the role that religion plays in moral discourse, specifically in relation to the life and practices of the professions.

Louis M. Smith is Professor of Education, Washington University, St. Louis, where he has taught for 38 years. He was trained at Oberlin College and the University of Minnesota and has held positions at the University of Minnesota Psychoeducational Clinic, the St. Paul Public Schools, and Cemrel, Inc. Through a mix of sabbaticals, fellowships, and smaller conferences, he has been fortunate to spend considerable time in New Zealand, Australia, Israel, and the United Kingdom. In the midst of all this, he and his colleagues have written half a dozen books and an array of articles and final reports.

Robert E. Stake is Professor of Education and Director of the Center for Instructional Research and Curriculum Evaluation at the University of Illinois at Urbana-Champaign. A specialist in the evaluation of educational programs, he was trained at Princeton University in psychology, and has taught at the University of Nebraska as well as having visiting appointments at universities in four countries. Among the honors that have been accorded him are the highest offices of two divisions of the American Educational Research Association and Fulbright fellowships to Sweden and Brazil. He is the author of *Quieting Reform,* a metaevaluation study of an urban youth program called Cities-in-Schools; *Evaluating the Arts in Education; Case Studies in Science Education* (with Jack Easley); *Evaluating Curriculum* (with Steven Kemmis); and *Custom and Cherishing: The Arts in Elementary Schools* (with Liora Bresler and Linda Mabry).

John H. Stanfield II was the Frances and Edwin Cummings Professor of American Studies and Sociology, Scholar in Residence for the Commonwealth Center for the Study of American Culture at the College of William and Mary from 1988 to 1993. He is currently Professor of African American and African Studies and Professor of Sociology at the University of California at Davis. His research interests and publications include studies in the sociology of knowledge, especially pertaining to race in sciences issues.

Anselm Strauss is Emeritus Professor, Department of Social and Behavioral Sciences, University of California, San Francisco. He coauthored, with Barney Glaser, *The Discovery of Grounded Theory* (1967), the foundational first book on this methodology, and he is also author of *Qualitative Analysis for Social Scientists* (1987) and (with Juliet Corbin) *Basics of Qualitative Research* (1990). He and his coworkers have published many research monographs, including *Psychiatric Ideologies and Institutions* (1964), *Awareness of Dying* (1965), *Time for Dying* (1968), and *The Social Organization of Medical Work* (1985). His theoretical writings include *Mirrors and Masks* (1958) and *Negotiations* (1978). A *Festschrift* edited by David Maines, titled *Social Organization and Social Processes* (1991), contains papers by ex-students and collegial friends that reflect his writings and teaching. He has been a visiting professor at various foreign universities, including the University of Paris and Cambridge University, and is known for both his theoretical and research writing. He is currently finishing a book on an interactionist theory of action titled the *Continual Permutations of Action.*

Gaye Tuchman is Professor of Sociology at the University of Connecticut, where she also serves on the graduate faculty of communication sciences. Her books include *Making News: A Study in the Construction of Reality* (1978) and (with Nina Fortin) *Edging Women Out: Victorian Novelists, Publishers, and Social Change* (1989). The 1990, 1991, and 1992 Distinguished Publication Committee of the American Sociological Association cited *Edging Women Out* as one of the 10 best books of the past three years. In the academic year 1994-1995, she will be President of the Eastern Sociological Society.

Arthur J. Vidich has conducted field research in Virogua, Wisconsin, Palau, the Western Carolines of Micronesia, Springdale, New York, Trujillo Alto, Puerto Rico, the Llanos region of Colombia, Kropa, Slovenia, and other sites in the United States, including in-depth studies of the Universities of Wisconsin, Michigan, Harvard, Cornell, and Connecticut, and the New School for Social Research. Employing an anthropological perspective and attitude, he has examined the functioning of American class and status systems and political, religious, and economic institutions. He continues his research on the American university and is writing a postscript for Thorstein Veblen's *Higher Learning in America.*